Algebra

Exponents

$$c^r c^s = c^{r+s}$$

$$\frac{c^r}{c^s} = c^{r-s}$$

$$(c^r)^s = c^{rs}$$

$$(cd)^r = c^r d^r$$

$$\left(\frac{c}{d}\right)^r = \frac{c^r}{d^r} \quad (d \neq 0)$$

$$c^{-r} = \frac{1}{c^r} \quad (c \neq 0)$$

Multiplication & Factoring

Difference of Squares: $\quad u^2 - v^2 = (u + v)(u - v)$

Perfect Squares: $\quad (u + v)^2 = u^2 + 2uv + v^2$
$$(u - v)^2 = u^2 - 2uv + v^2$$

Difference of Cubes: $\quad u^3 - v^3 = (u - v)(u^2 + uv + v^2)$

Sum of Cubes: $\quad u^3 + v^3 = (u + v)(u^2 - uv + v^2)$

Perfect Cubes: $\quad (u + v)^3 = u^3 + 3u^2v + 3uv^2 + v^3$
$$(u - v)^3 = u^3 - 3u^2v + 3uv^2 - v^3$$

The Quadratic Formula

If $a \neq 0$, then the solutions of $ax^2 + bx + c = 0$ are $\quad x = \dfrac{-b \pm \sqrt{b^2 - 4ac}}{2a}$.

Equations and Graphs

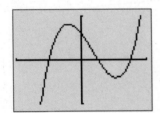

The solutions of the equation $f(x) = 0$ are the x-intercepts of the graph of $y = f(x)$.

Natural Logarithms

For $v, w > 0$ and any u:

$\ln v = u$ means $e^u = v$

$\ln (vw) = \ln v + \ln w$

$\ln \left(\dfrac{v}{w}\right) = \ln v - \ln w$

$\ln (v^k) = k(\ln v)$

Logarithms to Base b

For $v, w > 0$ and any u:

$\log_b v = u$ means $b^u = v$

$\log_b (vw) = \log_b v + \log_b w$

$\log_b \left(\dfrac{v}{w}\right) = \log_b v - \log_b w$

$\log_b (v^k) = k(\log_b v)$

Special Notation

$\ln v$ means $\log_e v$

$\log v$ means $\log_{10} v$

Change of Base Formula

$$\log_b v = \frac{\ln v}{\ln b}$$

Geometry

The Pythagorean Theorem

$$c^2 = a^2 + b^2$$

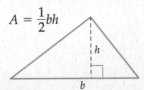

Area of a Triangle

$$A = \frac{1}{2}bh$$

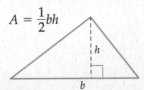

Circle

Diameter $= 2r$

Circumference $= 2\pi r$

Area $= \pi r^2$

Distance Formula

Length of segment PQ

$$d = \sqrt{(x_1 - x_2)^2 + (y_1 - y_2)^2}$$

Slope

Slope of line PQ, $x_1 \neq x_2$

$$m = \frac{y_2 - y_1}{x_2 - x_1}$$

Midpoint Formula

Midpoint M of segment PQ

$$M\left(\frac{x_1 + x_2}{2}, \frac{y_1 + y_2}{2}\right)$$

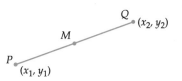

The equation of the straight line through (x_1, y_1) with slope m is $y - y_1 = m(x - x_1)$.
The equation of line with slope m and y-intercept b is $y = mx + b$.

Rectangular and Parametric Equations for Conic Sections

Circle
Center (h, k), radius r

$$(x - h)^2 + (y - k)^2 = r^2$$

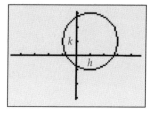

$x = r \cos t + h$
$y = r \sin t + k$ $\quad (0 \leq t \leq 2\pi)$

Ellipse
Center (h, k)

$$\frac{(x - h)^2}{a^2} + \frac{(y - k)^2}{b^2} = 1$$

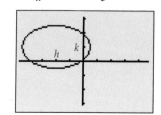

$x = a \cos t + h$
$y = b \sin t + k$ $\quad (0 \leq t \leq 2\pi)$

Parabola
Vertex (h, k)

$$(x - h)^2 = 4p(y - k)$$

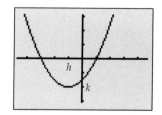

$x = t$
$y = \dfrac{(t - h)^2}{4p} + k$ $\quad (t \text{ any real})$

Parabola
Vertex (h, k)

$$(y - k)^2 = 4p(x - h)$$

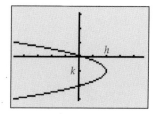

$x = \dfrac{(t - k)^2}{4p} + h$
$y = t$ $\quad (t \text{ any real})$

Hyperbola
Center (h, k)

$$\frac{(x - h)^2}{a^2} - \frac{(y - k)^2}{b^2} = 1$$

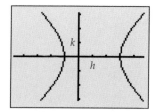

$x = \dfrac{a}{\cos t} + h$
$y = b \tan t + k$ $\quad (0 \leq t \leq 2\pi)$

Hyperbola
Center (h, k)

$$\frac{(y - k)^2}{a^2} - \frac{(x - h)^2}{b^2} = 1$$

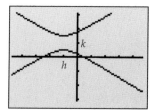

$x = b \tan t + h$
$y = \dfrac{a}{\cos t} + k$ $\quad (0 \leq t \leq 2\pi)$

Precalculus

A GRAPHING APPROACH

Precalculus

A GRAPHING APPROACH

HOLT, RINEHART AND WINSTON

A Harcourt Education Company

Orlando • **Austin** • New York • San Diego • Toronto • London

Acknowledgement: Portions of this text were previously published in *Contemporary Precalculus* by Thomas Hungerford, 2000, Saunders Publishing Co., and appear here with permission of the publisher.

Cover Credit: Humber River Bicycle Bridge, Toronto, Ontario, Canada; Architects: Montgomery & Sisam; Photography: Peter Griffith/Masterfile

(Acknowledgments appear on page 1057, which is an extension of the copyright page.)

STAFF CREDITS

Editors
Teresa Henry, *Editor*
Threasa Z. Boyar, *Editor*
Nancy Behrens, *Associate Editor*
Chris Rankin, *Associate Editor*

Editorial Staff
Patrick Ricci, *Copyeditor*
Jill Lawson, *Executive Assistant*

Book Design
Marc Cooper, *Design Director*
Lori Male, *Senior Designer*
Pronk & Associates, *Cover Design*

Image Acquisitions
Elaine Tate, *Art Buyer Supervisor*
Angela Parisi, *Senior Art Buyer*
Tim Taylor, *Photo Research Supervisor*

Manufacturing
Jevara Jackson, *Manufacturing Coordinator*

Production
Susan Mussey, *Production Manager*
Eddie Dawson, *Production Manager*
Sara Carroll-Downs, *Production Coordinator*
Rose Degollado, *Senior Production Coordinator*

Research and Curriculum
Kathy McKee, *Director Research and Curriculum*

AUTHORS

Thomas W. Hungerford

Dr. Hungerford, a leading authority in the use of technology in advanced mathematics instruction, is Professor of Mathematics at Cleveland State University. In addition to publishing numerous research articles, he has authored twelve mathematics textbooks, ranging from the high school to the graduate level. Dr. Hungerford is one of the founders of the Cleveland Collaborative for Mathematics Education, an ongoing project involving local universities, businesses, and mathematics teachers.

Irene "Sam" Jovell

An award winning teacher at Niskayuna High School, Niskayuna, New York, Ms. Jovell served on the writing team for the *New York State Mathematics, Science, and Technology Framework.* A popular presenter at state and national conferences, her workshops focus on technology-based innovative education. Ms. Jovell has served as president of the New York State Mathematics Teachers Association.

Betty Mayberry

Ms. Mayberry is the mathematics department chair at Gallatin High School, Gallatin, Tennessee. She has received the Presidential Award for Excellence in Teaching Mathematics and the Tandy Technology Scholar award. She is a Teachers Teaching with Technology instructor, is a popular speaker for the effective use of technology in mathematics instruction, and has served as president elect of the Tennessee Mathematics Teachers Associations.

CONTENT CONSULTANT

Martin Engelbrecht

A mathematics teacher at Culver Academies, Culver, Indiana, Mr. Engelbrecht also teaches statistics at Purdue University, North Central. An innovative teacher and writer, he integrates applied mathematics with technology to make mathematics accessible to all students.

REVIEWERS

J. Altonjy
  Montville High School
  Montville, NJ

Mark Budahl
  Mitchell Public Schools
  Mitchell, SD

Ronda Davis
  Sandia High School
  Albuquerque, NM

Renetta F. Deremer
  Hollidaysburg Area
  Senior High School
  Hollidaysburg, PA

James M. Harrington
  Omaha Public Schools
  Omaha, NE

Mary Meierotto
  Central High School
  Duluth, MN

Anita Morris
  Ann Arundel County
  Public Schools
  Annapolis, MD

Raymond Scacalossi Jr.
  Hauppauge Schools
  Hauppauge, NY

Harry Sirockman
  Central Catholic High School
  Pittsburgh, PA

Marilyn Wisler
  Hazelwood West High School
  Hazelwood, MO

Cathleen M. Zucco-Teveloff
  Trinity College
  Hartford, CT

Charlie Bialowas
  Anaheim Union High School
  Anaheim, CA

Marilyn Cobb
  Lake Travis High School
  Austin, TX

Jan Deibert
  Edison High School
  Huntington Beach, CA

Richard F. Dube
  Taunton Public Schools
  Taunton, MA

Jane La Voie
  Greece Arcadia
  High School
  Rochester, NY

Cheryl Mockel
  Mt. Spokane
  High School
  Mead, WA

Joseph Nidy
  Mayfield High School
  Mayfield Village, OH

Eli Shaheen
  Plum Senior High
  Pittsburgh, PA

Catherine S. Wood
  Chester High School
  Chester, PA

Janie Zimmer
  Research For Better Schools
  Philadelphia, PA

PREFACE

This book is intended to provide the mathematical background needed for calculus, and it assumes that students have taken a geometry course and two courses in algebra. The text integrates graphing technology into the course without losing the underlying mathematics, which is the crucial issue. Mathematics is presented in an informal manner that stresses meaningful motivation, careful explanations, and numerous examples, with an ongoing focus on real-world problem solving.

Representations

The concepts that play a central role in calculus are explored from algebraic, graphical, and numerical perspectives. Students are expected to participate actively in the development of these concepts by using graphing calculators or computers with suitable software, as directed in the *Graphing Explorations* and *Calculator Explorations*, either to complete a particular discussion or to explore appropriate examples.

A variety of examples and exercises based on real-world data are included in the text. Additionally, sections have been included covering linear, polynomial, exponential, and logarithmic models, which can be constructed from data by using the regression capabilities of a calculator.

Organization of Beginning Chapters

Chapter 1 begins with a review of basic terminology. Numerical patterns are discussed that lead to arithmetic sequences, lines, and linear models. Geometric sequences are then introduced. Some of this material may be new to many students.

Chapter 2 introduces solving equations graphically and then reviews techniques for finding algebraic solutions of various types of equations and inequalities.

Chapter 3 discusses functions in detail and stresses transformations of parent functions. Function notation is reviewed and used throughout the text. The difference quotient, a basic building block of differential calculus, is introduced as a rate-of-change function; several examples are given. There is an optional section on iterative real-valued functions.

Chapter 4 reviews polynomial and rational functions, introduces complex numbers, and includes an optional section on the Mandelbrot set. Finally, the Fundamental Theorem of Algebra is introduced.

Chapter 5 reviews and extends topics on exponential and logarithmic functions.

Trigonometry

Five full chapters offer extensive coverage of trigonometry. Chapter 6 introduces trigonometry as ratios in right triangles, expands the discussion to include to angle functions, and then presents trigonometric ratios as functions of real numbers. The basic trigonometric identities are given, and periodicity is discussed.

Chapter 7 introduces graphs of trigonometric functions and discusses amplitude and phase shift.

Chapter 8 deals with solving trigonometric equations by using graphical methods, as well as finding algebraic solutions by using inverse trigonometric functions. Algebraic methods for finding solutions to trigonometric equations are also discussed. The last section of Chapter 8 introduces simple harmonic motion and modeling.

Chapter 9 presents methods for proving identities and introduces other trigonometric identities.

Chapter 10 includes the Law of Cosines, the Law of Sines, polar form of complex numbers, de Moive's theorem, and nth roots of complex numbers. Vectors in the plane and applications of vectors are also presented.

Organization of Ending Chapters

Chapters 10 through 14 are independent of each other and may be presented in any order. Topics covered in these chapters include analytic geometry, systems of equations, statistics and probability, and limits and continuity.

Features

Chapter Openers Each chapter begins with a brief example of an application of the mathematics treated in that chapter, together with a reference to an appropriate exercise. The opener also lists the titles of the sections in the chapter and provides a diagram showing their interdependence.

Excursions Each Excursion is a section that extends or supplements material related to the previous section. Some present topics that illustrate mathematics developed with the use of technology, some are high-interest topics that are motivational, and some present material that is used in other areas of mathematics. Exercises are included at the end of every Excursion. Clearly marked exercises reflecting material contained in each Excursion are also in corresponding Chapter Reviews. Each Excursion is independent of the rest of the book and should be considered an extension or enrichment.

Cautions Students are alerted to common errors and misconceptions, both mathematical and technological, by clearly marked Caution boxes.

Notes Students are reminded of review topics or to direct their attention toward specific content.

Exercises Exercise sets proceed from routine calculations and drill to exercises requiring more complex thought, including graph interpretation and word problems. Problems labeled *Critical Thinking* present a question in a form different from what students may have seen before; a few of the *Critical Thinking* problems are quite challenging. Answers for selected problems are given in the back of the book.

Chapter Reviews Each chapter concludes with a list of important concepts (referenced by section and page number), a summary of important facts and formulas, and a set of review exercises.

Appendices

Technology Appendix The technology appendix presents an overview of the use of the graphing calculator. It is recommended that students who are unfamiliar with the use of a graphing calculator complete all examples, explorations, investigations, and exercises in this appendix. All students may use the appendix for reference.

Algebra Review This Appendix reviews basic algebra. It can be omitted by well-prepared students or treated as an introductory chapter. Exercises are included.

Geometry Review Frequently used facts from plane geometry are summarized, with examples, in this appendix.

Mathematical Induction and the Binomial Theorem Material relevant to these two topics is presented in an appendix with examples and exercises.

Technology

Minimal Technology Requirements It is assumed that each student has either a computer with appropriate software or a calculator at the level of a TI-82 or higher. Among current calculator models that meet or exceed this minimal requirement are TI-82 through TI-92, Sharp 9600, HP-38, and Casio 9850 and 9970. All students unfamiliar with graphing technology should complete the Technology Appendix before beginning the material.

Because either a graphing calculator or a computer with graphing software is required, several features are provided in the text to assist the student in the use of these tools.

Technology Tips Although the discussion of technology in the text is as generic as possible, some Technology Tips provide information and assistance in carrying out various procedures on specific calculators. Other Tips offer general information or helpful advice about performing a particular task on a calculator.

To avoid clutter, only a limited number of calculators are specifically mentioned in the Technology Tips. However, unless noted otherwise, observe the following guidelines.

- Technology Tips for the TI-83 also apply to TI-83 Plus and—except for some matrix operations—TI-82
- Technology Tips for the TI-86 also apply to TI-85
- Technology Tips for the Casio 9850 also apply to Casio 9970
- Technology Tips for the HP 38 also apply to HP 39 except for quartic regression not being available and LIB changing to APLET

There are no Tips specifically for HP-48 calculators, since they use entirely different operating systems than other calculators.

Graphing Explorations Students are directed to use a calculator or computer with suitable software to complete a particular discussion or to explore certain examples.

Calculator Investigation Students may not be aware of the full capabilities—or limitations— of a calculator. The Calculator Investigations, many of which appear in the Technology Appendix, will help students to become familiar with the calculator and to maximize mathematical power. Even if the instructor does not assign these investigations, students may want to read through them for enrichment purposes.

Can Do Calculus Features

Each chapter has a Can Do Calculus feature that connects a calculus topic to material included in that chapter. This feature gives the student the opportunity to briefly step into the world of calculus. Many of these features include topics that are typically solved by using calculus but can be solved by using precalculus skills that the student has recently acquired. Other Can Do Calculus features conceptually develop calculus topics by using tables and graphs.

Interdependence of Chapters and Sections

The chart on the next page shows the interdependence of chapters. A similar chart appears at the beginning of each chapter, showing the interdependence of sections within the chapter.

INTERDEPENDENCE OF CHAPTERS

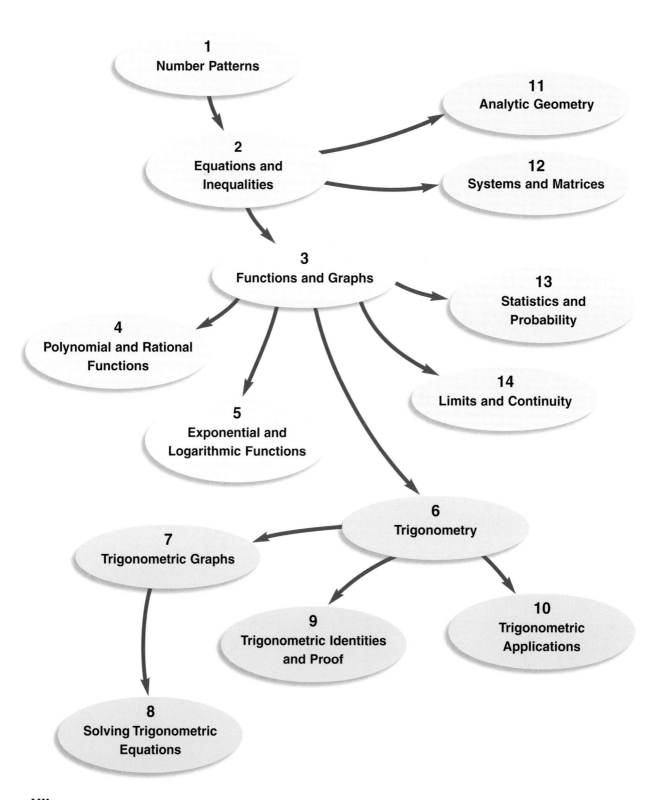

1 Number Patterns

2 Equations and Inequalities

11 Analytic Geometry

12 Systems and Matrices

3 Functions and Graphs

13 Statistics and Probability

4 Polynomial and Rational Functions

14 Limits and Continuity

5 Exponential and Logarithmic Functions

6 Trigonometry

7 Trigonometric Graphs

9 Trigonometric Identities and Proof

10 Trigonometric Applications

8 Solving Trigonometric Equations

TABLE OF CONTENTS

APPLICATIONS

Biology and Life Science

Animal populations, 21, 223, 233, 342, 344, 355, 388, 407

Bacteria, 198, 259, 344, 350, 355, 388

Birth rates, 344, 397

Blood flow, 221

Illness, 42, 55, 88, 273, 362

Food, 844, 897

Food web, 810, 813

Forest fires, 635

Genealogy, 64

Infant mortality rates, 398

Life expectancy, 71, 344

Medicine, 223, 292

Murder rates, 258, 278

Plant growth, 355, 873, 889

Population growth, 340, 349, 355, 382-3, 388, 391, 395, 397-8, 404, 407, 565

Business and Manufacturing

Art galleries, 883

Cash flows, 44

Clothing design, 883

Computer speed, 864

Cost functions, 123, 125, 149, 181, 183, 292, 319, 325, 831

Depreciation, 35, 42, 64, 72

Farming, 51, 399-400

Food, 49, 54, 105, 790, 803, 813, 833, 851, 883, 897

Furniture, 803, 808

Gift boxes, 820

Gross Domestic Product (GDP), 53

Managerial jobs, 73

Manufacturing, 136, 216, 221

Merchandise production, 20, 42, 126, 135, 400, 789, 831

Profits, 30, 42, 146, 170, 220, 222, 233, 237

Revenue functions, 125, 146, 171, 824

Sales, 20, 41, 45, 126, 171-2, 221, 344, 363, 404, 790, 803, 812, 833, 837

Telemarketing, 848

Textbook publication, 42

Chemistry, Physics, and Geology

Antifreeze, 104-5

Atmospheric pressure, 388

Boiling points, 41, 335

Bouncing balls, 16, 62, 64

Carbon dioxide, 387

Evaporation, 195

Fahrenheit v. Celsius, 214

Floating balloons, 70

Gas pressure, 148

Gravitational acceleration, 293

Gravity, 677, 680, 687

Halley's Comet, 700, 754

Light, 117, 602

Mixtures, 104-5, 790, 835, 837

Orbits of astronomical objects, 393, 697, 700

Ozone, 387

Pendulums, 335, 556, 602

Photography, 293, 538

Purification, 350, 355

Radio waves, 500

Radioactive decay, 340, 352, 355-6, 381, 387, 404, 407

Richter Scale, 370, 407

Rotating wheels, 442-3, 550, 556

Sinkholes, 623

Sledding, 678, 687

Springs, 551-2, 564

Swimming pool chlorine levels, 20

Vacuum pumps, 64

Weather, 105, 116, 407, 485, 553, 557-8, 897, 903

Weather balloons, 198

Weight, 116

Whispering Gallery, 696

Construction

Antenna towers, 620

Building a ramp, 40

Bus shelters, 635

Equipment, 30, 106, 428, 431, 442, 469, 636

Fencing, 149, 292, 325, 635

Highway spotlights, 538

Lifting beams, 442

Monument construction, 30

Paving, 102, 105, 473

Pool heaters, 789

Rain gutters, 468

Sub-plots, 126

Surveying, 284

Tunnels, 623

Consumer Affairs

Campaign contributions, 5

Cars, 20, 126

Catalogs, 879

College, 10, 75, 87, 149, 320, 813

Credit cards, 64, 353, 800

Energy use, 57, 125

Expenditures per student, 355

Gas prices, 11

Health care, 42

Inflation, 355

Lawsuits, 864

Libraries, 883

Life insurance premiums, 53, 72

Loans, 56, 72, 105, 353, 803

Lotteries, 881, 886

CHAPTER 1

Number Patterns

On a Clear Day

Hot-air balloons rise linearly as they ascend to the designated height. The distance they have traveled, as measured along the ground, is a function of time and can be found by using a linear function. See Exercise 58 in Chapter 1 Review.

Chapter Outline

Interdependence of Sections

1.1 ⟶ 1.2 ⟶ 1.3 ⟶ 1.4 ⟶ 1.5

↘ 1.6

Mathematics is the study of quantity, order, and relationships. This chapter defines the real numbers and the coordinate plane, and it uses the vocabulary of relations and functions to begin the study of mathematical relationships. The number patterns in recursive, arithmetic, and geometric sequences are examined numerically, graphically, and algebraically. Lines and linear models are reviewed.

Real Numbers, Relations, and Functions

Objectives

- Define key terms:
  - sets of numbers
  - the coordinate plane
  - relation
  - input and output
  - domain and range
  - function
- Use functional notation

Real number relationships, the points of a line, and the points of a plane are powerful tools in mathematics.

Real Numbers

You have been using **real numbers** most of your life. Some subsets of the real numbers are the **natural numbers,** 1, 2, 3, 4, … , and the **whole numbers,** which include 0 together with the set of natural numbers. The **integers** are the whole numbers and their opposites.

$$… , -5, -4, -3, -2, -1, 0, 1, 2, 3, 4, 5, …$$

The natural numbers are also referred to as the **counting numbers** and as the set of **positive integers,** and the whole numbers are also referred to as the set of **nonnegative integers.**

A real number is said to be a **rational number** if it can be expressed as a ratio, $\frac{r}{s}$, with r and s integers and $s \neq 0$. The following are rational numbers.

$$\frac{1}{2}, \quad -0.983 = -\frac{938}{1000}, \quad 47 = \frac{47}{1}, \quad \text{and} \quad 8\frac{3}{5} = \frac{43}{5}$$

Rational numbers may also be described as numbers that can be expressed as terminating decimals, such as $0.25 = \frac{1}{4}$, or as nonterminating repeating decimals in which a single digit or block of digits repeats, such as

$$\frac{5}{3} = 1.6666\ldots \quad \text{or} \quad \frac{53}{333} = 0.159159\ldots$$

A real number that cannot be expressed as a ratio with integer numerator and denominator is called an **irrational number.** Alternatively, an irrational number is one that can be expressed as a nonterminating, nonrepeating decimal in which no single digit or block of digits repeats. For example, the number π, which is used to calculate the area of a circle, is irrational.

Although Figure 1.1-1 does not represent the size of each set of numbers, it shows the relationship between subsets of real numbers.

- All natural numbers are whole numbers.
- All whole numbers are integers.
- All integers are rational numbers.
- All rational numbers are real numbers.
- All irrational numbers are real numbers.

Real Numbers

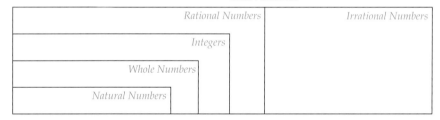

Figure 1.1-1

The Real Number Line

The real numbers are represented graphically as points on a number line, as shown in Figure 1.1-2. There is a one-to-one correspondence between the real numbers and the points of the line, which means that each real number corresponds to exactly one point on the line, and vice versa.

Figure 1.1-2

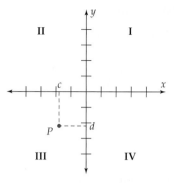

Figure 1.1-3

The Coordinate Plane

Just as real numbers correspond to points on a number line, ordered *pairs* of real numbers correspond to points in a plane. To sketch a coordinate plane, draw two number lines in the plane, one vertical and one horizontal, as shown in Figure 1.1-3.

The number lines, or **axes,** are often named the x-axis and the y-axis, but other letters may be used. The point where the axes intersect is the **origin,** and the axes divide the plane into four regions, called **quadrants,** indicated by Roman numerals in Figure 1.1-3. The plane is now said to have a **rectangular,** or **Cartesian, coordinate system.**

In Figure 1.1-3, point P is represented by an **ordered pair** that has **coordinates** (c, d), where c is the x-**coordinate** of P, and d is the y-**coordinate** of P.

Scatter Plots

In many application problems, data is plotted as points on the coordinate plane. This type of representation of data is called a **scatter plot.**

Example 1   Scatter Plot

Create a scatter plot of this data from the Federal Election Commission that shows the total amount of money, in millions of dollars, contributed to all congressional candidates in the years shown.

Year	1988	1990	1992	1994	1996
Amount	276	284	392	418	500

Solution

Let x be the number of years since 1988, so that $x = 0$ denotes 1988, $x = 2$ denotes 1990, and so on. Plot the points (0, 276), (2, 284), (4, 392), (6, 418), and (8, 500) to obtain a scatter plot. See Figure 1.1-4.

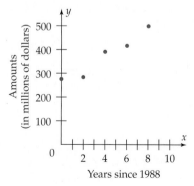

Years since 1988

Figure 1.1-4

A Relation and Its Domain and Range

Scientists and social scientists spend much time and money looking for how two quantities are related. These quantities might be a person's height and his shoe size or how much a person earns and how many years of college she has completed. In these examples, a **relation** exists between two variables. The first quantity, often called the x-variable, is said to be related to the second quantity, often called the y-variable. Mathematicians are interested in the types of relations that exist between two quantities, or how x and y are paired. Of interest is a relation's **domain,** or possible values that x can have, as well as a relation's **range,** possible values that y can have. Relations may be represented numerically by a set of ordered pairs, graphically by a scatter plot, or algebraically by an equation.

Example 2 Domain and Range of a Relation

The table below shows the heights and shoe sizes of twelve high school seniors.

Height (inches)	67	72	69	76	67	72
Shoe size	8.5	10	12	12	10	11

Height (inches)	67	62.5	64.5	64	62	62
Shoe Size	7.5	5.5	8	8.5	6.5	6

For convenience, the data table lists the height first, so the pairing (height, shoe size) is said to be ordered. Hence, the data is a relation. Find the relation's domain and range.

Solution

There are twelve ordered pairs.

$$(67, 8.5), (72, 10), (69, 12), (76, 12), (67, 10), (72, 11),$$
$$(67, 7.5), (62.5, 5.5), (64.5, 8), (64, 8.5), (62, 6.5), (62, 6)$$

Figure 1.1-5 shows the scatter plot of the relation.

The relation's domain is the set of x values: $\{62, 62.5, 64, 64.5, 67, 69, 72, 76\}$, and its range is the set of y values: $\{5.5, 6, 6.5, 7.5, 8, 8.5, 10, 11, 12\}$.

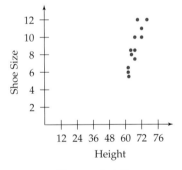

Figure 1.1-5

Sometimes a rule, which is a statement or an equation, expresses one quantity in a relation in terms of the other quantity.

Example 3   A Rule of a Relation

Given the relation

$$\{(0, 0), (1, 1), (1, -1), (4, 2), (4, -2), (9, 3), (9, -3)\},$$

state its domain and range. Create a scatter plot of the relation and find a rule that relates the value of the first coordinate to the value of the second coordinate.

Solution

The domain is $\{0, 1, 4, 9\}$, and the range is $\{-3, -2, -1, 0, 1, 2, 3\}$. The scatter plot is shown in Figure 1.1-6. One rule that relates the first coordinate to the second coordinate in each pair is $x = y^2$, where x is an integer.

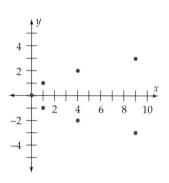

Figure 1.1-6

Functions

Much of mathematics focuses on special relations called **functions.** A **function** is a set of ordered pairs in which the first coordinate denotes the **input,** the second coordinate denotes the **output** that is obtained from the **rule of the function,** and

each *input* **corresponds to one and only one** *output.*

Think of a function as a calculator with only one key that provides the solution for the *rule of the function.* A number is *input* into the calculator, the rule key (which represents a set of operations) is pushed, and a single answer is *output* to the display. On the special "function calculator," shown in Figure 1.1-7, if you press 9 then $2x^2 + 1$, the display screen will show 163—twice the square of 9 plus 1. The number 9 is the input, the rule is given by $2x^2 + 1$, and the output is 163.

Figure 1.1-7

Example 4   Identifying a Function Represented Numerically

In each set of ordered pairs, the first coordinate represents input and the second coordinate represents its corresponding output. Explain why each set is, or is not, a function.

a. $\{(0, 0), (1, 1), (1, -1), (4, 2), (4, -2), (9, 3), (9, -3)\}$

b. $\{(0, 0), (1, 1), (-1, 1), (4, 2), (-4, 2), (9, 3), (-9, 3)\}$

c. $\{(0, 0), (1, 1), (-1, 1), (4, 2), (-4, -2), (9, 3), (-9, -3)\}$

Solution

The phrase "one and only one" in the definition of a function is the critical qualifier. To determine if a relation is a function, make sure that each input corresponds to exactly one output.

a. $\{(0, 0), (1, 1), (1, -1), (4, 2), (4, -2), (9, 3), (9, -3)\}$ is not a function because the input 1 has two outputs, 1 and -1. Two other inputs, 4 and 9, also have more than one output.

b. $\{(0, 0), (1, 1), (-1, 1), (4, 2), (-4, 2), (9, 3), (-9, 3)\}$ is a function. Although 1 appears as an output twice, each input has one and only one output.

c. $\{(0, 0), (1, 1), (-1, 1), (4, 2), (-4, -2), (9, 3), (-9, -3)\}$ is a function because each input corresponds to one and only one output. ∎

Calculator Exploration

Make a scatter plot of each set of ordered pairs in Example 4. Examine each scatter plot to determine if there is a graphical test that can be used to determine if each input produces one and only one output, that is, if the set represents a function.

Example 5   **Finding Function Values from a Graph**

The graph in Figure 1.1-8 defines a function whose rule is:

For input x, the output is the unique number y such that (x, y) is on the graph.

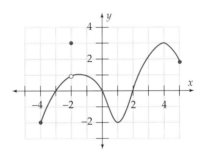

Figure 1.1-8

a. Find the output for the input 4.
b. Find the inputs whose output is 0.
c. Find the y-value that corresponds to $x = -2$.
d. State the domain and range of the function.

Solution

a. From the graph, if $x = 4$, then $y = 3$. Therefore, 3 is the output corresponding to the input 4.

b. When $y = 0$, $x = -3$ or $x = 0$ or $x = 2$. Therefore, $-3, 0$, and 2 are the inputs corresponding to the output 0.

c. The y-value that corresponds to $x = -2$ is $y = 3$.

d. The domain is all real numbers between -4 and 5, inclusive. The range is all real numbers between -2 and 3, inclusive.

Function Notation

Because functions are used throughout mathematics, **function notation** is a convenient shorthand developed to make their use and analysis easier. Function notation is easily adapted to mathematical settings, in which the particulars of a relationship are not mentioned. Suppose a function is given. Let f denote a given function and let a denote a number in the domain of f. Then

$f(a)$ **denotes the output of the function f produced by input a.**

For example, $f(6)$ denotes the output of the function f that corresponds to the input 6.

y is the output produced by input x according to
the rule of the function f

is abbreviated

$$y = f(x),$$

which is read "y equals f of x."

In actual practice, functions are seldom presented in the style of domain-rule-range, as they have been here. Usually, a phrase, such as "the function $f(x) = \sqrt{x^2 + 1}$," will be given. It should be understood as a set of directions, as shown in the following diagram.

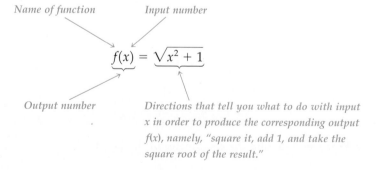

Name of function   *Input number*

$$f(x) = \sqrt{x^2 + 1}$$

Output number   *Directions that tell you what to do with input x in order to produce the corresponding output $f(x)$, namely, "square it, add 1, and take the square root of the result."*

For example, to find $f(3)$, the output of the function f for input 3, simply replace x by 3 in the rule's directions.

$$f(x) = \sqrt{x^2 + 1}$$
$$f(3) = \sqrt{(3)^2 + 1} = \sqrt{9 + 1} = \sqrt{10}$$

Similarly, replacing x by -5 and 0 produces the respective outputs.

$$f(-5) = \sqrt{(-5)^2 + 1} = \sqrt{26} \quad \text{and} \quad f(0) = \sqrt{0^2 + 1} = 1$$

CAUTION

The parentheses in $d(t)$ do not denote multiplication. The entire symbol $d(t)$ is part of the shorthand language that is convenient for representing a function, its input and its output; it is *not* the same as algebraic notation.

NOTE The choice of letters that represent the function and input may vary.

Technology Tip

One way to evaluate a function $f(x)$ is to enter its rule into the equation memory as $y = f(x)$ and use TABLE or EVAL. See the Technology Appendix for more detailed information.

NOTE Functions will be discussed in detail in Chapter 3.

Example 6 Function Notation

For $h(x) = x^2 + x - 2$, find each of the following:

a. $h(\sqrt{3})$ **b.** $h(-2)$ **c.** $h(-a)$

Solution

To find $h(\sqrt{3})$ and $h(-2)$, replace x by $\sqrt{3}$ and -2, respectively, in the rule of h.

a. $h(\sqrt{3}) = (\sqrt{3})^2 + \sqrt{3} - 2 = 3 + \sqrt{3} - 2 = 1 + \sqrt{3}$

b. $h(-2) = (-2)^2 + (-2) - 2 = 4 - 2 - 2 = 0$

The values of the function h at any quantity, such as $-a$, can be found by using the same procedure: *replace x in the formula for $h(x)$ by the quantity $-a$ and simplify*.

c. $h(-a) = (-a)^2 + (-a) - 2 = a^2 - a - 2$

Exercises 1.1

1. Find the coordinates of points A–I.

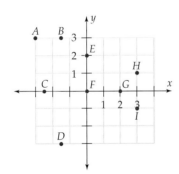

In Exercises 2–5, find the coordinates of the point P.

2. P lies 4 units to the left of the y-axis and 5 units below the x-axis.

3. P lies 3 units above the x-axis and on the same vertical line as $(-6, 7)$.

4. P lies 2 units below the x-axis and its x-coordinate is three times its y-coordinate.

5. P lies 4 units to the right of the y-axis and its y-coordinate is half its x-coordinate.

In Exercises 6–8, sketch a scatter plot of the given data. In each case, let the x-axis run from 0 to 10.

6. The maximum yearly contribution to an individual retirement account in 2003 is $3000. The table shows the maximum contribution in fixed 2003 dollars. Let $x = 0$ correspond to 2000.

Year	2003	2004	2005	2006	2007	2008
Amount	3000	2910	3764	3651	3541	4294

7. The table shows projected sales, in thousands, of personal digital video recorders. Let $x = 0$ correspond to 2000. (Source: eBrain Market Research)

Year	2000	2001	2002	2003	2004	2005
Sales	257	129	143	214	315	485

8. The tuition and fees at public four-year colleges in the fall of each year are shown in the table. Let $x = 0$ correspond to 1995. (Source: The College Board)

Year	Tuition & fees	Year	Tuition & fees
1995	$2860	1998	$3247
1996	$2966	1999	$3356
1997	$3111	2000	$3510

9. The graph, which is based on data from the U.S. Department of Energy, shows approximate average gasoline prices (in cents per gallon) between 1985 and 1996, with $x = 0$ corresponding to 1985.

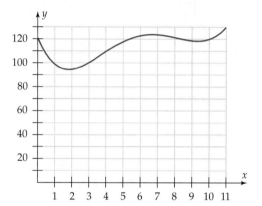

a. Estimate the average price in 1987 and in 1995.
b. What was the approximate percentage increase in the average price from 1987 to 1995?
c. In what year(s) was the average price at least $1.10 per gallon?

10. The graph, which is based on data from the U.S. Department of Commerce, shows the approximate amount of personal savings as a percent of disposable income between 1960 and 1995, with $x = 0$ corresponding to 1960.

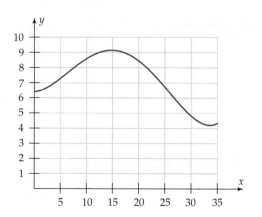

a. In what years during this period were personal savings largest and smallest (as a percent of disposable income)?
b. In what years were personal savings at least 7% of disposable income?

11. a. If the first coordinate of a point is greater than 3 and its second coordinate is negative, in what quadrant does it lie?
b. What is the answer to part **a** if the first coordinate is less than 3?

12. In which possible quadrants does a point lie if the product of its coordinates is
a. positive?   **b.** negative?

13. a. Plot the points $(3, 2)$, $(4, -1)$, $(-2, 3)$, and $(-5, -4)$.
b. Change the sign of the y-coordinate in each of the points in part **a**, and plot these new points.
c. Explain how the points (a, b) and $(a, -b)$ are related graphically.
Hint: What are their relative positions with respect to the x-axis?

14. a. Plot the points $(5, 3)$, $(4, -2)$, $(-1, 4)$, and $(-3, -5)$.
b. Change the sign of the x-coordinate in each of the points in part **a**, and plot these new points.
c. Explain how the points (a, b) and $(-a, b)$ are related graphically.
Hint: What are their relative positions with respect to the y-axis?

In Exercises 15–18, determine whether or not the given table could possibly be a table of values of a function. Give reasons for each answer.

15.

Input	−2	0	3	1	−5
Output	2	3	−2.5	2	14

16.

Input	−5	3	0	−3	5
Output	7	3	0	5	−3

17.

Input	−5	1	3	−5	7
Output	0	2	4	6	8

18.

Input	1	−1	2	−2	3
Output	1	−2	±5	−6	8

Exercises 19–22 refer to the following state income tax table.

Annual income	Amount of tax
Less than $2000	0
$2000–$6000	2% of income over $2000
More than $6000	$80 plus 5% of income over $6000

19. Find the output (tax amount) that is produced by each of the following inputs (incomes):
$500 $1509 $3754
$6783 $12,500 $55,342

20. Find four different numbers in the domain of this function that produce the same output (number in the range).

21. Explain why your answer in Exercise 20 does not contradict the definition of a function.

22. Is it possible to do Exercise 20 if all four numbers in the domain are required to be greater than 2000? Why or why not?

23. The amount of postage required to mail a first-class letter is determined by its weight. In this situation, is weight a function of postage? Or vice versa? Or both?

24. Could the following statement ever be the rule of a function?

> For input x, the output is the number whose square is x.

Why or why not? If there is a function with this rule, what is its domain and range?

Use the figure at the top of page 13 for Exercises 25–31. Each of the graphs in the figure defines a function.

25. State the domain and range of the function defined by graph **a.**

26. State the output (number in the range) that the function of Exercise 25 produces from the following inputs (numbers in the domain):
$-2, -1, 0, 1.$

27. Do Exercise 26 for these numbers in the domain: $\frac{1}{2}, \frac{5}{2}, -\frac{5}{2}.$

28. State the domain and range of the function defined by graph **b.**

29. State the output (number in the range) that the function of Exercise 28 produces from the following inputs (numbers in the domain): $-2, 0, 1, 2.5, -1.5.$

30. State the domain and range of the function defined by graph **c.**

31. State the output (number in the range) that the function of Exercise 30 produces from the following inputs (numbers in the domain): $-2, -1, 0, \frac{1}{2}, 1.$

32. Find the indicated values of the function by hand and by using the table feature of a calculator.
$g(x) = \sqrt{x + 4} - 2$
a. $g(-2)$ **b.** $g(0)$ **c.** $g(4)$
d. $g(5)$ **e.** $g(12)$

33. The rule of the function f is given by the graph. Find
a. the domain of f
b. the range of f
c. $f(-3)$
d. $f(-1)$
e. $f(1)$
f. $f(2)$

34. The rule of the function g is given by the graph. Find
a. the domain of g
b. the range of g
c. $g(-3)$
d. $g(-1)$
e. $g(1)$
f. $g(4)$

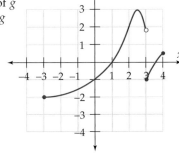

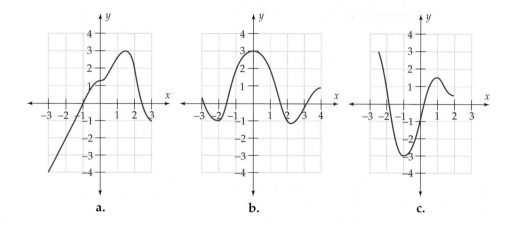

a.   b.   c.

1.2   Mathematical Patterns

Objectives

- Define key terms:
    sequence
    sequence notation
    recursive functions
- Create a graph of a sequence
- Apply sequences to real-world situations

Visual patterns exist all around us, and many inventions and discoveries began as ideas sparked by noticing patterns.

Consider the following lists of numbers.

$$-4, -1, 2, 5, 8, \underline{?} \qquad -1, 10, -3, 73, \underline{?}$$

Analyzing the lists above, many people would say that the next number in the list on the left is 11 because the pattern appears to be "add 3 to the previous term." In the list on the right, the next number is uncertain because there is no obvious pattern. Sequences may help in the visualization and understanding of patterns.

Definition of a Sequence

A *sequence* is an ordered list of numbers.
Each number in the list is called a *term* of the sequence.

An **infinite sequence** is a sequence with an infinite number of terms. Examples of infinite sequences are shown below.

$$2, 4, 6, 8, 10, 12, \ldots$$
$$1, -3, 5, -7, 9, -11, 13, \ldots$$
$$2, 1, \frac{2}{3}, \frac{2}{4}, \frac{2}{5}, \frac{2}{6}, \frac{2}{7}, \ldots$$

The three dots, or *points of ellipsis,* at the end of a sequence indicate that the same pattern continues for an infinite number of terms.

A special notation is used to represent a sequence.

Sequence Notation

The following notation denotes specific terms of a sequence:

- **The first term of a sequence is denoted u_1.**
- **The second term u_2.**
- **The term in the nth position, called the nth term, is denoted by u_n.**
- **The term before u_n is u_{n-1}.**

NOTE Any letter can be used to represent the terms of a sequence.

Example 1   **Terms of a Sequence**

Make observations about the pattern suggested by the diagrams below. Continue the pattern by drawing the next two diagrams, and write a sequence that represents the number of circles in each diagram.

		○○○ ○
	○○	○
○	○	○
Diagram 1	**Diagram 2**	**Diagram 3**
1 circle	*3 circles*	*5 circles*

Solution

Adding two additional circles to the previous diagram forms each new diagram. If the pattern continues, then the number of circles in Diagram 4 will be two more than the number of circles in Diagram 3, and the number of circles in Diagram 5 will be two more than the number in Diagram 4.

	○○○○○
○○○○	○
○	○
○	○
○	○
Diagram 4	**Diagram 5**
7 circles	*9 circles*

The number of circles in the diagrams is represented by the sequence

$$\{1, 3, 5, 7, 9, \ldots\},$$

which can be expressed using sequence notation.

$$u_1 = 1 \qquad u_2 = 3 \qquad u_3 = 5 \qquad u_4 = 7 \qquad u_5 = 9 \quad \ldots \quad u_n = u_{n-1} + 2$$ ∎

Technology Tip

If needed, review how to create a scatter plot in the Technology Appendix.

Graphs of Sequences

A sequence is a function, because each input corresponds to exactly one output.

- The domain of a sequence is a subset of the integers.
- The range is the set of terms of the sequence.

Because the domain of a sequence is discrete, the graph of a sequence consists of points and is a scatter plot.

Example 2 — Graph of a Sequence

Graph the first five terms of the sequence $\{1, 3, 5, 7, 9, \dots\}$.

Solution

The sequence can be written as a set of ordered pairs where the first coordinate is the position of the term in the sequence and the second coordinate is the term.

$$(1, 1) \quad (2, 3) \quad (3, 5) \quad (4, 7) \quad (5, 9)$$

The graph of the sequence is shown in Figure 1.2-1.

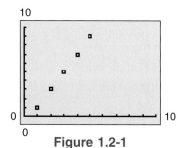

Figure 1.2-1

Recursive Form of a Sequence

In addition to being represented by a listing or a graph, a sequence can be denoted in recursive form.

Recursively Defined Sequence

> A sequence is defined *recursively* if the first term is given and there is a method of determining the nth term by using the terms that precede it.

Example 3 — Recursively Defined Sequence

Define the sequence $\{-7, -4, -1, 2, 5, \dots\}$ recursively and graph it.

Solution

The sequence can be expressed as

$$u_1 = -7 \quad u_2 = -4 \quad u_3 = -1 \quad u_4 = 2 \quad u_5 = 5$$

The first term is given. The second term is obtained by adding 3 to the first term, and the third term is obtained by adding 3 to the second term. Therefore, the recursive form of the sequence is

$$u_1 = -7 \text{ and } u_n = u_{n-1} + 3 \text{ for } n \geq 2.$$

The ordered pairs that denote the sequence are

$$(1, -7) \quad (2, -4) \quad (3, -1) \quad (4, 2) \quad (5, 5)$$

The graph is shown in Figure 1.2-2.

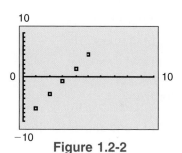

Figure 1.2-2

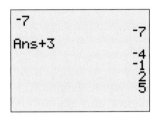

Figure 1.2-3

Technology Tip

The sequence graphing mode can be found in the TI-83/89 **MODE** menu, the HP-38 **LIB** menu, the **COORD** submenu of the Sharp 9600 **SETUP** menu, or the **RECUR** submenu of the Casio 9850 main menu. On such calculators, recursively defined function may be entered into the sequence memory, or **Y** = list. Check your instruction manual for the correct syntax and use.

Calculator Exploration

An alternative way to think about the sequence in Example 3 is

Each answer = Preceding answer + 3.

- Type -7 into your calculator and press **ENTER**. This establishes the first answer.
- To calculate the second answer, press + to automatically place ANS + at the beginning of the next line of the display.
- Now press 3 and **ENTER** to display the second answer.
- Pressing **ENTER** repeatedly will display subsequent answers. See Figure 1.2-3.

Alternate Sequence Notation

Sometimes it is more convenient to begin numbering the terms of a sequence with a number other than 1, such as 0 or 4.

$$u_0, u_1, u_2, \ldots \text{ or } b_4, b_5, b_6, \ldots$$

Example 4   **Using Alternate Sequence Notation**

A ball is dropped from a height of 9 feet. It hits the ground and bounces to a height of 6 feet. It continues to bounce, and on each rebound it rises to $\frac{2}{3}$ the height of the previous bounce.

a. Write a recursive formula for the sequence that represents the height of the ball on each bounce.

b. Create a table and a graph showing the height of the ball on each bounce.

c. Find the height of the ball on the fourth bounce.

Solution

a. The initial height, u_0, is 9 feet. On the first bounce, the rebound height, u_1, is 6 feet, which is $\frac{2}{3}$ the initial height of 9 feet. The recursive form of the sequence is given by

$$u_0 = 9 \text{ and } u_n = \frac{2}{3} u_{n-1} \text{ for } n \geq 1$$

b. Set the mode of the calculator to **Seq** instead of **Func** and enter the function as shown on the next page in Figure 1.2-4a. Figure 1.2-4b displays the table of values of the function, and Figure 1.2-4c displays the graph of the function.

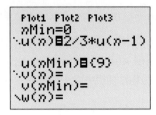

Figure 1.2-4a

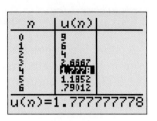

Figure 1.2-4b

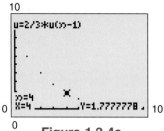

Figure 1.2-4c

c. As shown in Figures 1.2-4b and 1.2-4c, the height on the fourth bounce is approximately 1.7778 feet.

Applications using Sequences

Example 5   Salary Raise Sequence

If the starting salary for a job is $20,000 and a raise of $2000 is earned at the end of each year of work, what will the salary be at the end of the sixth year? Find a recursive function to represent this problem and use a table and a graph to find the solution.

Solution

The initial term, u_0, is 20,000. The amount of money earned at the end of the first year, u_1, will be 2000 more than u_0. The recursive function

$$u_0 = 20{,}000 \text{ and } u_n = u_{n-1} + 2000 \text{ for } n \geq 1$$

will generate the sequence that represents the salaries for each year. As shown in Figures 1.2-5a and 1.2-5b, the salary at the end of the sixth year will be $32,000.

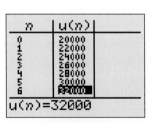

Figure 1.2-5a

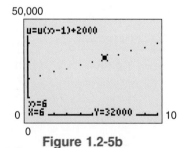

Figure 1.2-5b

In the previous examples, the recursive formulas were obtained by either adding a constant value to the previous term or by multiplying the previous term by a constant value. Recursive functions can also be obtained by adding different values that form a pattern.

Example 6   Sequence Formed by Adding a Pattern of Values

A chord is a line segment joining two points of a circle. The following diagram illustrates the maximum number of regions that can be formed by 1, 2, 3, and 4 chords, where the regions are not required to have equal areas.

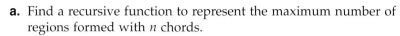

1 Chord	2 Chords	3 Chords	4 Chords
2 Regions	4 Regions	7 Regions	11 Regions

a. Find a recursive function to represent the maximum number of regions formed with n chords.

b. Use a table to find the maximum number of regions formed with 20 chords.

Solution

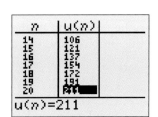

Figure 1.2-6a

Let the initial number of regions occur with 1 chord, so $u_1 = 2$. The maximum number of regions formed for each number or chords is shown in the following table.

Number of chords	Maximum number of regions
1	$u_1 = 2$
2	$u_2 = 4 = u_1 + 2$
3	$u_3 = 7 = u_2 + 3$
4	$u_4 = 11 = u_3 + 4$
…	…
n	$u_n = u_{n-1} + n$

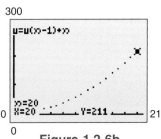

Figure 1.2-6b

The recursive function is shown as the last entry in the listing above, and the table and graph, as shown in Figures 1.2-6a and 1.2-6b, identify the 20th term of the sequence as 211. Therefore, the maximum number of regions that can be formed with 20 chords is 211. ∎

Example 7   Adding Chlorine to a Pool

Dr. Miller starts with 3.4 gallons of chlorine in his pool. Each day he adds 0.25 gallons of chlorine and 15% evaporates. How much chlorine will be in his pool at the end of the sixth day?

Solution

The initial amount of chlorine is 3.4 gallons, so $u_1 = 3.4$ and each day 0.25 gallons of chlorine are added. Because 15% evaporates, 85% of the mixture remains.

Figure 1.2-7a

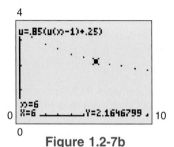

Figure 1.2-7b

The amount of chlorine in the pool at the end of the first day is obtained by adding 0.25 to 3.4 and then multiplying the result by 0.85.

$$0.85(3.4 + 0.25) = 3.1025$$

The procedure is repeated to yield the amount of chlorine in the pool at the end of the second day.

$$0.85(3.1025 + 0.25) = 2.85$$

Continuing with the same pattern, the recursive form for the sequence is

$$u_0 = 3.4 \text{ and } u_n = 0.85(u_{n-1} + 0.25) \text{ for } n \geq 1.$$

As shown in Figures 1.2-7a and 1.2-7b, approximately 2.165 gallons of chlorine will be in the pool at the end of the sixth day.

Exercises 1.2

In Exercises 1–4, graph the first four terms of the sequence.

1. $\{2, 5, 8, 11, \ldots\}$

2. $\{3, 6, 12, 24, \ldots\}$

3. $\{4, 5, 8, 13, \ldots\}$

4. $\{4, 12, 36, 108, \ldots\}$

In Exercises 5–8, define the sequence recursively and graph the sequence.

5. $\{-6, -4, -2, 0, 2, \ldots\}$

6. $\{-4, -8, -16, -32, -64, \ldots\}$

7. $\{6, 11, 16, 21, 26, \ldots\}$

8. $\left\{8, 4, 2, 1, \dfrac{1}{2}, \dfrac{1}{4}, \ldots\right\}$

In Exercises 9–12, find the first five terms of the given sequence.

9. $u_1 = 4$ and $u_n = 2u_{n-1} + 3$ for $n \geq 2$

10. $u_1 = 5$ and $u_n = \dfrac{1}{3}u_{n-1} - 4$ for $n \geq 2$

11. $u_1 = 1, u_2 = -2, u_3 = 3$, and $u_n = u_{n-1} + u_{n-2} + u_{n-3}$ for $n \geq 4$

12. $u_0 = 1, u_1 = 1$ and $u_n = nu_{n-1}$ for $n \geq 2$

13. A really big rubber ball will rebound 80% of its height from which it is dropped. If the ball is dropped from 400 centimeters, how high will it bounce after the sixth bounce?

14. A tree in the Amazon rain forest grows an average of 2.3 cm per week. Write a sequence that represents the weekly height of the tree over the course of 1 year if it is 7 meters tall today. Write a recursive formula for the sequence and graph the sequence.

15. If two rays have a common endpoint, one angle is formed. If a third ray is added, three angles are formed. See the figure below.

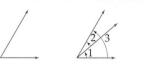
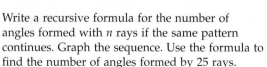

Write a recursive formula for the number of angles formed with n rays if the same pattern continues. Graph the sequence. Use the formula to find the number of angles formed by 25 rays.

16. Swimming pool manufacturers recommend that the concentration of chlorine be kept between 1 and 2 parts per million (ppm). They also warn that if the concentration exceeds 3 ppm, swimmers experience burning eyes. If the concentration drops below 1 ppm, the water will become cloudy. If it drops below 0.5 ppm, algae will begin to grow. During a period of one day 15% of the chlorine present in the pool dissipates, mainly due to evaporation.

   a. If the chlorine content is currently 2.5 ppm and no additional chlorine is added, how long will it be before the water becomes cloudy?

   b. If the chlorine content is currently 2.5 ppm and 0.5 ppm of chlorine is added daily, what will the concentration eventually become?

   c. If the chlorine content is currently 2.5 ppm and 0.1 ppm of chlorine is added daily, what will the concentration eventually become?

   d. How much chlorine must be added daily for the chlorine level to stabilize at 1.8 ppm?

17. An auditorium has 12 seats in the front row. Each successive row, moving towards the back of the auditorium, has 2 additional seats. The last row has 80 seats.

Write a recursive formula for the number of seats in the nth row and use the formula to find the number of seats in the 30th row.

18. In 1991, the annual dividends per share of a stock were approximately $17.50. The dividends were increasing by $5.50 each year. What were the approximate dividends per share in 1993, 1995, and 1998? Write a recursive formula to represent this sequence.

19. A computer company offers you a job with a starting salary of $30,000 and promises a 6% raise each year. Find a recursive formula to represent the sequence, and find your salary ten years from now. Graph the sequence.

20. Book sales in the United States (in billions of dollars) were approximated at 15.2 in the year 1990. The book sales increased by 0.6 billion each year. Find a sequence to represent the book sales for the next four years, and write a recursive formula to represent the sequence. Graph the sequence and predict the number of book sales in 2003.

21. The enrollment at Tennessee State University is currently 35,000. Each year, the school will graduate 25% of its students and will enroll 6,500 new students. What will be the enrollment 8 years from now?

22. Suppose you want to buy a new car and finance it by borrowing $7,000. The 12-month loan has an annual interest rate of 13.25%.

   a. Write a recursive formula that provides the declining balances of the loan for a monthly payment of $200.

   b. Write out the first five terms of this sequence.

   c. What is the unpaid balance after 12 months?

   d. Make the necessary adjustments to the monthly payment so that the loan can be paid off in 12 equal payments. What monthly payment is needed?

23. Suppose a flower nursery manages 50,000 flowers and each year sells 10% of the flowers and plants 4,000 new ones. Determine the number of flowers after 20 years and 35 years.

24. Find the first ten terms of a sequence whose first two terms are $u_1 = 1$ and $u_2 = 1$ and whose nth term (for $n \geq 3$) is the sum of the two preceding terms.

Exercises 25–29 deal with prime numbers. A positive integer greater than 1 is prime if its only positive integer factors are itself and 1. For example, 7 is prime because its only factors are 7 and 1, but 15 is not prime because it has factors other than 15 and 1, namely, 3 and 5.

25. *Critical Thinking* **a.** Let $\{u_n\}$ be the sequence of prime integers in their usual ordering. Verify that the first ten terms are 2, 3, 5, 7, 11, 13, 17, 19, 23, 29.

   b. Find $u_{17}, u_{18}, u_{19}, u_{20}$.

In Exercises 26–29, find the first five terms of the sequence.

26. *Critical Thinking* u_n is the nth prime integer larger than 10.

27. *Critical Thinking* u_n is the square of the nth prime integer.

28. *Critical Thinking* u_n is the number of prime integers less than n.

29. *Critical Thinking* u_n is the largest prime integer less than $5n$.

Exercises 30–34 deal with the Fibonacci sequence $\{u_n\}$ which is defined as follows:

$u_1 = 1, u_2 = 1$, and for $n \geq 3$, u_n is the sum of the two preceding terms, $u_n = u_{n-1} + u_{n-2}$. That is,

$$u_1 = 1$$
$$u_2 = 1$$
$$u_3 = u_1 + u_z = 1 + 1 = 2$$
$$u_4 = u_2 + u_3 = 1 + 2 = 3$$
$$u_5 = u_3 + u_4 = 2 + 3 = 5$$

and so on.

30. *Critical Thinking* Leonardo Fibonacci discovered the sequence in the thirteenth century in connection with the following problem: A rabbit colony begins with one pair of adult rabbits, one male and one female. Each adult pair produces one pair of babies, one male and one female, every month. Each pair of baby rabbits becomes adult and produces its first offspring at age two months. Assuming that no rabbits die, how many adult pairs of rabbits are in the colony at the end of n months, $n = 1, 2, 3, \ldots$? *Hint:* It may be helpful to make up a chart listing for each month the number of adult pairs, the number of one-month-old pairs, and the number of baby pairs.

31. *Critical Thinking* List the first ten terms of the Fibonacci sequence.

32. *Critical Thinking* Verify that every positive integer less than or equal to 15 can be written as a sum of Fibonacci numbers, with none used more than once.

33. *Critical Thinking* Verify that $5(u_n)^2 + 4(-1)^n$ is a perfect square for $n = 1, 2, \ldots, 10$.

34. *Critical Thinking* Verify that $(u_n)^2 = u_{n+1}u_{n-1} + (-1)^{n-1}$ for $n = 2, 3, \ldots, 10$.

1.3   Arithmetic Sequences

Objectives

- Identify and graph an arithmetic sequence

- Find a common difference

- Write an arithmetic sequence recursively and explicitly

- Use summation notation

- Find the nth term and the nth partial sum of an arithmetic sequence

An **arithmetic sequence,** which is sometimes called an *arithmetic progression,* is a sequence in which the difference between each term and the preceding term is always constant.

Example 1   **Arithmetic Sequence**

Are the following sequences arithmetic? If so, what is the difference between each term and the term preceding it?

a. $\{14, 10, 6, 2, -2, -6, -10, \ldots\}$

b. $\{3, 5, 8, 12, 17, \ldots\}$

Solution

a. The difference between each term and the preceding term is -4. So this is an arithmetic sequence with a difference of -4.

b. The difference between the 1st and 2nd terms is 2 and the difference between the 2nd and 3rd terms is 3. The differences are not constant, therefore this is not an arithmetic sequence. ∎

If $\{u_n\}$ is an arithmetic sequence, then for each $n \geq 2$, the term preceding u_n is u_{n-1} and the difference $u_n - u_{n-1}$ is some constant—usually called d. Therefore, $u_n - u_{n-1} = d$.

Recursive Form of an Arithmetic Sequence

In an arithmetic sequence $\{u_n\}$

$$u_n = u_{n-1} + d$$

for some constant d and all $n \geq 2$.

The number d is called the **common difference** of the arithmetic sequence.

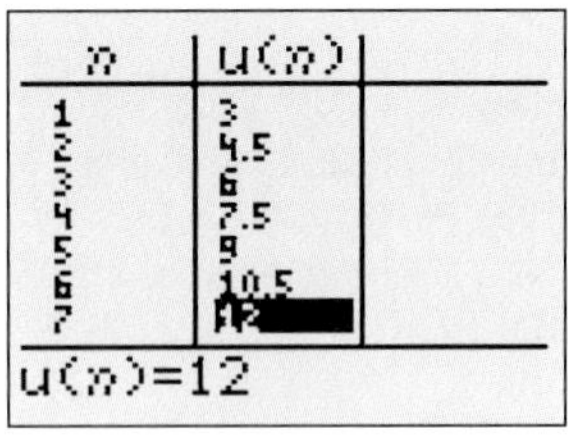

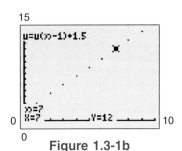

Figure 1.3-1a

15

u=u(n-1)+1.5

n=7
X=7   Y=12
0   10
0

Figure 1.3-1b

Example 2   Graph of an Arithmetic Sequence

If $\{u_n\}$ is an arithmetic sequence with $u_1 = 3$ and $u_2 = 4.5$ as its first two terms,

a. find the common difference.

b. write the sequence as a recursive function.

c. give the first seven terms of the sequence.

d. graph the sequence.

Solution

a. The sequence is arithmetic and has a common difference of

$$u_2 - u_1 = 4.5 - 3 = 1.5$$

b. The recursive function that describes the sequence is

$$u_1 = 3 \text{ and } u_n = u_{n-1} + 1.5 \text{ for } n \geq 2$$

c. The first seven terms are 3, 4.5, 6, 7.5, 9, 10.5, and 12, as shown in Figure 1.3-1a.

d. The graph of the sequence is shown in Figure 1.3-1b.   ∎

Explicit Form of an Arithmetic Sequence

Example 2 illustrated an arithmetic sequence expressed in recursive form in which a term is found by using preceding terms. Arithmetic sequences can also be expressed in a form in which a term of the sequence can be found based on its position in the sequence.

Example 3   Explicit Form of an Arithmetic Sequence

Confirm that the sequence $u_n = u_{n-1} + 4$ with $u_1 = -7$ can also be expressed as $u_n = -7 + (n - 1) \cdot 4$.

Solution

Use the recursive function to find the first few terms of the sequence.

$$u_1 = -7$$
$$u_2 = -7 + 4 = -3$$

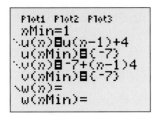

Figure 1.3-2a

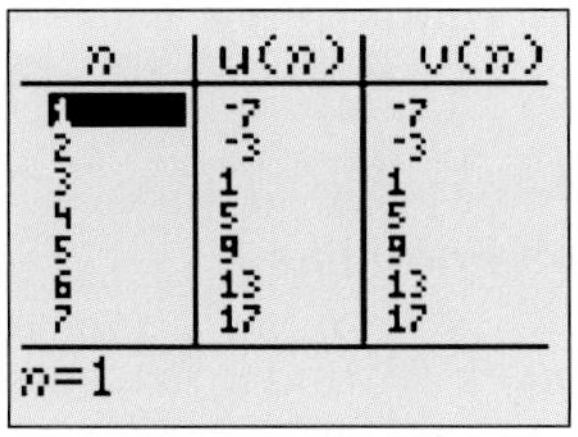

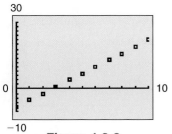

Figure 1.3-2b

$$u_3 = (-7 + 4) + 4 = -7 + 2 \cdot 4 = -7 + 8 = 1$$
$$u_4 = (-7 + 2 \cdot 4) + 4 = -7 + 3 \cdot 4 = -7 + 12 = 5$$
$$u_5 = (-7 + 3 \cdot 4) + 4 = -7 + 4 \cdot 4 = -7 + 16 = 9$$

Notice that u_3 is $-7 + 2 \cdot 4$, which is the first term of the sequence with the common difference of 4 added twice. Also, u_4 is $-7 + 3 \cdot 4$, which is the first term of the sequence with the common difference of 4 added three times. Because this pattern continues, $u_n = -7 + (n - 1) \cdot 4$. The table in Figure 1.3-2b confirms the equality of the two functions.

$$u_n = u_{n-1} + 4 \quad \text{with} \quad u_1 = -7 \qquad \text{and} \qquad u_n = -7 + (n - 1) \cdot 4$$

As shown in Example 3, if $\{u_n\}$ is an arithmetic sequence with common difference d, then for each $n \geq 2$, $u_n = u_{n-1} + d$ can be written as a function in terms of n, the position of the term.

Applying the procedure shown in Example 3 to the general case shows that

$$u_2 = u_1 + d$$
$$u_3 = u_2 + d = (u_1 + d) + d = u_1 + 2d$$
$$u_4 = u_3 + d = (u_1 + 2d) + d = u_1 + 3d$$
$$u_5 = u_4 + d = (u_1 + 3d) + d = u_1 + 4d$$

Notice that $4d$ is added to u_1 to obtain u_5. In general, adding $(n - 1)d$ to u_1 yields u_n. So u_n is the sum of n numbers: u_1 and the common difference, d, added $(n - 1)$ times.

Explicit Form of an Arithmetic Sequence

In an arithmetic sequence $\{u_n\}$ with common difference d,

$$u_n = u_1 + nd \qquad \text{for every } n \geq 1.$$

If the initial term of a sequence is denoted as u_0, the explicit form of an arithmetic sequence with common difference d is

$$u_n = u_0 + (n - 1)d \qquad \text{for every } n \geq 0.$$

Example 4   **Explicit Form of an Arithmetic Sequence**

Find the nth term of an arithmetic sequence with first term -5 and common difference of 3. Sketch a graph of the sequence.

Solution

Because $u_1 = -5$ and $d = 3$, the formula in the box states that

$$u_n = u_1 + (n - 1)d = -5 + (n - 1)3 = 3n - 8$$

The graph of the sequence is shown in Figure 1.3-3.

Figure 1.3-3

| **Example 5** | Finding a Term of an Arithmetic Sequence |

What is the 45th term of the arithmetic sequence whose first three terms are 5, 9, and 13?

Solution

The first three terms show that $u_1 = 5$ and that the common difference, d, is 4. Apply the formula with $n = 45$.

$$u_{45} = u_1 + (45 - 1)d = 5 + (44)(4) = 181$$

| **Example 6** | Finding Explicit and Recursive Formulas |

If $\{u_n\}$ is an arithmetic sequence with $u_6 = 57$ and $u_{10} = 93$, find u_1, a recursive formula, and an explicit formula for u_n.

Solution

The sequence can be written as

$$\ldots, \underset{u_6}{57}, \underset{u_7}{\underline{\quad}}, \underset{u_8}{\underline{\quad}}, \underset{u_9}{\underline{\quad}}, \underset{u_{10}}{93}, \ldots$$

The common difference, d, can be found by the difference between 93 and 57 divided by the number of times d must be added to 57 to produce 93 (i.e., the number of terms from 6 to 10).

$$d = \frac{93 - 57}{10 - 6} = \frac{36}{4} = 9$$

Note that $d = 9$ is the difference of the output values (terms of the sequence) divided by the difference of the input values (position of the terms of the sequence), which represents the change in output per unit change in input.

The value of u_1 can be found by using $n = 6$, $u_6 = 57$ and $d = 9$ in the equation

$$u_6 = u_1 + (n - 1)d$$
$$57 = u_1 + (6 - 1)9$$
$$u_1 = 57 - 5 \cdot 9 = 57 - 45 = 12$$

Because $u_1 = 12$ and $d = 9$, the recursive form of the arithmetic sequence is given by

$$u_1 = 12 \text{ and } u_n = u_{n-1} + 9, \text{ for } n \geq 2$$

The explicit form of the arithmetic sequence is given by

$$u_n = 12 + (n - 1)9$$
$$= 9n + 3, \text{ for } n \geq 1.$$

Summation Notation

It is sometimes necessary to find the sum of various terms in a sequence. For instance, we might want to find the sum of the first nine terms of the sequence $\{u_n\}$. Mathematicians often use the capital Greek letter sigma (Σ) to abbreviate such a sum as follows.

$$\sum_{i=1}^{9} u_i = u_1 + u_2 + u_3 + u_4 + u_5 + u_6 + u_7 + u_8 + u_9$$

Similarly, for any positive integer m and numbers $c_1, c_2, \dots, c_m,$

Summation Notation

$$\sum_{k=1}^{m} c_k \quad \textbf{means} \quad c_1 + c_2 + c_3 + \cdots + c_m$$

Example 7 Sum of a Sequence

Compute each sum.

a. $\displaystyle\sum_{n=1}^{5} (-7 + 3n)$ **b.** $\displaystyle\sum_{n=1}^{4} [-3 + (n-1)4]$

Solution

a. Substitute 1, 2, 3, 4, and 5 for n in the expression $-7 + 3n$ and add the terms.

$$\sum_{n=1}^{5} (-7 + 3n)$$

$$= (-7 + 3 \cdot 1) + (-7 + 3 \cdot 2) + (-7 + 3 \cdot 3)$$
$$\quad + (-7 + 3 \cdot 4) + (-7 + 3 \cdot 5)$$
$$= (-7 + 3) + (-7 + 6) + (-7 + 9) + (-7 + 12) + (-7 + 15)$$
$$= -4 - 1 + 2 + 5 + 8$$
$$= 10$$

b. Substitute 1, 2, 3, and 4 for n in the expression $-3 + (n-1)4$, and add the terms.

$$\sum_{n=1}^{4} [-3 + (n-1)4]$$

$$= [-3 + (1-1)4] + [-3 + (2-1)4]$$
$$\quad + [-3 + (3-1)4] + [-3 + (4-1)4]$$
$$= [-3 + 0 \cdot 4] + [-3 + 1 \cdot 4] + [-3 + 2 \cdot 4] + [-3 + 3 \cdot 4]$$
$$= -3 + (-3 + 4) + (-3 + 8) + (-3 + 12)$$
$$= -3 + 1 + 5 + 9$$
$$= 12$$

Technology Tip

SEQ is in the OPS sub-menu of the TI-83/86 LIST menu, in the LIST submenu of the TI-89 MATH menu, in the OPE submenu of the Sharp 9600 LIST menu, and in the LIST submenu of the Casio 9850 OPTN menu.

On TI-83 and Sharp 9600, SUM is in the MATH sub-menu of the LIST menu. On TI-86/89 and Casio 9850, SUM is in the same submenu as SEQ.

On an HP-38, MAKELIST and ΣLIST are used instead of SEQ and SUM, respectively. MAKELIST and ΣLIST are in the LIST submenu of HP-38 MATH menu.

Using Calculators to Compute Sequences and Sums

Calculators can aid in computing sequences and sums of sequences. The SEQ (or MAKELIST) feature on most calculators has the following syntax.

$$\textbf{SEQ}(\textit{expression, variable, begin, end, increment})$$

The last parameter, *increment,* is usually optional. When omitted, *increment* defaults to 1. Refer to the Technology Tip about which menus contain SEQ and SUM for different calculators.

The syntax for the SUM (or ΣLIST) feature is

$$\textbf{SUM}(\textit{list[, start, end]}),\text{ where } \textit{start} \text{ and } \textit{end} \text{ are optional. When } \textit{start} \text{ and }$$
end are omitted, the sum of the entire list is given.

Combining the two features of SUM and SEQ can produce sums of sequences.

$$\textbf{SUM(SEQ}(\textit{expression, variable, begin, end}))$$

Example 8   Calculator Computation of a Sum

Use a calculator to display the first 8 terms of the sequence $u_n = 7 - 3n$ and to compute the sum $\sum_{n=1}^{50} 7 - 3n.$

Solution

Using the Technology Tip, enter SEQ($7 - 3n, n, 1, 8$), which produces Figure 1.3-4. Additional terms can be viewed by using the right arrow key to scroll the display, as shown at right below.

```
seq(7-3n,n,1,8)
{4 1 -2 -5 -8 -...
```

```
seq(7-3n,n,1,8)
...-8 -11 -14 -17}
```

Figure 1.3-4

```
sum(seq(7-3n,n,1
,50))
                -3475
```

Figure 1.3-5

The first 8 terms of the sequence are 4, 1, -2, -5, -8, -11, -14, and -17. To compute the sum of the first 50 terms of the sequence, enter SUM(SEQ($7 - 3n, n, 1, 50$)). Figure 1.3-5 shows the resulting display. Therefore, $\sum_{n=1}^{50} 7 - 3n = -3475.$ ∎

Partial Sums

Suppose $\{u_n\}$ is a sequence and k is a positive integer. The sum of the first k terms of the sequence is called the ***k*th partial sum** of the sequence.

Calculator Exploration ●───

Write the sum of the first 100 counting numbers. Then find a pattern to help find the sum by developing a formula using the terms in the sequence.

---

*Partial Sums of
an Arithmetic
Sequence*

───────O

If $\{u_n\}$ is an arithmetic sequence with common difference d, then for each positive integer k, the kth partial sum can be found by using either of the following formulas.

1. $\displaystyle\sum_{n=1}^{k} u_n = \frac{k}{2}(u_1 + u_k)$

2. $\displaystyle\sum_{n=1}^{k} u_n = ku_1 + \frac{k(k-1)}{2}d$

Proof Let S_k represent the kth partial sum $u_1 + u_2 + \cdots + u_k$. Write the terms of the arithmetic sequence in two ways. In the first representation of S_k, repeatedly add d to the first term.

$$S_k = u_1 + u_2 + u_3 + \cdots + u_{k-2} + u_{k-1} + u_k$$
$$= u_1 + [u_1 + d] + [u_1 + 2d] + \cdots + [u_1 + (k-1)d]$$

In the second representation of S_k, repeatedly subtract d from the kth term.

$$S_k = u_k + u_{k-1} + u_{k-2} + \cdots + u_3 + u_2 + u_1$$
$$= u_k + [u_k - d] + [u_k - 2d] + \cdots + [u_k - (k-1)d]$$

If the two representations of S_k are added, the multiples of d add to zero and the following representation of $2S_k$ is obtained.

$$S_k = u_1 + [u_1 + d] + [u_1 + 2d] + \cdots + [u_1 + (k-1)d]$$
$$S_k = u_k + [u_k - d] + [u_k - 2d] + \cdots + [u_k - (k-1)d]$$

$\overbrace{}^{k \text{ terms}}$

$$2S_k = (u_1 + u_k) + (u_1 + u_k) + \cdots + (u_1 + u_k) = k(u_1 + u_k)$$

$$S_k = \frac{k}{2}(u_1 + u_k) \qquad\qquad\qquad \textit{Divide by 2.}$$

The second formula is obtained by letting $u_k = u_1 + (k-1)d$ in the last equation.

$$S_k = \frac{k}{2}(u_1 + u_k) = \frac{k}{2}[u_1 + u_1 + (k-1)d] = \frac{k}{2}[2u_1 + (k-1)d]$$

$$= ku_1 + \frac{k(k-1)}{2}d$$

Example 9   Partial Sum of a Sequence

Find the 12th partial sum of the arithmetic sequence below.

$$-8, -3, 2, 7, \ldots$$

Solution

First note that d, the common difference, is 5 and $u_1 = -8$.

$$
\begin{aligned}
u_{12} &= u_1 + (12 - 1)d \\
&= -8 + 11(5) = 47
\end{aligned}
$$

Using formula **1** from the box on page 27 yields the 12th partial sum.

$$\sum_{n=1}^{12} u_n = \frac{12}{2}(-8 + 47) = 234$$

■

Example 10   Partial Sum of a Sequence

Find the sum of all multiples of 3 from 3 to 333.

Solution

Note that the desired sum is the partial sum of the arithmetic sequence $3, 6, 9, 12, \ldots$. The sequence can be written in the form

$$3 \cdot 1, 3 \cdot 2, 3 \cdot 3, 3 \cdot 4, \ldots,$$

where $333 = 3 \cdot 111$ is the 111th term. The 111th partial sum of the sequence can be found by using formula **1** from the box on page 27 with $k = 111$, $u_1 = 3$, and $u_{111} = 333$.

$$\sum_{n=1}^{111} u_n = \frac{111}{2}(3 + 333) = \frac{111}{2}(336) = 18{,}648$$

■

Example 11   Application of Partial Sums

If the starting salary for a job is \$20,000 and you get a \$2000 raise at the beginning of each subsequent year, how much will you earn during the first ten years?

Solution

The yearly salary rates form an arithmetic sequence.

$$20{,}000 \quad 22{,}000 \quad 24{,}000 \quad 26{,}000 \quad \ldots$$

The tenth-year salary is found using $u_1 = 20{,}000$ and $d = 2000$.

$$
\begin{aligned}
u_{10} &= u_1 + (10 - 1)d \\
&= 20{,}000 + 9(2000) = \$38{,}000
\end{aligned}
$$

The ten-year total earnings are the tenth partial sum of the sequence.

$$\sum_{n=1}^{10} u_n = \frac{10}{2}(u_1 + u_{10}) = \frac{10}{2}(20{,}000 + 38{,}000)$$
$$= 5(58{,}000)$$
$$= \$290{,}000$$

Exercises 1.3

In Exercises 1–6, the first term, u_1, and the common difference, d, of an arithmetic sequence are given. Find the fifth term, the explicit form for the nth term, and sketch the graph of each sequence.

1. $u_1 = 5, d = 2$

2. $u_1 = -4, d = 5$

3. $u_1 = 4, d = \frac{1}{4}$

4. $u_1 = -6, d = \frac{2}{3}$

5. $u_1 = 10, d = -\frac{1}{2}$

6. $u_1 = \pi, d = \frac{1}{5}$

In Exercises 7–12, find the sum.

7. $\sum_{i=1}^{5} 3i$

8. $\sum_{i=1}^{4} \frac{1}{2^i}$

9. $\sum_{n=1}^{16} (2n - 3)$

10. $\sum_{n=1}^{75} (3n + 1)$

11. $\sum_{n=15}^{36} (2n - 8)$

12. $\sum_{n=1}^{31} (300 + (n - 1)2)$

In Exercises 13–18, find the kth partial sum of the arithmetic sequence $\{u_n\}$ with common difference d.

13. $k = 6, u_1 = 2, d = 5$

14. $k = 8, u_1 = \frac{2}{3}, d = -\frac{4}{3}$

15. $k = 7, u_1 = \frac{3}{4}, d = -\frac{1}{2}$

16. $k = 9, u_1 = 6, u_9 = -24$

17. $k = 6, u_1 = -4, u_6 = 14$

18. $k = 10, u_1 = 0, u_{10} = 30$

In Exercises 19–24, show that the sequence is arithmetic and find its common difference.

19. $\{3 - 2n\}$

20. $\left\{4 + \frac{n}{3}\right\}$

21. $\left\{\frac{5 + 3n}{2}\right\}$

22. $\left\{\frac{\pi - n}{2}\right\}$

23. $\{c + 2n\}$ (c constant)

24. $\{2b + 3nc\}$ (b, c constants)

In Exercises 25–30, use the given information about the arithmetic sequence with common difference d to find u_5 and a formula for u_n.

25. $u_4 = 12, d = 2$

26. $u_7 = -8, d = 3$

27. $u_2 = 4, u_6 = 32$

28. $u_7 = 6, u_{12} = -4$

29. $u_5 = 0, u_9 = 6$

30. $u_5 = -3, u_9 = -18$

In Exercises 31–34, find the sum.

31. $\sum_{n=1}^{20} (3n + 4)$

32. $\sum_{n=1}^{25} \left(\frac{n}{4} + 5\right)$

33. $\sum_{n=1}^{40} \frac{n + 3}{6}$

34. $\sum_{n=1}^{30} \frac{4 - 6n}{3}$

35. Find the sum of all the even integers from 2 to 100.

36. Find the sum of all the integer multiples of 7 from 7 to 700.

37. Find the sum of the first 200 positive integers.

38. Find the sum of the positive integers from 101 to 200 (inclusive). *Hint:* Recall the sum from 1 to 100. Use it and Exercise 37.

39. A business makes a $10,000 profit during its first year. If the yearly profit increases by $7500 in each subsequent year, what will the profit be in the tenth year? What will be the total profit for the first ten years?

40. If a man's starting salary is $15,000 and he receives a $1000 increase every six months, what will his salary be during the last six months of the sixth year? How much will he earn during the first six years?

41. A lecture hall has 6 seats in the first row, 8 in the second, 10 in the third, and so on, through row 12. Rows 12 through 20 (the last row) all have the same number of seats. Find the number of seats in the lecture hall.

42. A monument is constructed by laying a row of 60 bricks at ground level. A second row, with two fewer bricks, is centered on that; a third row, with two fewer bricks, is centered on the second; and so on. The top row contains ten bricks. How many bricks are there in the monument?

43. A ladder with nine rungs is to be built, with the bottom rung 24 inches wide and the top rung 18 inches wide. If the lengths of the rungs decrease uniformly from bottom to top, how long should each of the seven intermediate rungs be?

44. Find the first eight numbers in an arithmetic sequence in which the sum of the first and seventh terms is 40 and the product of the first and fourth terms is 160.

1.4 Lines

Objectives

- Find the slopes of lines, including parallel and perpendicular lines

- Describe the connection between arithmetic sequences and lines

- Graph lines

- Write the equations of lines, including horizontal and vertical lines

A **graph** is a set of points in a plane. Some graphs are based on data points, such as those shown in Section 1.3 where arithmetic sequences were graphed as scatter plots. Other graphs arise from equations.

A **solution of an equation** in two variables, say x and y, is a pair of numbers such that the substitution of the first number for x and the second for y produces a true statement. The **graph of an equation** in two variables is the set of points in a plane whose coordinates are solutions of the equation. Thus, the graph is a *geometric picture* of the solutions.

Recall that an arithmetic sequence is a sequence in which the difference between each term and the preceding term is constant.

For example, $\{3, 8, 13, 18, \dots\}$ is an arithmetic sequence.

Position (n)	1	2	3	4	5	...	n
Term (u_n)	3	8	13	18	23	...	$3 + (n-1) \cdot 5$

The graph of the sequence above has an infinite number of discrete points because the value of the sequence depends upon the term of the sequence, which must be a counting number. See Figure 1.4-1a. The graph of $y = 3 + (x - 1) \cdot 5$ is a continuous line that contains the discrete points of the arithmetic sequence, as shown in Figures 1.4-1a and 1.4-b on page 31.

NOTE If needed, review graphing functions on a graphing calculator in the Technology Appendix.

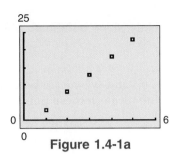

Figure 1.4-1a

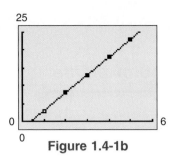

Figure 1.4-1b

As the positions within a sequence increase by one, the value of the terms increases by 5. Notice on the graph that as the x-values move to the right a distance of one, the y-values move up by a distance of 5. This common difference represents one of the most identifiable characteristics of a line, its slope.

Slope

When you move from a point P to a point Q on a line, two numbers are involved, as illustrated in Figure 1.4-2.

- The vertical distance you move is called the **change in y**, which is sometimes denoted Δy and read "delta y."
- The horizontal distance you move is called the **change in x**, which is sometimes denoted Δx and read "delta x."

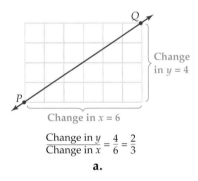

$$\frac{\text{Change in } y}{\text{Change in } x} = \frac{4}{6} = \frac{2}{3}$$

a.

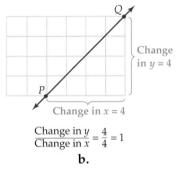

$$\frac{\text{Change in } y}{\text{Change in } x} = \frac{4}{4} = 1$$

b.

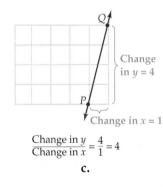

$$\frac{\text{Change in } y}{\text{Change in } x} = \frac{4}{1} = 4$$

c.

Figure 1.4-2

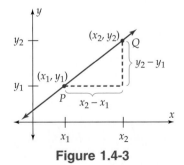

Figure 1.4-3

The fraction $\dfrac{\text{change in } y}{\text{change in } x} = \dfrac{\Delta y}{\Delta x}$ measures the steepness of the line. Suppose P has coordinates (x_1, y_1) and Q has coordinates (x_2, y_2), as shown in Figure 1.4-3.

- The change in y is the difference of the y-coordinates of P and Q.

$$\Delta y = y_2 - y_1$$

- The change in x is the difference of the x-coordinates of P and Q.

$$\Delta x = x_2 - x_1$$

Consequently, slope is defined as follows.

Slope of a Line

If (x_1, y_1) and (x_2, y_2) are points with $x_1 \neq x_2$, then the *slope* of the line through these points is the ratio

$$\frac{\text{change in } y}{\text{change in } x} = \frac{\Delta y}{\Delta x} = \frac{y_2 - y_1}{x_2 - x_1}$$

Example 1 Finding Slope Given Two Points

Find the slope of the line that passes through $(0, -1)$ and $(4, 1)$. See Figure 1.4-4.

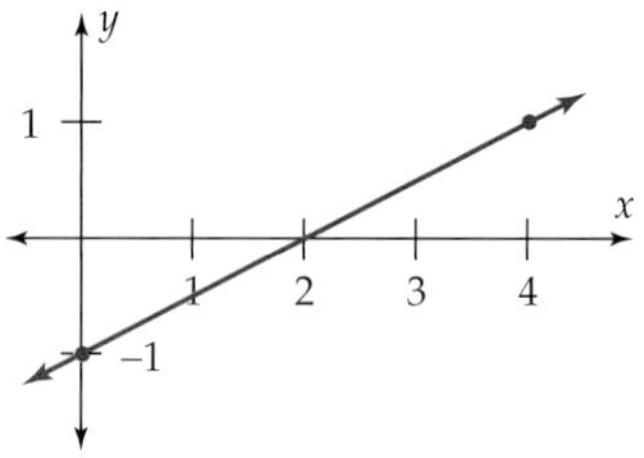

Solution

Apply the formula in the previous box with $x_1 = 0, y_1 = -1$ and $x_2 = 4, y_2 = 1$.

$$\text{Slope} = \frac{y_2 - y_1}{x_2 - x_1} = \frac{1 - (-1)}{4 - 0} = \frac{2}{4} = \frac{1}{2}$$

Figure 1.4-4

The order of the points makes no difference; if you use $(4, 1)$ for (x_1, y_1) and $(0, -1)$ for (x_2, y_2) in Example 1, the result is the same.

Example 2 Finding Slope From a Graph

Find the slope of each line shown in Figure 1.4-5. The lines shown are determined by the following points:

L_1: $(0, 2)$ and $(-1, -1)$ L_2: $(0, 2)$ and $(2, 4)$ L_3: $(-6, 2)$ and $(3, 2)$
L_4: $(-3, 5)$ and $(3, -1)$ L_5: $(1, 0)$ and $(2, -2)$

CAUTION

When finding slopes, you must subtract the y-coordinates and the x-coordinates in the same order. With the points $(3, 4)$ and $(1, 8)$, for instance, if you use $8 - 4$ in the numerator, you must write $1 - 3$ in the denominator, *not* $3 - 1$.

Solution

The slopes are as follows.

L_1: $\dfrac{2 - (-1)}{0 - (-1)} = \dfrac{3}{1} = 3$

L_2: $\dfrac{4 - 2}{2 - 0} = \dfrac{2}{2} = 1$

L_3: $\dfrac{2 - 2}{3 - (-6)} = \dfrac{0}{9} = 0$

L_4: $\dfrac{-1 - 5}{3 - (-3)} = \dfrac{-6}{6} = -1$

L_5: $\dfrac{-2 - 0}{2 - 1} = \dfrac{-2}{1} = -2$

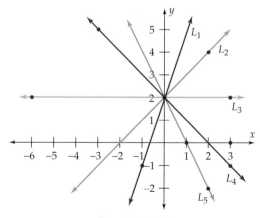

Figure 1.4-5

Example 2, page 32, illustrates how the slope measures the steepness of the line, summarized as follows. The lines referenced refer to Figure 1.4-5.

Properties of Slope

The slope of a nonvertical line is a number m that measures how steeply the line rises or falls.

- **If $m > 0$, the line rises from left to right; the larger m is, the more steeply the line rises. [*Lines L_1 and L_2*]**
- **If $m = 0$, the line is horizontal. [*Line L_3*]**
- **If $m < 0$, the line falls from left to right; the larger $|m|$ is, the more steeply the line falls. [*Lines L_4 and L_5*]**

Slope-Intercept Form

A nonvertical line intersects the y-axis at a point with coordinates $(0, b)$, because every point on the y-axis has first coordinate 0. The number b is called the y-intercept of the line. For example, the line in Figure 1.4-4 has y-intercept -1 because it crosses the y-axis at $(0, -1)$.

Let L be a nonvertical line with slope m and y-intercept b. Therefore, $(0, b)$ is a point on L. Let (x, y) be any other point on L, as shown in Figure 1.4-6. Use the points $(0, b)$ and (x, y) to compute the slope of L.

$$m = \frac{y - b}{x - 0} = \frac{y - b}{x}$$

Multiply both sides of the equation by x, and solve for y.

$$mx = y - b$$
$$y = mx + b$$

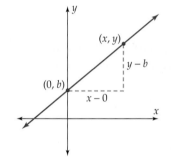

Figure 1.4-6

Thus, the coordinates of any point on L satisfy the equation $y = mx + b$, which leads to the following.

Slope-Intercept Form

The line with slope m and y-intercept b is the graph of the equation

$$y = mx + b.$$

Did you notice, as you recall your work with arithmetic sequences, that the explicit form of the sequence looks very similar to $y = mx + b$?

Example 3   Graphs of Arithmetic Sequences and Lines

The first three terms of an arithmetic sequence are $-2, 3$, and 8. Use the explicit form of the sequence to express the nth term, and compare it to the slope-intercept form of the equation of a line that passes through the points on the graph of the sequence. Graph both the sequence and the corresponding line on the same set of axes.

Solution

The common difference for the sequence is 5 and $u_1 = -2$. Therefore, the explicit form is

$$u_n = u_1 + (n - 1)d$$
$$= -2 + (n - 1)5$$
$$= -2 + 5n - 5$$
$$= 5n - 7$$

The last equation, $u_n = 5n - 7$, has the form $y = mx + b$, where

$$m = d = 5 \qquad b = u_0 = u_1 - d = -7 \qquad \text{and} \qquad x \text{ corresponds to } n.$$

Figure 1.4-7 shows graphs of the sequence and the line. ∎

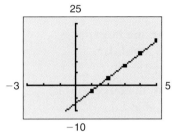

25

−3   5

−10

Figure 1.4-7

Below is an important summary connecting the explicit form of an arithmetic sequence to the slope-intercept form of a line.

Connection between Arithmetic Sequences and Lines

The connection between the explicit form of an arithmetic sequence, $u_n = u_1 + (n - 1)d$, and the slope-intercept form of a line, $y = mx + b$, is as follows.

- **The slope of the line corresponds to the common difference of the sequence, $m = d$.**

- **The y-intercept represents the value of the first term of the sequence minus the difference, $b = u_1 - d$.**

A linear equation expressed in slope-intercept form defines a relation for all the ordered pairs (x, y) on the line. The equation represents the rule and each x represents an input. For every input x there is one and only one output y, so y is a function of x. The graph of a linear function f is the graph of $y = f(x) = mx + b$.

Most graphing calculators are called *function graphers* because they graph a relation only if it can be expressed as a function $y = f(x)$. Thus, slope-intercept form is useful for graphing a line both on paper and with a graphing calculator.

Example 4   Graphing a Line

Sketch the graph of $2y - 5x = 2$, and confirm your sketch with a graphing calculator.

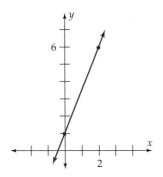

Figure 1.4-8a

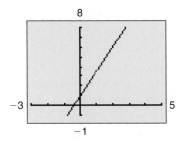

Figure 1.4-8b

Solution

Begin by solving the equation for y.

$$2y - 5x = 2$$
$$2y = 5x + 2$$
$$y = f(x) = \frac{5}{2}x + 1$$

Therefore, the graph is a line with slope $\frac{5}{2}$, the coefficient of x, and y-intercept 1, the constant term. Because the y-intercept is 1, the point $(0, 1)$ is on the line. When $x = 2$, then $f(2) = \frac{5}{2}(2) + 1 = 6$, so $(2, 6)$ is also on the line. Plotting and connecting the points $(0, 1)$ and $(2, 6)$ produces the line in Figure 1.4-8a. Figure 1.4-8b displays the same graph produced by a graphing calculator.

■

Example 5 Linear Depreciation

An office buys a new computer system for $7000. Five years later its value is $800. Assume that the system depreciates linearly.

a. Write the equation that represents value as a function of years.

b. Find its value two years after it was purchased, that is, the y-value when $x = 2$.

c. Graph the equation.

d. Find how many years before the system is worthless, that is, the x-value that corresponds to a y-value of 0.

Solution

a. Linear depreciation means that the equation that gives the value y of the computer system in year x has the form $y = mx + b$ for some constants m and b. Because the system is worth $7000 new (when $x = 0$) the y-intercept is 7000 and the equation can be written as

$$y = mx + b$$
$$y = mx + 7000$$

Because the system is worth $800 after 5 years (i.e., $y = 800$ when $x = 5$),

$$y = mx + 7000$$
$$800 = m \cdot 5 + 7000$$
$$-6200 = 5m$$
$$m = \frac{-6200}{5} = -1240$$

The depreciation equation is $y = -1240x + 7000$, where y represents the value of the system after x years.

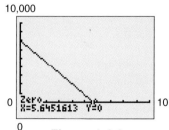

Figure 1.4-9

b. The value of the system after two years ($x = 2$) is

$$y = -1240(2) + 7000$$
$$= \$4520.$$

c. The graph of $y = -1240x + 7000$ is shown in Figure 1.4-9. Notice that the slope of the line, -1240, represents the depreciation of the system per year. That is, the value of the system decreases \$1240 each year.

d. The trace feature or the zero feature of a graphing calculator shows that the x-value corresponding to $y = 0$ is $x \approx 5.6$, as shown in Figure 1.4-9. That is, the system will be worthless in 5 years and $0.6 \cdot 12 \approx 7.2$ months. ∎

The Point-Slope Form

Suppose the line L passes through the point (x_1, y_1) and has slope m. Let (x, y) be any other point on L. Use the fixed point (x_1, y_1) and the variable point (x, y) to compute the slope m of L, and it will generate another useful form of a line called the **point-slope form.** For $x \neq x_1$,

$$\frac{y - y_1}{x - x_1} = m \qquad \textit{slope of L}$$

$$y - y_1 = m(x - x_1)$$

Thus, the coordinates of every point on L satisfy the equation

$$y - y_1 = m(x - x_1).$$

Point-Slope Form

> The line with slope m through the point (x_1, y_1) is the graph of the equation
>
> $$y - y_1 = m(x - x_1).$$

There are two interesting observations about point-slope form.

1. Although slope-intercept form and point-slope form can be used to write the equation of a line, the point-slope form is easier to use, unless you know the y-intercept.

2. The point-slope form can also be used to graph a line because any point of the line can be used as the initial point and the remaining points can be found by using the equation's slope. The slope determines how to find a second point from the initial point by moving vertically an amount equal to the numerator of the slope, which represents Δy, and then moving horizontally an amount equal to the denominator of the slope, which represents Δx.

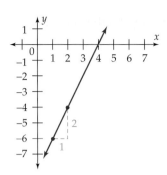

Figure 1.4-10

Example 6 Point-Slope Form of a Line

Sketch the graph and find the equation of the line that passes through the point $(1, -6)$ with slope 2. Write the equation in slope-intercept form.

Solution

To graph the line, start at the point $(1, -6)$ and identify another point on the line by moving 2 units vertically and 1 unit horizontally. The point $(2, -4)$ is also on the line. Because a unique line is determined by two points, connecting the points $(1, -6)$ and $(2, -4)$ produces the line, as shown in Figure 1.4-10.

To find the equation of the line, substitute 2 for m and $(1, -6)$ for (x_1, y_1) in the point-slope equation.

$$y - y_1 = m(x - x_1)$$
$$y - (-6) = 2(x - 1) \qquad \textit{Point-slope form}$$
$$y + 6 = 2x - 2$$
$$y = 2x - 8 \qquad \textit{Slope-intercept form}$$

Vertical and Horizontal Lines

When a line has 0 slope, it is called a **horizontal line,** and it can be written as $y = 0x + b = b$.

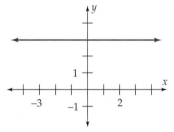

Figure 1.4-11

Example 7 Equation of a Horizontal Line

Describe and sketch the graph of the equation $y = 3$.

Solution

Because $y = 3$ can be written as $y = 0x + 3$, its graph is a line with slope 0 and y-intercept 3. This is sufficient information to obtain the graph shown in Figure 1.4-11.

Vertical Lines

The preceding discussion does not apply to vertical lines, whose equations have a different form than those examined earlier because a vertical line is not a function.

Example 8 Equation of a Vertical Line

Find the equation of the vertical line shown in Figure 1.4-12.

Solution

Every point on the vertical line in Figure 1.4-12 has first coordinate 2. Thus, every point on the line satisfies $x + 0y = 2$, and the line is the graph

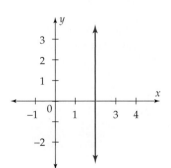

Figure 1.4-12

of the equation $x = 2$. If you try to compute the slope of the line, say using (2, 1) and (2, 4), you obtain $\frac{4-1}{2-2} = \frac{3}{0}$, which is not defined. ∎

Parallel and Perpendicular Lines

The slope of a line measures how steeply it rises or falls. Because parallel lines rise or fall equally steeply, their slopes are the same.

Two lines that meet in a right angle, that is, a 90° angle, are said to be **perpendicular.** There is a close relationship between the slopes of two perpendicular lines.

Parallel and Perpendicular Lines

Two nonvertical lines are parallel when they have exactly the same slope.

Two nonvertical lines are perpendicular when the product of their slopes is **−1**.

Example 9   Parallel and Perpendicular Lines

Given the line M whose equation is $3x - 2y + 6 = 0$, find the equation of the lines through the point $(2, -1)$

a. parallel to M.
b. perpendicular to M.

Solution

First find the slope of M by rewriting its equation in slope-intercept form.

$$3x - 2y + 6 = 0$$
$$-2y = -3x - 6$$
$$y = \frac{3}{2}x + 3$$

Therefore, M has slope $\frac{3}{2}$.

a. The line parallel to M must have the same slope, and because $(2, -1)$ is on the parallel line, use the point-slope form to find its equation.

$$y - y_1 = m(x - x_1)$$
$$y - (-1) = \frac{3}{2}(x - 2)$$
$$y + 1 = \frac{3}{2}x - 3$$
$$y = \frac{3}{2}x - 4$$

b. The line perpendicular to M must have slope $-\dfrac{1}{\frac{3}{2}} = -\dfrac{2}{3}$. Use point-slope form again to find the equation of the line perpendicular to M through $(2, -1)$.

$$y - (-1) = -\frac{2}{3}(x - 2)$$

$$y + 1 = -\frac{2}{3}x + \frac{4}{3}$$

$$y = -\frac{2}{3}x + \frac{1}{3}$$

Standard Form of a Line

The *standard form of a line* is

$$Ax + By = C,$$

where A, B, and C are integers, $A \geq 0$, and A and B are not both 0.

NOTE The standard form of a line is sometimes called the *general form* of a line and may also be written as $Ax + By + C = 0$.

Any line, including vertical lines, can be written in this form. The last equation shown in Example 9, for the perpendicular line, $y = -\frac{2}{3}x + \frac{1}{3}$, can be written in standard form by multiplying both sides by 3, the least common denominator of all the terms, and then adding $2x$ to both sides. The resulting equation is $2x + 3y = 1$.

The following box summarizes the different forms of the equation of a line and when each form is best used.

Forms of Linear Equations

The forms of the equation of a line are

$Ax + By = C$	*standard* form	
$y = mx + b$	*slope-intercept* form	Graphing
$y - y_0 = m(x - x_0)$	*point-slope* form	Write equations

A horizontal line has slope 0 and an equation of the form $y = b$.

A vertical line has undefined slope and an equation of the form $x = c$.

Exercises 1.4

1. For which of the line segments in the figure is the slope
   a. largest?
   b. smallest?
   c. largest in absolute value?
   d. closest to zero?

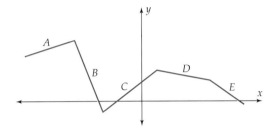

2. The doorsill of a campus building is 5 ft above ground level. To allow wheelchair access, the steps in front of the door are to be replaced by a straight ramp with constant slope $\frac{1}{12}$, as shown in the figure. How long must the ramp be? [The answer is not 60 ft.]

In Exercises 3–6, find the slope and y-intercept of the line whose equation is given.

3. $2x - y + 5 = 0$ 4. $3x + 4y = 7$

5. $3(x - 2) + y = 7 - 6(y + 4)$

6. $2(y - 3) + (x - 6) = 4(x + 1) - 2$

In Exercises 7–10, find the slope of the line through the given points.

7. $(1, 2); (3, 7)$ 8. $(-1, -2); (2, -1)$

9. $\left(\frac{1}{4}, 0\right); \left(\frac{3}{4}, 2\right)$ 10. $(\sqrt{2}, -1); (2, -9)$

In Exercises 11–14, find a number t such that the line passing through the two given points has slope -2.

11. $(0, t); (9, 4)$ 12. $(1, t); (-3, 5)$

13. $(t + 1, 5); (6, -3t + 7)$ 14. $(t, t); (5, 9)$

15. Let L be a nonvertical straight line through the origin. L intersects the vertical line through $(1, 0)$ at a point P. Show that the second coordinate of P is the slope of L.

16. On one graph, sketch five line segments, not all meeting at a single point, whose slopes are five different positive numbers.

In Exercises 17–20, find the equation of the line with slope m that passes through the given point.

17. $m = 1; (3, 5)$ 18. $m = 2; (-2, 1)$

19. $m = -1; (6, 2)$ 20. $m = 0; (-4, -5)$

In Exercises 21–24, find the equation of the line through the given points.

21. $(0, -5)$ and $(-3, -2)$ 22. $(4, 3)$ and $(2, -1)$

23. $\left(\frac{4}{3}, \frac{2}{3}\right)$ and $\left(\frac{1}{3}, 3\right)$ 24. $(6, 7)$ and $(6, 15)$

In Exercises 25–28, determine whether the line through P and Q is parallel or perpendicular to the line through R and S, or neither.

25. $P = (2, 5), Q = (-1, -1)$ and $R = (4, 2), S = (6, 1)$

26. $P = \left(0, \frac{3}{2}\right), Q = (1, 1)$ and $R = (2, 7), S = (3, 9)$

27. $P = \left(-3, \frac{1}{3}\right), Q = (1, -1)$ and $R = (2, 0),$
    $S = \left(4, -\frac{2}{3}\right)$

28. $P = (3, 3), Q = (-3, -1)$ and
    $R = (2, -2), S = (4, -5)$

In Exercises 29–31, determine whether the lines whose equations are given are parallel, perpendicular, or neither.

29. $2x + y - 2 = 0$ and $4x + 2y + 18 = 0$

30. $3x + y - 3 = 0$ and $6x + 2y + 17 = 0$

31. $y = 2x + 4$ and $0.5x + y = -3$

32. Use slopes to show that the points $(-4, 6), (-1, 12)$, and $(-7, 0)$ all lie on the same straight line.

33. Use slopes to determine if $(9, 6), (-1, 2)$, and $(1, -3)$ are the vertices of a right triangle.

34. Use slopes to show that the points $(-5, -2) (-3, 1), (3, 0)$, and $(5, 3)$ are the vertices of a parallelogram.

In Exercises 35–42, find an equation for the line satisfying the given conditions.

35. through $(-2, 1)$ with slope 3

36. y-intercept -7 and slope 1

37. through $(2, 3)$ and parallel to $3x - 2y = 5$

38. through $(1, -2)$ and perpendicular to $y = 2x - 3$

39. x-intercept 5 and y-intercept -5

40. through $(-5, 2)$ and parallel to the line through $(1, 2)$ and $(4, 3)$

41. through $(-1, 3)$ and perpendicular to the line through $(0, 1)$ and $(2, 3)$

42. y-intercept 3 and perpendicular to $2x - y + 6 = 0$

43. Find a real number k such that $(3, -2)$ is on the line $kx - 2y + 7 = 0$.

44. Find a real number k such that the line $3x - ky + 2 = 0$ has y-intercept -3.

45. Write the equation for the given arithmetic sequence in slope-intercept form.

1	2	3	4	5
-2	2	6	10	14

46. Write the equation for the given arithmetic sequence in slope-intercept form.

1	2	3	4	5
10	7	4	1	-2

47. The first three terms of an arithmetic sequence are 7, 1, and -5. Write the sequence's equation in slope-intercept form.

48. For a given arithmetic sequence, the common difference is -3 and $u_1 = 6$. Find the slope and y-intercept of the graph of this sequence.

49. For a given arithmetic sequence, the common difference is 8 and $u_1 = -2$. Find the slope and y-intercept of the graph of this sequence.

50. Let L be a line that is neither vertical nor horizontal and which does not pass through the origin. Show that L is the graph of $\frac{x}{a} + \frac{y}{b} = 1$, where a is the x-intercept and b is the y-intercept of L.

51. Let A, B, C, and D be nonzero real numbers. Show that the lines $Ax + By + C = 0$ and $Ax + By + D = 0$ are parallel.

52. Sales of a software company increased linearly from \$120,000 in 1996 to \$180,000 in 1999
   a. Find an equation that expresses the sales y in year x (where $x = 0$ corresponds to 1996).
   b. Estimate the sales in 2001.

53. The poverty level income for a family of four was \$9287 in 1981. Due to inflation and other factors, the poverty level income rose to approximately \$18,267 in 2001. (Source: U.S. Census Bureau)
   a. Find a linear equation that approximates the poverty level income y in year x (with $x = 0$ corresponding to 1981).
   b. Use the equation of part **a** to estimate the poverty level income in 1990 and 2005.

54. At sea level, water boils at 212° F. At a height of 1100 ft, water boils at 210° F. The relationship between boiling point and height is linear.
   a. Find an equation that gives the boiling point y of water at a height of x feet.

   Find the boiling point of water in each of the following cities (whose altitudes are given).

   b. Cincinnati, OH (550 ft)
   c. Springfield, MO (1300 ft)
   d. Billings, MT (3120 ft)
   e. Flagstaff, AZ (6900 ft)

55. A small plane costs $600,000 new. Ten years later, it is valued at $150,000. Assuming linear depreciation, find the value of the plane when it is 5 years old and when it is 12 years old.

56. In 1950, the age-adjusted death rate from heart disease was about 307.2 per 100,000 people. In 1998, the rate had decreased to 126.6 per 100,000.
   a. Assuming the rate decreased linearly, find an equation that gives the number y of deaths per 100,000 from heart disease in year x, with $x = 0$ corresponding to 1950. Round the slope of the line to one decimal place.
   b. Use the equation in part **a** to estimate the death rate in 1995 and in 2005.

57. According to the Center of Science in the Public Interest, the maximum healthy weight for a person who is 5 ft 5 in. tall is 150 pounds and for someone 6 ft 3 in. tall is 200 pounds. The relationship between weight and height here is linear.
   a. Find a linear equation that gives the maximum healthy weight y for a person whose height is x inches over 5 ft 5 in. ($x = 0$ corresponds to 5 ft 5 in., $x = 2$ to 5 ft 7 in., etc.).
   b. Use the equation of part **a** to estimate the maximum healthy weight for a person whose height is 5 ft and for a person whose height is 6 ft.

58. The profit p (in thousands of dollars) on x thousand units of a specialty item is $p = 0.6x - 14.5$. The cost c of manufacturing x items is given by $c = 0.8x + 14.5$.
   a. Find an equation that gives the revenue r from selling x items.
   b. How many items must be sold for the company to break even (i.e., for revenue to equal cost)?

59. A publisher has fixed costs of $110,000 for a mathematics text. The variable costs are $50 per book. The book sells for $72. Find equations that give the required information.
   a. the cost c of making x books
   b. the revenue r from selling x books
   c. the profit p from selling x books
   d. the publisher's break-even point (see Exercise 58**b**)

60. If the fixed costs of a manufacturer are $1000 and it costs $2000 to produce 40 items, find a linear equation that gives the total cost of making x items.

61. A hat company has fixed costs of $50,000 and variable costs of $8.50 per hat.
   a. Find an equation that gives the total cost y of producing x hats.
   b. What is the average cost per hat when 20,000 are made? 50,000? 100,000?

Use the graph and the following information for Exercises 62–64. Rocky is an "independent" ticket dealer who markets choice tickets for Los Angeles Lakers home games (California currently has no laws against scalping). Each graph shows how many tickets will be demanded by buyers at a particular price. For instance, when the Lakers play the Chicago Bulls, the graph shows that at a price of $160, no tickets are demanded. As the price (y-coordinate) gets lower, the number of tickets demanded (x-coordinate) increases.

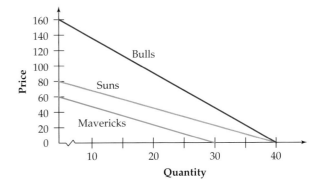

62. Write a linear equation expressing the quantity x of tickets demanded at price y when the Lakers play the indicated team.
   a. Dallas Mavericks
   b. Phoenix Suns
   c. Chicago Bulls
   Hint: In each case, use the points where the graph crosses the two axes to determine its slope.

63. Use the equations from Exercise 62 to find the number of tickets Rocky would sell at a price of $40 for a game against the indicated team.
   a. Mavericks   **b.** Bulls

64. Suppose Rocky has 20 tickets to sell. At what price could he sell them all when the Lakers play the indicated team.
   a. Mavericks   **b.** Suns

1.5 Linear Models

Objectives

- Algebraically fit a linear model
- Calculate finite differences and use residuals to determine the model of best fit
- Use a calculator to determine a linear model
- Find and interpret the correlation coefficient for a model
- Create and interpret a residual plot for a linear model

People working in business, medicine, agriculture, and other fields frequently want to know the relationship between two quantities. For instance,

How does money spent on advertising affect sales?

What effect does a fertilizer have on crop yield?

How much do large doses of certain vitamins lengthen life expectancy?

In many such situations there is sufficient data available to construct a **mathematical model,** such as an equation or graph, which demonstrates the desired relationship or predicts the likely outcome in cases not included in the data. In this section applications are considered in which the data can be modeled by a linear equation. More complicated models will be considered in later sections.

When you are given a set of data points, you should first determine whether a straight line would be a good model for the data. This can be done graphically by making a scatter plot of the data, as shown in Figures 1.5-1a and 1.5-1b. Visual inspection suggests that the data points in Figure 1.5-1a are approximately linear but that those in Figure 1.5-1b are not. So a line would be a good model for the data points in Figure 1.5-1a, but for those in Figure 1.5-1b a line is not a good model.

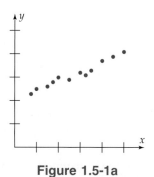

Figure 1.5-1a

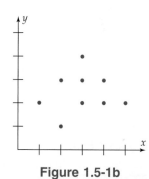

Figure 1.5-1b

You can also determine whether a line is a good model for a given set of data points, without graphing, by using **finite differences.** To understand the idea, consider the equation $y = 3x - 1$, whose graph is known to be a line. Consider the table of values shown on the next page and look at the difference between each y-entry and the preceding one.

The differences are the same; all of them are equal to the slope of the line $y = 3x - 1$. This fact suggests that if the successive differences of the y-coordinates of the data points are approximately equal, then a line should be a good model for the data.

x	$y = 3x - 1$	Difference
1	2	
2	5	$5 - 2 = 3$
3	8	$8 - 5 = 3$
4	11	$11 - 8 = 3$
5	14	$14 - 11 = 3$

Example 1   Linear Data

Estimated cash flows from a company over the five-year period 1988–1992 are shown in the table.

Year	1988	1989	1990	1991	1992
Cash flow per share ($)	2.38	2.79	3.23	3.64	4.06

Determine whether a line would be a good model for this data. Use two different methods.

a. Calculate the finite differences for the data points.

b. Draw a scatter plot of the data.

Solution

a. Subtract each cash flow from the preceding one and record the difference, as shown in Figure 1.5-2a.

Because the differences are approximately equal, a line is a good model for this data.

b. Let $x = 0$ correspond to 1988. The scatter plot for the data points is shown in Figure 1.5-2b, where the points appear to be linear. Therefore, a line is a reasonable model.

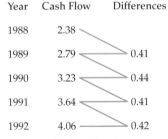

Year	Cash Flow	Differences
1988	2.38	
1989	2.79	0.41
1990	3.23	0.44
1991	3.64	0.41
1992	4.06	0.42

Figure 1.5-2a

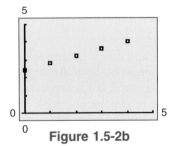

Figure 1.5-2b

Once it has been determined that a line would be a good model for a set of data points, there are several ways to determine an appropriate model. The simplest way is to choose two of the data points and find the equation of the line that includes the points. This may require some experimenting to see which two points appear to produce a line that fits the data well. The number of data points above the line should balance with the number of data points below the line. Of course, there are many choices of two points and many possible lines that model the data. So there must be some way of determining which line fits the data best.

Modeling Terminology

Suppose (x, r) is a data point and that the corresponding point on the model is (x, y). Then the difference $r - y$ is called a **residual.** Residuals are a measure of the error between the actual value of the data, r, and the value y given by the model. Graphically, the residual is the vertical distance between the data point (x, r) and the model point (x, y), as shown in Figure 1.5-3.

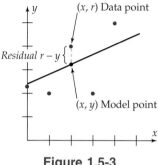

Figure 1.5-3

The residual represents a directed distance that is positive when the data point is above the model point and negative when the data point is below the model point. When the sum of the residuals is 0, which indicates that the positive and negative errors cancel out each other, the model is probably a reasonable one. However, this is not always enough to determine which of several models is best because their residuals may all have the same sum.

Consequently, to find which model among several fits the data best, use the sum of the *squares* of the residuals because this sum has no negative terms and no canceling. Using the sum of the squares as a measure of accuracy has the effect of emphasizing large errors, those with absolute value greater than 1, because the square is greater than the residual. It minimizes small errors, those with absolute value less than 1, because the square is less than the residual.

Example 2   **Modeling Data**

The data below shows the weekly amount spent on advertising and the weekly sales revenue of a small store over a seven-week period.

Advertising Expenditure x (in hundreds of dollars)	0	1	2	3	4	5	6
Sales revenue (in thousands of dollars)	1	2	2	3	3	5	5

Find two models for the data, each determined by a pair of data points. Then use residuals to see which model best fits the data.

Solution

Let the two models be denoted as A and B. For Model A, use the points (1, 2) and (3, 3). The slope of the line through these points is

$$m = \frac{3 - 2}{3 - 1} = \frac{1}{2} = 0.5$$

The equation of the line through (1, 2) and (3, 3) is

$$y - 2 = 0.5(x - 1)$$
$$y = 0.5x + 1.5$$

Model A is shown in Figure 1.5-4 and its residuals are shown in the table below. Notice that the sum of the squared residuals is 2.

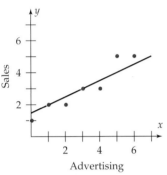

Figure 1.5-4

Data point (x, r)	Model point (x, y)	Residual r − y	Squared residual (r − y)²
(0, 1)	(0, 1.5)	−0.5	0.25
(1, 2)	(1, 2)	0	0
(2, 2)	(2, 2.5)	−0.5	0.25
(3, 3)	(3, 3)	0	0
(4, 3)	(4, 3.5)	−0.5	0.25
(5, 5)	(5, 4)	1	1
(6, 5)	(6, 4.5)	0.5	0.25
		Sum	**2.00**

For Model B, use the point (1, 2) and (6, 5). The slope of the line through these points is $\frac{5 - 2}{6 - 1} = \frac{3}{5} = 0.6$ and its equation is

$$y - 2 = 0.6(x - 1) \quad \text{or} \quad y = 0.6x + 1.4$$

Figure 1.5-5 shows the graph of Model B and the table below shows its residuals. The sum of the squared residuals is 1.56.

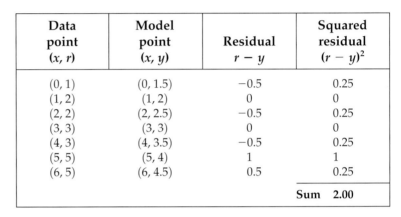

Figure 1.5-5

Data point (x, r)	Model point (x, y)	Residual r − y	Squared residual (r − y)²
(0, 1)	(0, 1.4)	−0.4	0.16
(1, 2)	(1, 2)	0	0
(2, 2)	(2, 2.6)	−0.6	0.36
(3, 3)	(3, 3.2)	−0.2	.04
(4, 3)	(4, 3.8)	−0.8	0.64
(5, 5)	(5, 4.4)	0.6	0.36
(6, 5)	(6, 5)	0	0
		Sums −1.4	**1.56**

Because this sum is smaller that the sum for Model A, conclude that Model B is the better of the two models.

NOTE If needed, review how to compute linear regression equations in the Technology Appendix.

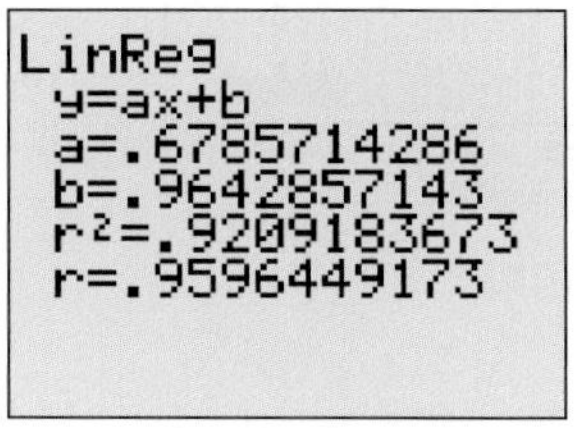

```
LinReg
 y=ax+b
 a=.6785714286
 b=.9642857143
 r²=.9209183673
 r=.9596449173
```

Figure 1.5-6

Least–Squares Regression Lines

It can be proved that for any set of data there is one and only one line for which the sum of the squares of the residuals is as small as possible. Such a line is called the **least–squares regression line,** and the computational process for finding it is called **linear regression.** Most graphing calculators have the linear regression process built-in. For example, Figure 1.5-6 shows the approximate least–squares regression line for the data in Example 2.

$$y = 0.679x + 0.964$$

The sum of the squared residuals for this model is approximately 1.107, slightly less than the corresponding sum for Model B in Example 2.

The number r in Figure 1.5-6, which is called the **correlation coefficient,** is a statistical measure of how well the least–squares regression line fits the data points. The value of r is always between -1 and 1, the closer the absolute value of r is to 1, the better the fit. When $|r| = 1$, the fit is perfect: all the data points are on the regression line. Conversely, a correlation coefficient near 0 indicates a poor fit.

r^2 is called the **coefficient of determination.** It is the proportion of variation in y that can be attributed to a linear relationship between x and y in the data.

Example 3   **Modeling Data**

A circle can be circumscribed around any regular polygon. The lengths of the radii of the circumscribed circles around regular polygons whose sides have length of one unit are given as follows.

Number of sides	3	4	5	6	7	8	9
Radius	0.577	0.707	0.851	1.00	1.152	1.306	1.462

a. Draw a scatterplot.

b. Calculate the finite differences for the data points.

c. Find the model that best fits the data using the regression feature on a calculator.

d. What does the correlation coefficient indicate about the data?

Technology Tip

Many calculators have a ΔList command that can be entered into the label cell of a list. This will automatically calculate the differences between the items of the list specified. For example, ΔList(L2) produces a list of differences between the items of list L2.

Solution

a. A scatter plot of the data is shown in Figure 1.5-7a.

b. Subtract each radius from the preceding one and record the differences in a list. Notice that the differences are approximately equal, as shown in Figure 1.5-7b.

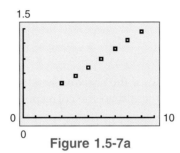

Figure 1.5-7a

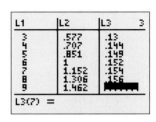

Figure 1.5-7b

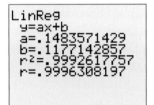

Figure 1.5-7c

c. Use the linear regression feature to obtain Figure 1.5-7c, which shows that the least–squares regression line is approximately $y = 0.15x + 0.12$.

d. The correlation coefficient, $r = 0.9996308197$, is very close to 1, which indicates that this linear model is a very good fit for the data.

Although only linear models are constructed in this section, you should always allow for the possibility that a linear model may not be the best choice for certain data. The least–squares regression line may give a reasonable model, which is the *line* that fits the data best, but there may be a nonlinear equation that is an even better model for the data. Polynomial models, for example, are presented in Chapter 4.

In addition to finding finite differences and a scatter plot of the data, another way to check that a linear model is appropriate is to construct a scatter plot of the residuals. In other words, plot the points $(x, r - y)$, where (x, r) is a data point and (x, y) is the corresponding point on the model. The general rule is two fold:

Use a linear model when the scatter plot of the residuals shows no obvious pattern, as shown in Figure 1.5-8.

Use a nonlinear model when the scatter plot of the residuals has a pattern, as shown in Figure 1.5-9.

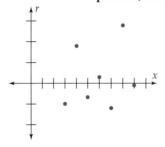

Figure 1.5-8

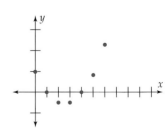

Figure 1.5-9

Technology Tip

The regression equation is stored in a variable that is usually called RegEQ each time the regression coefficients are calculated. The residuals are stored in a variable called RESID each time a regression is performed. See the Technology Appendix for specific instructions for graphing a regression line and residuals.

Example 4   **Linear Regression and Residuals**

A local resident owns an espresso cart and has asked you to provide an analysis based on last summer's data. To simplify things, only data for Mondays is provided. The data includes the amount the workers were paid each day, the number of cups sold, the cost of materials, and the total revenue for the day. The owner also must spend $40 each operating day on rent for her location and payment toward a business loan. Sales taxes have been removed from the data, so you need not consider them, and amounts have been rounded to the nearest dollar.

Date	Salaries ($)	Cups sold	Material cost ($)	Total revenue ($)
June 02	68	112	55	202
June 09	60	88	42	119
June 16	66	81	33	125
June 23	63	112	49	188
June 30	63	87	38	147
July 07	59	105	45	159
July 14	57	116	49	165
July 21	61	122	52	178
July 28	64	100	48	193
August 04	58	80	36	112
August 11	65	96	42	158
August 18	57	108	52	162
August 25	64	93	47	166

a. Find a linear regression model for the daily revenue as a function of the number of cups sold.

b. Use a scatter plot of the residuals to determine if the linear model is a good fit for revenue.

c. Find a linear regression model for the daily cost as a function of the number of cups sold. Be sure to include the pay for the workers, the fixed daily cost, and the cost of the material.

d. Draw a scatter plot of the residuals to determine if the proposed model is a good fit for cost.

e. Find the break-even point, that is, when revenue is equal to cost.

Solution

a. Enter two lists in your calculator, using the column labeled "Cups Sold" and "Total Revenue" in the chart. That is, the data points are (112, 202), (88, 119), and so on. Next, use the linear regression function on these lists to approximate the least–squares regression line.

$$y = 1.586x + 0.895$$

Store its equation as y_1 in the equation memory, as shown in Figure 1.5-10a and 1.5-10b.

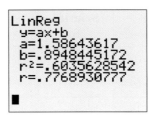

| Figure 1.5-10a | Figure 1.5-10b |

b. To obtain a scatter plot of the residuals for the least squares regression line for revenue, plot the points whose first coordinates are given by the CUPS list and whose second coordinates are given by the RESID, the variable that holds the residuals each time a regression is performed.

Technology Tip

Placing **RESID** into Ylist will use the last computed regression's residual values in a scatter plot.

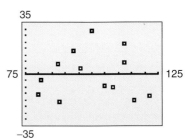

| Figure 1.5-11a | Figure 1.5-11b |

c. First, create a new list that shows the total cost each day. For June 2,

Salaries + Material Cost + Rent/Loan Costs = Daily Cost

$68   + $55   + $40   = $163

Compute the total daily cost for each date, as shown in Figure 1.5-12a, where the salaries list is called PAY, the materials cost list is called COST, and TOTCO is the total daily cost list.

To find a model for the total daily cost as a function of cups sold, use the data points given by the lists CUPS and TOTCO with the regression feature. Find the closest approximate least–squares regression line.

$$y = 0.395x + 107.659$$

Figure 1.5-12a

Technology Tip

A formula can be placed in the upper cell of a list to perform the operation on all the elements of the list.

Store this equation as y_2 in the equation memory, as shown in Figure 1.5-12b.

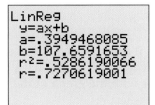
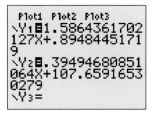

Figure 1.5-12b

d. Use the same procedure as in part **b** to obtain the scatter plot of the residuals for cost shown in Figure 1.5-12c. It shows no obvious pattern, which again indicates that a linear model is a good choice for this data.

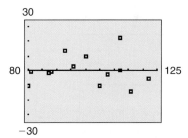

Figure 1.5-12c

e. The break-even point occurs when revenue is equal to cost. Plot the revenue equation found in part **a** and the cost equation found in part **c** on the same screen, and find the x-coordinate of their intersection (shown in Figure 1.5-13). Since 89.6 cups cannot be sold, 90 cups a day must be sold to break even. ∎

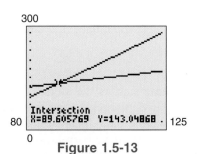

Figure 1.5-13

Example 5   **Prediction from a Model**

The total number of farm workers (in millions) in selected years is shown in the following table.

Year	Workers	Year	Workers	Year	Workers
1900	29.030	1950	59.230	1985	106.210
1920	42.206	1960	67.990	1990	117.490
1930	48.686	1970	79.802	1994	120.380
1940	51.742	1980	105.060		

a. Use linear regression to find an equation that models the data. Use the equation to estimate the number of farm workers in 1975 and in 2000.

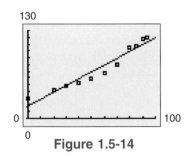

Figure 1.5-14

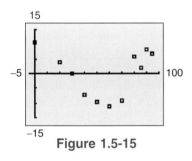

Figure 1.5-15

b. According to the model, when will the number of workers be 150 million?

c. Is a line the best model for the data?

Solution

Let $x = 0$ correspond to 1900 and enter the data into two lists. Perform linear regression on the data, and display the scatter plot of the data together with the graph of the least–squares regression line.

$$y \approx 1.0116x + 18.3315$$

As suggested by Figure 1.5-14, the regression line provides a reasonable model for approximating the number of farm workers in a given year.

a. If $x = 75$, then $y \approx 1.0116(75) + 18.3315 = 94.202$.
If $x = 100$, then $y \approx 1.0116(100) + 18.3315 = 119.492$.

Therefore, there were approximately 94,202,000 farm workers in 1975 and 119,492,000 in 2000.

b. To determine when the number of workers will be 150 million, solve the regression equation when $y = 150$.

$$1.0116x + 18.3315 = 150$$
$$1.0116x = 131.6685$$
$$x = \frac{131.6685}{1.0116} \approx 130.159$$

There will be 150 million farm workers in approximately 2030.

c. As shown in Figure 1.5-15, there seems to be a pattern in the residuals, so there is a better, nonlinear model for the data. Nonlinear models are discussed in Section 4.3.A.

Correlation and Slope

The **correlation coefficient,** r, always has the same sign as the slope of the least squares regression line. So when r is negative, the regression line slants downward from left to right. In other words, as x increases, y decreases. In such cases, we say that the data has a **negative correlation.** When r is positive, the regression line slopes upward from left to right, and the data is said to have a **positive correlation.** As x increases, y also increases. When r is close to 0 (regardless of sign), there is **no correlation** between the quantities.

Exercises 1.5

1. a. In Example 2, find the equation of the line through the data points (1, 2) and (5, 5).
  b. Compute the sum of the squares of the errors for this line. Is it a better model than any of the models in the example? Why?

2. The linear model in Example 5 is the least squares regression line with coefficients rounded. Find the correlation coefficient for this model.

3. a. In Example 5, find the slope of the line through the data points for 1920 and 1994.
  b. Find the equation of the line through these two data points.
  c. Which model predicts the higher number of farm workers in 2010: the line in part **b** or the regression line found in Example 5?

In Exercises 4–7, determine whether the given scatter plot of the data indicates that there is a positive correlation, negative correlation, or very little correlation.

4.
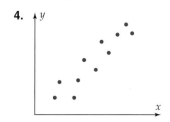

5.
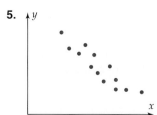

6.
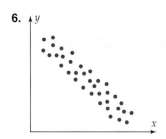

7.
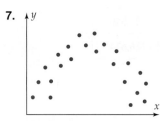

8. The U.S. gross domestic product (GDP) is the total value of all goods and services produced in the United States. The table shows the GDP in billions of 1996 dollars. Let $x = 0$ correspond to 1990. (Source: U.S. Bureau of Economic Analysis)
  a. Use a scatter plot to determine if the data appears to be linear.
  b. If so, is there a positive or negative correlation?

Year	GDP
1990	$6707.9
1992	$6880.0
1994	$7347.7
1996	$7813.2
1998	$8495.7
2000	$9318.5

In Exercises 9–13, construct a scatter plot for the data and answer these questions:
a. What are the finite differences for the data?
b. Do the finite differences confirm that the data is linear? If so, is there a positive or negative correlation?

9. The table shows the monthly premium (in dollars) for a term life insurance policy for a female nonsmoker. Let x represent age and y the amount of the premium.

Age	Premium
25	$11.57
30	$11.66
35	$11.83
40	$13.05
45	$16.18
50	$21.32
55	$29.58

10. The table shows the percent of persons in the United States below the U.S. poverty level in selected years. Let $x = 0$ correspond to 1960.

Year	Percent below poverty level
1960	22.2
1965	17.3
1970	12.6
1975	12.3
1980	13.0
1985	14.0
1990	13.5
1992	14.8
1994	14.5
1996	13.7
1997	13.3
1998	12.7
1999	11.8

11. The vapor pressure y of water depends on the temperature x, as given in the table.

Temperature (°C)	Pressure (mm Hg)
0	4.6
10	9.2
20	17.5
30	31.8
40	55.3
50	92.5
60	149.4
70	233.7
80	355.1
90	525.8
100	760.0

12. The table shows the U.S. Census Bureau's population data for St. Louis, Missouri in selected years. Let $x = 0$ correspond to 1950.

Year	Population
1950	856,796
1970	622,236
1980	452,801
1990	396,685
2000	348,189

13. The table shows the U.S. disposable income (personal income less personal taxes) in billions of dollars. (Source: Bureau of Economic Analysis, U.S. Dept. of Commerce). Let $x = 0$ correspond to 1990.

Year	Disposable personal income
1990	4166.8
1992	4613.7
1994	5018.9
1996	5534.7
1998	6320.0
1999	6618.0
2000	7031.0

14. The table gives the annual U.S. consumption of beef and poultry, in million of pounds. (Source: U.S. Dept. of Agriculture)

Year	Beef	Poultry
1990	24,031	22,151
1991	24,113	23,270
1992	24,261	24,394
1993	24,006	25,099
1994	25,125	25,754
1995	25,533	25,940
1996	25,875	26,614

a. Make scatter plots for both beef and poultry consumption, using the actual years (1990, 1991, etc.) as x in each case.

b. Without graphing, use your knowledge of slopes to determine which of the following equations models beef consumption and which one models poultry consumption. Confirm your answer by graphing.

$$y_1 = 717.44x - 1{,}405{,}160$$
$$y_2 = 329.86x - 632{,}699$$

15. The table at the bottom of the page gives the median weekly earnings of full-time workers 25 years and older by their amount of education. (Source: U.S. Bureau of Labor Statistics)

a. Make four scatter plots, one for each educational group, using $x = 0$ to correspond to 1990.

b. Four linear models are given below. Match each model with the appropriate data set.

$$y_1 = 20.74x + 392 \qquad y_2 = 12.31x + 238$$
$$y_3 = 34.86x + 543 \qquad y_4 = 15.17x + 354$$

In Exercises 16–22, use the linear regression feature of your calculator to find the required model.

16. The table shows the number of deaths per 100,000 people from heart disease.

Year	1950	1960	1970	1980	1990	1999
Deaths	510.8	521.8	496.0	436.4	368.3	265.9

a. Find a linear model for this data, using $x = 0$ to correspond to 1950.

b. In the unlikely event that the linear model in part **a** remains valid far into the future, will there be a time when death from heart disease has been completely eliminated? If so, when would this occur?

17. The table shows the share of total U.S. household income earned by the poorest 20% of households and the share received by the wealthiest 5% of households. (Source: U.S. Census Bureau)

Year	Lowest 20%	Top 5%
1985	4	17.0
1990	3.9	18.6
1995	3.7	21.0
1996	3.7	21.4

a. Find a linear model for the income share of the poorest 20% of households.

b. Find a linear model for the income share of the wealthiest 5% of households.

c. What do the slopes of the two models suggest of each?

d. Assuming that these models remain accurate, will the income gap between the wealthy and the poor grow, stay about the same, or decline in the year 2000?

Median Weekly Earnings By Amount of Education

Year	No High School Diploma	High School Graduate	Some College	College Graduate
1996	$317	$443	$518	$758
1997	$321	$461	$535	$779
1998	$337	$479	$558	$821
1999	$346	$490	$580	$860
2000	$360	$506	$598	$896
2001	$378	$520	$621	$924

18. The table shows what percent of federal aid is given in the form of loans to students at a particular college in selected years.

Year (in which school year begins)	Loans (%)
1975	18
1978	30
1984	54
1987	66
1990	78

a. Find a linear model for this data, with $x = 0$ corresponding to 1975.
b. Interpret the meaning of the slope and the y-intercept.
c. If the model remains accurate, what percentage of federal student aid were loans in 2000?

19. The table shows the percent of federal aid given in the form of grants or work-study programs to students at the college of Exercise 18.

Year (in which school year begins)	Grants and work-study (%)
1975	82
1978	70
1984	46
1987	34
1990	22

a. Find a linear model for this data, with $x = 0$ corresponding to 1975.
b. Graph the model from part **a** and the model from Exercise 18 on the same axes. What appears to be the trend in the federal share of financial aid to college students?
c. In what year is the percent of federal aid the same for loans as for grants and work-study?

20. The table gives the average number of takeout meals per person purchased at restaurants in selected years. (Source: NPD Group's Crest Service)
a. Make a scatter plot of the data, with $x = 0$ corresponding to 1980.

b. Find a linear model for the data.
c. According to the model, what was the average number of take-out meals purchased per person in 1993? in 2000?

Year	Average number of annual take-out meals per person
1984	43
1986	48
1988	53
1990	55
1992	57
1994	61
1996	65

21. The table shows the median time, in months, for the Food and Drug Administration to approve a new drug after the application has been made. (Source: U.S. Food and Drug Administration)

Year	Median time for approval
1990	24.3
1991	22.1
1992	22.6
1993	23.0
1994	17.5
1995	15.9
1996	14.3
1997	13.4
1998	12.0
1999	11.6
2000	15.6

a. Make a scatter plot of the data, with $x = 0$ corresponding to 1990.
b. Find a linear model for the data.
c. What are the limitations of this model? *Hint:* What does it say about approval time in the year 2009?

22. The ordered pairs below give production (x) and consumption (y) of primary energy in quadrillion BTUs for a sample of countries in 1995.

Australia (7.29, 4.43)   Mexico (8.15, 5.59)
Brazil (4.55, 6.76)   Poland (3.74, 3.75)
Canada (16.81, 11.72)   Russia (39.1, 26.75)
China (35.49, 35.67)   Saudi Arabia (20.34, 3.72)
France (4.92, 9.43)   South Africa (6.08, 5.51)
Germany (5.42, 13.71)   United States (69.1, 88.28)
India (8.33, 10.50)   United Kingdom (10.57,
Indonesia (6.65, 3.06)   9.85)
Iran (9.35, 3.90)   Venezuela (8.22, 2.53)
Japan (3.98, 21.42)

a. Make a scatter plot of the data.
b. Find a linear model for the data. Graph the model with the scatter plot.
c. In 1995, what three countries were the world's leading producers and consumers of energy?
d. As a general trend, what does it mean if a country's coordinates lie above the linear model?
e. As a general trend, what does it mean if a country's coordinates lie below the linear model?
f. Identify any countries whose coordinates appear to differ dramatically from most of the others.

23. The table shows the winning times, in minutes, for men's 1500-meter freestyle swimming at the Olympics in selected years.

Year	Time
1912	22.00
1924	20.11
1936	19.23
1948	19.31
1960	17.33
1972	15.88
1984	15.09
1996	14.94

a. Find a linear model for this data, with $x = 0$ corresponding to 1900.
b. Kieren Perkins of Australia set the Olympic record of 14.72 minutes in 1992. How accurately did your model estimate his time?
c. How long is this model likely to remain accurate? Why?
d. Find the correlation coefficient for the model.

e. Make a residual plot of the model. Is a linear model appropriate for the data?

24. The following table shows, for selected states, the percent of high school students in the class of 2001 who took the SAT and the average SAT math score.

State	Students who took SAT (%)	Average math score
Connecticut	82	510
Delaware	67	499
Georgia	63	489
Idaho	17	542
Indiana	60	501
Iowa	5	603
Montana	23	539
Nevada	33	515
New Jersey	81	513
New Mexico	13	542
North Dakota	4	599
Ohio	26	539
Pennsylvania	71	499
South Carolina	57	488
Washington	53	527

a. Make a scatter plot of the percent of students who took the SAT (x) versus the average SAT math score (y).
b. Find a linear model for the data.
c. What is the slope of your linear model? What does this mean in the context of the problem?
d. Below is the data on four additional states. How well does the model match the actual figures for these states?

State	Students taking SAT (%)	Average math score
Oklahoma	8	561
Arizona	34	525
Alaska	51	510
Hawaii	52	515

Geometric Sequences

Objectives

- Recognize a geometric sequence
- Find a common ratio
- Graph a geometric sequence
- Write a geometric sequence recursively and explicitly
- Find partial sums of a geometric sequence

Recall that in an arithmetic sequence, each term is obtained from the preceding term by adding a constant, d. A **geometric sequence,** which is sometimes called a *geometric progression,* is a sequence in which terms are found by multiplying a preceding term by a nonzero constant. Like an arithmetic sequence, where the difference between consecutive terms is the constant d, the quotient of consecutive terms in a geometric sequence is the constant r. The constant r is called the **common ratio** of the geometric sequence.

Example 1   **Recognizing a Geometric Sequence**

Are the following sequences geometric? If so, what is the common ratio? Write each sequence as a recursive function.

a. $\{3, 9, 27, 81, \dots\}$ **b.** $\left\{\dfrac{5}{2}, \dfrac{5}{4}, \dfrac{5}{8}, \dfrac{5}{16}, \dots\right\}$

Solution

a. The sequence $\{3, 9, 27, 81, \dots\}$ is geometric with a common ratio of 3.

$$\frac{u_2}{u_1} = \frac{9}{3} = 3 \qquad \frac{u_3}{u_2} = \frac{27}{9} = 3 \qquad \frac{u_4}{u_3} = \frac{81}{27} = 3$$

Because each term is obtained by multiplying the previous term by 3, the sequence may be denoted as a recursive function.

$$u_1 = 3 \text{ and } u_n = 3u_{n-1} \text{ for } n \geq 2$$

b. The sequence $\left\{\dfrac{5}{2}, \dfrac{5}{4}, \dfrac{5}{8}, \dfrac{5}{16}, \dots\right\}$ is geometric with a common ratio of $\dfrac{1}{2}$.

$$\frac{u_2}{u_1} = \frac{\frac{5}{4}}{\frac{5}{2}} = \frac{1}{2} \qquad \frac{u_3}{u_2} = \frac{\frac{5}{8}}{\frac{5}{4}} = \frac{1}{2} \qquad \frac{u_4}{u_3} = \frac{\frac{5}{16}}{\frac{5}{8}} = \frac{1}{2}$$

Each term is obtained by multiplying the previous term by $\dfrac{1}{2}$, which gives the following recursive function.

$$u_1 = \frac{5}{2} \text{ and } u_n = \frac{1}{2}u_{n-1} \text{ for } n \geq 2$$

If $\{u_n\}$ is a geometric sequence with common ratio r, then for each $n \geq 2$ the term preceding u_n is u_{n-1} and

$$\frac{u_n}{u_{n-1}} = r, \qquad \text{or equivalently,} \qquad u_n = ru_{n-1}.$$

Recursive Form of a Geometric Sequence

In a geometric sequence $\{u_n\}$,

$$u_n = ru_{n-1}$$

for some u_1 and some nonzero constant r and all $n \geq 2$.

Example 2　Graph of a Geometric Sequence

Find the common ratio of the geometric sequence with $u_1 = 2$ and $u_2 = 8$. List the first five terms of the sequence, write the sequence as a recursive function, and graph the function.

Solution

Because the sequence is geometric, the common ratio is $\dfrac{u_2}{u_1} = \dfrac{8}{2} = 4$.

Therefore, the sequence begins with $\{2, 8, 32, 128, 512, \dots\}$ and the recursive function is given below.

$$u_n = 4u_{n-1}, \text{ with } u_1 = 2$$

The graph of the function is shown in Figure 1.6-1.

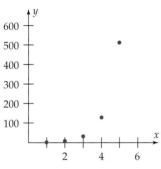

Figure 1.6-1

Notice that the graph of the geometric sequence in Example 2 does not appear to be linear. If the points were connected, the graph would be an *exponential function*, which is discussed in Chapter 5.

Explicit Form of a Geometric Sequence

Geometric sequences can also be expressed in a form where the value of the sequence can be determined by the position of the term.

Example 3　Writing a Geometric Sequence in Explicit Form

Confirm that the sequence defined by $u_n = 2u_{n-1}$ with $u_1 = 7$ can also be expressed as $u_n = 7(2)^{n-1}$ by listing the first seven terms produced by each form.

Solution

Using the recursive function, the sequence is

$$u_1 = 7$$
$$u_2 = u_1 \cdot 2 = 7 \cdot 2 = 14$$
$$u_3 = u_2 \cdot 2 = (7 \cdot 2) \cdot 2 = 7(2)^2 = 28$$
$$u_4 = u_3 \cdot 2 = (7 \cdot 2^2) \cdot 2 = 7(2)^3 = 56$$
$$u_5 = u_4 \cdot 2 = (7 \cdot 2^3) \cdot 2 = 7(2)^4 = 112$$
$$u_6 = u_5 \cdot 2 = (7 \cdot 2^4) \cdot 2 = 7(2)^5 = 224$$
$$u_7 = u_6 \cdot 2 = (7 \cdot 2^5) \cdot 2 = 7(2)^6 = 448$$

Figure 1.6-2a

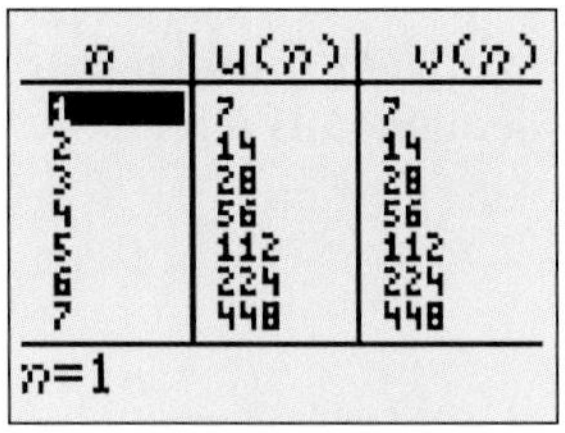

Figure 1.6-2b

Notice that u_3 is $7 \cdot 2^2$, which is the first term of the sequence multiplied by the common ratio twice, and that u_4 is $7 \cdot 2^3$, which is the first term of the sequence multiplied by the common ratio three times. u_n is the product of u_1 and the common ratio, r, raised to the $(n - 1)$ power. In general,

$$u_n = 7 \cdot 2^{n-1}.$$

The table in Figure 1.6-2b confirms the apparent equality of the two functions.

The recursive formula for $n = 2, 3, 4, \ldots$ implies that

$$u_2 = u_1 r$$
$$u_3 = u_2 r = (u_1 r)r = u_1 r^2$$
$$u_4 = u_3 r = (u_1 r^2)r = u_1 r^3$$
$$u_5 = u_4 r = (u_1 r^3)r = u_1 r^4$$

Explicit Form of a Geometric Sequence

If $\{u_n\}$ is a geometric sequence with common ratio r, then for all $n \geq 1$,

$$u_n = u_1 r^{n-1}$$

Example 4   Explicit Form of a Geometric Sequence

Write the explicit form of a geometric sequence where the first two terms are 2 and $-\dfrac{2}{5}$, and find the first five terms of the sequence.

Solution

The common ratio is $r = \dfrac{-\frac{2}{5}}{2} = \dfrac{-2}{5} \cdot \dfrac{1}{2} = -\dfrac{1}{5}$.

Using the explicit form, the geometric sequence can be written as

$$u_n = u_1 r^{n-1} = (2)\left(-\frac{1}{5}\right)^{n-1}$$

The sequence begins $2, \quad -\dfrac{2}{5}, \quad \dfrac{2}{5^2}, \quad -\dfrac{2}{5^3}, \quad \dfrac{2}{5^4}, \ldots$

Example 5   Explicit Form of a Geometric Sequence

The fourth and ninth terms of a geometric sequence are 20 and -640. Find the explicit form of the sequence.

Solution

The fourth term can be written as $u_4 = u_1 r^{n-1}$, or $20 = u_1 r^3$.

The ninth term can be written as $u_9 = u_1 r^{n-1}$, or $-640 = u_1 r^8$.

The ratio of the ninth term to the fourth term can be used to find r.

$$\frac{u_1 r^8}{u_1 r^3} = \frac{-640}{20}$$
$$r^5 = -32$$
$$r = -2$$

Substitute -2 for r into the equation defining the fourth term.

$$u_1(-2)^3 = 20$$
$$u_1 = \frac{20}{-8} = -\frac{5}{2}$$

Thus, $u_n = u_1 \cdot r^{n-1} = -\frac{5}{2}(-2)^{n-1}$.

Partial Sums

If the common ratio r of a geometric sequence is the number 1, then

$$u_n = 1^{n-1}u_1 \qquad \text{for every } n \geq 1.$$

Therefore, the sequence is just the constant sequence $u_1, u_2, u_3, \ldots$. For any positive integer k, the kth partial sum of this constant sequence is

$$\underbrace{u_1 + u_1 + \cdots + u_1}_{k \text{ terms}} = ku_1$$

In other words, the kth partial sum of a constant sequence is just k times the constant. If a geometric sequence is not constant (that is, $r \neq 1$), then its partial sums are given by the following formula.

Partial Sums of a Geometric Sequence

The kth partial sum of the geometric sequence $\{u_n\}$ with common ratio $r \neq 1$ is

$$\sum_{n=1}^{k} u_n = u_1\left(\frac{1 - r^k}{1 - r}\right)$$

Proof

If S denotes the kth partial sum, then using the formula for the nth term of a geometric sequence derives the expression for S.

$$S = u_1 + u_2 + \ldots + u_k = u_1 + u_1 r + u_1 r^2 + \ldots + u_1 r^{k-1}$$

Use this equation to compute $S - rS$, as shown on the next page.

$$S = u_1 + u_1r + u_1r^2 + \ldots + u_1r^{k-1}$$
$$rS = \qquad u_1r + u_1r^2 + \ldots + u_1r^{k-1} + u_1r^k$$
$$\overline{S - rS = u_1 \qquad\qquad\qquad\qquad\qquad - u_1r^k}$$
$$(1 - r)S = u_1(1 - r^k)$$

Because $r \neq 1$, both sides of the last equation can be divided by $1 - r$ to complete the proof.

$$S = \frac{u_1(1 - r^k)}{1 - r} = u_1\left(\frac{1 - r^k}{1 - r}\right)$$

∎

Example 6 Partial Sum

Find the sum

$$-\frac{3}{2} + \frac{3}{4} - \frac{3}{8} + \frac{3}{16} - \frac{3}{32} + \frac{3}{64} - \frac{3}{128} + \frac{3}{256} - \frac{3}{512}.$$

Solution

This is the ninth partial sum of the geometric sequence $\left\{\dfrac{-3}{2}\left(\dfrac{-1}{2}\right)^{n-1}\right\}$, where the common ratio is $r = -\dfrac{1}{2}$. The formula in the box shows that

$$\sum_{n=1}^{9} \frac{-3}{2}\left(\frac{-1}{2}\right)^{n-1} = u_1\left(\frac{1 - r^9}{1 - r}\right) = \left(\frac{-3}{2}\right)\left[\frac{1 - \left(\frac{-1}{2}\right)^9}{1 - \left(\frac{-1}{2}\right)}\right] = \left(\frac{-3}{2}\right)\left(\frac{1 + \left(\frac{1}{2}\right)^9}{\frac{3}{2}}\right)$$

$$= \left(\frac{-3}{2}\right)\left(\frac{2}{3}\right)\left(1 + \frac{1}{2^9}\right) = -1 - \frac{1}{2^9} = -1 - \frac{1}{512} = -\frac{513}{512}$$

∎

Example 7 calculates the distance traveled by the ball discussed in Section 1.2 Example 4 when it hits the ground for the seventh time by using a partial sum of a geometric sequence.

Example 7 Application of Partial Sum

A ball is dropped from a height of 9 feet. It hits the ground and bounces to a height of 6 feet. It continues to bounce up and down. On each bounce it rises to $\dfrac{2}{3}$ of the height of the previous bounce. How far has the ball traveled (both up and down) when it hits the ground for the seventh time?

Solution

First consider how far the ball travels on each bounce. On the first bounce, it rises 6 feet and falls 6 feets for a total of 12 feet. On the second bounce it rises and falls $\frac{2}{3}$ of the previous height, i.e., it travels $\frac{2}{3}$ of 12 feet. The distance traveled is a geometric sequence with $u_1 = 12$ and $r = \frac{2}{3}$. If u_n denotes the distance traveled on the nth bounce, then

$$u_n = 12\left(\frac{2}{3}\right)^{n-1}$$

So $\{u_n\}$ is a geometric sequence with common ratio $r = \left(\frac{2}{3}\right)$. When the ball hits the ground for the seventh time, it has completed six bounces. Therefore, the total distance it has traveled is the distance it was originally dropped, 9 feet, plus the distance traveled in six bounces.

$$9 + u_1 + u_2 + u_3 + u_4 + u_5 + u_6 = 9 + \sum_{n=1}^{6} u_n$$

$$= 9 + u_1\left(\frac{1 - r^6}{1 - r}\right)$$

$$= 9 + 12\left(\frac{1 - \left(\frac{2}{3}\right)^6}{1 - \frac{2}{3}}\right) \approx 41.84 \text{ feet}$$

Exercises 1.6

In Exercises 1–8, determine whether the sequence is arithmetic, geometric, or neither.

1. $2, 7, 12, 17, 22, \ldots$

2. $2, 6, 18, 54, 162, \ldots$

3. $13, \dfrac{13}{2}, \dfrac{13}{4}, \dfrac{13}{8}, \ldots$

4. $-1, -\dfrac{1}{2}, 0, \dfrac{1}{2}, \ldots$

5. $50, 48, 46, 44, \ldots$

6. $2, -3, \dfrac{9}{2}, -\dfrac{27}{4}, -\dfrac{81}{8}, \ldots$

7. $3, -\dfrac{3}{2}, \dfrac{3}{4}, -\dfrac{3}{8}, \dfrac{3}{16}, \ldots$

8. $-6, -3.7, -1.4, 9, 3.2, \ldots$

In Exercises 9–14, the first term, u_1, and the common ratio, r, of a geometric sequence are given. Find the sixth term and the recursive and explicit formulas for the nth term.

9. $u_1 = 5, r = 2$

10. $u_1 = 1, r = -2$

11. $u_1 = 4, r = \dfrac{1}{4}$

12. $u_1 = -6, r = \dfrac{2}{3}$

13. $u_1 = 10, r = -\dfrac{1}{2}$

14. $u_1 = \pi, r = \dfrac{1}{5}$

In Exercises 15–18, find the kth partial sum of the geometric sequence $\{u_n\}$ with common ratio r.

15. $k = 6, u_1 = 5, r = \dfrac{1}{2}$

16. $k = 8, u_1 = 9, r = \dfrac{1}{3}$

17. $k = 7, u_2 = 6, r = 2$ **18.** $k = 9, u_2 = 6, r = \dfrac{1}{4}$

In Exercises 19–22, show that the given sequence is geometric and find the common ratio.

19. $\left\{\left(-\dfrac{1}{2}\right)^n\right\}$

20. $\{2^{3n}\}$

21. $\{5^{n+2}\}$

22. $\{3^{\frac{n}{2}}\}$

In Exercises 23–28, use the given information about the geometric sequence $\{u_n\}$ to find u_5 and recursive and explicit formulas for u_n.

23. $u_1 = 256, u_2 = -64$

24. $u_1 = \dfrac{1}{6}, u_2 = -\dfrac{1}{18}$

25. $u_2 = 4, u_5 = \dfrac{1}{16}$

26. $u_3 = 4, u_6 = -32$

27. $u_4 = -\dfrac{4}{5}, r = \dfrac{2}{5}$

28. $u_2 = 6, u_7 = 192$

In Exercises 29–34, find the sum.

29. $\displaystyle\sum_{n=1}^{7} 2^n$

30. $\displaystyle\sum_{k=1}^{6} 3\left(\dfrac{1}{2}\right)^k$

31. $\displaystyle\sum_{n=1}^{9} \left(-\dfrac{1}{3}\right)^n$

32. $\displaystyle\sum_{n=1}^{5} 5 \cdot 3^{n-1}$

33. $\displaystyle\sum_{j=1}^{6} 4\left(\dfrac{3}{2}\right)^{j-1}$

34. $\displaystyle\sum_{t=1}^{8} 6(0.9)^{t-1}$

35. For 1987–1998, the annual revenue per share in year n of a company's stock are approximated by $u_n = 1.71(1.191)^n$, where $n = 7$ represents 1987.
   a. Show that the sequence $\{u_n\}$ is a geometric sequence.
   b. Approximate the total revenues per share for the period 1987–1998.

36. The annual dividends per share of a company's stock from 1989 through 1998 are approximated by the sequence $\{b_n\}$, where $n = 9$ corresponds to 1989 and $b_n = 0.0228(1.1999)^n$.
   a. Show that the sequence $\{b_n\}$ is a geometric sequence.
   b. Approximate the total dividends per share for the period 1989–1998.

37. A ball is dropped from a height of 8 feet. On each bounce it rises to half its previous height. When the ball hits the ground for the seventh time, how far has it traveled?

38. A ball is dropped from a height of 10 feet. On each bounce it rises to 45% of its previous height. When it hits the ground for the tenth time, how far has it traveled?

39. If you are paid a salary of 1¢ on the first day of March, 2¢ on the second day, and your salary continues to double each day, how much will you earn in the month of March?

40. Starting with your parents, how many ancestors do you have for the preceding ten generations?

41. A car that sold for $8000 depreciates in value 25% each year. What is it worth after five years?

42. A vacuum pump removes 60% of the air in a container at each stroke. What percentage of the original amount of air remains after six strokes?

43. *Critical Thinking* Suppose $\{u_n\}$ is a geometric sequence with common ratio $r > 0$ and each $u_n > 0$. Show that the sequence $\{\log u_n\}$ is an arithmetic sequence with common difference $\log r$.

44. *Critical Thinking* Suppose $\{u_n\}$ is an arithmetic sequence with common difference d. Let C be any positive number. Show that the sequence $\{C^{u_n}\}$ is a geometric sequence with common ratio C^d.

45. *Critical Thinking* In the geometric sequence $1, 2, 4, 8, 16, \ldots$ show that each term is 1 plus the sum of all preceding terms.

46. *Critical Thinking* In the geometric sequence $2, 6, 18, 54, \ldots$ show that each term is twice the sum of 1 and all preceding terms.

47. *Critical Thinking* The minimum monthly payment for a certain bank credit card is the larger of $5 or $\dfrac{1}{25}$ of the outstanding balance. If the balance is less than $5, then the entire balance is due. If you make only the minimum payment each month, how long will it take to pay off a balance of $200 (excluding any interest that might accrue)?

CHAPTER 1 REVIEW

Important Concepts

Important Facts and Formulas

A **sequence** is an ordered list of numbers.

A sequence is defined **recursively** if the first term is given and there is a method of determining the nth term by using the terms that precede it.

A sequence is defined **explicitly** if terms are determined by their position.

An **arithmetic sequence** is a sequence in which the difference between each term and the preceding term is a constant d.

Facts about an arithmetic sequence $\{u_n\}$ with common difference d:

- the recursive form of the sequence is
  $u_n = u_{n-1} + d$ for $n \geq 2$.

- the explicit form of the sequence is $u_n = u_1 + (n-1)d$.

- the kth partial sum is $\displaystyle\sum_{n=1}^{k} u_n = \frac{k}{2}(u_1 + u_k)$

The **slope** of a line that passes through (x_1, y_1) and (x_2, y_2) is given by

$$m = \frac{\Delta y}{\Delta x} = \frac{y_2 - y_1}{x_2 - x_1}.$$

The **slope-intercept form** of the equation of a line is $y = mx + b$, where m is the slope and b is the y-intercept.

The **point-slope form** of the equation of a line is $y - y_1 = m(x - x_1)$, where m is the slope and (x_1, y_1) is a given point on the line.

The **standard form** of the equation of a line is $Ax + By = C$, where A, B, and C are integers.

The equation of a **vertical line** has the form $x = h$.

The equation of a **horizontal line** has the form $y = k$.

Parallel lines have equal slopes.

The product of the slopes of **perpendicular lines** is -1.

The difference between an actual data value and a predicted data value is called a **residual.**

The **correlation coefficient** always has the same sign as the slope of the least squares regression line.

A **geometric sequence** is a sequence in which terms are found by multiplying a preceding term by a nonzero constant r.

Facts about the geometric sequence $\{u_n\}$ with common ratio $r \neq 0$:

- the recursive form is $u_n = ru_{n-1}$ for $n \geq 2$.

- the explicit form is $u_n = r^{n-1}u_1$ or $u_n = u_1 r^{n-1}$.

- if $r \neq 1$, the kth partial sum is $\displaystyle\sum_{n=1}^{k} u_n = u_1\left(\frac{1 - r^k}{1 - r}\right)$

Review Exercises

In Exercises 1–10, identify the smallest subset of the real numbers—natural numbers, whole numbers, integers, rational numbers, or irrational numbers—that contains the given number.

Section 1.1

1. $\sqrt{3}$ **2.** 0.255 **3.** e **4.** 11 **5.** 0

6. -3 **7.** $\sqrt{121}$ **8.** $\dfrac{4}{9}$ **9.** 5 **10.** $0.2\overline{55}$

11. List two real numbers that are *not* rational numbers.

In Exercises 12–15, which sets of points represent a function? Why?

12. $\{(2, 3), (3, 4), (4, 5), (5, 6), (6, 7)\}$

13. $\{(2, -3), (2, 4), (2, -5), (2, 6), (2, -7)\}$

14. $\{(2, 3), (3, 3), (4, 3), (5, 3), (6, 3)\}$

15. $\{(-2, 3), (3, 4), (-4, 5), (5, 6), (-6, 7)\}$

16. Let f be the function given by the rule $f(x) = 7 - 2x$. Complete the following table.

x	0	1	2	-4	t
$f(x)$					

17. What is the domain of the function g given by $g(t) = \dfrac{\sqrt{t-2}}{t-3}$?

18. If $f(x) = |3 - x|\sqrt{x-3} + 7$, then $f(7) - f(4) = $ ____ .

19. What is the domain of the function given by $g(r) = \sqrt{r-4} + \sqrt{r-2}$?

20. What is the domain of the function $f(x) = \sqrt{-x+2}$?

21. The radius of an oil spill (in meters) is 50 times the square root of the time t (in hours).
  a. Write the rule of a function f that gives the radius of the spill at time t.
  b. Write the rule of a function g that gives the area of the spill at time t.
  c. What are the radius and area of the spill after 9 hours?
  d. When will the spill have an area of 100,000 square meters?

22. The function whose graph is shown below gives the amount of money (in millions of dollars) spent on tickets for major concerts in selected years. (*Source:* Pollstar)

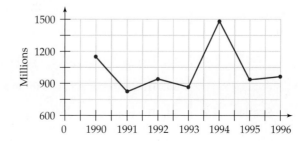

a. What is the domain of the function?

b. What is the approximate range of the function?

c. Over what one-year interval is the rate of change the largest?

Use the graph of the function f in the figure below to answer Exercises 23–26.

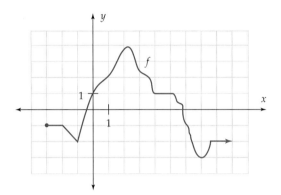

23. What is the domain of f?

24. What is the range of f?

25. Find all numbers x such that $f(x) = 1$.

26. Find a number x such that $f(x + 1) < f(x)$. (Many correct answers are possible.)

Use the graph of the function f in the figure to answer Exercises 27–33.

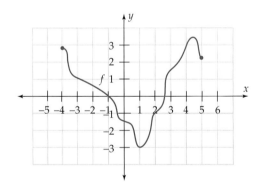

27. What is the domain of f?

28. $f(-3) = $ _____   **29.** $f(2 + 2) = $ _____   **30.** $f(-1) + f(1) = $ _____

31. True or false: $2f(2) = f(4)$.

32. True or false: $3f(2) = -f(4)$.

33. True or false: $f(x) = 3$ for exactly one number x.

Section 1.2   **34.** The population of Gallatin is growing at the rate of 2.75% per year. The present population is 20,000. Find a recursive sequence that represents

Gallatin's population each year. Represent the nth term of the sequence both explicitly and recursively. Find the first seven terms of the sequence.

35. Roberta had \$1525 in a savings account 2 years ago. What will be the value of her account 1 year from now, assuming that no deposits or withdrawals are made and the account earns 6.9% interest compounded annually? Find the solution using both a recursive and an explicit formula.

36. Suppose that \$3,000 is invested at 6.5% annual interest, compounded monthly.
   a. What is the balance after 6 years?
   b. Suppose \$150 is added to the account every month. What is the balance after 6 years?

37. The "biological" specimen *Geomeuricus sequencius* is 5 centimeters long when born. On the second day it grows 3 centimeters. The third day it grows 1.8 centimeters, and on each following day it grows 60% of the previous day's growth. What is its length after two weeks? What is the maximum length that it could grow?

In Exercises 38–39, let

$$u_n = \frac{\left(1 + \sqrt{5}\right)^n - \left(1 - \sqrt{5}\right)^n}{2^n \sqrt{5}}$$

38. a. Show that $u_1 = 1$ and $u_2 = 1$.
   b. Show that the first ten terms of $\{u_n\}$ are Fibonacci numbers. (See Exercises 30–32 Section 1.2)

39. a. For the first ten terms, compute the ratio

$$\frac{u_n}{u_{n-1}}$$

   b. As n gets large, what number does the ratio approach? This number is also referred to as the "golden ratio." This ratio is believed to have been used in the construction of the Great Pyramid in Egypt, where the ratio equals the sum of the areas of the four face triangles divided by the total surface area.

40. For the sequence $u_n = 3u_{n-1} + 1$ with $u_1 = 1.5$, write the first four terms.

41. For the sequence $u_n = 3u_{n-1} + 2$ with $u_n = -4$, write the first five terms.

42. For the sequence $u_n = 3u_{n-1}$ with $u_n = \frac{1}{9}$, write the first four terms.

Section 1.3   **In Exercises 43–46, find a formula for u_n; assume that the sequence is arithmetic.**

43. $u_1 = 3$ and the common difference is –6.

44. $u_2 = 4$ and the common difference is 3.

45. $u_1 = -5$ and $u_3 = 7$.   **46.** $u_3 = 2$ and $u_7 = -1$.

47. Find the 12th partial sum of the arithmetic sequence with $u_1 = -3$ and $u_{12} = 16$.

48. Find numbers b, c, and d such that 8, b, c, d, 23 are the first five terms of an arithmetic sequence.

Section 1.4

49. The national unemployment rates for 1990–1996 were as follows. (Source: U.S. Department of Labor, Bureau of Labor Statistics)

Year	1990	1991	1992	1993	1994	1995	1996
Rate (%)	5.6	6.8	7.5	6.9	6.1	5.6	5.4

Sketch a scatter plot and a line graph for the data, letting $x = 0$ correspond to 1990.

50. The table shows the average speed (mph) of the winning car in the Indianapolis 500 race in selected years.

Year	1980	1982	1984	1986	1988	1990	1992	1994	1996
Speed (mph)	143	162	164	171	145	186	134	161	148

Sketch a scatter plot and a line graph for these data, letting $x = 0$ correspond to 1980.

51. a. What is the y-intercept of the graph of the line defined by
$$y = x - \frac{x - 2}{5} + \frac{3}{5}?$$
b. What is the slope of the line?

52. Find the equation of the line passing through (1, 3) and (2, 5).

53. Find the equation of the line passing through (2, −1) with slope 3.

54. Find the equation of the line that crosses the y-axis at $y = 1$ and is perpendicular to the line $2y - x = 5$.

55. a. Find the y-intercept of the line defined by $2x + 3y - 4 = 0$.
b. Find the equation of the line through (1, 3) that has the same y-intercept as the line in part **a.**

56. Sketch the graph of the line defined by $3x + y - 1 = 0$.

57. Find the equation of the line through (−4, 5) that is parallel to the line through (1, 3) and (−4, 2).

58. As a balloon is launched from the ground, the wind blows it due east. The conditions are such that the balloon is ascending along a straight line with slope $\frac{1}{5}$. After 1 hour the balloon is 5000 ft directly above the ground. How far east has the balloon blown?

59. The point (u, v) lies on the line $y = 5x - 10$. What is the slope of the line passing through (u, v) and the point $(0, -10)$?

In Exercises 60–66, determine whether the statement is true or false.

60. The graph of $x = 5y + 6$ has y-intercept 6.

61. The graph of $2y - 8 = 3x$ has y-intercept 4.

62. The lines $3x + 4y = 12$ and $4x + 3y = 12$ are perpendicular.

63. Slope is not defined for horizontal lines.

64. The line in the figure at right has positive slope.

65. The line in the figure does not pass through Quadrant III.

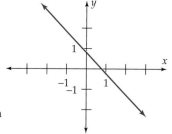

66. The y-intercept of the line in the figure is negative.

67. Which of the following lines rises most steeply from left to right?
    a. $y = -4x - 10$ **b.** $y = 3x + 4$
    c. $20x + 2y - 20 = 0$ **d.** $4x = y - 1$
    e. $4x = 1 - y$

68. Which of the following lines is not perpendicular to the line $y = x + 5$?
    a. $y = 4 - x$ **b.** $y + x = -5$
    c. $4 - 2x - 2y = 0$ **d.** $x = 1 - y$
    e. $y - x = \dfrac{1}{5}$

69. Which of the following lines does not pass through Quadrant III?
    a. $y = x$ **b.** $y = 4x - 7$
    c. $y = -2x - 5$ **d.** $y = 4x + 7$
    e. $y = -2x + 5$

70. Let a and b be fixed real numbers. Where do the lines $x = a$ and $y = b$ intersect?
    a. Only at (b, a).   **b.** Only at (a, b).
    c. These lines are parallel, so they don't intersect.
    d. If $a = b$, then these are the same line, so they have infinitely many points of intersection.
    e. Since these equations are not of the form $y = mx + b$, the graphs are not lines.

71. What is the y-intercept of the line $2x - 3y + 5 = 0$?

72. For what values of k will the graphs of $2y + x + 3 = 0$ and $3y + kx + 2 = 0$ be perpendicular lines?

73. The average life expectancy increased linearly from 62.9 years for a person born in 1940 to 75.4 years for a person born in 1990.
    a. Find an equation that gives the average life expectancy y of a person born in year x, with $x = 0$ corresponding to 1940.
    b. Use the equation in part **a** to estimate the average life expectancy of a person born in 1980.

74. The population of San Diego grew in an approximately linear fashion from 334,413 in 1950 to 1,151,977 in 1994.

a. Find an equation that gives the population y of San Diego in year x, with $x = 0$ corresponding to 1950.

b. Use the equation in part **a** to estimate the population of San Diego in 1975 and 2000.

In Exercises 75–78, match the given information with the graph, and determine the slope of each line.

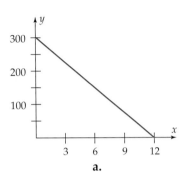

a.

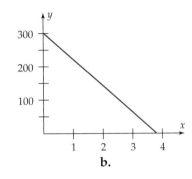

b.

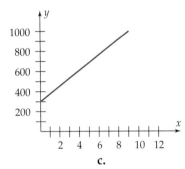

c.

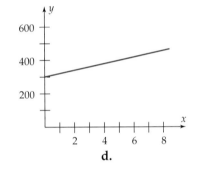

d.

75. A salesman is paid $300 per week plus $75 for each unit sold.

76. A person is paying $25 per week to repay a $300 loan.

77. A gold coin that was purchased for $300 appreciates $20 per year.

78. A CD player that was purchased for $300 depreciates $80 per year.

Section   1.5

79. The table shows the monthly premium (in dollars) for a term life insurance policy for women who smoke.

Age (years)	25	30	35	40	45	50	55	60
Premium	19.58	20.10	20.79	25.23	34.89	48.55	69.17	98.92

a. Make a scatter plot of the data, using x for age and y for amount of premium.

b. Does the data appear to be linear?

c. Calculate the finite differences. Do they confirm that the data is linear?

80. For which of the following scatter plots would a linear model be reasonable? Which sets of data show positive correlation, and which show negative correlation?

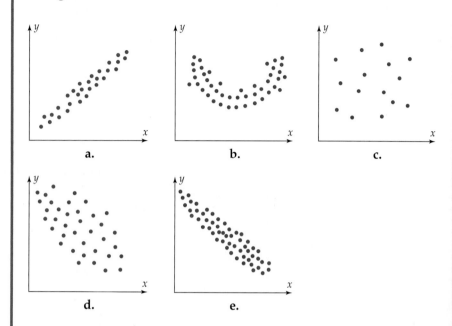

a.   b.   c.

d.   e.

Exercises 81–82 refer to the following table, which shows the percentage of jobs that are classified as managerial and the percentage of male and female employees who are managers.

Year (since 1990)	Managerial jobs (%)	Female managers (%)	Male managers (%)
−8	12.32	6.28	16.81
−5	12.31	6.85	16.67
−2	12.00	7.21	16.09
0	11.83	7.45	15.64
1	11.79	7.53	15.52
3	11.43	7.65	14.79
5	11.09	7.73	14.10

81. a. Make scatter plots of each data set (managerial jobs, female managers, male managers).
 b. Match the following linear models with the correct data set. Explain your choices.

$$y_1 = 0.11x + 7.34 \quad y_2 = -0.09x + 11.74 \quad y_3 = -0.21x + 15.48$$

82. a. According to the models in Exercise 81, is the percentage of female or male managers increasing at the greater rate?

b. Use the models to predict the percentage of female managers and the percentage of male managers in the year 2000.

c. What year do the models indicate that the percentage of female managers will surpass the percentage of male managers?

83. The table shows the average hourly earnings of production workers in manufacturing. (Source: U.S. Bureau of Labor Statistics)

Year	1991	1993	1995	1997	1999	2001
Hourly earnings ($)	11.18	11.74	12.37	13.17	13.90	14.84

a. Find a linear model for this data, with $x = 0$ corresponding to 1990.

b. Use the model to estimate the average hourly wage in 1993 and in 2000. The actual average in 1993 was $11.74 and in 2000 it was $14.38. How far off is the model?

c. Estimate the average hourly earnings in 2004.

84. The table shows the total amount of charitable giving (in billions of dollars) in the United States during recent years. (Source: Statistical Abstract of the U.S.: 2001)

Year	Total charitable giving
1990	101.4
1991	107.2
1992	110.4
1993	116.5
1994	119.2
1995	124.0
1996	138.6
1997	153.8
1998	172.1
1999	190.8
2000	203.5

a. Find a linear model for this data, with $x = 0$ corresponding to 1990.

b. Use your model to estimate the approximate total giving in 2002 and 2005.

c. Find the correlation coefficient for the model.

d. Make a residual plot of the model. Is a linear model appropriate for the data?

Section   1.6

In Exercises 85–88, find a formula for u_n. Assume that the sequence is geometric.

85. $u_1 = 2$ and the common ratio is 3.

86. $u_1 = 5$ and the common ratio is $-\dfrac{1}{2}$.

87. $u_2 = 192$ and $u_7 = 6$.

88. $u_3 = \dfrac{9}{2}$ and $u_6 = -\dfrac{243}{16}$.

89. Find the 11th partial sum of the arithmetic sequence with $u_1 = 5$ and common difference -2.

90. Find the fifth partial sum of the geometric sequence with $u_1 = \dfrac{1}{4}$ and common ratio 3.

91. Find the sixth partial sum of the geometric sequence with $u_1 = 5$ and common ratio $\dfrac{1}{2}$.

92. Find numbers c and d such that 8, c, d, 27 are the first four terms of a geometric sequence.

93. Is it better to be paid $5 per day for 100 days or to be paid 5¢ the first day, 10¢ the second day, 20¢ the third day, and have your salary increase in this fashion every day for 100 days?

94. Tuition at a university is now $3000 per year and will increase $150 per year in subsequent years. If a student starts school now, spends four years as an undergraduate, three years in law school, and five years earning a Ph.D., how much tuition will she have paid?

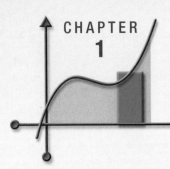

can do calculus

Infinite Geometric Series

Calculus is a branch of mathematics that deals with changing quantities. It is based on the concept of quantities that can be approached more and more closely. There are two related branches of calculus: differential calculus and integral calculus. Differential calculus is used to calculate the change in one variable produced by change in a related variable, and integral calculus is used to calculate quantities like the total change of a quantity given its rate of change, area, and volume.

The Can Do Calculus features found here and at the end of each chapter are short adventures into the world of calculus. This first Can Do Calculus explores infinite series, which is closely related to infinite sequences. It is an example of the limit process, the fundamental building block of both differential and integral calculus.

Infinite Geometric Series

Consider the sequence $2(0.6)^n$ and let S_k denote its kth partial sum.

$$S_1 = 2(0.6) = 1.2$$
$$S_2 = 2(0.6) + 2(0.6)^2 = 1.92$$
$$S_3 = 2(0.6) + 2(0.6)^2 + 2(0.6)^3 = 2.352$$
$$S_4 = 2(0.6) + 2(0.6)^2 + 2(0.6)^3 + 2(0.6)^4 = 2.6112$$

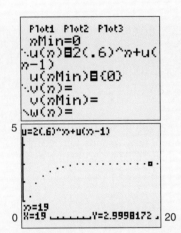

Figure 1.C-1

The partial sums $S_1, S_2, S_3, S_4, \ldots$ themselves form a sequence. This sequence is a function whose domain is the set of natural numbers. The sequence can be described by the following function:

$$u_n = \begin{cases} 2(0.6) & n = 1 \\ 2(0.6)^n + u_{n-1} & n > 1 \end{cases}$$

By using the trace feature to find large values of n, the graph in Figure 1C-1 suggests that the terms of the sequence of partial sums are getting closer and closer to 3. Consequently,

$$2(0.6) + 2(0.6)^2 + 2(0.6)^3 + 2(0.6)^4 + \cdots = 3,$$

where 3 is said to be sum of the *infinite series*.

NOTE Although TI, Sharp, and HP calculators use the letter "u" to denote terms of a sequence, the letter "a" is traditionally used.

In the general case, an **infinite series,** or simply **series,** is defined to be an expression of the form

$$a_1 + a_2 + a_3 + a_4 + a_5 + \cdots + a_n + \cdots$$

in which each a_n is a real number. This series is also denoted by the symbol $\displaystyle\sum_{n=1}^{\infty} a_n$.

The **partial sums** of the series $a_1 + a_2 + a_3 + a_4 + \cdots$ are

$$S_1 = a_1$$
$$S_2 = a_1 + a_2$$
$$S_3 = a_1 + a_2 + a_3$$
$$S_4 = a_1 + a_2 + a_3 + a_4$$

and in general, for any $k \geq 1$,

$$S_k = a_1 + a_2 + a_3 + a_4 + \cdots + a_k.$$

If it happens that the terms $S_1, S_2, S_3, S_4, \ldots$ of the *sequence* of partial sums get closer and closer to a particular real number S in such a way that the partial sum S_k is arbitrarily close to S when k is large enough, then the series **converges**. Additionally, S is called the **sum of the convergent series**. The series $2(0.6) + 2(0.6)^2 + 2(0.6)^3 + 2(0.6)^4 + \cdots$ converges, and its sum is 3. This series is an infinite geometric series because it has a common ratio of 0.6.

Definition of Infinite Geometric Series

> If $\{a_n\}$ is a geometric sequence with common ratio r, then the corresponding infinite series
>
> $$a_1 + a_2 + a_3 + a_4 + \cdots$$
>
> is called an *infinite geometric series*.

By using the formula for the nth term of a geometric sequence, the corresponding geometric series can be expressed in the form

$$a_1 + ra_1 + r^2a_1 + r^3a_1 + \cdots$$

Under certain circumstances, an infinite geometric series is convergent and has a sum.

Sum of an Infinite Geometric Series

> If $|r| < 1$, then the infinite geometric series
>
> $$a_1 + ra_1 + r^2a_1 + r^3a_1 + \cdots$$
>
> converges, and its sum is
>
> $$\frac{a_1}{1 - r}.$$

NOTE A series that is not convergent is said to be **divergent**. If $|r| \geq 1$, the series is divergent. Therefore, a geometric series is only convergent when $|r| < 1$.

Example 1   Sum of an Infinite Geometric Series

Determine whether the infinite geometric series converges.

a. $\displaystyle\sum_{n=1}^{\infty} 6(2)^n$

b. $\displaystyle\sum_{n=1}^{\infty} \frac{8}{5^n}$

Solution

a. The first term is 6 and the common ratio is 2. The sum of the first k terms is

$$S_k = a_1\left(\frac{1-r^k}{1-r}\right) = 6\left(\frac{1-2^k}{1-2}\right) = -6(1-2^k) = 6(2^k-1)$$

The graph of $S_k = 6(2^k - 1)$, as shown in Figure 1.C-2, does not approach a single value. In fact, the sums get larger for each subsequent term. So this series with a common ratio of 2 does not converge.

b. $\displaystyle\sum_{n=1}^{\infty}\frac{8}{5^n}$ is an infinite geometric series with $a_1 = \frac{8}{5}$ and $r = \frac{1}{5}$. The kth partial sum of this series is the same as the kth partial sum of the sequence $\left\{\dfrac{8}{5^n}\right\}$.

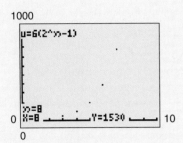

1000

u=6(2^n-1)

n=8 X=8   Y=1530

0   10

Figure 1.C-2

$$S_k = a_1\left(\frac{1-r^k}{1-r}\right) = \frac{8}{5}\left[\frac{1-\left(\frac{1}{5}\right)^k}{1-\frac{1}{5}}\right] = \frac{8}{5}\left(\frac{1-\frac{1}{5^k}}{\frac{4}{5}}\right) = \frac{8}{5}\cdot\frac{5}{4}\left(1-\frac{1}{5^k}\right) =$$

$$2\left(1-\frac{1}{5^k}\right) = 2 - \frac{2}{5^k}$$

The graph of S_k is shown in Figure 1.C-3. If you use the trace feature and move beyond approximately $n = 10$, the calculator will probably tell you that every partial sum is 2. Actually, the partial sums are slightly smaller than 2 but are rounded to 2 by the calculator. The graph gets very close to 2 as x gets larger, but it never reaches 2. According to the formula, the sum of the infinite series is

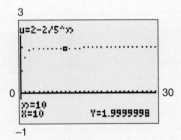

3

u=2-2/5^n

n=10 X=10   Y=1.9999998

0   30

−1

Figure 1.C-3

$$S = \frac{a_1}{1-r} = \frac{\frac{8}{5}}{1-\frac{1}{5}} = \frac{\frac{8}{5}}{\frac{4}{5}} = \frac{8}{4} = 2.$$

Example 1**b** is typical of the general case, as can be seen algebraically. Consider the geometric series $a_1 + a_2 + a_3 + \cdots$ with common ratio r such that $|r| < 1$. The kth partial sum S_k is the same as the kth partial sum of geometric sequence $\{a_n\}$, and hence

$$S_k = a_1\left(\frac{1-r^k}{1-r}\right).$$

As k gets very large, the number r^k gets very close to 0 because $|r| < 1$. Consequently, when k is very large, $1 - r^k$ is very close to $1 - 0$ so that

$$S_k = a_1\left(\frac{1-r^k}{1-r}\right) \quad \text{is very close to} \quad a_1\left(\frac{1-0}{1-r}\right) = \frac{a_1}{1-r}.$$

Infinite geometric series provide another way of writing an infinite repeating decimal as a rational number.

Example 2   Repeating Decimal as a Rational Number

Express $6.8573573573\cdots$ as a rational number.

Solution

First write the number as $6.8 + 0.0573573573\cdots$. Then consider $0.0573573573\cdots$ as an infinite series:

$$0.0573 + 0.0000573 + 0.0000000573 + 0.0000000000573 + \cdots,$$

which is the same as

$$0.0573 + (0.001)(0.0573) + (0.001)^2(0.0573) + (0.001)^3(0.0573) + \cdots$$

This is a convergent geometric series with $a_1 = 0.0573$ and $r = 0.001$. Its sum is

$$\frac{a_1}{1-r} = \frac{0.0573}{1-0.001} = \frac{0.0573}{0.999} = \frac{573}{9990}.$$

Therefore,

$$6.8573573573\cdots = 6.8 + [0.0573 + 0.0000573 + \cdots]$$

$$= 6.8 + \frac{573}{9990}$$

$$= \frac{68}{10} + \frac{573}{9990}$$

$$= \frac{68505}{9990} = \frac{4567}{666}$$

Exercises

In Exercises 1–8, find the sum of the infinite series, if it has one.

1. $\displaystyle\sum_{n=1}^{\infty} \frac{1}{2^n}$ **2.** $\displaystyle\sum_{n=1}^{\infty} \left(-\frac{3}{4}\right)^n$ **3.** $\displaystyle\sum_{n=1}^{\infty} (0.06)^n$

4. $1 - 0.5 + 0.25 - 0.125 + 0.0625 - \cdots$

5. $500 + 200 + 80 + 32 + \cdots$

6. $9 - 3\sqrt{3} + 3 - \sqrt{3} + 1 - \dfrac{1}{\sqrt{3}} + \cdots$

7. $2 + \sqrt{2} + 1 + \dfrac{1}{\sqrt{2}} + \dfrac{1}{2} + \cdots$

8. $\displaystyle\sum_{n=1}^{\infty} \left(\frac{1}{2^n} - \frac{1}{3^n}\right)$

In Exercises 9–14, express the repeating decimal as a rational number.

9. $0.22222\cdots$ **10.** $0.37373737\cdots$

11. $5.4272727\cdots$ **12.** $85.131313\cdots$

13. $2.1425425425\cdots$ **14.** $3.7165165165\cdots$

15. If $\{a_n\}$ is an arithmetic sequence with common difference $d > 0$ and each $a_i > 0$ explain why the infinite series $a_1 + a_2 + a_3 + a_4 + \cdots$ is not convergent.

16. Use the graphical approach illustrated in Example 1 to find the sum of the series in $\displaystyle\sum_{n=1}^{\infty} \left(\frac{-1}{2}\right)^n$. Does the graph get very close to the horizontal line through $-\dfrac{1}{3}$? Describe the behavior of the series.

CHAPTER
2 Equations and Inequalities

And the rockets' red glare . . .

Many Fourth of July firework displays are timed to coincide with patriotic music. To accomplish correct timing, each rocket must be detonated at precisely the correct height at the right moment. The time needed for a rocket to reach a specific height is the solution of an equation representing the height of the rocket as a function of time. See Exercise 24 of Section 2.3.

Chapter Outline

Interdependence of Sections

2.1

2.2 ⟶ 2.3

   2.4

   2.5 ⟶ 2.5.A

G raphing technology is useful for solving equations, but don't be misled into thinking that technology is always the best tool. For example, graphing technology is useless if you do not know enough algebra to understand the information displayed on the screen. When exact answers are required, algebraic techniques are usually needed. This chapter and the next two chapters develop both algebraic and graphical techniques for solving equations in one variable.

2.1 Solving Equations Graphically

Objectives

- Solve equations using the intersect method
- Solve equations using the *x*-intercept method

A **solution** of an equation is a number that, when substituted for the variable, produces a true statement. For example, 5 is a solution of $3x + 2 = 17$ because $3(5) + 2 = 17$ is a true statement. To **solve** an equation means to find all of its solutions.

Two equations are said to be **equivalent** if they have the same solutions. For example, $3x + 2 = 17$ and $x - 2 = 3$ are equivalent because 5 is the only solution of each equation.

Algebraic techniques provide exact solutions to linear and quadratic equations; however, there are no formulas that provide solutions to many other types of equations. For such equations, graphical approximation methods are practical alternatives.

NOTE If necessary, review the material on graphing in the Technology Appendix. Knowledge of a graphing calculator is assumed throughout the remainder of this book.

Complete Graphs

A viewing window is said to display a **complete graph** if it shows all the important features of the graph—including all peaks, valleys, and points where it touches an axis—and suggests the general shape of portions of the graph that are not in the window. Many different windows may show a complete graph, but it usually is best to use a window small enough to show as much detail as possible.

Later chapters develop algebraic facts that will enable you to know when graphs are complete. Until then try several different windows to see which, if any, appear to display a complete graph.

The Intersection Method

The following example illustrates a graphical method of approximating solutions of equations where both sides of an equation are algebraic expressions. Each side of the equation can be viewed as the output of a function, and the solutions of the equation represent inputs that produce equal outputs.

Example 1   Solving an Equation Using the Intersect Method

Solve $|x^2 - 4x - 3| = x^3 + x - 6$.

Solution

Set $y_1 = |x^2 - 4x - 3|$ and $y_2 = x^3 + x - 6$. Graph both equations on the same screen and find the *x-coordinate* of the point where the two graphs intersect. This coordinate can be approximated by zooming in and using the trace feature or by using a graphical intersection finder. As shown in Figure 2.1-1, $x \approx 2.207$ is an approximate solution.

$$|x^2 - 4x - 3| = x^3 + x - 6$$

Letting $x = 2.207$,

left side	*right side*
$|(2.207)^2 - 4(2.207) - 3|$	$(2.207)^3 + 2.207 - 6$
$|4.870849 - 8.828 - 3|$	$10.74996374 + 2.207 - 6$
6.957151	6.956963743

The difference between the value of the left side and the value of the right side is small. Therefore, the solution to the original equation is $x \approx 2.207$. ∎

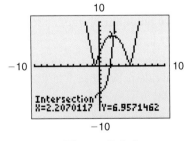

10

−10   10

Intersection
X=2.2070117 Y=6.9571462

−10

Figure 2.1-1

The Intersection Method

To solve an equation of the form $f(x) = g(x)$ by using the *intersection method*, follow two steps.

1. Graph $y_1 = f(x)$ and $y_2 = g(x)$ on the same screen.
2. Find the *x*-coordinate of each point of intersection.

> **CAUTION**
>
> Check several viewing windows to ensure that a complete graph is shown for each side of the equation. If the graphs do not intersect, then they have no common output value. Therefore, there are no real solutions to the equation.

The *x*-Intercept Method

A **zero of a function** f is an input that produces an output of 0. For example, 2 is a zero of the function $f(x) = x^3 - 8$ because $f(2) = 2^3 - 8 = 0$. Note that 2 is also a solution of the equation $x^3 - 8 = 0$. In other words, the zeros of the function f are the **solutions**, or **roots**, of the equation $f(x) = 0$. The zeros of a function also have a graphical interpretation.

Technology Tip

> A **decimal window** produces one-decimal-place values of the x-coordinates when using the trace feature.
>
> For a decimal window select **ZDECIMAL** or **ZOOMDEC** in the TI-83/86/89 **ZOOM** menu, **DECIMAL** in the Sharp 9600 **ZOOM** menu and the HP-38 **VIEWS** menu, and **INIT** in the Casio 9850 **V-WINDOW** menu. If needed, review the material on decimal windows in the Technology Appendix.

Graphing Exploration

1. Graph $y = x^4 - 2x^2 - 3x - 2$ using a decimal window. (See Technology Tip.) Find the points where the graph crosses the x-axis.

2. Verify that the x-coordinates found in Step 1 are zeros of the function f. That is, the x-coordinates are solutions of
$$x^4 - 2x^2 - 3x - 2 = 0.$$

A point where the graph of $y = f(x)$ intersects the x-axis is of the form $(a, 0)$ because every point on the x-axis has y-coordinate 0. The number a is called an x-**intercept** of the graph of f. In the preceding Exploration, the x-intercepts of $f(x) = x^4 - 2x^2 - 3x - 2$ were found to be $x = -1$ and $x = 2$. The x-intercepts of the graph are the zeros of the function f.

Zeros, x-Intercepts, and Solutions

> **Let f be a function. If r is a real number that satisfies any of the following statements, then r satisfies all the statements.**
>
> • r is a *zero* of the function f
> • r is an *x-intercept* of the graph of f
> • $x = r$ is a *solution*, or *root*, of the equation $f(x) = 0$

Because the x-intercepts of the graph of $y = f(x)$ are the zeros of f, and the zeros of f are solutions of the related equation $f(x) = 0$, the x-intercepts can be used to solve $f(x) = 0$.

The x-Intercept Method

Follow three steps to solve an equation by the *x*-intercept method.

1. **Write the equation in the equivalent form $f(x) = 0$.**
2. **Graph $y = f(x)$.**
3. **Find the *x*-intercepts of the graph. The *x*-intercepts of the graph are the real solutions of the equation.**

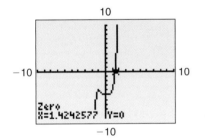

Figure 2.1-2

An advantage of using the *x*-intercept method is that solutions appear on the *x*-axis, and prior information about the range of the function is not needed.

Example 2   Solving an Equation by Using the *x*-Intercept Method

Solve the equation $x^5 + x^2 = x^3 + 5$.

Solution

Rewrite the equation so that one side is zero.

$$x^5 - x^3 + x^2 - 5 = 0$$

Graph $y = x^5 - x^3 + x^2 - 5$ in the **standard viewing window.**

Use the trace feature to find that the zero is between 1.3 and 1.5, then use zoom-in and trace features repeatedly, or use the **graphical zero finder,** to get a better approximation of 1.4242577. (See the Technology Tip for the location of the graphical zero finder.) Verify that 1.42 is an approximate solution by substituting $x = 1.42$ into the original equation. ∎

Technological Quirks

A graphical zero finder may fail to find some solutions of an equation, particularly when the graph of the equation touches, but does not cross, the *x*-axis. If the calculator does not show any *x*-intercepts on a graph or if its zero finder gives an error message, an alternative approach may be necessary, as illustrated in the next two examples.

Example 3   Solving $\sqrt{f(x)} = 0$ by Solving $f(x) = 0$

Solve $\sqrt{x^4 + x^2 - 2x - 1} = 0$.

Solution

Graph $y = \sqrt{x^4 + x^2 - 2x - 1}$. The trace feature may display no *y*-value for some points and the graphical zero finder may display an error message. See Figure 2.1-3 on the next page.

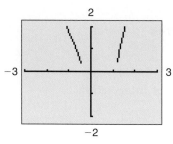

Figure 2.1-3

NOTE Solving radical and rational equations is presented in Section 2.4, and radical and rational functions are presented in Chapter 4.

This difficulty can be eliminated by using the fact that the only number whose square root is zero is zero itself.

That is, the solutions of $\sqrt{x^4 + x^2 - 2x - 1} = 0$ are the same as the solutions of $x^4 + x^2 - 2x - 1 = 0$.

As the graphs below display, the solutions of $x^4 + x^2 - 2x - 1 = 0$ are

$$x \approx -0.4046978 \qquad \text{and} \qquad x \approx 1.1841347,$$

which are also approximate solutions of $\sqrt{x^4 + x^2 - 2x - 1} = 0$.

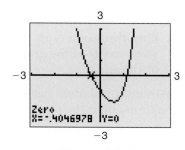

Figure 2.1-4a   **Figure 2.1-4b**

The solutions can be verified by substitution.

■

Example 4 Solving $\dfrac{f(x)}{g(x)} = 0$

Solve $\dfrac{2x^2 + x - 1}{9x^2 - 9x + 2} = 0.$

Solution

The graph of $y = \dfrac{2x^2 + x - 1}{9x^2 - 9x + 2}$ in Figure 2.1-5 is impossible to read.

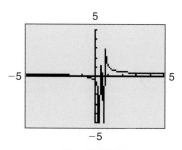

Figure 2.1-5

Using the zoom feature will display a better graph, but it may be easier to use the fact that a fraction is zero only when its numerator is zero and its denominator is nonzero.

The values that make the numerator zero can easily be found by finding the zeros of $y = 2x^2 + x - 1$. Discard any value that makes the denominator of the original equation zero because

an input that gives an undefined output is not in the domain.

Figure 2.1-6 shows that one x-intercept of $y = 2x^2 + x - 1$ is $x = 0.5$ and the other is $x = -1$ (not identified on the graph). Neither value makes the denominator zero, so they are the solutions to the given equation, which can be verified by substitution.

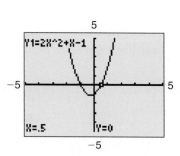

Figure 2.1-6

■

Summary of Solving Equations Graphically

To solve $h(x) = g(x)$ use one of the following.

- *The Intersection Method*
  1. Graph $y_1 = h(x)$ and $y_2 = g(x)$.
  2. Find the x-coordinate of each point of intersection.

- *The x-Intercept Method*
  1. Rewrite the equation as $f(x) = 0$, where

$$f(x) = h(x) - g(x).$$

  2. Graph $y = f(x)$.
  3. Find the x-intercepts of the graph of $f(x)$. The x-intercepts of the graph of $y = f(x)$ are the solutions of the equation.

The x-Intercept Method has the advantage of needing no information about the range of the functions.

Applications

Graphical solution methods can be helpful in dealing with applied problems because approximate solutions are adequate in most real-world contexts.

Example 5   Equal Populations

According to data from the U.S. Bureau of the Census, the approximate population y (in millions) of Chicago and Los Angeles between 1950 and 2000 are given by

Chicago	$y = 0.0000304x^3 - 0.0023x^2 + 0.02024x + 3.62$
Los Angeles	$y = 0.0000113x^3 - 0.000922x^2 + 0.0538x + 1.97$

where 0 corresponds to 1950. In what year did the two cities have the same population?

Solution

Graph both functions on the same screen, and find the x-value of their point(s) of intersection.

As shown in Figure 2.1-7, the populations were the same when $x \approx 28.75$, which represents September of 1978.

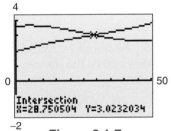

Figure 2.1-7

Exercises 2.1

In Exercises 1–6, determine graphically the number of solutions of the equation, but don't solve the equation. You may need a viewing window other than the standard one to find all of the x-intercepts.

1. $x^5 + 5 = 3x^4 + x$ **2.** $x^3 + 5 = 3x^2 + 24x$

3. $x^7 - 10x^5 + 15x + 10 = 0$

4. $x^5 + 36x + 25 = 13x^3$

5. $x^4 + 500x^2 - 8000x = 16x^3 - 32{,}000$

6. $6x^5 + 80x^3 + 45x^2 + 30 = 45x^4 + 86x$

In Exercises 7–34, use a graphical method to find all real solutions of the equation, approximating when necessary.

7. $x^3 + 4x^2 + 10x + 15 = 0$

8. $x^3 + 9 = 3x^2 + 6x$ **9.** $x^4 + x - 3 = 0$

10. $x^5 + 5 = 3x^4 + x$ **11.** $\sqrt{x^4 + x^3 - x - 3} = 0$

12. $\sqrt{8x^4 - 14x^3 - 9x^2 + 11x - 1} = 0$

13. $\sqrt{\dfrac{2}{5}x^5 + x^2 - 2x} = 0$

14. $\sqrt{x^4 + x^2 - 3x + 1} = 0$

15. $x^2 = \sqrt{x + 5}$

16. $\sqrt{x^2 - 1} - \sqrt{x + 9} = 0$

17. $\dfrac{2x^5 - 10x + 5}{x^3 + x^2 - 12x} = 0$

18. $\dfrac{3x^5 - 15x + 5}{x^7 - 8x^5 + 2x^2 - 5} = 0$

19. $\dfrac{x^3 - 4x + 1}{x^2 + x - 6} = 0$

20. $\dfrac{4}{x + 2} - \dfrac{3}{x + 1} = 0$ [Use parentheses correctly.]

21. $2x^3 - 4x^2 + x - 3 = 0$

22. $6x^3 - 5x^2 + 3x - 2 = 0$

23. $x^5 - 6x + 6 = 0$

24. $x^3 - 3x^2 + x - 1 = 0$

25. $10x^5 - 3x^2 + x - 6 = 0$

26. $\dfrac{1}{4}x^4 - x - 4 = 0$ **27.** $2x - \dfrac{1}{2}x^2 - \dfrac{1}{12}x^4 = 0$

28. $\dfrac{1}{4}x^4 + \dfrac{1}{3}x^2 + 3x - 1 = 0$

29. $\dfrac{5x}{x^2 + 1} - 2x + 3 = 0$ **30.** $\dfrac{2x}{x + 5} = 1$

31. $|x^2 - 4| = 3x^2 - 2x + 1$

32. $|x^3 + 2| = 5 + x - x^2$

33. $\sqrt{x^2 + 3} = \sqrt{x - 2} + 5$

34. $\sqrt{x^3 + 2} = \sqrt{x + 5} + 4$

In Exercises 35–40, find an exact solution of the equation in the interval shown to the right of each equation. For example, if the graphical approximation of a solution begins .3333, check to see if $\dfrac{1}{3}$ is the exact solution. Similarly, if your approximation begins 1.414, check to see if $\sqrt{2}$ is a solution because $\sqrt{2} \approx 1.414$.

35. $3x^3 - 2x^2 + 3x - 2 = 0$ $0 < x < 1$

36. $4x^3 - 3x^2 - 3x - 7 = 0$ $1 < x < 2$

37. $12x^4 - x^3 - 12x^2 + 25x - 2 = 0$ $0 < x < 1$

38. $8x^5 + 7x^4 - x^3 + 16x - 2 = 0$ $0 < x < 1$

39. $4x^4 - 13x^2 + 3 = 0$ $1 < x < 2$

40. $x^3 + x^2 - 2x - 2 = 0$ $1 < x < 2$

41. According to data from the U.S. Department of Education, the average cost y of tuition and fees at public four-year institutions in year x is approximated by the equation

$$y = 0.024x^4 - 0.87x^3 + 9.6x^2 + 97.2x + 2196$$

where $x = 0$ corresponds to 1990. If this model continues to be accurate, during what year will tuition and fees reach $4000?

42. Use the equation in Example 5 to determine the year in which the population of Los Angeles reached 2.6 million.

43. According to data from the U.S. Department of Health and Human Services, the cumulative number y of AIDS cases (in thousands) as of year x is approximated by

$$y = 0.062x^4 - 1.54x^3 + 9.21x^2 + 57.54x + 199.36$$
$$(0 \leq x \leq 11)$$

where $x = 0$ corresponds to 1990. During what year did the cumulative number of cases reach 750,000?

44. a. How many real solutions does the equation

$$0.2x^5 - 2x^3 + 1.8x + k = 0$$

have when $k = 0$?
b. How many real solutions does it have when $k = 1$?
c. Is there a value of k for which the equation has just one real solution?
d. Is there a value of k for which the equation has no real solution?

 2.2

Solving Quadratic Equations Algebraically

Objectives

- Solve equations by:
  factoring
  square root of both sides
  completing the square
  quadratic formula
- Solve equations in quadratic form

The basic strategy for solving equations is to use the basic properties of equality.

- **Add or subtract the same quantity from both *sides* of the equation.**
- **Multiply or divide both *sides* of the equation by the same *nonzero* quantity.**

The properties of equality apply to *all* equations. They, together with other techniques that are presented in this chapter, can be used to transform a given equation into one whose solutions are easily found. This section considers quadratic equations and techniques used to find their solutions.

Definition of a Quadratic Equation

A *quadratic*, or *second degree*, **equation is one that can be written in the form**

$$ax^2 + bx + c = 0$$

for real constants a, b, and c, with $a \neq 0$.

NOTE This chapter considers only **real solutions,** that is, solutions that are real numbers.

Techniques Used to Solve Quadratic Equations

There are four techniques normally used to algebraically find exact solutions of quadratic equations. Techniques that can be used to solve *some* quadratic equations include

- factoring
- taking the square root of both sides of an equation

Techniques that can be used to solve *all* quadratic equations include

- completing the square
- using the quadratic formula

Solving Quadratic Equations by Factoring

The factoring method of solving quadratic equations is based on the Zero Product Property of real numbers.

The Zero Product Property

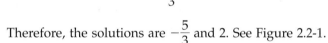

If a product of real numbers is zero, then at least one of the factors is zero. In other words,

If $ab = 0$, then $a = 0$ or $b = 0$ (or both).

NOTE If needed, review factoring in the Algebra Appendix.

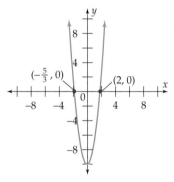

Figure 2.2-1

Example 1 **Solving a Quadratic Equation by Factoring**

Solve $3x^2 - x = 10$ by factoring.

Solution

Rearrange the terms so that one side is 0, and then factor.

$$3x^2 - x - 10 = 0 \qquad \text{\textit{Subtract 10 from each side}}$$
$$(3x + 5)(x - 2) = 0 \qquad \text{\textit{Factor the left side}}$$

Using the Zero Product Property, $3x + 5$ or $x - 2$ must be 0.

$$3x + 5 = 0 \qquad \text{or} \qquad x - 2 = 0$$
$$3x = -5 \qquad\qquad\qquad x = 2$$
$$x = -\frac{5}{3}$$

Therefore, the solutions are $-\dfrac{5}{3}$ and 2. See Figure 2.2-1.

CAUTION

To guard against mistakes, always check solutions by substituting each solution into the *original* equation to make sure it really *is* a solution.

Solving $x^2 = k$

The equation $x^2 = -5$ has no real solutions because the square of a number is never negative. The equation $x^2 = 0$ has only one solution, $x = 0$. The equation $x^2 = 7$ has two solutions, $\sqrt{7}$ and $-\sqrt{7}$, because these are the only numbers whose square is 7. Similar facts are true for equations of the form $x^2 = k$, where k is a real number.

Solutions of $x^2 = k$

For a real number k,

	Number of Solutions	Solutions
$k < 0$	0	
$k = 0$	1	0
$k > 0$	2	$\sqrt{k}$ and $-\sqrt{k}$

When k is positive, the two solutions of $x^2 = k$ are often written as $x = \pm\sqrt{k}$, which is read "x equals plus or minus the square root of k."

Taking the Square Root of Both Sides of an Equation

Example 2   Solving $ax^2 = b$

Solve $3x^2 = 9$.

Solution

$$3x^2 = 9$$
$$x^2 = 3 \qquad \text{\textit{Divide by 3}}$$
$$x = \pm\sqrt{3} \approx \pm1.732 \qquad \text{\textit{Take the square root}}$$

Substitute both solutions into the original equation to check. ∎

The method of taking the square root of both sides of an equation can be used to solve equations of the form $a(x - h)^2 = k$.

Example 3   Solving $a(x - h)^2 = k$

Solve $2(x + 4)^2 = 6$.

Solution

The equation is in the form $au^2 = k$, where u represents $x + 4$. Therefore, the procedure outlined above can be applied.

$$2(x + 4)^2 = 6$$
$$(x + 4)^2 = 3 \qquad \text{\textit{Divide by 2}}$$
$$x + 4 = \pm\sqrt{3} \qquad \text{\textit{Take square roots}}$$
$$x = -4 \pm\sqrt{3} \qquad \text{\textit{Subtract 4}}$$
$$x = -4 + \sqrt{3} \quad \text{or} \quad x = -4 - \sqrt{3} \qquad \text{\textit{Exact solutions}}$$
$$x \approx -2.27 \qquad\qquad x \approx -5.73 \qquad \text{\textit{Approximate solutions}}$$
∎

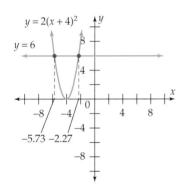

Figure 2.2-2

Completing the Square

A variation of the method of taking the square root of both sides can be used to solve *any* quadratic equation. It is based on the fact that an expression of the form $x^2 + bx$ can be changed into a perfect square by adding a suitable constant. For example, adding 9 to the expression $x^2 + 6x$ changes it into a perfect square.

$$x^2 + 6x + 9 = (x + 3)^2$$

The number added is 9, which is 3^2, and 3 is one-half of 6, the coefficient of x in the original expression, $x^2 + 6x$. This technique, which is called **completing the square,** works in every case.

Completing the Square

To *complete the square* of the expression $x^2 + bx$, add the square of one-half the coefficient of x, namely $\left(\dfrac{b}{2}\right)^2$. The addition produces a perfect square trinomial.

$$x^2 + bx + \left(\frac{b}{2}\right)^2 = \left(x + \frac{b}{2}\right)^2$$

NOTE The procedure of completing the square is used in other areas of mathematics, and knowledge of this procedure is important in later chapters.

Solving a Quadratic Equation by Completing the Square

To solve a quadratic equation by completing the square, follow the procedure below.

1. Write the equation in the form $x^2 + bx = c$.

2. Add $\left(\dfrac{b}{2}\right)^2$ to both sides so that the left side is a perfect square and the right side is a constant.

3. Take the square root of both sides.

4. Simplify.

CAUTION

Completing the square only works when the coefficient of x^2 is 1. In an equation such as

$$2x^2 - 6x + 1 = 0$$

first divide both sides by 2 and *then* complete the square.

Example 4   **Solving a Quadratic Equation by Completing the Square**

Solve $2x^2 - 6x + 1 = 0$ by completing the square.

Solution

$$2x^2 - 6x + 1 = 0$$
$$2x^2 - 6x = -1 \qquad \textit{Subtract 1}$$
$$x^2 - 3x = -\frac{1}{2} \qquad \textit{Divide by 2}$$
$$x^2 - 3x + \frac{9}{4} = \frac{9}{4} - \frac{1}{2} \qquad \textit{Add } \left(\frac{3}{2}\right)^2 = \frac{9}{4}$$
$$\left(x - \frac{3}{2}\right)^2 = \frac{7}{4} \qquad \textit{Rewrite as perfect square and simplify}$$
$$x - \frac{3}{2} = \pm\sqrt{\frac{7}{4}} \qquad \textit{Take square root}$$
$$x = \frac{3}{2} \pm \sqrt{\frac{7}{4}} \qquad \textit{Add } \frac{3}{2}$$
$$x = \frac{3}{2} + \sqrt{\frac{7}{4}} \approx 2.823 \qquad \text{or} \qquad x = \frac{3}{2} - \sqrt{\frac{7}{4}} \approx 0.177$$

There are two real solutions. See Figure 2.2-3.

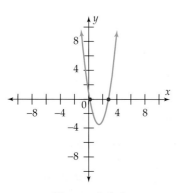

Figure 2.2-3

The technique of completing the square can be used to solve *any* quadratic equation.

Solving $ax^2 + bx + c = 0$ by Completing the Square

Solve $ax^2 + bx + c = 0$ by completing the square as follows:

1. Subtract c from both sides.

$$ax^2 + bx = -c$$

2. Divide both sides by a, the leading coefficient.

$$x^2 + \frac{b}{a}x = -\frac{c}{a}$$

3. Add the square of half of $\frac{b}{a}$, that is, $\left(\frac{b}{2a}\right)^2$, to both sides.

$$x^2 + \frac{b}{a}x + \left(\frac{b}{2a}\right)^2 = \left(\frac{b}{2a}\right)^2 - \frac{c}{a}$$

4. Write the left side of the equation as a perfect square.

$$\left(x + \frac{b}{2a}\right)^2 = \left(\frac{b}{2a}\right)^2 - \frac{c}{a}$$

5. Take the square root of both sides.

$$x + \frac{b}{2a} = \pm\sqrt{\left(\frac{b}{2a}\right)^2 - \frac{c}{a}}$$

6. Subtract $\frac{b}{2a}$ from both sides.

$$x = -\frac{b}{2a} \pm \sqrt{\left(\frac{b}{2a}\right)^2 - \frac{c}{a}}$$

The equation in step 6 can be simplified.

$$x = -\frac{b}{2a} \pm \sqrt{\frac{b^2}{4a^2} - \frac{c}{a}} \qquad \left(\frac{b}{2a}\right)^2 = \frac{b^2}{4a^2}$$

$$= \frac{-b}{2a} \pm \sqrt{\frac{b^2 - 4ac}{4a^2}} \qquad \frac{b^2}{4a^2} - \frac{c}{a} = \frac{b^2}{4a^2} - \frac{4ac}{4a^2}$$

$$= \frac{-b}{2a} \pm \frac{\sqrt{b^2 - 4ac}}{2a}$$

$$= \frac{-b \pm \sqrt{b^2 - 4ac}}{2a}$$

The final expression is known as the quadratic formula.

The Quadratic Formula

The solutions of the quadratic equation $ax^2 + bx + c = 0$ are

$$x = \frac{-b \pm \sqrt{b^2 - 4ac}}{2a}$$

Because the quadratic formula can be used to solve *any* quadratic equation, it should be memorized.

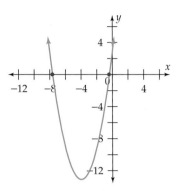

Figure 2.2-4

Example 5 Solving a Quadratic Equation by Using the Quadratic Formula

Solve $x^2 + 3 = -8x$ by using the quadratic formula.

Solution

Rewrite the equation as $x^2 + 8x + 3 = 0$, and apply the quadratic formula with $a = 1$, $b = 8$, and $c = 3$.

$$x = \frac{-8 \pm \sqrt{8^2 - 4(1)(3)}}{2(1)} = \frac{-8 \pm \sqrt{64 - 12}}{2} = \frac{-8 \pm \sqrt{52}}{2}$$

Therefore, $x = \dfrac{-8 + \sqrt{52}}{2} \approx -0.4$ or $x = \dfrac{-8 - \sqrt{52}}{2} \approx -7.6$.

The equation has two distinct real solutions, as confirmed in Figure 2.2-4.

The Discriminant

The expression $b^2 - 4ac$ in the quadratic formula, called the **discriminant,** can be used to determine the *number* of real solutions of the equation $ax^2 + bx + c = 0$.

Real Solutions of a Quadratic Equation

Discriminant Value	Number of Real Solutions of $ax^2 + bx + c = 0$
$b^2 - 4ac > 0$	2 distinct real solutions
$b^2 - 4ac = 0$	1 distinct real solution
$b^2 - 4ac < 0$	0 real solutions

The discriminant can be used to determine if an equation has no real solutions without completing all computations.

Example 6 Determining the Number of Solutions by Using the Discriminant

Solve $2x^2 = -x - 3$.

Solution

First, write the equation in general form.

$$2x^2 + x + 3 = 0$$
$$b^2 - 4ac = 1 - 4(2)(3) = -23 < 0$$

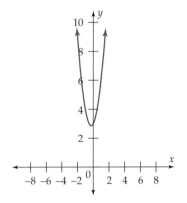

Figure 2.2-5

The discriminant of $2x^2 + x + 3 = 0$ is negative. Therefore, $2x^2 + x + 3 = 0$ has no real solutions.

You can confirm this fact because the graph of $y = 2x^2 + x + 3$ does not touch the x-axis, as shown in Figure 2.2-5. Since the graph has no x-intercepts, the equation has no real solutions. ∎

NOTE A quadratic equation with no x-intercepts has no real solution.

Polynomial Equations

Definition of Polynomial Equation

A polynomial equation of degree n is an equation that can be written in the form

$$a_n x^n + a_{n-1}x^{n-1} + \cdots + a_1 x + a_0 = 0,$$

where $a_n, \cdots, a_0$ are real numbers.

For instance, $4x^6 - 3x^5 + x^4 + 7x^3 - 8x^2 + 4x + 9 = 0$ is a polynomial equation of degree 6. Similarly, $4x^3 - 3x^2 + 4x - 5$ is a polynomial expression of degree 3. Notice that polynomials have the following traits.

- no variables in denominators
- no variables under radical signs

As a general rule, polynomial equations of degree 3 and above are best solved by the graphical methods presented in Section 2.1. However, some equations are quadratic in form and can be solved algebraically.

NOTE Polynomials are discussed in Chapter 4.

Polynomial Equations in Quadratic Form

Example 7 **Solving an Equation in Quadratic Form**

Solve $4x^4 - 13x^2 + 3 = 0$.

Solution

To write $4x^4 - 13x^2 + 3 = 0$ in quadratic form, substitute u for x^2.

$$4x^4 - 13x^2 + 3 = 0$$
$$4(x^2)^2 - 13x^2 + 3 = 0 \qquad \textit{Write } x^4 \textit{ as } (x^2)^2$$
$$4u^2 - 13u + 3 = 0 \qquad \textit{Substitute } u \textit{ for } x^2$$

Then solve the resulting quadratic equation.

$$(u - 3)(4u - 1) = 0 \qquad \textit{Factor}$$

$$u - 3 = 0 \quad \text{or} \quad 4u - 1 = 0 \qquad \textit{Zero-Product Property}$$

$$u = 3 \qquad\qquad\qquad u = \frac{1}{4}$$

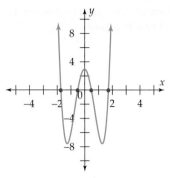

Because $u = x^2$,

$$x^2 = 3 \qquad \text{or} \qquad x^2 = \frac{1}{4}$$

$$x = \pm\sqrt{3} \qquad\qquad x = \pm\frac{1}{2}$$

Therefore, the original equation has four solutions, $x = \pm\sqrt{3}$ and $x = \pm\frac{1}{2}$, as shown in Figure 2.2-6.

Figure 2.2-6

Exercises 2.2

In Exercises 1–12, solve each equation by factoring.

1. $x^2 - 8x + 15 = 0$ **2.** $x^2 + 5x + 6 = 0$

3. $x^2 - 5x = 14$ **4.** $x^2 + x = 20$

5. $2y^2 + 5y - 3 = 0$ **6.** $3t^2 - t - 2 = 0$

7. $4t^2 + 9t + 2 = 0$ **8.** $9t^2 + 2 = 11t$

9. $3u^2 + u = 4$ **10.** $5x^2 + 26x = -5$

11. $12x^2 + 13x = 4$ **12.** $18x^2 = 23x + 6$

In Exercises 13–24, solve the equation by taking the square root of both sides. Give exact solutions and approximate solutions, if appropriate.

13. $x^2 = 9$ **14.** $x^2 = 12$

15. $x^2 = 40$ **16.** $-x^2 = -10$

17. $3x^2 = 12$ **18.** $\frac{1}{2}v^2 = 10$

19. $-5s^2 = -30$ **20.** $-3x^2 = 11$

21. $25x^2 - 4 = 0$ **22.** $4x^2 - 28 = 0$

23. $-3w^2 + 8 = -20$ **24.** $-2t^2 - 11 = 5$

In Exercises 25–28, solve the equation by completing the square.

25. $x^2 - 2x = 12$ **26.** $x^2 - 4x - 30 = 0$

27. $w^2 - w - 1 = 0$ **28.** $t^2 + 3t - 2 = 0$

In Exercises 29–40, use the quadratic formula to solve the equation.

29. $x^2 - 4x + 1 = 0$ **30.** $x^2 - 2x - 1 = 0$

31. $x^2 + 6x + 7 = 0$ **32.** $x^2 + 4x - 3 = 0$

33. $x^2 + 6 = 2x$ **34.** $x^2 + 11 = 6x$

35. $4x^2 - 4x = 7$ **36.** $4x^2 - 4x = 11$

37. $4x^2 - 8x + 1 = 0$ **38.** $2t^2 + 4t + 1 = 0$

39. $5u^2 + 8u = -2$ **40.** $4x^2 = 3x + 5$

In Exercises 41–46, find the number of real solutions of the equation by computing the discriminant.

41. $x^2 + 4x + 1 = 0$ **42.** $4x^2 - 4x - 3 = 0$

43. $9x^2 = 12x + 1$ **44.** $9t^2 + 15 = 30t$

45. $25t^2 + 49 = 70t$ **46.** $49t^2 + 5 = 42t$

In Exercises 47–56, solve the equation by any method.

47. $x^2 + 9x + 18 = 0$ **48.** $3t^2 - 11t - 20 = 0$

49. $4x(x + 1) = 1$ **50.** $25y^2 = 20y + 1$

51. $2x^2 = 7x + 15$ **52.** $2x^2 = 6x + 3$

53. $t^2 + 4t + 13 = 0$ **54.** $5x^2 + 2x = -2$

55. $\dfrac{7x^2}{3} = \dfrac{2x}{3} - 1$ **56.** $25x + \dfrac{4}{x} = 20$

In Exercises 57–60, use a calculator to find approximate solutions of the equation.

57. $4.42x^2 - 10.14x + 3.79 = 0$

58. $8.06x^2 + 25.8726x - 25.047256 = 0$

59. $3x^2 - 82.74x + 570.4923 = 0$

60. $7.63x^2 + 2.79x = 5.32$

In Exercises 61–68, find all exact real solutions of the equation.

61. $y^4 - 7y^2 + 6 = 0$

62. $x^4 - 2x^2 + 1 = 0$

63. $x^4 - 2x^2 - 35 = 0$

64. $x^4 - 2x^2 - 24 = 0$

65. $2y^4 - 9y^2 + 4 = 0$

66. $6z^4 - 7z^2 + 2 = 0$

67. $10x^4 + 3x^2 = 1$

68. $6x^4 - 7x^2 = 3$

In Exercises 69–72, find a number k such that the given equation has exactly one real solution.

69. $x^2 + kx + 25 = 0$

70. $x^2 - kx + 49 = 0$

71. $kx^2 + 8x + 1 = 0$

72. $kx^2 + 24x + 16 = 0$

73. Find a number k such that 4 and 1 are the solutions of $x^2 - 5x + k = 0$.

74. Suppose a, b, and c are fixed real numbers such that $b^2 - 4ac \geq 0$. Let r and s be the solutions of

$$ax^2 + bx + c = 0.$$

    a. Use the quadratic formula to show that
$$r + s = -\frac{b}{a} \text{ and } rs = \frac{c}{a}.$$

    b. Use part **a** to verify that
$$ax^2 + bx + c = a(x - r)(x - s).$$

    c. Use part **b** to factor $x^2 - 2x - 1$ and $5x^2 + 8x + 2$.

Applications of Equations

Objectives

- Solve application problems

Real-life situations are usually described verbally, but they must be interpreted and expressed as equivalent mathematical statements. The following guideline may be helpful.

Applied Problems Guideline

1. *Read* the problem carefully, and determine what is asked for.
2. *Label* the unknown quantities with variables.
3. *Draw* a picture of the situation, if appropriate.
4. *Translate* the verbal statements in the problem and the relationships between the known and unknown quantities into mathematical language.
5. *Consolidate* the mathematical information into an equation in one variable that can be solved or an equation in two variables that can be graphed.
6. *Solve* for at least one of the unknown quantities.
7. *Find* all remaining unknown quantities by using the relationships given in the problem.
8. *Check* and *interpret* all quantities found in the original problem.

Example 1   Number Relations

The average of two real numbers is 41.125, and their product is 1683. Find the two numbers.

Solution

1. *Read:*   Two numbers are asked for.

2. *Label:*   Let the numbers be a and b.

3. *Draw:*   A diagram is not appropriate in this problem.

4. *Translate:*

English Language	Mathematical Language	
two numbers	a and b	
Their average is 41.125.	$\dfrac{a + b}{2} = 41.125$	[1]
Their product is 1683.	$ab = 1683$	[2]

5. *Consolidate:* One technique to use when dealing with two unknowns is to express one in terms of the other, then substitute to obtain an equation in one variable. Solve equation [2] for b.

$$ab = 1683 \qquad\qquad [2]$$

$$b = \frac{1683}{a} \qquad \textit{Divide both sides by a}$$

Substitute the result into equation [1] and simplify.

$$\frac{a + b}{2} = 41.125 \qquad\qquad\qquad\qquad [1]$$

$$\frac{a + \dfrac{1683}{a}}{2} = 41.125 \qquad \textit{Substitute } \frac{1683}{a} \textit{ for } b$$

$$a + \frac{1683}{a} = 82.25 \qquad \textit{Multiply both sides by 2}$$

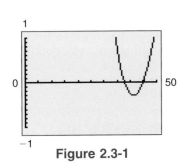

Figure 2.3-1

6. *Solve:*   Solve the equation by using the *x*-Intercept Method with the graph of $y_1 = x + \dfrac{1683}{x} - 82.25$, where *x* represents *a*. See Figure 2.3-1.

The solutions of $a + \dfrac{1683}{a} - 82.25$ are $a = 44$ and $a = 38.25$.

7. *Find:*   Find the other number, *b*, from the equation $ab = 1683$.

Let $a = 44$. $44b = 1683$

$$b = 38.25$$

Similarly, let $a = 38.25$ and use the same equation to find $b = 44$.

8. *Check:*   The average of 44 and 38.25 is $\dfrac{44 + 38.25}{2} = 41.125$.

The product of 44 and 38.25 is 1683.

The two numbers are 44 and 38.25. ∎

Solutions in Context

When solving an application problem, it is important to interpret answers in terms of the original problem. Each solution should

- make sense
- satisfy the given conditions
- answer the original question

In particular, an equation may have several solutions, some of which may not make sense in the context of the problem. For instance, distance cannot be negative, the number of people cannot be a fraction, etc.

Example 2   **Dimensions of a Rectangle**

A rectangle is twice as wide as it is high. If it has an area of 24.5 square inches, what are its dimensions?

$w = 2h$

Figure 2.3-2

Solution

1. *Read:*   The dimensions of the rectangle are asked for.

2. *Label:*   Let *w* denote the width and *h* denote the height.

3. *Draw:*   See Figure 2.3-2.

4. *Translate:* The area of a rectangle is width × height.

English Language	Mathematical Language	
Width is twice height.	$w = 2h$	[3]
The area is 24.5 in².	$wh = 24.5$	[4]

5. *Consolidate:* Substitute $2h$ for w in equation [4].

$$wh = 24.5$$
$$(2h)h = 24.5$$
$$2h^2 = 24.5$$

6. *Solve:* Solve by taking the square root of both sides.

$$h^2 = 12.25 \qquad \textit{Divide by 2}$$
$$h = \pm\sqrt{12.25} = \pm 3.5 \qquad \textit{Take square root of both sides}$$

Because height is never negative, only the positive root applies to this situation. Therefore, $h = 3.5$ in.

7. *Find:* Find the width by using equation [3] and $h = 3.5$.

$$w = 2(3.5) = 7 \text{ in.}$$

8. *Check:* The width is twice the height and the area is correct.

$$3.5(7) = 24.5 \text{ in}^2$$

Thus, the width is 7 inches and the height is 3.5 inches. ■

Example 3 **Volume of a Rectangular Box**

A rectangular box with a square base and no top is to have a volume of 30,000 cm³. If the surface area of the box is 6000 cm², what are the dimensions of the box?

Solution

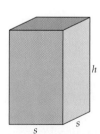

Figure 2.3-3

1. *Read:* The quantities to be found are the length, width, and height of the box.

2. *Label:* Notice that the two sides of the base have the same length. Let s denote a side of the square base of the box. Let h denote the height of the box.

3. *Draw:* See Figure 2.3-3.

4. *Translate:* The volume of a box is given by length × width × height and the surface area is the sum of the area of the base and the area of the four sides of the box.

English Language	Mathematical Language	
length, width, height	$s, s,$ and h	
surface area:		
base surface area	s^2	
each side surface area	sh	
total surface area	$s^2 + 4sh$	
Volume is 30,000 cm³	$s^2h = 30{,}000$	[5]
Surface area is 6000 cm²	$s^2 + 4sh = 6{,}000$	[6]

5. *Consolidate:* Solve equation [5] for h: $h = \dfrac{30{,}000}{s^2}$

Substitute the expression for h into equation [6].

$$s^2 + 4s\left(\frac{30{,}000}{s^2}\right) = 6000$$

$$s^2 + \frac{120{,}000}{s} = 6000$$

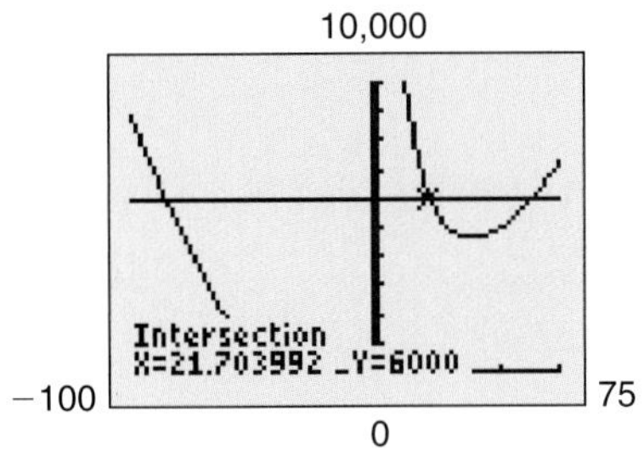

6. *Solve:* To solve by using the Intersection Method, graph $y_1 = s^2 + \dfrac{120{,}000}{s}$ and $y_2 = 6000$, as shown in Figure 2.3-4, and find the points of intersection. Therefore, $s \approx 21.70$ cm or $s \approx 64.29$ cm.

10,000

Intersection
X=21.703992 Y=6000

−100   0   75

Figure 2.3-4

7. *Find:* Use $h = \dfrac{30{,}000}{s^2}$ to find h.

$$h \approx \frac{30{,}000}{(21.70)^2}$$
$$\approx \frac{30{,}000}{470.89} \approx 63.71 \text{ cm}$$

$$h \approx \frac{30{,}000}{(64.29)^2}$$
$$\approx \frac{30{,}000}{4133.2041} \approx 7.26 \text{ cm}$$

8. *Check:* Volume
$\approx (21.7)^2(63.71)$
$\approx 30{,}000.4019$

$\approx (64.29)^2(7.26)$
$\approx 30{,}007.06177$

Surface Area
$\approx (21.7)^2 + 4(21.7)(63.71)$
≈ 6000.918

$\approx (64.29)^2 + 4(64.29)(7.26)$
≈ 6000.1857

One base is approximately 21.7 cm $\times$ 21.7 cm with a height of approximately 63.71 cm. Another base is approximately 64.29 cm $\times$ 64.29 cm with a height of approximately 7.26 cm. ∎

Interest Applications

Calculating interest is common in real-world applications. When an amount, P, is deposited or borrowed, P is referred to as the **principal.** **Interest** is the fee paid for the use of the money and is calculated as a percentage of the principal each year. When the duration of a loan or a bank balance is less than 1 year, **simple interest** is generally used. The basic rule of **simple interest** is

$$I = Prt$$

P represents the principal, r represents the *annual* interest rate, and t represents time in years.

Example 4   **Stock and Savings Returns**

A high-risk stock pays dividends at a rate of 12% per year, and a savings account pays 6% interest per year. How much of a $9000 investment should be put in the stock and how much should be put in savings to obtain a return of 8% per year on the total investment?

Solution

Read and Label: Let s be the amount invested in stock. Then the rest of the $9000, namely $9000 - s$, will be the amount in the savings account.

Translate:

$$\left(\begin{array}{l}\text{Return on } s \text{ dollars}\\\text{in stock at 12\%}\end{array}\right) + \left(\begin{array}{l}\text{Return on } 9000 - s\\\text{dollars in savings at 6\%}\end{array}\right) = 8\% \text{ of } \$9000$$

$$12\% \text{ of } s \quad + \quad 6\% \text{ of } (9000 - s) \quad = \quad 0.08(9000)$$

$$0.12s + 0.06(9000 - s) = 720$$
$$0.12s + 540 - 0.06s = 720$$
$$0.12s - 0.06s = 720 - 540$$
$$0.06s = 180$$
$$s = \frac{180}{0.06} = 3000$$

Therefore, the investment should be as follows:

• $3000 in stock

• $(9000 - 3000) = \$6000$ in the savings account

If this is done, the total return will be 12% of $3000 plus 6% of $6000, making a total return of $360 + $360 = $720—which is 8% of $9000.

Distance Applications

The basic formula for problems involving distance and a constant rate of velocity is

$$d = rt$$

where d represents the distance traveled at rate r for time t. The units for rate should be the distance units divided by the time units, such as miles per hour.

Example 5 **Distance**

A pilot wants to make an 840-mile round trip from Cleveland to Peoria and back in 5 hours flying time. There will be a headwind of 30 mph going to Peoria, and it is estimated that there will be a 40-mph tailwind returning to Cleveland. At what constant engine speed should the plane be flown?

Solution

Let r be the engine speed of the plane, and note that the headwind slows the velocity by 30 and the tailwind increases the velocity by 40.

	Distance	Actual Velocity	Time
Cleveland to Peoria	420	$r - 30$	$\dfrac{D}{r_P} = \dfrac{420}{r - 30}$
Peoria to Cleveland	420	$r + 40$	$\dfrac{D}{r_C} = \dfrac{420}{r + 40}$

The time traveling to Peoria plus the time traveling back to Cleveland is the total time traveled, or 5 hours.

$$(\text{Time to Peoria}) + (\text{Time to Cleveland}) = 5$$

$$\frac{420}{r - 30} + \frac{420}{r + 40} = 5$$

Multiply both sides by the common denominator $(r - 30)(r + 40)$, and simplify.

$$5(r - 30)(r + 40) = \frac{420}{r - 30}(r - 30)(r + 40) + \frac{420}{r + 40}(r - 30)(r + 40)$$

$$5(r - 30)(r + 40) = 420(r + 40) + 420(r - 30)$$

$$(r - 30)(r + 40) = 84(r + 40) + 84(r - 30)$$

$$r^2 + 10r - 1200 = 84r + 3360 + 84r - 2520$$

$$r^2 - 158r - 2040 = 0$$

$$(r - 170)(r + 12) = 0$$

$$r - 170 = 0 \qquad \text{or} \qquad r + 12 = 0$$

$$r = 170 \qquad\qquad r = -12$$

Obviously, the negative solution does not apply. Because both sides were multiplied by a quantity involving the variable, the positive solution, 170, should be checked in the original problem to make sure it *is* a solution.   ■

Other Applications

Example 6   Width of a Garden Walk

A landscaper wants to put a cement walk of uniform width around a rectangular garden that measures 24 by 40 feet. She has enough cement to cover 660 square feet. How wide should the walk be in order to use all the cement?

Solution

Let x denote the width of the walk in feet and draw a picture of the situation, as shown in Figure 2.3-5.

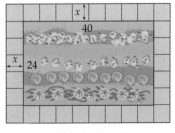

Figure 2.3-5

The length of the outer rectangle is the garden length plus walks on each end, or $40 + 2x$, and its width is the garden width plus walks on each end, or $24 + 2x$. The area of the walk is found by subtracting the area of the garden from the area of the outer rectangle.

$$(\text{Area of outer rectangle}) - (\text{Area of garden}) = \text{Area of the walk}$$

$$(40 + 2x)(24 + 2x) \quad - \quad (40)(24) = 660$$
$$960 + 128x + 4x^2 - 960 = 660$$
$$4x^2 + 128x - 660 = 0$$
$$x^2 + 32x - 165 = 0$$

$$x = \frac{-32 \pm \sqrt{(32)^2 - 4(1)(-165)}}{2(1)} \qquad \textit{Apply the quadratic formula}$$

$$x = \frac{-32 \pm \sqrt{1684}}{2}$$

$$x \approx 4.5 \text{ or } x \approx -36.5$$

Only the positive solution makes sense, so the walk should be approximately 4.5 feet wide. Check the solution in the original problem. ∎

Example 7   Box Construction

A box with no top that has a volume of 1000 cubic inches is to be constructed from a 22 × 30-inch sheet of cardboard by cutting squares of equal size from each corner and folding up the flaps, as shown in Figure 2.3-6. What size square should be cut from each corner?

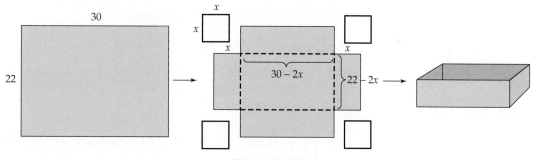

Figure 2.3-6

Solution

Let x represent the length of the side of the square to be cut from each corner. The dashed rectangle in Figure 2.3-6 is the bottom of the box. Its length is $30 - 2x$, as shown in the figure. Similarly, the width of the box will be $22 - 2x$, and its height will be x inches. Therefore,

$$\text{Length} \times \text{Width} \times \text{Height} = \text{Volume of the box}$$

$$(30 - 2x) (22 - 2x)x = 1000$$

Because the cardboard is 22 inches wide, x must be less than 11, and because x is a length, it must be positive. Therefore, the only meaningful solutions in this context are between 0 and 11.

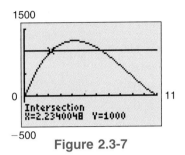

Figure 2.3-7

Graph $y_1 = (30 - 2x)(22 - 2x)x$ and $y_2 = 1000$. As shown in Figure 2.3-7, there are two points of intersection: one at approximately (2.23, 1000) and another at approximately (6.47, 1000), which is not identified on the graph. Because both are viable solutions, there are *two* boxes that meet the given conditions.

Find the dimensions of the box for each possible case.

	Case I	**Case II**
Height:	2.23 in.	6.47 in.
Length:	$30 - 2(2.23) = 25.54$ in.	$30 - 2(6.47) = 17.06$ in.
Width:	$22 - 2(2.23) = 17.54$ in.	$22 - 2(6.47) = 9.06$ in.

Figure 2.3-8

Example 8   Mixture Problem

A car radiator contains 12 quarts of fluid, 20% of which is antifreeze. How-much fluid should be drained and replaced with pure antifreeze so that the resulting mixture is 50% antifreeze?

Solution

Let x be the number of quarts of fluid to be replaced by pure antifreeze. When x quarts are drained, there are $12 - x$ quarts of fluid left in the radiator, 20% of which is antifreeze.

$$\begin{pmatrix} \text{Amount of antifreeze} \\ \text{in radiator after} \\ \text{draining } x \text{ quarts of} \\ \text{fluid} \end{pmatrix} + \begin{pmatrix} x \text{ quarts of} \\ \text{antifreeze} \end{pmatrix} = \begin{pmatrix} \text{Amount of} \\ \text{antifreeze in} \\ \text{final mixture} \end{pmatrix}$$

20% of $(12 - x)$ + x =   50% of 12

$$0.2(12 - x) + x = 0.5(12)$$
$$2.4 - 0.2x + x = 6$$
$$0.8x = 3.6$$
$$x = \frac{3.6}{0.8} = 4.5$$

Therefore, 4.5 quarts should be drained and replaced with pure antifreeze.

Exercises 2.3

In Exercises 1–4, a problem situation is given.
  a. Decide what is being asked for, and label the unknown quantities.
  b. Translate the verbal statements in the problem and the relationships between the known and unknown quantities into mathematical language, using a table like those in Examples 1–3. The table is provided in Exercises 1–2. You need not find an equation to be solved.

1. The sum of two numbers is 15 and the difference of their squares is 5. What are the numbers?

English Language	Mathematical Language
the two numbers	
Their sum is 15.	
The difference of their squares is 5.	

2. The sum of the squares of two consecutive integers is 4513. What are the integers?

English Language	Mathematical Language
the two integers	
The integers are consecutive.	
The sum of their squares is 4513.	

3. A rectangle has a perimeter of 45 centimeters and an area of 112.5 square centimeters. What are its dimensions?

4. A triangle has an area of 96 square inches, and its height is two-thirds of its base. What are the base and height of the triangle?

In Exercises 5–8, set up the problem by labeling the unknowns, translating the given information into mathematical language, and finding an equation that will produce the solution to the problem. You need not solve this equation.

5. A worker gets an 8% pay raise and now makes $1600 per month. What was the worker's old salary?

6. A merchant has 5 pounds of mixed nuts that cost $30. He wants to add peanuts that cost $1.50 per pound and cashews that cost $4.50 per pound to obtain 50 pounds of a mixture that costs $2.90 per pound. How many pounds of peanuts are needed?

7. The diameter of a circle is 16 cm. By what amount must the radius be decreased in order to decrease the area by 48π square centimeters?

8. A corner lot has dimensions 25 by 40 yards. The city plans to take a strip of uniform width along the two sides bordering the streets in order to widen these roads. How wide should the strip be if the remainder of the lot is to have an area of 844 square yards?

In Exercises 9–20, solve the problem.

9. You have already invested $550 in a stock with an annual return of 11%. How much of an additional $1100 should be invested at 12% and how much at 6% so that the total return on the entire $1650 is 9%?

10. If you borrow $500 from a credit union at 12% annual interest and $250 from a bank at 18% annual interest, what is the effective annual interest rate (that is, what single rate of interest on $750 would result in the same total amount of interest)?

11. A radiator contains 8 quarts of fluid, 40% of which is antifreeze. How much fluid should be drained and replaced with pure antifreeze so that the new mixture is 60% antifreeze?

12. A radiator contains 10 quarts of fluid, 30% of which is antifreeze. How much fluid should be drained and replaced with pure antifreeze so that the new mixture is 40% antifreeze?

13. Two cars leave a gas station at the same time, one traveling north and the other south. The northbound car travels at 50 mph. After 3 hours the cars are 345 miles apart. How fast is the southbound car traveling?

14. An airplane flew with the wind for 2.5 hours and returned the same distance against the wind in 3.5 hours. If the cruising speed of the plane was a constant 360 mph in air, how fast was the wind blowing? *Hint:* If the wind speed is r miles per hour, then the plane travels at $(360 + r)$ mph with the wind and at $(360 - r)$ mph against the wind.

15. The average of two real numbers is 41.375 and their product is 1668. What are the numbers?

16. A rectangle is four times as long as it is wide. If it has an area of 36 square inches, what are its dimensions?

17. A 13-foot-long ladder leans on a wall. The bottom of the ladder is 5 feet from the wall. If the bottom is pulled out 3 feet farther from the wall, how far does the top of the ladder move down the wall? *Hint:* The ladder, ground, and wall form a right triangle. Draw pictures of this triangle before and after the ladder is moved. Use the Pythagorean Theorem to set up an equation.

18. A factory that makes can openers has fixed costs for building, fixtures, machinery, etc. of $26,000. The variable cost for material and labor for making one can opener is $2.75.
  a. What is the total cost of making 1000 can openers? 20,000? 40,000?
  b. What is the average cost per can opener in each case?

19. Red Riding Hood drives the 432 miles to Grandmother's house in 1 hour less than it takes the Wolf to drive the same route. Her average speed is 6 mph faster than the Wolf's average speed. How fast does each drive?

20. To get to work Sam jogs 3 kilometers to the train, then rides the remaining 5 kilometers. If the train goes 40 km per hour faster than Sam's constant rate of jogging and the entire trip takes 30 minutes, how fast does Sam jog?

In Exercises 21–24, an object is thrown upward, dropped, or thrown downward and travels in a vertical line subject only to gravity with wind resistance ignored. The height h, in feet, of the object above the ground after t seconds is given by

$$h = -16t^2 + v_0 t + h_0$$

where h_0 is the initial height of the object at starting time $t = 0$, and v_0 is the initial velocity (speed) of the object at time $t = 0$. The value of v_0 is taken as positive if the object starts moving upward at time $t = 0$ and negative if the object starts moving downward at $t = 0$. An object that is dropped (rather than thrown downward) has initial velocity $v_0 = 0$.

21. How long does it take an object to reach the ground in each case?
  a. It is dropped from the top of a 640-foot-high building.

  b. It is thrown downward from the top of the same building, with an initial velocity of 52 feet per second.

22. You are standing on a cliff 200 feet high. How long will it take a rock to reach the ground at the bottom of the cliff in each case?
  a. You drop it.
  b. You throw it downward at an initial velocity of 40 feet per second.
  c. How far does the rock fall in 2 seconds if you throw it downward with an initial velocity of 40 feet per second.

23. A rocket is fired straight up from ground level with an initial velocity of 800 feet per second.
  a. How long does it take the rocket to rise 3200 feet?
  b. When will the rocket hit the ground?

24. A rocket loaded with fireworks is to be shot vertically upward from ground level with an initial velocity of 200 feet per second. When the rocket reaches a height of 400 feet on its upward trip, the fireworks will be detonated. How many seconds after lift-off will this take place?

25. The dimensions of a rectangular box are consecutive integers. If the box has volume of 13,800 cubic centimeters, what are its dimensions?

26. Find a real number that exceeds its cube by 2.

27. The lateral surface area S of the right circular cone at the left in the figure below is given by $S = \pi r \sqrt{r^2 + h^2}$. What radius should be used to produce a cone of height 5 inches and lateral surface area 100 square inches?

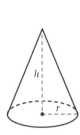 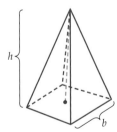

28. The lateral surface area of the right square pyramid at the right in the figure above is given by $S = b\sqrt{b^2 + 4h^2}$. If the pyramid has height 10 feet and lateral surface area 100 square feet, what is the length of a side b of its base?

29. Suppose that the open-top box being made from a sheet of cardboard in Example 7 is required to have at least one of its dimensions *greater* than 18 inches. What size square should be cut from each corner?

30. A homemade loaf of bread turns out to be a perfect cube. Five slices of bread, each 0.6 inch thick, are cut from one end of the loaf. The remainder of the loaf now has a volume of 235 cubic inches. What were the dimensions of the original loaf?

31. A rectangular bin with an open top and volume of 38.72 cubic feet is to be built. The length of its base must be twice the width and the bin must be at least 3 feet high. Material for the base of the bin costs $12 per square foot and material for the sides costs $8 per square foot. If it costs $538.56 to build the bin, what are its dimensions?

2.4   Other Types of Equations

Objectives

- Solve absolute-value equations
- Solve radical equations
- Solve fractional equations

Like linear and quadratic equations, other types of equations can be solved algebraically. This section outlines procedures for solving absolute-value, radical, and fractional equations.

Definition of Absolute Value

The **absolute value** of a number c is denoted $|c|$ and is defined as follows.

Algebraic Definition of Absolute Value

> If $c \geq 0$, then $|c| = c$.
>
> If $c < 0$, then $|c| = -c$.

For example, because 5 is positive, $|5| = 5$, and because -3 is negative, $|-3| = -(-3) = 3$. To determine $|\pi - 6|$, note that $\pi \approx 3.14$ and $\pi - 6 < 0$. Therefore, the second part of the definition applies.

$$|\pi - 6| = -(\pi - 6) = 6 - \pi$$

In all cases, the absolute value of a number is nonnegative.

Absolute value can also be interpreted geometrically as a distance. Observe that the distance between -5 and 3 on the number line is 8 units.

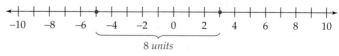

Figure 2.4-1

Notice that $|-5 - 3| = |-8| = 8$. This is an example of a key geometric property of absolute value.

Absolute Value and Distance

If c and d are real numbers, then

$|c - d|$ is the distance between c and d on the number line.

For example, the number $|5 + \sqrt{2}|$ can be written as $|5 - (-\sqrt{2})|$ and thus represents the distance between 5 and $-\sqrt{2}$ on the number line. See Figure 2.4-2.

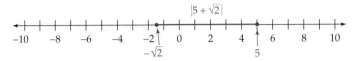

Figure 2.4-2

In the special case when $d = 0$, the distance formula shows that the distance from c to 0 is $|c - 0| = |c|$, which is an alternative definition of $|c|$.

Geometric Definition of Absolute Value

If c is a real number, then

$|c|$ is the distance from c to 0 on the number line.

For example, $|-3.5|$ denotes the distance from -3.5 to 0 on the number line, as shown below.

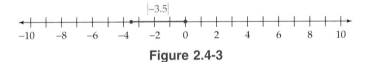

Figure 2.4-3

Properties of Absolute Value

The following properties are helpful in simplifying absolute value expressions.

Properties of Absolute Value

Let c and d represent real numbers.

1. $|c| \geq 0$ and $|c| > 0$ when $c \neq 0$
2. $|c| = |-c|$
3. $|cd| = |c| \cdot |d|$
4. $\left|\dfrac{c}{d}\right| = \dfrac{|c|}{|d|}$, where $d \neq 0$

CAUTION

When c and d have opposite signs, $|c + d|$ is *not equal* to $|c| + |d|$. For example, if $c = -3$ and $d = 5$, then

$$|c + d| = |-3 + 5|$$
$$= 2$$

But, $|c| + |d|$
$$= |-3| + |5|$$
$$= 3 + 8$$
$$= 8$$

Illustrations of Properties 2, 3, and 4 for absolute value are shown below.

Property 2: Let $c = 3$. Then $|c| = |3| = 3$ and $|-c| = |-3| = 3$.

Therefore, $|3| = |-3|$.

Property 3: Let $c = 6$ and $d = -2$.

$$|cd| = |6(-2)| = |-12| = 12$$
$$|c| \cdot |d| = |6| \cdot |-2| = 6 \cdot 2 = 12$$

Therefore, $|6(-2)| = |6| \cdot |-2|$.

Property 4: Let $c = -5$ and $d = 4$.

$$\left|\frac{c}{d}\right| = \left|\frac{-5}{4}\right| = \left|-\frac{5}{4}\right| = \frac{5}{4} \quad \text{and} \quad \frac{|c|}{|d|} = \frac{|-5|}{|4|} = \frac{5}{4}$$

Therefore, $\left|\frac{-5}{4}\right| = \frac{|5|}{|4|}$.

The caution shows that $|c + d| < |c| + |d|$ when $c = -3$ and $d = 5$. The general case is called the Triangle Inequality.

The Triangle Inequality

> **For any real numbers c and d,**
>
> $$|c + d| \le |c| + |d|.$$

Square Root of Squares

When c is a positive number, then $\sqrt{c^2} = c$. This is not true when c is negative. Consider the case when $c = -3$.

$$\sqrt{(-3)^2} = \sqrt{9} = 3, \text{ which is } not -3$$

But $\sqrt{c^2}$ is equal to the absolute value of c when c is any real number. That is, $\sqrt{(-3)^2} = \sqrt{9} = 3 = |-3|$.

Square Root of Squares

> **For every real number c,**
>
> $$\sqrt{c^2} = |c|.$$

Solving Absolute-Value Equations

Absolute-value equations can be solved by using the definitions. Some equations lend themselves to the geometric definition, while others are solved more easily using the algebraic definition. Graphing techniques can be used to check all solutions.

Technology Tip

To compute absolute values on a calculator, use the ABS feature. The ABS feature is on the keyboard of HP-38 and in the NUM submenu of the MATH menu of TI and SHARP 9600. It is in the NUM submenu of the Casio 9850 OPTN menu.

Example 1   Using the Geometric Definition of Absolute Value

Solve $|x - 4| = 8$ using the geometric definition of absolute value.

Solution

The equation $|x - 4| = 8$ can be interpreted as

the distance from x to 4 is 8 units.

See Figure 2.4-4.

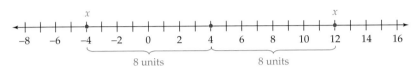

Figure 2.4-4

The two possible values of x that are solutions of the original equation are -4 and 12, as shown.

NOTE When dealing with long expressions inside absolute value bars, do the computations inside first, and then take the absolute value of the simplified expression.

Extraneous Solutions

As shown in Example 2 below, some solutions do not make the original equation true when checked by substitution. Such "fake" solutions are called **extraneous solutions,** or **extraneous roots.** Because extraneous solutions may occur when solving absolute-value equations, all solutions *must* be checked by substituting into the original equation or by graphing.

Example 2   Using the Algebraic Definition of Absolute Value

Solve $|x + 4| = 5x - 2$ by using the algebraic definition of absolute value.

Solution

The absolute value of any quantity is either the quantity itself or the opposite of the quantity, depending on whether the quantity is positive or negative. So, $|x - 4|$ is either $x - 4$ or $-(x - 4)$. Therefore, the original equation can be rewritten as two equations that do not involve absolute value.

$$|x + 4| = 5x - 2$$

$$x + 4 = 5x - 2 \qquad \text{or} \qquad -(x + 4) = 5x - 2$$
$$-4x = -6 \qquad\qquad\qquad -x - 4 = 5x - 2$$
$$x = \frac{6}{4} = \frac{3}{2} \qquad\qquad\qquad -6x = 2$$
$$x = -\frac{2}{6} = -\frac{1}{3}$$

Each solution must be checked in the original equation.

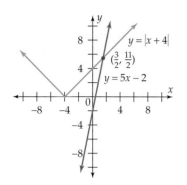

Figure 2.4-5

$x = \dfrac{3}{2}$ is a solution and checks in the original equation, as shown in Figure 2.4-5. However, $x = -\dfrac{1}{3}$ is an extraneous root because the graphs do not intersect when $x = -\dfrac{1}{3}$, which can be confirmed by substitution. Therefore, the only solution of $|x + 4| = 5x - 2$ is $x = \dfrac{3}{2}$. ∎

Example 3   Solving an Absolute Value Equation

Solve $|x^2 + 4x - 3| = 2$.

Solution

Use the algebraic definition of absolute value to rewrite the original equation as two equations.

$$|x^2 + 4x - 3| = 2$$

$$\begin{array}{c|c}
x^2 + 4x - 3 = 2 & -(x^2 + 4x - 3) = 2 \\
x^2 + 4x - 5 = 0 & -x^2 - 4x + 3 = 2 \\
 & -x^2 - 4x + 1 = 0
\end{array}$$

The equation on the left can be solved by factoring, and the equation on the right by using the quadratic formula.

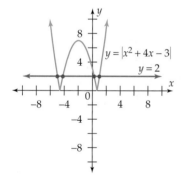

Figure 2.4-6

$$\begin{array}{c|c}
x^2 + 4x - 5 = 0 & x^2 + 4x - 1 = 0 \\
 & \\
(x + 5)(x - 1) = 0 & x = \dfrac{-4 \pm \sqrt{4^2 - 4(1)(-1)}}{2(1)} \\
 & \\
x = -5 \text{ or } x = 1 & x = \dfrac{-4 \pm \sqrt{20}}{2} = \dfrac{-4 \pm 2\sqrt{5}}{2} \\
 & x = -2 \pm \sqrt{5}
\end{array}$$

See Figure 2.4-6 to confirm that all four values are solutions. ∎

Solving Radical Equations

Radical equations are equations that contain expressions with a variable under a radical symbol. Although the approximate solutions of a radical equation can be found graphically, exact solutions can be found algebraically in many cases.

The algebraic solution method depends on the following fact.

<blockquote>

If A and B are algebraic expressions and $A = B$,
then $A^n = B^n$ for every positive integer n.

</blockquote>

NOTE Squaring both sides of an equation *may* introduce extraneous roots.

For example, if $x - 2 = 3$, then $(x - 2)^2 = 3^2$. Therefore, every solution of $x - 2 = 3$ is also a solution of $(x - 2)^2 = 9$. However, -1 is a solution of $(x - 2)^2 = 9$, but -1 is *not* a solution of $x - 2 = 3$.

Power Principle

If both sides of an equation are raised to the same positive integer power, then every solution of the original equation is a solution of the new equation. However, the new equation may have solutions that are not solutions of the original one.

CAUTION

Although it is always a good idea to verify solutions, solutions to radical equations *must* be checked in the original equation.

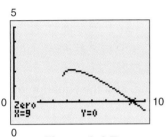

Figure 2.4-7

Example 4 Solving a Radical Equation

Solve $5 + \sqrt{3x - 11} = x$

Solution

Rearrange terms to get the radical expression alone on one side.

$$\sqrt{3x - 11} = x - 5$$

Square both sides to remove the radical sign and solve the resulting equation.

$$\left(\sqrt{3x - 11}\right)^2 = (x - 5)^2$$
$$3x - 11 = x^2 - 10x + 25$$
$$0 = x^2 - 13x + 36$$
$$0 = (x - 4)(x - 9)$$

$$x - 4 = 0 \qquad \text{or} \qquad x - 9 = 0$$
$$x = 4 \qquad\qquad\qquad x = 9$$

If these values are solutions of the original equation, they should be x-intercepts of the graph of $y = \sqrt{3x - 11} - (x - 5)$. But Figure 2.4-7 shows that the graph does not have an x-intercept at $x = 4$. That is, $x = 4$ is an extraneous solution.

The graph suggests that $x = 9$ is a solution of the original equation, which can be confirmed by substitution.

Sometimes the Power Principle must be applied more than once to eliminate all radicals.

Example 5 Using the Power Principle Twice

Solve $\sqrt{2x - 3} - \sqrt{x + 7} = 2$.

Solution

Rearrange terms so that one side contains only a single radical term.

$$\sqrt{2x - 3} = \sqrt{x + 7} + 2$$

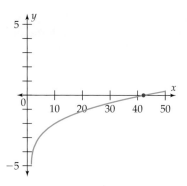

Figure 2.4-8

Square both sides and isolate the remaining radical.

$$\left(\sqrt{2x-3}\right)^2 = \left(\sqrt{x+7}+2\right)^2$$
$$2x - 3 = \left(\sqrt{x+7}\right)^2 + 2 \cdot 2\sqrt{x+7} + 2^2$$
$$2x - 3 = x + 7 + 4\sqrt{x+7} + 4$$
$$x - 14 = 4\sqrt{x+7}$$

Square both sides again, and solve the resulting equation.

$$(x-14)^2 = \left(4\sqrt{x+7}\right)^2$$
$$x^2 - 28x + 196 = 4^2\left(\sqrt{x+7}\right)^2$$
$$x^2 - 28x + 196 = 16(x+7)$$
$$x^2 - 28x + 196 = 16x + 112$$
$$x^2 - 44x + 84 = 0$$
$$(x-2)(x-42) = 0$$
$$x - 2 = 0 \qquad \text{or} \qquad x - 42 = 0$$
$$x = 2 \qquad\qquad\qquad x = 42$$

Verify by substitution that $x = 2$ is an extraneous root but that $x = 42$ is a solution. ∎

Technology Tip

Graphing calculators do not always show all solutions of a radical equation. See Example 3 in Section 2.1 for an illustration of a technological quirk.

Example 6   **Distance**

Stella is standing at point A on the bank of a river that is 2.5 kilometers wide. She wants to reach point B, which is 15 kilometers downstream on the opposite bank. She plans to row downstream to point C on the opposite shore and then run to B, as shown in Figure 2.4-9. She can row downstream at a rate of 4 kilometers per hour and can run at 8 kilometers per hour. If her trip is to take 3 hours, how far from B should she land?

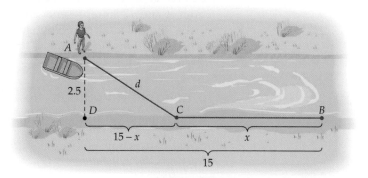

Figure 2.4-9

Solution

Refer to Figure 2.4-9. The basic formula for distance can be written in different ways.

$$d = rt \qquad \text{or} \qquad t = \frac{d}{r}$$

Let x represent the distance between C and B, t represent the time required to run from C to B, and r represent the rate Stella can run (8 kilometers per hour).

Therefore, $t = \dfrac{x}{8}$ denotes the time needed to run from C to B.

Similarly, $t = \dfrac{d}{4}$ can express the time required to row distance d.

Since $15 - x$ is the distance from D to C, the Pythagorean Theorem can be applied to right triangle ADC.

NOTE To review the Pythagorean Theorem, see the Geometry Review Appendix.

$$d^2 = (15 - x)^2 + 2.5^2 \qquad \text{or equivalently} \qquad d = \sqrt{(15 - x)^2 + 6.25}$$

Therefore, the total time for the trip is given by a function of x.

$$\begin{aligned} T(x) &= \text{rowing time} + \text{running time} \\ &= \frac{d}{4} + \frac{x}{8} \\ &= \frac{\sqrt{(x - 15)^2 + 6.25}}{4} + \frac{x}{8} \end{aligned}$$

If the trip is to take 3 hours, then $T(x) = 3$.

$$\frac{\sqrt{(x - 15)^2 + 6.25}}{4} + \frac{x}{8} = 3$$

Using the viewing window with $0 \le x \le 20$ and $-2 \le y \le 2$, graph this function.

$$f(x) = \frac{\sqrt{(x - 15)^2 + 6.25}}{4} + \frac{x}{8} - 3$$

Find the zeros of f and interpret their values in the context of the problem.

The zeros of f are $x \approx 6.74$ and $x \approx 17.26$. These represent the distances that Stella should land from B. 6.74 represents a downstream destination from A and 17.26 represents an upstream destination from A. Therefore, Stella should land approximately 6.74 kilometers from B to make the downstream trip in 3 hours. ∎

Fractional Equations

If $f(x)$ and $g(x)$ are algebraic expressions, the quotient $\dfrac{f(x)}{g(x)}$ is called a **fractional expression** with numerator $f(x)$ and denominator $g(x)$. As in all fractions, *the denominator, $g(x)$, cannot be zero.* That is, if $g(x) = 0$, the fraction $\dfrac{f(x)}{g(x)}$ is undefined. The following principle is used to solve fractional equations of the form $\dfrac{f(x)}{g(x)} = 0$.

Solving $\dfrac{f(x)}{g(x)} = 0$

Let $f(x)$ and $g(x)$ represent algebraic expressions. Then the solutions of the equation

$$\frac{f(x)}{g(x)} = 0$$

are all values of x such that $f(x) = 0$ and $g(x) \neq 0$.

Example 7   **Solving a Fractional Equation**

Solve $\dfrac{6x^2 - x - 1}{2x^2 + 9x - 5} = 0.$

Solution

Find all solutions to $6x^2 - x - 1 = 0$.

$$6x^2 - x - 1 = 0$$
$$(3x + 1)(2x - 1) = 0$$
$$3x + 1 = 0 \qquad \text{or} \qquad 2x - 1 = 0$$
$$x = -\frac{1}{3} \qquad\qquad\qquad x = \frac{1}{2}$$

Discard any solution that makes $2x^2 + 9x - 5 = 0$.

For $x = -\dfrac{1}{3}$: $\qquad 2\left(-\dfrac{1}{3}\right)^2 + 9\left(-\dfrac{1}{3}\right) - 5 = -\dfrac{70}{9} \neq 0$

For $x = \dfrac{1}{2}$: $\qquad 2\left(\dfrac{1}{2}\right)^2 + 9\left(\dfrac{1}{2}\right) - 5 = 0$

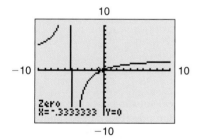

Figure 2.4-10a

Therefore, $x = -\dfrac{1}{3}$ is the solution of $\dfrac{6x^2 - x - 1}{2x^2 + 9x - 5} = 0$, and $x = \dfrac{1}{2}$ is not a solution. Figure 2.4-10a confirms that $x = -\dfrac{1}{3}$ is a solution and that $x = \dfrac{1}{2}$ is extraneous.

■

Technology Tip

In Figure 2.4-10a, the vertical line shown at $x = -5$ is not part of the graph but is a result of the calculator evaluating the function just to the left of $x = -5$ and just to the right of $x = -5$, but not at $x = -5$. The calculator erroneously connects these points with a near vertical segment. By choosing a window such as $-7.7 \leq x \leq 1.7$ and $-2.2 \leq y \leq 10.2$ on a TI-83 graphing calculator, the near vertical line will not be drawn. Using the trace feature in Figure 2.4-10b identifies a hole at $x = \dfrac{1}{2}$, where the function is not defined.

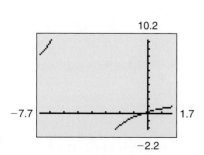

Figure 2.4-10b

Exercises 2.4

In Exercises 1–8, rewrite each statement using the geometric definition of absolute value. Represent each on a number line, and find the value(s) of the variable.

1. The distance between y and 2 is 4.

2. The distance between x and 4 is 6.

3. The distance between $3w$ and 2 is 8.

4. The distance between $4x$ and 3 is 6.

5. The distance between $-2x$ and 4 is 5.

6. The distance between $-4z$ and 3 is 11.

7. The distance between $-3x$ and -2 is 5.

8. The distance between $-4w$ and -6 is $\frac{5}{2}$.

In Exercises 9–20, find all real solutions of each equation.

9. $|2x + 3| = 9$

10. $|3x - 5| = 7$

11. $|6x - 9| = 0$

12. $|4x - 5| = -9$

13. $|2x + 3| = 4x - 1$

14. $|3x - 2| = 5x + 4$

15. $|x - 3| = x$

16. $|2x - 1| = 2x + 1$

17. $|x^2 + 4x - 1| = 4$

18. $|x^2 + 2x - 9| = 6$

19. $|x^2 - 5x + 1| = 3$

20. $|12x^2 + 5x - 7| = 4$

21. Explain why there are no real numbers that satisfy the equation $|2x^2 + 3x| = -12$.

22. Describe in words the meaning of the inequality.

$$|a + b| \le |a| + |b|$$

Make sure to consider positive and negative values of a and b.

23. Joan weighs 120 pounds and her doctor told her that her weight is 5 percent from her ideal weight. What are the possible values, to the nearest pound, for Joan's ideal body weight?

24. A tightrope walker is 8 feet from one end of the rope. If he takes 2 steps and each step is 10 inches long, how far is he from the same end of the rope? Give both possible answers.

25. An instrument measures a wind speed of 20 feet per second. The true wind speed is within 5 feet per second of the measured wind speed. What are the possible values for the true wind speed?

26. For two real numbers s and t, the notation $\min(s, t)$ represents the smaller of the two numbers. When $s = t$, $\min(s, t)$ represents the common value. It can be shown that $\min(s, t)$ can be expressed as shown.

$$\min(s, t) = \frac{s + t - |s - t|}{2}$$

For each of the following, verify the equation.
a. $s = 4$ and $t = 1$
b. $s = -2$ and $t = 3$
c. $s = t = -5$

27. In statistical quality control, one needs to find the proportion of the product that is not acceptable. The upper and lower control limits (CL) are found by solving the following equation in which p is the mean percent defective, and n is the sample size for CL.

$$|CL - p| = 3\sqrt{\frac{p(1 - p)}{n}}$$

Find CL when $p = 0.02$ and $n = 200$.

In Exercises 28–63, find all real solutions of each equation. Find exact solutions when possible, approximate solutions otherwise.

28. $\sqrt{x - 7} = 4$

29. $\sqrt{4x + 9} = 5$

30. $\sqrt{3x - 2} = 7$

31. $\sqrt[3]{5 - 11x} = 3$

32. $\sqrt[3]{6x - 10} = 2$

33. $\sqrt[3]{x^2 - 1} = 2$

34. $\sqrt[3]{(x + 1)^2} = 4$

35. $\sqrt{x^2 - x - 1} = 1$

36. $\sqrt{x^2 - 5x + 4} = 2$

37. $\sqrt{x + 7} = x - 5$

38. $\sqrt{x + 5} = x - 1$

39. $\sqrt{3x^2 + 7x - 2} = x + 1$

40. $\sqrt{4x^2 - 10x + 5} = x - 3$

41. $\sqrt[3]{x^3 + x^2 - 4x + 5} = x + 1$

42. $\sqrt[3]{x^3 - 6x^2 + 2x + 3} = x - 1$

43. $\sqrt[5]{9 - x^2} = x^2 + 1$

44. $\sqrt[4]{x^3 - x + 1} = x^2 - 1$

45. $\sqrt[3]{x^5 - x^3 - x} = x + 2$

46. $\sqrt{x^3 + 2x^2 - 1} = x^3 + 2x - 1$

47. $\sqrt{x^2 + 3x - 6} = x^4 - 3x^2 + 2$

48. $\sqrt[3]{x^4 + x^2 + 1} = x^2 - x - 5$

49. $\sqrt{5x + 6} = 3 + \sqrt{x + 3}$

50. $\sqrt{3y + 1} - 1 = \sqrt{y + 4}$

51. $\sqrt{2x - 5} = 1 + \sqrt{x - 3}$

52. $\sqrt{x - 3} + \sqrt{x + 5} = 4$

53. $\sqrt{3x + 5} + \sqrt{2x + 3} + 1 = 0$

54. $\sqrt{20 - x} = \sqrt{9 - x} + 3$

55. $\sqrt{6x^2 + x + 7} - \sqrt{3x + 2} = 2$

56. $\sqrt{x^3 + x^2 - 3} = \sqrt{x^3 - x + 3} - 1$

57. $\sqrt{x + 2} = 3$

58. $\dfrac{x^2 - 2x + 1}{x - 2} = 0$

59. $\dfrac{2x^2 - 3x - 4}{x - 4} = 0$

60. $\dfrac{x^2 - x - 2}{x^2 + 5x + 5} = 0$

61. $\dfrac{x^2 - 3x + 2}{x^2 + x - 6} = 0$

62. $\dfrac{2x^2 - 7x + 6}{3x^2 - 5x - 2} = 0$

63. $\dfrac{3x^2 + 4x + 1}{3x^2 - 5x - 2} = 0$

In Exercises 64–67, assume that all letters represent positive numbers. Solve each equation for the required letter.

64. $T = 2\pi\sqrt{\dfrac{m}{g}}$ for g

65. $K = \sqrt{1 - \dfrac{x^2}{u^2}}$ for u

66. $R = \sqrt{d^2 + k^2}$ for d

67. $A = \sqrt{1 + \dfrac{a^2}{b^2}}$ for b

68. A rope is to be stretched at uniform height from a tree to a fence, 20 feet from the tree, and then to the side of a building, 35 ft from the tree, at a point 30 ft from the fence, as shown in the figure.
a. If 63 ft of rope is to be used, how far from the building wall should the rope meet the fence?
b. How far from the building wall should the rope meet the fence if as little rope as possible is to be used? *Hint:* What is the x value of the lowest point on the graph?

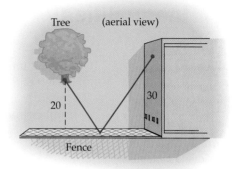

Tree   (aerial view)

20

30

Fence

69. A spotlight is to be placed on a building wall to illuminate a bench that is 32 feet from the base of the wall. The intensity of the light I at the bench is known to be $I = \dfrac{x}{d^3}$, where x is the spotlight's height above the ground and d is the distance from the bench to the spotlight.
a. Express I as a function of x. It may help to draw a picture.
b. How high should the spotlight be in order to provide maximum illumination at the bench? *Hint:* What is the x value of the highest point on the graph?

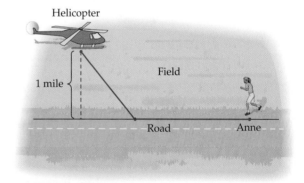

Helicopter

Field

1 mile

Road   Anne

70. Anne is standing on a straight road and wants to reach her helicopter, which is located 2 miles down the road from her and a mile off the road in a field. She can run 5 miles per hour on the road and 3 miles per hour in the field. She plans to run down the road, then cut diagonally across the field to reach the helicopter.
a. Where should she leave the road in order to reach the helicopter in exactly 42 minutes, that is, 0.7 hour?
b. Where should she leave the road in order to reach the helicopter as soon as possible? (see Exercise 68**b**)

2.5 Inequalities

Objectives

- Use interval notation
- Solve linear inequalities and extended linear inequalities
- Find exact solutions of quadratic and factorable inequalities

The statement $c < d$, which is read "c is less than d," means that c is to the left of d on the real number line. Similarly, the statement $c > d$, which is read "c is greater than d," means that c is to the right of d on the real number line.

In the set of real numbers, any pair of numbers can be compared because the set of real numbers is **ordered.** That is, for any two real numbers a and b, exactly one of the following statements is true.

$$a < b \qquad a = b \qquad a > b$$

The two statements $c < d$ and $d > c$ are equivalent, and both mean that $d - c$ is positive. The statement $c \leq d$, read "c is less than or equal to d," means either c is less than d or c is equal to d. A similar statement applies to $c \geq d$.

The statement $b < c < d$, called an **extended inequality,** means

$$b < c \quad \text{and simultaneously} \quad c < d.$$

Interval Notation

An **interval** of numbers is the set of all numbers lying between two fixed numbers. Such sets appear frequently enough to merit special notation.

Interval Notation

Let c and d be real numbers with $c < d$.

$[c, d]$ denotes the set of all real numbers x such that $c \leq x \leq d$.

(c, d) denotes the set of all real numbers x such that $c < x < d$.

$[c, d)$ denotes the set of all real numbers x such that $c \leq x < d$.

$(c, d]$ denotes the set of all real numbers x such that $c < x \leq d$.

All four sets above are called intervals from c to d, where c and d are the **endpoints** of the interval. The interval $[c, d]$ is called the **closed interval** from c to d because both endpoints are included, as indicated by brackets, and (c, d) is called the **open interval** from c to d because neither endpoint is included, as indicated by parentheses. The last two intervals in the box above are called **half-open intervals,** where the bracket indicates which endpoint is included.

The half-line extending to the right or left of b is also called an interval.

NOTE The symbol ∞ is read "infinity" but does *not* denote a real number. It is simply part of the notation used to denote half-lines.

- For the half-line to the right of b,
  $[b, \infty)$ denotes the set of all real numbers x such that $x \geq b$.
  (b, ∞) denotes the set of all real numbers x such that $x > b$.
- For the half-line to the left of b,
  $(-\infty, b]$ denotes the set of all real numbers x such that $x \leq b$.
  $(-\infty, b)$ denotes the set of all real numbers x such that $x < b$.

Similar notation is used for the entire number line.
$(-\infty, \infty)$ denotes the set of all real numbers.

Solving Inequalities

Solutions of inequalities in one variable are all values of the variable that make the inequality true. Such solutions may be found by using algebraic, geometric, and graphical methods, each of which is discussed in this section. Whenever possible, algebra will be used to obtain exact solutions. When algebraic methods are tedious or when no algebraic method exists, approximate graphical solutions will be found.

Equivalent Inequalities

Like equations, two inequalities are **equivalent** if they have the same solutions. The basic tools for solving inequalities are as follows.

Basic Principles for Solving Inequalities

Performing any of the following operations on an inequality produces an equivalent inequality.

1. **Add or subtract the same quantity on both sides of the inequality.**
2. **Multiply or divide both sides of the inequality by the same *positive* quantity.**
3. **Multiply or divide both sides of the inequality by the same *negative* quantity, and *reverse the direction of the inequality*.**

Note that Principles **1** and **2** are the same as the principles used in solving linear *equations*, but Principle **3** states that when an inequality is multiplied or divided by a negative number, the inequality sign must be reversed. For example,

$$2 < 5$$
$$(-1)(2) > (-1)(5) \quad \textit{Multiply by } -1 \textit{ and reverse the inequality}$$
$$-2 > -5$$

Solving Linear Inequalities

Example 1 Solving an Extended Linear Inequality

Solve $2 \leq 3x + 5 < 2x + 11$.

Solution

A solution of the inequality $2 \le 3x + 5 < 2x + 11$ is any number that is a solution of *both* of the following inequalities.

$$2 \le 3x + 5 \qquad \text{and} \qquad 3x + 5 < 2x + 11$$

Each of these inequalities can be solved by the principles listed above.

Subtract 5	*Subtract 2x and Subtract 5*
$2 - 5 \le 3x$	$3x - 2x < 11 - 5$
Simplify	*Simplify*
$-3 \le 3x$	$x < 6$
Divide by 3	
$-1 \le x$	

The solutions are all real numbers that satisfy *both* $-1 \le x$ *and* $x < 6$, that is, $-1 \le x < 6$. Therefore, the solutions are the numbers in the interval $[-1, 6)$, as shown in Figure 2.5-1.

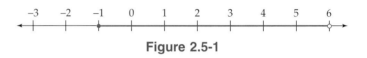

Figure 2.5-1

Example 2   Solving an Extended Inequality

Solve $4 < 3 - 5x < 18$.

Solution

When a variable appears only in the middle of an extended inequality, the process can be streamlined by performing any operation on each part of the extended inequality.

$$4 < 3-5x < 18$$
$$1 < -5x\ < 15 \qquad \text{\textit{Subtract 3 from each part}}$$
$$-\frac{1}{5} >\ x\ > -3 \qquad \text{\textit{Divide each part by} -5}$$
$$\text{\textit{and reverse direction of the}}$$
$$\text{\textit{inequalities}}$$

Intervals are usually written from the smaller to the larger, so the solution to the extended inequality is

$$-3 < x < -\frac{1}{5}.$$

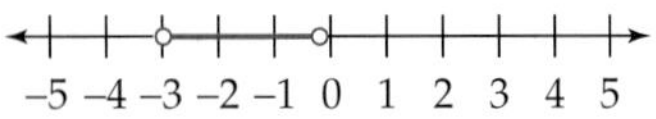

The solution of the extended inequality is the interval $\left(-3, -\frac{1}{5}\right)$, as shown in Figure 2.5-2, where open circles indicate that the endpoints are not included in the interval.

Figure 2.5-2

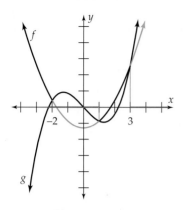

Figure 2.5-3a

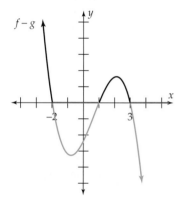

Figure 2.5-3b

Solving Other Inequalities

Although the basic principles play a role in the solution of nonlinear inequalities, geometrically the key to solving such inequalities is the following fact.

> **The solutions of an inequality of the form $f(x) < g(x)$ consist of intervals on the x-axis where the graph of f is below the graph of g.**

> **The solutions of $f(x) > g(x)$ consist of intervals on the x-axis where the graph of f is above the graph of g.**

In Figure 2.5-3a, the blue portion of the graph of f is below the graph of g. The solutions of $f(x) < g(x)$ correspond to the intervals on the x-axis denoted in red. In Figure 2.5-3a, $f(x) < g(x)$ when $-2 < x < 1$ and when $x > 3$.

Although the above procedure can always be used, solutions of an inequality expressed as $f(x) < g(x)$ are often easier to find by using an equivalent inequality in the form $f(x) - g(x) < 0$.

> **The graph of $y = f(x) - g(x)$ lies above the x-axis when $f(x) - g(x) > 0$ and below the x-axis when $f(x) - g(x) < 0$.**

Figure 2.5-3b shows the graph of $y = f(x) - g(x)$, the difference of the two functions shown in Figure 2.5-3a. This graph is below the x-axis in the same intervals where the graph of f is below the graph of g. Therefore, the solution of $f(x) < g(x)$ is the same as the solution of $f(x) - g(x) < 0$.

Any inequality of the form $f(x) < g(x)$ can be rewritten in the equivalent form $f(x) - g(x) < 0$ by subtracting $g(x)$ from both sides of the inequality. The procedure for solving $f(x) < g(x)$ is to graph $y = f(x) - g(x)$ and find the intervals on the x-axis where the graph is below the x-axis. A similar procedure applies when the inequality sign is reversed, except that the solution is determined by x-intervals where the graph is *above* the x-axis.

Example 3   Solving an Inequality

Solve $x^4 + 10x^3 + 21x^2 > 40x + 80$.

Solution

Rewrite the inequality as $(x^4 + 10x^3 + 21x^2) - (40x + 80) > 0$.

The graph of $f(x) = x^4 + 10x^3 + 21x^2 - 40x - 80$ is shown in Figure 2.5-4. The graph shows that $f(x)$ has two zeros, one between -2 and -1 and the other near 2. The portion of the graph above the x-axis is shown in red.

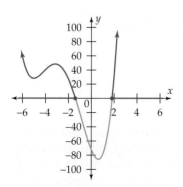

Figure 2.5-4

Graphing Exploration ●

Use the graphical root finder of a calculator to find approximate values of the x-intercepts.

The Exploration shows that the graph of f is above the x-axis approximately when $x < -1.53$ and when $x > 1.89$, so the approximate solutions of the original inequality are all numbers x such that $x < -1.53$ or $x > 1.89$.

Quadratic and Factorable Inequalities

The preceding example shows that solving an inequality depends only on knowing the zeros of a function and the places where its graph is above or below the x-axis. In the case of quadratic inequalities or completely factored expressions, exact solutions can by found algebraically.

Example 4   **Solving a Quadratic Inequality**

Solve $2x^2 + 3x - 4 \le 0$.

Solution

The solutions of $2x^2 + 3x - 4 \le 0$ are the numbers x where the graph of $f(x) = 2x^2 + 3x - 4$ lies on or below the x-axis. The zeros of f can be found by using the quadratic formula.

$$x = \frac{-3 \pm \sqrt{3^2 - 4(2)(-4)}}{2(2)} = \frac{-3 \pm \sqrt{41}}{4}$$

As shown in Figure 2.5-5, the graph lies below the x-axis *between* the two zeros. Therefore, the solutions of the original inequality are all numbers x such that

$$\frac{-3 - \sqrt{41}}{4} \le x \le \frac{-3 + \sqrt{41}}{4} \quad \text{\textit{Exact solution}}$$

$$-2.35 \le x \le 0.85 \quad \text{\textit{Approximate solution}}$$

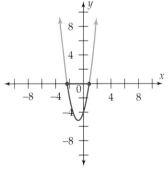

Figure 2.5-5

Example 5   **Solving an Inequality**

Solve $(x + 5)(x - 2)^6(x - 8) \le 0$.

Solution

The zeros of $f(x) = (x + 5)(x - 2)^6(x - 8)$ are easily read from the factored form to be $-5, 2$, and 8. Therefore, you need only determine where the graph of f is on or below the x-axis. A partial graph of f that clearly shows all three x-intercepts is shown in Figure 2.5-6a. A complete graph, which does not clearly show the x-intercept at 2, is shown in Figure

2.5-6b. Using both graphs, or using the trace feature on either one, confirms that the graph is on or below the x-axis between $x = -5$ and $x = 8$. Therefore, the solutions of the inequality are all numbers x such that $-5 \leq x \leq 8$.

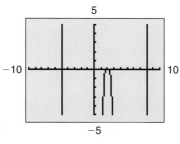

Figure 2.5-6a

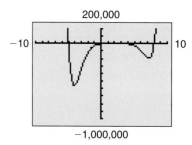

Figure 2.5-6b

The procedures used in the previous examples may be summarized as follows.

Solving Inequalities

1. Write the inequality in one of the following forms.

   $f(x) > 0 \qquad f(x) \geq 0 \qquad f(x) < 0 \qquad f(x) \leq 0$

2. Determine the zeros of f, exactly if possible, approximately otherwise.

3. Determine the interval, or intervals, on the x-axis where the graph of f is above (or below) the x-axis.

Applications

Example 6   Solving a Cost Inequality

A computer store has determined the cost C of ordering and storing x laser printers.

$$C = 2x + \frac{300{,}000}{x}$$

If the delivery truck can bring at most 450 printers per order, how many printers should be ordered at a time to keep the cost below \$1600?

Solution

To find the values of x that make C less than 1600, solve the inequality

$$2x + \frac{300{,}000}{x} < 1600 \quad \text{or equivalently,} \quad 2x + \frac{300{,}000}{x} - 1600 < 0.$$

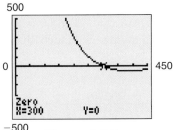

Figure 2.5-7

In this context, the only solutions that make sense are those between 0 and 450. Therefore, choose a viewing window, such as the one shown in Figure 2.5-7, and graph

$$f(x) = 2x + \frac{300{,}000}{x} - 1600.$$

The graph in Figure 2.5-7 shows that the zero of f is $x \approx 300$, and the graph of C is negative, i.e., below the x-axis, for values greater than 300. Therefore, to keep costs under \$1600, between 300 and 450 printers should be ordered per delivery. ■

Exercises 2.5

In Exercises 1–4, express the given statement in symbols.

1. x is nonnegative.   **2.** t is positive.

3. c is at most 3.   **4.** z is at least -17.

In Exercises 5–10, represent the given interval on a number line.

5. $(0, 8]$ **6.** $(0, \infty)$ **7.** $[-2, 1]$

8. $(-1, 1)$ **9.** $(-\infty, 0]$ **10.** $[-2, 7)$

In Exercises 11–16, use interval notation to denote the set of all real numbers x that satisfy the given inequality.

11. $5 \le x \le 8$ **12.** $-2 \le x \le 7$

13. $-3 < x < 14$ **14.** $7 < x < 135$

15. $x \ge -8$ **16.** $x \ge 12$

In Exercises 17–36, solve the inequality and express your answer in interval notation.

17. $2x + 4 \le 7$ **18.** $3x - 5 > -6$

19. $3 - 5x < 13$ **20.** $2 - 3x < 11$

21. $6x + 3 \le x - 5$ **22.** $5x + 3 \le 2x + 7$

23. $5 - 7x < 2x - 4$ **24.** $5 - 3x > 7x - 3$

25. $2 < 3x - 4 < 8$ **26.** $1 < 5x + 6 < 9$

27. $0 < 5 - 2x \le 11$ **28.** $-4 \le 7 - 3x < 0$

29. $2x + 7(3x - 2) < 2(x - 1)$

30. $x + 3(x - 5) \ge 3x + 2(x + 1)$

31. $\dfrac{x + 1}{2} - 3x \le \dfrac{x + 5}{3}$

32. $\dfrac{x - 1}{4} + 2x \ge \dfrac{2x - 1}{3} + 2$

33. $2x + 3 \le 5x + 6 < -3x + 7$

34. $4x - 2 < x + 8 < 9x + 1$

35. $3 - x < 2x + 1 \le 3x - 4$

36. $2x + 5 \le 4 - 3x < 1 - 4x$

In Exercises 37–40, the constants a, b, c, and d are positive. Solve each inequality for x.

37. $ax - b < c$ **38.** $d - cx > a$

39. $0 < x - c < a$ **40.** $-d < x - c < d$

In Exercises 41–70, solve the inequality. Find exact solutions when possible, and approximate them otherwise.

41. $x^2 - 4x + 3 \le 0$ **42.** $x^2 - 7x + 10 \le 0$

43. $x^2 + 9x + 15 \ge 0$ **44.** $x^2 + 8x + 20 \ge 0$

45. $8 + x - x^2 \le 0$ **46.** $4 - 3x - x^2 \ge 0$

47. $x^3 - x \ge 0$ **48.** $x^3 + 2x^2 + x > 0$

49. $x^3 - 2x^2 - 3x < 0$ **50.** $x^4 - 14x^3 + 48x^2 \ge 0$

51. $x^4 - 5x^2 + 4 < 0$

52. $x^4 - 10x^2 + 9 \le 0$

53. $x^3 - 2x^2 - 5x + 7 \ge 2x + 1$

54. $x^4 - 6x^3 + 2x^2 < 5x - 2$

55. $2x^4 + 3x^3 < 2x^2 + 4x - 2$

56. $x^5 + 5x^4 > 4x^3 - 3x^2 + 2$

57. $\dfrac{3x + 1}{2x - 4} > 0$ **58.** $\dfrac{2x - 1}{5x + 3} \ge 0$

59. $\dfrac{x^2 + x - 2}{x^2 - 2x - 3} < 0$ **60.** $\dfrac{2x^2 + x - 1}{x^2 - 4x + 4} \ge 0$

61. $\dfrac{x - 2}{x - 1} < 1$ **62.** $\dfrac{-x + 5}{2x + 3} \ge 2$

63. $\dfrac{x - 3}{x + 3} \le 5$ **64.** $\dfrac{2x + 1}{x - 4} > 3$

65. $\dfrac{2}{x + 3} \ge \dfrac{1}{x - 1}$ **66.** $\dfrac{1}{x - 1} < \dfrac{-1}{x + 2}$

67. $\dfrac{x^3 - 3x^2 + 5x - 29}{x^2 - 7} > 3$

68. $\dfrac{x^4 - 3x^3 + 2x^2 + 2}{x - 2} > 15$

69. $\dfrac{2x^2 + 6x - 8}{2x^2 + 5x - 3} < 1$ Be alert for hidden behavior.

70. $\dfrac{1}{x^2 + x - 6} + \dfrac{x - 2}{x + 3} > \dfrac{x + 3}{x - 2}$

In Exercises 71–73, read the solution of the inequality from the given graph.

71. $3 - 2x < 0.8x + 7$

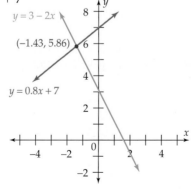

72. $8 - |7 - 5x| > 3$

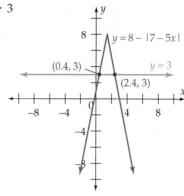

73. $x^2 + 3x + 1 \ge 4$

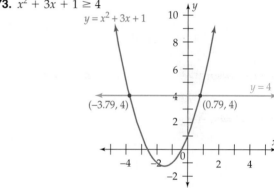

74. The graphs of the revenue and cost functions for a manufacturing firm are shown in the figure.
   a. What is the break-even point?
   b. Which region represents profit?

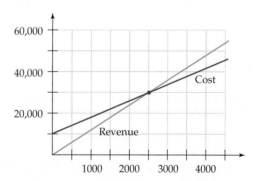

75. One freezer costs \$623.95 and uses 90 kilowatt hours (kwh) of electricity each month. A second freezer costs \$500 and uses 100 kwh of electricity each month. The expected life of each freezer is 12 years. What is the minimum electric rate in cents per kwh for which the 12-year total cost (purchase price + electricity costs) will be less for the first freezer?

76. A business executive leases a car for $300 per month. She decides to lease another brand for $250 per month, but has to pay a penalty of $1000 for breaking the first lease. How long must she keep the second car in order to come out ahead?

77. One salesperson is paid a salary of $1000 per month plus a commission of 2% of her total sales. A second salesperson receives no salary, but is paid a commission of 10% of her total sales. What dollar amount of sales must the second salesperson have in order to earn more per month than the first?

78. A developer subdivided 60 acres of a 100-acre tract, leaving 20% of the 60 acres as a park. Zoning laws require that at least 25% of the total tract be set aside for parks. For financial reasons the developer wants to have no more than 30% of the tract as parks. How many one-quarter-acre lots can the developer sell in the remaining 40 acres and still meet the requirements for the whole tract?

79. If $5000 is invested at 8%, how much more should be invested at 10% in order to guarantee a total annual interest income between $800 and $940?

80. How many gallons of a 12% salt solution should be added to 10 gallons of an 18% salt solution in order to produce a solution whose salt content is between 14% and 16%?

81. Find all pairs of numbers that satisfy these two conditions: Their sum is 20 and the sum of their squares is less than 362.

82. The length of a rectangle is 6 inches longer than its width. What are the possible widths if the area of the rectangle is at least 667 square inches?

83. It costs a craftsman $5 in materials to make a medallion. He has found that if he sells the medallions for $50 - x$ dollars each, where x is the number of medallions produced each week, then he can sell all that he makes. His fixed costs are $350 per week. If he wants to sell all he makes and show a profit each week, what are the possible numbers of medallions he should make?

84. A retailer sells file cabinets for $80 - x$ dollars each, where x is the number of cabinets she receives from the supplier each week. She pays $10 for each file cabinet and has fixed costs of $600 per week. How many file cabinets should she order from the supplier each week in order to guarantee that she makes a profit?

In Exercises 85–88, you will need the following formula for the height h of an object above the ground at time t seconds, where v_0 denotes initial velocity and h_0 denotes initial height. $h = -16t^2 + v_0 t + h_0$

85. A toy rocket is fired straight up from ground level with an initial velocity of 80 feet per second. During what time interval will it be at least 64 feet above the ground?

86. A projectile is fired straight up from ground level with an initial velocity of 72 feet per second. During what time interval is it at least 37 feet above the ground?

87. A ball is dropped from the roof of a 120-foot-high building. During what time period will it be strictly between 56 feet and 39 feet above the ground?

88. A ball is thrown straight up from a 40-foot-high tower with an initial velocity of 56 feet per second.
    a. During what time interval is the ball at least 8 feet above the ground?
    b. During what time interval is the ball between 53 feet and 80 feet above the ground?

Excursion: **Absolute-Value Inequalities**

Objectives

- Solve absolute-value inequalities by the Intersection Method

- Solve absolute-value inequalities by the *x*-Intercept Method

Polynomial and rational inequalities involving absolute value can be solved by either of two graphing methods.

Intersection Method

- Graph the expressions on each side of the inequality.

- Determine the intervals on the *x-axis* where the graph of the expression on one side of the inequality is above or below the graph of the expression on the other side of the inequality.

x-Intercept Method

- Rewrite the inequality in an equivalent form with 0 on one side of the inequality.

- Graph the function given by the nonzero side of the inequality.

- Determine the *x*-values where the graph is above or below the *x*-axis.

Example 1 **Solving an Absolute-Value Inequality Using the Intersection Method**

Solve $|x^4 + 2x^2 - x + 2| < 11x$.

Solution

The solutions of $|x^4 + 2x^2 - x + 2| < 11x$ can be found be determining the *x*-intervals for which the graph of $f(x) = |x^4 + 2x^2 - x + 2|$ is below the graph of $g(x) = 11x$.

A graphical intersection finder shows that the points of intersection occur when $x \approx 0.17$ and $x \approx 1.92$, and the graph of f is below the graph of g between them, as shown in Figure 2.5.A-1. Therefore, approximate solutions of the original inequality are all x such that

$$0.17 < x < 1.92.$$

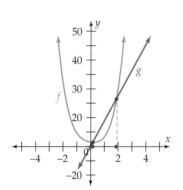

Figure 2.5.A-1

Example 2 **Solving an Absolute-Value Inequality Using the *x*-Intercept Method**

Solve $\left| \dfrac{x + 4}{x - 2} \right| > 3$.

Solution

Rewrite $\left| \dfrac{x + 4}{x - 2} \right| > 3$ as $\left| \dfrac{x + 4}{x - 2} \right| - 3 > 0$, graph $f(x) = \left| \dfrac{x + 4}{x - 2} \right| - 3$, and find the intervals on the *x*-axis where the graph is above the *x*-axis.

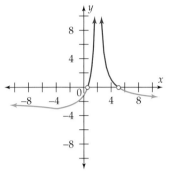

Figure 2.5.A-2

The graph of f is above the x-axis between the two zeros, which can be found algebraically or graphically to be $x = \dfrac{1}{2}$ and $x = 5$. Notice that the function is not defined at $x = 2$ because a fraction cannot have a zero denominator. Therefore, the solutions of

$$\left|\frac{x+4}{x-2}\right| - 3 > 0$$

are the x-intervals $\left(\dfrac{1}{2}, 2\right)$ and $(2, 5)$. The solution can also be written out.

$$\frac{1}{2} < x < 2 \quad \text{or} \quad 2 < x < 5$$

Algebraic Methods

Most linear and quadratic inequalities that contain absolute values can be solved exactly by using algebra. In fact, this is often the easiest way to solve such inequalities. The key to the algebraic method is to interpret the absolute value of a number as distance on the number line.

For example, the inequality $|r| \leq 5$ states that

the distance from r to 0 is less than or equal to 5 units.

A glance at the number line in Figure 2.5.A-3a shows that these are the numbers r such that $-5 \leq r \leq 5$.

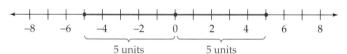

Figure 2.5.A-3a

Similarly, the inequality $|r| \geq 5$ states that

the distance from r to 0 is greater than or equal to 5 units.

These values are the numbers r such that $r \leq -5$ or $r \geq 5$, as shown in Figure 2.5.A-3b.

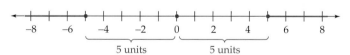

Figure 2.5.A-3b

Similar conclusions hold in the general cases, with 5 replaced by any number k.

Absolute-Value Inequalities

Let k be a positive real number and r any real number.

$\quad |r| \le k \qquad$ is equivalent to $\qquad -k \le r \le k.$

$\quad |r| \ge k \qquad$ is equivalent to $\qquad r \le -k \quad$ or $\quad r \ge k.$

Example 3   Solving an Absolute-Value Inequality

Solve $|3x - 7| \le 11$.

Solution

Apply the first fact in the box above, with $3x - 7$ in place of r and 11 in place of k, and conclude that $|3x - 7| \le 11$ is equivalent to

$$-11 \le 3x - 7 \le 11$$
$$-4 \le \quad 3x \quad \le 18 \qquad \textit{Add 7}$$
$$\frac{-4}{3} \le \quad x \quad \le 6 \qquad \textit{Divide by 3}$$

Therefore, the solution to $|3x - 7| \le 11$ is all numbers in the interval $\left[-\frac{4}{3}, 6\right]$, that is, all x such that $-\frac{4}{3} \le x \le 6$.

Example 4   Solving an Absolute-Value Inequality

Solve $|5x + 2| > 3$.

Solution

Apply the second fact in the box with $5x + 2$ in place of r, 3 in place of k, and $>$ in place of $\ge$.

$$5x + 2 < -3 \qquad \text{or} \qquad 5x + 2 > 3$$
$$x < -1 \qquad\qquad\qquad x > \frac{1}{5}$$

Therefore, the solutions of the original inequality are the numbers in *either* of the intervals $(-\infty, -1)$ or $\left(\frac{1}{5}, \infty\right)$, that is, $x < -1$ or $x > \frac{1}{5}$.

Example 5   Solving an Absolute-Value Inequality

Solve $|x^2 - x - 4| \ge 2$.

Solution

Rewrite the absolute-value inequality as two quadratic inequalities using the algebraic definition.

The inequality $|x^2 - x - 4| \geq 2$ is equivalent to two inequalities.

$$x^2 - x - 4 \leq -2 \quad \text{or} \quad x^2 - x - 4 \geq 2$$
$$x^2 - x - 2 \leq 0 \qquad\qquad x^2 - x - 6 \geq 0$$

The solutions are all numbers that are solutions of *either one* of the two inequalities shown above.

The solutions are the intervals on the x-axis that are determined by the following.

- $f(x) = x^2 - x - 2$ is on or below the x-axis
- $g(x) = x^2 - x - 6$ is on or above the x-axis

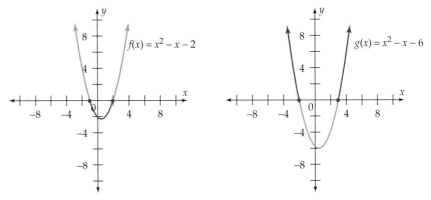

Figure 2.5.A-4a   **Figure 2.5.A-4b**

As shown in Figure 2.5.A-4a, the graph of $f(x) = x^2 - x - 2$ is on or below the x-axis when

$$-1 \leq x \leq 2.$$

As shown in Figure 2.5.A-4b, the graph of $g(x) = x^2 - x - 6$ is on or above the x-axis when

$$x \leq -2 \quad \text{or} \quad x \geq 3.$$

Therefore, the solutions of the original inequality are all numbers x such that $x \leq -2$ *or* $-1 \leq x \leq 2$ *or* $x \geq 3$, as shown in Figure 2.5.A-4c.

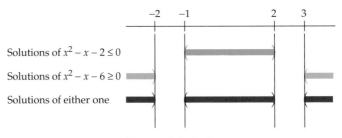

Figure 2.5.A-4c

| **Example 6** | Interpreting an Absolute-Value Inequality |

Let a and δ represent real numbers with δ positive.

a. Interpret $|x - a| < \delta$ geometrically.
b. Draw the interval represented.
c. Write the equivalent simplified extended inequality.
d. Interpret the last inequality.

Solution

a. Geometrically, $|x - a| < \delta$ means that

the distance from x to a is less than δ.

b.

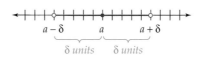

$$a - \delta \qquad a \qquad a + \delta$$
$$\delta\ units \qquad \delta\ units$$

Figure 2.5.A-5

c.
$$-\delta < x - a < \delta$$
$$a - \delta < x < a + \delta \qquad \textit{Add a to each term}$$

d. The solutions of the inequality are all numbers strictly between $a - \delta$ and $a + \delta$.

Exercises 2.5.A

In Exercises 1–32, solve the inequality. Find exact solutions when possible, and approximate values otherwise.

1. $|3x + 2| \le 2$

2. $|5x - 1| < 3$

3. $|3 - 2x| < \dfrac{2}{3}$

4. $|4 - 5x| \le 4$

5. $|2x + 3| > 1$

6. $|3x - 1| \ge 2$

7. $|5x + 2| \ge \dfrac{3}{4}$

8. $|2 - 3x| > 4$

9. $\left|\dfrac{12}{5} + 2x\right| > \dfrac{1}{4}$

10. $\left|\dfrac{5}{6} + 3x\right| < \dfrac{7}{6}$

11. $\left|\dfrac{x - 1}{x + 2}\right| \le 3$

12. $\left|\dfrac{x + 1}{3x + 5}\right| < 2$

13. $\left|\dfrac{2x - 1}{x + 5}\right| > 1$

14. $\left|\dfrac{x + 1}{x + 2}\right| \ge 2$

15. $\left|\dfrac{1 - 4x}{2 + 3x}\right| < 1$

16. $\left|\dfrac{3x + 1}{1 - 2x}\right| \ge 2$

17. $|x^2 - 2| < 1$

18. $|x^2 - 4| \le 3$

19. $|x^2 - 2| > 4$

20. $\left|\dfrac{1}{x^2 - 1}\right| \le 2$

21. $|x^2 + x - 1| \ge 1$

22. $|x^2 + x - 4| \le 2$

23. $|3x^2 - 8x + 2| < 2$

24. $|x^2 + 3x - 4| < 6$

25. $|x^5 - x^3 + 1| < 2$

26. $|4x - x^3| > 1$

27. $|x^4 - x^3 + x^2 - x + 1| > 4$

28. $|x^3 - 6x^2 + 4x - 5| < 3$

29. $\dfrac{x + 2}{|x - 3|} \le 4$

30. $\dfrac{x^2 - 9}{|x^2 - 4|} < -2$

31. $\left|\dfrac{2x^2 + 2x - 12}{x^3 - x^2 + x - 2}\right| > 2$

32. $\left|\dfrac{x^2 - x - 2}{x^2 + x - 2}\right| > 3$

33. *Critical Thinking* Let E be a fixed real number. Show that every solution of $|x - 3| < \dfrac{E}{5}$ is also a solution of $|(5x - 4) - 11| < E$.

34. *Critical Thinking* Let a and b be fixed real numbers with $a < b$. Show that the solutions of

$$\left| x - \frac{a + b}{2} \right| < \frac{b - a}{2}$$

are all x such that $a < x < b$.

CHAPTER 2 REVIEW

Important Concepts

Important Facts and Formulas

To solve an equation of the form $f(x) = g(x)$ with the **Intersection Method,** use two steps.

1. Graph $y_1 = f(x)$ and $y_2 = g(x)$

2. Find the x-coordinate of each point of intersection

When f is a function and a is a real number, the following are **equivalent statements:**

- a is a zero of the function $y = f(x)$

- a is an x-intercept of the graph of f

- a is a solution, or root, of the equation $f(x) = 0$

To solve an equation by the **x-Intercept Method,** use three steps.

1. Rewrite the equation in the form $f(x) = 0$

2. Graph f

3. Find the x-intercepts of the graph. The x-intercepts of the graph of f are the solutions of $f(x) = 0$.

The only number whose square root is zero is zero itself.

A fraction is zero only when its numerator is zero and its denominator is nonzero.

Quadratic Formula

If $a \neq 0$, then the solutions of $ax^2 + bx + c = 0$ are

$$x = \frac{-b \pm \sqrt{b^2 - 4ac}}{2a}$$

If $a \neq 0$, then the number of *real* solutions of $ax^2 + bx + c = 0$ is 0, 1, or 2, depending on whether the discriminant, $b^2 - 4ac$, is negative, zero, or positive, respectively.

Absolute Value

$$|x| = x \quad \text{if } x \geq 0$$
$$|x| = -x \text{ if } x < 0$$

$|c - d|$ represents the distance between c and d on the number line.

$|c|$ represents the distance between c and 0 on the number line.

Review Questions

In Questions 1–8, solve the equation graphically. You need only find solutions in the given interval.

Section **2.1**

1. $x^3 + 2x^2 = 11x + 6;$ $[0, \infty)$

2. $x^3 + 2x^2 = 11x + 6;$ $(-\infty, 0)$

3. $x^4 + x^3 - 10x^2 = 8x + 16;$ $[0, \infty)$

4. $2x^4 + x^3 - 2x^2 + 6x + 2 = 0;$ $(-\infty, -1)$

5. $\dfrac{x^3 + 2x^2 - 3x + 4}{x^2 + 2x - 15} = 0;$ $(-10, \infty)$

6. $\dfrac{3x^4 + x^3 - 6x^2 - 2x}{x^5 + x^3 + 2} = 0;$ $[0, \infty)$

7. $\sqrt{x^3 + 2x^2 - 3x - 5} = 0;$ $[0, \infty)$

8. $\sqrt{1 + 2x - 3x^2 + 4x^3 - x^4} = 0;$ $(-5, 5)$

Section **2.2**

9. Solve for x: $3x^2 - 2x + 5 = 0$

10. Solve for y: $3y^2 - 2y = 5$

11. Solve for z: $5z^2 + 6z = 7$

12. Solve for x: $325x^2 + 17x - 127 = 0$

13. Solve for x: $x^4 - 11x^2 + 18 = 0$

14. Solve for x: $x^6 - 4x^3 + 4 = 0$

15. Find the number of real solutions of the equation $20x^2 + 12 = 31x$.

16. For what value of k does the equation $kt^2 + 5t + 2 = 0$ have exactly one real solution for t?

Section **2.3**

17. A jeweler wants to make a 1-ounce ring composed of gold and silver, using $200 worth of metal. If gold costs $600 per ounce and silver $50 per ounce, how much of each metal should she use?

18. A calculator is on sale for 15% less than the list price. The sale price, plus a 5% shipping charge, totals $210. What is the list price?

19. Karen can do a job in 5 hours and Claire can do the same job in 4 hours. How long will it take them to do the job together?

20. A car leaves the city traveling at 54 mph. A half hour later, a second car leaves from the same place and travels at 63 mph along the same road. How long will it take for the second car to catch up to the first?

21. A 12-foot rectangular board is cut into two pieces so that one piece is four times as long as the other. How long is the bigger piece?

22. George owns 200 shares of stock, 40% of which are in the computer industry. How many more shares must he buy in order to have 50% of his total shares in computers?

23. A square region is changed into a rectangular one by making it 2 feet longer and twice as wide. If the area of the rectangular region is three times larger than the area of the original square region, what was the length of a side of the square before it was changed?

24. The radius of a circle is 10 inches. By how many inches should the radius be increased so that the area increases by 5π square inches?

25. If $c(x)$ is the cost of producing x units, then $\dfrac{c(x)}{x}$ is the *average cost* per unit. The cost of manufacturing x caseloads of ballpoint pens is given by

$$c(x) = \frac{600x^2 + 600x}{x^2 + 1}$$

where $c(x)$ is in dollars. How many caseloads should be manufactured in order to have an average cost of $25?

26. An open-top box with a rectangular base is to be constructed. The box is to be at least 2 inches wide, twice as long as it is wide, and must have a volume of 150 cubic inches. What should be the dimensions of the box if the surface area is 90 square inches?

Section 2.4

27. Simplify: $\left| b^2 - 2b + 1 \right|$

In Exercises 28–40, find all real exact solutions.

28. $\left| x + 2 \right| = 4$

29. $\left| x + 3 \right| = \dfrac{5}{2}$

30. $\left| x - 5 \right| = 3$

31. $\left| 3x - 1 \right| = 4$

32. $\left| 2x - 1 \right| = x + 4$

33. $\sqrt{x^2 - x - 2} = 0$

34. $\sqrt{6x^2 - 7x - 5} = 0$

35. $\dfrac{x^2 - 6x + 8}{x - 1} = 0$

36. $\dfrac{x^2 - x - 2}{x - 2} = 0$

37. $\sqrt{x - 1} = 2 - x$

38. $\sqrt[3]{1 - t^2} = -2$

39. $\sqrt{x + 1} + \sqrt{x - 1} = 1$

40. $\sqrt[3]{x^4 - 2x^3 + 6x - 7} = x + 3$

Section 2.5

41. Express in interval notation:
 a. The set of all real numbers that are strictly greater than -8
 b. The set of all real numbers that are less than or equal to 5.

42. Express in interval notation:
 a. The set of all real numbers that are strictly between -6 and 9;
 b. The set of all real numbers that are greater than or equal to 5, but strictly less than 14.

43. Solve for x: $-3(x - 4) \le 5 + x$.

44. Solve for x: $-4 < 2x + 5 < 9$.

45. On which intervals is $\dfrac{2x - 1}{3x + 1} < 1$?

46. On which intervals is $\dfrac{2}{x+1} < x$?

47. Solve for x: $(x-1)^2(x^2-1)x \leq 0$.

48. Solve for x: $x^2 + x > 12$.

49. If $\dfrac{x+3}{2x+3} > 1$, then which of these statements is true?

    a. $\dfrac{x-3}{2x+3} < -1$,   **b.** $\dfrac{2x-3}{x+3} < -1$

    c. $\dfrac{3-2x}{x+3} > 1$ **d.** $2x+3 < x-3$

    e. None of these

50. If $0 < r \leq s - t$, then which of these statements is false?

    a. $s \geq r + t$ **b.** $t - s \leq -r$

    c. $-r \geq s - t$ **d.** $\dfrac{s-t}{r} > 0$

    e. $s - r \geq t$

51. Solve and express your answer in interval notation:

$$2x - 3 \leq 5x + 9 < -3x + 4.$$

In Questions 52–61, solve the inequality.

52. $x^2 + x - 20 > 0$ **53.** $\dfrac{x-2}{x+4} \leq 3$

54. $(x+1)^2(x-3)^4(x+2)^3(x-7)^5 > 0$

55. $\dfrac{x^2+x-9}{x+3} < 1$ **56.** $\dfrac{x^2-x-6}{x-3} > 1$

57. $\dfrac{x^2-x-5}{x^2+2} > -2$ **58.** $\dfrac{x^4-3x^2+2x-3}{x^2-4} < -1$

Section **2.5.A**   **59.** $\left|\dfrac{y+2}{3}\right| \geq 5$ **60.** $\left|\dfrac{1}{1-x^2}\right| \geq \dfrac{1}{2}$

61. $|3x+2| \geq 2$

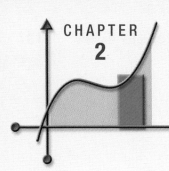

2

can do calculus
Maximum Area

There are two related branches of calculus: differential calculus and integral calculus. Differential calculus is a method of calculating the changes in one variable produced by changes in a related variable. It is often used to find maximum or minimum values of a function. Integral calculus is used to calculate quantities like distance, area, and volume. This Can Do Calculus finds the maximum area of the triangle formed by folding a piece of paper using different methods.

The Maximum Area of a Triangle Problem

One corner of an 8.5 × 11-inch piece of paper is folded over to the opposite side, as shown in Figure 2.C-1. A triangle is formed, and its area formula is $A = \frac{1}{2}$ (base)(height). The following Example will find the length of the base that will produce the maximum area of the triangle using numerical, graphical, and algebraic methods.

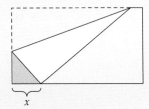

x

Figure 2.C-1

Example 1   **Numerical Method**

One corner of an 8.5 × 11-inch piece of paper is folded over to the opposite side, as shown in Figure 2.C-1. The area of the darkly shaded triangle at the lower left is the focus of this problem.

a. Determine the shortest and the longest base that will produce a triangle by folding the paper.

b. Measure the height when *x* has the lengths given in the chart, and calculate the area in each case.

c. Create a scatter plot of the data.

d. Estimate the length of the base that produces the maximum area, and state the approximate maximum area.

Solution

a. The base must be greater than 0 and less than 8.5 inches, and *nt* in the chart indicates that no triangle can be formed with a base length of 9 inches.

b. The values shown in the chart may vary from your data.

Base	1"	2"	3"	4"	5"	6"	7"	8"	9"
Height	4.25	4.1	3.6	3.3	2.75	2	1.5	0.5	*nt*
Area	2.125	4.1	5.4	6.6	6.875	6	5.25	2	-

138

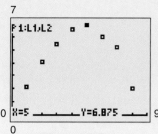

Figure 2.C-2

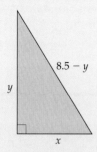

Figure 2.C-3

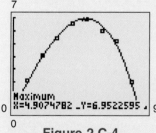

Figure 2.C-4

c. The graph of the data is shown in Figure 2.C-2.

d. A maximum area of 6.875 in^2 appears to occur when the base length is 5 in.

In Example 1, all calculations were accomplished with measurements. Notice that the hypotenuse is $8.5 - y$, where y is the height of the triangle. (Why?)

Because each triangle formed was a right triangle, the Pythagorean Theorem can be used to find an expression that gives the height as a function of the length of the base. That function can then be used to write a function that gives area in terms of the length of the base.

Example 2   Algebraic Method

Find a function of the base to represent the area of the triangle described in Example 1, graph the function along with the scatter plot of the data found in Example 1. Find the length of the base that produces maximum area. What is the maximum area?

Solution

The Pythagorean Theorem yields the following equation.

$$x^2 + y^2 = (8.5 - y)^2$$
$$x^2 + y^2 = 72.25 - 17y + y^2$$
$$x^2 = 72.25 - 17y$$
$$y = \frac{72.25 - x^2}{17} \text{ } \textit{Height as a function of the base}$$

Hence, the area is represented by $A = \frac{1}{2}(x)\left(\dfrac{72.25 - x^2}{17}\right)$. Using the maximum finder on a calculator indicates that the maximum area of 6.95 in^2 occurs at approximately $x = 4.9$ in.

To get exact values of x and the area, differential calculus is needed. However, graphing technology can provide very good approximations.

Exercises

In each problem, find the maximum by using a numerical method like the one shown in Example 1, and then by using an analytical and graphical method like the one shown in Example 2. Answer all questions given in the two examples.

1. Ten yards of wire is to be used to create a rectangle. What is the maximum possible area of the rectangle?

2. A rectangle is bounded by the x-axis and the semicircle $y = \sqrt{36 - x^2}$. What are the dimensions of the rectangle with maximum area?

3. A rectangle is bounded by the x- and y-axes and the line $y = \dfrac{(4 - x)}{2}$. What are the dimensions of the rectangle with maximum area?

CHAPTER

3

Functions and Graphs

This *is* rocket science!

If a rocket is fired straight up from the ground, its height is a function of time. This function can be adapted to give the height of any object that is falling or thrown along a vertical path. The shape of the graph of the function, a *parabola,* appears in applications involving motion, revenue, communications, and many other topics. See Exercise 50 of Section 3.3.

Chapter Outline

Interdependence of Sections

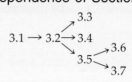

$$3.1 \rightarrow 3.2 \begin{array}{c} \nearrow 3.3 \\ \rightarrow 3.4 \\ \searrow 3.5 \end{array} \begin{array}{c} \nearrow 3.6 \\ \searrow 3.7 \end{array}$$

The concept of a function and function notation are central to modern mathematics and its applications. In this chapter you will review functions, operations on functions, and how to use function notation. Then you will develop skill in constructing and interpreting graphs of functions.

3.1 Functions

Objectives

• Determine whether a relation is a function

• Find the domain of functions

• Evaluate piecewise-defined and greatest integer functions

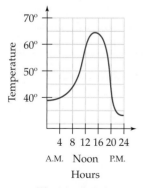

Figure 3.1-1

To understand the origin of the concept of a function it may help to consider some "real-life" situations in which one numerical quantity depends on, corresponds to, or determines another.

Example 1 **Determining Inputs and Outputs of Functions**

Describe the set of inputs, the set of outputs, and the rule for the following functions:

a. The amount of income tax you pay depends on your income.

b. Suppose a rock is dropped straight down from a high place. Physics tells us that the distance traveled by the rock in t seconds is $16t^2$ feet.

c. The weather bureau records the temperature over a 24-hour period in the form of a graph (Figure 3.1-1). The graph shows the temperature that corresponds to each given time.

141

Solution

The table below summarizes the features of each function.

	Set of inputs	Set of outputs	Function rule
a.	all incomes	all tax amounts	tax laws
b.	number of seconds, t, after dropping the rock	distance rock travels	Distance $= 16t^2$
c.	time	temperature	time/temperature graph

The formal definition of function incorporates the set of inputs, the function rule, and the set of outputs, with a slight change in terminology.

Definition of a Function

A *function* consists of

- a set of inputs, called the *domain*
- a rule by which each input determines one and only one output
- a set of outputs, called the *range*

The phrase "one and only one" means that for each input (element of the domain), the rule of a function determines exactly one output (element of the range). However, different inputs may produce the same output.

Example 2 Determining Whether a Relation is a Function

The tables below list the inputs and outputs for two relations. Determine whether each relation is a function.

a.

Inputs	1	1	2	3	3
Outputs	5	6	7	8	9

b.

Inputs	1	3	5	7	9
Outputs	5	5	7	8	5

Solution

In table **a,** the input 1 has two corresponding outputs, 5 and 6; and the input 3 has two corresponding outputs, 8 and 9. So the relation in table **a** is not a function.

In table **b,** each input determines exactly one output, so the relation in table **b** is a function. Notice that the inputs 1, 3, and 9 all produce the same output, 5, which is allowed in the definition of a function. ∎

The value of a function *f* that corresponds to a specific input value *a,* is found by substituting *a* into the function rule and simplifying the resulting expression. See Section 1.1 for a discussion of function notation.

Technology Tip

Function notation can be used directly on TI-82/83/86/89, Sharp 9600, and HP-38. For example, if a function is entered as Y$_1$, evaluate the function at $x = 3$, press Y$_1$ (3), then ENTER.

```
Y₁(3)
        3.16227766
Y₁(-5)
        5.099019514
Y₁(0)
                  1
```

Figure 3.1-2

Example 3   **Evaluating a Function**

Find the indicated values of $f(x) = \sqrt{x^2 + 1}$.

a. $f(3)$ **b.** $f(-5)$ **c.** $f(0)$

Solution

a. To find the output of the function *f* for input 3, simply replace *x* with 3 in the function rule and simplify the result.

$$f(3) = \sqrt{3^2 + 1} = \sqrt{10} \approx 3.162$$

Similarly, replace *x* with −5 and 0 for **b** and **c.**

b. $f(-5) = \sqrt{(-5)^2 + 1} = \sqrt{26} \approx 5.099$

c. $f(0) = \sqrt{0^2 + 1} = 1$ ∎

Example 4   **Finding a Difference Quotient**

For $f(x) = x^2 - x + 2$ and $h \neq 0$, find each output.

a. $f(x + h)$ **b.** $f(x + h) - f(x)$ **c.** $\dfrac{f(x + h) - f(x)}{h}$

Solution

When function notation is used in expressions such as $f(x + h)$, the basic rule applies: Replace *x* in the function rule with the entire expression within parentheses and simplify the resulting expression.

a. Replace *x* with $x + h$ in the rule of the function.

$$f(x + h) = (x + h)^2 - (x + h) + 2$$
$$= x^2 + 2xh + h^2 - x - h + 2$$

b. By part **a**,
$$f(x + h) - f(x) = [x^2 + 2xh + h^2 - x - h + 2] - [x^2 - x + 2]$$
$$= x^2 + 2xh + h^2 - x - h + 2 - x^2 + x - 2$$
$$= 2xh + h^2 - h$$

c. By part **b**,
$$\frac{f(x + h) - f(x)}{h} = \frac{2xh + h^2 - h}{h} = \frac{h(2x + h - 1)}{h} = 2x + h - 1$$

If f is a function, then the quantity $\dfrac{f(x + h) - f(x)}{h}$, as in Example 4, is called the **difference quotient** of f. Difference quotients, whose significance is explained in Section 3.7, play an important role in calculus.

Functions Defined by Equations

Equations in two variables can be used to define functions. However, not every equation in two variables represents a function.

Example 5 **Determining if an Equation Defines a Function**

Determine whether each equation defines y as a function of x.

a. $4x - 2y^3 + 5 = 0$
b. $y^2 - x + 1 = 0$

Solution

a. The equation $4x - 2y^3 + 5 = 0$ can be solved uniquely for y.
$$2y^3 = 4x + 5$$
$$y^3 = 2x + \frac{5}{2}$$
$$y = \sqrt[3]{2x + \frac{5}{2}}$$

If a number is substituted for x in this equation, then exactly one value of y is produced. So the equation defines a function whose domain is the set of all real numbers and whose rule is stated below.
$$f(x) = \sqrt[3]{2x + \frac{5}{2}}$$

b. The equation $y^2 - x + 1 = 0$ can *not* be solved uniquely for y:
$$y^2 = x - 1$$
$$y = \pm\sqrt{x - 1}$$
$$y = \sqrt{x - 1} \quad \text{or} \quad y = -\sqrt{x - 1}$$

This equation does not define y as a function of x because, for example, the input $x = 5$ produces two outputs, 2 and -2.

Domains

When the rule of a function is given by a formula, as in Examples 3–6, its domain (set of inputs) is determined by the following convention.

Domain Convention

> Unless information to the contrary is given, the domain of a function f consists of every real number input for which the function rule produces a real number output.

Thus, the domain of a polynomial function such as $f(x) = x^3 - 4x + 1$ is the set of all real numbers, since $f(x)$ is defined for every value of x. However, in cases where applying the rule of a function leads to one of the following, the domain may not consist of all real numbers.

- division by zero
- the square root of a negative number (or nth root, where n is even)

Example 6   **Finding Domains of Functions**

Find the domain for each function given below.

a. $k(x) = \dfrac{x^2 - 6x}{x - 1}$ **b.** $f(u) = \sqrt{u + 2}$

Solution

a. When $x = 1$, the denominator of $\dfrac{x^2 - 6x}{x - 1}$ is 0 and the output is not defined. When $x \neq 1$, however, the denominator is nonzero and the fraction *is* defined. Therefore, the domain of k consists of all real numbers *except* 1, which is written as $x \neq 1$.

b. Since negative numbers do not have real square roots, $\sqrt{u + 2}$ is a real number only when $u + 2 \geq 0$, that is, when $u \geq -2$. Therefore, the domain of f consists of all real numbers greater than or equal to -2, that is, the interval $[-2, \infty)$.

Applications and the Domain Convention

The domain convention does not always apply when dealing with applications. Consider the distance function for falling objects, $d(t) = 16t^2$. Since t represents time, only nonnegative values of t make sense here, even though the rule of the function is defined for all values of t. Analogous comments apply to other applications.

> A real-life situation may lead to a function whose domain does not include all the values for which the rule of the function is defined.

Example 7 Finding the Domain of a Profit Function

A glassware factory has fixed expenses (mortgage, taxes, machinery, etc.) of $12,000 per week. In addition, it costs 80 cents to make one cup (labor, materials, shipping). A cup sells for $1.95. At most, 18,000 cups can be manufactured each week. Let x represent the number of cups made per week.

a. Express the weekly revenue R as a function of x.

b. Express the weekly cost C as a function of x.

c. Find the rule and the domain of the weekly profit function P.

Solution

a. $R(x) = $ (price per cup) $\cdot$ (number sold)
$R(x) = 1.95x$

b. $C(x) = $ (cost per cup) $\cdot$ (number sold) + (fixed expenses)
$C(x) = 0.80x + 12{,}000$

c. $P(x) = $ revenue $-$ cost $= R(x) - C(x)$
$P(x) = 1.95x - (0.80x + 12{,}000)$
$P(x) = 1.15x - 12{,}000$

Although this rule is defined for all real numbers x, the domain of the function P consists of the possible number of cups that can be made each week. Since only whole cups can be made and the maximum production is 18,000, the domain of P consists of all integers from 0 to 18,000. ∎

Piecewise-Defined and Greatest Integer Functions

A piecewise-defined function is one whose rule includes several formulas. The formula for each piece of the function is applied to certain values of the domain, as specified in the definition of the function.

Example 8 Evaluating a Piecewise-Defined Function

For the piecewise-defined function

$$f(x) = \begin{cases} 2x + 3 & \text{if } x < 4 \\ x^2 - 1 & \text{if } 4 \le x \le 10 \end{cases}$$

find each of the following.

a. $f(-5)$ **b.** $f(8)$ **c.** the domain of f.

Solution

a. Since -5 is less than 4, the first part of the rule applies.
$f(-5) = 2(-5) + 3 = -7$

b. Since 8 is between 4 and 10, the second part of the rule applies.
$f(8) = 8^2 - 1 = 63$

c. The rule of f gives directions when $x < 4$ and when $4 \le x \le 10$, so the domain of f consists of all real numbers x such that $x \le 10$, that is, $(-\infty, 10]$. ∎

The **greatest integer function** is a piecewise-defined function with infinitely many pieces.

$$f(x) = \begin{cases} \vdots \\ -3 & \text{if } -3 \leq x < -2 \\ -2 & \text{if } -2 \leq x < -1 \\ -1 & \text{if } -1 \leq x < 0 \\ 0 & \text{if } 0 \leq x < 1 \\ 1 & \text{if } 1 \leq x < 2 \\ 2 & \text{if } 2 \leq x < 3 \\ \vdots \end{cases}$$

The rule can be written in words as follows:

Greatest Integer Function

For any number x, round *down* to the nearest integer less than or equal to x.

Technology Tip

The greatest integer function is denoted INT or FLOOR in the NUM submenu of the MATH menu of TI and Sharp 9600. It is denoted FLOOR in the REAL submenu of the HP-38 MATH menu, and INTG in the NUM submenu of the Casio 9850 OPTN menu.

The domain of the greatest integer function is all real numbers, and the range is the set of integers. It is written as $f(x) = [x]$.

Example 9   **Evaluating the Greatest Integer Function**

Let $f(x) = [x]$. Evaluate the following:

a. $f(-4.7)$ **b.** $f(-3)$ **c.** $f(0)$ **d.** $f\left(\dfrac{5}{4}\right)$ **e.** $f(\pi)$

Solution

a. $f(-4.7) = [-4.7] = -5$ **b.** $f(-3) = [-3] = -3$

c. $f(0) = [0] = 0$ **d.** $f\left(\dfrac{5}{4}\right) = \left[\dfrac{5}{4}\right] = [1.25] = 1$

e. $f(\pi) = [\pi] = 3$

Exercises 3.1

In Exercises 1–4, describe the set of inputs, the set of outputs, and the rule for each function.

1. The amount of your paycheck before taxes is a function of the number of hours worked.

2. Your shoe size is a function of the length of your foot.

3. In physics, the pressure P of a gas kept at a constant volume is a function of the temperature T, related by the formula $P \cdot T = k$ for some constant k.

4. The number of hours of daylight at a certain latitude is a function of the day of the year. The following graph shows the number of hours of daylight that corresponds to each day.

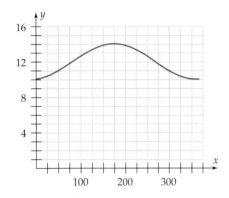

In Exercises 5–12, determine whether the equation defines y as a function of x.

5. $y = 3x^2 - 12$

6. $y = 2x^4 + 3x^2 - 2$

7. $y^2 = 4x + 1$

8. $5x - 4y^4 + 64 = 0$

9. $3x + 2y = 12$

10. $y - 4x^3 - 14 = 0$

11. $x^2 + y^2 = 9$

12. $y^2 - 3x^4 + 8 = 0$

Exercises 13–34 refer to the functions below. Find the indicated value of the function.

$$f(x) = \sqrt{x + 3} - x + 1$$
$$g(t) = t^2 - 1$$
$$h(x) = x^2 + \frac{1}{x} + 2$$

13. $f(0)$

14. $f(1)$

15. $f(\sqrt{2})$

16. $f(\sqrt{2} - 1)$

17. $f(-2)$

18. $f\left(-\frac{3}{2}\right)$

19. $h(3)$

20. $h(-4)$

21. $h\left(\frac{3}{2}\right)$

22. $h(\pi + 1)$

23. $h(a + k)$

24. $h(-x)$

25. $h(2 - x)$

26. $h(x - 3)$

27. $g(3)$

28. $g(-2)$

29. $g(0)$

30. $g(x)$

31. $g(s + 1)$

32. $g(1 - r)$

33. $g(-t)$

34. $g(t + h)$

In Exercises 35–42, compute and simplify the difference quotient (shown below). Assume $h \neq 0$.

$$\frac{f(x + h) - f(x)}{h}$$

35. $f(x) = x + 1$

36. $f(x) = -10x$

37. $f(x) = 3x + 7$

38. $f(x) = x^2$

39. $f(x) = x - x^2$

40. $f(x) = x^3$

41. $f(x) = \sqrt{x}$

42. $f(x) = \frac{1}{x}$

In Exercises 43–56, determine the domain of the function according to the domain convention.

43. $f(x) = x^2$

44. $g(x) = \frac{1}{x^2} + 2$

45. $h(t) = |t| - 1$

46. $k(u) = \sqrt{u}$

47. $k(x) = |x| + \sqrt{x} - 1$

48. $h(x) = \sqrt{(x + 1)^2}$

49. $g(u) = \frac{|u|}{u}$

50. $h(x) = \frac{\sqrt{x - 1}}{x^2 - 1}$

51. $g(y) = [-y]$

52. $f(t) = \sqrt{-t}$

53. $g(u) = \frac{u^2 + 1}{u^2 - u - 6}$

54. $f(t) = \sqrt{4 - t^2}$

55. $f(x) = -\sqrt{9 - (x - 9)^2}$

56. $f(x) = \sqrt{-x} + \frac{2}{x + 1}$

In Exercises 57–62, find the following:

a. $f(0)$ b. $f(1.6)$
c. $f(-2.3)$ d. $f(5 - 2\pi)$
e. The domain of f

57. $f(x) = [x]$

58. $f(x) = \begin{cases} -x & \text{if } x < 0 \\ x & \text{if } x \geq 0 \end{cases}$

59. $f(x) = \begin{cases} x^2 + 2x & \text{if } x < 2 \\ 3x - 5 & \text{if } 2 \leq x \leq 20 \end{cases}$

60. $f(x) = \begin{cases} x + 5 & \text{if } -3 < x \leq 0 \\ 3x & \text{if } 0 < x \leq 5 \end{cases}$

61. $f(x) = \begin{cases} 2x - 3 & \text{if } x < -1 \\ |x| - 5 & \text{if } -1 \leq x \leq 2 \\ x^2 & \text{if } x > 2 \end{cases}$

62. $f(x) = \begin{cases} x^2 & \text{if } -4 \leq x < -2 \\ x - 3 & \text{if } -2 \leq x \leq 1 \\ 2x + 1 & \text{if } x > 1 \end{cases}$

63. Find an equation that expresses the area A of a circle as a function of its
     a. radius r **b.** diameter d

64. Find an equation that expresses the area A of a square as a function of its
     a. side s **b.** diagonal d

65. A box with a square base of side x is four times higher than it is wide. Express the volume V of the box as a function of x.

66. The surface area of a cylindrical can of radius r and height h is $2\pi r^2 + 2\pi rh$. If the can is twice as high as the diameter of its top, express its surface area S as a function of r.

67. A rectangular region of 6000 square feet is to be fenced in on three sides with fencing that costs $3.75 per foot and on the fourth side with fencing that costs $2.00 per foot.
     a. Express the cost of the fence as a function of the length x of the fourth side.
     b. Find the domain of the function.

68. A box with a square base measuring $t \times t$ ft is to be made of three kinds of wood. The cost of the wood for the base is $0.85 per square foot; the wood for the sides costs $0.50 per square foot, and the wood for the top $1.15 per square foot. The volume of the box must be 10 cubic feet.

     a. Express the total cost of the box as a function of the length t.
     b. Find the domain of the function.

69. A man walks for 45 minutes at a rate of 3 mph, then jogs for 75 minutes at a rate of 5 mph, then sits and rests for 30 minutes, and finally walks for 90 minutes at a rate of 3 mph.
     a. Write a piecewise-defined function that expresses his distance traveled as a function of time.
     b. Find the domain of the function.

70. Average tuition and fees in private four-year colleges in recent years were as follows. (Source: The College Board)

Year	Tuition & fees
1995	$12,432
1996	$12,823
1997	$13,664
1998	$14,709
1999	$15,380
2000	$16,332

     a. Use linear regression to find the rule of a function f that gives the approximate average tuition in year x, where $x = 0$ corresponds to 1990.
     b. Find $f(6), f(8)$, and $f(10)$. How do they compare with the actual data?
     c. Use f to estimate tuition in 2003.

71. Suppose that a state income tax law reads as follows:

Annual income	Amount of tax
less than $2000	0
$2000–$6000	2% of income over $2000
more than $6000	$80 plus 5% of income over $6000

Write a piecewise-defined function that represents the income tax law. What is the domain of the function?

72. The table below shows the 2002 federal income tax rates for a single person.

Taxable income	Tax
not over $6000	10% of income
over $6000, but not over $27,950	$600 + 15% of amount over $6000
over $27,950, but not over $67,700	$3892.50 + 27% of amount over $27,950
over $67,700, but not over $141,250	$14,625 + 30% of amount over $67,700
over $141,250, but not over $307,050	$36,690 + 35% of amount over $141,250
over $307,050	$94,720 + 38.6% of amount over $307,050

a. Write a piecewise-defined function T such that $T(x)$ is the tax due on a taxable income of x dollars. What is the domain of the function?

b. Find $T(24,000)$, $T(35,000)$, and $T(100,000)$.

3.2   Graphs of Functions

Objectives

- Determine whether a graph represents a function
- Analyze graphs to determine domain and range, local maxima and minima, inflection points, and intervals where they are increasing, decreasing, concave up, and concave down
- Graph parametric equations

Functions Defined by Graphs

A graph may be used to define a function or relation. Suppose that f is a function defined by a graph in the coordinate plane. If the point (x, y) is on the graph of f, then y is the output produced by the input x, or $y = f(x)$.

Example 1   **A Function Defined by a Graph**

The graph in Figure 3.2.1 defines the function f. Determine the following.

a. $f(0)$ **b.** $f(3)$ **c.** the domain of f **d.** the range of f

NOTE An open circle on a graph indicates that the point is *not* a part of the graph, and a solid circle indicates that the point *is* a part of the graph.

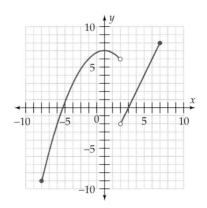

Figure 3.2-1

Solution

a. To find $f(0)$, notice that the point $(0, 7)$ is on the graph. Thus, 7 is the output produced by the input 0, or $f(0) = 7$.

b. To find $f(3)$, notice that the point $(3, 0)$ is on the graph. Thus, 0 is the output produced by the input 3, or $f(3) = 0$.

c. To find the domain of the function, find the x-coordinates of the point farthest to the left and farthest to the right. Then, determine whether there are any gaps in the function between these values. $(-8, -9)$ is the point farthest to the left, and $(7, 8)$ is farthest to the right. The function does not have a point with an x-coordinate of 2, so the domain of f is $[-8, 2)$ and $(2, 7]$.

d. To find the range of the function, find the y-coordinates of the highest and lowest points, then determine if there are any gaps between these values. The highest point is $(7, 8)$ and the lowest point is $(-8, -9)$, and there are no y-values between -9 and 8 that do not correspond to at least one x-value. Thus, the range of f is $[-9, 8]$.

The Vertical Line Test

If a graph represents a function, then each input determines one and only one output. Thus, no two points can have the same x-coordinate and different y-coordinates. Since any two such points would lie on the same vertical line, this fact provides a useful test for determining whether a graph represents a function.

Vertical Line Test

A graph in a coordinate plane represents a function if and only if no vertical line intersects the graph more than once.

Example 2 Determining Whether a Graph Defines a Function

Use the Vertical Line Test to determine whether the following graphs represent functions. If not, give an example of an input value that corresponds to more than one output value.

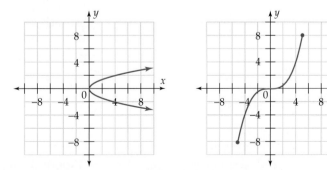

Figure 3.2-2

Solution

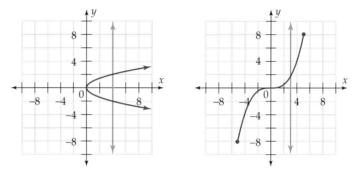

Figure 3.2-3

The vertical line $x = 4$ intersects the graph above at $(4, 2)$ and $(4, -2)$, so the graph is not a function. The input 4 has two corresponding outputs, 2 and -2.	There is no vertical line that intersects the graph above in more than one place, so this graph defines a function.

■

Analyzing Graphs

In order to discuss a graph or compare two graphs, it is important to be able to describe the features of different graphs. The most important features are the x- and y-intercepts, intervals where the graph is increasing or decreasing, local maxima and minima, intervals where the graph is concave up or concave down, and points of inflection.

Increasing and Decreasing Functions

A function is said to be **increasing** on an interval if its graph always rises as you move from left to right over the interval. It is **decreasing** on an interval if its graph always falls as you move from left to right over the interval. A function is said to be **constant** on an interval if its graph is a horizontal line over the interval.

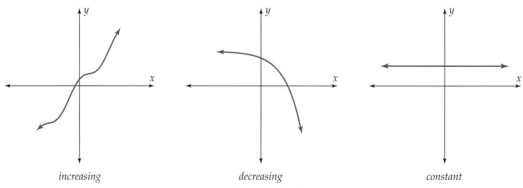

increasing   *decreasing*   *constant*

Figure 3.2-4

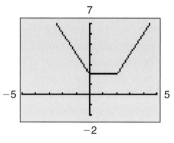

Figure 3.2-5

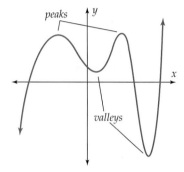

Figure 3.2-6

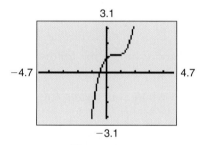

Figure 3.2-7

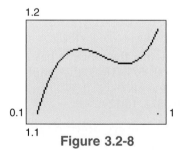

Figure 3.2-8

Example 3   Where a Function is Increasing/Decreasing

On what interval is the function $f(x) = |x| + |x - 2|$ increasing? decreasing? constant?

Solution

The graph of the function, shown in Figure 3.2-5, suggests that f is decreasing on the interval $(-\infty, 0)$, increasing on $(2, \infty)$, and constant on $[0, 2]$. Using the trace feature on a graphing calculator, you can confirm the function is constant between 0 and 2. For an algebraic proof that f is constant on $[0, 2]$, see Exercise 55.

Local Maxima and Minima

The graph of a function may include some peaks and valleys, as in Figure 3.2-6. A peak may not be the highest point on the graph, but it is the highest point in its neighborhood. Similarly, a valley is the lowest point in its neighborhood.

A function f has a **local maximum** (plural: **local maxima**) at $x = c$ if the graph of f has a peak at the point $(c, f(c))$. This means that $f(x) \leq f(c)$ for all x near c. Similarly, a function has a **local minimum** (plural: **local minima**) at $x = d$ if the graph of f has a valley at $(d, f(d))$. This means $f(x) \geq f(d)$ for all x near d.

Calculus is usually needed to find exact local maxima and minima. However, they can be approximated with a calculator.

Example 4   Finding Local Maxima and Minima

Graph $f(x) = x^3 - 1.8x^2 + x + 1$ and find all local maxima and minima.

Solution

In the decimal or standard window, the graph does not appear to have any local maxima or minima (see Figure 3.2-7). Select a viewing window such as the one in Figure 3.2-8 to see that the function actually has a local maximum and a local minimum (Figure 3.2-9). The calculator's minimum finder and maximum finder show that the local minimum occurs when $x \approx 0.763$ and the local maximum occurs when $x \approx 0.437$.

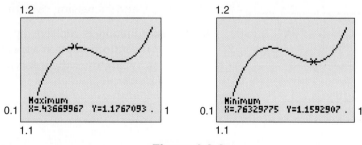

Figure 3.2-9

Concavity and Inflection Points

Concavity is used to describe the way that a curve bends. For any two points in a given interval that lie on a curve, if the segment that connects them is *above* the curve, then the curve is said to be **concave up** over the given interval. If the segment is *below* the curve, then the curve is said to be **concave down** over the interval (see Figure 3.2-10). A straight line is neither concave up nor concave down. A point where the curve changes concavity is called an **inflection point.**

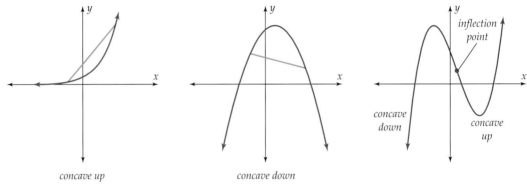

Figure 3.2-10

Example 5   Analyzing a Graph

Graph the function $f(x) = -2x^3 + 6x^2 - x + 3$ and estimate the following, using the graph and a maximum and minimum finder.

a. intervals where the function is increasing and where it is decreasing

b. all local maxima and minima of the function

c. intervals where the function is concave up and where it is concave down

d. all inflection points of the function

Solution

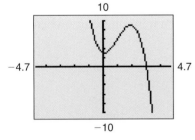

Figure 3.2-11

a.–b. The maximum and minimum finders show that the function has a maximum at $x \approx 1.9129$ and a minimum at $x \approx 0.0871$. Thus, the graph shows that the function is decreasing over the intervals $(-\infty, 0.0871)$ and $(1.9129, \infty)$, and increasing over the interval $(0.0871, 1.9129)$.

c.–d. The function is concave up on the left and concave down on the right, and the inflection point appears to be at about $x \approx 1$. Thus, the function is concave up over the interval $(-\infty, 1)$ and concave down over the interval $(1, \infty)$.   ∎

Graphs of Piecewise-Defined and Greatest Integer Functions

The graphs of piecewise-defined functions are often discontinuous, that is, they commonly have jumps or holes. To graph a piecewise-defined function, graph each piece separately.

Example 6   Graphing a Piecewise-Defined Function

Graph the piecewise-defined function below.

$$f(x) = \begin{cases} x^2 & \text{if } x \le 1 \\ x + 2 & \text{if } 1 < x \le 4 \end{cases}$$

Solution

The graph is made up of parts of two different graphs, corresponding to the different parts of the function.

For $x \le 1$, the graph of f coincides with the graph of $y = x^2$.

For $1 < x \le 4$, the graph of f coincides with the graph of $y = x + 2$.

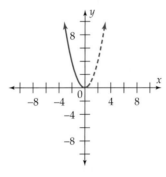
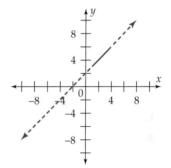

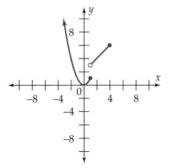

Combining these partial graphs produces the graph of f.

Figure 3.2-12

Piecewise-defined functions can be graphed on a calculator, provided that you use the correct syntax. However, the screen does not show which endpoints are included or excluded from the graph.

Technology Tip

Graphing Exploration

Graph the function f from Example 6 on a calculator as follows: On Sharp 9600 or HP-38 or TI-83/86 calculators, graph these two equations on the same screen:

$$Y_1 = X^2/(X \le 1)$$
$$Y_2 = X + 2/((X > 1)(X \le 4))$$

On a TI-89/92, graph these equations on the same screen:

$$Y_1 = X^2 \,|\, X \le 1$$
$$Y_2 = X + 2 \,|\, X > 1 \quad \text{and} \quad X \le 4$$

To graph f on a Casio 9850, graph these equations on the same screen (including commas and square brackets):

$$Y_1 = X^2, [-6, 1]$$
$$Y_2 = X + 2, [1, 4]$$

How does your graph compare with Figure 3.2-12?

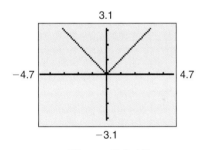

3.1

−4.7   4.7

−3.1

Figure 3.2-13

Example 7   The Absolute-Value Function

Graph $f(x) = |x|$.

Solution

The absolute-value function $f(x) = |x|$ is also a piecewise-defined function, since by definition

$$|x| = \begin{cases} -x & \text{if } x < 0 \\ x & \text{if } x \ge 0 \end{cases}$$

Its graph can be obtained by drawing the part of the line $y = x$ to the right of the origin and the part of the line $y = -x$ to the left of the origin or by graphing $Y_1 = $ **ABS X** on a calculator.

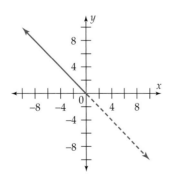
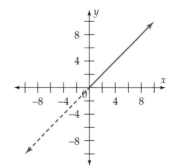
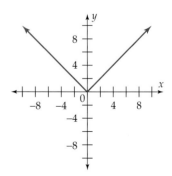

Figure 3.2-14

Example 8   The Greatest Integer Function

Graph the greatest integer function $f(x) = [x]$.

Solution

The greatest integer function can easily be graphed by hand, by considering the values of the function between each two consecutive integers. For instance, between $x = -2$ and $x = -1$ the value of $f(x) = [x]$ is always -2, so the graph there is a horizontal line segment, all of whose points have y-coordinate -2, with a solid circle on the left endpoint and an open circle on the right endpoint. The rest of the graph is obtained similarly.

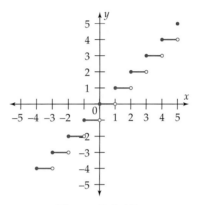

Figure 3.2-15

A function whose graph consists of horizontal line segments, such as Figure 3.2-15, is called a **step function.** Step functions can be graphed on a calculator, but some features of their graphs may not be shown.

Technology Tip

To change to dot mode, select **DOT** or **DRAW-DOT** in the TI-83 **MODE** menu, the **FORMT** submenu of the TI-86 **GRAPH** menu, the **STYLE** submenu of the TI-89 Y = menu, or the **STYLE1** submenu of the Sharp 9600 **FORMAT** menu. In the Casio 9850 **SETUP** menu, set the **DRAWTYPE** to **PLOT**. In the HP-38 **PLOT SETUP** menu, uncheck **CONNECT** on the second screen.

Graphing Exploration

Graph the greatest integer function $f(x) = [x]$ on your calculator (see the Technology Tip on page 147). Does your graph look like Figure 3.2-15? Change your calculator to "dot" rather than "connected" mode (see the Technology Tip at left) and graph again. How does this graph compare with Figure 3.2-15? Can you tell from the graph which endpoints are included and which are excluded?

Parametric Graphing

In **parametric graphing,** the x-coordinate and the y-coordinate of each point on a graph are each given as a function of a third variable, t, called a **parameter.** The functions that give the rules for the coordinates are called **parametric equations.**

A parametric graph can be thought of as representing the function

$$f(t) = (x, y)$$

where

$$x = x(t) \quad \text{and} \quad y = y(t)$$

are the rules for the x- and y-coordinates. Note that the graph will not necessarily pass the Vertical Line Test.

Example 9   Graphing a Parametric Equation

Graph the curve given by

$$x = 2t + 1$$
$$y = t^2 - 3$$

Solution

Make a table of values for t, x, and y. Then plot the points from the table and complete the graph.

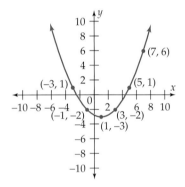

Figure 3.2-16

t	$x = 2t + 1$	$y = t^2 - 3$	(x, y)
-2	-3	1	$(-3, 1)$
-1	-1	-2	$(-1, -2)$
0	1	-3	$(1, -3)$
1	3	-2	$(3, -2)$
2	5	1	$(5, 1)$
3	7	6	$(7, 6)$

Technology Tip

To change to parametric mode, choose **PAR**, **PARAM**, **PARAMETRIC**, or **PARM** in the TI **MODE** menu, the HP-38 **LIB** menu, the **COORD** submenu of the Sharp 9600 **SETUP** menu, or the **TYPE** submenu of the Casio 9850 **GRAPH** menu (on the main menu).

Graphing Exploration

Graph the equations from Example 9 on a calculator in parametric mode in the standard viewing window. Set the range so that $-10 \le t \le 10$, with t-step $= 0.1$. Use the trace feature to find at least three points on the graph that are not given in the table in Example 9.

Parametric mode can be used to graph equations of the form $y = f(x)$ or the form $x = f(y)$.

Graphing y = f(x) or x = f(y) in Parametric Mode

To graph $y = f(x)$ in parametric mode, let

$$x = t$$
$$y = f(t)$$

To graph $x = f(y)$ in parametric mode, let

$$x = f(t)$$
$$y = t$$

Example 10   **Graphing in Parametric Mode**

Graph the following equations in parametric mode on a calculator.

a. $y = \left(\dfrac{x-1}{2}\right)^2 - 3$ **b.** $x = y^2 - 3y + 1$

Solution

a. Let $x = t$ and $y = \left(\dfrac{t-1}{2}\right)^2 - 3$.   **b.** Let $x = t^2 - 3t + 1$ and $y = t$.

NOTE The graph in part **a** is the same as in Example 9. To obtain the equation in part **a** from the parametric equations in Example 9, solve the first equation for t and substitute the result into the second equation.

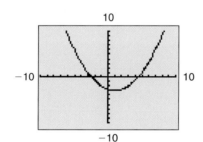

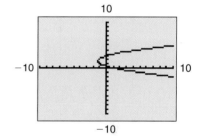

Figure 3.2-17

Notice that the graph in part **b** does not pass the Vertical Line Test. The equation does not represent y as a function of x.

Parametric equations will be studied more thoroughly in Chapter 11.

Exercises 3.2

In Exercises 1–4, the graph below defines a function, f. Determine the following:

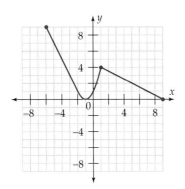

1. $f(-5)$ **2.** $f(1)$

3. the domain of f **4.** the range of f

In Exercises 5–8, the graph below defines a function, g. Determine the following:

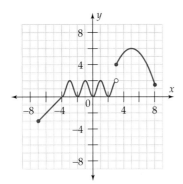

5. $g(1)$ **6.** $g(5)$

7. the domain of g **8.** the range of g

In Exercises 9–14, use the Vertical Line Test to determine whether the graph defines a function. If not, give an example of an input value that corresponds to more than one output value.

9.

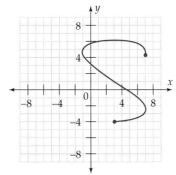

10.

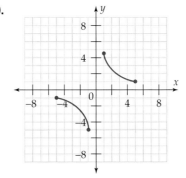

11.

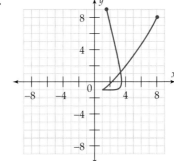

12.

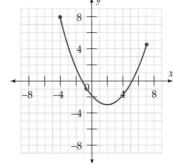

13.

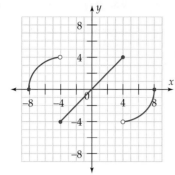

14.

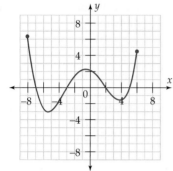

In Exercises 15 and 16, the graph of a function is shown. Find the approximate intervals on which the function is increasing and on which it is decreasing.

15.

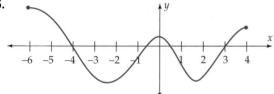

16.

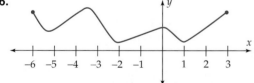

In Exercises 17–22, graph each function. Find the approximate intervals on which the function is increasing, decreasing, and constant.

17. $f(x) = |x - 1| - |x + 1|$

18. $g(x) = |x - 1| + |x + 2|$

19. $f(x) = -x^3 - 8x^2 + 8x + 5$

20. $f(x) = x^4 - 0.7x^3 - 0.6x^2 + 1$

21. $g(x) = 0.2x^4 - x^3 + x^2 - 2$

22. $g(x) = x^4 + x^3 - 4x^2 + x - 1$

In Exercises 23–28, graph each function. Estimate all local maxima and minima of the function.

23. $f(x) = x^3 - x$

24. $g(t) = -\sqrt{16 - t^2}$

25. $h(x) = \dfrac{x}{x^2 + 1}$

26. $k(x) = x^3 - 3x + 1$

27. $f(x) = x^3 - 1.8x^2 + x + 2$

28. $g(x) = 2x^3 + x^2 + 1$

29. a. A rectangle has a perimeter of 100 inches, and one side has length x. Express the area of the rectangle as a function of x.
　b. Use the function in part **a** to find the dimensions of the rectangle with perimeter 100 inches and the largest possible area.

30. a. A rectangle has an area of 240 in^2, and one side has length x. Express the perimeter of the rectangle as a function of x.
　b. Use the function in part **a** to find the dimensions of the rectangle with area 240 in^2 and the smallest possible perimeter.

31. a. A box with a square base has a volume of 867 in^3. Express the surface area of the box as a function of the length x of a side of the base. (Be sure to include the top of the box.)
　b. Use the function in part **a** to find the dimensions of the box with volume 867 in^3 and the smallest possible surface area.

32. a. A cylindrical can has a surface area of 60 in^2. Express the volume of the can as a function of the radius r.
　b. Use the function in part **a** to find the radius and height of the can with surface area 60 in^2 and the largest possible volume.

In Exercises 33–36, graph each function. Find the approximate intervals on which the function is concave up and concave down, and estimate all inflection points.

33. $f(x) = x^3$

34. $f(x) = x^3 - 2x$

35. $h(x) = x^4 - 2x^2$

36. $g(x) = x^3 - 3x^2 + 2x + 1$

In Exercises 37–40,

a. Graph each function.

b. Find the approximate intervals on which the function is increasing, decreasing, and constant.

c. Estimate all local maxima and minima.

d. Find the approximate intervals on which the function is concave up and concave down.

e. Estimate the coordinates of any inflection points.

37. $f(x) = x^2 - 2x + 1$ **38.** $f(x) = -x^2 - 4x - 3$

39. $g(x) = x^3 - 3x^2 + 2$ **40.** $g(x) = -x^3 + 4x - 2$

In Exercises 41–44, sketch the graph of the function. Be sure to indicate which endpoints are included and which are excluded.

41. $f(x) = \begin{cases} 2x + 3 & \text{if } x < -1 \\ x^2 & \text{if } x \geq -1 \end{cases}$

42. $g(x) = \begin{cases} |x| & \text{if } x < 1 \\ -3x + 4 & \text{if } x \geq 1 \end{cases}$

43. $k(u) = \begin{cases} -2u - 2 & \text{if } u < -3 \\ u - [u] & \text{if } -3 \leq u \leq 1 \\ 2u^2 & \text{if } u > 1 \end{cases}$

44. $f(x) = \begin{cases} x^2 & \text{if } x < -2 \\ x & \text{if } -2 \leq x < 4 \\ \sqrt{x} & \text{if } x \geq 4 \end{cases}$

In Exercises 45–49,

a. Use the fact that the absolute-value function is piecewise-defined (see Example 7) to write the rule of the given function as a piecewise-defined function whose rule does not include any absolute value bars.

b. Graph the function.

45. $f(x) = |x| + 2$ **46.** $g(x) = |x| - 4$

47. $h(x) = \dfrac{|x|}{2} - 2$ **48.** $g(x) = |x + 3|$

49. $f(x) = |x - 5|$

In Exercises 50–53, sketch the graph of the function. Be sure to indicate which endpoints are included and which are excluded.

50. $f(x) = -[x]$

51. $g(x) = [-x]$ (This is not the same function as in Exercise 50.)

52. $h(x) = [x] + [-x]$ **53.** $f(x) = 2[x]$

54. A common mistake is to graph the function f in Example 6 by graphing both $y = x^2$ and $y = x + 2$ on the same screen, with no restrictions on x. Explain why this graph could not possibly be the graph of a function.

55. Show that the function $f(x) = |x| + |x - 2|$ is constant on the interval $[0, 2]$. *Hint:* Use the piecewise definition of absolute value in Example 7 to compute $f(x)$ when $0 \leq x \leq 2$.

In Exercises 56–59, use your calculator to estimate the domain and range of the function by tracing its graph.

56. $g(x) = x^2 - 4$ **57.** $h(x) = \sqrt{x^2 - 4}$

58. $k(x) = \sqrt{x^2 + 4}$ **59.** $f(x) = 3x - 2$

In Exercises 60 and 61, draw the graph of a function f that satisfies the given conditions. The function does not need to be given by an algebraic rule.

60. • $f(-1) = 2$

• $f(x) \geq 2$ when x is in the interval $\left(-1, \dfrac{1}{2}\right)$

• $f(x)$ starts decreasing when $x = 1$
• $f(3) = 3 = f(0)$
• $f(x)$ starts increasing when $x = 5$

61. • domain $f = [-2, 4]$
• range $f = [-5, 6]$
• $f(-1) = f(3)$
• $f\left(\dfrac{1}{2}\right) = 0$

In Exercises 62–67, graph the curve determined by the parametric equations.

62. $x = 0.1t^3 - 0.2t^2 - 2t + 4$
$y = 1 - t \quad (-5 \leq t \leq 6)$

63. $x = t^2 - 3t + 2$
$y = 8 - t^3 \quad (-4 \leq t \leq 4)$

64. $x = t^2 - 6t$
$y = \sqrt{t + 7} \quad (-5 \leq t \leq 9)$

65. $x = 1 - t^2$
$y = t^3 - t - 1 \quad (-4 \leq t \leq 4)$

66. $x = t^2 - t - 1$
$y = 1 - t - t^2$

67. $x = 3t^2 - 5$
$y = t^2 \quad (-4 \leq t \leq 4)$

In Exercises 68–71, graph the equation in parametric mode. Give the rule for x and for y in terms of t.

68. $y = x^3 + x^2 - 6x$

69. $y = x^4 - 3x^3 + x^2$

70. $x = y^3 + 5y^2 - 4y - 5$

71. $x = y^4 - 3y^2 - 5$

3.3 Quadratic Functions

Objectives

- Define three forms for quadratic functions

- Find the vertex and intercepts of a quadratic function and sketch its graph

- Convert one form of a quadratic function to another

Parabolas

The rule of a **quadratic function** is a polynomial of degree 2. The shape of the graph of a quadratic function is a **parabola.** Three parabolas are shown in Figure 3.3-1, with important points labeled.

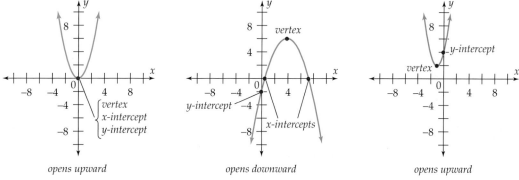

opens upward   opens downward   opens upward

Figure 3.3-1

Notice that the graph of a quadratic function

- can open either upward or downward
- always has a vertex which is either the maximum or minimum
- always has exactly 1 y-intercept
- can have 0, 1, or 2 x-intercepts

A parabola is symmetric about a line through the vertex called the **axis of symmetry.**

Quadratic Functions

Quadratic functions can be written in several forms.

Three Forms of a Quadratic Function

A quadratic function can be written in any of the following forms:

Transformation form: $f(x) = a(x - h)^2 + k$

Polynomial form: $f(x) = ax^2 + bx + c$

x-Intercept form: $f(x) = a(x - s)(x - t)$

where $a, b, c, h, k, s,$ and t are real numbers and $a \neq 0$. If a is positive, the graph opens upward; and if a is negative, the graph opens downward.

NOTE It is not necessary to memorize the formulas for the vertex and intercept forms. The method of finding these points is the most important thing to learn.

Transformation Form

The transformation form is the most useful form for finding the vertex. For a quadratic function written in transformation form, $f(x) = a(x - h)^2 + k$, the vertex is the point with coordinates (h, k).

Since the y-intercept of a function is $f(0)$,

$$f(0) = a(0 - h)^2 + k = ah^2 + k$$

shows the y-intercept is $ah^2 + k$.

Since the x-intercepts occur when $y = 0$, the x-intercepts are the solutions of the quadratic equation $a(x - h)^2 + k = 0$.

$$a(x - h)^2 + k = 0$$
$$a(x - h)^2 = -k$$
$$(x - h)^2 = \frac{-k}{a}$$
$$x - h = \pm\sqrt{\frac{-k}{a}}$$
$$x = h \pm \sqrt{\frac{-k}{a}}$$

The x-intercepts are $h + \sqrt{\frac{-k}{a}}$ and $h - \sqrt{\frac{-k}{a}}$.

Example 1   Transformation Form

For the function $f(x) = 2(x - 3)^2 - 4$, find the vertex and the x- and y-intercepts. Then sketch the graph.

Solution

In $f(x) = 2(x - 3)^2 - 4 = 2(x - 3)^2 + (-4), a = 2, h = 3$ and $k = -4$. The vertex is

$$(h, k) = (3, -4)$$

the y-intercept is

$$ah^2 + k = 2(3^2) + (-4) = 14$$

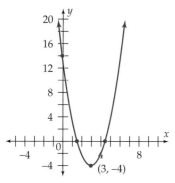

Figure 3.3-2

and the x-intercepts are

$$h + \sqrt{\frac{-k}{a}} = 3 + \sqrt{\frac{-(-4)}{2}} = 3 + \sqrt{2} \approx 4.4$$

$$h - \sqrt{\frac{-k}{a}} = 3 - \sqrt{\frac{-(-4)}{2}} = 3 - \sqrt{2} \approx 1.6$$

To graph the function, plot the vertex and intercepts, then draw the parabola. Since a is positive, the parabola opens upward. ∎

Polynomial Form

The polynomial form is the most useful form for finding the y-intercept. Since the y-intercept of a function is $f(0)$, the y-intercept is c.

$$f(0) = a(0)^2 + b(0) + c = 0 + 0 + c = c$$

The x-intercepts are the solutions of the quadratic equation $ax^2 + bx + c = 0$, which can be solved either by factoring or by the quadratic formula. In general, the x-intercepts are

$$\frac{-b + \sqrt{b^2 - 4ac}}{2a} \qquad \text{and} \qquad \frac{-b - \sqrt{b^2 - 4ac}}{2a}$$

for values which make $b^2 - 4ac$ positive. If $b^2 - 4ac = 0$, then there is only one x-intercept. If $b^2 - 4ac$ is negative, then there are no x-intercepts.

To find the vertex of the graph of a quadratic function in polynomial form, compare the transformation form to the polynomial form. First, multiply and distribute the terms in the transformation form, so the coefficients can be compared.

$$\begin{aligned}
f(x) &= a(x - h)^2 + k & \textit{transformation form} \\
&= a(x^2 - 2hx + h^2) + k & \textit{multiply} \\
&= ax^2 - 2ahx + ah^2 + k & \textit{distribute the a} \\
&= ax^2 - 2ahx + (ah^2 + k)
\end{aligned}$$

Match the second coefficient in each of the two equivalent forms.

$$b = -2ah$$

$$\frac{-b}{2a} = h$$

Since h is the x-coordinate of the vertex in the transformation form, $\dfrac{-b}{2a}$ is the x-coordinate of the vertex in the polynomial form. The y-coordinate of the vertex can be found by substituting $\dfrac{-b}{2a}$ into the function. Thus, the vertex of the graph of a quadratic function is

$$\left(\frac{-b}{2a}, f\left(\frac{-b}{2a} \right) \right)$$

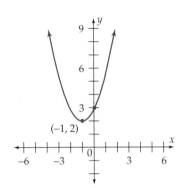

(−1, 2)

Figure 3.3-3

Example 2 Polynomial Form

For the function $f(x) = x^2 + 2x + 3$, find the vertex and the x- and y-intercepts. Then sketch the graph.

Solution

In $f(x) = x^2 + 2x + 3$, $a = 1$, $b = 2$, and $c = 3$. Thus, the y-intercept is

$$c = 3$$

and the vertex is

$$\left(\frac{-b}{2a}, f\left(\frac{-b}{2a}\right)\right) = \left(\frac{-2}{2(1)}, f\left(\frac{-2}{2(1)}\right)\right) = (-1, 2)$$

Since $b^2 - 4ac = -8$, the quadratic equation $x^2 + 2x + 3 = 0$ has no solutions, so there are no x-intercepts.

To graph the function, plot the vertex and y-intercept, then draw the parabola. Since a is positive, the parabola opens upward. ∎

NOTE Not all quadratic functions can be written in x-intercept form. If the graph of a quadratic function has no x-intercepts, then there are no real values of s and t for which $f(x) = a(x - s)(x - t)$.

x-Intercept Form

The x-intercept form is the most useful form for finding the x-intercepts. For a quadratic function written in x-intercept form, $f(x) = a(x - s)(x - t)$, the x-intercepts of the graph are s and t. Notice that both of these values are solutions to the equation $f(x) = 0$.

$$f(s) = a(s - s)(s - t) = a(0)(s - t) = 0$$
$$\text{and}$$
$$f(t) = a(t - s)(t - t) = a(t - s)(0) = 0$$

Since the y-intercept of a function is $f(0)$,

$$f(0) = a(0 - s)(0 - t) = ast$$

so the y-intercept is ast.

To find the vertex of a graph of a quadratic function in x-intercept form, recall that a parabola is symmetric about a line through the vertex. Thus, the vertex is exactly halfway between the x-intercepts. The x-coordinate of the vertex is the average of the x-intercepts, or $\left(\frac{s + t}{2}\right)$. To find the y-coordinate of the vertex, substitute this value into the function. The vertex is

$$\left(\frac{s + t}{2}, f\left(\frac{s + t}{2}\right)\right)$$

Example 3 x-Intercept Form

For the graph of the function $f(x) = -\frac{1}{2}(x - 4)(x + 2)$, find the vertex and the x- and y-intercepts. Then sketch the graph.

Solution

In $f(x) = -\dfrac{1}{2}(x - 4)(x + 2)$, $a = -\dfrac{1}{2}$, $s = 4$, and $t = -2$. The x-intercepts are

$$s = 4, \text{ and } t = -2$$

and the y-intercept is

$$ast = -\dfrac{1}{2}(4)(-2) = 4$$

and the vertex is

$$\left(\dfrac{s+t}{2}, f\left(\dfrac{s+t}{2}\right)\right) = \left(\dfrac{4 + (-2)}{2}, f\left(\dfrac{4 + (-2)}{2}\right)\right) = (1, 4.5)$$

To graph the function, plot the vertex and intercepts, then draw the parabola. Since a is negative, the parabola opens downward.

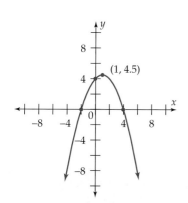

Figure 3.3-4

Changing from One Form to Another

It is sometimes necessary to change a quadratic function from one form to another. To change either transformation or x-intercept form to polynomial form, distribute and collect like terms. To change either polynomial or transformation form to x-intercept form, factor out the leading coefficient, then factor or use the quadratic formula to find the x-intercepts.

Example 4   Changing to Polynomial and *x*-Intercept Form

Write the following functions in polynomial and x-intercept form, if possible.

a. $f(x) = 0.4(x - 3)^2 + 2$
b. $g(x) = 3x^2 - 3.9x - 43.2$
c. $h(x) = -2(x - 4)(x + 2)$

Solution

a. To change the function f to polynomial form, distribute and collect like terms.

$$f(x) = 0.4(x - 3)^2 + 2$$
$$f(x) = 0.4(x^2 - 6x + 9) + 2$$
$$f(x) = 0.4x^2 - 2.4x + 5.6$$

Since $b^2 - 4ac = -3.2$ is negative, there are no x-intercepts. Thus, the function f cannot be written in x-intercept form.

b. The function g is already given in polynomial form. To find the x-intercept form, first factor out $a = 3$, then use the quadratic formula on the remaining expression.

$$g(x) = 3x^2 - 3.9x - 43.2$$

$$g(x) = 3(x^2 - 1.3x - 14.4)$$

x-intercepts:

$$\frac{1.3 \pm \sqrt{(-1.3)^2 - 4(1)(-14.4)}}{2} = \frac{1.3 \pm 7.7}{2} = 4.5 \text{ and } -3.2$$

So the x-intercept form is

$$g(x) = 3(x - 4.5)(x + 3.2)$$

c. The function h is already given in x-intercept form. To change the function to polynomial form, distribute and collect like terms.

$$h(x) = -2(x - 4)(x + 2)$$

$$h(x) = -2(x^2 - 2x - 8)$$

$$h(x) = -2x^2 + 4x + 16$$

To convert a quadratic function to transformation form, it may be necessary to complete the square.

Example 5   **Changing to Transformation Form**

Write the following functions in transformation form.

a. $f(x) = -3x^2 + 4x - 1$

b. $g(x) = 0.3(x - 2)(x + 1)$

Solution

a. Factor $a = -3$ out of the first two terms, then complete the square as shown below.

$$f(x) = -3x^2 + 4x - 1$$

$$= -3\left(x^2 - \frac{4}{3}x\right) - 1 \qquad \textit{Factor 3 out of first two terms}$$

$$= -3\left(x^2 - \frac{4}{3}x + \frac{4}{9} - \frac{4}{9}\right) - 1 \qquad \textit{Add and subtract } \left(\frac{b}{2}\right)^2$$

$$= -3\left(\left(x - \frac{2}{3}\right)^2 - \frac{4}{9}\right) - 1 \qquad \textit{Write } x^2 - \frac{4}{3}x + \frac{4}{9} \textit{ as a perfect}$$
$$\textit{square}$$

$$= -3\left(x - \frac{2}{3}\right)^2 + \frac{4}{3} - 1 \qquad \textit{Distribute the } -3 \textit{ over the } -\frac{4}{9}$$

$$f(x) = -3\left(x - \frac{2}{3}\right)^2 + \frac{1}{3} \qquad \textit{Combine like terms}$$

b. Multiply the terms in parentheses, then complete the square as shown below.

$$g(x) = 0.3(x - 2)(x + 1)$$
$$= 0.3(x^2 - x - 2) \qquad \textit{Multiply}$$
$$= 0.3(x^2 - x + 0.25 - 0.25 - 2) \qquad \textit{Add and subtract } \left(\frac{b}{2}\right)^2$$
$$= 0.3((x - 0.5)^2 - 0.25 - 2) \qquad \textit{Write } x^2 - x + 0.25 \textit{ as a perfect square}$$
$$= 0.3((x - 0.5)^2 - 2.25) \qquad \textit{Combine like terms}$$
$$g(x) = 0.3(x - 0.5)^2 - 0.675 \qquad \textit{Distribute the 0.3 over the } -2.25$$

> **CAUTION**
>
> When completing the square of an expression that is part of a function, it is not possible to divide by the leading coefficient or add a term to both sides. It is necessary to factor out the leading coefficient, then add and subtract the $\left(\frac{b}{2}\right)^2$ term.

Summary of Quadratic Forms

Below is a summary of the basic forms and the important points of a quadratic function. You should memorize the highlighted items.

Summary of Quadratic Functions

Name	Transformation	Polynomial	x-Intercept
Form	$f(x) = a(x - h)^2 + k$	$f(x) = ax^2 + bx + c$	$f(x) = a(x - s)(x - t)$
Vertex	(h, k)	$\left(\frac{-b}{2a}, f\left(\frac{-b}{2a}\right)\right)$	$\left(\frac{s + t}{2}, f\left(\frac{s + t}{2}\right)\right)$
***x*-Intercepts**	$h + \sqrt{\frac{-k}{a}}$ and $h - \sqrt{\frac{-k}{a}}$	$\dfrac{-b + \sqrt{b^2 - 4ac}}{2a}$ and $\dfrac{-b - \sqrt{b^2 - 4ac}}{2a}$	s and t
***y*-Intercept**	$ah^2 + k$	c	ast

Applications

In the graph of a quadratic function, the vertex of the parabola is either a maximum or a minimum of the function. Thus, the solution of many applications depends on finding the vertex of the parabola.

Example 6 **Maximum Area for a Fixed Perimeter**

Find the dimensions of a rectangular field that can be enclosed with 3000 feet of fence and that has the largest possible area.

Solution

Let x denote the length and y the width of the field, as shown in Figure 3.3-5.

$$\text{Perimeter} = x + x + y + y = 2x + 2y$$
$$\text{Area} = xy$$

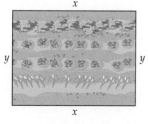

Figure 3.3-5

The perimeter is the length of the fence, or 3000.

$$2x + 2y = 3000$$
$$y = 1500 - x$$

The area of the field is

$$A(x) = xy = x(1500 - x) = -x^2 + 1500x$$

The graph of the function A is a parabola that opens downward, so the maximum occurs at the vertex. The function is in polynomial form, so the vertex occurs when $x = \dfrac{-b}{2a} = \dfrac{-1500}{2(-1)} = 750.$

The largest possible area is 562,500 ft^2, which occurs when $x = 750$ and $y = 1500 - 750 = 750$. The dimensions of the field are 750 by 750 ft. ∎

Example 7   Maximizing Profit

A vendor can sell 275 souvenirs per day at a price of $2 each. The cost to the vendor is $1.50 per souvenir. Each 10¢ price increase decreases sales by 25 per day. What price should be charged to maximize profit?

Solution

Let x be the number of 10¢ price increases. Then the profit on each souvenir is $0.50 + $0.10x$, and the number of souvenirs sold per day is $275 - 25x$. Thus, the profit per day is

$$P(x) = (0.1x + 0.5)(-25x + 275)$$

or, in x-intercept form,

$$P(x) = -2.5(x + 5)(x - 11)$$

The graph is a parabola that opens downward, so the maximum occurs at the vertex. The function is in x-intercept form, so the vertex occurs when

$$x = \frac{s + t}{2} = \frac{-5 + 11}{2} = 3.$$

The maximum profit of $160 per day occurs for 3 price increases, so the price should be $2 + 3($0.10) = $2.30 per souvenir. ∎

Exercises 3.3

In Exercises 1–4, determine the vertex of the given quadratic function and state whether its graph opens upward or downward.

1. $f(x) = 3(x - 5)^2 + 2$ **2.** $g(x) = -6(x - 2)^2 - 5$

3. $f(x) = -(x - 1)^2 + 2$ **4.** $h(x) = -x^2 + 1$

In Exercises 5–8, determine the y-intercept of the given quadratic function and state whether its graph opens upward or downward.

5. $f(x) = x^2 - 6x + 3$ **6.** $g(x) = x^2 + 8x - 1$

7. $h(x) = -3x^2 + 4x + 5$ **8.** $g(x) = 2x^2 - x - 1$

In Exercises 9–12, determine the x-intercepts of the given quadratic function and state whether its graph opens upward or downward.

9. $f(x) = (x - 2)(x + 3)$

10. $h(x) = -2(x + 3)(x + 1)$

11. $g(x) = \dfrac{1}{3}\left(x - \dfrac{3}{4}\right)\left(x - \dfrac{1}{2}\right)$

12. $f(x) = -0.4(x + 2.1)(x - 0.7)$

In Exercises 13–21, determine the vertex and x- and y-intercepts of the given quadratic function, and sketch a graph.

13. $f(x) = 2(x + 3)^2 - 4$ **14.** $g(x) = -\dfrac{1}{2}(x + 4)^2 + 2$

15. $h(x) = (x + 1)^2 + 4$ **16.** $f(x) = x^2 - 6x + 3$

17. $h(x) = -x^2 + 8x - 2$ **18.** $f(x) = 2x^2 - 4x + 2$

19. $g(x) = (x + 1)(x - 3)$ **20.** $h(x) = -(x + 2)(x + 6)$

21. $g(x) = 2(x - 3)(x + 4)$

Write the following functions in polynomial form.

22. $f(x) = 3(x - 2)(x + 1)$

23. $g(x) = -2(x - 5)(x - 2)$

24. $h(x) = 3(x - 4)^2 - 47$

25. $f(x) = -\dfrac{1}{2}(x + 4)^2 - 5$

Write the following functions in x-intercept form.

26. $f(x) = x^2 - 3x - 4$ **27.** $h(x) = -2x^2 + 13x + 7$

28. $g(x) = 3(x + 3)^2 - 3$ **29.** $f(x) = 6\left(x - \dfrac{2}{3}\right)^2 - \dfrac{2}{3}$

Write the following functions in transformation form.

30. $g(x) = x^2 + 4x - 5$ **31.** $f(x) = -3x^2 + 6x - 1$

32. $h(x) = -(x - 4)(x + 2)$

33. $g(x) = 2(x - 1)(x + 6)$

34. Write a rule in transformation form for the quadratic function whose graph is the parabola with vertex at the origin that passes through (2, 12).

35. Write a rule in transformation form for the quadratic function whose graph is the parabola with vertex (0, 1) that passes through (2, −7).

36. Find the number c such that the vertex of $f(x) = x^2 + 8x + c$ lies on the x-axis.

37. If the vertex of $f(x) = x^2 + bx + c$ is at (2, 4), find b and c.

38. If the vertex of $f(x) = -x^2 + bx + 8$ has y-coordinate 17 and is in the second quadrant, find b.

39. Find the number b such that the vertex of $f(x) = x^2 + bx + c$ lies on the y-axis.

40. If the vertex of $f(x) = a(x - s)(x - 4)$ has x-coordinate 7, find s.

41. If the y-intercept of $f(x) = a(x - 3)(x + 2)$ is 3, find a.

42. Find two numbers whose sum is −18 and whose product is the maximum.

43. Find two numbers whose difference is 4 and whose product is the minimum.

44. The sum of the height h and the base b of a triangle is 30. What height and base will produce a triangle of maximum area?

45. A field bounded on one side by a river is to be fenced on three sides to form a rectangular enclosure. If the total length of fence is 200 feet, what dimensions will give an enclosure of maximum area?

46. A salesperson finds that her sales average 40 cases per store when she visits 20 stores per week. If she visits an additional store per week, her average sales per store decrease by one case. How many stores per week should she visit to maximize her sales?

47. A potter can sell 120 bowls per week at $4 per bowl. For each 50¢ decrease in price, 20 more bowls are sold. What price should be charged in order to maximize revenue?

48. When a basketball team charges $4 per ticket, average attendance is 400 people. For each 20¢ decrease in ticket price, average attendance increases by 40 people. What should the ticket price be to maximize revenue?

49. A ballpark concessions manager finds that each vendor sells an average of 40 boxes of popcorn per game when 20 vendors are working. For every additional vendor, each averages 1 fewer box sold per game. How many vendors should be hired to maximize sales?

In Exercises 50–53, use the following equation for the height (in feet) of an object moving along a vertical line after t seconds:

$$s = -16t^2 + v_0t + s_0$$

where s_0 is the initial height (in ft) and v_0 is the initial velocity (in ft/sec). The velocity is positive if it is traveling upward, and negative if it is traveling downward.

50. A rocket is fired upward from ground level with an initial velocity of 1600 ft/sec. When does the rocket reach its maximum height and how high is it at that time?

51. A ball is thrown upward from a height of 6 ft with an initial velocity of 32 ft/sec. When does the ball reach its maximum height and how high is it at that time?

52. A ball is thrown upward from the top of a 96-ft tower with an initial velocity of 80 ft/sec. When does the ball reach its maximum height and how high is it at that time?

53. A bullet is fired upward from ground level with an initial velocity of 1500 ft/sec. When does the bullet reach its maximum height and how high is it at that time?

54. *Critical Thinking* The *discriminant* of a quadratic function $f(x) = ax^2 + bx + c$ is the value $b^2 - 4ac$. For each value of the discriminant listed, state which graphs below could possibly be the graph of f.
   a. $b^2 - 4ac = 25$ **b.** $b^2 - 4ac = 0$
   c. $b^2 - 4ac = -49$ **d.** $b^2 - 4ac = 72$

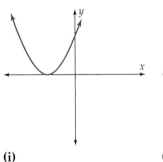

(i)

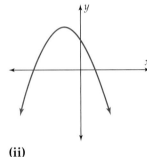

(ii)

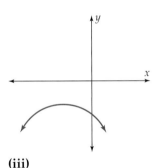

(iii)

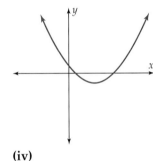

(iv)

3.4 # Graphs and Transformations

Objectives

- Define parent functions
- Transform graphs of parent functions

When the rule of a function is algebraically changed in certain ways to produce a new function, then the graph of the new function can be obtained from the graph of the original function by a simple geometric transformation.

Parent Functions

The functions on the next page are often called **parent functions**. A parent function is a function with a certain shape that has the simplest algebraic rule for that shape. For example, $f(x) = x^2$ is the simplest rule for a parabola. You should memorize the basic shapes of the parent functions.

> **NOTE** The points $(0, 0)$ and $(1, 1)$ are labeled for reference in each case. The origin is not on the graph of the constant or reciprocal function.

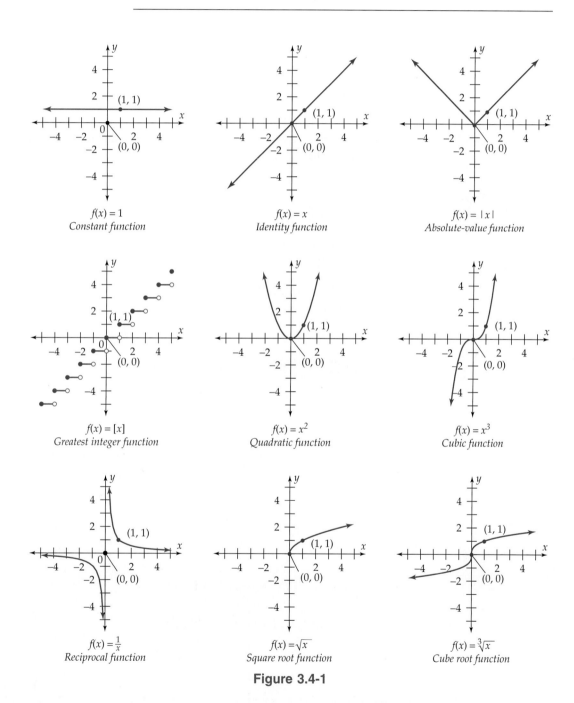

$f(x) = 1$
Constant function

$f(x) = x$
Identity function

$f(x) = |x|$
Absolute-value function

$f(x) = [x]$
Greatest integer function

$f(x) = x^2$
Quadratic function

$f(x) = x^3$
Cubic function

$f(x) = \frac{1}{x}$
Reciprocal function

$f(x) = \sqrt{x}$
Square root function

$f(x) = \sqrt[3]{x}$
Cube root function

Figure 3.4-1

The parent functions will be used to illustrate the rules for the basic transformations. Remember, however, that these transformation rules work for *all* functions.

Technology Tip

● If the function f is entered as Y_1, then the function

$$g(x) = f(x) + c$$

can be entered in Y_2 as Y_1 + C and the function

$$g(x) = f(x) - c$$

can be entered in Y_3 as Y_1 − C.

Vertical Shifts

Vertical Shifts

> ── **Graphing Exploration** ●──────
>
> Graph these functions on the same screen and describe your results.
>
> $$f(x) = \sqrt[3]{x} \qquad g(x) = \sqrt[3]{x} + 2 \qquad h(x) = \sqrt[3]{x} - 3$$

Notice that when a value is added to $f(x)$, the effect is to add the value to the y-coordinate of each point. The result is to shift every point on the graph upward by the same amount. A similar result is true for subtracting a value from $f(x)$.

> Let c be a positive number.
>
> **The graph of $g(x) = f(x) + c$ is the graph of f shifted upward c units.**
>
> **The graph of $g(x) = f(x) - c$ is the graph of f shifted downward c units.**

Example 1 Shifting a Graph Vertically

Graph $g(x) = |x| + 4$ and $h(x) = |x| - 3$.

Solution

The parent function is $f(x) = |x|$. The graph of $g(x)$ is the graph of $f(x) = |x|$ shifted upward 4 units, and the graph of $h(x)$ is the graph of $f(x) = |x|$ shifted downward 3 units.

$$g(x) = |x| + 4 \qquad\qquad h(x) = |x| - 3$$

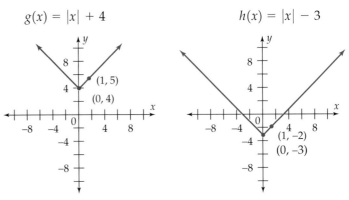

Figure 3.4-2

Technology Tip

If the function f is entered as Y_1, then the function

$$g(x) = f(x + c)$$

can be entered in Y_2 as $Y_1(X + C)$ and the function

$$g(x) = f(c - x)$$

can be entered in Y_3 as $Y_1(X - C)$.

Horizontal Shifts

Graphing Exploration

Graph these functions on the same screen and describe your results.

$$f(x) = x^2 \qquad g(x) = (x - 1)^2 \qquad h(x) = (x + 3)^2$$

A table of values is helpful in visualizing the direction of a horizontal shift.

x	-3	-2	-1	0	1	2	3	4	5
$x - 1$	-4	-3	-2	-1	0	1	2	3	4
x^2	9	4	1	0	1	4	9	16	25
$(x - 1)^2$	16	9	4	1	0	1	4	9	16

When 1 is subtracted from the x-values, the result is that the entries in the table shift 1 position to the right. Thus, the entire graph is shifted 1 unit to the right. Construct a table for $h(x) = (x + 3)^2$ to see that the entries shift 3 positions to the left.

Horizontal Shifts

Let c be a positive number.

The graph of $g(x) = f(x + c)$ is the graph of f shifted c units to the left.

The graph of $g(x) = f(x - c)$ is the graph of f shifted c units to the right.

Example 2   Shifting a Graph Horizontally

Graph $g(x) = \dfrac{1}{x - 3}$ and $h(x) = \dfrac{1}{x + 4}$.

Solution

The parent function is $f(x) = \dfrac{1}{x}$. The graph of $g(x)$ is the graph of $f(x) = \dfrac{1}{x}$ shifted 3 units to the right and the graph of $h(x)$ is the graph of $f(x) = \dfrac{1}{x}$ shifted 4 units to the left.

$$g(x) = \frac{1}{x - 3} \qquad\qquad h(x) = \frac{1}{x + 4}$$

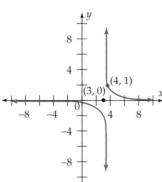
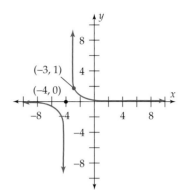

Figure 3.4-3

Reflections

> **Graphing Exploration** ●
>
> Graph these functions on the same screen.
>
> $$f(x) = \sqrt{x} \qquad g(x) = -\sqrt{x}$$
>
> Use the **TRACE** feature to verify that for every point on the graph
> of f there is a point on the graph of g with the same x-coordinate
> and opposite y-coordinate.
>
> Graph these functions on the same screen.
>
> $$f(x) = \sqrt{x} \qquad h(x) = \sqrt{-x}$$
>
> Use the **TRACE** feature to verify that for every point on the graph
> of f there is a point on the graph of h with the same y-coordinate
> and opposite x-coordinate.

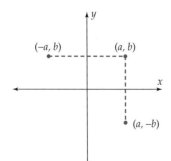

Figure 3.4-4

The results of the first part of the Graphing Exploration show that in the
functions $f(x) = \sqrt{x}$ and $g(x) = -\sqrt{x}$, if the point (a, b) is on the graph of
f, then the point $(a, -b)$ is on the graph of g. These two points are reflections of each other across the x-axis, as shown in Figure 3.4-4.

In the second part of the Graphing Exploration, the results show that in
the functions $f(x) = \sqrt{x}$ and $h(x) = \sqrt{-x}$, if the point (a, b) is on the graph
of f, then the point $(-a, b)$ is on the graph of h. These two points are reflections of each other across the y-axis, as shown in Figure 3.4-4.

Reflections

The graph of $g(x) = -f(x)$ is the graph of f reflected across the *x*-axis.

The graph of $g(x) = f(-x)$ is the graph of f reflected across the *y*-axis.

Example 3   Reflecting a Graph Across the *x*- or *y*-Axis

Graph $g(x) = -[x]$ and $h(x) = [-x]$.

Solution

The parent function is $f(x) = [x]$. The graph of $g(x)$ is the graph of $f(x) = [x]$ reflected across the *x*-axis, and the graph of $h(x)$ is the graph of $f(x) = [x]$ reflected across the *y*-axis. One difference in the reflections is whether the endpoint of each segment is included on the left or on the right. Study the functions closely, along with the parent function, to determine another difference in the two reflections.

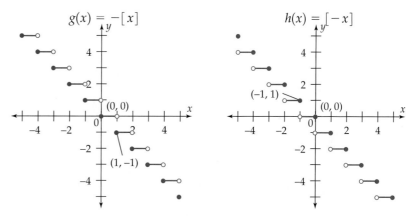

Figure 3.4-5

Technology Tip

If the function *f* is entered as Y_1, then the function

$$g(x) = c \cdot f(x)$$

can be entered in Y_2 as $C \cdot Y_1$ and the function

$$g(x) = f(c \cdot x)$$

can be entered in Y_3 as $Y_1(C \cdot X)$.

Stretches and Compressions

Graphing Exploration

Graph these functions on the same screen.

$$f(x) = \sqrt{x} \qquad g(x) = \sqrt{3x} \qquad h(x) = 3\sqrt{x}$$

Use the **TRACE** feature to locate the *y*-value on each graph when $x = 1$. Describe your results. Predict the graph of $j(x) = 4\sqrt{x}$.

In addition to reflections and shifts, graphs of functions may be stretched or compressed, either vertically or horizontally. The following example illustrates the difference between a vertical stretch and compression.

Example 4 Vertically Stretching and Compressing a Graph

Graph $g(x) = 2x^3$ and $h(x) = \dfrac{1}{4}x^3$.

Solution

The parent function is $f(x) = x^3$. For the function $g(x) = 2x^3$, every y-coordinate of the parent function is multiplied by 2, stretching the graph of the function in the vertical direction, away from the x-axis. For the function $h(x) = \dfrac{1}{4}x^3$, every y-coordinate of the parent function is multiplied by $\dfrac{1}{4}$, compressing the graph of the function in the vertical direction, toward the x-axis.

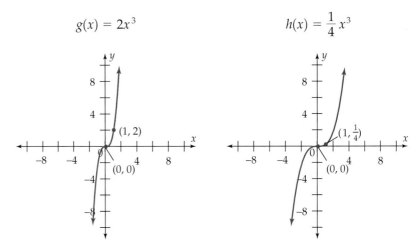

$$g(x) = 2x^3 \qquad\qquad h(x) = \dfrac{1}{4}x^3$$

Figure 3.4-6

The following example illustrates the difference between a vertical and a horizontal stretch.

Example 5 Stretching a Function Vertically and Horizontally

Graph $g(x) = 2[x]$ and $h(x) = [2x]$.

Solution

The parent function is $f(x) = [x]$. In $g(x) = 2[x]$, the y-values are multiplied by 2, and in $h(x) = [2x]$, the x-values are multiplied by 2. The result is that in the graph of the first function, the "steps" get higher, and in the graph of the second function, they get narrower.

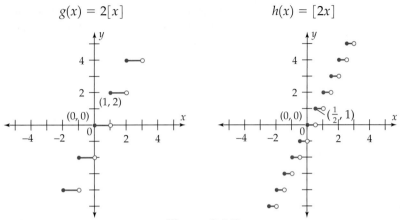

Figure 3.4-7

Stretches and Compressions

Let c be a positive number.

Vertical Stretches and Compressions

If (x, y) is a point on the graph of $f(x)$, then (x, cy) is a point on the graph of $g(x) = c \cdot f(x)$.

If $c > 1$, the graph of $g(x) = c \cdot f(x)$ is the graph of f stretched vertically, away from the x-axis, by a factor of c.

If $c < 1$, the graph of $g(x) = c \cdot f(x)$ is the graph of f compressed vertically, toward the x-axis, by a factor of c.

Horizontal Stretches and Compressions

If (x, y) is a point on the graph of $f(x)$, then $\left(\dfrac{1}{c} x, y\right)$ is a point on the graph of $g(x) = f(c \cdot x)$.

If $c > 1$, the graph of $g(x) = f(c \cdot x)$ is the graph of f compressed horizontally, toward the y-axis, by a factor of $\dfrac{1}{c}$.

If $c < 1$, the graph of $g(x) = f(c \cdot x)$ is the graph of f stretched horizontally, away from the y-axis, by a factor of $\dfrac{1}{c}$.

NOTE Some horizontal compressions can be expressed as vertical stretches, and vice versa. The graph of the function g below can be obtained from a horizontal compression of $f(x) = x^2$ by a factor of $\dfrac{1}{3}$ or from a vertical stretch by a factor of 9.

$$g(x) = (3x)^2 = 3^2 x^2 = 9x^2$$

This is not possible for the greatest integer function (see Example 5) or trigonometric functions, which you will study in later chapters.

Transformations can be combined to produce many different functions. There is often more than one correct order in which to perform these transformations; however, *not every possible order is correct*. One method is shown below.

Combining Transformations

For a function of the form $g(x) = c \cdot f(a(x - b)) + d$, first graph $f(x)$.

1. If $a < 0$, reflect the graph across the y-axis.
2. Stretch or compress the graph horizontally by a factor of $\left|\dfrac{1}{a}\right|$.
3. Shift the graph horizontally by b units: right if $b > 0$, and left if $b < 0$.
4. If $c < 0$, reflect the graph across the x-axis.
5. Stretch or compress the graph vertically by a factor of $|c|$.
6. Shift the graph vertically by d units: up if $d > 0$, and down if $d < 0$.

Example 6   **Combining Transformations**

Graph the following function.

$$g(x) = -|2x - 1| + 4$$

Solution

Rewrite $g(x) = -|2x - 1| + 4$ as $g(x) = -\left|2\left(x - \dfrac{1}{2}\right)\right| + 4$. The parent function is $f(x) = |x|$.

| Compress the graph horizontally by a factor of $\dfrac{1}{2}$. | Shift the graph $\dfrac{1}{2}$ unit to the right. | Reflect the graph across the x-axis. | Shift the graph upward 4 units. |

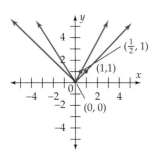 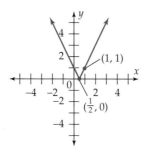 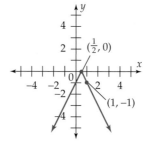 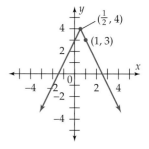

Figure 3.4-8

Graphing Exploration ●———

For the function $g(x) = -3\sqrt{-2x + 4} + 1$, list several different possible orders of the transformations performed on the graph of $f(x) = \sqrt{x}$ to produce the graph of $g(x)$. Then graph $g(x)$ on a calculator. Did any orders of transformations that you listed produce an incorrect graph? Try to determine some rules about the order in which the transformations may be performed. Compare your rules with those of your classmates.

Example 7   **Package Delivery**

An overnight delivery service charges $18 for a package weighing less than 1 pound, $21 for one weighing at least 1 pound, but less than 2 pounds, $24 for one weighing at least 2 pounds, but less than 3 pounds, and so on. The cost $c(x)$ of shipping a package weighing x pounds is given by $c(x) = 18 + 3[x]$. Graph $c(x)$ and interpret the result.

Solution

The parent function of $c(x)$ is $f(x) = [x]$. The parent function is stretched vertically by a factor of 3, then shifted upward 18 units. Note: although this rule is defined for all real numbers, the domain of this cost function is $x > 0$.

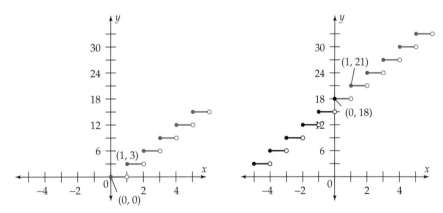

Figure 3.4-9

The function is stretched vertically by a factor of 3 because the increment from one step to the next is $3, and the function is shifted 18 units upward because the lowest rate for any package is $18.

Exercises 3.4

In Exercises 1–9, identify the parent function that can be used to graph each function. Do not graph the function.

1. $f(x) = -(x + 2)^3$

2. $g(x) = 4|x| - 3$

3. $f(x) = 7$

4. $h(x) = \sqrt{-2x + 4}$

5. $g(x) = \dfrac{2}{x - 1} + 4$

6. $f(x) = -3x + 2$

7. $h(x) = -6\left[\dfrac{1}{2}x + 3\right] + \dfrac{2}{3}$

8. $g(x) = 2\sqrt[3]{x} + 5$

9. $h(x) = 2(3 - x)^2 + 4$

In Exercises 10–21, graph each function and its parent function on the same set of axes.

10. $f(x) = -x^2$

11. $h(x) = -\dfrac{1}{x}$

12. $g(x) = |-x|$

13. $h(x) = \sqrt[3]{-x}$

14. $f(x) = x - 5$

15. $g(x) = [x] + 1$

16. $f(x) = \sqrt{x + 4}$

17. $h(x) = |x - 2|$

18. $g(x) = 3x$

19. $f(x) = \dfrac{1}{2}$

20. $g(x) = \left(\dfrac{1}{4}x\right)^3$

21. $h(x) = \dfrac{1}{3x}$

In Exercises 22–27, write a rule for the function whose graph can be obtained from the given parent function by performing the given transformations.

22. parent function: $f(x) = x^3$
transformations: shift the graph 5 units to the left and upward 4 units

23. parent function: $f(x) = \sqrt{x}$
transformations: reflect the graph across the x-axis and shift it upward 3 units

24. parent function: $f(x) = [x]$
transformations: shift the graph 6 units to the right, stretch it vertically by a factor of 2, and shift it downward 3 units

25. parent function: $f(x) = |x|$
transformations: shift the graph 3 units to the left, reflect it across the x-axis, and shrink it vertically by a factor of $\dfrac{1}{2}$

26. parent function: $f(x) = \dfrac{1}{x}$
transformations: shift the graph 2 units to the right, stretch it horizontally by a factor of 2, and shift it upward 2 units

27. parent function: $f(x) = x^2$
transformations: shift the graph 3 units to the left, reflect it across the y-axis, and stretch it vertically by a factor of 1.5

In Exercises 28–33, describe a sequence of transformations that transform the graph of the parent function f into the graph of the function g. Do not graph the functions.

28. $f(x) = \sqrt{x}$ $g(x) = -\sqrt{-\dfrac{1}{2}x + 3}$

29. $f(x) = x$ $g(x) = -3(x - 4) + 1$

30. $f(x) = [x]$ $g(x) = 2\left[\dfrac{1}{3}x\right] + 5$

31. $f(x) = x^3$ $g(x) = 4(2 - x)^3 - 3$

32. $f(x) = \dfrac{1}{x}$ $g(x) = \dfrac{3}{4 - 2x}$

33. $f(x) = \sqrt[3]{x}$ $g(x) = \sqrt[3]{1.3x - 4.2} + 0.4$

In Exercises 34–41, graph each function and its parent function on the same graph.

34. $f(x) = -2(x + 1)^2 + 3$

35. $g(x) = \dfrac{1}{4}\sqrt[3]{x + 3} - 1$

36. $f(x) = -\dfrac{3}{4}\left[-\dfrac{1}{3}x\right]$

37. $h(x) = 3(x - 1) + 5$

38. $g(x) = |-x + 5| - 3$

39. $f(x) = \dfrac{-3}{2 - x} + 4$

40. $h(x) = \sqrt{-4x + 3} - 1$

41. $g(x) = \dfrac{2}{5}(5 - x)^3 - \dfrac{3}{5}$

In Exercises 42–45, use the graph of the function *f* in the figure to sketch the graph of the function *g*.

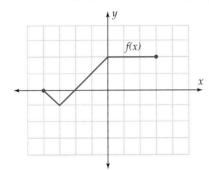

42. $g(x) = f(x) - 1$ **43.** $g(x) = 3f(x)$

44. $g(x) = 0.25f(x)$ **45.** $g(x) = f(x) + 3$

In Exercises 46–49, use the graph of the function *f* in the figure to sketch the graph of the function *h*.

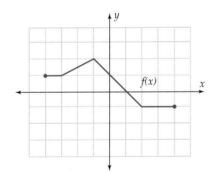

46. $h(x) = -4f(x)$ **47.** $h(x) = -f(x)$

48. $h(x) = f(-x)$ **49.** $h(x) = f(-2x)$

In Exercises 50–55, use the graph of the function *f* in the figure to sketch the graph of the function *g*.

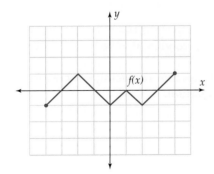

50. $g(x) = f(x - 2)$ **51.** $g(x) = f(x - 2) + 3$

52. $g(x) = f(x + 1) - 3$ **53.** $g(x) = 2 - f(x)$

54. $g(x) = f(-x) + 2$ **55.** $g(x) = f(x + 3)$

Exercises 56–61 refer to the parent function

$$f(x) = \sqrt{1 - x^2}$$

The graph of *f* is a semicircle with radius 1, as shown below.

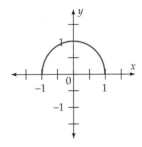

Use the graph of *f* to sketch the graph of the function *g*.

56. $g(x) = -\sqrt{1 - x^2}$ **57.** $g(x) = \sqrt{1 - x^2} + 4$

58. $g(x) = \sqrt{1 - (x - 3)^2}$ **59.** $g(x) = 3\sqrt{1 - x^2}$

60. $g(x) = \sqrt{1 - (x + 2)^2} + 1$

61. $g(x) = 5\sqrt{1 - \left(\frac{1}{5}x\right)^2}$

62. In 2002, the cost of sending first-class mail was $0.37 for a letter weighing less than 1 ounce, $0.60 for a letter weighing at least one ounce, but less than 2 ounces, $0.83 for a letter weighing at least 2 ounces, but less than 3 ounces, and so on.
   a. Write a function $c(x)$ that gives the cost of mailing a letter weighing *x* ounces (see Example 7).
   b. Graph $c(x)$ and interpret the result.

63. A factory has a linear cost function $f(x) = ax + b$, where *b* represents fixed costs and *a* represents the labor and material costs of making one item, both in thousands of dollars.
   a. If property taxes (part of the fixed costs) are increased by $28,000 per year, what effect does this have on the graph of the cost function?
   b. If labor and material costs for making 100,000 items increase by $12,000, what effect does this have on the graph of the cost function?

3.4.A   *Excursion:* Symmetry

Objectives

*   Determine whether a graph has *y*-axis, *x*-axis, or origin symmetry

*   Determine whether a function is even, odd, or neither

This section presents three kinds of symmetry that a graph can have and ways to identify these symmetries both geometrically and algebraically.

y-Axis Symmetry

A graph of a function or relation is **symmetric with respect to the *y*-axis** if the part of the graph on the right side of the *y*-axis is the mirror image of the part on the left side of the *y*-axis, as shown in Figure 3.4.A-1.

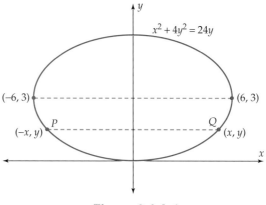

Figure 3.4.A-1

Each point P on the left side of the graph has a mirror image point Q on the right side of the graph, as indicated by the dashed lines. Note that

*   their *y*-coordinates are the same
*   their *x*-coordinates are opposites of each other
*   the *y*-axis is the perpendicular bisector of $\overline{PQ}$

y-Axis Symmetry

A graph is symmetric with respect to the *y*-axis if whenever (x, y) is on the graph, then $(-x, y)$ is also on it.

In algebraic terms, this means that replacing *x* by $-x$ produces an equivalent equation.

Example 1   *y*-Axis Symmetry

Verify that $y = x^4 - 5x^2 + 3$ is symmetric with respect to the *y*-axis.

Solution

Replace x by $-x$ in the equation.

$$y = x^4 - 5x^2 + 3$$
$$y = (-x)^4 - 5(-x)^2 + 3$$

which is equivalent to the original equation because $(-x)^2 = x^2$ and $(-x)^4 = x^4$. Therefore, the graph is symmetric with respect to the y-axis.

◼

Graphing Exploration ●

Graph the equation $y = x^4 - 5x^2 + 3$ from Example 1. Use the TRACE feature to locate at least three points (x, y) on the graph and show that for each point, $(-x, y)$ is also on the graph.

---

x-Axis Symmetry

A graph of a relation is symmetric with respect to the x-axis if the part of the graph above the x-axis is the mirror image of the part below the x-axis, as shown in Figure 3.4.A-2.

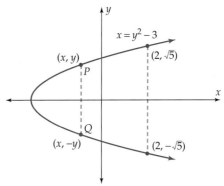

Figure 3.4.A-2

Each point P on the top of the graph has a mirror image point Q on the bottom of the graph, as indicated by the dashed lines. Note that

- their x-coordinates are the same
- their y-coordinates are opposites of each other
- the x-axis is the perpendicular bisector of $\overline{PQ}$

x-Axis Symmetry

A graph is symmetric with respect to the x-axis if whenever (x, y) is on the graph, then $(x, -y)$ is also on it.

In algebraic terms, this means that replacing y by $-y$ produces an equivalent equation.

NOTE Except for $f(x) = 0$, the graph of a function is never symmetric with respect to the x-axis. By the Vertical Line Test, a function's graph cannot contain points that lie on a vertical line, such as (x, y) and $(x, -y)$.

Example 2 *x*-Axis Symmetry

Verify that $y^2 = 4x - 12$ is symmetric with respect to the x-axis.

Solution

Replacing y by $-y$ in the equation gives

$$(-y)^2 = 4x - 12$$

which is equivalent to the original equation because $(-y)^2 = y^2$. Therefore, the graph is symmetric with respect to the x-axis. ∎

Graphing Exploration ●—

Graph the equation $y^2 = 4x - 12$ from Example 2 in parametric mode by entering the parametric equations below.

$$x_1 = \frac{1}{4}t^2 + 3$$

$$y_1 = t$$

Use the **TRACE** feature to locate at least three points (x, y) on the graph and show that for each point, $(x, -y)$ is also on the graph.

Origin Symmetry

A graph is **symmetric with respect to the origin** if a line through the origin and any point P on the graph also intersects the graph at a point Q such that the origin is the midpoint of $\overline{PQ}$, as shown in Figure 3.4.A-3.

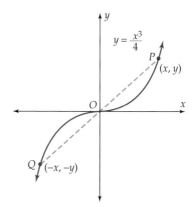

Figure 3.4.A-3

Using Figure 3.4.A-3, symmetry with respect to the origin can also be described in terms of coordinates and equations.

Origin Symmetry

> A graph is **symmetric with respect to the origin** if whenever (x, y) is on the graph, then $(-x, -y)$ is also on it.
>
> In algebraic terms, this means that replacing x by $-x$ and y by $-y$ produces an equivalent equation.

Example 3   Origin Symmetry

Verify that $y = \dfrac{x^3}{10} - x$ is symmetric with respect to the origin.

Solution

Replace x by $-x$ and y by $-y$ in the equation.

$$-y = \frac{(-x)^3}{10} - (-x)$$

$$-y = \frac{-x^3}{10} + x \qquad \textit{Simplify}$$

$$-1(-y) = -1\left(\frac{-x^3}{10} + x\right) \qquad \textit{Multiply both sides by } -1$$

$$y = \frac{x^3}{10} - x \qquad \textit{Simplify}$$

Therefore, the graph is symmetric with respect to the origin. ∎

Graphing Exploration

Graph the equation $y = \dfrac{x^3}{10} - x$ from Example 3. Use the **TRACE** feature to locate at least three points (x, y) on the graph and show that for each point, $(-x, -y)$ is also on the graph.

Summary

There are a number of techniques used to understand the fundamental features of a graph. Symmetry, whether line or point, is beneficial when graphing a function. Knowing a graph's symmetry prior to graphing reduces the necessary number of coordinates needed to display a complete graph; thus, the graph can be sketched more quickly and easily.

Here is a summary of the various tests for line and point symmetry:

Symmetry Tests

Symmetry with respect to	Coordinate test	Algebraic test
y-Axis	If (x, y) is on the graph, then $(-x, y)$ is on the graph.	Replacing x by $-x$ produces an equivalent equation.
x-Axis	If (x, y) is on the graph, then $(x, -y)$ is on the graph.	Replacing y by $-y$ produces an equivalent equation.
Origin	If (x, y) is on the graph, then $(-x, -y)$ is on the graph.	Replacing x by $-x$ and y by $-y$ produces an equivalent equation.

Even and Odd Functions

For relations that are *functions,* the algebraic description of symmetry can take a different form.

Even Functions

A function f whose graph is symmetric with respect to the y-axis is called an **even function.**

Even Functions

A function f is even if

$$f(-x) = f(x) \text{ for every value } x \text{ in the domain of } f.$$

The graph of an even function is symmetric with respect to the y-axis.

NOTE If the rule of a function is a polynomial in which all terms have even degree, then the function is even. (A constant term has degree 0, which is even.)

For example, $f(x) = x^4 + x^2$ is even because

$$f(-x) = (-x)^4 + (-x)^2 = x^4 + x^2 = f(x)$$

Thus, the graph of f is symmetric with respect to the y-axis, as you can verify with your calculator.

Odd Functions

A function f whose graph is symmetric with respect to the origin is called an **odd function.** If both (x, y) and $(-x, -y)$ are on the graph of such a function f, then

$$y = f(x) \quad \text{and} \quad -y = f(-x)$$
$$-y = -f(x)$$

so $f(-x) = -f(x)$.

Odd Functions

> A function f is **odd** if
>
> $$f(-x) = -f(x) \text{ for every value } x \text{ in the domain of } f.$$
>
> The graph of an odd function is symmetric with respect to the origin.

NOTE If the rule of a function is a polynomial in which all terms have odd degree, then the function is odd.

For example, $f(x) = x^3 + 2x$ is an odd function because

$$f(-x) = (-x)^3 + 2(-x) = -x^3 - 2x$$
$$-f(x) = -(x^3 + 2x) = -x^3 - 2x$$

Hence, the graph of f is symmetric with respect to the origin, as you can verify with your calculator.

Exercises 3.4.A

In Exercises 1–6, graph the equation and state whether the graph has symmetry. If so, is it symmetric with respect to the x-axis, the y-axis, or the origin?

1. $y = x^2 + 2$ **2.** $x = (y - 3)^2$

3. $y = x^3 + 2$ **4.** $y = (x + 2)^3$

5. $y = \dfrac{\sqrt[3]{x}}{x^2}$ **6.** $|y| = x$

In Exercises 7–10, determine algebraically whether or not the graph of the given equation is symmetric with respect to the y-axis.

7. $x^2 + y^2 = 1$ **8.** $y = x^3 - x^2$

9. $4x^2 - 3y + y^2 = 7$ **10.** $x^4 + x^2 - x = y^3 + 1$

In Exercises 11–14, determine algebraically whether the graph of the given equation is symmetric with respect to the x-axis.

11. $x^2 - 6x + y^2 + 8 = 0$ **12.** $x^2 + 8x + y^2 = -15$

13. $x^2 - 2x + y^2 + 2y = 2$ **14.** $x^2 - x + y^2 - y = 0$

In Exercises 15–18, determine algebraically whether the graph of the given equation is symmetric with respect to the origin.

15. $4x^2 - 3y^2 + xy = 6$ **16.** $x^3 + y^3 = x$

17. $|x| + |y| = x^2 + y^2$ **18.** $3x^2 = 4y - 2x + 6$

In Exercises 19–24, determine whether the given graph is symmetric with respect to the y-axis, the x-axis, the origin, or any combination of the three.

19.

20.

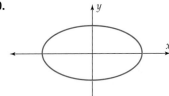

21.

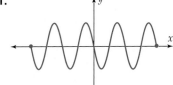

22.

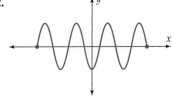

23.

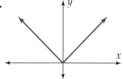

24.

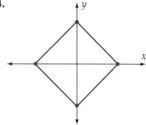

In Exercises 25–34, determine whether the given function is even, odd, or neither.

25. $f(x) = 4x$

26. $k(t) = -5t$

27. $f(x) = x^2 - |x|$

28. $h(u) = |3u|$

29. $k(t) = t^4 - 6t^2 + 5$

30. $f(x) = x(x^4 - x^2) + 4$

31. $f(t) = \sqrt{t^2 - 5}$

32. $h(x) = \sqrt{7 - 2x^2}$

33. $f(x) = \dfrac{x^2 + 2}{x - 7}$

34. $g(x) = \dfrac{x^2 + 1}{x^2 - 1}$

In Exercises 35–38, complete the graph of the given function, assuming that it satisfies the given symmetry condition.

35. Even

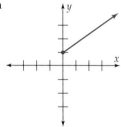

36. Even

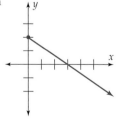

37. Odd

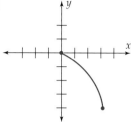

38. Odd

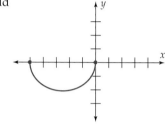

39. a. Plot the points $(0, 0)$, $(2, 3)$, $(3, 4)$, $(5, 0)$, $(7, -3)$, $(-1, -1)$, $(-4, -1)$, and $(-6, 1)$.

b. Suppose the points in part **a** lie on the graph of an odd function f. Plot the points $(-2, f(-2))$, $(-3, f(-3))$, $(-5, f(-5))$, $(-7, f(-7))$, $(1, f(1))$, $(4, f(4))$, and $(6, f(6))$.

40. a. Plot the points $(1, -3)$, $(-5, 2)$, $(-3, 5)$, $(2, 3)$, and $(4, 1)$.

b. Suppose the points in part **a** lie on the graph of an even function f. Plot the points $(-1, f(-1))$, $(5, f(5))$, $(3, f(3))$, $(-2, f(-2))$, and $(-4, f(-4))$.

41. Show that any graph that has two of the three types of symmetry (x-axis, y-axis, origin) always has the third type.

42. Use the midpoint formula (see the Algebra Review Appendix) to show that $(0, 0)$ is the midpoint of the segment joining (x, y) and $(-x, -y)$.

3.5 **Operations on Functions**

Objectives

- Form sum, difference, product, and quotient functions and find their domains
- Form composite functions and find their domains

There are several ways in which two or more given functions can be used to create new functions.

Sums and Differences of Functions

If f and g are functions, their **sum** is the function h defined by this rule.

$$h(x) = f(x) + g(x)$$

For example, if $f(x) = 3x^2 + x$ and $g(x) = 4x - 2$, then

$$h(x) = f(x) + g(x) = (3x^2 + x) + (4x - 2) = 3x^2 + 5x - 2$$

Instead of using a different letter h for the sum function, we shall usually denote it by $f + g$. Thus, the sum $f + g$ is defined by the rule

$$(f + g)(x) = f(x) + g(x)$$

NOTE This rule is not just a formal manipulation of symbols. If x is a number, then so are $f(x)$ and $g(x)$. The plus sign in $f(x) + g(x)$ is addition of numbers, and the result is a number. But the plus sign in $f + g$ is addition of functions, and the result is a new function.

The **difference** function $f - g$ is the function defined by a similar rule.

$$(f - g)(x) = f(x) - g(x)$$

The domain of the sum and difference functions is the set of all real numbers that are in both the domain of f and the domain of g.

Technology Tip

If two functions are entered as Y_1 and Y_2, their sum function can be graphed by entering $Y_3 = Y_1 + Y_2$.

Difference, product, and quotient functions can be graphed similarly.

Example 1 **Sum and Difference Functions**

For $f(x) = \sqrt{9 - x^2}$ and $g(x) = \sqrt{x - 2}$

a. write the rule for $f + g$ and $f - g$.

b. find the domain of $f + g$ and $f - g$.

Solution

a. $(f + g)(x) = \sqrt{9 - x^2} + \sqrt{x - 2}$
   $(f - g)(x) = \sqrt{9 - x^2} - \sqrt{x - 2}$

b. The domain of f consists of all x such that $9 - x^2 \geq 0$, that is, $-3 \leq x \leq 3$. Similarly, the domain of g consists of all x such that $x - 2 \geq 0$, that is, $x \geq 2$. The domain of $f + g$ and $f - g$ consists of all real numbers in both the domain of f and the domain of g, namely, all x such that $2 \leq x \leq 3$.

Products and Quotients of Functions

The **product** and **quotient** of functions f and g are the functions defined by the following rules.

$$(fg)(x) = f(x) \cdot g(x) \qquad \text{and} \qquad \left(\frac{f}{g}\right)(x) = \frac{f(x)}{g(x)}$$

The domain of fg consists of all real numbers in both the domain of f and the domain of g. The domain of $\left(\dfrac{f}{g}\right)$ consists of all real numbers x in both the domain of f and the domain of g such that $g(x) \neq 0$.

Example 2   **Product and Quotient Functions**

For $f(x) = \sqrt{3x}$ and $g(x) = \sqrt{x^2 - 1}$

a. write the rule for fg and $\dfrac{f}{g}$

b. find the domain of fg and $\dfrac{f}{g}$

Solution

a. $(fg)(x) = \sqrt{3x} \cdot \sqrt{x^2 - 1} = \sqrt{3x^3 - 3x}$

$\left(\dfrac{f}{g}\right)(x) = \dfrac{\sqrt{3x}}{\sqrt{x^2 - 1}} = \dfrac{\sqrt{3x^3 - 3x}}{x^2 - 1}$

b. The domain of f consists of all x such that $3x \geq 0$, that is, $x \geq 0$. Similarly, the domain of g consists of all x such that $x^2 - 1 \geq 0$, that is, $x \leq -1$ or $x \geq 1$. The domain of fg consists of all real numbers in both the domain of f and the domain of g, that is, $x \geq 1$. The domain of $\left(\dfrac{f}{g}\right)$ consists of all these x for which $g(x) \neq 0$, so the value $x = 1$ must also be excluded. Thus, the domain of $\left(\dfrac{f}{g}\right)$ is $x > 1$.

> **CAUTION**
>
> The function with the rule $\sqrt{3x^3 - 3x}$ is defined for values that are not in the domain of f and g. The domain of a sum, difference, product, or quotient function must be determined before the function is simplified.

Products with Constant Functions

If c is a real number and f is a function, then the product of f and the constant function $g(x) = c$ is

$$(cf)(x) = c \cdot f(x)$$

The domain of cf is the same as the domain of f. For example, if $f(x) = x^3 - x + 2$ and $c = 5$, then $5f$ is the function

$$(5f)(x) = 5 \cdot f(x) = 5(x^3 - x + 2) = 5x^3 - 5x + 10$$

and the domain of $5f$ is still all real numbers.

Composition of Functions

Another way of combining functions is to use the output of one function as the input of another. This operation is called **composition of functions.** The idea can be expressed in function notation as shown below.

$$\text{input of } f \qquad \begin{array}{c}\text{output of } f = \\ f(x) \\ = \text{input of } g\end{array} \qquad \text{output of } g$$

$$x \;\rightarrow\; \boxed{f} \qquad \rightarrow \qquad \boxed{g} \;\rightarrow\; g(f(x))$$

Composite Functions

If f and g are functions, then the *composite function* of f and g is

$$(g \circ f)(x) = g(f(x))$$

The expression $g \circ f$ is read "g circle f" or "f followed by g." Note the order carefully; the functions are applied right to left.

Technology Tip

To evaluate or graph composite functions on TI-82/83/86/89, Sharp 9600, and HP-38, enter the equations as Y_1 and Y_2. Then enter $Y_1(Y_2(X))$ or $Y_2(Y_1(X))$.

On other calculators, such as TI-85, this does not produce the correct value of the composite functions.

Example 3 Composite Functions

If $f(x) = 4x^2 + 1$ and $g(x) = \dfrac{1}{x + 2}$, find the following.

a. $(g \circ f)(2)$ **b.** $(f \circ g)(-1)$

c. $(g \circ f)(x)$ **d.** $(f \circ g)(x)$

Solution

a. To find $(g \circ f)(2)$, first find $f(2)$.

$$f(2) = 4(2)^2 + 1 = 17$$

Next, use the result as an input in g.

$$g(17) = \frac{1}{17 + 2} = \frac{1}{19}$$

So $(g \circ f)(2) = \dfrac{1}{19}$.

b. To find $(f \circ g)(-1)$, first find $g(-1)$.

$$g(-1) = \frac{1}{-1 + 2} = 1$$

Next, use the result as an input in f.

$$f(1) = 4(1)^2 + 1 = 5$$

So $(f \circ g)(-1) = 5$.

c. To find $(g \circ f)(x) = g(f(x))$, replace x with the rule for $f(x)$ in g.

$$(g \circ f)(x) = g(f(x)) = \frac{1}{f(x) + 2} = \frac{1}{(4x^2 + 1) + 2} = \frac{1}{4x^2 + 3}$$

d. To find $(f \circ g)(x) = f(g(x))$, replace x with the rule for $g(x)$ in f.

$$(f \circ g)(x) = f(g(x)) = 4(g(x))^2 + 1 = 4\left(\frac{1}{x+2}\right)^2 + 1 = \frac{4}{(x+2)^2} + 1$$

Notice that $(g \circ f)(x) \neq (f \circ g)(x)$.

Domains of Composite Functions

The domain of $g \circ f$ is determined by the following convention.

Domain of $g \circ f$

Let f and g be functions. The domain of $g \circ f$ is the set of all real numbers x such that

- x is in the domain of f
- $f(x)$ is in the domain of g

Example 4   **Finding the Domain of a Composite Function**

If $f(x) = \sqrt{x}$ and $g(x) = x^2 - 5$,

a. find $g \circ f$ and $f \circ g$

b. find the domain of each composite function

Solution

a. $(g \circ f)(x) = g(f(x)) = (f(x))^2 - 5 = \left(\sqrt{x}\right)^2 - 5 = x - 5$
   $(f \circ g)(x) = f(g(x)) = \sqrt{g(x)} = \sqrt{x^2 - 5}$

b. Domain of $g \circ f$: even though the rule $x - 5$ is defined for every real number x, the domain of $g \circ f$ is *not* the set of all real numbers.

- The domain of f is $x \geq 0$
- The domain of g is all real numbers, so all values of $f(x)$ are in the domain of g.

Thus, the domain of $g \circ f$ is $x \geq 0$.

Domain of $f \circ g$:

- The domain of g is all real numbers.
- The values of $g(x)$ that are in the domain of f are

$$x^2 - 5 \geq 0$$
$$x \leq -\sqrt{5} \text{ or } x \geq \sqrt{5}$$

Thus, the domain of $f \circ g$ is $x \leq -\sqrt{5}$ or $x \geq \sqrt{5}$.

Expressing Functions as Composites

In calculus, it is often necessary to write a function as the composition of two simpler functions. For a function with a complicated rule, this can usually be done in several ways.

Example 5   **Writing a Function as a Composite**

Let $h(x) = \sqrt{3x^2 + 1}$. Write h as a composition of functions in two different ways.

Solution

The function h can be written as the composite $g \circ f$, where $f(x) = 3x^2 + 1$ and $g(x) = \sqrt{x}$.

$$(g \circ f)(x) = g(f(x)) = g(3x^2 + 1) = \sqrt{3x^2 + 1}$$

Additionally, h can be written as the composite $j \circ k$, where $j(x) = \sqrt{x + 1}$ and $k(x) = 3x^2$.

$$(j \circ k)(x) = j(k(x)) = j(3x^2) = \sqrt{3x^2 + 1}$$

Applications

Composition of functions arises in applications involving several functional relationships. In such cases, one quantity may have to be expressed as a function of another.

Example 6   **The Area of a Circular Puddle**

A circular puddle of liquid is evaporating and slowly shrinking in size. After t minutes, the radius r of the surface of the puddle measures $r(t) = \dfrac{18}{2t + 3}$ inches. The area A of the surface of the puddle is given by $A(r) = \pi r^2$.

Express the area as a function of time by finding $(A \circ r)(t) = A(r(t))$, and compute the area of the surface of the puddle at $t = 12$ minutes.

Solution

Substitute $r(t) = \dfrac{18}{2t + 3}$ into the area function $A(r)$.

$$(A \circ r)(t) = A\left(\frac{18}{2t + 3}\right) = \pi \left(\frac{18}{2t + 3}\right)^2$$

At $t = 12$ minutes, the area of the surface of the puddle is

$$(A \circ r)(12) = \pi \left(\frac{18}{2 \cdot 12 + 3}\right)^2 = \frac{4\pi}{9} \approx 1.396 \text{ square inches.}$$

Example 7 Manufacturing

Suppose that a manufacturer produces n telephones. The unit cost for producing each telephone is

$$U(n) = \frac{\text{total cost}}{\text{number of phones}} = \frac{12,000 + 15n}{n}$$

If the price of each telephone is the unit cost, u, plus a 30% markup, or

$$p(U) = U + 0.30U$$

find $(p \circ U)(n)$ and interpret the result.

Solution

$$(p \circ U)(n) = p(U(n)) = U(n) + 0.30U(n)$$
$$= \frac{12,000 + 15n}{n} + 0.30\left(\frac{12,000 + 15n}{n}\right)$$
$$= \frac{15,600 + 19.5n}{n}$$

The function $(p \circ U)(n)$ represents the unit price as a function of n, the number of telephones produced. For example, if 10,000 telephones were produced, the price of each phone would be

$$(p \circ U)(10,000) = \frac{15,600 + 19.5(10,000)}{10,000} = \$21.06$$

Exercises 3.5

In Exercises 1–4, find $(f + g)(x)$, $(f - g)(x)$, $(g - f)(x)$, and their domains.

1. $f(x) = -3x + 2 \quad g(x) = x^3$

2. $f(x) = x^2 + 2 \quad g(x) = -4x + 7$

3. $f(x) = \dfrac{1}{x} \quad g(x) = x^2 + 2x - 5$

4. $f(x) = \sqrt{x} \quad g(x) = x^2 + 1$

In Exercises 5–8, find $(fg)(x)$, $\left(\dfrac{f}{g}\right)(x)$, and $\left(\dfrac{g}{f}\right)(x)$.

5. $f(x) = -3x + 2 \quad g(x) = x^3$

6. $f(x) = 4x^2 + x^4 \quad g(x) = \sqrt{x^2 + 4}$

7. $f(x) = x^2 - 3 \quad g(x) = \sqrt{x - 3}$

8. $f(x) = \sqrt{x^2 - 1} \quad g(x) = \sqrt{x - 1}$

In Exercises 9–12, find the domains of fg and $\dfrac{f}{g}$.

9. $f(x) = x^2 + 1 \quad g(x) = \dfrac{1}{x}$

10. $f(x) = x + 2 \quad g(x) = \dfrac{1}{x + 2}$

11. $f(x) = \sqrt{4 - x^2} \quad g(x) = \sqrt{3x + 4}$

12. $f(x) = 3x^2 + x^4 + 2 \quad g(x) = 4x - 3$

In Exercises 13–16, find $(g \circ f)(3)$, $(f \circ g)(1)$, and $(f \circ f)(0)$.

13. $f(x) = 3x - 2 \quad g(x) = x^2$

14. $f(x) = |x + 2| \quad g(x) = -x^2$

15. $f(x) = x \quad g(x) = -3$

16. $f(x) = x^2 - 1 \quad g(x) = \sqrt{x}$

In Exercises 17–20, find the indicated values, where

$$g(t) = t^2 - t \text{ and } f(x) = 1 + x.$$

17. $g(f(0)) + f(g(0))$ **18.** $(f \circ g)(3) - 2f(1)$

19. $g(f(2) + 3)$ **20.** $f(2g(1))$

In Exercises 21–24, find the rule of the function $g \circ f$ and its domain and the rule of $f \circ g$ and its domain.

21. $f(x) = x^2$ $g(x) = x + 3$

22. $f(x) = -3x + 2$ $g(x) = x^3$

23. $f(x) = \dfrac{1}{x}$ $g(x) = \sqrt{x}$

24. $f(x) = \dfrac{1}{2x + 1}$ $g(x) = x^2 - 1$

In Exercises 25–28, find the rules of the functions ff and $f \circ f$.

25. $f(x) = x^3$ **26.** $f(x) = (x - 1)^2$

27. $f(x) = \dfrac{1}{x}$ **28.** $f(x) = \dfrac{1}{x - 1}$

In Exercises 29–32, verify that $(f \circ g)(x) = x$ and $(g \circ f)(x) = x$ for the given functions f and g.

29. $f(x) = 9x + 2$ $g(x) = \dfrac{x - 2}{9}$

30. $f(x) = \sqrt[3]{x - 1}$ $g(x) = x^3 + 1$

31. $f(x) = \sqrt[3]{x} + 2$ $g(x) = (x - 2)^3$

32. $f(x) = 2x^3 - 5$ $g(x) = \sqrt[3]{\dfrac{x + 5}{2}}$

In Exercises 33–38, write the given function as the composite of two functions, neither of which is the identity function, $f(x) = x$. (There may be more than one possible answer.)

33. $f(x) = \sqrt[3]{x^2 + 2}$

34. $g(x) = \sqrt{x + 3} - \sqrt[3]{x + 3}$

35. $h(x) = (7x^3 - 10x + 17)^7$

36. $k(x) = \sqrt[3]{(7x - 3)^2}$

37. $f(x) = \dfrac{1}{3x^2 + 5x - 7}$ **38.** $g(t) = \dfrac{3}{\sqrt{t - 3}} + 7$

In Exercises 39 and 40, graph both $g \circ f$ and $f \circ g$ on the same screen. Use the graphs to show that $g \circ f \neq f \circ g$.

39. $f(x) = x^5 - x^3 - x$ $g(x) = x - 2$

40. $f(x) = x^3 + x$ $g(x) = \sqrt[3]{x - 1}$

For Exercises 41–44, complete the given tables by using the values of the functions f and g given below.

x	$f(x)$
1	3
2	5
3	1
4	2
5	3

x	$g(x)$
1	5
2	4
3	4
4	3
5	2

41.

x	$(g \circ f)(x)$
1	4
2	?
3	5
4	?
5	?

42.

x	$(f \circ g)(x)$
1	?
2	2
3	?
4	?
5	?

43.

x	$(f \circ f)(x)$
1	?
2	?
3	3
4	?
5	?

44.

x	$(g \circ g)(x)$
1	?
2	?
3	?
4	4
5	?

In Exercises 45–49, let $g(x) = |x|$. Graph the function f and the composite function $g \circ f = |f(x)|$ on the same graph.

45. $f(x) = 0.5x^2 - 5$

46. $f(x) = x^3 - 4x^2 + x + 3$

47. $f(x) = x + 3$ **48.** $f(x) = |x| - 2$

49. a. Use the piecewise definition of absolute value to explain why the following statement is true:

$$(g \circ f)(x) = \begin{cases} -f(x) & \text{if } f(x) < 0 \\ f(x) & \text{if } f(x) \geq 0 \end{cases}$$

b. Use part **a** and your knowledge of transformations to explain why the graph of $g \circ f$ consists of the parts of the graph of f that lie above the x-axis together with the reflection across the x-axis of those parts of the graph of f that lie below the x-axis.

In Exercises 50–54, let $g(x) = |x|$. Graph the function f and the composite function $f \circ g = f(|x|)$ on the same graph.

50. $f(x) = x - 4$ **51.** $f(x) = x^3 - 3$

52. $f(x) = 0.5(x - 4)^2 - 9$ **53.** $f(x) = \sqrt{x - 1}$

54. Based on the results of Exercises 50–53, describe the relationship between the graph of f and the graph of $f \circ g$ in terms of transformations.

55. If f is any function and I is the identity function $I(x) = x$, what are $f \circ I$ and $I \circ f$?

56. Give an example of a function f such that

$$f\left(\frac{1}{x}\right) \neq \frac{1}{f(x)}.$$

57. If $f(x) = 2x^3 + 5x - 1$,
  a. find $f(x^2)$
  b. find $(f(x))^2$
  c. Using your answers to parts **a** and **b** what can you conclude about $f(x^2)$ and $(f(x))^2$?

58. In a laboratory culture, the number $N(d)$ of bacteria (in thousands) at temperature d degrees Celsius is given by the function

$$N(d) = \frac{-90}{d + 1} + 20 \quad (4 \leq d \leq 32)$$

and the temperature $D(t)$ at time t hours is given by the function $D(t) = 2t + 4 \quad (0 \leq t \leq 14)$
  a. What does the composite function $N \circ D$ represent?
  b. How many bacteria are in the culture after 4 hours? after 10 hours?

59. As a weather balloon is inflated, its radius increases at the rate of 4 cm per second. Express the volume of the balloon as a function of time, and determine the volume of the balloon after 4 seconds. *Hint:* the volume of a sphere of radius r is $\frac{4}{3}\pi r^3$.

60. Express the surface area of the weather balloon in Exercise 59 as a function of time. *Hint:* the surface area of a sphere of radius r is $4\pi r^2$.

61. Brandon, who is 6 ft tall, walks away from a streetlight that is 15 ft high at a rate of 5 ft per second, as shown in the figure. Express the length s of Brandon's shadow as a function of time. *Hint:* first use similar triangles to express s as a function of the distance d from the streetlight to Brandon.

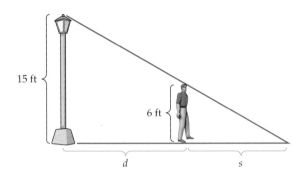

62. A water-filled balloon is dropped from a window 120 ft above the ground. Its height above the ground after t seconds is $120 - 16t^2$ ft. Laura is standing on the ground 40 ft from the point where the balloon will hit the ground, as shown in the figure.
  a. Express the distance d between Laura and the balloon as a function of time.
  b. When is the balloon exactly 90 ft from Laura?

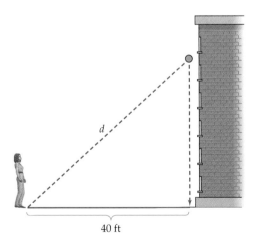

63. *Critical Thinking* Find a function f (other than the identity function) such that $(f \circ f \circ f)(x) = x$ for every value of x in the domain of f. (More than one correct answer is possible.)

Excursion: Iterations and Dynamical Systems

Discrete dynamical systems, which deal with growth and change, occur in economics, biology, and a variety of other scientific fields. Compound interest provides a simple example of a discrete dynamical system. As discussed in Chapter 5, an investment of P dollars at 8% interest compounded annually for one year grows by a factor of 1.08 each year. For example, an investment of $1000 grows like this:

$$\$1000.00 \qquad \textit{Initial amount}$$
$$1.08(1000) = \$1080.00 \qquad \textit{Amount after one year}$$
$$1.08(1080) = \$1166.40 \qquad \textit{Amount after two years}$$
$$1.08(1166.40) = \$1259.71 \qquad \textit{Amount after three years}$$

This process can be described in function notation as follows. Let $f(x) = 1.08x$.

$$\$1000.00 \qquad \textit{Initial amount}$$
$$\$1080 = 1.08(1000) = f(1000) \qquad \textit{After one year}$$
$$\$1166.40 = 1.08(1080) = f(1080) = f(f(1000)) \qquad \textit{After two years}$$
$$\$1259.71 = 1.08(1166.40) = f(1166.40) = f(f(f(1000))) \qquad \textit{After three years}$$

In each step after the first one the output of the function f becomes the input for the next step, and the final result can be expressed in terms of a composite function.

Iteration

Iterations of a function are the repeated compositions of a function with itself.

1. Select a number k as the initial input.
2. Compute the output $f(k)$.
3. Using the output from Step 2 as input, compute the output $f(f(k))$.
4. Continue the process repeatedly, using the output from each step as the input for the next step.

CAUTION

Do not confuse this notation with exponents. $f^2(x)$ does *not* represent the product of two output values, $f(x) \cdot f(x)$.

Iterated Function Notation

Because function notation becomes cumbersome after several steps, the following abbreviated notation is used for iterations of functions:

$$x \text{ is the initial value}$$
$$f(x) \text{ denotes } f(x), \text{ the first iteration}$$
$$f^2(x) \text{ denotes } f(f(x)), \text{ the second iteration}$$
$$f^3(x) \text{ denotes } f(f(f(x))), \text{ the third iteration}$$

and in general

$$f^n(x) \text{ denotes the } n\text{th iteration.}$$

Example 1   Iterated Function Notation

Write the first four iterations of the function $f(x) = \sqrt{x}$ with $x = 0.25$ using iterated function notation.

Solution

$$f(0.25) = \sqrt{0.25} = 0.5$$
$$f^2(0.25) = \sqrt{\sqrt{0.25}} \approx 0.7071$$

$$f^3(0.25) = \sqrt{\sqrt{\sqrt{0.25}}} \approx 0.8409$$

$$f^4(0.25) = \sqrt{\sqrt{\sqrt{\sqrt{0.25}}}} \approx 0.9170$$

Orbits

For a given function, the **orbit** of a number, c, is the sequence of output values produced by starting with c and then iterating the function. That is, the orbit of a number c for a given function f is the sequence

$$c, f(c), f^2(c), f^3(c), f^4(c), f^5(c), \ldots$$

Example 2   Orbits

Find the orbit of $x = 0.25$ for $f(x) = \sqrt{x}$.

Solution

Enter $Y_1 = \sqrt{X}$ in the equation memory. Using the Technology Tip in the margin yields the orbit of $x = 0.25$.

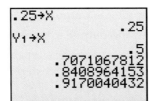 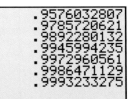

Figure 3.5.A-1

Technology Tip

If a function has been entered as Y_1 in the equation memory, it can be iterated as follows:
• Store the initial value as X.
• Key in Y_1 STO▸ X.
Pressing **ENTER** repeatedly produces the iterated values of the function.

Converging Orbits

Notice that the orbit of $x = 0.25$ in Example 2 has the property that as n gets larger, the terms of the orbit get closer and closer to 1. The orbit is said to **converge** to 1.

Let $f(x) = \sqrt{x}$ and compute the first twelve terms of the orbit of $x = 100$. To what number does the orbit appear to converge?

Choose another positive number and compute its orbit. Does the orbit appear to converge? To what number?

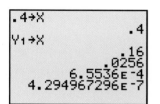

Figure 3.5.A-2

Example 2 and the preceding Exploration suggest that the orbit of every positive number under the function $f(x) = \sqrt{x}$ converges to 1. The following notation is sometimes used to express this fact.

$$\text{For } f(x) = \sqrt{x} \text{ and } x > 0,$$
$$f^n(x) \rightarrow 1 \text{ as } n \rightarrow \infty$$

Example 3 Orbits

Find the orbits of $x = 0.4$ and $x = 2$ for the function $f(x) = x^2$.

Solution

Let $Y_1 = X^2$ and $x = 0.4$. Figure 3.5.A-2 shows that the orbit begins

$$0.4, 0.16, 0.0256, 0.0006554, 0.0000004295, \ldots$$

and that the orbit appears to converge to 0.

Now let $x = 2$. Figure 3.5.A-3 shows that the orbit begins

$$2, 4, 16, 256, 65536, 4294967296, \ldots$$

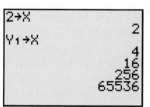

Figure 3.5.A-3

In this case, the orbit is not converging: its terms get larger and larger without bound as n increases. The fact is expressed by saying that the orbit diverges or that the orbit **approaches infinity.** ■

Choose a number strictly between -1 and 1 and find its orbit under the function $f(x) = x^2$. Does the orbit converge? To what number?

Choose another number with absolute value greater than 1 and find its orbit. How would you describe the behavior of the orbit?

Example 3 and the preceding Exploration suggest that the orbit of a number x converges to 0 when $-1 < x < 1$, but that the orbit of x approaches infinity when $|x| > 1$. This fact is expressed as follows.

$$\text{For } f(x) = x^2 \text{ and } |x| < 1, f^n(x) \rightarrow 0 \text{ as } n \rightarrow \infty$$
$$\text{For } f(x) = x^2 \text{ and } |x| > 1, f^n(x) \rightarrow \infty \text{ as } n \rightarrow \infty$$

Fixed Points and Periodic Orbits

In addition to orbits that converge and orbits that approach infinity, there are several other possibilities, some of which are illustrated in the next example.

Example 4   Orbits

Describe the orbit of each of the following.

a. $x = 1$ under the function $f(x) = \sqrt{x}$

b. $x = -1$ under $f(x) = x^2$

c. $x = 4$ under $f(x) = \dfrac{1}{x}$

d. $x = \sqrt{2}$ under $f(x) = x^2 - 1$

Solution

a. Because $f(1) = \sqrt{1} = 1$, the orbit is $1, 1, 1, \ldots$. Consequently, 1 is said to be a **fixed point** of the function $f(x) = \sqrt{x}$.

b. The orbit is $-1, 1, 1, 1, \ldots$ because $f(-1) = (-1)^2 = 1$. Hence, -1 is said to be an **eventually fixed point** of the function $f(x) = x^2$.

c. Because $f(4) = \dfrac{1}{4}$ and $f\left(\dfrac{1}{4}\right) = \dfrac{1}{\frac{1}{4}} = 4$, the orbit is $4, \dfrac{1}{4}, 4, \dfrac{1}{4}, 4, \ldots$.

Since it repeats the same values, the orbit is said to be **periodic** and 4 is said to be a **periodic point.**

d. Direct computation shows that

$$f(\sqrt{2}) = (\sqrt{2})^2 - 1 = 1$$
$$f^2(\sqrt{2}) = 1^2 - 1 = 0$$
$$f^3(\sqrt{2}) = 0^2 - 1 = -1$$
$$f^4(\sqrt{2}) = (-1)^2 - 1 = 0.$$

Therefore, the orbit is $\sqrt{2}, 1, 0, -1, 0 - 1, 0, -1, \ldots$. Because the orbit begins to repeat its values after a few steps, it is said to be **eventually periodic** and $\sqrt{2}$ is said to be an **eventually periodic point.**

Example 5   Orbit Analysis

Analyze all the orbits of $f(x) = x^2$ and illustrate them graphically.

Solution

Example 3 and the Calculator Exploration after it suggest two possibilities.
   When $|x| < 1$, the orbit of x converges to 0.
   When $|x| > 1$, the orbit of x approaches infinity.

The orbit of 1 is 1, 1, 1, ..., so 1 is a fixed point.
The orbit of 0 is 0, 0, 0, ..., so 0 is a fixed point.
The orbit of -1 is -1, 1, 1, ..., so -1 is an eventually fixed point.

Figure 3.5.A-4 illustrates the orbits of $f(x) = x^2$.

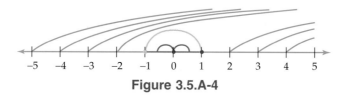

Red: Fixed points

Orange: Eventually fixed point

Green: Orbits that converge to 0

Figure 3.5.A-4

Blue: Orbits that approach ∞

For a function f, if $f(a) = a$, for some value a, then a is called a fixed point of the function.

Exercises 3.5.A

In Exercises 1–6, find the first eight terms of the orbit of the given number under the given function.

1. $x = 2$ and $f(x) = 1.08x$

2. $x = 0.8$ and $f(x) = -2.5x$

3. $x = 0.2$ and $f(x) = 4x(1 - x)$

4. $x = 1.2$ and $f(x) = 4x(1 - x)$

5. $x = 0.5$ and $f(x) = x^3 - x$

6. $x = 0.1$ and $f(x) = x^3 + x^2$

In Exercises 7–12, determine whether the orbit of the point under the function $f(x) = 4x(1 - x)$ converges or approaches infinity or neither.

7. $x = -1$ **8.** $x = -0.5$

9. $x = 0$ **10.** $x = 0.5$

11. $x = 1$ **12.** $x = 1.5$

In Exercises 13–18, find the real number fixed points of the function (if any) by solving the equation $g(x) = x$.

13. $g(x) = x^2 - 6$ **14.** $g(x) = x^2 - 3x - 3$

15. $g(x) = x^3$ **16.** $g(x) = x^3 - 2x^2 + 2x$

17. $g(x) = x^2 - x - 1$ **18.** $g(x) = x^2 - x + 2$

19. Determine all the fixed points and all the eventually fixed points of the function $f(x) = |x|$.

20. Let $f(x) = |x - 2|$.
   a. Find the orbit of x for every integer value of x such that $-4 \le x \le 4$. Classify each point as fixed, eventually fixed, periodic, or eventually periodic.
   b. Describe a pattern in the classifications you made in part **a**.

21. Let $f(x) = |x - 1|$ and perform an orbit analysis as follows.
   a. Show that $x = 0.5$ is a fixed point and that $x = -0.5$ is an eventually fixed point.
   b. Show that $x = 0$ and $x = 1$ are periodic points.

Inverse Functions

3.6

Objectives

- Define inverse relations and functions

- Find inverse relations from tables, graphs, and equations

- Determine whether an inverse relation is a function

- Verify inverses using composition

Inverse Relations and Functions

Consider the following question:

What was the world population in 1997?

The answer to the question can be thought of as the output of a function. The input of the function is a year, 1997, and the output is a number of people. The function can be represented by a table of values or a scatter plot, as shown below. From the table, the output corresponding to the input of 1997 was a world population of 5.85 billion people.

Year	Population (in billions)
1995	5.69
1996	5.77
1997	5.85
1998	5.92
1999	6.00
2000	6.08

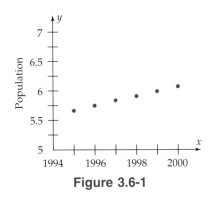

Figure 3.6-1

Now consider another question:

In what year was the world population 6 billion people?

In this question, the input and output are reversed. The input is a population, 6 billion, and the output is a year. To create a function to answer this question, exchange the columns in the table, or the axes of the scatter plot. From the table, the output corresponding to the input of 6 billion people was the year 1999.

Population (in billions)	Year
5.69	1995
5.77	1996
5.85	1997
5.92	1998
6.00	1999
6.08	2000

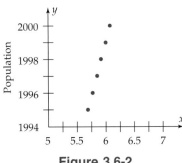

Figure 3.6-2

The result of exchanging the input and output values of a function or relation is called an **inverse relation.** If the inverse is a function, it is called the **inverse function.**

Graphs of Inverse Relations

Suppose that (x, y) is a point on the graph of a function. Then (y, x) is a point on its inverse function or relation. This fact can be used to graph the inverse of a function.

Example 1   Graphing an Inverse Relation

The graph of a function f is shown below. Graph the inverse, and describe the relationship between the function and its inverse.

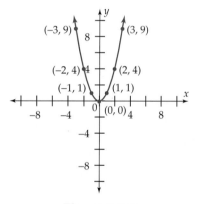

Figure 3.6-3

Solution

Start by reversing the coordinates of each labeled point. Plot these points, then sketch the relation.

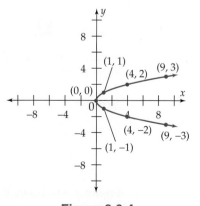

Figure 3.6-4

Exercise 55 shows that the line $y = x$ is the perpendicular bisector of the segment from (a, b) to (b, a), which means that the two points are reflections of each other across the line $y = x$. Thus, the graph of the inverse of $f(x) = x^2$ in Example 1 is a reflection of the original graph across the line $y = x$.

CAUTION

When using a calculator to verify that an inverse is a reflection over the line $y = x$, it is important to use a square viewing window.

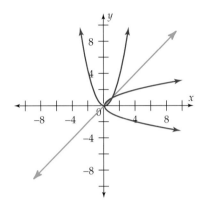

Figure 3.6-5

Graphs of Inverse Relations

Let f be a function. If (a, b) is a point on the graph of f, then (b, a) is a point on the graph of its inverse.

The graph of the inverse of f is a reflection of the graph of f across the line

$$y = x$$

The definition of an inverse makes it very easy to graph an inverse by using parametric graphing mode. Recall that to graph the function $y = f(x)$ in parametric mode, let $x_1 = t$ and $y_1 = f(t)$. To graph the inverse, let $x_2 = f(t)$ and $y_2 = t$.

Example 2 Graphing an Inverse in Parametric Mode

Graph the function $f(x) = 0.7x^5 + 0.3x^4 - 0.2x^3 + 2x + 0.5$ and its inverse in parametric mode.

Solution

To graph f, let $x_1 = t$ and $y_1 = 0.7t^5 + 0.3t^4 - 0.2t^3 + 2t + 0.5$.

To graph the inverse of f, exchange x and y by letting $x_2 = 0.7t^5 + 0.3t^4 - 0.2t^3 + 2t + 0.5$ and $y_2 = t$.

Figure 3.6-6 shows the graph of f and its inverse on the same screen with the graph of $y = x$.

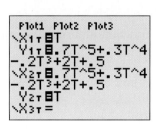
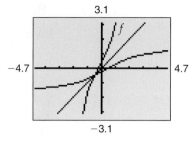

Figure 3.6-6

Algebraic Representations of Inverses

Suppose that a function is represented by an equation in x and y. Then the inverse of the function is found by exchanging the input and output values, that is, by exchanging x and y.

Example 3   **Finding an Inverse from an Equation**

Find $g(x)$, the inverse of $f(x) = 3x - 2$.

Solution

First, write the function in terms of x and y.

$$y = 3x - 2$$

Exchange the x and the y.

$$x = 3y - 2$$

Thus, the inverse relation is $x = 3y - 2$. It is common to solve for y, so that the relation can be represented in function notation.

$$y = \frac{x + 2}{3}$$

$$g(x) = \frac{x + 2}{3}$$

Graphing Exploration ●

Graph the functions f and g from Example 3 together on the same screen with the line $y = x$, and describe your results. Be sure to use a square viewing window.

Example 4   **Finding an Inverse from an Equation**

Find the inverse of $f(x) = x^2 + 4x$.

Solution

Write the function in terms of x and y.

$$y = x^2 + 4x$$

Exchange x and y.

$$x = y^2 + 4y$$

Thus, the inverse is $x = y^2 + 4y$. To solve for y, write the relation as a quadratic equation in y.

$$y^2 + 4y - x = 0$$

Then use the quadratic formula with $a = 1$, $b = 4$, and $c = -x$.

$$y = \frac{-4 \pm \sqrt{16 + 4x}}{2}$$

$$y = -2 \pm \sqrt{4 + x}$$

Notice that the inverse is not a function, so it cannot be written in function notation. ∎

Determining Whether an Inverse is a Function

The inverse of a function is also a function if every input of the inverse corresponds to exactly one output. This means that in the original function, every output corresponds to exactly one input. A function that has this property is called a **one-to-one** function.

One-to-One Functions

A function f is one-to-one if

$$f(a) = f(b)$$

implies that $a = b$.

If a function is one-to-one, then its inverse is also a function.

NOTE By the definition of a function, $a = b$ implies that $f(a) = f(b)$.

Determining Whether a Graph is One-to-One

In Example 1, the points $(2, 4)$ and $(-2, 4)$ are both on the graph of f. These two points have different inputs and the same output, so f is not one-to-one. Also, the points $(2, 4)$ and $(-2, 4)$ lie on the same horizontal line, which suggests a graphical test for whether a function is one-to-one.

Horizontal Line Test

A function f is one-to-one if and only if no horizontal line intersects the graph of f more than once.

Example 5   Using the Horizontal Line Test

Graph each function below and determine whether the function is one-to-one. If so, graph its inverse function.

a. $f(x) = 7x^5 + 3x^4 - 2x^3 + 2x + 1$

b. $g(x) = x^3 - 3x - 1$

c. $h(x) = 1 - 0.2x^3$

Solution

Complete graphs of each function are shown below.

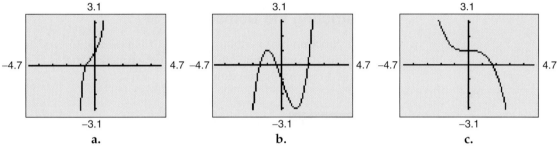

a.   b.   c.

Figure 3.6-7

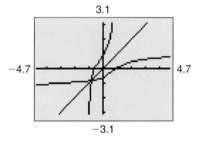

Figure 3.6-8

a. The graph of f passes the Horizontal Line Test, since no horizontal line intersects the graph more than once. Hence, f is one-to-one. The inverse function is the reflection of f across the line $y = x$, shown in Figure 3.6–8.

b. The graph of g fails the Horizontal Line Test because many horizontal lines, including the x-axis, intersect the graph more than once. Therefore, g is not one-to-one, and its inverse is not a function.

c. The graph of h appears to contain a horizontal line segment, so h appears to fail the Horizontal Line Test. In this case, it is helpful to use the trace feature to see that the points on the segment that appears horizontal do not have the same y-value. Thus, the graph of h passes the Horizontal Line Test, and so it is one-to-one. The function and its inverse are shown in Figure 3.6–9.

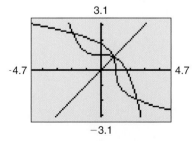

Figure 3.6-9

NOTE The function f in Example 5 is always increasing and the function h is always decreasing. Every increasing or decreasing function is one-to-one because its graph can never touch the same horizontal line twice—it would have to change from increasing to decreasing, or vice versa, to do so.

Inverse Functions

Let f be a function. The following statements are equivalent.

- The inverse of f is a function.
- f is one-to-one.
- The graph of f passes the Horizontal Line Test.

The inverse function, if it exists, is written as f^{-1}, where

$$\text{if } y = f(x), \text{ then } x = f^{-1}(y).$$

The notation f^{-1} does not mean $\dfrac{1}{f}$.

Restricting the Domain

For a function that is not one-to-one, it is possible to produce an inverse function by considering only a part of the function that is one-to-one. This is called **restricting the domain.**

Example 6　Restricting the Domain

Find an interval on which the function $f(x) = x^2$ is one-to-one, and find f^{-1} on that interval.

Solution

The graph of f is one-to-one on the interval $[0, \infty)$, as shown in the graph. To find a rule for f^{-1}, first write the function in terms of x and y.

$$y = x^2$$

Exchange x and y in the equation, and solve for y.

$$x = y^2$$
$$y = \pm \sqrt{x}$$

$$y = \sqrt{x} \qquad \text{or} \qquad y = -\sqrt{x}$$

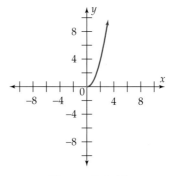

Figure 3.6-10

Because every point on the graph of the restricted function f has non-negative coordinates, the inverse function must be $y = \sqrt{x}$. Thus,

$$f^{-1}(x) = \sqrt{x}$$

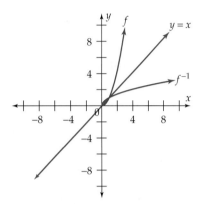

Figure 3.6-11

Composition of a Function and its Inverse

The inverse of a function f is designed to send each output of f back to the input it came from, that is,

$$f(a) = b \qquad \text{exactly when} \qquad f^{-1}(b) = a$$

Consequently, if you first apply f and then apply f^{-1} to the result, you obtain the number you started with.

$$f^{-1}(f(a)) = f^{-1}(b) = a$$

Similarly,

$$f(f^{-1}(b)) = f(a) = b$$

The results above can be generalized to all values in the domains of f and f^{-1}.

Composition of Inverse Functions

A one-to-one function f and its inverse function f^{-1} have these properties.

$$(f^{-1} \circ f)(x) = x \qquad \text{for every } x \text{ in the domain of } f$$
$$(f \circ f^{-1})(x) = x \qquad \text{for every } x \text{ in the domain of } f^{-1}$$

Also, any two functions having both properties are one-to-one and are inverses of each other.

Example 7 Verifying the Inverse of a Function

Let

$$f(x) = \frac{5}{2x - 4} \quad \text{and} \quad g(x) = \frac{4x + 5}{2x}$$

Use composition to verify that f and g are inverses of each other.

Solution

$$(g \circ f)(x) = \frac{4(f(x)) + 5}{2(f(x))} = \frac{4\left(\dfrac{5}{2x - 4}\right) + 5}{2\left(\dfrac{5}{2x - 4}\right)} = \frac{\dfrac{20 + 5(2x - 4)}{2x - 4}}{\dfrac{10}{2x - 4}}$$

$$= \frac{20 + 5(2x - 4)}{10} = \frac{20 + 10x - 20}{10} = \frac{10x}{10} = x$$

$$(f \circ g)(x) = \frac{5}{2(g(x)) - 4} = \frac{5}{2\left(\dfrac{4x + 5}{2x}\right) - 4} = \frac{5}{\dfrac{4x + 5}{x} - 4}$$

$$= \frac{5}{\dfrac{4x + 5 - 4x}{x}} = \frac{5}{\dfrac{5}{x}} = x$$

Thus, f and g are inverses of each other. ∎

Exercises 3.6

In Exercises 1 and 2, write a table that represents the inverse of the function given by the table.

1.

x	$f(x)$
1	4
2	2
3	3
4	6
5	1

2.

x	$g(x)$
-1	4
0	3
1	4
2	1
3	5

In Exercises 3 and 4, the graph of a function f is given. Sketch the graph of the inverse function of f and give the coordinates of three points on the inverse.

3.

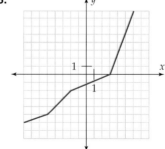

4.

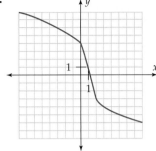

In Exercises 5–8, graph f and its inverse in parametric mode (see Example 2).

5. $f(x) = x^3 - 3x^2 + 2$ **6.** $f(x) = \sqrt[3]{x^2 - 1}$

7. $f(x) = x^4 - 3x^2$ **8.** $f(x) = \sqrt{x^2 + 1}$

In Exercises 9–22, find the rule for the inverse of the given function. Solve your answers for y and, if possible, write in function notation (see Examples 3 and 4).

9. $f(x) = -x$ **10.** $f(x) = -x + 1$

11. $f(x) = 5x^2 - 4$ **12.** $f(x) = -3x^2 + 5$

13. $f(x) = 5 - 2x^3$ **14.** $f(x) = (x^5 + 1)^3$

15. $f(x) = \sqrt{4x - 7}$ **16.** $f(x) = 5 + \sqrt{3x - 2}$

17. $f(x) = \dfrac{1}{x}$ **18.** $f(x) = \dfrac{1}{\sqrt{x}}$

19. $f(x) = \dfrac{1}{2x^2 + 1}$ **20.** $f(x) = \dfrac{x}{x^2 + 1}$

21. $f(x) = \dfrac{x^3 - 1}{x^3 + 5}$ **22.** $f(x) = \sqrt[5]{\dfrac{3x - 1}{x - 2}}$

In Exercises 23–30, use a calculator and the Horizontal Line Test to determine whether the function f is one-to-one.

23. $f(x) = x^4 - 4x^2 + 3$

24. $f(x) = x^4 - 4x + 3$

25. $f(x) = x^3 + x - 5$

26. $f(x) = \begin{cases} x - 3 & \text{for } x \le 3 \\ 2x - 6 & \text{for } x > 3 \end{cases}$

27. $f(x) = x^5 + 2x^4 - x^2 + 4x - 5$

28. $f(x) = x^3 - 4x^2 + x - 10$

29. $f(x) = 0.1x^3 - 0.1x^2 - 0.005x + 1$

30. $f(x) = 0.1x^3 + 0.005x + 1$

In Exercises 31–36, each given function has an inverse function. Sketch the graph of the inverse function.

31. $f(x) = \sqrt{x + 3}$

32. $f(x) = \sqrt{3x - 2}$

33. $f(x) = 0.3x^5 + 2$

34. $f(x) = \sqrt[3]{x + 3}$

35. $f(x) = \sqrt[5]{x^3 + x - 2}$

36. $f(x) = \begin{cases} x^2 - 1 & \text{for } x \le 0 \\ -0.5x - 1 & \text{for } x > 0 \end{cases}$

In Exercises 37–44, none of the functions is one-to-one. State at least one way of restricting the domain of the function so that the restricted function has an inverse that is a function. Then find the rule of the inverse function (see Example 6).

37. $f(x) = |x|$ **38.** $f(x) = |x - 3|$

39. $f(x) = -x^2$ **40.** $f(x) = x^2 + 4$

41. $f(x) = \dfrac{x^2 + 6}{2}$ **42.** $f(x) = \sqrt{4 - x^2}$

43. $f(x) = \dfrac{1}{x^2 + 1}$

44. $f(x) = 3(x + 5)^2 + 2$

In Exercises 45–50, use composition to show that f and g are inverses of each other (see Example 7).

45. $f(x) = x + 1$ $g(x) = x - 1$

46. $f(x) = 2x - 6$ $g(x) = \dfrac{x}{2} + 3$

47. $f(x) = \dfrac{1}{x + 1}$ $g(x) = \dfrac{1 - x}{x}$

48. $f(x) = \dfrac{-3}{2x + 5}$ $g(x) = \dfrac{-3 - 5x}{2x}$

49. $f(x) = x^5$ $g(x) = \sqrt[5]{x}$

50. $f(x) = x^3 - 1$ $g(x) = \sqrt[3]{x + 1}$

51. Show that the inverse function of the function f whose rule is $f(x) = \dfrac{2x + 1}{3x - 2}$ is f itself.

52. List three different functions (other than the one in Exercise 51), each of which is its own inverse. Many correct answers are possible.

53. *Critical Thinking* Let m and b be constants with $m \neq 0$. Show that the function $f(x) = mx + b$ is one-to-one, and find the rule of the inverse function f^{-1}.

54. *Critical Thinking* Prove that the function $h(x) = 1 - 0.2x^3$ of Example 5c is one-to-one by showing that it satisfies the definition:
If $a \neq b$, then $f(a) \neq f(b)$.
Hint: Use the rule of f to show that when $f(a) = f(b)$ then $a = b$. If this is the case, then it is impossible to have $f(a) = f(b)$ when $a \neq b$.

55. *Critical Thinking* Show that the points $P = (a, b)$ and $Q = (b, a)$ are symmetric with respect to the line $y = x$ as follows:
a. Find the slope of the line through P and Q.
b. Use slopes to show that the line through P and Q is perpendicular to $y = x$.
c. Let R be the point where the line $y = x$ intersects $\overline{PQ}$. Since R is on $y = x$, it has coordinates (c, c) for some number c, as shown in the figure. Use the distance formula to show that $\overline{PR}$ has the same length as $\overline{RQ}$. Conclude that the line $y = x$ is the perpendicular bisector of $\overline{PQ}$. Therefore, P and Q are symmetric with respect to the line $y = x$.

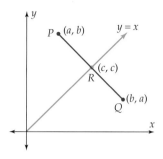

56. Let C be the temperature in degrees Celsius. Then the temperature in degrees Fahrenheit is given by

$$f(C) = \frac{9}{5}C + 32.$$

Let g be the function that converts degrees Fahrenheit to degrees Celsius. Find the rule of g and show that g is the inverse function of f.

3.7   **Rates of Change**

Objectives

- Find the average rate of change of a function over an interval

- Represent average rate of change geometrically as the slope of a secant line

- Use the difference quotient to find a formula for the average rate of change of a function

Rates of change play a central role in calculus. They also have an important connection with the difference quotient of a function, which was introduced in Section 3.1.

Average Rates of Change

When a rock is dropped from a high place, the distance the rock travels (ignoring wind resistance) is given by the function

$$d(t) = 16t^2$$

with distance $d(t)$ measured in feet and time t in seconds. The following table shows the distance the rock has fallen at various times.

Time t	0	1	2	3	3.5	4	4.5	5
Distance $d(t)$	0	16	64	144	196	256	324	400

To find the distance the rock falls from time $t = 1$ to $t = 3$, note that at the end of three seconds, the rock has fallen $d(3) = 144$ feet, whereas it had only fallen $d(1) = 16$ feet at the end of one second.

$$d(3) - d(1) = 144 - 16 = 128 \text{ feet}$$

So during this time interval the rock traveled 128 feet. The distance traveled by the rock during other time intervals can be found the same way.

In general,

the distance traveled from time $t = a$ to time $t = b$ is $d(b) - d(a)$ feet.

From the chart, the length of each time interval can be computed by taking the difference between the two times. For example, from $t = 1$ to $t = 4$ is a time interval of length $4 - 1 = 3$ seconds. Similarly, the interval from $t = 2$ to $t = 3.5$ is of length $3.5 - 2 = 1.5$ seconds. In general,

the length of the time interval from $t = a$ to $t = b$ is $b - a$ seconds.

Since distance traveled = average speed $\cdot$ time interval,

$$\text{average speed} = \frac{\text{distance traveled}}{\text{time interval}}$$

so the average speed over the time interval from $t = a$ to $t = b$ is

$$\text{average speed} = \frac{\text{distance traveled}}{\text{time interval}} = \frac{d(b) - d(a)}{b - a}.$$

Example 1   Average Speed over a Given Interval

Find the average speed of the falling rock

a. from $t = 1$ to $t = 4$ and

b. from $t = 2$ to $t = 4.5$.

Solution

a. Apply the average speed formula with $a = 1$ and $b = 4$.

$$\text{average speed} = \frac{d(4) - d(1)}{4 - 1} = \frac{256 - 16}{4 - 1} = \frac{240}{3}$$

$$= 80 \text{ feet per second}$$

b. Similarly, from $t = 2$ to $t = 4.5$ the average speed is

$$\frac{d(4.5) - d(2)}{4.5 - 2} = \frac{324 - 64}{4.5 - 2} = \frac{260}{2.5} = 104 \text{ feet per second.}$$

The units in which average speed is measured in Example 1 (feet per second) indicate the rate of change of distance (feet) with respect to time (seconds). The average speed, or **average rate of change** of distance with respect to time, as time changes from $t = a$ to $t = b$ is given by

$$\text{average speed} = \text{average rate of change}$$

$$= \frac{\text{change in distance}}{\text{change in time}} = \frac{d(b) - d(a)}{b - a}.$$

Although speed is the most familiar example, rates of change play a role in many other situations as well, as illustrated in Examples 2–4 below. The average rate of change of any function is defined below.

Average Rate of Change

Let f be a function. The *average rate of change* of $f(x)$ with respect to x as x changes from a to b is the value

$$\frac{\text{change in } f(x)}{\text{change in } x} = \frac{f(b) - f(a)}{b - a}$$

Example 2 Rate of Change of Volume

A balloon is being filled with water. Its approximate volume in gallons is

$$V(x) = \frac{x^3}{55}$$

where x is the radius of the balloon in inches. Find the average rate of change of the volume of the balloon as the radius increases from 5 to 10 inches.

Solution

$$\frac{\text{change in volume}}{\text{change in radius}} = \frac{V(10) - V(5)}{10 - 5} \approx \frac{18.18 - 2.27}{10 - 5} \approx \frac{15.91}{5}$$
$$\approx 3.18 \text{ gallons per inch}$$

NOTE Analyzing units is helpful in interpreting the meaning of a rate of change. In Example 2, the units of the answer are gallons per inch. This means that for every inch that the radius increases between 5 and 10 inches, the volume increases by an average of 3.18 gallons.

Example 3 Manufacturing Costs

A small manufacturing company makes specialty office desks. The cost (in thousands of dollars) of producing x desks is given by the function

$$c(x) = 0.0009x^3 - 0.06x^2 + 1.6x + 5$$

Find the average rate of change of the cost

a. from 0 to 10 desks

b. from 10 to 30 desks

c. from 30 to 50 desks.

Solution

a. As production increases from 0 to 10 desks, the average rate of change of cost is

$$\frac{\text{change in cost}}{\text{change in production}} = \frac{c(10) - c(0)}{10 - 0} = \frac{15.9 - 5}{10} = \frac{10.9}{10} = 1.09$$

This means that costs are rising at an average rate of 1.09 thousand dollars (that is, $1090) per desk.

b. As production goes from 10 to 30 desks, the average rate of change of cost is

$$\frac{c(30) - c(10)}{30 - 10} = \frac{23.3 - 15.9}{30 - 10} = \frac{7.4}{20} = 0.37$$

so costs are rising at an average rate of only $370 per desk.

c. As production goes from 30 to 50 desks

$$\frac{c(50) - c(30)}{50 - 30} = \frac{47.5 - 23.3}{50 - 30} = \frac{24.2}{20} = 1.21$$

so the rate increases to $1210 per desk.

■

Example 4   **Rate of Change of Temperature**

The graph of the temperature function f during a particular day is given below. The temperature at x hours after midnight is $f(x)$. What is the average rate of change of the temperature

a. from 4 a.m. to noon?

b. from 3 p.m. to 8 p.m.?

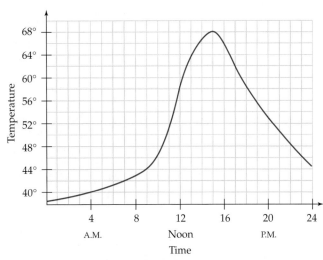

Figure 3.7-1

Solution

a. The graph shows that the temperature at 4 a.m. is $f(4) = 40°$ and the temperature at noon is $f(12) = 58°$. Thus, the average rate of change of temperature is

$$\frac{\text{change in temperature}}{\text{change in time}} = \frac{f(12) - f(4)}{12 - 4} = \frac{58 - 40}{12 - 4} = \frac{18}{8}$$

$$= 2.25° \text{ per hour}$$

Notice that the rate of change is positive. This is because the temperature is *increasing* at an average rate of 2.25° per hour.

b. The time 3 p.m. corresponds to $x = 15$ and 8 p.m. to $x = 20$. The graph shows that $f(15) = 68°$ and $f(20) = 53°$. Thus, the average rate of change of temperature is

$$\frac{\text{change in temperature}}{\text{change in time}} = \frac{f(20) - f(15)}{20 - 15} = \frac{53 - 68}{20 - 15} = \frac{-15}{5}$$

$$= -3° \text{ per hour}$$

The rate of change is negative because the temperature is *decreasing* at an average rate of 3° per hour. ∎

Geometric Interpretation of Average Rate of Change

If P and Q are points on the graph of a function f, then the straight line determined by P and Q is called a **secant line**. Figure 3.7-2 shows the secant line joining the points (4, 40) and (12, 58) on the graph of the temperature function f of Example 3.

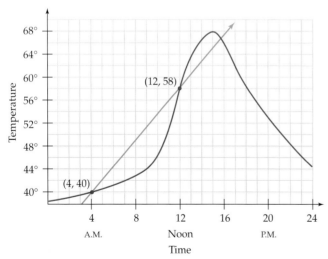

Figure 3.7-2

Using the points (4, 40) and (12, 58), the slope of this secant line is $\dfrac{58 - 40}{12 - 4} = \dfrac{18}{8} = 2.25$. To say that (4, 40) and (12, 58) are on the graph of f means that $f(4) = 40$ and $f(12) = 58$. Thus,

slope of secant line = 2.25

$$= \frac{58 - 40}{12 - 4}$$

$$= \frac{f(12) - f(4)}{12 - 4}$$

= average rate of change as x goes from 4 to 12.

The same thing happens in the general case.

Secant Lines and Average Rates of Change

Let f be a function.

$$\text{average rate of change of } f \text{ from } x = a \text{ to } x = b = \frac{f(b) - f(a)}{b - a} = \text{slope of secant line joining } (a, f(a)) \text{ and } (b, f(b)) \text{ on the graph of } f$$

The Difference Quotient

Average rates of change are often computed for very small intervals, such as the rate from 4 to 4.01 or from 4 to 4.001. Since $4.01 = 4 + 0.01$ and $4.001 = 4 + 0.001$, both cases are essentially the same: computing the rate of change over the interval from 4 to $4 + h$ for some small quantity h. Furthermore, it is often possible to define a formula to determine the average rate for all possible values of h.

Example 5   Computing Average Speed by using a Formula

Find a formula for the average speed of a falling rock from time x to time $x + h$. Use the formula to find the average speed from 3 to 3.1 seconds.

Solution

Recall that the distance the rock travels is given by the function $d(t) = 16t^2$ with distance $d(t)$ measured in feet and time t in seconds.

$$\text{average speed} = \frac{d(x + h) - d(x)}{(x + h) - x} = \frac{16(x + h)^2 - 16x^2}{h}$$

$$= \frac{16(x^2 + 2xh + h^2) - 16x^2}{h} = \frac{16x^2 + 32xh + 16h^2 - 16x^2}{h}$$

$$= \frac{32xh + 16h^2}{h} = \frac{h(32x + 16h)}{h} = 32x + 16h$$

To find the average speed from 3 to 3.1 seconds, apply the formula above, with $x = 3$ and $h = 0.1$.

$$\text{average speed} = 32x + 16h$$

$$= 32(3) + 16(0.1) = 96 + 1.6 = 97.6 \text{ feet per second}$$

In general, the average rate of change of any function f over the interval from x to $x + h$ can be computed as in Example 5: Apply the definition of average rate of change with $a = x$ and $b = x + h$.

$$\text{average rate of change} = \frac{f(b) - f(a)}{b - a} = \frac{f(x + h) - f(x)}{(x + h) - x} = \frac{f(x + h) - f(x)}{h}$$

This last quantity is just the difference quotient of f (see page 144).

Difference Quotients and Rates of Change

Let f be a function. The average rate of change of f over the interval from x to $x + h$ is given by the difference quotient.

$$\frac{f(x + h) - f(x)}{h}$$

Example 6   Using a Rate of Change Formula

Find the difference quotient of $V(x) = \dfrac{x^3}{55}$ and use it to find the average rate of change of V as x changes from 8 to 8.01.

Solution

Find the difference quotient of $V(x)$ and simplify.

$$\frac{V(x + h) - V(x)}{h} = \frac{\overbrace{\dfrac{(x + h)^3}{55}}^{V(x + h)} - \overbrace{\dfrac{x^3}{55}}^{V(x)}}{h} = \frac{\dfrac{1}{55}\left((x + h)^3 - x^3\right)}{h}$$

$$= \frac{1}{55} \cdot \frac{(x + h)^3 - x^3}{h} = \frac{1}{55} \cdot \frac{x^3 + 3x^2h + 3xh^2 + h^3 - x^3}{h}$$

$$= \frac{3x^2 + 3xh + h^2}{55}$$

To find the average rate of change as x changes from 8 to $8.01 = 8 + 0.01$, let $x = 8$ and $h = 0.01$. So the average rate of change is

$$\frac{3x^2 + 3xh + h^2}{55} = \frac{3 \cdot 8^2 + 3 \cdot 8(0.01) + (0.01)^2}{55} \approx 3.495$$

Exercises 3.7

1. A car moves along a straight test track. The distance traveled by the car at various times is shown in the table below. Find the average speed of the car over each interval.
  a. 0 to 10 seconds
  b. 10 to 20 seconds
  c. 20 to 30 seconds
  d. 15 to 30 seconds

2. The yearly profit of a small manufacturing firm is shown in the tables below. What is the average rate of change of profits over the given time span?
  a. 1996–2000   **b.** 1996–2003
  c. 1999–2002   **d.** 1998–2002

Year	1996	1997	1998	1999
Profit	$5000	$6000	$6500	$6800

Year	2000	2001	2002	2003
Profit	$7200	$6700	$6500	$7000

Time (seconds)	0	5	10	15	20	25	30
Distance (feet)	0	20	140	400	680	1400	1800

3. Find the average rate of change of the volume of the balloon in Example 2 as the radius increases
   a. from 2 to 5 inches.   **b.** from 4 to 8 inches.

4. Find the average rate of change of cost for the company in Example 3 when production increases from
   a. 5 to 25 desks.   **b.** 0 to 40 desks.

5. The graph in the figure shows the monthly sales of floral pattern ties (in thousands of ties) made by a company over a 48-month period. Sales are very low when the ties are first introduced; then they increase significantly, hold steady for a while, and then drop off as the ties go out of fashion. Find the average rate of change of sales (in ties per month) over the given interval.
   a. 0 to 12   **b.** 8 to 24
   c. 12 to 24   **d.** 20 to 28
   e. 28 to 36   **f.** 32 to 44
   g. 36 to 40   **h.** 40 to 48

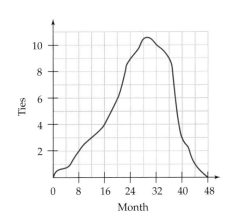

6. A certain company has found that its sales are related to the amount of advertising it does in trade magazines. The graph in the figure shows the sales (in thousands of dollars) as a function of the amount of advertising (in number of magazine ad pages). Find the average rate of change of sales when the number of ad pages increases from
   a. 10 to 20.   **b.** 20 to 60.
   c. 60 to 100.   **d.** 0 to 100.
   e. Is it worthwhile to buy more than 70 pages of ads if the cost of a one-page ad is $2000? if the cost is $5000? if the cost is $8000?

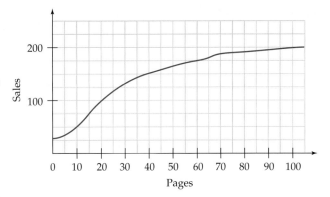

7. When blood flows through an artery (which can be thought of as a cylindrical tube) its velocity is greatest at the center of the artery. Because of friction along the walls of the tube, the blood's velocity decreases as the distance r from the center of the artery increases, finally becoming 0 at the wall of the artery. The velocity (in centimeters per second) is given by the function

$$v = 18{,}500(0.000065 - r^2)$$

where r is measured in centimeters. Find the average rate of change of the velocity as the distance from the center changes from
   a. $r = 0.001$ to $r = 0.002$.
   b. $r = 0.002$ to $r = 0.003$.
   c. $r = 0$ to $r = 0.025$.

8. A car is stopped at a traffic light and begins to move forward along a straight road when the light turns green. The distance (in feet) traveled by the car in t seconds is given by $s(t) = 2t^2$ for $0 \le t \le 30$ What is the average speed of the car from
   a. $t = 0$ to $t = 5$?   **b.** $t = 5$ to $t = 10$?
   c. $t = 10$ to $t = 30$?   **d.** $t = 10$ to $t = 10.1$?

In Exercises 9–14, find the average rate of change of the function f over the given interval.

9. $f(x) = 2 - x^2$
   from $x = 0$ to $x = 2$

10. $f(x) = 0.25x^4 - x^2 - 2x + 4$
   from $x = -1$ to $x = 4$

11. $f(x) = x^3 - 3x^2 - 2x + 6$
   from $x = -1$ to $x = 3$

12. $f(x) = -\sqrt{2x^2 - x + 4}$
   from $x = 0$ to $x = 3$

13. $f(x) = \sqrt{x^3 + 2x^2 - 6x + 5}$
from $x = 1$ to $x = 2$

14. $f(x) = \dfrac{x^2 - 3}{2x - 4}$
from $x = 3$ to $x = 6$

In Exercises 15–22, compute the difference quotient of the function.

15. $f(x) = x + 5$ **16.** $f(x) = 7x + 2$

17. $f(x) = x^2 + 3$ **18.** $f(x) = x^2 + 3x - 1$

19. $f(t) = 160,000 - 8000t + t^2$

20. $V(x) = x^3$ **21.** $A(r) = \pi r^2$

22. $V(p) = \dfrac{5}{p}$

23. Water is draining from a large tank. After t minutes there are $160,000 - 8000t + t^2$ gallons of water in the tank.
   a. Use the results of Exercise 19 to find the average rate at which the water runs out in the interval from 10 to 10.1 minutes.
   b. Do the same for the interval from 10 to 10.01 minutes.
   c. Estimate the rate at which the water runs out after exactly 10 minutes.

24. Use the results of Exercise 20 to find the average rate of change of the volume of a cube whose side has length x as x changes from
   a. 4 to 4.1.   **b.** 4 to 4.01.   **c.** 4 to 4.001.
   d. Estimate the rate of change of the volume at the instant when $x = 4$.

25. Use the results of Exercise 21 to find the average rate of change of the area of a circle of radius r as r changes from
   a. 3 to 3.5.   **b.** 3 to 3.2.   **c.** 3 to 3.1.
   d. Estimate the rate of change at the instant when $r = 3$.
   e. How is your answer in part **d** related to the circumference of a circle of radius 3?

26. Under certain conditions, the volume V of a quantity of air is related to the pressure p (which is measured in kilopascals) by the equation $V = \dfrac{5}{p}$. Use the results of Exercise 22 to estimate the rate at which the volume is changing at the instant when the pressure is 50 kilopascals.

27. Two cars race on a straight track, beginning from a dead stop. The distance (in feet) each car has covered at each time during the first 16 seconds is shown in the figure below.
   a. What is the average speed of each car during this 16-second interval?
   b. Find an interval beginning at $t = 4$ during which the average speed of car D was approximately the same as the average speed of car C from $t = 2$ to $t = 10$.
   c. Use secant lines and slopes to justify the statement "car D traveled at a higher average speed than car C from $t = 4$ to $t = 10$."

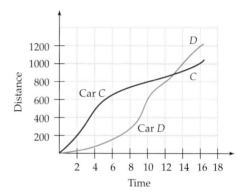

28. The figure below shows the profits earned by a certain company during the last quarter of three consecutive years.
   a. Explain why the average rate of change of profits from October 1 to December 31 was the same in all three years.
   b. During what month in what year was the average rate of change of profits the greatest?

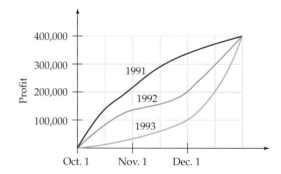

29. The graph in the figure shows the chipmunk population in a certain wilderness area. The population increases as the chipmunks reproduce, but then decreases sharply as predators move into the area.

a. During what approximate time period (beginning on day 0) is the average growth rate of the chipmunk population positive?

b. During what approximate time period, beginning on day 0, is the average growth rate of the chipmunk population 0?

c. What is the average growth rate of the chipmunk population from day 50 to day 100? What does this number mean?

d. What is the average growth rate from day 45 to day 50? from day 50 to day 55? What is the approximate average growth rate from day 49 to day 51?

30. Lucy has a viral flu. How bad she feels depends primarily on how fast her temperature is rising at that time. The figure shows her temperature during the first day of the flu.

a. At what average rate does her temperature rise during the entire day?

b. During what 2-hour period during the day does she feel worst?

c. Find two time intervals, one in the morning and one in the afternoon, during which she feels about the same (that is, during which her temperature is rising at the same average rate).

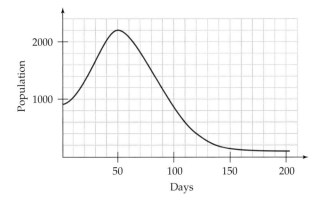

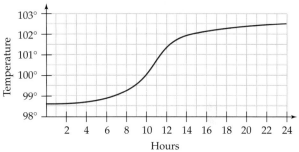

CHAPTER

3

REVIEW

Important Concepts

Important Facts and Formulas

Vertical Line Test: A graph in a coordinate plane represents a function if and only if no vertical line intersects the graph more than once.

A quadratic function can be written in any of the following forms:

Transformation form: $f(x) = a(x - h)^2 + k$

- vertex (h, k)

- x-intercepts $h \pm \sqrt{\dfrac{-k}{a}}$

- y-intercept $ah^2 + k$

Polynomial form: $f(x) = ax^2 + bx + c$

- vertex $\left(\dfrac{-b}{2a}, f\left(\dfrac{-b}{2a}\right) \right)$

- x-intercepts $\dfrac{-b \pm \sqrt{b^2 - 4ac}}{2a}$

- y-intercept c

x-Intercept form: $f(x) = a(x - s)(x - t)$

- vertex $\left(\dfrac{s + t}{2}, f\left(\dfrac{s + t}{2}\right) \right)$

- x-intercepts s and t

- y-intercept ast

The graph of $g(x) = f(x) + c$ is the graph of f shifted upward c units.

The graph of $g(x) = f(x) - c$ is the graph of f shifted downward c units.

The graph of $g(x) = f(x + c)$ is the graph of f shifted c units to the left.

The graph of $g(x) = f(x - c)$ is the graph of f shifted c units to the right.

The graph of $g(x) = -f(x)$ is the graph of f reflected across the x-axis.

The graph of $g(x) = f(-x)$ is the graph of f reflected across the y-axis.

The graph of $g(x) = c \cdot f(x)$ is the graph of f stretched or compressed vertically by a factor of c.

The graph of $g(x) = f(c \cdot x)$ is the graph of f stretched or compressed horizontally by a factor of $\frac{1}{c}$.

Horizontal Line Test: A function is one-to-one if and only if no horizontal line intersects the graph more than once.

A one-to-one function f and its inverse f^{-1} have these properties.

- $(f^{-1} \circ f)(x) = x$
- $(f \circ f^{-1})(x) = x$

The average rate of change of a function f as x changes from a to b is the number

$$\frac{f(b) - f(a)}{b - a}$$

The average rate of change of a function f as x changes from x to $x + h$ is given by the difference quotient of the function,

$$\frac{f(x + h) - f(x)}{h}$$

Review Exercises

Section 3.1

1. Let f be the function given by the rule $f(x) = 7 - 2x$. Complete the table below.

x	-2	-1	0	1	2	t	$b + 1$	$x + h$
$f(x)$								

2. If $h(x) = x^2 - 3x$, then $h(t + 2) = $ ___?___

3. If $f(x) = 2x^3 + x + 1$, then $f\left(\dfrac{x}{2}\right) = $ ___?___

4. What is the domain of the function $f(x) = \sqrt{-x + 2}$?

5. What is the domain of the function $g(t) = \dfrac{\sqrt{t-2}}{t-3}$?

6. What is the domain of the function $h(r) = \sqrt{r-4} + \sqrt{r-2}$?

7. The cost of renting a limousine for 24 hours is given by

$$C(x) = \begin{cases} 150 & \text{if } 0 < x \le 25 \\ 1.75x + 150 & \text{if } x > 25 \end{cases}$$

where x is the number of miles driven.
a. What is the cost if the limo is driven 20 miles? 30 miles?
b. If the cost is \$218.25, how many miles were driven?

8. Let $[x]$ denote the greatest integer function and evaluate

a. $\left[\dfrac{-5}{2}\right] = $ ___?___

b. $[1755] = $ ___?___

c. $[18.7] + [-15.7] = $ ___?___

d. $[-7] - [7] = $ ___?___

9. If $f(x) = x + |x| + [x]$, then find $f(0)$, $f(-1)$, $f\left(\dfrac{1}{2}\right)$, and $f\left(\dfrac{-3}{2}\right)$.

Section 3.2

Use the graph of the function f in the figure to answer Exercises 10–13.

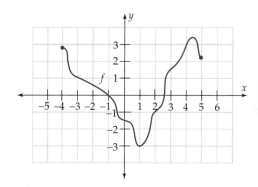

10. What is the domain of f?

11. What is the range of f?

12. $f(-3) = $ ___?___

13. $f(-1) + f(1) = $ ___?___

14. The function whose graph is shown gives the amount of money (in millions of dollars) spent on tickets for major concerts in selected years. [*Source: Pollstar*]

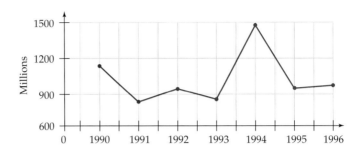

a. What is the domain of the function?
b. What is the approximate range of the function?
c. Over what one-year interval is the rate of change the largest?

In Exercises 15–18, determine the local maxima and minima of the function and the intervals on which the function is increasing and decreasing. Estimate the intervals on which it is concave up and concave down, and the inflection points.

15. $g(x) = \sqrt{x^2 + x + 1}$

16. $f(x) = 2x^3 - 5x^2 + 4x - 3$

17. $g(x) = x^3 + 8x^2 + 4x - 3$

18. $f(x) = 0.5x^4 + 2x^3 - 6x^2 - 16x + 2$

19. State whether the graphs below represent functions of x. Explain your reasoning.

a.  **b.**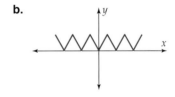

20. Draw the graph of a function f that satisfies the given conditions. The function does not need to be given by an algebraic rule.
- domain of $f = [-3, 4]$ • range of $f = [-2, 5]$
- $f(-2) = 0$ • $f(1) > 2$

21. Sketch the graph of the function $f(x) = \begin{cases} x^2 & \text{if } x \le 0 \\ x + 1 & \text{if } 0 < x < 4 \\ \sqrt{x} & \text{if } x \ge 4 \end{cases}$

In Exercises 22 and 23, sketch the graph of the curve given by the parametric equations.

22. $x = t^3 + 3t^2 - 1$
$y = t^2 + 1 \quad (-3 \le t \le 2)$

23. $x = t^2 - 4$
$y = 2t + 1 \quad (-3 \le t \le 3)$

Section   **3.3**

In Exercises 24–29, find the vertex, *y*-intercept, and *x*-intercepts (if any) of the quadratic function. Sketch the graph, with these points labeled.

24. $f(x) = 3(x + 4)^2 - 5$

25. $g(x) = (x - 4)^2 + 1$

26. $h(x) = 2x^2 - 4x - 3$

27. $f(x) = -x^2 - 2x - 7$

28. $g(x) = -2(x - 1)(x + 2)$

29. $h(x) = (x + 2.4)(x - 1.7)$

30. Write the function $f(x) = (x - 1)^2 - 1$ in polynomial and *x*-intercept form.

31. Write the function $f(x) = x^2 - 3x - 4$ in transformation and *x*-intercept form.

32. Write the function $f(x) = -2(x - 3)(x + 1)$ in transformation and polynomial from.

Section   **3.4**

In Exercises 33–38, graph each function with its parent function on the same graph.

33. $f(x) = -\sqrt{x}$

34. $h(x) = \dfrac{1}{x + 2}$

35. $g(x) = 1.5|x|$

36. $h(x) = [-x]$

37. $f(x) = x^2 - 3$

38. $g(x) = \sqrt[3]{2x}$

In Exercises 39–42, list the transformations, in the order they should be performed on the graph of $g(x) = x^2$, to produce a graph of the function f.

39. $f(x) = 0.25x^2 + 2$

40. $f(x) = -(x + 4)^2 - 5$

41. $f(x) = -3(x - 7)^2 + 2$

42. $f(x) = (x - 2)^2$

43. The figure shows the graph of a function f. If g is the function $g(x) = f(x + 2)$, then which of these statements is true?
   a. The graph of g touches, but does not cross, the *x*-axis.
   b. The graph of g touches, but does not cross, the *y*-axis.
   c. The graph of g crosses the *y*-axis at $y = 4$.
   d. The graph of g crosses the *y*-axis at the origin.
   e. The graph of g crosses the *x*-axis at $x = -3$.

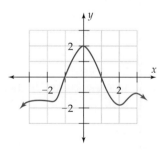

44. The graph of a function f is shown in the figure. On the same coordinate plane, carefully draw the graphs of the functions g and h whose rules are:

$$g(x) = -f(x) \qquad \text{and} \qquad h(x) = 1 - f(x)$$

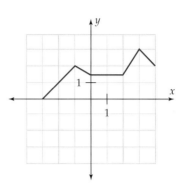

45. U.S. Express Mail rates in 2002 are shown in the following table. Sketch the graph of the function e, whose rule is $e(x) = $ cost of sending a package weighing x pounds by Express Mail.

Express Mail

Letter Rate—Post Office to Addressee Service

Up to 8 ounces	$13.65
Over 8 ounces to 2 pounds	17.85
Up to 3 pounds	21.05
Up to 4 pounds	24.20
Up to 5 pounds	27.30
Up to 6 pounds	30.40
Up to 7 pounds	33.45

Section 3.4.A

In Exercises 46–48, determine algebraically whether the graph of the given equation is symmetric with respect to the x-axis, the y-axis, or the origin.

46. $5y = 7x^2 - 2x$ **47.** $x^2 = y^2 + 2$ **48.** $x^2 + y^2 + 6y = -5$

In Exercises 49–51, determine whether the given function is even, odd, or neither.

49. $g(x) = 9 - x^2$ **50.** $f(x) = |x|x + 1$ **51.** $h(x) = 3x^5 - x(x^4 - x^2)$

52. Plot the points $(-2, 1), (-1, 3), (0, 1), (3, 2)$, and $(4, 1)$ on coordinate axes.
   a. Suppose the points lie on the graph of an even function f. Plot the points $(2, f(2)), (1, f(1)), (0, f(0)), (-3, f(-3))$, and $(-4, f(-4))$.
   b. Suppose the points lie on the graph of an odd function g. Plot the points $(2, g(2)), (1, g(1)), (0, g(0)), (-3, g(-3))$, and $(-4, g(-4))$.

Section 3.5

53. If $f(x) = 3x + 2$ and $g(x) = x^3 + 1$, find each value.

    a. $(f + g)(-1)$ **b.** $(f - g)(2)$ **c.** $(fg)(0)$

54. If $f(x) = \dfrac{1}{x - 1}$ and $g(x) = \sqrt{x^2 + 5}$, find the rule of each function and state its domain.

    a. $(f + g)(x)$ **b.** $(f - g)(x)$ **c.** $(fg)(x)$ **d.** $\left(\dfrac{f}{g}\right)(x)$

55. If $g(x) = x^2 - 1$ then $g(x - 1) - g(x + 1) = $ ___?___

Exercises 56–61 refer to the functions $f(x) = \dfrac{1}{x + 1}$ and $g(x) = x^3 + 3$.

56. $(f \circ g)(1) = $ ___?___   **57.** $(g \circ f)(2) = $ ___?___

58. $g(f(-2)) = $ ___?___   **59.** $(g \circ f)(x - 1) = $ ___?___

60. $g(2 + f(0)) = $ ___?___   **61.** $f(g(1) - 1) = $ ___?___

62. If $f(x) = \dfrac{1}{1 - x}$ and $g(x) = \sqrt{x}$, find the domain of the composite function $f \circ g$.

63. Find two functions f and g such that neither is the identity function and $(f \circ g)(x) = (2x + 1)^2$

64. The radius of an oil spill (in meters) is 50 times the square root of the time t (in hours).

    a. Write the rule of a function f that gives the radius of the spill at time t.

    b. Write the rule of a function g that gives the area of the spill at time t.

    c. What are the radius and area of the spill after 9 hours?

    d. When will the spill have an area of 100,000 square meters?

Section 3.5.A

65. Find the first eight terms of the orbit of $x = 2$ under the function $f(x) = (1 - x)^2$.

66. Describe the set of fixed points of the function $f(x) = [x]$.

Section 3.6

67. The graph of a function f is shown in the figure. Sketch the graph of the inverse of f.

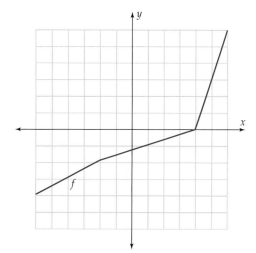

In Exercises 68–73, find the inverse relation of each function. If the inverse is a function, write its rule in function notation.

68. $f(x) = x^3$ **69.** $f(x) = 1 - x^2$

70. $f(x) = |x|$ **71.** $f(x) = 2x + 1$

72. $f(x) = \sqrt{5 - x} + 7$ **73.** $f(x) = \sqrt[5]{x^3 + 1}$

In Exercises 74–76, determine whether or not the given function is one-to-one. Give reasons for your answer. If so, graph the inverse function.

74. $f(x) = 0.02x^3 - 0.04x^2 + 0.6x - 4$ **75.** $f(x) = \dfrac{1}{x}$

76. $f(x) = 0.2x^3 - 4x^2 + 6x - 15$

In Exercises 77–80, use composition to verify that f and g are inverses.

77. $f(x) = 4x - 6$ $g(x) = 0.25x + 1.5$

78. $f(x) = x^3 - 1$ $g(x) = \sqrt[3]{x + 1}$

79. $f(x) = \dfrac{2x + 1}{x - 3}$ $g(x) = \dfrac{3x + 1}{x - 2}$

80. $f(x) = \dfrac{x + 1}{x - 1}$ $g(x) = \dfrac{x + 1}{x - 1}$

Section 3.7

81. Find the average rate of change of the function $g(x) = \dfrac{x^3 - x + 1}{x + 2}$ as x changes from
    a. -1 to 1 **b.** 0 to 2

82. Find the average rate of change of the function $f(x) = \sqrt{x^2 - x + 1}$ as x changes from
    a. -3 to 0 **b.** -3 to 3.5 **c.** -3 to 5

83. If $f(x) = 2x + 1$ and $g(x) = 3x - 2$, find the average rate of change of the composite function $f \circ g$ as x changes from 3 to 5.

84. If $f(x) = x^2 + 1$ and $g(x) = x - 2$, find the average rate of change of the composite function $f \circ g$ as x changes from -1 to 1.

In Exercises 85–88, find the difference quotient of the function and simplify.

85. $f(x) = 3x + 4$ **86.** $g(x) = 4x - 1$

87. $g(x) = x^2 - 1$ **88.** $f(x) = x^2 + x$

89. The graph of the function g in the figure consists of straight line segments. Find an interval over which the average rate of change of g is

 a. 0   **b.** -3 **c.** 0.5

 d. Explain why the average rate of change of g is the same from -3 to -1 as it is from -2.5 to 0.

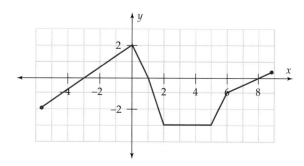

90. The graph in the figure below shows the population of fruit flies during a 50-day experiment in a controlled atmosphere.

 a. During what 5-day period is the average rate of population growth the slowest?

 b. During what 10-day period is the average rate of population growth the fastest?

 c. Find an interval beginning at the 30th day during which the average rate of population growth is the same as the average rate from day 10 to day 20.

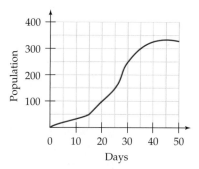

91. The profit (in hundreds of dollars) from selling x tons of an industrial chemical is given by $P(x) = 0.2x^2 + 0.5x - 1$. What is the average rate of change in profit when the number of tons of the chemical sold increases from

 a. 4 to 8 tons?   **b.** 4 to 5 tons?   **c.** 4 to 4.1 tons?

92. On the planet Mars, the distance traveled by a falling rock (ignoring atmospheric resistance) in t seconds is $6.1t^2$ feet. How far must a rock fall in order to have an average speed of 25 feet per second over that time interval?

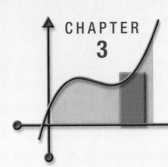

CHAPTER 3

can do calculus

Instantaneous Rates of Change

Rates of change are a major theme in differential calculus—not just the average rate of change discussed in Section 3.7, but the **instantaneous rate of change** of a function. Instantaneous rate of change is the rate of change at a particular instant, which is like a policeman finding the speed of a car at a particular moment by using radar. Even without calculus, however, quite accurate approximations of instantaneous rates of change can be obtained by using average rates appropriately.

The equation of the position (in feet) above the ground of a falling object after t seconds is given by the equation

$$s = -16t^2 + v_0t + s_0,$$

where s_0 is the initial height in feet and v_0 is the initial velocity in feet per second. The object must be moving straight upward or straight downward.

Example 1   Instantaneous Velocity

A ball is thrown straight up from a rooftop with an initial height of 160 feet and an initial velocity of 48 feet per second. The ball misses the rooftop on its way down and falls to the ground. Find the instantaneous velocity of the ball at $t = 2$ seconds.

Solution

The height of the ball is given by the equation

$$s(t) = -16t^2 + 48t + 160.$$

The exact speed of the ball at $t = 2$ can be approximated by finding the average speed over very small time intervals, say 2 to 2.01 or even shorter intervals. Over a very short time span, such as a hundredth of a second, the ball cannot change speed very much, so these average speeds should be a reasonable approximation of its speed at the instant $t = 2$.

The difference quotient of the function s, which represents the average velocity of the function s, is

NOTE Δ is often used to denote change in the value of a quantity. $\dfrac{\Delta s}{\Delta t}$, which is read "change in s divided by change in t," represents the ratio of the change in position to the change in time, which is velocity.

$$\frac{\Delta s}{\Delta t} = \frac{s(t + h) - s(t)}{h}$$

$$= \frac{(-16(t + h)^2 + 48(t + h) + 160) - (-16t^2 + 48t + 160)}{h}$$

$$= \frac{(-16(t^2 + 2th + h^2) + 48(t + h) + 160) - (-16t^2 + 48t + 160)}{h}$$

$$= \frac{-16t^2 - 32th - 16h^2 + 48t + 48h + 160 + 16t^2 - 48t - 160}{h}$$

234

$$= \frac{-32th - 16h^2 + 48h}{h}$$

$$= -32t - 16h + 48 \qquad \textit{General expression of average velocity}$$

When $t = 2$, the expression for average velocity is

$$-32(2) - 16h + 48 = -16 - 16h.$$

The values of the average velocity at times close to $t = 2$ are shown in the following table.

Change in Time 2 to 2 + h	h	Average Velocity at $t = 2$ $-16 - 16h$
2 to 2.1	0.1	-17.6
2 to 2.01	0.01	-16.16
2 to 2.001	0.001	-16.016
2 to 2.0001	0.0001	-16.0016
2 to 2.00001	0.00001	-16.00016

As the value of h gets very small, the values of the average velocity approach the value of the instantaneous velocity. Since these values approach -16, the instantaneous velocity at $t = 2$ is -16 feet per second.

In the table in Example 1, notice that when h is small, the term $-16h$ contributes very little to the average rate of change. Therefore, the instantaneous velocity is the remaining term of the difference quotient at $t = 2$, namely -16. In a similar fashion, the general expression of the difference quotient, $-32t - 16h + 48$, becomes

$$-32t + 48 \qquad \textit{Instantaneous rate of change expression}$$

when h is very small. Instantaneous rate of change can be found by using $-32t + 48$ for different values of t.

Slope of the Tangent Line

In Example 1, the instantaneous rate of change was found by calculating the average rate of change over smaller and smaller intervals. This technique can also be represented on a graph. The average rate of change over an interval is the slope of the secant line that contains the points $(x, f(x))$ and $(x + h, f(x + h))$. If h is very small, the slope of the secant line approaches the slope of the **tangent line,** a line that touches the graph at only one point. The slope of the tangent line to a curve at a point is equal to the instantaneous rate of change of the function at that point.

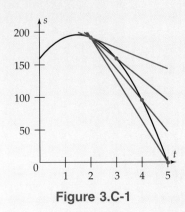

Figure 3.C-1

The graph in Figure 3.C-1 shows secant lines that contain the fixed point $(2, f(2))$ and the points $(3, f(3)), (4, f(4))$, and $(5, f(5))$ for the function in Example 1. As the second point approaches the fixed point, the secant lines approach the tangent line, and the slopes of the secant lines approach the slope of the **tangent line.** The slope of the tangent line, shown in red, is the instantaneous rate of change of the function at the point $x = 2$. The tangent line can be used to determine when the instantaneous rate of change is 0, that is, when the object changes direction.

Example 2   Instantaneous Rate of Change Equal Zero

When is the instantaneous rate of change of the ball in Example 1 equal to zero? What is the maximum height reached by the ball?

Solution

The expression for instantaneous rate of change for $s(t) = -16t^2 + 48t + 160$ was found to be $-32t + 48$. Set this expression equal to zero and solve for t.

$$-32t + 48 = 0$$

$$t = \frac{48}{32} = 1.5 \text{ seconds}$$

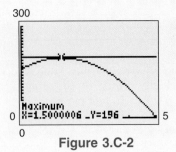

Figure 3.C-2

Therefore, 1.5 seconds after the ball is thrown upward, its rate of change is zero. That is, the ball stops moving upward 1.5 seconds after being thrown, it will be at its highest at that time. Maximum height is given by $s(1.5)$.

$$s(1.5) = -16(1.5)^2 + 48(1.5) + 160$$
$$= -16(2.25) + 48(1.5) + 160$$
$$= -36 + 72 + 160$$
$$= 196 \text{ feet.}$$

The graph of s and the tangent line to the curve at $t = 1.5$ are shown in Figure 3.C-2. Notice that the tangent line is horizontal when $t = 1.5$. ∎

Writing the Equation of a Tangent Line

The equation of the tangent line to a curve at a point can be found by using the instantaneous rate of change at that point and the point-slope form of a line.

Example 3   Equation of a Tangent Line

Write the equation of the tangent line to the function given in Example 1 when $t = 2$.

Solution

When $t = 2$, the position of the ball is $s(2) = -16(2)^2 + 48(2) + 160 = 192$, therefore, the point on the graph is $(2, 192)$. From Example 1, the instantaneous rate of change when $t = 2$ is -16. So, the slope of the tangent line is -16.

236

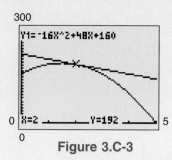

Figure 3.C-3

By using the point-slope form of a line with $m = -16$ and $(2, 192)$, the equation of the tangent line is

$$
\begin{aligned}
y - y_1 &= m(x - x_1) \qquad &\textit{Point-slope form} \\
y - 192 &= -16(x - 2) \\
y - 192 &= -16x + 32 \\
y &= -16x + 224 \qquad &\textit{Tangent line at } (2, 192)
\end{aligned}
$$

The graph of s and the tangent line at $t = 2$ is shown in figure 3.C-3. ■

Numerical Derivatives

Most graphing calculators will give you the value of the instantaneous rate of change of functions at particular input values. The instantaneous rate of change at a particular input value is usually called a **numerical derivative** and is denoted as nDeriv, nDer, d/dx, dY/dX, or ∂. On Sharp 9600, HP 38G, and most TI calculators, numerical derivatives are found in the MATH or CALC menu. On a Casio CFX-9850G, numerical derivatives are displayed when using the TRACE, Graph-to-Table, and Table & Graph features if the Derivative item is On in the SET UP screen for graphs. Check your calculator's manual for the syntax.

Exercises

1. Write an equation for the height of a ball after t seconds that is thrown straight up from a bridge at an initial height of 75 ft with an initial velocity of 20 ft/sec. Find the instantaneous velocity of the ball at $t = 2$ seconds.

2. Find when the instantaneous velocity of the ball in Exercise 1 is 0 feet per second, and interpret the result.

3. Write an equation for the height of a ball after t seconds that is dropped from a tower at an initial height of 300 ft. Find the instantaneous velocity of the ball at $t = 3$ seconds. [*Hint*: When an object is dropped, and not thrown upward or downward, the initial velocity is 0.]

In Exercises 4–7, find the instantaneous rate of change of the function at the given value.

4. $f(t) = t^2 + 4t - 7$ at $t = 5$

5. $f(t) = \dfrac{1}{t}$ at $t = 3$

6. $f(x) = x^3 + 1$ at $x = 1$

7. $f(u) = u^2$ at $u = a$

8. Find the instantaneous rate of change of $f(t) = -4t^2 + 16t + 12$ at $t = 4$ and use it to find the equation of the tangent line. Graph $f(t)$ and the tangent line on the same graph.

9. The surface area of a sphere of radius r is given by the formula $S(r) = 4\pi r^2$. Find the instantaneous rate of change of the surface area at $r = 1$ and interpret the result.

10. The profit, in dollars, of a manufacturer selling digital phones is given by the equation $P(x) = -0.05x^2 + 200x - 30{,}000$ where x is the number of phones sold. Find the instantaneous rate of change at $x = 1000$. What are the units of the rate of change? What does the instantaneous rate of change at $x = 1000$ tell you about the profit of the manufacturer?

Polynomial and Rational Functions

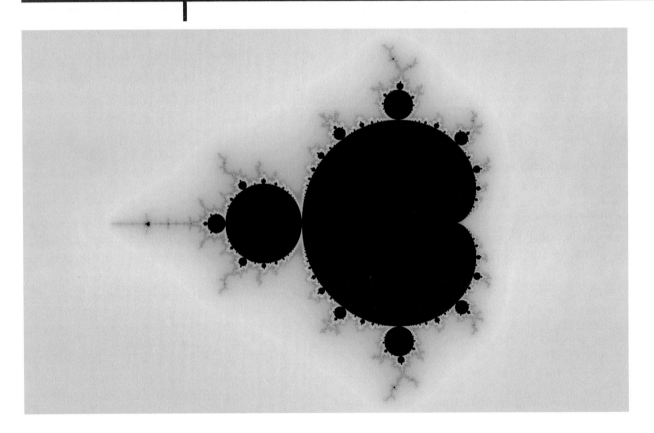

Beauty between order and chaos!

Everyday life abounds in apparently random phenomena: changing weather, traffic clusters on the freeway, lightning paths, ocean turbulence, and many others. Chaos theory is an area of mathematics that analyzes such chaotic behavior. The Mandelbrot set, which is shown above, is a fascinating mathematical object derived from the complex numbers. Its beautiful boundary illustrates chaotic behavior. See *Excursion* 4.5.A.

Chapter Outline

Interdependence of Sections

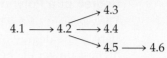

Polynomial functions arise naturally in many applications. Many complicated functions can be approximated by polynomial functions or their quotients, rational functions.

Polynomial Functions

Objectives

- Define a polynomial
- Divide polynomials
- Apply the Remainder Theorem, the Factor Theorem, and the connections between remainders and factors
- Determine the maximum number of zeros of a polynomial

A **polynomial** is an algebraic expression that can be written in the form

$$a_n x^n + a_{n-1} x^{n-1} + \cdots + a_3 x^3 + a_2 x^2 + a_1 x + a_0$$

where n is a nonnegative integer, x is a variable, and each of $a_0, a_1, \ldots, a_n$ is a constant, called a **coefficient.** The coefficient a_0 is called the **constant term.** Note the characteristics of a polynomial.

- all exponents are whole numbers
- no variable is contained in a denominator
- no variable is under a radical

Any letter may be used as the variable in a polynomial. Examples of **polynomials** include the following.

$$x^3 - 6x^2 + \frac{1}{2} \qquad y^{15} + y^{10} + 7 \qquad w - 6.7 \qquad 12$$

239

Constant and Zero Polynomials

A polynomial that consists of only a constant term, such as the polynomial 12, is called a **constant polynomial.** The **zero polynomial** is the constant polynomial 0.

Degree of a Polynomial

The *exponent* of the highest power of x that appears with *nonzero* coefficient is the **degree** of the polynomial, and the nonzero coefficient of this highest power of the variable is the **leading coefficient.**

Polynomial	Degree	Leading coefficient	Constant term
$6x^7 + 4x^3 + 5x^2 - 7x + 10$	7	6	10
x^3	3	1	0
12	0	12	12
$0x^9 + 2x^6 + 3x^7 + x^8 - 2x - 4$	8	1	-4

The degree of the zero polynomial is *not defined* because in that case no power of x occurs with a *nonzero* coefficient.

Definition of a Polynomial Function

A *polynomial function* is a function whose rule is given by a polynomial

$$f(x) = a_n x^n + a_{n-1} x^{n-1} + \cdots + a_1 x + a_0$$

where $a_n, a_{n-1}, \ldots, a_1, a_0$ are real numbers with $a_n \neq 0$, and n is a nonnegative integer.

NOTE The term *polynomial* may refer to a polynomial expression or a polynomial function. The context should clarify the meaning.

Review addition, subtraction, and multiplication of polynomials in the Algebra Review Appendix, if needed.

Polynomial functions of degree less than 5 are often referred to by special names.

- First-degree polynomial functions are called **linear functions.**
- Second-degree polynomial functions are called **quadratic functions.**
- Third-degree polynomial functions are called **cubic functions.**
- Fourth-degree polynomial functions are called **quartic functions.**

Polynomial Division

Long division of polynomials is similar to long division of real numbers, as shown in Example 1.

Example 1   Polynomial Division

Divide $3x^4 - 8x^2 - 11x + 1$ by $x - 2$.

Solution

Expand the dividend to accommodate the missing term, $0x^3$, and write the problem as division.

$$Divisor \rightarrow \quad x - 2 \overline{)3x^4 + 0x^3 - 8x^2 - 11x + 1} \quad \leftarrow Dividend$$

Divide the first term of the divisor, x, into the first term of the dividend, $3x^4$, and put the result, $\dfrac{3x^4}{x} = 3x^3$, on the top line. Then multiply $3x^3$ times the entire divisor, put the result on the third line, and subtract.

$$
\begin{array}{r}
3x^3 \\
x - 2 \overline{)3x^4 + 0x^3 - 8x^2 - 11x + 1} \\
\underline{3x^4 - 6x^3} \\
6x^3 - 8x^2 - 11x + 1
\end{array}
$$

Next, divide the first term of the divisor, x, into the leading term of the difference, $6x^3$, and put the result, $\dfrac{6x^3}{x} = 6x^2$, on the top line. Then multiply $6x^2$ times the entire divisor, put the result on the fifth line, and subtract.

Repeat the process until the remainder has a *smaller degree* than the divisor. Because the degree of the divisor in this case is 1, the process will stop when the subtraction results in a constant.

$$
\begin{array}{rl}
& 3x^3 + 6x^2 + 4x - 3 \leftarrow Quotient \\
Divisor \rightarrow \quad x - 2 \overline{)3x^4 + 0x^3 - 8x^2 - 11x + 1} & \leftarrow Dividend \\
\underline{3x^4 - 6x^3} & \\
6x^3 - 8x^2 - 11x + 1 & \\
\underline{6x^3 - 12x^2} & \\
4x^2 - 11x + 1 & \\
\underline{4x^2 - 8x} & \\
-3x + 1 & \\
\underline{-3x + 6} & \leftarrow Remainder \\
-5 &
\end{array}
$$

Synthetic Division

CAUTION

Synthetic division can be used *only* when the divisor is $x - c$.

When the divisor is a first-degree polynomial such as $x - 2$ or $x + 5$, there is a convenient shorthand method of division called **synthetic division.** The problem from Example 1 is reconsidered below, where it is used to illustrate the procedure used in synthetic division.

Step 1 In the first row, list the 2 from the divisor and the coefficients of the dividend in order of decreasing powers of x, inserting 0 for missing powers of x.

$$
\begin{array}{c|ccccc}
 & Divisor & & & & Dividend \\
 & \downarrow & & & & \\
2\rfloor & 3 & 0 & -8 & -11 & 1
\end{array}
$$

Step 2 Skip a line, draw a line, and draw a partial box under the line beneath the last coefficient in the first row. Bring the first coefficient of the dividend below the line.

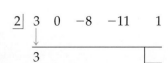

Step 3 Multiply the divisor constant, 2, and the number below the line, 3. Place the product, 6, under the dividend's next coefficient.

$$\begin{array}{r|rrrrr} 2 & 3 & 0 & -8 & -11 & 1 \\ & & 6 & & & \\ \hline & 3 & & & & \boxed{} \end{array}$$

Step 4 Add the numbers in that column and write the sum below the column under the line.

$$\begin{array}{r|rrrrr} 2 & 3 & 0 & -8 & -11 & 1 \\ & & 6 & & & \\ \hline & 3 & 6 & & & \boxed{} \end{array}$$

Step 5 Multiply the divisor and the last entry of the last row. Place the product under the dividend's next coefficient.

$$\begin{array}{r|rrrrr} 2 & 3 & 0 & -8 & -11 & 1 \\ & & 6 & 12 & & \\ \hline & 3 & 6 & & & \boxed{} \end{array}$$

Step 6 Add the numbers in that column and write the sum below the column under the line.

$$\begin{array}{r|rrrrr} 2 & 3 & 0 & -8 & -11 & 1 \\ & & 6 & 12 & & \\ \hline & 3 & 6 & 4 & & \boxed{} \end{array}$$

Step 7 Repeat steps **5** and **6** until a number appears in the box under the last column.

$$\begin{array}{r|rrrrr} 2 & 3 & 0 & -8 & -11 & 1 \\ & & 6 & 12 & 8 & -6 \\ \hline & 3 & 6 & 4 & -3 & \boxed{-5} \end{array}$$

The last number in the third row is the remainder. The other numbers in the third row are the coefficients of the quotient, arranged in order of decreasing powers of x. Because a *fourth*-degree polynomial was divided by a *first*-degree polynomial, the quotient is a *third*-degree polynomial. Therefore, the quotient is $3x^3 + 6x^2 + 4x - 3$ and the remainder is -5.

Example 2   Synthetic Division

Divide $x^5 + 5x^4 + 6x^3 - x^2 + 4x + 29$ by $x + 3$ and check the result.

Solution

To divide $x^5 + 5x^4 + 6x^3 - x^2 + 4x + 29$ by $x + 3$, write the divisor as $x - (-3)$ and perform synthetic division.

$$\begin{array}{r|rrrrrr} -3 & 1 & 5 & 6 & -1 & 4 & 29 \\ & & -3 & -6 & 0 & 3 & -21 \\ \hline & 1 & 2 & 0 & -1 & 7 & \boxed{8} \end{array}$$

The last row shows that the quotient is $x^4 + 2x^3 - x + 7$ and the remainder is 8. ∎

Checking Polynomial Division

Recall how to check a long division problem. When 4509 is divided by 31, the quotient is 145 and the remainder is 14. To check the division, multiply the quotient by the divisor and add the remainder,

$$4509 = 145 \cdot 31 + 14$$

Checking polynomial division uses the same process.

$$\textbf{Dividend} = \textbf{Divisor} \cdot \textbf{Quotient} + \textbf{Remainder}$$

Check the division in Example 2.

$$(x^4 + 2x^3 - x + 7)(x + 3) + 8 = (x^5 + 5x^4 + 6x^3 - x^2 + 4x + 21) + 8$$
$$= x^5 + 5x^4 + 6x^3 - x^2 + 4x + 29$$

The Division Algorithm

If a polynomial $f(x)$ is divided by a nonzero polynomial $h(x)$, then there is a quotient polynomial $q(x)$ and a remainder polynomial $r(x)$ such that

$$Dividend = Divisor \cdot Quotient + Remainder$$

$$f(x) = h(x) \cdot q(x) + r(x)$$

where either $r(x) = 0$ or $r(x)$ has degree less than the degree of the divisor, $h(x)$.

The Division Algorithm can be used to determine if one polynomial is a factor of another polynomial.

Remainders and Factors

If the remainder is 0 when one polynomial is divided by another polynomial, the divisor and the quotient are factors of the dividend.

Example 3   Factors Determined by Division

Determine if $2x^2 + 1$ is a factor of $6x^3 - 4x^2 + 3x - 2$.

Solution

Divide $6x^3 - 4x^2 + 3x - 2$ by $2x^2 + 1$, and see if the remainder is 0.

$$
\begin{array}{r}
3x - 2 \\
2x^2 + 1 \overline{)\, 6x^3 - 4x^2 + 3x - 2} \\
\underline{6x^3 \qquad\quad + 3x} \\
-4x^2 \qquad\quad\ -2 \\
\underline{-4x^2 \qquad\quad\ -2} \\
0
\end{array}
$$

The remainder is 0, and the Division Algorithm confirms the factorization.

$$Dividend = Divisor \cdot Quotient + Remainder$$
$$6x^3 - 4x^2 + 3x - 2 = (2x^2 + 1)(3x - 2) + 0$$
$$= (2x^2 + 1)(3x - 2)$$

Therefore, $(2x^2 + 1)$ is a factor of $6x^3 - 4x^2 + 3x - 2$, and the other factor is the quotient, $(3x - 2)$.

Remainders

When a polynomial $f(x)$ is divided by a first-degree polynomial, such as $x - 3$ or $x + 5$, the remainder is a constant. For example, when

$$f(x) = x^3 - 2x^2 - 4x + 5 \text{ is divided by } x - 3,$$

the quotient is $x^2 + x - 1$ and the remainder is 2.

$$x^3 - 2x^2 - 4x + 5 = (x - 3)(x^2 + x - 1) + 2$$

Notice that $f(3) = (3 - 3)(3^2 + 3 - 1) + 2$
$$= (0)(11) + 2 = 2.$$

That is, the number $f(3)$ is the same as the remainder when $f(x)$ is divided by $x - 3$, as stated in the Remainder Theorem.

Remainder
Theorem

> If a polynomial $f(x)$ is divided by $x - c$, then the remainder is $f(c)$.

Example 4   The Remainder When Dividing by $x - c$

Find the remainder when $x^{79} + 3x^{24} + 5$ is divided by $x - 1$.

Solution

Let $f(x) = x^{79} + 3x^{24} + 5$ and apply the Remainder Theorem with $c = 1$.

$$f(1) = 1^{79} + 3(1)^{24} + 5 = 1 + 3 + 5 = 9$$

Therefore, the remainder when $x^{79} + 3x^{24} + 5$ is divided by $x - 1$ is 9.

Example 5   The Remainder When Dividing by $x + k$

Find the remainder when $3x^4 - 8x^2 + 11x + 1$ is divided by $x + 2$.

Solution

The divisor, $x + 2$, is not in the form $x - a$, so the Remainder Theorem must be applied *carefully*. Rewrite the divisor as $x - (-2)$, and find $f(-2)$.

$$\begin{aligned} f(-2) &= 3(-2)^4 - 8(-2)^2 + 11(-2) + 1 \\ &= 3(16) - 8(4) + 11(-2) + 1 \\ &= 48 - 32 - 22 + 1 \\ &= -5 \end{aligned}$$

By the Remainder Theorem, when $3x^4 - 8x^2 + 11x + 1$ is divided by $x + 2$, the remainder is -5, which can be verified by division. ∎

Zeros and Factors

Recall that if $f(x)$ is a polynomial, then solutions of the equation $f(x) = 0$ are called **zeros** of the function. A zero that is a real number is called a **real zero**. The connection between zeros of a polynomial function and factors of the polynomial is given below.

Factor Theorem

A polynomial function $f(x)$ has a linear factor $x - a$ if and only if

$$f(a) = 0.$$

The Factor Theorem states

If a is a solution of $f(x) = 0$, then $x - a$ is a factor of $f(x)$.

and

If $x - a$ is a factor of $f(x)$, then a is a solution of $f(x) = 0$.

You can see why the Factor Theorem is true by noting that the remainder when $f(x)$ is divided by $x - a$ is $f(a)$ according to the Remainder Theorem. Therefore, by the Division Algorithm

$$f(x) = (x - a)q(x) + f(a).$$

Thus, when $f(a) = 0$, $f(x) = (x - a)q(x)$, so that $x - a$ is a factor. Conversely, when $x - a$ is a factor, the remainder $f(a)$ must be 0.

Example 6 The Factor Theorem

Show that $x - 3$ is a factor of $x^3 - 4x^2 + 2x + 3$ by using the Factor Theorem. Find $q(x)$ such that $(x - 3)q(x) = x^3 - 4x^2 + 2x + 3$.

Solution

Let $f(x) = x^3 - 4x^2 + 2x + 3$ and find $f(3)$.

$$\begin{aligned} f(3) &= 3^3 - 4(3^2) + 2(3) + 3 \\ &= 27 - 4(9) + 2(3) + 3 \\ &= 27 - 36 + 6 + 3 \\ &= 0 \end{aligned}$$

By the Factor Theorem, $x - 3$ is a factor of $x^3 - 4x^2 + 2x + 3$ because $f(3) = 0$.

Dividing $x^3 - 4x^2 + 2x + 3$ by $x - 3$ yields a quotient of $x^2 - x - 1$, and $f(x)$ can be written in factored form.

$$Dividend = Divisor \cdot Quotient$$

$$x^3 - 4x^2 + 2x + 3 = (x - 3)(x^2 - x - 1)$$

The product can be verified by multiplication. ∎

Fundamental Polynomial Connections

Section 2.1 described the connection among the x-intercepts of the graph of $y = f(x)$, the zeros of the function f, and the solutions of $f(x) = 0$. This connection can be extended to include linear factors of $f(x)$, when $f(x)$ is a polynomial.

Zeros, x-Intercepts, Solutions, and Factors of Polynomials

Let $f(x)$ be a polynomial. If r is a real number that satisfies any of the following statements, then r satisfies all the statements.

- **r is a zero of the function f**
- **r is an x-intercept of the graph of the function f**
- **$x = r$ is a solution, or root, of the equation $f(x) = 0$**
- **$x - r$ is a factor of the polynomial $f(x)$**

There is a one-to-one correspondence between the linear factors of $f(x)$ that have real coefficients and the x-intercepts of the graph of f.

The box above states that a zero, an x-intercept, a solution, and the value of r in a linear factor of the form $x - r$ are all the same for a polynomial. Additionally, the x-intercepts correspond to the linear factors of $f(x)$ of the form $x - r$, where r is a real number.

Example 7   Fundamental Polynomial Connections

For $f(x) = 15x^3 - x^2 - 114x + 72$, find the following:

a. the x-intercepts of the graph of f

b. the zeros of f

c. the solutions to $15x^3 - x^2 - 114x + 72 = 0$

d. the linear factors with real coefficients of $15x^3 - x^2 - 114x + 72$

Solution

Graph $f(x) = 15x^3 - x^2 - 114x + 72$ in a standard viewing window, as shown in Figure 4.1-1.

a. Using the zero finder, find the x-intercepts.

$$-3, \frac{2}{3} \approx 0.6667, \text{ and } \frac{12}{5} = 2.4$$

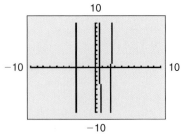

Figure 4.1-1

b. The zeros of f are $-3, \frac{2}{3} \approx 0.6667$, and $\frac{12}{5} = 2.4$.

c. The solutions of $15x^3 - x^2 - 114x + 72 = 0$ are $x = -3$, $x = \frac{2}{3} \approx 0.6667$, and $x = \frac{12}{5} = 2.4$, which can be verified by substitution.

d. The linear factors of $15x^3 - x^2 - 114x + 72$ are $(x - (-3))$, $\left(x - \frac{2}{3}\right)$, and $\left(x - \frac{12}{5}\right)$.

The product $(x + 3)\left(x - \frac{2}{3}\right)\left(x - \frac{12}{5}\right)$ is *not* the original polynomial. There is a constant, a, such that

$$a(x + 3)\left(x - \frac{2}{3}\right)\left(x - \frac{12}{5}\right) = 15x^3 - x^2 - 114x + 72.$$

The leading coefficient of the original polynomial, 15, must be the leading coefficient of the product of the factors. So, $a = 15$.

$$15x^3 - x^2 - 114x + 72 = 15(x + 3)\left(x - \frac{2}{3}\right)\left(x - \frac{12}{5}\right)$$

$$= 3 \cdot 5(x + 3)\left(x - \frac{2}{3}\right)\left(x - \frac{12}{5}\right)$$

$$= (x + 3) \cdot 3\left(x - \frac{2}{3}\right) \cdot 5\left(x - \frac{12}{5}\right)$$

$$= (x + 3)(3x - 2)(5x - 12)$$

Example 8   A Polynomial with Specific Zeros

Find three polynomials of different degrees that have 1, 2, 3, and -5 as zeros.

Solution

A polynomial that has 1, 2, 3, and -5 as zeros must have $x - 1, x - 2, x - 3$, and $x - (-5) = x + 5$ as factors. Many polynomials satisfy these conditions, such as

$$g(x) = (x - 1)(x - 2)(x - 3)(x + 5)$$
$$h(x) = 8(x - 1)(x - 2)(x - 3)^2(x + 5)$$
$$k(x) = 2(x + 4)^2(x - 1)(x - 2)(x - 3)(x + 5)(x^2 + x + 1)$$

Notice that g has degree 4, h had degree 5, and k has degree 8.

The Number of Zeros of a Polynomial

If a polynomial $f(x)$ has four real zeros, say $a, b, c,$ and d, then by the same argument used in Example 8, $f(x)$ must have

$$(x - a), (x - b), (x - c), \text{ and } (x - d)$$

as linear factors. Because its leading term is x^4, $(x - a)(x - b)(x - c)$ $(x - d)$ has degree 4. Since $f(x)$ must have all four factors, its degree must be at least 4. In particular, this means that no polynomial of degree 3 can have four or more zeros. A similar argument holds in the general case.

Number of Zeros

> A polynomial of degree n has at most n distinct real zeros.

Example 9   Maximum Number of Distinct Real Zeros

State the maximum number of distinct real zeros of f.

$$f(x) = 18x^4 - 51x^3 - 187x^2 - 56x + 80$$

Solution

The degree of f is 4. Therefore, the maximum number of distinct real zeros of f is 4.

Exercises 4.1

In Exercises 1–8, determine whether the given algebraic expression is a polynomial. If it is, list its leading coefficient, constant term, and degree.

1. $1 + x^3$ **2.** -7 **3.** $(x - 1)(x^2 + 1)$

4. $7^x + 2x + 1$ **5.** $(x + \sqrt{3})(x - \sqrt{3})$

6. $4x^2 + 3\sqrt{x} + 5$ **7.** $\dfrac{7}{x^2} + \dfrac{5}{x} - 15$

8. $(x - 1)^k$ (where k is a fixed positive integer)

In Exercises 9–16, use synthetic division to find the quotient and remainder.

9. $(3x^4 - 8x^3 + 9x + 5) \div (x - 2)$

10. $(4x^3 - 3x^2 + x + 7) \div (x - 2)$

11. $(2x^4 + 5x^3 - 2x - 8) \div (x + 3)$

12. $(3x^3 - 2x^2 - 8) \div (x + 5)$

13. $(5x^4 - 3x^2 - 4x + 6) \div (x - 7)$

14. $(3x^4 - 2x^3 + 7x - 4) \div (x - 3)$

15. $(x^4 - 6x^3 + 4x^2 + 2x - 7) \div (x - 2)$

16. $(x^6 - x^5 + x^4 - x^3 + x^2 - x + 1) \div (x + 3)$

In Exercises 17–22, state the quotient and remainder when the first polynomial is divided by the second. Check your division by calculating (Divisor)(Quotient) + Remainder

17. $3x^4 + 2x^2 - 6x + 1;$ $x + 1$

18. $x^5 - x^3 + x - 5;$ $x - 2$

19. $x^5 + 2x^4 - 6x^3 + x^2 - 5x + 1;$ $x^3 + 1$

20. $3x^4 - 3x^3 - 11x^2 + 6x - 1;$ $x^3 + x^2 - 2$

21. $5x^4 + 5x^2 + 5;$ $x^2 - x + 1$

22. $x^5 - 1;$ $x - 1$

In Exercises 23–26, determine whether the first polynomial is a factor of the second.

23. $x^2 + 3x - 1;$ $x^3 + 2x^2 - 5x - 6$

24. $x^2 + 9;$ $x^5 + x^4 - 81x - 81$

25. $x^2 + 3x - 1$; $x^4 + 3x^3 - 2x^2 - 3x + 1$

26. $x^2 - 5x + 7$; $x^3 - 3x^2 - 3x + 9$

In Exercises 27–30, determine which of the given numbers are zeros of the given polynomial.

27. $2, 3, 0, -1$; $g(x) = x^4 + 6x^3 - x^2 - 30x$

28. $1, \dfrac{1}{2}, 2, -\dfrac{1}{2}, 3$; $f(x) = 6x^2 + x - 1$

29. $2\sqrt{2}, \sqrt{2}, -\sqrt{2}, 1, -1$; $h(x) = x^3 + x^2 - 8x - 8$

30. $\sqrt{3}, -\sqrt{3}, 1, -1$; $k(x) = 8x^3 - 12x^2 - 6x + 9$

In Exercises 31–40, find the remainder when $f(x)$ is divided by $g(x)$, without using division.

31. $f(x) = x^{10} + x^8$; $g(x) = x - 1$

32. $f(x) = x^6 - 10$; $g(x) = x - 2$

33. $f(x) = 3x^4 - 6x^3 + 2x - 1$; $g(x) = x + 1$

34. $f(x) = x^5 - 3x^2 + 2x - 1$; $g(x) = x - 2$

35. $f(x) = x^3 - 2x^2 + 5x - 4$; $g(x) = x + 2$

36. $f(x) = 10x^{75} - 8x^{65} + 6x^{45} + 4x^{32} - 2x^{15} + 5$;
$\qquad\qquad\qquad\qquad\qquad g(x) = x - 1$

37. $f(x) = 2x^5 - 3x^4 + x^3 - 2x^2 + x - 8; g(x) = x - 10$

38. $f(x) = x^3 + 8x^2 - 29x + 44$; $g(x) = x + 11$

39. $f(x) = 2x^5 - 3x^4 + 2x^3 - 8x - 8$; $g(x) = x - 20$

40. $f(x) = x^5 - 10x^4 + 20x^3 - 5x - 95$; $g(x) = x + 10$

In Exercises 41–46, use the Factor Theorem to determine whether $h(x)$ is a factor of $f(x)$.

41. $h(x) = x - 1$; $f(x) = x^5 + 1$

42. $h(x) = x - \dfrac{1}{2}$; $f(x) = 2x^4 + x^3 + x - \dfrac{3}{4}$

43. $h(x) = x + 2$; $f(x) = x^3 - 3x^2 - 4x - 12$

44. $h(x) = x + 1$; $f(x) = x^3 - 4x^2 + 3x + 8$

45. $h(x) = x - 1$; $f(x) = 14x^{99} - 65x^{56} + 51$

46. $h(x) = x - 2$; $f(x) = x^3 + x^2 - 4x + 4$

In Exercises 47–50, use the Factor Theorem and a calculator to factor the polynomial, as in Example 7.

47. $f(x) = 6x^3 - 7x^2 - 89x + 140$

48. $g(x) = x^3 - 5x^2 - 5x - 6$

49. $h(x) = 4x^4 + 4x^3 - 35x^2 - 36x - 9$

50. $f(x) = x^5 - 5x^4 - 5x^3 + 25x^2 + 6x - 30$

In Exercises 51–54, each graph is of a polynomial function $f(x)$ of degree 5 whose leading coefficient is 1, but the graph is not drawn to scale. Use the Factor Theorem to find the polynomial. *Hint:* What are the zeros of $f(x)$? What does the Factor Theorem tell you?

51.

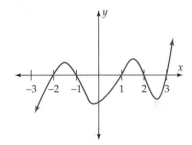

52.

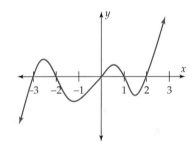

53.

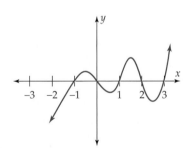

54.

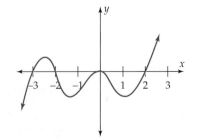

In Exercises 55–58, find a polynomial with the given degree n, the given zeros, and no other zeros.

55. $n = 3$; zeros, $1, 7, -4$ **56.** $n = 3$; zeros, $1, -1$

57. $n = 6$; zeros $1, 2, \pi$ **58.** $n = 5$; zero 2

59. Find a polynomial function f of degree 3 such that $f(10) = 17$ and the zeros of $f(x)$ are 0, 5, and 8.

60. Find a polynomial function g of degree 4 such that the zeros of g are $0, -1, 2, -3$, and $g(3) = 288$.

In Exercises 61–64, find a number k satisfying the given condition.

61. $x + 2$ is a factor of $x^3 + 3x^2 + kx - 2$.

62. $x - 3$ is a factor of $x^4 - 5x^3 - kx^2 + 18x + 18$.

63. $x - 1$ is a factor of $k^2 x^4 - 2kx^2 + 1$.

64. $x + 2$ is a factor of $x^3 - kx^2 + 3x + 7k$.

65. Use the Factor Theorem to show that for every real number c, $x - c$ is not a factor of $x^4 + x^2 + 1$.

66. Let c be a real number and n a positive integer.
   a. Show that $x - c$ is a factor of $x^n - c^n$.
   b. If n is even, show that $x + c$ is a factor of $x^n - c^n$. [Remember: $x + c = x - (-c)$.]

67. a. If c is a real number and n an odd positive integer, give an example to show that $x + c$ may not be a factor of $x^n - c^n$.
   b. If c and n are as in part **a,** show that $x + c$ is a factor of $x^n + c^n$.

68. *Critical Thinking* For what value of k is the difference quotient of $g(x) = kx^2 + 2x + 1$ equal to $7x + 2 + 3.5h$?

69. *Critical Thinking* For what value of k is the difference quotient of $f(x) = x^2 + kx$ equal to $2x + 5 + h$?

70. *Critical Thinking* When $x^3 + cx + 4$ is divided by $x + 2$, the remainder is 4. Find c.

71. *Critical Thinking* If $x - d$ is a factor of $2x^3 - dx^2 + (1 - d^2)x + 5$, what is d?

4.2   Real Zeros

Objectives

- Find all rational zeros of a polynomial function
- Use the Factor Theorem
- Factor a polynomial completely
- Find lower and upper bounds of zeros

Finding the real zeros of a polynomial $f(x)$ is the same as solving the related polynomial equation, $f(x) = 0$. The zero of a first-degree polynomial, such as $5x - 3$, can always be found by solving the equation $5x - 3 = 0$. Similarly, the zeros of any second-degree polynomial can be found by using the quadratic formula, as discussed in Section 2.2. Although the zeros of higher degree polynomials can always be approximated graphically as in Section 2.1, it is better to find exact values, if possible.

Rational Zeros

When a polynomial has *integer* coefficients, all of its **rational zeros** (zeros that are rational numbers) can be found exactly by using the following test.

The Rational Zero Test

If a rational number $\frac{r}{s}$ (written in lowest terms) is a zero of the polynomial function

$$f(x) = a_n x^n + \ldots + a_1 x + a_0$$

where the coefficients $a_n, \cdots, a_1$ are *integers* with $a_n \neq 0$ and $a_0 \neq 0$, then

- r is a factor of the constant term a_0 and
- s is a factor of the leading coefficient a_n.

The test states that every rational zero of a polynomial function with integer coefficients must meet the conditions that

- the numerator is a factor of the constant term, and
- the denominator is a factor of the leading coefficient.

By finding all the numbers that satisfy these conditions, a list of *possible* rational zeros is produced. The polynomial must be evaluated at each number in the list to see if the number actually is a zero. Using a calculator can considerably shorten this testing process, as shown in the next example.

Example 1 The Rational Zeros of a Polynomial

Find the rational zeros of $f(x) = 2x^4 + x^3 - 17x^2 - 4x + 6$.

Solution

If $f(x)$ has a rational zero $\frac{r}{s}$, then by the Rational Zero Test r must be a factor of the constant term, 6. Therefore, r must be one of the integers $\pm 1, \pm 2, \pm 3,$ or ± 6. Similarly, s must be a factor of the leading coefficient, 2. Therefore, s must be one of the integers ± 1 or ± 2. Consequently, the only *possibilities* for $\frac{r}{s}$, are $\dfrac{\pm 1}{\pm 1}, \dfrac{\pm 2}{\pm 1}, \dfrac{\pm 3}{\pm 1}, \dfrac{\pm 6}{\pm 1}, \dfrac{\pm 1}{\pm 2}, \dfrac{\pm 2}{\pm 2}, \dfrac{\pm 3}{\pm 2}, \dfrac{\pm 6}{\pm 2}.$

Eliminating duplications leaves a list of the only *possible* rational zeros.

$$1, -1, 2, -2, 3, -3, 6, -6, \frac{1}{2}, -\frac{1}{2}, \frac{3}{2}, -\frac{3}{2}$$

Graph $f(x)$ in a viewing window that includes all of these numbers on the x-axis, such as $-7 \leq x \leq 7$ and $-7 \leq y \leq 7$. A complete graph is not necessary because only the x-intercepts are of interest.

The graph in Figure 4.2-1a shows that the only numbers in the list that could possibly be zeros are -3, $-\frac{1}{2}$, and $\frac{1}{2}$, so these are the only ones that need to be tested. The table feature can be used to evaluate $f(x)$ at

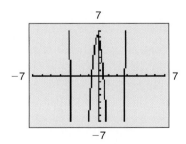

Figure 4.2-1a

these three numbers, as shown in Figure 4.2-1b, where the function is entered in the $Y =$ editor and the independent variable is set to **Ask**.

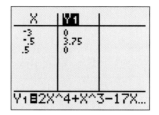

Figure 4.2-1b

The table shows that -3 and $\frac{1}{2}$ are the rational zeros of f and $-\frac{1}{2}$ is not a zero. Therefore, the two other zeros shown in Figure 4.2-1a cannot be rational numbers, that is, the two other zeros must be irrational.

Zeros and the Factor Theorem

Once some zeros of a polynomial have been found, the Factor Theorem can be used to factor the polynomial, which may lead to additional zeros.

Example 2   Finding All Real Zeros of a Polynomial

Find all the real zeros of the function given in Example 1.

$$f(x) = 2x^4 + x^3 - 17x^2 - 4x + 6$$

Solution

The graph of f, shown in Figure 4.2-1a, shows that there are four x-intercepts, and therefore, four real zeros. The rational zeros, -3 and $\frac{1}{2}$, were found in Example 1. By the Factor Theorem, $x - (-3) = x + 3$ and $x - \frac{1}{2}$ are factors of $f(x)$. The other factors can be found by using synthetic division twice. First, factor $x + 3$ out of $f(x)$.

$$
\begin{array}{r|rrrrr}
-3 & 2 & 1 & -17 & -4 & 6 \\
   &   & -6 & 15 & 6 & -6 \\
\hline
   & 2 & -5 & -2 & 2 & \boxed{0}
\end{array}
$$

$$f(x) = (x + 3)(2x^3 - 5x^2 - 2x + 2)$$

Then factor $x - \frac{1}{2}$ out of $2x^3 - 5x^2 - 2x + 2$.

$$\frac{1}{2} \begin{array}{|rrrr} 2 & -5 & -2 & 2 \\ & 1 & -2 & -2 \\ \hline 2 & -4 & -4 & \boxed{0} \end{array}$$

$$f(x) = (x + 3)\left(x - \frac{1}{2}\right)(2x^2 - 4x - 4)$$

Therefore, $2x^4 + x^3 - 17x^2 - 4x + 6 = (x + 3)\left(x - \frac{1}{2}\right)(2x^2 - 4x - 4)$

$$= 2(x + 3)\left(x - \frac{1}{2}\right)(x^2 - 2x - 2)$$

The two remaining zeros of f are the solutions of $x^2 - 2x - 2 = 0$, which can be found by using the quadratic formula.

$$x = \frac{-(-2) \pm \sqrt{(-2)^2 - 4(1)(-2)}}{2(1)} = \frac{2 \pm \sqrt{12}}{2}$$

Therefore, $f(x)$ has two rational zeros, -3 and $\frac{1}{2}$, and two irrational zeros,

$\frac{2 + \sqrt{12}}{2}$ and $\frac{2 - \sqrt{12}}{2}$. ∎

NOTE Recall from algebra that $\frac{2 \pm \sqrt{12}}{2}$ can be simplified as follows:

$$\frac{2 \pm \sqrt{12}}{2} = \frac{2 \pm 2\sqrt{3}}{2}$$
$$= 1 \pm \sqrt{3}.$$

Irreducible and Completely Factored Polynomials

A polynomial that cannot be written as the product of polynomials of lesser degree is said to be **irreducible.** When a polynomial is written as the product of irreducible factors with real coefficients, it is said to be **completely factored over the set of real numbers.** All linear polynomials are irreducible, and some quadratic polynomials are irreducible over the set of real numbers.

Example 2 shows that $\frac{2 + \sqrt{12}}{2}$ and $\frac{2 - \sqrt{12}}{2}$ are zeros of $2x^2 - 4x - 4$.

By the Factor Theorem $x - \left(\frac{2 + \sqrt{12}}{2}\right)$ and $x - \left(\frac{2 - \sqrt{12}}{2}\right)$ are factors. You can verify that

$$2x^2 - 4x - 4 = 2\left[x - \left(\frac{2 + \sqrt{12}}{2}\right)\right]\left[x - \left(\frac{2 - \sqrt{12}}{2}\right)\right].$$

Therefore, the original polynomial can be written as

$$f(x) = 2x^4 + x^3 - 17x^2 - 4x + 6$$
$$= 2(x + 3)\left(x - \frac{1}{2}\right)\left[x - \left(\frac{2 + \sqrt{12}}{2}\right)\right]\left[x - \left(\frac{2 - \sqrt{12}}{2}\right)\right].$$

Notice that the Factor Theorem applies to irrational zeros as well as to rational zeros. That is, because $\frac{2 + \sqrt{12}}{2}$ is a zero, $x - \left(\frac{2 + \sqrt{12}}{2}\right)$ is a factor.

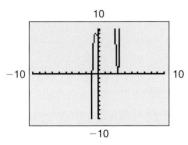

Figure 4.2-2

Example 3   Factoring a Polynomial Completely

Factor $f(x) = 2x^5 - 10x^4 + 7x^3 + 13x^2 + 3x + 9$ completely.

Solution

Begin by finding as many rational zeros as possible. By the Rational Zero Test, every rational zero is of the form $\frac{r}{s}$, where $r = \pm 1, \pm 3,$ or ± 9 and $s = \pm 1$ or ± 2. Thus, the possible rational zeros are

$$\pm 1, \pm 3, \pm 9, \pm \frac{1}{2}, \pm \frac{3}{2}, \pm \frac{9}{2}$$

The graph of f shows that the only possible zeros are -1 and 3. It is easily verified that both numbers *are* zeros of $f(x)$. Consequently, $x - (-1) = x + 1$ and $x - 3$ are factors of $f(x)$ by the Factor Theorem. Division shows other factors.

$$2x^5 - 10x^4 + 7x^3 + 13x^2 + 3x + 9 = (x + 1)(2x^4 - 12x^3 + 19x^2 - 6x + 9)$$
$$= (x + 1)(x - 3)(2x^3 - 6x^2 + x - 3)$$

The other zeros of f are the zeros of $g(x) = 2x^3 - 6x^2 + x - 3$.

Because every zero of $g(x)$ is also a zero of $f(x)$, and the only rational zeros of f are -1 and 3, check if either is a zero of g by using substitution.

$$g(-1) = 2(-1)^3 - 6(-1)^2 + (-1) - 3 = -12$$
$$g(3) = 2(3)^3 - 6(3)^2 + (3) - 3 = 0$$

So 3 is a zero of g, but -1 is not. By the Factor Theorem, $x - 3$ is a factor of $g(x)$. Division shows that

$$f(x) = (x + 1)(x - 3)(2x^3 - 6x^2 + x - 3)$$
$$= (x + 1)(x - 3)(x - 3)(2x^2 + 1)$$

Because $2x^2 + 1$ has no real zeros, it cannot be factored further. So $f(x)$ is completely factored in the last statement above.   ∎

Bounds

In some cases, special techniques may be needed to guarantee that all zeros of a polynomial are located.

Example 4   Finding All Real Zeros of a Polynomial

Show that all the real zeros of $g(x) = x^5 - 2x^4 - x^3 + 3x + 1$ lie between -1 and 3, and find all the real zeros of $g(x)$.

Solution

First show that g has no zero larger than 3, as follows. Use synthetic division to divide $g(x)$ by $x - 3$.

$$
\begin{array}{r|rrrrrr}
3 & 1 & -2 & -1 & 0 & 3 & 1 \\
  &   & 3 & 3 & 6 & 18 & 63 \\
\hline
  & 1 & 1 & 2 & 6 & 21 & \boxed{64}
\end{array}
$$

Thus, the quotient is $x^4 + x^3 + 2x^2 + 6x + 21$ and the remainder is 64. Applying the Division Algorithm,

$$
\begin{aligned}
g(x) &= x^5 - 2x^4 - x^3 + 3x + 1 \\
&= (x - 3)(x^4 + x^3 + 2x^2 + 6x + 21) + 64
\end{aligned}
$$

When $x > 3$, the factor $x - 3$ is positive and $x^4 + x^3 + 2x^2 + 6x + 21$, the quotient, is also positive because all its coefficients are positive. The remainder, 64, is also positive. Therefore, $g(x)$ is positive whenever $x > 3$. In particular, $g(x)$ is never 0 when $x > 3$, and so there are no zeros of g greater than 3.

A similar procedure shows that g has no zero less than -1. Divide $g(x)$ by $x - (-1) = x + 1$ and rewrite $g(x)$ by applying the Division Algorithm.

$$
\begin{aligned}
g(x) &= x^5 - 2x^4 - x^3 + 3x + 1 \\
&= (x + 1)(x^4 - 3x^3 + 2x^2 - 2x + 5) - 4
\end{aligned}
$$

When $x < -1$, the factor $x + 1$ is negative. When x is negative, all odd powers of x are negative and all even powers are positive. Consequently, the quotient, $x^4 - 3x^3 + 2x^2 - 2x + 5$, is positive when $x < -1$ because all odd powers are multiplied by negative coefficients. The positive quotient multiplied by the negative factor $x + 1$ produces a negative product. The remainder, -4, is also negative. Hence, $g(x)$ is negative whenever $x < -1$, and there are no real zeros of g less than -1. Therefore, all the real zeros of $g(x)$ lie between -1 and 3.

Finally, find all the real zeros of $g(x) = x^5 - 2x^4 - x^3 + 3x + 1$. The only possible rational zeros are ± 1, and it is easy to verify that neither is actually a zero. The graph of g in Figure 4.2-3 shows that there are exactly three real zeros between -1 and 3. Because all real zeros of g lie between -1 and 3, g has only these three real zeros. They can be approximated by using a calculator's zero finder.

$$
x \approx -0.3361 \qquad x \approx 1.4268 \qquad \text{and} \qquad x \approx 2.1012
$$

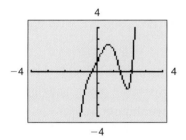

Figure 4.2-3

Upper Bound and Lower Bound

Suppose $f(x)$ is a polynomial and m and n are real numbers with $m < n$. If all the real zeros of $f(x)$ are between m and n, m is called a **lower bound** and n is called an **upper bound** for the real zeros of $f(x)$. Example 4 shows that -1 is a lower bound and 3 is an upper bound for the real zeros of $g(x) = x^5 - 2x^4 - x^3 + 3x + 1$.

If you know lower and upper bounds for the real zeros of a polynomial, you can usually determine the number of real zeros the polynomial has, as shown in Example 4. The technique used in Example 4 to test possible lower and upper bounds works in the general case.

Bounds Test

Let $f(x)$ be a polynomial with positive leading coefficient.

- If $d > 0$ and every number in the last row in the synthetic division of $f(x)$ by $x - d$ is nonnegative, then d is an upper bound for the real zeros of f.
- If $c < 0$ and the numbers in the last row of the synthetic division of $f(x)$ by $x - c$ are alternately positive and negative, with 0 considered as either, then c is a lower bound for the real zeros of f.

Example 5 Finding All Real Zeros of a Polynomial

Find all real zeros of $f(x) = x^6 + x^3 - 7x^2 - 3x + 1$.

Solution

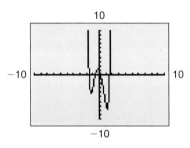

Figure 4.2-4

By the Rational Zero Test, the only possible rational zeros are ± 1, but neither is a zero of f. Hence, the real zeros are irrational. Figure 4.2-4 shows four x-intercepts between -2 and 2, but because f has degree 6, there may be two more zeros that are not shown. Use the Bounds Test to see if all the zeros are between -2 and 2.

To see if 2 is an upper bound, divide $f(x)$ by $x - 2$.

$$
\begin{array}{r|rrrrrrr}
2 & 1 & 0 & 0 & 1 & -7 & -3 & 1 \\
  &   & 2 & 4 & 8 & 18 & 22 & 38 \\
\hline
  & 1 & 2 & 4 & 9 & 11 & 19 & \boxed{39}
\end{array}
$$

All nonnegative

Because the divisor and every term in the last row are positive, 2 is an upper bound for the real zeros of f.

Now divide $f(x)$ by $x - (-2)$ to see if -2 is a lower bound.

$$
\begin{array}{r|rrrrrrr}
-2 & 1 & 0 & 0 & 1 & -7 & -3 & 1 \\
   &   & -2 & 4 & -8 & 14 & -14 & 34 \\
\hline
   & 1 & -2 & 4 & -7 & 7 & -17 & \boxed{35}
\end{array}
$$

Alternating signs

Because the divisor number is negative and the signs in the last row of the synthetic division alternate, -2 is a lower bound.

Therefore, all real zeros of f are between -2 and 2, and all zeros of f are shown in Figure 4.2-4. Using a zero finder, there are four zeros.

$$x \approx -1.5837 \qquad x \approx -0.6180 \qquad x \approx 0.2220 \qquad \text{and} \qquad x \approx 1.6180$$

The examples in this section illustrate the following guidelines for finding all the real zeros of a polynomial.

Finding
Real Zeros
of
Polynomials

1. **Use the Rational Zero Test to find all the rational zeros of *f*.** [*Examples 1, 3, and 6*]
2. **Write *f*(*x*) as the product of linear factors, one for each rational zero, and another factor *g*(*x*).** [*Examples 2 and 3*]
3. **If *g*(*x*) has degree 2, find its zeros by factoring or by using the quadratic formula.** [*Example 2*]
4. **If *g*(*x*) has degree 3 or greater, use the Bounds Test, if possible, to find lower and upper bounds for the zeros of *g*. Approximate the remaining zeros graphically.** [*Examples 4 and 5*]

Shortcuts and variations are always possible. For instance, if the graph of a cubic polynomial shows three *x*-intercepts, then it has three real zeros, which is the maximum number of zeros, and there is no point in finding bounds of the zeros. In order to find as many exact zeros as possible in Guideline 4 above, check to see if the rational zeros of *f* are also zeros of *g*. Factor *g*(*x*) accordingly, as in Example 3.

Example 6   **Finding All Real Zeros of a Polynomial**

Find all real zeros of

$$f(x) = x^7 - 6x^6 + 9x^5 + 7x^4 - 28x^3 + 33x^2 - 36x + 20.$$

Solution

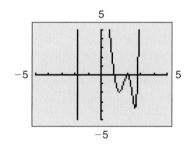

Figure 4.2-5

The graph of *f* shown in Figure 4.2-5 indicates 4 possible real zeros. By the Rational Zero Test, the only possible rational zeros are:

$$\pm 1, \pm 2, \pm 4, \pm 5, \pm 10, \text{ and } \pm 20.$$

It can be verified that both 1 and 2 are zeros of *f*. The graph also suggests that all the real zeros lie between -2 and 6. The Bounds Test shows that this is indeed the case.

Negative Divisor

-2	1	-6	9	7	-28	33	-36	20
		-2	16	-50	86	-116	166	-260
	1	-8	25	-43	58	-83	130	-240

Alternating signs

Positive Divisor

6	1	-6	9	7	-28	33	-36	20
		6	0	54	366	2028	12,366	73,980
	1	0	9	61	338	2061	12,330	74,000

All nonnegative

Therefore, all the real zeros of *f* are between -2 and 6, and the four *x*-intercepts shown in Figure 4.2-5 are the only real zeros of *f*: two are rational zeros, 1 and 2, and two are irrational, $x \approx -1.7913$ and $x \approx 2.7913$, as determined by using a zero finder.

Exercises 4.2

When asked to find the zeros of a polynomial, find exact zeros whenever possible and approximate the other zeros.

In Exercises 1–12, find all the rational zeros of the polynomial.

1. $x^3 + 3x^2 - x - 3$ **2.** $x^3 - x^2 - 3x + 3$

3. $x^3 + 5x^2 - x - 5$ **4.** $3x^3 + 8x^2 - x - 20$

5. $2x^5 + 5x^4 - 11x^3 + 4x^2$ *Hint:* The Rational Zero Test can only be used on polynomials with nonzero constant terms. Factor $f(x)$ as a product of a power of x and a polynomial $g(x)$ with nonzero constant term. Then use the Rational Zero Test on $g(x)$.

6. $2x^6 - 3x^5 - 7x^4 - 6x^3$

7. $\frac{1}{12}x^3 - \frac{1}{12}x^2 - \frac{2}{3}x + 1$ *Hint:* The Rational Zero Test can only be used on polynomials with integer coefficients. Note that $f(x)$ and $12f(x)$ have the same zeros. (Why?)

8. $\frac{2}{3}x^4 + \frac{1}{2}x^3 - \frac{5}{4}x^2 - x - \frac{1}{6}$

9. $\frac{1}{3}x^4 - x^3 - x^2 + \frac{13}{3}x - 2$

10. $\frac{1}{3}x^7 - \frac{1}{2}x^6 - \frac{1}{6}x^5 + \frac{1}{6}x^4$

11. $0.1x^3 - 1.9x + 3$

12. $0.05x^3 + 0.45x^2 - 0.4x + 1$

In Exercises 13–18, factor the polynomial as a product of linear factors and a factor $g(x)$ such that $g(x)$ is either a constant or a polynomial that has no rational zeros.

13. $2x^3 - 4x^2 + x - 2$ **14.** $6x^3 - 5x^2 + 3x - 1$

15. $x^6 + 2x^5 + 3x^4 + 6x^3$

16. $x^5 - 2x^4 + 2x^3 - 3x + 2$

17. $x^5 - 4x^4 + 8x^3 - 14x^2 + 15x - 6$

18. $x^5 + 4x^3 + x^2 + 6x$

In Exercises 19–22, use the Bounds Test to find lower and upper bounds for the real zeros of the polynomial.

19. $x^3 + 2x^2 - 7x + 20$ **20.** $x^3 - 15x^2 - 16x + 12$

21. $-x^5 - 5x^4 + 9x^3 + 18x^2 - 68x + 176$ *Hint:* The Bounds Test applies only to polynomials with a positive leading coefficient. The polynomial $f(x)$ has the same zeros as $-f(x)$. Why?

22. $-0.002x^3 - 5x^2 + 8x - 3$

In Exercises 23–36, find all real zeros of the polynomial.

23. $2x^3 - 5x^2 + x + 2$ **24.** $t^4 - t^3 + 2t^2 - 4t - 8$

25. $6x^3 - 11x^2 + 6x - 1$ **26.** $z^3 + z^2 + 2z + 2$

27. $x^4 + x^3 - 19x^2 + 32x - 12$

28. $3x^5 + 2x^4 - 7x^3 + 2x^2$

29. $2x^5 - x^4 - 10x^3 + 5x^2 + 12x - 6$

30. $x^5 - x^3 + x$

31. $x^6 - 4x^5 - 5x^4 - 9x^2 + 36x + 45$

32. $x^5 + 3x^4 - 4x^3 - 11x^2 - 3x + 2$

33. $3x^4 + 2x^3 - 4x^2 + 4x - 1$

34. $x^5 + 8x^4 + 20x^3 + 9x^2 - 27x - 27$

35. $x^4 - 48x^3 - 101x^2 + 49x + 50$

36. $3x^7 + 8x^6 - 13x^5 - 36x^4 - 10x^3 + 21x^2 + 41x + 10$

37. a. Show that $\sqrt{2}$ is an irrational number. *Hint:* $\sqrt{2}$ is a zero of $x^2 - 2$. Does this polynomial have any rational zeros?
     b. Show that $\sqrt{3}$ is irrational.

38. Graph $f(x) = 0.001x^3 - 0.199x^2 - 0.23x + 6$ in the standard viewing window.
     a. How many zeros does $f(x)$ appear to have? Without changing the viewing window, explain why $f(x)$ must have an additional zero. *Hint:* Each zero corresponds to a factor of $f(x)$. What does the rest of the factorization consist of?
     b. Find all the zeros of $f(x)$.

39. According to the FBI, the number of people murdered each year per 100,000 population can be approximated by the polynomial function $f(x) = 0.0011x^4 - 0.0233x^3 + 0.1144x^2 + 0.0126x + 8.1104$ $(0 \le x \le 10)$, where $x = 0$ corresponds to 1987.

a. What was the murder rate in 1990?
b. In what year was the rate 8 people per 100,000?
c. In what year was the rate the highest?

40. During the first 150 hours of an experiment, the growth rate of a bacteria population at time t hours is $g(t) = -0.0003t^3 + 0.04t^2 + 0.3t + 0.2$ bacteria per hour.

a. What is the growth rate at 50 hours? at 100 hours?
b. What is the growth rate at 145 hours? What does this mean?
c. At what time is the growth rate 0?
d. At what time is the growth rate -50 bacteria per hour?
e. Approximately at what time does the highest growth rate occur?

41. An open-top reinforced box is to be made from a 12-by-36-inch piece of cardboard by cutting along the marked lines, discarding the shaded pieces, and folding as shown in the figure. If the box must be less than 2.5 inches high, what size squares should be cut from the corners in order for the box to have a volume of 448 cubic inches?

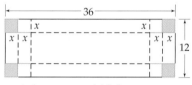

cut along ——— fold along – – – –

42. A box with a lid is to be made from a 48-by-24-inch piece of cardboard by cutting and folding, as shown in the figure. If the box must be at least 6 inches high, what size squares should be cut from the two corners in order for the box to have a volume of 1000 cubic inches?

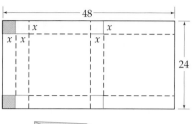

43. In a sealed chamber where the temperature varies, the instantaneous rate of change of temperature with respect to time over an 11-day period is given by $F(t) = 0.0035t^4 - 0.4t^2 - 0.2t + 6$, where time is measured in days and temperature in degrees Fahrenheit (so that rate of change is in degrees per day).

a. At what rate is the temperature changing at the beginning of the period ($t = 0$)? at the end of the period ($t = 11$)?
b. When is the temperature increasing at a rate of 4°F per day?
c. When is the temperature decreasing at a rate of 3°F per day?
d. When is the temperature decreasing at the fastest rate?

44. *Critical Thinking*
a. If c is a zero of

$$f(x) = 5x^4 - 4x^3 + 3x^2 - 4x + 5,$$

show that $\dfrac{1}{c}$ is also a zero.

b. Do part **a** with $f(x)$ replaced by $g(x)$.

$$g(x) = 2x^6 + 3x^5 + 4x^4 - 5x^3 + 4x^2 + 3x + 2$$

c. Let

$$f(x) = a_{12}x^{12} + a_{11}x^{11} + \cdots + a_2x^2 + a_1x + a_0.$$

If c is a zero of f, what conditions must the coefficients a_i satisfy so that $\dfrac{1}{c}$ is also a zero?

4.3 Graphs of Polynomial Functions

Objectives

- Recognize the shape of basic polynomial functions

- Describe the graph of a polynomial function

- Identify properties of general polynomial functions: Continuity, End Behavior, Intercepts, Local Extrema, Points of Inflection

- Identify complete graphs of polynomial functions

The graph of a first-degree polynomial function is a straight line, as discussed in Section 1.4. The graph of a second-degree, or quadratic, polynomial function is a parabola, as discussed in Section 3.3. The emphasis in this section is on higher degree polynomial functions.

Basic Polynomial Shapes

The simplest polynomial functions are those of the form $f(x) = ax^n$, where a is a constant and n is a nonnegative integer. The graphs of polynomial functions of the form $f(x) = ax^n$, with $n \geq 2$, are of two basic types. The different types are determined by whether n is even or odd.

Polynomial Functions of Odd Degree

When the degree of a polynomial function in the form $f(x) = ax^n$, is *odd*, its graph has the basic form shown is Figures 4.3-1a and 4.3-1b. Notice that the graph shown in Figure 4.3-1b has the same shape as the graph shown in Figure 4.3-1a, but it is the reflection of the Figure 4.3-1a across either the x-axis or the y-axis.

$$f(x) = ax^n, \, n \text{ odd}$$

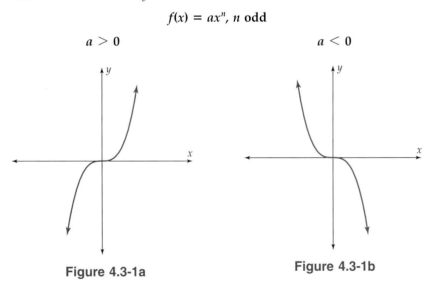

Figure 4.3-1a

Figure 4.3-1b

Graphing Exploration ●

Graph each of the following functions of odd degree in the window with $-5 \leq x \leq 5$ and $-30 \leq y \leq 30$, and compare each shape with those shown in Figure 4.3-1a and 4.3-1b.

- $f(x) = 2x^3$
- $h(x) = -x^3$
- $g(x) = 0.01x^5$
- $k(x) = -2x^7$

Polynomial Functions of Even Degree

When the degree of a polynomial function in the form $f(x) = ax^n$ is even, its graph has the form shown in Figures 4.3-2a or 4.3-2b. Again, the graph of $f(x) = ax^n$, when a is negative, is the reflection of Figure 4.3-2a across the x-axis.

$$f(x) = ax^n, \text{ } n \text{ even}$$

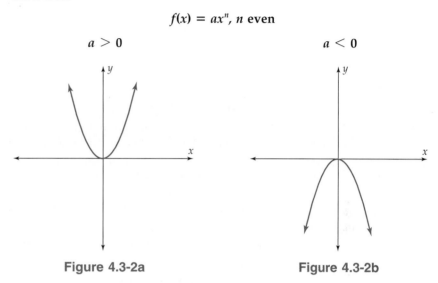

$a > 0$	$a < 0$
Figure 4.3-2a	**Figure 4.3-2b**

Graphing Exploration ⬤

Graph each of the following functions of even degree in the window with $-5 \le x \le 5$ and $-30 \le y \le 30$, and compare each shape with those shown in Figure 4.3-2a or 4.3-2b.

- $f(x) = 2x^4$
- $h(x) = -2x^2$
- $g(x) = 6x^6$
- $k(x) = -3x^4$

Properties of General Polynomial Functions

The graphs of other polynomial functions can vary considerably in shape. Understanding the properties that follow should assist you in interpreting graphs correctly and in determining when a graph of a polynomial function is complete.

Continuity

Every graph of a polynomial function is **continuous,** that is, it is an un-broken curve, with no jumps, gaps, or holes. Furthermore, graphs of polynomial functions have no sharp corners. Thus, *neither* of the graphs shown in Figure 4.3-3 represents a polynomial function. Note: some calculator graphs of polynomial functions may appear to have sharp corners; however, zooming in on the area in question will show a smooth curve.

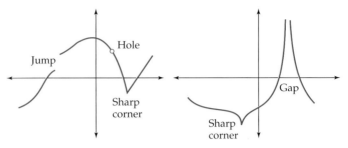

Figure 4.3-3

End Behavior

The shape of a polynomial graph at the far left and far right of the coordinate plane, that is, when $|x|$ is large, is called the **end behavior** of the graph. End behavior of graphs of functions of the form $f(x) = ax^n$ have common characteristics when n is odd and when n is even. The Graphing Exploration below asks you to find a generalization about the end behavior of polynomial functions of odd degree.

Graphing Exploration

Consider the function $f(x) = 2x^3 + x^2 - 6x$ and the function determined by its leading term $g(x) = 2x^3$.

- In a standard viewing window, graph f and g. Describe how the graphs look different and how they look the same.
- In the viewing window $-20 \le x \le 20$ and $-10{,}000 \le y \le 10{,}000$, graph f and g. Do the graphs look almost the same?
- In the viewing window

$$-100 \le x \le 100 \text{ and } -1{,}000{,}000 \le y \le 1{,}000{,}000,$$

graph f and g. Do the graphs look virtually identical?

The reason that the answer to the last question is "yes" can be understood by observing which term contributes the most to the output value $f(x)$ when x is large, as shown in the following chart.

Values of Specific Terms of $f(x) = 2x^3 + x^2 - 6x$

x	-100	-50	70	100
$-6x$	600	300	-420	-600
x^2	$10{,}000$	$2{,}500$	$4{,}900$	$10{,}000$
$g(x) = 2x^3$	$-2{,}000{,}000$	$-250{,}000$	$686{,}000$	$2{,}000{,}000$
$f(x) = 2x^3 + x^2 - 6x$	$-1{,}989{,}400$	$-247{,}200$	$690{,}480$	$2{,}009{,}400$

The chart shows that when $|x|$ is large, the terms x^2 and $-6x$ are insignificant compared with $2x^3$, and they play a very minor role in determining the end behavior of $f(x)$. Hence, the values of $f(x)$ and $g(x)$ are relatively close for large values of x.

End Behavior of Polynomial Functions

When $|x|$ is large, the graph of a polynomial function closely resembles the graph of its highest degree term.

When a polynomial function has *odd* degree, one end of its graph shoots upward and the other end downward.

When a polynomial function has *even* degree, both ends of its graph shoot upward or both ends shoot downward.

Following are some illustrations of the facts listed in the preceding box. In Figures 4.3-4a–d, the graph of a polynomial function is shown on the left and the graph of its leading term is shown on the right. The end behavior of the graph of the polynomial is the same as the end behavior of the graph of the leading term. Note the degree of each set of graphs and whether the leading coefficient is positive or negative.

$$f(x) = 2x^4 - 5x^2 + 2 \qquad\qquad g(x) = 2x^4$$

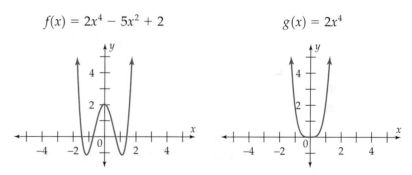

Figure 4.3-4a

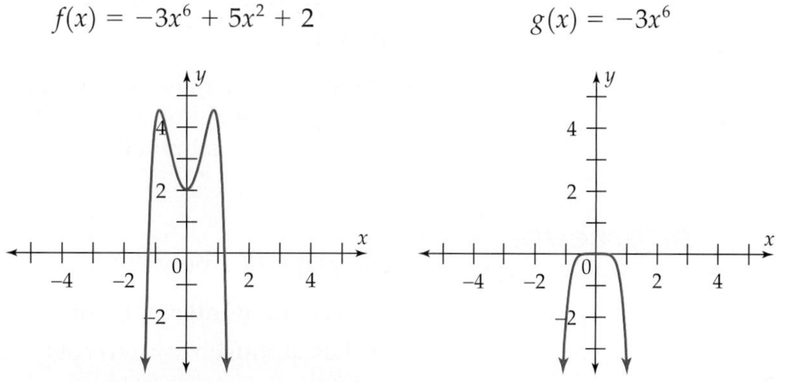

$$f(x) = -3x^6 + 5x^2 + 2 \qquad\qquad g(x) = -3x^6$$

Figure 4.3-4b

$$f(x) = 0.4x^3 - x^2 - 2x + 3 \qquad\qquad g(x) = 0.4x^3$$

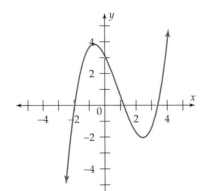 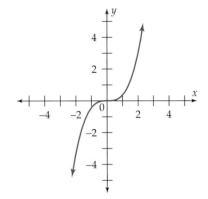

Figure 4.3-4c

$$f(x) = -0.6x^5 + 4x^2 + x - 4 \qquad\qquad g(x) = -0.6x^5$$

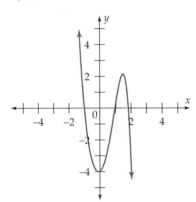 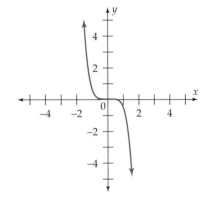

Figure 4.3-4d

Intercepts

Consider a polynomial function written in polynomial form.

$$f(x) = a_n x^n + a_{n-1} x^{n-1} + \ \ldots \ + a_1 x + a_0$$

- The y-intercept of the graph of f is the constant term, a_0.
- The x-intercepts of the graph of f are the real zeros of f.

The graph of every polynomial function has exactly one y-intercept, and because a polynomial of degree n has at most n distinct zeros, the number of x-intercepts is limited.

Intercepts

The graph of a polynomial function of degree n

- **has one y-intercept, which is equal to the constant term.**
- **has at most n x-intercepts.**

That is, the number of x-intercepts can be no greater than the degree of the polynomial function.

Multiplicity

There is another connection between zeros and graphs. If $x - r$ is a factor that occurs m times in the complete factorization of a polynomial expression, then r is called a zero with **multiplicity** m of the related polynomial function.

For example, -3, -1 and 1 are zeros of $f(x) = (x + 3)^2(x + 1)(x - 1)^3$. The multiplicity of each zero is shown in the following chart.

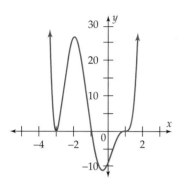

Figure 4.3-5

Zero	-3	-1	1
Multiplicity	2	1	3

Observe in Figure 4.3-5 that the graph of f does not cross the x-axis at -3, a zero of *even* multiplicity, but does cross the x-axis at -1 and 1, zeros of *odd* multiplicity.

Multiplicity and Graphs

> Let c be a zero of multiplicity k of a polynomial f.
>
> - **If k is odd, the graph of f crosses the x-axis at c.**
> - **If k is even, the graph of f touches, but does not cross, the x-axis at c.**

Example 1   Multiplicity of Zeros

Find all zeros of $f(x) = (x + 1)^2(x - 2)(x - 3)^3$. State the multiplicity of each zero, and state whether the graph of f touches or crosses the x-axis at each corresponding x-intercept.

Solution

The following chart lists the zeros of f, the multiplicity of each, and whether the graph touches or crosses the x-axis at the corresponding x-intercept.

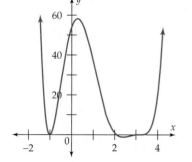

Figure 4.3-6

Zero	Multiplicity	x-Intercept
-1	2	touches
2	1	crosses
3	3	crosses

The graph of f, shown in Figure 4.3-6, verifies that the graph touches but does not cross the x-axis at -1 and crosses the x-axis at 2 and 3.

Local Extrema

The term **local extremum** (plural, extrema) refers to either a local maximum or a local minimum, that is, a point where the graph has a peak or a valley. Local extrema occur when the output values change from increasing to decreasing, or vice versa, as discussed in Section 3.2.

Graphing Exploration

- Graph $f(x) = 0.5x^5 + 1.5x^4 - 2.5x^3 - 7.5x^2 + 2x + 5$ in the standard viewing window. What is the total number of local extrema on the graph? What is the degree of f?

- Graph $g(x) = x^4 - 3x^3 - 2x^2 + 4x + 5$ in the standard viewing window. What is the total number of local extrema on the graph? What is the degree of $g(x)$?

The two polynomials graphed in the Exploration are illustrations of the following fact.

Number of Local Extrema

A polynomial function of degree n has at most $n - 1$ local extrema.

That is, that total number of peaks and valleys on the graph is at most one less than the degree of the function.

Points of Inflection

Recall from Section 3.2 that an inflection point occurs where the concavity of a graph of a function changes. The number of inflection points on the graph of a polynomial is governed by the degree of the function.

Number of Points of Inflection

- The graph of a polynomial function of degree n, with $n \geq 2$, has at most $n - 2$ points of inflection.
- The graph of a polynomial function of odd degree has at least one point of inflection.

Thus, the graph of a quadratic function, which has degree 2, has no points of inflection because it can have at most $n - 2 = 2 - 2 = 0$. The graph of a cubic has exactly one point of inflection because it has at least 1 and at most $3 - 2 = 1$.

Technology Tip

Points of inflection may be found by using INFLC in the TI-86/89 GRAPH MATH menu or INFLEC in the Sharp 9600 CALC menu.

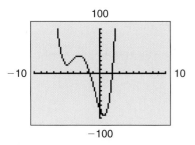

Figure 4.3-7

Complete Graphs of Polynomial Function

By using the facts discussed in this section, you can often determine whether or not the graph of a polynomial function is complete, that is, shows all the important features.

Example 2   A Complete Graph of a Polynomial

Find a complete graph of $f(x) = x^4 + 10x^3 + 21x^2 - 40x - 80$.

Solution

Because the y-intercept is -80, graph f in the window with $-10 \le x \le 10$ and $-100 \le y \le 100$, as shown in Figure 4.3-7.

The three peaks and valleys shown are the only local extrema because a fourth-degree polynomial graph has at most three local extrema.

There cannot be more x-intercepts than the two shown because if the graph turned toward the x-axis farther to the right or farther to the left, there would be an additional peak, which is impossible.

Finally, the end behavior of the graph resembles the graph of $y = x^4$, the highest degree term.

Figure 4.3-7 includes all the important features of the graph and is therefore complete. ∎

Example 3   A Complete Graph of a Polynomial

Find a complete graph of $f(x) = x^3 - 1.8x^2 + x + 2$.

Solution

The graph of f, shown in Figure 4.3-8a on the next page, is similar to the graph of its leading term $y = x^3$, but it does not appear to have any local extrema. However, if you use the trace feature on the flat portion of the graph to the right of the y-axis, you should see that the y-coordinates increase, then decrease, and then increase again.

Zoom in on the portion of the graph between 0 and 1, as shown in Figure 4.3-8b. Observe that the graph actually has two local extrema, one peak and one valley, which is the maximum possible number of local extrema for a cubic function. Figures 4.3-8a and 4.3-8b together provide a complete graph of f.

NOTE No polynomial graph contains horizontal line segments like those shown in Figure 4.3-8a. Always investigate such segments by using trace or zoom-in to determine any hidden behavior.

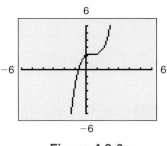

| Figure 4.3-8a | Figure 4.3-8b |

Example 4 **A Complete Graph of a Polynomial**

Determine if the graph shown in Figure 4.3-9a is a complete graph of

$$f(x) = 0.01x^5 + x^4 - x^3 - 6x^2 + 5x + 4.$$

Solution

The graph shown in Figure 4.3-9a cannot be a complete graph because, when $|x|$ is large, the graph of f must resemble the graph of $g(x) = 0.01x^5$, whose left end goes downward.

So the graph of f must turn downward and cross the x-axis somewhere to the left of the origin. Therefore, the graph must have one more peak, where the graph turns downward, and must have another x-intercept.

One additional peak and the ones shown in Figure 4.3-9a make a total of four, the maximum possible for a polynomial of degree 5. Similarly, the additional x-intercept makes a total of 5 x-intercepts. Because f has degree 5, there are no other x-intercepts.

A viewing window that includes the local maximum and the x-intercept shown in Figure 4.3-9b will not display the local extrema and x-intercepts shown in Figure 4.3-9a. Consequently, a complete graph of f requires both Figure 4.3-9a and Figure 4.3-9b to illustrate the important features of the graph.

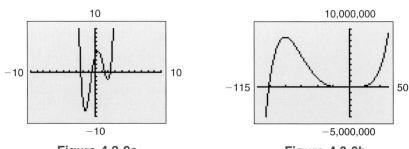

| Figure 4.3-9a | Figure 4.3-9b |

The graphs shown in Examples 2–4 were known to be complete because they included the maximum possible number of local extrema. Many graphs, however, may have fewer than the maximum number of possible peaks and valleys. In such cases, use any available information and try several viewing windows to obtain the most complete graph.

Exercises 4.3

In Exercises 1–6, decide whether the given graph could possibly be the graph of a polynomial function.

1.

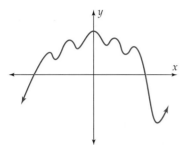

2.

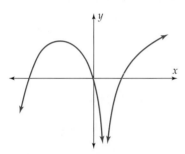

3.

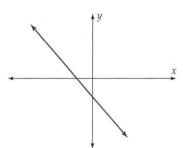

4.

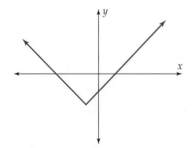

5.

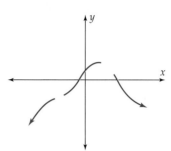

6.

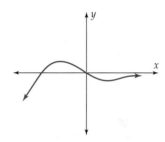

In Exercises 7–12, determine whether the given graph could possibly be the graph of a polynomial function of degree 3, degree 4, or degree 5.

7.

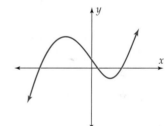

8.

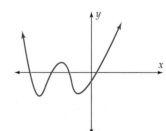

9.

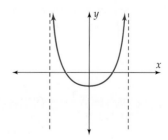

10.

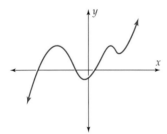

11.

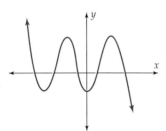

12.

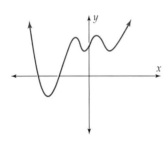

In Exercises 13 and 14, find a viewing window in which the graph of the given polynomial function f appears to have the same general shape as the graph of its leading term.

13. $f(x) = x^4 - 6x^3 + 9x^2 - 3$

14. $f(x) = x^3 - 5x^2 + 4x - 2$

In Exercises 15–18, the graph of a polynomial function is shown. List each zero of the polynomial and state whether its multiplicity is even or odd.

15.

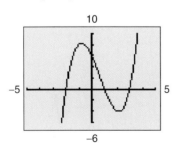

16.

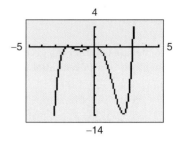

17.

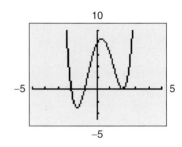

18.

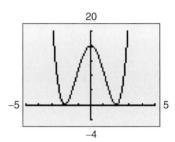

In Exercises 19–24, use your knowledge of polynomial graphs, *not* a calculator, to match the given function with one of graphs a–f.

a.

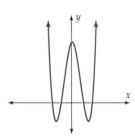

b.

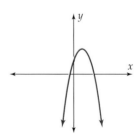

c.

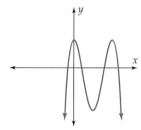

d.

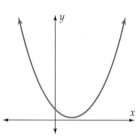

e.

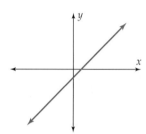

f.

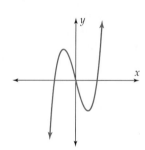

19. $f(x) = 2x - 3$ **20.** $g(x) = x^2 - 4x + 7$

21. $g(x) = x^3 - 4x$ **22.** $f(x) = x^4 - 5x^2 + 4$

23. $f(x) = -x^4 + 6x^3 - 9x^2 + 2$

24. $g(x) = -2x^2 + 3x + 1$

In Exercises 25–28, graph the function in the standard viewing window and explain why that graph cannot possibly be complete.

25. $f(x) = 0.01x^3 - 0.2x^2 - 0.4x + 7$

26. $g(x) = 0.01x^4 + 0.1x^3 - 0.8x^2 - 0.7x + 9$

27. $h(x) = 0.005x^4 - x^2 + 5$

28. $f(x) = 0.001x^5 - 0.01x^4 - 0.2x^3 + x^2 + x - 5$

In Exercises 29–34, find a single viewing window that shows a complete graph of the function.

29. $f(x) = x^3 + 8x^2 + 5x - 14$

30. $g(x) = x^3 - 3x^2 - 4x - 5$

31. $g(x) = -x^4 - 3x^3 + 24x^2 + 80x + 15$

32. $f(x) = x^4 - 10x^3 + 35x^2 - 50x + 24$

33. $f(x) = 2x^5 - 3.5x^4 - 10x^3 + 5x^2 + 12x + 6$

34. $g(x) = x^5 + 8x^4 + 20x^3 + 9x^2 - 27x - 7$

In Exercises 35–40, find a complete graph of the function and list the viewing window(s) that show(s) this graph.

35. $f(x) = 0.1x^5 + 3x^4 - 4x^3 - 11x^2 + 3x + 2$

36. $g(x) = x^4 - 48x^3 - 101x^2 + 49x + 50$

37. $g(x) = 0.03x^3 - 1.5x^2 - 200x + 5$

38. $f(x) = 0.25x^6 + 0.25x^5 - 35x^4 - 7x^3 + 823x^2 + 25x - 2750$

39. $g(x) = 2x^3 - 0.33x^2 - 0.006x + 5$

40. $f(x) = 0.3x^5 + 2x^4 - 7x^3 + 2x^2$

41. a. Explain why the graph of a cubic polynomial function has either two local extrema or none at all. *Hint:* If it had only one, what would the graph look like when $|x|$ is very large?

b. Explain why the general shape of the graph of a cubic polynomial function must be one of the following.

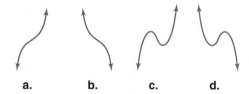

a.   **b.**   **c.**   **d.**

42. The figure shows an incomplete graph of an even polynomial function f of fourth degree. (Even functions were defined in *Excursion* 3.4.A.)
a. Find the zeros of f.
b. Explain why
$$f(x) = k(x - a)(x - b)(x - c)(x - d)$$
where a, b, c, d are the zeros of f.

c. Experiment with your calculator to find the value of k that produces the graph in the figure.
d. Find all local extrema of f.
e. List the approximate intervals on which f is increasing and those on which it is decreasing.

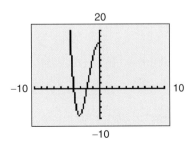

43. A complete graph of a polynomial function g is shown below.
a. Is the degree of $g(x)$ even or odd?
b. Is the leading coefficient of $g(x)$ positive or negative?
c. What are the real zeros of $g(x)$?
d. What is the smallest possible degree of $g(x)$?

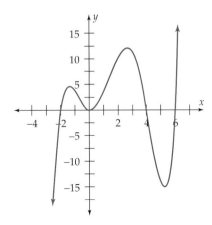

44. Do Exercise 43 for the polynomial function g whose complete graph is shown here.

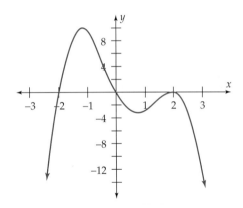

45. The figure below is a partial view of the graph of a cubic polynomial whose leading coefficient is negative. Which of the patterns shown in Exercise 41 does this graph have?

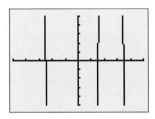

46. The figure below is a partial view of the graph of a fourth-degree polynomial. Sketch the general shape of the graph and state whether the leading coefficient is positive or negative.

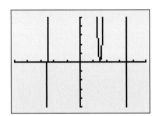

In Exercises 47–56, sketch a complete graph of the function. Label each x-intercept and the coordinates of each local extremum; find intercepts and coordinates exactly when possible, otherwise approximate them.

47. $f(x) = x^3 - 3x^2 + 4$ **48.** $g(x) = 4x - \dfrac{4x^3}{3}$

49. $h(x) = 0.25x^4 - 2x^3 + 4x^2$

50. $f(x) = 0.25x^4 - \dfrac{2x^3}{3}$

51. $g(x) = 3x^3 - 18.5x^2 - 4.5x - 45$

52. $h(x) = 2x^3 + x^2 - 4x - 2$

53. $f(x) = x^5 - 3x^3 + x + 1$

54. $g(x) = 0.25x^4 - x^2 + 0.5$

55. $h(x) = 8x^4 + 22.8x^3 - 50.6x^2 - 94.8x + 138.6$

56. $f(x) = 32x^6 - 48x^4 + 18x^2 - 1$

57. *Critical Thinking*
a. Graph $g(x) = 0.01x^3 - 0.06x^2 + 0.12x + 3.92$ in the viewing window with $-3 \le x \le 3$ and $0 \le y \le 6$ and verify that the graph appears to coincide with the horizontal line $y = 4$ between

$x = 1$ and $x = 3$. In other words, it appears that every x with $1 \le x \le 3$ is a solution of the equation

$$0.01x^3 - 0.06x^2 + 0.12x + 3.92 = 4.$$

Explain why this is impossible. Conclude that the actual graph is not horizontal between $x = 1$ and $x = 3$.

b. Use the trace feature to verify that the graph is actually rising from left to right between $x = 1$ and $x = 3$. Find a viewing window that shows this.

c. Show that it is not possible for the graph of a polynomial $f(x)$ to contain a horizontal segment. *Hint:* A horizontal line segment is part of the horizontal line $y = k$ for some constant k. Adapt the argument in part **a**, which is the case $k = 4$.

58. *Critical Thinking*
a. Let $f(x)$ be a polynomial of odd degree. Explain why $f(x)$ must have at least one real zero. *Hint:* Why must the graph of f cross the x-axis, and what does this mean?

b. Let $g(x)$ be a polynomial of even degree, with a negative leading coefficient and a positive constant term. Explain why $g(x)$ must have at least one positive and at least one negative zero.

59. *Critical Thinking* The graph of

$$f(x) = (x + 18)(x^2 - 20)(x - 2)^2(x - 10)$$

has x-intercepts at each of its zeros, that is, at $x = -18, \pm\sqrt{20} \approx \pm4.472, 2,$ and 10. It is also true that $f(x)$ has a relative minimum at $x = 2$.

a. Draw the x-axis and mark the zeros of $f(x)$. Then use the fact that $f(x)$ has degree 6 (Why?) to sketch the general shape of the graph, as was done for cubics in Exercise 41.

b. Now graph $f(x)$ in the standard viewing window. Does the graph resemble your sketch? Does it even show all the x-intercepts between -10 and 10?

c. Graph $f(x)$ in the viewing window with $-19 \le x \le 11$ and $-10 \le y \le 10$. Does this window include all the x-intercepts, as it should?

d. List viewing windows that give a complete graph of $f(x)$.

Excursion: Polynomial Models

Objectives

- Fit a polynomial model to data

Linear regression was used in Section 1.5 to construct a linear function that modeled a set of data points. When the scatter plot of the data points looks more like a higher degree polynomial graph than a straight line, similar least squares regression procedures are available on most calculators for constructing quadratic, cubic, and quartic polynomial functions to model the data.

Example 1   **A Polynomial Model**

The following data, which is based on statistics from the Department of Health and Human Services, gives the *cumulative* number of reported cases of AIDS in the United States from 1982 through 2000. Find a quadratic, a cubic, and a quartic regression equation and determine which equation best models the data.

Year	Cases	Year	Cases	Year	Cases
1982	1563	1991	232,383	1996	595,559
1984	10,845	1992	278,189	1997	652,439
1986	41,662	1993	380,601	1998	698,527
1988	105,489	1994	457,789	1999	743,418
1990	188,872	1995	528,421	2000	784,518

Solution

Let $x = 0$ correspond to 1980 and plot the data points (2, 1563), (4, 10845), etc., to obtain the scatter plot shown in Figure 4.3.A-1a. The points are not in a straight line, but could be part of a polynomial graph of degree 2 or more.

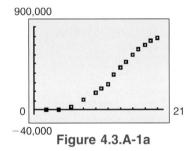

Figure 4.3.A-1a

Using the same procedure as for linear regression, find a quadratic, a cubic, and a quartic regression equation for the data. See the Technology Tip in the margin on this page for the specific calculator procedure needed. The polynomial functions shown below have rounded coefficients, but the graph in Figure 4.3.A-1b shows the data points along with the quadratic regression equation and was produced using full coefficients.

$f(x) = 1758.0x^2 + 9893.3x - 59,024.3$ *Quadratic*

$g(x) = -219.18x^3 + 9111.66x^2 - 59,991.75x + 103,255.32$ *Cubic*

$h(x) = -20.29x^4 + 681.94x^3 - 4318.57x^2 + 15,550.81x - 17,877.25$ *Quartic*

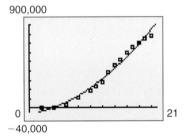

Figure 4.3.A-1b

The graphs of f, g, and h are virtually identical in the viewing window shown. Although any one of f, g, or h provides a reasonable model for the given data, knowledge of polynomial graphs suggests that the cubic and quartic models, should not be used for predicting future results. As x gets larger, the graphs of g and h will resemble respectively those of $y = -219.2x^3$ and $y = -20.3x^4$, which turn downward. However, the cumulative number of cases cannot decrease because even when there are no new cases, the cumulative total stays the same.

Graphing Exploration ●

Graph the functions f, g, and h in the window with $0 \le x \le 27$ and $0 \le y \le 1,800,000$. In this window, can you distinguish the graphs of f and g? Assuming no medical breakthroughs or changes in the current social situation, does the graph of f seem to be a plausible model for the next few years? What about the graph of g?

Example 2   **Estimating Data Values**

The population of San Francisco in selected years is given in the table.

Year	1950	1960	1970	1980	1990	2000
Population	775,357	740,316	715,674	678,974	723,959	776,733

[*Source: U.S. Census Bureau*]

Let $x = 0$ correspond to 1950. Find a polynomial regression model that is a reasonably good fit and estimate the population of San Francisco in 1995 and in 2004.

900,000

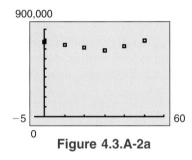

−5   60
0
Figure 4.3.A-2a

Solution

The scatter plot of the data shown in Figure 4.3.A-2a suggests a parabola. However, the data points do not climb quite so steeply in the later years, so a higher-degree polynomial graph might fit the data better. The quadratic, cubic, and quartic regression models are shown below.

$f(x) \approx 128.14x^2 - 6632.39x + 783{,}517.18$ *Quadratic*

$g(x) \approx 2.48x^3 - 58.10x^2 - 3230.49x + 776{,}067.76$ *Cubic*

$h(x) \approx -0.11x^4 + 13.20x^3 - 387.24x^2 - 168.65x + 774{,}230.65$ *Quartic*

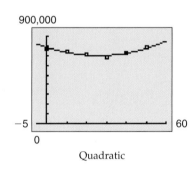

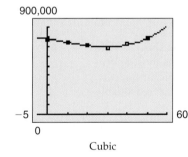

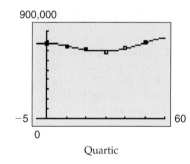

Quadratic   Cubic   Quartic

Figure 4.3.A-2b

The quartic appears to be the best fitting function. Use h to estimate the population in 1995 and 2004 by finding $h(45)$ and $h(54)$.

$$h(45) \approx 745{,}843.98 \quad \text{and} \quad h(54) \approx 803{,}155.18$$

That is, the estimated population of San Francisco in 1995 was approximately 745,844 and the estimated population of San Francisco in 2004 was approximately 803,155. ∎

In Example 2, a model may not be accurate when applied outside the range of points used to construct it. For instance, $f(-174) \approx 5{,}817{,}115$, suggesting that the population of San Francisco in 1776 was about 5,817,115.

NOTE The following table lists the minimum number of data points required for polynomial regression. In each case, the minimum number of data points required is the number of coefficients in the polynomial function modeling the data. If you have exactly the required minimum number of data points, no two of them can have the same first coordinate.

Model	Minimum number of data points
Quadratic Regression	3
Cubic Regression	4
Quartic Regression	5

When using the minimum number of data points, the polynomial regression function will pass through all the data points and will fit exactly. When using more than the minimum number of data points required, the fit will generally be approximate rather than exact.

Exercises 4.3.A

In Exercises 1–4, a scatter plot of data is shown. State the type of polynomial model that seems most appropriate for the data (linear, quadratic, cubic, or quartic). If none of them is likely to provide a reasonable model, say so.

1.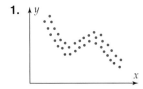

2.

3.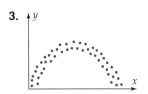

4.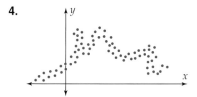

5. The table, which is based on the United States FBI Uniform Crime Report, shows the rate of property crimes per 100,000 population.

Year	Crimes	Year	Crimes
1982	5032.5	1994	4660.0
1984	4492.1	1996	4450.1
1986	4862.6	1997	4318.7
1988	5027.1	1998	4051.8
1990	5088.5	1999	3743.6
1992	4902.7	2000	3617.9

a. Use cubic regression to find a polynomial function that models this data, with $x = 0$ corresponding to 1980.
b. According to this model, what was the property crime rate in 1987 and 1995?

c. The actual crime rate was about 3698 in 2001. What does the model predict?

d. Is this model a reasonable one?

6. The table, which is based on the U.S. National Center for Educational Statistics, shows actual and projected enrollment (in millions) in public high schools in selected years.

Year	Enrollment	Year	Enrollment
1975	14.3	1995	12.5
1980	13.2	2000	13.5
1985	12.4	2005	14.4
1990	11.3	2010	14.1

a. Use quartic regression to find a polynomial function that models this data, with $x = 0$ corresponding to 1975.

b. According to this model, what was the enrollment in 1998 and 1999?

c. According to the model, in what year between 1975 and 2000 was enrollment at its lowest level?

d. Does this estimate appear to be accurate?

7. The table shows the air temperature at various times during a spring day in Gainesville, Florida.

Time	Temp (F°)	Time	Temp (F°)
6 a.m.	52	1 p.m.	82
7 a.m.	56	2 p.m.	86
8 a.m.	61	3 p.m.	85
9 a.m.	67	4 p.m.	83
10 a.m.	72	5 p.m.	78
11 a.m.	77	6 p.m.	72
noon	80		

a. Sketch a scatter plot of the data, with $x = 0$ corresponding to midnight.

b. Find a quadratic polynomial model for the data.

c. What is the predicted temperature for noon? for 9 a.m.? for 2 p.m.?

8. The table, which is based on data from the Association of Departments of Foreign Languages, shows the fall enrollment (in thousands) in college level Spanish classes.

Year	Enrollment	Year	Enrollment
1970	389.2	1986	411.3
1974	362.2	1990	533.9
1977	376.7	1995	606.3
1980	379.4	1998	656.6
1983	386.2		

a. Sketch a scatter plot of the data, with $x = 0$ corresponding to 1970.

b. Find a cubic polynomial model for this data.

Use the following table for Exercises 9–10. It shows the median income of U.S. households in 1999 dollars.

Year	Median Income	Year	Median Income
1985	$36,568	1993	$36,019
1987	38,220	1995	37,251
1989	38,836	1997	38,411
1991	36,850	1999	40,816

[*Source: U.S. Census Bureau*]

9. a. Sketch a scatter plot of the data from 1985 to 1999, with $x = 0$ corresponding to 1985.

b. Decide whether a quadratic or quartic model seems more appropriate.

c. Find an appropriate polynomial model.

d. Use the model to predict the median income in 2002.

e. Does this model seem reasonable after 2002?

10. a. Sketch a scatter plot of the data from 1989 to 1999, with $x = 0$ corresponding to 1989.

b. Find both a cubic and a quartic model for this data.

c. Is there any significant difference between the models from 1989 to 1999? What about from 1999 to 2005?

d. According to these models, when will the median income reach $45,000?

11. The table shows the U.S. public debt per person, in dollars, in selected years.

Year	Debt	Year	Debt
1981	$4,338	1993	$17,105
1983	5,870	1995	18,930
1985	7,598	1997	20,026
1987	9,615	1999	20,746
1989	11,545	2001	20,353
1991	14,436		

[*Source: U.S. Department of Treasury, Bureau of Public Debt*]

a. Sketch a scatter plot of the data with $x = 0$ corresponding to 1980.

b. Find a quartic model for the data.

c. Use the model to estimate the public debt per person in 1996. How does your estimate compare with the actual figure of $19,805?

12. The table shows the total advertising expenditures, in billions of dollars, in selected years.

Year	Expenditures	Year	Expenditures
1990	$129.59	1996	$175.23
1992	132.65	1998	201.59
1994	151.68	2000	236.33

[*Source: Statistical abstract of the United States 2001*]

a. Sketch a scatter plot of the data with $x = 0$ corresponding to 1990.

b. Find a quadratic model for the data.

c. Use the model to estimate expenditures in 1995 and 2002.

d. If this model remains accurate, when will expenditures reach $350 billion?

4.4

Rational Functions

Objectives

- Find the domain of a rational function

- Find intercepts, vertical asymptotes, and horizontal asymptotes

- Identify holes

- Describe end behavior

- Sketch complete graphs

Recall that a polynomial is an algebraic expression that can be written as

$$a_n x^n + a_{n-1}x^{n-1} + \cdots + a_2 x^2 + a_1 x + a_0$$

where n is a nonnegative integer.

A **rational function** is a function whose rule is the quotient of two polynomials, such as

$$f(x) = \frac{1}{x} \qquad t(x) = \frac{4x - 3}{2x + 1} \qquad k(x) = \frac{2x^3 + 5x + 2}{x^2 - 7x + 6}$$

Although a polynomial function is defined for every real number x, a rational function is defined only when its denominator is nonzero.

Domain of Rational Functions

> The domain of a rational function is the set of all real numbers that are *not* zeros of its denominator.

Example 1 The Domain of a Rational Function

Find the domain of each rational function.

a. $f(x) = \dfrac{1}{x^2}$

b. $g(x) = \dfrac{x^2 + 3x + 1}{x^2 - x - 6}$

Solution

a. The domain of $f(x) = \dfrac{1}{x^2}$ is the set of all real numbers except $x = 0$, because the denominator is 0 when $x = 0$, making the fraction undefined.

b. The domain of $g(x) = \dfrac{x^2 + 3x + 1}{x^2 - x - 6}$ is the set of all real numbers except the solutions of $x^2 - x - 6 = 0$. Because $x^2 - x - 6$ factors into $(x + 2)(x - 3)$, the solutions to $x^2 - x - 6 = 0$ are $x = -2$ and $x = 3$. Therefore, the domain of g is the set of all real numbers except $x = -2$ and $x = 3$.

Properties of Rational Graphs

Because calculators often do a poor job of graphing rational functions, the emphasis in this section is on the algebraic analysis of rational functions. Such analysis should enable you to interpret misleading screen images.

Intercepts

As with any function, the y-intercept of the graph of a rational function f occurs at $f(0)$, provided that f is defined at $x = 0$. The x-intercepts of the graph of a rational function occur when its numerator is 0 and its denominator is nonzero.

Intercepts of Rational Functions

> If f has a y-intercept, it occurs at $f(0)$.
>
> The x-intercepts of the graph of a rational function occur at the numbers that
>
> • are zeros of the numerator
> • are *not* zeros of the denominator

Locating the intercepts can help you determine if you correctly entered the parentheses when graphing a rational function on a graphing calculator.

Example 2 Intercepts of a Rational Graph

Find the intercepts of $f(x) = \dfrac{x^2 - x - 2}{x - 1}$.

Solution

The y-intercept is $f(0) = \dfrac{0^2 - 0 - 2}{0 - 1} = \dfrac{-2}{-1} = 2$.

The x-intercepts are solutions of $x^2 - x - 2 = 0$ that are not solutions of $x - 1 = 0$. Solutions of $x^2 - x - 2 = 0$ can be found by factoring.

$$x^2 - x - 2 = 0$$
$$(x + 1)(x - 2) = 0$$
$$x = -1 \quad \text{or} \quad x = 2.$$

Neither -1 nor 2 is a solution of $x - 1 = 0$, so both are x-intercepts of the graph of f, as shown in Figure 4.4-1.

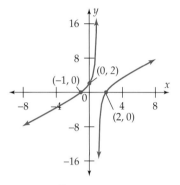

Figure 4.4-1

Continuity

There are breaks in the graph of a rational function wherever the function is not defined, that is, at the zeros of the denominator. Except for breaks, the graph is a continuous unbroken curve. Additionally, the graph has no sharp corners.

Vertical Asymptotes

Unlike polynomial functions, a rational function has breaks in its graph at all points where the function is not defined. Vertical asymptotes occur at every number that is a zero of the denominator but not of the numerator. The key to understanding the behavior of a rational function near these asymptotes is a fact from arithmetic.

The Big-Little Concept

If c is a number far from 0, then $\dfrac{1}{c}$ is a number close to 0.

If c is close to 0, then $\dfrac{1}{c}$ is far from 0.

In less precise, but more suggestive terms

$$\frac{1}{big} = little \quad \text{and} \quad \frac{1}{little} = big$$

For example, 5000 is big and $\dfrac{1}{5000}$ is little. Similarly, $\dfrac{-1}{1000}$ is little and

$\dfrac{1}{\frac{-1}{1000}} = -1000$ is big. Note that even though -1000 is negative, it is far

from zero and therefore is large in absolute value. The role played by the Big-Little Concept when graphing rational functions is illustrated in Example 3.

Example 3   A Rational Function Near a Vertical Asymptote

Without using a calculator, describe the graph of $f(x) = \dfrac{x+1}{2x-4}$ near $x = 2$. Then sketch the graph for values near $x = 2$.

Solution

The function is not defined at $x = 2$ because the denominator is 0 there. When x is greater than 2 but very close to 2,

- The numerator, $x + 1$, is very close to $2 + 1 = 3$.
- The denominator, $2x - 4$, is a positive number very close to $2(2) - 4 = 0$.

By the Big-Little Concept,

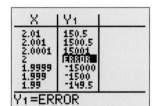

Figure 4.4-2a

$$f(x) = \frac{x+1}{2x-4} = \frac{3}{little} = 3 \cdot \frac{1}{little} = 3(big) = very\ big$$

This fact can be confirmed by a table of values for $f(x)$ near $x = 2$ when $x = 2.01, 2.001, 2.0001$, etc., as shown in Figure 4.4-2a. In graphical terms, the points with x-coordinates slightly greater than 2 have very large y-coordinates, so the graph shoots upward just to the right of $x = 2$. That is,

f increases without bound as x approaches 2 from the right.

A similar analysis when x is less than 2 but very close to 2 shows that the numerator, $x + 1$, is very close to 3 and the denominator is negative and very close to 0. Using the Big-Little Concept, the quotient is a negative number far from 0. As x approaches 2 from values less than 2, the quotient becomes a larger and larger negative number. Therefore, the graph of f shoots downward just to left of $x = 2$. That is,

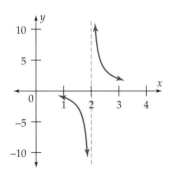

Figure 4.4-2b

f decreases without bound as x approaches 2 from the left.

The portion of the graph of f near $x = 2$ is shown in Figure 4.4–2b. ∎

The dashed vertical line in Figure 4.4-2b is included for easier visualization, but it is *not* part of the graph. Such a line is called a **vertical asymptote** of the graph. The graph approaches a vertical asymptote very closely, but never touches or crosses it because the function is not defined at that value of x.

All rational functions have vertical asymptotes at values that are zeros of their denominators but not zeros of their numerators.

Vertical Asymptotes

> A rational function has a vertical asymptote at $x = c$, provided
> - c is a zero of the denominator
> - c is *not* a zero of the numerator

Near a vertical asymptote, the graph of a rational fraction may look like the graph in Figure 4.4-2b, or like one of the graphs in Figure 4.4-3.

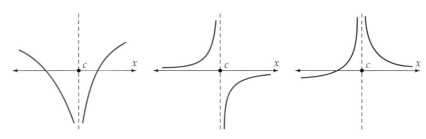

vertical asymptotes at $x = c$

Figure 4.4-3

Holes

When a number c is a zero of both the numerator and denominator of a rational function, the function might have a vertical asymptote at $x = c$, or it might behave differently.

You have often cancelled factors to reduce fractions.

$$\frac{x^2 - 4}{x - 2} = \frac{(x + 2)(x - 2)}{x - 2} = x + 2$$

But the functions

$$p(x) = \frac{x^2 - 4}{x - 2} \qquad \text{and} \qquad q(x) = x + 2$$

are *not* the same, because when $x = 2$

$$p(2) = \frac{2^2 - 4}{2 - 2} = \frac{0}{0}, \text{ which is not defined, but}$$

$$q(x) = 2 + 2 = 4.$$

For any number other than 2, the two functions have the same values, and hence, the same graphs. The graph of $q(x) = x + 2$ is a straight line that includes the point (2, 4), as shown in Figure 4.4-4a. The graph of $p(x)$ is the same straight line, but with the point (2, 4) omitted. That is, there is a **hole** in the graph of p at $x = 2$ because p is not defined there. The graph of p is shown in Figure 4.4-4b.

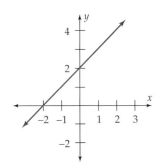

Figure 4.4-4a

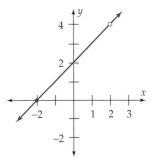

Figure 4.4-4b

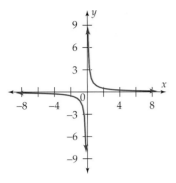

Figure 4.4-5

The graph of $g(x) = \dfrac{x^2}{x^3}$, shown in Figure 4.4-5, is the same as the graph of $f(x) = \dfrac{1}{x}$. At $x = 0$ neither function is defined. There is a vertical asymptote rather than a hole at $x = 0$. Note that the vertical asymptote occurs at $x = 0$, which is a zero of multiplicity 2 in the numerator, but of larger multiplicity 3 in the denominator.

Holes

Let $f(x) = \dfrac{g(x)}{h(x)}$ be a rational function and let d denote a zero of both g and h.

- **If the multiplicity of d as a zero of g is greater than or equal to its multiplicity as a zero of h, then the graph of f has a hole at $x = d$.**
- **Otherwise, the graph has a vertical asymptote at $x = d$.**

Accurate Rational Function Graphs

Getting an accurate graph of a rational function on a calculator often depends on choosing an appropriate viewing window. For example, the following are graphs of $f(x) = \dfrac{x + 1}{2x - 4}$ in different viewing windows.

Technology Tip

To avoid erroneous vertical lines, use a window with a vertical asymptote in the center of the screen. In Figure 4.4-6b, the asymptote at $x = 2$ is halfway between -8 and 12. See the Technology Appendix for further information.

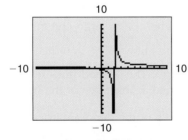

Figure 4.4-6a

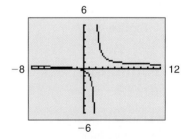

Figure 4.4-6b

The vertical segment shown in Figure 4.4-6a is *not* a vertical asymptote. It is a result of the calculator evaluating f just to the left of $x = 2$ and just to the right of $x = 2$, but not at $x = 2$, and then erroneously connecting these points with a near vertical segment that looks like an asymptote. In the accurate graph shown in Figure 4.4-6b, the calculator attempted to plot a point with $x = 2$ and when it found that $f(2)$ was not defined, skipped a pixel and did not join the points on either side of the one skipped.

A calculator graph may also fail to show holes in graphs that should have them. Even if a window is chosen so that the graph skips a pixel where the hole should be, the hole may be difficult to see.

End Behavior

As with polynomials, the behavior of a rational function when $|x|$ is large is called its **end behavior.** Known facts about the end behavior of polynomial functions make it easy to determine the end behavior of rational functions in which the degree of the numerator is less than or equal to the degree of the denominator.

Example 4   **End Behavior of Rational Functions**

List the vertical asymptotes and describe the end behavior of the following functions. Then sketch each graph.

a. $f(x) = \dfrac{3x - 6}{5 - 2x}$ **b.** $g(x) = \dfrac{x}{x^2 - 4}$ **c.** $h(x) = \dfrac{2x^3 - x}{x^3 + 1}$

Solution

a. The zero of the denominator of $f(x) = \dfrac{3x - 6}{5 - 2x}$ is $\dfrac{5}{2}$ and it is not a

zero of the numerator. So the vertical asymptote occurs at $x = \dfrac{5}{2}$.

When $|x|$ is large, a polynomial function behaves like its highest degree term, as shown in Section 4.3. The highest degree term of the numerator of f is $3x$ and the highest degree term of the denominator is $-2x$. Therefore, when $|x|$ is large, the function reduces to $-\dfrac{3}{2}$.

$$f(x) = \frac{3x - 6}{5 - 2x} = \frac{3x - 6}{-2x + 5} \approx \frac{3x}{-2x} = -\frac{3}{2}$$

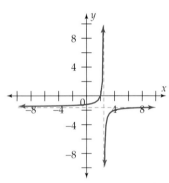

Figure 4.4-7

Thus, when $|x|$ is large, the graph of f gets very close to the horizontal line $y = -\dfrac{3}{2}$, which is called a **horizontal asymptote** of the graph. The dashed lines in Figure 4.4-7 indicate the vertical and horizontal asymptotes of the graph.

b. The zeros of the denominator of $g(x) = \dfrac{x}{x^2 - 4}$ are ± 2 and neither is a zero of the numerator. So the graph has vertical asymptotes at $x = -2$ and at $x = 2$.

When $|x|$ is large,

$$g(x) = \frac{x}{x^2 - 4} \approx \frac{x}{x^2} = \frac{1}{x}$$

and $\dfrac{1}{x}$ is very close to 0 by the Big-Little Concept. Therefore, the graph of g approaches the horizontal line $y = 0$ (the x-axis) when $|x|$ is large and this line is a horizontal asymptote of the graph, as shown in Figure 4.4-8.

Technology Tip

When the vertical asymptotes of a rational function occur at numbers such as $-2.1, -2, -1.9, \ldots, 2.9, 3$, etc., a decimal window normally produces an accurate graph because the calculator actually evaluates the function at the asymptotes, finds that it is undefined, and skips a pixel.

CAUTION

Unlike a vertical asymptote that is never crossed by a graph, a graph may cross a horizontal or oblique asymptote at some values of $|x|$.

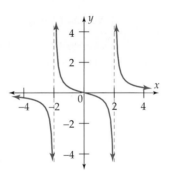

Figure 4.4-8

c. The only real zero of the denominator of $h(x) = \dfrac{2x^3 - x}{x^3 + 1}$ is $x = -1$, which is not a zero of the numerator. So, the graph has a vertical asymptote at $x = -1$.

When $|x|$ is large,

$$h(x) = \frac{2x^3 - x}{x^3 + 1} \approx \frac{2x^3}{x^3} = \frac{2}{1} = 2$$

Therefore, the graph of h has a horizontal asymptote at $y = 2$, as shown in Figure 4.4-9. ∎

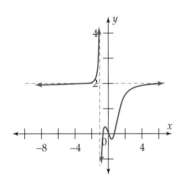

Figure 4.4-9

The function in Example **4b** illustrates a useful fact. When the degree of the numerator is less than the degree of the denominator of a rational function, the x-axis is the horizontal asymptote of the graph.

When the numerator and denominator have the same degree, as in Examples **4a** and **4c**, the horizontal asymptote is determined by the leading coefficients of the numerator and denominator:

Function	Horizontal asymptote
$f(x) = \dfrac{3x - 6}{-2x + 5}$	$y = -\dfrac{3}{2}$
$h(x) = \dfrac{2x^3 - x}{x^3 + 1}$	$y = \dfrac{2}{1} = 2$

Other Asymptotes

When the degree of the numerator of a rational function is greater than the degree of its denominator, the graph will not have a horizontal asymptote. To determine the end behavior in this case, the Division Algorithm must be used.

Example 5   A Slant Asymptote

Describe the end behavior of the graph of $f(x) = \dfrac{x^2 - x - 2}{x - 5}$.

Solution

Use synthetic or long division to divide the denominator into the numerator, and rewrite the rational expression by using the Division Algorithm.

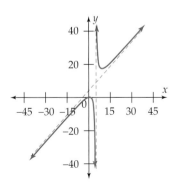

Figure 4.4-10

Dividend = Divisor Quotient + Remainder

$$x^2 - x - 2 = (x - 5)(x + 4) + 18$$

$$f(x) = \frac{x^2 - x - 2}{x - 5}$$

$$= \frac{(x - 5)(x + 4) + 18}{x - 5}$$

$$= \frac{(x - 5)(x + 4)}{x - 5} + \frac{18}{x - 5}$$

$$= (x + 4) + \frac{18}{x - 5}$$

When $|x|$ is large, $x - 5$ is also large, and by the Big-Little Concept $\frac{18}{x - 5}$ is very close to 0. Therefore, $f(x) \approx x + 4$, and the graph of f approaches the line $y = x + 4$ as $|x|$ gets large (see Figure 4.4-10). The line $y = x + 4$ is called a **slant** or **oblique asymptote** of the graph. Note that $x + 4$ is the quotient without the remainder in the division of the numerator by the denominator.

Example 6   A Parabolic Asymptote

Describe the end behavior of the graph of $f(x) = \dfrac{x^3 + 3x^2 + x + 1}{x - 1}$.

Solution

Divide the denominator into the numerator and rewrite the function.

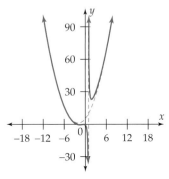

Figure 4.4-11

$$Quotient + \frac{Remainder}{Divisor}$$

$$f(x) = \frac{x^3 + 3x^2 + x + 1}{x - 1} = (x^2 + 4x + 5) + \frac{6}{x - 1}$$

When $|x|$ is large, so is $x - 1$ and by the Big-Little Concept $\frac{6}{x - 1}$ is very close to 0. Therefore, $f(x) \approx x^2 + 4x + 5$ for large values of $|x|$. The graph of f approaches the parabola $y = x^2 + 4x + 5$, as shown in Figure 4.4-11. The curve $y = x^2 + 4x + 5$ is called a **parabolic asymptote.** Note that $x^2 + 4x + 5$ is the quotient in the division.

End Behavior of Rational Functions

Let $f(x) = \dfrac{ax^n + \cdots}{cx^k + \cdots}$ be a rational function whose numerator has degree n and whose denominator has degree k.

- If $n < k$, then the x-axis is a horizontal asymptote.

- If $n = k$, then the line $y = \dfrac{a}{c}$ is a horizontal asymptote.

- If $n > k$, then the quotient polynomial when the numerator is divided by the denominator is the asymptote that describes the end behavior of the graph.

Notice that when the degree of the numerator and the denominator are the same, the horizontal asymptote is the horizontal line determined by the quotient of the leading coefficients of the numerator and denominator.

Graphs of Rational Functions

The facts presented in this section can be used in conjunction with a calculator to find accurate, complete graphs of rational functions.

Graphing Rational Functions

1. Analyze the function algebraically to determine its vertical asymptotes, holes, and intercepts.

2. Determine the end behavior of the graph.

   If the degree of the numerator is less than or equal to the degree of the denominator, find the horizontal asymptote by using the facts in the box above.

   Otherwise, divide the numerator by the denominator. The quotient is the nonvertical asymptote of the graph.

3. Use the preceding information to select an appropriate viewing window, or windows, to interpret the calculator's version of the graph, and display a complete graph of the function.

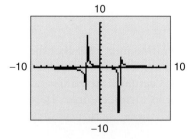

Figure 4.4-12a

Example 7   A Complete Graph of a Rational Function

Find a complete graph of $f(x) = \dfrac{x - 1}{x^2 - x - 6}$.

Solution

The graph of f is shown in Figure 4.4-12a. It is hard to determine whether or not the graph is complete, so analyze the function algebraically.

Begin by writing the function in factored form. Then read off the relevant information.

$$f(x) = \frac{x-1}{x^2 - x - 6} = \frac{x-1}{(x+2)(x-3)}$$

Vertical Asymptotes: $x = -2$ and $x = 3$ *zeros of the denominator but not the numerator*

Intercepts:

y-intercept: $f(0) = \dfrac{0-1}{0^2 - 0 - 6} = \dfrac{1}{6}$

x-intercept: $x = 1$ *zero of numerator but not of denominator*

Horizontal Asymptote: $y = 0$ *degree of numerator is less than degree of denominator*

Interpreting the above information suggests that a complete graph of f looks similar to Figure 4.4-12b.

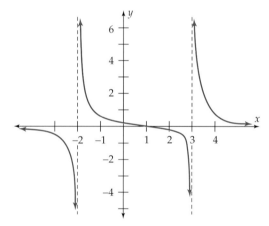

Figure 4.4-12b

Example 8   **A Complete Graph of a Rational Function**

Find a complete graph of $f(x) = \dfrac{x^3 - 2x^2 - 5x + 6}{x^2 + 3x + 2}$.

Solution

The denominator is easily factored. To factor the numerator, note that the only possible rational zeros of $x^3 - 2x^2 - 5x + 6$ are ±1, ±2, ±3, and ±6 by the Rational Zeros Test. Verify that $-2, 1$ and 3 actually are zeros and use the Factor Theorem to write the numerator in factored form. Then reduce the fraction.

Holes:

$$f(x) = \frac{x^3 - 2x^2 - 5x + 6}{x^2 + 3x + 2} = \frac{(x + 2)(x - 1)(x - 3)}{(x + 2)(x + 1)}$$

$$= \frac{(x - 1)(x - 3)}{x + 1}, \text{ where } x \neq -2.$$

Therefore, the graph of *f* is the same as the graph of

$$g(x) = \frac{(x - 1)(x - 3)}{x + 1} = \frac{x^2 - 4x + 3}{x + 1}$$

except there is a hole when $x = -2$. Because

$$g(-2) = \frac{(-2 - 1)(-2 - 3)}{-2 + 1} = \frac{(-3)(-5)}{-1} = -15,$$

the hole occurs at $(-2, -15)$.

Intercepts:

      y-intercept: $g(0) = \dfrac{(0 - 1)(0 - 3)}{0 + 1} = \dfrac{(-1)(-3)}{1} = 3$

      x-intercepts: The *x*-intercepts of *f* are the same as the *x*-intercepts of *g*. Solving $(x - 1)(x - 3) = 0$ yields $x = 1$ or $x = 3$.

Vertical Asymptote: The vertical asymptote is $x = -1$.

End Behavior: Dividing the numerator by the denominator produces a quotient of $x - 5$. Therefore, the slant asymptote that describes the end behavior of the function is the line $y = x - 5$.

The graph of *f* is shown in Figure 4.4-13.

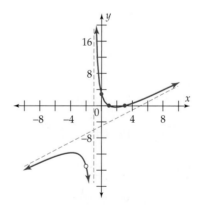

Figure 4.4-13

Exercises 4.4

In Exercises 1–6, find the domain of the function.

1. $f(x) = \dfrac{-3x}{2x + 5}$

2. $g(x) = \dfrac{x^3 + x + 1}{2x^2 - 5x - 3}$

3. $h(x) = \dfrac{6x - 5}{x^2 - 6x + 4}$

4. $g(x) = \dfrac{x^3 - x^2 - x - 1}{x^5 - 36x}$

5. $f(x) = \dfrac{x^5 - 2x^3 + 7}{x^3 - x^2 - 2x + 2}$

6. $h(x) = \dfrac{x^5 - 5}{x^4 + 12x^3 + 60x^2 + 50x - 125}$

In Exercises 7–12, use algebra to determine the location of the vertical asymptotes and holes in the graph of the function.

7. $f(x) = \dfrac{x^2 + 4}{x^2 - 5x - 6}$

8. $g(x) = \dfrac{x - 5}{x^3 + 7x^2 + 2x}$

9. $f(x) = \dfrac{x}{x^3 + 2x^2 + x}$

10. $g(x) = \dfrac{x}{x^3 + 5x}$

11. $f(x) = \dfrac{x^2 - 4x + 4}{(x + 2)(x - 2)^3}$

12. $h(x) = \dfrac{x - 3}{x^2 - x - 6}$

In Exercises 13–22, find the horizontal or other asymptote of the graph of the function when $|x|$ is large, and find a viewing window in which the ends of the graph are within 0.1 of this asymptote.

13. $f(x) = \dfrac{3x - 2}{x + 3}$

14. $g(x) = \dfrac{3x^2 + x}{2x^2 - 2x + 4}$

15. $h(x) = \dfrac{5 - x}{x - 2}$

16. $f(x) = \dfrac{4x^2 - 5}{2x^3 - 3x^2 + x}$

17. $g(x) = \dfrac{5x^3 - 8x^2 + 4}{2x^3 + 2x}$

18. $h(x) = \dfrac{8x^5 - 6x^3 + 2x - 1}{0.5x^5 + x^4 + 3x^2 + x}$

19. $f(x) = \dfrac{x^3 - 1}{x^2 - 4}$

20. $g(x) = \dfrac{x^3 - 4x^2 + 6x + 5}{x - 2}$

21. $h(x) = \dfrac{x^3 + 3x^2 - 4x + 1}{x + 4}$

22. $f(x) = \dfrac{x^3 + 3x^2 - 4x + 1}{x^2 - x}$

In Exercises 23–50, analyze the function algebraically: list its vertical asymptotes, holes, and horizontal asymptote. Then sketch a complete graph of the function.

23. $f(x) = \dfrac{1}{x + 5}$

24. $q(x) = \dfrac{-7}{x - 6}$

25. $k(x) = \dfrac{-3}{2x + 5}$

26. $g(x) = \dfrac{-4}{2 - x}$

27. $f(x) = \dfrac{3x}{x - 1}$

28. $p(x) = \dfrac{x - 2}{x}$

29. $f(x) = \dfrac{2 - x}{x - 3}$

30. $g(x) = \dfrac{3x - 2}{x + 3}$

31. $f(x) = \dfrac{1}{x(x + 1)^2}$

32. $g(x) = \dfrac{x}{2x^2 - 5x - 3}$

33. $f(x) = \dfrac{x - 3}{x^2 + x - 2}$

34. $g(x) = \dfrac{x + 2}{x^2 - 1}$

35. $h(x) = \dfrac{(x^2 + 6x + 5)(x + 5)}{(x + 5)^3(x - 1)}$

36. $f(x) = \dfrac{x^2 - 1}{x^3 - 2x^2 + x}$

37. $f(x) = \dfrac{-4x^2 + 1}{x^2}$

38. $k(x) = \dfrac{x^2 + 1}{x^2 - 1}$

39. $q(x) = \dfrac{x^2 + 2x}{x^2 - 4x - 5}$

40. $F(x) = \dfrac{x^2 + x}{x^2 - 2x + 4}$

41. $p(x) = \dfrac{(x + 3)(x - 3)}{(x - 5)(x + 4)(x + 3)}$

42. $p(x) = \dfrac{x^3 + 3x^2}{x^4 - 4x^2}$

43. $f(x) = \dfrac{x^2 - x - 6}{x - 2}$

44. $k(x) = \dfrac{x^2 + x - 2}{x}$

45. $Q(x) = \dfrac{4x^2 + 4x - 3}{2x - 5}$

46. $K(x) = \dfrac{3x^2 - 12x + 15}{3x + 6}$

47. $f(x) = \dfrac{x^3 - 2}{x - 1}$

48. $p(x) = \dfrac{x^3 + 8}{x + 1}$

49. $q(x) = \dfrac{x^3 - 1}{x - 2}$

50. $f(x) = \dfrac{x^4 - 1}{x^2}$

In Exercises 51–60, find a viewing window or windows that show(s) a complete graph of the function using asymptotes, intercepts, end behavior, and holes. Be alert for hidden behavior.

51. $f(x) = \dfrac{x^3 + 4x^2 - 5x}{(x^2 - 4)(x^2 - 9)}$

52. $g(x) = \dfrac{x^2 + x - 6}{x^3 - 19x + 30}$ **53.** $h(x) = \dfrac{2x^2 - x - 6}{x^3 + x^2 - 6x}$

54. $f(x) = \dfrac{x^3 - x + 1}{x^4 - 2x^3 - 2x^2 + x - 1}$

55. $f(x) = \dfrac{2x^4 - 3x^2 + 1}{3x^4 - x^2 + x - 1}$ **56.** $g(x) = \dfrac{x^4 + 2x^3}{x^5 - 25x^3}$

57. $h(x) = \dfrac{3x^2 + x - 4}{2x^2 - 5x}$ **58.** $f(x) = \dfrac{2x^2 - 1}{3x^3 + 2x + 1}$

59. $g(x) = \dfrac{x - 4}{2x^3 - 5x^2 - 4x + 12}$

60. $h(x) = \dfrac{x^2 - 9}{x^3 + 2x^2 - 23x - 60}$

In Exercises 61–66, find a viewing window or windows that show(s) a complete graph of the function—if possible, with no erroneous vertical line segments. Be alert for hidden behavior.

61. $f(x) = \dfrac{2x^2 + 5x + 2}{2x + 7}$ **62.** $g(x) = \dfrac{2x^3 + 1}{x^2 - 1}$

63. $h(x) = \dfrac{x^3 - 2x^2 + x - 2}{x^2 - 1}$

64. $f(x) = \dfrac{3x^3 - 11x - 1}{x^2 - 4}$

65. $g(x) = \dfrac{2x^4 + 7x^3 + 7x^2 + 2x}{x^3 - x + 50}$

66. $h(x) = \dfrac{2x^3 + 7x^2 - 4}{x^2 + 2x - 3}$

67. a. Graph $f(x) = \dfrac{1}{x}$ in the viewing window with $-6 \le x \le 6$ and $-6 \le y \le 6$.
  b. Without using a calculator, describe how the graph of $g(x) = \dfrac{2}{x}$ can be obtained from the graph of $f(x)$. *Hint:* $g(x) = 2f(x)$
  c. Without using a calculator, describe how the graphs of each of the following functions can be obtained from the graph of $f(x)$.

$$h(x) = \frac{1}{x} + 4 \qquad k(x) = \frac{1}{x - 3} \qquad t(x) = \frac{1}{x + 2}$$

  d. Without using a calculator, describe how the graph of $p(x) = \dfrac{2}{x - 3} + 4$ can be obtained from the graph of $f(x) = \dfrac{1}{x}$.
  e. Show that the function $p(x)$ of part **d** is a rational function by rewriting its rule as the quotient of two first-degree polynomials.
  f. If r, s, and t are constants, describe how the graph of $q(x) = \dfrac{r}{x + s} + t$ can be obtained from the graph of $f(x) = \dfrac{1}{x}$.
  g. Show that the function $q(x)$ of part **f** is a rational function by rewriting its rule as the quotient of two first-degree polynomials.

68. The graph of $f(x) = \dfrac{2x^3 - 2x^2 - x + 1}{3x^3 - 3x^2 + 2x - 1}$ has a vertical asymptote. Find a viewing window that demonstrates this fact.

69. a. Find the difference quotient of $f(x) = \dfrac{1}{x}$ and express it as a single fraction in lowest terms.
  b. Use the difference quotient in part **a** to determine the average rate of change of $f(x)$ as x changes from 2 to 2.1, from 2 to 2.01, and from 2 to 2.001. Estimate the instantaneous rate of change of $f(x)$ at $x = 2$.
  c. Use the different quotient in part **a** to determine the average rate of change of $f(x)$ as x changes from 3 to 3.1, from 3 to 3.01, and from 3 to 3.001. Estimate the instantaneous rate of change of $f(x)$ at $x = 3$.
  d. How are the estimated instantaneous rates of change of $f(x)$ at $x = 2$ and $x = 3$ related to the values of $g(x) = \dfrac{-1}{x^2}$ at $x = 2$ and $x = 3$?

70. Do Exercise 69 for the functions $f(x) = \dfrac{1}{x^2}$ and $g(x) = \dfrac{-2}{x^3}$.

71. a. When $x \ge 0$, what rational function has the same graph as $f(x) = \dfrac{x - 1}{|x| - 2}$? *Hint:* Use the definition of absolute value.
  b. When $x < 0$, what rational function has the same graph as $f(x) = \dfrac{x - 1}{|x| - 2}$? See the hint for part **a**.

c. Use parts **a** and **b** to explain why the graph of $f(x) = \dfrac{x - 1}{|x| - 2}$ has two vertical asymptotes. What are they? Confirm your answer by graphing the function.

72. The percentage c of a drug in a person's bloodstream t hours after its injection is approximated by $c(t) = \dfrac{5t}{4t^2 + 5}$.

   a. Approximately what percentage of the drug is in the person's bloodstream after four and a half hours?

   b. Graph the function c in an appropriate window for this situation.

   c. What is the horizontal asymptote of the graph? What does it tell you about the amount of the drug in the bloodstream?

   d. At what time is the percentage the highest? What is the percentage at that time?

73. A box with a square base and a volume of 1000 cubic inches is to be constructed. The material for the top and bottom of the box costs $3 per 100 square inches and the material for the sides costs $1.25 per 100 square inches.

   a. If x is the length of a side of the base, express the cost of constructing the box as a function of x.

   b. If the side of the base must be at least 6 inches long, for what value of x will the cost of the box be $20?

74. A truck traveling at a constant speed on a reasonably straight, level road burns fuel at the rate of $g(x)$ gallons per mile, where x is the speed of the truck in miles per hour and $g(x)$ is given by $g(x) = \dfrac{800 + x^2}{200x}$.

   a. If fuel costs $1.40 per gallon, find the rule of the cost function $c(x)$ that expresses the cost of fuel for a 500-mile trip as a function of the speed. *Hint:* $500 \cdot g(x)$ gallons of fuel are needed to go 500 miles. (Why?)

   b. What driving speed will make the cost of fuel for the trip $250?

   c. What driving speed will minimize the cost of fuel for the trip?

75. Pure alcohol is being added to 50 gallons of a coolant mixture that is 40% alcohol.

   a. Find the rule of the concentration function $c(x)$ that expresses the percentage of alcohol in the resulting mixture as a function of the number x of gallons of pure alcohol that are added. *Hint:* The final mixture contains $50 + x$ gallons.

(Why?) So $c(x)$ is the amount of alcohol in the final mixture divided by the total amount $50 + x$. How much alcohol is in the original 50-gallon mixture? How much is in the final mixture?

   b. How many gallons of pure alcohol should be added to produce a mixture that is at least 60% alcohol and no more than 80% alcohol?

   c. Determine algebraically the exact amount of pure alcohol that must be added to produce a mixture that is 70% alcohol.

76. A rectangular garden with an area of 250 square meters is to be located next to a building and fenced on three sides, with the building acting as a fence on the fourth side.

   a. If the side of the garden parallel to the building has length x meters, express the amount of fencing needed as a function of x.

   b. For what values of x will less than 60 meters of fencing be needed?

77. A certain company has fixed costs of $40,000 and variable costs of $2.60 per unit.

   a. Let x be the number of units produced. Find the rule of the average cost function. (The average cost is the cost of the units divided by the number of units.)

   b. Graph the average cost function in a window with $0 \leq x \leq 100{,}000$ and $0 \leq y \leq 20$.

   c. Find the horizontal asymptote of the average cost function. Explain what the asymptote means in this situation, that is, how low can the average cost possibly be?

78. Radioactive waste is stored in a cylindrical tank, whose exterior has radius r and height h as shown in the figure. The sides, top, and bottom of the tank are one foot thick and the tank has a volume of 150 cubic feet including top, bottom, and walls.

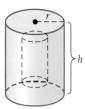

   a. Express the interior height h_1 (that is, the height of the storage area) as a function of h.

   b. Express the interior height as a function of r.

   c. Express the volume of the interior as a function of r.

   d. Explain why r must be greater than 1.

79. The relationship between the fixed focal length F of a camera, the distance u from the object being photographed to the lens, and the distance v from the lens to the film is given by $\dfrac{1}{F} = \dfrac{1}{u} + \dfrac{1}{v}$.

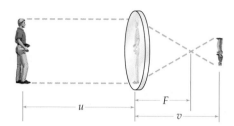

a. If the focal length is 50 mm, express v as a function of u.

b. What is the horizontal asymptote of the graph of the function in part **a**?

c. Graph the function in part **a** when 50 mm $< u <$ 35,000 mm.

d. When you focus the camera on an object, the distance between the lens and the film is changed. If the distance from the lens to the camera changes by less than 0.1 millimeter, the object will remain in focus. Explain why you have more latitude in focusing on distant objects than on very close ones.

80. The formula for the gravitational acceleration in units of meters per second squared of an object relative to the earth is

$$g(r) = \frac{3.987 \times 10^{14}}{(6.378 \times 10^6 + r)^2}$$

where r is the distance in meters above the earth's surface.

a. What is the gravitational acceleration at the earth's surface?

b. Graph the function $g(r)$ for $r \geq 0$.

c. Can you ever escape the pull of gravity? Does the graph have any r-intercepts?

Complex Numbers

Objectives

- Write complex numbers in standard form
- Perform arithmetic operations on complex numbers
- Find the conjugate of a complex number
- Simplify square roots of negative numbers
- Find all solutions of polynomial equations

If restricted to nonnegative numbers, you cannot solve the equation $x + 5 = 0$. Enlarging the number system to include negative integers makes it possible to find the solution to this equation. By enlarging the number system to include rational numbers, it is possible to solve equations that have no integer solution, such as $3x = 7$. Similarly, the equation $x^2 = 2$ has no rational solution, but $x = \sqrt{2}$ and $x = -\sqrt{2}$ are real number solutions. The idea of enlarging a number system to include solutions to equations that cannot be solved in a particular number system is a natural one.

Complex Numbers

Equations such as $x^2 = -1$ and $x^2 = -4$ have no solutions in the real number system because $\sqrt{-1}$ and $\sqrt{-4}$ are not real numbers. In order to solve such equations, that is, to find the square roots of negative numbers, the number system must be enlarged again. There is a number system, called the **complex number system,** with the desired properties.

Properties of the Complex Number System

1. **The complex number system contains all real numbers.**
2. **Addition, subtraction, multiplication, and division of complex numbers obey the same rules of arithmetic that hold in the real number system, with one exception:**

   the exponent laws hold for *integer* exponents, but not necessarily for fractional ones (see p. 297).

3. **The complex number system contains a number, denoted *i*, such that**
$$i^2 = -1.$$
4. **Every complex number can be written in the *standard form***
$$a + bi,$$
   where *a* and *b* are real numbers.
5. **$a + bi = c + di$ if and only if $a = c$ and $b = d$.**

Numbers of the form bi, where b is a real number, are called **imaginary numbers.** Sums of real and imaginary numbers, numbers of the form $a + bi$, are called **complex numbers.** For example,

$$5 + 2i \qquad 7 - 4i \qquad 18 + \frac{3}{2}i \qquad 3 - 12i$$

are all complex numbers.

Just as every integer is a rational number because it can be written as a fraction with denominator of 1, every real number a is a complex number because it can be written as $a + 0i$. Similarly, every imaginary number bi is a complex number because it can be written as $0 + bi$.

NOTE The mathematicians who invented the complex numbers in the seventeenth century were very uneasy about a number i such that $i^2 = -1$. Consequently, they called numbers of the form bi, where b is a real number and $i = \sqrt{-1}$, imaginary numbers.

The existence of imaginary numbers is as *real* as any of the familiar numbers that are called real numbers, such as $3, \frac{2}{3}$ or $-\sqrt{2}$.

Example 1 **Equating Two Complex Numbers**

Find x and y if $2x - 3i = -6 + 4yi$.

Solution

Property 5 of the Complex Number System states that two complex numbers $a + bi$ and $c + di$ are equal exactly when $a = c$ and $b = d$. So,

$$2x = -6 \qquad \text{and} \qquad -3 = 4y$$
$$x = -3 \qquad\qquad\qquad y = -\frac{3}{4}$$

Direct substitution verifies the solution.

$$2(-3) - 3i = -6 + 4\left(-\frac{3}{4}\right)i$$
$$-6 - 3i = -6 - 3i$$

Arithmetic of Complex Numbers

Because the usual laws of arithmetic hold, it is easy to add, subtract, and multiply complex numbers. As the following examples demonstrate,

all symbols can be treated as if they were real numbers, provided that i^2 is replaced by -1.

Example 2 **Adding, Subtracting, and Multiplying Complex Numbers**

Perform the indicated operation and write the result in the form $a + bi$.

a. $(1 + i) + (3 - 7i)$

b. $(4 + 3i) - (8 - 6i)$

c. $4i\left(2 + \dfrac{1}{2}i\right)$

d. $(2 + i)(3 - 4i)$

Solution

a. $(1 + i) + (3 - 7i) = 1 + i + 3 - 7i = (1 + 3) + (1 - 7)i = 4 - 6i$

b. $(4 + 3i) - (8 - 6i) = 4 + 3i - 8 + 6i = (4 - 8) + (3 + 6)i = -4 + 9i$

c. $4i\left(2 + \dfrac{1}{2}i\right) = 4i(2) + 4i\left(\dfrac{1}{2}i\right) = 8i + 2i^2 = 8i + 2(-1) = -2 + 8i$

d. $(2 + i)(3 - 4i) = 2(3 - 4i) + i(3 - 4i) = 6 - 8i + 3i - 4i^2$
$= 6 - 5i - 4(-1) = 6 + 4 - 5i = 10 - 5i$

The familiar multiplication patterns and exponent laws for integer exponents hold in the complex number system.

Example 3 **Products and Powers of Complex Numbers**

Perform the indicated operation and write the result in the form $a + bi$.

a. $(3 + 2i)(3 - 2i)$

b. $(4 + i)^2$

Solution

a. $(3 + 2i)(3 - 2i) = 3^2 - (2i)^2 = 9 - 4i^2 = 9 - 4(-1) = 9 + 4 = 13$

b. $(4 + i)^2 = 4^2 + 2(4)(i) + i^2 = 16 + 8i + i^2 = 16 + 8i - 1 = 15 + 8i$

Powers of *i*

Observe that

$$i^1 = i$$
$$i^2 = -1 \qquad \textit{Definition of i}$$
$$i^3 = i^2 \cdot i = -1 \cdot i = -i$$
$$i^4 = i^2 \cdot i^2 = (-1)(-1) = 1$$
$$i^5 = i^4 \cdot i = 1 \cdot i = i$$

The powers of i form a cycle. Any power of i must be one of four values: $i, -1, -i,$ or 1. To find higher powers of i, such as i^n, divide n by 4 and match the *remainder* to one of the powers listed above.

Example 4 Powers of *i*

Find i^{54}.

Solution

The remainder when 54 is divided by 4 is 2, so $i^{54} = i^2 = -1$.

NOTE The result of Example 4 can also be seen by rewriting i^{54} using exponent rules.

$$i^{54} = i^{52} \cdot i^2$$
$$= i^{4 \cdot 13} i^2$$
$$= (i^4)^{13} i^2$$
$$= 1^{13}(-1)$$
$$= -1.$$

Complex Conjugates

The **conjugate** of the complex number $a + bi$ is the number $a - bi$, and the conjugate of $a - bi$ is $a + bi$. For example, the conjugate of $3 + 4i$ is $3 - 4i$, and the conjugate of $-3i = 0 - 3i$ is $0 + 3i = 3i$. The numbers $3 + 4i$ and $3 - 4i$ are called **conjugate pairs**. Because $a + 0i = a - 0i$ for each real number a, *every real number is its own conjugate.*

The product of conjugate pairs is a real number, as shown below.

Let $a + bi$ be a complex number. Then the product of $a + bi$ and its conjugate $a - bi$ is

$$(a + bi)(a - bi) = a^2 - (bi)^2 = a^2 - b^2 i^2 = a^2 - b^2(-1) = a^2 + b^2$$

Because a^2 and b^2 are nonnegative real numbers, so is $a^2 + b^2$.

Quotients of Complex Numbers

The procedure used to find the quotient of two complex numbers uses the fact that the product of conjugate pairs is a real number.

Example 5 Quotients of Two Complex Numbers

Express the quotient $\dfrac{3 + 4i}{1 + 2i}$ in standard form.

Solution

To find the quotient $\dfrac{3 + 4i}{1 + 2i}$, multiply both the numerator and denominator by the *conjugate* of the denominator, $1 - 2i$.

$$\frac{3 + 4i}{1 + 2i} = \frac{3 + 4i}{1 + 2i} \cdot \frac{1 - 2i}{1 - 2i}$$

$$= \frac{(3 + 4i)(1 - 2i)}{(1 + 2i)(1 - 2i)} = \frac{3(1 - 2i) + 4i(1 - 2i)}{1^2 - (2i)^2} = \frac{3 - 6i + 4i - 8i^2}{1 - 4i^2}$$

$$= \frac{3 - 6i + 4i - 8(-1)}{1 - 4(-1)} = \frac{3 + 8 - 6i + 4i}{1 + 4} = \frac{11 - 2i}{5} = \frac{11}{5} - \frac{2}{5}i$$

Square Roots of Negative Numbers

Because $i^2 = -1$, $\sqrt{-1}$ is defined to be i. Similarly, because

$$(5i)^2 = 5^2 i^2 = 25(-1) = -25,$$

$\sqrt{-25}$ is define to be $5i$. In general,

Square Roots of Negative Numbers

> **Let b be a positive real number.**
> $$\sqrt{-b} \text{ is defined to be } i\sqrt{b}$$
> **because $(i\sqrt{b})^2 = i^2(\sqrt{b})^2 = -1 \cdot b = -b$**

Example 6 **Square Roots of Negative Numbers**

Write each of the following as a complex number.

a. $\sqrt{-3}$ **b.** $\dfrac{1 - \sqrt{-7}}{3}$ **c.** $(7 - \sqrt{-4})(5 + \sqrt{-9})$

Solution

a. $\sqrt{-3} = \sqrt{(3)(-1)} = \sqrt{3} \cdot \sqrt{-1} = i\sqrt{3}$

b. $\dfrac{1 - \sqrt{-7}}{3} = \dfrac{1 - i\sqrt{7}}{3} = \dfrac{1}{3} - \dfrac{\sqrt{7}}{3}i$

c. $(7 - \sqrt{-4})(5 + \sqrt{-9}) = (7 - i\sqrt{4})(5 + i\sqrt{9})$

$$= (7 - 2i)(5 + 3i)$$
$$= 35 + 21i - 10i - 6i^2$$
$$= 35 + 11i - 6(-1)$$
$$= 41 + 11i$$

Technology Tip

Most calculators that do complex number arithmetic automatically return a complex number when asked for the square root of a negative number. On TI-83/89, however, the MODE must be set to "rectangular" or "$a + bi$."

NOTE When i is multiplied by a radical, it is customary to write $i\sqrt{b}$ instead of $\sqrt{b}\,i$ to make clear that i is *not* under the radical.

CAUTION

The property $\sqrt{cd} = \sqrt{c} \cdot \sqrt{d}$—or equivalently in exponential notation $(cd)^{\frac{1}{2}} = c^{\frac{1}{2}} d^{\frac{1}{2}}$—which is valid for positive real numbers, *does not hold* when both c and d are negative. To avoid difficulty,

always write square roots of negative numbers in terms of i before doing any simplification.

For example,

$$\sqrt{-20} \cdot \sqrt{-5} = i\sqrt{20} \cdot i\sqrt{5} = i^2 \sqrt{20 \cdot 5} = -\sqrt{100} = -10.$$

Therefore, $\sqrt{-20} \cdot \sqrt{-5} = -\sqrt{20 \cdot 5}$.

Because every negative real number has two square roots in the complex number system, complex solutions can be found for equations that have no real solutions. For example, the solutions of $x^2 = -25$ are

$$x = \pm\sqrt{-25} = \pm 5i$$

Every quadratic equation with real coefficients has solutions in the complex number system.

Example 7 Complex Solutions to a Quadratic Equation

Find all solutions to $2x^2 + x + 3 = 0$.

Solution

Apply the quadratic formula.

$$x = \frac{-1 \pm \sqrt{1^2 - 4 \cdot 2 \cdot 3}}{2 \cdot 2} = \frac{-1 \pm \sqrt{-23}}{4}$$

Because $\sqrt{-23}$ is not a real number, this equation has no real number solutions. However, $\sqrt{-23}$ *is* an imaginary number, namely, $\sqrt{-23} = i\sqrt{23}$. Thus, the equation has solutions in the complex number system.

$$x = \frac{-1 \pm \sqrt{-23}}{4} = \frac{-1 \pm i\sqrt{23}}{4} = -\frac{1}{4} \pm \frac{\sqrt{23}}{4}i$$

Note that the two solutions, $-\dfrac{1}{4} + \dfrac{\sqrt{23}}{4}i$ and $-\dfrac{1}{4} - \dfrac{\sqrt{23}}{4}i$, are complex conjugates.

Example 8 Zeros of Unity

Find all solutions of $x^3 = 1$.

Solution

NOTE See the Algebra Review Appendix to review factoring the difference of two cubes.

Rewrite the equation as $x^3 - 1 = 0$ and use the difference of cubes pattern to factor the left side.

$$x^3 = 1$$
$$x^3 - 1 = 0$$
$$(x - 1)(x^2 + x + 1) = 0$$
$$x - 1 = 0 \qquad \text{or} \qquad x^2 + x + 1 = 0$$

$$x = 1 \quad \text{or} \quad x = \frac{-1 \pm \sqrt{1^2 - 4 \cdot 1 \cdot 1}}{2 \cdot 1} \qquad \textit{Quadratic formula}$$

$$= \frac{-1 \pm \sqrt{-3}}{2}$$

$$= \frac{-1 \pm i\sqrt{3}}{2} = -\frac{1}{2} \pm \frac{\sqrt{3}}{2}i$$

Therefore, the equation $x^3 = 1$ has one real solution, $x = 1$, and two non-real complex solutions, $x = -\dfrac{1}{2} + \dfrac{\sqrt{3}}{2}i$ and $x = -\dfrac{1}{2} - \dfrac{\sqrt{3}}{2}i$. Each of the solutions is said to be a **cube root of one** or a **cube root of unity.** Observe that the two nonreal cube roots of unity are complex conjugates.   ■

Examples 7 and 8 illustrated the following useful fact.

Conjugate Solutions

If $a + bi$ is a solution of a polynomial equation with *real* coefficients, then its conjugate, $a - bi$, is also a solution of the equation.

Calculator Investigation

The following investigation of complex number arithmetic is for use with TI-81/82 and other calculators that do not do complex number arithmetic, but do have matrix capabilities. Before doing it, look up "matrix" or "matrices" in your instruction manual and learn how to enter and store 2×2 matrices and how to do addition, subtraction, and multiplication with them.

1. The complex number $a + bi$ is expressed in matrix notation as the matrix $\begin{pmatrix} a & b \\ -b & a \end{pmatrix}$. For example, $-3 + 6i$ is written as $\begin{pmatrix} -3 & 6 \\ -6 & -3 \end{pmatrix}$.

   a. Write $3 + 4i$, $1 + 2i$, and $1 - i$ in matrix form and enter them in your calculator as $[A]$, $[B]$, $[C]$.

   b. We know that $(3 + 4i) + (1 + 2i) = 4 + 6i$. Verify that $[A] + [B]$ is $\begin{pmatrix} 4 & 6 \\ -6 & 4 \end{pmatrix}$, which represents the complex number $4 + 6i$.

   c. Use matrix addition, subtraction, and multiplication to find the following. Interpret the answers as complex numbers.
   $$[A] - [C], \ [B] + [C], \ [A][B], \ [B][C]$$

   d. In Example 5 we saw that $\dfrac{3 + 4i}{1 + 2i} = \dfrac{11}{5} - \dfrac{2}{5}i = 2.2 - 0.4i$. Do this problem in matrix form by computing $[A] \cdot [B]^{-1}$. Use the x^{-1} key for the exponent.

   e. Do each of the following calculations and interpret the answer in terms of complex numbers.
   $$[A] \cdot [C]^{-1}, \ [B][A]^{-1}, \ [B][C]^{-1}$$

Exercises 4.5

In Exercises 1–54, perform the indicated operation and write the result in the form $a + bi$.

1. $(2 + 3i) + (6 - i)$
2. $(-5 + 7i) + (14 + 3i)$

3. $(2 - 8i) - (4 + 2i)$
4. $(3 + 5i) - (3 - 7i)$

5. $\frac{5}{4} - \left(\frac{7}{4} + 2i\right)$
6. $\left(\sqrt{3} + i\right) + \left(\sqrt{5} - 2i\right)$

7. $\left(\frac{\sqrt{2}}{2} + i\right) - \left(\frac{\sqrt{3}}{2} - i\right)$

8. $\left(\frac{1}{2} + \frac{\sqrt{3}}{2}i\right) + \left(\frac{3}{4} - \frac{5\sqrt{3}}{2}i\right)$

9. $(2 + i)(3 + 5i)$
10. $(2 - i)(5 + 2i)$

11. $(-3 + 2i)(4 - i)$
12. $(4 + 3i)(4 - 3i)$

13. $(2 - 5i)^2$
14. $(1 + i)(2 - i)i$

15. $\left(\sqrt{3} + i\right)\left(\sqrt{3} - i\right)$
16. $\left(\frac{1}{2} - i\right)\left(\frac{1}{4} + 2i\right)$

17. i^{15}
18. i^{26}
19. i^{33}
20. $(-i)^{53}$

21. $(-i)^{107}$
22. $(-i)^{213}$
23. $\frac{1}{5 - 2i}$
24. $\frac{1}{i}$

25. $\frac{1}{3i}$
26. $\frac{i}{2 + i}$
27. $\frac{3}{4 + 5i}$
28. $\frac{2 + 3i}{i}$

29. $\frac{1}{i(4 + 5i)}$
30. $\frac{1}{(2 - i)(2 + i)}$

31. $\frac{2 + 3i}{i(4 + i)}$
32. $\frac{2}{(2 + 3i)(4 + i)}$

33. $\frac{2 + i}{1 - i} + \frac{1}{1 + 2i}$
34. $\frac{1}{2 - i} + \frac{3 + i}{2 + 3i}$

35. $\frac{i}{3 + i} - \frac{3 + i}{4 + i}$
36. $6 + \frac{2i}{3 + i}$

37. $\sqrt{-36}$
38. $\sqrt{-81}$

39. $\sqrt{-14}$
40. $\sqrt{-50}$

41. $-\sqrt{-16}$
42. $-\sqrt{-12}$

43. $\sqrt{-16} + \sqrt{-49}$
44. $\sqrt{-25} - \sqrt{-9}$

45. $\sqrt{-15} - \sqrt{-18}$
46. $\sqrt{-12} \sqrt{-3}$

47. $\frac{\sqrt{-16}}{\sqrt{-36}}$
48. $\frac{-\sqrt{-64}}{\sqrt{-4}}$

49. $\left(\sqrt{-25} + 2\right)\left(\sqrt{-49} - 3\right)$

50. $\left(5 - \sqrt{-3}\right)\left(-1 + \sqrt{-9}\right)$

51. $\left(2 + \sqrt{-5}\right)\left(1 - \sqrt{-10}\right)$
52. $\sqrt{-3}\left(3 - \sqrt{-27}\right)$

53. $\frac{1}{1 + \sqrt{-2}}$
54. $\frac{1 + \sqrt{-4}}{3 - \sqrt{-9}}$

In Exercises 55–58, find x and y.

55. $3x - 4i = 6 + 2yi$
56. $8 - 2yi = 4x + 12i$

57. $3 + 4xi = 2y - 3i$
58. $8 - xi = \frac{1}{2}y + 2i$

In Exercises 59–70, solve the equation and express each solution in the form $a + bi$.

59. $3x^2 - 2x + 5 = 0$
60. $5x^2 + 2x + 1 = 0$

61. $x^2 + x + 2 = 0$
62. $5x^2 - 6x + 2 = 0$

63. $2x^2 - x = -4$
64. $x^2 + 1 = 4x$

65. $2x^2 + 3 = 6x$
66. $3x^2 + 4 = -5x$

67. $x^3 - 8 = 0$
68. $x^3 + 125 = 0$

69. $x^4 - 1 = 0$
70. $x^4 - 81 = 0$

71. Simplify: $i + i^2 + i^3 + \cdots + i^{15}$

72. Simplify: $i - i^2 + i^3 - i^4 + i^5 - \cdots + i^{15}$

73. *Critical Thinking* If $z = a + bi$ is a complex number, then its conjugate is usually denoted $\bar{z}$, that is, $\bar{z} = a - bi$. Prove that for any complex number $z = a + bi$, z is a real number exactly when $\bar{z} = z$.

74. *Critical Thinking* The **real part** of the complex number $a + bi$ is defined to be the real number a. The **imaginary part** of $a + bi$ is defined to be the real number b (not bi). See Exercise 73 for notation.

    a. Show that the real part of $z = a + bi$ is $\frac{z + \bar{z}}{2}$.

    b. Show that the imaginary part of z is $\frac{z - \bar{z}}{2i}$.

75. *Critical Thinking* If $z = a + bi$ (with a and b real numbers, not both 0), express $\frac{1}{z}$ in standard form.

Excursion: The Mandelbrot Set

Chapter 1 introduced the recursive process of beginning with a value and adding a specific number repeatedly, and Section 3.5.A discussed iterating real-valued functions. This section will extend the iterative process to the set of complex numbers and complex-valued functions and will illustrate the Mandelbrot set, which is used to produce many fractal images. Before reading this section, review Section 3.5.A for terminology and processes, if needed.

The Complex Plane

Every complex number $a + bi$, where a and b are real numbers, corresponds to the point (a, b) in the coordinate plane. Therefore, complex numbers can be plotted in a coordinate plane, where the horizontal axis represents the real axis and the vertical axis represents the imaginary axis. For example, several complex numbers are plotted in Figure 4.5.A-1.

NOTE The complex plane is discussed in detail in Section 10.3.

When dealing with functions that have the complex numbers as their domains, the input variable is usually denoted as z, not x.

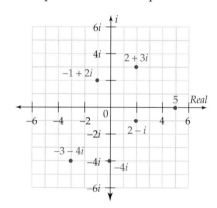

Figure 4.5.A-1

Orbits of Complex Numbers

The concepts and processes described in Section 3.5.A apply equally well to functions with complex number inputs. For instance, the process of finding the orbit of a complex number under a complex-valued function is the same as finding the orbit of a real number under a real-valued function. For example, the orbit of i under $f(z) = iz$ was illustrated in Section 4.5, where it was shown that the powers of i form an orbit of period 4.

$$z = i$$
$$f(i) = i \cdot i = i^2 = -1$$
$$f^2(i) = i \cdot (-1) = -i \qquad f^2(i) = f[f(i)]$$
$$f^3(i) = i \cdot (-i) = -i^2 = -(-1) = 1$$
$$f^4(i) = i \cdot 1 = i$$

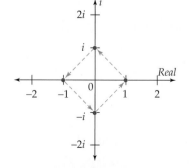

Figure 4.5.A-2

The orbit of i under $f(z) = iz$ is shown graphically in Figure 4.5.A-2.

Orbits of complex numbers of many functions are very interesting, but the discussion that follows will be limited to the orbit of 0 under $f(z) = z^2 + c$ for different values of c.

Example 1   The Orbit of 0 for $f(z) = z^2 + c$

Describe the orbit of 0 under $f(z) = z^2 + c$ for the given complex number c.

a. $c = -0.25 + 0.25i$ **b.** $c = -1.2 + 0.05i$

Solution

a. For $c = -0.25 + 0.25i$,
$$f(z) = z^2 + (-0.25 + 0.25i) = z^2 - 0.25 + 0.25i.$$

The orbit of 0 under $f(z) = z^2 - 0.25 + 0.25i$ is as follows.

$$f^1(0) = 0^2 - 0.25 + 0.25i = -0.25 + 0.25i$$

$$f^2(0) = (-0.25 + 0.25i)^2 + (-0.25 + 0.25i) = -0.25 + 0.125i$$

$$f^3(0) = f(-0.25 + 0.125i) = -0.203125 + 0.187500i$$

$$f^4(0) = f(-0.203125 + 0.187500i) = -0.2439 + 0.1738i$$

$$f^5(0) = f(-0.243896 + 0.173828i) = -0.2207 + 0.1652i$$

$$f^6(0) = f(-0.220731 + 0.165208i) = -0.2286 + 0.1771i$$

Use iteration on your calculator to find $f^{15}(0)$. It suggests that the orbit of 0 is approaching a number near $-0.2277 + 0.1718i$. In fact, it can be shown that for $c = -0.25 + 0.25i$,

$$f^n(0) \rightarrow -0.2276733451 + 0.1717803749i \text{ as } n \rightarrow \infty$$

b. For $c = -1.2 + 0.05i$, $f(z) = z^2 + (-1.2 + 0.05i) = z^2 - 1.2 + 0.05i$.

The orbit of 0 under $f(z) = z^2 - 1.2 + 0.05i$ is as follows.

$f^1(0) = -1.2 + 0.05i$	$f^2(0) = 0.2375 - 0.0700i$
$f^3(0) = -1.1485 + 0.0168i$	$f^4(0) = 0.1188 + 0.0115i$
$f^5(0) = -1.1860 + 0.0527i$	$f^6(0) = 0.2039 - 0.0751i$
$f^7(0) = -1.1641 + 0.0194i$	$f^8(0) = 0.1547 + 0.0049i$
$f^9(0) = -1.1761 + 0.0515i$	$f^{10}(0) = 0.1805 - 0.0712i$
$f^{11}(0) = -1.1725 + 0.0243i$	$f^{12}(0) = 0.1741 - 0.0070i$
$f^{13}(0) = -1.1697 + 0.0476i$	$f^{14}(0) = 0.1660 - 0.0613i$
$f^{15}(0) = -1.1762 + 0.0296i$	$f^{16}(0) = 0.1825 - 0.0197i$

NOTE All decimals are shown rounded to four decimal places, but calculations are done using the decimal capacity of the calculator.

Viewing additional iterations, the orbit of 0 when $c = -1.2 + 0.05i$ appears to oscillate between two values that are close to $-1.17 + 0.04i$ and $0.17 - 0.04i$ as illustrated in Figure 4.5.A-3.

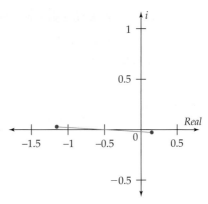

Figure 4.5.A-3

Example 2   The Orbit of 0 for $f(z) = z^2 + c$

Describe the orbit of 0 under $f(z) = z^2 + c$ for the given complex number c.

a. $c = 1 + i$ **b.** $c = 0.25 + 0.625i$

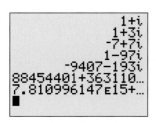

Figure 4.5.A-4

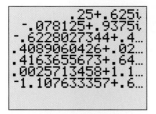

Figure 4.5.A-5a

Figure 4.5.A-5b

Solution

a. The first seven iterations of $f(z) = z^2 + (1 + i)$ are shown in Figure 4.5.A-4. If each of these numbers is plotted in the complex plane, successive iterations get farther and farther from the origin at a very fast rate. For instance,

$$f^5(0) = -9407 - 193i$$
$$f^6(0) = 88{,}454{,}401 + 3{,}631{,}103i$$
$$f^7(0) = (7.81 \times 10^{15}) + (6.42 \times 10^{14})i$$

The distance formula shows that after only five iterations, the distance to the origin is about 9509 and after seven iterations, it is *gigantic.* In this case, the orbit of 0 is said to **approach infinity,** which is sometimes expressed as follows.

If $f(z) = z^2 + (1 + i)$, then $f^n(0) \to \infty$ as $n \to \infty$.

b. The iterations $f^1(0)$ through $f^7(0)$ are shown in Figure 4.5.A-5a and $f^{15}(0)$ through $f^{21}(0)$ are shown in Figure 4.5.A-5b. As you can see, successive iterations stay fairly close to the origin through the 16th iteration and then quickly move farther and farther away.

$$f^{20}(20) = -167.4 - 522.8i$$
$$f^{21}(0) = -254{,}270 + 175{,}058i$$
$$f^{22}(0) = (2.95 \times 10^{10}) - (8.59 \times 10^{10})i$$

Therefore, the orbit of 0 approaches infinity. In other words,

if $f(z) = z^2 + (0.25 + 0.625i)$, then $f^n(0) \to \infty$ as $n \to \infty$.

The Mandelbrot Set

The Mandelbrot set is defined by whether or not the orbit of 0 under the function $f(z) = z^2 + c$ approaches infinity for each complex number c.

The Mandelbrot Set

> The *Mandelbrot set* is the set of complex numbers c such that the orbit of 0 under the function $f(z) = z^2 + c$ does not approach infinity.

To avoid awkward repetition in the following discussion, the orbit of 0 under the function $f(z) = z^2 + c$ will be referred to as "the orbit of c."

Example 1 shows that the orbit of $c = -0.25 + 0.25i$ converges and the orbit of $c = -1.2 + 0.05i$ oscillates. Neither orbit approaches infinity, so both numbers are in the Mandelbrot set. Example 2 shows that the orbits of $c = 1 + i$ and $c = 0.25 + 0.625i$ approach infinity, so these numbers are not in the Mandelbrot set.

Diagram of the Mandelbrot Set

Although the Mandelbrot set is defined analytically, it is usually viewed geometrically by plotting the numbers in the Mandelbrot set as points in the complex plane. The Mandelbrot set is the white region in Figure 4.5.A-6, in which the tick marks on each axis are $\frac{1}{2}$ unit apart. Note that the Mandelbrot set is symmetric with respect to the real axis, but not with respect to the imaginary axis.

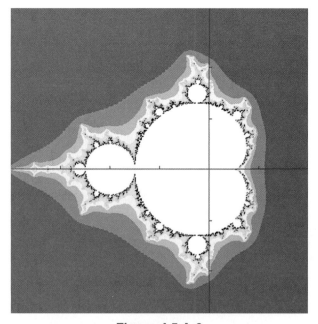

Figure 4.5.A-6

Figure 4.5.A-6 illustrates the following fact in which the complex numbers are considered as points in the complex plane.

> If c lies outside the circle of radius 2 with center at the origin, then c is not in the Mandelbrot set.

Furthermore, it can be proved that

> **If c lies inside the circle of radius 2 with center at the origin, but some number in its orbit lies outside the circle, then c is not in the Mandelbrot set.**

Determining whether a particular point c is in the Mandelbrot set can be quite difficult, particularly if the numbers in its orbit move away from the origin very slowly. Even after hundreds of iterations, it may not be clear whether or not the orbit approaches infinity. Because of round-off errors, a calculator is inadequate for such calculations, and even computers have their limitations.

Border of the Mandelbrot Set

The border of the Mandelbrot set, which consists of the points just outside of the set, is shown in various colors in Figure 4.5.A-6. The colors indicate how quickly the orbit of the point approaches infinity. The colors are determined by the number of iterations n needed for a number in the orbit of the point to be more than 3 units from the origin, as indicated in the following table.

Red	Medium Red	Light Red	Light Yellow	Yellow	Blue	Black
$n \leq 5$	$6 \leq n \leq 7$	$8 \leq n \leq 9$	$10 \leq n \leq 12$	$13 \leq n \leq 19$	$20 \leq n \leq 49$	$n \geq 50$

Example 2 shows that $1 + i$ is in the red region because the second iteration produces a point more than 3 units from the origin and that $0.25 + 0.625i$ is in the yellow region.

The border of the Mandelbrot set is very jagged and chaotic. The varying rates at which the orbits of these border points approach infinity produce some interesting patterns of great complexity. When specific areas are magnified, you can see shapes that resemble islands, seahorse tails, and elephant trunks. The most fascinating aspect of the set is that some of these islands have the same shape as the entire set. Consequently, the Mandelbrot set is said to be **self-similar under magnification.**

The following figures show the region near the point $-0.75 + 0.3i$ under increasing magnification.

The purple points in Figure 4.5.A-7a indicate the Mandelbrot set. Each subsequent image is the magnification of the region denoted by the white square in the previous image. The image shown in Figure 4.5.A-7d is a copy of the set that is contained within the set, and even though the graphs shown do not indicate that all of the purple regions are connected, they are.

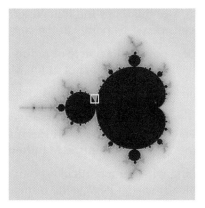

Figure 4.5.A-7a

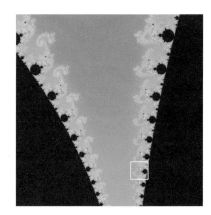

Figure 4.5.A-7b

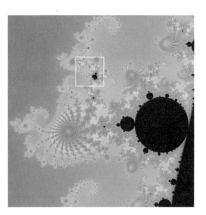

Figure 4.5.A-7c

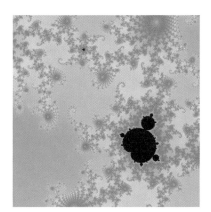

Figure 4.5.A-7d

Exercises 4.5.A

In Exercises 1–6, compute $f(0), f^1(0)$, and $f^2(0)$ where $f(z) = z^2 + c$. Then determine the distance from $f^3(0)$ to the origin in the complex plane, where the distance from a point $a + bi$ to the origin is given by

$$\sqrt{a^2 + b^2}.$$

1. $c = 0.3$

2. $c = 0.5i$

3. $c = 0.5 + 0.5i$

4. $c = 1 + 0.5i$

5. $c = -1.2 + 0.5i$

6. $c = -0.75 + 0.25i$

In Exercises 7–12, show that c is *not* in the Mandelbrot set by finding a number in its orbit that is more than 2 units from the origin. How many iterations are needed to find the first such number?

7. $c = 0.4$

8. $c = -1.1 + 0.4i$

9. $c = 0.7i$

10. $c = 0.2 + 0.8i$

11. $c = -0.5 - 0.7i$

12. $c = 0.4 - 0.6i$

In Exercises 13–18, determine whether or not c is in the Mandelbrot set.

13. $c = i$

14. $c = -i$

15. $c = 1$

16. $c = 0.1 - 0.3i$

17. $c = -0.2 + 0.6i$

18. $-0.1 + 0.8i$

4.6   The Fundamental Theorem of Algebra

Objectives

- Use the Fundamental Theorem of Algebra
- Find complex conjugate zeros
- Find the number of zeros of a polynomial
- Give the complete factorization of polynomial expressions

The complex numbers were constructed in order to obtain a solution for the equation $x^2 = -1$, that is, a zero of the polynomial $f(x) = x^2 + 1$. *Every quadratic equation with real coefficients has solutions in the complex number system*, as discussed in Section 4.5. A natural question arises:

Does the complex number system need to be enlarged, perhaps many times, to find zeros of higher degree polynomial functions?

This section explains why the answer is no.

In order to give the full answer, the discussion will not be limited to polynomials with real coefficients but will consider polynomials with complex coefficients, such as

$$x^3 - ix^2 + (4 - 3i)x + 1 \quad \text{or} \quad (-3 + 2i)x^6 - 3x + (5 - 4i).$$

The discussion of polynomial division in Section 4.1 can easily be extended to include polynomials with complex coefficients. In fact,

All of the results in Section 4.1 are valid for polynomials with complex coefficients.

For example, for $f(x) = x^2 + (-1 + i)x + (2 + i)$, it is easy to verify that i is a zero of f and that $x - i$ is a factor of $f(x)$. Both statements can be checked using the same procedures as before.

$$f(i) = i^2 + (-1 + i)i + (2 + i) = i^2 - i + i^2 + 2 + i$$
$$= -1 - i - 1 + 2 + i = 0$$

Therefore, i is a zero of f.

NOTE The graph of a polynomial with complex coefficients cannot be drawn on a coordinate plane.

$$
\begin{array}{r}
x + (-1 + 2i) \\
x - i \overline{)x^2 + (-1 + i)x + 2 + i} \\
\underline{x^2 \qquad\quad - ix} \\
(-1 + 2i)x + 2 + i \\
\underline{(-1 + 2i)x + 2 + i} \\
0
\end{array}
$$

Therefore, $x - i$ is a factor of $f(x)$ and

$$f(x) = x^2 + (-1 + i)x + (2 + i) = (x - i)[x + (-1 + 2i)].$$

Because every real number is also a complex number, polynomials with real coefficients are just special cases of polynomials with complex coefficients. In the rest of this section, "polynomial" means "polynomial with complex, possibly real, coefficients" unless specified otherwise.

Fundamental Theorem of Algebra

Every nonconstant polynomial has a zero in the complex number system.

Although this is a powerful result, neither the Fundamental Theorem nor its proof provides a practical method for *finding* a zero of a given polynomial. You may think it strange that you can prove a zero exists without actually finding one, but such "existence" proofs are quite common in mathematics.

Factorization over the Complex Numbers

> Let $f(x)$ be a polynomial of degree $n > 0$ with leading coefficient a. Then there are n, not necessarily distinct, complex numbers $c_1, c_2, \ldots, c_n$ such that
>
> $$f(x) = a(x - c_1)(x - c_2) \ldots (x - c_n)$$
>
> Furthermore, $c_1, c_2 \ldots, c_n$ are the only zeros of f.

That is, every polynomial of degree $n > 0$ can be written as the product of n linear factors. The statement follows from the Fundamental Theorem and the Factor Theorem. By the Fundamental Theorem, $f(x)$ has a complex zero c_1, and by the Factor Theorem $x - c_1$ is a factor, so

$$f(x) = (x - c_1)g(x).$$

If $g(x)$ is nonconstant, then it has a complex zero c_2 by the Fundamental Theorem and a factor $x - c_2$ so that

$$f(x) = (x - c_1)(x - c_2)(h(x)).$$

This process can be continued until the final factor is a constant a, at which point you have the factorization shown in the preceding box.

Because the n zeros $c_1, c_2, \ldots, c_n$ of f may not all be distinct, the number of distinct zeros may be less than n.

Number of Zeros

> Every polynomial of degree $n > 0$ has at most n different zeros in the complex number system.

Suppose f has repeated zeros, meaning that some of the $c_1, c_2, \ldots, c_n$ are the same in the factorization of $f(x)$. Recall that a zero c is said to have multiplicity k if $(x - c)^k$ is a factor of $f(x)$, but no higher power of $(x - c)$ is a factor. Consequently, *if every zero is counted as many times as its multiplicity*, then the statement in the preceding box implies that

A polynomial of degree n has exactly n complex zeros.

Example 1   Finding a Polynomial Given Its Zeros

Find a polynomial $f(x)$ of degree 5 such that 1, -2, and 5 are zeros, 1 is a zero of multiplicity 3, and $f(2) = -24$.

Solution

Because 1 is a zero of multiplicity 3, $(x - 1)^3$ must be a factor of $f(x)$. There are two other factors corresponding to the zeros -2 and 5.

$$x - (-2) = x + 2 \text{ and } x - 5$$

The product of these factors has degree 5, as does $f(x)$ so

$$f(x) = a(x - 1)^3(x + 2)(x - 5)$$

where a is the leading coefficient.

Because $f(2) = -24$,

$$a(2 - 1)^3(2 + 2)(2 - 5) = -24$$
$$-12a = -24$$
$$a = 2$$

Therefore, $f(x) = 2(x - 1)^3(x + 2)(x - 5)$

$$= 2x^5 - 12x^4 + 4x^3 + 40x^2 - 54x + 20$$

The graph of f is shown in Figure 4.6-1.

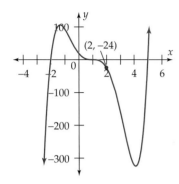

Figure 4.6-1

Polynomials with Real Coefficients

Recall that the **conjugate** of the complex number $a + bi$ is the number $a - bi$. We usually write a complex number as a single letter, say z, and indicate its conjugate by $\bar{z}$, sometimes read "z bar." For instance, if $z = 3 + 7i$, then $\bar{z} = 3 - 7i$. Conjugates play a role whenever a quadratic polynomial with real coefficients has complex zeros.

Example 2 **Conjugate Zeros**

Find the zeros of $f(x) = x^2 - 6x + 13$.

Solution

The quadratic formula shows that f has two complex zeros.

$$\frac{-(-6) \pm \sqrt{(-6)^2 - 4 \cdot 1 \cdot 13}}{2 \cdot 1} = \frac{6 \pm \sqrt{-16}}{2} = \frac{6 \pm 4i}{2} = 3 \pm 2i$$

The complex roots are $z = 3 + 2i$ and its conjugate $\bar{z} = 3 - 2i$. Notice that f has no real zeros, as shown in Figure 4.6-2.

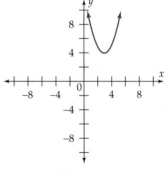

Figure 4.6-2

The preceding example is a special case of a more general theorem.

Conjugate Zero Theorem

Let $f(x)$ be a polynomial with *real* coefficients. If the complex number z is a zero of f, then its conjugate $\bar{z}$ is also a zero of f.

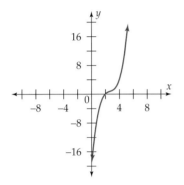

Figure 4.6-3

Example 3   **A Polynomial with Specific Zeros**

Find a polynomial with real coefficients whose zeros include the numbers 2 and $3 + i$.

Solution

Because $3 + i$ is a zero, its conjugate, $3 - i$, must also be a zero. By the Factor Theorem, $x - (3 + i)$ and $x - (3 - i)$ are factors. Similarly, because 2 is a zero, $x - 2$ is a factor. So, consider the polynomial

$$f(x) = (x - 2)[x - (3 + i)][x - (3 - i)].$$

Obviously, $2, 3 + i$, and $3 - i$ are zeros of f. Multiplying out the factored form shows that $f(x)$ has real coefficients.

$$\begin{aligned} f(x) &= (x - 2)[x^2 - (3 - i)x - (3 + i)x + (3 + i)(3 - i)] \\ &= (x - 2)(x^2 - 3x + ix - 3x - ix + 9 - i^2) \\ &= (x - 2)(x^2 - 6x + 10) \\ &= x^3 - 8x^2 + 22x - 20 \end{aligned}$$

The next-to-last line of the calculation also shows that $f(x)$ can be factored as a product of a linear and a quadratic polynomial, each with *real* coefficients. The graph of f is shown in Figure 4.6-3. ∎

The technique used in Example 3 works because the product,

$$[x - (3 + i)][x - (3 - i)] = x^2 - 6x + 10,$$

has real coefficients. The proof of the following result shows why this must always be the case.

Factorization over the Real Numbers

Every nonconstant polynomial with real coefficients can be factored as a product of linear and irreducible quadratic polynomials with real coefficients in such a way that the quadratic factors, if any, have no real zeros.

That is, every nonconstant polynomial with real coefficients can be written as the product of factors in the form $x - k$ or $ax^2 + bx + c$, where each quadratic factor is irreducible over the set of real numbers.

Proof The box on page 308 shows that for any polynomial $f(x)$,

$$f(x) = a(x - c_1)(x - c_2)\dots(x - c_n)$$

where $c_1, c_2, \dots, c_n$ are the zeros of f. If some c_r is a real number, then the factor $x - c$, is a linear polynomial with real coefficients. If some c_j is a nonreal complex zero, then its conjugate must also be a zero. Thus, some c_k is the conjugate of c_j, say, $c_j = a + bi$ and $c_k = a - bi$, with a and b real numbers. Thus,

$$(x - c_j)(x - c_k) = [x - (a + bi)][x - (a - bi)]$$
$$= x^2 - (a - bi)x - (a + bi)x + (a + bi)(a - bi)$$
$$= x^2 - ax + bix - ax - bix + a^2 - (bi)^2$$
$$= x^2 - 2ax + (a^2 + b^2)$$

Therefore, the factor $(x - c_j)(x - c_k)$ is a quadratic expression with real coefficients because a and b are real numbers. Its zeros, c_j and c_k, are nonreal. By taking the real zeros of f one at a time and the nonreal ones in conjugate pairs in this fashion, the desired factorization of $f(x)$ is obtained.

Example 4   **Completely Factoring a Polynomial over the Real Numbers**

Completely factor $f(x) = x^4 - 2x^3 - x^2 + 6x - 6$ over the set of real numbers given that $1 + i$ is a zero of f.

Solution

Because $1 + i$ is a zero of f, its conjugate, $1 - i$, is also a zero of f, and $f(x)$ has the following quadratic factor.

$$[x - (1 + i)][x - (1 - i)] = x^2 - 2x + 2$$

Dividing $f(x)$ by $x^2 - 2x + 2$ shows that the other factor is $x^2 - 3$, which factors as $(x + \sqrt{3})(x - \sqrt{3})$. Therefore,

$$f(x) = (x + \sqrt{3})(x - \sqrt{3})(x^2 - 2x + 2)$$

is the complete factorization of $x^4 - 2x^3 - x^2 + 6x - 6$ over the real numbers. The graph of f is shown in Figure 4.6-4.

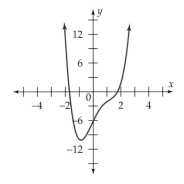

Figure 4.6-4

Complete Factorization of Polynomials

The techniques illustrated in this chapter can be used to completely factor some polynomials into linear factors.

Example 5   **Completely Factoring a Polynomial over the Complex Numbers**

Completely factor $f(x) = x^4 - 5x^3 + 4x^2 + 2x - 8$ over the set of real numbers and then over the set of complex numbers.

Solution

Because the degree of the polynomial is 4, there are exactly 4 complex zeros.

Find all rational zeros: The possible rational zeros are factors of 8.

$$\pm 1, \pm 2, \pm 4, \pm 8$$

Graph $f(x) = x^4 - 5x^3 + 4x^2 + 2x - 8$ and determine which of the possible zeros are the rational zeros.

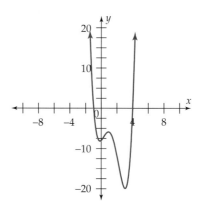

Figure 4.6-5

The graph suggests that -1 and 4 are zeros and you can easily verify that they are. The graph shows that there are no other real zeros.

Find all rational factors: Two linear factors of $f(x)$ are $x + 1$ and $x - 4$.

Find remaining factors: Use synthetic division twice to find another factor of $f(x)$.

$$
\begin{array}{r|rrrrr}
4 & 1 & -5 & 4 & 2 & -8 \\
  &   & 4 & -4 & 0 & 8 \\
\hline
  & 1 & -1 & 0 & 2 & \boxed{0}
\end{array}
$$

$$f(x) = (x - 4)(x^3 - x^2 + 2)$$

$$
\begin{array}{r|rrrr}
-1 & 1 & -1 & 0 & 2 \\
   &   & -1 & 2 & -2 \\
\hline
   & 1 & -2 & 2 & \boxed{0}
\end{array}
$$

$$f(x) = (x - 4)(x + 1)(x^2 - 2x + 2)$$

So, $x^4 - 5x^3 + 4x^2 + 2x - 8 = (x + 1)(x - 4)(x^2 - 2x + 2)$.

Use the quadratic formula to find the two zeros of $g(x) = x^2 - 2x + 2$.

$$x = \frac{2 \pm \sqrt{(-2)^2 - 4(1)(2)}}{2(1)}$$

$$= \frac{2 \pm \sqrt{-4}}{2} = \frac{2 \pm 2i}{2} = 1 \pm i$$

The complex factors are $x - (1 + i)$ and $x - (1 - i)$.

The complete factorizations of $f(x)$ over the set of real numbers and over the set of complex numbers are shown below.

$$x^4 - 5x^3 + 4x^2 + 2x - 8 = (x + 1)(x - 4)(x^2 - 2x + 2)$$
$$= (x + 1)(x - 4)[x - (1 + i)][x - (1 - i)]$$

Both products can be verified by multiplication.

An expression that has *even* degree of 4 or greater may have only complex roots. Zeros and factors of such functions and expressions may be difficult to find, and the techniques illustrated in this chapter are of little use. However, functions of *odd* degree must have at least one real zero, and the corresponding expression must have at least one real linear factor. Therefore, a cubic expression can easily be approximately factored by estimating one zero, which yields the real linear factor, using synthetic division to determine the quadratic factor, and then using the quadratic formula to estimate the remaining two zeros.

Exercises 4.6

In Exercises 1–6, determine if $g(x)$ is a factor of $f(x)$ without using synthetic or long division.

1. $f(x) = x^{10} + x^8$ $g(x) = x - 1$

2. $f(x) = x^6 - 10$ $g(x) = x - 2$

3. $f(x) = 3x^4 - 6x^3 + 2x - 1$ $g(x) = x + 1$

4. $f(x) = x^5 - 3x^2 + 2x - 1$ $g(x) = x - 2$

5. $f(x) = x^3 - 2x^2 + 5x - 4$ $g(x) = x + 2$

6. $f(x) = 10x^{75} - 8x^{65} + 6x^{45} + 4x^{32} - 2x^{15} + 5$
$g(x) = x - 1$

In Exercises 7–10, list the zeros of the polynomial and state the multiplicity of each zero.

7. $f(x) = x^{54}\left(x + \dfrac{4}{5}\right)$

8. $g(x) = 3\left(x + \dfrac{1}{6}\right)\left(x - \dfrac{1}{5}\right)\left(x + \dfrac{1}{4}\right)$

9. $h(x) = 2x^{15}(x - \pi)^{14}[x - (\pi + 1)]^{13}$

10. $k(x) = \left(x - \sqrt{7}\right)^7\left(x - \sqrt{5}\right)^5(2x - 1)$

In Exercises 11–22, find all the zeros of f in the complex number system; then write $f(x)$ as a product of linear factors.

11. $f(x) = x^2 - 2x + 5$ **12.** $f(x) = x^2 - 4x + 13$

13. $f(x) = 3x^2 + 2x + 7$ **14.** $f(x) = 3x^2 - 5x + 2$

15. $f(x) = x^3 - 27$ *Hint:* Factor first.

16. $f(x) = x^3 + 125$ **17.** $f(x) = x^3 + 8$

18. $f(x) = x^6 - 64$
  Hint: Let $u = x^3$ and factor $u^2 - 64$ first.

19. $f(x) = x^4 - 1$ **20.** $f(x) = x^4 - x^2 - 6$

21. $f(x) = x^4 - 3x^2 - 10$ **22.** $f(x) = 2x^4 - 7x^2 - 4$

In Exercises 23–44, find a polynomial $f(x)$ with real coefficients that satisfies the given conditions. Some of the problems have many correct answers.

23. degree 3; only zeros are $1, 7, -4$

24. degree 3; only zeros are 1 and -1

25. degree 6; only zeros are $1, 2, \pi$

26. degree 5; only zero is 2

27. degree 3; zeros $-3, 0, 4$; $f(5) = 80$

28. degree 3; zeros $-1, \dfrac{1}{2}, 2$; $f(0) = 2$

29. zeros include $2 + i$ and $2 - i$

30. zeros include $1 + 3i$ and $1 - 3i$

31. zeros include 2 and $2 + i$

32. zeros include 3 and $4i - 1$

33. zeros include $-3, 1 - i, 1 + 2i$

34. zeros include $1, 2 + i, 3i - 1$

35. degree 2; zeros $1 + 2i$ and $1 - 2i$

36. degree 4; zeros $3i$ and $-3i$, each of multiplicity 2

37. degree 4; only zeros are $4, 3 + i$, and $3 - i$

38. degree 5; zeros 2 of multiplicity 3, i, and $-i$

39. degree 6; zeros 0 of multiplicity 3 and $3, 1 + i$, $1 - i$, each of multiplicity 1

40. degree 6; zeros include i of multiplicity 2 and 3

41. degree 2; zeros include $1 + i$; $f(0) = 6$

42. degree 2; zeros include $3 + i$; $f(2) = 3$

43. degree 3; zeros include i and 1; $f(-1) = 8$

44. degree 3; zeros include $2 + 3i$ and -2; $f(2) = -3$

In Exercises 45–48, find a polynomial with complex coefficients that satisfies the given conditions.

45. degree 2; zeros i and $1 - 2i$

46. degree 2; zeros $2i$ and $1 + i$

47. degree 3; zeros $3, i$, and $2 - i$

48. degree 4; zeros $\sqrt{2}, -\sqrt{2}, 1 + i$, and $1 - i$

In Exercises 49–56, one zero of the polynomial is given; find all the zeros.

49. $x^3 - 2x^2 - 2x - 3$; zero 3

50. $x^3 + x^2 + x + 1$; zero i

51. $x^4 + 3x^3 + 3x^2 + 3x + 2$; zero i

52. $x^4 - x^3 - 5x^2 - x - 6$; zero i

53. $x^4 - 2x^3 + 5x^2 - 8x + 4$; zero 1 of multiplicity 2

54. $x^4 - 6x^3 + 29x^2 - 76x + 68$; zero 2 of multiplicity 2

55. $x^4 - 4x^3 + 6x^2 - 4x + 5$; zero $2 - i$

56. $x^4 - 5x^3 + 10x^2 - 20x + 24$; zero $2i$

57. Let $z = a + bi$ and $w = c + di$ be complex numbers (a, b, c, d are real numbers). Prove the given equality by computing each side and comparing the results.
   a. $\overline{z + w} = \overline{z} + \overline{w}$ (The left side says: "First find $z + w$ and then take the conjugate." The right side says: "First take the conjugates of z and w and then add.")
   b. $\overline{z \cdot w} = \overline{z} \cdot \overline{w}$

58. Let $g(x)$ and $h(x)$ be polynomials of degree n and assume that there are $n + 1$ numbers $c_1, c_2, ..., c_n,$ c_{n+1} such that
$$g(c_i) = h(c_i) \quad \text{for every } i.$$
Prove that $g(x) = h(x)$. Hint: Show that each c_i is a zero of $f(x) = g(x) - h(x)$. If $f(x)$ is nonzero, what is its largest possible degree? To avoid a contradiction, conclude that $f(x) = 0$.

59. Suppose $f(x) = ax^3 + bx^2 + cx + d$ has real coefficients and z is a complex zero of f.
   a. Use Exercise 57 and the fact that $\overline{r} = r$, when r is a real number, to show that
$$\overline{f(z)} = \overline{az^3 + bz^2 + cz + d}$$
$$= a\overline{z}^3 + b\overline{z}^2 + c\overline{z} + d = f(\overline{z}).$$
   b. Conclude that $\overline{z}$ is also a zero of f. Note: $f(\overline{z}) = \overline{f(z)} = \overline{0} = 0$.

60. Let $f(x)$ be a polynomial with real coefficients and z a complex zero of f. Prove that the conjugate $\overline{z}$ is also a zero of f. Hint: Exercise 59 is the case when $f(x)$ has degree 3; the proof in the general case is similar.

61. Use the Factorization over the Real Numbers statement to show that every polynomial with real coefficients and odd degree must have at least one real zero.

62. Give an example of a polynomial $f(x)$ with complex, nonreal coefficients and a complex number z such that z is a zero of f but its conjugate is not. Therefore, the conclusion of the Conjugate Roots Theorem may be false if $f(x)$ doesn't have real coefficients.

CHAPTER 4 REVIEW

Important Concepts

Important Facts and Formulas

When f is a polynomial and r is a real number that satisfies any of the following statements, then r satisfies all the statements.

- r is a zero of the polynomial function $y = f(x)$
- r is an x-intercept of the graph of f
- r is a solution, or root, of the equation $f(x) = 0$
- $x - r$ is a factor of the polynomial expression $f(x)$
- There is a one-to-one correspondence between the linear factors of $f(x)$ that have real coefficients and the x-intercepts of the graph of f.

A polynomial of degree n has at most n distinct real zeros.

All rational zeros of a polynomial have the form $\frac{r}{s}$, where r is a factor of the constant term and s is a factor of the leading coefficient.

The end behavior of the graph of a polynomial function is similar to the end behavior of the graph of the highest degree term of the polynomial.

Zeros of even multiplicity touch but do not cross the x-axis. Zeros of odd multiplicity cross the x-axis.

The number of local extrema of the graph of a polynomial function is at most one less than the degree of a polynomial.

The number of points of inflection of the graph of a polynomial function is at most two less than the degree of the polynomial.

The graph of a rational function has a vertical asymptote at every number that is a zero of the denominator and not a zero of the numerator.

The x-intercepts of the graph of a rational function occur at the numbers that are zeros of the numerator but are not zeros of the denominator.

Every complex number can be written in the standard form $a + bi$.

$i^2 = -1$ and $i = \sqrt{-1}$

If $a + bi$ is a zero of a polynomial with real coefficients, then its conjugate $a - bi$ is also a zero.

A polynomial of degree n has exactly n complex zeros counting multiplicities.

Every polynomial expression with real coefficients can be factored into linear and irreducible quadratic factors with real coefficients.

Every polynomial expression can be factored into linear factors with complex coefficients.

Review Exercises

Section 4.1

1. Which of the following are polynomials?

   a. $2^3 + x^2$ **b.** $x + \dfrac{1}{x}$ **c.** $x^3 - \dfrac{1}{\sqrt{2}}$

   d. $\sqrt[3]{x^4}$ **e.** $\pi^3 - x$ **f.** $\sqrt{2} + 2x^2$

   g. $\sqrt{x} + 2x^2$ **h.** $|x|$

2. What is the remainder when $x^4 + 3x^3 + 1$ is divided by $x^2 + 1$?

3. What is the remainder when $x^{112} - 2x^8 + 9x^5 - 4x^4 + x - 5$ is divided by $x - 1$?

4. Is $x - 1$ a factor of $f(x) = 14x^{87} - 65x^{56} + 51$? Justify your answer.

5. Use synthetic division to show that $x - 2$ is a factor of $x^6 - 5x^5 + 8x^4 + x^3 - 17x^2 + 16x - 4$, and find the other factor.

6. Find a polynomial f of degree 3 such that $f(-1) = 0$, $f(1) = 0$, and $f(0) = 5$.

Section 4.2

7. Find the zero(s) of $2\left(\dfrac{x}{5} + 7\right) - 3x - \dfrac{x + 2}{5} + 4$.

8. Find the zeros of $3x^2 - 2x - 5$.

9. Factor the polynomial $x^3 - 8x^2 + 9x + 6$. *Hint:* 2 is a zero.

10. Find all real zeros of $x^6 - 4x^3 + 4$.

11. Find all real zeros of $9x^3 - 6x^2 - 35x + 26$. *Hint:* Try $x = -2$.

12. Find all real zeros of $3y^3(y^4 - y^2 - 5)$.

13. Find the rational zeros of $x^4 - 2x^3 - 4x^2 + 1$.

14. Consider the polynomial $2x^3 - 8x^2 + 5x + 3$.
   a. List the only possible rational zeros.
   b. Find one rational zero.
   c. Find all the zeros of the polynomial.

15. a. Find all rational zeros of $x^3 + 2x^2 - 2x - 2$.
   b. Find two consecutive integers such that an irrational zero of $x^3 + 2x^2 - 2x - 2$ lies between them.

16. How many distinct real zeros does $x^3 + 4x$ have?

17. How many distinct real zeros does $x^3 - 6x^2 + 11x - 6$ have?

18. Find the zeros of $x^4 - 11x^2 + 18$.

19. The polynomial $x^3 - 2x + 1$ has
   a. no real zeros.
   b. only one real zero.
   c. three rational zeros.
   d. only one rational zero.
   e. none of the above.

20. Show that 5 is an upper bound for the real zeros of $x^4 - 4x^3 + 16x - 16$.

21. Show that -1 is a lower bound for the real zeros of $x^4 - 4x^3 + 15$.

In Exercises 22 and 23, find the real zeros of the polynomial.

22. $x^6 - 2x^5 - x^4 + 3x^3 - x^2 - x + 1$

23. $x^5 - 3x^4 - 2x^3 - x^2 - 23x - 20$

Section 4.3

24. List the zeros of the polynomial and the multiplicity of each zero.
$f(x) = 5(x - 4)^3(x - 2)(x + 17)^3(x^2 - 4)$

25. List the zeros of the polynomial and the multiplicity of each zero.
$f(x) = -2(x + 3)^2(x - 4)(x^2 - 9)$

26. Draw the graph of a function that could not possibly be the graph of a polynomial function, and explain why.

27. Draw a graph that could be the graph of a polynomial function of degree 5. You need not list a specific polynomial nor do any computation.

28. Which of the statements is not true about the polynomial function f whose graph is shown in the figure on the next page?

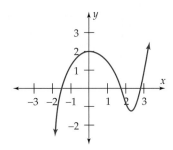

a. f has three zeros between -2 and 3
b. $f(x)$ could possibly be a fifth-degree polynomial
c. $(f \circ f)(0) > 0$
d. $f(2) - f(-1) < 3$
e. $f(x)$ is positive for all x in the interval $[-1, 0]$

29. Which of the statements **i–v** about the polynomial function f whose graph is shown in the figure below are false?

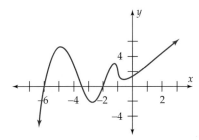

i f has 2 zeros in the interval $(-6, -3)$ **iv** $f(2) - 2 = 0$
ii $f(-3) - f(-6) < 0$ **v** f has degree ≤ 4
iii $f(0) < f(1)$

In Exercises 30–33, find a viewing window (or windows) that shows a complete graph of the function. Be alert for hidden behavior.

30. $f(x) = 0.5x^3 - 4x^2 + x + 1$

31. $g(x) = 0.3x^5 - 4x^4 + x^3 - 4x^2 + 5x + 1$

32. $h(x) = 4x^3 - 100x^2 + 600x$

33. $f(x) = 32x^3 - 99x^2 + 100x + 2$

In Exercises 34–37, sketch a complete graph of the function.

34. $f(x) = x^3 - 9x$ **35.** $g(x) = x^3 - 2x^2 + 3$

36. $h(x) = x^4 - x^3 - 4x^2 + 4x + 2$ **37.** $f(x) = x^4 - 3x - 2$

Section 4.3.A

38. HomeArt makes plastic replicas of famous statues. Their total cost to produce copies of a particular statue is shown in the table on the next page.
a. Sketch a scatter plot of the data.
b. Use cubic regression to find a function $C(x)$ that models the data—that

is, the cost of making x statues. Assume C is reasonably accurate when $x \leq 100$.

c. Use C to estimate the cost of making the seventy-first statue.

d. Use C to approximate the average cost per statue when 35 are made and when 75 are made. Recall that the average cost of x statues is $\dfrac{C(x)}{x}$.

Number of statues	Total cost
0	$2,000
10	2,519
20	2,745
30	2,938
40	3,021
50	3,117
60	3,269
70	3,425

39. The following table gives the estimated cost of a college education at a public institution. Costs include tuition, fees, books, and room and board for four years.

a. Sketch a scatter plot of the data (with $x = 0$ corresponding to 1990).

b. Use quartic regression to find a function C that models the data. Estimate the cost of a college education in 2007 and in 2015.

Enrollment Year	Costs	Enrollment Year	Costs
1998	$46,691	2008	$ 83,616
2000	52,462	2010	93,951
2002	58,946	2012	105,564
2004	66,232	2014	118,611
2006	74,418		

Source: Teachers Insurance and Annuity Association College Retirement Equities Fund

Section 4.4

In Exercises 40–43, sketch a complete graph of the function. Label the x-intercepts, all local extrema, holes, and asymptotes.

40. $g(x) = \dfrac{-2}{x + 4}$

41. $h(x) = \dfrac{3 - x}{x - 2}$

42. $k(x) = \dfrac{4x + 10}{3x - 9}$

43. $f(x) = \dfrac{x + 1}{x^2 - 1}$

In Exercises 44 and 45, list all asymptotes of the graph of the function.

44. $f(x) = \dfrac{x^2 - 1}{x^3 - 2x^2 - 5x + 6}$

45. $g(x) = \dfrac{x^4 - 6x^3 + 2x^2 - 6x + 2}{x^2 - 3}$

In Exercises 46–49, find a viewing window (or windows) that shows a complete graph of the function. Be alert for hidden behavior.

46. $f(x) = \dfrac{x - 3}{x^2 + x - 2}$

47. $g(x) = \dfrac{x^2 - x - 6}{x^3 - 3x^2 + 3x - 1}$

48. $h(x) = \dfrac{x^4 + 4}{x^4 - 99x^2 - 100}$

49. $k(x) = \dfrac{x^3 - 2x^2 - 4x + 8}{x - 10}$

50. Which of these statements is true about the graph of

$$f(x) = \frac{(x - 1)(x + 3)}{(x^2 + 1)(x^2 - 1)} ?$$

  a. The graph has two vertical asymptotes.
  b. The graph touches the x-axis at $x = 3$.
  c. The graph lies above the x-axis when $x < -1$.
  d. The graph has a hole at $x = 1$.
  e. The graph has no horizontal asymptotes.

Section 4.5

In Exercises 51–58, solve the equation in the complex number system.

51. $x^2 + 3x + 10 = 0$

52. $x^2 + 2x + 5 = 0$

53. $5x^2 + 2 = 3x$

54. $-3x^2 + 4x - 5 = 0$

55. $3x^4 + x^2 - 2 = 0$

56. $8x^4 + 10x^2 + 3 = 0$

57. $x^3 + 8 = 0$

58. $x^3 - 27 = 0$

59. One zero of $x^4 - x^3 - x^2 - x - 2$ is i. Find all zeros.

60. One zero of $x^4 + x^3 - 5x^2 + x - 6$ is i. Find all zeros.

61. Give an example of a fourth-degree polynomial with real coefficients whose zeros include 0 and $1 + i$.

62. Find a fourth-degree polynomial f whose only zeros are $2 + i$ and $2 - i$ such that $f(-1) = 50$.

Section 4.5.A

63. Find the orbit of 1 for $f(z) = \left(\dfrac{3}{5} + \dfrac{4}{5}i\right) z$.

64. Find the orbit of 0 for $f(z) = z^2 + c$ using the following values of c. State whether c is in the Mandelbrot set.

  a. $c = -1$ **b.** $c = -0.5 + 0.6i$ **c.** $c = 0.3 + 0.5i$

Section 4.6

Factor each of the following over the set of real numbers and over the set of complex numbers.

65. $x^3 - 6x^2 + 11x - 6$

66. $x^3 + 3x^2 + 3x + 2$

67. $x^4 - x^3 - x^2 - x - 2$

68. $2x^3 + 3x^2 + 9x + 4$

69. $x^4 + 2x^2 + 1$

70. $9x^5 + 30x^4 + 43x^3 + 114x^2 + 28x - 24$

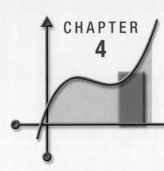

can do calculus

Optimization Applications

Many real-world situations require you to find the largest or smallest quantity satisfying certain conditions. For instance, automotive engineers want to design engines with maximum fuel efficiency. Similarly, a cereal manufacturer who needs a box of volume 300 cubic inches might want to know the dimensions of the box that requires the least amount of cardboard, which is the cheapest to make. The exact solutions of such minimum/maximum problems require calculus. However, graphing technology can provide very accurate approximate solutions.

Example 1 Maximum of a Rational Function

Find two negative numbers whose product is 50 and whose sum is as large as possible.

Solution

Let x and z be the two negative numbers, and let y be their sum. Then $xz = 50$ and $y = x + z$. Solving $xz = 50$ for z yields $z = \dfrac{50}{x}$ so that

$$y = x + z = x + \frac{50}{x}.$$

The desired quantity is the value of x that makes y as large as possible. Since x must be negative, graph $y = x + \dfrac{50}{x}$ in a window with $-20 \le x \le 0$.

Each point (x, y) on the graph represents the following:

- x represents one of the two negative number, and $\dfrac{50}{x}$ represents the other negative number

- y is the sum of the two negative numbers

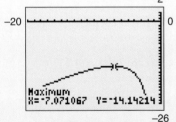

Figure 4.C-1

The largest y possible is the point on the graph with largest y-coordinate, that is, the highest point on this part of the graph. Either zoom-in or use the maximum finder to approximate the highest point. As shown in Figure 4.C-1, the largest value of y is approximately -14.14214 which occurs when $x \approx -7.071067$. Therefore, the numbers are approximately -7.071067 and $\dfrac{50}{-7.071067} \approx -7.071069$. The exact solution, as found by using calculus, is $\sqrt{50}$—which is approximately -7.071068 and is very close to the graphical solution.

Example 2 Largest Volume of a Box

A box with no top is to be made from a 22 × 30 inch sheet of cardboard by cutting squares of equal size from each corner and bending up the flaps, as shown in Figure 4.C-2. To the nearest hundredth of an inch, what size square should be cut from each corner in order to obtain a box with the largest possible volume? What is the volume of this box?

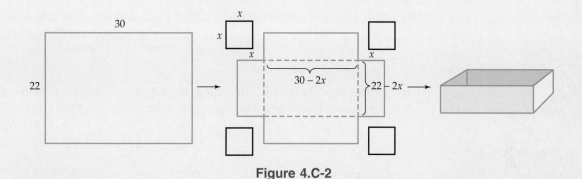

Figure 4.C-2

Solution

Let x denote the length of the side of the square to be cut from each corner. Then,

$$\text{Volume of box} = \text{Length} \times \text{Width} \times \text{Height}$$
$$= (30 - 2x)(22 - 2x)x$$
$$= 4x^3 - 104x^2 + 660x$$

Thus, the equation $y = 4x^3 - 104x^2 + 660x$ gives the volume y of the box that results from cutting an $x \times x$ square from each corner. Because the shortest side of the cardboard is 22 inches, the length x of the side of the cut-out square must be less than 11. (Why?)

On the graph of $f(x) = 4x^3 - 104x^2 + 660x$,

- the x-coordinate of each point is the size of the square to be cut from each corner.
- the y-coordinate of each point is the volume of the resulting box.

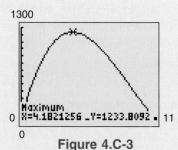

Figure 4.C-3

The box with the largest volume corresponds to the point with the largest y-coordinate, that is, the highest point in the viewing window. A maximum find shows that the highest point is approximately (4.182, 1233.809), as shown in Figure 4.C-3. Therefore, a square measuring approximately 4.18 × 4.18 inches should be cut from each corner, producing a box of approximately 1233.81 cubic inches.

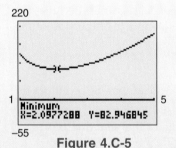

Example 3   Minimum Surface Area of a Cylinder

A cylindrical can of volume 58 cubic inches (approximately 1 quart) is to be designed. For convenient handling, it must be at least 1 inch high and 2 inches in diameter. What dimensions will use the least amount of material?

Solution

The cylinder can be constructed by rolling a rectangular sheet of metal into a tube and then attaching the top and bottom, as shown in Figure 4.C-4. The surface area of the can, which determines the amount of material needed, has the following formula:

Surface Area = Area of rectangular sheet + Area of top + Area of bottom

$$= \quad Ch \quad + \pi r^2 \quad + \pi r^2$$
$$= Ch + 2\pi r^2$$

When the sheet is rolled into a tube, the width c of the sheet is the circumference of the ends of the can, so $C = 2\pi r$.

$$\text{Surface Area} = Ch + 2\pi r^2$$
$$= 2\pi rh + 2\pi r^2$$

The volume of the cylinder of radius r and height h is $\pi r^2 h$. Since the can is to have volume 58 cubic inches,

$$\pi r^2 h = 58, \qquad \text{or equivalently,} \qquad h = \frac{58}{\pi r^2}.$$

Therefore,

$$\text{surface area} = 2\pi rh + 2\pi r^2 = 2\pi r\left(\frac{58}{\pi r^2}\right) + 2\pi r^2 = \frac{116}{r} + 2\pi r^2.$$

Note that r must be 1 or greater because the diameter $2r$ must be at least 2. Furthermore, r cannot be more than 5 because if $r > 5$ and $h \geq 1$, then the volume $\pi r^2 h$ would be at least $\pi(25)(1)$, which is greater than 58.

The situation can be represented by the graph of the equation $y = \frac{116}{x} + 2\pi x^2$.

The x-coordinate of each point represents a possible radius, and the y-coordinate represents the surface area of the corresponding can. A graphical minimum finder shows that the coordinates of the lowest point are approximately (2.098, 82.947), as shown in Figure 4.C-5.

If the radius is 2.098, then the height is $\dfrac{58}{2.098^2 \cdot \pi} \approx 4.19$.

The dimensions of can that uses the least amount of materials are approximately a radius of 2.1 inches and a height of 4.2 inches.

Figure 4.C-4

Figure 4.C-5

Exercises

1. Find the highest point on the part of the graph of $y = x^3 - 3x + 2$ that is shown in the given window. The answers are not all the same.
   a. $-2 \leq x \leq 0$ **b.** $-2 \leq x \leq 2$
   c. $-2 \leq x \leq 3$

2. Find the lowest point on the part of the graph of $y = x^3 - 3x + 2$ that is shown in the given window.
   a. $0 \leq x \leq 2$ **b.** $-2 \leq x \leq 2$
   c. $-3 \leq x \leq 2$

3. An open-top box with a square base is to be constructed from 120 square centimeters of material. What dimensions will produce a box
   a. of volume 100 cm³?
   b. with largest possible volume?

4. A 20-inch square piece of metal is to be used to make an open-top box by cutting equal-sized squares from each corner and folding up the sides (as in Example 2). The length, width, and height of the box are each to be less than 12 inches. What size squares should be cut out to produce a box with
   a. volume 550 in³?
   b. largest possible volume?

5. A cylindrical waste container with no top, a diameter of at least 2 feet, and a volume of 25 cubic feet is to be constructed. What should its radius be under the given conditions?
   a. 65 square feet of material will be used to construct it
   b. the smallest possible amount of material will be used to construct it (how much material is needed?)

6. If $c(x)$ is the cost of producing x units, then $\dfrac{c(x)}{x}$ is the average cost per unit. Suppose the cost of producing x units is given by $c(x) = 0.13x^3 - 70x^2 + 10{,}000x$ and that no more than 300 units can be produced per week.
   a. If the average cost is $1100 per unit, how many units are being produced?
   b. What production level should be used in order to minimize the average cost per unit? What is the minimum average cost?

7. If the cost of material to make the can in Example 3 is 5 cents per square inch for the top and bottom and 3 cents per square inch for the sides, what dimensions should be used to minimize the cost of making the can? [The answer is not the same as in Example 3.]

8. A certain type of fencing comes in rigid 10-foot segments. Four uncut segments are used to fence in a garden on the side of a building, as shown in the figure. What value of x will result in a garden of the largest possible area? What is that area?

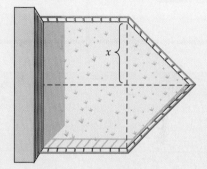

9. A rectangle is to be inscribed in a semicircle of radius 2, as shown in the figure. What is the largest possible area of such a rectangle? *Hint:* The width of the rectangle is the second coordinate of the point P (Why?), and P is on the top half of the circle $x^2 + y^2 = 4$.

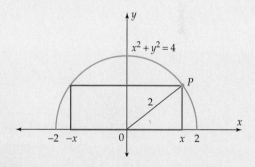

10. Find the point on the graph of $y = 5 - x^2$ that is closest to the point $(0, 1)$ and has positive coordinates. *Hint:* The distance from the point (x, y) on the graph to $(0, 1)$ is $\sqrt{(x - 0)^2 + (y - 1)^2}$; express y in terms of x.

CHAPTER 5

Exponential and Logarithmic Functions

Doorway to the past

The image above is of Pueblo Benito in Chaco Canyon, New Mexico. It was the home of the Anasazi people of the desert southwest for several centuries, and it includes timbers (shown above the doorway) that were used to date the buildings by using carbon-14 dating, which involves an exponential equation. See Exercise 55 Section 5.6.

Chapter Outline

Chapter Review

can do calculus Tangents to Exponential Functions

Interdependence of Sections

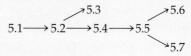

Section 5.1 contains prerequisite review material for this chapter. If students are familiar enough with the objectives of this section, it may be skipped.

E xponential and logarithmic functions are essential for the mathematical description of a variety of phenomena in the physical sciences, engineering, and economics. Although a calculator is necessary to evaluate these functions for most values, you will not be able to use your calculator efficiently or interpret its answers unless you understand the properties of these functions. When calculations can readily be done by hand, you will be expected to do them without a calculator.

Radicals and Rational Exponents

Objectives

- Define and apply rational and irrational exponents

- Simplify expressions containing radicals or rational exponents

---

NOTE All constants, variables, and solutions in this chapter are real numbers.

---

*n*th Roots

Recall that when $c \geq 0$, the square root of c is the nonnegative solution of the equation $x^2 = c$. Cube roots, fourth roots, and higher roots are defined in a similar fashion as solutions of the equation $x^n = c$.

This equation can be solved graphically by finding the x-coordinate of the intersection points of the graphs of $y = x^n$ and $y = c$. (Review finding solutions graphically in Section 2.1 and the shape of the graph of $y = ax^n$ in Section 4.3, if needed.)

Depending on whether n is even or odd and whether c is positive or negative, $x^n = c$ may have two, one, or no solutions, as shown in the following figures.

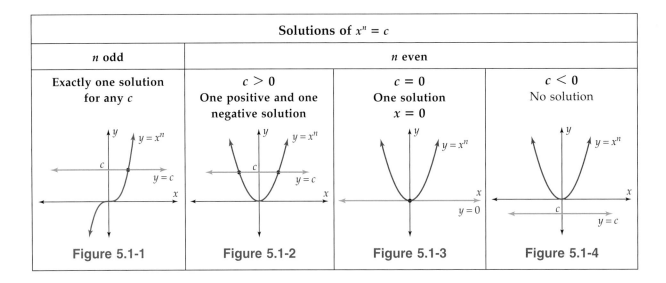

Solutions of $x^n = c$			
***n* odd**	***n* even**		
Exactly one solution for any c	$c > 0$ One positive and one negative solution	$c = 0$ One solution $x = 0$	$c < 0$ No solution

Figure 5.1-1   Figure 5.1-2   Figure 5.1-3   Figure 5.1-4

The figures illustrate the following definition of *n*th roots.

*n*th Roots

Let c be a real number and n a positive integer. The ***n*th root** of c is denoted by either of the symbols

$$\sqrt[n]{c} \quad \text{or} \quad c^{\frac{1}{n}}$$

and is defined to be

- the solution of $x^n = c$ when n is odd; or
- the nonnegative solution of $x^n = c$ when n is even and $c \geq 0$.

Examples of *n*th roots are shown below.

$$\sqrt[3]{-8} = (-8)^{\frac{1}{3}} = -2 \text{ because } -2 \text{ is the solution of } x^3 = -8.$$
$$\sqrt[4]{81} = (81)^{\frac{1}{4}} = 3 \text{ because } 3 \text{ is the nonnegative solution of } x^4 = 81.$$

Expressions involving *n*th roots can often be simplified or written in a variety of ways by using a basic fact of exponents.

$$\sqrt[n]{cd} = \sqrt[n]{c}\,\sqrt[n]{d} \quad \text{or equivalently,} \quad (cd)^{\frac{1}{n}} = c^{\frac{1}{n}}d^{\frac{1}{n}}$$

Example 1   Operations on *n*th Roots

Simplify each expression.

a. $\sqrt{8} \cdot \sqrt{12}$

b. $\sqrt{12} - \sqrt{75}$

c. $\sqrt[3]{8x^6y^4}$

d. $(5 + \sqrt{c})(5 - \sqrt{c})$, where $c > 0$

Solution

a. $\sqrt{8} \cdot \sqrt{12} = \sqrt{8 \cdot 12} = \sqrt{96} = \sqrt{16 \cdot 6} = \sqrt{16} \cdot \sqrt{6} = 4\sqrt{6}$

b. $\sqrt{12} - \sqrt{75} = \sqrt{4 \cdot 3} - \sqrt{25 \cdot 3} = \sqrt{4}\sqrt{3} - \sqrt{25}\sqrt{3}$
$$= 2\sqrt{3} - 5\sqrt{3} = -3\sqrt{3}$$

c. $\sqrt[3]{8x^6y^4} = \sqrt[3]{8} \cdot \sqrt[3]{x^3 \cdot x^3} \cdot \sqrt[3]{y^3 \cdot y} = 2x^2y\sqrt[3]{y}$

d. $\left(5 + \sqrt{c}\right)\left(5 - \sqrt{c}\right) = 5^2 - \left(\sqrt{c}\right)^2 = 25 - c$

When using a calculator, exponent notation for nth roots is usually preferred over radical notation.

■

<table>
<tr><td>

CAUTION

When using exponent notation to evaluate nth roots with a calculator, be sure to use parentheses when raising to the fractional power. Example: To enter $\sqrt[3]{9}$, press 9^(1/3).

</td></tr>
</table>

$$\boxed{\text{Example 2}}\quad \text{Evaluating } n\text{th Roots}$$

Use a calculator to approximate each expression to the nearest ten-thousandth.

a. $40^{\frac{1}{5}}$ b. $225^{\frac{1}{11}}$

Solution

a. Because $\dfrac{1}{5} = 0.2$, the expressions $40^{\frac{1}{5}}$ and $40^{0.2}$ are equivalent, as shown at right.

$$40^{\frac{1}{5}} \approx 2.0913$$

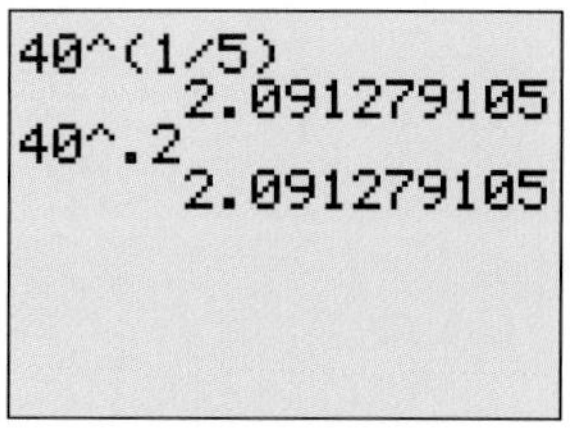

```
40^(1/5)
        2.091279105
40^.2
        2.091279105
```

Figure 5.1-5

b. The fraction $\dfrac{1}{11}$ is equivalent to the repeating decimal $0.090909\cdots$. The fraction $\dfrac{1}{11}$ is not equivalent to this decimal if it is rounded off, as shown at left. Therefore, it is better to leave the exponent in fractional form.

$$225^{\frac{1}{11}} \approx 1.6362$$

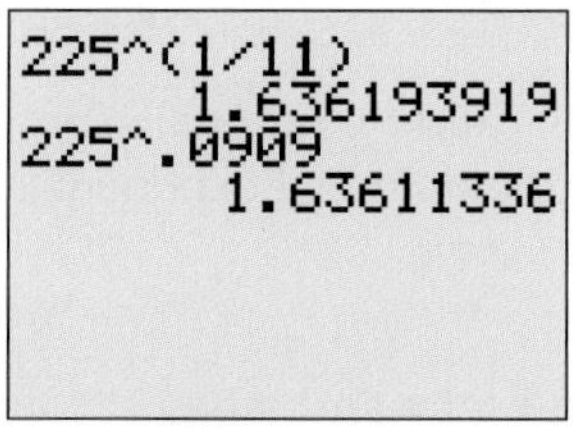

■

```
225^(1/11)
        1.636193919
225^.0909
        1.63611336
```

Figure 5.1-6

Rational Exponents

Rational exponents of the form $\dfrac{1}{n}$ are called nth roots. Rational exponents can also be of the form $\dfrac{m}{n}$, such as $4^{\frac{3}{2}}$. Rational exponents of the form $\dfrac{m}{n}$ can be defined in such a way that the laws of exponents, such as $c^{rs} = (c^r)^s$, are still valid. For example, because $\dfrac{3}{2} = (3)\dfrac{1}{2} = \left(\dfrac{1}{2}\right)3$, it is reasonable to say that $4^{\frac{3}{2}} = (4^3)^{\frac{1}{2}} = (4^{\frac{1}{2}})^3$. These expressions are equivalent.

$$4^{\frac{3}{2}} = (4^3)^{\frac{1}{2}} = (64)^{\frac{1}{2}} = \sqrt{64} = 8$$
$$4^{\frac{3}{2}} = (4^{\frac{1}{2}})^3 = \left(\sqrt{4}\right)^3 = (2)^3 = 8$$

This illustrates the definition of rational exponents.

Definition of Rational Exponents

Let c be a positive real number and let $\frac{t}{k}$ be a rational number with positive denominator.

$c^{\frac{t}{k}}$ is defined to be the number $(c^t)^{\frac{1}{k}} = (c^{\frac{1}{k}})^t$

In radical notation, $c^{\frac{t}{k}} = \sqrt[k]{c^t} = (\sqrt[k]{c})^t$.

Every terminating decimal is a rational number; therefore, expressions such as $13^{3.78}$ can be expressed as $13^{\frac{378}{100}}$. Although the definition of rational exponents requires c to be positive, it remains valid when c is negative, *provided that* the exponent is in lowest terms with an odd denominator, such as $(-8)^{\frac{2}{3}}$. In Exercise 89, you will explore why these restrictions are necessary when c is negative.

CAUTION

Although $(-8)^{\frac{2}{3}} = \sqrt[3]{(-8)^2} = \sqrt[3]{64} = 4$, and 4 is a real number, entering $(-8)^{\frac{2}{3}}$ on some calculators may produce either an error message or a complex number. If this occurs, you can get the correct answer by entering one of the equivalent expressions below.

$$[(-8)^2]^{\frac{1}{3}} \quad \text{or} \quad [(-8)^{\frac{1}{3}}]^2$$

Laws of Exponents

You have seen that the law of exponents $c^{rs} = (c^r)^s$ is valid for rational exponents. In fact, all of the laws of exponents are valid for rational exponents.

Laws of Exponents

Let c and d be nonnegative real numbers and let r and s be rational numbers. Then

1. $c^r c^s = c^{r+s}$

2. $\dfrac{c^r}{c^s} = c^{r-s}$ $(c \neq 0)$

3. $(c^r)^s = c^{rs}$

4. $(cd)^r = c^r d^r$

5. $\left(\dfrac{c}{d}\right)^r = \dfrac{c^r}{d^r}$ $(d \neq 0)$

6. $c^{-r} = \dfrac{1}{c^r}$ $(c \neq 0)$

If $c \neq 1$ and $d \neq 1$,

- $c^r = c^s$ if and only if $r = s$.

- $c^r = d^r$ if and only if $c = d$.

Example 3   **Simplifying Expressions with Rational Exponents**

Write the expression $(8r^{\frac{3}{4}}s^{-3})^{\frac{2}{3}}$ using only positive exponents.

Solution

$$(8r^{\frac{3}{4}}s^{-3})^{\frac{2}{3}} = 8^{\frac{2}{3}}(r^{\frac{3}{4}})^{\frac{2}{3}}(s^{-3})^{\frac{2}{3}} \qquad (cd)^r = c^r d^r$$
$$= \sqrt[3]{8^2}(r^{\frac{6}{12}})(s^{-\frac{6}{3}}) \qquad \text{definition and } (c^r)^s = c^{rs}$$
$$= \sqrt[3]{64}(r^{\frac{1}{2}})(s^{-2}) \qquad \text{simplify}$$
$$= \frac{4r^{\frac{1}{2}}}{s^2} \qquad \text{simplify and } c^{-r} = \frac{1}{c^r}$$

The expression $\dfrac{4r^{\frac{1}{2}}}{s^2}$ can also be written as $= \dfrac{4\sqrt{r}}{s^2}$ if it is more convenient.

Example 4 Simplifying Expressions with Rational Exponents

Simplify the expression $x^{\frac{1}{2}}(x^{\frac{3}{4}} - x^{\frac{3}{2}})$.

Solution

$$x^{\frac{1}{2}}(x^{\frac{3}{4}} - x^{\frac{3}{2}}) = x^{\frac{1}{2}}x^{\frac{3}{4}} - x^{\frac{1}{2}}x^{\frac{3}{2}} \qquad a(b-c) = ab - ac$$
$$= x^{\frac{1}{2}+\frac{3}{4}} - x^{\frac{1}{2}+\frac{3}{2}} \qquad c^r c^s = c^{r+s}$$
$$= x^{\frac{5}{4}} - x^{\frac{4}{2}}$$
$$= x^{\frac{5}{4}} - x^2$$

Example 5 Simplifying Expressions with Rational Exponents

Simplify the expression $(x^{\frac{5}{2}}y^4)(xy^{\frac{7}{4}})^{-2}$.

Solution

$$(x^{\frac{5}{2}}y^4)(xy^{\frac{7}{4}})^{-2} = (x^{\frac{5}{2}}y^4)(x^{-2})(y^{\frac{7}{4}})^{-2} \qquad (cd)^r$$
$$= (x^{\frac{5}{2}}y^4)(x^{-2})(y^{-\frac{14}{4}}) \qquad (c^r)^s$$
$$= x^{\frac{5}{2}}x^{-2}y^4 y^{-\frac{7}{2}} \qquad \text{commutative}$$
$$= x^{\frac{5}{2}-2}y^{4-\frac{7}{2}} \qquad c^r c^s = c^{r+s}$$
$$= x^{\frac{1}{2}}y^{\frac{1}{2}} \qquad \text{simplify}$$

Example 6 Simplifying Expressions with Rational Exponents

Let k be a positive rational number. Write the expression $\sqrt[10]{c^{5k}}\sqrt{(c^{-k})^{\frac{1}{2}}}$ without radicals, using only positive exponents.

Solution

$$\sqrt[10]{c^{5k}}\sqrt{(c^{-k})^{\frac{1}{2}}} = (c^{5k})^{\frac{1}{10}}[(c^{-k})^{\frac{1}{2}}]^{\frac{1}{2}} \qquad \text{definition}$$
$$= c^{\frac{5k}{10}}(c^{-\frac{k}{2}})^{\frac{1}{2}} \qquad (c^r)^s = c^{rs}$$
$$= c^{\frac{k}{2}}c^{-\frac{k}{4}} \qquad \text{simplify and } (c^r)^s = c^{rs}$$
$$= c^{\frac{k}{2}-\frac{k}{4}} \qquad c^r c^s = c^{r+s}$$
$$= c^{\frac{k}{4}} \qquad \text{simplify}$$

Rationalizing Denominators and Numerators

Transforming fractions with radicals in the denominator to equivalent fractions with no radicals in the denominator is called *rationalizing the denominator*. Before the common use of calculators, fractions with rational denominators were preferred because they were easier to calculate or estimate. With calculators today there is no computational advantage to rationalizing denominators. However, the skill of rationalizing numerators or denominators is useful in calculus.

Example 7 **Rationalizing the Denominator**

Rationalize the denominator of each fraction.

a. $\dfrac{7}{\sqrt{5}}$ **b.** $\dfrac{2}{3 + \sqrt{6}}$

Solution

a. Multiply the fraction by 1 using a suitable radical fraction.

$$\frac{7}{\sqrt{5}} = \frac{7}{\sqrt{5}} \cdot 1 = \frac{7}{\sqrt{5}} \cdot \frac{\sqrt{5}}{\sqrt{5}} = \frac{7\sqrt{5}}{5}$$

b. Use the multiplication pattern $(a + b)(a - b) = a^2 - b^2$ to determine a suitable radical fraction equivalent to 1.

$$\frac{2}{3 + \sqrt{6}} = \frac{2}{3 + \sqrt{6}} \cdot 1$$

$$= \frac{2}{3 + \sqrt{6}} \cdot \frac{3 - \sqrt{6}}{3 - \sqrt{6}}$$

$$= \frac{2(3 - \sqrt{6})}{(3 + \sqrt{6})(3 - \sqrt{6})}$$

$$= \frac{6 - 2\sqrt{6}}{9 - 6}$$

$$= \frac{6 - 2\sqrt{6}}{3}$$

NOTE When rationalizing a denominator or numerator which contains a radical expression, use a suitable radical fraction, equal to one, that contains the conjugate of the expression.

Example 8 **Rationalizing the Numerator**

Assume $h \neq 0$. Rationalize the numerator of $\dfrac{\sqrt{x + h} - \sqrt{x}}{h}$.

Solution

Multiply the fraction by 1 using a suitable radical fraction.

$$\frac{\sqrt{x+h}-\sqrt{x}}{h} = \frac{\sqrt{x+h}-\sqrt{x}}{h}\cdot 1$$

$$= \frac{\sqrt{x+h}-\sqrt{x}}{h}\cdot\frac{\sqrt{x+h}+\sqrt{x}}{\sqrt{x+h}+\sqrt{x}}$$

$$= \frac{\left(\sqrt{x+h}\right)^2-\left(\sqrt{x}\right)^2}{h\left(\sqrt{x+h}+\sqrt{x}\right)}$$

$$= \frac{x+h-x}{h\left(\sqrt{x+h}+\sqrt{x}\right)}$$

$$= \frac{h}{h\left(\sqrt{x+h}+\sqrt{x}\right)}$$

$$= \frac{1}{\sqrt{x+h}+\sqrt{x}}$$

Irrational Exponents

The example (not proof) below illustrates how a^t is defined when t is an irrational number.

To compute $10^{\sqrt{2}}$, the exponent could be replaced with the equivalent non-terminating decimal $1.414213562\ldots$. Each of the decimal approximations of $\sqrt{2}$ given below is a more accurate approximation than the preceding one.

$$1.4,\ 1.41,\ 1.414,\ 1.4142,\ 1.41421,\ \ldots .$$

We can raise 10 to each of these rational numbers.

$$10^{1.4} \approx 25.1189$$
$$10^{1.41} \approx 25.7040$$
$$10^{1.414} \approx 25.9418$$
$$10^{1.4142} \approx 25.9537$$
$$10^{1.41421} \approx 25.9543$$
$$10^{1.414213} \approx 25.9545$$

The pattern suggests that as the exponent r gets closer and closer to $\sqrt{2}$, 10^r gets closer and closer to a real number whose decimal expansion begins $25.954\ldots$. So $10^{\sqrt{2}}$ is defined to be this number.

Similarly, for any $a > 0$,

a^t **is a well-defined positive number for each real exponent t.**

The fact below shall be assumed.

The laws of exponents are valid for *all* real exponents.

Exercises 5.1

Note: Unless directed otherwise, assume all letters represent positive real numbers.

In Exercises 1–15, evaluate each expression without using a calculator.

1. $\sqrt{144}$ 2. $\sqrt[3]{64}$ 3. $\sqrt[4]{16}$

4. $\sqrt[3]{-27}$ 5. $\sqrt{0.0081}$ 6. $\sqrt{0.000169}$

7. $\sqrt[3]{0.008}$ 8. $\sqrt[3]{-0.125}$ 9. $\sqrt{0.5^6}$

10. $\sqrt{(-3)^4}$ 11. $27^{\frac{4}{3}}$ 12. $81^{-\frac{1}{4}}$

13. $(-64)^{\frac{2}{3}}$ 14. $\left(-\dfrac{1}{64}\right)^{-\frac{2}{3}}$ 15. $16^{-\frac{3}{2}}$

In Exercises 16–40, simplify each expression without using a calculator.

16. $\sqrt{3^{15}}$ 17. $\sqrt[3]{12^{16}}$

18. $\sqrt{0.08^{12}}$ 19. $\sqrt{(-11)^{28}}$

20. $\sqrt[3]{(-0.05)^{24}}$ 21. $\sqrt[3]{0.4^{18}}$

22. $\sqrt{6} \cdot \sqrt{12}$ 23. $\sqrt{8} \cdot \sqrt{96}$

24. $\sqrt[3]{18} \cdot \sqrt[3]{12}$ 25. $\sqrt[3]{-32} \cdot \sqrt[3]{16}$

26. $\dfrac{\sqrt{10}}{\sqrt{8} \cdot \sqrt{5}}$ 27. $\dfrac{\sqrt{6}}{\sqrt{14} \cdot \sqrt{63}}$

28. $\dfrac{\sqrt[3]{324}}{\sqrt[3]{6} \cdot \sqrt[3]{2}}$ 29. $\dfrac{\sqrt[3]{54}}{\sqrt[3]{32} \cdot \sqrt[3]{-4}}$

30. $\sqrt{27} + 2\sqrt{3}$ 31. $4\sqrt{5} - \sqrt{20}$

32. $(1 + \sqrt{3})(2 - \sqrt{3})$

33. $(3 + \sqrt{2})(3 - \sqrt{2})$

34. $(4 - \sqrt{3})(5 + 2\sqrt{3})$

35. $(2\sqrt{5} - 4)(3\sqrt{5} + 2)$

36. $(3\sqrt{2} - 4\sqrt{6})^2$

37. $5\sqrt{20} - \sqrt{45} + 2\sqrt{80}$

38. $\sqrt[3]{40} + 2\sqrt[3]{135} - 5\sqrt[3]{320}$

39. $\dfrac{2^{\frac{11}{2}} \cdot 2^{-7} \cdot 2^{-5}}{2^3 \cdot 2^{\frac{1}{2}} \cdot 2^{-10}}$ 40. $\dfrac{(3^2)^{-\frac{1}{2}}(9^4)^{-1}}{27^{-3}}$

In Exercises 41–56, simplify each expression.

41. $\sqrt{16a^8 b^{-2}}$ 42. $\sqrt{24x^6 y^{-4}}$

43. $\dfrac{\sqrt{c^2 d^6}}{\sqrt{4c^3 d^{-4}}}$ 44. $\dfrac{\sqrt{a^{-10} b^{-12}}}{\sqrt{a^{14} d^{-4}}}$

45. $\sqrt[9]{(4x + 2y)^8}$

46. $\sqrt[3]{a + b} \cdot \sqrt[3]{-(a + b)^2} + \sqrt[3]{a + b}$

47. $\sqrt{x^7} \cdot x^{\frac{5}{2}} \cdot x^{-\frac{3}{2}}$ 48. $\left(x^{\frac{1}{2}} y^3\right)\left(x^0 y^7\right)^{-2}$

49. $\left(c^{\frac{2}{5}} d^{-\frac{2}{3}}\right)\left(c^6 d^3\right)^{\frac{4}{3}}$ 50. $\left(\dfrac{r^{\frac{2}{3}}}{s^{\frac{1}{5}}}\right)^{\frac{15}{9}}$

51. $\dfrac{(7a)^2 (5b)^{\frac{3}{2}}}{(5a)^{\frac{3}{2}}(7b)^4}$ 52. $\dfrac{(6a)^{\frac{1}{2}} \sqrt{ab}}{a^2 b^{\frac{3}{2}}}$

53. $\dfrac{(2a)^{\frac{1}{2}}(3b)^{-2}(4a)^{\frac{3}{5}}}{(4a)^{-\frac{3}{2}}(3b)^2 (2a)^{\frac{1}{5}}}$ 54. $\dfrac{\left(a^{\frac{3}{4}} b\right)^2 \left(ab^{\frac{1}{4}}\right)^3}{(ab)^{\frac{1}{2}}(bc)^{-\frac{1}{4}}}$

55. $\left(a^{x^2}\right)^{\frac{1}{x}}$ 56. $\dfrac{(b^x)^{x-1}}{b^{-x}}$

In Exercises 57–66, write each expression without radicals, using only positive exponents.

57. $\sqrt[3]{a^2 + b^2}$ 58. $\sqrt[4]{a^3 - b^3}$

59. $\sqrt[4]{\sqrt[4]{a^3}}$ 60. $\sqrt{\sqrt[3]{a^3 b^4}}$

61. $\sqrt[5]{t} \cdot \sqrt{16t^5}$ 62. $\sqrt{x} \cdot \sqrt[3]{x^2} \cdot \sqrt[4]{x^3}$

63. $\left(\sqrt[3]{xy^2}\right)^{-\frac{3}{5}}$ 64. $\left(\sqrt[4]{r^{14} s^{-\frac{21}{5}}}\right)^{-\frac{3}{7}}$

65. $\dfrac{c}{(c^{\frac{5}{6}})^{42}(c^{51})^{-\frac{2}{3}}}$ 66. $\left(c^{\frac{5}{6}} - c^{-\frac{5}{6}}\right)^2$

In Exercises 67–72, simplify each expression.

67. $x^{\frac{1}{2}}\left(x^{\frac{2}{3}} - x^{\frac{4}{3}}\right)$ 68. $x^{\frac{1}{2}}\left(3x^{\frac{3}{2}} + 2x^{-\frac{1}{2}}\right)$

69. $\left(x^{\frac{1}{2}} + y^{\frac{1}{2}}\right)\left(x^{\frac{1}{2}} - y^{\frac{1}{2}}\right)$ 70. $\left(x^{\frac{1}{3}} + y^{\frac{1}{2}}\right)\left(2x^{\frac{1}{3}} - y^{\frac{1}{2}}\right)$

71. $(x + y)^{\frac{1}{2}}\left[(x + y)^{\frac{1}{2}} - (x + y)\right]$

72. $\left(x^{\frac{1}{3}} + y^{\frac{1}{3}}\right)\left(x^{\frac{2}{3}} - x^{\frac{1}{3}}y^{\frac{1}{3}} + y^{\frac{2}{3}}\right)$

In Exercises 73–78, rationalize the denominator and simplify your answer.

73. $\dfrac{3}{\sqrt{8}}$ 74. $\dfrac{2}{\sqrt{6}}$ 75. $\dfrac{3}{2 + \sqrt{12}}$

76. $\dfrac{1 + \sqrt{3}}{5 + \sqrt{10}}$ 77. $\dfrac{2}{\sqrt{x} + 2}$ 78. $\dfrac{\sqrt{x}}{\sqrt{x} - \sqrt{c}}$

In Exercises 79–84, factor the given expression. For example, $x - x^{\frac{1}{2}} - 2 = (x^{\frac{1}{2}} - 2)(x^{\frac{1}{2}} + 1)$.

79. $x^{\frac{2}{3}} + x^{\frac{1}{3}} - 6$ **80.** $x^{\frac{2}{5}} + 11x^{\frac{1}{5}} + 30$

81. $x + 4x^{\frac{1}{2}} + 3$ **82.** $x^{\frac{1}{3}} + 7x^{\frac{1}{6}} + 10$

83. $x^{\frac{4}{5}} - 81$ **84.** $x^{\frac{2}{3}} - 6x^{\frac{1}{3}} + 9$

In Exercises 85–88, rationalize the numerator and simplify your answer. Assume $h \neq 0$.

85. $\dfrac{\sqrt{x + h + 1} - \sqrt{x + 1}}{h}$

86. $\dfrac{2\sqrt{x + h + 3} - 2\sqrt{x + 3}}{h}$

87. $\dfrac{\sqrt{(x + h)^2 + 1} - \sqrt{x^2 + 1}}{h}$

88. $\dfrac{\sqrt{(x + h)^2 - (x + h)} - \sqrt{x^2 - x}}{h}$

89. Some restrictions are necessary when defining fractional powers of a negative number.
   a. Explain why the equations $x^2 = -4$, $x^4 = -4$, $x^6 = -4$, etc., have no real solutions. Conclude that $c^{\frac{1}{2}}, c^{\frac{1}{4}}, c^{\frac{1}{6}}$ cannot be defined when $c = -4$.
   b. Since $\dfrac{1}{3}$ is the same as $\dfrac{2}{6}$, it should be true that $c^{\frac{1}{3}} = c^{\frac{2}{6}}$, that is, that $\sqrt[3]{c} = \sqrt[6]{c^2}$. Show that this is false when $c = -8$.

90. a. Suppose r is a solution of the equation $x^n = c$ and s is a solution of $x^n = d$. Verify that rs is a solution of $x^n = cd$.
   b. Explain why part **a** shows that $\sqrt[n]{cd} = \sqrt[n]{c} \cdot \sqrt[n]{d}$.

91. Write laws 3, 4, and 5 of exponents in radical notation in the case when $r = \dfrac{1}{m}$ and $s = \dfrac{1}{n}$.

92. a. Graph $f(x) = x^5$ and explain why this function has an inverse function.
   b. Show algebraically that the inverse function is $g(x) = x^{\frac{1}{5}}$.

93. If n is an odd positive integer, show that $f(x) = x^n$ has an inverse function and find the rule of the inverse function. *Hint:* Exercise 92 is the case when $n = 5$.

94. A long pendulum swings more slowly than a short pendulum. The time it takes for a pendulum to complete one full swing, or cycle,

is called its period. The relationship between the period T (in seconds) of the pendulum and its length x (in meters) is given by the function $T(x) = 2\pi\sqrt{\dfrac{x}{9.8}}$. Find the period for pendulums whose lengths are 0.5 m and 1.0 m.

95. In meteorology, the wind chill C can be calculated by using the formula $C = 0.0817(3.71\sqrt{V} + 5.81 - 0.25V)(t - 91.4) + 91.4$, where V is the wind speed in miles per hour and t is the air temperature in degrees Fahrenheit. Find the wind chill when the wind speed is 12 miles per hour and the temperature is 35°F.

96. The elevation E in meters above sea level and the boiling point of water, T, in degrees Celsius at that elevation are related by the equation $E \approx 1000(100 - T) + 580(100 - T)^2$. Find the approximate boiling point of water at an elevation of 1600 meters.

97. Accident investigators can usually estimate a motorist's speed s in miles per hour by examining the length d in feet of the skid marks on the road. The estimate of the speed also depends on the road surface and weather conditions. If f represents the coefficient of friction between rubber and the road surface, then $s = \sqrt{30fd}$ gives an estimate of the motorist's speed. The coefficient of friction f between rubber and concrete under wet conditions is 0.4. Estimate, to the nearest mile per hour, a motorist's speed under these conditions if the skid marks are 200 feet long.

98. Using a viewing window with $0 \leq x \leq 4$ and $0 \leq y \leq 2$, graph the following functions on the same screen.
$$f(x) = x^{\frac{1}{2}} \quad g(x) = x^{\frac{1}{4}} \quad h(x) = x^{\frac{1}{6}}$$
In each of the following cases, arrange $x^{\frac{1}{2}}, x^{\frac{1}{4}}$, and $x^{\frac{1}{6}}$ in order of increasing size and justify your answer by using the graphs.
   a. $0 < x < 1$ **b.** $x > 1$

99. Using a viewing window with $-3 \leq x \leq 3$ and $-1.5 \leq y \leq 1.5$, graph the following functions on the same screen.
$$f(x) = x^{\frac{1}{3}} \quad g(x) = x^{\frac{1}{5}} \quad h(x) = x^{\frac{1}{7}}$$
In each of the following cases, arrange $x^{\frac{1}{3}}, x^{\frac{1}{5}}$, and $x^{\frac{1}{7}}$ in order of increasing size and justify your answer by using the graphs.
   a. $x < -1$ **b.** $-1 < x < 0$
   c. $0 < x < 1$ **d.** $x > 1$

100. Graph $f(x) = \sqrt{x}$ in the standard viewing window. Then, without doing any more graphing, describe the graphs of these functions.

a. $g(x) = \sqrt{x + 3}$ *Hint:* $g(x) = f(x + 3)$; see Section 3.4.

b. $h(x) = \sqrt{x} - 2$
c. $k(x) = \sqrt{x + 3} - 2$

101. Do Exercise 100 with $\sqrt[3]{}$ in place of $\sqrt{}$.

5.2 Exponential Functions

Objectives

• Graph and identify transformations of exponential functions

• Use exponential functions to solve application problems

Graphs of Exponential Functions

For each positive real number a, $a \neq 1$, there is an **exponential function with base a** whose domain is all real numbers and whose rule is $f(x) = a^x$. Some examples are shown below.

$$f(x) = 10^x \qquad g(x) = 2^x \qquad h(x) = \left(\frac{1}{2}\right)^x \qquad k(x) = \left(\frac{3}{2}\right)^x$$

The shape of the graph of an exponential function $f(x) = a^x$ depends only on the size of a, as shown in the following figures.

Graph of
$f(x) = a^x$

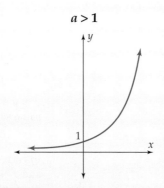

$a > 1$

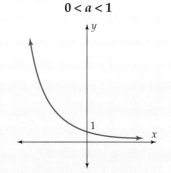

$0 < a < 1$

• graph is above x-axis
• y-intercept is 1
• $f(x)$ is increasing
• $f(x)$ approaches the negative x-axis as x approaches $-\infty$

• graph is above x-axis
• y-intercept is 1
• $f(x)$ is decreasing
• $f(x)$ approaches the positive x-axis as x approaches ∞

For $a = 0$ or $a = 1$, the function $f(x) = a^x$ is a constant function, not exponential. Even roots of negative numbers are not defined in the set of real numbers, so when $a < 0$, a^x is not defined for any rational exponent that has an even number as its denominator. Because within any interval there are infinitely many rational numbers that have an even denominator, $f(x) = a^x$ has an infinite number of holes in every interval when $a < 0$. Therefore, the function is not *well-behaved* for $a < 0$, so it is not defined for those values.

The following two Graphing Explorations illustrate the effect that the value of a has on the shape of the graph of an exponential function for $a > 1$ and for $0 < a < 1$.

Graphing Exploration ●

a. Using a viewing window with $-3 \le x \le 7$ and $-2 \le y \le 18$, graph each function below on the same screen, and observe the behavior of each to the right of the y-axis.

$$f(x) = 1.3^x \quad g(x) = 2^x \quad h(x) = 10^x$$

As the graphs continue to the right, which graph rises least steeply? most steeply?

How does the steepness of the graph of $f(x) = a^x$ to the right of the y-axis seem to be related to the size of the base a?

b. Using the graphs of the same three functions in the viewing window with $-4 \le x \le 2$ and $-0.5 \le y \le 2$, observe the behavior to the *left* of the y-axis.

As the graph continues to the left, how does the size of the base a seem to be related to how quickly the graph of $f(x) = a^x$ falls toward the x-axis?

Graphing Exploration ●

Using a viewing window with $-4 \le x \le 4$ and $-1 \le y \le 4$, graph each function below on the same screen, and observe the behavior of each.

$$f(x) = 0.2^x \quad g(x) = 0.4^x \quad h(x) = 0.6^x \quad k(x) = 0.8^x$$

Notice that the bases of the exponential functions are increasing in size: $0 < 0.2 < 0.4 < 0.6 < 0.8 < 1$

As the graphs continue to the right, which graph falls least steeply? most steeply?

How does the steepness of the graph of $f(x) = a^x$ seem to be related to the size of the base a?

The graphing explorations above show that the graph of $f(x) = a^x$ rises or falls less steeply as the base a gets closer to 1.

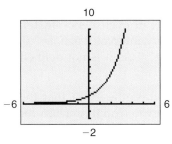

Figure 5.2-1

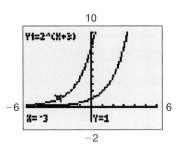

Figure 5.2-2

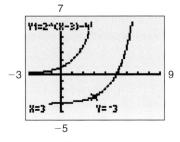

Figure 5.2-3

Example 1   Translations

The graph of $f(x) = 2^x$ is shown in Figure 5.2-1. Without graphing, describe the transformation from the graph of f to the graph of each function below. Verify by graphing.

a. $g(x) = 2^{x+3}$ **b.** $h(x) = 2^{x-3} - 4$

Solution

a. If $f(x) = 2^x$, then $g(x) = 2^{x+3} = f(x + 3)$. So the graph of g is the graph of f shifted horizontally 3 units to the left, as shown in Figure 5.2-2.

b. If $f(x) = 2^x$, then $h(x) = 2^{x-3} - 4 = f(x - 3) - 4$. So the graph of $h(x)$ is the graph of $f(x) = 2^x$ shifted horizontally 3 units to the right and vertically 4 units downward, as shown in Figure 5.2-3. ∎

The graphs of exponential functions of the form $f(x) = a^x$ increase at an explosive rate. To see this, consider the graph of $f(x) = 2^x$ in Figure 5.2-3. If the x-axis were extended to the right, then $x = 50$ would be at the right edge of the page. At this point, the graph of $f(x) = 2^x$ is 2^{50} units high. The scale of the y-axis in Figure 5.2-3 is about 12 units per inch, or 144 units per foot, or 760,320 units per mile. Therefore, the height of the graph at $x = 50$ is

$$\frac{2^{50}}{760,320} = 1{,}480{,}823{,}741 \text{ miles,}$$

which would put that part of the graph well beyond the planet Saturn!

Since most quantities that grow exponentially do not change as dramatically as the graph of $f(x) = 2^x$, exponential functions that model real-life growth or decay are usually modified by the insertion of appropriate constants. These functions are generally of the form

$$f(x) = Pa^{kx},$$

such as the functions shown below.

$$f(x) = \frac{1}{2}(5.2^{0.45x}) \qquad g(x) = 3.5(10^{-0.03x}) \qquad h(x) = (-6)(1.076^{2x})$$

Their graphs have the same shape as the graph of $f(x) = a^x$, but may rise or fall more or less steeply, depending on the constants P, k, and a.

Example 2   Horizontal Stretches

The graph of $f(x) = 3^x$ is shown in Figure 5.2-4. Without graphing, describe the transformation from the graph of f to the graph of each function below. Verify by graphing.

$$g(x) = 3^{0.2x} \qquad h(x) = 3^{0.8x} \qquad k(x) = 3^{-x} \qquad p(x) = 3^{-0.4x}$$

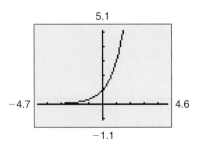

Figure 5.2-4

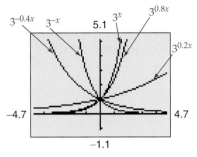

Figure 5.2-5

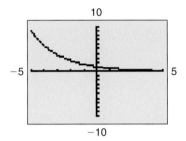

Figure 5.2-6

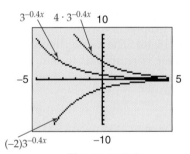

Figure 5.2-7

Solution

The graphs of $g(x) = 3^{0.2x}$ and $h(x) = 3^{0.8x}$ are the graph of f stretched horizontally by a factor of $\dfrac{1}{0.2} = 5$ and $\dfrac{1}{0.8} = 1.25$, respectively. The graph of $k(x) = 3^{-x}$ is the graph of f reflected across the y-axis. The graph of $p(x) = 3^{-0.4x}$ is the graph of f stretched horizontally by a factor of $\dfrac{1}{0.4} = 2.5$ and reflected across the y-axis. The graphs are identified in Figure 5.2.5. ■

Example 3   **Vertical Stretches**

The graph of $p(x) = 3^{-0.4x}$ is shown in Figure 5.2-6. Without graphing, describe the transformation from the graph of p to the graph of each function below. Verify by graphing.

$$q(x) = 4 \cdot 3^{-0.4x} \qquad r(x) = (-2)3^{-0.4x}$$

Solution

The graph of $q(x) = 4 \cdot 3^{-0.4x}$ is the graph of $p(x) = 3^{-0.4x}$ stretched vertically by a factor of 4. The graph of $r(x) = (-2)3^{-0.4x}$ is the graph of $p(x) = 3^{-0.4x}$ stretched vertically by a factor of 2 and reflected across the x-axis. The graphs are identified in Figure 5.2-7. ■

Exponential Growth and Decay

In this section, you will see that exponential functions are useful for modeling situations in which a quantity increases or decreases by a fixed factor. In Section 5.3 you will learn how to construct these types of functions.

Example 4   **Finance**

If you invest $5000 in a stock that is increasing in value at the rate of 3% per year, then the value of your stock is given by the function $f(x) = 5000(1.03)^x$, where x is measured in years.

a. Assuming that the value of your stock continues growing at this rate, how much will your investment be worth in 4 years?

b. When will your investment be worth $8000?

Solution

a. Letting $x = 4$, $f(4) = 5000(1.03)^4 \approx 5627.54$.
In 4 years your stock is worth about $5627.54.

b. Find the value of x for which $f(x) = 8000$. In other words, solve the equation $5000(1.03)^x = 8000$.

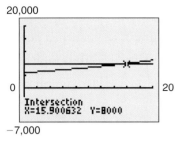

20,000

0 |_____| 20

Intersection
X=15.900632 Y=8000

−7,000

Figure 5.2-8

The point of intersection of the graphs of $f(x) = 5000(1.03)^x$ and $y = 8000$ is approximately (15.901, 8000).

Therefore, the stock will be worth $8000 in about 16 years. ■

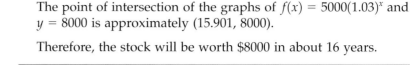

Example 5   Population Growth

Based on data from the past 50 years, the world population, in billions, can be approximated by the function $g(x) = 2.5(1.0185)^x$, where $x = 0$ corresponds to 1950.

a. Estimate the world population in 2015.

b. In what year will the population be double what it is in 2015?

Solution

a. Since $x = 0$ corresponds to 1950, $x = 1$ to 1951, and so on, the year 2015 corresponds to $x = 65$. Find g(65).

$$g(65) = 2.5(1.0185)^{65} \approx 8.23$$

The world population in 2015 will be about 8.23 billion people.

b. Twice the population in 2015 is 2(8.23) = 16.46 billion. Find the number x such that $g(x) = 16.46$; that is, solve $2.5(1.0185)^x = 16.46$.

A graphical intersection finder shows that the approximate coordinates of the point of intersection of the graphs of $g(x) = 2.5(1.0185)^x$ and $y = 16.46$ are (102.81, 16.46). The x-coordinate 102.81, or 103 when rounded to the nearest year, corresponds to the year 2053. Notice that it takes only 38 years for the world population to double. ■

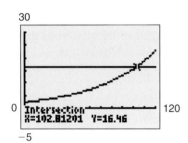

30

0 |_____| 120

Intersection
X=102.81201 Y=16.46

−5

Figure 5.2-9

Example 6   Radioactive Decay

The amount from one kilogram of plutonium (^{239}Pu) that remains after x years can be approximated by the function $M(x) = 0.99997^x$. Estimate the amount of plutonium remaining after 10,000 years.

Solution

Because M is an exponential function with a base smaller than 1 but very close to 1, its graph falls very slowly from left to right. The fact that the graph falls so slowly as x gets large means that even after an extremely long time, a substantial amount of plutonium will remain.

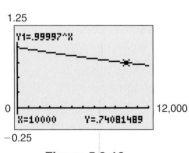

1.25

Y1=.99997^X

0 |_____| 12,000

X=10000   Y=.74081489

−0.25

Figure 5.2-10

When $x = 10,000$, $M(x) \approx 0.74$. Therefore, almost three-fourths of the original plutonium remains after 10,000 years! This is the reason that nuclear waste disposal is such a serious concern. ■

The Number *e* and the Natural Exponential Function

There is an irrational number, denoted *e*, that arises naturally in a variety of phenomena and plays a central role in the mathematical description of the physical universe. Its decimal expansion begins as shown below.

$$e = 2.718281828459045\ldots$$

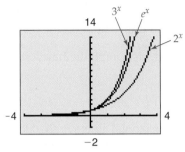

Figure 5.2-11

Most calculators have an e^x key that can be used to evaluate the natural exponential function $f(x) = e^x$. When you evaluate e^1 using a calculator, the display will show the first part of the decimal expansion of *e*.

Figure 5.2-11 shows that the graph of $f(x) = e^x$ has the same shape as the graphs of $y = 2^x$ and $y = 3^x$, but it climbs more steeply than the graph of $y = 2^x$ and less steeply than the graph of $y = 3^x$.

Example 7   **Population Growth**

If the population of the United States continues to grow as it has since 1980, then the approximate population, in millions, of the United States in year *t*, where $t = 0$ corresponds to the year 1980, will be given by the function $P(t) = 227e^{0.0093t}$.

a. Estimate the population in 2015.

b. When will the population reach half a billion?

Solution

a. The year 2015 corresponds to $t = 35$. Find $P(35)$.

$$P(35) = 227e^{0.0093(35)} \approx 314.3$$

Therefore, the population in 2015 will be approximately 314.3 million people.

b. Half a billion is 500 million. Find the value of *t* for which $P(t) = 500$. A graphical intersection finder shows that the approximate coordinates of the point of intersection of the graphs of $P(t) = 227e^{0.0093t}$ and $y = 500$ are approximately (85, 500). A *t*-value of 85 corresponds to the year 2065. Therefore, the population will reach half a billion approximately by the year 2065. ■

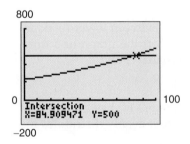

Figure 5.2-12

Other Exponential Functions

In most real-world applications, populations cannot grow infinitely large. The population growth models shown previously do not take into account factors that may limit population growth in the future. Example 8 illustrates a function, called a **logistic model,** which is designed to model situations that have limited future growth due to a fixed area, food supply, or other factors.

25,000

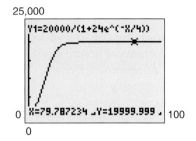

Y1=20000/(1+24e^(-X/4))

0

0 X=79.787234 Y=19999.999 100

Figure 5.2-13

Example 8 Logistic Model

The population of fish in a certain lake at time t months is given by the function $p(t) = \dfrac{20{,}000}{1 + 24e^{-\frac{t}{4}}}$, where $t \geq 0$. There is an upper limit on the fish population due to the oxygen supply, available food, etc. Graph the function, and find the upper limit on the fish population.

Solution

The graph of $p(t)$ at the left suggests that the horizontal line $y = 20{,}000$ is a horizontal asymptote of the graph. If so, the upper limit on the fish population is 20,000.

You can verify this by rewriting the rule of p as shown below.

$$p(t) = \frac{20{,}000}{1 + 24e^{-\frac{t}{4}}} = \frac{20{,}000}{1 + \dfrac{24}{e^{\frac{t}{4}}}}$$

As t increases, $\dfrac{t}{4}$ increases and $e^{\frac{t}{4}}$ grows very large. As $e^{\frac{t}{4}}$ grows very large, $\dfrac{24}{e^{\frac{t}{4}}}$ gets very close to 0. As $\dfrac{24}{e^{\frac{t}{4}}}$ gets closer and closer to 0, $p(t)$ gets closer and closer to $\dfrac{20{,}000}{1 + 0}$, or 20,000. Because $e^{\frac{t}{4}}$ is positive and $\dfrac{24}{e^{\frac{t}{4}}}$ never quite reaches 0, the denominator of $p(t)$ is always slightly larger than 1 and $p(t)$ is always less than 20,000. ∎

When a cable, such as a power line, is suspended between towers of equal height, it forms a curve called a catenary, which is the graph of a function of the form shown below for suitable constants A and k.

$$f(x) = A(e^{kx} + e^{-kx})$$

The Gateway Arch in St. Louis, shown in Figure 5.2-14, has the shape of an inverted catenary, which was chosen because it evenly distributes the internal structural forces.

Figure 5.2-14

Graphing Exploration ●

Using the viewing window with $-5 \leq x \leq 5$ and $-10 \leq y \leq 80$, graph each function below on the same screen, and observe their behavior.

$$Y_1 = 10(e^{0.4x} + e^{-0.4x}) \quad Y_2 = 10(e^{2x} + e^{-2x}) \quad Y_3 = 10(e^{3x} + e^{-3x})$$

How does the coefficient of x affect the shape of the graph?
Predict the shape of the graph of $y = -Y_1 + 80$. Confirm your answer by graphing.

Exercises 5.2

In Exercises 1–6, list the transformations needed to transform the graph of $h(x) = 2^x$ into the graph of the given function. (Section 3.4 may be helpful.)

1. $f(x) = 2^x - 5$

2. $g(x) = -(2^x)$

3. $k(x) = 3(2^x)$

4. $g(x) = 2^{x-1}$

5. $f(x) = 2^{x+2} - 5$

6. $g(x) = -5(2^{x-1}) + 7$

In Exercises 7–13, list the transformations needed to transform the graph of $h(x) = 3^x$ into the graph of the given function. (Section 3.4 may be helpful.)

7. $f(x) = 3^x + 4$

8. $g(x) = 3^{-x}$

9. $k(x) = \frac{1}{4}(3^x)$

10. $g(x) = 3^{0.4x}$

11. $f(x) = 3^{2-x}$

12. $f(x) = 8 + 5(3^x)$

13. $g(x) = 4(3^{-0.15x})$

In Exercises 14–19, sketch a complete graph of the function.

14. $f(x) = 4^{-x}$

15. $f(x) = \left(\frac{5}{2}\right)^{-x}$

16. $f(x) = 2^{3x}$

17. $g(x) = 3^{\frac{x}{2}}$

18. $f(x) = 2^{5-x}$

19. $g(x) = 2^{x-5}$

In Exercises 20–21, match the functions to the graphs. Assume $a > 1$ and $c > 1$.

20. $f(x) = a^x$
$g(x) = a^x + 3$
$h(x) = a^{x+5}$

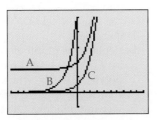

21. $f(x) = c^x$
$g(x) = -3c^x$
$h(x) = c^{x+5}$
$k(x) = -3c^x - 2$

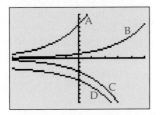

In Exercises 22–29, find a viewing window (or windows) that shows a complete graph of the function.

22. $k(x) = e^{-x}$

23. $f(x) = e^{-x^2}$

24. $f(x) = \frac{e^x + e^{-x}}{2}$

25. $h(x) = \frac{e^x - e^{-x}}{2}$

26. $g(x) = 2^x - x$

27. $k(x) = \frac{2}{e^x + e^{-x}}$

28. $f(x) = \frac{5}{1 + e^{-x}}$

29. $g(x) = \frac{10}{1 + 9e^{-\frac{x}{2}}}$

In Exercises 30–34, determine whether the function is even, odd, or neither. (See *Excursion* 3.4A.)

30. $f(x) = 10^x$

31. $g(x) = 2^x - x$

32. $f(x) = \frac{e^x + e^{-x}}{2}$

33. $f(x) = \frac{e^x - e^{-x}}{2}$

34. $f(x) = e^{-x^2}$

35. Use the Big-Little concept (see Section 4.4) to explain why $e^x + e^{-x}$ is approximately equal to e^x when x is large.

In Exercises 36–39, find the average rate of change of the function. (See Section 3.7.)

36. $f(x) = x(2^x)$ as x goes from 1 to 3

37. $g(x) = 3^{x^2 - x}$ as x goes from -1 to 1

38. $h(x) = 5^{-x^2}$ as x goes from -1 to 0

39. $f(x) = e^x - e^{-x}$ as x goes from -3 to -1

In Exercises 40–43, find the difference quotient of the function. (See Section 3.7.)

40. $f(x) = 10^x$

41. $g(x) = 5^{x^2}$

42. $f(x) = 2^x + 2^{-x}$

43. $f(x) = e^x - e^{-x}$

In Exercises 44–49, list all asymptotes of the graph of the function and the approximate coordinates of each local extremum. (See Section 4.3.)

44. $f(x) = x(2^x)$

45. $g(x) = x(2^{-x})$

46. $h(x) = e^{\frac{x^2}{2}}$

47. $k(x) = 2^{x^2 - 6x + 2}$

48. $f(x) = e^{-x^2}$

49. $g(x) = -xe^{\frac{x^2}{20}}$

50. If you deposit $750 at 2.2% interest, compounded annually and paid from the day of deposit to the day of withdrawal, your balance at time t is given by $B(t) = 750(1.022)^t$. How much will you have after 2 years? after 3 years and 9 months?

51. The population of a colony of fruit flies t days from now is given by the function $p(t) = 100 \cdot 3^{\frac{t}{10}}$.
   a. What will the population be in 15 days? in 25 days?
   b. When will the population reach 2500?

52. A certain type of bacteria grows according to the function $f(x) = 5000e^{0.4055x}$, where the time x is measured in hours.
   a. What will the population be in 8 hours?
   b. When will the population reach 1 million?

53. According to data from the National Center for Health Statistics, the life expectancy at birth for a person born in year x is approximated by the function below.

$$D(x) = \frac{79.257}{1 + 9.7135 \times 10^{24} \cdot e^{-0.0304x}}$$

$$(1900 \le x \le 2050)$$

   a. What is the life expectancy of someone born in 1980? in 2000?
   b. In what year was life expectancy at birth 60 years?

54. The number of subscribers, in millions, to basic cable TV can be approximated by the function

$$g(x) = \frac{76.7}{1 + 16 \cdot 0.8444^x}$$

where $x = 0$ corresponds to 1970. (Source: The Cable TV Financial Datebook and The Pay TV Newsletter)
   a. Estimate the number of subscribers in 1995 and in 2005.
   b. When does the number of subscribers reach 70 million?
   c. According to this model, will the number of subscribers ever reach 90 million?

55. The estimated number of units that will be sold by a certain company t months from now is given by $N(t) = 100{,}000e^{-0.09t}$.
   a. What are the current sales ($t = 0$)? What will sales be in 2 months? in 6 months?

   b. From examining the graph, do you think that sales will ever start to increase again? Explain.

56. a. The function $g(t) = 1 - e^{-0.0479t}$ gives the percentage of the population (expressed as a decimal) that has seen a new TV show t weeks after it goes on the air. What percentage of people have seen the show after 24 weeks?
   b. Approximately when will 90% of the people have seen it?

57. a. The beaver population near a certain lake in year t is approximated by the function

$$p(t) = \frac{2000}{1 + 199e^{-0.5544t}}.$$ What is the population

now (when $t = 0$) and what will it be in 5 years?
   b. Approximately when will there be 1000 beavers?

58. *Critical Thinking* Look back at Section 4.3, where the basic properties of graphs of polynomial functions were discussed. Then review the basic properties of the graph of $f(x) = a^x$ discussed in this section. Using these various properties, give an argument to show that for any fixed positive number a, where $a \ne 1$, it is not possible to find a polynomial function $g(x) = c_n x^n + \cdots + c_1 x + c_0$ such that $a^x = g(x)$ for all numbers x. In other words, *no exponential function is a polynomial function.*

59. *Critical Thinking* For each positive integer n, let f_n be the polynomial function below.

$$f_n(x) = 1 + x + \frac{x^2}{2!} + \frac{x^3}{3!} + \frac{x^4}{4!} + \cdots + \frac{x^n}{n!}$$

   a. Using the viewing window with $-4 \le x \le 4$ and $-5 \le y \le 55$, graph $g(x) = e^x$ and $f_4(x)$ on the same screen. Do the graphs appear to coincide?
   b. Replace the graph of $f_4(x)$ by that of $f_5(x)$, then by $f_6(x)$, $f_7(x)$, and so on until you find a polynomial $f_n(x)$ whose graph appears to coincide with the graph of $g(x) = e^x$ in this viewing window. Use the trace feature to move from graph to graph at the same value of x to see how accurate this approximation is.
   c. Change the viewing window so that $-6 \le x \le 6$ and $-10 \le y \le 400$. Is the polynomial you found in part **b** a good approximation for $g(x)$ in this viewing window? If not, what polynomial is a good approximation?

5.3 Applications of Exponential Functions

Objective

- Create and use exponential models for a variety of exponential growth or decay application problems

In Section 5.2, you used several exponential functions that modeled exponential growth and decay. In this section you will learn how to construct such exponential models in a variety of real-life situations.

Compound Interest

When interest is paid on a balance that includes interest accumulated from the previous time periods it is called **compound interest.**

> ### Example 1   Compounding Annually
>
> If you invest $6000 at 8% interest, compounded annually, how much is in the account at the end of 10 years?
>
> ### Solution
>
> After one year the account balance is
>
> *Principal + Interest*
> $$6000 + 0.08(6000) = 6000(1 + 0.08) = 6000(1.08).$$
>
> The account balance has changed by a factor of 1.08. If this amount is left in the account, the balance will again change by a factor of 1.08 after the second year.
>
> $$[6000(1.08)](1.08), \text{ or } 6000(1.08)^2$$
>
> Because the balance will change by a factor of 1.08 every year, the balance in the account at the end of year x is given by
>
> $$B(x) = 6000 \cdot (1.08)^x.$$
>
> Therefore, the balance (to the nearest penny) in the account after 10 years is
>
> $$B(10) = 6000 \cdot (1.08)^{10} = \$12,953.55.$$

The pattern illustrated in Example 1 can be generalized as shown below.

Compound Interest

> If P dollars is invested at interest rate r (expressed as a decimal) per time period t, then A is the amount after t periods.
>
> $$A = P(1 + r)^t$$

Notice that in Example 1, $P = 6000$, $r = 0.08$, and the number of periods, or years, is $t = 10$.

Example 2 Different Compounding Periods

Determine the amount that a $4000 investment over three years at an annual interest rate of 6.4% is worth for each compounding period.

a. annually   **b.** quarterly   **c.** monthly   **d.** daily

Solution

a. Use $P = 4000$, $r = 0.064$, and $t = 3$ in the compound interest formula.

$$A = 4000(1.064)^3 \approx \$4818.20$$

b. Quarterly compounding means that interest is compounded every one-fourth of a year or 4 times a year. Therefore,

- the interest rate per period is $r = \dfrac{0.064}{4}$, and
- the number of periods in 3 years is $t = 4(3)$.

$$A = 4000\left(1 + \frac{0.064}{4}\right)^{4(3)} \approx \$4839.32$$

c. Monthly compounding means that interest is compounded every $\dfrac{1}{12}$ of a year or 12 times a year. Therefore,

- the interest rate per period is $r = \dfrac{0.064}{12}$, and
- the number of periods in 3 years is $t = 12(3)$.

$$A = 4000\left(1 + \frac{0.064}{12}\right)^{12(3)} \approx \$4844.21$$

d. Daily compounding means that interest is compounded every $\dfrac{1}{365}$ of a year, or 365 times a year. Therefore,

- the interest rate per period is $r = \dfrac{0.064}{365}$, and
- the number of periods in 3 years is $t = 365(3)$.

$$A = 4000\left(1 + \frac{0.064}{365}\right)^{365(3)} \approx \$4846.60$$

Notice in Example 2 that the more often interest is compounded, the larger the final amount will be. Example 3 shows you how to write and solve an exponential equation to determine how long it will take for an investment to be worth a given amount.

Example 3 Solving for the Time Period

If $5000 is invested at 7% annual interest, compounded daily, when will the investment be worth $6800?

Solution

Use the compound interest formula with the final amount $A = 6800$ and $P = 5000$. Because the interest is compounded every $\frac{1}{365}$ of a year, the interest rate per period is $r = \frac{0.07}{365}$.

$$A = P(1 + r)^t$$
$$6800 = 5000\left(1 + \frac{0.07}{365}\right)^t$$

The point of intersection of the graphs of $y_1 = 5000\left(1 + \frac{0.07}{365}\right)^t$ and $y_2 = 6800$ is approximately $(1603.5, 6800)$. Therefore, the investment will be worth $6800 after about 1603 days, or about 4.4 years.

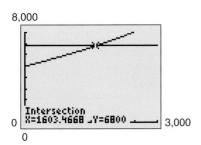

Figure 5.3-1

Continuous Compounding and the Number *e*

As you have seen in previous examples, the more often interest is compounded, the larger the final amount will be. However, there is a limit that is reached, as you will see in Example 4.

Example 4 The Number *e*

Suppose you invest $1 for one year at 100% annual interest, compounded *n* times per year. Find the maximum value of the investment in one year.

Solution

Use the compound interest formula. The annual interest rate is 1.00, so the interest rate per period is $\frac{1}{n}$, and the number of periods is *n*.

$$A = P(1 + r)^t$$
$$= 1\left(1 + \frac{1}{n}\right)^n$$
$$= \left(1 + \frac{1}{n}\right)^n$$

Observe what happens to the final amount as *n* grows larger and larger.

Compounding period	n	$\left(1 + \dfrac{1}{n}\right)^n$
Annually	1	$\left(1 + \dfrac{1}{1}\right)^1 = 2$
Semiannually	2	$\left(1 + \dfrac{1}{2}\right)^2 = 2.25$
Quarterly	4	$\left(1 + \dfrac{1}{4}\right)^4 \approx 2.4414$
Monthly	12	$\left(1 + \dfrac{1}{12}\right)^{12} \approx 2.6130$
Daily	365	$\left(1 + \dfrac{1}{365}\right)^{365} \approx 2.71457$
Hourly	8760	$\left(1 + \dfrac{1}{8760}\right)^{8760} \approx 2.718127$
Every minute	525,600	$\left(1 + \dfrac{1}{525,600}\right)^{525,600} \approx 2.7182792$
Every second	31,536,000	$\left(1 + \dfrac{1}{31,536,000}\right)^{31,536,000} \approx 2.7182825$

The maximum amount of the $1 investment after one year is approximately $2.72, no matter how large n is.

When the number of compounding periods increases without bound, the process is called **continuous compounding.** Note that the last entry in the preceding table is the same as the number e to five decimal places. Example 4 is the case when $P = 1$, $r = 100\%$, and $t = 1$. A similar result occurs in the general case and leads to the following formula.

Continuous Compounding

> If P dollars is invested at an annual interest rate of r, compounded continuously, then A is the amount after t years.
>
> $$A = Pe^{rt}$$

Example 5   Continuous Compounding

If you invest $4000 at 5% annual interest compounded continuously, how much is in the account at the end of 3 years?

Solution

Use the continuous compounding formula with $P = 4000$, $r = 0.05$, and $t = 3$.

$$A = Pe^{rt}$$
$$= 4000e^{0.05(3)}$$
$$\approx 4647.34$$

After 3 years the investment will be worth $4647.34.

Exponential Growth

Compound interest is one type of exponential growth; other exponential growth functions are very similar to the compound interest formula, as you will see in Example 6.

Example 6   Population Growth

The world population in 1950 was about 2.5 billion people and has been increasing at approximately 1.85% per year. Write the function that gives the world population in year x, where $x = 0$ corresponds to 1950.

Solution

If the population increases each year by 1.85%, then it increases each year by a factor of 1.0185. Notice that this pattern of population growth is the same as that of compound interest.

Year	1950	1951	1952	1953	...	1950 + x
Population (in billions)	2.5	2.5(1.0185)	2.5(1.0185)²	2.5(1.0185)³	...	2.5(1.0185)ˣ

So, the function that gives the world population, in billions, in year x, where $x = 0$ corresponds to 1950 is $f(x) = 2.5(1.0185)^x$.

Exponential Growth

Exponential growth can be described by a function of the form

$$f(x) = Pa^x,$$

where $f(x)$ is the quantity at time x, P is the initial quantity when $x = 0$ and $a > 1$ is the factor by which the quantity changes when x increases by 1. If the quantity $f(x)$ is growing at rate r per time period, then $a = 1 + r$ and

$$f(x) = Pa^x = P(1 + r)^x.$$

Example 7 Bacteria Growth

At the beginning of an experiment, a culture contains 1000 bacteria. Five hours later, there are 7600 bacteria. Assuming that the bacteria grow exponentially, how many bacteria will there be after 24 hours?

Solution

Use the exponential growth formula with $P = 1000$.

$$f(x) = 1000a^x$$

Because there are 7600 bacteria after 5 hours, $f(5) = 7600$ and $1000a^5 = 7600$. Solve for a to find the factor by which the bacteria population grows.

$$1000a^5 = 7600$$
$$a^5 = 7.6$$
$$a = \sqrt[5]{7.6}$$
$$a = 7.6^{\frac{1}{5}} = 7.6^{0.2}$$

Therefore, the function's growth factor is $7.6^{0.2}$.

$$f(x) = 1000 \cdot 7.6^{0.2x}$$

Find $f(24)$, the bacteria population after 24 hours.

$$f(24) = 1000 \cdot 7.6^{0.2(24)} \approx 16{,}900{,}721$$

After 24 hours, the bacteria population will be approximately 16,900,721.

Exponential Decay

Sometimes a quantity decreases by a fixed factor as time goes on, as shown in Example 8.

Example 8 Filtering

When tap water is filtered through a layer of charcoal and other purifying agents, 30% of the chemical impurities in the water are removed. If the water is filtered through a second purifying layer, 30% of the remaining impurities in the water are removed. How many layers are needed to ensure that 95% of the impurities are removed from the water?

Solution

With the first layer, 30% of the impurities are removed and 70% of the impurities remain. With the second layer, 70% of the 70% of the impurities remain. The table below shows this pattern of exponential decay.

Layer	Impurities remaining
1	$0.7 = 70\%$
2	$0.7^2 = 0.49,\ \ \text{or } 49\%$
3	$0.7^3 = 0.343,\ \text{or } 34.3\%$
$\vdots$	$\vdots$
x	0.7^x

Therefore, the percentage of impurities remaining in the water after it passes through x layers of purifying material is given by the function

$$f(x) = 0.7^x.$$

When 95% of the impurities are removed, 5% remain. So, find the value of x for which $f(x) = 0.05$.

The point of intersection of the graphs of $y_1 = 0.7^x$ and $y_2 = 0.05$ is approximately $(8.4, 0.05)$. Because you cannot have a fractional part of a filter, 9 layers are needed to ensure that 95% of the impurities are removed from the water.

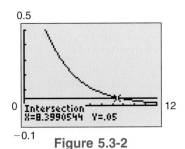

Figure 5.3-2

Example 8 illustrates **exponential decay.** Notice that the impurities were removed at a rate of $30\% = 0.3$ and that the amount of impurities remaining in the water was changing by a factor of $1 - 0.3 = 0.7$. This pattern is true in general for exponential decay.

Exponential Decay

Exponential decay can be described by a function of the form

$$f(x) = Pa^x,$$

where $f(x)$ is the quantity at time x, P is the initial quantity when $x = 0$ and $0 < a < 1$ is the factor by which the quantity changes when x increases by 1. If the quantity $f(x)$ is decaying at rate r per time period then $a = 1 - r$ and

$$f(x) = Pa^x = P(1 - r)^x.$$

The half-life of a radioactive substance is the time it takes a given quantity of the substance to decay to one-half of its original mass. The half-life depends only on the substance, not on the size of the sample. Because radioactive substances decay exponentially, their decay can be described by a function of the form $f(x) = Pa^x$, where x is measured in the same time units as the half-life. The constant a can be determined from the half-life of the substance.

For example, suppose that the half-life of a substance is 25 years. Then after 25 years, the initial amount P decays to $0.5P$, or $f(25) = 0.5P$.

$$f(25) = 0.5P$$
$$Pa^{25} = 0.5P$$
$$a^{25} = 0.5$$
$$a = 0.5^{\frac{1}{25}}$$

The function for this radioactive decay is

$$f(x) = Pa^x = P(0.5^{\frac{1}{25}})^x = P(0.5)^{\frac{x}{25}}.$$

Radioactive Decay

The amount of a radioactive substance that remains is given by the function

$$f(x) = P(0.5)^{\frac{x}{h}},$$

where P is the initial amount of the substance, $x = 0$ corresponds to the time when the radioactive decay began, and h is the half-life of the substance.

Example 9 Radioactive Decay

When a living organism dies, its carbon-14 decays exponentially. An archeologist determines that the skeleton of a mastodon has lost 64% of its carbon-14. The half-life of carbon-14 is 5730 years. Estimate how long ago the mastodon died.

Solution

Use the exponential decay formula for radioactive decay, with $h = 5730$.

$$f(x) = P(0.5^{\frac{x}{5730}})$$

Because the mastodon has lost 64% of its carbon-14, 36% of its carbon-14, or $0.36P$, remains. So, find the value of x for which $f(x) = 0.36P$.

$$0.36P = P(0.5^{\frac{x}{5730}})$$
$$0.36 = 0.5^{\frac{x}{5730}}$$

The point of intersection of the graphs of $y_1 = 0.5^{\frac{x}{5730}}$ and $y_2 = 0.36$ is approximately $(8445.6, 0.36)$ as shown in Figure 5.3-3. Therefore, the mastodon died about 8445.6 years ago. ∎

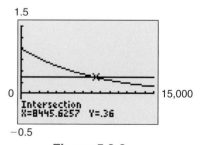

Figure 5.3-3

Exercises 5.3

1. If $1,000 is invested at 8% interest, find the value of the investment after 5 years for each compounding period.
   a. annually   **b.** quarterly
   c. monthly   **d.** weekly

2. If $2500 is invested at 11.5% interest, what is the value of the investment after 10 years for each compounding period?
   a. annually   **b.** monthly   **c.** daily

In Exercises 3–12, determine how much money will be in a savings account with an initial deposit of $500 and the interest rate indicated below.

3. 2% compounded annually for 8 years

4. 2% compounded annually for 10 years

5. 2% compounded quarterly for 10 years

6. 2.3% compounded monthly for 9 years

7. 2.9% compounded daily for 8.5 years

8. 3.5% compounded weekly for 7 years and 7 months

9. 3% compounded continuously for 4 years

10. 3.5% compounded continuously for 10 years

11. 2.45% compounded continuously for 6.2 years

12. 3.25% compounded continuously for 11.6 years

A sum of money P that can be deposited today to yield some larger amount A in the future is called the *present value* of A. **In Exercises 13–18, find the present value of the given amount A. *Hint:* Substitute the given amount A, the interest rate r per period, and the number of periods t into the compound interest formula, and solve for P.**

13. $A = $5000 at 6% compounded annually for 7 years

14. $A = $3500 at 5.5% compounded annually for 4 years

15. $A = $4800 at 7.2% compounded quarterly for 5 years

16. $A = $7400 at 5.9% compounded quarterly for 8 years

17. $A = $8900 at 11.3% compounded monthly for 3 years

18. $A = $9500 at 9.4% compounded monthly for 6 years

In Exercises 19–26, use the compound interest formula. Given three of the quantities, A, P, r, and t, find the remaining one.

19. A typical credit card company charges 18% annual interest, compounded monthly, on the unpaid balance. If your current balance is $520 and you do not make any payments for 6 months, how much will you owe?

20. When his first child was born, a father put $3000 in a savings account that pays 4% annual interest, compounded quarterly. How much will be in the account on the child's 18th birthday?

21. You have $10,000 to invest for 2 years. Fund A pays 13.2% interest, compounded annually. Fund B pays 12.7% interest, compounded quarterly, and Fund C pays 12.6% interest, compounded monthly. Which fund will return the most money?

22. If you invest $7400 for 5 years, which will return more money: an interest rate of 5% compounded quarterly or an interest rate of 4.8% compounded continuously?

23. If you borrow $1200 at 14% interest, compounded monthly, and pay off the loan (principle and interest) at the end of 2 years, how much interest will you have paid?

24. A developer borrows $150,000 at 6.5% interest, compounded quarterly, and agrees to pay off the loan in 4 years. How much interest will she owe?

25. A manufacturer has settled a lawsuit out of court by agreeing to pay 1.5 million dollars 4 years from now. How much should the company put in an account paying 6.4% annual interest, compounded monthly, in order to have $1.5 million in 4 years? *Hint:* See Exercises 13–18.

26. Ellen wants to have $30,000 available in 5 years for a down payment on a house. She has inherited $25,000. How much of the inheritance should be invested at 5.7% interest, compounded quarterly, in order for the investment to reach a value of $30,000?

27. Suppose you win a contest and have a choice of prizes. You can take $3000 now or you can receive $4000 in 4 years. If money can be invested at 6% interest, compounded annually, which prize is more valuable in the long run?

28. If money can be invested at 7% interest, compounded quarterly, which is worth more: $9000 now or $12,500 in 5 years?

29. If an investment of $1000 grows to $1407.10 in seven years with interest compounded annually, what is the interest rate?

30. If an investment of $2000 grows to $2700 in $3\frac{1}{2}$ years, with an annual interest rate that is compounded quarterly, what is the annual interest rate?

31. If you put $3000 in a savings account today, what interest rate (compounded annually) must you receive in order to have $4000 after 5 years?

32. If interest is compounded continuously, what annual rate must you receive if your investment of $1500 is to grow to $2100 in 6 years?

33. a. At an interest rate of 8%, compounded annually, how long will it take to double an investment of $100? of $500? of $1200?
b. What conclusion does part **a** suggest about doubling time?

34. At an interest rate of 6%, compounded annually, how long will it take to double an investment of P dollars?

35. How long will it take to double an investment of $500 at 7% interest, compounded continuously?

36. How long will it take to triple an investment of $5000 at 8% interest, compounded continuously?

37. a. Suppose P dollars is invested for 1 year at 12% interest, compounded quarterly. What interest rate r would yield the same amount in 1 year with annual compounding? r is called the **effective rate of interest.** *Hint:* Solve the equation $P\left(1 + \dfrac{0.12}{4}\right)^4 = P(1 + r)$ for r. The left side of the equation is the yield after 1 year at 12% interest, compounded quarterly, and the right side is the yield after 1 year at r% interest, compounded annually.
b. Complete the following table:

12% interest compounding period	Effective rate
annually	12%
quarterly	
monthly	
daily	

38. This exercise investigates the continuous compounding formula, using a realistic interest rate. Consider the value of $4000 deposited for 3 years at 5% interest, compounded n times per year, for increasing values of n. In this case, the interest rate per period is $\dfrac{0.05}{n}$, and the number of periods in 3 years is $3n$. So, the value at the end of 3 years is given by:

$$A = 4000\left(1 + \frac{0.05}{n}\right)^{3n} = 4000\left[\left(1 + \frac{0.05}{n}\right)^n\right]^3$$

a. Complete the following table:

n	$\left(1 + \dfrac{0.05}{n}\right)^n$
1000	
10,000	
500,000	
1,000,000	
5,000,000	
10,000,000	

b. Compare the entries in the second column of the table in part **a** to the number $e^{0.05}$, and complete the following sentence:
As n gets larger and larger, the value of $\left(1 + \dfrac{0.05}{n}\right)^n$ gets closer and closer to the number ___?___.
c. Use your answer to part **b** to complete the following sentence:
As n gets larger and larger, the value of $A = 4000\left[\left(1 + \dfrac{0.05}{n}\right)^n\right]^3$ gets closer and closer to the number ___?___.
d. Compare your answer to part **c** with the value given by the continuous compounding formula.

39. A weekly census of the tree-frog population in a state park is given below.

Week	1	2	3	4	5	6
Population	18	54	162	486	1458	4374

a. Find a function of the form $f(x) = Pa^x$ that describes the frog population at time x weeks.

b. What is the growth factor in this situation (that is, by what number must this week's population be multiplied to obtain next week's population)?

c. Each tree frog requires 10 square feet of space and the park has an area of 6.2 square miles. Will the space required by the frog population exceed the size of the park in 12 weeks? in 14 weeks? (1 square mile = 5280^2 square feet)

40. The fruit fly population in a certain laboratory triples every day. Today there are 200 fruit flies.

a. Make a table showing the number of fruit flies present for the first 4 days (today is day 0, tomorrow is day 1, etc.).

b. Find a function of the form $f(x) = Pa^x$ that describes the fruit fly population at time x days.

c. What is the growth factor here (that is, by what number must each day's population be multiplied to obtain the next day's population)?

d. How many fruit flies will there be a week from now?

41. The population of Mexico was 100.4 million in 2000 and is expected to grow by approximately 1.4% each year.

a. If $g(x)$ is the population, in millions, of Mexico in year x, where $x = 0$ corresponds to the year 2000, find the rule of the function g. (See Example 6.)

b. Estimate the population of Mexico in the year 2010.

42. The number of dandelions in your lawn increases by 5% a week, and there are 75 dandelions now.

a. If $f(x)$ is the number of dandelions in week x, find the rule of the function f.

b. How many dandelions will there be in 16 weeks?

43. Average annual expenditure per pupil in elementary and secondary schools was $5550 in 1989–1990 and has been increasing at about 3.68% each year.

a. Write the rule of a function that gives the expenditure per pupil in year x, where $x = 0$

corresponds to the 1989–1990 school year.

b. According to this model, what are the expenditures per pupil in 1999–2000?

c. In what year did expenditures first exceed $7000 per pupil?

44. There are now 3.2 million people who play bridge and the number increases by 3.5% a year.

a. Write the rule of a function that gives the number of bridge players x years from now.

b. How many people will be playing bridge 15 years from now?

c. When will there be 10 million bridge players?

45. At the beginning of an experiment a culture contains 200 *h-pylori* bacteria. An hour later there are 205 bacteria. Assuming that the *h-pylori* bacteria grow exponentially, how many will there be after 10 hours? after 2 days? (See Example 7.)

46. The population of India was approximately 1030 million in 2001 and was 865 million a decade earlier. What will the population be in 2006 if it continues to grow exponentially at the same rate?

47. Use graphical methods to estimate the following values.

a. $3^{\sqrt{3}}$ **b.** $4^{\sqrt{3}}$ **c.** $5^{\sqrt{3}}$

48. Kerosene is passed through a pipe filled with clay in order to remove various pollutants. Each foot of pipe removes 25% of the pollutants.

a. Write the rule of a function that gives the percentage of pollutants remaining in the kerosene after it has passed through x feet of pipe. (See Example 8.)

b. How many feet of pipe are needed to ensure that 90% of the pollutants have been removed from the kerosene?

49. If inflation runs at a steady 3% per year, then the amount that a dollar is worth today decreases by 3% each year.

a. Write the function rule that gives the value of a dollar x years from today.

b. How much will the dollar be worth in 5 years? in 10 years?

c. How many years will it take before today's dollar is worth only a dime?

50. a. The half-life of radium is 1620 years. Find the rule of the function that gives the amount remaining from an initial quantity of 100 milligrams of radium after x years.

b. How much radium is left after 800 years? after 1600 years? after 3200 years?

51. a. The half-life of polonium-210 is 140 days. Find the rule of the function that gives the amount of polonium-210 remaining from an initial 20 milligrams after t days.

b. How much polonium-210 is left after 15 weeks? after 52 weeks?

c. How long will it take for the 20 milligrams to decay to 4 milligrams?

52. How old is a piece of ivory that has lost 58% of its carbon-14? (See Example 9.)

53. How old is a mummy that has lost 49% of its carbon-14?

5.4 Common and Natural Logarithmic Functions

Objectives

- Evaluate common and natural logarithms with and without a calculator

- Solve common and natural exponential and logarithmic equations by using an equivalent equation

- Graph and identify transformations of common and natural logarithmic functions

From their invention in the seventeenth century until the development of computers and calculators, logarithms were the only effective tools for numerical computation in astronomy, chemistry, physics, and engineering. Although they are no longer needed for computation, logarithmic functions still play an important role in the sciences and engineering. In this section you will examine the two most important types of logarithms, those to base 10 and those to base e. Logarithms to other bases are considered in *Excursion 5.5A*.

Common Logarithms

The graph of the exponential function $f(x) = 10^x$ is shown in Figure 5.4-1. Because it is an increasing function, it is a one-to-one function, as explained in Section 3.6. Recall that the graphs of inverse functions are reflections of one another across the line $y = x$. The exponential function $f(x) = 10^x$ and its inverse function are graphed in Figure 5.4-2.

Technology Tip

The graph of $f(x) = 10^x$ can be obtained in parametric mode by letting

$$x = t \quad \text{and} \quad y = 10^t,$$

where t is any real number.

The graph of the inverse function g can then be obtained by letting

$$x = 10^t \quad \text{and} \quad y = t,$$

where t is any real number.

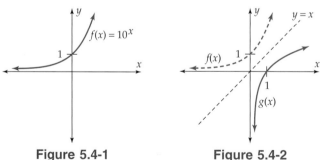

Figure 5.4-1   Figure 5.4-2

The inverse function of the exponential function $f(x) = 10^x$ is called the **common logarithmic function.** The value of this function at the number x is denoted as log x and called the common logarithm of the number x.

The functions $f(x) = 10^x$ and $g(x) = \log x$ are inverse functions.

$$\log v = u \quad \text{if and only if} \quad 10^u = v$$

Because logarithms are a special kind of exponent, every statement about logarithms is equivalent to a statement about exponents.

Logarithmic statement $\log v = u$	Equivalent exponential statement $10^u = v$
$\log 29 = 1.4624$	$10^{1.4624} = 29$
$\log 378 = 2.5775$	$10^{2.5775} = 378$

Example 1   Evaluating Common Logarithms

Without using a calculator, find each value.

a. $\log 1000$ **b.** $\log 1$ **c.** $\log \sqrt{10}$ **d.** $\log(-3)$

Solution

a. If $\log 1000 = x$, then $10^x = 1000$. Because $10^3 = 1000$, $\log 1000 = 3$.

b. If $\log 1 = x$, then $10^x = 1$. Because $10^0 = 1$, $\log 1 = 0$.

c. If $\log \sqrt{10} = x$, then $10^x = \sqrt{10}$. Because $10^{\frac{1}{2}} = \sqrt{10}$, $\log \sqrt{10} = \dfrac{1}{2}$.

d. If $\log(-3) = x$, then $10^x = -3$. Because there is no real number exponent of 10 that produces -3, $\log(-3)$ is not defined for real numbers.

NOTE Logarithms are rounded to four decimal places and an equal sign is used rather than the "approximately equal" sign. The word "common" will be omitted except when it is necessary to distinguish the common logarithm from another type of logarithm.

Every scientific and graphing calculator has a **LOG** key for evaluating logarithms. For example,

$$\log 0.6 = -0.2218 \quad \text{and} \quad \log 327 = 2.5145$$

A calculator is necessary to evaluate most logarithms, but you can get a rough estimate mentally. For example, because $\log 795$ is greater than $\log 100 = 2$ and less than $\log 1000 = 3$, you can estimate that $\log 795$ is between 2 and 3 and closer to 3.

Example 2   Using Equivalent Statements

Solve each equation by using an equivalent statement.

a. $\log x = 2$ **b.** $10^x = 29$

Solution

a. If $\log x = 2$, then $10^2 = x$. Therefore, $x = 100$.

b. If $10^x = 29$, then $\log 29 = x$. Therefore, $x = 1.4624$, as shown in Figure 5.4-3.

```
log(29)
        1.462397998
```

Figure 5.4-3

Natural Logarithms

The exponential function $f(x) = e^x$ is very useful in science and engineering. Consequently, another type of logarithm exists, based on the number e instead of 10.

The graph of the exponential function $f(x) = e^x$ is shown in Figure 5.4-4. Because it is an increasing function, it is one-to-one. The function $f(x) = e^x$ and its inverse function are graphed in Figure 5.4-5.

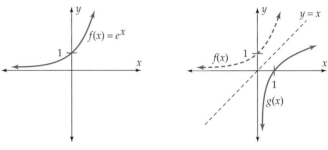

Figure 5.4-4   Figure 5.4-5

This inverse function of the exponential function $f(x) = e^x$ is called the **natural logarithmic function.** The value of this function at the number x is denoted as $\ln x$ and called the **natural logarithm** of the number x.

The functions $f(x) = e^x$ and $g(x) = \ln x$ are inverse functions.

$$\ln v = u \quad \textbf{if and only if} \quad e^u = v$$

Again, as with common logarithms, every statement about natural logarithms is equivalent to a statement about exponents.

Logarithmic statement $\ln v = u$	Equivalent exponential statement $e^u = v$
$\ln 14 = 2.6391$	$e^{2.6391} = 14$
$\ln 0.2 = -1.6094$	$e^{-1.6094} = 0.2$

```
ln(.15)
       -1.897119985
ln(186)
       5.225746674
```

Figure 5.4-6

Example 3   Evaluating Natural Logarithms

Use a calculator to find each value.

a. $\ln 0.15$ **b.** $\ln 186$ **c.** $\ln (-5)$

Solution

a. $\ln 0.15 = -1.8971$, which means that $e^{-1.8971} = 0.15$.

b. $\ln 186 = 5.2257$, which means that $e^{5.2257} = 186$.

c. $\ln(-5)$ is undefined for real numbers because there is no exponent of e that produces -5.

In a few cases you can evaluate ln x without a calculator.

$$\ln e = 1 \qquad \text{because} \qquad e^1 = e$$
$$\ln 1 = 0 \qquad \text{because} \qquad e^0 = 1$$

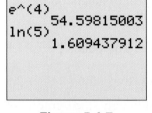

Figure 5.4-7

Example 4   Solving by Using an Equivalent Statement

Solve each equation by using an equivalent statement.

a. $\ln x = 4$ **b.** $e^x = 5$

Solution

a. If $\ln x = 4$, then $e^4 = x$. Therefore, $x = 54.5982$.
b. If $e^x = 5$, then $\ln 5 = x$. Therefore, $x = 1.6094$.

Graphs of Logarithmic Functions

Because the graphs of exponential functions have the same basic shape and each logarithmic function is the inverse of an exponential function, the graphs of logarithmic functions have common characteristics.

The following table compares the graphs of exponential and logarithmic functions.

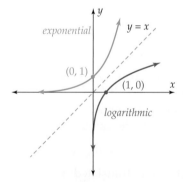

Figure 5.4-8

	Exponential functions	**Logarithmic functions**
Examples	$f(x) = 10^x; f(x) = e^x$	$g(x) = \log x; g(x) = \ln x$
Domain	all real numbers	all positive real numbers
Range	all positive real numbers	all real numbers
	$f(x)$ increases as x increases	$g(x)$ increases as x increases
	$f(x)$ approaches the x-axis as x decreases	$g(x)$ approaches the y-axis as x approaches 0
Reference points	$f(x) = 10^x$ $\left(-1, \dfrac{1}{10}\right), (0, 1), (1, 10)$	$g(x) = \log x$ $\left(\dfrac{1}{10}, -1\right), (1, 0), (10, 1)$
	$f(x) = e^x$ $\left(-1, \dfrac{1}{e}\right), (0, 1), (1, e)$	$g(x) = \ln x$ $\left(\dfrac{1}{e}, -1\right), (1, 0), (e, 1)$

Example 5   Transforming Logarithmic Functions

Describe the transformation from the graph of $g(x) = \log x$ to the graph of $h(x) = 2 \log(x - 3)$. Give the domain and range of h.

Solution

The graph of $h(x) = 2 \cdot g(x - 3)$ is the graph of $g(x) = \log x$ after a horizontal translation of 3 units right and a vertical stretch by a factor of 2.

Domain of h: The domain of $g(x) = \log x$ is all positive real numbers. The horizontal translation of 3 units to the right changes the domain to all real numbers greater than 3.

Range of h: The range of $g(x) = \log x$ is all real numbers, so the vertical stretch has no affect on the range.

The graphs of g and h are shown in Figure 5.4-9. The points $\left(\frac{1}{10}, -1\right)$, $(1, 0)$, and $(10, 1)$ on the graph of g are translated to the points $\left(3\frac{1}{10}, -2\right)$, $(4, 0)$, and $(13, 2)$ on the graph of h. Although the graph of $h(x) = 2 \log(x - 3)$ appears to stop abruptly at $x = 3$, you know that it continues to approach the asymptote at $x = 3$.

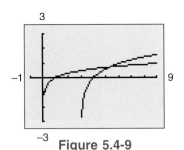

Figure 5.4-9

Example 6 **Transforming Logarithmic Functions**

Describe the transformation from $g(x) = \ln x$ to $h(x) = \ln(2 - x) - 3$. Give the domain and range of h.

Solution

Because $h(x) = g(-(x - 2)) - 3$, its graph is that of $g(x) = \ln x$ after a horizontal reflection across the y-axis followed by a horizontal translation of 2 units to the right and a vertical translation of 3 units downward.

Domain of h: The domain of $g(x) = \ln x$ is all positive real numbers. The reflection across the y-axis first changes the domain to all negative real numbers. Then the translation of 2 units to the right changes the domain from all negative real numbers to all real numbers less than 2.

Range of h: The range of $g(x) = \ln x$ is all real numbers, so the vertical translation does not affect the range.

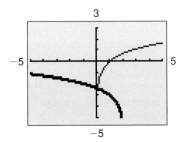

Figure 5.4-10

The graphs of g and h are shown in Figure 5.4-10. The points $\left(\frac{1}{e}, -1\right)$, $(1, 0)$, and $(e, 1)$ on the graph of g are translated to points $\left(2 - \frac{1}{e}, -4\right)$, $(1, -3)$, and $(2 - e, -2)$ on the graph of h.

Example 7 **Solving Logarithmic Equations Graphically**

If you invest money at an interest rate r, compounded annually, then $D(r)$ gives the time in years that it would take to double.

$$D(r) = \frac{\ln 2}{\ln(1 + r)}$$

a. How long will it take to double an investment of $2500 at 6.5% annual interest?

b. What annual interest rate is needed in order for the investment in part **a** to double in 6 years?

Solution

a. The annual interest rate r is 0.065. Find $D(0.065)$.

$$D(0.065) = \frac{\ln 2}{\ln(1 + 0.065)} = 11.0067$$

Therefore, it will take approximately 11 years to double an investment of $2500 at 6.5% annual interest.

b. If the investment doubles in 6 years, then $D(r) = 6$. To find the annual interest rate r, solve $\dfrac{\ln 2}{\ln(1 + r)} = 6$ by graphing. The point of intersection of the graphs of $Y_1 = \dfrac{\ln 2}{\ln(1 + r)}$ and $Y_2 = 6$ is approximately (0.1225, 6). Therefore, an annual interest rate of 12.25% is needed for the investment to double in 6 years. See Figure 5.4-11.

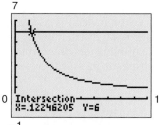

Figure 5.4-11

Exercises 5.4

Unless stated otherwise, all letters represent positive numbers.

In Exercises 1–4, find the value of each logarithm.

1. log 10,000

2. log 0.001

3. $\log \dfrac{\sqrt{10}}{1000}$

4. $\log \sqrt[3]{0.01}$

In Exercises 5–14, translate the given logarithmic statement into an equivalent exponential statement.

5. log 1000 = 3

6. log 0.001 = −3

7. log 750 = 2.8751

8. log 0.8 = −0.0969

9. ln 3 = 1.0986

10. ln 10 = 2.3026

11. ln 0.01 = −4.6052

12. ln s = r

13. $\ln(x^2 + 2y) = z + w$

14. $\log(a + c) = d$

In Exercises 15–24, translate the given exponential statement into an equivalent logarithmic statement.

15. $10^{-2} = 0.01$

16. $10^3 = 1000$

17. $10^{0.4771} = 3$

18. $10^{7k} = r$

19. $e^{3.25} = 25.79$

20. $e^{-4} = 0.0183$

21. $e^{\frac{12}{7}} = 5.5527$

22. $e^k = t$

23. $e^{\frac{2}{r}} = w$

24. $e^{4uv} = m$

In Exercises 25–36, evaluate the given expression without using a calculator.

25. $\log 10^{\sqrt{43}}$

26. $\log 10^{\sqrt{x^2+y^2}}$

27. $\ln e^{15}$

28. $\ln e^{3.78}$

29. $\ln \sqrt{e}$

30. $\ln \sqrt[5]{e}$

31. $e^{\ln 931}$

32. $e^{\ln 34.17}$

33. $\ln e^{x+y}$

34. $\ln e^{x^2 + 2y}$

35. $e^{\ln x^2}$

36. $e^{\ln \sqrt{x+3}}$

In Exercises 37–40, find the domain of the given function.

37. $f(x) = \ln(x + 1)$

38. $g(x) = \ln(x + 2)$

39. $h(x) = \log(-x)$

40. $k(x) = \log(2 - x)$

41. Compare the graphs of $f(x) = \log x^2$ and $g(x) = 2 \log x$. How are they alike? How are they different?

42. Compare the graphs of $h(x) = \log x^3$ and $k(x) = 3 \log x$. How are they alike? How are they different?

In Exercises 43–48, describe the transformation from $g(x) = \ln x$ to the given function. Give the domain and range of the given function.

43. $f(x) = 2 \ln x$

44. $f(x) = \ln x - 7$

45. $h(x) = \ln(x - 4)$

46. $k(x) = \ln(x + 2)$

47. $h(x) = \ln(x + 3) - 4$

48. $k(x) = \ln(x - 2) + 2$

In Exercises 49–52, sketch the graph of the function.

49. $f(x) = \log(x - 3)$

50. $g(x) = 2 \ln x + 3$

51. $h(x) = -2 \log x$

52. $f(x) = \ln(-x) - 3$

In Exercises 53–58, find a viewing window (or windows) that shows a complete graph of the function.

53. $f(x) = \dfrac{x}{\ln x}$

54. $g(x) = \dfrac{\ln x}{x}$

55. $h(x) = \dfrac{\ln x^2}{x}$

56. $k(x) = e^{\frac{2}{\ln x}}$

57. $f(x) = 10 \log x - x$

58. $f(x) = \dfrac{\log x}{x}$

In Exercises 59–62, find the average rate of change of the function. (See Section 3.7.)

59. $f(x) = \ln(x - 2)$, as x goes from 3 to 5

60. $g(x) = x - \ln x$, as x goes from 0.5 to 1

61. $g(x) = \log(x^2 + x + 1)$, as x goes from -5 to -3

62. $f(x) = x \log |x|$, as x goes from 1 to 4

63. a. What is the average rate of change of $f(x) = \ln x$, as x goes from 3 to $3 + h$?
   b. What is the value of h when the average rate of change of $f(x) = \ln x$, as x goes from 3 to $3 + h$, is 0.25?

64. a. Find the average rate of change of $f(x) = \ln x^2$, as x goes from 0.5 to 2.
   b. Find the average rate of change of $g(x) = \ln(x - 3)^2$, as x goes from 3.5 to 5.
   c. What is the relationship between your answers in parts **a** and **b**? Explain why this is so.

65. a. Use the doubling function D from Example 7 to find the time it takes to double your money at each of these interest rates: 4%, 6%, 8%, 12%, 18%, 24%, and 36%.
   b. Round the answers in part **a** to the nearest year and compare them with these numbers: $\dfrac{72}{4}, \dfrac{72}{6}, \dfrac{72}{8}, \dfrac{72}{12}, \dfrac{72}{18}, \dfrac{72}{24}$, and $\dfrac{72}{36}$. Use this evidence to state a "rule of thumb" for determining approximate doubling time, without using the function D. This rule of thumb, which has long been used by bankers, is called the Rule of 72.

66. The height h above sea level (in meters) is related to air temperature t (in degrees Celsius), the atmospheric pressure p (in centimeters of mercury at height h), and the atmospheric pressure c at sea level by:

$$h = (30t + 8000) \ln\left(\frac{c}{p}\right)$$

If the pressure at the top of Mount Rainier is 44 centimeters on a day when sea level pressure is 75.126 centimeters and the temperature is $7°$, what is the height of Mount Rainier?

67. A class is tested at the end of the semester and weekly thereafter on the same material. The average score on the exam taken after t weeks is given by the following "forgetting function".

$$g(t) = 77 - 10 \ln(t + 1)$$

   a. What was the average score on the original exam?
   b. What was the average score after 2 weeks? after 5 weeks?

68. Students in a precalculus class were given a final exam. Each month thereafter, they took an equivalent exam. The class average on the exam taken after t months is given by the following function.

$$F(t) = 82 - 8 \cdot \ln(t + 1)$$

   a. What was the average score on the original exam?
   b. What was the average score after 6 months? after 10 months?

69. One person with a flu virus visited the campus. The number T of days it took for the virus to infect x people is given by T.

$$T = -0.93 \ln\left(\frac{7000 - x}{6999x}\right)$$

a. How many days did it take for 6000 people to become infected?

b. After 2 weeks, how many people were infected?

70. *Critical Thinking* For each positive integer n, let f_n be the polynomial function whose rule is

$$f_n(x) = x - \frac{x^2}{2} + \frac{x^3}{3} - \frac{x^4}{4} + \frac{x^5}{5} - \cdots \pm \frac{x^n}{n}$$

where the sign of the last term is $+$ if n is odd and $-$ if n is even. In the viewing window with $-1 \le x \le 1$ and $-4 \le y \le 1$, graph $g(x) = \ln(1 + x)$ and $f_4(x)$ on the same screen. For what values of x does f_4 appear to be a good approximation of g?

71. *Critical Thinking* Using the viewing window in Exercise 70, find a value of n for which the graph of the function f_n (as defined in Exercise 70)

appears to coincide with the graph of $g(x) = \ln(1 + x)$. Use the trace feature to move from graph to graph to see how good this approximation actually is.

72. A bicycle store finds that N the number of bikes sold, is related to d, the number of dollars spent on advertising.

$$N = 51 + 100 \cdot \ln\left(\frac{d}{100} + 2\right)$$

a. How many bikes will be sold if nothing is spent on advertising? if $1000 is spent? if $10,000 is spent?

b. If the average profit is $25 per bike, is it worthwhile to spend $1000 on advertising? What about $10,000?

c. What are the answers in part **b** if the average profit per bike is $35?

5.5   Properties and Laws of Logarithms

Objectives

• Use properties and laws of logarithms to simplify and evaluate expressions

The definitions of common and natural logarithms differ only in their bases. Therefore, common and natural logarithms share the same basic properties and laws.

Basic Properties of Logarithms

Logarithms are only defined for positive real numbers. That is,

log v and ln v are defined only when $v > 0$.

The graphs of $y = \log x$ and $y = \ln x$ both contain the point $(1, 0)$ because $10^0 = 1$ and $e^0 = 1$.

log 1 = 0   and   ln 1 = 0

The values of $\log 10^4$ and $\ln e^9$ can be found by writing equivalent exponential statements.

If $\log 10^4 = x$, then $10^x = 10^4$. So $x = 4$.
If $\ln e^9 = x$, then $e^x = e^9$. So $x = 9$.

In general,

log $10^k = k$,   for every real number k.
ln $e^k = k$,   for every real number k.

NOTE Any number raised to the zero power, except zero, is 1.

$$x^0 = 1, \text{ where } x \ne 0$$

By definition, log 678 is the exponent to which 10 must be raised to produce 678.

$$10^{\log 678} = 678$$

Similarly, ln 54 is the exponent to which e must be raised to produce 54.

$$e^{\ln 54} = 54$$

In general,

$$10^{\log v} = v \quad \text{and} \quad e^{\ln v} = v, \qquad \text{for every } v > 0.$$

The facts presented above are summarized in the table below.

Basic Properties of Logarithms

Common logarithms	Natural logarithms
1. log v is defined only when $v > 0$	1. ln v is defined only when $v > 0$
2. log 1 = 0 and log 10 = 1	2. ln 1 = 0 and ln e = 1
3. log $10^k = k$ for every real number k	3. ln $e^k = k$ for every real number k
4. $10^{\log v} = v$ for every $v > 0$	4. $e^{\ln v} = v$ for every $v > 0$

Properties 3 and 4 are restatements of the fact that the composition of inverse functions produces the identity function.

That is, if $f(x) = 10^x$ and $g(x) = \log x$, then

$$(f \circ g)(x) = f(\log x) = 10^{\log x} = x \text{ for all } x > 0$$
$$(g \circ f)(x) = g(10^x) = \log 10^x = x \text{ for all } x$$

Analogous statements are true for $f(x) = e^x$ and $g(x) = \ln x$.

The properties of logarithms can be used to simplify expressions and solve equations. For example, applying Property 3 with $k = 2x^2 + 7x + 9$ allows you to rewrite the expression $\ln e^{2x^2+7x+9}$ as $2x^2 + 7x + 9$.

Example 1 Solving Equations by Using Properties of Logarithms

Use the basic properties of logarithms to solve the equation $\ln(x + 1) = 2$.

Solution

Because $f(x) = e^x$ is a function, if $\ln(x + 1) = 2$, then $e^{\ln(x+1)} = e^2$.

$$e^{\ln(x+1)} = e^2$$
$$x + 1 = e^2 \qquad \textit{Apply Property 4 with } v = x + 1$$
$$x = e^2 - 1$$
$$x \approx 6.3891$$

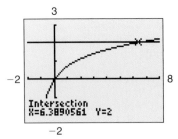

Figure 5.5-1

The intersection of the graphs of $Y_1 = \ln(x + 1)$ and $Y_2 = 2$, shown in Figure 5.5-1, confirms the solution.

Laws of Logarithms

The Product Law of Exponents states that $b^m b^n = b^{m+n}$. Because logarithms are exponents, the following law holds.

Product Law of Logarithms

> For all $v, w > 0$,
>
> $$\log (vw) = \log v + \log w$$
>
> $$\ln (vw) = \ln v + \ln w.$$

Proof According to Property 4 of logarithms, $10^{\log v} = v$ and $10^{\log w} = w$. Then, by the Product Law of Exponents:

$$vw = 10^{\log v} \cdot 10^{\log w} = 10^{\log v + \log w}$$

Again by Property 4 of logarithms:

$$10^{\log vw} = vw$$

Therefore, $10^{\log vw} = 10^{\log v + \log w}$; and because exponential functions are one-to-one, $\log vw = \log v + \log w$. A similar argument can be made for natural logarithms.

Example 2   Using the Product Law of Logarithms

Use the Product Law of Logarithms to evaluate each logarithm.

a. Given that $\log 3 = 0.4771$ and $\log 11 = 1.0414$, find $\log 33$.

b. Given that $\ln 7 = 1.9459$ and $\ln 9 = 2.1972$, find $\ln 63$.

Solution

a. $\log 33 = \log(3 \cdot 11) = \log 3 + \log 11 = 0.4771 + 1.0414 = 1.5185$

b. $\ln 63 = \ln(7 \cdot 9) = \ln 7 + \ln 9 = 1.9459 + 2.1972 = 4.1431$ ∎

CAUTION

A common error in applying the Product Law of Logarithms is to write the false statement

$$\ln 7 + \ln 9 = \ln(7 + 9) = \ln 16$$

instead of the correct statement

$$\ln 7 + \ln 9 = \ln (7 \cdot 9) = \ln 63.$$

Graphing Exploration

Using the viewing window with $-10 \le x \le 10$ and $-8 \le y \le 8$, graph both functions below on the same screen.

$$f(x) = \ln x + \ln 9 \qquad g(x) = \ln(x + 9)$$

Explain how the graph illustrates the caution in the margin.

The Quotient Law of Exponents states that $\dfrac{b^m}{b^n} = b^{m-n}$. When the exponents are logarithms, the Quotient Law is still valid.

Quotient Law of Logarithms

For all $v, w > 0$,

$$\log\left(\frac{v}{w}\right) = \log v - \log w$$

$$\ln\left(\frac{v}{w}\right) = \ln v - \ln w.$$

The proof of the Quotient Law of Logarithms is similar to the proof of the Product Law of Logarithms.

Example 3   Using the Quotient Law of Logarithms

Use the Quotient Law of Logarithms to evaluate each logarithm.

a. Given that $\log 28 = 1.4472$ and $\log 7 = 0.8451$, find $\log 4$.

b. Given that $\ln 18 = 2.8904$ and $\ln 6 = 1.7918$, find $\ln 3$.

Solution

a. $\log 4 = \log\left(\frac{28}{7}\right) = \log 28 - \log 7 = 1.4472 - 0.8451 = 0.6021$

b. $\ln 3 = \ln\left(\frac{18}{6}\right) = \ln 18 - \ln 6 = 2.8904 - 1.7918 = 1.0986$

CAUTION

Do not confuse $\ln\left(\frac{7}{9}\right) = -0.2513$ with the quotient $\frac{\ln 7}{\ln 9} = 0.8856$. They are *different* numbers.

Graphing Exploration

Using the viewing window with $0 \le x \le 8$ and $-4 \le y \le 2$, graph both functions below on the same screen.

$$f(x) = \ln\left(\frac{x}{9}\right) \qquad g(x) = \frac{\ln x}{\ln 9}$$

Explain how the graph illustrates the caution in the margin.

The Power Law of Exponents, which states that $(b^m)^k = b^{mk}$, can also be translated into a logarithmic statement.

Power Law of Logarithms

For all k and $v > 0$,

$$\log v^k = k \log v,$$

$$\ln v^k = k \ln v.$$

Proof

According to Property 4 of logarithms, $10^{\log v} = v$. Then, by the Power Law of Exponents:

$$v^k = (10^{\log v})^k = 10^{k \log v}$$

Again by Property 4 of logarithms:

$$10^{\log v^k} = v^k$$

So, $10^{\log v^k} = 10^{k \log v}$ and therefore, $\log v^k = k \log v$. A similar argument can be made for natural logarithms.

Example 4   Using the Power Law of Logarithms

Use the Power Law of Logarithms to evaluate each logarithm.

a. Given that $\log 6 = 0.7782$, find $\log \sqrt{6}$.
b. Given that $\ln 50 = 3.9120$, find $\ln \sqrt[3]{50}$.

Solution

a. $\log \sqrt{6} = \log 6^{\frac{1}{2}} = \dfrac{1}{2} \log 6 = \dfrac{1}{2}(0.7782) = 0.3891$

b. $\ln \sqrt[3]{50} = \ln 50^{\frac{1}{3}} = \dfrac{1}{3} \ln 50 = \dfrac{1}{3}(3.9120) = 1.3040$

The laws of logarithms can be used to simplify various expressions.

Example 5   Simplifying Expressions

Write $\ln 3x + 4 \ln x - \ln 3xy$ as a single logarithm.

Solution

$$\begin{aligned}
\ln 3x + 4 \ln x - \ln 3xy &= \ln 3x + \ln x^4 - \ln 3xy && \textit{Power Law} \\
&= \ln(3x \cdot x^4) - \ln 3xy && \textit{Product Law} \\
&= \ln\left(\frac{3x^5}{3xy}\right) && \textit{Quotient Law} \\
&= \ln\left(\frac{x^4}{y}\right)
\end{aligned}$$

Example 6   Simplifying Expressions

Simplify $\ln\left(\dfrac{\sqrt{x}}{x}\right) + \ln(\sqrt[4]{ex^2})$.

Solution

$$\ln\left(\frac{\sqrt{x}}{x}\right) + \ln\left(\sqrt[4]{ex^2}\right) = \ln\left(\frac{x^{\frac{1}{2}}}{x}\right) + \ln\left(ex^2\right)^{\frac{1}{4}}$$

$$= \ln\left(x^{-\frac{1}{2}}\right) + \ln\left(ex^2\right)^{\frac{1}{4}}$$

$$= -\frac{1}{2}\ln x + \frac{1}{4}\ln\left(ex^2\right) \qquad \textit{Power Law}$$

$$= -\frac{1}{2}\ln x + \frac{1}{4}(\ln e + \ln x^2) \qquad \textit{Product Law}$$

$$= -\frac{1}{2}\ln x + \frac{1}{4}(\ln e + 2\ln x) \qquad \textit{Power Law}$$

$$= -\frac{1}{2}\ln x + \frac{1}{4}\ln e + \frac{1}{2}\ln x$$

$$= \frac{1}{4}\ln e$$

$$= \frac{1}{4} \qquad \ln e = 1$$

Applications

NOTE The **zero earthquake** has ground motion amplitude of less than 1 micron on a standard seismograph 100 kilometers from the epicenter.

A logarithmic scale is a scale that is determined by a logarithmic function. Because logarithmic growth is slow, measurements on a logarithmic scale can sometimes be deceptive. The Richter scale is an illustration of this.

The magnitude $R(i)$ of an earthquake on the Richter scale is given by $R(i) = \log\left(\frac{i}{i_0}\right)$, where i is the amplitude of the ground motion of the earthquake and i_0 is the amplitude of the ground motion of the *zero earthquake*. A moderate earthquake might have 1000 times the ground motion of the zero earthquake, or $i = 1000i_0$. Its magnitude would be

$$\log\left(\frac{1000i_0}{i_0}\right) = \log 1000 = 3$$

An earthquake with 10 times this ground motion, or $i = 10{,}000i_0$, would have a magnitude of

$$\log\left(\frac{10{,}000i_0}{i_0}\right) = \log 10{,}000 = 4$$

So a tenfold increase in ground motion produces only a 1-point change on the Richter scale. In general,

increasing the ground motion by a factor of 10^k increases the Richter magnitude by k units.

Example 7   Richter Scale

The 1989 World Series earthquake in San Francisco measured 7.0 on the Richter scale, and the great earthquake of 1906 measured 8.3. How much more intense was the ground motion of the 1906 earthquake than that of the 1989 earthquake?

Solution

The difference in Richter magnitude is $8.3 - 7.0 = 1.3$. Therefore, the 1906 earthquake was $10^{1.3} \approx 20$ times more intense than the 1989 earthquake in terms of ground motion. ∎

Exercises 5.5

In Exercises 1–4, solve each equation by using the basic properties of logarithms.

1. $\log(x - 3) = 2$

2. $\log(2x) = 3$

3. $\ln(x + 4) = -1$

4. $5 + \ln(x - 1) = 8$

In Exercises 5–10, use laws of logarithms and the values given below to evaluate each logarithmic expression.

$$\log 7 = 0.8451 \quad \log 5 = 0.6990$$
$$\log 3 = 0.4771 \quad \log 2 = 0.3010$$

5. $\log 8$

6. $\log 12$

7. $\log\left(\dfrac{5}{7}\right)$

8. $\log\left(\dfrac{3}{14}\right)$

9. $\log 0.6$

10. $\log 1.5$

In Exercises 11–20, write the given expression as a single logarithm.

11. $\ln x^2 + 3\ln y$

12. $\ln 2x + 2\ln x - \ln 3y$

13. $\log(x^2 - 9) - \log(x + 3)$

14. $\log 3x - 2[\log x - \log(2 + y)]$

15. $2\ln x - 3(\ln x^2 + \ln x)$

16. $\ln\left(\dfrac{e}{\sqrt{x}}\right) - \ln\left(\sqrt{ex}\right)$ **17.** $3\ln(e^2 - e) - 3$

18. $2 - 2\log 20$

19. $\log 10x + \log 20y - 1$

20. $\ln(e^2 x) + \ln(ey) - 3$

In Exercises 21–26, let $u = \ln x$ and $v = \ln y$. Write the given expression in terms of u and v. For example,
$$\ln x^3 y = \ln x^3 + \ln y = 3\ln x + \ln y = 3u + v.$$

21. $\ln(x^2 y^5)$

22. $\ln(x^3 y^2)$

23. $\ln\left(\sqrt{x} \cdot y^2\right)$

24. $\ln\left(\dfrac{\sqrt{x}}{y}\right)$

25. $\ln\left(\sqrt[3]{x^2}\sqrt{y}\right)$

26. $\ln\left(\dfrac{\sqrt{x^2 y}}{\sqrt[3]{y}}\right)$

27. a. Graph $y = x$ and $y = e^{\ln x}$ in separate viewing windows. For what values of x are the graphs identical?
b. Use the properties of logarithms to explain your answer in part **a**.

28. a. Graph $y = x$ and $y = \ln e^x$ in separate viewing windows. For what values of x are the graphs identical?
b. Use the properties of logarithms to explain your answer in part **a**.

In Exercises 29–34, use graphical or algebraic means to determine whether the statement is true or false.

29. $\ln|x| = |\ln x|$

30. $\ln\left(\dfrac{1}{x}\right) = \dfrac{1}{\ln x}$

31. $\log x^5 = 5\log x$

32. $e^{x \ln x} = x^x \ (x > 0)$

33. $\ln x^3 = (\ln x)^3$

34. $\log \sqrt{x} = \sqrt{\log x}$

In Exercises 35 and 36, find values of a and b for which the statement is false.

35. $\dfrac{\log a}{\log b} = \log\left(\dfrac{a}{b}\right)$

36. $\log(a + b) = \log a + \log b$

37. If $\ln b^7 = 7$, what is b?

38. Suppose $f(x) = A \ln x + B$, where A and B are constants. If $f(1) = 10$ and $f(e) = 1$, what are A and B?

39. If $f(x) = A \ln x + B$ and $f(e) = 5$ and $f(e^2) = 8$, find A and B.

40. Show that $g(x) = \ln\left(\dfrac{x}{1 - x}\right)$ is the inverse function of $f(x) = \dfrac{1}{1 + e^{-x}}$. (See Section 3.6.)

In Exercises 41–44, state the magnitude on the Richter scale of an earthquake that satisfies the given condition.

41. 100 times stronger than the zero quake

42. $10^{4.7}$ times stronger than the zero quake

43. 350 times stronger than the zero quake

44. 2500 times stronger than the zero quake

Exercises 45–48 deal with the energy intensity i of a sound, which is related to the loudness of the sound by the function $L(i) = 10 \cdot \log\left(\dfrac{i}{i_0}\right)$, where i_0 is the minimum intensity detectable by the human ear and $L(i)$ is measured in decibels. Find the decibel measure of the sound.

45. ticking watch (intensity is 100 times i_0)

46. soft music (intensity is 10,000 times i_0)

47. loud conversation (intensity is 4 million times i_0)

48. Victoria Falls in Africa (intensity is 10 billion times i_0)

49. How much louder is the sound in Exercise 46 than the sound in Exercise 45?

50. The perceived loudness L of a sound of intensity I is given by $L = k \cdot \ln I$, where k is a certain constant. By how much must the intensity be increased to double the loudness? (That is, what must be done to I to produce $2L$?)

51. Compute each of the following pairs of numbers:
a. $\log 18$ and $\dfrac{\ln 18}{\ln 10}$ **b.** $\log 8950$ and $\dfrac{\ln 8950}{\ln 10}$
c. What do the results in parts **a** and **b** suggest?

52. Find each of the following logarithms.
a. $\log 8.753$ **b.** $\log 87.53$ **c.** $\log 875.3$
d. $\log 8753$ **e.** $\log 87{,}530$
f. How are the numbers 8.753, 87.53, 875.3, 8753, and 87,530 related to one another? How are their logarithms related? State a general conclusion that this evidence suggests.

Excursion: Logarithmic Functions to Other Bases

Objectives

- Evaluate logarithms to any base with and without a calculator

- Solve exponential and logarithmic equations to any base by using an equivalent equation

- Identify transformations of logarithmic functions to any base

- Use properties and laws of logarithms to simplify and evaluate logarithmic expressions to any base

Common and natural logarithms were defined by considering the inverse functions of the exponential functions $f(x) = 10^x$ and $f(x) = e^x$. In this section, you will see that a similar procedure can be carried out with any positive number b in place of 10 and e.

Throughout this excursion, b is a fixed positive number with $b > 1$.

Defining Logarithmic Functions to Other Bases

Because $f(x) = b^x$, is an increasing function, it is a one-to-one function and therefore has an inverse function. (See Section 3.6) Recall that the graphs of inverse functions are reflections of one another across the line $y = x$. An exponential function $f(x) = b^x$ and its inverse function are graphed in Figure 5.5.A-1.

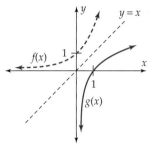

Figure 5.5.A-1

This inverse function g is called the **logarithmic function to the base b.**
The value of $g(x)$ at the number x is denoted $\log_b x$ and is called the **logarithm to the base b** of the number x.

Because the functions $f(x) = b^x$ and $g(x) = \log_b x$ are inverse functions,

$$\log_b v = u \quad \text{if and only if} \quad b^u = v.$$

Because all logarithms are exponents, every statement about logarithms is equivalent to a statement about exponents.

Logarithmic statement $\log_b v = u$	Equivalent exponential statement $b^u = v$
$\log_3 81 = 4$	$3^4 = 81$
$\log_4 64 = 3$	$4^3 = 64$
$\log_{125} 5 = \dfrac{1}{3}$	$125^{\frac{1}{3}} = 5$
$\log_8\left(\dfrac{1}{4}\right) = -\dfrac{2}{3}$	$8^{-\frac{2}{3}} = \dfrac{1}{4}$

NOTE The discussion in this section on exponents and logarithms to base b is also valid for $0 < b < 1$, but in that case the graphs have a different shape.

Example 1 Evaluating Logarithms to Other Bases

Without using a calculator, find each value.

a. $\log_2 16$ **b.** $\log_{\frac{1}{3}} 9$ **c.** $\log_5(-25)$

Solution

a. If $\log_2 16 = x$, then $2^x = 16$. Because $2^4 = 16$, $\log_2 16 = 4$.

b. If $\log_{\frac{1}{3}} 9 = x$, then $\left(\dfrac{1}{3}\right)^x = 9$. Because $\left(\dfrac{1}{3}\right)^{-2} = 9$, $\log_{\frac{1}{3}} 9 = -2$

c. If $\log_5(-25) = x$, then $5^x = -25$. Because there is no real number exponent of 5 that produces a negative number, $\log_5(-25)$ is not defined.

Example 2 Solving Logarithmic Equations

Solve each equation for x.

a. $\log_5 x = 3$ **b.** $\log_6 1 = x$ **c.** $\log_{\frac{1}{6}}(-3) = x$ **d.** $\log_6 6 = x$

Solution

a. If $\log_5 x = 3$, then $5^3 = x$. Therefore, $x = 125$.

b. If $\log_6 1 = x$, then $6^x = 1$. Therefore, $x = 0$.

c. If $\log_{\frac{1}{6}} (-3) = x$, then $\left(\dfrac{1}{6}\right)^x = -3$. Because no real power of $\dfrac{1}{6}$ is a negative number, $\log_{\frac{1}{6}} (-3) = x$ has no real solution.

d. If $\log_6 6 = x$, then $6^x = 6$. Therefore, $x = 1$.

Basic Properties of Logarithms to Other Bases

Logarithms are only defined for positive real numbers. That is,

$$\log_b v \text{ is defined only when } v > 0.$$

The graph of $y = \log_b x$ contains the point $(1, 0)$ because $b^0 = 1$ for any $b > 0$. That is,

$$\log_b 1 = 0$$

The value of $\log_5 5^4$ can be found by writing an equivalent exponential statement.

$$\text{If } \log_5 5^4 = x, \text{ then } 5^x = 5^4. \text{ So } x = 4.$$

In general,

$$\log_b b^k = k \quad \text{for every real number } k.$$

By definition, $\log_3 104$ is the exponent to which 3 must be raised to produce 104. Therefore,

$$3^{\log_3 104} = 104.$$

In general,

$$b^{\log_b v} = v \text{ for every } v > 0.$$

The facts presented above are summarized in the table below.

Basic Properties of Logarithms

For $b > 0$ and $b \neq 1$,

1. $\log_b v$ is defined only when $v > 0$
2. $\log_b 1 = 0$ and $\log_b b = 1$
3. $\log_b b^k = k$ for every real number k
4. $b^{\log_b v} = v$ for every $v > 0$

Properties 3 and 4 are restatements of the fact that the composition of inverse functions produces the identity function.

If $f(x) = b^x$ and $g(x) = \log_b x$, then

$$(f \circ g)(x) = f(\log_b x) = b^{\log_b x} = x \text{ for all } x > 0$$
$$(g \circ f)(x) = g(b^x) = \log_b b^x = x \text{ for all } x$$

Equations that involve both logarithmic and constant terms may be solved by using basic properties of logarithms.

$$b^{\log_b v} = v \text{ for } b > 0 \text{ and } b \neq 1$$

Example 3   Solving Logarithmic Equations

Solve the equation $\log_3(x - 1) = 4$.

Solution

$$\log_3(x - 1) = 4$$
$$3^{\log_3(x-1)} = 3^4 \qquad \textit{exponentiate both sides}$$
$$x - 1 = 3^4 \qquad b^{\log_b v} = v$$
$$x = 82$$

Laws of Logarithms to Other Bases

Because all logarithms are a form of exponents, the laws of exponents translate to the corresponding laws of logarithms to any base.

Laws of Logarithms

For all b, v, w, and k, with b, v, and w positive and $b \neq 1$:

Product Law: $\log_b(vw) = \log_b v + \log_b w$

Quotient Law: $\log_b\left(\dfrac{v}{w}\right) = \log_b v - \log_b w$

Power Law: $\log_b(v^k) = k \log_b v$

Example 4   Using the Laws of Logarithms

Use the Laws of Logarithms to evaluate each expression, given that $\log_7 2 = 0.3562$, $\log_7 3 = 0.5646$, and $\log_7 5 = 0.8271$.

a. $\log_7 10$ **b.** $\log_7 2.5$ **c.** $\log_7 48$

Solution

a. Use the Product Law.

$$\log_7 10 = \log_7(2 \cdot 5) = \log_7 2 + \log_7 5 = 0.3562 + 0.8271 = 1.1833$$

b. Use the Quotient Law.

$$\log_7 2.5 = \log_7\left(\frac{5}{2}\right) = \log_7 5 - \log_7 2 = 0.8271 - 0.3562 = 0.4709$$

c. Use the Product and Power Laws.

$$\log_7 48 = \log_7(3 \cdot 2^4)$$
$$= \log_7 3 + \log_7 2^4$$
$$= \log_7 3 + 4\log_7 2$$
$$= 0.5646 + 4(0.3562)$$
$$= 1.9894$$

Example 5   **Using the Laws of Logarithms**

Simplify and write each expression as a single logarithm.

a. $\log_3(x + 2) + \log_3 y - \log_3(x^2 - 4)$

b. $3 - \log_5(125x)$

Solution

a. $\log_3(x + 2) + \log_3 y - \log_3(x^2 - 4) = \log_3[(x + 2)y] - \log_3(x^2 - 4)$

$$= \log_3\left[\frac{(x + 2)y}{x^2 - 4}\right]$$

$$= \log_3\left[\frac{(x + 2)y}{(x + 2)(x - 2)}\right]$$

$$= \log_3\frac{y}{x - 2}$$

> **NOTE** $-\log_5 x$ can also be expressed as $\log_5 x^{-1}$ or $\log_5\left(\frac{1}{x}\right)$.

b. $3 - \log_5(125x) = 3 - (\log_5 125 + \log_5 x)$

$$= 3 - 3 - \log_5 x$$

$$= -\log_5 x$$

Change-of-Base Formula

Scientific and graphing calculators have a **LOG** key and a **LN** key for calculating logarithms. No calculators have a key for logarithms to other bases. One way to evaluate logarithms to other bases is to use the formula below.

Change-of-Base Formula

For any positive number v,

$$\log_b v = \frac{\log v}{\log b} \quad \text{and} \quad \log_b v = \frac{\ln v}{\ln b}$$

Proof By Property 4 of the Basic Properties of Logarithms $b^{\log_b v} = v$.

$$b^{\log_b v} = v$$

$$\ln(b^{\log_b v}) = \ln v \qquad \textit{take logarithms of both sides}$$

$$\log_b v(\ln b) = \ln v \qquad \textit{apply the Power Law}$$

$$\log_b v = \frac{\ln v}{\ln b}$$

A similar argument can be made by taking common logarithms of both sides.

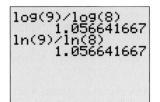

Figure 5.5A-2

Example 6 Evaluating Logarithms to Other Bases

Evaluate $\log_8 9$.

Solution

Use the change-of-base formula and a calculator.

$$\log_8 9 = \frac{\log 9}{\log 8} = 1.0566 \qquad \text{or} \qquad \log_8 9 = \frac{\ln 9}{\ln 8} = 1.0566$$

Graphing Logarithmic Functions to Other Bases

The graph of a logarithmic function to any base b shares characteristics with the graphs of natural logarithms and common logarithms. The following table compares the graphs of exponential and logarithmic functions for base b, where b is any real number, $b > 0$, and $b \neq 1$.

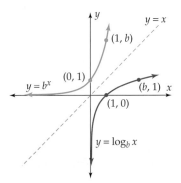

Figure 5.5A-3

	Exponential function $f(x) = b^x$	Logarithmic function $g(x) = \log_b x$
Domain	all real numbers	all positive real numbers
Range	all positive real numbers	all real numbers
	$f(x)$ increases as x increses	$g(x)$ increases as x increases
	$f(x)$ approaches the x-axis as x decreases	$g(x)$ approaches the y-axis as x approaches 0
Reference points	$\left(-1, \frac{1}{b}\right), (0, 1), (1, b)$	$\left(\frac{1}{b}, -1\right), (1, 0), (b, 1)$

Example 7 Transforming Logarithmic Functions

Describe the transformation from $g(x) = \log_2 x$ to $h(x) = \log_2(x + 1) - 3$. Give the domain and range of h.

Solution

Because $h(x) = g(x + 1) - 3$, its graph is the graph of $g(x) = \log_2 x$ after a horizontal translation of 1 unit to the left and a vertical translation of 3 units down.

Domain of h: The domain of $g(x) = \log_2 x$ is all positive real numbers. The horizontal translation of 1 unit to the left changes the domain to all real numbers greater than -1.

Range of h: The range of $g(x) = \log_2 x$ is all real numbers, so the vertical translation has no affect on the range.

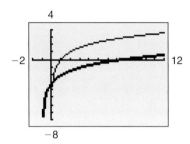

Figure 5.5A-4

The points $\left(\dfrac{1}{2}, -1\right)$, $(1, 0)$, and $(2, 1)$ on the graph of g are translated to the points $\left(-\dfrac{1}{2}, -4\right)$, $(0, -3)$, and $(1, -2)$ on the graph of h. To graph these functions with a calculator, graph $Y_1 = \dfrac{\ln x}{\ln 2}$ for $g(x) = \log_2 x$ and $Y_2 = \dfrac{\ln(x + 1)}{\ln 2} - 3$ for $h(x) = \log_2(x + 1) - 3$. The graphs of g and h are shown in Figure 5.5A-4.   ∎

Exercises 5.5.A

Note: Unless stated otherwise, all letters represent positive numbers and $b \neq 1$.

In Exercises 1–10, translate the given exponential statement into an equivalent logarithmic statement.

1. $10^{-2} = 0.01$ **2.** $10^3 = 1000$ **3.** $\sqrt[3]{10} = 10^{\frac{1}{3}}$

4. $10^{0.4771} \approx 3$ **5.** $10^{7k} = r$ **6.** $10^{(a + b)} = c$

7. $7^8 = 5{,}764{,}801$ **8.** $2^{-3} = \dfrac{1}{8}$

9. $3^{-2} = \dfrac{1}{9}$ **10.** $b^{14} = 3379$

In Exercises 11–20, translate the given logarithmic statement into an equivalent exponential statement.

11. $\log 10{,}000 = 4$ **12.** $\log 0.001 = -3$

13. $\log 750 = 2.8751$ **14.** $\log 0.8 = -0.0969$

15. $\log_5 125 = 3$ **16.** $\log_8\left(\dfrac{1}{4}\right) = -\dfrac{2}{3}$

17. $\log_2\left(\dfrac{1}{4}\right) = -2$ **18.** $\log_2 \sqrt{2} = \dfrac{1}{2}$

19. $\log(x^2 + 2y) = z + w$

20. $\log(a + c) = d$

In Exercises 21–28, evaluate the given expression without using a calculator.

21. $\log 10^{\sqrt{43}}$ **22.** $\log_{17}(17^{17})$ **23.** $\log 10^{\sqrt{x^2 + y^2}}$

24. $\log_{3.5}(3.5^{(x^2 - 1)})$ **25.** $\log_{16} 4$ **26.** $\log_2 64$

27. $\log_{\sqrt{3}}(27)$ **28.** $\log_{\sqrt{3}}\left(\dfrac{1}{9}\right)$

In Exercises 29–36, find the missing entries in each table.

29.

x	0	1	2	4
$f(x) = \log_4 x$	?	?	?	?

30.

x	$\dfrac{1}{25}$	5	25	$\sqrt{5}$
$g(x) = \log_5 x$	?	?	?	?

31.

x	?	$\dfrac{1}{6}$	1	216
$h(x) = \log_6 x$	-2	?	?	?

32.

x	$\dfrac{10}{3}$	4	6	12
$k(x) = \log_3 (x - 3)$	?	?	?	?

33.

x	0	$\dfrac{1}{7}$	$\sqrt{7}$	49
$f(x) = 2 \log_7 x$	?	?	?	?

34.

x	?	?	100	1000
$g(x) = 3 \log x$	6	3	?	?

35.

x	-2.75	-1	1	29
$h(x) = 3 \log_2 (x + 3)$	?	?	?	?

36.

x	$\dfrac{1}{e}$	1	e	e^2
$k(x) = 2 \ln x$	?	?	?	?

In Exercises 37–40, a graph or a table of values is given for the function $f(x) = \log_b x$. Find b.

37.

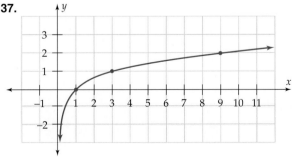

38.

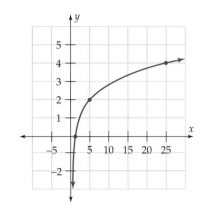

39.

x	0.05	1	400	$2\sqrt{5}$
$f(x)$	-1	0	2	$\dfrac{1}{2}$

40.

x	$\dfrac{1}{25}$	1	5	125
$f(x)$	-4	0	2	6

In Exercises 41–46, solve each equation for x.

41. $\log_3 243 = x$ **42.** $\log_{81} 27 = x$

43. $\log_{27} x = \dfrac{1}{3}$ **44.** $\log_5 x = -4$

45. $\log_x 64 = 3$ **46.** $\log_x \left(\dfrac{1}{9}\right) = -\dfrac{2}{3}$

In Exercises 47–60, write the given expression as the logarithm of a single quantity. (See Example 5.)

47. $2 \log x + 3 \log y - 6 \log z$

48. $5 \log_8 x - 3 \log_8 y + 2 \log_8 z$

49. $\log x - \log(x + 3) + \log(x^2 - 9)$

50. $\log_3 (y + 2) + \log_3 (y - 3) - \log_3 y$

51. $\dfrac{1}{2} \log_2 (25c^2)$ **52.** $\dfrac{1}{3} \log_2 (27b^6)$

53. $-2 \log_4 (7c)$ **54.** $\dfrac{1}{3} \log_5 (x + 1)$

55. $2 \ln(x + 1) - \ln(x + 2)$

56. $\ln(z - 3) + 2 \ln(z + 3)$

57. $\log_2 (2x) - 1$

58. $2 - \log_5 (25z)$

59. $2 \ln(e^2 - e) - 2$

60. $4 - 4 \log_5 (20)$

In Exercises 61–68, use a calculator and the change-of-base formula to evaluate the logarithm.

61. $\log_2 10$

62. $\log_2 22$

63. $\log_7 5$

64. $\log_5 7$

65. $\log_{500} 1000$

66. $\log_{500} 250$

67. $\log_{12} 56$

68. $\log_{12} 725$

In Exercises 69–72, describe the transformation from f to g, and give the domain and range of g.

69. $f(x) = \log_5 x$ and $g(x) = \log_5 (3x - 4)$

70. $f(x) = \log_7 x$ and $g(x) = -2 \cdot \log_7 (x + 5)$

71. $f(x) = \log_2 x$ and $g(x) = \dfrac{1}{3} \cdot \log_2 (x - 1) + 7$

72. $f(x) = \log_4 x$ and $g(x) = 3 \log_4 (-2x)$

In Exercises 73–78, answer true or false. Explain your answer.

73. $\log_b \left(\dfrac{r}{5}\right) = \log_b r - \log_b 5$

74. $\dfrac{\log_b a}{\log_b c} = \log_b \left(\dfrac{a}{c}\right)$

75. $\dfrac{\log_b r}{t} = \log_b (r^{\frac{1}{t}})$

76. $\log_b (cd) = \log_b c + \log_b d$

77. $\log_5 (5x) = 5(\log_5 x)$

78. $\log_b (ab)^t = t(\log_b a) + t$

79. Which is larger: 397^{398} or 398^{397}? *Hint:* $\log 397 \approx 2.5988$ and $\log 398 \approx 2.5999$ and $f(x) = 10^x$ is an increasing function.

80. If $\log_b 9.21 = 7.4$ and $\log_b 359.62 = 19.61$, then what is $\dfrac{\log_b 359.62}{\log_b 9.21}$?

In Exercises 81–84, assume that a and b are positive, with $a \neq 1$ and $b \neq 1$.

81. Express $\log_b u$ in terms of logarithms to the base a.

82. Show that $\log_b a = \dfrac{1}{\log_a b}$.

83. How are $\log u$ and $\log_{100} u$ related?

84. Show that $a^{\log b} = b^{\log a}$.

85. If $\log_b x = \dfrac{1}{2} \log_b v + 3$, show that $x = (b^3) \sqrt{v}$.

86. Graph the functions $f(x) = \log x + \log 7$ and $g(x) = \log (x + 7)$ on the same screen. For what values of x is it true that $f(x) = g(x)$? What do you conclude about the statement $\log 6 + \log 7 = \log (6 + 7)$?

87. Graph the functions $f(x) = \log \left(\dfrac{x}{4}\right)$ and $g(x) = \dfrac{\log x}{\log 4}$. Are they the same? What does this say about a statement such as $\log \left(\dfrac{48}{4}\right) = \dfrac{\log 48}{\log 4}$?

In Exercises 88–90, sketch a complete graph of the function, labeling any holes, asymptotes, or local extrema.

88. $f(x) = \log_5 x + 2$

89. $h(x) = x \log x^2$

90. $g(x) = \log_{20} x^2$

5.6　Solving Exponential and Logarithmic Equations

Objectives

- Solve exponential and logarithmic equations
- Solve a variety of application problems by using exponential and logarithmic equations

Exponential and logarithmic equations have been solved in this chapter so far by using the graphing method or by writing equivalent statements that can be easily solved. Most of them could also have been solved algebraically by using the techniques presented in this section, which depend primarily on the properties and laws of logarithms.

By definition of a function, if $u = v$ and f is a function, then $f(u) = f(v)$. This results in two statements.

If $u = v$, then $b^u = b^v$ for all real numbers $b > 0$.

If $u = v$, then $\log_b u = \log_b v$ for all real numbers $b > 0$.

Because exponential and logarithmic functions are one-to-one functions, the converse is also true.

If $b^u = b^v$, then $u = v$.

If $\log_b u = \log_b v$, then $u = v$.

Exponential Equations

The easiest exponential equations to solve are those in which both sides are powers of the same base.

Example 1　Powers of the Same Base

Solve the equation $8^x = 2^{x+1}$. Confirm your solution with a graph.

Solution

Write the equation so that each side is a power of the same base.

$$8^x = 2^{x+1}$$
$$(2^3)^x = 2^{x+1}$$
$$2^{3x} = 2^{x+1}$$
$$3x = x + 1 \qquad \textit{If } b^u = b^v, \textit{ then } u = v.$$
$$2x = 1$$
$$x = \frac{1}{2}$$

To find a window for the graphs of $Y_1 = 8^x$ and $Y_2 = 2^{x+1}$, consider the basic shapes of the graphs and any transformations. Because both bases of these exponential functions are greater than 1, the graphs are increasing. Because there is no vertical shift on either function, both graphs are asymptotic to the x-axis. The intersection of the graphs of $Y_1 = 8^x$ and $Y_2 = 2^{x+1}$, shown at the left, confirms the solution.

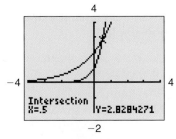

Figure 5.6-1

CAUTION

$$\frac{\ln 2}{\ln 5} \neq \ln\left(\frac{2}{5}\right) \text{ and}$$

$$\frac{\ln 2}{\ln 5} \neq \ln 2 - \ln 5$$

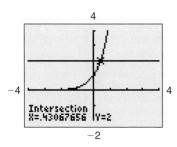

Figure 5.6-2

Example 2   **Powers of Different Bases**

Solve the equation $5^x = 2$. Confirm your solution with a graph.

Solution

$$5^x = 2$$
$$\ln 5^x = \ln 2 \qquad \textit{take logarithms on each side}$$
$$x \ln 5 = \ln 2 \qquad \textit{use the Power Law}$$
$$x = \frac{\ln 2}{\ln 5}$$
$$x = \frac{0.6931}{1.6094} = 0.4307$$

The intersection of the graphs of $Y_1 = 5^x$ and $Y_2 = 2$, shown at the left, confirms the solution. ∎

Example 3   **Powers of Different Bases**

Solve the equation $2^{4x-1} = 3^{1-x}$. Confirm your solution with a graph.

Solution

$$2^{4x-1} = 3^{1-x}$$
$$\ln(2^{4x-1}) = \ln(3^{1-x}) \qquad \textit{Take logarithms on each side}$$
$$(4x - 1)\ln 2 = (1 - x)\ln 3 \qquad \textit{Power Law}$$
$$4x \ln 2 - \ln 2 = \ln 3 - x \ln 3 \qquad \textit{Distributive Property}$$
$$4x \ln 2 + x \ln 3 = \ln 3 + \ln 2 \qquad \textit{Rearrange terms and isolate } x$$
$$x(4 \ln 2 + \ln 3) = \ln 3 + \ln 2$$
$$x = \frac{\ln 3 + \ln 2}{4 \ln 2 + \ln 3}$$
$$x = 0.4628$$

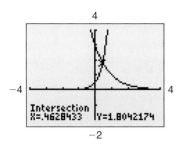

Figure 5.6-3

The intersection of the graphs of $Y_1 = 2^{4x-1}$ and $Y_2 = 3^{1-x}$, shown at the left, confirms the solution. ∎

When you multiply each side of an equation by the same expression, extraneous solutions may be introduced, as shown in Example 4.

Example 4   **Using Substitution**

Solve the equation $e^x - e^{-x} = 4$. Confirm your solution with a graph.

Solution

First multiply each side by e^x to eliminate negative exponents.

$$e^x - e^{-x} = 4$$
$$e^x(e^x - e^{-x}) = e^x(4)$$
$$e^x e^x - e^x e^{-x} = 4e^x$$
$$e^{2x} - 1 = 4e^x \qquad \textit{Product Law.}$$
$$e^{2x} - 4e^x - 1 = 0$$

Let $u = e^x$ and substitute.

$$u^2 - 4u - 1 = 0$$
$$u = \frac{-(-4) \pm \sqrt{(-4)^2 - 4(1)(-1)}}{2(1)}$$
$$u = \frac{4 \pm \sqrt{20}}{2}$$
$$u = \frac{4 \pm 2\sqrt{5}}{2}$$
$$u = 2 \pm \sqrt{5}$$

Replace u with e^x to get $e^x = 2 + \sqrt{5}$ or $e^x = 2 - \sqrt{5}$. Because e^x can only be positive and $2 - \sqrt{5}$ is negative, $e^x = 2 - \sqrt{5}$ has no solution.

$$e^x = 2 + \sqrt{5}$$
$$\ln e^x = \ln(2 + \sqrt{5})$$
$$x \cdot \ln e = \ln(2 + \sqrt{5})$$
$$x = 1.4436 \qquad \ln e = 1$$

The intersection of the graphs of $Y_1 = e^x - e^{-x}$ and $Y_2 = 4$, shown in Figure 5.6-4, confirms that there is exactly one solution ∎

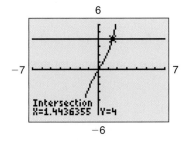

Figure 5.6-4

Applications of Exponential Equations

When a living organism dies, its carbon-14 decays. The half-life of carbon-14 is 5730 years, so the amount of carbon-14 remaining at time t is given by $M(t) = P(0.5)^{\frac{t}{5730}}$, where P is the mass of carbon-14 that was present initially. The function M can be used to determine the age of fossils and some relics.

Example 5 Radiocarbon Dating

The skeleton of a mastodon has lost 58% of its original carbon-14. When did the mastodon die?

Solution

If the mastodon has lost 58% of its original carbon-14, then 42% of the initial amount, or $0.42P$, remains and $M(t) = 0.42P$. To determine when the mastodon died, solve $0.42P = P(0.5)^{\frac{t}{5730}}$ for t.

$$0.42P = P(0.5)^{\frac{t}{5730}}$$
$$0.42 = (0.5)^{\frac{t}{5730}}$$
$$\ln 0.42 = \ln(0.5)^{\frac{t}{5730}}$$
$$\ln 0.42 = \frac{t}{5730}(\ln 0.5)$$
$$t = \frac{5730(\ln 0.42)}{\ln 0.5}$$
$$t = 7171.3171$$

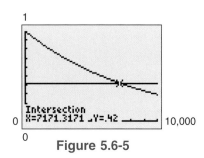

Figure 5.6-5

Therefore, the mastodon died approximately 7200 years ago. The intersection of the graphs of $Y_1 = 0.42$ and $Y_2 = (0.5)^{\frac{x}{5730}}$, shown in Figure 5.6-5, confirms the solution.

Example 6   Compound Interest

If $3000 is to be invested at 8% per year, compounded quarterly, in how many years will the investment be worth $10,680?

Solution

The interest rate per quarter r is $\frac{0.08}{4}$, or 0.02. To find the time t that it will take the investment to be worth $10,680 use the compound interest formula $A = P(1 + r)^t$.

$$10,680 = 3000(1 + 0.02)^t$$
$$10,680 = 3000(1.02)^t$$
$$3.56 = (1.02)^t$$
$$\ln 3.56 = \ln(1.02)^t$$
$$\ln 3.56 = t(\ln 1.02)$$
$$t = \frac{\ln 3.56}{\ln 1.02} = 64.1208 \text{ quarters}$$

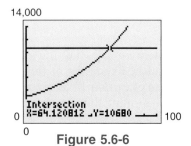

Figure 5.6-6

Therefore, it will take 64.12 quarters, or $\frac{64.12}{4} = 16.03$ years. The intersection of the graphs of $Y_1 = 10,680$ and $Y_2 = 3000(1 + 0.02)^x$, shown in Figure 5.6-6, confirms the solution.

Example 7   Population Growth

A biologist knows that if there are no inhibiting or stimulating factors, the population of a certain type of bacteria will increase exponentially. The population at time t is given by the function

$$S(t) = Pe^{rt},$$

where P is the initial population and r is the continuous growth rate. The biologist has a culture that contains 1000 bacteria, and 7 hours later there are 5000 bacteria.

a. Write the function for this population.

b. When will the population reach 1 billion?

Solution

a. The initial population P is 1000. To find the growth rate r, use the fact that $S(7) = 5000$.

$$S(t) = 1000e^{rt}$$
$$5000 = 1000e^{r\,(7)}$$
$$5 = e^{7r}$$
$$\ln 5 = \ln e^{7r}$$
$$\ln 5 = 7r \ln e$$
$$\ln 5 = 7r \qquad\qquad \ln e = 1$$
$$r = \frac{\ln 5}{7} = 0.2299$$

Therefore, the function for this population is

$$S(t) = 1000e^{0.2299t}$$

The intersection of the graphs of $Y_1 = 5000$ and $Y_2 = 1000e^{7x}$, shown in Figure 5.6-7, confirms the value of r.

b. Find the value of t when $S(t)$ is 1 billion.

$$1000e^{0.2299t} = 1{,}000{,}000{,}000$$
$$e^{0.2299t} = 1{,}000{,}000$$
$$\ln e^{0.2299t} = \ln 1{,}000{,}000$$
$$0.2299t \ln e = \ln 1{,}000{,}000$$
$$0.2299t = \ln 1{,}000{,}000 \qquad\qquad \ln e = 1$$
$$t = \frac{\ln 1{,}000{,}000}{0.2299} = 60.0936 \text{ hours}$$

The bacteria population will reach 1 billion after about 60 hours. The intersection of the graphs of $Y_1 = 1000e^{0.2299x}$ and $Y_2 = 1{,}000{,}000{,}000$, shown in Figure 5.6-8, confirms the solution.   ■

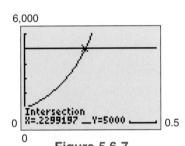

Figure 5.6-7

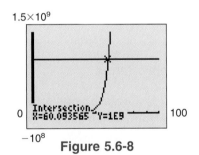

Figure 5.6-8

Example 8   **Inhibited Population Growth**

A population of fish in a lake at time t months is given by the function F.

$$F(t) = \frac{20{,}000}{1 + 24e^{-\frac{t}{4}}}$$

How long will it take for the fish population to reach 15,000?

Solution

Find the value of t when $F(t)$ is 15,000.

$$15,000 = \frac{20,000}{1 + 24e^{-\frac{t}{4}}}$$

$$15,000(1 + 24e^{-\frac{t}{4}}) = 20,000$$

$$1 + 24e^{-\frac{t}{4}} = \frac{20,000}{15,000}$$

$$24e^{-\frac{t}{4}} = \frac{4}{3} - 1$$

$$e^{-\frac{t}{4}} = \frac{1}{3} \cdot \frac{1}{24}$$

$$\ln e^{-\frac{t}{4}} = \ln \frac{1}{72}$$

$$-\frac{t}{4}\ln e = \ln 1 - \ln 72$$

$$-\frac{t}{4} = 0 - \ln 72 \qquad \textit{ln } e = 1 \textit{ and } \ln 1 = 0$$

$$t = 4 \ln 72 = 17.1067$$

Therefore, it will take a little more than 17 months for the population to reach 15,000. The intersection of the graphs of $Y_1 = 15,000$ and $Y_2 = \dfrac{20,000}{1 + 24e^{-\frac{x}{4}}}$ shown in Figure 5.6-9 confirms the solution. ∎

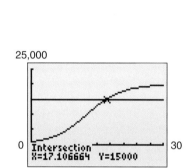

Figure 5.6-9

Logarithmic Equations

Properties of one-to-one functions are useful when solving logarithmic equations, as shown in Example 9.

Example 9   **Equations with Only Logarithmic Terms**

Solve the equation $\ln(x - 3) + \ln(2x + 1) = 2(\ln x)$. Confirm your solution with a graph.

Solution

First use the Product and Power Laws to rewrite the equation.

$$\ln(x - 3) + \ln(2x + 1) = 2(\ln x)$$

$$\ln[(x - 3)(2x + 1)] = \ln x^2$$

$$\ln(2x^2 - 5x - 3) = \ln x^2$$

$$2x^2 - 5x - 3 = x^2 \qquad y = \textit{ln } x \textit{ is a one-to-one function}$$

$$x^2 - 5x - 3 = 0$$

Use the Quadratic Formula to solve for x.

$$x = \frac{-(-5) \pm \sqrt{(-5)^2 - 4(1)(-3)}}{2(1)}$$

$$x = \frac{5 + \sqrt{37}}{2} \approx 5.5414 \quad \text{or} \quad x = \frac{5 - \sqrt{37}}{2} \approx -0.5414$$

Because $\ln(x - 3)$ is undefined for $x \le 3$, $x = \dfrac{5 - \sqrt{37}}{2} \approx -0.5414$ cannot be a solution. Therefore, the only solution of the original equation is $x = \dfrac{5 + \sqrt{37}}{2} \approx 5.5414$. The intersection of the graphs of $Y_1 = \ln(x - 3) + \ln(2x + 1)$ and $Y_2 = 2(\ln x)$, shown in Figure 5.6-10, confirms the solution. ∎

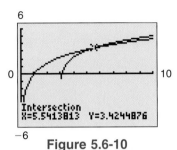

Figure 5.6-10

Equations that involve both logarithmic and constant terms may be solved by using the basic property of logarithms.

$$10^{\log v} = v \quad \text{and} \quad e^{\ln v} = v$$

Example 10   **Equations with Logarithmic and Constant Terms**

Solve the equation $\ln(x - 3) = 5 - \ln(x - 3)$. Confirm your solution with a graph.

Solution

First get all the logarithmic terms on one side of the equal sign and the constants on the other. Then rewrite the side that contains the logarithms as a single logarithm.

$$\ln(x - 3) = 5 - \ln(x - 3)$$
$$\ln(x - 3) + \ln(x - 3) = 5$$
$$2 \ln(x - 3) = 5$$
$$\ln(x - 3) = \frac{5}{2}$$
$$e^{\ln(x-3)} = e^{\frac{5}{2}}$$
$$x - 3 = e^{\frac{5}{2}}$$
$$x = e^{\frac{5}{2}} + 3 \approx 15.1825$$

The intersection of the graphs of $Y_1 = \ln(x - 3)$ and $Y_2 = 5 - \ln(x - 3)$, shown in Figure 5.6-11, confirms the solution. ∎

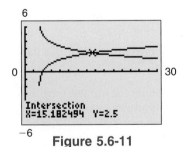

Figure 5.6-11

Example 11   **Equations with Logarithmic and Constant Terms**

Solve the equation $\log(x - 16) = 2 - \log(x - 1)$. Confirm your solution with a graph.

Solution

$$\log(x - 16) = 2 - \log(x - 1)$$
$$\log(x - 16) + \log(x - 1) = 2$$
$$\log[(x - 16)(x - 1)] = 2$$
$$\log(x^2 - 17x + 16) = 2$$
$$10^{\log(x^2 - 17x + 16)} = 10^2$$
$$x^2 - 17x + 16 = 100$$
$$x^2 - 17x - 84 = 0$$
$$(x + 4)(x - 21) = 0$$
$$x + 4 = 0 \quad \text{or} \quad x - 21 = 0$$
$$x = -4 \qquad x = 21$$

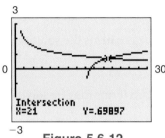

Figure 5.6-12

Because $\log(x - 16)$ and $\log(x - 1)$ are not defined for $x = -4$, it cannot be a solution. Therefore, the only solution is $x = 21$. The intersection of the graphs of $Y_1 = \log(x - 16)$ and $Y_2 = 2 - \log(x - 1)$, shown in Figure 5.6-12, confirms the solution. ∎

Exercises 5.6

In Exercises 1–8, solve the equation without using logarithms.

1. $3^x = 81$

2. $3^x + 3 = 30$

3. $3^{x+1} = 9^{5x}$

4. $4^{5x} = 16^{2x-1}$

5. $3^{5x}9^{x^2} = 27$

6. $2^{x^2+5x} = \dfrac{1}{16}$

7. $9^{x^2} = 3^{-5x-2}$

8. $4^{x^2-1} = 8^x$

In Exercises 9–29, solve the equation. Give exact answers (in terms of natural logarithms). Then use a calculator to find an approximate answer.

9. $3^x = 5$

10. $5^x = 4$

11. $2^x = 3^{x-1}$

12. $4^{x+2} = 2^{x-1}$

13. $3^{1-2x} = 5^{x+5}$

14. $4^{3x-1} = 3^{x-2}$

15. $2^{1-3x} = 3^{x+1}$

16. $3^{z+3} = 2^z$

17. $e^{2x} = 5$

18. $e^{-3x} = 2$

19. $6e^{-1.4x} = 21$

20. $3.4e^{-\frac{x}{3}} = 5.6$

21. $2.1e^{\frac{x}{2}\ln 3} = 5$

22. $7.8e^{\frac{x}{3}\ln 5} = 14$

23. $9^x - 4 \cdot 3^x + 3 = 0$ *Hint:* Note that $9^x = (3^x)^2$; let $u = 3^x$.

24. $4^x - 6 \cdot 2^x = -8$

25. $e^{2x} - 5e^x + 6 = 0$ *Hint:* Let $u = e^x$.

26. $2e^{2x} - 9e^x + 4 = 0$

27. $6e^{2x} - 16e^x = 6$

28. $8e^{2x} + 8e^x = 6$

29. $4^x + 6 \cdot 4^{-x} = 5$

In Exercises 30–32, solve the equation for x.

30. $\dfrac{e^x + e^{-x}}{e^x - e^{-x}} = t$

31. $\dfrac{e^x - e^{-x}}{2} = t$

32. $\dfrac{e^x - e^{-x}}{e^x + e^{-x}} = t$

33. Prove that if $\ln u = \ln v$, then $u = v$. *Hint:* Use the basic property of inverses $e^{\ln v} = v$.

34. a. Solve $7^x = 3$ using natural logarithms. Give an exact answer, not an approximation.
b. Solve $7^x = 3$ using common logarithms. Give an exact answer, not an approximation.
c. Use the change-of-base formula in *Excursion* 5.5.A to show that your answers in parts **a** and **b** are the same.

In Exercises 35–44, solve the equation. (See Example 9.)

35. $\ln(3x - 5) = \ln 11 + \ln 2$

36. $\log(4x - 1) = \log(x + 1) + \log 2$

37. $\log(3x - 1) + \log 2 = \log 4 + \log(x + 2)$

38. $\ln(x + 6) - \ln 10 = \ln(x - 1) - \ln 2$

39. $2 \ln x = \ln 36$ **40.** $2 \log x = 3 \log 4$

41. $\ln x + \ln(x + 1) = \ln 3 + \ln 4$

42. $\ln(6x - 1) + \ln x = \dfrac{1}{2} \ln 4$

43. $\ln x = \ln 3 - \ln(x + 5)$

44. $\ln(2x + 3) + \ln x = \ln e$

In Exercises 45–52, solve the equation.

45. $\ln(x + 9) - \ln x = 1$

46. $\ln(2x + 1) - 1 = \ln(x - 2)$

47. $\log x + \log(x - 3) = 1$

48. $\log(x - 1) + \log(x + 2) = 1$

49. $\log \sqrt{x^2 - 1} = 2$ **50.** $\log \sqrt[3]{x^2 + 21x} = \dfrac{2}{3}$

51. $\ln(x^2 + 1) - \ln(x - 1) = 1 + \ln(x + 1)$

52. $\dfrac{\ln(x + 1)}{\ln(x - 1)} = 2$

Exercises 53–62 deal with the half-life function $M(x) = c(0.5)^{\frac{x}{h}}$, which was discussed in Section 5.3 and used in Example 5 of this section.

53. How old is a piece of ivory that has lost 36% of its carbon-14?

54. How old is a mummy that has lost 49% of its carbon-14?

55. Find when part of the Pueblo Benito ruins was built if the doorway timbers have 89.14% of their original carbon-14. (See the image on the first page of this chapter.)

56. How old is a wooden statue that has only one-third of its original carbon-14?

57. A quantity of uranium decays to two-thirds of its original mass in 0.26 billion years. Find the half-life of uranium.

58. A certain radioactive substance loses one-third of its original mass in 5 days. Find its half-life.

59. Krypton-85 loses 6.44% of its mass each year. What is its half-life?

60. Strontium-90 loses 2.5% of its mass each year. What is its half-life?

61. The half-life of a certain substance is 3.6 days. How long will it take for 20 grams to decay to 3 grams?

62. The half-life of cobalt-60 is 4.945 years. How long will it take for 25 grams to decay to 15 grams?

Exercises 63–68 deal with the compound interest formula $A = P(1 + r)^t$, which was discussed in Section 5.3 and used in Example 6 of this section.

63. At what annual rate of interest should $1000 be invested so that it will double in 10 years, if interest is compounded quarterly?

64. Find how long it takes $500 to triple if it is invested at 6% in each compounding period.
a. annually   **b.** quarterly   **c.** daily

65. a. How long will it take to triple your money if you invest $500 at a rate of 5% per year compounded annually?
b. How long will it take at 5% compounded quarterly?

66. At what rate of interest compounded annually should you invest $500 if you want to have $1500 in 12 years?

67. How much money should be invested at 5% interest compounded quarterly so that 9 years later the investment will be worth $5000? This answer is called the present value of $5000 at 5% interest.

68. Find a formula that gives the time needed for an investment of P dollars to double, if the interest rate is r% compounded annually. *Hint:* Solve the compound interest formula for t, when $A = 2P$.

Exercises 69–76 deal with functions of the form $f(x) = Pe^{kx}$, where k is the continuous exponential growth rate. See Example 7.

69. The present concentration of carbon dioxide in the atmosphere is 364 parts per million (ppm) and is increasing exponentially at a continuous yearly rate of 0.4% (that is, $k = 0.004$). How many years will it take for the concentration to reach 500 ppm?

70. The amount P of ozone in the atmosphere is currently decaying exponentially each year at a continuous rate of $\frac{1}{4}$% (that is, $k = -0.0025$). How long will it take for half the ozone to disappear $\left(\text{that is, when will the amount be } \frac{P}{2}\right)$? Your answer is the half-life of ozone.

71. The population of Brazil increased exponentially from 151 million in 1990 to 173 million in 2000.
   a. At what continuous rate was the population growing during this period?
   b. Assuming that Brazil's population continues to increase at this rate, when will it reach 250 million?

72. Outstanding consumer debt increased exponentially from $781.5 billion in 1990 to $1765.5 billion in 2002. (Source: Federal Reserve Bulletin)
   a. At what continuous rate is consumer debt growing?
   b. Assuming this rate continues, when will consumer debt reach $2500 billion?

73. The probability P percent of having an accident while driving a car is related to the alcohol level of the driver's blood by the formula $P = e^{kt}$, where k is a constant. Accident statistics show that the probability of an accident is 25% when the blood alcohol level is $t = 0.15$.
   a. Find k. Use $P = 25$, not 0.25.
   b. At what blood alcohol level is the probability of having an accident 50%?

74. Under normal conditions, the atmospheric pressure (in millibars) at height h feet above sea level is given by $P(h) = 1015e^{-kh}$, where k is a positive constant.
   a. If the pressure at 18,000 feet is half the pressure at sea level, find k.
   b. Using the information from part **a**, find the atmospheric pressure at 1000 feet, 5000 feet, and 15,000 feet.

75. One hour after an experiment begins, the number of bacteria in a culture is 100. An hour later there are 500.
   a. Find the number of bacteria at the beginning of the experiment and the number 3 hours later.
   b. How long does it take the number of bacteria at any given time to double?

76. If the population at time t is given by $S(t) = ce^{kt}$, find a formula that gives the time it takes for the population to double.

77. The spread of a flu virus in a community of 45,000 people is given by the function

$$f(t) = \frac{45{,}000}{1 + 224e^{-0.889t}},$$

where $f(t)$ is the number of people infected in week t.
   a. How many people had the flu at the outbreak of the epidemic? after 3 weeks?
   b. When will half the town be infected?

78. The beaver population near a certain lake in year t is approximately $p(t) = \dfrac{2000}{1 + 199e^{-0.5544t}}$.
   a. When will the beaver population reach 1000?
   b. Will the population ever reach 2000? Why?

79. *Critical Thinking* According to one theory of learning, the number of words per minute N that a person can type after t weeks of practice is given by $N = c(1 - e^{-kt})$, where c is an upper limit that N cannot exceed and k is a constant that must be determined experimentally for each person.
   a. If a person can type 50 wpm (words per minute) after 4 weeks of practice and 70 wpm after 8 weeks, find the values of k and c for this person. According to the theory, this person will never type faster than c wpm.
   b. Another person can type 50 wpm after 4 weeks of practice and 90 wpm after 8 weeks. How many weeks must this person practice to be able to type 125 wpm?

80. *Critical Thinking* Wendy has been offered two jobs, each with the same starting salary of $24,000 and identical benefits. Assuming satisfactory performance, she will receive a $1200 raise each year at the company A, whereas the company B will give her a 4% raise each year.
   a. In what year (after the first year) would her salary be the same at either company? Until then, which company pays better? After that, which company pays better?
   b. Answer the questions in part **a** assuming that the annual raise at company A is $1800.

Exponential, Logarithmic, and Other Models

Objectives

• Model real data sets with power, exponential, logarithmic, and logistic functions

Many data sets can be modeled by suitable exponential, logarithmic, and related functions. Most calculators have regression procedures for constructing the models described in the table below.

Model	Equation	Examples	
Power	$y = ax^r$	$y = 5x^{2.7}$	$y = 3.5x^{-0.45}$
Exponential	$y = ab^x$ or $y = ae^{kx}$	$y = 2(1.64)^x$	$y = 2e^{0.4947x}$
Logarithmic	$y = a + b \ln x$	$y = 5 + 4.2 \ln x$	$y = 2 - 3 \ln x$
Logistic	$y = \dfrac{a}{1 + be^{-kx}}$	$y = \dfrac{20{,}000}{1 + 24e^{-0.25x}}$	$y = \dfrac{650}{1 + 6e^{-0.3x}}$

Exponential Models

In the table of values for the exponential model $y = 3 \cdot 2^x$ that follows, examine the patterns in the ratios of successive y-values.

x	0	4	8	12	16
y	3	48	768	12,288	196,608

$$\frac{48}{3} = 16 \qquad \frac{768}{48} = 16 \qquad \frac{12{,}288}{768} = 16 \qquad \frac{196{,}608}{12{,}288} = 16$$

At each step, x changes from x to $x + 4$, y changes from $3 \cdot 2^x$ to $3 \cdot 2^{x+4}$, and the ratio of successive y-values is always the same.

$$\frac{3 \cdot 2^{x+4}}{3 \cdot 2^x} = \frac{3 \cdot 2^x \cdot 2^4}{3 \cdot 2^x} = 2^4 = 16$$

A similar argument applies to any exponential model $y = ab^x$ and shows that if x changes by a fixed amount k, then the ratio of the corresponding y-values is the constant b^k. In the exponential model $y = 3 \cdot 2^x$ above, b is 2 and k is 4. This fact identifies the model that would best represent the data.

> **When the ratio of successive entries in a table of data is approximately constant, an exponential model is appropriate.**

Example 1 U.S. Population Before the Civil War

In the years before the Civil War, the population of the United States grew rapidly, as shown in the following table. Find a model for this growth.

Year	Population in millions		Year	Population in millions
1790	3.93		1830	12.86
1800	5.31		1840	17.07
1810	7.24		1850	23.19
1820	9.64		1860	31.44

[*Source: U.S. Bureau of the Census*]

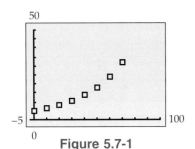

Figure 5.7-1

Solution

The data points, with $x = 0$ corresponding to 1790, are shown in Figure 5.7-1. Their shape suggests either a polynomial graph of even degree or an exponential graph. Since populations generally grow exponentially, an exponential model is likely to be a good choice. This can be confirmed by looking at the successive entries in the table.

Year	Population		Year	Population
1790	3.93		1830	12.86
	$\dfrac{5.31}{3.93} \approx 1.351$			$\dfrac{17.07}{12.86} \approx 1.327$
1800	5.31		1840	17.07
	$\dfrac{7.24}{5.31} \approx 1.363$			$\dfrac{23.19}{17.07} \approx 1.359$
1810	7.24		1850	23.19
	$\dfrac{9.64}{7.24} \approx 1.331$			$\dfrac{31.44}{23.19} \approx 1.356$
1820	9.64		1860	31.44
	$\dfrac{12.86}{9.64} \approx 1.334$			
1830	12.86			

NOTE Throughout this section, coefficients are rounded for convenient reading, but the full expansion is used for calculations and graphs.

Because the ratios are almost constant, as they would be in an exponential model, use regression to find an exponential model. The procedure is the same as for linear and polynomial regression. An exponential regression produces this model.

$$y = 3.9572(1.0299^x)$$

The graph of the exponential model in Figure 5.7-2 appears to fit the data well. In fact, you can readily verify that the model has an error of less than 1% for each of the data points. Furthermore, as discussed before this example, when x changes by 10, the value of y changes by approximately $1.0299^{10} \approx 1.343$, which is very close to the successive ratios of the data.

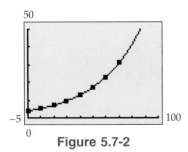

Figure 5.7-2

Logistic Models

A logistic model represents growth that has a limiting factor, such as food supplies, war, new diseases, etc. Logistic models are often used to model population growth, as shown in Example 2.

Example 2 U.S. Population After the Civil War

After the Civil War, the population of the United States continued to increase, as shown in the following table. Find a model for this growth.

Year	Population in millions	Year	Population in millions	Year	Population in millions
1870	38.56	1920	106.02	1960	179.32
1880	50.19	1930	123.20	1970	202.30
1890	62.98	1940	132.16	1980	226.54
1900	76.21	1950	151.33	1990	248.72
1910	92.23			2000	281.42

Solution

The model from Example 1 does not remain valid, as can be seen in Figure 5.7-3, which shows its graph together with all the data points from 1790 through 2000, where $x = 0$ corresponds to 1790.

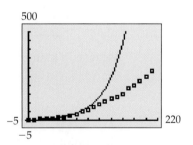

Figure 5.7-3

The *rate* of growth has steadily decreased since the Civil War. For instance, the ratio of the first two entries is $\frac{50.19}{38.56} \approx 1.302$ and the ratio of the last two is $\frac{281.42}{248.72} \approx 1.131$. So an exponential model may not be the best choice.

Other possibilities are polynomial models, which grow at a slower rate, or logistic models, in which the growth rate decreases with time. Figure 5.7-4 on the next page shows these models compared to an exponential model.

Exponential Model	Quartic Model	Logistic Model
$y = 6.0662 \cdot 1.02039^x$	$y = (7.94 \times 10^{-8})x^4 - (2.76 \times 10^{-5})x^3$ $+ 0.0093x^2 - 0.1621x + 5.462$	$y = \dfrac{442.10}{1 + 56.329e^{-0.022x}}$

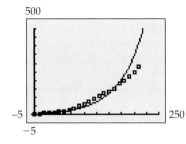
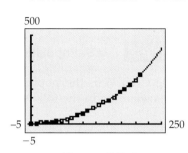
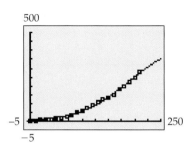

Figure 5.7-4

The quartic and logistic models fit the data better than does the exponential model. The quartic model indicates unlimited future growth, but the logistic model has the population growing more slowly in the future. ∎

Exponential versus Power Models

In Example 1, the ratios of successive entries of the data table were used to determine that an exponential model was appropriate. Another way to determine if an exponential model might be to consider the exponential function $y = ab^x$, as shown below.

$$y = ab^x$$
$$\ln y = \ln (ab^x) \qquad \textit{Take the natural logarithm of each side}$$
$$\ln y = \ln a + \ln b^x \qquad \textit{Product Law}$$
$$\ln y = \ln a + x \ln b \qquad \textit{Power Law}$$

Because $\ln a$ and $\ln b$ are constants, let $k = \ln a$ and $m = \ln b$.

$$\ln y = \ln a + x \ln b$$
$$\ln y = (\ln b)x + \ln a$$
$$\ln y = mx + k$$

The points $(x, \ln y)$ lie on a straight line with slope m and y-intercept k. Consequently, a guideline for determining if an exponential model is appropriate is as follows.

> **If (x, y) are data points and if the points $(x, \ln y)$ are approximately linear, then an exponential model may be appropriate for the data.**

Similarly, consider the power function $y = ax^r$

$$y = ax^r$$
$$\ln y = \ln (ax^r) \qquad \textit{Take the natural logarithm of each side}$$
$$\ln y = \ln a + \ln x^r \qquad \textit{Product Law}$$
$$\ln y = \ln a + r \ln x \qquad \textit{Power Law}$$

Because r and $\ln a$ are constants, let $k = \ln a$. Then:

$$\ln y = \ln a + r \ln x$$
$$\ln y = r \ln x + \ln a$$
$$\ln y = r \ln x + k$$

Thus, the points $(\ln x, \ln y)$ lie on the straight line with slope r and y-intercept k. Consequently, a guideline for determining if a power model is appropriate is as follows

> **If (x, y) are data points and if the points $(\ln x, \ln y)$ are approximately linear, then a power model may be appropriate for the data.**

Example 3   Different Planet Years

The length of time that a planet takes to make one complete rotation around the sun is that planet's "year." The table below shows the length of each planet's year, relative to an Earth year, and the average distance of that planet from the Sun in millions of miles. Find a model for this data in which x is the length of the year and y is the distance from the Sun.

Planet	Year	Distance	Planet	Year	Distance
Mercury	0.24	36.0	Saturn	29.46	886.7
Venus	0.62	67.2	Uranus	84.01	1783.0
Earth	1.00	92.9	Neptune	164.79	2794.0
Mars	1.88	141.6	Pluto	247.69	3674.5
Jupiter	11.86	483.6			

Technology Tip

Solution

Figure 5.7-5 shows the data points for the five planets with the shortest years. Figure 5.7-6 shows all of the data points, but on this scale, the first four points look like a single large point near the origin.

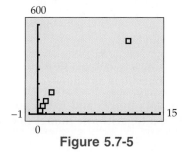

Figure 5.7-5

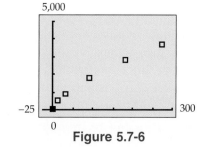

Figure 5.7-6

Plotting the point $(x, \ln y)$ for each data point (x, y) produces the graph shown in Figure 5.7-7. Its points do not form a linear pattern, so an exponential model is not appropriate. The points $(\ln x, \ln y)$ shown in Figure 5.7-8 do form a linear pattern, which suggests that a power model will work.

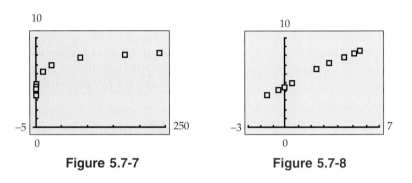

Figure 5.7-7   Figure 5.7-8

A power regression produces this model:

$$y = 92.8932x^{0.6669}$$

Its graph in Figures 5.7-9 and 5.7-10 show that it fits the original data points well.

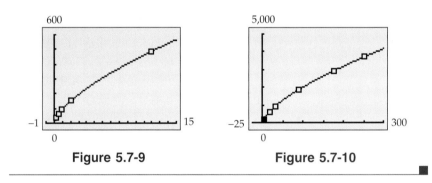

Figure 5.7-9   Figure 5.7-10

Logarithmic Models

Consider the logarithmic function $y = b \ln x + a$

Because a and b are constants, let $m = b$ and $k = a$. Then:

$$y = m(\ln x) + k$$

The points $(\ln x, y)$ lie on the straight line with slope m and y-intercept k. Consequently, a guideline for determining if a logarithmic model is appropriate is as follows.

If (x, y) are data points and if the points $(\ln x, y)$ are approximately linear, then a logarithmic model may be appropriate for the data.

Example 4   Logarithmic Population Growth

Find a model for population growth in El Paso, Texas, given the information in the following table.

Year	1950	1970	1980	1990	2000
Population	130,485	322,261	425,259	515,342	563,662

[*Source: U.S. Bureau of the Census.*]

Solution

The scatter plot of the data, where $x = 50$ corresponds to 1950, shown in Figure 5.7-11, suggests a logarithmic curve with a very slight bend.

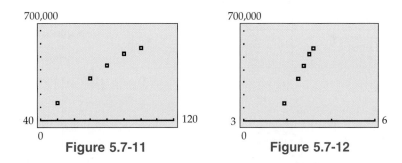

Figure 5.7-11   **Figure 5.7-12**

To determine whether a logarithmic model is appropriate for this data, plot points $(\ln x, y)$; that is $(\ln 50, 130,485) \ldots (\ln 100, 563,662)$. Because these points, shown in Figure 5.7-12, appear to be approximately linear, a logarithmic model seems appropriate.

Using logarithmic regression, the model is:

$$y = -2,382,368.345 + 640,666.815 \ln x$$

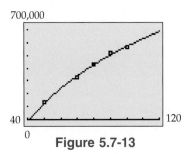

Figure 5.7-13

CAUTION

When using logarithmic models, you must have data points with positive first coordinates because logarithms of negative numbers and 0 are not defined.

The graph of this model, shown in Figure 5.7-13, shows that it is a good fit for the data.   ■

Exercises 5.7

In Exercises 1–10, state which of the following models might be appropriate for the given scatter plot of data. More than one model may be appropriate.

Model	Corresponding function
A. Linear	$y = ax + b$
B. Quadratic	$y = ax^2 + bx + c$
C. Power	$y = ax^r$
D. Cubic	$y = ax^3 + bx^2 + cx + d$
E. Exponential	$y = ab^x$
F. Logarithmic	$y = a + b \ln x$
G. Logistic	$y = \dfrac{a}{1 + be^{-kx}}$

1.

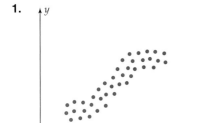

2.

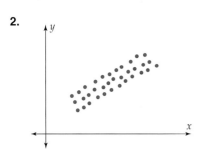

3.

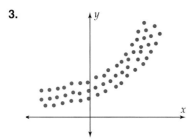

4.

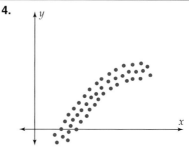

5.

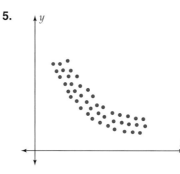

6.

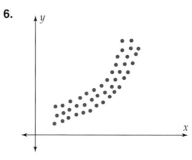

7.

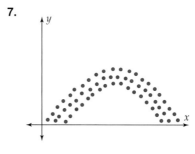

8.

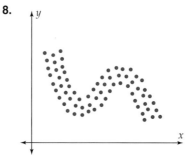

9.

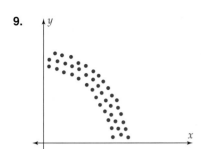

10.

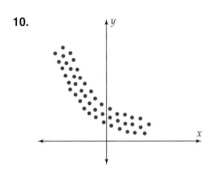

In Exercises 11 and 12, compute the ratios of successive entries in the table to determine whether an exponential model is appropriate for the data.

11.

x	0	2	4	6	8	10
y	3	15.2	76.9	389.2	1975.5	9975.8

12.

x	1	3	5	7	9	11
y	3	21	55	105	171	253

13. a. Show algebraically that in the logistic model for the U.S. population in Example 2, the population can never exceed 442.10 million people.
   b. Confirm your answer in part **a** by graphing the logistic model in a window that includes the next three centuries.

14. According to estimates by the U.S. Bureau of the Census, the U.S. population was 287.7 million in 2002. Based on this information, which of the models in Example 2 appears to be the most accurate predictor?

15. Graph each of the following power functions in a window with $0 \le x \le 20$.
   a. $f(x) = x^{-1.5}$ **b.** $g(x) = x^{0.75}$ **c.** $h(x) = x^{2.4}$

16. Based on your graphs in Exercise 15, describe the general shape of the graph of $y = ax^r$, when $a > 0$ and r is as described below.
   a. $r < 0$ **b.** $0 < r < 1$ **c.** $r > 1$

In Exercises 17–20, determine whether an exponential, power, or logarithmic model (or none or several of these) is appropriate for the data by determining which (if any) of the following sets of points are approximately linear, where the given data set consists of the points $\{(x, y)\}$.

$$\{(x, \ln y)\} \qquad \{(\ln x, \ln y)\} \qquad \{(\ln x, y)\}$$

17.

x	1	3	5	7	9	11
y	2	25	81	175	310	497

18.

x	3	6	9	12	15	18
y	385	74	14	2.75	0.5	0.1

19.

x	5	10	15	20	25	30
y	17	27	35	40	43	48

20.

x	5	10	15	20	25	30
y	2	110	460	1200	2500	4525

21. The table shows the number of babies born as twins, triplets, quadruplets, etc., in recent years.

Year	Multiple births
1989	92,916
1990	96,893
1991	98,125
1992	99,255
1993	100,613
1994	101,658
1995	101,709

a. Sketch a scatter plot of the data, with $x = 1$ corresponding to 1989.
b. Plot both of the following models on the same screen with the scatter plot:

$$f(x) = 93,201.973 + 4,545.977 \ln x$$

and

$$g(x) = \frac{102,519.98}{1 + 0.1536e^{-0.4263x}}$$

c. Use the table feature to estimate the number of multiple births in 2000 and 2005.
d. Over the long run, which model do you think is the better predictor?

22. The graph shows the Census Bureau's estimates of future U.S. population.

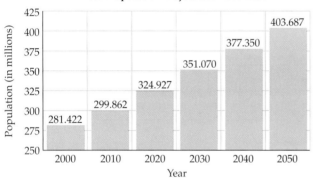

U.S. Population Projections: 2000–2050

a. How well do the projections in the graph compare with those given by the logistic model in Example 2?
b. Find a logistic model of the U.S. population, using the data given in Example 2 for the years from 1900 to 2000, with $x = 0$ corresponding to 1900.
c. How well do the projections in the graph compare with those given by the model in part **b**?

23. Infant mortality rates in the United States are shown in the following table.

Year	Infant mortality rate*	Year	Infant mortality rate*
1920	76.7	1980	12.6
1930	60.4	1985	10.6
1940	47.0	1990	9.2
1950	29.2	1995	7.6
1960	26.0	2000	6.9
1970	20.0		

*Rates are infant (under 1 year) deaths per 1000 live births.

a. Sketch a scatter plot of the data, with $x = 0$ corresponding to 1900.
b. Verify that the set of points $(x, \ln y)$, where (x, y) are the original data points, is approximately linear.
c. Based on part **b**, what type of model would be appropriate for this data? Find such a model.

24. The average number of students per computer in the U.S. public schools (elementary through high school) is shown in the table below.

Fall of school year	Students per computer
1987	32
1988	25
1989	22
1990	20
1991	18
1992	16
1993	14
1994	10.5
1995	10
1996	7.8
1997	6.1
1998	5.7
1999	5.4

a. Sketch a scatter plot of the data, with $x = 1$ corresponding to 1987.
b. Find an exponential model for the data.
c. Use the model to estimate the number of students per computer in 2003.
d. In what year, according to this model, will each student have his or her own computer in school?
e. What are the limitations of this model?

25. The number of children who were home-schooled in the United States in selected years is shown in the table below.

Fall of school year	Number of children (in 1000s)
1985	183
1988	225
1990	301
1992	470
1993	588
1994	735
1995	800
1996	920
1997	1100
1999	1400
2000	1700

[*Source: National Home Education Research Institute*]

a. Sketch a scatter plot of the data, with $x = 0$ corresponding to 1980.
b. Find a quadratic model for the data.
c. Find a logistic model for the data.
d. What is the number of home-schooled children predicted by each model for the year 2003?
e. What are the limitations of each model?

26. a. Find an exponential model for the federal debt, based on the data in the following table. Let $x = 0$ correspond to 1960.

Accumulated gross federal debt	
Year	Amount (in billions of dollars)
1960	284.1
1965	313.8
1970	370.1
1975	533.2
1980	907.7
1985	1823.1
1990	3233.3
1995	4974.0
2000	5674.2

b. Use the model to estimate the federal debt in 2003.

27. The table gives the life expectancy of a woman born in each given year.

Year	Life Expectancy (in years)	Year	Life Expectancy (in years)
1910	51.8	1960	73.1
1920	54.6	1970	74.7
1930	61.6	1980	77.5
1940	65.2	1990	78.8
1950	71.1	2000	79.4

[*Source: National Center for Health Statistics*]

a. Find a logarithmic model for the data, with $x = 10$ corresponding to 1910.
b. Use the model to find the life expectancy of a woman born in 1986. For comparison, the actual expectancy is 78.3 years.
c. Assume the model remains accurate. In what year will the life expectancy of a woman born in that year be at least 81 years?

28. The table gives the death rate in motor vehicle accidents, per 100,000 population, in selected years.

Year	Death Rate
1970	26.8
1980	23.4
1985	19.3
1990	18.8
1995	16.5
2000	15.6

    a. Find an exponential model for the data, with $x = 0$ corresponding to 1970.
    b. Use the model to predict the death rate in 1998 and in 2002.
    c. Assuming the model remains accurate, when will the death rate drop to 13 per 100,000?

29. Worldwide production of computers has grown dramatically, as shown in the first two columns of the following table.
    a. Sketch a scatter plot of the data, with $x = 1$ corresponding to 1985.
    b. Find an exponential model for the data.
    c. Use the model to complete column 3 of the table.
    d. Fill in column 4 of the table by dividing each entry in column 2 by the preceding one.
    e. What does column 4 tell you about the appropriateness of the model?

Year	Worldwide shipments (in thousands)	Predicted number of shipment (in thousands)	Ratio
1985	14.7		✕
1986	15.1		
1987	16.7		
1988	18.1		
1989	21.3		
1990	23.7		
1991	27		
1992	32.4		
1993	38.9		
1994	47.9		
1995	60.2		
1996	70.9		
1997	84.3		

[*Source: Dataquest*]

CHAPTER 5 REVIEW

401

Important Facts and Formulas

- *Rational Exponents:*

$$c^{\frac{1}{n}} = \sqrt[n]{c}$$

$$(c^t)^{\frac{1}{k}} = (c^{\frac{1}{k}})^t = c^{\frac{t}{k}}$$

- *Laws of Exponents:*

$$c^r c^s = c^{r+s} \qquad (cd)^r = c^r d^r$$

$$\frac{c^r}{c^s} = c^{r-s} \qquad \left(\frac{c}{d}\right)^r = \frac{c^r}{d^r}$$

$$(c^r)^s = c^{rs} \qquad c^{-r} = \frac{1}{c^r}$$

- $g(x) = \log x$ is the inverse function of $f(x) = 10^x$:

$$10^{\log v} = v \text{ for all } v > 0 \quad \text{and} \quad \log 10^u = u \text{ for all } u$$

- $g(x) = \ln x$ is the inverse function of $f(x) = e^x$:

$$e^{\ln v} = v \text{ for all } v > 0 \quad \text{and} \quad \ln e^u = u \text{ for all } u$$

- $h(x) = \log_b x$ is the inverse function of $k(x) = b^x$:

$$b^{\log_b v} = v \text{ for all } v > 0 \quad \text{and} \quad \log_b (b^u) = u \text{ for all } u$$

- *Logarithm Laws:* For all $v, w > 0$ and any k:

$$\ln(vw) = \ln v + \ln w \qquad \log_b (vw) = \log_b v + \log_b w$$

$$\ln\left(\frac{v}{w}\right) = \ln v - \ln w \qquad \log_b\left(\frac{v}{w}\right) = \log_b v - \log_b w$$

$$\ln(v^k) = k \ln v \qquad \log_b (v^k) = k \log_b v$$

- *Exponential Growth Functions:*

$$f(x) = P(1 + r)^x \quad (0 < r < 1)$$
$$f(x) = Pa^x \quad (a > 1)$$
$$f(x) = Pe^{kx} \quad (k > 0)$$

- *Exponential Decay Functions:*

$$f(x) = P(1 - r)^x \quad (0 < r < 1)$$
$$f(x) = Pa^x \quad (0 < a < 1)$$
$$f(x) = Pe^{kx} \quad (k < 0)$$

- *Logistic Function:* $f(x) = \dfrac{a}{1 + be^{-kx}}$

- *Compound Interest Formula:* $A = P(1 + r)^t$

- *Continuous Compounding:* $A = Pe^{rt}$

- *Radioactive Decay Function:* $f(x) = P(0.5)^{\frac{x}{h}}$

- *Change of Base Formula:* $\log_b v = \dfrac{\ln v}{\ln b}$

Review Exercises

Section 5.1

In Exercises 1–6, simplify the expression.

1. $\sqrt{\sqrt[3]{c^{12}}}$

2. $\left(\sqrt[3]{4c^3 d^2}\right)^3 \left(c\sqrt{d}\right)^2$

3. $\left(a^{-\frac{2}{3}} b^{\frac{2}{5}}\right)\left(a^3 b^6\right)^{\frac{4}{3}}$

4. $\dfrac{(3c)^{\frac{3}{5}}(2d)^{-2}(4c)^{\frac{1}{2}}}{(4c)^{\frac{1}{5}}(2d)^4(2c)^{-\frac{3}{2}}}$

5. $\left(u^{\frac{1}{4}} - v^{\frac{1}{4}}\right)\left(u^{\frac{1}{4}} + v^{\frac{1}{4}}\right)$

6. $c^{\frac{3}{2}}\left(2c^{\frac{1}{2}} + 3c^{-\frac{3}{2}}\right)$

In Exercises 7 and 8, simplify and write the expression without radicals or negative exponents.

7. $\dfrac{\sqrt[3]{6c^4 d^{14}}}{\sqrt[3]{48c^{-2} d^2}}$

8. $\dfrac{(8u^5)^{\frac{1}{4}} 2^{-1} u^{-3}}{2u^8}$

9. Rationalize the numerator and simplify: $\dfrac{\sqrt{2x + 2h + 1} - \sqrt{2x + 1}}{h}$

10. Rationalize the denominator: $\dfrac{5}{\sqrt{x} - 3}$

Section 5.2

In Exercises 11–16, list the transformations needed to transform the graph of $f(x) = 5^x$ into the graph of the given function.

11. $g(x) = -2 \cdot 5^x$

12. $h(x) = 5^{3x}$

13. $k(x) = 5^{-\frac{1}{2}x}$

14. $g(x) = 5^{2-x}$

15. $h(x) = 5^x + 4$

16. $h(x) = -5^{x+2}$

In Exercises 17 and 18, find a viewing window (or windows) that shows a complete graph of the function.

17. $f(x) = 2^{x^3 - x - 2}$

18. $g(x) = \dfrac{850}{1 + 5e^{-0.4x}}$

19. Compunote offers a starting salary of $60,000 with $1000 yearly raises. Calcuplay offers a starting salary of $30,000 with a 6% raise each year.
 a. Complete the following table for each company.

Year	Compunote	Year	Calcuplay
1	$60,000	1	$30,000
2	$61,000	2	$31,800
3		3	
4		4	
5		5	

 b. For each company write a function that gives your salary in terms of years employed.
 c. If you plan on staying with the company for only five years, which job should you take to earn the most money?
 d. If you plan on staying with the company for 20 years, which is your best choice?

20. A computer software company claims that the following function models the "learning curve" for their software.

$$P(t) = \frac{100}{1 + 48.2e^{-0.52t}}$$

where t is measured in months and $P(t)$ is the average percent of the software program's capabilities mastered after t months.
  a. Initially what percent of the program is mastered?
  b. After 6 months what percent of the program is mastered?
  c. Roughly, when can a person expect to "learn the most in the least amount of time"?
  d. If the company's claim is true, how many months will it take to have completely mastered the program?

Section 5.3

21. Phil borrows $800 at 9% annual interest, compounded annually.
  a. How much does he owe after 6 years?
  b. If he pays off the loan at the end of 6 years, how much interest will he owe?

22. If you invest $5000 for 5 years at 9% annual interest, how much more will you make if interest is compounded continuously than if it is compounded quarterly?

23. Mary Karen invests $2000 at 5.5% annual interest, compounded monthly.
  a. How much is her investment worth in 3 years?
  b. When will her investment be worth $12,000?

24. If a $2000 investment grows to $5000 in 14 years, with interest compounded annually, what is the interest rate?

25. Company sales are increasing at 6.5% per year. If sales this year are $56,000, write the rule of a function that gives the sales in year x (where $x = 0$ corresponds to the present year).

26. The population of Potterville is decreasing at an annual rate of 1.5%. If the population is 38,500 now, what will be the population x years from now?

27. The half-life of carbon-14 is 5730 years. How much carbon-14 remains from an original 16 grams after 12,000 years?

28. How long will it take for 4 grams of carbon-14 to decay to 1 gram?

Section 5.4

In Exercises 29–34, translate the given exponential statement into an equivalent logarithmic one.

29. $e^{6.628} = 756$ **30.** $e^{5.8972} = 364$ **31.** $e^{r^2-1} = u + v$

32. $e^{a-b} = c$ **33.** $10^{2.8785} = 756$ **34.** $10^{c+d} = t$

In Exercises 35–38, translate the given logarithmic statement into an equivalent exponential one.

35. $\ln 1234 = 7.118$ **36.** $\ln(ax + b) = y$ **37.** $\ln(rs) = t$

38. $\log 1234 = 3.0913$

39. Find $\log(-0.01)$.

In Exercises 40–43, describe the transformation from $f(x) = \log x$ or $g(x) = \ln x$ to the given function. Give the domain and range of the given function.

40. $h(x) = -\dfrac{1}{2}\log(x + 3)$ **41.** $k(x) = \log(4 - x)$

42. $h(x) = \ln(3x)$ **43.** $k(x) = 3\ln x - 5$

44. You are conducting an experiment about memory. The people who participate agree to take a test at the end of your course and every month thereafter for a period of two years. The average score for the group is given by the model $M(t) = 91 - 14\ln(t + 1)$, $0 \le t \le 24$, where t is time in months after the first test.
  a. What is the average score on the initial exam?
  b. What is the average score after three months?
  c. When will the average drop below 50%?
  d. Is the magnitude of the rate of memory loss greater in the first month after the course (from $t = 0$ to $t = 1$) or after the first year (from $t = 12$ to $t = 13$)?
  e. Hypothetically, if the model could be extended past $t = 24$ months, would it be possible for the average score to be 0%?

Section   5.5

In Exercises 45–48, evaluate the given expression without using a calculator.

45. $\ln e^3$ **46.** $\ln e$ **47.** $e^{\ln \frac{3}{4}}$ **48.** $e^{\ln(x + 2y)}$

49. Simplify: $3\ln \sqrt{x} + \dfrac{1}{2}\ln x$ **50.** Simplify: $\ln(e^{4e})^{-1} + 4e$

In Exercises 51 and 52, write the given expression as a single logarithm.

51. $\ln 3x - 3\ln x + \ln 3y$ **52.** $4\ln x - 2(\ln x^3 + 4\ln x)$

53. Which of the following statements is *true*?
  a. $\ln 10 = (\ln 2)(\ln 5)$ **b.** $\ln\left(\dfrac{e}{6}\right) = \ln e + \ln 6$
  c. $\ln\left(\dfrac{1}{7}\right) + \ln 7 = 0$ **d.** $\ln(-e) = -1$
  e. None of the above is true.

54. Which of the following statements is *false*?
  a. $10(\log 5) = \log 50$ **b.** $\log 100 + 3 = \log 10^5$
  c. $\log 1 = \ln 1$ **d.** $\dfrac{\log 6}{\log 3} = \log 2$
  e. All of the above are false.

55. What is the domain of the function $f(x) = \ln\left(\dfrac{x}{x - 1}\right)$?

Section   5.5.A

In Exercises 56 and 57, translate the given logarithmic statement into an equivalent exponential one.

56. $\log_5(cd - k) = u$ **57.** $\log_d(uv) = w$

58. Write $\log_7 7x + \log_7 y - 1$ as a single logarithm.

59. $\log_{20} 400 = $?   **60.** If $\log_3 9^{x^2} = 4$, what is x?

Use the following six graphs for Exercises 61 and 62.

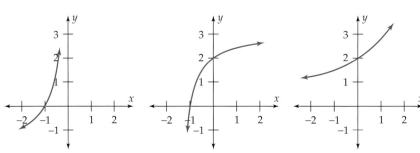

Figure I   Figure II   Figure III

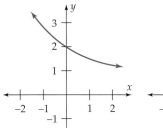 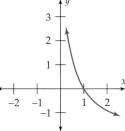 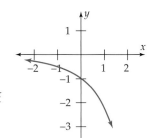

Figure IV   Figure V   Figure VI

61. If $b > 1$, then the graph of $f(x) = -\log_b x$ could possibly be

   a. I   **c.** V   **e.** none of these

   b. IV   **d.** VI

62. If $0 < b < 1$ then the graph of $g(x) = b^x + 1$ could possibly be

   a. II   **c.** IV   **e.** none of these

   b. III   **d.** VI

Section 5.6

In Exercises 63–71, solve the equation for x.

63. $8^x = 4^{x^2-3}$ **64.** $e^{3x} = 4$ **65.** $2 \cdot 4^x - 5 = -4$

66. $725e^{-4x} = 1500$ **67.** $u = c + d \ln x$ **68.** $2^x = 3^{x+3}$

69. $\ln x + \ln(3x - 5) = \ln 2$ **70.** $\ln(x + 8) - \ln x = 1$

71. $\log(x^2 - 1) = 2 + \log(x + 1)$

72. At a small community college the spread of a rumor through the population of 500 faculty and students can be modeled by

$$\ln n - \ln(1000 - 2n) = 0.65t - \ln 998,$$

where n is the number of people who have heard the rumor after t days.

   a. How many people know the rumor initially (at $t = 0$)?

   b. How many people have heard the rumor after four days?

   c. Roughly, in how many weeks will the entire population have heard the rumor?

   d. Use the properties of logarithms to write n as a function of t; in other words solve the model above for n in terms of t.

    e. Enter the function you found in part **d** into your calculator and use the table feature to check your answers to parts **a**, **b**, and **c**. Do they agree?

    f. Graph the function. Over what time interval does the rumor seem to "spread" the fastest?

73. The half-life of polonium (^{210}Po) is 140 days. If you start with 10 milligrams, how much will be left at the end of a year?

74. An insect colony grows exponentially from 200 to 2000 in 3 months. How long will it take for the insect population to reach 50,000?

75. Hydrogen-3 decays at a rate of 5.59% per year. Find its half-life.

76. The half-life of radium-88 is 1590 years. How long will it take for 10 grams to decay to 1 gram?

77. How much money should be invested at 8% per year, compounded quarterly, in order to have $1000 in 10 years?

78. At what annual interest rate should you invest your money if you want to double it in 6 years?

79. One earthquake measures 4.6 on the Richter scale. A second earthquake is 1000 times more intense than the first. What does it measure on the Richter scale?

Section 5.7 **80.** The table below gives the population of Austin, Texas.

Year	1950	1970	1980	1990	2000
Population	132,459	253,539	345,890	465,622	656,562

    a. Sketch a scatter plot of the data, with $x = 0$ corresponding to 1950.
    b. Find an exponential model for the data.
    c. Use the model to estimate the population of Austin in 1960 and 2005.

81. The wind-chill factor is the temperature that would produce the same cooling effect on a person's skin if there were no wind. The table shows the wind-chill factors for various wind speeds when the temperature is 25°F.

Wind speed (mph)	0	5	10	15	20	25	30	35	40	45
Wind chill temperature (°F)	25	19	15	13	11	9	8	7	6	5

[*Source: National Weather Service*]

    a. What does a 20-mph wind make 25°F feel like?
    b. Sketch a scatter plot of the data, with $x = 0$ corresponding to 0 mph.
    c. Explain why an exponential model would be appropriate.
    d. Find an exponential model for the data.
    e. According to the model, what is the wind-chill factor for a 23-mph wind?

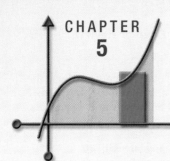

can do calculus

Tangents to Exponential Functions

Tangent lines to a curve are important in calculus—where they are used to approximate function values close to a specific point and used for finding the zeros of general functions. The procedure developed in the Can Do Calculus for Chapter 3 will be used here to develop the equations of the tangent lines to exponential functions.

Slopes of Secant Lines and Tangent Lines

Recall that the difference quotient of f at the specific value $x = b$ is given by

$$\frac{f(b + h) - f(b)}{h},$$

where h is the amount of change in the x values from one point to another. The difference quotient can be interpreted as the slope of the secant line that passes through the points $(b, f(b))$ and $(b + h, f(b + h))$. As h gets very small, the value of $\dfrac{f(b + h) - f(b)}{h}$ approaches the value of the slope of the tangent line at $(b, f(b))$.

Also, if f is any function, then the slope of the secant line through $(b, f(b))$ and any other point $(x, f(x))$ on the graph of f is given by

$$\frac{f(x) - f(b)}{x - b}.$$

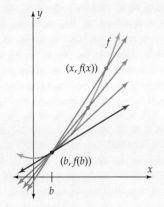

Figure 5.C-1

As the point $(x, f(x))$ approaches the point $(b, f(b))$, the value of $\dfrac{f(x) - f(b)}{x - b}$ approaches the value of the slope of the tangent line to the curve at $(b, f(b))$. Figure 5.C-1 shows four secant lines that pass through the point $(b, f(b))$. The tangent line to f at $(b, f(b))$ is shown in red.

Tangent Lines to the Exponential Function

Consider the function $f(x) = e^x$ and the values of the slopes of secant lines that pass through $(0, e^0)$, that is, $(0, 1)$. Find the values of

$$\frac{f(x) - f(0)}{x - 0} = \frac{e^x - e^0}{x} = \frac{e^x - 1}{x}$$

when x is near 0.

x	−0.01	−0.001	0.001	0.01
$\dfrac{e^x - 1}{x}$	0.99502	0.9995	1.0005	1.005

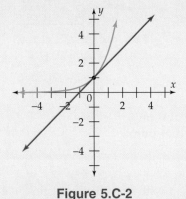

Figure 5.C-2

The table suggests that the slope of the tangent line to $f(x) = e^x$ at $x = 0$ is 1. The tangent line to the curve at $x = 0$ contains the point $(0, 1)$ and has slope $m = 1$. Therefore, the equation of the tangent line to $f(x) = e^x$ at $x = 0$ can be found by using the point-slope form of a line.

$$y - y_0 = m(x - x_0) \qquad \text{\textit{Point-slope form of a line}}$$
$$y - 1 = 1\,(x - 0)$$
$$y - 1 = x$$
$$y = x + 1 \qquad \text{\textit{Equation of tangent line}}$$

The graph of $f(x) = e^x$ and the tangent line to the curve at $(0, 1)$ is shown in Figure 5.C-2.

Example 1   Tangent Line to the Exponential Function

Find the tangent line to $f(x) = e^x$ when $x = 1$. Graph f and the tangent line.

Solution

When $x = 1, f(1) = e^1 = e$, so the point $(1, e)$ is the point where the tangent line will touch the graph. To find the slope of the tangent line, look at values of the difference quotient near $x = 1$.

$$\frac{f(x) - f(1)}{x - 1} = \frac{e^x - e^1}{x - 1} = \frac{e^x - e}{x - 1}$$

Alternately, you may use the numerical derivative feature of your calculator to find an approximate value of the slope of the tangent line for $f(x) = e^x$ at $x = 1$. You should find that the value of the slope of the tangent line is approximately 2.718282282.

Recall that $e \approx 2.71828$. It appears that the slope of the tangent line to $f(x) = e^x$ at $(1, e)$ is e, which can be proved using calculus. Therefore, the tangent line's equation is

$$y - e = e\,(x - 1) \qquad \text{or equivalently} \qquad y = ex$$

and the graphs of f and the tangent line are in Figure 5.C-3b.

Figure 5.C-3a

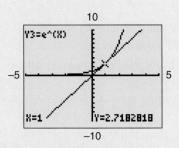

Figure 5.C-3b

Calculator Exploration ●

Find the slope of the tangent lines to $f(x) = e^x$ when $x = -3, -2, -1, 2, 3, 4$. Plot the points (x, y), where y is the slope of the tangent line, along with the corresponding points for $x = 0, 1$. What function would represent the graph of these points?

In the Calculator Exploration, you should have found the values and plotted the points shown in Figure 5.C-4. Also shown in Figure 5.C-4 are all the points on the graph of $f(x) = e^x$.

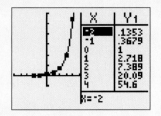

Figure 5.C-4

Slope of the Tangent line to $y = e^x$

> **The slope of the tangent line at any point on $y = e^x$ has the same value as the y coordinate, e^x, at that point.**

The exponential function is the only function with this characteristic.

Example 2   Slope of $y = e^x$

a. Find the x-value where the slope of $y = e^x$ is e^3.
b. Write the equation of the tangent line at $x = 3$.
c. Graph $y = e^x$ and the tangent line at $x = 3$ on the same screen.

Solution

a. The slope of $y = e^x$ at $x = 3$ is e^3.
b. Using the point-slope form of a line with $m = e^3$ and $(3, e^3)$, the equation of the tangent line to $y = e^x$ at $x = 3$ is

$$y - e^3 = e^3(x - 3)$$
$$y = e^3x - 2e^3 = e^3(x - 2)$$

c. The graphs of $y = e^x$ and $y = e^3(x - 2)$ are shown in Figure 5.C-5. ∎

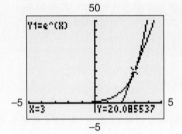

Figure 5.C-5

Exponential Functions with Bases Other Than e

The procedure for finding the equation of the tangent line at a specific value of x for exponential functions with bases other than e is the same as that for finding the equation of the tangent line at a specific value of x for any function.

1. Find the values of slopes of secant lines by using the difference quotient and several values of x near the point in question.
2. Find the slope of the tangent line by determining the value of the slope suggested by the values found in Step 1.
3. Write the equation of the tangent line using the point-slope form of a linear equation.
4. Confirm your finding by graphing the function and the tangent line.

Find the values of the slope of the tangent line for $y = 2^x$ at $x = -2, -1,$ 0, 1, 2, 3. Graph the ordered pairs (x, slope of tangent) and find an equation to represent the graph by using exponential regression.

The points to be graphed in the Calculator Exploration are

$$(-2, 0.17329)\ (-1, 0.34657)\ (0, 0.69315)\ (1, 1.3863)\ (2, 2.7726)\ (3, 5.5452)$$

and the regression equation is

$$y = 0.6931471806(2^x).$$

Notice that $\ln 2 \approx 0.6931471806$. In fact, the slope of the tangent line at any point $(c, f(c))$ on the graph of $f(x) = 2^x$ is given by $\ln 2 \cdot f(c)$, or $\ln 2\ (2^c)$.

Example 3   Tangent Line of $y = 2^x$

Find the equation of the tangent line to the curve $y = 2^x$ at $x = 4$, and confirm your result by graphing.

Solution

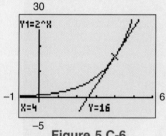

Figure 5.C-6

The point on the curve at $x = 4$ is $(4, 2^4)$, or (4, 16). The slope of the tangent line at that point is $(\ln 2)(16) \approx 11.09$, so the equation of the tangent line of $f(x) = 2^x$ at (4, 16) is

$$y - 16 = 11.09(x - 4)$$
$$y = 11.09(x - 4) + 16$$

The graph of $f(x) = 2^x$ and $y = 11.09(x - 4) + 16$ are shown in Figure 5.C-6.

Exercises

In Exercises 1–4, write the equation of the tangent line at the following values of x for the function $f(x) = e^{-x}$. Graph the function along with the tangent at each point.

1. $x = 0$ **2.** $x = 1$

3. $x = 2$ **4.** $x = -2$

In Exercises 5–8, write the equation of the tangent line at the following values of x for the function $f(x) = e^x + 2$. Graph the function along with the tangent at each point.

5. $x = 0$ **6.** $x = 1$

7. $x = 2$ **8.** $x = -2$

In Exercises 9–12, write the equation of the tangent line at the following values of x for the function $f(x) = 3^x$. Graph the function along with the tangent at each point.

9. $x = 0$ **10.** $x = 1$

11. $x = 2$ **12.** $x = -2$

Trigonometry

Where are we?

Navigators at sea must determine their location. Surveyors need to determine the height of a mountain or the width of a canyon when direct measurement is not feasible. A fighter plane's computer must set the course of a missile so that it will hit a moving target. Many phenomena such as the tides, seasonal change, and radio waves, have cycles that repeat. All of the situations can be described mathematically using trigonometry.

Chapter Outline

Interdependence of Sections

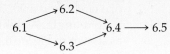

T**rigonometry,** which means "triangle measurement," was developed in ancient times for determining the angles and sides of triangles in order to solve problems in astronomy, navigation, and surveying. With the development of calculus and physics in the 17th century, a different viewpoint toward trigonometry arose, and trigonometry was used to model all kinds of periodic behavior, such as sound waves, vibrations, and planetary orbits. In this chapter, you will be introduced to both types of trigonometry, beginning with right-triangle trigonometry.

Right-Triangle Trigonometry

Objectives

- Define the six trigonometric ratios of an acute angle in terms of a right triangle

- Evaluate trigonometric ratios, using triangles and on a calculator

Angles and Degree Measure

Recall from geometry that an **angle** is a figure formed by two rays with a common endpoint, called the **vertex.** The rays are called the **sides** of the angle. An angle may be labeled by the angle symbol ($\angle$) and the vertex. The angle in Figure 6.1-1 may be labeled $\angle A$.

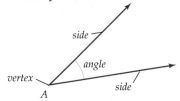

Figure 6.1-1

Angles may be measured in *degrees*, where 1 **degree** (°) is $\frac{1}{360}$ of a circle. (See Figure 6.1-2.) Thus, a 360° angle is an entire circle, a 180° angle is half of a circle, and a 90° angle is a quarter of a circle. A 90° angle is also called a **right angle.** A right angle is indicated on a diagram by a small square, as shown in Figure 6.1-3. An angle of less than 90° is called an **acute angle.** The measure of an angle is indicated by the letter m in front of the angle symbol, such as $m\angle A = 36°$.

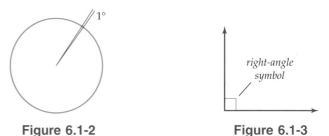

Figure 6.1-2   Figure 6.1-3

Minutes and Seconds

Fractional parts of a degree are usually expressed in decimal form or in *minutes* and *seconds*. A **minute** (') is $\frac{1}{60}$ of a degree, and a **second** (") is $\frac{1}{60}$ of a minute, or $\frac{1}{3600}$ of a degree. This form is often called **DMS form,** for degrees, minutes, seconds.

Example 1   **Converting Between Decimal Form and DMS Form**

a. Write 35° 15′ 27″ in decimal form.

b. Write 48.3625° in DMS form.

Solution

a. $35° \, 15′ \, 27″ = 35° + \left(\frac{15}{60}\right)° + \left(\frac{27}{3600}\right)°$

$= 35° + 0.25° + 0.0075°$

$= 35.2575°$

b. First, convert the entire decimal part to minutes by writing it in terms of $\frac{1}{60}$ of a degree.

$$48.3625° = 48° + 0.3625° = 48° + \left(\frac{60}{60}\right)0.3625°$$

$$= 48° + \left(\frac{21.75}{60}\right)° = 48° + 21.75′$$

Second, convert the decimal part of the minutes to seconds by writing it in terms of $\frac{1}{60}$ of a minute.

$$48° + 21.75' = 48° + 21' + \left(\frac{60}{60}\right)0.75'$$

$$= 48° + 21' + \left(\frac{45}{60}\right)'$$

$$= 48° \ 21' \ 45''$$

Similar Triangles and Trigonometric Ratios

Examine the following right triangles.

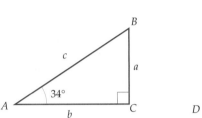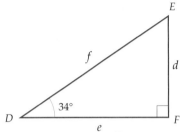

Figure 6.1-4

$$\frac{a}{c} = \frac{d}{f} \qquad\qquad \frac{b}{c} = \frac{e}{f} \qquad\qquad \frac{a}{b} = \frac{d}{e}$$

Since all right triangles that contain a 34° angle are similar, the corresponding ratios would be the same. Thus, the ratio is dependent only on the measure of the angle. These ratios, which can be determined for any angle between 0° and 90°, are the basis of trigonometry.

The **hypotenuse** (hyp) of a right triangle is the side across from the right angle. The hypotenuse is always the longest side of the triangle. The remaining sides are labeled by their relationship to the given angle, as shown in Figure 6.1-5. The **adjacent** (adj) side is the side of the given angle that is *not* the hypotenuse, and the **opposite** (opp) side is the side of the triangle that is across from the given angle.

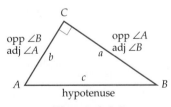

Figure 6.1-5

In the figure, if $\angle A$ is the given angle, the adjacent side is b and the opposite side is a. If $\angle B$ is the given angle, the adjacent side is a and the opposite side is b.

There are six possible ratios for the three sides of a triangle. These ratios are called **trigonometric ratios.**

Trigonometric Ratios

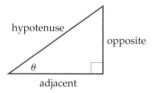

Figure 6.1-6

For a given acute angle θ in a right triangle:

The *sine* of θ, written as sin θ, is the ratio

$$\sin \theta = \frac{\text{opposite}}{\text{hypotenuse}}$$

The *cosine* of θ, written as cos θ, is the ratio

$$\cos \theta = \frac{\text{adjacent}}{\text{hypotenuse}}$$

The *tangent* of θ, written as tan θ, is the ratio

$$\tan \theta = \frac{\text{opposite}}{\text{adjacent}}$$

In addition, the reciprocal of each ratio above is also a trigonometric ratio.

cosecant of θ	*secant* of θ	*cotangent* of θ
$\csc \theta = \dfrac{\text{hypotenuse}}{\text{opposite}}$	$\sec \theta = \dfrac{\text{hypotenuse}}{\text{adjacent}}$	$\cot \theta = \dfrac{\text{adjacent}}{\text{opposite}}$
$= \dfrac{1}{\sin \theta}$	$= \dfrac{1}{\cos \theta}$	$= \dfrac{1}{\tan \theta}$

NOTE The Greek letter θ (theta) is commonly used to label the measure of an angle in trigonometry.

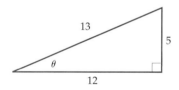

Figure 6.1-7

Example 2   Evaluating Trigonometric Ratios

Evaluate the six trigonometric ratios of the angle θ shown in Figure 6.1-7.

Solution

The opposite side has length 5, the adjacent side has length 12, and the hypotenuse has length 13.

$$\sin \theta = \frac{\text{opposite}}{\text{hypotenuse}} = \frac{5}{13} \approx 0.3846 \qquad \csc \theta = \frac{\text{hypotenuse}}{\text{opposite}} = \frac{13}{5} = 2.6$$

$$\cos \theta = \frac{\text{adjacent}}{\text{hypotenuse}} = \frac{12}{13} \approx 0.9231 \qquad \sec \theta = \frac{\text{hypotenuse}}{\text{adjacent}} = \frac{13}{12} \approx 1.0833$$

$$\tan \theta = \frac{\text{opposite}}{\text{adjacent}} = \frac{5}{12} \approx 0.4167 \qquad \cot \theta = \frac{\text{adjacent}}{\text{opposite}} = \frac{12}{5} = 2.4$$

Example 3   Evaluating Trigonometric Ratios

Evaluate the six trigonometric ratios of 62° by using the triangle in Figure 6.1-8. (Side lengths given are approximate.)

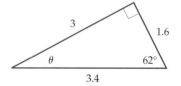

Figure 6.1-8

Solution

$$\sin 62° = \frac{\text{opposite}}{\text{hypotenuse}} \approx \frac{3}{3.4} \approx 0.8824 \quad \csc 62° = \frac{\text{hypotenuse}}{\text{opposite}} \approx \frac{3.4}{3} \approx 1.1333$$

$$\cos 62° = \frac{\text{adjacent}}{\text{hypotenuse}} \approx \frac{1.6}{3.4} \approx 0.4706 \quad \sec 62° = \frac{\text{hypotenuse}}{\text{adjacent}} \approx \frac{3.4}{1.6} \approx 2.1250$$

$$\tan 62° = \frac{\text{opposite}}{\text{adjacent}} \approx \frac{3}{1.6} \approx 1.8750 \quad \cot 62° = \frac{\text{adjacent}}{\text{opposite}} \approx \frac{1.6}{3} \approx 0.5333$$

Evaluating Trigonometric Ratios Using a Calculator

If the measure of an angle is given without a corresponding triangle, it may be difficult to accurately evaluate the trigonometric ratios of that angle. For example, to find sin 20°, it would be possible to draw a right triangle with an angle of 20° and measure its sides. However, there may be inaccuracies in drawing and measuring the triangle. Tables of trigonometric ratios are available, but it is usually most convenient to use a calculator.

Technology Tip

The following facts will be helpful in evaluating trigonometric ratios on a calculator.

- Scientific and graphing calculators have modes for different units of angle measurements. When using degrees, make sure that your calculator is set in degree mode.
- The functions $\sin^{-1}$, $\cos^{-1}$, and $\tan^{-1}$ on a calculator *do not* indicate the reciprocal functions. These functions will be discussed in Section 8.2.
- Some calculators automatically insert an opening parenthesis "(" after sin, cos, or tan. Be sure to place the closing parenthesis ")" in the appropriate place.

In trigonometry, many of the values used are approximate, and answers are usually rounded to 4 decimal places. However, in calculations involving trigonometric ratios, the values should not be rounded until the end of the problem.

Example 4 Evaluating Trigonometric Ratios on a Calculator

Evaluate the six trigonometric ratios of 20°.

Solution

Your calculator should have buttons for sine, cosine, and tangent. To find the cosecant, secant, and cotangent, take the reciprocal of each answer.

```
sin(20)
        .3420201433
cos(20)
        .9396926208
tan(20)
        .3639702343
```

Figure 6.1-9

$\sin 20° \approx 0.3420$

$\cos 20° \approx 0.9397$

$\tan 20° \approx 0.3640$

$\csc 20° = \dfrac{1}{\sin 20°} \approx \dfrac{1}{0.3420} \approx 2.9238$

$\sec 20° = \dfrac{1}{\cos 20°} \approx \dfrac{1}{0.9397} \approx 1.0642$

$\cot 20° = \dfrac{1}{\tan 20°} \approx \dfrac{1}{0.3640} \approx 2.7475$

■

Special Angles

Properties of 30-60-90 and 45-45-90 triangles can be used to find exact values of the trigonometric ratios for 30°, 60°, and 45°. These angles are called **special angles**.

NOTE For a review of the properties of 30-60-90 and 45-45-90 triangles, see the Geometry Review in the Appendix.

Example 5   **Evaluating Trigonometric Ratios of Special Angles**

Evaluate the six trigonometric ratios of 30°, 60°, and 45°.

Solution

A 30-60-90 and a 45-45-90 triangle are shown below.

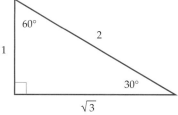

Figure 6.1-10

In the 30-60-90 triangle:

- the hypotenuse is 2
- for the 30° angle, 1 is opposite and $\sqrt{3}$ is adjacent
- for the 60° angle, $\sqrt{3}$ is opposite and 1 is adjacent

In the 45-45-90 triangle:

- the hypotenuse is $\sqrt{2}$
- for either 45° angle, 1 is both opposite and adjacent

The following table summarizes the values of the trigonometric ratios for the special angles.

NOTE The exact values of the trigonometric ratios of the special angles will be needed regularly. You should memorize the sine and cosine values for all three angles. The other ratios are easily derived from the sine and cosine.

θ		$30°$	$45°$	$60°$
$\sin\theta =$	$\dfrac{\text{opposite}}{\text{hypotenuse}}$	$\dfrac{1}{2}$	$\dfrac{1}{\sqrt{2}} = \dfrac{\sqrt{2}}{2}$	$\dfrac{\sqrt{3}}{2}$
$\cos\theta =$	$\dfrac{\text{adjacent}}{\text{hypotenuse}}$	$\dfrac{\sqrt{3}}{2}$	$\dfrac{1}{\sqrt{2}} = \dfrac{\sqrt{2}}{2}$	$\dfrac{1}{2}$
$\tan\theta =$	$\dfrac{\text{opposite}}{\text{adjacent}}$	$\dfrac{1}{\sqrt{3}} = \dfrac{\sqrt{3}}{3}$	$\dfrac{1}{1} = 1$	$\dfrac{\sqrt{3}}{1} = \sqrt{3}$
$\csc\theta =$	$\dfrac{\text{hypotenuse}}{\text{opposite}}$	$\dfrac{2}{1} = 2$	$\dfrac{\sqrt{2}}{1} = \sqrt{2}$	$\dfrac{2}{\sqrt{3}} = \dfrac{2\sqrt{3}}{3}$
$\sec\theta =$	$\dfrac{\text{hypotenuse}}{\text{adjacent}}$	$\dfrac{2}{\sqrt{3}} = \dfrac{2\sqrt{3}}{3}$	$\dfrac{\sqrt{2}}{1} = \sqrt{2}$	$\dfrac{2}{1} = 2$
$\cot\theta =$	$\dfrac{\text{adjacent}}{\text{opposite}}$	$\dfrac{\sqrt{3}}{1} = \sqrt{3}$	$\dfrac{1}{1} = 1$	$\dfrac{1}{\sqrt{3}} = \dfrac{\sqrt{3}}{3}$

Exercises 6.1

In Exercises 1–4, write the DMS degree measurement in decimal form.

1. $47°\ 15'\ 36''$ **2.** $38°\ 33'\ 9''$

3. $15°\ 24'\ 45''$ **4.** $20°\ 51'\ 54''$

In Exercises 5–8, write the decimal degree measurement in DMS form.

5. $23.16°$ **6.** $50.3625°$

7. $4.2075°$ **8.** $85.655°$

In Exercises 9–14, find the six trigonometric ratios for θ.

9.

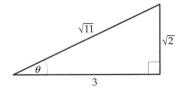

10.

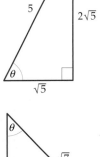

11.

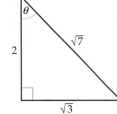

12.

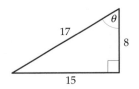

13.

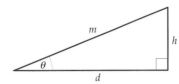

14.

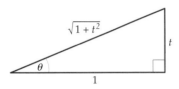

In Exercises 15–20, use a calculator in degree mode to find the following. Round your answers to four decimal places.

15. $\sin 32°$

16. $\cos 68°$

17. $\tan 6°$

18. $\csc 25°$

19. $\sec 47°$

20. $\cot 39°$

In Exercises 21–26, use the exact values of the trigonometric ratios for the special angles to find a value of θ that is a solution of the given equation. (See Example 5.)

21. $\sin \theta = \dfrac{1}{2}$

22. $\tan \theta = 1$

23. $\csc \theta = \sqrt{2}$

24. $\cot \theta = \sqrt{3}$

25. $\cos \theta = \dfrac{1}{2}$

26. $\sec \theta = 2$

In Exercises 27–32, refer to the figure below. Find the exact value of the trigonometric ratio for the given values of a, b, and c.

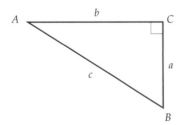

27. $a = 4, b = 2, \tan B = $ _____?_____

28. $a = 5, c = 7, \sin A = $ _____?_____

29. $b = 3, c = 8, \cos A = $ _____?_____

30. $a = 12, b = 15, \cot A = $ _____?_____

31. $a = 7, c = 16, \sec B = $ _____?_____

32. $b = 2, c = 3, \csc B = $ _____?_____

In Exercises 33–38, use a calculator in degree mode to determine whether the equation is true or false, and explain your answer.

33. $\sin 50° = 2 \sin 25°$

34. $\sin 50° = 2 \sin 25° \cos 25°$

35. $(\cos 28°)^2 = 1 - (\sin 28°)^2$

36. $(\cos 28°)^2 = (1 - \sin 28°)^2$

37. $\tan 75° = \tan 30° + \tan 45°$

38. $\tan 75° = \dfrac{\tan 30° + \tan 45°}{1 - \tan 30° \tan 45°}$

39. *Critical Thinking* Complete the table below.

θ	$\sin \theta$	$\cos \theta$
1°	?	?
0.1°	?	?
0.01°	?	?
0.001°	?	?

Based on the values in the table, what do you think would be a reasonable value for $\sin 0°$ and $\cos 0°$? Verify your answers with a calculator. Why can't these values be found by using the definition on page 416?

40. *Critical Thinking* Complete the table below.

θ	$\sin \theta$	$\cos \theta$
89°	?	?
89.9°	?	?
89.99°	?	?
89.999°	?	?

Based on the values in the table, what do you think would be a reasonable value for $\sin 90°$ and $\cos 90°$? Verify your answers with a calculator. Why can't these values be found by using the definition on page 416?

41. *Critical Thinking* Use the diagram below to show that the area of a triangle with acute angle θ that has sides a and b is

$$A = \frac{1}{2}\,ab\,\sin\theta.$$

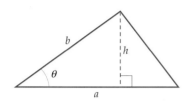

In Exercises 42–45, use the result of Exercise 41 to find the area of the given triangle.

42.

43.

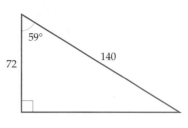

44.

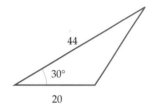

45.

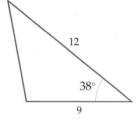

Trigonometric Applications

6.2

Objectives

- Solve triangles using trigonometric ratios
- Solve applications using triangles

Solving Right Triangles

Many applications in trigonometry involve **solving a triangle.** This means finding the lengths of all three sides and the measures of all three angles when only some of these quantities are known. Solving right triangles by using trigonometric ratios involves two theorems from geometry:

> **Triangle Sum Theorem: The sum of the measures of the angles in a triangle is 180°.**
>
> **Pythagorean Theorem: In a right triangle with legs a and b and hypotenuse c, $a^2 + b^2 = c^2$.**

If the measures of two angles are known, the Triangle Sum Theorem can be used to find the measure of the third. If the lengths of two sides of a right triangle are known, the Pythagorean Theorem can be used to find the length of the third.

Trigonometric ratios are used to solve right triangles when the measure of an angle and the length of a side or when the lengths of two sides are given. The underlying idea is that the definition of each trigonometric ratio involves three quantities:

- the measure of an angle   •   the lengths of two sides of the triangle

When two of the three quantities are known, the third can always be found, as illustrated in the next two examples.

Example 1　Finding a Side of a Triangle

Find side x of the right triangle in Figure 6.2-1.

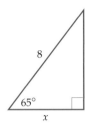

Figure 6.2-1

Solution

The 65° angle and the hypotenuse are known. The adjacent side x must be found, so use the cosine ratio.

$$\cos 65° = \frac{\text{adjacent}}{\text{hypotenuse}} = \frac{x}{8}$$

Solve this equation for x and then use a calculator to evaluate $\cos 65°$.

$$\cos 65° = \frac{x}{8}$$
$$x = 8\cos 65° \qquad \textit{Multiply both sides by 8}$$
$$\approx 3.3809 \qquad \textit{Use a calculator}$$

Example 2　Finding an Angle of a Triangle

Find the measure of angle θ in Figure 6.2-2.

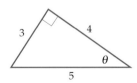

Figure 6.2-2

Solution

Note that

$$\sin \theta = \frac{\text{opposite}}{\text{hypotenuse}} = \frac{3}{5} = 0.6.$$

Before calculators were available, θ was found by using a table of sine values. You can do the same thing by having your calculator generate a table for $Y_1 = \sin(X)$ by using the settings shown in Figure 6.2-3a and Figure 6.2-3b.

View the table, shown in Figure 6.2-3c, and look through the column of sine values for the closest one to 0.6. Then look in the first column for the corresponding value of θ. The closest entry to 0.6 in the sine column is 0.060042, which corresponds to an angle of 36.9°. Hence, $\theta \approx 36.9°$.

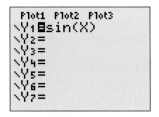

Figure 6.2-3a

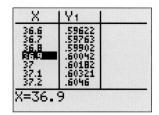

Figure 6.2-3b

Figure 6.2-3c

> **NOTE** Make sure your calculator is in degree mode.

A faster and more accurate method of finding θ is to use the SIN^{-1} key on your calculator. (SIN^{-1} is labeled ASIN on some models.) When you key in $\text{SIN}^{-1}(0.6)$, as in Figure 6.2-3d, the calculator produces an acute angle whose sine is 0.6, namely, $\theta \approx 36.8699°$.

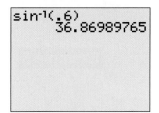

Figure 6.2-3d

Thus, the SIN^{-1} key provides the electronic equivalent of searching the sine table, without actually having to construct the table. ∎

> **NOTE** In this chapter, the SIN^{-1} key and the analogous COS^{-1} and TAN^{-1} keys will be used as they were in Example 2 to find an angle θ. The other uses of these keys are discussed in Section 8.2, which deals with inverse trigonometric functions.

Here is a summary of how these techniques can be used to solve any right triangle.

Solving Right Triangles

A right triangle can be solved if the following information is given.	
Case 1: an acute angle and a side	**Case 2:** two sides
Sketch the triangle and label the acute angle, the right angle, and the given side. Find the remaining acute angle by subtracting the known angles from 180°. Write a trigonometric equation that has an unknown side as the variable, and solve it with a calculator to evaluate the trigonometric ratio of the angle. Repeat the previous step or use the Pythagorean Theorem to find the third side.	Sketch the triangle and label the right angle and the two given sides. Find the third side by using the Pythagorean Theorem. Write a trigonometric equation that has an unknown angle as the variable. If the angle is a special angle, you can solve it by recognizing the value of the trigonometric ratio. If the angle is not one of the special angles, use the technique explained in Example 2.

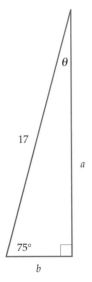

Figure 6.2-4

Example 3 Solving a Right Triangle

Solve the right triangle in Figure 6.2-4.

Solution

One side and one angle are given, so use the first case above. To solve the triangle, it is necessary to find θ, a, and b.

To find θ, subtract the measures of the given angles from 180°.

$$\theta = 180° - 75° - 90° = 15°$$

Write a trigonometric equation that has a as the variable. Since a is opposite the given angle and the hypotenuse is given, the sine is used.

$$\sin 75° = \frac{a}{17} \qquad \frac{opposite}{hypotenuse}$$
$$a = 17 \sin 75°$$
$$a \approx 17(0.9659) \approx 16.42$$

Next, write a trigonometric equation that has b as the variable. Since b is adjacent to the given angle, cosine is used. Evaluate $\cos 75°$ by using a calculator, and solve.

$$\cos 75° = \frac{b}{17} \qquad \frac{adjacent}{hypotenuse}$$
$$b = 17 \cos 75°$$
$$b \approx 4.40$$

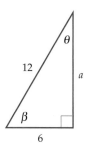

Figure 6.2-5

Example 4   **Solving a Right Triangle**

Solve the right triangle in Figure 6.2-5.

Solution

Two sides are given, so use the second case above. To solve the triangle, it is necessary to find a, θ, and β.

To find a, use the Pythagorean Theorem.

$$a^2 + 6^2 = 12^2$$
$$a^2 = 108$$
$$a = \sqrt{108} = 6\sqrt{3}$$

To find β, use trigonometric ratios. The adjacent side and the hypotenuse are given, so cosine is used.

$$\cos \beta = \frac{6}{12} = \frac{1}{2} \qquad \frac{adjacent}{hypotenuse}$$

From the table of trigonometric ratios of special angles on page 419, $\cos 60° = \frac{1}{2}$. Since 60° is the only acute angle with a cosine of $\frac{1}{2}$,

$$\beta = 60° \qquad \text{and} \qquad \theta = 180° - 60° - 90° = 30°$$

Applications

The following examples illustrate a variety of applications of the trigonometric ratios.

Example 5   **Height Above Sea Level**

A straight road leads from an ocean beach at a constant upward angle of 3°. How high above sea level is the road at a point 1 mile from the beach?

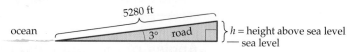

Figure 6.2-6

Technology Tip

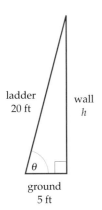

ladder
20 ft
wall
h

θ

ground
5 ft

Figure 6.2-7

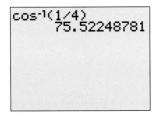

Figure 6.2-8

Solution

Figure 6.2-6 shows a right triangle with the road as the hypotenuse (1 mi = 5280 ft) and the opposite side h as the height above sea level. Write a trigonometric equation that uses sine.

$$\sin 3° = \frac{h}{5280} \qquad \frac{opposite}{hypotenuse}$$

$$h = 5280 \sin 3° \qquad Solve\ for\ h$$

$$h \approx 5280(0.0523) \qquad Use\ a\ calculator\ to\ evaluate\ \sin 3°$$

$$h \approx 276.33\ ft \qquad Simplify$$

At one mile, the road is about 276 feet above sea level.

Example 6   Ladder Safety

According to the safety sticker on a 20-foot ladder, the distance from the bottom of the ladder to the base of the wall on which it leans should be one-fourth of the length of the ladder: 5 feet.

a. How high up the wall will the ladder reach?

b. If the ladder is in this position, what angle does it make with the ground?

Solution

Draw the right triangle formed by the ladder, the wall, and the ground. Label the sides and angles as shown in Figure 6.2-7.

a. Since the length of the ladder and the distance from the wall are known, find the third side by using the Pythagorean Theorem.

$$h^2 + 5^2 = 20^2$$

$$h^2 = 375$$

$$h \approx 19.36$$

The ladder will safely reach a height of a little more than 19 feet up the wall.

b. The hypotenuse and the side adjacent to angle θ are known, so use the cosine ratio.

$$\cos \theta = \frac{\text{adjacent}}{\text{hypotenuse}} = \frac{5}{20} = \frac{1}{4}$$

Use the COS^{-1} key to find that $\theta \approx 75.5°$, as shown in Figure 6.2-8.

Angles of Elevation and Depression

In many applications the angle between a horizontal line and another line is used, such as the line of sight from an observer to a distant object. If the line is above the horizontal, the angle is called the **angle of elevation**.

If the line is below the horizontal, the angle is called the **angle of depression.**

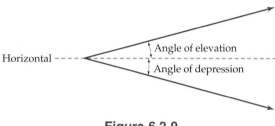

Horizontal — — — — — —
Angle of elevation
Angle of depression

Figure 6.2-9

Example 7 **Indirect Measurement**

A flagpole casts a 60-foot shadow when the angle of elevation of the sun is 35°, as shown in Figure 6.2-10. Find the height of the flagpole.

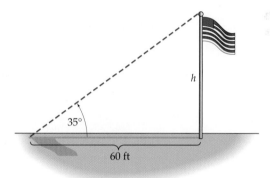

35°

h

60 ft

Figure 6.2-10

Solution

A right triangle is formed by the flagpole and its shadow. The opposite side is unknown and the adjacent side is given, so the tangent is used.

$$\tan 35° = \frac{h}{60} \qquad \textit{opposite} \atop \textit{adjacent}$$

$$h = 60 \tan 35° \qquad \textit{Solve for h}$$

$$h \approx 42.012 \qquad \textit{Use a calculator}$$

Thus, the flagpole is about 42 feet high.

Example 8 **Indirect Measurement**

A wire needs to reach from the top of a building to a point on the ground. The building is 10 m tall, and the angle of depression from the top of the building to the point on the ground is 22°. How long should the wire be?

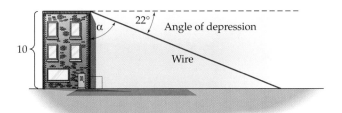

Figure 6.2-11

Solution

Figure 6.2-11 shows that the sum of the angle of depression and the angle α formed by the wall of the building and the wire is 90°.

$$\alpha = 90° - 22° = 68°$$

The wall, wire, and ground form a right triangle where the wall is the side adjacent to α and the wire is the hypotenuse. Thus,

$$\cos 68° = \frac{10}{w} \qquad \frac{adjacent}{hypotenuse}$$

$$w = \frac{10}{\cos 68°}$$

$$w \approx 26.7 \text{ m}$$

Thus, the wire should be about 27 m long. ∎

Example 9 **Indirect Measurement**

A person on the edge of a canal observes a lamp post on the other side with an angle of elevation of 12° to the top of the lamp post and an angle of depression of 7° to the bottom of the lamp post from eye level. The person's eye level is 152 cm (about 5 ft).

a. Find the width of the canal.

b. Find the height of the lamp post.

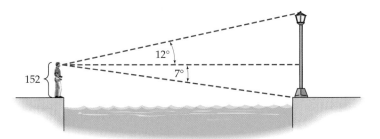

Figure 6.2-12

Solution

The essential information is shown in Figure 6.2-13 below. Note that $\overline{AC}$ is parallel to $\overline{DE}$, so CD is also 152 cm.

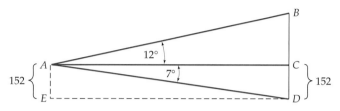

Figure 6.2-13

a. The width of the canal AC is adjacent to the $7°$ angle, and 152 is opposite the $7°$ angle.

$$\tan 7° = \frac{152}{AC} \qquad \frac{opposite}{adjacent}$$

$$AC = \frac{152}{\tan 7°} \approx 1237.94 \text{ cm, or about 12.38 m wide}$$

b. The height BC can be represented in terms of the width of the canal found in part **a.**

$$\tan 12° = \frac{BC}{AC} \qquad \frac{opposite}{adjacent}$$

$$BC = AC \tan 12° \approx (1237.94)(\tan 12°) \approx 263.13 \text{ cm}$$

The height of the lamp post is $BC + CD$.

$$BC + CD \approx 263.13 + 152 \approx 415.13 \text{ cm}$$

Exercises 6.2

In Exercises 1–6, find side c in the figure below by using the given conditions.

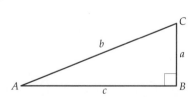

1. $\cos A = \dfrac{12}{13}$ $\qquad b = 39$

2. $\sin C = \dfrac{3}{4}$ $\qquad b = 12$

3. $\tan A = \dfrac{5}{12}$ $\qquad a = 15$

4. $\sec A = 2$ $\qquad b = 8$

5. $\cot A = 6$ $\qquad a = 1.4$

6. $\csc C = 1.5$ $\qquad b = 4.5$

In Exercises 7–12, find the exact value of h without using a calculator.

7.

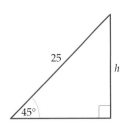

8.

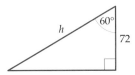

9.

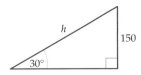

10.

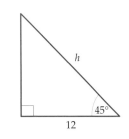

11.

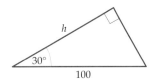

12.

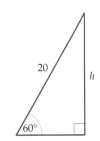

Use the figure below for Exercises 13–24.

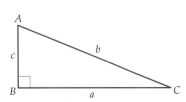

In Exercises 13–16, find the indicated value without using a calculator.

13. $a = 4$ $m\angle A = 60°$ Find c.

14. $c = 5$ $m\angle A = 60°$ Find a.

15. $c = 10$ $m\angle A = 30°$ Find a.

16. $a = 12$ $m\angle A = 30°$ Find c.

In Exercises 17–24, solve the triangle with the given conditions.

17. $b = 10$ $m\angle C = 50°$

18. $c = 12$ $m\angle C = 37°$

19. $a = 6$ $m\angle A = 14°$

20. $a = 8$ $m\angle A = 40°$

21. $c = 5$ $m\angle A = 65°$

22. $c = 4$ $m\angle C = 28°$

23. $b = 3.5$ $m\angle A = 72°$

24. $a = 4.2$ $m\angle C = 33°$

In Exercises 25–28, find angle θ.

25.

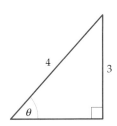

26.

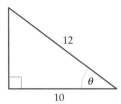

27.

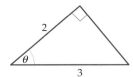

28.

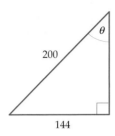

In Exercises 29–36, use the figure for Exercises 13–24 to find angles *A* and *C* under the given conditions.

29. $a = 4$ and $c = 6$

30. $b = 14$ and $c = 5$

31. $a = 7$ and $b = 10$

32. $a = 5$ and $c = 3$

33. $b = 18$ and $c = 12$

34. $a = 4$ and $b = 9$

35. $a = 2.5$ and $c = 1.4$

36. $b = 3.7$ and $c = 2.2$

37. A 24-ft ladder positioned against a wall forms an angle of 75° with the ground.
   a. How high up the wall does the ladder reach?
   b. How far is the base of the ladder from the wall?

38. A guy wire stretches from the top of an antenna tower to a point on level ground 18 feet from the base of the tower. The angle between the wire and the ground is 63°. How high is the tower?

39. A plane takes off at an angle of 5°. After traveling 1 mile along this flight path, how high (in feet) is the plane above the ground? (1 mi = 5280 ft)

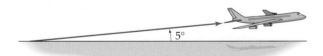

40. A plane takes off at an angle of 6° traveling at the rate of 200 feet/second. If it continues on this flight path at the same speed, how many minutes will it take to reach an altitude of 8000 feet?

41. The Ohio Turnpike has a maximum uphill slope of 3°. How long must a straight uphill segment of the road be in order to allow a vertical rise of 450 feet?

42. Ruth is flying a kite. Her hand is 3 feet above ground level and is holding the end of a 300-ft kite string, which makes an angle of 57° with the horizontal. How high is the kite above the ground?

43. Suppose that a person with a reach of 27 inches and a shoulder height of 5 feet is standing upright on a mountainside that makes a 62° angle with the horizontal, as shown in the figure below. Can the person touch the mountain?

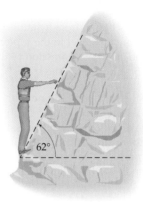

44. A swimming pool is 3 feet deep in the shallow end. The bottom of the pool has a steady downward drop of 12° toward the deep end. If the pool is 50 feet long, how deep is the deep end?

45. A wire from the top of a TV tower makes an angle of 49.5° with the ground and touches the ground 225 feet from the base of the tower. How high is the tower?

46. A plane flies a straight course. On the ground directly below the flight path, observers 2 miles apart spot the plane at the same time. The plane's angle of elevation is 46° from one observation point and 71° from the other. How high is the plane?

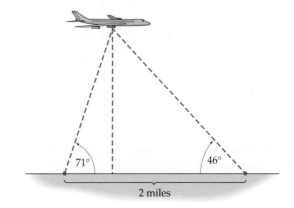

47. A buoy in the ocean is observed from the top of a 40-meter-high radar tower on shore. The angle of depression from the top of the tower to the base of the buoy is 6.5°. How far is the buoy from the base of the radar tower?

48. A plane passes directly over your head at an altitude of 500 feet. Two seconds later you observe that its angle of elevation is 42°. How far did the plane travel during those 2 seconds?

49. A man stands 12 feet from a statue. The angle of elevation from eye level to the top of the statue is 30°, and the angle of depression to the base of the statue is 15°. How tall is the statue?

50. Two boats lie on a straight line with the base of a lighthouse. From the top of the lighthouse, 21 meters above water level, it is observed that the angle of depression of the nearest boat is 53° and the angle of depression of the farthest boat is 27°. How far apart are the boats?

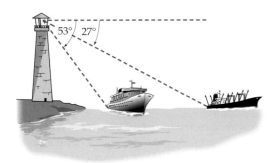

51. A rocket shoots straight up from the launch pad. Five seconds after lift-off, an observer 2 miles away notes that the rocket's angle of elevation is 3.5°. Four seconds after that, the angle of elevation is 41°. How far did the rocket rise during those 4 seconds?

52. From a window 35 meters high, the angle of depression to the top of a nearby streetlight is 55°. The angle of depression to the base of the streetlight is 57.8°. How tall is the streetlight?

53. A 60-foot drawbridge is 24 feet above water level when closed. When open, the bridge makes an angle of 33° with the horizontal.
  a. How high is the tip P of the open bridge above the water?
  b. When the bridge is open, what is the distance from P to Q?

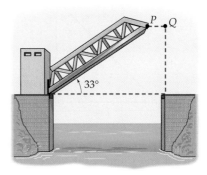

54. A drinking glass 5 inches tall has a 2.5-inch diameter base. Its sides slope outward at a 4° angle as shown. What is the diameter of the top of the glass?

55. In aerial navigation, directions are given in degrees clockwise from north, called *headings*. Thus east is 90°, south is 180°, and so on, as shown below. A plane travels from an airport for 200 miles at a heading of 300°. How far west of the airport is the plane?

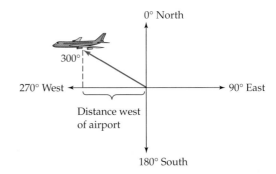

56. A plane travels from an airport at a constant 300 mph at a heading of 65°. (See Exercise 55.)
  a. How far east of the airport is the plane after half an hour?
  b. How far north of the airport is the plane after 2 hours and 24 minutes?

57. A car on a straight road passes under a bridge. Two seconds later an observer on the bridge, 20 feet above the road, notes that the angle of depression to the car is 7.4°. How fast, in miles per hour, is the car traveling? (Note: 60 mph is equivalent to 88 feet/second.)

58. A pedestrian overpass is shown in the figure below. If you walk on the overpass from one end to the other, how far have you walked?

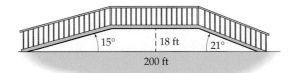

59. *Critical Thinking* A 50-ft flagpole stands on top of a building. From a point on the ground the angle of elevation to the top of the pole is 43° and the angle of elevation to the bottom of the pole is 40°. How high is the building?

60. *Critical Thinking* Two points on level ground are 500 meters apart. The angles of elevation from these points to the top of a nearby hill are 52° and 67°, respectively. The two points and the ground-level point directly below the top of the hill lie on a straight line. How high is the hill?

 # 6.3 Angles and Radian Measure

Objectives

- Use a rotating ray to extend the definition of angle measure to negative angles and angles greater than 180°

- Define radian measure and convert angle measures between degrees and radians

Extending Angle Measure

In geometry and triangle trigonometry, an angle is a static figure consisting of two rays that meet at a point. But in modern trigonometry, which will be introduced in the next section, an angle is thought of as being formed dynamically by *rotating* a ray around its endpoint, the **vertex.** The starting position of the ray is called the **initial side** and its final position after the rotation is called the **terminal side.**

The amount the ray is rotated is the measure of the angle. Counterclockwise rotations have positive measure and clockwise rotations have negative measure.

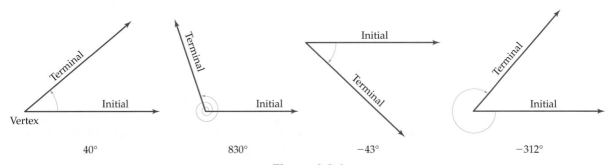

Figure 6.3-1

An angle in the coordinate plane is said to be in **standard position** if its vertex is at the origin and its initial side is on the positive x-axis.

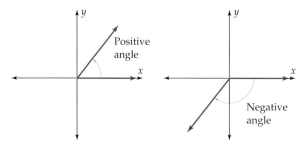

Figure 6.3-2

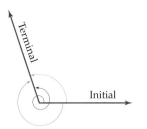

Figure 6.3-3

Angles formed by different rotations that have the same initial and terminal sides are called **coterminal.** (See Figure 6.3-3.) For example, $0°$ and $360°$ are coterminal angles.

Example 1   Coterminal Angles

Find three angles coterminal with an angle of $60°$ in standard position.

Solution

To find an angle that is coterminal with a given angle, add or subtract a complete revolution, or $360°$. To find additional angles, add or subtract any multiple of $360°$. Three possible angles are shown below.

$$60° + 360° = 420° \qquad 60° - 360° = -300° \qquad 60° + 2(360°) = 780°$$

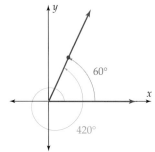 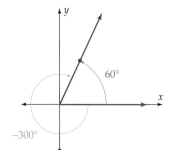 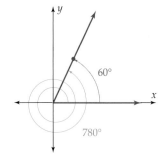

Figure 6.3-4

Arc Length

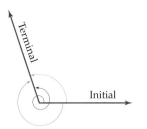

Figure 6.3-5

Recall from geometry that an **arc** is a part of a circle and that a **central angle** is an angle whose vertex is the center of the circle. The length of an arc depends on the radius of the circle and the measure of the central angle θ that it intercepts, as shown in Figure 6.3-5.

Arc length can be calculated by considering an arc as a fraction of the entire circle. Suppose an arc in a circle of radius r has a central angle measure of θ. Since there are $360°$ in a full circle, the arc is $\dfrac{\theta}{360}$ of the circle. The circumference of the circle is $2\pi r$, so, the length ℓ of the arc is

$$\ell = \frac{\theta}{360} \cdot 2\pi r = \frac{\theta \pi r}{180}$$

Example 2   **Finding an Angle Given an Arc Length**

An arc in a circle has an arc length ℓ which is equal to the radius r. Find the measure of the central angle that the arc intercepts.

Solution

$$r = \ell$$
$$r = \frac{\theta \pi r}{180}$$
$$180r = \theta \pi r$$
$$180 = \theta \pi$$
$$\frac{180}{\pi} = \theta$$

The central angle measure is $\left(\dfrac{180}{\pi}\right)^{\circ}$, or about $57.3°$.

Radian Measure

The angle found in Example 2 leads to another unit used in finding angle measure called a *radian*. Because it simplifies many formulas in calculus and physics, radians are used as a unit of angle measurement in mathematical and scientific applications.

Angle measurement in radians can be described in terms of the **unit circle,** which is the circle of radius 1 centered at the origin, whose equation is $x^2 + y^2 = 1$. When an angle is in standard position, its initial side lies on the x-axis and passes through $(1, 0)$. Its terminal side intersects the unit circle at some point P, as shown in Figure 6.3-6.

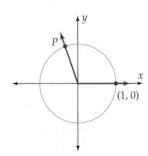

Figure 6.3-6

Definition of Radian Measure

The radian measure of an angle is the distance traveled along the unit circle in a counterclockwise direction by the point P, as it moves from its starting position on the initial side to its final position on the terminal side of the angle.

$$1 \text{ radian} = \left(\frac{180}{\pi}\right)^{\circ} \approx 57.3°$$

If the vertex of an angle is the center of a circle of radius r, then an angle of 1 radian intercepts an arc of length r.

Movement along the unit circle is counterclockwise for positive measure and clockwise for negative measure.

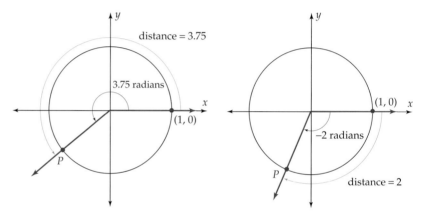

Figure 6.3-7

Consider an angle in standard position, with its terminal side rotating around the origin. In degree measure, one full revolution produces a 360° angle. The radian measure of this angle is the circumference of the unit circle, namely 2π. Other angles can be considered as a fraction of a full revolution, as shown in Figure 6.3-8.

1 revolution
2π radians

3/4 revolution
$\frac{3}{4} \cdot 2\pi = \frac{3\pi}{2}$ radians

1/2 revolution
$\frac{1}{2} \cdot 2\pi = \pi$ radians

1/4 revolution
$\frac{1}{4} \cdot 2\pi = \frac{\pi}{2}$ radians

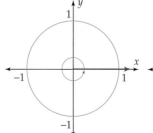 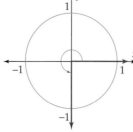 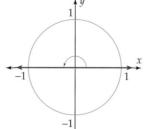 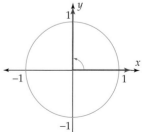

Figure 6.3-8

Radian Measure of Special Angles

The special angles of 30°, 60°, and 45° can also be considered as a fraction of a full revolution. Note that

- $\dfrac{360}{12} = 30$, so 30° is $\dfrac{1}{12}$ of a complete revolution: $30° = \dfrac{1}{12} \cdot 2\pi = \dfrac{\pi}{6}$ rad

- $\dfrac{360}{6} = 60$, so 60° is $\dfrac{1}{6}$ of a complete revolution: $60° = \dfrac{1}{6} \cdot 2\pi = \dfrac{\pi}{3}$ rad

- $\dfrac{360}{8} = 45$, so 45° is $\dfrac{1}{8}$ of a complete revolution: $45° = \dfrac{1}{8} \cdot 2\pi = \dfrac{\pi}{4}$ rad

Figure 6.3-9 shows a unit circle with radian and degree measures for important values. The radian measures for the angles shown in the first quadrant and on the x- and y-axes should be memorized.

NOTE Radian measurements are usually given in terms of π; however, it is useful to know the decimal equivalents for common measurements when using a calculator.

$$\pi \approx 3.14 \quad 2\pi \approx 6.28$$

$$\dfrac{\pi}{2} \approx 1.57 \quad \dfrac{\pi}{4} \approx 0.79$$

$$\dfrac{\pi}{6} \approx 0.52 \quad \dfrac{\pi}{3} \approx 1.05$$

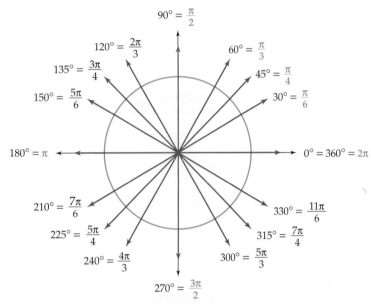

Figure 6.3-9

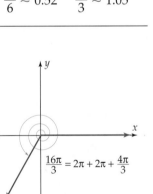

$$\dfrac{16\pi}{3} = 2\pi + 2\pi + \dfrac{4\pi}{3}$$

Figure 6.3-10

As shown in Figure 6.3-9, 2π radians corresponds to a full revolution of the terminal side of an angle in standard position. So an angle of radian measure t is coterminal with the angles whose radian measures are $t \pm 2\pi$, $t \pm 4\pi$, and so on, as shown in Figure 6.3-10.

Increasing or decreasing the radian measure of an angle by an integer multiple of 2π results in a coterminal angle.

Converting Between Degrees and Radians

As shown in Figure 6.3-9,

$$\pi \text{ radians} = 180°.$$

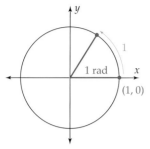

Figure 6.3-11

Dividing both sides by π shows that

$$1 \text{ radian} = \left(\frac{180}{\pi}\right)^{\circ} \approx 57.3^{\circ},$$

which agrees with the definition of radian.

Similarly, both sides of the original equation can be divided by 180.

$$\frac{\pi}{180} \text{ radians} = 1^{\circ}$$

These two equations give the conversion factors for radians to degrees and degrees to radians.

Radian/Degree Conversion

To convert radians to degrees, multiply by $\frac{180}{\pi}$.

To convert degrees to radians, multiply by $\frac{\pi}{180}$.

Example 3   Converting From Radians to Degrees

Convert the following radian measurements to degrees.

a. $\frac{\pi}{5}$ **b.** $\frac{4\pi}{9}$ **c.** 6π

Solution

a. $\frac{\pi}{5} \cdot \frac{180}{\pi} = 36^{\circ}$ **b.** $\frac{4\pi}{9} \cdot \frac{180}{\pi} = 80^{\circ}$ **c.** $6\pi \cdot \frac{180}{\pi} = 1080^{\circ}$

> **NOTE** One radian, which is illustrated in Figure 6.3-11, is close to 60°. There are about 6 radians ($2\pi \approx 6.28$) in a complete circle.

Example 4   Converting From Degrees to Radians

Convert the following degree measurements to radians.

a. 75°   **b.** 220°   **c.** 400°

Solution

a. $75^{\circ} \cdot \frac{\pi}{180} = \frac{5\pi}{12}$ **b.** $220^{\circ} \cdot \frac{\pi}{180} = \frac{11\pi}{9}$ **c.** $400^{\circ} \cdot \frac{\pi}{180} = \frac{20\pi}{9}$

> **NOTE** To help you remember which conversion factor to use, it may be helpful to notice that radians are *usually* written in terms of π.
>
> Degrees to radians: to get π in final answer, multiply by $\frac{\pi}{180}$
>
> Radians to degrees: to cancel π in final answer, multiply by $\frac{180}{\pi}$

Arc Length and Angular Speed

The formula for arc length can also be written in terms of radians.

Arc Length

> An arc with central angle measure θ radians has length
>
> $$\ell = r\theta$$
>
> In other words, the arc length is the radius times the radian measure of the central angle of the arc.

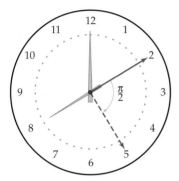

Figure 6.3-12

Example 5   Arc Length

The second hand on a clock is 6 inches long. How far does the tip of the second hand move in 15 seconds?

Solution

The second hand makes a full revolution every 60 seconds, that is, it moves through an angle of 2π radians. During a 15-second interval it will make $\dfrac{15}{60} = \dfrac{1}{4}$ of a revolution, moving through an angle of $\dfrac{1}{4}(2\pi) = \dfrac{\pi}{2}$ radians (Figure 6.3-12), so the tip of the second hand travels along an arc with central angle measure of $\dfrac{\pi}{2}$. Therefore, the distance that the tip moves in 15 seconds is the arc length

$$\ell = r\theta = 6\left(\frac{\pi}{2}\right) = 3\pi \approx 9.4 \text{ inches.}$$

Example 6   Central Angle Measure

Find the central angle measure (in radians) of an arc of length 5 cm on a circle with a radius of 3 cm.

Solution

Solve the arc length formula $\ell = r\theta$ for θ.

$$\theta = \frac{\ell}{r} = \frac{5}{3} \text{ radians}$$

This is a little more than one-quarter of a complete revolution, as shown in Figure 6.3-13.

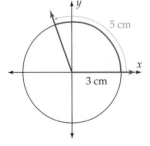

Figure 6.3-13

Linear and Angular Speed

Suppose that a wheel is rotating at a constant rate around its center, O, and P is a point on the outer edge of the wheel. There are two ways to measure the speed of point P, in terms of the distance traveled or in terms of the angle of rotation. The two measures of speed are called *linear speed* and *angular speed*.

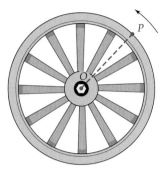

Figure 6.3-14

NOTE The angular speed of an object traveling in a circular path is the same, regardless of its distance from the center of the circle. When the angular speed of the object stays the same, the linear speed increases as the object moves farther from the center.

Recall that the speed of a moving object is $\dfrac{\text{distance}}{\text{time}}$. If the object is traveling in a circular path with radius r, the **linear speed** is given by

$$\text{linear speed} = \frac{\text{arc length}}{\text{time}} = \frac{r\theta}{t}$$

and the **angular speed** is given by

$$\text{angular speed} = \frac{\text{angle}}{\text{time}} = \frac{\theta}{t}$$

where θ is the radian measure of the angle through which the object travels in time t. Notice the relationship between linear speed and angular speed:

$$\text{linear speed} = r \cdot \text{angular speed}$$

Example 7   **Linear and Angular Speed**

A merry-go-round makes 8 revolutions per minute.

a. What is the angular speed of the merry-go-round in radians per minute?

b. How fast is a horse 12 feet from the center traveling?

c. How fast is a horse 4 feet from the center traveling?

Solution

a. Each revolution of the merry-go-round corresponds to a central angle of 2π radians, so the merry-go-round travels through an angle of $8 \cdot 2\pi = 16\pi$ radians in one minute.

$$\text{angular speed} = \frac{\theta}{t} = \frac{16\pi}{1} = 16\pi \text{ radians per minute}$$

b. The horse 12 feet from the center travels along a circle of radius 12. From part **a**,

$$\text{linear speed} = r \cdot \text{angular speed} = 12 \cdot 16\pi = 192\pi \text{ ft/min}$$

which is about 6.9 mph.

c. The horse 4 feet from the center travels along a circle of radius 4. From part **a**,

$$\text{linear speed} = r \cdot \text{angular speed} = 4 \cdot 16\pi = 64\pi \text{ ft/min}$$

which is about 2.3 mph. ∎

NOTE The units ft/min in Example 7 can be converted to mph as follows:

$$\frac{192\pi \text{ ft}}{1 \text{ min}} \cdot \frac{60 \text{ min}}{1 \text{ hr}} \cdot \frac{1 \text{ mi}}{5280 \text{ ft}} \approx \frac{6.9 \text{ mi}}{1 \text{ hr}}$$

Exercises 6.3

In Exercises 1–10, find the degree and radian measure of the angle in standard position formed by rotating the terminal side by the given amount.

1. $\dfrac{1}{9}$ of a circle

2. $\dfrac{1}{24}$ of a circle

3. $\dfrac{1}{18}$ of a circle

4. $\dfrac{1}{72}$ of a circle

5. $\dfrac{1}{36}$ of a circle

6. $\dfrac{1}{5}$ of a circle

7. $\dfrac{2}{3}$ of a circle

8. $\dfrac{7}{12}$ of a circle

9. $\dfrac{4}{5}$ of a circle

10. $\dfrac{5}{36}$ of a circle

In Exercises 11–22, convert the given radian measure to degrees.

11. $\dfrac{\pi}{5}$ **12.** $-\dfrac{\pi}{6}$ **13.** $-\dfrac{\pi}{10}$ **14.** $\dfrac{2\pi}{5}$

15. $\dfrac{3\pi}{4}$ **16.** $-\dfrac{5\pi}{3}$ **17.** $\dfrac{\pi}{45}$ **18.** $-\dfrac{\pi}{60}$

19. $-\dfrac{5\pi}{12}$ **20.** $\dfrac{7\pi}{15}$ **21.** $\dfrac{27\pi}{5}$ **22.** $-\dfrac{41\pi}{6}$

In Exercises 23–34, convert the given degree measure to radians. Write your answer in terms of π.

23. $6°$ **24.** $-10°$ **25.** $-12°$ **26.** $36°$

27. $75°$ **28.** $-105°$ **29.** $135°$ **30.** $-165°$

31. $-225°$ **32.** $252°$ **33.** $930°$ **34.** $-585°$

In Exercises 35–42, state the radian measure of an angle in standard position between 0 and 2π that is coterminal with the given angle in standard position.

35. $-\dfrac{\pi}{3}$ **36.** $-\dfrac{3\pi}{4}$ **37.** $\dfrac{19\pi}{4}$ **38.** $\dfrac{16\pi}{3}$

39. $-\dfrac{7\pi}{5}$ **40.** $\dfrac{45\pi}{8}$ **41.** 7 **42.** 18.5

In Exercises 43–46, find the radian measure of four angles in standard position that are coterminal with the given angle in standard position.

43. $\dfrac{\pi}{4}$ **44.** $\dfrac{7\pi}{5}$ **45.** $-\dfrac{\pi}{6}$ **46.** $-\dfrac{9\pi}{7}$

In Exercises 47–52, determine the positive radian measure of the angle that the second hand of a clock travels through in the given time.

47. 40 seconds

48. 50 seconds

49. 35 seconds

50. 2 minutes 15 seconds

51. 3 minutes 25 seconds

52. 1 minute 55 seconds

53. The second hand on a clock is 6 cm long. How far does its tip travel in 40 seconds?

54. The second hand on a clock is 5 cm long. How far does its tip travel in 2 minutes and 15 seconds?

55. If the radius of the circle in the figure is 20 cm and $\ell = 85$ cm, what is the radian measure of the angle θ?

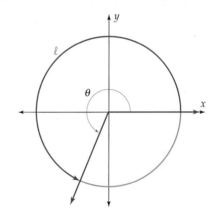

56. Find the radian measure of the angle θ in the preceding figure if the diameter of the circle is 150 cm and $\ell = 360$ cm.

In Exercises 57–60, assume that a wheel on a car has radius 36 cm. Find the angle (in radians) that the wheel turns while the car travels the given distance.

57. 2 meters (200 cm)

58. 5 meters

59. 720 meters

60. 1 kilometer (1000 meters)

In Exercises 61–64, find the length of the circular arc with the central angle whose radian measure is given. Assume that the circle has diameter 10.

61. 1 radian

62. 2 radians

63. 1.75 radians

64. 2.2 radians

The *latitude* of a point P on Earth is the degree measure of the angle θ between the point and the plane of the equator, with Earth's center as the vertex, as shown in the figure below.

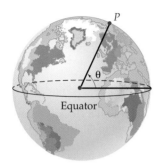

In Exercises 65–68, the latitudes of a pair of cities are given. Assume that one city is directly south of the other and that the earth is a perfect sphere of radius 4000 miles. Use the arc length formula in terms of degrees to find the distance between the two cities.

65. The North Pole: latitude 90° north
Springfield, Illinois: latitude 40° north

66. San Antonio, Texas: latitude 29.5° north
Mexico City, Mexico: latitude 20° north

67. Cleveland, Ohio: latitude 41.5° north
Tampa, Florida: latitude 28° north

68. Rome, Italy: latitude 42° north
Copenhagen, Denmark: latitude 54.3° north

In Exercises 69–76, a wheel is rotating around its axle. Find the angle (in radians) through which the wheel turns in the given time when it rotates at the given number of revolutions per minute (rpm). Assume $t > 0$ and $k > 0$.

69. 3.5 minutes, 1 rpm   **70.** t minutes, 1 rpm

71. 1 minute, 2 rpm   **72.** 3.5 minutes, 2 rpm

73. 4.25 minutes, 5 rpm   **74.** t minutes, 5 rpm

75. 1 minute, k rpm   **76.** t minutes, k rpm

77. One end of a rope is attached to a circular drum of radius 2 feet and the other to a steel beam. When the drum is rotated, the rope wraps around it and pulls the object upward (see figure). Through what angle must the drum be rotated in order to raise the beam 6 feet?

78. A circular saw blade has an angular speed of 15,000 radians per minute.
  a. How many revolutions per minute does the saw make?
  b. How long will it take the saw to make 6000 revolutions?

79. A circular gear rotates at the rate of 200 revolutions per minute (rpm).
  a. What is the angular speed of the gear in radians per minute?
  b. What is the linear speed of a point on the gear 2 inches from the center in inches per minute? in feet per minute?

80. A wheel in a large machine is 2.8 feet in diameter and rotates at 1200 rpm.
  a. What is the angular speed of the wheel?
  b. How fast is a point on the circumference of the wheel traveling in feet per minute? in miles per hour?

81. A riding lawn mower has wheels that are 15 inches in diameter, which are turning at 2.5 revolutions per second.
  a. What is the angular speed of a wheel?
  b. How fast is the lawn mower traveling in miles per hour?

82. A bicycle has wheels that are 26 inches in diameter. If the bike is traveling at 14 mph, what is the angular speed of each wheel?

83. A merry-go-round horse is traveling at 10 feet per second when the merry-go-round is making 6 revolutions per minute. How far is the horse from the center of the merry-go-round?

84. The pedal sprocket of a bicycle has radius 4.5 inches and the rear wheel sprocket has radius 1.5 inches (see figure). If the rear wheel has a radius of 13.5 inches and the cyclist is pedaling at the rate of 80 rpm, how fast is the bicycle traveling in feet per minute? in miles per hour?

85. A spy plane on a practice run over the Midwest takes a picture that shows Cleveland, Ohio, on the eastern horizon and St. Louis, Missouri, 520 miles away on the western horizon. (The figure is not to scale.) Assuming that the radius of the earth is 3950 miles, how high was the plane when the picture was taken? *Hint:* The sight lines from the plane to the horizons are tangent to the earth and a tangent line to a circle is perpendicular to the radius at that point. The arc of the earth between St. Louis and Cleveland is 520 miles long. Use this fact and the arc length formula to find angle θ. Your answers will be in radians. Note that

$$\alpha = \frac{\theta}{2} \text{ (why?).}$$

6.4   Trigonometric Functions

Objectives

- Define the trigonometric ratios in the coordinate plane
- Define the trigonometric functions in terms of the unit circle

---

NOTE P can be any point on the terminal side of the angle, except for the origin, since different choices for P generate similar right triangles. Thus, the value of a trigonometric ratio depends only on the angle.

Extending the Trigonometric Ratios

Trigonometric ratios were defined for acute angles in Section 6.1. The next step is to develop a definition of these ratios that applies to angles of any measure.

To do this, first consider an acute angle θ in standard position. Choose a point P, with coordinates (x, y), on the terminal side, and draw a right triangle, as shown in Figure 6.4-1. The side adjacent to θ has length x and the side opposite θ has length y. The length of the hypotenuse, r, is the distance from the origin, which may be found by using the Pythagorean Theorem.

$$x^2 + y^2 = r^2$$
$$r = \sqrt{x^2 + y^2}$$

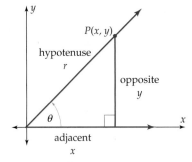

Figure 6.4-1

The trigonometric ratios can now be written in terms of x, y, and r. For example,

$$\sin\theta = \frac{\text{opposite}}{\text{hypotenuse}} = \frac{y}{r} \qquad \text{and} \qquad \cos\theta = \frac{\text{adjacent}}{\text{hypotenuse}} = \frac{x}{r}$$

Thus, the trigonometric ratios can be described without triangles by using a point on the terminal side of the angle. More importantly, this process can be carried out for *any* angle, not just acute angles. Therefore, the following definition applies to any angle and agrees with the previous definition when the angle is acute.

Trigonometric Ratios in the Coordinate Plane

Let θ be an angle in standard position and let $P(x, y)$ be any point on the terminal side of θ. Let r be the distance from (x, y) to the origin:

$$r = \sqrt{x^2 + y^2}$$

Then the trigonometric ratios of θ are defined as follows:

$$\sin\theta = \frac{y}{r} \qquad \csc\theta = \frac{r}{y}$$

$$\cos\theta = \frac{x}{r} \qquad \sec\theta = \frac{r}{x}$$

$$\tan\theta = \frac{y}{x} \qquad \cot\theta = \frac{x}{y}$$

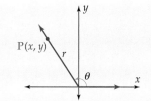

Example 1   Trigonometric Ratios in the Coordinate Plane

Find the sine, cosine, and tangent of the angle θ, whose terminal side passes through the point $(-3, -2)$.

Solution

Using the values $x = -3$, $y = -2$, and $r = \sqrt{(-3)^2 + (-2)^2} = \sqrt{13}$,

$$\sin\theta = \frac{-2}{\sqrt{13}} \qquad \cos\theta = \frac{-3}{\sqrt{13}} \qquad \tan\theta = \frac{-2}{-3} = \frac{2}{3}$$

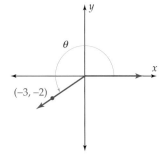

Figure 6.4-2

Trigonometric Functions

Trigonometric ratios have been defined for all *angles*. But modern applications of trigonometry deal with *functions* whose domains consist of real numbers. The basic idea is quite simple: If t is a real number, then

sin t is defined to be the sine of an angle of t radians;

cos t is defined to be the cosine of an angle of t radians;

and so on. Instead of starting with angles, as was done up until now, this new approach starts with a number and only then moves to angles, as summarized below.

Trigonometric Functions of Real Numbers

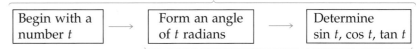

Trigonometric Ratios of Angles

Adapting earlier definitions of ratios to this new viewpoint produces the following definition of trigonometric functions of real numbers. Use Figure 6.4-3 for reference.

Trigonometric Functions of a Real Variable

Let t be a real number. Choose any point (x, y) on the terminal side of an angle of t radians in standard position. Then

$$\sin t = \frac{y}{r} \qquad \cos t = \frac{x}{r} \qquad \tan t = \frac{y}{x}$$

$$\csc t = \frac{r}{y} \qquad \sec t = \frac{r}{x} \qquad \cot t = \frac{x}{y}$$

where $r = \sqrt{x^2 + y^2}$ is the distance from (x, y) to the origin.

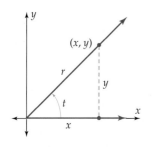

Figure 6.4-3

Although this definition is essential for developing various facts about the trigonometric functions, the values of these functions are usually approximated by a calculator in *radian mode*, as shown in Figure 6.4-4.

NOTE Unless stated otherwise, use radian mode when evaluating trigonometric functions of real numbers.

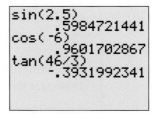

Figure 6.4-4

Trigonometric Functions and the Unit Circle

Recall that the **unit circle** is the circle of radius 1 centered at the origin, whose equation is $x^2 + y^2 = 1$. The unit circle is the basis for the most useful description of trigonometric functions of real numbers.

Let t be any real number. Construct an angle of t radians in standard position. Let $P(x, y)$ be the point where the terminal side of this angle meets the unit circle, as shown in Figure 6.4-5.

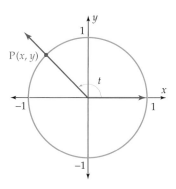

Figure 6.4-5

NOTE The length of the arc from $(1, 0)$ to P is t.

The distance from P to the origin is 1 because the unit circle has radius 1. Using the point P, $r = 1$, and the definition of trigonometric functions of real numbers shows that

$$\sin t = \frac{y}{r} = \frac{y}{1} = y \qquad \text{and} \qquad \cos t = \frac{x}{r} = \frac{x}{1} = x$$

Unit Circle Description of Trigonometric Functions

Let t be a real number and let P be the point where the terminal side of an angle of t radians in standard position meets the unit circle. Then

$$P \text{ has coordinates } (\cos t, \sin t)$$

and

$$\tan t = \frac{y}{x} = \frac{\sin t}{\cos t} \qquad \cot t = \frac{x}{y} = \frac{\cos t}{\sin t}$$

$$\sec t = \frac{1}{x} = \frac{1}{\cos t} \qquad \csc t = \frac{1}{y} = \frac{1}{\sin t}$$

Graphing Exploration

With your calculator in radian mode and parametric graphing mode, set the range values as follows:

$$0 \le t \le 2\pi \qquad -1.8 \le x \le 1.8 \qquad -1.2 \le y \le 1.2$$

Then, graph the curve given by these parametric equations:

$$x = \cos t \qquad y = \sin t$$

The graph is the unit circle. Use the trace to move around the circle. At each point, the screen will display three numbers: the values of t, x, and y. For each t, the cursor is on the point where the terminal side of an angle of t radians meets the unit circle, so the corresponding x is the number $\cos t$ and the corresponding y is the number $\sin t$.

The coordinates of points on a circle of radius r that is centered at the origin can be written by using r and t with the definition of the trigonometric ratios in the coordinate plane. See Exercise 61.

Domain and Range

By the domain convention in Section 3.1, the domain of a function is all real numbers for which the function is defined. For any real number t, an appropriate angle of t radians and its intersection point with the unit circle are always defined, so

> **the domain of the sine function and of the cosine function is the set of all real numbers.**

The range of a function is the set of all possible outputs. Because $\sin t$ and $\cos t$ are the coordinates of a point on the unit circle, they take on all values between -1 and 1 and no other values. Thus,

> **the range of the sine function and of the cosine function is the set of all real numbers between -1 and 1, that is, the interval $[-1, 1]$.**

The tangent function is defined as $\tan t = \frac{y}{x}$, whenever $x \neq 0$, that is, for all points on the unit circle except $(0, 1)$ and $(0, -1)$. The point $(0, 1)$ is on the terminal side of an angle of $\frac{\pi}{2}$ radians or any angle obtained by adding integer multiples of 2π (a complete circle) to it, that is,

$$\ldots, -\frac{7\pi}{2}, -\frac{3\pi}{2}, \frac{\pi}{2}, \frac{5\pi}{2}, \frac{9\pi}{2}, \ldots$$

The point $(0, -1)$ is on the terminal side of an angle of $\frac{3\pi}{2}$ radians or any angle obtained by adding integer multiples of 2π to it, that is,

$$\ldots, -\frac{5\pi}{2}, -\frac{\pi}{2}, \frac{3\pi}{2}, \frac{7\pi}{2}, \frac{11\pi}{2}, \ldots$$

Combining these facts shows that

> **the domain of the tangent function consists of all real numbers except $\pm\frac{\pi}{2} + 2k\pi$, where $k = 0, \pm1, \pm2, \pm3, \ldots$.**

In contrast to sine and cosine,

> **the range of the tangent function is the set of all real numbers.**

A proof of this fact is found in Exercise 60. Figure 6.4-6 shows that values of the tangent can be very large positives, very large negatives, or in between.

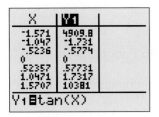

Figure 6.4-6

Signs of the Trigonometric Functions

It is often important to know whether the value of a trigonometric function is positive or negative. For any real number t, the point $(\cos t, \sin t)$ is on the terminal side of an angle of t radians in standard position. The

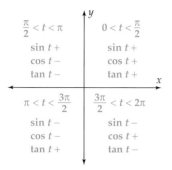

$\frac{\pi}{2} < t < \pi$

$\sin t +$
$\cos t -$
$\tan t -$

$0 < t < \frac{\pi}{2}$

$\sin t +$
$\cos t +$
$\tan t +$

$\pi < t < \frac{3\pi}{2}$

$\sin t -$
$\cos t -$
$\tan t +$

$\frac{3\pi}{2} < t < 2\pi$

$\sin t -$
$\cos t +$
$\tan t -$

Figure 6.4-7

quadrant in which this point lies determines the signs of sine and cosine, as well as those of the other trigonometric functions, as summarized in Figure 6.4-7.

Exact Values of Trigonometric Functions

Although a calculator is used to evaluate trigonometric functions approximately, there are a few special numbers for which exact values can be found. Recall that 30°, 45°, and 60° are the same as $\frac{\pi}{6}, \frac{\pi}{4}$, and $\frac{\pi}{3}$, respectively. Therefore, the chart on page 419 can be translated as follows.

t	$\dfrac{\pi}{6}$	$\dfrac{\pi}{4}$	$\dfrac{\pi}{3}$
$\sin t$	$\dfrac{1}{2}$	$\dfrac{1}{\sqrt{2}} = \dfrac{\sqrt{2}}{2}$	$\dfrac{\sqrt{3}}{2}$
$\cos t$	$\dfrac{\sqrt{3}}{2}$	$\dfrac{1}{\sqrt{2}} = \dfrac{\sqrt{2}}{2}$	$\dfrac{1}{2}$
$\tan t$	$\dfrac{1}{\sqrt{3}} = \dfrac{\sqrt{3}}{3}$	1	$\sqrt{3}$
$\csc t$	$\dfrac{2}{1} = 2$	$\dfrac{\sqrt{2}}{1} = \sqrt{2}$	$\dfrac{2}{\sqrt{3}} = \dfrac{2\sqrt{3}}{3}$
$\sec t$	$\dfrac{2}{\sqrt{3}} = \dfrac{2\sqrt{3}}{3}$	$\dfrac{\sqrt{2}}{1} = \sqrt{2}$	$\dfrac{2}{1} = 2$
$\cot t$	$\dfrac{\sqrt{3}}{1} = \sqrt{3}$	$\dfrac{1}{1} = 1$	$\dfrac{1}{\sqrt{3}} = \dfrac{\sqrt{3}}{3}$

The exact values of the trigonometric functions can also be found for any number that is an integer multiple of $\frac{\pi}{6}, \frac{\pi}{4}$, and $\frac{\pi}{3}$. The technique for doing this depends on the concept of a *reference angle*.

Example 2   **Exact Values of Trigonometric Functions**

Find the exact value of the sine, cosine, and tangent functions when $t = 0$, $\frac{\pi}{2}, \pi, \frac{3\pi}{2}$, and 2π.

Solution

If the measure of an angle is a multiple of $\frac{\pi}{2}$, then its terminal side lies on an axis. Thus, the only possible values of the sine and cosine functions

of such angles are -1, 0 and 1. The following chart shows the value of
the sine, cosine, and tangent functions for these angles between 0 and 2π.

t	$\sin t$	$\cos t$	$\tan t$
0	0	1	0
$\frac{\pi}{2}$	1	0	undefined
π	0	-1	0
$\frac{3\pi}{2}$	-1	0	undefined
2π	0	1	0

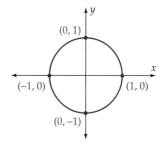

Figure 6.4-8

Reference Angles

**Definition of
Reference
Angle**

For an angle θ in standard position, the *reference angle* is the
positive acute angle formed by the terminal side of θ and the
x-axis.

In the following figure, the reference angle t' for an angle of t radians in
standard position is shown in two ways.

Definition of Reference Angle

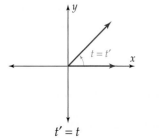

$t' = t$

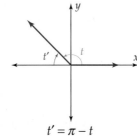

$t' = \pi - t$

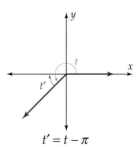

$t' = t - \pi$

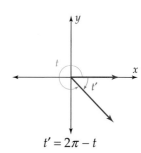

$t' = 2\pi - t$

Unit Circle with Reference Angle Placed in Quadrant I

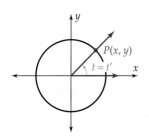

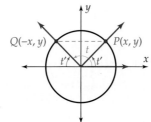

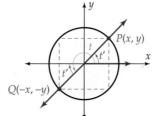

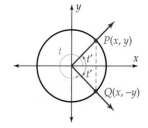

Figure 6.4-9

In every case, the figure that references the unit circle illustrates the following fact that can be proved by using congruent triangles:

$$x\text{-coordinate of } Q = \pm(x\text{-coordinate of } P)$$
$$y\text{-coordinate of } Q = \pm(y\text{-coordinate of } P)$$

By definition, the values of the trigonometric functions for t are given by the coordinates of Q and the values of these functions for t' are given by the coordinates of P. So, these values will be the same, except for a plus or minus sign. The correct sign is determined by the quadrant in which the terminal side of an angle of t radians lies, as shown in Figure 6.4-7 on page 448.

Finding Trigonometric Function Values

To find the sine, cosine, or tangent of t radians,

- **Sketch an angle of t radians in standard position and determine the quadrant in which the terminal side lies.**
- **Find the reference angle, which has measure t' radians.**
- **Find the sine, cosine, and tangent of t' and append the appropriate sign.**

Example 3 Using Reference Angles

Use reference angles to find the exact value of $\sin t$, $\cos t$, and $\tan t$.

a. $t = \dfrac{3\pi}{4}$ **b.** $t = \dfrac{4\pi}{3}$ **c.** $t = \dfrac{11\pi}{6}$

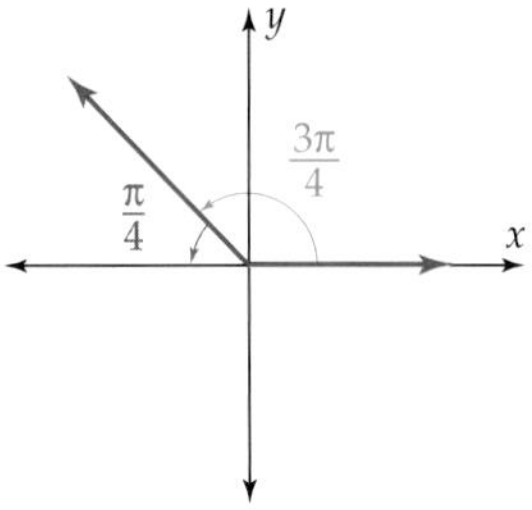

Solution

a. Sketch the angle, as shown in Figure 6.4-10. The terminal side is in the second quadrant, so the reference angle is $\pi - t$.

$$\pi - \frac{3\pi}{4} = \frac{\pi}{4}$$

Because the terminal side of the angle of $\dfrac{3\pi}{4}$ radians lies in the second quadrant, $\sin \dfrac{3\pi}{4}$ is positive, and $\cos \dfrac{3\pi}{4}$ and $\tan \dfrac{3\pi}{4}$ are negative.

$$\sin \frac{3\pi}{4} = \sin \frac{\pi}{4} = \frac{\sqrt{2}}{2} \qquad \cos \frac{3\pi}{4} = -\cos \frac{\pi}{4} = -\frac{\sqrt{2}}{2}$$

$$\tan \frac{4\pi}{3} = -\tan \frac{\pi}{4} = -1$$

b. Sketch the angle, as shown in Figure 6.4-11. The terminal side is in quadrant III, so the reference angle is $t - \pi$.

$$\frac{4\pi}{3} - \pi = \frac{\pi}{3}$$

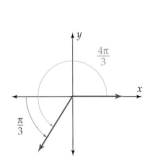

Figure 6.4-10

Figure 6.4-11

Thus, the sine, cosine, and tangent functions are

$$\sin \frac{4\pi}{3} = -\sin \frac{\pi}{3} = -\frac{\sqrt{3}}{2} \qquad \cos \frac{4\pi}{3} = -\cos \frac{\pi}{3} = -\frac{1}{2}$$

$$\tan \frac{3\pi}{4} = \tan \frac{\pi}{3} = \sqrt{3}$$

c. Sketch the angle, as shown in Figure 6.4-12. The terminal side is in quadrant IV, so the reference angle is $2\pi - t$.

$$2\pi - \frac{11\pi}{6} = \frac{\pi}{6}$$

Thus, the sine, cosine, and tangent functions are

$$\sin \frac{11\pi}{6} = -\sin \frac{\pi}{6} = -\frac{1}{2} \qquad \cos \frac{11\pi}{6} = \cos \frac{\pi}{6} = \frac{\sqrt{3}}{2}$$

$$\tan \frac{11\pi}{6} = -\tan \frac{\pi}{6} = -\frac{\sqrt{3}}{3}$$

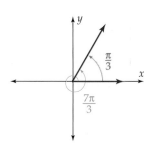

Figure 6.4-12

If an angle is less than 0 or greater than 2π, it is possible to find a coterminal angle between 0 and 2π by adding or subtracting multiples of 2π. Thus, the trigonometric functions of a real variable have the following property.

Trigonometric Ratios of Coterminal Angles

Any trigonometric function of a real number t is equal to the same trigonometric function of all numbers $t \pm 2k\pi$, where k is an integer.

Example 4   **Trigonometric Functions Where $t > 2\pi$**

Find the sine, cosine, and tangent of $\frac{7\pi}{3}$.

Solution

$\frac{7\pi}{3}$ can be written as $\frac{\pi}{3} + 2\pi$. Therefore, $\frac{7\pi}{3}$ is coterminal with $\frac{\pi}{3}$.

$$\sin \frac{7\pi}{3} = \sin \frac{\pi}{3} = \frac{\sqrt{3}}{2}$$

$$\cos \frac{7\pi}{3} = \cos \frac{\pi}{3} = \frac{1}{2}$$

$$\tan \frac{7\pi}{3} = \tan \frac{\pi}{3} = \sqrt{3}$$

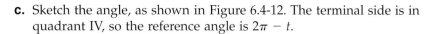

Figure 6.4-13

Exercises 6.4

Note: Unless stated otherwise, all angles are in standard position.

In Exercises 1–6, find sin t, cos t, and tan t when the terminal side of an angle of t radians passes through the given point.

1. $(2, 7)$ **2.** $(-3, 2)$ **3.** $(-5, -6)$

4. $(4, -3)$ **5.** $(\sqrt{3}, -10)$ **6.** $(-\pi, 2)$

In Exercises 7–10, find sin t, cos t, and tan t when the terminal side of an angle of t radians passes through the given point on the unit circle.

7. $\left(-\dfrac{2}{\sqrt{5}}, \dfrac{1}{\sqrt{5}}\right)$ **8.** $\left(\dfrac{1}{\sqrt{10}}, -\dfrac{3}{\sqrt{10}}\right)$

9. $\left(-\dfrac{3}{5}, -\dfrac{4}{5}\right)$ **10.** $(0.6, -0.8)$

In Exercises 11–14, identify an angle $0 \le t' \le \pi$ that is coterminal with the given angle, and find the sine and cosine of the given angle.

11. $\dfrac{13\pi}{6}$ **12.** $\dfrac{9\pi}{2}$ **13.** 16π **14.** $-\dfrac{7\pi}{4}$

In Exercises 15–23,

a. Use a calculator in radian mode to find the sine, cosine, and tangent of each number. Round your answers to four decimal places.

b. Use the signs of the functions to identify the quadrant of the terminal side of an angle of t radians. If the terminal side lies on an axis, identify which axis and whether it is on the positive or negative side of the axis. Explain your reasoning.

15. $\dfrac{7\pi}{5}$ **16.** 11 **17.** $-\dfrac{14\pi}{9}$

18. -23π **19.** $\dfrac{10\pi}{3}$ **20.** 6.4π

21. 9.5π **22.** $\dfrac{\pi}{17}$ **23.** -17

In Exercises 24–29, sketch each angle whose radian measure is given and find its reference angle.

24. $\dfrac{7\pi}{3}$ **25.** $\dfrac{17\pi}{6}$ **26.** $\dfrac{6\pi}{5}$

27. 1.75π **28.** $-\dfrac{3\pi}{4}$ **29.** $-\dfrac{\pi}{7}$

In Exercises 30–47, find the exact value of the sine, cosine, and tangent of the number without using a calculator.

30. $\dfrac{7\pi}{6}$ **31.** $\dfrac{7\pi}{3}$ **32.** $\dfrac{17\pi}{3}$ **33.** $\dfrac{11\pi}{4}$

34. $\dfrac{5\pi}{4}$ **35.** $-\dfrac{3\pi}{2}$ **36.** 3π **37.** $-\dfrac{23\pi}{6}$

38. $\dfrac{11\pi}{6}$ **39.** $-\dfrac{19\pi}{3}$ **40.** $-\dfrac{10\pi}{3}$ **41.** $-\dfrac{15\pi}{4}$

42. $-\dfrac{25\pi}{4}$ **43.** $\dfrac{5\pi}{6}$ **44.** $-\dfrac{17\pi}{2}$ **45.** $\dfrac{9\pi}{2}$

46. $-\pi$ **47.** 4π

In Exercises 48–53, write the expression as a single real number. Do not use decimal approximations.

48. $\sin\left(\dfrac{\pi}{6}\right)\cos\left(\dfrac{\pi}{2}\right) - \cos\left(\dfrac{\pi}{6}\right)\sin\left(\dfrac{\pi}{2}\right)$

49. $\cos\left(\dfrac{\pi}{2}\right)\cos\left(\dfrac{\pi}{4}\right) - \sin\left(\dfrac{\pi}{2}\right)\sin\left(\dfrac{\pi}{4}\right)$

50. $\cos\left(\dfrac{2\pi}{3}\right)\cos\pi + \sin\left(\dfrac{2\pi}{3}\right)\sin\pi$

51. $\sin\left(\dfrac{3\pi}{4}\right)\cos\left(\dfrac{5\pi}{6}\right) - \cos\left(\dfrac{3\pi}{4}\right)\sin\left(\dfrac{5\pi}{6}\right)$

52. $\sin\left(\dfrac{-7\pi}{3}\right)\cos\left(\dfrac{5\pi}{4}\right) + \cos\left(\dfrac{-7\pi}{3}\right)\sin\left(\dfrac{5\pi}{4}\right)$

53. $\sin\left(\dfrac{\pi}{3}\right)\cos\pi + \sin\pi\cos\left(\dfrac{\pi}{3}\right)$

In Exercises 54–59, the terminal side of an angle of t radians lies in the given quadrant on the given line. Find sin t, cos t, and tan t. (*Hint:* Find a point on the terminal side of the angle.)

54. Quadrant III; line $2y - 4x = 0$

55. Quadrant IV; line through $(-3, 5)$ and $(-9, 15)$

56. Quadrant III; line through the origin parallel to $7x - 2y = -6$

57. Quadrant II; line through the origin parallel to $2y + x = 6$

58. Quadrant I; line through the origin perpendicular to $3y + x = 6$

59. Quadrant IV; line $y = -3x$

60. The terminal side of an angle of t radians lies on a straight line through the origin, and therefore, has an equation of the form $y = mx$, where m is the slope of the line.

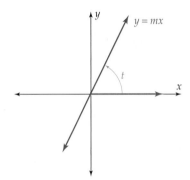

a. Prove that $m = \tan t$. *Hint:* a point on the terminal side of the angle has coordinates (x, mx)

b. Explain why $\tan t$ approaches infinity as t approaches $\frac{\pi}{2}$ from below. *Hint:* What happens to the slope of the terminal side when t is close to $\frac{\pi}{2}$?

c. Explain why $\tan t$ approaches negative infinity as t approaches $\frac{\pi}{2}$ from above. *Hint:* When t is a bit larger than $\frac{\pi}{2}$, is the slope of its terminal side positive or negative?

d. Use parts **b** and **c** to show that the range of the tangent function is the set of all real numbers.

61. The figure below shows an angle of t radians. Use trigonometric functions to write the coordinates of point P in terms of r and t.

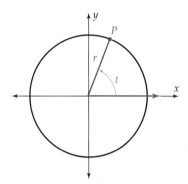

62. Complete the following table by writing each value as a fraction with denominator 2 and a radical in the numerator. You may find the resulting pattern an easy way to remember these function values.

t	0	$\dfrac{\pi}{6}$	$\dfrac{\pi}{4}$	$\dfrac{\pi}{3}$	$\dfrac{\pi}{2}$
$\sin t$	$\dfrac{\sqrt{?}}{2}$	$\dfrac{\sqrt{?}}{2}$	$\dfrac{\sqrt{?}}{2}$	$\dfrac{\sqrt{?}}{2}$	$\dfrac{\sqrt{?}}{2}$
$\cos t$	$\dfrac{\sqrt{?}}{2}$	$\dfrac{\sqrt{?}}{2}$	$\dfrac{\sqrt{?}}{2}$	$\dfrac{\sqrt{?}}{2}$	$\dfrac{\sqrt{?}}{2}$

63. Find the domain and range of the cosecant function.

64. Find the domain and range of the secant function.

65. Find the domain and range of the cotangent function.

66. *Critical Thinking* Using only the definition and no calculator, determine which number is larger: $\sin(\cos 0)$ or $\cos(\sin 0)$.

6.5 **Basic Trigonometric Identities**

Objectives

- Develop basic trigonometric identities

NOTE TI-83 and HP-38 automatically insert an opening parenthesis when a trigonometric function key is pushed. The display cos(5 + 3) is interpreted as cos(5 + 3). If you want cos 5 + 3, you must insert a parenthesis after the 5: cos(5) + 3 .

Technology Tip

Calculators do not use the convention of writing an exponent between the trigonometric function and its argument. In order to obtain $\sin^3 4$, you must enter sin (4)^3.

The algebra of trigonometric functions is just like that of other functions. They may be added, subtracted, composed, etc. However, two notational conventions are normally used with trigonometric functions.

Parentheses can be omitted whenever no confusion can result.

Figure 6.5-1 shows, however, that parentheses *are* needed to distinguish

$$\cos(t + 3) \qquad \text{and} \qquad \cos t + 3.$$

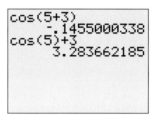

Figure 6.5-1

When dealing with powers of trigonometric functions,

exponents (other than −1) are written between the function symbol and the variable.

For example,

$$(\cos t)^3 \qquad \text{is written} \qquad \cos^3 t.$$

Furthermore,

$$\sin t^3 \qquad \text{means } \sin(t^3) \qquad \textit{not } (\sin t)^3 \text{ or } \sin^3 t,$$

as illustrated in Figure 6.5-2.

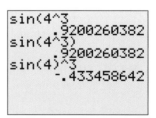

Figure 6.5-2

Identities

Trigonometric functions have numerous relationships that can be expressed as *identities*. An **identity** is an equation that is true for all values of the variables for which every term of the equation is defined. For example,

$$(a + b)^2 = a^2 + 2ab + b^2$$

is an identity because it is true for all possible values of a and b.

The unit circle description of trigonometric functions (see the box on page 446) leads to the following **quotient identities.**

Quotient Identities

$$\tan t = \frac{\sin t}{\cos t} \qquad \cot t = \frac{\cos t}{\sin t}$$

Example 1 Quotient Identities

Simplify the expression below.

$$\tan t \cos t$$

Solution

By the quotient identity,

$$\tan t \cos t = \frac{\sin t}{\cos t} \cos t = \sin t$$

Reciprocal Identities

The **reciprocal identities** follow immediately from the definitions of the trigonometric functions.

Reciprocal Identities

$$\sin t = \frac{1}{\csc t} \qquad \cos t = \frac{1}{\sec t} \qquad \tan t = \frac{1}{\cot t}$$

$$\csc t = \frac{1}{\sin t} \qquad \sec t = \frac{1}{\cos t} \qquad \cot t = \frac{1}{\tan t}$$

CAUTION

An identity may not be true for a value of the variable that makes a term of the equation undefined. For example, if $t = 0$, then $\tan t = 0$ while $\cot t$ is undefined.

Thus, $\tan t \neq \frac{1}{\cot t}$ for $t = 0$.

Example 2 Reciprocal Identities

Given that $\sin t = 0.28$ and $\cos t = 0.96$, find $\csc t$ and $\sec t$.

Solution

By the reciprocal identities,

$$\csc t = \frac{1}{\sin t} = \frac{1}{0.28} \approx 3.57 \qquad \sec t = \frac{1}{\cos t} = \frac{1}{0.96} \approx 1.04$$

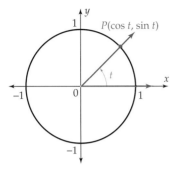

Figure 6.5-3

Pythagorean Identities

For any real number t, the coordinates of the point P where the terminal side of an angle of t radians meets the unit circle are $(\cos t, \sin t)$, as shown in Figure 6.5-3. Since P is on the unit circle, its coordinates must satisfy $x^2 + y^2 = 1$, which is the equation of the unit circle. That is,

$$\cos^2 t + \sin^2 t = 1$$

This identity, which is usually written $\sin^2 t + \cos^2 t = 1$, is called the **Pythagorean identity.** It can be used as follows to derive two other identities, which are also called **Pythagorean identities.**

$$\sin^2 t + \cos^2 t = 1$$
$$\frac{\sin^2 t}{\cos^2 t} + \frac{\cos^2 t}{\cos^2 t} = \frac{1}{\cos^2 t} \qquad \textit{Divide by } \cos^2 t$$
$$\tan^2 t + 1 = \sec^2 t \qquad \textit{Simplify}$$

Similarly, dividing both sides of $\sin^2 t + \cos^2 t = 1$ by $\sin^2 t$ shows that

$$1 + \cot^2 t = \csc^2 t$$

Pythagorean Identities

$$\sin^2 t + \cos^2 t = 1$$
$$\tan^2 t + 1 = \sec^2 t$$
$$1 + \cot^2 t = \csc^2 t$$

In addition to the version shown above, the following forms of the Pythagorean identity are also commonly used.

$$\sin^2 t = 1 - \cos^2 t$$
$$\cos^2 t = 1 - \sin^2 t$$

Example 3   Pythagorean Identities

Simplify the expression below.

$$\tan^2 t \cos^2 t + \cos^2 t$$

Solution

By the quotient and Pythagorean identities,

$$\tan^2 t \cos^2 t + \cos^2 t = \frac{\sin^2 t}{\cos^2 t} \cos^2 t + \cos^2 t = \sin^2 t + \cos^2 t = 1$$

Periodicity Identities

Let t be any real number. Construct two angles in standard position of measure t and $t + 2\pi$ radians, as shown in Figure 6.5-4. Since both of these angles have the same terminal side, the point P where the terminal side intersects the unit circle is the same for both angles.

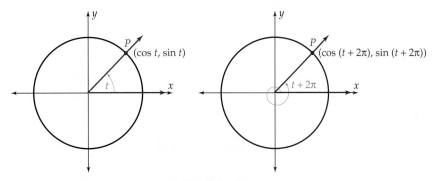

Figure 6.5-4

In both cases, the sine is the y-coordinate of P, so

$$\sin t = \sin(t + 2\pi)$$

In addition, the terminal side of the angle is the same for measures of t, $t \pm 2\pi$, $t \pm 4\pi$, $t \pm 6\pi$, and so on. Thus,

$$\sin t = \sin(t \pm 2\pi) = \sin(t \pm 4\pi) = \sin(t \pm 6\pi) = \ldots$$

Similarly in both cases, the cosine is the x-coordinate of P, so

$$\cos t = \cos(t \pm 2\pi) = \cos(t \pm 4\pi) = \cos(t \pm 6\pi) = \ldots$$

The identities above show that sine and cosine functions repeat their values at regular intervals. Such functions are called *periodic*. A function is said to be **periodic** if there exists some constant k such that

$$f(t) = f(t + k)$$

for every number t in the domain of f. The smallest value of k that has this property is called the **period** of the function f.

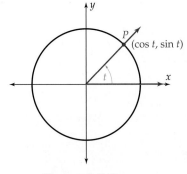

Figure 6.5-5

Since the tangent function is the quotient of the sine and cosine functions, it must also be true that $\tan t = \tan(t + 2\pi)$. However, there is a number smaller than 2π that has this property. Figure 6.5-5 shows the angles t and $t + \pi$. A rotation of π radians is the same as a rotation of $180°$, so the image of the point (x, y) is $(-x, -y)$. Thus,

$$\tan(t + \pi) = \frac{-y}{-x} = \frac{y}{x} = \tan t$$

Graphing Exploration ●

Use your calculator to verify the following:

$$\sin 3 = \sin(3 + 2\pi) = \sin(3 - 4\pi)$$
$$\cos 4 = \cos(4 + 2\pi) = \cos(4 + 6\pi)$$
$$\tan 1 = \tan(1 + \pi) = \tan(1 - 5\pi)$$

Periodicity Identities

> The sine and cosine functions are periodic with period 2π. For every real number t,
>
> $$\sin t = \sin(t \pm 2\pi) \quad \text{and} \quad \cos t = \cos(t \pm 2\pi)$$
>
> The tangent function is periodic with period π. For every number t in the domain of the tangent function,
>
> $$\tan t = \tan(t \pm \pi)$$

Example 4 Periodicity Identities

Find the exact value of $\sin \dfrac{13\pi}{6}$.

Solution

By the periodicity identity for sine,

$$\sin \frac{13\pi}{6} = \sin \left(\frac{\pi}{6} + \frac{12\pi}{6} \right) = \sin \left(\frac{\pi}{6} + 2\pi \right) = \sin \frac{\pi}{6} = \frac{1}{2}$$

Negative Angle Identities

Let t be any real number and construct two angles in standard position of measure t and $-t$ radians, as shown in Figure 6.5-6.

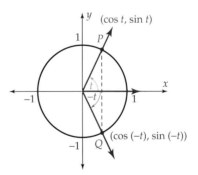

Figure 6.5-6

Since the point Q is the reflection of the point P across the x-axis, the x-coordinates of P and Q are the same, and the y-coordinates are opposites of each other. Thus,

$$\cos t = \cos(-t) \quad \text{and} \quad \sin t = -\sin(-t)$$

Also,

$$\tan(-t) = \frac{\sin(-t)}{\cos(-t)} = \frac{-\sin t}{\cos t} = -\frac{\sin t}{\cos t} = -\tan t$$

Negative Angle Identities

$$\sin t = -\sin(-t)$$
$$\cos t = \cos(-t)$$
$$\tan t = -\tan(-t)$$

Example 5   Negative Angle Identities

Find the exact value of $\sin\left(-\dfrac{\pi}{6}\right)$ and of $\cos\left(-\dfrac{\pi}{6}\right)$.

Solution

By the negative angle identities,

$$\sin\left(-\frac{\pi}{6}\right) = -\sin\frac{\pi}{6} = -\frac{1}{2} \qquad \text{and} \qquad \cos\left(-\frac{\pi}{6}\right) = \cos\frac{\pi}{6} = \frac{\sqrt{3}}{2}$$

Other Identities

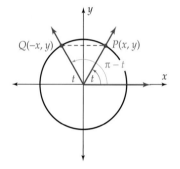

Figure 6.5-7

Let t be any real number. Figure 6.5-7 shows the angles of t and $\pi - t$ radians in standard position. The terminal side of the angle of t radians meets the unit circle at P, and the terminal side of the angle of $\pi - t$ radians meets the unit circle at Q. Congruent triangles can be used to prove what the figure illustrates:

The y-coordinates of P and Q are the same, and their x-coordinates are opposites.

This leads to the following identities.

Identities Involving $\pi - t$

$$\sin t = \sin(\pi - t)$$
$$\cos t = -\cos(\pi - t)$$
$$\tan t = -\tan(\pi - t)$$

Example 6   Identities Involving $\pi - t$

Find the exact value of $\sin\left(\dfrac{5\pi}{6}\right)$.

Solution

By the identity $\sin t = \sin(\pi - t)$,

$$\sin\left(\frac{5\pi}{6}\right) = \sin\left(\frac{6\pi}{6} - \frac{\pi}{6}\right) = \sin\left(\pi - \frac{\pi}{6}\right) = \sin\left(\frac{\pi}{6}\right) = \frac{1}{2}$$

NOTE The identity $\sin t = \sin(\pi - t)$ is used in solving basic trigonometric equations. (See Section 8.3.)

Summary of Identities

Quotient Identities:

$$\tan t = \frac{\sin t}{\cos t} \qquad \cot t = \frac{\cos t}{\sin t}$$

Reciprocal Identities:

$$\sin t = \frac{1}{\csc t} \qquad \cos t = \frac{1}{\sec t} \qquad \tan t = \frac{1}{\cot t}$$

$$\csc t = \frac{1}{\sin t} \qquad \sec t = \frac{1}{\cos t} \qquad \cot t = \frac{1}{\tan t}$$

Pythagorean Identities:

$$\sin^2 t + \cos^2 t = 1 \qquad \tan^2 t + 1 = \sec^2 t \qquad 1 + \cot^2 t = \csc^2 t$$

Periodicity Identities:

$$\sin (t \pm 2\pi) = \sin t \quad \cos(t \pm 2\pi) = \cos t \quad \tan(t \pm \pi) = \tan t$$

Negative Angle Identities:

$$\sin (-t) = -\sin t \qquad \cos(-t) = \cos t \qquad \tan (-t) = -\tan t$$

Identities Involving $\pi - t$:

$$\sin t = \sin(\pi - t) \quad \cos t = -\cos(\pi - t) \quad \tan t = -\tan(\pi - t)$$

Exercises 6.5

In Exercises 1–4, use the quotient and reciprocal identities to simplify the given expression.

1. $\cot t \sin t$

2. $\tan t \cot t$

3. $\csc t \sin t$

4. $\cot t \sec t$

In Exercises 5–8, use the Pythagorean identities to simplify the given expression.

5. $\sin^2 t + \cot^2 t \sin^2 t$

6. $1 - \sec^2 t$

7. $\dfrac{\csc^2 t - \cot^2 t}{\sin^2 t}$

8. $\dfrac{\sin^2 t - \cos^2 t \sin^2 t}{\sin^2 t}$

In Exercises 9–14, the value of one trigonometric function is given for $0 < t < \dfrac{\pi}{2}$. Use quotient, reciprocal, and Pythagorean identities to find the values of the remaining five trigonometric functions. Round your answers to four decimal places.

9. $\sin t = 0.3251$

10. $\cos t = 0.4167$

11. $\tan t = 3.6294$

12. $\sec t = 2.5846$

13. $\csc t = 6.2474$

14. $\cot t = 1.8479$

In Exercises 15–25, use basic identities and algebra to simplify the expression. Assume all denominators are nonzero.

15. $(\sin t + \cos t)(\sin t - \cos t)$

16. $(\sin t - \cos t)^2$

17. $\dfrac{\sin t}{\tan t}$

18. $(\tan t + 2)(\tan t - 3) - (6 - \tan t) + 2 \tan t$

19. $\left(\dfrac{4 \cos^2 t}{\sin^2 t}\right)\left(\dfrac{\sin t}{4 \cos t}\right)^2$

20. $\dfrac{5\cos t}{\sin^2 t} \cdot \dfrac{\sin^2 t - \sin t \cos t}{\sin^2 t - \cos^2 t}$

21. $\dfrac{\cos^2 t + 4\cos t + 4}{\cos t + 2}$

22. $\dfrac{\sin^2 t - 2\sin t + 1}{\sin t - 1}$

23. $\dfrac{1}{\cos t} - \sin t \tan t$

24. $\dfrac{1 - \tan^2 t}{1 + \tan^2 t} + 2\sin^2 t$

25. $\sqrt{\sin^3 t \cos t} \cdot \sqrt{\cos t}$

Recall that a function is even if

$$f(x) = f(-x)$$

and a function is odd if

$$f(-x) = -f(x)$$

for every value of x in the domain of f. In Exercises 26–32, use the negative angle identities to determine whether the function is even, odd, or neither.

26. $f(t) = \sin t$ **27.** $f(t) = \cos t$

28. $f(t) = \tan t$ **29.** $f(t) = \sec t$

30. $f(t) = t \sin t$ **31.** $f(t) = t + \tan t$

32. $f(t) = t + \cos t$

In Exercises 33–36, use the Pythagorean identities to find $\sin t$ for the given value of $\cos t$. Make sure that the sign is correct for the given quadrant.

33. $\cos t = -0.5$ $\pi < t < \dfrac{3\pi}{2}$

34. $\cos t = -\dfrac{3}{\sqrt{10}}$ $\dfrac{\pi}{2} < t < \pi$

35. $\cos t = \dfrac{1}{2}$ $0 < t < \dfrac{\pi}{2}$

36. $\cos t = \dfrac{2}{\sqrt{5}}$ $\dfrac{3\pi}{2} < t < 2\pi$

In Exercises 37–44, $\sin t = \dfrac{3}{5}$ and $0 < t < \dfrac{\pi}{2}$. Use basic identities and the signs of the trigonometric functions in each quadrant to find each value.

37. $\sin(-t)$ **38.** $\sin(t + 10\pi)$

39. $\sin(2\pi - t)$ **40.** $\cos t$

41. $\tan t$ **42.** $\cos(-t)$

43. $\tan(2\pi - t)$ **44.** $\sin(\pi - t)$

In Exercises 45–50, $\cos t = -\dfrac{2}{5}$ and $\pi < t < \dfrac{3\pi}{2}$. Use basic identities and the signs of the trigonometric functions in each quadrant to find each value.

45. $\sin t$ **46.** $\tan t$

47. $\cos(2\pi - t)$ **48.** $\cos(-t)$

49. $\sin(4\pi + t)$ **50.** $\tan(4\pi - t)$

In Exercises 51–54, it is given that

$$\sin \frac{\pi}{8} = \frac{\sqrt{2 - \sqrt{2}}}{2}$$

Use basic identities to find each value.

51. $\cos \dfrac{\pi}{8}$ **52.** $\tan \dfrac{\pi}{8}$

53. $\sin \dfrac{17\pi}{8}$ **54.** $\tan \dfrac{-15\pi}{8}$

In Exercises 55–60, use the Pythagorean identities to determine if it is possible for a number t to satisfy the given conditions.

55. $\sin t = \dfrac{5}{13}$ and $\cos t = \dfrac{12}{13}$

56. $\sin t = -2$ and $\cos t = 1$

57. $\sin t = -1$ and $\cos t = 1$

58. $\sin t = \dfrac{1}{\sqrt{2}}$ and $\cos t = \dfrac{1}{\sqrt{2}}$

59. $\sin t = 1$ and $\tan t = 1$

60. $\cos t = \dfrac{8}{17}$ and $\tan t = \dfrac{15}{8}$

61. Use the periodicity identities for sine, cosine, and tangent to write periodicity identities for cosecant, secant, and cotangent.

62. Use the negative angle identities for sine, cosine, and tangent to write negative angle identities for cosecant, secant, and cotangent.

CHAPTER 6 REVIEW

Important Concepts

Important Facts and Formulas

For a given acute angle θ:

$$\sin\theta = \frac{\text{opposite}}{\text{hypotenuse}} \qquad \cos\theta = \frac{\text{adjacent}}{\text{hypotenuse}} \qquad \tan\theta = \frac{\text{opposite}}{\text{adjacent}}$$

$$\csc\theta = \frac{\text{hypotenuse}}{\text{opposite}} \qquad \sec\theta = \frac{\text{hypotenuse}}{\text{adjacent}} \qquad \cot\theta = \frac{\text{adjacent}}{\text{opposite}}$$

θ	$\sin\theta$	$\cos\theta$	$\tan\theta$	$\csc\theta$	$\sec\theta$	$\cot\theta$
30°	$\frac{1}{2}$	$\frac{\sqrt{3}}{2}$	$\frac{\sqrt{3}}{3}$	2	$\frac{2\sqrt{3}}{3}$	$\sqrt{3}$
60°	$\frac{\sqrt{3}}{2}$	$\frac{1}{2}$	$\sqrt{3}$	$\frac{2\sqrt{3}}{3}$	2	$\frac{\sqrt{3}}{3}$
45°	$\frac{\sqrt{2}}{2}$	$\frac{\sqrt{2}}{2}$	1	$\sqrt{2}$	$\sqrt{2}$	1

To convert radians to degrees, multiply by $\frac{180}{\pi}$.

To convert degrees to radians, multiply by $\frac{\pi}{180}$.

Quotient Identities:

$$\tan t = \frac{\sin t}{\cos t} \qquad \cot t = \frac{\cos t}{\sin t}$$

Reciprocal Identities:

$$\sin t = \frac{1}{\csc t} \qquad \cos t = \frac{1}{\sec t} \qquad \tan t = \frac{1}{\cot t}$$

$$\csc t = \frac{1}{\sin t} \qquad \sec t = \frac{1}{\cos t} \qquad \cot t = \frac{1}{\tan t}$$

Pythagorean Identities:

$$\sin^2 t + \cos^2 t = 1 \qquad \tan^2 + 1 = \sec^2 t \qquad 1 + \cot^2 t = \sec^2 t$$

**Important Facts
and Formulas**

Periodicity Identities:

$$\sin(t \pm 2\pi) = \sin t \qquad \cos(t \pm 2\pi) = \cos t \qquad \tan(t \pm \pi) = \tan t$$

Negative Angle Identities:

$$\sin(-t) = -\sin t \qquad \cos(-t) = \cos t \qquad \tan(-t) = -\tan(t)$$

Identities Involving $\pi - t$:

$$\sin t = \sin(\pi - t) \qquad \cos t = -\cos(\pi - t) \qquad \tan t = -\tan(\pi - t)$$

Review Exercises

Section 6.1

1. Write $41° 6' 54''$ in decimal form.

2. Write $10.5625°$ in DMS form.

3. Which of the following statements about the angle θ is true?

a. $\sin \theta = \dfrac{3}{4}$ **b.** $\cos \theta = \dfrac{5}{4}$

c. $\tan \theta = \dfrac{3}{5}$ **d.** $\sin \theta = \dfrac{4}{5}$

e. $\sin \theta = \dfrac{4}{3}$

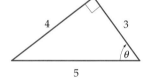

In Exercises 4–9, use the right triangle in the figure to find each ratio.

4. $\sin \theta$ **5.** $\cos \theta$ **6.** $\tan \theta$

7. $\csc \theta$ **8.** $\sec \theta$ **9.** $\cot \theta$

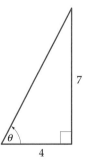

10. Find the length of side h in the triangle, given that angle A measures $40°$ and the distance from C to A is 25.

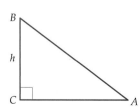

Section 6.2

In Exercises 11–14, solve triangle *ABC*.

11. $A = 40°$ $b = 10$

12. $C = 35°$ $a = 12$

13. $A = 56°$ $a = 11$

14. $a = 3$ $c = 3$

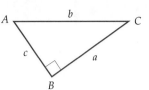

15. From a point on level ground 145 feet from the base of a tower, the angle of elevation to the top of the tower is 57.3°. How high is the tower?

16. A pilot in a plane at an altitude of 22,000 feet observes that the angle of depression to a nearby airport is 26°. How many miles is the airport from the point on the ground directly below the plane?

17. A lighthouse keeper 100 feet above the water sees a boat sailing in a straight line directly toward her. As she watches, the angle of depression to the boat changes from 25° to 40°. How far has the boat traveled during this time?

Section 6.3

18. $\dfrac{9\pi}{5}$ radians = ___?___ degrees

19. $\dfrac{17\pi}{12}$ radians = ___?___ degrees

20. $-\dfrac{11\pi}{4}$ radians = ___?___ degrees

21. $36° = $ ___?___ radians

22. $220° = $ ___?___ radians

23. $-135° = $ ___?___ radians

24. Find a number θ between 0 and 2π such that an angle of θ radians in standard position is coterminal with an angle of $-\dfrac{23\pi}{3}$ radians in standard position.

25. Through how many radians does the second hand of a clock move in 2 minutes and 40 seconds?

26. 10 revolutions per minute = ___?___ radians per minute

27. 4π radians per minute = ___?___ revolutions per minute

Section 6.4

28. If the terminal side of an angle of t radians in standard position passes through the point $(-2, 3)$, then $\tan t = $ ___?___ .

29. If the terminal side of an angle of t radians in standard position passes through the point $(6, -8)$, then $\cos t = $ ___?___ .

30. If the terminal side of an angle of t radians in standard position passes through the point $(1.2, 3.5)$, then $\sin t = $ ___?___ .

In Exercises 31–42, give the exact values.

31. $\cos \dfrac{47\pi}{2}$

32. $\sin(-13\pi)$

33. $\sin \dfrac{7\pi}{6}$

34. $\cos \dfrac{3\pi}{4}$

35. $\tan \dfrac{8\pi}{3}$

36. $\sin\left(-\dfrac{7\pi}{4}\right)$

37. $\cot \dfrac{4\pi}{3}$ \hspace{2em} **38.** $\cos\left(-\dfrac{\pi}{6}\right)$ \hspace{2em} **39.** $\sec \dfrac{2\pi}{3}$

40. $\sin\left(-\dfrac{11\pi}{6}\right)$ \hspace{2em} **41.** $\sin \dfrac{\pi}{3}$ \hspace{2em} **42.** $\csc \dfrac{5\pi}{2}$

43. The value of $\cos t$ is negative when the terminal side of an angle of t radians in standard position lies in which quadrants?

In Exercises 44–46, express as a single real number (no decimal approximations allowed).

44. $\cos \dfrac{3\pi}{4} \sin \dfrac{5\pi}{6} - \sin \dfrac{3\pi}{4} \cos \dfrac{5\pi}{6}$ \hspace{2em} **45.** $\left(\sin \dfrac{\pi}{6} + 1\right)^2$

46. $\sin\left(\dfrac{\pi}{2}\right) + \sin 0 + \cos 0$

Section 6.5

47. Write $\dfrac{\tan t}{\cot t}$ entirely in terms of $\sin t$ and $\cos t$, then simplify.

48. $\left[3 \sin\left(\dfrac{\pi}{5^{500}}\right)\right]^2 + \left[3 \cos\left(\dfrac{\pi}{5^{500}}\right)\right]^2 = ?$

49. Which of the following could possibly be a true statement about a real number t?
 a. $\sin t = -2$ and $\cos t = 1$
 b. $\sin t = \dfrac{1}{2}$ and $\cos t = \dfrac{\sqrt{2}}{2}$
 c. $\sin t = -1$ and $\cos t = 1$
 d. $\sin t = \dfrac{\pi}{2}$ and $\cos t = 1 - \dfrac{\pi}{2}$
 e. $\sin t = \dfrac{3}{5}$ and $\cos t = \dfrac{4}{5}$

50. If $\dfrac{\pi}{2} < t < \pi$ and $\sin t = \dfrac{5}{13}$, then $\cos t = ?$

51. If $\sin t = -\dfrac{4}{5}$ and the terminal side of an angle of t radians in standard position lies in the third quadrant, then $\cos t = $ __?__ .

52. Simplify $\dfrac{\tan (t + \pi)}{\sin (t + 2\pi)}$.

53. If $\sin\left(-\dfrac{101\pi}{2}\right) = -1$, then $\sin\left(-\dfrac{105\pi}{2}\right) = ?$

54. Which of the statements **(i)**–**(iii)** are true?
 (i) $\sin (-x) = -\sin x$
 (ii) $\cos (-x) = -\cos x$
 (iii) $\tan (-x) = -\tan x$
 a. **(i)** and **(ii)** only
 b. **(ii)** only
 c. **(i)** and **(iii)** only
 d. all of them
 e. none of them

55. Suppose θ is a real number. Consider the right triangle with sides as shown in the figure. Then:

   a. $x = 1$
   b. $x = 2$
   c. $x = 4$
   d. $x = 2(\cos \theta + \sin \theta)$
   e. none of the above

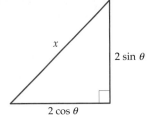

56. Determine the following segment lengths in terms of a single trigonometric function of t.

   a. OR **b.** PR **c.** SQ **d.** OQ

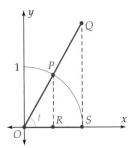

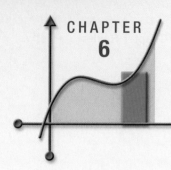

can do calculus
Optimization with Trigonometry

Optimization problems involve finding a solution that is either a maximum or a minimum value of a function. Calculus is needed to find exact solutions to most optimization problems, but tables or graphs can often be used to find approximate solutions.

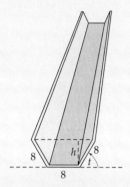

Figure 6.C-1

Example 1 Maximum Area

A gutter is to be made from a strip of metal 24 inches wide by bending up the sides to form a trapezoid, as shown in Figure 6.C-1.

a. Express the area of the cross-section of the gutter as a function of the angle t.

b. For what value of t will this area be as large as possible?

Solution

a. The cross-section of the gutter is a trapezoid, shown in Figure 6.C-2.

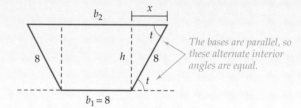

The bases are parallel, so these alternate interior angles are equal.

Figure 6.C-2

The area of a trapezoid is $\dfrac{h(b_1 + b_2)}{2}$.

The top base $b_2 = 8 + 2x$, where
$$\cos t = \frac{x}{8}.$$
So $x = 8 \cos t$.

The height is h, where
$$\sin t = \frac{h}{8}.$$
So $h = 8 \sin t$.

Thus, the area of the cross-section is

$$A = \frac{8 \sin t(8 + 8 + 2(8 \cos t))}{2} = 4 \sin t(16 + 16 \cos t) = 64 \sin t(1 + \cos t).$$

b. To find the value of t that makes the area be as large as possible, first notice that t must be between 0 and $\dfrac{\pi}{2} \approx 1.57$. By examining a table of values, it is possible to estimate the maximum value of A over this interval.

A good starting interval for the table is $\frac{\pi}{12} \approx 0.26$. The table in Figure 6.C-3 shows the highest value at about 1.05, or $\frac{4\pi}{12} = \frac{\pi}{3}$.

Figure 6.C-3

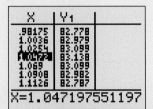

Figure 6.C-4

It is possible to confirm this value or get a better estimate by using a table with a smaller step size, such as $\frac{\pi}{144} \approx 0.02$. Figure 6.C-4 confirms that $\frac{\pi}{3}$ appears to be the value of t that corresponds to the largest area, about 83.1 in^2.

Example 2   Maximum Length

Two corridors meet at a right angle. One corridor is 6 ft wide, and the other is 8 ft wide. A ladder is being carried horizontally along the corridor. What is the maximum length of a ladder that can fit around the corner?

Solution

The length of the longest ladder that fits around the corner is the same as the *shortest* length of the red segment in Figure 6.C-5 as it pivots about the corner. Let the part of the segment from the corner to the opposite wall of the 6-ft corridor be d_1, and the part to the wall of the 8-ft corridor be d_2. Then the desired length is $d_1 + d_2$.

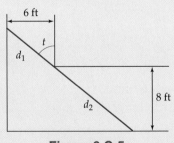

Figure 6.C-5

For the angle t in Figure 6.C-5,

$$\sin t = \frac{6}{d_1} \qquad\qquad \sin\left(\frac{\pi}{2} - t\right) = \frac{8}{d_2}$$

$$d_1 = \frac{6}{\sin t} \qquad\qquad d_2 = \frac{8}{\sin\left(\frac{\pi}{2} - t\right)}$$

The function that describes the desired length is $L = \dfrac{6}{\sin t} + \dfrac{8}{\sin\left(\frac{\pi}{2} - t\right)}$.

To find the minimum of the function, note that t is between 0 and $\frac{\pi}{2}$. Construct a table with an increment of $\frac{\pi}{12}$, then use the minimum value to construct a table with an increment of $\frac{\pi}{144}$. The minimum appears to be at $t \approx 0.74$, which corresponds to a length of about 19.7 ft.

Figure 6.C-6

In Examples 1 and 2, an area and a length were represented in terms of an angle to find the optimal solution. In the following example, the angle is the quantity to be maximized.

Example 3   Maximum Viewing Angle

The best view of a statue is where the viewing angle is a maximum. In Figure 6.C-7, the height of the statue is 24 ft and the height of the pedestal is 8 ft. Find the distance from the statue where the viewing angle is optimal.

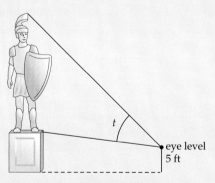

Figure 6.C-7

Solution

In Figure 6.C-8, the angle $t = t_1 - t_2$. The important quantities are opposite and adjacent to the angles, so the tangent function is used to describe the relationship.

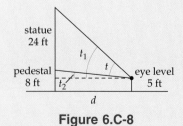

Figure 6.C-8

$$\tan t_1 = \frac{27}{d} \qquad\qquad \tan t_2 = \frac{3}{d}$$

$$t_1 = \tan^{-1}\frac{27}{d} \qquad\qquad t_2 = \tan^{-1}\frac{3}{d}$$

$$t = \tan^{-1}\frac{27}{d} - \tan^{-1}\frac{3}{d}$$

To create a table, first notice that $d > 0$. Start with a large increment, such as 5 ft, and narrow the increment to refine your estimate, as shown in Figure 6.C-9.

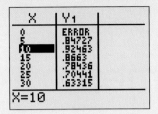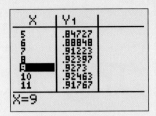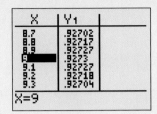

Figure 6.C-9

The best distance to view the statue is at about 9 ft away. The viewing angle at this distance is about 0.93 radians, which is about 53°.

Exercises

Estimate the maximum value of the given function between 0 and $\frac{\pi}{2}$ by using tables with increments of $\frac{\pi}{12}$ and $\frac{\pi}{144}$.

1. $f(t) = \sin t \cos t$

2. $f(t) = \sin t + 2 \cos t$

3. $f(t) = 3 \sin t + \sin\left(\frac{\pi}{2} - t\right)$

4. $f(t) = 2 \cos t - \dfrac{1}{1 + \sin t}$

5. The cross section of a tunnel is a semicircle with radius 10 meters. The interior walls of the tunnel form a rectangle.

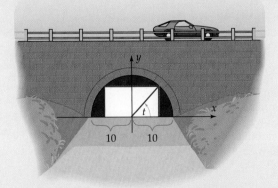

a. Express the area of the rectangular cross-section of the tunnel opening as a function of angle t.

b. For what value of t is the cross-sectional area of the tunnel opening as large as possible? What are the dimensions of the tunnel opening in this case?

6. A 30-ft statue stands on a 10-ft pedestal. Find the best distance to view the statue, assuming eye level is 5 ft (see Example 3).

7. Two towns lie 10 miles apart on opposite sides of a mile-wide straight river, as shown. A road is to be built along one side of the river from town A to point X, then across the river to town B. The cost of building on land is $10,000 per mile, and the cost of building over the water is $20,000 per mile.

a. Express the cost of building the road as a function of the angle t.

b. Find the minimum cost of the road.

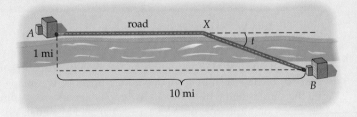

471

CHAPTER 7

Trigonometric Graphs

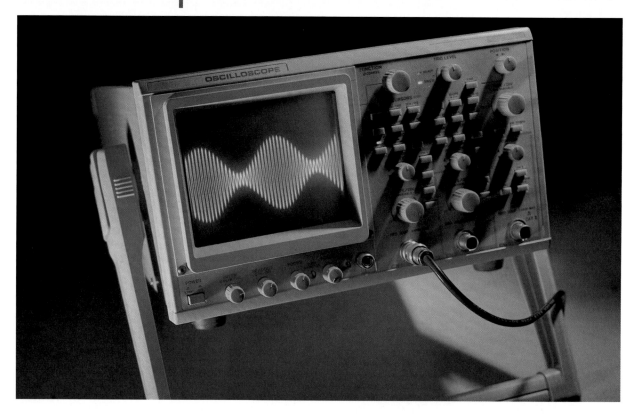

Stay tuned for more!

Radio stations transmit by sending out a signal in the form of an electromagnetic wave that can be described by a trigonometric function. The shape of this signal is modified by the sounds being transmitted. AM radio signals are modified by varying the "height," or amplitude, of the waves, whereas FM signals are modified by varying the frequency of the waves. The signal displayed in the photo is from an AM radio station found at 900 on the broadcast dial. See Exercise 65 of Section 7.3.

Chapter Outline

Interdependence of Sections

$$7.1 \longrightarrow 7.3 \longrightarrow 7.4$$
$$\nearrow 7.2$$

G raphs of trigonometric functions often make it very easy to see the essential properties of these functions, particularly the fact that they repeat their values at regular intervals. Because of the repeating, or periodic, nature of trigonometric functions, they are used to model a variety of phenomena that involve cyclic behavior, such as sound waves, electron orbitals, planetary orbits, radio transmissions, vibrating strings, pendulums, and many more.

7.1   Graphs of the Sine, Cosine, and Tangent Functions

Objectives

- Graph the sine, cosine, and tangent functions

- State all values in the domain of a basic trigonometric function that correspond to a given value of the range

- Graph transformations of the sine, cosine, and tangent graphs

Although a graphing calculator will quickly sketch the graphs of the sine, cosine, and tangent functions, it will not give you much insight into why these graphs have the shapes they do and why these shapes are important. So the emphasis in this section is the connection between the functions' definitions and their graphs.

Using radians and the unit circle, you learned in Chapter 6 that trigonometric functions can be defined as functions of real numbers. Using this definition, you will see that the graphs of trigonometric functions are directly related to angles in the unit circle.

Graph of the Sine Function

Consider an angle of t radians in standard position. Let P be the point where the terminal side of the angle meets the unit circle. Then the y-coordinate of P is the number $\sin t$. As t increases, the graph of $f(t) = \sin t$ can be sketched from the corresponding y-coordinates of P.

473

Change in t	Movement of point P	$\sin t$ (y-coordinate of P)	Corresponding graph
from 0 to $\dfrac{\pi}{2}$	from $(1, 0)$ to $(0, 1)$ 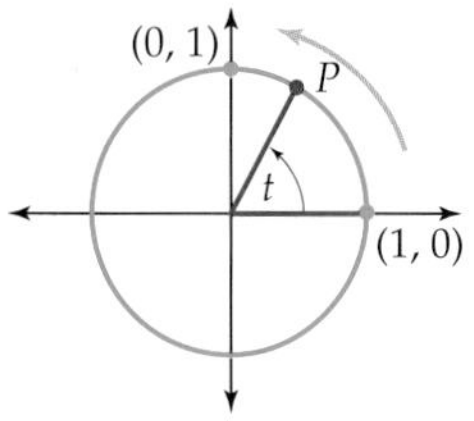	increases from 0 to 1	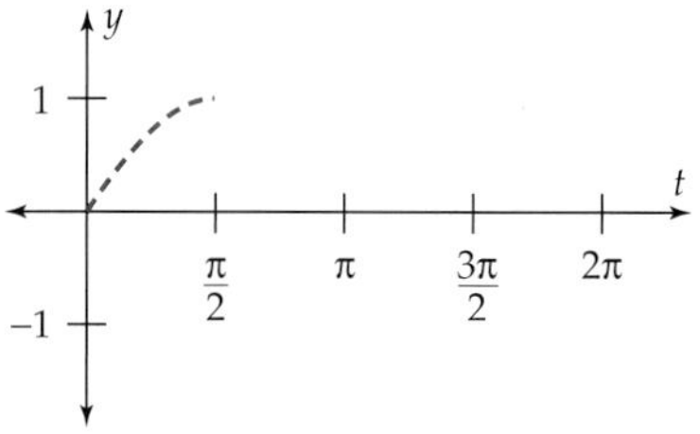
from $\dfrac{\pi}{2}$ to π	from $(0, 1)$ to $(-1, 0)$ 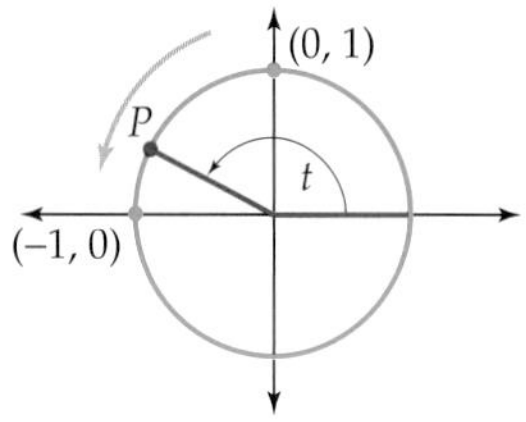	decreases from 1 to 0	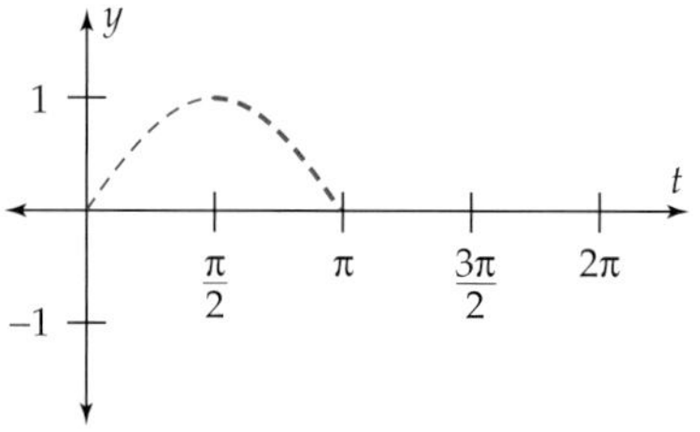
from π to $\dfrac{3\pi}{2}$	from $(-1, 0)$ to $(0, -1)$ 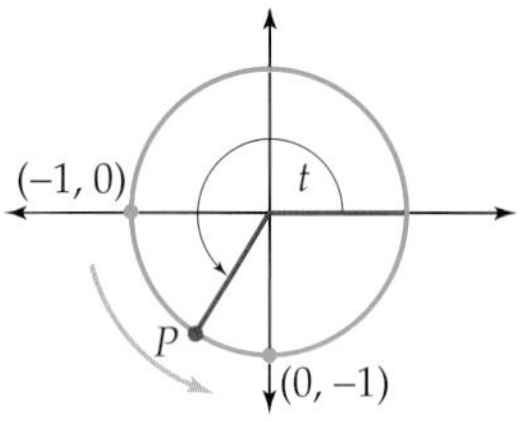	decreases from 0 to -1	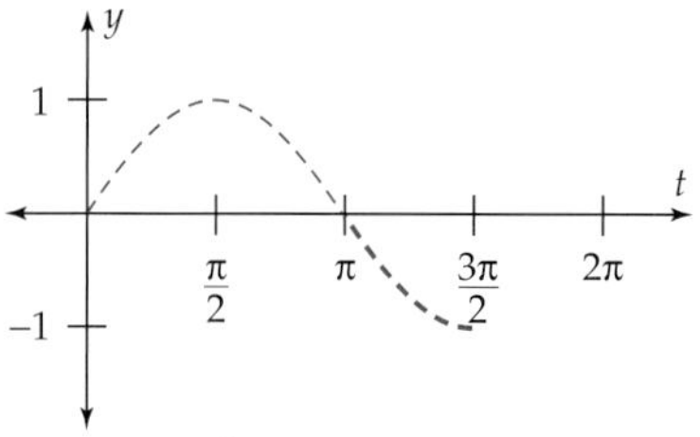
from $\dfrac{3\pi}{2}$ to 2π	from $(0, -1)$ to $(1, 0)$ 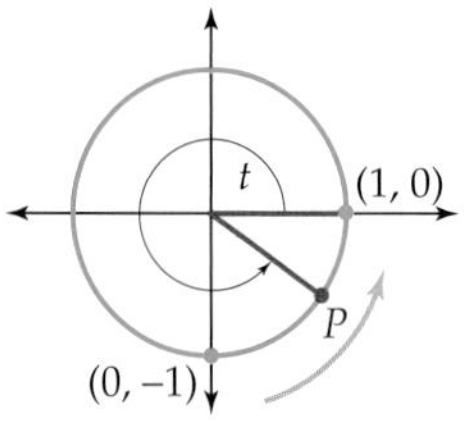	increases from -1 to 0	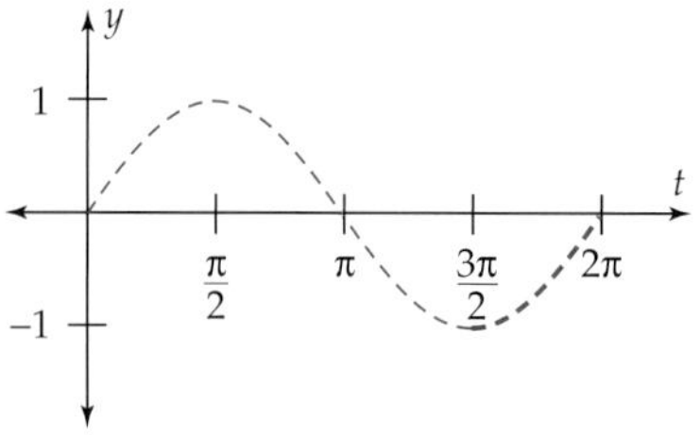

CAUTION

Throughout this chapter, the independent variable used for trigonometric functions will be t to avoid any confusion with the x and y that are part of the definition of these functions. However, using a graphing calculator in function mode, you must enter x as the independent variable.

Your graphing calculator can provide a dynamic view of the graph of the sine function and its relationship to points on the unit circle.

Graphing Exploration ●

With your graphing calculator in parametric mode, set the viewing window as shown below, with a *t*-step of 0.1.

$$0 \le t \le 2\pi \qquad -\frac{\pi}{3} \le x \le 2\pi \qquad -2.5 \le y \le 2.5$$

On the same screen, graph the two functions given below.

$$X_1 = \cos t, Y_1 = \sin t \qquad X_2 = t, Y_2 = \sin t$$

Use the trace feature to move the cursor along the first graph, which is the unit circle. Stop at a point, and note the values of *t* and *y*.

Use the up or down key to move the cursor to the second graph, which is the graph of the sine function. The value of *t* will remain the same. What are the *x*- and *y*-coordinates of this point?

How does the *y*-coordinate of the new point compare with the *y*-coordinate of the original point on the unit circle?

To complete the graph of the sine function, note that as *t* goes from 2π to 4π, the point *P* on the unit circle *retraces* the path it took from 0 to 2π, so *the same curve will repeat* on the graph. This repetition occurs each 2π units along the horizontal axis, therefore the sine function has a period of 2π. That is, for any real number *t*,

$$\sin(t \pm 2\pi) = \sin t.$$

Graph of the Sine Function

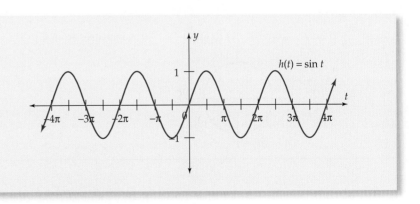

Graph of the Cosine Function

Let *P* be the point where the terminal side of an angle of *t* radians in standard position meets the unit circle. Then the *x*-coordinate of *P* is the number $\cos t$. To obtain the graph of $f(t) = \cos(t)$, the same process as that used for the sine function is followed, except the x-coordinate is observed. The following chart illustrates the graph of the cosine function.

Change in t	Movement of point P	cos t (x-coordinate of P)	Corresponding graph
from 0 to $\frac{\pi}{2}$	from (1, 0) to (0, 1) 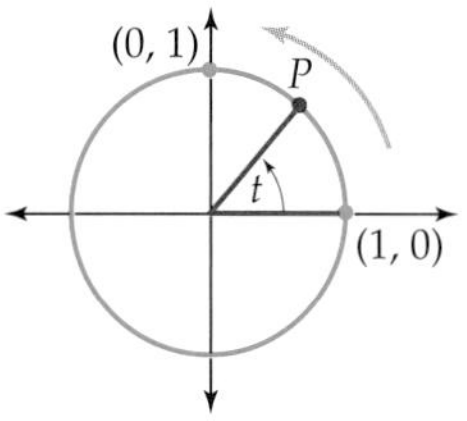	x decreases from 1 to 0	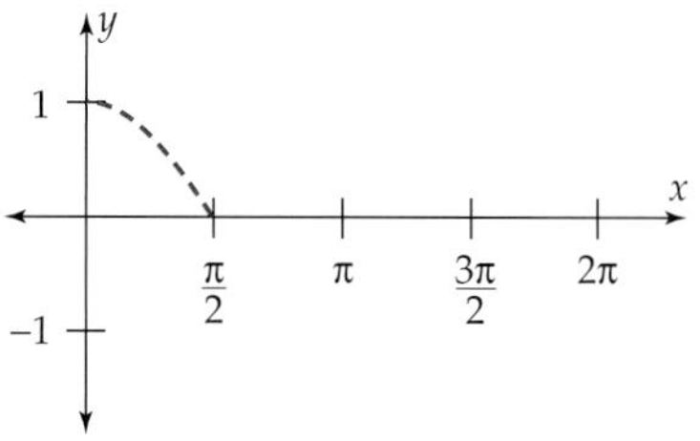
from $\frac{\pi}{2}$ to π	from (0, 1) to (−1, 0) 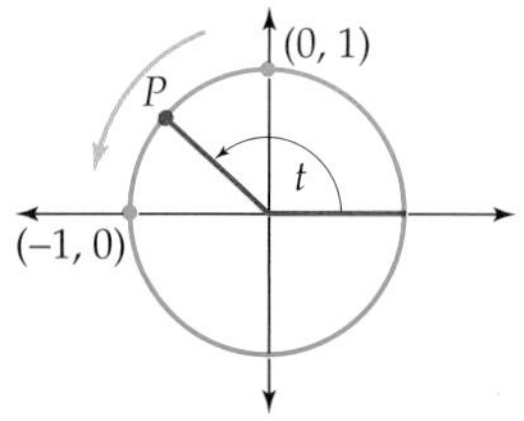	x decreases from 0 to −1	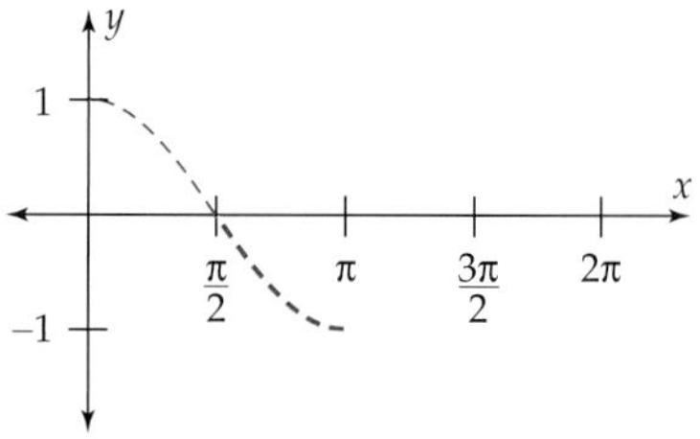
from π to $\frac{3\pi}{2}$	from (−1, 0) to (0, −1) 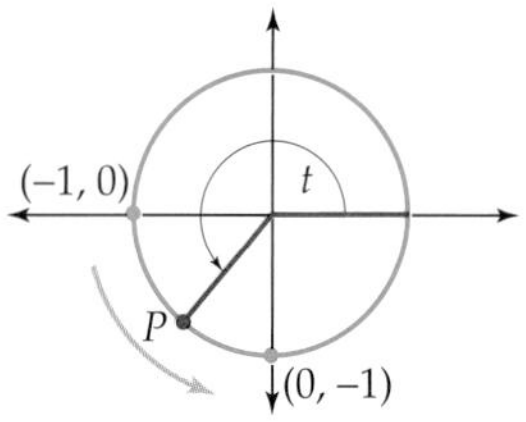	x increases from −1 to 0	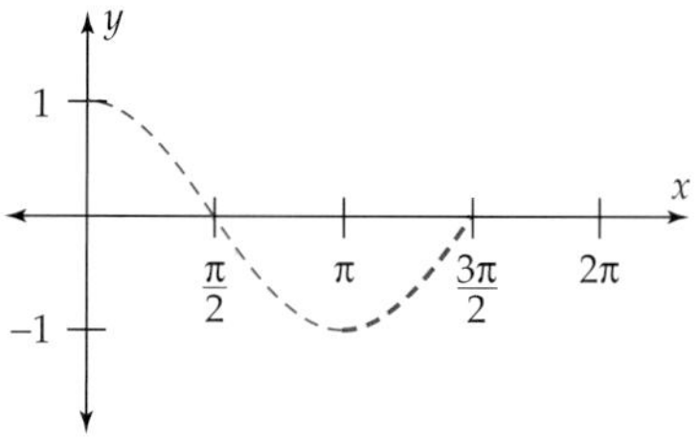
from $\frac{3\pi}{2}$ to 2π	from (0, −1) to (1, 0) 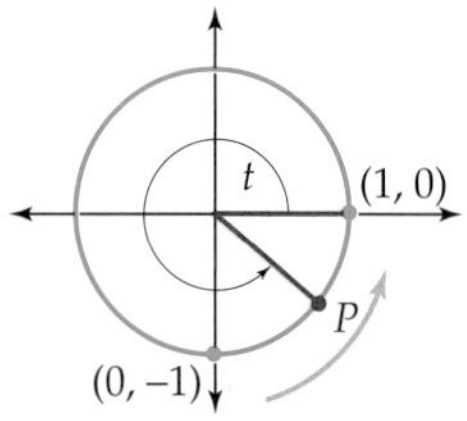	x increases from 0 to 1	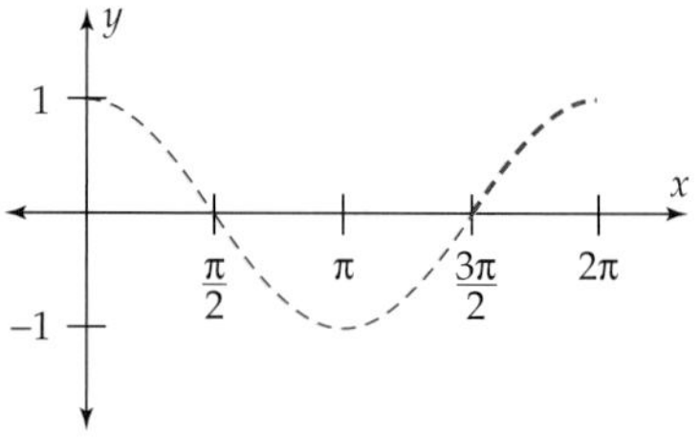

As the value of t increases, the point P on the unit circle *retraces* its path along the unit circle, so the graph of $f(t) = \cos(t)$ repeats the same curve at intervals of length 2π. Because the cosine function also has a period of 2π, for any number t,

$$\cos t = \cos(t \pm 2\pi).$$

Graph of the Cosine Function

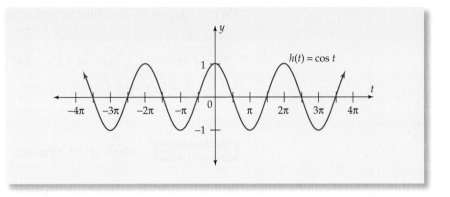

The graphs of the sine and cosine functions visually illustrate two basic facts about these functions. Because the graphs extend infinitely to the right and to the left,

> **the domain of the sine and cosine functions is the set of all real numbers.**

Also, the y-coordinate of every point on these graphs lies between -1 and 1 (inclusive), so that

> **the range of the sine and cosine functions is the interval $[-1, 1]$.**

You can use the period of the function to state all values of t for which $\sin t$ or $\cos t$ is a given number, as shown in Examples 1 and 2.

Example 1   Finding All t-values

State all values of t for which $\sin t$ is -1.

Solution

The sine function oscillates between -1 and 1 and has a period of 2π (i.e., it repeats the pattern every 2π units on the horizontal axis), so there are an *infinite* number of t-values for which $\sin t$ is -1. These points occur every 2π units on the horizontal axis, and a few are highlighted in red on the graph $y = \sin t$ shown in Figure 7.1.1.

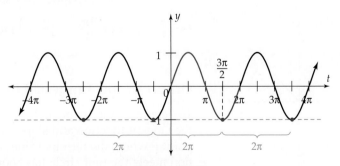

Figure 7.1-1

On the interval $[0, 2\pi)$, highlighted in red on the graph above, the graph of $y = \sin t$ has only one point, $\left(\dfrac{3\pi}{2}, -1\right)$, at which the y-coordinate is -1. Therefore, all values of t for which $\sin t$ is -1 can be expressed as $t = \dfrac{3\pi}{2} + 2k\pi$, where k is any integer.

Example 2   Finding All *t*-values

State all values of t for which $\cos t$ is $\dfrac{1}{2}$.

Solution

The cosine function repeats its pattern of y-values at intervals of 2π, so there are an *infinite* number of t-values for which $\cos t$ is $\dfrac{1}{2}$. The graph of $y = \cos t$ shown in Figure 7.1-2 highlights a few points with a y-coordinate of $\dfrac{1}{2}$.

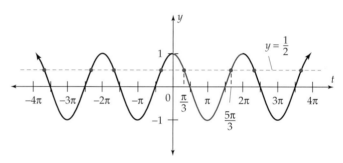

Figure 7.1-2

On the interval $[0, 2\pi)$, highlighted in red on the graph above, the graph of $y = \cos t$ has two points, $\left(\dfrac{\pi}{3}, \dfrac{1}{2}\right)$ and $\left(\dfrac{5\pi}{3}, \dfrac{1}{2}\right)$, at which the y-coordinate is $\dfrac{1}{2}$. Therefore, all values of t for which $\cos t$ is $\dfrac{1}{2}$ can be expressed as $t = \dfrac{\pi}{3} + 2k\pi$ or $\dfrac{5\pi}{3} + 2k\pi$, where k is any integer.

Graph of the Tangent Function

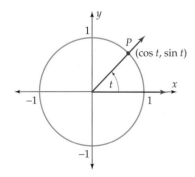

Figure 7.1-3

To determine the shape of the graph of $f(t) = \tan t$, a connection between the tangent function and slope can be used. As shown in Figure 7.1-3, the point P where the terminal side of an angle of t radians in standard position meets the unit circle has coordinates $(\cos t, \sin t)$. This point and the point $(0, 0)$ can be used to compute the *slope* of the line containing the terminal side.

$$\text{slope} = \frac{\sin t - 0}{\cos t - 0} = \frac{\sin t}{\cos t} = \tan t$$

The graph of $f(t) = \tan t$ can be sketched by noting the slope of the terminal side of an angle of t radians, as t takes different values.

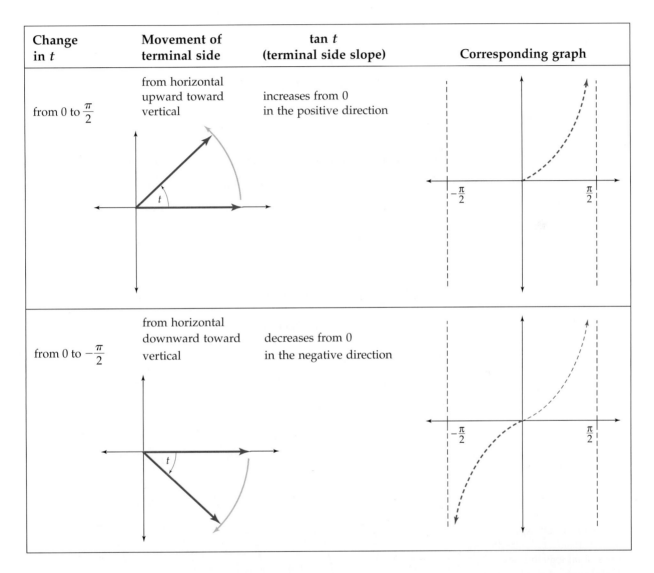

Change in t	Movement of terminal side	tan t (terminal side slope)	Corresponding graph
from 0 to $\frac{\pi}{2}$	from horizontal upward toward vertical	increases from 0 in the positive direction	
from 0 to $-\frac{\pi}{2}$	from horizontal downward toward vertical	decreases from 0 in the negative direction	

When $t = \pm\frac{\pi}{2}$, the terminal side of the angle is vertical, so its slope is not defined. The graph of the tangent function has vertical asymptotes at the values of t for which the function is undefined.

To complete the graph of the tangent function, note that as t goes from $\frac{\pi}{2}$ to $\frac{3\pi}{2}$, the terminal side goes from almost vertical with negative slope to almost vertical with positive slope, exactly as it does from $-\frac{\pi}{2}$ to $\frac{\pi}{2}$. So the graph repeats this pattern at intervals of length π.

Graph of the Tangent Function

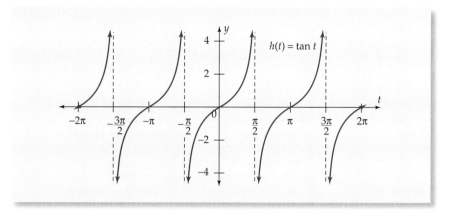

Notice that the **domain of the tangent function** is all real numbers except *odd* multiples of $\frac{\pi}{2}$. The **range of the tangent function** is all real numbers. Because the tangent function has a period of π, for any number t in its domain,

$$\tan t = \tan(t \pm \pi).$$

Example 3 Finding All *t*-values

State all values of t for which $\tan t$ is -1.

Solution

The tangent function repeats its pattern of y-values at intervals of π, so there are an *infinite* number t-values for which $\tan t$ is -1. The graph of $y = \tan t$ shown in Figure 7.1-4 highlights a few points with a y-coordinate of -1.

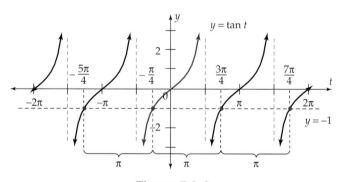

Figure 7.1-4

Technology Tip

Most calculators have a window setting that automatically rescales the horizontal axis in fractional units of π when in radian mode. On TI models, select ZTRIG in the ZOOM menu; on Sharp 9600, select E TRIG in the ZOOM menu; on Casio 9850, select F3 (V-Window) then F2 (TRIG) from GRAPH mode; and on the HP-38, select Trig from the VIEWS menu.

On the interval $\left[-\frac{\pi}{2}, \frac{\pi}{2}\right)$, highlighted in red on the graph above, the graph of $y = \tan t$ has only one point, $\left(-\frac{\pi}{4}, -1\right)$, at which the y-coordinate is

−1. Therefore, all values of t for which $\tan t$ is −1 can be expressed as $t = -\dfrac{\pi}{4} + k\pi$, where k is any integer. ∎

Basic Transformations of Sine, Cosine, and Tangent

The graphical transformations (such as shifting and stretching) that were considered in Section 3.4 also apply to trigonometric graphs.

Example 4   Vertical Stretch

List the transformation needed to change the graph of $f(t) = \cos t$ into the graph of $h(t) = 4\cos t$. Graph both equations on the same screen.

Solution

Because $h(t) = 4 \cdot f(t)$, the graph of h is the graph of f after a vertical stretch by a factor of 4. Both graphs are identified in Figure 7.1-5. ∎

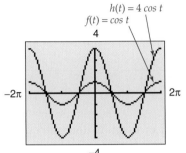

$h(t) = 4\cos t$
$f(t) = \cos t$

Figure 7.1-5

Example 5   Reflection and Vertical Stretch

Graph $g(t) = -\dfrac{1}{2}\sin t$ on the interval $[-2\pi, 2\pi]$.

Solution

The graph of g is the graph of $f(t) = \sin t$ reflected across the x-axis and compressed vertically by a factor of $\dfrac{1}{2}$, as shown in Figure 7.1-6.

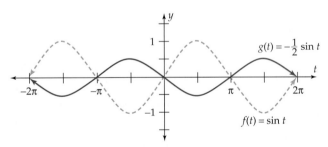

$g(t) = -\dfrac{1}{2}\sin t$

$f(t) = \sin t$

Figure 7.1-6

Example 6   Vertical Shift

Graph $h(t) = \tan t + 5$ on the interval $[-3\pi, 3\pi]$.

Solution

The graph of h is the graph of $f(t) = \tan t$ shifted up 5 units.

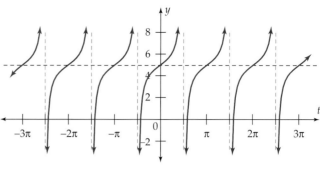

Figure 7.1-7

NOTE For a complete discussion of symmetry and odd and even functions, see *Excursion* 3.4.A.

Even and Odd Functions

Trigonometric functions can be classified as odd or even as determined by their symmetry.

Even Functions

A graph is *symmetric with respect to the y-axis* if the part of the graph on the right side of the y-axis is the mirror image of the part on the left side of the y-axis.

> ┌─── **Graphing Exploration** ●───
>
> **1.** For each pair of functions f and g below, answer the following questions.
>
> $$f(t) = \cos t \quad \text{and} \quad g(t) = \cos(-t)$$
> $$f(t) = \sin t \quad \text{and} \quad g(t) = \sin(-t)$$
> $$f(t) = \tan t \quad \text{and} \quad g(t) = \tan(-t)$$
>
> - Is f symmetric with respect to the y-axis?
> - Does the graph of g appear to coincide with the graph of f?
>
> **2.** If a graph is symmetric with respect to the y-axis, describe the graph after a reflection across the y-axis.

A function f whose graph is symmetric with respect to the y-axis is called an **even function.**

Even Function

> A function f is *even* if
>
> $$f(-x) = f(x) \text{ for every } x \text{ in the domain of } f.$$
>
> The graph of an even function is symmetric with respect to the y-axis.

For example, $f(t) = \cos t$ is an even function because

$$\cos(-t) = \cos t \text{ for every } t \text{ in the domain of } f(t) = \cos t.$$

Odd Functions

If a graph is *symmetric with respect to the origin*, then whenever (x, y) is on the graph, then $(-x, -y)$ is also on the graph. A function f whose graph is symmetric with respect to the origin is called an **odd function.**

Odd Function

A function f is *odd* if

$$f(-x) = -f(x) \text{ for every } x \text{ in the domain of } f.$$

The graph of an odd function is symmetric with respect to the origin.

For example, $f(t) = \sin t$ and $g(t) = \tan t$ are odd functions because

$$\sin(-t) = -\sin t \text{ for every } t \text{ in the domain of } f(t) = \sin t.$$
$$\tan(-t) = -\tan t \text{ for every } t \text{ in the domain of } g(t) = \tan t.$$

Summary of the Properties of Sine, Cosine, and Tangent Functions					
Function	Symbol	Domain	Range	Period	Even/Odd
sine	$f(t) = \sin t$	all real numbers	all real numbers from -1 to 1, inclusive	2π	odd
cosine	$f(t) = \cos t$	all real numbers	all real numbers from -1 to 1, inclusive	2π	even
tangent	$f(t) = \tan t$	all real numbers except odd multiples of $\frac{\pi}{2}$	all real numbers	π	odd

Exercises 7.1

Graph each function on the given interval.

1. $f(t) = \sin t; [2\pi, 6\pi]$

2. $g(t) = \cos t; [\pi, 3\pi]$

3. $h(t) = \tan t; [\pi, 2\pi]$

4. $f(t) = \sin t; [-5\pi, -3\pi]$

5. $g(t) = \cos t; \left[\dfrac{7\pi}{6}, \dfrac{7\pi}{2}\right]$

6. $h(t) = \tan t; \left[\dfrac{5\pi}{3}, 3\pi\right]$

7. For what values of t on the interval $[-2\pi, 2\pi]$ is $\sin t = 1$?

8. For what values of t on the interval $[-2\pi, 2\pi]$ is $\cos t = 0$?

9. What is the maximum value of $g(t) = \cos t$?

10. What is the minimum value of $f(t) = \sin t$?

11. For what values of t on the interval $[-2\pi, 2\pi]$ does the graph of $h(t) = \tan t$ have vertical asymptotes?

12. What is the y-intercept of the graph of $f(t) = \sin t$?

13. What is the y-intercept of the graph of $g(t) = \cos t$?

14. What is the y-intercept of the graph of $h(t) = \tan t$?

15. For what values of t on the interval $[-\pi, \pi]$ is $f(t) = \sin t$ increasing?

16. For what values of t on the interval $[-3\pi, -\pi]$ is $g(t) = \cos t$ decreasing?

17. For what values of t on the interval $[-2\pi, 2\pi]$ is $\tan t$ greater than 1?

18. For what values of t on the interval $[-2\pi, 2\pi]$ is $\tan t$ less than 0?

19. For what values of t on the interval $[\pi, 2\pi]$ is $h(t) = \tan t$ increasing?

In Exercises 20–33, find all the exact t-values for which the given statement is true.

20. $\tan t = 0$

21. $\sin t = \dfrac{\sqrt{2}}{2}$

22. $\sin t = 0$

23. $\cos t = -\dfrac{1}{2}$

24. $\tan t = 1$

25. $\sin t = -\dfrac{\sqrt{3}}{2}$

26. $\cos t = 0$

27. $\cos t = \dfrac{\sqrt{3}}{2}$

28. $\sin t = 1$

29. $\sin t = \dfrac{1}{2}$

30. $\tan t = -\dfrac{\sqrt{3}}{3}$

31. $\cos t = -\dfrac{\sqrt{2}}{2}$

32. $\cos t = -1$

33. $\tan t = \sqrt{3}$

In Exercises 34–43, list the transformations that change the graph of f into the graph of g. State the domain and range of g.

34. $f(t) = \cos t;$ $\quad g(t) = \cos t - 2$

35. $f(t) = \cos t;$ $\quad g(t) = -\cos t$

36. $f(x) = \sin t;$ $\quad g(t) = -3 \sin t$

37. $f(t) = \tan t;$ $\quad g(t) = \tan t + 5$

38. $f(t) = \tan t;$ $\quad g(t) = -\tan t$

39. $f(t) = \cos t;$ $\quad g(t) = 3 \cos t$

40. $f(t) = \sin t;$ $\quad g(t) = -2 \sin t$

41. $f(t) = \sin t;$ $\quad g(t) = 3 \sin t + 2$

42. $f(t) = \cos t;$ $\quad g(t) = 5 \cos t + 3$

43. $f(t) = \sin t;$ $\quad g(t) = \sin t + 3$

In Exercises 44–48, sketch the graph of each function.

44. $f(t) = -2 \cos t$

45. $f(t) = 5 \sin t + 1$

46. $f(t) = 4 \tan t$

47. $f(t) = -\dfrac{1}{4} \cos t$

48. $f(t) = 3 \sin t - \dfrac{1}{2}$

In Exercises 49–54, match a graph to a function. Only one graph is possible for each function.

49. $h(t) = -2 \tan t$

50. $g(t) = 2.5 \cos t$

51. $h(t) = -\sin t + 1$

52. $f(t) = -2.5 \sin t$

53. $g(t) = 3 \tan t - 1$

54. $f(t) = -\cos t + 1$

a.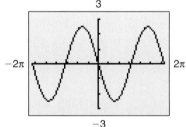

b.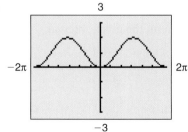

c.

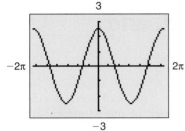

d.

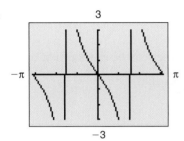

e.

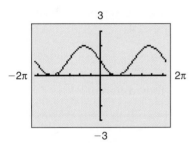

f.

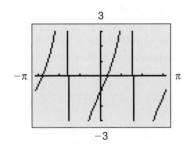

55. Fill the blanks with "even" or "odd" so that the resulting statement is true. Then prove the statement by using an appropriate identity. *Excursion 3.4.A* may be helpful.
  a. $f(t) = \sin t$ is an ____ function.
  b. $g(t) = \cos t$ is an ____ function.
  c. $h(t) = \tan t$ is an ____ function.
  d. $f(t) = t \sin t$ is an ____ function.
  e. $g(t) = t + \tan t$ is an ____ function.

In Exercises 56–59, find tan t, where the terminal side of an angle of t radians lies on the given line.

56. $y = 1.5x$ **57.** $y = 1.4x$

58. $y = 0.32x$ **59.** $y = 11x$

60. Scientists theorize that the average temperature at a specific location fluctuates from cooler to warmer and then to cooler again over a long period of time. The graph shows a theoretical prediction of the average summer temperature for the last 150,000 years for a location in Alaska.

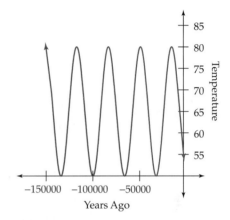

  a. Find the highest and lowest temperature represented.
  b. Over what time interval does the temperature repeat the cycle?
  c. What is the estimated average summer temperature at the present time?

61. A rotating beacon is located at point P, 5 yards from a wall. The distance d, as measured along the wall, where the light shines is given by

$$d = 5 \tan 2\pi t$$

where t is time measured in seconds since the beacon began to rotate. When $t = 0$, the light is aimed at point A. When the beacon is aimed to the right of A, the distance d is positive, and when it is aimed to the left of A, the value of d is negative.

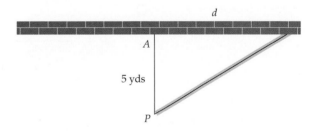

Graph the function and estimate the value of d for the following times.
  a. $t = 0$ **b.** $t = 0.5$
  c. $t = 0.7$ **d.** $t = 1.4$
  e. Determine the position of the beacon when $t = 0.25$ and discuss the corresponding value of d for that value of t.

7.2 Graphs of the Cosecant, Secant, and Cotangent Functions

Objectives

- Graph the cosecant, secant, and cotangent functions

- Graph transformations of the cosecant, secant, and cotangent graphs

The graphs of $y = \sin t$, $y = \cos t$, and $y = \tan t$ that were developed in Section 7.1 are closely related to the graphs of the reciprocal functions $y = \csc t$, $y = \sec t$, and $y = \cot t$ that are studied in this section.

Graph of the Cosecant Function

The general shape of the graph of $f(t) = \csc t$ can be determined by using the graph of the sine function and the fact that $\csc t = \dfrac{1}{\sin t}$.

Graphing Exploration ●

Graph the two functions below on the same screen in a viewing window with $-2\pi \le t \le 2\pi$ and $-4 \le y \le 4$

$$f(t) = \sin t \qquad g(t) = \frac{1}{\sin t}$$

How are the graphs alike and how are they different?

Because $\sin t$ and $\csc t$ are reciprocals, $\csc t$ is not defined when $\sin t = 0$; that is, when t is an integer multiple of π. Therefore, the **domain of $f(t) = \csc t$** is all real numbers except integer multiples of π, and the graph of $f(t) = \csc t$ has vertical asymptotes at integer multiples of π.

Graph of the Cosecant Function ——○

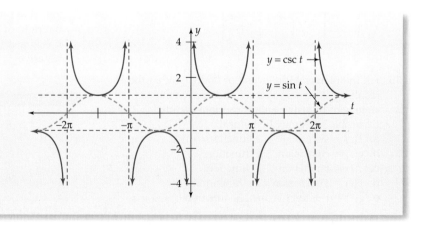

Notice that as the graph of $y = \sin t$ *increases* to a height of 1, the graph of $f(t) = \csc t$ *decreases* to a height of 1, and as the graph of $y = \sin t$ *decreases* to a height of -1, the graph of $f(t) = \csc t$ *increases* to a height of -1. The **range of** $f(t) = \csc t$ is all real numbers greater than or equal to 1 or less than or equal to -1. The period of the cosecant function is 2π.

<hr>

Example 1   Reflection and Vertical Stretch

Graph $h(t) = -3 \csc t$.

Solution

First consider the graph of $y = -3 \sin t$, which is the graph of $y = \sin t$ stretched vertically by a factor of 3 and reflected across the horizontal axis. The relationship between the graph of $y = -3 \sin t$ and that of $h(t) = -3 \csc t$ is similar to that between $y = \csc t$ and $y = \sin t$, as shown in Figure 7.2-1.

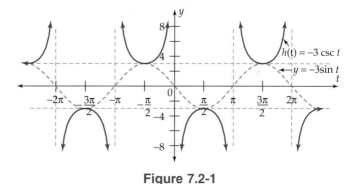

Figure 7.2-1

<hr>

Graph of the Secant Function

The graph of $f(t) = \sec t$ is related to the cosine graph in the same way that the graph of $f(t) = \csc t$ is related to the sine graph.

Graphing Exploration ●

Graph the two functions below on the same screen in a viewing window with $-2\pi \le t \le 2\pi$ and $-4 \le y \le 4$.

$$f(t) = \cos t \qquad g(t) = \frac{1}{\cos t}$$

How are the graphs alike and how are they different?

Because $\cos t$ and $\sec t$ are reciprocals, $\sec t$ is not defined when $\cos t = 0$; that is, when t is an odd multiple of $\frac{\pi}{2}$. Therefore, the **domain of** $f(t) = \sec t$ is all real numbers except odd multiples of $\frac{\pi}{2}$, and the **range of** $f(t) = \sec t$ is all real numbers greater than or equal to 1 or less than or equal to -1. The period of the secant function is 2π.

Graph of the Secant Function

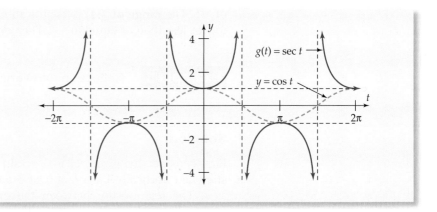

Example 2   Vertical Stretch and Vertical Shift

Graph $g(t) = 2 \sec t - 3$.

Solution

First graph $y = 2 \cos t - 3$, which is the graph of $y = \cos t$ stretched vertically by a factor of 2 and shifted down 3 units. The graphs of $g(t) = 2 \sec t - 3$ and $y = 2 \cos t - 3$ are related in the same way as the graphs of $y = \sec t$ and $y = \cos t$, as shown in Figure 7.2-2.

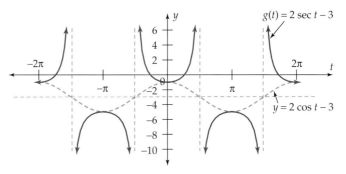

Figure 7.2-2

Graph of the Cotangent Function

Because $\cot t = \dfrac{\cos t}{\sin t}$, the graph of $f(t) = \cot t$ can be obtained by graphing the quotient

$$y = \frac{\cos t}{\sin t}.$$

The cotangent function is not defined when $\sin t = 0$, and this occurs whenever t is an integer multiple of π. Therefore the **domain of $f(t) = \cot t$** consists of all real numbers except integer multiples of π, and the **range of $f(t) = \cot t$** is the set of real numbers. The graph of $f(t) = \cot t$ has vertical asymptotes at integer multiples of π.

Graph of the Cotangent Function

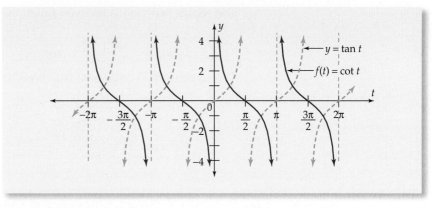

Notice that as the graph of $y = \tan t$ *increases*, the graph of $f(t) = \cot t$ *decreases*, and as the graph of $y = \tan t$ *decreases*, the graph of $f(t) = \cot t$ *increases*. The period of the cotangent function is π.

Example 3   Reflection, Vertical Stretch, and Horizontal Shift

Graph $k(t) = -3 \cot\left(t - \dfrac{\pi}{4}\right)$.

Solution

The graph of $k(t) = -3 \cot\left(t - \dfrac{\pi}{4}\right)$ is the graph of $y = \cot t$ after a horizontal shift of $\dfrac{\pi}{4}$ units to the right, a reflection across the horizontal axis, and a vertical stretch by a factor of 3. The graph of $k(t) = -3 \cot\left(t - \dfrac{\pi}{4}\right)$ is shown with the graph of $y = \cot t$ in Figure 7.2-3 below.

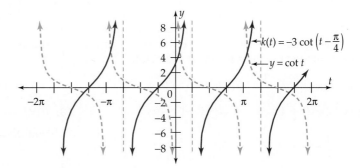

Figure 7.2-3

Even and Odd Functions

The fact that the cosecant, secant, and cotangent functions are reciprocals of the sine, cosine, and tangent functions, respectively, can be used to determine whether the functions are even or odd.

The secant function is an even function, as shown below.

$$\sec(-t) = \frac{1}{\cos(-t)} = \frac{1}{\cos t} = \sec t$$

The cosecant and cotangent functions are odd functions.

$$\csc(-t) = \frac{1}{\sin(-t)} = \frac{1}{-\sin t} = -\frac{1}{\sin t} = -\csc t$$

$$\cot(-t) = \frac{\cos(-t)}{\sin(-t)} = \frac{\cos t}{-\sin t} = -\frac{\cos t}{\sin t} = -\cot t$$

Summary of the Properties of Secant, Cosecant, and Cotangent Functions					
Function	**Symbol**	**Domain**	**Range**	**Period**	**Even/Odd**
secant	$f(t) = \sec t$	all real numbers except odd multiples of $\frac{\pi}{2}$	all real numbers less than or equal to -1 or greater than or equal to 1	2π	even
cosecant	$f(t) = \csc t$	all real numbers except multiples of π	all real numbers less than or equal to -1 or greater than or equal to 1	2π	odd
cotangent	$f(t) = \cot t$	all real numbers except multiples of π	all real numbers	π	odd

Exercises 7.2

In Exercises 1–10, describe the transformations that change the graph of $f(t) = \csc t$, $g(t) = \sec t$, or $h(t) = \cot t$ into the graph of the given function.

1. $s(t) = 3 \sec t - 2$

2. $q(t) = 5 \cot(t - 3)$

3. $m(t) = \csc(t) + 4$

4. $r(t) = -2 \cot(t)$

5. $p(t) = \frac{1}{2} \sec t + 1$

6. $k(t) = -2 \csc t$

7. $q(t) = \sec(-t) - 8$

8. $s(t) = 5 + \cot(t + 2)$

9. $v(t) = \pi \csc t$

10. $j(t) = -\frac{1}{4} \sec(t)$

In Exercises 11–17, state the rule of a function g whose graph is the given transformation of the graph of f.

11. $f(t) = \sec t$ stretched vertically by a factor of 3 and shifted 1 unit to the left

12. $f(t) = \csc t$ compressed vertically by a factor of 0.5 and shifted 1 unit up

13. $f(t) = \sec t$ reflected across the horizontal axis and compressed vertically by a factor of $\frac{1}{4}$

14. $f(t) = \cot t$ reflected across the vertical axis and shifted down 2 units

15. $f(t) = \csc t$ shifted $\frac{\pi}{2}$ units to the right and 5 units down

16. $f(t) = \csc t$ compressed vertically by a factor of 0.75

17. $f(t) = \cot t$ reflected across the vertical axis and across the horizontal axis

18. $f(t) = \frac{1}{2} \cot t - 1$

19. $f(t) = \frac{1}{2} \cot t + 1$

20. $f(t) = 2 \cot t + 1$

21. $f(t) = 2 \cot t - 1$

In Exercises 18–21, match graph a, b, c, or d with each function.

a.

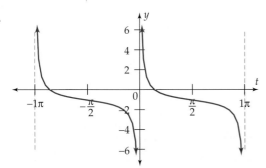

b.

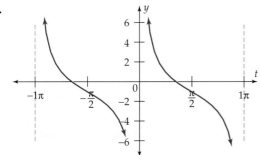

c.

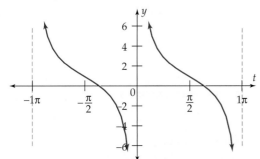

d.

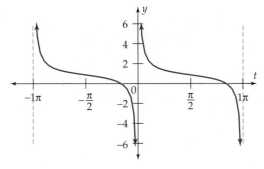

In Exercises 22–25, match graph a or b with each function.

a.

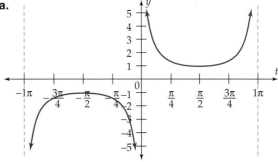

b.

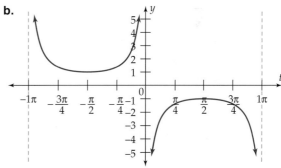

22. $f(t) = -\csc t$

23. $f(t) = \csc t$

24. $f(t) = \csc(-t)$

25. $f(t) = -\csc(-t)$

In Exercises 26–29, match graph a or b with each function.

a.

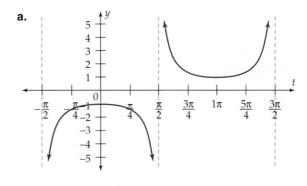

b.

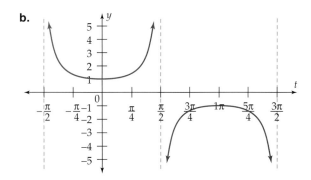

26. $f(t) = -\sec(-t)$

27. $f(t) = \sec(-t)$

28. $f(t) = \sec(t)$

29. $f(t) = -\sec(t)$

In Exercises 30–33, match graph **a** or **b** with each function.

a.

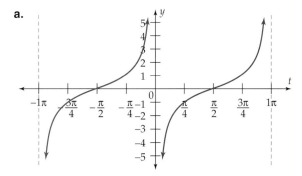

b.

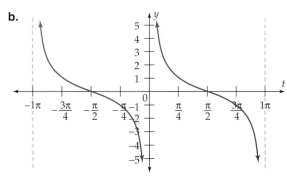

30. $f(t) = -\cot(-t)$

31. $f(t) = \cot(-t)$

32. $f(t) = -\cot(t)$

33. $f(t) = \cot(t)$

In Exercises 34–38, graph at least one cycle of the given function.

34. $f(t) = \sec 2t$

35. $f(t) = -\cot 3t + 4$

36. $f(t) = 5\csc\left(t - \dfrac{\pi}{2}\right)$

37. $f(t) = \dfrac{3}{4}\csc\dfrac{t}{2}$

38. $f(t) = -3\sec(t + \pi)$

39. *Critical Thinking* Show graphically that the equation $\sec t = t$ has infinitely many solutions, but none between $-\dfrac{\pi}{2}$ and $\dfrac{\pi}{2}$.

40. *Critical Thinking* A rotating beacon is positioned 5 yards from a wall at P. In the figure, the distance a is given by

$$a = 5\,|\sec 2\pi t|,$$

where t is the number of seconds since the beacon began to rotate.

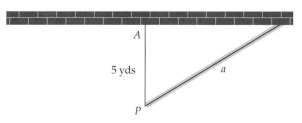

a. Use the graph of a as a function of t to find a for the following times.

$$t = 0 \qquad t = 0.75 \qquad t = 1$$

b. For what values of t is $a = 5$?
c. How fast is the beacon rotating?

7.3 Periodic Graphs and Amplitude

Objectives

- State the period and amplitude (if any) given the function rule or the graph of a sine, cosine, or tangent function

- Use the period and amplitude (if any) to sketch the graph of a sine, cosine, or tangent function

A surprisingly large number of physical phenomena can be described by functions like the following:

$$f(t) = 5 \sin(3t + 4) \quad \text{and} \quad g(t) = -4 \cos(0.5t + 1) + 3$$

In this section and in the next, the graphs of such functions will be analyzed. All of these functions are periodic and their graphs consist of a series of identical *waves*. A single *wave* of the graph is called a **cycle.** The length of each cycle is the period of the function.

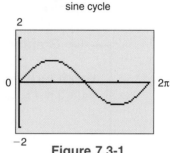

sine cycle

Figure 7.3-1

Every cycle for the sine function resembles the graph of $f(t) = \sin t$ from 0 to 2π, as shown in Figure 7.3-1.

- beginning at a point midway between its maximum and minimum value
- rising to its maximum value
- falling to its minimum value
- returning to the beginning point

Every cycle repeats the same pattern.

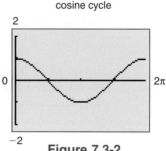

cosine cycle

Figure 7.3-2

Similarly, every cycle for the cosine function resembles the graph of $g(t) = \cos t$ from 0 to 2π, as shown in Figure 7.3-2.

- beginning at its maximum value
- falling to its minimum value
- returning to the beginning point

Again, every cycle repeats the same pattern.

Period

Before proceeding to the discussion about functions that have different periods, it will be helpful to consider functions of the form

$$f(t) = \sin bt \qquad \text{and} \qquad g(t) = \cos bt$$

where b is a constant. The constant b changes the period of the sine or cosine function. Its effect on the graph is to increase or decrease the length of each cycle.

Graphing Exploration ●

Graph each function below, one at a time, in a viewing window with $0 \le t \le 2\pi$. Answer the questions that follow for each function.

$$f(t) = \cos 4t \qquad h(t) = \sin 5t$$

Determine the number of complete cycles between 0 and 2π.

Find the period, or length of one complete cycle. *Hint:* Use division.

The exploration above suggests the following rule.

***Period of
sin bt and
cos bt***

○

If $b > 0$, then the graph of either

$$f(t) = \sin bt \qquad \text{or} \qquad g(t) = \cos bt$$

makes b complete cycles between 0 and 2π, and each function has a period of $\dfrac{2\pi}{b}$.

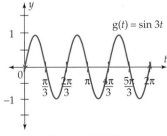

Figure 7.3-3

The graph of $h(t) = \sin t$ completes one cycle as t takes on values from 0 to 2π. Similarly, the graph of $g(t) = \sin 3t$ completes one cycle as $3t$ takes on values from 0 to 2π.

$$\text{When } 3t = 0, t \text{ must be } 0.$$

$$\text{When } 3t = 2\pi, t \text{ must be } \frac{2\pi}{3}.$$

Therefore, the graph of $g(t) = \sin 3t$ completes one cycle as t takes on values from 0 to $\dfrac{2\pi}{3}$, as shown in Figure 7.3-3.

Example 1   Determining Period

Determine the period of each function.

a. $k(t) = \cos 3t$

b. $f(t) = \sin \dfrac{t}{2}$

Solution

a. The function $k(t) = \cos 3t$ has a period of $\dfrac{2\pi}{b} = \dfrac{2\pi}{3}$, as shown in Figure 7.3-4.

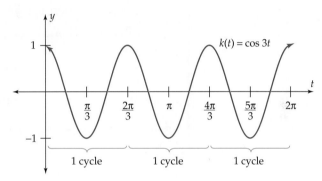

Figure 7.3-4

b. Rewrite $f(t) = \sin \dfrac{t}{2}$ as $f(t) = \sin\left(\dfrac{1}{2}t\right)$. The function $f(t) = \sin\left(\dfrac{1}{2}t\right)$ has a period of $\dfrac{2\pi}{b} = \dfrac{2\pi}{\frac{1}{2}} = 4\pi$, as shown in Figure 7.3-5.

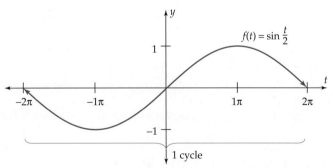

Figure 7.3-5

CAUTION

A calculator may not produce an accurate graph of $f(t) = \sin bt$ or $g(t) = \cos bt$ for large values of b. For instance, the graph of

$$f(t) = \sin 50t$$

has 50 complete cycles between 0 and 2π, but that is not what your calculator will show. (try it!)

Graphing Exploration ●━━━━━

Graph each function below, one at a time, in a viewing window with $-\dfrac{\pi}{2} \le t \le \dfrac{\pi}{2}$. Answer the questions that follow for each function.

$$f(t) = \tan 3t \qquad g(t) = \tan 4t$$

Determine the number of complete cycles between $-\dfrac{\pi}{2}$ and $\dfrac{\pi}{2}$.

Find the period, that is, the length of one complete cycle.

The exploration above suggests the following rule.

Period of
tan bt
━━━━━━━━━━○

If $b > 0$, then the graph of

$$f(t) = \tan bt$$

makes b complete cycles between $-\dfrac{\pi}{2}$ and $\dfrac{\pi}{2}$, and the function has a period of $\dfrac{\pi}{b}$.

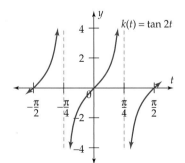

Figure 7.3-6

Example 2 **Determining Period**

Determine the period of each function.

a. $k(t) = \tan 2t$ **b.** $f(t) = \tan \dfrac{t}{3}$

Solution

a. The function $k(t) = \tan 2t$ has a period of $\dfrac{\pi}{b} = \dfrac{\pi}{2}$. It completes one cycle between $-\dfrac{\pi}{4}$ and $\dfrac{\pi}{4}$, as shown in Figure 7.3-6.

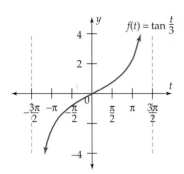

Figure 7.3-7

b. Rewrite as $f(t) = \tan \dfrac{t}{3}$ as $f(t) = \tan\left(\dfrac{1}{3}t\right)$. The function has a period

of $\dfrac{\pi}{b} = \dfrac{\pi}{\frac{1}{3}} = 3\pi$, as shown in Figure 7.3-7.

Amplitude

Recall from Section 3.4 that multiplying the rule of a function by a positive constant has the effect of stretching or compressing its graph vertically.

Example 3   **Vertical and Horizontal Stretches or Compressions**

Graph each function.

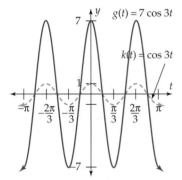

Figure 7.3-8

a. $g(t) = 7 \cos 3t$ **b.** $h(t) = \dfrac{1}{3} \sin \dfrac{t}{2}$

Solution

a. The function $g(t) = 7 \cos 3t$ is the function $k(t) = \cos 3t$ multiplied by 7. Consequently, the graph of g is the graph of k (see Example 1**a**) stretched vertically by a factor of 7.

As Figure 7.3-8 shows, stretching the graph affects only the height of the waves in the graph, not the period of the function. So the period of g is the same as that of $k(t) = \cos 3t$, namely $\dfrac{2\pi}{b} = \dfrac{2\pi}{3}$.

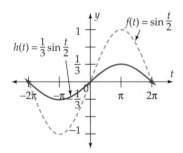

Figure 7.3-9

b. The function $h(t) = \dfrac{1}{3} \sin \dfrac{t}{2}$ is the function $f(t) = \sin \dfrac{t}{2}$ multiplied by $\dfrac{1}{3}$. Consequently, the graph of h is the graph of f (see Example 1**b**) vertically compressed by a factor of $\dfrac{1}{3}$. The period of h is the same as the period of f, namely $\dfrac{2\pi}{b} = \dfrac{2\pi}{\frac{1}{2}} = 4\pi$.

As the graphs in Example 3 illustrate, vertically stretching or compressing the graph affects only the height, not the period of the function.

The graph of $g(t) = 7 \cos 3t$ in Example 3 reaches a maximum value of 7 units above the horizontal axis and a minimum value of 7 units below the horizontal axis. In general, the graph of $f(t) = a \sin bt$ or $g(t) = a \cos bt$ reaches a distance of $|a|$ units above and below the horizontal axis, and is said to have an **amplitude** of $|a|$. The graph of $g(t) = 7 \cos 3t$ has an amplitude of 7.

Amplitude and Period

If $a \neq 0$ and $b > 0$, then each of the functions

$$f(t) = a \sin bt \qquad \text{or} \qquad g(t) = a \cos bt$$

has an amplitude of $|a|$ and a period of $\dfrac{2\pi}{b}$.

Example 4   Determining Amplitude and Period

Determine the amplitude and period of $f(t) = -2 \sin 4t$. Then graph f on the interval $\left[-\dfrac{\pi}{2}, \dfrac{\pi}{2}\right]$.

Solution

The amplitude of $f(t) = -2 \sin 4t$ is $|a| = |-2| = 2$, and the period of $f(t) = -2 \sin 4t$ is $\dfrac{2\pi}{b} = \dfrac{2\pi}{4} = \dfrac{\pi}{2}$. So the graph of f consists of cycles that are $\dfrac{\pi}{2}$ long and rise and fall between the heights of -2 and 2. To graph this function, be sure to notice that its graph is the reflection of $h(t) = 2 \sin 4t$ across the horizontal axis, as shown in Figure 7.3-10. ∎

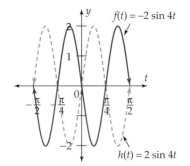

Figure 7.3-10

Although the graph of any function can be vertically stretched or compressed, amplitude only applies to bounded periodic functions.

Exercises 7.3

In Exercises 1–15, state the amplitude (if any) and period of each function.

1. $f(t) = -\cos t$

2. $f(t) = \sin 2t$

3. $f(t) = \cos 3t$

4. $f(t) = 2.5 \tan t$

5. $f(t) = 4 \cos t$

6. $f(t) = -3 \sin t$

7. $f(t) = 5 \tan 2t$

8. $f(t) = 1.2 \cos 0.5t$

9. $f(t) = -0.3 \sin \dfrac{t}{3}$

10. $f(t) = -\tan 0.4t$

11. $f(t) = \dfrac{1}{2} \sin 3t$

12. $f(t) = -\dfrac{1}{2} \tan 3t$

13. $f(t) = 5 \cos 1.7t$

14. $f(t) = 2 \sin \dfrac{2\pi t}{3}$

15. $f(t) = \dfrac{1}{3} \tan \dfrac{\pi t}{4}$

16. a. What is the period of $f(t) = \sin 2\pi t$?
  b. For what values of t (with $0 \le t \le 2\pi$) is $f(t) = 0$?
  c. For what values of t (with $0 \le t \le 2\pi$) is $f(t) = 1$?
  d. For what values of t (with $0 \le t \le 2\pi$) is $f(t) = -1$?

17. a. What is the period of $f(t) = \cos \pi t$?
  b. For what values of t (with $0 \le t \le 2\pi$) is $f(t) = 0$?
  c. For what values of t (with $0 \le t \le 2\pi$) is $f(t) = 1$?
  d. For what values of t (with $0 \le t \le 2\pi$) is $f(t) = -1$?

18. a. What is the period of $f(t) = \tan \pi t$?
  b. For what values of t $\left(\text{with } -\dfrac{\pi}{2} \le t \le \dfrac{\pi}{2}\right)$ is $f(t) = 0$?

c. For what values of t $\left(\text{with } -\dfrac{\pi}{2} \le t \le \dfrac{\pi}{2}\right)$ is

$f(t) = 1$?

d. For what values of t $\left(\text{with } -\dfrac{\pi}{2} \le t \le \dfrac{\pi}{2}\right)$ is

$f(t) = -1$?

In Exercises 19–38, describe the transformations that change the graph of f into the graph of g. State the amplitude (if any) and the period of g.

19. $f(t) = \sin t; g(t) = \sin 5t$

20. $f(t) = \tan t; g(t) = \tan 3t$

21. $f(t) = \cos t; g(t) = \cos 8t$

22. $f(t) = \cos t; g(t) = \cos(-t)$

23. $f(t) = \tan t; g(t) = \tan(-t)$

24. $f(t) = \sin t; g(t) = \sin(-t)$

25. $f(t) = \sin t; g(t) = \sin 1.6t$

26. $f(t) = \cos t; g(t) = \cos 2.6t$

27. $f(t) = \sin t; g(t) = 3 \sin t$

28. $f(t) = \cos t; g(t) = \dfrac{1}{2} \cos t$

29. $f(t) = \tan t; g(t) = \dfrac{1}{3} \tan t$

30. $f(t) = \sin t; g(t) = 4 \sin \dfrac{t}{2}$

31. $f(t) = \sin t; g(t) = 5 \sin 2t$

32. $f(t) = \tan t; g(t) = -2 \tan \dfrac{t}{2}$

33. $f(t) = \tan t; g(t) = -2 \tan 0.2t$

34. $f(t) = \cos t; g(t) = 3 \cos 6t$

35. $f(t) = \cos t; g(t) = \dfrac{2}{5} \cos 8t$

36. $f(t) = \sin t; g(t) = -2 \sin \dfrac{3\pi t}{5}$

37. $f(t) = \tan t; g(t) = \dfrac{1}{3} \tan \pi t$

38. $f(t) = \cos t; g(t) = \dfrac{5}{3} \cos \dfrac{\pi t}{3}$

In Exercises 39–44, sketch at least one cycle of the graph of each function.

39. $f(t) = 4 \cos \dfrac{t}{2}$

40. $f(t) = \dfrac{2}{3} \sin 2t$

41. $f(t) = 2 \tan 3t$

42. $f(t) = -0.8 \cos \pi t$

43. $f(t) = 3.5 \sin 2\pi t$

44. $f(t) = \tan \dfrac{\pi t}{2}$

In Exercises 45–50, match a graph to a function. Only one graph is possible for each function.

a.

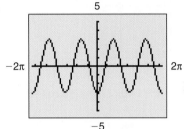

b.

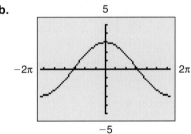

c.

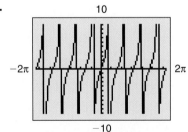

d.

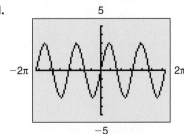

e.

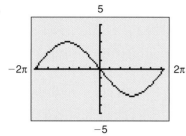

f.

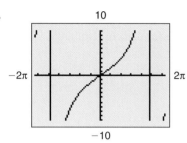

45. $f(t) = 3 \sin 2t$ **46.** $f(t) = -3 \cos 2t$

47. $f(t) = 3 \cos \dfrac{t}{2}$ **48.** $f(t) = -3 \sin \dfrac{t}{2}$

49. $f(t) = 5 \tan \dfrac{t}{3}$ **50.** $f(t) = 3 \tan 2t$

In Exercises 51–56, write an equation for a sine function with the given information.

51. amplitude $= 2$, period $= 4\pi$

52. amplitude $= \dfrac{1}{2}$, period $= \dfrac{\pi}{2}$

53. amplitude $= 1.8$, period $= \dfrac{3\pi}{2}$

54. amplitude $= 1$, period $= 2$

55. amplitude $= \dfrac{3}{2}$, period $= 4$

56. amplitude $= 6$, period $= \dfrac{1}{2}$

In Exercises 57–59, state the rule of a sine function whose graph appears to be identical to the given graph.

57.

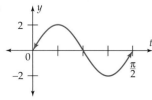

58.

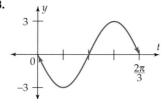

59.

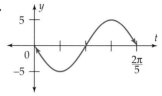

In Exercises 60–64, state all local minima and maxima of the function on the given interval.

60. $f(t) = \sin 2t; \ 0 \leq t \leq \pi$

61. $f(t) = \cos 3t; \ 0 \leq t \leq \pi$

62. $f(t) = \cos \dfrac{t}{2}; \ -2\pi \leq t \leq \pi$

63. $f(t) = \sin \dfrac{t}{3}; \ -2\pi \leq t \leq \pi$

64. $f(t) = 3 \sin 2\pi t; \ -1.5 \leq t \leq 1.5$

65. The current generated by an AM radio transmitter is given by a function of the form $f(t) = A \sin 2000 \, \pi m t$, where $550 \leq m \leq 1600$ is the location on the broadcast dial and t is measured in seconds. For example, a station at 900 on the AM dial has a function of the form

$$f(t) = A \sin 2000\pi(900) \, t = A \sin 1{,}800{,}000\pi t$$

Sound information is added to this signal by modulating A, that is, by changing the amplitude of the waves being transmitted. AM means amplitude modulation. For a station at 900 on the dial, what is the period of function f?

66. Find the function f, its period, and its frequency for a radio station at 1440 on the dial. (See Exercise 65.)

7.4 Periodic Graphs and Phase Shifts

Objectives

• State the period, amplitude, vertical shift, and phase shift given the function rule or graph of a sine or cosine function

• Use graphs to determine whether an equation could possibly be an identity

In Section 7.3, you studied graphs of functions of the form

$$f(t) = a \sin bt \qquad \text{and} \qquad g(t) = a \cos bt$$

and learned how the constants a and b affect the amplitudes and periods of the functions. In this section, you will consider functions of the form

$$f(t) = a \sin[b(t + c)] + d \qquad \text{and} \qquad g(t) = a \cos[b(t + c)] + d$$

where a, b, c, and d are constants, and you will determine how these constants affect the graphs of the functions.

Vertical Shifts

Recall from Section 3.4 that adding a constant to the rule of a function shifts the graph vertically. Example 1 illustrates a vertical shift in combination with a reflection and a change in amplitude.

Example 1   Reflection, Vertical Stretch, and Vertical Shift

Describe the graph of $k(t) = -2 \cos t + 3$. Then graph k on the interval $[-2\pi, 2\pi]$.

Solution

The graph of $k(t) = -2 \cos t + 3$ is the graph of $g(t) = \cos t$ reflected across the horizontal axis, vertically stretched by a factor of 2, and shifted 3 units upward, as shown in Figure 7.4-1.

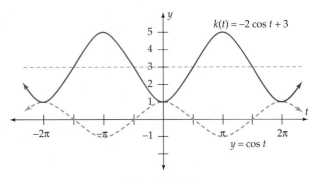

Figure 7.4-1

After the vertical shift, the graph of $k(t) = -2 \cos t + 3$ is vertically centered on the horizontal line $y = 3$.

Phase Shifts

Recall from Section 3.4 that when the independent variable t in the rule of a function is replaced by $t - c$ or $t + c$, where c is a constant, the graph is shifted horizontally. For periodic functions, the number c is the **phase shift** associated with the graph.

Example 2   Phase Shift

Describe the graph of each function.

a. $g(t) = \sin\left(t + \dfrac{\pi}{2}\right)$ **b.** $h(t) = \cos\left(t - \dfrac{2\pi}{3}\right)$

Solution

a. The graph of $g(t) = \sin\left(t + \dfrac{\pi}{2}\right)$ is the graph of $f(t) = \sin t$ shifted to the left $\dfrac{\pi}{2}$ units, as shown in Figure 7.4-2.

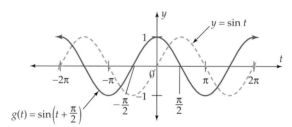

Figure 7.4-2

When the graph of $f(t) = \sin t$ is shifted to become the graph of $g(t) = \sin\left(t + \dfrac{\pi}{2}\right)$, the cycle of f that begins at $t = 0$ becomes a cycle of g that begins at $t = -\dfrac{\pi}{2}$. Thus, g has a phase shift of $-\dfrac{\pi}{2}$.

b. The graph of $h(t) = \cos\left(t - \dfrac{2\pi}{3}\right)$ is the graph of $f(t) = \cos t$ shifted to the right $\dfrac{2\pi}{3}$ units, as shown in Figure 7.4-3.

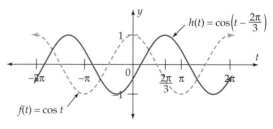

Figure 7.4-3

The cycle of $f(t) = \cos t$ that begins at $t = 0$ becomes a cycle of $h(t) = \cos\left(t - \dfrac{2\pi}{3}\right)$ that begins at $t = \dfrac{2\pi}{3}$. Thus, the function h has a phase shift of $\dfrac{2\pi}{3}$.

Combined Transformations

Now that you are familiar with the effects of various transformations on the sine and cosine functions, you are ready for some examples that simultaneously include changes in amplitude, period, and phase shift.

Example 3   Combined Transformations

State the amplitude, period, and phase shift of $f(t) = 3\sin(2t + 5)$.

Solution

Rewrite the function rule.

$$f(t) = 3\sin(2t + 5) = 3\sin\left[2\left(t + \dfrac{5}{2}\right)\right]$$

When the rule of f is written in this form, you can see that it is obtained from the rule of $k(t) = 3\sin 2t$ by replacing t with $t + \dfrac{5}{2}$. Therefore, the graph of f can be obtained by horizontally shifting the graph of k to the left $\dfrac{5}{2}$ units, as shown in Figure 7.4-4.

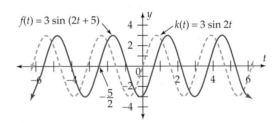

Figure 7.4-4

The cycle of k that begins at $t = 0$ becomes a cycle of f that begins at $t = -\dfrac{5}{2}$; so the function f has a phase shift of $-\dfrac{5}{2}$.

The amplitude of f is 3 and its period is $\dfrac{2\pi}{2} = \pi$.

The procedure that is used in Examples 1–3 can be used to analyze any function whose rule is of the form

$$f(t) = a \sin(bt + c) + d.$$

First rewrite the function rule as follows.

$$f(t) = a \sin(bt + c) + d = a \sin\left[b\left(t + \frac{c}{b}\right)\right] + d$$

Thus, the graph of f is obtained from the graph of $k(t) = a \sin bt$ by shifting it d units vertically and $-\dfrac{c}{b}$ units horizontally. The cycle of k that begins at $t = 0$ becomes the cycle of f that begins at $t = -\dfrac{c}{b}$, so f has phase shift $-\dfrac{c}{b}$. The amplitude of both f and k is $|a|$ and both have period $\dfrac{2\pi}{b}$. A similar analysis applies to the function $g(t) = a \cos(bt + c) + d$.

Combined Transformations

If $a \neq 0$ and $b > 0$, then each of the functions

$$f(t) = a \sin(bt + c) + d \qquad \text{and} \qquad g(t) = a \cos(bt + c) + d$$

has the following characteristics:

$$\textbf{amplitude} = |a| \qquad\qquad \textbf{period} = \frac{2\pi}{b}$$

$$\textbf{phase shift} = -\frac{c}{b} \qquad \textbf{vertical shift} = d$$

Example 4 Combined Transformations

Describe the graph of $g(t) = 2 \cos(3t - 4) - 1$.

Solution

Identify the amplitude, period, vertical shift and phase shift.

$$g(t) = 2 \cos(3t - 4) - 1 = 2 \cos[3t + (-4)] + (-1)$$

$$\text{amplitude } |a| = 2 \qquad \text{period} = \frac{2\pi}{b} = \frac{2\pi}{3}$$

$$\text{phase shift} = -\frac{c}{b} = -\left(\frac{-4}{3}\right) = \frac{4}{3} \qquad \text{vertical shift} = -1$$

The graph of $g(t) = 2 \cos(3t - 4) - 1$, shown in Figure 7.4-5, is vertically centered on the horizontal line $y = -1$. The waves reach a maximum of 2 units above that horizontal line and a minimum of 2 units below that horizontal line. The graph begins a cosine wave at $t = \dfrac{4}{3}$ and completes one cycle in $\dfrac{2\pi}{3}$ units.

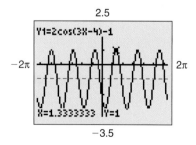

Figure 7.4-5

Example 5 **Combined Transformations**

Identify the amplitude, period, vertical shift, and phase shift of $f(t) = -4\sin\left(\dfrac{t}{2} + 1\right) + 3$. Then graph at least one complete cycle of f.

Solution

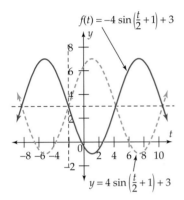

$f(t) = -4\sin\left(\dfrac{t}{2}+1\right)+3$

$y = 4\sin\left(\dfrac{t}{2}+1\right)+3$

Figure 7.4-6

The function rule $f(t)$ is of the form $a\sin(bt + c) + d$, with $a = -4$, $b = \dfrac{1}{2}$, $c = 1$, and $d = 3$.

$$\text{amplitude } |a| = |-4| = 4 \qquad \text{period} = \dfrac{2\pi}{b} = \dfrac{2\pi}{\frac{1}{2}} = 4\pi$$

$$\text{phase shift} = -\dfrac{c}{b} = -\dfrac{1}{\frac{1}{2}} = -2 \qquad \text{vertical shift} = 3$$

The waves of the graph are vertically centered on the horizontal line $y = 3$ reaching a maximum of 7 and a minimum of -1. The graph begins a sine wave at $t = -2$ and completes one cycle in $4\pi \approx 12.6$ units. The graph of f is the graph of $y = 4\sin\left(\dfrac{t}{2} + 1\right) + 3$ reflected across the horizontal line $y = 3$, as shown in Figure 7.4-6. ∎

Example 6 **Identifying Graphs**

Find a sine function and a cosine function whose graphs look like the graph shown in Figure 7.4-7.

Solution

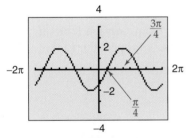

Figure 7.4-7

This graph appears to have an amplitude of 2 and to be centered vertically on the horizontal axis. The period appears to be 2π, so $b = 1$. Therefore, the graph looks like the graph of $f(t) = 2\sin t$ or $g(t) = 2\cos t$ shifted horizontally.

The graph of $f(t) = 2\sin t$ intercepts the x-axis at $t = 0$. The graph in Figure 7.4-7 intercepts the x-axis at $t = \dfrac{\pi}{4}$, so it looks like the graph of $f(t) = 2\sin t$ shifted $\dfrac{\pi}{4}$ units to the right. Therefore, this graph closely resembles the graph of $h(t) = 2\sin\left(t - \dfrac{\pi}{4}\right)$.

At $t = 0$, the graph of $g(t) = 2\cos t$ reaches its maximum of 2. The graph in Figure 7.4-7 reaches its maximum of 2 at $t = \dfrac{3\pi}{4}$, so it looks like the graph of $g(t) = 2\cos t$ shifted $\dfrac{3\pi}{4}$ units to the right. Therefore, this graph closely resembles the graph of $k(t) = 2\cos\left(t - \dfrac{3\pi}{4}\right)$.

NOTE Identities are proved algebraically in Chapter 9.

Graphs and Identities

Graphing calculators can be used to determine equations that could possibly be identities. A calculator cannot *prove* that such an equation is an identity, but it can provide evidence that it *might* be one. On the other hand, a calculator can prove that a particular equation is not an identity.

Example 7 Possible Identities

Which of the following equations could possibly be an identity?

a. $\cos\left(\dfrac{\pi}{2} + t\right) = \sin t$ **b.** $\cos\left(\dfrac{\pi}{2} - t\right) = \sin t$

Solution

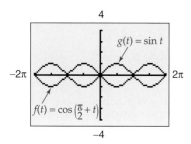

Figure 7.4-8

a. If $\cos\left(\dfrac{\pi}{2} + t\right) = \sin t$ is an identity, then

$$f(t) = \cos\left(\frac{\pi}{2} + t\right) \text{ and } g(t) = \sin t$$

are equivalent functions and have the same graph. The graphs of f and g, shown in Figure 7.4-8 are obviously different. Therefore, $\cos\left(\dfrac{\pi}{2} + t\right) = \sin t$ is not an identity.

b. In Figure 7.4-9, the graphs of

$$f(t) = \cos\left(\frac{\pi}{2} - t\right) \text{ and } g(t) = \sin t$$

appear to coincide on the interval $[-2\pi, 2\pi]$. Comparing a table of values for f and g, shown in Figure 7.4-10, also supports the idea that $f(t) = \cos\left(\dfrac{\pi}{2} - t\right)$ and $g(t) = \sin t$ are equivalent functions.

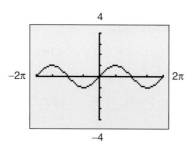 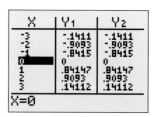

Figure 7.4-9 Figure 7.4-10

This evidence strongly suggests that the equation $\cos\left(\dfrac{\pi}{2} - t\right) = \sin t$ is an identity, but does not prove it. Therefore, $\cos\left(\dfrac{\pi}{2} - t\right) = \sin t$ could possibly be an identity.

Example 8   Possible Identities

Which of the following equations could possibly be an identity?

a. $\dfrac{\cot t}{\cos t} = \sin t$ **b.** $\dfrac{\sin t}{\tan t} = \cos t$

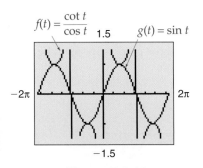

$f(t) = \dfrac{\cot t}{\cos t}$ 1.5 $g(t) = \sin t$

−2π   2π

−1.5

Figure 7.4-11

Solution

a. Rewrite f as $f(t) = \dfrac{\dfrac{1}{\tan t}}{\cos t}$ and compare its graph with the graph of $g(t) = \sin t$. The graphs of f and g, shown in Figure 7.4-11 are obviously different. Therefore, $\dfrac{\cot t}{\cos t} = \sin t$ is not an identity.

However, it does appear from the graph that $\dfrac{\cot t}{\cos t} = \csc t$ could possibly be an identity.

b. In Figure 7.4-12a, the graphs of $f(t) = \dfrac{\sin t}{\tan t}$ and $g(t) = \cos t$ appear to coincide. Comparing a table of values for f and g, shown in Figure 7.4-12b, also supports the idea that $f(t) = \dfrac{\sin t}{\tan t}$ and $g(t) = \cos t$ are equivalent functions for all values of t for which f is defined; that is, all values of t except those that make $\tan t = 0$.

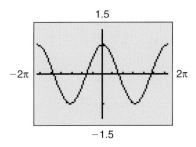

1.5

−2π   2π

−1.5

Figure 7.4-12a

X	Y₁	Y₂
-4	-.6536	-.6536
-3	-.99	-.99
-2	-.4161	-.4161
-1	.5403	.5403
0	ERROR	1
1	.5403	.5403
2	-.4161	-.4161

X=0

Figure 7.4-12b

Therefore, $\dfrac{\sin t}{\tan t} = \cos t$ could possibly be an identity for $\tan t \neq 0$.

CAUTION

Do not assume that two graphs that look the same on a calculator screen actually are the same. Depending on the viewing window, two graphs that are actually quite different may appear identical.

Exercises 7.4

In Exercises 1–20, state the amplitude, period, phase shift, and vertical shift of the function.

1. $h(t) = \cos(t + 1)$ **2.** $m(t) = 7\cos(t + 3)$

3. $f(t) = -5\sin 2t$ **4.** $k(t) = \cos\left(\dfrac{2\pi t}{3}\right)$

5. $k(t) = \sin(t - \pi) - 4$ **6.** $g(t) = 3\sin(2t - \pi)$

7. $p(t) = 6\cos(3\pi t + 1)$

8. $f(t) = 4.5\sin(12t - 6) - 5$

9. $h(t) = -4\cos\left(3t - \dfrac{\pi}{6}\right) + 1$

10. $p(t) = -5\sin\left(\dfrac{t}{4} + 3\right) - 1$

11. $q(t) = -7\sin\left(7t + \dfrac{1}{7}\right)$ **12.** $h(t) = 16\sin\left(\dfrac{2t}{3} - 4\right)$

13. $d(t) = -3\sin\left(2t - \dfrac{5\pi}{4}\right)$

14. $c(t) = -\cos\left(\dfrac{3t}{2} - \dfrac{\pi}{3}\right) - 5$

15. $g(t) = 97\cos(14t + 5)$ **16.** $f(t) = 3 - 2\cos(4t + 1)$

17. $s(t) = 7 - \cos 2\pi t$ **18.** $m(t) = 4\cos(t - 5) + 2$

19. $k(t) = 3\cos\left(\dfrac{\pi t}{3} - 1\right) + 5$

20. $h(t) = -4 - \sin\left(\dfrac{t}{3} + \dfrac{\pi}{4}\right)$

In Exercises 21–30, state the rule of a sine function with the given amplitude, period, phase shift, and vertical shift, respectively.

21. $3, \dfrac{\pi}{4}, \dfrac{\pi}{5}, 0$ **22.** $1, 2, 3, 4$

23. $\dfrac{2}{3}, 3\pi, -\dfrac{2\pi}{3}, -2$ **24.** $8, \dfrac{1}{2}, \dfrac{2}{3}, 4$

25. $0.5, 2.5, 1.5, -0.6$ **26.** $1, 5, 0, 3$

27. $6, \dfrac{5\pi}{3}, 0, -1$ **28.** $2, 8\pi, 1, 1$

29. $\dfrac{5}{2}, 1.8, 0.2, 0$ **30.** $1, 1, -1, -1$

In Exercises 31–40,

a. State the rule of a function of the form $f(t) = a\sin(bt + c) + d$ whose graph appears to be identical to the given graph.

b. State the rule of a function of the form $f(t) = a\cos(bt + c) + d$ whose graph appears to be identical to the given graph.

31.

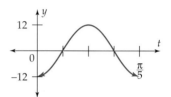

32.

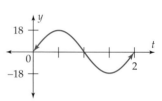

33.

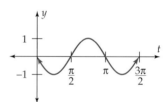

34.

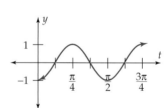

35.

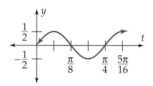

36.

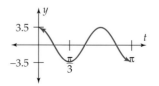

37.

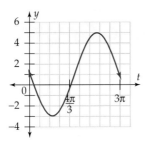

38.

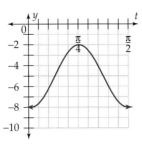

39.

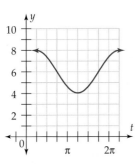

40.

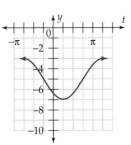

In Exercises 41–48, sketch the graph of at least one cycle of the function.

41. $k(t) = -3 \sin t$

42. $y(t) = -2 \cos 3t$

43. $p(t) = -\dfrac{1}{2} \sin 2t$

44. $q(t) = \dfrac{2}{3} \cos \dfrac{3}{2} t$

45. $h(t) = 3 \sin\left(2t + \dfrac{\pi}{2}\right)$

46. $p(t) = 3 \cos(3t - \pi)$

47. $f(t) = -\sin(2t - 3) + 1$

48. $g(t) = 5 \cos\left(t - \dfrac{\pi}{3}\right) + 2$

In Exercises 49–52, graph the function over the interval $(0, 2\pi)$, and determine the location of all local maxima and minima.

49. $f(t) = \dfrac{1}{2} \sin\left(t - \dfrac{\pi}{3}\right)$

50. $g(t) = 2 \sin\left(\dfrac{2t}{3} - \dfrac{\pi}{9}\right)$

51. $f(t) = -2 \sin(3t - \pi)$

52. $h(t) = \dfrac{1}{2} \cos\left(\dfrac{\pi}{2} t - \dfrac{\pi}{8}\right) + 1$

53. Describe the graph of $f(t) = \sin^2 t + \cos^2 t$.

In Exercises 54–57, use graphs to determine whether the equation could possibly be an identity or is definitely not an identity.

54. $\dfrac{\cos t}{\cos\left(t - \dfrac{\pi}{2}\right)} = \cot t$

55. $\dfrac{\sin t}{1 - \cos t} = \cot t$

56. $\dfrac{\sec t + \csc t}{1 + \tan t} = \csc t$

57. $\tan t = \cot\left(\dfrac{\pi}{2} - t\right)$

In Exercises 58–61, graph f in a viewing window with $-2\pi \le t \le 2\pi$. Use the trace feature to determine constants a, b, and c such that the graph of f appears to coincide with the graph of $g(t) = a \sin(bt + c)$.

58. $f(t) = -3 \sin t + 2 \cos t$

59. $f(t) = 3 \sin(4t + 2) + 2 \cos(4t - 1)$

60. $f(t) = 2 \sin(3t - 5) - 3 \cos(3t + 2)$

61. $f(t) = 2 \sin t + 5 \cos t$

In Exercises 62–63, explain why there could not possibly be constants a, b, and c such that the graph of $g(t) = a \sin(bt + c)$ coincides with the graph of f.

62. $f(t) = 2 \sin(3t - 1) + 3 \cos(4t + 1)$

63. $f(t) = \sin 2t + \cos 3t$

7.4.A — *Excursion*: Other Trigonometric Graphs

Objectives

- Write a sine function whose graph looks like the graph of another given sinusoidal function

- Find viewing windows for the graphs of other trigonometric functions

A graphing calculator enables you to explore with ease a wide variety of trigonometric functions.

Graphing Exploration ⬤

Graph each function on the same screen in a viewing window with $0 \leq t \leq 2\pi$.

$$g(t) = \cos t \qquad f(t) = \sin\left(t + \frac{\pi}{2}\right)$$

How do the two graphs compare? Do they appear to coincide?

The exploration above suggests that the equation

$$\cos t = \sin\left(t + \frac{\pi}{2}\right)$$

is an identity and that the graph of the cosine function can be obtained by horizontally shifting the graph of the sine function. This is true, and it will be proved in Section 9.2. Consequently, every cosine function, such as $g(t) = 3\cos(4t + 5) + 6$, can be expressed as a sine function of the form $f(t) = a\sin(bt + c) + d$. The shape of the graph of such a function is called a **sinusoid.**

Other Sinusoidal Graphs

The exploration below suggests that other trigonometric functions can be expressed in the form $f(t) = a\sin(bt + c)$.

Graphing Exploration ⬤

1. Graph $g(t) = -2\sin(t + 7) + 3\cos(t + 2)$ in a viewing window with $-2\pi \leq t \leq 2\pi$. Does the function appear to be periodic?

2. Using the calculator's minimum and maximum finders, determine the approximate amplitude of this function.

3. Using the calculator's zero finder, estimate the period of this function (find the length of a complete cycle).

4. What is the smallest positive t-value at which a sine cycle begins?

5. Use the information from Questions 2–4 to write a function of the form $f(t) = a\sin(bt + c)$ whose graph looks very much like the graph of $g(t) = -2\sin(t + 7) + 3\cos(t + 2)$. Graph the new function on the same screen with g. Do the graphs appear to coincide?

The results of the preceding graphing exploration suggest that the graph of $g(t) = -2 \sin(t + 7) + 3 \cos(t + 2)$ looks like the graph of $f(t) = 4.95 \sin(t - 2.60)$.

These results illustrate the following facts.

Sinusoidal Graphs

If b, d, k, r, and s are constants, then the graph of the function

$$g(t) = d \sin(bt + r) + k \cos(bt + s)$$

is a sinusoid and there are constants a and c such that

$$d \sin(bt + r) + k \cos(bt + s) = a \sin(bt + c).$$

Example 1   Sinusoidal Graphs

Find a sine function whose graph looks like the graph of

$$g(t) = 4 \sin(3t + 2) + 2 \cos(3t - 4).$$

Solution

The graph of $g(t) = 4 \sin(3t + 2) + 2 \cos(3t - 4)$ is shown in Figure 7.4.A-1.

By using a graphing calculator's minimum and maximum finders with the graph of $g(t) = 4 \sin(3t + 2) + 2 \cos(3t - 4)$, you see that g has an amplitude of approximately 3.94.

The function g has period $\dfrac{2\pi}{3}$ because this is the period of both $\sin(3t + 2)$ and $\cos(3t - 4)$. The function $f(t) = a \sin(bt + c)$ has period $\dfrac{2\pi}{b} = \dfrac{2\pi}{3}$. So $b = 3$.

By using a graphing calculator's zero finder, you can see that a sine cycle in the graph of g begins at approximately $t = -0.84$, so the phase shift $-\dfrac{c}{b}$ is approximately -0.84. Find c.

$$-\frac{c}{b} \approx -0.84$$

$$-\frac{c}{3} \approx -0.84 \qquad \textit{Substitute 3 for b}$$

$$-c \approx -2.52$$

$$c \approx 2.52$$

Therefore, $a \approx 3.94$, $b = 3$, $c \approx 2.52$, and the graph of

$$f(t) = 3.94 \sin(3t + 2.52)$$

looks like the graph of

$$g(t) = 4 \sin(3t + 2) + 2 \cos(3t - 4).$$

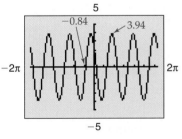

Figure 7.4.A-1

Other Trigonometric Graphs

In Example 1, the variable t has the same coefficient b in both the sine and cosine terms of the function's rule. When this is not the case, the graph will consist of waves of varying size and shape, as shown in Figure 7.4.A-2.

$$f(t) = \sin 3t + \cos 2t \qquad g(t) = -2 \sin(3t + 5) + 4 \cos(t + 2) \qquad h(t) = 2 \sin 2t - 3 \cos 3t$$

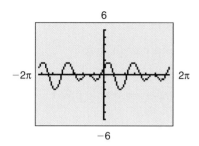 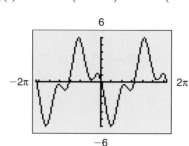 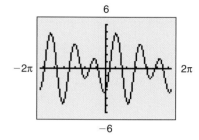

Figure 7.4.A-2

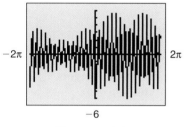

Figure 7.4.A-3

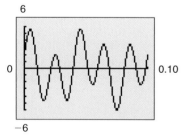

Figure 7.4.A-4

Example 2 Finding a Viewing Window

Find a viewing window for one complete cycle of

$$f(t) = 4 \sin 100\pi t + 2 \cos 40\pi t.$$

Solution

A graph of f in a viewing window with $-2\pi \le t \le 2\pi$ includes so many cycles that the calculator cannot display an accurate graph, as shown in Figure 7.4.A-3.

Instead, find the period of f by using the following method:

$$\text{Let } h(t) = 4 \sin 100\pi t \qquad \text{and} \qquad g(t) = 2 \cos 40\pi t.$$

The period of h is $\dfrac{2\pi}{100\pi} = \dfrac{1}{50} = 0.02$. The period of g is $\dfrac{2\pi}{40\pi} = \dfrac{1}{20} = 0.05$. The period of f is the least common multiple of 0.02 and 0.05, which is 0.10.

Therefore, the viewing window with $0 \le t \le 0.10$ in Figure 7.4.A-4 shows one complete cycle of $f(t) = 4 \sin 100\pi t + 2 \cos 40\pi t$. ∎

Damped and Compressed Trigonometric Graphs

Suppose a weight hanging from a spring is set in motion by an upward push. No spring is perfectly elastic, and friction acts to slow the motion of the weight as time goes on. Consequently, the graph showing the height of the spring above or below its equilibrium point at time t will consist of waves that get smaller and smaller as t gets larger. Many other physical situations can be described by functions whose graphs consist of waves of diminishing or increasing heights. Other situations, such as sound waves in FM radio transmission, are modeled by functions whose graphs consist of waves of uniform height and varying frequency.

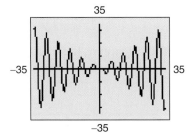

35

−35   35

−35

Figure 7.4.A-5

Example 3   Analyzing a Damped Graph

Analyze the graph of $f(t) = t \cos t$.

Solution

Graph f in a viewing window with $-35 \le t \le 35$ and $-35 \le y \le 35$, as shown in Figure 7.4.A-5.

Recall that $-1 \le \cos t \le 1$. Multiply each term of the inequality by t considering the cases $t \ge 0$ and $t < 0$. (Remember to reverse the inequality sign when $t < 0$.)

$$-t \le t \cos t \le t \quad \text{when } t \ge 0$$
$$-t \ge t \cos t \ge t \quad \text{when } t < 0$$

In graphical terms, this means that the graph of $f(t) = t \cos t$ lies between the straight lines $y = t$ and $y = -t$, with the waves growing larger or smaller to fit the space between the lines. The graph touches the lines $y = t$ and $y = -t$ exactly when $t \cos t = \pm t$, that is, when $\cos t = \pm 1$. This occurs when $t = 0 + k\pi$, where k is an integer.

Therefore, the graph of $f(t) = t \cos t$ consists of waves that diminish in amplitude as t approaches 0 from both negative and positive values, and the waves are bounded by the lines $y = \pm t$. ∎

> ┌── **Graphing Exploration** ●───
>
> Illustrate the analysis of the graph $f(t) = t \cos t$ by graphing $f(t) = t \cos t$, $y = t$, and $y = -t$ on the same screen.

Example 4   Analyzing a Damped Graph

Analyze the graph of $g(t) = 0.5^t \sin t$.

Solution

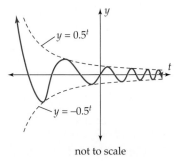

$y = 0.5^t$

$y = -0.5^t$

not to scale

Figure 7.4.A-6

No single viewing window gives a completely readable graph of g. To the left of the y-axis, the graph gets quite large; but to the right, it almost coincides with the t-axis. To get a better mental picture, note that $0.5^t > 0$ for every t. To find the bounds of $0.5^t \sin t$, multiply each term of the known inequality $-1 \le \sin t \le 1$ by 0.5^t.

$$-1 \le \sin t \qquad \le 1$$
$$-0.5^t \le 0.5^t \sin t \qquad \le 0.5^t \qquad \text{for every } t$$

Therefore, the graph of g lies between the graphs of the exponential functions $y = -0.5^t$ and $y = 0.5^t$. The graph of g will consist of sine waves rising and falling between the graph of the exponential functions $y = -0.5^t$ and $y = 0.5^t$, as indicated in Figure 7.4.A-6 (which is not to scale). ∎

Graphing Exploration ●

Find viewing window ranges that clearly show the graph in Example 4 when t is in the following domains.

$$-2\pi \le t \le 0 \qquad 0 \le t \le 2\pi \qquad 2\pi \le t \le 4\pi$$

Example 5   Oscillating Behavior

Analyze the graph of $f(t) = \sin\left(\dfrac{\pi}{t}\right)$.

Solution

Using a wide viewing window, it is clear that the t-axis is an asymptote of the graph of $f(t) = \sin\left(\dfrac{\pi}{t}\right)$, as shown in Figure 7.4.A-7a. Near the origin, however, the graph is not readable, even in a very narrow viewing window like Figure 7.4.A-7b.

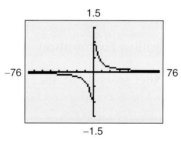

Figure 7.4.A-7a

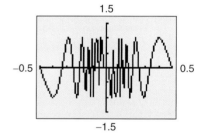

Figure 7.4.A-7b

Consider what happens to the graph between $t = \dfrac{1}{2}$, and $t = 0$.

As t goes from $\dfrac{1}{2}$ to $\dfrac{1}{4}$, $\sin\left(\dfrac{\pi}{t}\right)$ goes from $\sin\left(\dfrac{\pi}{\frac{1}{2}}\right)$ to $\sin\left(\dfrac{\pi}{\frac{1}{4}}\right)$, that is from $\sin 2\pi$ to $\sin 4\pi$. Therefore, the graph of f makes one complete sine wave for $\dfrac{1}{4} \le t \le \dfrac{1}{2}$. Similarly, for $\dfrac{1}{6} \le t \le \dfrac{1}{4}$, the graph of f makes another complete sine wave. The same pattern continues so that the graph of f makes a complete wave for $\dfrac{1}{8} \le t \le \dfrac{1}{6}$, for $\dfrac{1}{10} \le t \le \dfrac{1}{8}$, and so on. A similar phenomenon occurs as t takes values between $-\dfrac{1}{2}$ and 0. Consequently, the graph of f near 0 oscillates infinitely often between -1 and 1, with the waves becoming more and more compressed as t gets closer to 0, as indicated in Figure 7.4.A-8. Because the function is not defined at $t = 0$, the left and right halves of the graph are not connected.

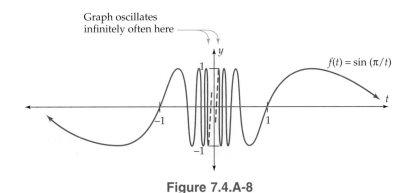

Figure 7.4.A-8

Exercises 7.4.A

In Exercises 1–6, find a sine function whose graph looks like the graph of the given function f.

1. $f(t) = \sin t + 2 \cos t$

2. $f(t) = 3 \sin t + 2 \cos t$

3. $f(t) = 2 \sin 4t - 5 \cos 4t$

4. $f(t) = 3 \sin(2t - 1) + 4 \cos(2t + 3)$

5. $f(t) = -5 \sin(3t + 2) + 2 \cos(3t - 1)$

6. $f(t) = 0.3 \sin(2t + 4) - 0.4 \cos(2t - 3)$

In Exercises 7–16, find a viewing window that shows a complete graph of the function.

7. $g(t) = (5 \sin 2t)(\cos 5t)$

8. $h(t) = e^{\sin t}$

9. $f(t) = \dfrac{t}{2} + \cos 2t$

10. $g(t) = \sin\left(\dfrac{t}{3} - 2\right) + 2 \cos\left(\dfrac{t}{4} - 2\right)$

11. $h(t) = \sin 300t + \cos 500t$

12. $f(t) = 3 \sin(200t + 1) - 2 \cos(300t + 2)$

13. $g(t) = -5 \sin(250\pi t + 5) + 2 \cos(400\pi t - 7)$

14. $h(t) = 4 \sin(600\pi t + 3) - 6 \cos(500\pi t - 3)$

15. $f(t) = 4 \sin 0.2\pi t - 5 \cos 0.4\pi t$

16. $g(t) = 6 \sin 0.05\pi t + 2 \cos 0.04\pi t$

In Exercises 17–24, describe the graph of the function verbally, including such features as asymptotes, undefined points, amplitude and number of waves between 0 and 2π. Find viewing windows that illustrate the main features of the graph.

17. $g(t) = \sin e^t$

18. $h(t) = \dfrac{\cos 2t}{1 + t^2}$

19. $f(t) = \sqrt{|t|} \cos t$

20. $g(t) = e^{-\frac{t^2}{8}} \sin 2\pi t$

21. $h(t) = \dfrac{1}{t} \sin t$

22. $f(t) = t \sin \dfrac{1}{t}$

23. $h(t) = \ln|\cos t|$

24. $h(t) = \ln|\sin t + 1|$

CHAPTER 7 REVIEW

Important Concepts

Important Facts and Formulas

If $a \neq 0$ and $b > 0$, then each of the functions $f(t) = a \sin(bt + c) + d$ and $g(t) = a \cos(bt + c) + d$ has:

$$\text{amplitude } |a|, \quad \text{period } \frac{2\pi}{b},$$

$$\text{phase shift } -\frac{c}{b} \quad \text{vertical shift } d$$

If $b > 0$, then the function $h(t) = \tan bt$ has period $\frac{\pi}{b}$.

Review Exercises

Section 7.1

1. Which of the following is not true about the graph of $f(t) = \sin t$?
   a. It has no sharp corners.
   b. It crosses the horizontal axis more than once.
   c. It rises higher and higher as t gets larger.
   d. It is periodic.
   e. It has no vertical asymptotes.

In Exercises 2–4, graph each function on the given interval.

2. $f(t) = \sin t \quad \left[\dfrac{7\pi}{2}, 7\pi\right]$

3. $g(t) = \cos t \quad \left[-5\pi, -\dfrac{7\pi}{2}\right]$

4. $h(t) = \tan t \quad [2\pi, 3\pi]$

In Exercises 5–7, find all the exact t-values for which the given statement is true.

5. $\cos t = 1$

6. $\sin t = -\dfrac{1}{2}$

7. $\tan t = -\sqrt{3}$

In Exercises 8–10, list the transformations that change the graph of f into the graph of g. State the domain and range of g.

8. $f(t) = \sin t \quad g(t) = -\dfrac{1}{2}\sin t$

9. $f(t) = \tan t \quad g(t) = -\tan 2t$

10. $f(t) = \cos t \quad g(t) = \cos\left(-\dfrac{1}{2}t\right) - 1$

In Exercises 11–13, sketch the graph of each function.

11. $g(t) = -3\cos t$

12. $h(t) = \tan t - 4$

13. $k(t) = 2\sin t + 3$

14. Which of the following functions has the graph shown below between $-\pi$ and π?
   a. $f(x) = \begin{cases} \sin x, & \text{if } x \geq 0 \\ \cos x, & \text{if } x < 0 \end{cases}$
   b. $g(x) = \cos x - 1$
   c. $h(x) = \begin{cases} \sin x, & \text{if } x \geq 0 \\ \sin(-x), & \text{if } x < 0 \end{cases}$
   d. $k(x) = |\cos x|$
   e. $p(x) = \sqrt{1 - \sin^2 x}$

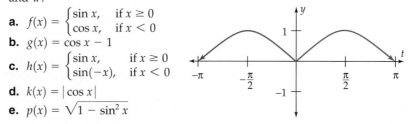

15. Between (and including) 0 and 2π, the function $h(t) = \tan t$ has ___?___ .
   a. 3 zeros and is undefined at 2 places
   b. 2 zeros and is undefined at 3 places
   c. 2 zeros and is undefined at 2 places
   d. 3 zeros and is defined everywhere
   e. no zeros and is undefined at 3 places

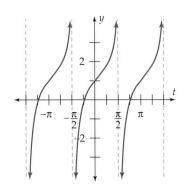

16. Which of the statements **i–iii** are true?
  i. The sine function is an odd function.
  ii. The cosine function is an odd function.
  iii. The tangent function is an odd function.
  a. i and ii only
  b. ii only
  c. i and iii only
  d. all of them
  e. none of them

17. Which of the following functions has the graph shown at left?
  a. $f(t) = \tan t$
  b. $g(t) = \tan\left(t + \dfrac{\pi}{2}\right)$
  c. $h(t) = 1 + \tan t$
  d. $k(t) = 3 \tan t$
  e. $p(t) = -\tan t$

Section 7.2

18. Which of the following is true about $\sec t$?
  a. $\sec(0) = 0$
  b. $\sec t = \dfrac{1}{\sin t}$
  c. Its graph has no asymptotes.
  d. It is a periodic function.
  e. It is never negative.

In Exercises 19–21, sketch the graph of each function.

19 $g(t) = \cot t + 2$

20. $f(t) = 3 \sec t - 2$

21. $h(t) = -\csc\left(\dfrac{1}{2}t\right)$

In Exercises 22–23, complete the statement with "odd" or "even."

22. The cosecant function is an _____ function.

23. The secant function is an _____ function.

Section 7.3

24. Let $f(t) = \dfrac{3}{2} \sin 5t$.

  a. What is the largest possible value of $f(t)$?
  b. Find the smallest positive number t such that $f(t) = 0$.

25. Sketch the graph of $g(t) = -2 \cos t$.

26. Sketch the graph of $f(t) = -\dfrac{1}{2} \sin 2t$ on the interval $-2\pi \le t \le 2\pi$.

27. Sketch the graph of $f(t) = \sin 4t$ on the interval $0 \le t \le 2\pi$.

28. What is the period of the function $g(t) = \sin 4\pi t$?

29. If $g(t) = 20 \sin(200t)$, for how many values of t with $0 \le t \le 2\pi$ is it true that $g(t) = 1$?

30. What is the period of $f(t) = -\tan\left(\dfrac{t}{2}\right)$?

31. Which of the following statements is true?
   a. The amplitude of $f(t) = 3 \sin 2t + 1$ is 2.
   b. The period of $g(t) = -\dfrac{1}{2} \cos 2t$ is 4π.
   c. The period of $h(t) = 3 \tan 2t$ is $\dfrac{\pi}{2}$.
   d. The amplitude of $k(t) = -3 \tan t$ is 3.

Section 7.4

32. What are the amplitude, period, and phase shift of the function $h(t) = 13 \cos(14t + 15)$?

33. State the rule of a sine function with amplitude 8, period 5, and phase shift 14.

34. State the rule of a sine function with amplitude 3, period π, and phase shift $\dfrac{\pi}{3}$.

35. State the rule of a periodic function whose graph from $t = 0$ to $t = 2\pi$ closely resembles the graph at left.

In Exercises 36–38, sketch the graph of at least one cycle of each function.

36. $f(t) = \dfrac{1}{2} \cos(2t - \pi) + 3$

37. $g(t) = -\sin\left(\dfrac{1}{3}t + \pi\right)$

38. $g(t) = 4 \cos\left(\dfrac{2t}{3}\right) - 5$

In Exercises 39–42, determine graphically whether the given equation could possibly be an identity.

39. $\cos t = \sin\left(t - \dfrac{\pi}{2}\right)$

40. $\tan \dfrac{t}{2} = \dfrac{\sin t}{1 + \cos t}$

41. $\dfrac{\sin t - \sin 3t}{\cos t + \cos 3t} = -\tan t$

42. $\cos 2t = \dfrac{1}{1 - 2 \sin^2 t}$

Section 7.4.A

In Exercises 43 and 44, find a sine function whose graph looks like the graph of the given function.

43. $f(t) = 6 \sin(4t + 7) - 5 \cos(4t + 8)$

44. $f(t) = -5 \sin(5t - 3) + 2 \cos(5t + 2)$

In Exercises 45 and 46, find a viewing window that shows a complete graph of the function.

45. $f(t) = 3 \sin(300t + 5) - 2 \cos(500t + 8)$

46. $g(t) = -5 \sin(400\pi t + 1) + 2 \cos(150\pi t - 6)$

(graph at left, with y-axis marks at 2, 1, -1, -2 and t-axis marks at $\dfrac{2\pi}{5}$, $\dfrac{4\pi}{5}$, π, $\dfrac{6\pi}{5}$, $\dfrac{8\pi}{5}$, 2π)

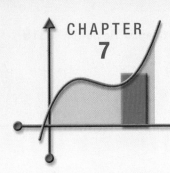

CHAPTER 7

can do calculus

Approximations with Infinite Series

In the Chapter 1 Can Do Calculus, it was shown that the infinite geometric series $a + ar + ar^2 + ar^3 + \ldots = \dfrac{a}{1 - r}$ when $|r| < 1$. This section will investigate certain functions that can be represented by an infinite series, a topic considered in depth in calculus.

Example 1   Representing a Function as a Series

Write $f(x) = \dfrac{1}{1 - x}$ as an infinite series.

Solution

The expression $\dfrac{1}{1 - x}$ is in the form $\dfrac{a}{1 - r}$, where $a = 1$ and $r = x$. Because

$$\frac{a}{1 - r} = a + ar + ar^2 + ar^3 + \ldots \text{ when } |r| < 1,$$

$$\frac{1}{1 - x} = 1 + x + x^2 + x^3 + \ldots, \text{ when } |x| < 1.$$

■

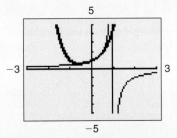

Figure 7.C-1

To confirm that $\dfrac{1}{1 - x} = 1 + x + x^2 + x^3 + \ldots$ when $|x| < 1$, graph $y = \dfrac{1}{1 - x}$ and $y = 1 + x + x^2 + x^3 + x^4$ on the same screen, as shown in Figure 7.C-1 where $y = 1 + x + x^2 + x^3 + x^4$ is drawn with a heavy line. The graphs of the function and the series are very close when $|x| < 1$, but they diverge when $x < -1$ and when $x > 1$. When more terms are used in graphing the series, the series approximates the function more closely when $|x| < 1$. The set of all values of x for which the series converges to the function is called the **interval of convergence**. The function $\dfrac{1}{1 - x}$ has interval of convergence $-1 < x < 1$. It is not defined when $x = 1$, and when $x = -1$ the infinite series does not converge to a single value.

Technology Tip

The factorial feature is found in the PROB (or PRB) submenu of the MATH or OPTN menu on most calculators.

Other Types of Series

Many interesting functions that can be represented by a series include the product of all the integers from 1 to n. Such a product is written as $n!$, which is read "n factorial."

$$n! = 1 \cdot 2 \cdot 3 \cdot 4 \cdots (n - 2)(n - 1)n$$

0! is defined to be the number 1.

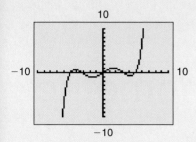

Figure 7.C-2a

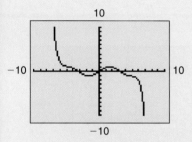

Figure 7.C-2b

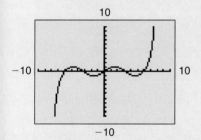

Figure 7.C-2c

A Series that Approximates a Function

Find a function that is approximated by the following series in the interval $-\pi \le x \le \pi$.

$$x - \frac{x^3}{3!} + \frac{x^5}{5!} - \frac{x^7}{7!} + \frac{x^9}{9!} + \cdots + (-1)^{n-1} \frac{x^{2n-1}}{(2n-1)!}$$

Solution

Begin by graphing the function formed by the first five terms of the series, as shown in Figure 7.C-2a. Next graph the functions formed by first six terms of the series and then the first seven terms, as shown in Figures 7.C-2b and 7.C-2c.

The graph of the series is beginning to resemble the graph of the sine function. To test the hypothesis that the series converges to the sine function, graph both the sine function and the function formed by series on the same screen using several terms of the series. In Figure 7.C-2d, the series is displayed with the heavier line, and $y = \sin x$ is shown as the lighter line. In calculus it will be shown that the *infinite* series converges to the sine function, and the interval of convergence is the entire set of real numbers.

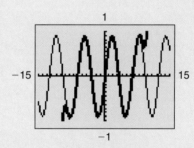

Figure 7.C-2d

Exercises

Find an infinite geometric series that represents the given function, and state the interval of convergence.

1. $y = \dfrac{2}{1 - 3x}$

2. $y = \dfrac{3}{1 - 2x}$

3. $y = \dfrac{-2}{1 + x}$

4. $y = \dfrac{-3}{1 + 2x}$

Find a function that is approximated by the following series. State the interval of convergence.

5. $1 - \dfrac{x^2}{2!} + \dfrac{x^4}{4!} - \dfrac{x^6}{6!} + \cdots$

6. $1 - (x - 1) + (x - 1)^2 - (x - 1)^3 + (x - 1)^4 - \cdots$

7. $1 + x + \dfrac{x^2}{2!} + \dfrac{x^3}{3!} + \dfrac{x^4}{4!} + \cdots$

521

CHAPTER

8 Solving Trigonometric Equations

Round and round we go!

Trigonometric functions are used to analyze periodic phenomena, because simple harmonic motion models circular motion or any phenomenon that is "back and forth." Some examples of simple harmonic motion include a vibrating prong of a tuning fork, a buoy bobbing up and down in water, seismic and ocean waves, spring-mass systems, a piston in a running engine, a particle of air during the passage of a simple sound wave, or a turning Ferris wheel. See Exercise 1 of Section 8.4.

Chapter Outline

Interdependence of Sections

8.1

8.2 $\longrightarrow$ 8.3 $\longrightarrow$ 8.4

There are two kinds of trigonometric equations. _Identities,_ which will be studied more in Chapter 9, are equations that are valid for all values of the variable for which the equation is defined, such as

$$\sin^2 x + \cos^2 x = 1 \qquad \text{and} \qquad \cot x = \frac{1}{\tan x}.$$

In this chapter, _conditional equations_ will be studied. Conditional equations are valid only for certain values of the variable, such as

$$\sin x = 0, \qquad \cos x = \frac{1}{2}, \qquad \text{and} \qquad 3\sin^2 x - \sin x = 2.$$

If a trigonometric equation is conditional, solutions are found by using techniques similar to those used to solve algebraic equations. Graphs were used to solve some simple trigonometric equations in Chapter 7. This chapter will extend graphical solution techniques and introduce analytic solution methods.

Graphical solution methods are presented in 8.1. Inverse trigonometric functions are discussed in Section 8.2. Methods that use inverse functions, basic identities, and algebra to solve trigonometric equations are considered in Section 8.3. Skills from the Sections 8.1 through 8.3 are applied to problem-solving and real-world applications in Section 8.4.

NOTE In Chapter 7, the variable t was used for trigonometric functions to avoid confusion with the x's and y's that appear in their definitions. Now that you are comfortable with these functions, the letter x, or occasionally y, will be used for the variable. Unless otherwise stated, all trigonometric functions in this chapter are considered as functions of real numbers, rather than functions of angles in degree measure.

8.1 Graphical Solutions to Trigonometric Equations

Objectives

- Solve trigonometric equations graphically
- State the complete solution of a trigonometric equation

Any equation involving trigonometric functions can be solved graphically. To solve trigonometric equations graphically, the same methods of graphical solutions are used here as have been used previously to solve polynomial equations, except that trigonometric equations typically have an infinite number of solutions. These solutions are systematically determined by using the periodicity of the function.

Basic Trigonometric Equations

An equation that involves a single trigonometric function set equal to a number is called a **basic equation.** Some examples include the following:

$$\sin x = 0.39, \qquad \cos x = 0.5, \qquad \text{and} \qquad \tan x = -3$$

Examples 1 and 2 show how they can be solved graphically.

Example 1   The Intersection Method

Solve $\tan x = 2$.

Solution

The equation can be solved by graphing $Y_1 = \tan x$ and $Y_2 = 2$ on the same screen and finding intersection points. The x-coordinate of every such point is a number whose tangent is 2; or a solution of $\tan x = 2$. Figure 8.1-1 indicates that there are infinitely many intersection points, so the equation has an infinite number of solutions.

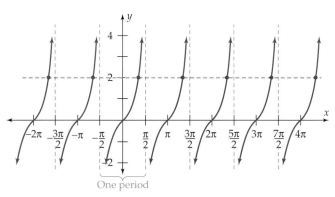

Figure 8.1-1

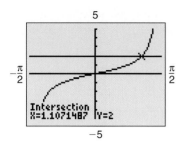

Figure 8.1-2

The function $f(x) = \tan x$ completes one cycle on the interval $\left(-\dfrac{\pi}{2}, \dfrac{\pi}{2}\right)$, and there is one solution of $\tan x = 2$ in this interval. Using the intersection finder on a graphing calculator gives the approximate solution in this interval.

$$x = 1.1071$$

Because the graph of $f(x) = \tan x$ repeats its pattern to the left and to the right, the other solutions will differ from this first solution by multiples of π, the period of the tangent function. The other solutions are

$$1.1071 \pm \pi, \qquad 1.1071 \pm 2\pi, \qquad \text{and} \qquad 1.1071 \pm 3\pi,$$

and so on. All solutions can be expressed as

$$1.1071 + k\pi,$$

where k is any integer.

NOTE Solutions in this chapter are often rounded, but the full decimal expansion given by the calculator is used in all computations. The symbol = is used rather than ≈ even though these calculator solutions are approximations of the actual solutions.

Example 2   The x-Intercept Method

Solve $\sin x = -0.75$.

Solution

Rewrite the equation $\sin x = -0.75$ as

$$\sin x + 0.75 = 0.$$

Recall from Section 2.1 that the solutions of this equation are the x-intercepts of the graph of

$$f(x) = \sin x + 0.75.$$

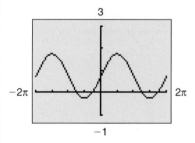

Figure 8.1-3

The graph of f is shown in Figure 8.1-3. The function has a period of 2π and the viewing window can be modified to show one period of $f(x) = \sin x + 0.75$. Figures 8.1-4a and 8.1-4b show that there are two zeros of f on the interval $[0, 2\pi]$, so the equation has two solutions on that interval.

The calculator's zero finder calculates the zeros:

$$x = 3.9897 \qquad\qquad\qquad x = 5.4351$$

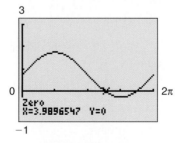

Figure 8.1-4a

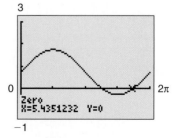

Figure 8.1-4b

Because the graph repeats its pattern every 2π, the other solutions will differ from these two by multiples of 2π, the period of $f(x) = \sin x + 0.75$. Therefore, all solutions of $\sin x = -0.75$ are

$$x = 3.9897 + 2k\pi \qquad \text{and} \qquad x = 5.4351 + 2k\pi,$$

where k is any integer.

Other Trigonometric Equations

The procedures in Examples 1 and 2 can be used to solve any trigonometric equation graphically.

Example 3 **The x-intercept Method**

Solve $3\sin^2 x - \cos x - 2 = 0$.

Solution

Both sine and cosine have period 2π, so the period of $f(x) = 3\sin^2 x - \cos x - 2$ is at most 2π. The graph of f, which is shown in two viewing windows in Figure 8.1-5, does not repeat its pattern over any interval of less than 2π, so you can conclude that f has a period of 2π.

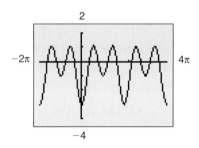

Figure 8.1-5a

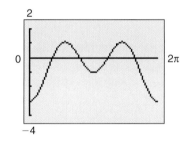

Figure 8.1-5b

The function f makes one complete period on the interval $[0, 2\pi)$, as shown in Figure 8.1-5b. The equation has four solutions between 0 and 2π, namely, the four x-intercepts of the graph in that interval. A graphical zero finder shows these four solutions.

$$x \approx 1.1216 \qquad x \approx 2.4459 \qquad x \approx 3.8373 \qquad x \approx 5.1616$$

Because the graph repeats its pattern every 2π, all solutions of the equation are given by

$$x \approx 1.1216 + 2k\pi, \qquad x \approx 2.4459 + 2k\pi,$$
$$x \approx 3.8373 + 2k\pi, \qquad x \approx 5.1616 + 2k\pi,$$

where k is any integer.

The solution methods in Examples 1 through 3 depend only on knowing the period of a function and all the solutions of the equation in one period. A similar procedure can be used to solve any trigonometric equation graphically.

Solving Trigonometric Equations Graphically

1. **Write the equation in the form $f(x) = 0$.**
2. **Determine the period p of f.**
3. **Graph f over an interval of length p.**
4. **Use a calculator's zero finder to determine the x-intercepts of the graph in this interval.**
5. **For each x-intercept u, all of the numbers**

$$u + kp \text{ where } k \text{ is any integer}$$

are solutions of the equation.

In Example 1, for example, p was π. In Examples 2 and 3, p was 2π.

Example 4   Solving Any Trigonometric Equation

Solve $\tan x = 3 \sin 2x$.

Solution

First rewrite the equation

$$\tan x - 3 \sin 2x = 0$$

Next, determine the period of $f(x) = \tan x - 3 \sin 2x$. Recall from Section 7.3 that $y = 3 \sin 2x$ has a period of $\dfrac{2\pi}{2} = \pi$, which is also the period of $y = \tan x$. Therefore, the period of f is π. Figure 8.1-6 shows the graph of f on the interval $\left(-\dfrac{\pi}{2}, \dfrac{\pi}{2} \right)$, an interval of length π.

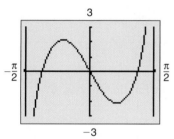

Figure 8.1-6

Even without the graph, it can be easily verified that there is an x-intercept at 0.

$$f(0) = \tan 0 - 3 \sin(2 \cdot 0) = 0$$

Using the calculator's zero finder gives the other x-intercepts of the graph of f on this interval.

$$x = -1.1503 \quad \text{and} \quad x = 1.1503$$

Because f has a period of π, all solutions of the equation $\tan x = 3 \sin 2x$ are

$$x = -1.1503 + k\pi, \quad x = 0 + k\pi, \quad \text{and} \quad x = 1.1503 + k\pi,$$

where k is any integer.

Trigonometric Equations in Degree Measure

Some real-world applications of trigonometric equations require solutions to be expressed as angles in degree measure. The graphical solution procedure is the same, except that you must set the mode of your calculator to "degree."

Example 5 Trigonometric Equations in Degree Measure

Solve $2 \sin^2\theta - 3 \sin \theta - 3 = 0$.

Solution

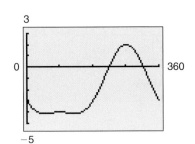

Figure 8.1-7

The period of the function $f(\theta) = 2 \sin^2\theta - 3 \sin \theta - 3$ is 360°, and Figure 8.1-7 shows the graph of f on the interval $[0°, 360°)$.

A graphical zero finder determines the approximate x-intercepts.

$$\theta \approx 223.33° \qquad \text{and} \qquad \theta \approx 316.67°$$

Using the fact that the period of f is 360°, all solutions of the equation are

$$\theta \approx 223.33° + 360°k \qquad \text{and} \qquad \theta \approx 316.67° + 360°k,$$

where k is any integer. ∎

Exercises 8.1

In Exercises 1–12, solve the equation graphically.

1. $4 \sin 2x - 3 \cos 2x = 2$

2. $5 \sin 3x + 6 \cos 3x = 1$

3. $3 \sin^3 2x = 2 \cos x$

4. $\sin^2 2x - 3 \cos 2x + 2 = 0$

5. $\tan x + 5 \sin x = 1$

6. $2 \cos^2 x + \sin x + 1 = 0$

7. $\cos^3 x - 3 \cos x + 1 = 0$

8. $\tan x = 3 \cos x$

9. $\cos^4 x - 3 \cos^3 x + \cos x = 1$

10. $\sec x + \tan x = 3$

11. $\sin^3 x + 2 \sin^2 x - 3 \cos x + 2 = 0$

12. $\csc^2 x + \sec x = 1$

13. Use the graph of the sine function to show the following.

a. The solutions of $\sin x = 1$ are

$$x = \frac{\pi}{2}, \frac{5\pi}{2}, \frac{9\pi}{2}, \ldots \text{ and}$$

$$x = \frac{-3\pi}{2}, \frac{-7\pi}{2}, \frac{-11\pi}{2}, \ldots .$$

b. The solutions of $\sin x = -1$ are

$$x = \frac{3\pi}{2}, \frac{7\pi}{2}, \frac{11\pi}{2}, \ldots \text{ and}$$

$$x = \frac{-\pi}{2}, \frac{-5\pi}{2}, \frac{-9\pi}{2}, \ldots .$$

14. Use the graph of the cosine function to show the following.

a. The solutions of $\cos x = 1$ are
$$x = 0, \pm 2\pi, \pm 4\pi, \pm 6\pi, \ldots .$$

b. The solutions of $\cos x = -1$ are
$$x = \pm \pi, \pm 3\pi, \pm 5\pi, \ldots .$$

In Exercises 15–18, approximate all solutions of the given equation in $(0, 2\pi)$.

15. $\sin x = 0.119$ **16.** $\cos x = 0.958$

17. $\tan x = 5$ **18.** $\tan x = 17.65$

In Exercises 19–28, find all angles θ with $0° \leq \theta < 360°$ that are solutions of the given equation.

19. $\tan \theta = 7.95$ **20.** $\tan \theta = 69.4$

21. $\cos \theta = -0.42$ **22.** $\cot \theta = -2.4$

23. $2 \sin^2 \theta + 3 \sin \theta + 1 = 0$

24. $4 \cos^2\theta + 4 \cos \theta - 3 = 0$

25. $\tan^2\theta - 3 = 0$ **26.** $2 \sin^2\theta = 1$

27. $4 \cos^2\theta + 4 \cos \theta + 1 = 0$

28. $\sin^2\theta - 3 \sin \theta = 10$

At the instant you hear a sonic boom from an airplane overhead, your angle of elevation α to the plane is given by the equation

$$\sin \alpha = \frac{1}{m}$$

where m is the Mach number for the speed of the plane (Mach 1 is the speed of sound, Mach 2.5 is 2.5 times the speed of sound, etc.). In Exercises 29–32, find the angle of elevation (in degrees) for the given Mach number. Remember that an angle of elevation must be between 0° and 90°.

29. $m = 1.1$ **30.** $m = 1.6$

31. $m = 2$ **32.** $m = 2.4$

33. *Critical Thinking* Under what conditions (on the constant) does a basic equation involving the sine and cosine function have no solutions?

34. *Critical Thinking* Under what conditions (on the constant) does a basic equation involving the secant and cosecant function have no solutions?

8.2 Inverse Trigonometric Functions

Objectives

- Define the domain and range of the inverse trigonometric functions
- Use inverse trigonometric function notation

Many trigonometric equations can be solved without graphing. Nongraphical solution methods make use of the *inverse trigonometric functions* that are introduced in this section.

Recall from Section 3.6 that a function cannot have an inverse function unless its graph has the following property.

> No horizontal line intersects the graph more than once.

You have seen that the graphs of trigonometric functions do not have this property. However, restricting their domains can modify the trigonometric functions so that they do have inverse functions.

NOTE Other ways of restricting the domains of trigonometric functions are possible. Those presented here for sine, cosine, and tangent are the ones universally agreed upon by mathematicians.

Inverse Sine Function

The *restricted sine function* is $f(x) = \sin x$, when its domain is restricted to the interval $\left[-\dfrac{\pi}{2}, \dfrac{\pi}{2}\right]$. Its graph in Figure 8.2-1 shows that for each number v in the interval $[-1, 1]$, there is exactly one number u in the interval $\left[-\dfrac{\pi}{2}, \dfrac{\pi}{2}\right]$ such that $\sin u = v$.

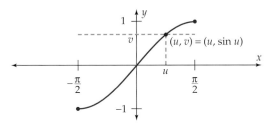

Figure 8.2-1

Because the graph of the restricted sine function passes the Horizontal Line Test, it has an inverse function. This inverse function is called the **inverse sine** (or **arcsine**) **function** and is denoted by

$$g(x) = \sin^{-1} x \text{ or } g(x) = \arcsin x.$$

It is convenient to think of a value of an inverse trigonometric function as an angle; $\sin^{-1}\dfrac{\sqrt{3}}{2}$ represents an angle in the interval $\left[-\dfrac{\pi}{2}, \dfrac{\pi}{2}\right]$ whose sine is $\dfrac{\sqrt{3}}{2}$. Since $\sin\dfrac{\pi}{3} = \dfrac{\sqrt{3}}{2}$, then $\sin^{-1}\dfrac{\sqrt{3}}{2} = \dfrac{\pi}{3}$.

The graph of the inverse sine function, shown in Figure 8.2-2, is readily obtained from a calculator. Because $g(x) = \sin^{-1} x$ is the inverse of the restricted sine function, its graph is the reflection of the graph of the restricted sine function across the line $y = x$.

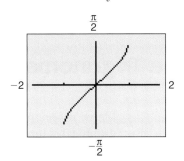

Figure 8.2-2

The domain of $g(x) = \sin^{-1} x$ is the interval $[-1, 1]$, and its range is the interval $\left[-\dfrac{\pi}{2}, \dfrac{\pi}{2}\right]$.

Inverse Sine Function

For each v with $-1 \le v \le 1$,

$\sin^{-1} v$ is the unique number u in the interval $\left[-\dfrac{\pi}{2}, \dfrac{\pi}{2}\right]$ whose sine is v; that is,

$$\sin^{-1} v = u \quad \text{exactly when} \quad \sin u = v.$$

Technology Tip

Unless otherwise noted, make sure your calculator is in radian mode.

Technology Tip

If you attempt to use a calculator to evaluate the inverse sine function at a number not in its domain, such as $\sin^{-1}(2)$, you will get an error message.

The inverse sine function can be evaluated by using the SIN^{-1} key (sometimes labeled ASIN) on a calculator. For example,

$$\sin^{-1}(-0.67) = -0.7342 \quad \text{and} \quad \sin^{-1} 0.42 = 0.4334.$$

For many special values, however, you can evaluate the inverse sine function without using a calculator.

Example 1 **Special Values**

Evaluate:

a. $\sin^{-1} \dfrac{1}{2}$ **b.** $\sin^{-1}\left(-\dfrac{\sqrt{2}}{2}\right)$

Solution

a. $\sin^{-1} \dfrac{1}{2}$ is the number in the interval $\left[-\dfrac{\pi}{2}, \dfrac{\pi}{2}\right]$ whose sine is $\dfrac{1}{2}$. From your study of special values, you know that $\sin \dfrac{\pi}{6} = \dfrac{1}{2}$. Because $\dfrac{\pi}{6}$ is in the interval $\left[-\dfrac{\pi}{2}, \dfrac{\pi}{2}\right]$, $\sin^{-1} \dfrac{1}{2} = \dfrac{\pi}{6}$.

b. $\sin^{-1}\left(-\dfrac{\sqrt{2}}{2}\right) = -\dfrac{\pi}{4}$ because $\sin\left(-\dfrac{\pi}{4}\right) = -\dfrac{\sqrt{2}}{2}$ *and* $-\dfrac{\pi}{4}$ is in the interval $\left[-\dfrac{\pi}{2}, \dfrac{\pi}{2}\right]$.

■

CAUTION

The notation $\sin^{-1} x$ is *not* exponential notation. It does *not* mean $(\sin x)^{-1}$ or $\dfrac{1}{\sin x}$. For instance, Example 1 shows that

$$\sin^{-1} \dfrac{1}{2} = \dfrac{\pi}{6} \approx 0.5236,$$

but this is not equivalent to

$$\left(\sin \dfrac{1}{2}\right)^{-1} = \dfrac{1}{\sin \dfrac{1}{2}} \approx \dfrac{1}{0.4794} \approx 2.0858.$$

Suppose $-1 \leq v \leq 1$ and $\sin^{-1} v = u$. Then by definition of the inverse sine function, $-\dfrac{\pi}{2} \leq u \leq \dfrac{\pi}{2}$ and $\sin u = v$. Therefore,

$$\sin^{-1}(\sin u) = \sin^{-1}(v) = u \quad \text{and} \quad \sin(\sin^{-1} v) = \sin(u) = v.$$

This shows that the restricted sine function and the inverse sine function have the usual composition properties of other inverse functions.

Properties of Inverse Sine

$$\sin^{-1}(\sin u) = u \quad \text{if} \quad -\frac{\pi}{2} \leq u \leq \frac{\pi}{2}$$

$$\sin(\sin^{-1} v) = v \quad \text{if} \quad -1 \leq v \leq 1$$

Example 2 Composition of Inverse Functions

Explain why $\sin^{-1}\left(\sin\frac{\pi}{6}\right) = \frac{\pi}{6}$ is true but $\sin^{-1}\left(\sin\frac{5\pi}{6}\right) = \frac{5\pi}{6}$ is *not* true.

Solution

You know that $\sin\frac{\pi}{6} = \frac{1}{2}$, so by substitution

$$\sin^{-1}\left(\sin\frac{\pi}{6}\right) = \sin^{-1}\left(\frac{1}{2}\right) = \frac{\pi}{6}$$

because $\frac{\pi}{6}$ is in the interval $\left[-\frac{\pi}{2}, \frac{\pi}{2}\right]$.

Although $\sin\frac{5\pi}{6}$ is also $\frac{1}{2}$, by substitution

$$\sin^{-1}\left(\sin\frac{5\pi}{6}\right) = \sin^{-1}\left(\frac{1}{2}\right) = \frac{\pi}{6},$$

not $\frac{5\pi}{6}$, because $\frac{5\pi}{6}$ is not in the interval $\left[-\frac{\pi}{2}, \frac{\pi}{2}\right]$. ∎

Inverse Cosine Function

The *restricted cosine function* is $f(x) = \cos x$, when its domain is restricted to the interval $[0, \pi]$. Its graph in Figure 8.2-3 shows that for each number v in the interval $[-1, 1]$, there is exactly one number u in the interval $[0, \pi]$ such that $\cos u = v$.

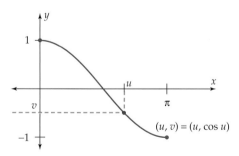

Figure 8.2-3

Because the graph of the restricted cosine function passes the horizontal line test, it has an inverse function. This inverse function is called the **inverse cosine** (or **arccosine**) **function** and is denoted by

$$g(x) = \cos^{-1} x \text{ or } g(x) = \arccos x.$$

The graph of the inverse cosine function, which is the reflection of the graph of the restricted cosine function (Figure 8.2-3) across the line $y = x$, is shown in Figure 8.2-4.

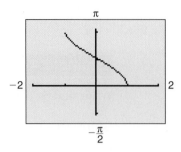

Figure 8.2-4

The domain of $g(x) = \cos^{-1} x$ is the interval $[-1, 1]$ and its range is $[0, \pi]$.

Inverse Cosine Function

For each v with $-1 \leq v \leq 1$,

$\cos^{-1}v$ is the unique number u in the interval $[0, \pi]$ whose cosine is v; that is,

$$\cos^{-1}v = u \quad \text{exactly when} \quad \cos u = v.$$

The properties of the inverse cosine function are similar to the properties of the inverse sine function.

Properties of Inverse Cosine

$$\cos^{-1}(\cos u) = u \quad \text{if} \quad 0 \leq u \leq \pi$$
$$\cos(\cos^{-1}v) = v \quad \text{if} \quad -1 \leq v \leq 1$$

Example 3 **Evaluating Inverse Cosine Expressions**

Evaluate the following.

a. $\cos^{-1}\dfrac{1}{2}$ **b.** $\cos^{-1}0$ **c.** $\cos^{-1}(-0.63)$

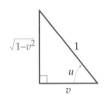

CAUTION

$\cos^{-1}$ does *not* mean $(\cos x)^{-1}$ or $\dfrac{1}{\cos x}$.

Solution

a. $\cos^{-1} \dfrac{1}{2} = \dfrac{\pi}{3}$ because $\dfrac{\pi}{3}$ is the unique number in the interval $[0, \pi]$ whose cosine is $\dfrac{1}{2}$.

b. $\cos^{-1} 0 = \dfrac{\pi}{2}$ because $\cos \dfrac{\pi}{2} = 0$ and $0 \le \dfrac{\pi}{2} \le \pi$.

c. The COS^{-1} command on a calculator shows that $\cos^{-1}(-0.63) = 2.2523$.

Example 4 **Equivalent Algebraic Expressions**

Write $\sin(\cos^{-1} v)$ as an algebraic expression in v.

Solution

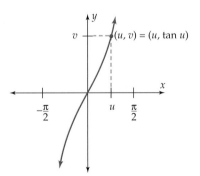

Figure 8.2-5

Let $\cos^{-1} v = u$, where $0 \le u \le \pi$. Construct a right triangle containing an angle of u radians where $\cos u = \dfrac{\text{adjacent}}{\text{hypotenuse}} = v$, as shown in Figure 8.2-5. By the Pythagorean Theorem, the length of the side opposite u is $\sqrt{1 - v^2}$. By the definition of sine,

$$\sin u = \frac{\text{opposite}}{\text{hypotenuse}} = \frac{\sqrt{1 - v^2}}{1} = \sqrt{1 - v^2}$$

Therefore, $\sin(\cos^{-1} v) = \sqrt{1 - v^2}$.

Inverse Tangent Function

The *restricted tangent function* is $f(x) = \tan x$, when its domain is restricted to the interval $\left(-\dfrac{\pi}{2}, \dfrac{\pi}{2}\right)$. Its graph in Figure 8.2-6 shows that for every real number v, there is exactly one number u between $-\dfrac{\pi}{2}$ and $\dfrac{\pi}{2}$ such that $\tan u = v$.

Figure 8.2-6

Because the graph of the restricted tangent function passes the horizontal line test, it has an inverse function. This inverse function is called the **inverse tangent** (or **arctangent**) **function** and is denoted

$$g(x) = \tan^{-1} x \text{ or } g(x) = \arctan x.$$

The graph of the inverse tangent function, which is the reflection of the graph of the restricted tangent function (Figure 8.2-6) across the line $y = x$, is shown in Figure 8.2-7.

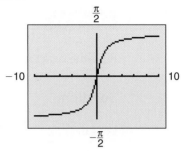

Figure 8.2-7

The domain of $g(x) = \tan^{-1} x$ is the set of all real numbers and its range is the interval $\left(-\dfrac{\pi}{2}, \dfrac{\pi}{2}\right)$.

Inverse Tangent Function

For each real number v,

$\tan^{-1} v$ is the unique number u in the interval $\left(-\dfrac{\pi}{2}, \dfrac{\pi}{2}\right)$ whose tangent is v; that is,

$$\tan^{-1} v = u \qquad \text{exactly when} \qquad \tan u = v.$$

The properties of the inverse tangent function are similar to the properties of the inverse sine and inverse cosine functions.

Properties of Inverse Tangent

$$\tan^{-1}(\tan u) = u \qquad \text{if} \quad -\dfrac{\pi}{2} \le u \le \dfrac{\pi}{2}$$

$$\tan(\tan^{-1} v) = v \text{ for every real number } v.$$

CAUTION

$\tan^{-1}$ does *not* mean $(\tan x)^{-1}$ or $\dfrac{1}{\tan x}$.

Example 5 Evaluating Inverse Tangent Expressions

Evaluate:

a. $\tan^{-1} 1$ **b.** $\tan^{-1} 136$

Solution

a. $\tan^{-1} 1 = \dfrac{\pi}{4}$ because $\dfrac{\pi}{4}$ is the unique number in the interval $\left(-\dfrac{\pi}{2}, \dfrac{\pi}{2}\right)$ such that $\tan \dfrac{\pi}{4} = 1$.

b. The TAN^{-1} key on a calculator shows that $\tan^{-1}(136) = 1.5634$.

Example 6   **Exact Values**

Find the exact value of $\cos\left(\tan^{-1} \dfrac{\sqrt{5}}{2}\right)$.

Solution

Let $\tan^{-1} \dfrac{\sqrt{5}}{2} = u$. Then $\tan u = \dfrac{\sqrt{5}}{2}$ and $-\dfrac{\pi}{2} \le u \le \dfrac{\pi}{2}$.

Because $\tan u = \dfrac{\sqrt{5}}{2}$ is positive, u must be between 0 and $\dfrac{\pi}{2}$. Draw a right triangle containing an angle of u radians whose tangent is $\dfrac{\sqrt{5}}{2}$.

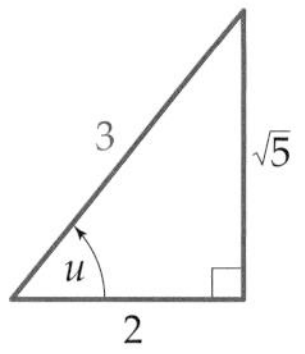

$$\tan u = \frac{\text{opposite}}{\text{hypotenuse}} = \frac{\sqrt{5}}{2}$$

Figure 8.2-8

The hypotenuse has length $\sqrt{2^2 + (\sqrt{5})^2} = \sqrt{4 + 5} = 3$. Therefore,

$$\cos\left(\tan^{-1} \frac{\sqrt{5}}{2}\right) = \cos u = \frac{\text{adjacent}}{\text{hypotenuse}} = \frac{2}{3}.$$

Exercises 8.2

In Exercises 1–14, find the exact functional value without using a calculator.

1. $\sin^{-1} 1$ **2.** $\cos^{-1} 0$ **3.** $\tan^{-1}(-1)$

4. $\sin^{-1}(-1)$ **5.** $\cos^{-1} 1$ **6.** $\tan^{-1} 1$

7. $\tan^{-1} \dfrac{\sqrt{3}}{3}$ **8.** $\cos^{-1} \dfrac{\sqrt{3}}{2}$

9. $\sin^{-1}\left(-\dfrac{\sqrt{2}}{2}\right)$ **10.** $\sin^{-1} \dfrac{\sqrt{3}}{2}$

11. $\tan^{-1}(-\sqrt{3})$ **12.** $\cos^{-1}\left(-\dfrac{\sqrt{2}}{2}\right)$

13. $\cos^{-1}\left(-\dfrac{1}{2}\right)$ **14.** $\sin^{-1}\left(-\dfrac{1}{2}\right)$

In Exercises 15–24, use a calculator in radian mode to approximate the functional value.

15. $\sin^{-1} 0.35$ **16.** $\cos^{-1} 0.76$

17. $\tan^{-1}(-3.256)$ **18.** $\sin^{-1}(-0.795)$

19. $\sin^{-1}(\sin 7)$ *Hint:* the answer is not 7.

20. $\cos^{-1}(\cos 3.5)$

21. $\tan^{-1}\left[\tan(-4)\right]$

22. $\sin^{-1}\left[\sin(-2)\right]$

23. $\cos^{-1}\left[\cos(-8.5)\right]$

24. $\tan^{-1}(\tan 12.4)$

25. Given that $u = \sin^{-1}\left(-\dfrac{\sqrt{3}}{2}\right)$, find the exact value of $\cos u$ and $\tan u$.

26. Given that $u = \tan^{-1}\left(\dfrac{4}{3}\right)$, find the exact value of $\sin u$ and $\sec u$.

In Exercises 27–42, find the exact functional value without using a calculator.

27. $\sin^{-1}(\cos 0)$

28. $\cos^{-1}\left(\sin \dfrac{\pi}{6}\right)$

29. $\cos^{-1}\left(\sin \dfrac{4\pi}{3}\right)$

30. $\tan^{-1}(\cos \pi)$

31. $\sin^{-1}\left(\cos \dfrac{7\pi}{6}\right)$

32. $\cos^{-1}\left(\tan \dfrac{7\pi}{4}\right)$

33. $\sin^{-1}\left(\sin \dfrac{2\pi}{3}\right)$ (See Exercise 19.)

34. $\cos^{-1}\left(\cos \dfrac{5\pi}{4}\right)$

35. $\cos^{-1}\left[\cos\left(-\dfrac{\pi}{6}\right)\right]$

36. $\tan^{-1}\left[\tan\left(-\dfrac{4\pi}{3}\right)\right]$

37. $\sin\left[\cos^{-1}\left(\dfrac{3}{5}\right)\right]$ (See Example 6.)

38. $\tan\left[\sin^{-1}\left(\dfrac{3}{5}\right)\right]$

39. $\cos\left[\tan^{-1}\left(-\dfrac{3}{4}\right)\right]$

40. $\cos\left[\sin^{-1}\left(\dfrac{\sqrt{3}}{5}\right)\right]$

41. $\tan\left[\sin^{-1}\left(\dfrac{5}{13}\right)\right]$

42. $\sin\left[\cos^{-1}\left(\dfrac{\sqrt{3}}{13}\right)\right]$

In Exercises 43–46, write the expression as an algebraic expression in v, as in Example 4.

43. $\cos(\sin^{-1}v)$

44. $\cot(\cos^{-1}v)$

45. $\tan(\sin^{-1}v)$

46. $\sin(2\sin^{-1}v)$

In Exercises 47–50, graph the function.

47. $f(x) = \cos^{-1}(x + 1)$

48. $g(x) = \tan^{-1}x + \pi$

49. $h(x) = \sin^{-1}(\sin x)$

50. $k(x) = \sin(\sin^{-1}x)$

51. A model plane 40 feet above the ground is flying away from an observer.

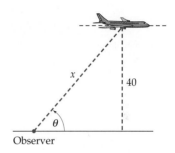

a. Express the angle of elevation θ of the plane as a function of the distance x from the observer to the plane.

b. What is θ when the plane is 250 feet from the observer?

52. Show that the restricted secant function, whose domain consists of all numbers x such that
$0 \le x \le \pi$ and $x \ne \dfrac{\pi}{2}$, has an inverse function.
Sketch its graph.

53. Show that the restricted cosecant function, whose domain consists of all numbers x such that
$-\dfrac{\pi}{2} \le x \le \dfrac{\pi}{2}$ and $x \ne 0$, has an inverse function.
Sketch its graph.

54. Show that the restricted cotangent function, whose domain is the interval $(0, \pi)$, has an inverse function. Sketch its graph.

55. a. Show that the inverse cosine function actually has the two properties listed in the box on page 533.

b. Show that the inverse tangent function actually has the two properties listed in the box on page 535.

56. *Critical Thinking* A 15-foot-wide highway sign is placed 10 feet from a road, perpendicular to the road. A spotlight at the edge of the road is aimed at the sign, as shown in the figure below.

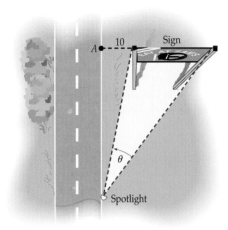

a. Express θ as a function of the distance x from point A to the spotlight.
b. How far from point A should the spotlight be placed so that the angle θ is as large as possible?

57. *Critical Thinking* A camera on a 5-foot-high tripod is placed in front of a 6-foot-high picture that is mounted 3 feet above the floor, as shown in figure below.

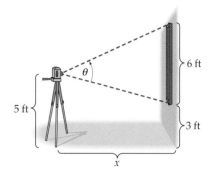

a. Express angle θ as a function of the distance x from the camera to the wall.
b. The photographer wants to use a particular lens, for which $\theta = 36° \left(\dfrac{\pi}{5} \text{ radians} \right)$. How far should she place the camera from the wall to be sure the entire picture will show in the photograph?

Algebraic Solutions of Trigonometric Equations

Objective

• Solve trigonometric equations algebraically

Trigonometric equations were solved graphically in Section 8.1. In this section you will learn how to use algebra with inverse trigonometric functions and identities to solve trigonometric equations.

Recall from Section 8.1 that equations such as

$$\sin x = -0.75, \quad \cos x = 0.6, \quad \text{and} \quad \tan x = 3$$

are called **basic equations.** Algebraic solution methods for basic equations are illustrated in Examples 1 through 3.

Example 1   **Solving Basic Cosine Equations**

Solve $\cos x = 0.6$.

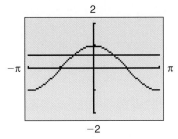

2

$-\pi$ ⎯⎯⎯⎯⎯⎯⎯⎯⎯ π

-2

Figure 8.3-1

Solution

The graphs of $Y_1 = \cos x$ and $Y_2 = 0.6$ in Figure 8.3-1 show that there are just two solutions (intersection points) on the interval $[-\pi, \pi]$, which is one full period of the cosine function.

The definition of the inverse cosine function states that

$\cos^{-1}0.6$ is the number in the interval $[0, \pi]$ whose cosine is 0.6.

Using the inverse cosine function, $x = \cos^{-1}0.6 = 0.9273$ is one solution of $\cos x = 0.6$ on the interval $[-\pi, \pi]$. The second solution can be found by using the identity $\cos(-x) = \cos x$, with $x = 0.9273$.

$$\cos(-0.9273) = \cos 0.9273 = 0.6$$

Therefore, the solutions of $\cos x = 0.6$ on the interval $[-\pi, \pi]$ are

$$x = \cos^{-1}0.6 = 0.9273 \qquad \text{and} \qquad x = -\cos^{-1}0.6 = -0.9273$$

Because the interval $[-\pi, \pi]$ is one complete period of the cosine function, all solutions of $\cos x = 0.6$ are given by

$$x = 0.9273 + 2k\pi \qquad \text{and} \qquad x = -0.9273 + 2k\pi,$$

where k is any integer. ∎

Example 2   **Solving Basic Sine Equations**

Solve $\sin x = -0.75$.

Solution

The definition of the inverse sine function states that

$\sin^{-1}(-0.75)$ is the number in the interval $\left[-\dfrac{\pi}{2}, \dfrac{\pi}{2}\right]$ whose sine is -0.75.

Using the inverse sine function, $x = \sin^{-1}(-0.75) = -0.8481$ is the solution of $\sin x = -0.75$ on the interval $\left[-\dfrac{\pi}{2}, \dfrac{\pi}{2}\right]$. A second solution can be found by using the identity $\sin(\pi - x) = \sin x$, with $x = -0.8481$.

$$\sin[\pi - (-0.8481)] = \sin(3.9897) = -0.75$$

Therefore, $x = \pi - (-0.8481) = 3.9897$ is also a solution of $\sin x = -0.75$, and all solutions are given by

$$x = -0.8481 + 2k\pi \qquad \text{and} \qquad x = 3.9897 + 2k\pi,$$

where k is any integer.

Recall that there are an infinite number of solutions to many trigonometric equations. Figure 8.3-2 indicates that there are two solutions in the interval $[-\pi, \pi]$: $x = -2.2935$ and $x = -0.8481$. The solution $x = -2.2935$ can be found by letting $k = -1$ in the solution $x = 3.9897 + 2\pi k$. ∎

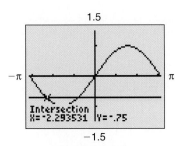

1.5

$-\pi$ ⎯⎯⎯⎯⎯⎯⎯⎯⎯ π

Intersection
X=-2.293531 Y=-.75

-1.5

Figure 8.3-2

Example 3 Solving Basic Tangent Equations

Solve $\tan x = 3$.

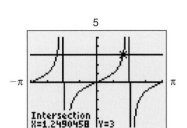

Figure 8.3-3

Solution

The definition of the inverse tangent function states that

$\tan^{-1} 3$ is the number in the interval $\left(-\dfrac{\pi}{2}, \dfrac{\pi}{2}\right)$ whose tangent is 3.

Using the inverse tangent function, $x = \tan^{-1} 3 = 1.2490$ is the solution of $\tan x = 3$ on the interval $\left(-\dfrac{\pi}{2}, \dfrac{\pi}{2}\right)$. Because $\left(-\dfrac{\pi}{2}, \dfrac{\pi}{2}\right)$ is one full period of the tangent function, all solutions are given by

$$x = 1.2490 + k\pi,$$

where k is any integer.

The solution method used in Examples 1–3 is summarized in the following table, where k is any integer.

Solutions of Basic Trigonometric Equations		
Equation	**Possible values of c**	**Solutions**
$\sin x = c$	$-1 < c < 1$	$x = \sin^{-1} c + 2k\pi$ and $x = (\pi - \sin^{-1} c) + 2k\pi$
	$c = 1$	$x = \dfrac{\pi}{2} + 2k\pi$
	$c = -1$	$x = -\dfrac{\pi}{2} + 2k\pi$
	$c > 1$ or $c < -1$	no solution
$\cos x = c$	$-1 < c < 1$	$x = \cos^{-1} c + 2k\pi$ and $x = -\cos^{-1} c + 2k\pi$
	$c = 1$	$x = 0 + 2k\pi = 2k\pi$
	$c = -1$	$x = \pi + 2k\pi$
	$c > 1$ or $c < -1$	no solution
$\tan x = c$	all real numbers	$x = \tan^{-1} c + k\pi$

Example 4   Using the Solution Algorithm

Solve $8 \cos x - 1 = 0$.

Solution

First rewrite the equation as an equivalent basic equation.

$$8 \cos x - 1 = 0$$

$$\cos x = \frac{1}{8}$$

Then solve the basic equation using the inverse cosine function. One solution is in Quadrant I.

$$x = \cos^{-1} \frac{1}{8} = 1.4455$$

The other solution on the interval $[-\pi, \pi]$ is in Quadrant IV.

$$x = -\cos^{-1} \frac{1}{8} = -1.4455$$

All solutions are given by

$$x = 1.4455 + 2k\pi \qquad \text{and} \qquad x = -1.4455 + 2k\pi,$$

where k is any integer.

Example 5   Solving Basic Equations with Special Values

Solve $\sin u = \dfrac{\sqrt{2}}{2}$ exactly, without using a calculator.

Solution

Because $\sin \dfrac{\pi}{4} = \dfrac{\sqrt{2}}{2}$, $u = \dfrac{\pi}{4}$ is one solution of $\sin u = \dfrac{\sqrt{2}}{2}$ on the interval $[-\pi, \pi]$. Another solution is in Quadrant II.

$$u = \pi - \frac{\pi}{4} = \frac{3\pi}{4}$$

Therefore, the exact solution is given by

$$u = \frac{\pi}{4} + 2k\pi \qquad \text{and} \qquad u = \frac{3\pi}{4} + 2k\pi,$$

where k is any integer.

Sometimes trigonometric equations can be solved by using substitution to make them into basic equations.

Example 6 Using Substitution and Basic Equations

Solve $\sin 2x = \dfrac{\sqrt{2}}{2}$ exactly, without using a calculator.

Solution

First, let $u = 2x$, and solve the basic equation $\sin u = \dfrac{\sqrt{2}}{2}$. From Example 5, you know the complete exact solution of $\sin u = \dfrac{\sqrt{2}}{2}$ is given by

$$u = \frac{\pi}{4} + 2k\pi \quad \text{and} \quad u = \frac{3\pi}{4} + 2k\pi,$$

where k is any integer.

Because $u = 2x$, each of these solutions leads to a solution of the original equation. Substitute $2x$ for u, and solve for x.

$$u = \frac{\pi}{4} + 2k\pi \qquad\qquad u = \frac{3\pi}{4} + 2k\pi$$

$$2x = \frac{\pi}{4} + 2k\pi \quad \text{and} \quad 2x = \frac{3\pi}{4} + 2k\pi$$

$$x = \frac{\pi}{8} + k\pi \qquad\qquad x = \frac{3\pi}{8} + k\pi$$

Therefore, all solutions of $\sin 2x = \dfrac{\sqrt{2}}{2}$ are given by

$$x = \frac{\pi}{8} + k\pi \quad \text{and} \quad x = \frac{3\pi}{8} + k\pi,$$

where k is any integer.

Algebraic Techniques

Many trigonometric equations can be solved algebraically—by using factoring, the quadratic formula, and basic identities to write an equivalent equation that involves only basic equations, as shown in the following examples.

Example 7 Factoring Trigonometric Equations

Find the solutions of $3 \sin^2 x - \sin x - 2 = 0$ in the interval $[-\pi, \pi]$.

Solution

Let $u = \sin x$.

$$3 \sin^2 x - \sin x - 2 = 0$$
$$3u^2 - u - 2 = 0 \qquad \textit{Substitution}$$

This quadratic equation can be solved by factoring.

$$3u^2 - u - 2 = 0$$
$$(3u + 2)(u - 1) = 0$$
$$u = -\frac{2}{3} \quad \text{or} \quad u = 1$$

Substituting $\sin x$ for u results in two basic equations.

$$\sin x = -\frac{2}{3} \quad \text{or} \quad \sin x = 1$$

If $\sin x = \left(-\dfrac{2}{3}\right)$, then

$$x = \sin^{-1}\left(-\frac{2}{3}\right) \qquad\qquad x = \pi - \sin^{-1}\left(-\frac{2}{3}\right)$$

or

$$= -0.7297 + 2k\pi \qquad\qquad = 3.8713 + 2k\pi$$

If $\sin x = 1$, then $x = \dfrac{\pi}{2} + 2k\pi$

Therefore, the solutions of $3 \sin^2 x - \sin x - 2 = 0$ are

$$x = -0.7297 + 2k\pi, \qquad x = \frac{\pi}{2} + 2k\pi, \qquad \text{and} \qquad x = 3.8713 + 2k\pi,$$

where k is any integer.

Figure 8.3-4 indicates that there are three solutions in the interval $[-\pi, \pi]$, which is marked with vertical lines. The solution $x = 3.8713$ is outside the interval, but the corresponding solution within the interval can be found by letting $k = -1$ in $x = 3.8713 + 2k\pi$. Within $[-\pi, \pi]$, the solutions are

$$x = 3.8713 - 2\pi = -2.4119, \qquad x = -0.7297, \qquad \text{and} \qquad x = \frac{\pi}{2}.$$

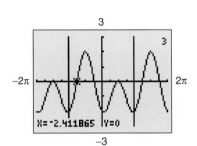

X=-2.411865 Y=0

Figure 8.3-4

Example 8 Factoring Trigonometric Equations

Solve $\tan x \cos^2 x = \tan x$.

Solution

Write an equivalent equation as an expression equal to zero, and factor.

$$\tan x \cos^2 x - \tan x = 0$$
$$\tan x (\cos^2 x - 1) = 0$$

$$\tan x = 0 \qquad \text{or} \qquad \cos^2 x - 1 = 0$$
$$x = 0 + k\pi \qquad\qquad \cos^2 x = 1$$
$$\sqrt{\cos^2 x} = \sqrt{1}$$
$$\cos x = \pm 1$$
$$x = 0 + 2k\pi \quad \text{or} \quad x = \pi + 2k\pi$$

CAUTION

$$\cos^2 x - 1 \neq \sin^2 x$$

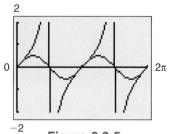

Figure 8.3-5

More simply stated, the solution of $\tan x \cos^2 x = \tan x$ is

$$x = 0 + k\pi = k\pi,$$

where k is any integer. The graphs of $Y_1 = \tan x \cos^2 x$ and $Y_2 = \tan x$ are shown in Figure 8.3-5.

■

Many trigonometric equations can be solved if trigonometric identities are used to rewrite the original equation, as shown in Examples 9 and 10.

Example 9 **Identities and Factoring**

Solve $-10 \cos^2 x - 3 \sin x + 9 = 0$.

Solution

Use the Pythagorean identity to rewrite the equation in terms of the sine function.

$$-10 \cos^2 x - 3 \sin x + 9 = 0$$
$$-10(1 - \sin^2 x) - 3 \sin x + 9 = 0$$
$$-10 + 10 \sin^2 x - 3 \sin x + 9 = 0$$
$$10 \sin^2 x - 3 \sin x - 1 = 0$$

Factor the left side and solve.

$$(2 \sin x - 1)(5 \sin x + 1) = 0$$

$$2 \sin x - 1 = 0 \qquad\qquad 5 \sin x + 1 = 0$$

$$\sin x = \frac{1}{2} \qquad\qquad \text{or} \qquad\qquad \sin x = -\frac{1}{5}$$

$$x = \sin^{-1}\left(\frac{1}{2}\right) \qquad\qquad x = \sin^{-1}\left(-\frac{1}{5}\right)$$

$$x = \frac{\pi}{6} + 2k\pi \quad \text{or} \qquad\qquad x = -0.2014 + 2k\pi \quad \text{or}$$

$$x = \pi - \frac{\pi}{6} + 2k\pi \qquad\qquad x = \pi - (-0.2014) + 2k\pi$$

$$= \frac{5\pi}{6} + 2k\pi \qquad\qquad = 3.3430 + 2k\pi$$

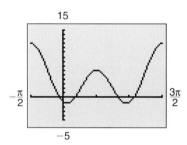

Figure 8.3-6

Therefore, all solutions of $-10 \cos^2 x - 3 \sin x + 9 = 0$ are

$$x = \frac{\pi}{6} + 2\,k\pi, \qquad x = \frac{5\pi}{6} + 2k\pi,$$

$$x = -0.2014 + 2k\pi, \qquad \text{and} \qquad x = 3.3430 + 2k\pi,$$

where k is any integer. The graph of $Y_1 = -10 \cos^2 x - 3 \sin x + 9$ shown in Figure 8.3-6 confirms the solution.

■

Example 10 **Identities and Quadratic Formula**

Solve $\sec^2 x + 5 \tan x = -2$.

Solution

Use a Pythagorean identity to rewrite the equation in terms of the tangent function.

$$\sec^2 x + 5 \tan x = -2$$
$$\sec^2 x + 5 \tan x + 2 = 0$$
$$(1 + \tan^2 x) + 5 \tan x + 2 = 0$$
$$\tan^2 x + 5 \tan x + 3 = 0$$

Use the quadratic formula to solve for $\tan x$.

$$\tan x = \frac{-5 \pm \sqrt{5^2 - 4(1)(3)}}{2(1)} = \frac{-5 \pm \sqrt{13}}{2}$$

$$\tan x = \frac{-5 + \sqrt{13}}{2} = -0.6972 \quad \text{or} \quad \tan x = \frac{-5 - \sqrt{13}}{2} = -4.3028$$

$$x = \tan^{-1}(-0.6972) \qquad\qquad\qquad x = \tan^{-1}(-4.3028)$$

$$= -0.6088 + k\pi \qquad\qquad\qquad = -1.3424 + k\pi$$

Therefore, the solution set of $\sec^2 x + 5 \tan x = -2$ is

$$x = -0.6089 + \pi k \quad \text{and} \quad x = -1.3424 + \pi k,$$

where k is any integer. The graphs of $Y_1 = \sec^2 x + 5 \tan x$ and $Y_2 = -2$ in Figure 8.3-7 confirm the solution. ∎

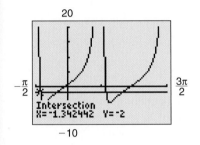

Figure 8.3-7

Exercises 8.3

In Exercises 1–8, find the exact solutions.

1. $\sin x = \dfrac{\sqrt{3}}{2}$

2. $2 \cos x = \sqrt{2}$

3. $\tan x = -\sqrt{3}$

4. $\tan x = 1$

5. $2 \cos x = -\sqrt{3}$

6. $\sin x = 0$

7. $2 \sin x + 1 = 0$

8. $\csc x = \sqrt{2}$

In the following exercises, find exact solutions if possible and approximate solutions otherwise. When a calculator is used, round to four decimal places.

Use the following information in Exercises 9–12.

When a light beam passes from one medium to another (for instance, from air to water), it changes both its speed and direction. According to Snell's Law of Refraction,

$$\frac{\sin \theta_1}{\sin \theta_2} = \frac{v_1}{v_2},$$

where v_1 is the speed of light in the first medium, v_2 its speed in the second medium, θ_1 the angle of incidence, and θ_2 the angle of refraction, as shown in the figure. The number $\dfrac{v_1}{v_2}$ is called the index of refraction.

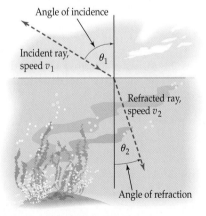

9. The index of refraction of light passing from air to water is 1.33. If the angle of incidence is 38°, find the angle of refraction.

10. The index of refraction of light passing from air to ordinary glass is 1.52. If the angle of incidence is 17°, find the angle of refraction.

11. The index of refraction of light passing from air to dense glass is 1.66. If the angle of incidence is 24°, find the angle of refraction.

12. The index of refraction of light passing from air to quartz is 1.46. If the angle of incidence is 50°, find the angle of refraction.

In Exercises 13–32, find all the solutions of each equation.

13. $\sin x = -0.465$

14. $\sin x = -0.682$

15. $\cos x = -0.564$

16. $\cos x = -0.371$

17. $\tan x = -0.237$

18. $\tan x = -12.45$

19. $\cot x = 2.3 \left[\text{Hint: } \cot x = \dfrac{1}{\tan x} \cdot \right]$

20. $\cot x = -3.5$

21. $\sec x = -2.65$

22. $\csc x = 5.27$

23. $\sin 2x = -\dfrac{\sqrt{3}}{2}$

24. $\cos 2x = \dfrac{\sqrt{2}}{2}$

25. $2 \cos \dfrac{x}{2} = \sqrt{2}$

26. $2 \sin \dfrac{x}{3} = 1$

27. $\tan 3x = -\sqrt{3}$

28. $5 \sin 2x = 2$

29. $5 \cos 3x = -3$

30. $2 \tan 4x = 16$

31. $4 \tan \dfrac{x}{2} = 8$

32. $5 \sin \dfrac{x}{4} = 4$

In Exercises 33–53, use factoring, the quadratic formula, or identities to solve the equation. Find all solutions in the interval $[0, 2\pi)$.

33. $3 \sin^2 x - 8 \sin x - 3 = 0$

34. $5 \cos^2 x + 6 \cos x = 8$

35. $2 \tan^2 x + 5 \tan x + 3 = 0$

36. $3 \sin^2 x + 2 \sin x = 5$

37. $\cot x \cos x = \cos x$

38. $\tan x \cos x = \cos x$ **39.** $\cos x \csc x = 2 \cos x$

40. $\tan x \sec x + 3 \tan x = 0$

41. $4 \sin x \tan x - 3 \tan x + 20 \sin x - 15 = 0$
Hint: One factor is $\tan x + 5$.

42. $25 \sin x \cos x - 5 \sin x + 20 \cos x = 4$

43. $\sin^2 x + 2 \sin x - 2 = 0$

44. $\cos^2 x + 5 \cos x = 1$ **45.** $\tan^2 x + 1 = 3 \tan x$

46. $4 \cos^2 x - 2 \cos x = 1$ **47.** $2 \tan^2 x - 1 = 3 \tan x$

48. $6 \sin^2 x + 4 \sin x = 1$ **49.** $\sec^2 x - 2 \tan^2 x = 0$

50. $9 - 12 \sin x = 4 \cos^2 x$

51. $\sec^2 x + \tan x = 3$

52. $\cos^2 x - \sin^2 x + \sin x = 0$

53. $2 \tan^2 x + \tan x = 5 - \sec^2 x$

54. The number of hours of daylight in Detroit on day t of a non-leap year (with $t = 0$ being January 1) is given by the following function.

$$d(t) = 3 \sin \left[\frac{2\pi}{365} (t - 80) \right] + 12$$

a. On what days of the year are there exactly 11 hours of daylight?

b. What day has the maximum amount of daylight?

55. A weight hanging from a spring is set into motion moving up and down. Its distance d (in centimeters) above or below the equilibrium point at time t seconds is given by

$$d = 5(\sin 6t - 4 \cos 6t).$$

At what times during the first 2 seconds is the weight at the equilibrium position ($d = 0$)?

In Exercises 56–59, use the following information.

When a projectile (such as a ball or a bullet) leaves its starting point at angle of elevation θ with velocity v, the horizontal distance d it travels is given by the equation

$$d = \frac{v^2}{32} \sin 2\theta,$$

where d is measured in feet and v in feet per second. Note that the horizontal distance traveled may be the same for two different angles of elevation, so that some of these exercises may have more than one correct answer.

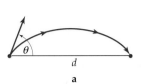

a

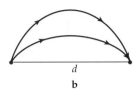

b

where V_{max} is the maximum voltage, f is the frequency (in cycles per second), t is the time in seconds, and ϕ is the phase angle.

a. If the phase angle is 0, solve the voltage equation for t.

b. If $\phi = 0$, $V_{max} = 20$, $V = 8.5$, and $f = 120$, find the smallest positive value of t.

56. If muzzle velocity of a rifle is 300 feet per second, at what angle of elevation (in radians) should it be aimed in order for the bullet to hit a target 2500 feet away?

57. Is it possible for the rifle in Exercise 56 to hit a target that is 3000 feet away? At what angle of elevation would it have to be aimed?

58. A fly ball leaves the bat at a velocity of 98 miles per hour and is caught by an outfielder 288 feet away. At what angle of elevation (in degrees) did the ball leave the bat?

59. An outfielder throws the ball at a speed of 75 miles per hour to the catcher who is 200 feet away. At what angle of elevation was the ball thrown?

60. In an alternating current circuit, the voltage is given by the formula

$$V = V_{max} \cdot \sin(2\pi ft + \phi),$$

61. *Critical Thinking* Find all solutions of $\sin^2 x + 3\cos^2 x = 0$ in the interval $[0, 2\pi)$.

62. *Critical Thinking* What is wrong with this "solution"?

$$\sin x \tan x = \sin x$$
$$\tan x = 1$$
$$x = \frac{\pi}{4} \quad \text{or} \quad \frac{5\pi}{4}$$

Hint: Solve the original equation by moving all terms to one side and factoring. Compare your answers with the ones above.

63. *Critical Thinking* Let n be a fixed positive integer. Describe all solutions of the equation $\sin nx = \frac{1}{2}$.

8.4

Simple Harmonic Motion and Modeling

Objective

- Write a sinusoidal function whose graph resembles a given graph

- Write a sinusoidal function to represent a given simple harmonic motion, and use the function to solve problems

- Find a sinusoidal model for a set of data, and use the model to make predictions

In Section 7.4, graphs of functions of the form

$$f(t) = a \sin(bt + c) + d \quad \text{and} \quad g(t) = a \cos(bt + c) + d,$$

were studied; and the constants a, b, c, and d were examined to see how they affect the graphs of the functions. In this section, trigonometric functions of this form are used to model real-world phenomena.

Recall that if $a \neq 0$ and $b > 0$, then each of the functions

$$f(t) = a \sin(bt + c) + d \quad \text{and} \quad g(t) = a \cos(bt + c) + d$$

has the following characteristics.

$$\text{amplitude} = |a| \qquad\qquad \text{period} = \frac{2\pi}{b}$$

$$\text{phase shift} = -\frac{c}{b} \qquad\qquad \text{vertical shift} = d$$

Recall the shapes of sine and cosine waves.

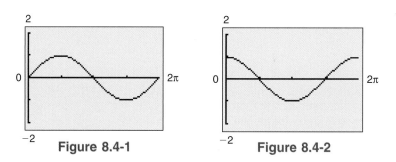

Figure 8.4-1   **Figure 8.4-2**

The wave shape of the graphs of these functions is called a **sinusoid** and the functions are called **sinusoidal functions.**

Recall that the amplitude of the function $f(t) = a \sin(bt)$ is the number $|a|$, and that its graph consists of waves that rise to $|a|$ units above the horizontal axis and fall to $-|a|$ units below the horizontal axis. In other words, the amplitude is half the distance from the maximum value to the minimum value of the function. This number remains the same when the graph is shifted vertically or horizontally. Thus the amplitude of the sinusoidal function $f(t) = a \sin(bt + c) + d$ or $g(t) = a \cos(bt + c) + d$ is the number

$$a = \frac{1}{2}(f_{max} - f_{min}),$$

where f_{max} and f_{min} denote the maximum and minimum values of f.

The vertical shift d of a sinusoidal function can be determined by averaging the maximum and minimum values as shown below.

$$\text{vertical shift} = d = \frac{f_{max} + f_{min}}{2}$$

Example 1   **Constructing Sinusoidal Functions**

Write a sine function and a cosine function whose graph resembles the sinusoidal graph below.

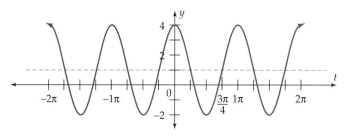

Figure 8.4-3

Solution

The graph shows that the function has a maximum of 4 and a minimum of -2. Therefore, the amplitude is

$$a = \frac{1}{2}(f_{max} - f_{min}) = \frac{1}{2}(4 - (-2)) = 3.$$

The graph shows one complete cosine cycle between 0 and π, so the period is π. Therefore,

$$\frac{2\pi}{b} = \pi$$
$$b = 2$$

The vertical shift d is one unit.

$$d = \frac{f_{max} + f_{min}}{2} = \frac{4 + (-2)}{2} = 1$$

The variable c depends on whether the function is described in terms of sine or cosine. If $g(t) = \cos t$ is used, there is no phase shift because a cosine wave's maximum occurs at $t = 0$. So the phase shift is 0, and a function for the sinusoidal graph in Figure 8.4-3 has a value of 0 for c.

$$g(t) = 3\cos 2t + 1$$

The graph indicates that a sine wave begins at $t = \frac{3\pi}{4}$, so the phase shift for a function using $f(t) = \sin t$ is $\frac{3\pi}{4}$.

$$\frac{3\pi}{4} = -\frac{c}{b} \qquad \textit{phase shift is } -\frac{c}{b}$$
$$\frac{3\pi}{4} = -\frac{c}{2} \qquad \qquad b = 2$$
$$c = -\frac{3\pi}{2} \qquad \qquad \textit{Solve for } c.$$

Therefore, a function for the sinusoidal graph in Figure 8.4-3 is

$$f(t) = 3\sin\left(2t - \frac{3\pi}{2}\right) + 1.$$

> **NOTE** The function that represents the graph, $g(t) = 3\cos 2t + 1$, is not unique because infinitely many functions can name the graph, such as $h(t) = 3\cos(2(t + \pi)) + 1$. They can be written using different phase shifts. The first function above is the representative answer because it uses the phase shift that is closest to zero.

Simple Harmonic Motion

Motion that can be described by a function of the form

$$f(t) = a\sin(bt + c) + d \qquad \text{or} \qquad g(t) = a\cos(bt + c) + d$$

is called **simple harmonic motion.** Many kinds of physical motion are simple harmonic motions.

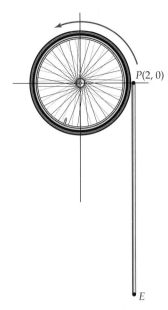

Figure 8.4-4

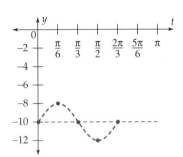

Figure 8.4-5

| Example 2 | Rotating Wheel |

A wheel with a radius of 2 centimeters is rotating counterclockwise at 3 radians per second. A free-hanging rod 10 centimeters long is connected to the edge of the wheel at point P and remains vertical as the wheel rotates (Figure 8.4-4).

a. Assuming that the center of the wheel is at the origin and that P is at $(2, 0)$ at time $t = 0$, find a function that describes the y-coordinate of the tip E of the rod at time t.

b. What is the first time that the tip E of the rod will be at a height of -9 centimeters?

Solution

a. The wheel is rotating at 3 radians per second. After t seconds, the point P has moved through an angle of $3t$ radians and is 2 units from the origin.

To find the time t that it takes to complete one revolution (i.e., 2π), solve $3t = 2\pi$.

$$t = \frac{2\pi}{3}$$

After $\frac{1}{4}$ of a revolution, or $\frac{1}{4} \times \frac{2\pi}{3} = \frac{\pi}{6}$, the height of P reaches its maximum of 2 centimeters, so the y-coordinate of E is $2 - 10 = -8$. After $\frac{1}{2}$ of a revolution, or $\frac{1}{2} \times \frac{2\pi}{3} = \frac{\pi}{3}$, the height of P is at 0, so the y-coordinate of E is -10. Continuing this process, it can be found that at $\frac{\pi}{2}$ the y-coordinate of E is -12 and at $\frac{2\pi}{3}$ the y-coordinate of E is -10.

Plotting these key points shows the main features of the graph.

The amplitude is

$$a = \frac{1}{2}(f_{max} - f_{min}) = \frac{1}{2}(-8 - (-12)) = 2.$$

Use the period to find b.

$$\frac{2\pi}{3} = \frac{2\pi}{b}$$
$$b = 3$$

The sine wave begins at $t = 0$, so there is no phase shift and $c = 0$. The vertical shift, d, is -10 units.

$$d = \frac{f_{max} + f_{min}}{2} = \frac{-8 + (-12)}{2} = -10$$

Thus, the function giving the y-coordinate of E at time t is

$$f(t) = 2 \sin 3t - 10.$$

b. To find the first time that the tip E of the rod will be at a height of -9 centimeters, solve $2 \sin 3t - 10 = -9$ for t.

$$2 \sin 3t - 10 = -9$$
$$2 \sin 3t = 1$$
$$\sin 3t = \frac{1}{2}$$
$$3t = \sin^{-1}\left(\frac{1}{2}\right)$$
$$3t = \frac{\pi}{6} + 2k\pi \; (k \text{ is any integer})$$
$$t = \frac{\pi}{18} + \frac{2k\pi}{3} = 0.1745 + \frac{2k\pi}{3}$$

The first time that the tip E of the rod will be at a height of -9 cm is when $k = 0$, that is, $t = \dfrac{\pi}{18} \approx 0.1745$ seconds.

Example 3   Bouncing Spring

Suppose that a weight hanging from a spring is set in motion by an upward push (Figure 8.4-6). It takes 5 seconds for it to complete one cycle of moving from its equilibrium position to 8 centimeters above, then dropping to 8 centimeters below, and finally returning to its equilibrium position. (This is an idealized situation in which the spring has perfect elasticity, and friction, air resistance, etc., are negligible.)

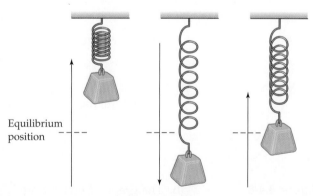

Equilibrium position

Figure 8.4-6

a. Find a sinusoidal function to represent the motion of the moving spring.

b. Sketch a graph of the function you wrote in part **a**.

c. Use the function from part **a** to predict the height of the weight after 3 seconds.

d. In the first 5 seconds, when will the height of the weight be 6 centimeters below the equilibrium position?

Solution

a. Let $h(t)$ denote the distance of the weight above (+) or below (−) its equilibrium position at time t. Then $h(t)$ is 0 when t is 0. As t increases from 0 to 5, $h(t)$ increases from 0 to 8, decreases to −8, and increases again to 0. In the next 5 seconds it repeats the same pattern, and so on. Therefore, the graph of h is periodic and has some kind of wave shape. Two possibilities are shown in Figures 8.4-7a and 8.4-7b.

 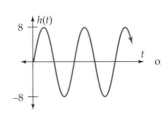 or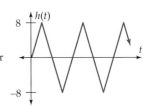

Figure 8.4-7a   **Figure 8.4-7b**

Careful physical experiment suggests that the curve in Figure 8.4-7a, which resembles the sine graphs you have studied, is a reasonably accurate model of this process. Facts from physics and calculus show that the rule of the function h is the form $h(t) = a \sin(bt + c)$ for some constants a, b, and c.

The function h has an amplitude of 8, a period of 5, and a phase shift 0, so the constants a, b, and c must satisfy

$$|a| = 8, \qquad \frac{2\pi}{b} = 5, \qquad \text{and} \qquad -\frac{c}{b} = 0,$$

or equivalently,

$$a = 8, \qquad b = \frac{2\pi}{5}, \qquad \text{and} \qquad c = 0.$$

Therefore, the motion of the moving spring can be described by this function:

$$h(t) = 8 \sin \frac{2\pi}{5}t$$

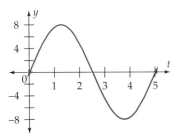

Figure 8.4-8

b. The graph of $h(t) = 8 \sin \frac{2\pi}{5}t$ is shown in Figure 8.4-8.

c. The value of $h(3)$ gives the height of the weight after 3 seconds.

$$h(3) = 8 \sin\left(\frac{2\pi}{5} \cdot 3\right) = 8 \sin \frac{6\pi}{5} \approx -4.7$$

The height of the weight after 3 seconds is approximately 4.7 centimeters below the equilibrium point.

d. To find the times in the first 5 seconds when the weight is 6 centimeters below the equilibrium, you must solve the equation

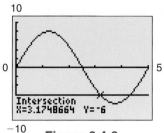

Figure 8.4-9

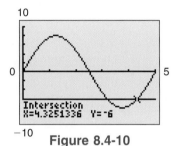

Figure 8.4-10

$$8 \sin\left(\frac{2\pi}{5} t\right) = -6 \quad (0 \le t \le 5)$$

The graphs of $Y_1 = 8 \sin\left(\frac{2\pi}{5} t\right)$ and $Y_2 = -6$ in a window with $0 \le t \le 5$ are shown in Figure 8.4-9 and 8.4-10. The points of intersection show that the weight will be 6 centimeters below the equilibrium at two times between 0 and 5 seconds.

$$t \approx 3.1749 \quad \text{and} \quad t \approx 4.3251$$

Modeling Trigonometric Data

Periodic data that appears to resemble a sinusoidal curve when plotted can often be modeled by a sine function, as shown in Example 4.

Example 4 **Temperature Data**

The following table shows the average monthly temperature in Cleveland, Ohio, based on data from 1971 to 2000. Since average temperatures are not likely to vary much from year to year, the data essentially repeats the same pattern in subsequent years. So, a periodic model is appropriate.

Month	Temperature (°F)		Month	Temperature (°F)
Jan.	25.7		July	71.9
Feb.	28.4		Aug.	70.2
Mar.	37.5		Sep.	63.3
Apr.	47.6		Oct.	52.2
May	58.5		Nov.	41.8
June	67.5		Dec.	31.1

[*Source: National Climatic Data Center*]

a. Make a scatter plot of the data.

b. Find a sinusoidal function that models the temperature data.

c. Use the sine regression feature on a calculator to find another sinusoidal model for the data.

d. How do the models in parts **b** and **c** differ from one another?

e. Use one of the models to predict time(s) of year in which the average temperature is 45°F.

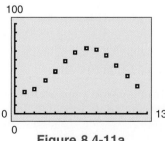

Figure 8.4-11a

Solution

a. Let $t = 1$ represent January. Enter 1 through 12 in List 1 and the temperatures in List 2. The scatter plot is shown in Figure 8.4-11a.

b. To find a sinusoidal function to represent the temperature data, examine the properties of the scatter plot.

The minimum value is 25.7 and the maximum value is 71.9, so the amplitude is

$$a = \frac{1}{2}(f_{max} - f_{min}) = \frac{1}{2}(71.9 - 25.7) = 23.1.$$

One complete cycle is 12 months, so the period, $\frac{2\pi}{b}$, is 12.

$$\frac{2\pi}{b} = 12$$

$$b = \frac{\pi}{6}$$

The vertical shift is

$$d = \frac{f_{max} + f_{min}}{2} = \frac{71.9 + 25.7}{2} = 48.8.$$

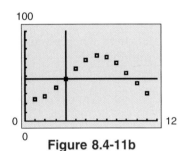

Figure 8.4-11b

A sine wave begins close to the data point (4, 47.6), as shown in Figure 8.4-11b, so the phase shift $-\frac{c}{b}$ is approximately 4. Find c.

$$-\frac{c}{b} = 4$$

$$-\frac{c}{\frac{\pi}{6}} = 4$$

$$c = -\frac{2\pi}{3}$$

Therefore, a sinusoidal function to represent the temperature data is approximately

$$f(t) = 23.1 \sin\left(\frac{\pi}{6}t - \frac{2\pi}{3}\right) + 48.8.$$

The graph of this function is shown with the scatter plot of the data in Figure 8.4-12.

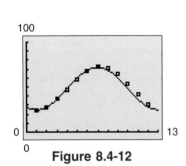

Figure 8.4-12

c. Using the 12 given data points, the regression feature on a calculator produces the following model.

$$f(t) = 23.1202 \sin(0.5018t - 2.0490) + 48.6927$$

The period of this function is approximately

$$\frac{2\pi}{0.5018} = 12.52,$$

which is not a very good approximation for a 12-month cycle.

Because the data repeats the same pattern from year to year, a more accurate model can be obtained by using the same data repeated for

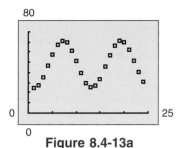

Figure 8.4-13a

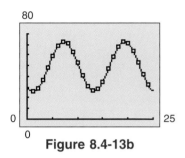

Figure 8.4-13b

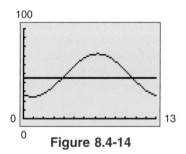

Figure 8.4-14

the second year. The data for a two-year period is plotted in Figure 8.4-13a. The sine regression feature on a calculator produces this model from the 24 data points:

$$f(t) = 22.7000 \sin(0.5219t - 2.1842) + 49.5731$$

The period of this function is

$$\frac{2\pi}{0.5219} \approx 12.04,$$

which is slightly off from the expected 12-month period. However, its graph in Figure 8.4-13b appears to fit the data well.

d. Using the decimal approximation of π, the rule of the function found in part **b** becomes

$$f(t) \approx 23.1 \sin(0.5236t - 2.0944) + 48.8.$$

This model differs only slightly from the second model in part **c**.

$$f(t) = 22.7000 \sin(0.5219t - 2.1842) + 49.5731$$

Visually, however, the model shown in Figure 8.4-12 does not seem to fit the data points quite as well as the model shown in Figure 8.4-13b. Nevertheless, considering that the model found in part **b** can be obtained without technology, it is remarkably close.

e. The model from part **c** will be used to predict the times of year in which the average temperature is 45°F.

There are two points of intersection of the graphs of

$$y = 45 \text{ and } f(t) = 22.7000 \sin(0.5219t - 2.1842) + 49.5731,$$

as shown in Figure 8.4-14. Their approximate coordinates are (3.8, 45) and (10.6, 45). Therefore, according to this model, the temperature would be around 45°F in late March and late October. ∎

Exercises 8.4

1. The original Ferris wheel, built by George Ferris for the Columbian Exposition of 1893, was much larger and slower than its modern counterparts: It had a diameter of 250 feet and contained 36 cars, each of which held 40 people; it made one revolution every 10 minutes. Suppose that the Ferris wheel revolves counterclockwise in the x-y plane with its center at the origin. Car D in the figure had coordinates (125, 0) at time $t = 0$. Find the rule of a function that gives the y-coordinate of car D at time t.

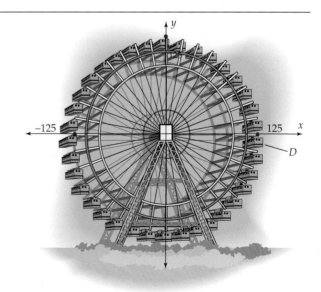

2. Do Exercise 1 if the wheel turns at 2 radians per minute and car D is at $(0, -125)$ at time $t = 0$.

3. A circular wheel with a radius of 1 foot rotates counterclockwise. A 4-foot rod has one end attached to the edge of this wheel and the other end to the base of a piston (see figure). It transfers the rotary motion of the wheel into a back-and-forth linear motion of the piston. If the wheel is rotating at 10 revolutions per second, point W is at $(1, 0)$ at time $t = 0$, and point P is always on x-axis, find the rule of a function that gives the x-coordinate of P at time t.

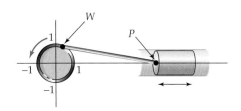

4. Do Exercise 3 if the wheel has a radius of 2 feet, rotates at 50 revolutions per second, and is at $(2, 0)$ when $t = 0$.

In Exercises 5–8, suppose a weight is hanging from a spring (under the same conditions as in Example 3). The weight is pushed to start it moving. At time t, let $h(t)$ be the distance of the weight above or below its equilibrium point. Assume the maximum distance the weight moves in either direction from the equilibrium point is 6 cm and that it moves through a complete cycle every 4 seconds. Express $h(t)$ in terms of the sine or cosine function under the given conditions.

5. There is an initial push upward from the equilibrium point.

6. There is an initial pull downward from the equilibrium point. *Hint:* What does the graph of $y = a \sin bt$ look like when $a < 0$?

7. The weight is pulled 6 cm above the equilibrium point, and the initial movement (at $t = 0$) is downward. *Hint:* Think of the cosine graph.

8. The weight is pulled 6 cm below its equilibrium point, and the initial movement is upward.

9. A pendulum swings uniformly back and forth, taking 2 seconds to move from the position directly above point A to the position directly above point B, as shown in the figure. The distance from A to B is 20 centimeters. Let $d(t)$ be the horizontal distance

from the pendulum to the (dashed) center line at time t seconds (with distances to the right of the line measured by positive numbers and distances to the left by negative ones). Assume that the pendulum is on the center line at time $t = 0$ and moving to the right. Assume the motion of the pendulum is simple harmonic motion. Find the rule of the function $d(t)$.

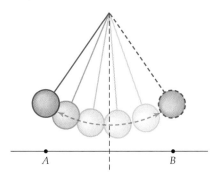

10. The following figure shows a diagram of a merry-go-round that is turning counterclockwise at a constant rate, making 2 revolutions in 1 minute. On the merry-go-round are horses A, B, C, and D 4 meters from the center and horses E, F, and G 8 meters from the center. There is a function $a(t)$ that gives the distance the horse A is from the y-axis (this is the x-coordinate of A's position) as a function of time t measured in minutes. Similarly, $b(t)$ gives the x-coordinate for B as a function of time, and so on. Assume the diagram shows the situation at time $t = 0$.

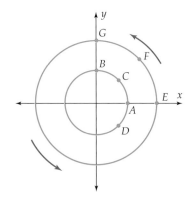

a. Which of the following function rules does $a(t)$ have?
   $4 \cos t$, $4 \cos \pi t$, $4 \cos 2t$, $4 \cos 2\pi t$,
   $4 \cos\left(\dfrac{1}{2}t\right)$, $4 \cos\left(\dfrac{\pi}{2}t\right)$, $4 \cos 4\pi t$

b. Describe the function $b(t)$, $c(t)$, $d(t)$, $e(t)$, $f(t)$, and $g(t)$ using the cosine function.

c. Suppose the x-coordinate of a horse S is given by the function $s(t) = 4\cos\left(4\pi t - \dfrac{5\pi}{6}\right)$ and the x-coordinate of another horse R is given by $r(t) = 8\cos\left(4\pi t - \dfrac{\pi}{3}\right)$. Where are these horses located in relation to the rest of the horses? Copy the diagram and mark the positions of R and S at $t = 0$.

11. The following table shows the number, in millions, of unemployed people in the labor force for 1991–2002.

Year	Unemployed	Year	Unemployed
1991	8.628	1997	6.739
1992	9.613	1998	6.210
1993	8.940	1999	5.880
1994	7.996	2000	5.655
1995	7.404	2001	6.742
1996	7.236	2002	8.234

a. Sketch a scatter plot of the data, with $x = 0$ corresponding to 1990.
b. Does the data appear to be periodic? If so, find an appropriate model.
c. Do you think this model is likely to be accurate much beyond the year 2002? Why?

In Exercises 12 and 13, do the following:

a. Use 12 data points (with $x = 1$ corresponding to January) to find a periodic model of the data.
b. What is the period of the function found in part **a**? Is this reasonable?
c. Plot 24 data points (two years) and graph the function from part **a** on the same screen. Is the function a good model in the second year?
d. Use the 24 data points in part **c** to find another periodic model for the data.
e. What is the period of the function in part **d**? Does its graph fit the data well?

12. The table shows the average monthly temperature in Chicago, IL, based on data from 1971 to 2000.

Month	Temperature (°F)
Jan.	22.0
Feb.	27.0
Mar.	37.3
Apr.	47.8
May	58.7
June	68.2
July	73.3
Aug.	71.7
Sep.	63.8
Oct.	52.1
Nov.	39.3
Dec.	27.4

[*Source: National Climatic Data Center*]

13. The table shows the average monthly precipitation, in inches, in San Francisco, CA, based on data from 1971 to 2000.

Month	Precipitation
Jan.	4.45
Feb.	4.01
Mar.	3.26
Apr.	1.17
May	0.38
June	0.11
July	0.03
Aug.	0.07
Sep.	0.2
Oct.	1.04
Nov.	2.49
Dec.	2.89

[*Source: National Climatic Data Center*]

14. *Critical Thinking* A grandfather clock has a pendulum length of k meters. Its swing is given (as in Exercise 9) by the function

$$f(t) = 0.25 \sin(\omega t), \text{ where } \omega = \sqrt{\frac{9.8}{k}}.$$

a. Find k such that the period of the pendulum is 2 seconds.

b. The temperature in the summer months causes the pendulum to increase its length by 0.01%. How much time will the clock lose in June, July, and August? *Hint:* These three months have a total of 92 days (7,948,800 seconds). If k is increased by 0.01%, what is $f(2)$?

8.4.A

Excursion: Sound Waves

Objectives

- Find the frequency of a sound wave using a tuning fork and a data collection device

- Model sound wave data with sinusoidal functions and graphs

Sound travels through the air like small ripples traveling across a body of water. Throwing a rock into a calm body of water causes the water to begin to move up and down around the entry point. The movement of the water causes ripples to move outward. If a flower is floating in this body of water, the ripples will cause the flower to move up and down on the water.

Sound is produced by a vibrating object that disturbs the surrounding air molecules and causes them to vibrate. These vibrations cause a periodic change in air pressure that travels through the air much like the ripples in a body of water. When the air pressure waves reach the eardrum, they cause it to vibrate at the same frequency as the source. These air pressure waves are more commonly called **sound waves.** The voices and sounds heard each day are generally a combination of many different sound waves. The sound from a tuning fork is a single tone that can be described mathematically using a sinusoidal function, $f(t) = a \sin(bt + c) + d$ or $g(t) = a \cos(bt + c) + d$.

Recall from Sections 7.4 and 8.4 that if $a \neq 0$ and $b > 0$, then each of the functions

$$f(t) = a \sin(bt + c) + d \quad \text{and} \quad g(t) = a \cos(bt + c) + d$$

has the following characteristics:

$$\text{amplitude} = |a| \qquad \text{period} = \frac{2\pi}{b}$$

$$\text{phase shift} = -\frac{c}{b} \qquad \text{vertical shift} = d$$

The period of a sound wave determines the sound's *frequency.* The **frequency** f of a sound wave is the reciprocal of its period.

$$f = \frac{b}{2\pi}$$

Frequency gives the number of cycles (periods) that the sound wave completes in one second. Frequencies are measured in units called **Hertz** (Hz), where one Hertz is one cycle per second. Most tuning forks have their frequency and corresponding musical note listed on them.

A tuning fork, a microphone connected to a data collection device (such as a CBL or CBR), and a calculator with a tuning program can be used to simulate the sounds heard through the eardrum.

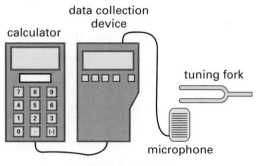

Figure 8.4.A-1

Example 1   Frequency

Confirm with a sinusoid graph that the frequency of a sound wave formed by striking a C tuning fork is 262 Hz.

Solution

Connect the calculator to the data collection device, connect the microphone to the data collection device, and run the program needed to calculate the pressure for the sound waves. Follow the directions on the screen of your calculator to obtain a graph like the one shown in Figure 8.4.A-2.

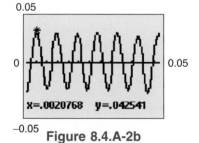

Figure 8.4.A-2b

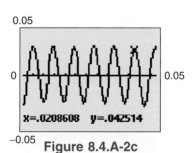

Figure 8.4.A-2c

Figure 8.4.A-2a

The period of the data can be found by dividing the differences between the x-value of the first maximum and the x-value for the last maximum by the number of complete cycles between the maximums. For the data shown in Figure 8.4.A-2a, Figures 8.4.A-2b and 8.4.A-2c show that the first maximum occurs when $x = 0.0020768$, the last maximum occurs when $x = 0.0208608$, and there are five complete cycles between the first and last maximum. Therefore, the period of the data is given by the following.

$$\frac{0.0208608 - 0.0020768}{5} = 0.0037568 \qquad \textit{cycle length}$$

The frequency is the reciprocal of the period.

$$\frac{1}{0.0037568} \approx 266.184$$

Therefore, the graph indicates a frequency of about 266.184, which is very close to the actual frequency of 262 Hz.

■

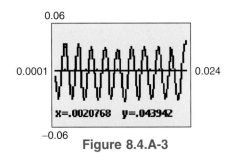

0.06

0.0001   0.024

x=.0020768   y=.043942

−0.06

Figure 8.4.A-3

Example 2   Sinusoidal Model

Find a sinusoidal model to fit the sound waves produced by a tuning fork with the note G.

Solution

Use a data collection device, a G tuning fork, and a tuning program to obtain a graph similar to the one shown in Figure 8.4.A-3.

Find the amplitude a by finding half the difference between the maximum value and minimum value. The data graphed in Figure 8.4-3 has a maximum value of 0.043942 and a minimum value of −0.045618.

$$a = \frac{0.043942 - (-0.045618)}{2} = 0.04478 \qquad \textit{amplitude}$$

To find the period, find the x-value of the first maximum of the graph, find the x-value of the last maximum of the graph, and divide the difference between the two x-values by 8 (the number of cycles between the first and last maximum). The first maximum shown on the graph occurs when $x = 0.0020768$, and the last maximum occurs when $x = 0.0221088$.

$$p = \frac{0.0221088 - 0.0020768}{8} = 0.002504 \qquad \textit{period}$$

Use the period to find b.

$$\frac{2\pi}{b} = 0.002504$$

$$b = \frac{2\pi}{0.002504}$$

The graph has a maximum at $x = 0.0020768$, so the phase shift for a function using cosine is 0.0020768.

Use the phase shift and b to find c.

$$-\frac{c}{b} = \text{phase shift}$$

$$c = -0.0020768\left(\frac{2\pi}{0.002504}\right) = -1.658786\pi$$

Find the vertical shift d by finding the average of the maximum and minimum values. In this example, $d = 0$.

Therefore, the sinusoidal model to fit the sound waves produced by a tuning fork with the note G is

$$y = 0.04478 \cos\left(\frac{2\pi}{0.002504} x - 1.658786\pi\right).$$

Notice that the frequency, the reciprocal of the period, is 399.361, which is very close to the actual frequency of 392 Hz for the note G. ∎

When two sounds of slightly different frequency are produced simultaneously, a *beat* is heard. A **beat** is a single sound that gets louder and softer at periodic intervals. By using more than one tuning fork, a beat can be displayed.

| **Example 3** | **Chord Frequency** |

Place tuning forks with notes of C and G close to a microphone.
a. Find a graphical representation for the sound waves produced by playing the two notes simultaneously.
b. Find the period of the function.
c. How does the frequency of this sound compare with the actual frequencies of C and G?

Solution

a. Using a data collection device, the graph in Figure 8.4.A-4 is obtained.

b. The graph appears to be periodic. By finding the length of one complete cycle, the period of this graph appears to be approximately 0.0077632.

c. The frequency of this sound is the reciprocal of the period of the function.

$$\frac{1}{0.0077632} = 128.8128607 \text{ Hz}$$

The frequency of this sound is very close to the difference between the actual frequency of C, 262 Hz, and the actual frequency of G, 392 Hz.

$$392 - 262 = 130$$

∎

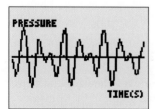

PRESSURE

TIME(S)

Figure 8.4.A-4

NOTE The intensity of the strike on the tuning fork determines the amplitude.

Graphing Exploration ●

Find a sinusoidal function to model the graph produced by the C tuning fork.

Add the sinusoidal models for C and G notes. (Use the model from Example 2.) Graph this sum.

What is the frequency of the graph? How does the frequency of this sound compare with the sum of the actual frequencies of C and G?

Most sounds are more complex than those produced by tuning forks. A tuning fork produces a graph of a single note. Most musical instruments produce a sound that is a combination of several different sounds.

A C-G chord was produced with the tuning forks in Example 3. The exploration above indicates that this sound can be modeled by the sum of the models for the C note and the G note.

Exercises 8.4.A

Bottles of water can be tuned using a microphone and data collection device. Place some water in the bottle and blow air over the top of the bottle to produce a sound. Use the frequency of the graph formed from the sound to approximate the frequency. If a higher note is needed, place more water in the bottle and calculate the frequency again. Display the graph of the following notes using the chart below.

Note	Frequency in Hz
C	262
C# or Db	277
D	294
D# or Eb	311
E	330
F	349
F# or Gb	370
G	392

Note	Frequency in Hz
G# or Ab	415
A	440
A# or Bb	466
B	494
C (next octave)	524

1. D   **2.** B   **3.** A   **4.** C#

5. Using only one tuning fork at a time and the sum of three functions, sketch a graph of the C-major chord (C + E + G).

6. Using three tuning forks for the notes C, E, and G at one time, find a graph of the C-major chord (C + E + G).

CHAPTER 8

REVIEW

Important Concepts

**Important Facts
and Formulas**

$$\sin^{-1} v = u \quad \text{exactly when} \quad \sin u = v \left(-\frac{\pi}{2} \le u \le \frac{\pi}{2}, -1 \le v \le 1 \right)$$

$$\cos^{-1} v = u \quad \text{exactly when} \quad \cos u = v \left(0 \le u \le \pi, -1 \le v \le 1 \right)$$

$$\tan^{-1} v = u \quad \text{exactly when} \tan u = v \left(-\frac{\pi}{2} < u < \frac{\pi}{2}, v \text{ a real number} \right)$$

Let $a \ne 0$ and $b > 0$. The following functions have the given characteristics.

$$f(t) = a\sin(bt + c) + d \text{ and } g(t) = a\cos(bt + c) + d$$

$$\text{amplitude} |a| = \frac{1}{2}(f_{\max} - f_{\min})$$

$$\text{period} \frac{2\pi}{b}, \quad \text{phase shift} -\frac{c}{b}$$

$$\text{vertical shift } d = \frac{1}{2}(f_{\max} + f_{\min})$$

Review Exercises

Section 8.1

In Exercises 1–6, solve each equation graphically.

1. $5 \tan x = 2 \sin 2x$

2. $\sin^3 x + \cos^2 x - \tan x = 2$

3. $\sin x + \sec^2 x = 3$

4. $\cos^2 x - \csc^2 x + \tan\left(x - \dfrac{\pi}{2}\right) + 5 = 0$

5. $\cos 2x = \sin x$

6. $3 \sin 2x = -\cos x$

7. A weight hanging from a spring is set into motion, moving up and down. (See Figure 8.4-6 in Example 3 of Section 8.4.) Its distance in centimeters above or below the equilibrium point at time t seconds is given by $d = 5 \sin 3t - 3 \cos 3t$. At what times during the first two seconds is the weight at the equilibrium position ($d = 0$)?

In Exercises 8–17, find the exact value without using a calculator.

Section 8.2

8. $\cos^{-1}\left(\dfrac{\sqrt{2}}{2}\right) = ?$

9. $\sin^{-1}\left(\dfrac{\sqrt{3}}{2}\right) = ?$

10. $\tan^{-1}\sqrt{3} = ?$

11. $\sin^{-1}\left(\cos \dfrac{11\pi}{6}\right) = ?$

12. $\cos^{-1}\left(\sin \dfrac{5\pi}{3}\right) = ?$

13. $\tan^{-1}\left(\cos \dfrac{7\pi}{2}\right) = ?$

14. $\sin^{-1}(\sin 0.75) = ?$

15. $\cos^{-1}(\cos 2) = ?$

16. $\sin^{-1}\left(\sin \dfrac{8\pi}{3}\right) = ?$

17. $\cos^{-1}\left(\cos \dfrac{13\pi}{4}\right) = ?$

18. Sketch the graph of $f(x) = \tan^{-1} x - \pi$.

19. Sketch the graph of $g(x) = \sin^{-1}(x - 2)$.

20. Find the exact value of $\sin\left(\cos^{-1}\dfrac{1}{4}\right)$.

21. Find the exact value of $\sin\left(\tan^{-1}\dfrac{1}{2} - \cos^{-1}\dfrac{4}{5}\right)$.

Section 8.3

22. Find all angles θ with $0° \le \theta \le 360°$ such that $\sin \theta = -0.7133$.

23. Find all angles θ with $0° \le \theta \le 360°$ such that $\tan \theta = 3.7321$.

In Exercises 24–38, solve the equation by any means. Find exact solutions when possible and approximate solutions otherwise.

24. $2 \sin x = 1$

25. $\cos x = \dfrac{\sqrt{3}}{2}$

26. $\tan x = -1$

27. $\sin 3x = -\dfrac{\sqrt{3}}{2}$

28. $\sin x = 0.7$

29. $\cos x = -0.8$

30. $\tan x = 13$

31. $\cot x = 0.4$

32. $2 \sin^2 x + 5 \sin x = 3$

33. $4 \cos^2 x - 2 = 0$

34. $2 \sin^2 x - 3 \sin x = 2$ **35.** $\sec^2 x + 3 \tan^2 x = 13$

36. $\sec^2 x = 4 \tan x - 2$ **37.** $2 \sin^2 x + \sin x - 2 = 0$

38. $\cos^2 x - 3 \cos x - 2 = 0$

39. A cannon has a muzzle velocity of 600 feet per second. At what angle of elevation should it be fired in order to hit a target 3500 feet away? *Hint:* Use the projectile equation given for Exercises 56–59 of Section 8.3.

Section **8.4**

40. The following table gives the average population, in thousands, of a southern town for each month throughout the year. The population is greater in the winter and smaller in the summer, and it repeats this pattern from year to year.

Month	Population	Month	Population
Jan.	10.5	July	4.7
Feb.	9.3	Aug.	5.8
Mar.	7.8	Sep.	7.6
Apr.	6.0	Oct.	9.4
May	4.9	Nov.	10.6
June	4.5	Dec.	10.9

  a. Make a scatter plot of the data.
  b. Find a sinusoidal function to represent the population data.
  c. Use the sine regression feature on a calculator to find a periodic model for the data.
  d. Use the model from part **c** to predict time(s) of year in which the average population is 6200.

41. The paddle wheel of a steamboat is 22 feet in diameter and is turning at 3 revolutions per minute. The axle of the wheel is 8 feet above the surface of the water. Assume that the center of the wheel is at the origin and that a point P on the edge of the paddle wheel is at $(0, 19)$ at time $t = 0$ seconds.
  a. What maximum height above the water does point P reach?
  b. How far below the water does point P reach?
  c. In how many seconds does the wheel complete one revolution?
  d. Write a cosine function for the height of point P at time t.
  e. Write a sine function for the height of point P at time t.
  f. Use the function from part **d** or **e** to find the time(s) at which point P will be at a height of 10 feet.

Section **8.4.A**

42. Confirm with a sinusoid graph that the frequency of a sound wave formed by striking an F tuning fork is 349 Hz.

43. Find a sinusoidal model to fit the sound waves produced by striking an E tuning fork.

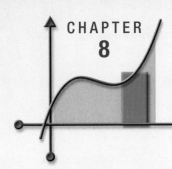

CHAPTER 8

can do calculus
Limits of Trigonometric Functions

A main focus of calculus is the behavior of the output of a function as the input approaches a specific value. The value that the function approaches, if it exists, is called a **limit.** In this section an informal description of a limit is illustrated with some interesting trigonometric functions, but the discussion is not intended to be complete. See Chapter 14 for a detailed discussion of limits.

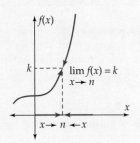

Figure 8.C-1

If the output of a function approaches a single real number k as the input approaches the real number n, then the function is said to have a *limit* of k as the input approaches n.

This is written as

$$\lim_{x \to n} f(x) = k,$$

and is read "the limit of $f(x)$ as x approaches n is k". See Figure 8.C-1.

If the outputs of the function do not approach a single real number as the inputs approach n, the limit does not exist.

Calculus is needed to find limits analytically, but a calculator's table feature and a graph can approximate a limit, if it exists. A table or a graph will also indicate when a limit does not exist. The following two limits are very important in calculus and are used in future can do calculus features.

Example 1 Limit of $\dfrac{\sin x}{x}$

Find $\displaystyle\lim_{x \to 0} \dfrac{\sin x}{x}$, if it exists, by using a table and a graph.

Solution

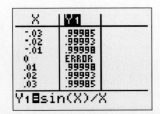

Figure 8.C-2a

Enter $Y_1 = \dfrac{\sin x}{x}$ into the function editor of a calculator and produce the table shown in Figure 8.C-2a and the graph shown in Figure 8.C-2b.

The table confirms that $\dfrac{\sin 0}{0} = \dfrac{0}{0}$ is undefined, but it also suggests that the values of $\dfrac{\sin x}{x}$ are approaching 1 for x-values near 0, both positive and negative.

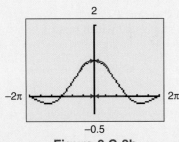

Figure 8.C-2b

The graph confirms that the values of $\dfrac{\sin x}{x}$ are approaching 1 as x approaches 0 from the positive side and from the negative side. Therefore,

$$\lim_{x \to 0} \dfrac{\sin x}{x} = 1$$

There is another trigonometric limit that is often used in calculus.

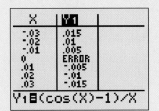

Figure 8.C-3a

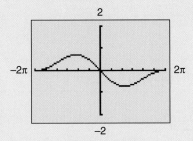

Figure 8.C-3b

NOTE $\frac{\pi}{2} \approx 1.57.$

Example 2 Limit of $\frac{\cos x - 1}{x}$

Find $\lim\limits_{x \to 0} \dfrac{\cos x - 1}{x}$, if it exists, by using a table and a graph.

Solution

Figure 8.C-3a confirms that $\dfrac{\cos x - 1}{x} = \dfrac{0}{0}$ is undefined, but that the values of $\dfrac{\cos x - 1}{x}$ are approaching 0 when x is near 0. The graph shown in Figure 8.C-3b also illustrates this. Therefore,

$$\lim_{x \to 0} \frac{\cos x - 1}{x} = 0.$$

There are two ways in which a limit may not exist, as shown in the next examples. The first example illustrates a function that does not have a limit as x approaches $\frac{\pi}{2}$ because function values on either side of $\frac{\pi}{2}$ do not approach a *single* real number. The second example illustrates a function that does not have a limit as x approaches 0 because the function values oscillate wildly.

Example 3 Determining the Behavior of a Function Near an x-Value

Discuss the behavior of $f(x) = \dfrac{1}{\cos x}$ as x approaches $\dfrac{\pi}{2}$. Find $\lim\limits_{x \to \frac{\pi}{2}} \dfrac{1}{\cos x}$, if it exists, by using a table and a graph.

Solution

As shown in Figure 8.C-4a, the values of $f(x) = \dfrac{1}{\cos x}$ when $x < \dfrac{\pi}{2}$ are large positive numbers, and the values are large negative numbers when $x > \dfrac{\pi}{2}$. Figure 8.C-4b shows that the graph of $f(x) = \dfrac{1}{\cos x}$ has a vertical asymptote at $\dfrac{\pi}{2}$. Because the values of $f(x)$ do not approach a single real number as x approaches $\dfrac{\pi}{2}$, $\lim\limits_{x \to \frac{\pi}{2}} \dfrac{1}{\cos x}$ does not exist.

567

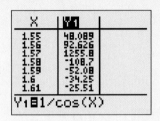

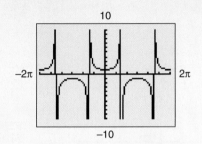

Figure 8.C-4a   **Figure 8.C-4b**

■

Example 4 **Oscillating Function Values**

Discuss the behavior of $f(x) = \cos\left(\dfrac{1}{x}\right)$ near $x = 0$ and find $\lim\limits_{x \to 0} \cos\left(\dfrac{1}{x}\right)$, if it exists.

Solution

A table of values of $f(x) = \cos\left(\dfrac{1}{x}\right)$ near $x = 0$ is shown in Figure 8.C-5a.

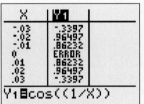

Figure 8.C-5a

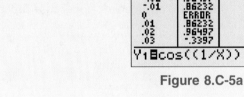

Figure 8.C-5b

The table suggests that the function values near $x = 0$ may be near 0.86232, but using the trace feature on the graph shown in Figure 8.C-5b indicates that the function value is near 0.365 when x is near 0.

Using a window where $-0.01 \le x \le 0.01$, you can see that the graph oscillates wildly around $x = 0$. See Figure 8.C-5c.

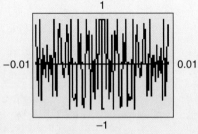

Figure 8.C-5c

Because the values of $f(x) = \cos\left(\dfrac{1}{x}\right)$ oscillate as x approaches 0, $\lim\limits_{x \to 0} \cos\left(\dfrac{1}{x}\right)$ does not exist.

■

Exercises

Discuss the behavior of the function around the given *x*-value by using a table and a graph. Find the limit of each function, if it exists.

1. $\lim\limits_{x \to 0} \dfrac{1}{\cos x}$

2. $\lim\limits_{x \to \frac{\pi}{2}} \dfrac{x}{\tan x}$

3. $\lim\limits_{x \to \frac{\pi}{2}} \dfrac{\tan x}{x}$

4. $\lim\limits_{x \to 0} \dfrac{\tan x}{x}$

5. $\lim\limits_{x \to 0} \dfrac{\sin 3x}{3x}$

6. $\lim\limits_{x \to 0} \dfrac{\sin 2x}{2x}$

7. $\lim\limits_{x \to 0} \dfrac{x}{\tan^2 x}$

8. $\lim\limits_{x \to 0} \dfrac{x}{\sin^2 x}$

9. $\lim\limits_{x \to 0} \dfrac{3x}{\sin 3x}$

10. $\lim\limits_{x \to 0} \dfrac{x}{\sin x}$

11. $\lim\limits_{x \to 0} \dfrac{\sin 3x}{\sin 4x}$

12. $\lim\limits_{x \to 0} \dfrac{\sin 8x}{\sin 7x}$

13. $\lim\limits_{x \to 0} \sin\left(\dfrac{1}{x}\right)$

14. $\lim\limits_{x \to 0} \dfrac{2x + \sin x}{x}$

15. $\lim\limits_{x \to \frac{\pi}{2}} \dfrac{x}{\cos x}$

16. $\lim\limits_{x \to 0} \tan\left(\dfrac{1}{x}\right)$

17. $\lim\limits_{x \to 2} 3x$

18. $\lim\limits_{x \to 2} -2x$

19. $\lim\limits_{x \to 1} \dfrac{x}{1 - x}$

20. $\lim\limits_{x \to -1} \dfrac{x}{1 - x}$

21. $\lim\limits_{x \to 3} \dfrac{x^2 - x - 6}{x - 3}$

22. $\lim\limits_{x \to 1} \dfrac{x^2 + 2x - 3}{x - 1}$

23. $\lim\limits_{x \to 1} \dfrac{x^3 - 1}{x - 1}$

24. $\lim\limits_{x \to -1} \dfrac{x^3 + x^2 + x + 1}{x - 1}$

25. Make a conjecture about the $\lim\limits_{x \to 0} \dfrac{\sin bx}{\sin cx}$, where b and c are real numbers.

Trigonometric Identities and Proof

Time.

To find the exact period of the oscillations of a simple pendulum, a trigonometric expression must be written in an alternate form, which is obtained by using trigonometric identities. See Exercise 75 in Section 9.3.

Chapter Outline

Interdependence of Sections

The basic trigonometric identities, which were discussed in Chapter 6 and used in Chapter 8, are not the only identities that are useful in rewriting trigonometric expressions and in solving trigonometric equations. This chapter presents many widely used trigonometric identities and specific methods for solving particular forms of trigonometric equations.

9.1   Identities and Proofs

Objectives

• Identify possible identities by using graphs

• Apply strategies to prove identities

Recall that an identity is an equation that is true for all values of the variable for which every term of the equation is defined. Several trigonometric identities have been discussed in previous sections. This section will introduce other identities and discuss techniques used to verify that an equation is an identity.

Trigonometric identities can be used for simplifying expressions, rewriting the rules of trigonometric functions, and performing numerical calculations. There are no hard and fast rules for dealing with identities, but some suggestions follow. The phrases "prove the identity" and "verify the identity" mean "prove that the given equation is an identity."

571

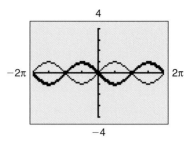

Figure 9.1-1

Graphical Testing

When presented with a trigonometric equation that *might* be an identity, it is a good idea to determine graphically whether or not this is possible. For instance, the equation $\cos\left(\dfrac{\pi}{2} + x\right) = \sin t$ can be tested to determine if it is possibly an identity by graphing $Y_1 = \cos\left(\dfrac{\pi}{2} + x\right)$ and $Y_2 = \sin x$ on the same screen, as shown in Figure 9.1-1 where the graph of Y_1 is darker than the graph of Y_2. Because the graphs are different, it can be concluded that the equation is not an identity.

Any equation can be tested by simultaneously graphing the two functions whose rules are given by the left and right sides of the equation. If the graphs are different, the equation is not an identity. If the graphs appear to be the same, then it is possible that the equation is an identity. However,

> **The fact that the graphs of both sides of an equation appear identical does not prove that the equation is an identity, as the following exploration demonstrates.**

Graphing Exploration ●

In the viewing window with $-\pi \le x \le \pi$ and $-2 \le y \le 2$, graph both sides of the equation

$$\cos x = 1 - \frac{x^2}{2} + \frac{x^4}{24} - \frac{x^6}{720} + \frac{x^8}{40{,}320}$$

Do the graphs appear identical? Now change the viewing window so that $-2\pi \le x \le 2\pi$. Is the equation an identity?

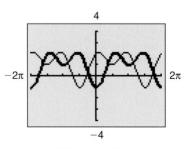

Figure 9.1-2a

Example 1   **Graphical Identity Testing**

Is either of the following equations an identity?

a. $2\sin^2 x - \cos x = 2\cos^2 x + \sin x$

b. $\dfrac{1 + \sin x - \sin^2 x}{\cos x} = \cos x + \tan x$

Solution

Test each equation graphically to see if it might be an identity by graphing each side of the equation.

a. Graph $Y_1 = 2\sin^2 x - \cos x$ and $Y_2 = 2\cos^2 x + \sin x$ on the same screen, as shown in Figure 9.1-2a. The graph of Y_1 is shown darker than Y_2. Because the graphs are *not* the same, the equation $2\sin^2 x - \cos x = 2\cos^2 x + \sin x$ is not an identity.

b. The graph shown in Figure 9.1-2b suggests that

$$\frac{1 + \sin x - \sin^2 x}{\cos x} = \cos x + \tan x$$

may be an identity, but the proof that it actually is an identity must be done algebraically.

<table>
<tr>
<td>
CAUTION

Be sure to use parentheses correctly when entering each function to be graphed.
</td>
</tr>
</table>

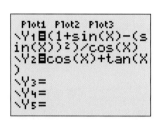

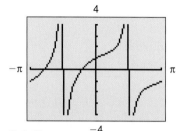

Figure 9.1-2b

Example 2   **Finding an Identity**

Find an equation involving $2 \sin x \cos x$ that could possibly be an identity.

Solution

The graph of $y = 2 \sin x \cos x$ is shown in Figure 9.1-3a. Does it look familiar? At first it looks like the graph of $y = \sin x$, but there is an important difference. The function graphed in Figure 9.1-3a has a period of π. As was shown in Section 7.3, the graph of $y = \sin 2x$ looks like the sine graph but has a period of π.

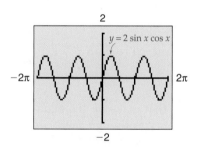

Figure 9.1-3a

The graphs $Y_1 = 2 \sin x \cos x$ and $Y_2 = \sin 2x$ are shown in Figures 9.1-3a and 9.1-3b. Because the graphs appear identical, $2 \sin x \cos x = \sin 2x$ may be an identity.

Figure 9.1-3b

Proving Identities

A useful feature of trigonometric functions is that they can be written in many ways. One form may be easier to use in one situation, and a different form of the same function may be more useful in another.

The elementary identities that were given in Section 6.5 are summarized for your reference on the following page. Memorizing these identities will benefit you greatly in the future.

NOTE The definitions of the basic trigonometric ratios may help you remember the quotient and reciprocal identities. The shapes of the graphs of sine, cosine, and tangent may help you remember the periodicity and negative angle identities. Also, if you can remember the first of the Pythagorean identities, which is based on the Pythagorean Theorem, the other two can easily be derived from it.

Basic Trigonometry Identities

Quotient Identities

$$\tan x = \frac{\sin x}{\cos x} \qquad \cot x = \frac{\cos x}{\sin x}$$

Reciprocal Identities

$$\sin x = \frac{1}{\csc x} \qquad \cos x = \frac{1}{\sec x}$$

$$\csc x = \frac{1}{\sin x} \qquad \sec x = \frac{1}{\cos x}$$

$$\cot x = \frac{1}{\tan x} \qquad \tan x = \frac{1}{\cot x}$$

Periodicity Identities

$$\sin(x \pm 2\pi) = \sin x \qquad \cos(x \pm 2\pi) = \cos x$$

$$\csc(x \pm 2\pi) = \csc x \qquad \sec(x \pm 2\pi) = \sec x$$

$$\tan(x \pm \pi) = \tan x \qquad \cot(x \pm \pi) = \cot x$$

Pythagorean Identities

$$\sin^2 x + \cos^2 x = 1 \qquad \tan^2 x + 1 = \sec^2 x \qquad 1 + \cot^2 x = \csc^2 x$$

Negative Angle Identities

$$\sin(-x) = -\sin x \qquad \cos(-x) = \cos x \qquad \tan(-x) = -\tan x$$

Just looking at the graphs of the two expressions that make up the equation is not enough to guarantee that it is an identity. Although there are no exact rules for simplifying trigonometric expressions or proving identities, there are some common strategies that are often helpful.

Strategies for Proving Trigonometric Identities

1. Use algebra and *previously* proven identities to transform one side of the equation into the other.
2. If possible, write the entire equation is terms of one trigonometric function.
3. Express everything in terms of sine and cosine.
4. Deal separately with each side of the equation $A = B$. First use identities and algebra to transform A into some expression C, then use (possibly different) identities and algebra to transform B into the *same* expression C. Conclude that $A = B$.
5. Prove that $AD = BC$, with $B \neq 0$ and $D \neq 0$. You can then conclude that $\frac{A}{B} = \frac{C}{D}$.

There are often a variety of ways to proceed, and it will take some practice before you can easily decide which strategies are likely to be the most efficient in a particular case. Keep these two purposes of working with trigonometric identities in mind:

- to learn the relationships among the trigonometric functions
- to simplify an expression by using an equivalent form

CAUTION

Proving identities is not the same as solving equations. Properties that apply to equations, such as adding the same value to both sides, are not valid when verifying identities because the beginning statement (to be verified) may not be true.

In the following example, the Pythagorean identity is used to replace $1 - \sin^2 x$ with $\cos^2 x$. Consider using one of the Pythagorean identities whenever a squared trigonometric function appears.

replace	*with*	*replace*	*with*
$\sin^2 x$	$1 - \cos^2 x$	$\csc^2 x$	$1 + \cot^2 x$
$\cos^2 x$	$1 - \sin^2 x$	$\sec^2 x$	$\tan^2 x + 1$
$\tan^2 x$	$\sec^2 x - 1$	$\cot^2 x$	$\csc^2 x - 1$

Example 3 **Transform One Side into the Other Side**

Verify that $\dfrac{1 + \sin x - \sin^2 x}{\cos x} = \cos x + \tan x$.

Solution

The graph of each side of the equation is shown in Figure 9.1-2b of Example 1, where it was noted that the equation *might* be an identity. Begin with the left side of the equation.

$$\frac{1 + \sin x - \sin^2 x}{\cos x} = \frac{(1 - \sin^2 x) + \sin x}{\cos x} \qquad \textit{regrouping terms}$$

$$= \frac{\cos^2 x + \sin x}{\cos x} \qquad \textit{Pythagorean identity}$$

$$= \frac{\cos^2 x}{\cos x} + \frac{\sin x}{\cos x} \qquad \frac{a + b}{c} = \frac{a}{c} + \frac{b}{c}$$

$$= \cos x + \frac{\sin x}{\cos x} \qquad \frac{a^2}{a} = a$$

$$= \cos x + \tan x \qquad \textit{quotient identity}$$

Strategies for proving identities can also be used to simplify complex expressions.

Example 4 Write Everything in Terms of Sine and Cosine

Simplify $(\csc x + \cot x)(1 - \cos x)$.

Solution

$(\csc x + \cot x)(1 - \cos x)$

$$= \left(\frac{1}{\sin x} + \frac{\cos x}{\sin x}\right)(1 - \cos x) \qquad \text{reciprocal and quotient identities}$$

$$= \frac{(1 + \cos x)}{\sin x}(1 - \cos x) \qquad \frac{a}{c} + \frac{b}{c} = \frac{a + b}{c}$$

$$= \frac{(1 + \cos x)(1 - \cos x)}{\sin x} \qquad \frac{a}{c} \cdot b = \frac{ab}{c}$$

$$= \frac{1 - \cos^2 x}{\sin x} \qquad (a + b)(a - b) = a^2 - b^2$$

$$= \frac{\sin^2 x}{\sin x} \qquad \text{Pythagorean identity}$$

$$= \sin x \qquad \frac{x^2}{x} = x$$

The strategies presented above and those to be considered are "plans of attack." By themselves they are not much help unless you also have some techniques for carrying out these plans. In the previous examples, the techniques of basic algebra and the use of known identities were used to change trigonometric expressions into equivalent expressions. There is another technique that is often useful when dealing with fractions.

> **Rewrite a fraction in equivalent form by multiplying its numerator and denominator by the same quantity.**

Example 5 Transform One Side into the Other Side

Prove that $\dfrac{\sin x}{1 + \cos x} = \dfrac{1 - \cos x}{\sin x}$.

Solution

Beginning with the left side, multiply the numerator and denominator by $1 - \cos x$.

$$\frac{\sin x}{1 + \cos x} = \frac{\sin x}{1 + \cos x} \cdot \frac{1 - \cos x}{1 - \cos x}$$

$$= \frac{\sin x(1 - \cos x)}{(1 + \cos x)(1 - \cos x)}$$

$$= \frac{\sin x(1 - \cos x)}{1 - \cos^2 x}$$

$$= \frac{\sin x(1 - \cos x)}{\sin^2 x} \qquad \text{Pythagorean identity}$$

$$= \frac{1 - \cos x}{\sin x}$$

NOTE If a denominator is of the form $1 + \cos x$, multiplying by $1 - \cos x$ gives $1 - \cos^2 x = \sin^2 x$. Similarly, if a denominator is of the form $1 + \sin x$, multiplying by $1 - \sin x$ gives $1 - \sin^2 x = \cos^2 x$. Compare this with earlier techniques used to rationalize denominators and simplify numbers with complex denominators.

Alternate Solution

The numerators of the given equation, $\sin x$ and $1 - \cos x$, look similar to the Pythagorean identity—except the squares are missing. So begin with the left side and introduce some squares by multiplying it by $\dfrac{\sin x}{\sin x} = 1$.

$$
\begin{aligned}
\frac{\sin x}{1 + \cos x} &= \frac{\sin x}{\sin x} \cdot \frac{\sin x}{1 + \cos x} \\[1mm]
&= \frac{\sin^2 x}{\sin x(1 + \cos x)} \\[1mm]
&= \frac{1 - \cos^2 x}{\sin x(1 + \cos x)} \qquad \textit{Pythagorean identity} \\[1mm]
&= \frac{(1 - \cos x)(1 + \cos x)}{\sin x(1 + \cos x)} \qquad a^2 - b^2 = (a - b)(a + b) \\[1mm]
&= \frac{1 - \cos x}{\sin x}
\end{aligned}
$$

Example 6   Dealing with Each Side Separately

Prove that $\csc x - \cot x = \dfrac{\sin x}{1 + \cos x}$.

Solution

Begin with the left side.

$$
\begin{aligned}
\csc x - \cot x &= \frac{1}{\sin x} - \frac{\cos x}{\sin x} \\[1mm]
&= \frac{1 - \cos x}{\sin x} \qquad\qquad\qquad [1]
\end{aligned}
$$

Example 5 shows that the right side of the identity to be proved can also be transformed into this same expression.

$$
\frac{\sin x}{1 + \cos x} = \frac{1 - \cos x}{\sin x} \qquad\qquad\qquad [2]
$$

Combining the equalities [1] and [2] proves the identity.

$$
\csc x - \cot x = \frac{1 - \cos x}{\sin x} = \frac{\sin x}{1 + \cos x}
$$

Proving identities involving fractions can sometimes be quite complicated. It often helps to approach a fractional identity indirectly, as in the following example.

Example 7 Proving Identities that Involve Fractions

Prove the first identity below, then use the first identity to prove the second identity.

a. $\sec x(\sec x - \cos x) = \tan^2 x$ **b.** $\dfrac{\sec x}{\tan x} = \dfrac{\tan x}{\sec x - \cos x}$

Solution

a. Begin by transforming the left side.

$$\sec x(\sec x - \cos x) = \sec^2 x - \sec x \cos x$$

$$= \sec^2 x - \frac{1}{\cos x}\cos x \qquad \textit{reciprocal identity}$$

$$= \sec^2 x - 1$$

$$= \tan^2 x \qquad\qquad \textit{Pythagorean identity}$$

Therefore, $\sec x(\sec x - \cos x) = \tan^2 x$.

b. By part **a,**

$$\sec x(\sec x - \cos x) = \tan^2 x$$

Divide both sides of this equation by $\tan x(\sec x - \cos x)$.

$$\frac{\sec x(\sec x - \cos x)}{\tan x(\sec x - \cos x)} = \frac{\tan^2 x}{\tan x(\sec x - \cos x)}$$

$$\frac{\sec x(\sec x - \cos x)}{\tan x(\sec x - \cos x)} = \frac{\tan x \tan x}{\tan x(\sec x - \cos x)}$$

$$\frac{\sec x}{\tan x} = \frac{\tan x}{\sec x - \cos x}$$

∎

Look carefully at how identity **b** was proved in Example 7. First prove identity **a,** which is of the form $AD = BC$ (with $A = \sec x$, $B = \tan x$, $C = \tan x$, and $D = \sec x - \cos x$). Then divide both sides by BD, that is, by $\tan x(\sec x - \cos x)$, to conclude that $\dfrac{A}{B} = \dfrac{C}{D}$. This property provides a useful strategy for dealing with identities involving fractions.

Example 8 If $AD = BC$, with $B \ne 0$ and $D \ne 0$, then $\dfrac{A}{B} = \dfrac{C}{D}$.

Prove that $\dfrac{\cot x - 1}{\cot x + 1} = \dfrac{1 - \tan x}{1 + \tan x}$.

Solution

Use the same strategy used in Example 7. First prove $AD = BC$, with $A = \cot x - 1$, $B = \cot x + 1$, $C = 1 - \tan x$, and $D = 1 + \tan x$.

$$AD = BC$$

$$(\cot x - 1)(1 + \tan x) = (\cot x + 1)(1 - \tan x) \qquad\qquad [3]$$

Multiply out the left side of [3].

$$(\cot x - 1)(1 + \tan x) = \cot x + \cot x \tan x - 1 - \tan x$$
$$= \cot x + \frac{1}{\tan x} \tan x - 1 - \tan x$$
$$= \cot x + 1 - 1 - \tan x$$
$$= \cot x - \tan x.$$

Similarly, multiply the right side of [3].

$$(\cot x + 1)(1 - \tan x) = \cot x - \cot x \tan x + 1 - \tan x$$
$$= \cot x - 1 + 1 - \tan x$$
$$= \cot x - \tan x.$$

Because the left and right sides are equal to the same expression, [3] has been proven to be an identity. Therefore, conclude that

$$\frac{\cot x - 1}{\cot x + 1} = \frac{1 - \tan x}{1 + \tan x}$$

is also an identity.

CAUTION

Strategy 5 does *not* say that you begin with a fractional equation $\frac{A}{B} = \frac{C}{D}$ and cross multiply to eliminate the fractions. If you did that, you would be assuming that the statement was true, which is what has to be proved. What the strategy says is that to prove an identity involving fractions, you need only prove a different identity that does not involve fractions. In other words, if you prove that $AD = BC$ whenever $B \neq 0$ and $D \neq 0$, then you can conclude that $\frac{A}{B} = \frac{C}{D}$. Note that you do not *assume* that $AD = BC$; you use some other strategy to *prove* this statement.

It takes a good deal of practice, as well as *much* trial and error, to become proficient at proving identities. The more practice you have, the easier it will become. Because there are many correct methods, your proofs may be quite different from those of your classmates, instructor, or text answers.

If you do not see what to do immediately, try something and see where it leads: multiply out, factor, or multiply numerator and denominator by the same nonzero quantity. Even if this does not lead anywhere, it may give you some ideas on other strategies to try. When you do obtain a proof, check to see if it can be done more efficiently. Do not include the "side trips" in your final proof—they may have given you some ideas, but they are not part of the proof.

Exercises 9.1

In Exercises 1–4, test the equation graphically to determine whether it might be an identity. You need not prove those equations that appear to be identities.

1. $\dfrac{\sec x - \cos x}{\sec x} = \sin^2 x$

2. $\tan x + \cot x = \sin x \cos x$

3. $\dfrac{1 - \cos 2x}{2} = \sin^2 x$

4. $\dfrac{\tan x + \cot x}{\csc x} = \sec x$

In Exercises 5–8, insert one of a–f on the right of the equal sign so that the resulting equation appears to be an identity when you test it graphically. You need not prove the identity.

a. $\cos x$ **b.** $\sec x$ **c.** $\sin^2 x$

d. $\sec^2 x$ **e.** $\sin x - \cos x$ **f.** $\dfrac{1}{\sin x \cos x}$

5. $\csc x \tan x = $ ——

6. $\dfrac{\sin x}{\tan x} = $ ——

7. $\dfrac{\sin^4 x - \cos^4 x}{\sin x + \cos x} = $ ——

8. $\tan^2(-x) - \dfrac{\sin(-x)}{\sin x} = $ ——

In Exercises 9–18, prove the identity.

9. $\tan x \cos x = \sin x$ **10.** $\cot x \sin x = \cos x$

11. $\cos x \sec x = 1$ **12.** $\sin x \csc x = 1$

13. $\tan x \csc x = \sec x$ **14.** $\sec x \cot x = \csc x$

15. $\dfrac{\tan x}{\sec x} = \sin x$ **16.** $\dfrac{\cot x}{\csc x} = \cos x$

17. $(1 + \cos x)(1 - \cos x) = \sin^2 x$

18. $(\csc x - 1)(\csc x + 1) = \cot^2 x$

In Exercises 19–48, state whether or not the equation is an identity. If it is an identity, prove it.

19. $\sin x = \sqrt{1 - \cos^2 x}$

20. $\cot x = \dfrac{\csc x}{\sec x}$

21. $\dfrac{\sin(-x)}{\cos(-x)} = -\tan x$

22. $\tan x = \sqrt{\sec^2 x - 1}$

23. $\cot(-x) = -\cot x$

24. $\sec(-x) = \sec x$

25. $1 + \sec^2 x = \tan^2 x$

26. $\sec^4 x - \tan^4 x = 1 + 2\tan^2 x$

27. $\sec^2 x - \csc^2 x = \tan^2 x - \cot^2 x$

28. $\sec^2 x + \csc^2 x = \sec^2 x \csc^2 x$

29. $\sin^2 x(\cot x + 1)^2 = \cos^2 x(\tan x + 1)^2$

30. $\cos^2 x(\sec x + 1)^2 = (1 + \cos x)^2$

31. $\sin^2 x - \tan^2 x = -\sin^2 x \tan^2 x$

32. $\cot^2 x - 1 = \csc^2 x$

33. $(\cos^2 x - 1)(\tan^2 x + 1) = -\tan^2 x$

34. $(1 - \cos^2 x)\csc x = \sin x$

35. $\tan x = \dfrac{\sec x}{\csc x}$

36. $\dfrac{\cos(-x)}{\sin(-x)} = -\cot x$

37. $\cos^4 x - \sin^4 x = \cos^2 x - \sin^2 x$

38. $\cot^2 x - \cos^2 x = \cos^2 x \cot^2 x$

39. $(\sin x + \cos x)^2 = \sin^2 x + \cos^2 x$

40. $(1 + \tan x)^2 = \sec^2 x$

41. $\dfrac{\sec x}{\csc x} + \dfrac{\sin x}{\cos x} = 2\tan x$

42. $\dfrac{1 + \cos x}{\sin x} + \dfrac{\sin x}{1 + \cos x} = 2\csc x$

43. $\dfrac{\sec x + \csc x}{1 + \tan x} = \csc x$

44. $\dfrac{\cot x - 1}{1 - \tan x} = \dfrac{\csc x}{\sec x}$

45. $\dfrac{1}{\csc x - \sin x} = \sec x \tan x$

46. $\dfrac{1 + \csc x}{\csc x} = \dfrac{\cos^2 x}{1 - \sin x}$

47. $\dfrac{\sin x - \cos x}{\tan x} = \dfrac{\tan x}{\sin x + \cos x}$

48. $\dfrac{\cot x}{\csc x - 1} = \dfrac{\csc x + 1}{\cot x}$

In Exercises 49–52, half of an identity is given. Graph this half in a viewing window with $-2\pi \le x \le 2\pi$ and write a conjecture as to what the right side of the identity is. Then prove your conjecture.

49. $1 - \dfrac{\sin^2 x}{1 + \cos x} = ?$ *Hint:* What familiar function has a graph that looks like this?

50. $\dfrac{1 + \cos x - \cos^2 x}{\sin x} - \cot x = ?$

51. $(\sin x + \cos x)(\sec x + \csc x) - \cot x - 2 = ?$

52. $\cos^3 x(1 - \tan^4 x + \sec^4 x) = ?$

In Exercises 53–66, prove the identity.

53. $\dfrac{1 - \sin x}{\sec x} = \dfrac{\cos^3 x}{1 + \sin x}$

54. $\dfrac{\sin x}{1 - \cot x} = \dfrac{\cos x}{1 - \tan x} = \cos x + \sin x$

55. $\dfrac{\cos x}{1 - \sin x} = \sec x + \tan x$

56. $\dfrac{1 + \sec x}{\tan x + \sin x} = \csc x$

57. $\dfrac{\cos x \cot x}{\cot x - \cos x} = \dfrac{\cot x + \cos x}{\cos x \cot x}$

58. $\dfrac{\cos^3 x - \sin^3 x}{\cos x - \sin x} = 1 + \sin x \cos x$

59. $\log_{10}(\cot x) = -\log_{10}(\tan x)$

60. $\log_{10}(\sec x) = -\log_{10}(\cos x)$

61. $\log_{10}(\csc x + \cot x) = -\log_{10}(\csc x - \cot x)$

62. $\log_{10}(\sec x + \tan x) = -\log_{10}(\sec x - \tan x)$

63. $\tan x - \tan y = -\tan x \tan y(\cot x - \cot y)$

64. $\dfrac{\tan x - \tan y}{\cot x - \cot y} = -\tan x \tan y$

65. $\dfrac{\cos x - \sin y}{\cos y - \sin x} = \dfrac{\cos y + \sin x}{\cos x + \sin y}$

66. $\dfrac{\tan x + \tan y}{\cot x + \cot y} = \dfrac{\tan x \tan y - 1}{1 - \cot x \cot y}$

9.2

Addition and Subtraction Identities

Objectives

- Use the addition and subtraction identities for sine, cosine, and tangent functions

- Use the cofunction identities

Many times, the input, or *argument*, of the sine or cosine function is the sum or difference of two angles, and you may need to simplify the expression. Be careful not to make this common student error.

$$\sin\left(x + \dfrac{\pi}{6}\right) \text{ is not } \sin x + \sin\dfrac{\pi}{6}$$

Graphing Exploration ●

Verify graphically that the expressions above do NOT form an identity by graphing $Y_1 = \sin\left(x + \dfrac{\pi}{6}\right)$ and $Y_2 = \sin x + \sin\dfrac{\pi}{6}$.

The exploration shows that $\sin(x + y) \neq \sin x + \sin y$ because it is false when $y = \frac{\pi}{6}$. So, is there an identity involving $\sin(x + y)$?

Graphing Exploration ●

Graph $Y_1 = \sin\left(x + \frac{\pi}{6}\right)$ and $Y_2 = \frac{\sqrt{3}}{2}\sin x + \frac{1}{2}\cos x$ on the same screen. Do the graphs appear identical?

The exploration suggests that $\sin\left(x + \frac{\pi}{2}\right) = \frac{\sqrt{3}}{2}\sin x + \frac{1}{2}\cos x$ may be an identity. Furthermore, note that the coefficients on the right side can be expressed in terms of $\frac{\pi}{6}$: $\cos\frac{\pi}{6} = \frac{\sqrt{3}}{2}$ and $\sin\frac{\pi}{6} = \frac{1}{2}$. In other words, the following equation appears to be an identity.

$$\sin\left(x + \frac{\pi}{6}\right) = \sin x \cos\frac{\pi}{6} + \cos x \sin\frac{\pi}{6}$$

Graphing Exploration ●

Graph $Y_1 = \sin(x + 5)$ and $Y_2 = \sin x \cos 5 + \cos x \sin 5$ on the same screen. Do the graphs appear identical? What identity does this suggest? Repeat the process with some other number in place of 5. Are the results the same?

The equations examined in the discussion and exploration above are examples of the first identity listed below. Each identity can be confirmed by assigning a constant value to y and then graphing each side of the equation, as in the Graphing Exploration above.

Addition and Subtraction Identities for Sine and Cosine

$$\sin(x + y) = \sin x \cos y + \cos x \sin y$$
$$\sin(x - y) = \sin x \cos y - \cos x \sin y$$
$$\cos(x + y) = \cos x \cos y - \sin x \sin y$$
$$\cos(x - y) = \cos x \cos y + \sin x \sin y$$

The addition and subtraction identities are important trigonometric identities. You should become familiar with the examples and special cases that follow.

Example 1   Addition Identities

Use the addition identities to find the *exact* values of $\sin \dfrac{5\pi}{12}$ and $\cos \dfrac{5\pi}{12}$.

Solution

NOTE In order to use addition or subtraction identities to find exact values, first write the argument as a sum or difference of two terms for which exact values are known, such as $\dfrac{\pi}{6}, \dfrac{\pi}{4}, \dfrac{\pi}{3}$, $\dfrac{\pi}{2}$, and π.

Because $\dfrac{5\pi}{12} = \dfrac{2\pi}{12} + \dfrac{3\pi}{12} = \dfrac{\pi}{6} + \dfrac{\pi}{4}$, apply the addition identities with $x = \dfrac{\pi}{6}$ and $y = \dfrac{\pi}{4}$.

$$\sin \frac{5\pi}{12} = \sin\left(\frac{\pi}{6} + \frac{\pi}{4}\right) = \sin \frac{\pi}{6} \cos \frac{\pi}{4} + \cos \frac{\pi}{6} \sin \frac{\pi}{4}$$

$$= \frac{1}{2} \cdot \frac{\sqrt{2}}{2} + \frac{\sqrt{3}}{2} \cdot \frac{\sqrt{2}}{2} = \frac{\sqrt{2}(1 + \sqrt{3})}{4}$$

$$\cos \frac{5\pi}{12} = \cos\left(\frac{\pi}{6} + \frac{\pi}{4}\right) = \cos \frac{\pi}{6} \cos \frac{\pi}{4} - \sin \frac{\pi}{6} \sin \frac{\pi}{4}$$

$$= \frac{\sqrt{3}}{2} \cdot \frac{\sqrt{2}}{2} - \frac{1}{2} \cdot \frac{\sqrt{2}}{2} = \frac{\sqrt{2}(\sqrt{3} - 1)}{4}$$

Example 2   Subtraction Identity

Find $\sin(\pi - y)$.

Solution

Apply the subtraction identity for the sine function with $x = \pi$.

$$\sin(\pi - y) = \sin \pi \cos y - \cos \pi \sin y = 0 \cos y - (-1)\sin y = \sin y$$

Example 3   Addition Identity

Prove that $\cos x \cos y = \dfrac{1}{2}[\cos(x + y) + \cos(x - y)]$.

Solution

Begin with the more complicated right side and use the addition and subtraction identities for cosine to transform it into the left side.

$$\frac{1}{2}[\cos(x + y) + \cos(x - y)]$$

$$= \frac{1}{2}[(\cos x \cos y - \sin x \sin y) + (\cos x \cos y + \sin x \sin y)]$$

$$= \frac{1}{2}(\cos x \cos y + \cos x \cos y) = \frac{1}{2}(2 \cos x \cos y)$$

$$= \cos x \cos y$$

NOTE Recall that the difference quotient of a function *f* is

$$\frac{f(x + h) - f(x)}{h}.$$

Simplifying the Difference Quotient of a Trigonometric Function

The difference quotient is very important in calculus, and the addition identities are needed to simplify difference quotients of trigonometric functions.

Example 4   The Difference Quotient of $f(x) = \sin x$

Show that for the function $f(x) = \sin x$ and any number $h \neq 0$,

$$\frac{f(x + h) - f(x)}{h} = \sin x\left(\frac{\cos h - 1}{h}\right) + \cos x\left(\frac{\sin h}{h}\right).$$

Solution

Use the addition identity for $\sin(x + y)$ with $y = h$.

$$\frac{f(x + h) - f(x)}{h} = \frac{\sin(x + h) - \sin x}{h}$$

$$= \frac{\sin x \cos h + \cos x \sin h - \sin x}{h}$$

$$= \frac{\sin x(\cos h - 1) + \cos x \sin h}{h}$$

$$= \sin x\left(\frac{\cos h - 1}{h}\right) + \cos x\left(\frac{\sin h}{h}\right)$$

Addition and Subtraction Identities for the Tangent Function

The addition and subtraction identities for sine and cosine can be used to obtain the addition and subtraction identities for the tangent function.

Addition and Subtraction Identities for Tangent

$$\tan(x + y) = \frac{\tan x + \tan y}{1 - \tan x \tan y}$$

$$\tan(x - y) = \frac{\tan x - \tan y}{1 + \tan x \tan y}$$

A proof of these identities is outlined in Exercise 36.

Example 5   Addition and Subtraction Identities for Tangent

Find the exact values of $\sin(x + y)$ and $\tan(x + y)$ if x and y are numbers such that $0 < x < \dfrac{\pi}{2}$, $\pi < y < \dfrac{3\pi}{2}$, $\sin x = \dfrac{3}{4}$, and $\cos y = -\dfrac{1}{3}$. Determine in which of the following intervals $x + y$ lies: $\left(0, \dfrac{\pi}{2}\right)$, $\left(\dfrac{\pi}{2}, \pi\right)$, $\left(\pi, \dfrac{3\pi}{2}\right)$, or $\left(\dfrac{3\pi}{2}, 2\pi\right)$.

Solution

NOTE See Figure 6.4-7 for the signs of the functions in each quadrant.

Use the Pythagorean identity and the fact that $\cos x$ and $\tan x$ are positive in the first quadrant to obtain the following. See Figure 9.2-1a.

$$\cos x = \sqrt{1 - \sin^2 x} = \sqrt{1 - \left(\dfrac{3}{4}\right)^2} = \sqrt{1 - \dfrac{9}{16}} = \sqrt{\dfrac{7}{16}} = \dfrac{\sqrt{7}}{4}$$

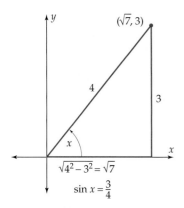

$$\tan x = \dfrac{\sin x}{\cos x} = \dfrac{\dfrac{3}{4}}{\dfrac{\sqrt{7}}{4}} = \dfrac{3}{\sqrt{7}} = \dfrac{3\sqrt{7}}{7}$$

Because y lies between π and $\dfrac{3\pi}{2}$, its sine is negative. See Figure 9.2-1b.

$$\sin y = -\sqrt{1 - \cos^2 y} = -\sqrt{1 - \left(-\dfrac{1}{3}\right)^2} = -\sqrt{\dfrac{8}{9}} = -\dfrac{\sqrt{8}}{3} = -\dfrac{2\sqrt{2}}{3}$$

Figure 9.2-1a

$$\tan y = \dfrac{\sin y}{\cos y} = \dfrac{\dfrac{-2\sqrt{2}}{3}}{\dfrac{-1}{3}} = \dfrac{-2\sqrt{2}}{3} \cdot \dfrac{3}{-1} = 2\sqrt{2}$$

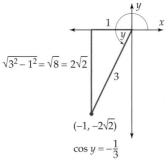

The addition identities for sine and tangent show exact values.

$$\sin(x + y) = \sin x \cos y + \cos x \sin y$$
$$= \dfrac{3}{4} \cdot \dfrac{-1}{3} + \dfrac{\sqrt{7}}{4} \cdot \dfrac{-2\sqrt{2}}{3} = \dfrac{-3}{12} - \dfrac{2\sqrt{14}}{12} = \dfrac{-3 - 2\sqrt{14}}{12}$$

Figure 9.2-1b

$$\tan(x + y) = \dfrac{\tan x + \tan y}{1 - \tan x \tan y}$$

$$= \dfrac{\dfrac{3\sqrt{7}}{7} + 2\sqrt{2}}{1 - \left(\dfrac{3\sqrt{7}}{7}\right)(2\sqrt{2})} = \dfrac{\dfrac{3\sqrt{7} + 14\sqrt{2}}{7}}{\dfrac{7 - 6\sqrt{14}}{7}}$$

$$= \dfrac{3\sqrt{7} + 14\sqrt{2}}{7 - 6\sqrt{14}} = -\dfrac{27\sqrt{7} + 32\sqrt{2}}{65}$$

Both the sine and tangent of $x + y$ are negative numbers. Therefore $x + y$ must be in the interval $\left(\dfrac{3\pi}{2}, 2\pi\right)$ because it is the only one of the four intervals in which both sine and tangent are negative. ∎

Cofunction Identities

Special cases of the addition and subtraction identities are the cofunction identities.

Cofunction Identities

$$\sin x = \cos\left(\frac{\pi}{2} - x\right) \qquad\qquad \cos x = \sin\left(\frac{\pi}{2} - x\right)$$

$$\tan x = \cot\left(\frac{\pi}{2} - x\right) \qquad\qquad \cot x = \tan\left(\frac{\pi}{2} - x\right)$$

$$\sec x = \csc\left(\frac{\pi}{2} - x\right) \qquad\qquad \csc x = \sec\left(\frac{\pi}{2} - x\right)$$

The first cofunction identity is proved by using the identity for $\cos(x - y)$ with $\frac{\pi}{2}$ in place of x and x in place of y.

$$\cos\left(\frac{\pi}{2} - x\right) = \cos\frac{\pi}{2}\cos x + \sin\frac{\pi}{2}\sin x = 0 \cdot \cos x + 1 \cdot \sin x = \sin x$$

Because the first cofunction identity is valid for *every* number x, it is also valid with the number $\frac{\pi}{2} - x$ in place of x.

$$\sin\left(\frac{\pi}{2} - x\right) = \cos\left[\frac{\pi}{2} - \left(\frac{\pi}{2} - x\right)\right] = \cos x$$

Thus, the second cofunction identity is proved. The others now follow from these previous two. For instance,

$$\tan\left(\frac{\pi}{2} - x\right) = \frac{\sin\left(\dfrac{\pi}{2} - x\right)}{\cos\left(\dfrac{\pi}{2} - x\right)} = \frac{\cos x}{\sin x} = \cot x$$

Also,

$$\csc\left(\frac{\pi}{2} - x\right) = \frac{1}{\sin\left(\dfrac{\pi}{2} - x\right)} = \frac{1}{\cos x} = \sec x$$

Example 6 Cofunction Identities

Verify that $\dfrac{\cos\left(x - \dfrac{\pi}{2}\right)}{\cos x} = \tan x$.

Solution

Beginning with the left side, the term $\cos\left(x - \dfrac{\pi}{2}\right)$ looks almost, but not quite, like the term $\cos\left(\dfrac{\pi}{2} - x\right)$ in the cofunction identity. But note that $-\left(x - \dfrac{\pi}{2}\right) = \dfrac{\pi}{2} - x$. Therefore,

$$\frac{\cos\left(x - \frac{\pi}{2}\right)}{\cos x} = \frac{\cos\left[-\left(x - \frac{\pi}{2}\right)\right]}{\cos x} \qquad \begin{array}{l} \textit{negative angle identity with} \\ x - \frac{\pi}{2} \textit{ in place of } x \end{array}$$

$$= \frac{\cos\left(\frac{\pi}{2} - x\right)}{\cos x}$$

$$= \frac{\sin x}{\cos x} \qquad \textit{cofunction identity}$$

$$= \tan x \qquad \textit{quotient identity}$$

Exercises 9.2

In Exercises 1–12, find the exact value.

1. $\sin\dfrac{\pi}{12}$

2. $\cos\dfrac{\pi}{12}$

3. $\tan\dfrac{\pi}{12}$

4. $\sin\dfrac{5\pi}{12}$

5. $\cot\dfrac{5\pi}{12}$

6. $\cos\dfrac{7\pi}{12}$

7. $\tan\dfrac{7\pi}{12}$

8. $\cos\dfrac{11\pi}{12}$

9. $\cot\dfrac{11\pi}{12}$

10. $\sin 75°$ *Hint:* $75° = 45° + 30°$.

11. $\sin 105°$

12. $\cos 165°$

In Exercises 13–18, rewrite the given expression in terms of $\sin x$ and $\cos x$.

13. $\sin\left(\dfrac{\pi}{2} + x\right)$

14. $\cos\left(x + \dfrac{\pi}{2}\right)$

15. $\cos\left(x - \dfrac{3\pi}{2}\right)$

16. $\csc\left(x + \dfrac{\pi}{2}\right)$

17. $\sec(x - \pi)$

18. $\cot(x + \pi)$

In Exercises 19–24, simplify the given expression.

19. $\sin 3 \cos 5 - \cos 3 \sin 5$

20. $\sin 37° \sin 53° - \cos 37° \cos 53°$

21. $\cos(x + y)\cos y + \sin(x + y)\sin y$

22. $\sin(x - y)\cos y + \cos(x - y)\sin y$

23. $\cos(x + y) - \cos(x - y)$

24. $\sin(x + y) - \sin(x - y)$

25. If $\sin x = \dfrac{1}{3}$ and $0 < x < \dfrac{\pi}{2}$, then $\sin\left(\dfrac{\pi}{4} + x\right) = ?$

26. If $\cos x = -\dfrac{1}{4}$ and $\dfrac{\pi}{2} < x < \pi$, then $\cos\left(\dfrac{\pi}{6} - x\right) = ?$

27. If $\cos x = -\dfrac{1}{5}$ and $\pi < x < \dfrac{3\pi}{2}$, then $\sin\left(\dfrac{\pi}{3} - x\right) = ?$

28. If $\sin x = -\dfrac{3}{4}$ and $\dfrac{3\pi}{2} < x < 2\pi$, then

$$\cos\left(\dfrac{\pi}{4} + x\right) = ?$$

In Exercises 29–34, assume that $\sin x = 0.8$ and $\sin y = \sqrt{0.75}$ and that x and y lie between 0 and $\dfrac{\pi}{2}$. Evaluate the given expressions.

29. $\cos(x + y)$

30. $\sin(x + y)$

31. $\cos(x - y)$

32. $\sin(x - y)$

33. $\tan(x + y)$

34. $\tan(x - y)$

35. If $f(x) = \cos x$ and h is a fixed nonzero number, prove that the difference quotient is

$$\frac{f(x + h) - f(x)}{h} = \cos x\left(\frac{\cos h - 1}{h}\right) - \sin x\left(\frac{\sin h}{h}\right).$$

36. Prove the addition and subtraction identities for the tangent function. *Hint:*

$$\tan(x + y) = \frac{\sin(x + y)}{\cos(x + y)}$$

Use the addition identities on the numerator and denominator; then divide both numerator and denominator by $\cos x \cos y$, and simplify.

37. If x is in the first quadrant and y is in the second quadrant, $\sin x = \dfrac{24}{25}$, and $\sin y = \dfrac{4}{5}$, find the exact value of $\sin(x + y)$ and $\tan(x + y)$ and the quadrant in which $x + y$ lies.

38. If x and y are in the second quadrant, $\sin x = \dfrac{1}{3}$, and $\cos y = -\dfrac{3}{4}$, find the exact value of $\sin(x + y)$, $\cos(x + y)$, and $\tan(x + y)$ and the quadrant in which $x + y$ lies.

39. If x is in the first quadrant and y is in the second quadrant, $\sin x = \dfrac{4}{5}$, and $\cos y = -\dfrac{12}{13}$, find the exact value of $\cos(x + y)$ and $\tan(x + y)$ and the quadrant in which $x + y$ lies.

40. If x is in the fourth quadrant and y is in the first quadrant, $\cos x = \dfrac{1}{3}$, and $\cos y = \dfrac{2}{3}$, find the exact value of $\sin(x - y)$ and $\tan(x - y)$ and the quadrant in which $x - y$ lies.

41. Express $\sin(u + v + w)$ in terms of sines and cosines of u, v, and w. *Hint:* First apply the addition identity with $x = u + v$ and $y = w$.

42. Express $\cos(x + y + z)$ in terms of sines and cosines of x, y, and z.

43. If $x + y = \dfrac{\pi}{2}$, show that $\sin^2 x + \sin^2 y = 1$.

44. Prove that $\cot(x + y) = \dfrac{\cot x \cot y - 1}{\cot x + \cot y}$.

In Exercises 45–56, prove the identity.

45. $\sin(x - \pi) = -\sin x$

46. $\cos(x - \pi) = -\cos x$

47. $\cos(\pi - x) = -\cos x$

48. $\tan(\pi - x) = -\tan x$

49. $\sin(x + \pi) = -\sin x$

50. $\cos(x + \pi) = -\cos x$

51. $\tan(x + \pi) = \tan x$

52. $\sin x \cos y = \dfrac{1}{2}[\sin(x + y) + \sin(x - y)]$

53. $\sin x \sin y = \dfrac{1}{2}[\cos(x - y) - \cos(x + y)]$

54. $\cos x \sin y = \dfrac{1}{2}[\sin(x + y) - \sin(x - y)]$

55. $\cos(x + y) \cos(x - y) = \cos^2 x \cos^2 y - \sin^2 x \sin^2 y$

56. $\sin(x + y) \sin(x - y) = \sin^2 x \cos^2 y - \cos^2 x \sin^2 y$

In Exercises 57–66, determine graphically whether the equation could not possibly be an identity (by choosing a numerical value for y and graphing both sides), or write a proof that it is.

57. $\dfrac{\cos(x - y)}{\sin x \cos y} = \cot x + \tan y$

58. $\dfrac{\cos(x + y)}{\sin x \cos y} = \cot x - \tan y$

59. $\sin(x - y) = \sin x - \sin y$

60. $\cos(x + y) = \cos x + \cos y$

61. $\dfrac{\sin(x + y)}{\sin(x - y)} = \dfrac{\tan x + \tan y}{\tan x - \tan y}$

62. $\dfrac{\sin(x + y)}{\sin(x - y)} = \dfrac{\cot y + \cot x}{\cot y - \cot x}$

63. $\dfrac{\cos(x + y)}{\cos(x - y)} = \dfrac{\cot x + \tan y}{\cot x - \tan y}$

64. $\dfrac{\cos(x - y)}{\cos(x + y)} = \dfrac{\cot y + \tan x}{\cot y - \tan x}$

65. $\tan(x + y) = \tan x + \tan y$

66. $\cot(x - y) = \cot x - \cot y$

Excursion: Lines and Angles

Objectives

- Find the angle of inclination of a line with a given slope

- Find the angle between two lines

Several interesting concepts dealing with lines are defined in terms of trigonometry. They lead to useful facts whose proofs are based on the addition and subtraction identities for sine, cosine, and tangent.

If L is a nonhorizontal straight line, the **angle of inclination** of L is the positive angle θ formed by the part of L above the x-axis and the x-axis, as shown in Figure 9.2.A-1.

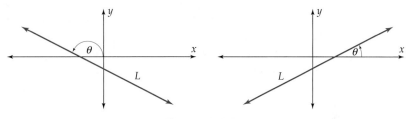

Figure 9.2.A-1

The angle of inclination of a horizontal line is defined to be $\theta = 0$. Thus, the radian measure of the angle of inclination of any line satisfies $0 \le \theta < \pi$. Furthermore,

Angle of Inclination Theorem

> If L is a nonvertical line with angle of inclination θ, then $\tan \theta = $ slope of L.

Proof

If L is horizontal, then L has slope 0 and angle of inclination $\theta = 0$. Hence, $\tan \theta = \tan 0 = 0$, so $\tan \theta = $ slope of $L = 0$.

If L is not horizontal, then it intersects the x-axis at some point $(x_1, 0)$, as shown for two possible cases in Figure 9.2.A-2.

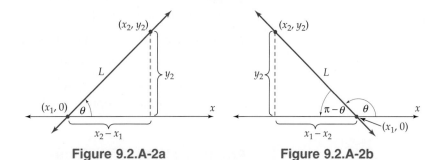

Figure 9.2.A-2a   **Figure 9.2.A-2b**

The right triangle in Figure 9.2.A-2a shows that

$$\text{slope of } L = \frac{y_2 - 0}{x_2 - x_1} = \frac{y_2}{x_2 - x_1} = \frac{opposite}{adjacent} = \tan\theta.$$

The right triangle in Figure 9.2.A-2b shows that

$$\text{slope of } L = \frac{0 - y_2}{x_1 - x_2} = -\frac{y_2}{x_1 - x_2} = -\frac{opposite}{adjacent} = -\tan(\pi - \theta). \quad [1]$$

Use the fact that the tangent function has period π and the negative angle identity for tangent to obtain

$$-\tan(\pi - \theta) = -\tan(-\theta) = -(-\tan\theta) = \tan\theta.$$

Combining this fact with [1] shows that slope of $L = \tan\theta$ in this case also.

Example 1 Angle of Inclination

Find the angle of inclination of a line of slope $\frac{5}{3}$.

Solution

By the Angle of Inclination Theorem, $\tan\theta = \frac{5}{3}$. The TAN^{-1} key on a calculator shows that $\theta \approx 1.0304$ radians, or $\theta \approx 59.04°$.

Example 2 Angle of Inclination

Find the angle of inclination of a line L with slope -2.

Solution

Because line L has slope -2, its angle of inclination is a solution of $\tan\theta = -2$ that lies between $\frac{\pi}{2}$ and π. A calculator gives the approximate solution -1.1071. Because an angle of inclination must be between 0 and π, another solution is needed.

Recall that $\tan t = \tan(t + \pi)$, for every t. So

$$\theta \approx -1.1071 + \pi \approx 2.0344$$

is the solution of $\tan\theta = -2$ in the interval from 0 to π. Therefore, the angle of inclination is approximately 2.03 radians, or about 116.57°.

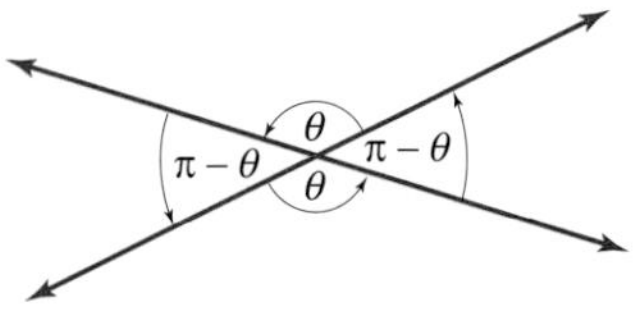

Figure 9.2.A-3

Angles Between Two Lines

If two lines intersect, then they determine four angles with vertices at the point of intersection, as shown in Figure 9.2.A-3. If one of these angles measures θ radians, then each of the two angles adjacent to it measures $\pi - \theta$ radians. (Why?) The fourth angle also measures θ radians by the vertical angle theorem from plane geometry.

The angles formed by intersecting lines can be determined from the angles of inclination of the lines. Suppose L and M have angles of inclination α and β, respectively, such that $\beta \geq \alpha$. Basic facts about parallel lines, as illustrated in Figure 9.2.A-4, show that $\beta - \alpha$ is one angle between L and M, and $\pi - (\beta - \alpha)$ is the other.

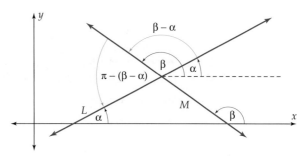

Figure 9.2.A-4

The angle between two lines can also be found from their slopes by using the following fact.

Angle Between Two Lines

> If two nonvertical, nonperpendicular lines have slopes m and k, then one angle θ between them satisfies
>
> $$\tan \theta = \left| \frac{m - k}{1 + mk} \right|.$$

Proof

Suppose L has slope k and angle of inclination α and that M has slope m and angle of inclination β. By the definition of absolute value

$$\left| \frac{m - k}{1 + mk} \right| = \frac{m - k}{1 + mk} \quad \text{or} \quad \left| \frac{m - k}{1 + mk} \right| = -\frac{m - k}{1 + mk}$$

whichever is positive. It will be shown that one angle between L and M has tangent $\dfrac{m - k}{1 + mk}$, and that the other has tangent $-\dfrac{m - k}{1 + mk}$. Thus, one of them necessarily has tangent $\left| \dfrac{m - k}{1 + mk} \right|$. If $\beta \geq \alpha$, then $\beta - \alpha$ is one angle between L and M. By the subtraction identity for tangent,

$$\tan(\beta - \alpha) = \frac{\tan \beta - \tan \alpha}{1 + \tan \beta \tan \alpha} = \frac{m - k}{1 + mk}$$

The other angle between L and M is $\pi - (\beta - \alpha)$ and by periodicity, the negative angle identity, and the addition identity

$$\tan[\pi - (\beta - \alpha)] = \tan[-(\beta - \alpha)]$$
$$= -\tan(\beta - \alpha)$$
$$= -\frac{\tan \beta - \tan \alpha}{1 + \tan \beta \tan \alpha}$$
$$= -\frac{m - k}{1 + mk}.$$

This completes the proof when $\beta \geq \alpha$. The proof in the case $\alpha \geq \beta$ is similar.

Example 3   **The Angle Between Two Lines**

If the slopes of lines L and M are 8 and -3, respectively, then find one angle between them.

Solution

Substitute 8 for m and -3 for k to find the tangent values.

$$\tan \theta = \left| \frac{8 - (-3)}{1 + 8(-3)} \right|$$
$$= \left| \frac{11}{-23} \right| = \frac{11}{23}$$

Solving the equation yields $\theta \approx 0.4461$ radians, or $25.56°$.

Exercises 9.2.A

In Exercises 1–6, find the angle of inclination of the straight line through the given points.

1. $(-1, 2)$, $(3, 5)$ **2.** $(0, 4)$, $(5, -1)$

3. $(1, 4)$, $(6, 0)$ **4.** $(4, 2)$, $(-3, -2)$

5. $(3, -7)$, $(3, 5)$ **6.** $(0, 0)$, $(-4, -5)$

In Exercises 7–12, find one of the angles between the straight lines L and M.

7. L has slope $\frac{3}{2}$ and M has slope -1.

8. L has slope 1 and M has slope 3.

9. L has slope -1 and M has slope 0.

10. L has slope -2 and M has slope -3.

11. $(3, 2)$ and $(5, 6)$ are on L; $(0, 3)$ and $(4, 0)$ are on M.

12. $(-1, 2)$ and $(3, -3)$ are on L; $(3, -3)$ and $(6, 1)$ are on M.

9.3   Other Identities

Objectives

*   Use the following identities:

    double-angle

    power-reducing

    half-angle

    product-to-sum

    sum-to-product

A variety of identities that are special cases of the addition and subtraction identities of Section 9.2 are presented in this section. These identities include double-angle identities, power-reducing identities, half-angle identities, product-to-sum identities, and sum-to-product identities.

Double-Angle Identities

Special cases of the addition identities occur when two angles have the same measure. These identities are called the **double-angle identities.**

Double-Angle Identities

$$\sin 2x = 2 \sin x \cos x$$

$$\cos 2x = \cos^2 x - \sin^2 x$$

$$\tan 2x = \frac{2 \tan x}{1 - \tan^2 x}$$

Proof Substitute x for y in the addition identities.

$$\sin 2x = \sin(x + x) = \sin x \cos x + \cos x \sin x = 2 \sin x \cos x$$
$$\cos 2x = \cos(x + x) = \cos x \cos x - \sin x \sin x = \cos^2 x - \sin^2 x$$
$$\tan 2x = \tan(x + x) = \frac{\tan x + \tan x}{1 - \tan x \tan x} = \frac{2 \tan x}{1 - \tan^2 x}$$

Example 1   Use Double-Angle Identities

If $\pi < x < \dfrac{3\pi}{2}$ and $\cos x = -\dfrac{8}{17}$, find $\sin 2x$ and $\cos 2x$, and show that $\dfrac{5\pi}{2} < 2x < 3\pi$.

Solution

In order to use the double-angle identities, first determine $\sin x$, which can be found by using the Pythagorean identity.

$$\sin^2 x = 1 - \cos^2 x = 1 - \left(-\frac{8}{17}\right)^2 = 1 - \frac{64}{289} = \frac{225}{289}$$

Thus, $\sin x = \pm\sqrt{\dfrac{225}{289}}$. Since $\pi < x < \dfrac{3\pi}{2}$, x must be in the third quadrant, and $\sin x$ is negative there.

$$\sin x = -\sqrt{\frac{225}{289}} = -\frac{15}{17}$$

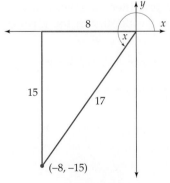

Figure 9.3-1

Now substitute these values in the double-angle identities to find $\sin 2x$ and $\cos 2x$.

$$\sin 2x = 2 \sin x \cos x = 2\left(-\frac{15}{17}\right)\left(-\frac{8}{17}\right) = \frac{240}{289} \approx 0.8304$$

$$\cos 2x = \cos^2 x - \sin^2 x = \left(-\frac{8}{17}\right)^2 - \left(-\frac{15}{17}\right)^2 = \frac{64}{289} - \frac{225}{289} = -\frac{161}{289} \approx -0.5571$$

You know that x lies in the third quadrant. Multiply the inequality $\pi < x < \frac{3\pi}{2}$ by 2 to find that $2\pi < 2x < 3\pi$. That is, $2x$ is in either the first or second quadrant. The calculations above show that at $2x$, sine is positive and cosine is negative. This can occur only if $2x$ lies in the second quadrant, so $\frac{5\pi}{2} < 2x < 3\pi$.

■

Example 2   Use Double-Angle Identities

Express the rule of the function $f(x) = \sin 3x$ in terms of powers of $\sin x$ and constants.

Solution

First use the addition identity for $\sin(x + y)$ with $y = 2x$.

$$
\begin{aligned}
f(x) = \sin 3x = \sin(x + 2x) &= \sin x \cos 2x + \cos x \sin 2x \\
&= \sin x(\cos^2 x - \sin^2 x) + \cos x(2 \sin x \cos x) \\
&\qquad \textit{identity for } \cos 2x \qquad\qquad \textit{identity for } \sin 2x \\
&= \sin x \cos^2 x - \sin^3 x + 2 \sin x \cos^2 x \\
&= 3 \sin x \cos^2 x - \sin^3 x \\
&= 3 \sin x(1 - \sin^2 x) - \sin^3 x \\
&\qquad \textit{Pythagorean identity} \\
&= 3 \sin x - 3 \sin^3 x - \sin^3 x \\
&= 3 \sin x - 4 \sin^3 x
\end{aligned}
$$

■

Forms of cos 2x

The double-angle identity for $\cos 2x$ can be rewritten in several useful ways. For instance, we can use the Pythagorean identity in the form of $\cos^2 x = 1 - \sin^2 x$ to obtain the following.

$$\cos 2x = \cos^2 x - \sin^2 x = (1 - \sin^2 x) - \sin^2 x = 1 - 2 \sin^2 x$$

Similarly, use the Pythagorean identity in the form $\sin^2 x = 1 - \cos^2 x$ to obtain the following.

$$\cos 2x = \cos^2 x - \sin^2 x = \cos^2 x - (1 - \cos^2 x) = 2 \cos^2 x - 1$$

Forms of cos 2x

$$\cos 2x = 1 - 2\sin^2 x$$
$$\cos 2x = 2\cos^2 x - 1$$

Example 3   Use Forms of cos 2x

Prove that $\dfrac{1 - \cos 2x}{\sin 2x} = \tan x$.

Solution

Use the first identity in the preceding box and the double-angle identity for sine.

$$\frac{1 - \cos 2x}{\sin 2x} = \frac{1 - (1 - 2\sin^2 x)}{2\sin x \cos x} = \frac{2\sin^2 x}{2\sin x \cos x} = \frac{\sin x}{\cos x} = \tan x$$

Power-Reducing Identities

If the first equation in the preceding box is solved for $\sin^2 x$ and the second one for $\cos^2 x$, alternate forms for these identities are obtained. The new forms are called the **power-reducing identities.**

Power-Reducing Identities

$$\sin^2 x = \frac{1 - \cos 2x}{2}$$

$$\cos^2 x = \frac{1 + \cos 2x}{2}$$

Example 4   Use Power-Reducing Identities

Express the function $f(x) = \sin^4 x$ in terms of constants and first powers of cosine functions.

Solution

Begin by applying the power-reducing identity.

$$f(x) = \sin^4 x = \sin^2 x \cdot \sin^2 x$$
$$= \frac{1 - \cos 2x}{2} \cdot \frac{1 - \cos 2x}{2}$$
$$= \frac{1 - 2\cos 2x + \cos^2 2x}{4}$$

NOTE To write $\cos^2 2x$ in terms of first powers of cosine functions, use $2x$ in place of x in the power-reducing identity for cosine.

$$\cos^2 2x = \frac{1 + \cos 2(2x)}{2}$$
$$= \frac{1 + \cos 4x}{2}$$

Next apply the power-reducing identity for cosine to $\cos^2 2x$. (See Note.)

$$\frac{1 - 2\cos 2x + \cos^2 2x}{4} = \frac{1 - 2\cos 2x + \dfrac{1 + \cos 4x}{2}}{4}$$

$$= \frac{1}{4} - \frac{1}{2}\cos 2x + \frac{1}{8}(1 + \cos 4x)$$

$$= \frac{3}{8} - \frac{1}{2}\cos 2x + \frac{1}{8}\cos 4x \qquad \blacksquare$$

Half-Angle Identities

The power-reducing identities with $\frac{x}{2}$ in place of x can be used to obtain the **half-angle identities.**

$$\sin^2\left(\frac{x}{2}\right) = \frac{1 - \cos 2\left(\dfrac{x}{2}\right)}{2} = \frac{1 - \cos x}{2}$$

$$\sin\left(\frac{x}{2}\right) = \pm\sqrt{\frac{1 - \cos x}{2}}$$

This proves the first of the half-angle identities.

Half-Angle Identities

$$\sin\frac{x}{2} = \pm\sqrt{\frac{1 - \cos x}{2}} \qquad \cos\frac{x}{2} = \pm\sqrt{\frac{1 + \cos x}{2}}$$

$$\tan\frac{x}{2} = \pm\sqrt{\frac{1 - \cos x}{1 + \cos x}}$$

The sign in front of the radical depends upon the quadrant in which $\frac{x}{2}$ lies.

The half-angle identity for cosine is derived from a power-reducing identity, as was the half-angle identity for sine. The half-angle identity for tangent then follows immediately since $\tan\left(\dfrac{x}{2}\right) = \dfrac{\sin\left(\dfrac{x}{2}\right)}{\cos\left(\dfrac{x}{2}\right)}$.

Example 5 **Half-Angle Identities**

Find the exact value of

a. $\cos\dfrac{5\pi}{8}$

b. $\sin\dfrac{\pi}{12}$

Solution

a. Because $\dfrac{5\pi}{8} = \dfrac{1}{2}\left(\dfrac{5\pi}{4}\right)$, use the half-angle identity with $x = \dfrac{5\pi}{4}$ and the fact that $\cos\dfrac{5\pi}{4} = -\dfrac{\sqrt{2}}{2}$. The sign chart given in Section 6.4 shows that $\cos\dfrac{5\pi}{8}$ is negative because $\dfrac{5\pi}{8}$ is in the second quadrant. So, use the negative sign in front of the radical.

$$\cos\frac{5\pi}{8} = \cos\frac{\frac{5\pi}{4}}{2} = -\sqrt{\frac{1 + \cos\left(\frac{5\pi}{4}\right)}{2}}$$

$$= -\sqrt{\frac{1 + \left(-\dfrac{\sqrt{2}}{2}\right)}{2}}$$

$$= -\sqrt{\frac{\dfrac{(2 - \sqrt{2})}{2}}{2}}$$

$$= -\sqrt{\frac{2 - \sqrt{2}}{4}}$$

$$= -\frac{\sqrt{2 - \sqrt{2}}}{2}$$

b. Because $\dfrac{\pi}{12} = \dfrac{1}{2}\left(\dfrac{\pi}{6}\right)$ and $\dfrac{\pi}{12}$ is in the first quadrant, where sine is positive,

$$\sin\frac{\pi}{12} = \sin\frac{\frac{\pi}{6}}{2} = \sqrt{\frac{1 - \cos\left(\frac{\pi}{6}\right)}{2}}$$

$$= \sqrt{\frac{1 - \dfrac{\sqrt{3}}{2}}{2}}$$

$$= \sqrt{\frac{\dfrac{2 - \sqrt{3}}{2}}{2}}$$

$$= \sqrt{\frac{2 - \sqrt{3}}{4}}$$

$$= \frac{\sqrt{2 - \sqrt{3}}}{2}$$

The problem of determining signs in the half-angle formulas can be eliminated for the tangent by using the following formulas.

Half-Angle Identities for Tangent

$$\tan \frac{x}{2} = \frac{1 - \cos x}{\sin x}$$

$$\tan \frac{x}{2} = \frac{\sin x}{1 + \cos x}$$

Proof

The proof of the first of these identities follows from the identity $\tan x = \dfrac{1 - \cos 2x}{\sin 2x}$, which was proved in Example 3. Replace x by $\dfrac{x}{2}$ in this identity.

$$\tan \frac{x}{2} = \frac{1 - \cos 2\left(\frac{x}{2}\right)}{\sin 2\left(\frac{x}{2}\right)} = \frac{1 - \cos x}{\sin x}$$

The second identity in the box is proved in Exercise 71.

Example 6 Use Half-Angle Identity for Tangent

If $\tan x = \dfrac{3}{2}$ and $\pi < x < \dfrac{3\pi}{2}$, find $\tan \dfrac{x}{2}$.

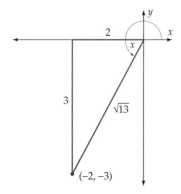

Figure 9.3-2

Solution

The terminal side of an angle of x radians in standard position lies in the third quadrant, as shown in Figure 9.3-2. The tangent of the angle in standard position whose terminal side passes through the point $(-2, -3)$ is $\dfrac{-3}{-2} = \dfrac{3}{2}$. Because there is only one angle in the third quadrant with tangent $\dfrac{3}{2}$, the point $(-2, -3)$ must lie on the terminal side of the angle of x radians.

The distance from $(-2, -3)$ to the origin is the hypotenuse of the triangle.

$$\sqrt{(-2 - 0)^2 + (-3 - 0)^2} = \sqrt{13}$$

Therefore,

$$\sin x = \frac{-3}{\sqrt{13}} \qquad \cos x = \frac{-2}{\sqrt{13}}$$

By the first of the half-angle identities for tangent,

$$\tan \frac{x}{2} = \frac{1 - \cos x}{\sin x} = \frac{1 - \left(\frac{-2}{\sqrt{13}}\right)}{\frac{-3}{\sqrt{13}}} = \frac{\frac{\sqrt{13} + 2}{\sqrt{13}}}{\frac{-3}{\sqrt{13}}} = -\frac{\sqrt{13} + 2}{3}$$

Product-to-Sum Identities

Use the addition and subtraction identities to rewrite $\sin(x+y)+\sin(x-y)$.

$$\sin(x+y)+\sin(x-y)=\sin x\cos y+\cos x\sin y+\sin x\cos y-\cos x\sin y$$
$$=2\sin x\cos y$$

Dividing both sides of the equation by 2 produces the first of the following identities.

Product-to-Sum Identities

$$\sin x\cos y=\frac{1}{2}\,[\sin(x+y)+\sin(x-y)]$$

$$\sin x\sin y=\frac{1}{2}\,[\cos(x-y)-\cos(x+y)]$$

$$\cos x\cos y=\frac{1}{2}\,[\cos(x+y)+\cos(x-y)]$$

$$\cos x\sin y=\frac{1}{2}\,[\sin(x+y)-\sin(x-y)]$$

The proofs of the second and fourth product-to-sum identities are similar to the proof of the first. The third product-to-sum identity was proved in Example 3 of Section 9.2.

Sum-to-Product Identities

Use the first product-to-sum identity with $\dfrac{x+y}{2}$ in place of x and $\dfrac{x-y}{2}$ in place of y to obtain the first sum-to-product identity.

$$\sin\frac{x+y}{2}\cos\frac{x-y}{2}$$
$$=\frac{1}{2}\left[\sin\!\left(\frac{x+y}{2}+\frac{x-y}{2}\right)+\sin\!\left(\frac{x+y}{2}-\frac{x-y}{2}\right)\right]$$
$$=\frac{1}{2}(\sin x+\sin y)$$

Multiplying both sides of the equation by 2 produces the identity.

Sum-to-Product Identities

$$\sin x+\sin y=2\sin\frac{x+y}{2}\cos\frac{x-y}{2}$$

$$\sin x-\sin y=2\cos\frac{x+y}{2}\sin\frac{x-y}{2}$$

$$\cos x+\cos y=2\cos\frac{x+y}{2}\cos\frac{x-y}{2}$$

$$\cos x-\cos y=-2\sin\frac{x+y}{2}\sin\frac{x-y}{2}$$

The other sum-to-product identities are proved the same way as the first.

Example 7 Use Sum-to-Product Identities

Prove the identity below.

$$\frac{\sin t + \sin 3t}{\cos t + \cos 3t} = \tan 2t$$

Solution

Use the first sum-to-product identity with $x = t$ and $y = 3t$.

$$\sin t + \sin 3t = 2 \sin\left(\frac{t + 3t}{2}\right) \cos\left(\frac{t - 3t}{2}\right) = 2 \sin 2t \cos(-t)$$

Similarly,

$$\cos t + \cos 3t = 2 \cos\left(\frac{t + 3t}{2}\right) \cos\left(\frac{t - 3t}{2}\right) = 2 \cos 2t \cos(-t).$$

Therefore,

$$\frac{\sin t + \sin 3t}{\cos t + \cos 3t} = \frac{2 \sin 2t \cos(-t)}{2 \cos 2t \cos(-t)} = \frac{\sin 2t}{\cos 2t} = \tan 2t.$$

Exercises 9.3

In Exercises 1–12, use the half-angle identities to evaluate the given expression exactly.

1. $\cos \dfrac{\pi}{8}$ **2.** $\tan \dfrac{\pi}{8}$ **3.** $\sin \dfrac{3\pi}{8}$ **4.** $\cos \dfrac{3\pi}{8}$

5. $\tan \dfrac{\pi}{12}$ **6.** $\sin \dfrac{5\pi}{8}$ **7.** $\cos \dfrac{\pi}{12}$ **8.** $\tan \dfrac{5\pi}{8}$

9. $\sin \dfrac{7\pi}{8}$ **10.** $\cos \dfrac{7\pi}{8}$ **11.** $\tan \dfrac{7\pi}{8}$ **12.** $\cot \dfrac{\pi}{8}$

In Exercises 13–18, write each expression as a sum or difference.

13. $\sin 4x \cos 6x$ **14.** $\sin 5x \sin 7x$

15. $\cos 2x \cos 4x$ **16.** $\sin 3x \cos 5x$

17. $\sin 17x \sin(-3x)$ **18.** $\cos 13x \cos(-5x)$

In Exercises 19–22, write each expression as a product.

19. $\sin 3x + \sin 5x$ **20.** $\cos 2x + \cos 6x$

21. $\sin 9x - \sin 5x$ **22.** $\cos 5x - \cos 7x$

In Exercises 23–30, find $\sin 2x$, $\cos 2x$, and $\tan 2x$ under the given conditions.

23. $\sin x = \dfrac{5}{13}$, for $0 < x < \dfrac{\pi}{2}$

24. $\sin x = -\dfrac{4}{5}$, for $\pi < x < \dfrac{3\pi}{2}$

25. $\cos x = -\dfrac{3}{5}$, for $\pi < x < \dfrac{3\pi}{2}$

26. $\cos x = -\dfrac{1}{3}$, for $\dfrac{\pi}{2} < x < \pi$

27. $\tan x = \dfrac{3}{4}$, for $\pi < x < \dfrac{3\pi}{2}$

28. $\tan x = -\dfrac{3}{2}$, for $\dfrac{\pi}{2} < x < \pi$

29. $\csc x = 4$, for $0 < x < \dfrac{\pi}{2}$

30. $\sec x = -5$, for $\pi < x < \dfrac{3\pi}{2}$

In Exercises 31–36, find $\sin \frac{x}{2}$, $\cos \frac{x}{2}$, and $\tan \frac{x}{2}$ under the given conditions.

31. $\cos x = 0.4$, for $0 < x < \frac{\pi}{2}$

32. $\sin x = 0.6$, for $\frac{\pi}{2} < x < \pi$

33. $\sin x = -\frac{3}{5}$, for $\frac{3\pi}{2} < x < 2\pi$

34. $\cos x = 0.8$, for $\frac{3\pi}{2} < x < 2\pi$

35. $\tan x = \frac{1}{2}$, for $\pi < x < \frac{3\pi}{2}$

36. $\cot x = 1$, for $-\pi < x < -\frac{\pi}{2}$

In Exercises 37–42, assume $\sin x = 0.6$ and $0 < x < \frac{\pi}{2}$ and evaluate the given expression.

37. $\sin 2x$ **38.** $\cos 4x$ **39.** $\cos 2x$

40. $\sin 4x$ **41.** $\sin \frac{x}{2}$ **42.** $\cos \frac{x}{2}$

43. Express $\cos 3x$ in terms of $\cos x$.

44. a. Express the function $f(x) = \cos^3 x$ in terms of constants and first powers of the cosine function, as in Example 4.
  b. Do the same for $f(x) = \cos^4 x$.

In Exercises 45–50, simplify the given expression.

45. $\dfrac{\sin 2x}{2 \sin x}$ **46.** $1 - 2\sin^2\left(\dfrac{x}{2}\right)$

47. $2 \cos 2y \sin 2y$

48. $\cos^2\left(\dfrac{x}{2}\right) - \sin^2\left(\dfrac{x}{2}\right)$

49. $(\sin x + \cos x)^2 - \sin 2x$

50. $2 \sin x \cos^3 x - 2 \sin^3 x \cos x$

In Exercises 51–64, determine graphically whether the equation could not possibly be an identity, or write a proof showing that it is.

51. $\sin 16x = 2 \sin 8x \cos 8x$

52. $\cos 8x = \cos^2 4x - \sin^2 4x$

53. $\cos^4 x - \sin^4 x = \cos 2x$

54. $\sec 2x = \dfrac{1}{1 - 2\sin^2 x}$

55. $\cos 4x = 2 \cos 2x - 1$

56. $\sin^2 x = \cos^2 x - 2 \sin x$

57. $\dfrac{1 + \cos 2x}{\sin 2x} = \cot x$

58. $\sin 2x = \dfrac{2 \cot x}{\csc^2 x}$

59. $\sin 3x = (\sin x)(3 - 4 \sin^2 x)$

60. $\sin 4x = (4 \cos x \sin x)(1 - 2 \sin^2 x)$

61. $\cos 2x = \dfrac{2 \tan x}{\sec^2 x}$

62. $\cos 3x = (\cos x)(3 - 4 \cos^2 x)$

63. $\csc^2\left(\dfrac{x}{2}\right) = \dfrac{2}{1 - \cos x}$

64. $\sec^2\left(\dfrac{x}{2}\right) = \dfrac{2}{1 + \cos x}$

In Exercises 65–70, prove the identity.

65. $\dfrac{\sin x - \sin 3x}{\cos x + \cos 3x} = -\tan x$

66. $\dfrac{\sin x - \sin 3x}{\cos x - \cos 3x} = -\cot 2x$

67. $\dfrac{\sin 4x + \sin 6x}{\cos 4x - \cos 6x} = \cot x$

68. $\dfrac{\cos 8x + \cos 4x}{\cos 8x - \cos 4x} = -\cot 6x \cot 2x$

69. $\dfrac{\sin x + \sin y}{\cos x - \cos y} = -\cot\left(\dfrac{x - y}{2}\right)$

70. $\dfrac{\sin x - \sin y}{\cos x + \cos y} = \tan\left(\dfrac{x - y}{2}\right)$

71. a. Prove that $\dfrac{1 - \cos x}{\sin x} = \dfrac{\sin x}{1 + \cos x}$.
  b. Use part **a** and the half-angle identity proved in the text to prove that $\tan \dfrac{x}{2} = \dfrac{\sin x}{1 + \cos x}$.

72. If $x = \cos 2t$ and $y = \sin x$, find the relation between x and y by eliminating t.

73. The horizontal range of a projectile R is given by the equation

$$R = vt \cos \alpha,$$

where v is the initial velocity of the projectile, t is the time of flight, and α is the angle between the line of fire and the horizontal. If $t = \dfrac{2v \sin \alpha}{g}$, where g is acceleration due to gravity, show that $R = \dfrac{v^2 \sin 2\alpha}{g}$.

74. The expression $\sin\left(\dfrac{\pi}{2} - 2\theta\right)$ occurs in the theory of reflection of light waves. Show that this expression can be written as $1 - 2 \sin^2\theta$.

75. The expression $2\left(\sin^2 \dfrac{1}{2}\alpha - \sin^2 \dfrac{1}{2}\theta\right)$ is used in the theory of the motion of a pendulum. Show that this equation can be written as $\cos \theta - \cos \alpha$.

76. A batter hits a baseball that is caught by a fielder. If the ball leaves the bat at an angle of θ radians to the horizontal, with an initial velocity of v feet per second, then the approximate horizontal distance d traveled by the ball is given by

$$d = \frac{v^2 \sin \theta \cos \theta}{16}.$$

a. If the initial velocity is 90 ft/sec, find the horizontal distance traveled by the ball when $\theta = 0.5$ radian and when $\theta = 0.75$ radian.

b. Use an identity to show that $d = \dfrac{v^2 \sin 2\theta}{32}$.

Using Trigonometric Identities

Objectives

- Use identities to solve trigonometric equations

Recall that the basic identities are used to simplify expressions and to algebraically solve trigonometric equations. The trigonometric identities introduced in Section 9.3 can also be used with the techniques shown in Section 8.3, where equations were rewritten into a basic form and then solved.

Example 1   Use Double-Angle Identities

Solve $5 \cos x + 3 \cos 2x = 3$.

Solution

Use a double-angle identity to rewrite $\cos 2x$ in terms of $\cos^2 x$.

$$5 \cos x + 3 \cos 2x = 3$$
$$5 \cos x + 3(2 \cos^2 x - 1) = 3 \qquad \textit{double-angle identity}$$
$$5 \cos x + 6 \cos^2 x - 3 = 3$$
$$6 \cos^2 x + 5 \cos x - 6 = 0$$
$$(2 \cos x + 3)(3 \cos x - 2) = 0 \qquad \textit{factor the quadratic expression}$$
$$2 \cos x + 3 = 0 \qquad \text{or} \qquad 3 \cos x - 2 = 0$$
$$\cos x = -\frac{3}{2} \qquad\qquad\qquad \cos x = \frac{2}{3}$$

The equation $\cos x = -\dfrac{3}{2}$ has no solutions because $\cos x$ always lies between -1 and 1. A calculator shows that the solutions of $\cos x = \dfrac{2}{3}$ are

$$x \approx 0.8411 + 2k\pi \quad \text{and} \quad x \approx -0.8411 + 2k\pi$$

for any integer k.

Example 2   **Use Double-Angle Identities**

Solve the equation $\sin x \cos x = 1$.

Solution

Use the double-angle identity to rewrite $\sin x \cos x$.

$$2 \sin x \cos x = \sin 2x$$
$$\sin x \cos x = \frac{1}{2} \sin 2x$$

Replace $\sin x \cos x$ with $\dfrac{1}{2} \sin 2x$ and multiply both sides by 2.

$$\frac{1}{2} \sin 2x = 1$$
$$\sin 2x = 2$$

Because the sine of any number must be between -1 and 1, there is no solution to the last equation. Therefore, there is no solution to the original equation.

Example 3   **Use Double-Angle Identities**

Find exact solutions of $\cos^2 x - \sin^2 x = \dfrac{1}{2}$

Solution

Because $\cos^2 x - \sin^2 x = \cos 2x$, the equation can be rewritten

$$\cos 2x = \frac{1}{2}$$
$$2x = \cos^{-1}\frac{1}{2}$$

$$2x = \frac{\pi}{3} + 2\pi k \qquad \text{or} \qquad 2x = \frac{5\pi}{3} + 2\pi k$$

$$x = \frac{\pi}{6} + \pi k \qquad\qquad x = \frac{5\pi}{6} + \pi k$$

for any integer k.

Example 4 Use Addition Identities

Find the exact solutions of $\sin 2x \cos x + \cos 2x \sin x = 1$.

Solution

The left side of the equation is similar to the right side of the addition identity for sine.

$$\sin(x + y) = \sin x \cos y + \cos x \sin y.$$

Substitute $2x$ for x and x for y.

$$\sin 2x \cos x + \cos 2x \sin x = \sin(2x + x) = 1$$
$$\sin 3x = 1$$
$$3x = \sin^{-1} 1$$

For any integer k,

$$3x = \frac{\pi}{2} + 2\pi k$$

$$x = \frac{\pi}{6} + \frac{2\pi k}{3}$$

∎

Example 5 Use Half-Angle Identities

Find the solutions of $\sin x = \sin \dfrac{x}{2}$, where $0 \le x \le 2\pi$.

Solution

$$\sin x = \sin \frac{x}{2}$$

$$\sin x = \pm\sqrt{\frac{1 - \cos x}{2}} \qquad \textit{half-angle identity}$$

$$\sin^2 x = \frac{1 - \cos x}{2} \qquad \textit{square both sides}$$

$$1 - \cos^2 x = \frac{1 - \cos x}{2} \qquad \textit{Pythagorean identity}$$

$$2 - 2\cos^2 x = 1 - \cos x$$

$$2\cos^2 x - \cos x - 1 = 0$$

$$(2\cos x + 1)(\cos x - 1) = 0$$

$$2\cos x + 1 = 0 \qquad \text{or} \qquad \cos x - 1 = 0$$

$$\cos x = -\frac{1}{2} \qquad\qquad \cos x = 1$$

CAUTION

Squaring both sides of an equation may introduce extraneous solutions. Be sure to check all solutions in the original equation.

For any integer k,

$$x = \frac{2\pi}{3} + 2\pi k \qquad x = \frac{4\pi}{3} + 2\pi k \qquad x = 0 + 2\pi k$$

For $0 \le x \le 2\pi$, $x = 0, \dfrac{2\pi}{3}, \dfrac{4\pi}{3}$, or 2π.

Solving *a* sin *x* + *b* cos *x* = *c* (Optional)

Equations of the form $a \sin x + b \cos x = c$ occur often.

For the case when $c = 0$, the equations can be rewritten as

$$a \sin x = -b \cos x$$

$$\frac{\sin x}{\cos x} = -\frac{b}{a}$$

$$\tan x = -\frac{b}{a}$$

The last equation can be solved by methods discussed in Section 8.3.

For the case when $c \neq 0$, a very different approach is needed to find the solutions to

$$a \sin x + b \cos x = c$$

The procedure involves rewriting the equation as

$$\sin (x + \alpha) = k,$$

where α is the angle whose terminal side contains the point (a, b), and then using the addition identity for the sine function.

To find α, construct a right triangle in the coordinate plane with sides a and b, where a lies on the positive x-axis and α is the angle with its vertex at the origin.

Begin by writing the equation so that the coefficient of sin x, a, is positive. The position of the point (a, b) depends on whether b is positive or negative. If b is positive, the point is in the first quadrant; if b is negative, the point is in the fourth quadrant. Both possibilities are shown in Figures 9.4-1 and 9.4-2.

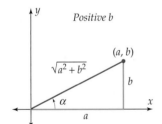

Figure 9.4-1

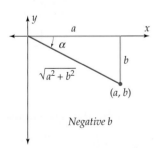

Figure 9.4-2

In both cases, $\sin \alpha = \dfrac{b}{\sqrt{a^2 + b^2}}$ and $\cos \alpha = \dfrac{a}{\sqrt{a^2 + b^2}}$.   [1]

Divide each side of the original equation by $\sqrt{a^2 + b^2}$ to obtain

$$a \sin x \quad + \quad b \cos x \quad = \quad c$$

$$\frac{a}{\sqrt{a^2 + b^2}} \sin x + \frac{b}{\sqrt{a^2 + b^2}} \cos x = \frac{c}{\sqrt{a^2 + b^2}} \qquad [2]$$

Substitute the equivalent expressions from [1] into equation [2].

$$\cos \alpha \sin x + \sin \alpha \cos x = \frac{c}{\sqrt{a^2 + b^2}}$$

Use the addition identity for sine to rewrite the left side of the equation.

$$\sin(x + \alpha) = \frac{c}{\sqrt{a^2 + b^2}}$$

The last equation can be solved by using the methods from Section 8.3. The steps of the procedure are summarized in the following box.

Solving *a* sin *x* + *b* cos *x* = *c*, *where c ≠ 0*

Let a, b, and c be nonzero real numbers. To solve

$$a \sin x + b \cos x = c$$

1. Multiply by -1, if needed, to make a positive.
2. Plot the point (a, b) and let α be the angle in standard position that contains (a, b) on its terminal side.
3. Find

   - the length of the hypotenuse of the reference triangle
   - expressions that represent $\sin \alpha$ and $\cos \alpha$
   - the measure of α

4. Divide each side of the equation by $\sqrt{a^2 + b^2}$ yielding

$$\frac{a}{\sqrt{a^2 + b^2}} \sin x + \frac{b}{\sqrt{a^2 + b^2}} \cos x = \frac{c}{\sqrt{a^2 + b^2}}$$

5. Use the addition identity for sine to rewrite the equation.

$$\sin(x + \alpha) = \frac{c}{\sqrt{a^2 + b^2}}$$

6. Solve the equation using techniques previously discussed.

Example 6   Solve $a \sin x + b \cos x = c$

Solve the equation $-\sqrt{3} \sin x + \cos x = -\sqrt{3}$.

Solution

Step 1   Make the coefficient of $\sin x$ positive by multiplying both sides of the equation by -1.

$$\sqrt{3} \sin x - \cos x = \sqrt{3} \qquad \text{so } a = \sqrt{3} \text{ and } b = -1$$

Step 2   Sketch a diagram of the angle α that has $(\sqrt{3}, -1)$ on its terminal side. See Figure 9.4-3.

Step 3   The length of the hypotenuse is $\sqrt{(\sqrt{3})^2 + (-1)^2} = 2$.

Find $\sin \alpha$ and $\cos \alpha$ from the figure.

$$\cos \alpha = \frac{\sqrt{3}}{2} \text{ and } \sin \alpha = \frac{-1}{2}$$

Find α.

$$\alpha = -\frac{\pi}{6} \qquad \text{or} \qquad \alpha = \frac{11\pi}{6}$$

Step 4   Divide both sides of the equation in Step 1 by the hypotenuse, $\sqrt{(\sqrt{3})^2 + (-1)^2} = 2$.

$$\frac{\sqrt{3}}{2} \sin x - \frac{1}{2} \cos x = \frac{\sqrt{3}}{2}$$

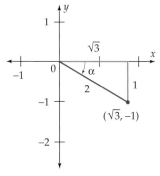

Figure 9.4-3

CAUTION

When substituting $-\sin\dfrac{11\pi}{6}$ for $\dfrac{1}{2}$, the sign between the terms changes to $+$.

Step 5 Rewrite the equation by substituting

$$\cos\frac{11\pi}{6} \text{ for } \frac{\sqrt{3}}{2} \quad \text{and} \quad -\sin\frac{11\pi}{6} \text{ for } \frac{1}{2}$$

and then use the addition identity for sine.

$$\cos\frac{11\pi}{6}\sin x + \sin\frac{11\pi}{6}\cos x = \frac{\sqrt{3}}{2}$$

$$\sin\left(x + \frac{11\pi}{6}\right) = \frac{\sqrt{3}}{2}$$

Step 6 Solve the equation.

$$x + \frac{11\pi}{6} = \sin^{-1}\left(\frac{\sqrt{3}}{2}\right)$$

$$x + \frac{11\pi}{6} = \frac{\pi}{3} + 2\pi k \qquad \text{or} \qquad x + \frac{11\pi}{6} = \frac{2\pi}{3} + 2\pi k$$

$$x = \frac{\pi}{3} - \frac{11\pi}{6} + 2\pi k \qquad\qquad x = \frac{2\pi}{3} - \frac{11\pi}{6} + 2\pi k$$

$$x = -\frac{3\pi}{2} + 2\pi k \qquad\qquad x = -\frac{7\pi}{6} + 2\pi k$$

$$x = \frac{\pi}{2} + 2\pi k \qquad\qquad x = \frac{5\pi}{6} + 2\pi k$$

for any integer k.

Maxima and Minima of $f(x) = a\sin x + b\cos x$

For functions of the form $f(x) = a\sin x + b\cos x$, maximum and minimum values can be found by using a technique similar to that described in the algorithm to solve equations of the form $a\sin x + b\cos x = c$.

Example 7 Maximum and Minimum of $f(x) = a\sin x + b\cos x$

Find the maximum and minimum of the function

$$f(x) = 3\sin x + 4\cos x.$$

Solution

NOTE The value of α is not needed to find the maximum or minimum of the function.

Note that $\sqrt{3^2 + 4^2} = \sqrt{25} = 5$. Let $\alpha = \cos^{-1}\dfrac{3}{5}$, or equivalently $\alpha = \sin^{-1}\dfrac{4}{5}$, and write the function in the form $f(x) = k\sin(x + \alpha)$.

$$f(x) = 5\left(\frac{3}{5}\sin x + \frac{4}{5}\cos x\right) = 5(\cos\alpha\sin x + \sin\alpha\cos x)$$

$$= 5\sin(x + \alpha)$$

Because the sine function varies between -1 and 1, the maximum of $5\sin(x + \alpha)$ is 5 and the minimum is -5.

To find the values of x that produce the maximum or minimum values of the function, solve the equation

$$a \sin x + b \cos x = c,$$

where c is the maximum or minimum value. In Example 6, the maximum value of 5 occurs when

$$3 \sin x + 4 \cos x = 5$$

$$\frac{3}{5} \sin x + \frac{4}{5} \cos x = 1$$

$$\sin(x + \alpha) = 1$$

$$x + \alpha = \sin^{-1} 1 = \frac{\pi}{2}$$

$$x = \frac{\pi}{2} - \alpha$$

$$\approx 1.5708 - 0.9273 \qquad \alpha = \cos^{-1}\frac{3}{5} \approx 0.9273$$

$$\approx 0.6435$$

In one revolution, the maximum occurs at approximately 0.6435.

Where the minimum value occurs is found in a similar manner.

Exercises 9.4

In Exercises 1–27, find all solutions of the equation in the interval $[0, 2\pi]$.

1. $\sin^2 x + 3 \cos^2 x = 0$

2. $\sin 2x + \cos x = 0$

3. $\cos 2x - \sin x = 1$

4. $\sin \frac{x}{2} = 1 - \cos x$

5. $4 \sin^2\left(\frac{x}{2}\right) + \cos^2 x = 2$

6. $\sin 4x - \sin 2x = 0$

7. $\sin x \sin \frac{1}{2} x = 1 - \cos x$

8. $\sin 2t \cos t - \cos 2t \sin t = 0$

9. $\sin 2x \sin x + \cos x = 0$

10. $\cos x = \cos \frac{1}{2} x$ (Check for extraneous solutions.)

11. $\sin 2x + \cos 2x = 0$

12. $\cos 4x \cos x - \sin 4x \sin x = 0$

13. $\sin 4x = \cos 2x$

14. $\cos 2x + \sin^2 x = 0$

15. $2 \cos^2 x - 2 \cos 2x = 1$

16. $\cos\left(x + \frac{\pi}{2}\right) - \sin x = 1$

17. $\sin\left(x + \frac{\pi}{2}\right) + \cos x = 1$

18. $\sin x - \sqrt{3} \cos x = 0$

19. $\sin x + \cos x = 0$

20. $\sin 2x - \cos x = 0$

21. $\cos 2x + \cos x = 0$

22. $(\sin x - \cos x)^2 = 1$

23. $\sin x \cos x + \dfrac{1}{2} = 0$

24. $\sin^2\left(\dfrac{x}{2}\right) + \cos x = 0$

25. $\csc^2 \dfrac{x}{2} = 2 \sec x$

26. $-\sqrt{2} \sin x + \sqrt{2} \cos x = 1$

27. $2 \sin x - 2 \cos x = \sqrt{2}$

In Exercises 28–31, find the solution to each equation in the interval $[-\pi, \pi]$.

28. $\sin x + \cos x = 1$

29. $\sin^2 x + \cos 2x = 1$

30. $\sin 2x + \cos x = 0$

31. $-\cos x + \sqrt{3} \sin x = 1$

In Exercises 32–35, solve each equation in $[0, 2\pi)$.

32. $\sin 4x - \sin 2x = \sin x$

33. $\sin 2x = \sin \dfrac{1}{2} x$

34. $\cos 3x + \cos x = 0$

35. $\sin 3x - \sin x = 0$

In Exercises 36–40,

a. Express each function in the form $f(x) = k \sin(x + \alpha)$.
b. Find the maximum value that $f(x)$ can assume.
c. Find all values of x in $[0, 2\pi]$ that give the maximum value of $f(x)$.

36. $f(x) = \sqrt{3} \sin x - \cos x$

37. $f(x) = \sin x + \sqrt{3} \cos x$

38. $f(x) = 2 \sin x + 2 \cos x$

39. $f(x) = \sin x - \cos x$

40. $f(x) = 4 \sin x - 3 \cos x$

Important Concepts

Important Facts and Formulas

Addition and Subtraction Identities

$$\sin(x + y) = \sin x \cos y + \cos x \sin y$$
$$\sin(x - y) = \sin x \cos y - \cos x \sin y$$
$$\cos(x + y) = \cos x \cos y - \sin x \sin y$$
$$\cos(x - y) = \cos x \cos y + \sin x \sin y$$
$$\tan(x + y) = \frac{\tan x + \tan y}{1 - \tan x \tan y}$$
$$\tan(x - y) = \frac{\tan x - \tan y}{1 + \tan x \tan y}$$

Cofunction Identities

$$\sin x = \cos\left(\frac{\pi}{2} - x\right) \qquad \cos x = \sin\left(\frac{\pi}{2} - x\right)$$

$$\tan x = \cot\left(\frac{\pi}{2} - x\right) \qquad \cot x = \tan\left(\frac{\pi}{2} - x\right)$$

$$\sec x = \csc\left(\frac{\pi}{2} - x\right) \qquad \csc x = \sec\left(\frac{\pi}{2} - x\right)$$

Double-Angle Identities

$$\sin 2x = 2 \sin x \cos x$$
$$\cos 2x = \cos^2 x - \sin^2 x = 2 \cos^2 x - 1 = 1 - 2 \sin^2 x$$
$$\tan 2x = \frac{2 \tan x}{1 - \tan^2 x}$$

Half-Angle Identities

$$\sin\frac{x}{2} = \pm\sqrt{\frac{1 - \cos x}{2}}$$

$$\cos\frac{x}{2} = \pm\sqrt{\frac{1 + \cos x}{2}}$$

$$\tan\frac{x}{2} = \frac{1 - \cos x}{\sin x} = \frac{\sin x}{1 + \cos x}$$

Review Exercises

In Exercises 1–4, simplify the given expression.

Section 9.1

1. $\dfrac{\sin^2 t + (\tan^2 t + 2 \tan t - 4) + \cos^2 t}{3 \tan^2 t - 3 \tan t}$

2. $\dfrac{\sec^2 t \csc t}{\csc^2 t \sec t}$

3. $\dfrac{\tan^2 x - \sin^2 x}{\sec^2 x}$

4. $\dfrac{(\sin x + \cos x)(\sin x - \cos x) + 1}{\sin^2 x}$

In Exercises 5–11, determine graphically whether the equation could not possibly be an identity, or write a proof showing that it is.

5. $\sin^4 t - \cos^4 t = 2 \sin^2 t - 1$

6. $1 + 2 \cos^2 t + \cos^4 t = \sin^4 t$

7. $\dfrac{\sin t}{1 - \cos t} = \dfrac{1 + \cos t}{\sin t}$

8. $\dfrac{\sin^2 t}{\cos^2 t} + 1 = \dfrac{1}{\cos^2 t}$

9. $\dfrac{\cos^2(\pi + t)}{\sin^2(\pi + t)} - 1 = \dfrac{1}{\sin^2 t}$

10. $\tan x + \cot x = \sec x \csc x$

11. $(\sin x + \cos x)^2 - \sin 2x = 1$

In Exercises 12–16, prove the given identity.

12. $\dfrac{\sec x + 1}{\tan x} = \dfrac{\tan x}{\sec x - 1}$

13. $\dfrac{\cos^4 x - \sin^4 x}{1 - \tan^4 x} = \cos^4 x$

14. $\dfrac{1 + \tan^2 x}{\tan^2 x} = \csc^2 x$

15. $\sec x - \cos x = \sin x \tan x$

16. $\tan^2 x - \sec^2 x = \cot^2 x - \csc^2 x$

17. $\sqrt{\dfrac{1 - \cos^2 x}{1 - \sin^2 x}} = ?$

    a. $|\tan x|$ **b.** $|\cot x|$

    c. $\sqrt{\dfrac{1 - \sin^2 x}{1 - \cos^2 x}}$ **d.** $\sec x$

    e. undefined

18. $\dfrac{1}{(\csc x)(\sec^2 x)} = ?$

    a. $\dfrac{1}{(\sin x)(\cos^2 x)}$ **b.** $\sin x - \sin^3 x$

    c. $\dfrac{1}{(\sin x)(1 + \tan^2 x)}$ **d.** $\sin x - \dfrac{1}{1 + \tan^2 x}$

    e. $1 + \tan^3 x$

Section 9.2

In Exercises 19–20, prove the given identity.

19. $\cos(x + y)\cos(x - y) = \cos^2 x - \sin^2 y$

20. $\dfrac{\cos(x - y)}{\cos x \cos y} = 1 + \tan x \tan y$

21. Evaluate the following in exact form, where the angles α and β satisfy the conditions:

$$\sin \alpha = \frac{4}{5} \text{ for } \frac{\pi}{2} < \alpha < \pi \qquad \tan \beta = \frac{7}{24} \text{ for } \pi < \beta < \frac{3\pi}{2},$$

    a. $\sin(\beta + \alpha)$ **b.** $\tan(\beta - \alpha)$ **c.** $\cos(\alpha - \beta)$

22. If $\tan x = \dfrac{4}{3}$ and $\pi < x < \dfrac{3\pi}{2}$, and $\cot y = -\dfrac{5}{12}$ with $\dfrac{3\pi}{2} < y < 2\pi$, find $\sin(x - y)$.

23. If $\sin x = -\dfrac{12}{13}$ with $\pi < x < \dfrac{3\pi}{2}$, and $\sec y = \dfrac{13}{12}$ with $\dfrac{3\pi}{2} < y < 2\pi$, find $\cos(x + y)$.

24. If $\sin x = \dfrac{1}{4}$ and $0 < x < \dfrac{\pi}{2}$, then $\sin\left(\dfrac{\pi}{3} + x\right) = ?$

25. If $\sin x = -\dfrac{2}{5}$ and $\dfrac{3\pi}{2} < x < 2\pi$, then $\cos\left(\dfrac{\pi}{4} + x\right) = ?$

26. Find the exact value of $\sin \dfrac{5\pi}{12}$.

27. Express $\sec(x - \pi)$ in terms of $\sin x$ and $\cos x$.

Section **9.2.A**

28. Find the angle of inclination of the straight line through the points $(2, 6)$ and $(-2, 2)$.

29. Find one of the angles between the line L through the points $(-3, 2)$ and $(5, 1)$ and the line M, which has slope 2.

Section **9.3**

30. Evaluate the following in exact form, where the angles α and β satisfy the conditions:

$$\sin \alpha = \frac{44}{125} \text{ for } \frac{\pi}{2} < \alpha < \pi \qquad \tan \beta = -\frac{15}{112} \text{ for } \frac{3\pi}{2} < \beta < 2\pi$$

a. $\sin \dfrac{\beta}{2}$

b. $\cos 2\alpha$

c. $\tan 2\alpha$

d. $\cos(\alpha - \beta) + \cos(\alpha + \beta)$

In Exercises 31–34, prove the given identity.

31. $\dfrac{1 - \cos 2x}{\tan x} = \sin 2x$

32. $\dfrac{\tan x - \sin x}{2 \tan x} = \sin^2 \dfrac{x}{2}$

33. $2 \cos x - 2 \cos^3 x = \sin x \sin 2x$

34. $\sin 2x = \dfrac{1}{\tan x + \cot 2x}$

35. If $\tan x = \dfrac{5}{12}$ and $\sin x > 0$, find $\sin 2x$.

36. If $\cos x = \dfrac{15}{17}$ and $0 < x < \dfrac{\pi}{2}$, find $\sin \dfrac{x}{2}$.

37. If $\sin x = 0$, is it true that $\sin 2x = 0$? Justify your answer.

38. If $\cos x = 0$, is it true that $\cos 2x = 0$? Justify your answer.

39. Show $\sqrt{2 + \sqrt{3}} = \dfrac{\sqrt{2} + \sqrt{6}}{2}$ by computing $\cos \dfrac{\pi}{12}$ in two ways, using the half-angle identity and the subtraction identity for cosine.

40. True or false: $2 \sin x = \sin 2x$. Justify your answer.

41. If $\sin x = 0.6$ and $0 < x < \dfrac{\pi}{2}$, find $\sin 2x$.

42. If $\sin x = 0.6$ and $0 < x < \dfrac{\pi}{2}$, find $\sin \dfrac{x}{2}$.

Section **9.4**

Solve the equation. Find exact solutions when possible and approximate ones otherwise.

43. $5 \tan x = 2 \sin 2x$

44. $\cos 2x = \cos x$

45. $2 \cos x + \sin x = 0$

46. $\sin 2x + \cos x = 0$

can do calculus

Rates of Change in Trigonometry

As discussed in Section 3.7, the difference quotient represents the average rate of change of a function over the interval from x to $x + h$.

$$\frac{f(x + h) - f(x)}{h} \qquad \textit{average rate of change}$$

As the value of h becomes smaller and smaller, the average rate of change approaches the instantaneous rate of change at x as discussed in the Chapter 3 Can Do Calculus.

Another way to represent the instantaneous rate of change is with limit notation, shown in the Can Do Calculus in Chapter 8. That is, instantaneous rate of change of a function f at x is the limit of the difference quotient.

$$\lim_{h \to 0} \frac{f(x + h) - f(x)}{h} \qquad \textit{instantaneous rate of change}$$

The instantaneous rate of change of a particular function is given by the expression in x that is the simplified form of the limit given above.

Example 1   Instantaneous Rate of Change of $f(x) = \sin x$

Find an expression for the instantaneous rate of change of $f(x) = \sin x$.

Solution

The difference quotient of $f(x) = \sin x$ can be simplified by using the addition identity for the sine function.

$$\sin(x + y) = \sin x \cos y + \cos x \sin y$$

Let $y = h$.

$$\sin(x + h) = \sin x \cos h + \cos x \sin h$$

Therefore, the difference quotient for the sine function can be simplified as follows. (See Example 4 of Section 9.2 for details of the simplification.)

$$\frac{\sin(x + h) - \sin x}{h} = \sin x \left(\frac{\cos h - 1}{h} \right) + \cos x \left(\frac{\sin h}{h} \right)$$

The expression that represents the instantaneous rate of change is found by finding the limit of $\sin x \left(\dfrac{\cos h - 1}{h} \right) + \cos x \left(\dfrac{\sin h}{h} \right)$ as h approaches 0.

$$\lim_{h \to 0} \left(\sin x \left(\frac{\cos h - 1}{h} \right) + \cos x \left(\frac{\sin h}{h} \right) \right) \qquad \textit{instantaneous rate of change}$$

The two fractional expressions in the limit above were evaluated in the Chapter 8 Can Do Calculus as follows:

NOTE See Chapter 14 for a complete discussion of limits.

$$\lim_{h \to 0} \frac{\sin h}{h} = 1 \qquad \text{and} \qquad \lim_{h \to 0} \frac{\cos h - 1}{h} = 0$$

Substitute the values above into the expression for instantaneous rate of change to find a simpler expression.

$$\lim_{h \to 0} \left(\sin x \left(\frac{\cos h - 1}{h} \right) + \cos x \left(\frac{\sin h}{h} \right) \right) = (\sin x)(0) + (\cos x)(1)$$

$$= \cos x \quad \textit{instantaneous rate of change}$$

The expression for the instantaneous rate of change for $f(x) = \sin x$ can be used to find the instantaneous rate of change at any particular value of x.

Example 2   Finding Instantaneous Rate of Change at $x = k$

Find the instantaneous rate of change of $f(x) = \sin x$ when $x = \frac{\pi}{3}$. Interpret the result.

Solution

Because the instantaneous rate of change of $f(x) = \sin x$ is given by $g(x) = \cos x$, the instantaneous rate of change at $x = \frac{\pi}{3}$ is $g\left(\frac{\pi}{3}\right) = \cos \frac{\pi}{3}$, or $\frac{1}{2}$. When $x = \frac{\pi}{3}$, $\sin x$ is changing $\frac{1}{2}$ unit per unit increase in x.

Exercises

1. What is the instantaneous rate of change of $f(x) = \sin x$ for the following values of x. Interpret each result.

   a. $x = 0$ **b.** $x = \frac{\pi}{4}$

   c. $x = \frac{\pi}{2}$ **d.** $x = \frac{\pi}{6}$

2. Find the expression for the instantaneous rate of change of $f(x) = \cos x$.

3. What is the instantaneous rate of change of $f(x) = \cos x$ for the following values of x? Interpret each result.

   a. $x = 0$ **b.** $x = \frac{\pi}{4}$

   c. $x = \frac{\pi}{2}$ **d.** $x = \frac{\pi}{6}$

10 Trigonometric Applications

A Bridge over Troubled Waters

When planning a bridge or building, architects and engineers must determine the stress on cables and other parts of the structure to be sure that all parts are adequately supported. Problems like these can be modeled and solved by using vectors. See Exercise 50 in Section 10.6.

Chapter Outline

Interdependence of Sections

Trigonometry has a variety of useful applications in geometry, algebra, and the physical sciences. Several applications are discussed in this chapter.

10.1   The Law of Cosines

Objectives

- Solve oblique triangles by using the Law of Cosines.

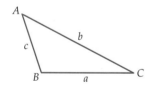

Figure 10.1-1

Sections 6.1 and 6.2 presented right triangle trigonometry and its applications. In this section, the solutions to **oblique triangles,** ones that do not contain a right angle, are considered.

Standard notation of triangles, which is used in this section and the next, is shown in Figure 10.1-1 and is described below.

Each vertex is labeled with a capital letter, and the length of the side opposite that vertex is denoted by the same letter in lower case. The letter *A* will also be used to label the angle at vertex *A*, and similarly for *B* and *C*. Thus, statements such as

$$A = 37° \qquad \text{or} \qquad \cos B = 0.326$$

will be made.

The first fact needed to solve oblique triangles is the Law of Cosines, whose proof is given at the end of this section.

Law of Cosines

In any triangle *ABC*, with lengths *a*, *b*, *c*, as in Figure 10.1-1,

$$a^2 = b^2 + c^2 - 2bc \cos A$$
$$b^2 = a^2 + c^2 - 2ac \cos B$$
$$c^2 = a^2 + b^2 - 2ab \cos C$$

617

You need only memorize one of these equations since each of them provides essentially the same information: the square of the length of one side of a triangle is given in terms of the angle opposite it and the other two sides.

Solving the first equation in the Law of Cosines for cos A results in the alternate form of the Law of Cosines, given below.

Alternate Form: Law of Cosines

In any triangle ABC, with sides of lengths a, b, and c, as in Figure 10.1-1,

$$\cos A = \frac{b^2 + c^2 - a^2}{2bc}.$$

NOTE When C is a right angle, then c is the hypotenuse and

$$\cos C = \cos 90° = 0,$$

so that the third equation in the Law of Cosines becomes the Pythagorean theorem.

$$c^2 = a^2 + b^2$$

The other two equations in the Law of Cosines can be similarly rewritten in an alternate form. In this form, the Law of Cosines provides a description of each angle of a triangle in terms of the three sides. Consequently, the Law of Cosines can be used to solve triangles in the following cases.

1. Two sides and the angle between them are known (SAS)
2. Three sides are known (SSS)

Example 1   Solve a Triangle with SAS Information

Solve triangle ABC shown in Figure 10.1-2.

Solution

Because c is the unknown quantity, use the third equation in the Law of Cosines.

$$c^2 = a^2 + b^2 - 2ab \cos C$$
$$c^2 = 16^2 + 10^2 - 2(16)(10) \cos 110°$$
$$c^2 = 356 - 320 \cos 110°$$
$$c = \sqrt{356 - 320 \cos 110°} \qquad \textit{Take the square root of each side.}$$
$$c \approx 21.6$$

Use the alternate form of the Law of Cosines to find the measure of angle A.

$$\cos A = \frac{b^2 + c^2 - a^2}{2bc}$$
$$\cos A \approx \frac{10^2 + 21.6^2 - 16^2}{2(10)(21.6)}$$
$$\cos A \approx 0.7172$$
$$A \approx \cos^{-1} 0.7172 \qquad \textit{Use the COS}^{-1} \textit{ key with the}$$
$$A \approx 44.2° \qquad\qquad \textit{calculator in degree mode.}$$

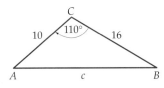

Figure 10.1-2

NOTE Throughout this chapter, no rounding is done in the actual computation until the final quantity is obtained.

Because the sum of the angle measures in a triangle is 180°,

$$B \approx 180° - (44.2° + 110°) = 25.8°.$$

Thus, $c \approx 21.6$, $A \approx 44.2°$, and $B \approx 25.8°$.

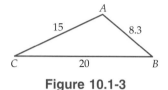

15   8.3

C 20 B

Figure 10.1-3

Example 2   Solve a Triangle with SSS Information

Find the angles of triangle ABC shown in Figure 10.1-3.

Solution

The given information is $a = 20$, $b = 15$, and $c = 8.3$. To find angles, use the alternate form of the Law of Cosines.

$$\cos A = \frac{b^2 + c^2 - a^2}{2bc} \qquad\qquad \cos B = \frac{a^2 + c^2 - b^2}{2ac}$$

$$\cos A = \frac{15^2 + 8.3^2 - 20^2}{2(15)(8.3)} \qquad \cos B = \frac{20^2 + 8.3^2 - 15^2}{2(20)(8.3)}$$

$$\cos A \approx -0.4261 \qquad\qquad \cos B \approx 0.7346$$

$$A \approx 115.2° \qquad\qquad\qquad B \approx 42.7°$$

Use the sum of angle measures in a triangle to find the third angle.

$$C \approx 180° - (115.2° + 42.7°) = 22.1°$$

Thus, $A \approx 115.2°$, $B \approx 42.7°$, and $C \approx 22.1°$.

Example 3   The Distance Between Two Vehicles

Two trains leave a station on different tracks. The tracks make an angle of 125° with the station as the vertex. The first train travels at an average speed of 100 kilometers per hour, and the second train travels at an average speed of 65 kilometers per hour. How far apart are the trains after 2 hours?

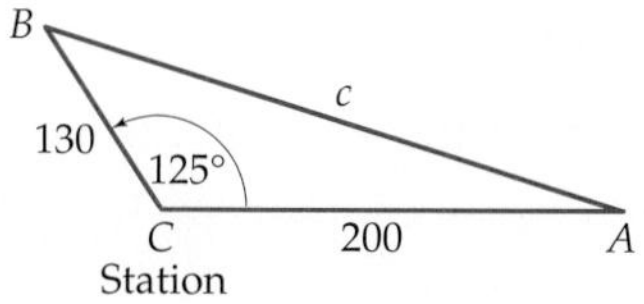

B

130   c

125°

C 200 A
Station

Figure 10.1-4

Solution

The first train, A, traveling at 100 kilometers per hour for 2 hours, goes a distance of $100 \times 2 = 200$ kilometers. The second train, B, travels a distance of $65 \times 2 = 130$ kilometers. The situation is shown in Figure 10.1-4.

By the Law of Cosines:

$$c^2 = a^2 + b^2 - 2ab \cos C$$
$$c^2 = 130^2 + 200^2 - 2(130)(200)\cos 125°$$
$$c^2 = 56{,}900 - 52{,}000 \cos 125°$$
$$c = \sqrt{56{,}900 - 52{,}000 \cos 125°}$$
$$c \approx 294.5$$

The trains are about 294.5 kilometers apart after 2 hours.

| Example 4 | Find Angles with the Horizontal |

A 100-foot tall antenna tower is to be placed on a hillside that makes an angle of 12° with the horizontal. It is to be anchored by two cables from the top of the tower to points 85 feet uphill and 95 feet downhill from the base. How much cable is needed?

Solution

The situation is shown in Figure 10.1-5, where AB represents the tower and AC and AD represent the cables.

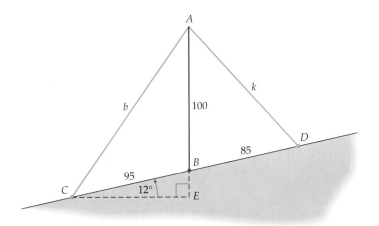

Figure 10.1-5

If the hillside makes an angle of 12° with the horizontal, then in triangle BEC, angle E is a right angle and angle C measures 12°. Use the sum of the angle measures in the triangle.

$$m\angle CBE = 180° - (90° + 12°) = 78°$$

As shown in Figure 10.1-5, adjacent angles ABC and CBE form a straight angle, which measures 180°.

$$m\angle ABC = 180° - 78° = 102°$$

Using the SAS information in triangle ABC, apply the Law of Cosines.

$$b^2 = a^2 + c^2 - 2ac \cos B$$
$$b^2 = 95^2 + 100^2 - 2(95)(100) \cos 102°$$
$$b^2 = 19{,}025 - 19{,}000 \cos 102°$$
$$b = \sqrt{19{,}025 - 19{,}000 \cos 102°}$$
$$b \approx 151.58$$

The length of the downhill cable is about 151.58 feet.

To find the length of the uphill cable, notice that adjacent angles ABC and ABD form a straight angle.

$$m\angle ABD = 180° - m\angle ABC = 180° - 102° = 78°$$

Using the SAS information in triangle ABD, apply the Law of Cosines.

$$k^2 = 100^2 + 85^2 - 2(100)(85) \cos 78°$$
$$k^2 = 17{,}225 - 17{,}000 \cos 78°$$
$$k = \sqrt{17{,}225 - 17{,}000 \cos 78°}$$
$$k \approx 117.01$$

The length of the uphill cable is about 117.01 feet.

The amount of cable needed is the sum of the lengths of the uphill and downhill cables.

$$151.58 + 117.01 = 268.59$$

Therefore, the length of the cable needed is about 268.59 feet.

Proof of the Law of Cosines

Given triangle ABC, position it on a coordinate plane so that angle A is in standard position with initial side c and terminal side b. Depending on the size of angle A, there are two possibilities, as shown in Figure 10.1-6.

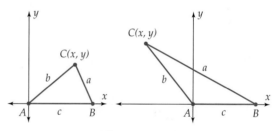

Figure 10.1-6

The coordinates of B are $(c, 0)$. Let (x, y) be the coordinates of C. Now C is a point on the terminal side of angle A, and the distance from C to the origin A is b. Therefore, according to the definitions of sine and cosine, the following statements are true.

$$\frac{x}{b} = \cos A, \qquad \text{or equivalently,} \qquad x = b \cos A$$

$$\frac{y}{b} = \sin A, \qquad \text{or equivalently,} \qquad y = b \sin A$$

Use the distance formula to find a, the distance from C to B.

$$a = \sqrt{(x - c)^2 + (y - 0)^2}$$

$a = \sqrt{(b \cos A - c)^2 + (b \sin A - 0)^2}$	*Substitute for x and y.*
$a^2 = (b \cos A - c)^2 + (b \sin A)^2$	*Square each side.*
$a^2 = b^2 \cos^2 A - 2bc \cos A + c^2 + b^2 \sin^2 A$	*Simplify.*
$a^2 = b^2 \cos^2 A + b^2 \sin^2 A + c^2 - 2bc \cos A$	*Rearrange terms.*
$a^2 = b^2(\cos^2 A + \sin^2 A) + c^2 - 2bc \cos A$	*Factor out b^2.*
$a^2 = b^2 + c^2 - 2bc \cos A$	*Pythagorean identity*

This proves the first equation in the Law of Cosines. Similar arguments beginning with angles B or C in standard position prove the other two equations.

Exercises 10.1

Standard notation for triangle ABC is used throughout. Use a calculator and round your answers to one decimal place at the end of each computation.

In Exercises 1–16, solve the triangle ABC under the given conditions.

1. $A = 20°, b = 10, c = 7$

2. $B = 40°, a = 12, c = 20$

3. $C = 118°, a = 6, b = 10$

4. $C = 52.5°, a = 6.5, b = 9$

5. $A = 140°, b = 12, c = 14$

6. $B = 25.4°, a = 6.8, c = 10.5$

7. $C = 78.6°, a = 12.1, b = 20.3$

8. $A = 118.2°, b = 16.5, c = 10.7$

9. $a = 7, b = 3, c = 5$

10. $a = 8, b = 5, c = 10$

11. $a = 16, b = 20, c = 32$

12. $a = 5.3, b = 7.2, c = 10$

13. $a = 7.2, b = 6.5, c = 11$

14. $a = 6.8, b = 12.4, c = 15.1$

15. $a = 12, b = 16.5, c = 21.3$

16. $a = 5.7, b = 20.4, c = 16.8$

17. Find the angles of the triangle whose vertices are $(0, 0), (5, -2)$, and $(1, -4)$.

18. Find the angles of the triangle whose vertices are $(-3, 4), (6, 1)$, and $(2, -1)$.

19. Two trains leave a station on different tracks. The tracks make a 112° angle with the station as vertex. The first train travels at an average speed of 90 kilometers per hour and the second at an average speed of 55 kilometers per hour. How far apart are the trains after 2 hours and 45 minutes?

20. One plane flies west from Cleveland at 350 miles per hour. A second plane leaves Cleveland at the same time and flies southeast at 200 miles per hour. How far apart are the planes after 1 hour and 36 minutes?

21. The pitcher's mound on a standard baseball diamond (which is actually a square) is 60.5 feet from home plate. How far is the pitcher's mound from first base?

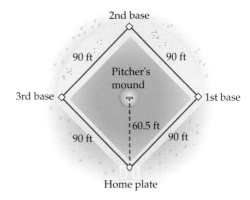

22. If the straight-line distance from home plate over second base to the center field wall in a baseball stadium is 400 feet, how far is it from first base to the same point in center field? Adapt the figure above.

23. A stake is located 10.8 feet from the end of a closed gate that is 8 feet long. The gate swings open, and its end hits the stake. Through what angle does the gate swing?

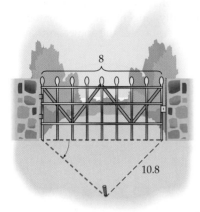

24. The distance from Chicago to St. Louis is 440 kilometers, from St. Louis to Atlanta 795 kilometers, and from Atlanta to Chicago 950 kilometers. What are the angles in the triangle with these three cities as vertices?

25. A boat runs in a straight line for 3 kilometers, then makes a 45° turn and goes for another 6 kilometers. How far is the boat from its starting point?

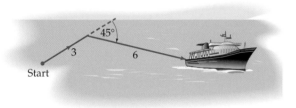

26. A plane flies in a straight line at 400 miles per hour for 1 hour and 12 minutes. It makes a 15° turn and flies at 375 miles per hour for 2 hours and 27 minutes. How far is it from its starting point?

27. The side of a hill makes an angle of 12° with the horizontal. A wire is to be run from the top of a 175-foot tower on the top of the hill to a stake located 120 feet down the hillside from the base of the tower. What length of wire is needed?

28. Two ships leave port, one traveling in a straight course at 22 miles per hour and the other traveling a straight course at 31 miles per hour. Their courses diverge by 38°. How far apart are they after 3 hours?

29. An engineer wants to measure the width *CD* of a sinkhole. He places a stake *B* and determines the

measurements shown in the figure below. How wide is the sinkhole?

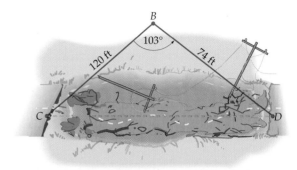

30. A straight tunnel is to be dug through a hill. Two people stand on opposite sides of the hill where the tunnel entrances are to be located. Both can see a stake located 530 meters from the first person and 755 meters from the second. The angle determined by the two people and the stake (the vertex) is 77°. How long must the tunnel be?

31. One diagonal of a parallelogram is 6 centimeters long, and the other is 13 centimeters long. They form an angle of 42° with each other. How long are the sides of the parallelogram? *Hint:* The diagonals of a parallelogram bisect each other.

32. A parallelogram has diagonals of lengths 12 and 15 inches that intersect at an angle of 63.7°. How long are the sides of the parallelogram?

33. A ship is traveling at 18 miles per hour from Corsica to Barcelona, a distance of 350 miles. To avoid bad weather, the ship leaves Corsica on a route 22° south of the direct route (see the figure below). After 7 hours the bad weather has been bypassed. Through what angle should the ship now turn to head directly to Barcelona?

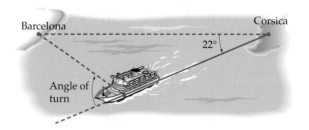

34. In aerial navigation, directions are given in degrees clockwise from north. Thus east is 90°, south is 180°, and so on, as shown in the following figure. A plane leaves South Bend for Buffalo, 400 miles away, intending to fly a straight course in the direction 70°. After flying 180 miles, the pilot realizes that an error has been made and that he has actually been flying in the direction 55°.

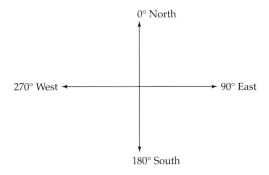

a. At that time, how far is the plane from Buffalo?
b. In what direction should the plane now go to reach Buffalo?

35. Assume that the earth is a sphere of radius 3980 miles. A satellite travels in a circular orbit around the earth, 900 miles above the equator, making one full orbit every 6 hours. If it passes directly over a tracking station at 2 P.M., what is the distance from the satellite to the tracking station at 2:05 P.M.?

36. Two planes at the same altitude approach an airport. One plane is 16 miles from the control tower and the other is 22 miles from the tower. The angle determined by the planes and the tower, with the tower as the vertex, is 11°. How far apart are the planes?

37. Assuming that the circles in the following figure are mutually tangent, find the lengths of the sides and the measures of the angles in triangle *ABC*.

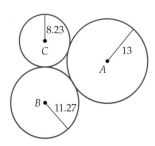

38. Assuming that the circles in the following figure are mutually tangent, find the lengths of the sides and the measures of the angles in triangle *ABC*.

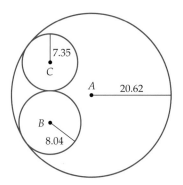

39. *Critical Thinking* A rope is attached at points *A* and *B* and taut around a pulley whose center is at *C*, as shown in the following figure. The rope lies on the pulley from *D* to *E* and the radius of the pulley is 1 meter. How long is the rope?

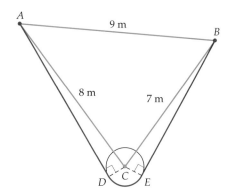

40. *Critical Thinking* Use the Law of Cosines to prove that the sum of the squares of the lengths of the two diagonals of a parallelogram equals the sum of the squares of the lengths of the four sides.

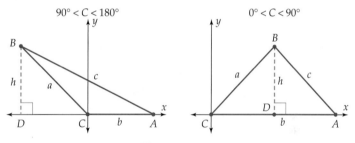

The Law of Sines

10.2

Objectives

- Solve oblique triangles by using the Law of Sines
- Use area formulas to find areas of triangles

In Section 10.1, the Law of Cosines was used to solve oblique triangles when SAS or SSS information was given. When different information is given about the triangle, the Law of Cosines may not be sufficient to solve them. In this case, the **Law of Sines** may be used.

Law of Sines

In any triangle ABC (in standard notation)

$$\frac{a}{\sin A} = \frac{b}{\sin B} = \frac{c}{\sin C}.$$

Proof Position triangle ABC on a coordinate plane so that angle C is in standard position, with initial side b and terminal side a, as shown in Figure 10.2-1.

Figure 10.2-1

In each case, $\sin C$ can be computed by using the point B on the terminal side of angle C. The second coordinate of B is h, and the distance from B to the origin is a. Therefore, by the definition of sine,

$$\sin C = \frac{h}{a}, \quad \text{or equivalently,} \quad h = a \sin C.$$

In each case, right triangle ADB shows that

$$\sin A = \frac{\text{opposite}}{\text{hypotenuse}} = \frac{h}{c}, \quad \text{or equivalently,} \quad h = c \sin A.$$

Combine these two expressions for h.

$$a \sin C = c \sin A$$

Because angles in a triangle are nonzero, $\sin A \neq 0$ and $\sin C \neq 0$. Divide each side of the last equation by $(\sin A)(\sin C)$.

$$\frac{a}{\sin A} = \frac{c}{\sin C}$$

This proves one proportion in the Law of Sines. Similar arguments beginning with angles A or B in standard position prove the other proportions.

The Law of Sines can be used to solve triangles in the following cases.

1. Two angles and one side are known (AAS)

2. Two sides and the angle opposite one of them are known (SSA)

Example 1   **Solve a Triangle with AAS Information**

If $B = 20°$, $C = 31°$, and $b = 210$, find the other angle measure and side lengths. See Figure 10.2-2.

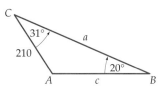

Figure 10.2-2

Solution

Because the sum of the angle measures of a triangle is $180°$,

$$A = 180° - (20° + 31°) = 129°.$$

In order to find a, notice that three of the four quantities in one of the Law of Sines proportions are known.

$$\frac{a}{\sin A} = \frac{b}{\sin B}$$

$$\frac{a}{\sin 129°} = \frac{210}{\sin 20°}$$

$$a = \frac{210 \sin 129°}{\sin 20°} \qquad \textit{Multiply each side by sin 129°.}$$

$$a \approx 477.2$$

c is found in a similar manner. Use a Law of Sines proportion involving c and the three known quantities.

$$\frac{c}{\sin C} = \frac{b}{\sin B}$$

$$\frac{c}{\sin 31°} = \frac{210}{\sin 20°}$$

$$c = \frac{210 \sin 31°}{\sin 20°} \qquad \textit{Multiply each side by sin 31°.}$$

$$c \approx 316.2$$

Therefore, $A = 129°$, $a \approx 477.2$, and $c \approx 316.2$.

The Ambiguous Case

Given AAS information, such as in Example 1, there is exactly one triangle satisfying the given data (see note). But when two sides of a triangle and the angle opposite one of them are known, as in the SSA case, there may be one, two, or no triangles that satisfy the given data. This is called the **ambiguous case.**

NOTE The four Triangle Congruence Theorems—AAS, SAS, SSS, and ASA—state that a unique triangle can be formed that is congruent to a given triangle. However, SSA is *not* a triangle congruence theorem because a unique triangle congruent to the given one is not guaranteed; zero, one, or two triangles can be formed from the side-side-angle information.

To see why the ambiguous case occurs, suppose sides a and b and angle A are given. Place angle A in standard position with terminal side b. If angle A is less than 90°, then there are four possibilities for side a.

Ambiguous Case: SSA Information with $A < 90°$	
(i) $a < b$, and side a is too short to reach the third side: *no solution.* 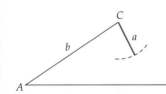 **Figure 10.2-3**	(ii) $a < b$, and side a just reaches the third side and is perpendicular to it: *one solution.* 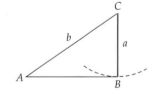 **Figure 10.2-4**
(iii) $a < b$, and an arc of radius a meets the third side at 2 points to the right of A: *two solutions.* 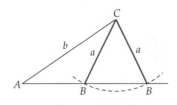 **Figure 10.2-5**	(iv) $a \geq b$, so that an arc of radius a meets the third side at just one point to the right of A: *one solution.* 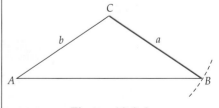 **Figure 10.2-6**

If angle A is greater than 90°, then there are only two possibilities.

Ambiguous Case: SSA Information with $A > 90°$	
(i) $a \leq b$, so that side a is too short to reach the third side: *no solution*.	(ii) $a > b$, so that an arc of radius a meets the third side at just one point to the right of A: *one solution*.
Figure 10.2-7	**Figure 10.2-8**

Recall from Section 8.3 that when finding all solutions of a trigonometric equation involving the sine function, the identity $\sin x = \sin(\pi - x)$ is used. This same identity, stated in terms of degrees rather than radians, is used to deal with the ambiguous SSA case.

Supplementary Angle Identity

If $0° \leq \theta \leq 90°$, then

$$\sin \theta = \sin(180° - \theta).$$

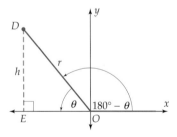

Figure 10.2-9

Proof   Place the angle $180° - \theta$ in standard position and choose a point D on its terminal side. Let r be the distance from D to the origin. The situation is shown in Figure 10.2-9.

Because h is the second coordinate of D, then $\sin(180° - \theta) = \dfrac{h}{r}$. Right triangle OED shows that

$$\sin \theta = \frac{\text{opposite}}{\text{hypotenuse}} = \frac{h}{r} = \sin(180° - \theta).$$

Example 2   Solve a Triangle with SSA Information

Given a possible triangle ABC with $a = 6$, $b = 7$, and $A = 65°$, find angle B.

Solution

Use a proportion of the Law of Sines involving angle B and three known quantities.

$$\frac{b}{\sin B} = \frac{a}{\sin A}$$

$$\frac{7}{\sin B} = \frac{6}{\sin 65°}$$

$$\sin B = \frac{7 \sin 65°}{6}$$

$$\sin B \approx 1.06$$

There is no angle B whose sine is greater than 1. Therefore, there is no triangle satisfying the given data.

■

Example 3 Solve a Triangle with SSA Information

An airplane A takes off from carrier B and flies in a straight line for 12 kilometers. At that instant, an observer on destroyer C, located 5 kilometers from the carrier, notes that the angle determined by the carrier, the destroyer (the vertex), and the plane is 37°. How far is the plane from the destroyer?

Solution

The given information is organized in Figure 10.2-10.

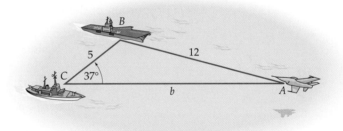

Figure 10.2-10

Because there is no proportion of the Law of Sines that can be written using B, use a proportion involving A to find a second angle of the triangle. This will provide you with enough information to find angle B and hence allowing you to use the Law of Sines to find b.

$$\frac{a}{\sin A} = \frac{c}{\sin C}$$

$$\frac{5}{\sin A} = \frac{12}{\sin 37°}$$

$$\sin A = \frac{5 \sin 37°}{12}$$

$$\sin A \approx 0.2508$$

$$A \approx 14.5° \quad \text{or} \quad A \approx 180° - 14.5° = 165.5°$$

If $A = 165.5°$ and $C = 37°$, then the sum of angles A, B, and C would be greater than $180°$. Because that is impossible, $14.5°$ is the only possible measure of angle A. Therefore,

$$B = 180° - (37° + 14.5°) = 128.5°.$$

All of the angles are known, and b can be found using either the Law of Cosines or the Law of Sines.

$$\frac{b}{\sin B} = \frac{c}{\sin C}$$

$$\frac{b}{\sin 128.5°} = \frac{12}{\sin 37°}$$

$$b = \frac{12 \sin 128.5°}{\sin 37°}$$

$$b \approx 15.6$$

The plane is approximately 15.6 kilometers from the destroyer. ∎

Example 4   **Solve a Triangle with SSA Information**

Solve triangle ABC when $a = 7.5$, $b = 12$, and $A = 35°$.

Solution

Use a proportion of the Law of Sines involving the known quantities.

$$\frac{b}{\sin B} = \frac{a}{\sin A}$$

$$\frac{12}{\sin B} = \frac{7.5}{\sin 35°}$$

$$\sin B = \frac{12 \sin 35°}{7.5}$$

$$\sin B \approx 0.9177$$

$$B \approx 66.6° \quad \text{or} \quad B \approx 180° - 66.6° = 113.4°$$

Because the sum of angles A and B is less than $180°$ in each case, there are two possible cases, as shown in Figure 10.2-11.

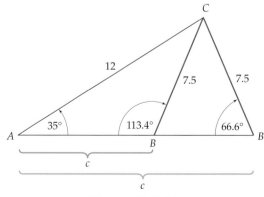

Figure 10.2-11

Case 1 $B = 66.6°$

$C = 180° - (35° + 66.6°) = 78.4°$

Use the Law of Sines.

$$\frac{c}{\sin C} = \frac{a}{\sin A}$$

$$\frac{c}{\sin 78.4°} = \frac{7.5}{\sin 35°}$$

$$c = \frac{7.5 \sin 78.4°}{\sin 35°}$$

$$c \approx 12.8$$

Case 2 $B = 113.4°$

$C = 180° - (35° + 113.4°) = 31.6°$

Use the Law of Sines.

$$\frac{c}{\sin C} = \frac{a}{\sin A}$$

$$\frac{c}{\sin 31.6°} = \frac{7.5}{\sin 35°}$$

$$c = \frac{7.5 \sin 31.6°}{\sin 35°}$$

$$c \approx 6.9$$

Thus, in Case 1, $B \approx 66.6°$, $C \approx 78.4°$, and $c \approx 12.8$; and in Case 2, $B \approx 113.4°$, $C \approx 31.6°$, and $c \approx 6.9$.

Example 5   **Solve a Triangle with ASA Information**

A plane flying in a straight line passes directly over point A on the ground and later directly over point B, which is 3 miles from A. A few minutes after the plane passes over B, the angle of elevation from A to the plane is 43° and the angle of elevation from B to the plane is 67°. How high is the plane at that moment?

Solution

If C represents the plane, then the situation is represented in Figure 10.2-12. The height of the plane is h.

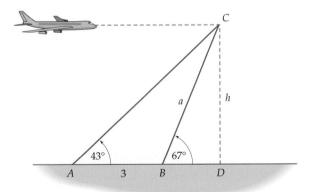

Figure 10.2-12

Angle ABC measures $180° - 67° = 113°$. So

$$m\angle BCA = 180° - (43° + 113°) = 24°.$$

Use the Law of Sines to find side a of triangle ABC.

$$\frac{a}{\sin 43°} = \frac{3}{\sin 24°}$$

$$a = \frac{3 \sin 43°}{\sin 24°}$$

$$a \approx 5.03$$

Now use $\sin 67° = \dfrac{h}{a}$ to find h in right triangle CBD.

$$\sin 67° = \frac{h}{5.03}$$

$$h = 5.03 \sin 67°$$

$$h \approx 4.63$$

The plane is about 4.63 miles high.

The Area of a Triangle

The proof of the Law of Sines leads to the following formula for the area of a triangle.

Area of a Triangle

The area of a triangle containing an angle C with adjacent sides of lengths a and b is

$$\frac{1}{2} ab \sin C.$$

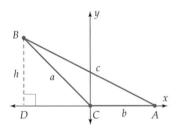

Figure 10.2-13

Proof Place the vertex of angle C at the origin, with side b on the positive x-axis, as in Figure 10.2-13. Then b is the base and h is the height of the triangle.

$$\text{area of triangle } ABC = \frac{1}{2} \cdot \text{base} \cdot \text{height} = \frac{1}{2} bh.$$

The proof of the Law of Sines shows that $h = a \sin C$. Therefore,

$$\text{area of triangle } ABC = \frac{1}{2} bh = \frac{1}{2} ab \sin C.$$

Figure 10.2-13 is the case when C is greater than 90°; the argument when C is less than 90° is similar.

Example 6 **Find Area with SAS Information**

Find the area of the triangle shown in Figure 10.2-14.

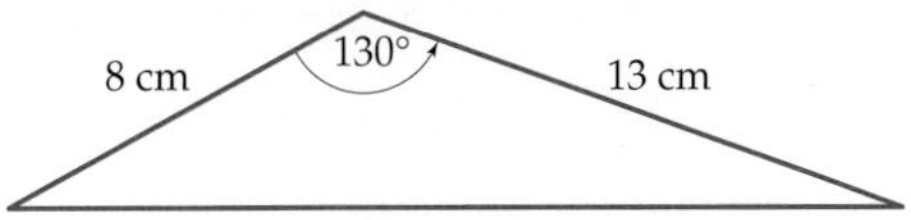

Figure 10.2-14

Solution

Use the new formula for the area of a triangle.

$$\frac{1}{2} ab \sin C = \frac{1}{2}(8)(13) \sin 130° \approx 39.83$$

Thus, the area is about 39.83 square centimeters.

An alternate formula for the area of a triangle, **Heron's formula,** gives the area in terms of its sides.

Heron's Formula

The area of a triangle with sides a, b, and c is

$$\sqrt{s(s - a)(s - b)(s - c)},$$

where $s = \frac{1}{2}(a + b + c)$.

This formula is proved in Exercise 62.

Example 7   **Find Area with SSS Information**

Find the area of the triangle whose sides have lengths 7, 9, and 12.

Solution

Let $a = 7, b = 9$, and $c = 12$. To use the Heron's formula, first find s.

$$s = \frac{1}{2}(a + b + c) = \frac{1}{2}(7 + 9 + 12) = 14$$

Now, use Heron's formula.

$$\sqrt{s(s - a)(s - b)(s - c)} = \sqrt{14(14 - 7)(14 - 9)(14 - 12)}$$
$$= \sqrt{980} \approx 31.3$$

The area is about 31.3 square units.

Exercises 10.2

Standard notation for triangle ABC is used through-out. Use a calculator and round off your answers to one decimal place at the end of each computation.

In Exercises 1–8, solve triangle ABC under the given conditions.

1. $A = 48°, B = 22°, a = 5$

2. $B = 33°, C = 46°, b = 4$

3. $A = 116°, C = 50°, a = 8$

4. $A = 105°, B = 27°, b = 10$

5. $B = 44°, C = 48°, b = 12$

6. $A = 67°, C = 28°, a = 9$

7. $A = 102.3°, B = 36.2°, a = 16$

8. $B = 97.5°, C = 42.5°, b = 7$

In Exercises 9–16, find the area of triangle ABC under the given conditions.

9. $a = 4, b = 8, C = 27°$

10. $b = 10, c = 14, A = 36°$

11. $c = 7, a = 10, B = 68°$

12. $a = 9, b = 13, C = 75°$

13. $a = 11, b = 15, c = 18$

14. $a = 4, b = 12, c = 14$

15. $a = 7, b = 9, c = 11$

16. $a = 17, b = 27, c = 40$

In Exercises 17–36, solve the triangle. The Law of Cosines may be needed in Exercises 27–36.

17. $b = 15, c = 25, B = 47°$

18. $b = 30, c = 50, C = 60°$

19. $a = 12, b = 5, B = 20°$

20. $b = 12.5, c = 20.1, B = 37.3°$

21. $a = 5, c = 12, A = 102°$

22. $a = 9, b = 14, B = 95°$

23. $b = 11, c = 10, C = 56°$

24. $a = 12.4, c = 6.2, A = 72°$

25. $A = 41°, B = 67°, a = 10.5$

26. $a = 30, b = 40, A = 30°$

27. $b = 4, c = 10, A = 75°$

28. $a = 50, c = 80, C = 45°$

29. $a = 6, b = 12, c = 16$

30. $B = 20.67°, C = 34°, b = 185$

31. $a = 16.5, b = 18.2, C = 47°$

32. $a = 21, c = 15.8, B = 71°$

33. $b = 17.2, c = 12.4, B = 62.5°$

34. $b = 24.1, c = 10.5, C = 26.3°$

35. $a = 10.1, b = 18.2, A = 50.7°$

36. $b = 14.6, c = 7.8, B = 40.4°$

In Exercises 37 and 38, find the area of the triangle with the given vertices.

37. $(0, 0), (2, -5), (-3, 1)$

38. $(-4, 2), (5, 7), (3, 0)$

In Exercises 39 and 40, find the area of the polygonal region. *Hint:* **Divide the region into triangles.**

39.

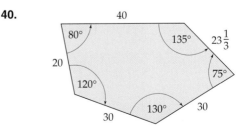

40.

41. A surveyor marks points A and B 200 meters apart on one bank of a river. She sights a point C on the opposite bank and determines the angles shown in the figure below. What is the distance from A to C?

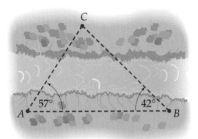

42. A forest fire is spotted from two fire towers. The triangle determined by the two towers and the fire has angles of 28° and 37° at the tower vertices. If the towers are 3000 meters apart, which one is closer to the fire?

43. A visitor to the Leaning Tower of Pisa observed that the tower's shadow was 40 meters long and that the angle of elevation from the tip of the shadow to the top of the tower was 57°. The tower is now 54 meters tall, measured from the ground to the top along the center line of the tower (see the figure). Approximate the angle α that the center line of the tower makes with the vertical.

44. A pole tilts at an angle 9° from the vertical, away from the sun, and casts a shadow 24 feet long. The

angle of elevation from the end of the pole's shadow to the top of the pole is 53°. How long is the pole?

45. A side view of a bus shelter is shown in the following figure. The brace d makes an angle of 37.25° with the back and an angle of 34.85° with the top of the shelter. How long is the brace?

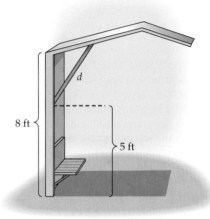

46. A straight path makes an angle of 6° with the horizontal. A statue at the higher end of the path casts a 6.5-meter shadow straight down the path. The angle of elevation from the end of the shadow to the top of the statue is 32°. How tall is the statue?

47. A vertical statue 6.3 meters high stands on top of a hill. At a point on the side of the hill 35 meters from the statue's base, the angle between the hillside and a line from the top of the statue is 10°. What angle does the side of the hill make with the horizontal?

48. A fence post is located 36 feet from one corner of a building and 40 feet from the adjacent corner. Fences are put up between the post and the building corners to form a triangular garden area. The 40-foot fence makes a 58° angle with the building. What is the area of the garden?

49. Two straight roads meet at an angle of 40° in Harville, one leading to Eastview and the other to Wellston (see the figure on the next page). Eastview is 18 kilometers from Harville and 20 kilometers from Wellston. What is the distance from Harville to Wellston?

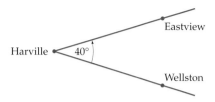

50. Each of two observers 400 feet apart measures the angle of elevation to the top of a tree that sits on the straight line between them. These angles are 51° and 65° respectively. How tall is the tree? How far is the base of its trunk from each observer?

51. From the top of the 800-foot-tall Cartalk Tower, Tom sees a plane; the angle of elevation is 67°. At the same instant, Ray, who is on the ground 1 mile from the building, notes that his angle of elevation to the plane is 81° and that his angle of elevation to the top of Cartalk Tower is 8.6°. Assume that Tom, Ray, and the airplane are in a plane perpendicular to the ground. (See the following figure.) How high is the airplane?

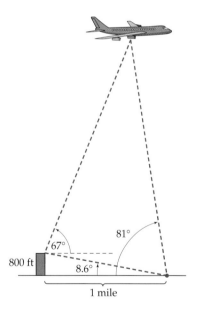

52. A plane flies in a direction of 105° from airport A. [Note: Aerial navigation directions are explained in Exercise 34 of Section 10.1.] After a time, it turns and proceeds in a direction of 267°. Finally, it lands at airport B, 120 miles directly south of airport A. How far has the plane traveled?

53. Charlie is afraid of water; he can't swim and refuses to get in a boat. However, he must measure the width of a river for his geography

class. He has a long tape measure, but no way to measure angles. While pondering what to do, he paces along the side of the river using the five paths joining points A, B, C, and D (see the following figure). If he does not determine the width of the river, he will not pass the course.

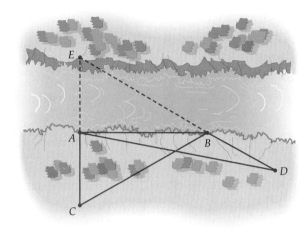

a. Save Charlie from disaster by explaining how he can determine the width AE simply by measuring the lengths AB, AC, AD, BC, and BD and using trigonometry.
b. Charlie determines that AB = 75 feet, AC = 25 feet, AD = 90 feet, BC = 80 feet, and BD = 22 feet. How wide is the river between A and E?

54. A plane flies in a direction of 85° from Chicago. [Note: Aerial navigation directions are explained in Exercise 34 of Section 10.1.] It then turns and flies in the direction of 200° for 150 miles. It is then 195 miles from its starting point. How far did the plane fly in the direction of 85°?

55. A hinged crane makes an angle of 50° with the ground. A malfunction causes the lock on the hinge to fail and the top part of the crane swings down (see the figure). How far from the base of the crane does the top hit the ground?

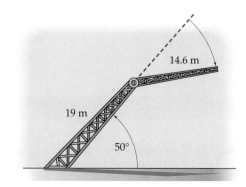

56. A triangular lot has sides of 120 feet and 160 feet. The angle between these sides is 42°. Adjacent to this lot is a rectangular lot whose longest side is 200 feet and whose shortest side is the same length as the shortest side of the triangular lot. What is the total area of both lots?

57. If a gallon of paint covers 400 square feet, how many gallons are needed to paint a triangular deck with sides of 65 feet, 72 feet, and 88 feet?

58. *Critical Thinking* Find the volume of the prism in the figure below. The volume is given by the formula $V = \frac{1}{3} Bh$, where B is the area of the base and h is the height.

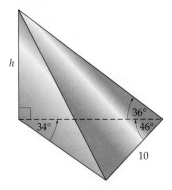

59. *Critical Thinking* A rigid plastic triangle *ABC* rests on three vertical rods, as shown in the figure. What is its area?

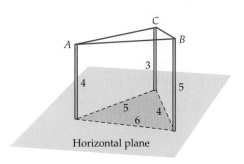

Horizontal plane

60. *Critical Thinking* Prove that the area of triangle *ABC*, in standard notation is given by
$$\frac{a^2 \sin B \sin C}{2 \sin A}.$$

61. *Critical Thinking* What is the area of a triangle whose sides have lengths 12, 20, and 36? *Hint:* Drawing a diagram may be helpful.

62. *Critical Thinking* Use the area formula $\frac{1}{2} ab \sin C$ and the Pythagorean identity $\sin^2 C = 1 - \cos^2 C$ to show that
$$\frac{1}{2} ab \sin C = \sqrt{\frac{1}{2} ab(1 + \cos C) \frac{1}{2} ab(1 - \cos C)}.$$
Then use the Law of Cosines to show that $\frac{1}{2} ab(1 + \cos C) = s(s - c)$, where $s = \frac{1}{2}(a + b + c)$ and $\frac{1}{2} ab(1 - \cos C) = (s - a)(s - b)$. Combine the facts to prove Heron's Formula.

The Complex Plane and Polar Form for Complex Numbers*

Objectives

- Graph a complex number in the complex plane
- Find the absolute value of a complex number
- Express a complex number in polar form
- Perform polar multiplication and division

The real number system is represented geometrically by the number line. The complex number system can be represented geometrically by the coordinate plane:

The complex number $a + bi$ corresponds to the point (a, b) in the plane.

For example, the point (2, 3) shown in Figure 10.3-1 is labeled by $2 + 3i$. The other points shown are labeled similarly.

*Section 4.5 is a prerequisite for this section.

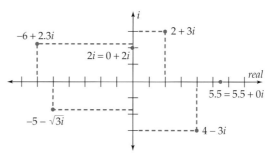

Figure 10.3-1

When the coordinate plane is used to graph complex numbers in this way, it is called the **complex plane.** Each real number $a = a + 0i$ corresponds to the point $(a, 0)$ on the horizontal axis; so this axis is called the **real axis.** The vertical axis is called the **imaginary axis** because every imaginary number $bi = 0 + bi$ corresponds to the point $(0, b)$ on the vertical axis.

The absolute value of a real number c is the distance from c to 0 on the number line. So the **absolute value** (or **modulus**) of the complex number $a + bi$ is defined to be the distance from $a + bi$ to the origin in the complex plane.

$|a + bi|$ represents the distance from (a, b) to $(0, 0)$, which is given by $\sqrt{(a - 0)^2 + (b - 0)^2} = \sqrt{a^2 + b^2}$.

Absolute Value of a Complex Number

The *absolute value* (or *modulus*) of the complex number $a + bi$ is

$$|a + bi| = \sqrt{a^2 + b^2}.$$

Example 1   Find Absolute Value of a Complex Number

Find the absolute value of each complex number.

a. $3 + 2i$ **b.** $4 - 5i$

Solution

a. $|3 + 2i| = \sqrt{3^2 + 2^2} = \sqrt{13}$ **b.** $|4 - 5i| = \sqrt{4^2 + (-5)^2} = \sqrt{41}$

Absolute values and trigonometry lead to a useful way of representing complex numbers. Let $a + bi$ be a nonzero complex number and denote $|a + bi|$ by r. Then r is the length of the line segment joining (a, b) and $(0, 0)$ in the plane. Let θ be the angle in standard position with this line segment as terminal side, as shown in Figure 10.3-2.

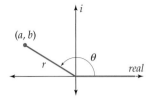

Figure 10.3-2

NOTE It is customary to place i in front of $\sin \theta$ rather than after it. Some books abbreviate $r(\cos \theta + i \sin \theta)$ as $r \operatorname{cis} \theta$.

Using the definitions of sine and cosine, the coordinates a and b can be expressed in terms of r and θ.

$$\cos \theta = \frac{a}{r} \qquad \text{and} \qquad \sin \theta = \frac{b}{r}$$
$$a = r \cos \theta \qquad\qquad b = r \sin \theta$$

Consequently,

$$a + bi = r \cos \theta + (r \sin \theta)i = r(\cos \theta + i \sin \theta).$$

When a complex number $a + bi$ is written in this way, it is said to be in **polar form** or **trigonometric form**. The angle θ is called the **argument** and is usually expressed in radian measure. The number $r = |a + bi|$ is called the **modulus** (plural, moduli). The number 0 can also be written in polar notation by letting $r = 0$ and θ be any angle.

Polar Form of a Complex Number

> Every complex number $a + bi$ can be written in polar form
> $$r(\cos \theta + i \sin \theta)$$
> where $r = |a + bi| = \sqrt{a^2 + b^2}$, $a = r \cos \theta$, and $b = r \sin \theta$.

When a complex number is written in polar form, the argument θ is not uniquely determined because $\theta, \theta \pm 2\pi, \theta \pm 4\pi$, and so on, all satisfy the conditions in the box.

Example 2 **Find Polar Form**

Express $-\sqrt{3} + i$ in polar form.

Solution

In this case, $a = -\sqrt{3}$ and $b = 1$. Therefore,

$$r = \sqrt{a^2 + b^2} = \sqrt{(-\sqrt{3})^2 + 1^2} = \sqrt{3 + 1} = 2.$$

The angle θ must satisfy the following two conditions.

$$\cos \theta = \frac{a}{r} = \frac{-\sqrt{3}}{2} \qquad \text{and} \qquad \sin \theta = \frac{b}{r} = \frac{1}{2}$$

Because $-\sqrt{3} + i$ is represented by the point $(-\sqrt{3}, 1)$ in the complex plane, it lies in the second quadrant, as shown in Figure 10.3-3. Therefore, θ must be a second-quadrant angle. So, $\theta = \dfrac{5\pi}{6}$ satisfies these conditions.

Thus, $-\sqrt{3} + i = 2\left(\cos \dfrac{5\pi}{6} + i \sin \dfrac{5\pi}{6}\right).$

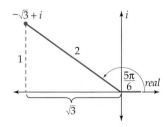

Figure 10.3-3

Example 3 Find Polar Form

Express $-2 + 5i$ in polar form.

Solution

In this case, $a = -2$ and $b = 5$. Therefore,

$$r = \sqrt{a^2 + b^2} = \sqrt{(-2)^2 + 5^2} = \sqrt{29}.$$

The angle θ must satisfy

$$\cos \theta = \frac{a}{r} = \frac{-2}{\sqrt{29}} \qquad \text{and} \qquad \sin \theta = \frac{b}{r} = \frac{5}{\sqrt{29}},$$

so that

$$\tan \theta = \frac{\sin \theta}{\cos \theta} = \frac{\frac{5}{\sqrt{29}}}{\frac{-2}{\sqrt{29}}} = -\frac{5}{2} = -2.5.$$

Because $-2 + 5i$ lies in the second quadrant (see Figure 10.3-4), θ lies between $\frac{\pi}{2}$ and π. Using the TAN^{-1} key, the calculator indicates that a solution to $\tan \theta = -2.5$ is $\theta = -1.1903$. Because that angle is in the fourth quadrant, the only solution between $\frac{\pi}{2}$ and π is

$$\theta = -1.1903 + \pi = 1.9513.$$

Thus, $-2 + 5i = \sqrt{29}(\cos 1.9513 + i \sin 1.9513)$.

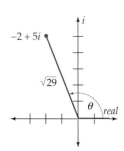

Figure 10.3-4

Multiplication and Division of Complex Numbers

Polar Multiplication and Division

> If $z_1 = r_1(\cos \theta_1 + i \sin \theta_1)$ and $z_2 = r_2(\cos \theta_2 + i \sin \theta_2)$ are any two complex numbers, then
>
> $$z_1 z_2 = r_1 r_2 [\cos(\theta_1 + \theta_2) + i \sin(\theta_1 + \theta_2)]$$
>
> and
>
> $$\frac{z_1}{z_2} = \frac{r_1}{r_2} [\cos(\theta_1 - \theta_2) + i \sin(\theta_1 - \theta_2)], \; z_2 \neq 0.$$

That is, given two complex numbers written in polar form,

- to multiply the two numbers
  multiply the moduli and add the arguments.

- to divide the two numbers
  divide the moduli and subtract the arguments.

The proof of the multiplication statement, which is given at the end of this section, uses the addition identities for sine and cosine.

Example 4   Multiplication of Numbers in Polar Form

Find z_1z_2 when $z_1 = 2\left(\cos\dfrac{5\pi}{6} + i\sin\dfrac{5\pi}{6}\right)$ and $z_2 = 3\left(\cos\dfrac{7\pi}{4} + i\sin\dfrac{7\pi}{4}\right)$.

Solution

In this case, $r_1 = 2$, $\theta_1 = \dfrac{5\pi}{6}$, $r_2 = 3$, and $\theta_2 = \dfrac{7\pi}{4}$. Therefore,

$$z_1z_2 = r_1r_2[\cos(\theta_1 + \theta_2) + i\sin(\theta_1 + \theta_2)]$$
$$= (2)(3)\left[\cos\left(\frac{5\pi}{6} + \frac{7\pi}{4}\right) + i\sin\left(\frac{5\pi}{6} + \frac{7\pi}{4}\right)\right]$$
$$= 6\left[\cos\left(\frac{10\pi}{12} + \frac{21\pi}{12}\right) + i\sin\left(\frac{10\pi}{12} + \frac{21\pi}{12}\right)\right]$$
$$= 6\left(\cos\frac{31\pi}{12} + i\sin\frac{31\pi}{12}\right)$$

NOTE A complex number written in polar form can be written in rectangular form by evaluating each term and simplifying. For example,

$$2\left(\cos\frac{5\pi}{6} + i\sin\frac{5\pi}{6}\right)$$
$$= 2\left(\frac{-\sqrt{3}}{2} + \frac{1}{2}i\right)$$
$$= -\sqrt{3} + i$$

Example 5   Division of Numbers in Polar Form

Find $\dfrac{z_1}{z_2}$ when $z_1 = 10\left(\cos\dfrac{\pi}{3} + i\sin\dfrac{\pi}{3}\right)$ and $z_2 = 2\left(\cos\dfrac{\pi}{4} + i\sin\dfrac{\pi}{4}\right)$.

Solution

In this case, $r_1 = 10$, $\theta_1 = \dfrac{\pi}{3}$, $r_2 = 2$, and $\theta_2 = \dfrac{\pi}{4}$. Therefore,

$$\frac{z_1}{z_2} = \frac{10}{2}\left[\cos\left(\frac{\pi}{3} - \frac{\pi}{4}\right) + i\sin\left(\frac{\pi}{3} - \frac{\pi}{4}\right)\right]$$
$$= 5\left(\cos\frac{\pi}{12} + i\sin\frac{\pi}{12}\right)$$

Proof of the Polar Multiplication Rule

Let $z_1 = r_1(\cos\theta_1 + i\sin\theta_1)$ and $z_2 = r_2(\cos\theta_2 + i\sin\theta_2)$.

$$z_1z_2 = [r_1(\cos\theta_1 + i\sin\theta_1)][r_2(\cos\theta_2 + i\sin\theta_2)]$$
$$= r_1r_2(\cos\theta_1 + i\sin\theta_1)(\cos\theta_2 + i\sin\theta_2)$$
$$= r_1r_2(\cos\theta_1\cos\theta_2 + i\sin\theta_1\cos\theta_2 + i\sin\theta_2\cos\theta_1 + i^2\sin\theta_1\sin\theta_2)$$
$$= r_1r_2[(\cos\theta_1\cos\theta_2 - \sin\theta_1\sin\theta_2) + i(\sin\theta_1\cos\theta_2 + \sin\theta_2\cos\theta_1)]$$

Recall from Section 9.2 that

$$\cos(\theta_1 + \theta_2) = \cos\theta_1\cos\theta_2 - \sin\theta_1\sin\theta_2$$

and

$$\sin(\theta_1 + \theta_2) = \sin \theta_1 \cos \theta_2 + \cos \theta_1 \sin \theta_2.$$

Therefore,

$$z_1 z_2 = r_1 r_2 [(\cos \theta_1 \cos \theta_2 - \sin \theta_1 \sin \theta_2) + i(\sin \theta_1 \cos \theta_2 + \sin \theta_2 \cos \theta_1)]$$
$$= r_1 r_2 [\cos(\theta_1 + \theta_2) + i \sin(\theta_1 + \theta_2)]$$

This completes the proof of the multiplication rule. The division rule is proved similarly. See Exercise 51.

Exercises 10.3

In Exercises 1–8, plot the point in the complex plane that corresponds to each number.

1. $3 + 2i$ **2.** $-7 + 6i$ **3.** $-\dfrac{8}{3} - \dfrac{5}{3}i$

4. $\sqrt{2} - 7i$ **5.** $(1 + i)(1 - i)$ **6.** $(2 + i)(1 - 2i)$

7. $2i\left(3 - \dfrac{5}{2}i\right)$ **8.** $\dfrac{4}{3}i(-6 - 3i)$

In Exercises 9–14, find each absolute value.

9. $|5 - 12i|$ **10.** $|2i|$ **11.** $|1 + i\sqrt{2}|$

12. $|2 - 3i|$ **13.** $|-12i|$ **14.** $|i^7|$

15. Give an example of complex numbers z and w such that $|z + w| = |z| + |w|$.

16. If $z = 3 - 4i$, find $|z|^2$ and $z\bar{z}$ where $\bar{z}$ is the conjugate of z. See Section 4.5 for the definition of a complex conjugate.

In Exercises 17–24, sketch the graph of the equation in the complex plane (z denotes a complex number of the form $a + bi$).

17. $|z| = 4$ *Hint:* The graph consists of all points that lie 4 units from the origin.

18. $|z| = 1$

19. $|z - 1| = 10$ *Hint:* 1 corresponds to (1, 0) in the complex plane. What does the equation say about the distance from z to 1?

20. $|z + 3| = 1$ **21.** $|z - 2i| = 4$

22. $|z - 3i + 2| = 3$ *Hint:* Rewrite it as $|z - (-2 + 3i)| = 3$.

23. $\text{Re}(z) = 2$ [The **real part** of the complex number $z = a + bi$ is defined to be the number a and is denoted $\text{Re}(z)$.]

24. $\text{Im}(z) = -\dfrac{5}{2}$ [The **imaginary part** of $z = a + bi$ is defined to be the number b (not bi) and is denoted $\text{Im}(z)$.]

In Exercises 25–32, express each number in polar form.

25. $3 + 4i$ **26.** $-4 + 3i$ **27.** $5 - 12i$

28. $-\sqrt{7} - 3i$ **29.** $1 + 2i$ **30.** $3 - 5i$

31. $-\dfrac{5}{2} + \dfrac{7}{2}i$ **32.** $\sqrt{5} + i\sqrt{11}$

In Exercises 33–38, perform the indicated multiplication or division. Express your answer in both rectangular form $a + bi$ and polar form $r(\cos \theta + i \sin \theta)$.

33. $3\left(\cos \dfrac{\pi}{12} + i \sin \dfrac{\pi}{12}\right) \cdot 2\left(\cos \dfrac{7\pi}{12} + i \sin \dfrac{7\pi}{12}\right)$

34. $3\left(\cos \dfrac{\pi}{8} + i \sin \dfrac{\pi}{8}\right) \cdot 12\left(\cos \dfrac{3\pi}{8} + i \sin \dfrac{3\pi}{8}\right)$

35. $12\left(\cos \dfrac{11\pi}{12} + i \sin \dfrac{11\pi}{12}\right) \cdot \dfrac{7}{2}\left(\cos \dfrac{\pi}{4} + i \sin \dfrac{\pi}{4}\right)$

36. $\dfrac{8\left(\cos \dfrac{5\pi}{18} + i \sin \dfrac{5\pi}{18}\right)}{4\left(\cos \dfrac{\pi}{9} + i \sin \dfrac{\pi}{9}\right)}$

37. $\dfrac{6\left(\cos \dfrac{7\pi}{20} + i \sin \dfrac{7\pi}{20}\right)}{4\left(\cos \dfrac{\pi}{10} + i \sin \dfrac{\pi}{10}\right)}$

38. $$\dfrac{\sqrt{54}\left(\cos\dfrac{9\pi}{4}+i\sin\dfrac{9\pi}{4}\right)}{\sqrt{6}\left(\cos\dfrac{7\pi}{12}+i\sin\dfrac{7\pi}{12}\right)}$$

In Exercises 39–46, convert to polar form and then multiply or divide. Express your answer in polar form.

39. $(1+i)(1+i\sqrt{3})$

40. $(1-i)(3-3i)$

41. $\dfrac{1+i}{1-i}$

42. $\dfrac{2-2i}{-1-i}$

43. $3i(2\sqrt{3}+2i)$

44. $\dfrac{-4i}{\sqrt{3}+i}$

45. $i(i+1)(-\sqrt{3}+i)$

46. $(1-i)(2\sqrt{3}-2i)(-4-4i\sqrt{3})$

47. Explain what is meant by saying that multiplying a complex number $z=r(\cos\theta+i\sin\theta)$ by i amounts to rotating z 90° counterclockwise around the origin. *Hint:* Express i and iz in polar form; what are their relative positions in the complex plane?

48. Describe what happens geometrically when you multiply a complex number by 2.

49. *Critical Thinking* The sum of two distinct complex numbers, $a+bi$ and $c+di$, can be found geometrically by means of the so-called **parallelogram rule:** Plot the points $a+bi$ and $c+di$ in the complex plane and form the parallelogram, three of whose vertices are 0, $a+bi$ and $c+di$ as in the figure below. Then the fourth vertex of the parallelogram is the point whose coordinate is the sum

$$(a+bi)+(c+di)=(a+c)+(b+d)i.$$

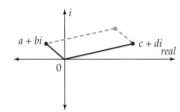

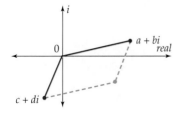

Complete the following *proof* of the parallelogram rule when $a\neq0$ and $c\neq0$.

a. Find the slope of the line K from 0 to $a+bi$. *Hint:* K contains the points $(0,0)$ and (a,b).

b. Find the slope of the line N from 0 to $c+di$.

c. Find the equation of the line L, through $a+bi$ and parallel to line N of part **b**. *Hint:* The point (a,b) is on L; find the slope of L by using part **b** and facts about the slope of parallel lines.

d. Find the equation of the line M, through $c+di$ and parallel to line K of part **a**.

e. Label the lines K, L, M, and N in each figure.

f. Show by using substitution that the point $(a+c,b+d)$ satisfies both the equation of line L and the equation of line M. Therefore, $(a+c,b+d)$ lies on both L and M. Because the only point on both L and M is the fourth vertex of the parallelogram, this vertex must be $(a+c,b+d)$. Hence, this vertex has coordinate

$$(a+c)+(b+d)i=(a+bi)+(c+di).$$

50. *Critical Thinking* Let $z=a+bi$ be a complex number and denote its conjugate $a-bi$ by $\bar{z}$. Prove that $|z|^2=z\bar{z}$.

51. *Critical Thinking* *Proof of the polar division rule.* Let $z_1=r_1(\cos\theta_1+i\sin\theta_1)$ and $z_2=r_2(\cos\theta_2+i\sin\theta_2)$.

$$\dfrac{z_1}{z_2}=\dfrac{r_1(\cos\theta_1+i\sin\theta_1)}{r_2(\cos\theta_2+i\sin\theta_2)}$$

$$=\dfrac{r_1(\cos\theta_1+i\sin\theta_1)}{r_2(\cos\theta_2+i\sin\theta_2)}\cdot\dfrac{\cos\theta_2-i\sin\theta_2}{\cos\theta_2-i\sin\theta_2}$$

a. Multiply the denominators and use the Pythagorean identity to show that it is the number r_2.

b. Multiply the numerators; use the subtraction identities for sine and cosine (Section 9.2) to show that it is

$$r_1[\cos(\theta_1-\theta_2)+i\sin(\theta_1-\theta_2)].$$

Therefore,

$$\dfrac{z_1}{z_2}=\left(\dfrac{r_1}{r_2}\right)[\cos(\theta_1-\theta_2)+i\sin(\theta_1-\theta_2)].$$

52. *Critical Thinking*

a. If $s(\cos\beta+i\sin\beta)=r(\cos\theta+i\sin\theta)$, explain why $s=r$ must be true. *Hint:* Think distance.

b. If $r(\cos\beta+i\sin\beta)=r(\cos\theta+i\sin\theta)$, explain why $\cos\beta=\cos\theta$ and $\sin\beta=\sin\theta$. *Hint:* See Property 5 of the complex numbers in Section 4.5.

c. If $\cos \beta = \cos \theta$ and $\sin \beta = \sin \theta$, show that angles β and θ in standard position have the same terminal side. *Hint:* $(\cos \beta, \sin \beta)$ and $(\cos \theta, \sin \theta)$ are points on the unit circle.

d. Use parts **a–c** to prove this equality rule for polar form:

$$s(\cos \beta + i \sin \beta) = r(\cos \theta + i \sin \theta)$$

exactly when $s = r$ and $\beta = \theta + 2k\pi$ for some integer k. *Hint:* Angles with the same terminal side must differ by an integer multiple of 2π.

10.4

DeMoivre's Theorem and nth Roots of Complex Numbers

Objectives

- Calculate powers and roots of complex numbers

- Find and graph roots of unity

Polar form provides a convenient way to calculate both powers and roots of complex numbers. If $z = r(\cos \theta + i \sin \theta)$, then the multiplication formula from Section 10.3 shows the following:

$$z^2 = z \cdot z = r \cdot r[\cos(\theta + \theta) + i \sin(\theta + \theta)]$$
$$= r^2(\cos 2\theta + i \sin 2\theta)$$

and

$$z^3 = z^2 \cdot z = r^2 \cdot r[\cos(2\theta + \theta) + i \sin(2\theta + \theta)]$$
$$= r^3(\cos 3\theta + i \sin 3\theta)$$

and so on. Repeated application of the multiplication formula proves **DeMoivre's Theorem.**

DeMoivre's Theorem

For any complex number $z = r(\cos \theta + i \sin \theta)$ and any positive integer n,

$$z^n = r^n(\cos n\theta + i \sin n\theta).$$

Example 1   **Find Powers of Complex Numbers**

Evaluate $\left(-\sqrt{3} + i\right)^5$.

Solution

First express the complex number $-\sqrt{3} + i$ in polar form. (See Example 2 of Section 10.3.)

$$-\sqrt{3} + i = 2\left(\cos \frac{5\pi}{6} + i \sin \frac{5\pi}{6}\right)$$

NOTE

$$\tan^{-1} \frac{1}{-\sqrt{3}} = \frac{5\pi}{6}$$

Apply DeMoivre's Theorem.

$$(-\sqrt{3} + i)^5 = 2^5\left[\cos\left(5 \cdot \frac{5\pi}{6}\right) + i\sin\left(5 \cdot \frac{5\pi}{6}\right)\right]$$

$$= 32\left(\cos\frac{25\pi}{6} + i\sin\frac{25\pi}{6}\right)$$

Because $\dfrac{25\pi}{6} = \dfrac{\pi}{6} + \dfrac{24\pi}{6} = \dfrac{\pi}{6} + 4\pi$, $\dfrac{\pi}{6}$ can be substituted for $\dfrac{25\pi}{6}$.

$$(-\sqrt{3} + i)^5 = 32\left(\cos\frac{25\pi}{6} + i\sin\frac{25\pi}{6}\right)$$

$$= 32\left(\cos\frac{\pi}{6} + i\sin\frac{\pi}{6}\right) \qquad \text{\textit{polar form}}$$

$$= 32\left(\frac{\sqrt{3}}{2} + \frac{1}{2}i\right)$$

$$= 16\sqrt{3} + 16i \qquad \text{\textit{rectangular form}}$$

Example 2   **Find Powers of Complex Numbers**

Evaluate $(1 + i)^{10}$.

Solution

Express the complex number $1 + i$ in polar form.

$$1 + i = \sqrt{2}\left(\cos\frac{\pi}{4} + i\sin\frac{\pi}{4}\right)$$

Apply DeMoivre's Theorem.

$$(1 + i)^{10} = (\sqrt{2})^{10}\left(\cos\frac{10\pi}{4} + i\sin\frac{10\pi}{4}\right)$$

$$= 32\left(\cos\frac{5\pi}{2} + i\sin\frac{5\pi}{2}\right) \qquad \text{\textit{polar form}}$$

$$= 32(0 + i)$$

$$= 32i \qquad \text{\textit{rectangular form}}$$

Nth Roots

NOTE With complex numbers, it is not possible to choose the positive root as the *n*th root of $a + bi$, as is done with real numbers, because "positive" and "negative" are not meaningful terms in the complex numbers. For instance, should $3 - 2i$ be called positive or negative?

If $a + bi$ is a complex number and n is a positive integer, the equation $z^n = a + bi$ may have n different solutions in the complex numbers. Furthermore, there is no obvious way to designate one of these solutions as *the* nth root of $a + bi$ (see note). Consequently, *any* solution of the equation $z^n = a + bi$ is called an ***n*th root** of $a + bi$.

Every real number is a complex number. When the definition of nth root of a complex number is applied to a real number, the terminology for real numbers no longer applies. For instance, in the complex numbers, 16 has *four* fourth roots because each of 2, -2, $2i$, and $-2i$ is a solution of $z^4 = 16$, whereas in the real numbers, 2 is the fourth root of 16.

Although nth roots are not unique in the complex numbers, the radical symbol will be used only for nonnegative real numbers and will have the same meaning as before. That is, if r is a nonnegative real number, then $\sqrt[n]{r}$ denotes the unique nonnegative real number whose nth power is r.

Example 3   **Find Roots of Complex Numbers**

Find the fourth roots of $-8 + 8i\sqrt{3}$.

Solution

Express the complex number $-8 + 8i\sqrt{3}$ in polar form.

$$-8 + 8i\sqrt{3} = 16\left(\cos\frac{2\pi}{3} + i\sin\frac{2\pi}{3}\right)$$

To solve $z^4 = 16\left(\cos\frac{2\pi}{3} + i\sin\frac{2\pi}{3}\right)$, find s and β such that $z = s(\cos\beta + i\sin\beta)$ is a solution. In other words, find s and β such that

$$[s(\cos\beta + i\sin\beta)]^4 = 16\left(\cos\frac{2\pi}{3} + i\sin\frac{2\pi}{3}\right).$$

Use DeMoivre's Theorem to rewrite the left side.

$$s^4(\cos 4\beta + i\sin 4\beta) = 16\left(\cos\frac{2\pi}{3} + i\sin\frac{2\pi}{3}\right)$$

The equality rules for complex numbers (proved in Exercise 52 of Section 10.3) show that the above equation is true if

$$s^4 = 16 \qquad \text{and} \qquad 4\beta = \frac{2\pi}{3} + 2k\pi$$

$$s = \sqrt[4]{16} = 2 \qquad\qquad \beta = \frac{\pi}{6} + \frac{k\pi}{2}$$

Therefore, the solutions of $z^4 = 16\left(\cos\frac{2\pi}{3} + i\sin\frac{2\pi}{3}\right)$ are

$$z = 2\left[\cos\left(\frac{\pi}{6} + \frac{k\pi}{2}\right) + i\sin\left(\frac{\pi}{6} + \frac{k\pi}{2}\right)\right],$$

where k is any integer. Letting $k = 0, 1, 2,$ and 3 produces four distinct solutions.

$$k = 0: \quad z = 2\left(\cos\frac{\pi}{6} + i\sin\frac{\pi}{6}\right) = \sqrt{3} + i$$

$$k = 1: \quad z = 2\left[\cos\left(\frac{\pi}{6} + \frac{\pi}{2}\right) + i\sin\left(\frac{\pi}{6} + \frac{\pi}{2}\right)\right]$$
$$= 2\left(\cos\frac{2\pi}{3} + i\sin\frac{2\pi}{3}\right) = -1 + i\sqrt{3}$$

$$k = 2: \quad z = 2\left[\cos\left(\frac{\pi}{6} + \pi\right) + i\sin\left(\frac{\pi}{6} + \pi\right)\right]$$
$$= 2\left(\cos\frac{7\pi}{6} + i\sin\frac{7\pi}{6}\right) = -\sqrt{3} - i$$

$$k = 3: \quad z = 2\left[\cos\left(\frac{\pi}{6} + \frac{3\pi}{2}\right) + i\sin\left(\frac{\pi}{6} + \frac{3\pi}{2}\right)\right]$$

$$= 2\left(\cos\frac{5\pi}{3} + i\sin\frac{5\pi}{3}\right) = 1 - i\sqrt{3}$$

Any other value of k produces an angle β with the same terminal side as one of the four angles already used and is the same solution. For instance, when $k = 4$, then $\beta = \frac{\pi}{6} + \frac{4\pi}{2} = \frac{\pi}{6} + 2\pi$, so β has the same terminal side as $\frac{\pi}{6}$. Therefore, all fourth roots of $-8 + 8i\sqrt{3}$ have been found.

■

The general equation $z^n = r(\cos\theta + i\sin\theta)$ can be solved exactly by the same method used in Example 3: substitute n for 4, r for 16, and θ for $\frac{2\pi}{3}$, as follows. A solution is a number $s(\cos\beta + i\sin\beta)$ such that:

$$[s(\cos\beta + i\sin\beta)]^n = r(\cos\theta + i\sin\theta)$$
$$s^n(\cos n\beta + i\sin n\beta) = r(\cos\theta + i\sin\theta)$$

Therefore,

$$s^n = r \qquad\qquad n\beta = \theta + 2k\pi$$
$$\text{and}$$
$$s = \sqrt[n]{r} \qquad\qquad \beta = \frac{\theta + 2k\pi}{n}$$

where k is any integer. Letting $k = 0, 1, 2, \ldots, n - 1$ produces n distinct angles β. This is stated in the following **formula for *n*th roots.**

Formula for nth Roots

For each positive integer n, the nonzero complex number

$$r(\cos\theta + i\sin\theta)$$

has exactly n distinct nth roots. They are given by

$$\sqrt[n]{r}\left[\cos\left(\frac{\theta + 2k\pi}{n}\right) + i\sin\left(\frac{\theta + 2k\pi}{n}\right)\right],$$

where $k = 0, 1, 2, 3, \ldots, n - 1.$

Example 4   Find Roots of Complex Numbers

Find the fifth roots of $4 + 4i$.

Solution

Express the complex number $4 + 4i$ in polar form.

$$4 + 4i = 4\sqrt{2}\left(\cos\frac{\pi}{4} + i\sin\frac{\pi}{4}\right)$$

Apply the root formula with $n = 5$, $r = 4\sqrt{2}$, $\theta = \frac{\pi}{4}$, and $k = 0, 1, 2, 3$, and 4.

$$\sqrt[n]{r} = \sqrt[5]{4\sqrt{2}} = \left(4\sqrt{2}\right)^{\frac{1}{5}} = \left(2^2 2^{\frac{1}{2}}\right)^{\frac{1}{5}} = \left(2^{\frac{5}{2}}\right)^{\frac{1}{5}} = 2^{\frac{5}{10}} = 2^{\frac{1}{2}} = \sqrt{2}$$

The fifth roots have the following form.

$$\sqrt{2}\left[\cos\left(\frac{\frac{\pi}{4} + 2k\pi}{5}\right) + i\sin\left(\frac{\frac{\pi}{4} + 2k\pi}{5}\right)\right], \text{ for } k = 0, 1, 2, 3, \text{ and } 4$$

Therefore, the five distinct roots are as follows.

$$k = 0: \quad \sqrt{2}\left[\cos\left(\frac{\frac{\pi}{4}}{5}\right) + i\sin\left(\frac{\frac{\pi}{4}}{5}\right)\right] = \sqrt{2}\left[\cos\left(\frac{\pi}{20}\right) + i\sin\left(\frac{\pi}{20}\right)\right]$$

$$k = 1: \quad \sqrt{2}\left[\cos\left(\frac{\frac{\pi}{4} + 2\pi}{5}\right) + i\sin\left(\frac{\frac{\pi}{4} + 2\pi}{5}\right)\right]$$
$$= \sqrt{2}\left[\cos\left(\frac{9\pi}{20}\right) + i\sin\left(\frac{9\pi}{20}\right)\right]$$

$$k = 2: \quad \sqrt{2}\left[\cos\left(\frac{\frac{\pi}{4} + 4\pi}{5}\right) + i\sin\left(\frac{\frac{\pi}{4} + 4\pi}{5}\right)\right]$$
$$= \sqrt{2}\left[\cos\left(\frac{17\pi}{20}\right) + i\sin\left(\frac{17\pi}{20}\right)\right]$$

$$k = 3: \quad \sqrt{2}\left[\cos\left(\frac{\frac{\pi}{4} + 6\pi}{5}\right) + i\sin\left(\frac{\frac{\pi}{4} + 6\pi}{5}\right)\right]$$
$$= \sqrt{2}\left[\cos\left(\frac{5\pi}{4}\right) + i\sin\left(\frac{5\pi}{4}\right)\right]$$

$$k = 4: \quad \sqrt{2}\left[\cos\left(\frac{\frac{\pi}{4} + 8\pi}{5}\right) + i\sin\left(\frac{\frac{\pi}{4} + 8\pi}{5}\right)\right]$$
$$= \sqrt{2}\left[\cos\left(\frac{33\pi}{20}\right) + i\sin\left(\frac{33\pi}{20}\right)\right]$$

Roots of Unity

The n distinct nth roots of 1 (the solutions of $z^n = 1$) are called the nth **roots of unity.** Because $\cos 0 = 1$ and $\sin 0 = 0$, the polar form of the number 1 is $\cos 0 + i\sin 0$. Applying the root formula with $r = 1$ and $\theta = 0$ produces a formula for roots of unity.

Formula for
Roots of Unity

For each positive integer n, there are n distinct nth roots of unity, which have the following form.

$$\cos\frac{2k\pi}{n} + i\sin\frac{2k\pi}{n}, \text{ for } k = 0, 1, 2, \dots, n - 1.$$

Example 5   **Find Roots of Unity**

Find the cube roots of unity.

Solution

Apply the formula for roots of unity with $n = 3$ and $k = 0, 1,$ and 2.

$$k = 0: \quad \cos 0 + i \sin 0 = 1$$

$$k = 1: \quad \cos \frac{2\pi}{3} + i \sin \frac{2\pi}{3} = -\frac{1}{2} + \frac{\sqrt{3}}{2} i$$

$$k = 2: \quad \cos \frac{4\pi}{3} + i \sin \frac{4\pi}{3} = -\frac{1}{2} - \frac{\sqrt{3}}{2} i$$

All roots of unity can be found from the first nonreal root. Let the first nonreal cube root of unity obtained in Example 5 be denoted by ω.

$$\omega = \cos \frac{2\pi}{3} + i \sin \frac{2\pi}{3}$$

Using DeMoivre's Theorem to find ω^2 and ω^3 produces the other two cube roots of unity.

$$\omega^2 = \left(\cos \frac{2\pi}{3} + i \sin \frac{2\pi}{3} \right)^2 = \cos \frac{4\pi}{3} + i \sin \frac{4\pi}{3}$$

$$\omega^3 = \left(\cos \frac{2\pi}{3} + i \sin \frac{2\pi}{3} \right)^3 = \cos \frac{6\pi}{3} + i \sin \frac{6\pi}{3} = \cos 2\pi + i \sin 2\pi = 1$$

In other words, all the cube roots of unity are powers of ω. The same is true in the general case, as stated below.

All Roots of Unity

Let n be a positive integer with $n > 1$. Then the number

$$z = \cos \frac{2\pi}{n} + i \sin \frac{2\pi}{n}$$

is an *n*th root of unity and all the *n*th roots of unity are

$$z, z^2, z^3, z^4, \ldots, z^{n-1}, z^n = 1.$$

The *n*th roots of unity have an interesting geometric interpretation. Every *n*th root of unity has absolute value of 1:

$$\left| \cos \frac{2k\pi}{n} + i \sin \frac{2k\pi}{n} \right| = \sqrt{\left(\cos \frac{2k\pi}{n} \right)^2 + \left(\sin \frac{2k\pi}{n} \right)^2}$$

$$= \sqrt{\cos^2 \frac{2k\pi}{n} + \sin^2 \frac{2k\pi}{n}}$$

$$= \sqrt{1}$$

$$= 1$$

Therefore, in the complex plane, every nth root of unity is exactly 1 unit from the origin. That is, the nth roots of unity all lie on the unit circle in the complex plane.

Example 6   Find nth Roots of Unity

Find the fifth roots of unity.

Solution

The fifth roots of unity have the following form.

$$\cos \frac{2k\pi}{5} + i \sin \frac{2k\pi}{5}, \text{ for } k = 0, 1, 2, 3, \text{ and } 4$$

Therefore, the five roots of unity are

$$k = 0: \quad \cos 0 + i \sin 0 = 1$$

$$k = 1: \quad \cos \frac{2\pi}{5} + i \sin \frac{2\pi}{5}$$

$$k = 2: \quad \cos \frac{4\pi}{5} + i \sin \frac{4\pi}{5}$$

$$k = 3: \quad \cos \frac{6\pi}{5} + i \sin \frac{6\pi}{5}$$

$$k = 4: \quad \cos \frac{8\pi}{5} + i \sin \frac{8\pi}{5}$$

These five roots can be plotted in the complex plane by starting at $1 = 1 + 0i$, and moving counterclockwise around the unit circle, moving through an angle of $\frac{2\pi}{5}$ at each step, as shown in Figure 10.4-1. If you connect these five roots, they form the vertices of a regular pentagon, as shown in Figure 10.4-2.

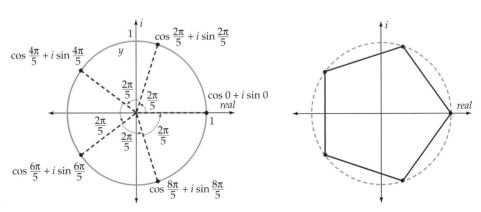

Figure 10.4-1   Figure 10.4-2

NOTE On wide screen calculators, you may choose to use $-2 \leq x \leq 2$ or $-1.7 \leq x \leq 1.7$ so that the unit circle looks like a circle.

Graphing Exploration

With your calculator in parametric graphing mode, use the following window settings.

$$0 \leq t \leq 2\pi \quad t\text{-step} \approx 0.067 \quad -2.2 \leq x \leq 2.2 \quad -1.5 \leq y \leq 1.5$$

Graph the unit circle, whose parametric equations are

$$x = \cos t \quad \text{and} \quad y = \sin t$$

Reset the *t*-step to be $\dfrac{2\pi}{5}$, and graph again. Your screen should now look exactly like the solid lines in Figure 10.4-2 because the calculator plotted only the five points corresponding to $t = 0, \dfrac{2\pi}{5}, \dfrac{4\pi}{5}, \dfrac{6\pi}{5}$, and $\dfrac{8\pi}{5}$, and connected them with the shortest possible segments.

Use the trace feature to move along the graph. The cursor will jump from vertex to vertex, that is, from one fifth root of unity to the next.

Example 7   Graph Roots of Unity

Graph the tenth roots of unity, and estimate the two tenth roots of unity in the first quadrant.

Solution

With a graphing calculator in parametric mode, set the range values as in the graphing exploration above.

Because $n = 10$, reset the *t*-step to $\dfrac{2\pi}{10} = \dfrac{\pi}{5}$ and graph. The result is a regular decagon whose vertices are the tenth roots of unity. By using the trace feature, you can approximate each tenth root of unity.

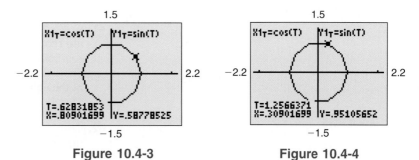

Figure 10.4-3   Figure 10.4-4

Figures 10.4-3 and 10.4-4 show the two approximate tenth roots of unity in the first quadrant.

$$0.8090 + 0.5878i \quad \text{and} \quad 0.3090 + 0.9511i.$$

Exercises 10.4

In Exercises 1–10, calculate each given product and express your answer in the form $a + bi$.

1. $\left(\cos\dfrac{\pi}{12} + i\sin\dfrac{\pi}{12}\right)^6$ **2.** $\left(\cos\dfrac{\pi}{5} + i\sin\dfrac{\pi}{5}\right)^{20}$

3. $\left[3\left(\cos\dfrac{7\pi}{30} + i\sin\dfrac{7\pi}{30}\right)\right]^5$

4. $\left[\sqrt[3]{4}\left(\cos\dfrac{7\pi}{36} + i\sin\dfrac{7\pi}{36}\right)\right]^{12}$

5. $(1 - i)^{12}$ *Hint:* Use polar form and DeMoivre's theorem.

6. $(2 + 2i)^8$

7. $\left(\dfrac{\sqrt{3}}{2} + \dfrac{1}{2}i\right)^{10}$

8. $\left(-\dfrac{1}{2} + \dfrac{\sqrt{3}}{2}i\right)^{20}$

9. $\left(\dfrac{-1}{\sqrt{2}} + \dfrac{i}{\sqrt{2}}\right)^{14}$

10. $(-1 + 3i)^8$

In Exercises 11 and 12, find all indicated roots of unity and express your answers in the form $a + bi$.

11. fourth roots of unity

12. sixth roots of unity

In Exercises 13–22, find the nth roots of each given number in polar form.

13. $64\left(\cos\dfrac{\pi}{5} + i\sin\dfrac{\pi}{5}\right); n = 3$

14. $8\left(\cos\dfrac{\pi}{10} + i\sin\dfrac{\pi}{10}\right); n = 3$

15. $81\left(\cos\dfrac{\pi}{12} + i\sin\dfrac{\pi}{12}\right); n = 4$

16. $16\left(\cos\dfrac{\pi}{7} + i\sin\dfrac{\pi}{7}\right); n = 5$

17. $-1; n = 5$ **18.** $1; n = 7$ **19.** $i; n = 5$

20. $-i; n = 6$ **21.** $1 + i; n = 2$ **22.** $1 - i\sqrt{3}; n = 3$

In Exercises 23–30, solve the given equation in the complex number system.

23. $x^6 = -1$ **24.** $x^6 + 64 = 0$ **25.** $x^3 = i$

26. $x^4 = i$ **27.** $x^3 + 27i = 0$ **28.** $x^6 + 729 = 0$

29. $x^4 = -1 + i\sqrt{3}$ **30.** $x^4 = -8 - 8i\sqrt{3}$

In Exercises 31–35, represent the roots of unity graphically. Then use the trace feature to obtain approximations of the form $a + bi$ for each root (round to four places).

31. seventh roots of unity

32. fifth roots of unity   **33.** eighth roots of unity

34. twelfth roots of unity   **35.** ninth roots of unity

36. Solve the equation $x^3 + x^2 + x + 1 = 0$. *Hint:* First find the quotient when $x^4 - 1$ is divided by $x - 1$, then consider solutions of $x^4 - 1 = 0$.

37. Solve $x^5 + x^4 + x^3 + x^2 + x + 1 = 0$ *Hint:* Consider $x^6 - 1$ and $x - 1$ and see Exercise 36.

38. What are the solutions of $x^{n-1} + x^{n-2} + \cdots + x^3 + x^2 + x + 1 = 0$? (See Exercises 36 and 37.)

39. *Critical Thinking* In the complex plane, the unit circle consists of all numbers (points) z such that $|z| = 1$. Suppose v and w are two points (numbers) that move around the unit circle in such a way that $v = w^{12}$ at all times. When w has made one complete trip around the circle, how many trips has v made? *Hint:* Think polar and DeMoivre.

40. *Critical Thinking* Suppose u is an nth root of unity. Show that $\dfrac{1}{u}$ is also an nth root of unity. *Hint:* Use the definition, not polar form.

41. *Critical Thinking* Let $u_1, u_2, \ldots, u_n$ be the distinct nth roots of unity and suppose v is a nonzero solution of the equation $z^n = r(\cos\theta + i\sin\theta)$. Show that $vu_1, vu_2, \ldots, vu_n$ are n distinct solutions of the equation. *Hint:* Each u_i is a solution of $x^n = 1$.

42. *Critical Thinking* Use the formula for nth roots and the identities

$$\cos(x + \pi) = -\cos x \qquad \sin(x + \pi) = -\sin x$$

to show that the nonzero complex number $r(\cos\theta + i\sin\theta)$ has two square roots and that these square roots are negatives of each other.

10.5   Vectors in the Plane

Objectives

- Find the components and magnitude of a vector

- Perform scalar multiplication of vectors, vector addition, and vector subtraction

Once a unit of measure has been agreed upon, quantities such as area, length, time, and temperature can be described by a single number. Other quantities, such as an east wind of 10 miles per hour, require two numbers to describe them because they involve both *magnitude* and *direction*. Quantities that have magnitude and direction are called **vectors** and are represented geometrically by a directed line segment or arrow, as shown in Figures 10.5-1 and 10.5-2.

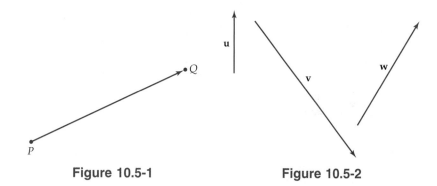

Figure 10.5-1   **Figure 10.5-2**

When a vector extends from a point P to a point Q, as in Figure 10.5-1, P is called the **initial point** of the vector, and Q is called the **terminal point,** and the vector is written $\overrightarrow{PQ}$. Its **length** is denoted by $\|\overrightarrow{PQ}\|$.

When the endpoints are not specified, as in Figure 10.5-2, vectors are denoted by boldface letters such as **u**, **v**, and **w**. The length of a vector **u** is denoted by $\|\mathbf{u}\|$ and is called the **magnitude of u**.

If **u** and **v** are vectors with the same magnitude and direction, the vectors **u** and **v** are said to be **equivalent,** written **u = v**. Some examples and nonexamples are shown in Figure 10.5-3.

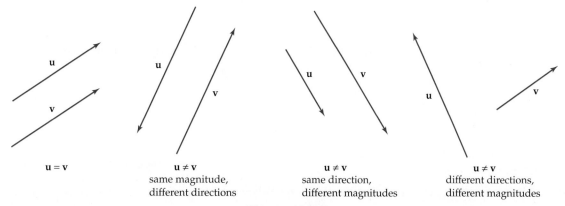

u = v   **u ≠ v**   **u ≠ v**   **u ≠ v**
                    same magnitude,   same direction,   different directions,
                    different directions   different magnitudes   different magnitudes

Figure 10.5-3

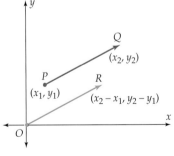

Figure 10.5-4

| Example 1 | Confirm Equivalent Vectors |

Let $P = (1, 2)$, $Q = (5, 4)$, $O = (0, 0)$, and $R = (4, 2)$, as in Figure 10.5-4. Show that $\overrightarrow{PQ} = \overrightarrow{OR}$.

Solution

The distance formula shows that $\overrightarrow{PQ}$ and $\overrightarrow{OR}$ have the same length.

$$\|\overrightarrow{PQ}\| = \sqrt{(5 - 1)^2 + (4 - 2)^2} = \sqrt{4^2 + 2^2} = \sqrt{20}$$
$$\|\overrightarrow{OR}\| = \sqrt{(4 - 0)^2 + (2 - 0)^2} = \sqrt{4^2 + 2^2} = \sqrt{20}$$

The lines containing $\overrightarrow{PQ}$ and $\overrightarrow{OR}$ have the same slope:

$$\text{slope } \overleftrightarrow{PQ} = \frac{4 - 2}{5 - 1} = \frac{2}{4} = \frac{1}{2} \qquad \text{slope } \overleftrightarrow{OR} = \frac{2 - 0}{4 - 0} = \frac{2}{4} = \frac{1}{2}$$

Because $\overrightarrow{PQ}$ and $\overrightarrow{OR}$ both point to the upper right on lines of the same slope, $\overrightarrow{PQ}$ and $\overrightarrow{OR}$ have the same direction. Therefore, $\overrightarrow{PQ} = \overrightarrow{OR}$. ∎

According to the definition of equivalence, if two vectors are equivalent, then one of the vectors may be moved from one location to another, provided that its magnitude and direction are not changed, and the two vectors will remain equivalent.

Equivalent Vectors

Every vector $\overrightarrow{PQ}$ is equivalent to a vector $\overrightarrow{OR}$ with initial point at the origin. If $P = (x_1, y_1)$ and $Q = (x_2, y_2)$, then

$$\overrightarrow{PQ} = \overrightarrow{OR}, \qquad \text{where } R = (x_2 - x_1, y_2 - y_1).$$

Proof The proof is similar to the one used in Example 1. It follows from the fact that $\overrightarrow{PQ}$ and $\overrightarrow{OR}$ have the same length:

$$\|\overrightarrow{OR}\| = \sqrt{[(x_2 - x_1) - 0]^2 + [(y_2 - y_1) - 0]^2}$$
$$= \sqrt{(x_2 - x_1)^2 + (y_2 - y_1)^2}$$
$$= \|\overrightarrow{PQ}\|$$

and either the lines containing $\overrightarrow{PQ}$ and $\overrightarrow{OR}$ are both vertical or they have the same slope:

$$\text{slope } \overleftrightarrow{OR} = \frac{(y_2 - y_1) - 0}{(x_2 - x_1) - 0}$$
$$= \frac{y_2 - y_1}{x_2 - x_1}$$
$$= \text{slope } \overleftrightarrow{PQ},$$

Figure 10.5-5

as shown in Figure 10.5-5.

Every vector can be written as a vector with the origin as its initial point. The magnitude and direction of a vector with the origin as its initial point are completely determined by the coordinates of its terminal point. Consequently, the vector with initial point $(0, 0)$ and terminal point (a, b) is denoted by $\langle a, b \rangle$. The numbers a and b are called the **components** of the vector $\langle a, b \rangle$.

Because the length of the vector $\langle a, b \rangle$ is the distance from $(0, 0)$ to (a, b), the distance formula gives its **magnitude,** which is also called its norm.

Magnitude

The *magnitude* (or *norm*) of the vector $\mathbf{v} = \langle a, b \rangle$ is

$$\|\mathbf{v}\| = \sqrt{a^2 + b^2}.$$

CAUTION

The order in which the coordinates of the initial point and terminal point are subtracted to obtain $\langle a, b \rangle$ is significant. For the points $P(x_1, y_1)$ and $Q(x_2, y_2)$:

$$\overrightarrow{PQ} = \langle x_2 - x_1, y_2 - y_1 \rangle$$
$$\overrightarrow{QP} = \langle x_1 - x_2, y_1 - y_2 \rangle$$

Example 2   **Find Components and Magnitude of a Vector**

Find the components and the magnitude of the vector with initial point $P = (-2, 6)$ and terminal point $Q = (4, -3)$.

Solution

According to the properties of equivalent vectors, where $x_1 = -2, y_1 = 6,$ $x_2 = 4,$ and $y_2 = -3$:

$$\overrightarrow{PQ} = \overrightarrow{OR}, \quad \text{where } R = (4 - (-2), -3 - 6) = (6, -9).$$

In other words,

$$\overrightarrow{PQ} = \overrightarrow{OR} = \langle 6, -9 \rangle.$$

Therefore, the magnitude is

$$\|\overrightarrow{PQ}\| = \|\overrightarrow{OR}\| = \sqrt{6^2 + (-9)^2} = \sqrt{36 + 81} = \sqrt{117}$$

Vector Arithmetic

Vectors can be added, can be subtracted, and can be multiplied in three different ways. Addition, subtraction, and one type of multiplication are discussed in this section. Another type of multiplication is presented in the *Excursion* 10.6.A.

Scalar Multiplication

When dealing with vectors, it is customary to refer to ordinary real numbers as **scalars. Scalar multiplication** is an operation in which a scalar k is "multiplied" by a vector $\mathbf{v}$ to produce another vector denoted by $k\mathbf{v}$.

Scalar Multiplication

If k is a real number and $\mathbf{v} = \langle a, b \rangle$ is a vector, then

$$k\mathbf{v} \text{ is the vector } \langle ka, kb \rangle.$$

The vector $k\mathbf{v}$ is called a *scalar multiple* of $\mathbf{v}$.

Example 3   Perform Scalar Multiplication

Let $\mathbf{v} = \langle 3, 1 \rangle$. Find the components of $3\mathbf{v}$ and $-2\mathbf{v}$.

Solution

$$
\begin{aligned}
3\mathbf{v} &= 3\langle 3, 1 \rangle & -2\mathbf{v} &= -2\langle 3, 1 \rangle \\
&= \langle 3 \cdot 3, 3 \cdot 1 \rangle & &= \langle -2 \cdot 3, -2 \cdot 1 \rangle \\
&= \langle 9, 3 \rangle & &= \langle -6, -2 \rangle
\end{aligned}
$$

The graphs of $\mathbf{v}$, $3\mathbf{v}$, and $-2\mathbf{v}$ from Example 3, shown in Figure 10.5-6, illustrates that $3\mathbf{v}$ has the same direction as $\mathbf{v}$ and $-2\mathbf{v}$ has the opposite direction.

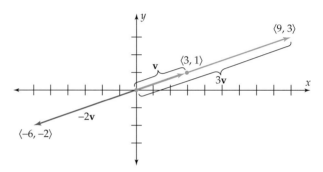

Figure 10.5-6

Also note that

$$
\|\mathbf{v}\| = \|\langle 3, 1 \rangle\| = \sqrt{3^2 + 1^2} = \sqrt{10}
$$
$$
\|-2\mathbf{v}\| = \|\langle -6, 2 \rangle\| = \sqrt{(-6)^2 + 2^2} = \sqrt{40} = 2\sqrt{10}
$$

Therefore,

$$
\|-2\mathbf{v}\| = 2\sqrt{10} = 2\|\mathbf{v}\| = |-2| \cdot \|\mathbf{v}\|
$$

Similarly, it can be verified that $\|3\mathbf{v}\| = |3| \cdot \|\mathbf{v}\| = 3\|\mathbf{v}\|$. Figure 10.5-6 is an illustration of the following facts.

Geometric Interpretation of Scalar Multiplication

The *magnitude* of the vector $k\mathbf{v}$ is $|k|$ times the length of $\mathbf{v}$, that is,

$$
\|k\mathbf{v}\| = |k| \cdot \|\mathbf{v}\|.
$$

The *direction of $k\mathbf{v}$* is the same as that of $\mathbf{v}$ when k is positive and opposite that of $\mathbf{v}$ when k is negative.

Vector Addition

Vector addition is an operation in which two vectors **u** and **v** are added, resulting in a new vector denoted **u** + **v**.

Vector Addition

> If **u** = $\langle a, b \rangle$ and **v** = $\langle c, d \rangle$, then
>
> $$\mathbf{u} + \mathbf{v} = \langle a + c, b + d \rangle.$$

Example 4   **Perform Vector Addition**

Let **u** = $\langle -5, 2 \rangle$ and **v** = $\langle 3, 1 \rangle$. Find the components of **u** + **v**.

Solution

$$\begin{aligned} \mathbf{u} + \mathbf{v} &= \langle -5, 2 \rangle + \langle 3, 1 \rangle \\ &= \langle -5 + 3, 2 + 1 \rangle \\ &= \langle -2, 3 \rangle \end{aligned}$$

Geometric Interpretation of u + v

The graph of **u** + **v** from Example 4 is shown in Figure 10.5-7.

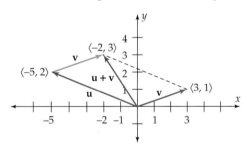

Figure 10.5-7

Figure 10.5-7 illustrates the following geometric interpretation of vector addition.

Geometric Interpretation of Vector Addition

> 1. If u and v are vectors with the same initial point P, then u + v is the vector $\overrightarrow{PQ}$, where $\overrightarrow{PQ}$ is the diagonal of the parallelogram with adjacent sides u and v.
> 2. If the vector v is moved without changing its magnitude or direction so that its initial point lies on the endpoint of the vector u, then u + v is the vector with the same initial point P as u and the same terminal point Q as v.

Exercise 33 asks for the proof of the geometric interpretation of vector addition stated above.

Vector Subtraction

The **negative** (or **opposite**) of a vector $\mathbf{v} = \langle c, d \rangle$ is defined to be the vector $(-1)\mathbf{v} = (-1)\langle c, d \rangle = \langle -c, -d \rangle$, and is denoted $-\mathbf{v}$. **Vector subtraction** is defined using the negative of a vector as follows.

Vector Subtraction

> If $\mathbf{u} = \langle a, b \rangle$ and $\mathbf{v} = \langle c, d \rangle$, then $\mathbf{u} - \mathbf{v}$ is the vector
> $$\mathbf{u} + (-\mathbf{v}) = \langle a, b \rangle + \langle -c, -d \rangle$$
> $$= \langle a - c, b - d \rangle$$

Example 5   Perform Vector Subtraction

Let $\mathbf{u} = \langle 2, 5 \rangle$ and $\mathbf{v} = \langle 6, 1 \rangle$. Find the components of $\mathbf{u} - \mathbf{v}$.

Solution
$$\mathbf{u} - \mathbf{v} = \langle 2, 5 \rangle - \langle 6, 1 \rangle$$
$$= \langle 2 - 6, 5 - 1 \rangle$$
$$= \langle -4, 4 \rangle$$

NOTE The vectors $\mathbf{v}$ and $-\mathbf{v}$ have the same magnitude, and lines that contain them have the same slope, but $\mathbf{v}$ and $-\mathbf{v}$ have opposite directions.

Geometric Interpretation of $\mathbf{u} - \mathbf{v}$

The graph of $\mathbf{u} - \mathbf{v}$ from Example 5 is shown in Figure 10.5-8.

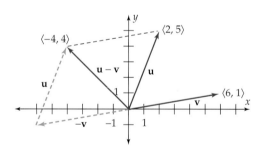

Figure 10.5-8

The Zero Vector

The vector $\langle 0, 0 \rangle$ is called the **zero vector** and is denoted $\mathbf{0}$.

Example 6   Perform Combined Vector Operations

Let $\mathbf{u} = \langle -1, 6 \rangle$, $\mathbf{v} = \left\langle \dfrac{2}{3}, -4 \right\rangle$, and $\mathbf{w} = \left\langle 2, \dfrac{5}{2} \right\rangle$. Find the components of each vector.

a. $2\mathbf{u} + 3\mathbf{v}$ **b.** $4\mathbf{w} - 2\mathbf{u}$

Solution

a. $2\mathbf{u} + 3\mathbf{v} = 2\langle -1, 6\rangle + 3\left\langle \dfrac{2}{3}, -4\right\rangle$ **b.** $4\mathbf{w} - 2\mathbf{u} = 4\left\langle 2, \dfrac{5}{2}\right\rangle - 2\langle -1, 6\rangle$

$\qquad\qquad\quad = \langle -2, 12\rangle + \langle 2, -12\rangle \qquad\qquad\qquad\quad = \langle 8, 10\rangle + \langle 2, -12\rangle$

$\qquad\qquad\quad = \langle -2 + 2, 12 - 12\rangle \qquad\qquad\qquad\quad = \langle 8 + 2, 10 - 12\rangle$

$\qquad\qquad\quad = \langle 0, 0\rangle \qquad\qquad\qquad\qquad\qquad\quad = \langle 10, -2\rangle$

$\qquad\qquad\quad = \mathbf{0}$

Vector Properties

Operations on vectors share many of the same properties as arithmetical operations on numbers.

Properties of Vector Addition and Scalar Multiplication

For any vectors **u**, **v**, and **w** and any scalars r and s,

1. $\mathbf{u} + (\mathbf{v} + \mathbf{w}) = (\mathbf{u} + \mathbf{v}) + \mathbf{w}$	*associative for addition*
2. $\mathbf{u} + \mathbf{v} = \mathbf{v} + \mathbf{u}$	*commutative*
3. $\mathbf{v} + \mathbf{0} = \mathbf{v} = \mathbf{0} + \mathbf{v}$	*additive identity*
4. $\mathbf{v} + (-\mathbf{v}) = \mathbf{0}$	*additive inverse*
5. $r(\mathbf{u} + \mathbf{v}) = r\mathbf{u} + r\mathbf{v}$	*distributive*
6. $(r + s)\mathbf{v} = r\mathbf{v} + s\mathbf{v}$	*distributive*
7. $(rs)\mathbf{v} = r(s\mathbf{v}) = s(r\mathbf{v})$	*associative for multiplication*
8. $1\mathbf{v} = \mathbf{v}$	*multiplicative identity*
9. $0\mathbf{v} = \mathbf{0}$ and $r\mathbf{0} = \mathbf{0}$	*multiplication by 0*

Proof Let $\mathbf{u} = \langle a, b\rangle$ and $\mathbf{v} = \langle c, d\rangle$. Addition of real numbers is commutative; therefore,

$$\begin{aligned} \mathbf{u} + \mathbf{v} &= \langle a, b\rangle + \langle c, d\rangle \\ &= \langle a + c, b + d\rangle \\ &= \langle c + a, d + b\rangle \\ &= \langle c, d\rangle + \langle a, b\rangle \\ &= \mathbf{v} + \mathbf{u} \end{aligned}$$

The other properties are proved similarly. See Exercises 26–31.

Exercises 10.5

In Exercises 1–4, find the magnitude of the vector $\overrightarrow{PQ}$.

1. $P = (2, 3), Q = (5, 9)$

2. $P = (-3, 5), Q = (7, -11)$

3. $P = (-7, 0), Q = (-4, -5)$

4. $P = (30, 12), Q = (25, 5)$

In Exercises 5–10, find a vector equivalent to the vector $\overrightarrow{PQ}$ with its initial point at the origin.

5. $P = (1, 5), Q = (7, 11)$

6. $P = (2, 7), Q = (-2, 9)$

7. $P = (-4, -8), Q = (-10, 2)$

8. $P = (-5, 6), Q = (-7, -9)$

9. $P = \left(\frac{4}{5}, -2\right), Q = \left(\frac{17}{5}, -\frac{12}{5}\right)$

10. $P = \left(\sqrt{2}, 4\right), Q = \left(\sqrt{3}, -1\right)$

In Exercises 11–15, find $u + v$, $u - v$, and $3u - 2v$.

11. $u = \langle -2, 4 \rangle, v = \langle 6, 1 \rangle$

12. $u = \langle 4, 0 \rangle, v = \langle 1, -3 \rangle$

13. $u = \langle 3, 3\sqrt{2} \rangle, v = \langle 4\sqrt{2}, 1 \rangle$

14. $u = \left\langle \frac{2}{3}, 4 \right\rangle, v = \left\langle -7, \frac{19}{3} \right\rangle$

15. $u = 2\langle -2, 5 \rangle, v = \frac{1}{4}\langle -7, 12 \rangle$

In Exercises 16–23, let $u = \langle 3, 1 \rangle, v = \langle -8, 4 \rangle$, and $w = \langle -6, -2 \rangle$. Find the magnitude of each vector.

16. $u + v$

17. $u - v$

18. $3u + v$

19. $v + w$

20. $2(v - w)$

21. $-2(w + 2u)$

22. $u + \frac{1}{2}w$

23. $\frac{7}{6}v - \frac{2}{3}v$

If forces $u_1, u_2, \ldots, u_k$ act on an object at the origin, the resultant force is the sum $u_1 + u_2 + \cdots + u_k$. The forces are said to be in equilibrium if their resultant force is 0. In Exercises 24 and 25, find the resultant force and find an additional force v, which, if added to the system, produces equilibrium.

24. $u_1 = \langle 2, 5 \rangle, u_2 = \langle -6, 1 \rangle, u_3 = \langle -4, -8 \rangle$

25. $u_1 = \langle 3, 7 \rangle, u_2 = \langle 8, -2 \rangle, u_3 = \langle -9, 0 \rangle, u_4 = \langle -5, 4 \rangle$

In Exercises 26–31, let $u = \langle a, b \rangle, v = \langle c, d \rangle$ and $w = \langle e, f \rangle$, and let r and s be scalars. Prove that the stated property holds.

26. $v + 0 = v = 0 + v$

27. $v + (-v) = 0$

28. $r(u + v) = ru + rv$

29. $(r + s)v = rv + sv$

30. $(rs)v = r(sv) = s(rv)$

31. $1v = v$ and $0v = 0$

32. Let v be the vector with initial point (x_1, y_1) and terminal point (x_2, y_2) and let k be any real number.
   a. Find the component form of v and kv.
   b. Calculate $\|v\|$ and $\|kv\|$.
   c. Use the fact that $\sqrt{k^2} = |k|$ to verify the following equation: $\|kv\| = |k| \cdot \|v\|$

33. Let $u = \langle a, b \rangle$ and $v = \langle c, d \rangle$. Verify the accuracy of the two geometric interpretations of vector addition given on page 657 as follows:
   a. Show that the distance from (a, b) to $(a + c, b + d)$ is the same as $\|v\|$.
   b. Show that the distance from (c, d) to $(a + c, b + d)$ is the same as $\|u\|$.
   c. Show that the line through (a, b) and $(a + c, b + d)$ is parallel to v by showing that they have the same slope.
   d. Show that the line through (c, d) and $(a + c, b + d)$ is parallel to u.

34. Let $u = \langle a, b \rangle$ and $v = \langle c, d \rangle$. Show that $\|u - v\| = \|w\|$.

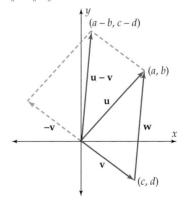

Applications of Vectors in the Plane

Objectives

- Perform operations with linear combinations of vectors
- Determine the direction angle of a vector
- Determine resultant forces in physical applications

In the previous section, vectors were introduced and vector arithmetic was defined. In this section, vectors are applied to real-world situations.

Unit Vectors

A vector with length 1 is called a **unit vector**. For instance, $\left\langle \frac{3}{5}, \frac{4}{5} \right\rangle$ is a unit vector because

$$\left\| \left\langle \frac{3}{5}, \frac{4}{5} \right\rangle \right\| = \sqrt{\left(\frac{3}{5}\right)^2 + \left(\frac{4}{5}\right)^2} = \sqrt{\frac{9}{25} + \frac{16}{25}} = \sqrt{\frac{25}{25}} = 1.$$

Example 1   Unit Vectors

Find a unit vector $\mathbf{u}$ with the same direction as the vector $\mathbf{v} = \langle 5, 12 \rangle$.

Solution

Multiplying vector $\mathbf{v}$ by a scalar that is the reciprocal of its length produces a unit vector. The length of $\mathbf{v}$ is

$$\|\mathbf{v}\| = \|\langle 5, 12 \rangle\| = \sqrt{5^2 + 12^2} = \sqrt{169} = 13.$$

Let

$$\mathbf{u} = \frac{1}{13}\mathbf{v} = \frac{1}{13}\langle 5, 12 \rangle = \left\langle \frac{5}{13}, \frac{12}{13} \right\rangle.$$

The vector $\mathbf{u} = \left\langle \frac{5}{13}, \frac{12}{13} \right\rangle$ is a unit vector because

$$\|\mathbf{u}\| = \left\| \frac{1}{13}\mathbf{v} \right\| = \left| \frac{1}{13} \right| \cdot \|\mathbf{v}\| = \frac{1}{13} \cdot 13 = 1$$

Multiplying a vector by a positive scalar produces a vector with the same direction. Thus, $\mathbf{u} = \left\langle \frac{5}{13}, \frac{12}{13} \right\rangle$ is a unit vector with the same direction as the vector $\mathbf{v} = \langle 5, 12 \rangle$.

Multiplying a vector by the reciprocal of its length to produce a unit vector, as in Example 1, works in the general case, as stated below.

Unit Vectors

> If v is a nonzero vector, then $\frac{1}{\|\mathbf{v}\|} \cdot$ v is a unit vector with the same direction as v.

Alternate Vector Notation

It can be verified that the vectors $\mathbf{i} = \langle 1, 0 \rangle$ and $\mathbf{j} = \langle 0, 1 \rangle$ are unit vectors. The vectors $\mathbf{i}$ and $\mathbf{j}$ play a special role because they lead to a useful alternate notation for vectors. For example, if $\mathbf{u} = \langle 5, -7 \rangle$, then

$$\mathbf{u} = \langle 5, 0 \rangle + \langle 0, -7 \rangle = 5\langle 1, 0 \rangle - 7\langle 0, 1 \rangle = 5\mathbf{i} - 7\mathbf{j}.$$

Similarly, if $\mathbf{v} = \langle a, b \rangle$ is any vector, then

$$\mathbf{v} = \langle a, b \rangle = \langle a, 0 \rangle + \langle 0, b \rangle = a\langle 1, 0 \rangle + b\langle 0, 1 \rangle = a\mathbf{i} + b\mathbf{j}.$$

The vector $\mathbf{v} = a\mathbf{i} + b\mathbf{j}$ is said to be a **linear combination** of $\mathbf{i}$ and $\mathbf{j}$. When vectors are written as linear combinations of $\mathbf{i}$ and $\mathbf{j}$, then the properties of vector addition and scalar multiplication, given in Section 10.5, can be used to write the rules for vector addition and scalar multiplication in terms of $\mathbf{i}$ and $\mathbf{j}$.

$$(a\mathbf{i} + b\mathbf{j}) + (c\mathbf{i} + d\mathbf{j}) = (a + c)\mathbf{i} + (b + d)\mathbf{j}$$

and

$$c(a\mathbf{i} + b\mathbf{j}) = ca\mathbf{i} + cb\mathbf{j}$$

Example 2   **Perform Operations with Linear Combinations**

If $\mathbf{u} = 2\mathbf{i} - 6\mathbf{j}$ and $\mathbf{v} = -5\mathbf{i} + 2\mathbf{j}$, find $3\mathbf{u} - 2\mathbf{v}$.

Solution

$$\begin{aligned}
3\mathbf{u} - 2\mathbf{v} &= 3(2\mathbf{i} - 6\mathbf{j}) - 2(-5\mathbf{i} + 2\mathbf{j}) \\
&= 6\mathbf{i} - 18\mathbf{j} + 10\mathbf{i} - 4\mathbf{j} \\
&= 16\mathbf{i} - 22\mathbf{j}
\end{aligned}$$

Direction Angles

If $\mathbf{v} = \langle a, b \rangle = a\mathbf{i} + b\mathbf{j}$ is a vector, then the direction of $\mathbf{v}$ is completely determined by the standard position angle θ between $0°$ and $360°$, whose terminal side is $\mathbf{v}$, as shown in Figure 10.6-1.

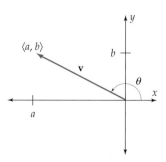

Figure 10.6-1

The angle θ is called the **direction angle** of the vector **v**. According to the definitions of the trigonometric functions,

$$\cos \theta = \frac{a}{\|\mathbf{v}\|} \quad \text{and} \quad \sin \theta = \frac{b}{\|\mathbf{v}\|}.$$

Rewriting each of these equations gives the following fact.

Components of the Direction Angle

If $\mathbf{v} = \langle a, b \rangle = a\mathbf{i} + b\mathbf{j}$, then

$$a = \|\mathbf{v}\| \cos \theta \quad \text{and} \quad b = \|\mathbf{v}\| \sin \theta$$

where θ is the direction angle of v.

Example 3 Find Velocity Vectors

Find the component form of the vector that represents the velocity of an airplane at the instant its wheels leave the ground, if the plane is going 60 miles per hour and the body of the plane makes a 7° angle with the horizontal.

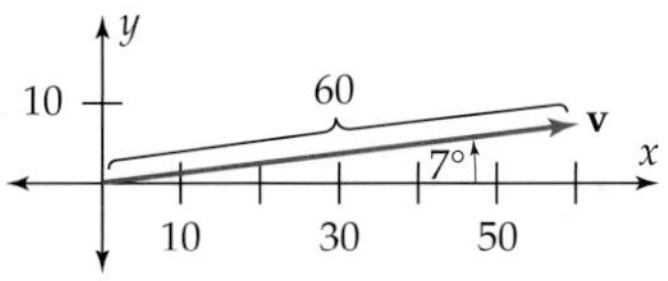

Figure 10.6-2

Solution

The velocity vector $\mathbf{v} = a\mathbf{i} + b\mathbf{j}$ has magnitude 60 and direction angle $\theta = 7°$, as shown in Figure 10.6-2. Therefore,

$$\begin{aligned}
\mathbf{v} &= (\|\mathbf{v}\| \cos \theta)\mathbf{i} + (\|\mathbf{v}\| \sin \theta)\mathbf{j} \\
&= (60 \cos 7°)\mathbf{i} + (60 \sin 7°)\mathbf{j} \\
&\approx 59.55\mathbf{i} + 7.31\mathbf{j} \\
&\approx \langle 59.55, 7.31 \rangle
\end{aligned}$$

If $\mathbf{v} = a\mathbf{i} + b\mathbf{j}$ is a nonzero vector with direction angle θ, then

$$\tan \theta = \frac{\sin \theta}{\cos \theta} = \frac{\dfrac{b}{\|\mathbf{v}\|}}{\dfrac{a}{\|\mathbf{v}\|}} = \frac{b}{a}.$$

This fact provides a convenient way to find the direction angle of a vector.

Figure 10.6-3

Example 4 Find Direction Angles

Find the direction angle of each vector.
a. $\mathbf{u} = 5\mathbf{i} + 13\mathbf{j}$ **b.** $\mathbf{v} = -10\mathbf{i} + 7\mathbf{j}$

Solution

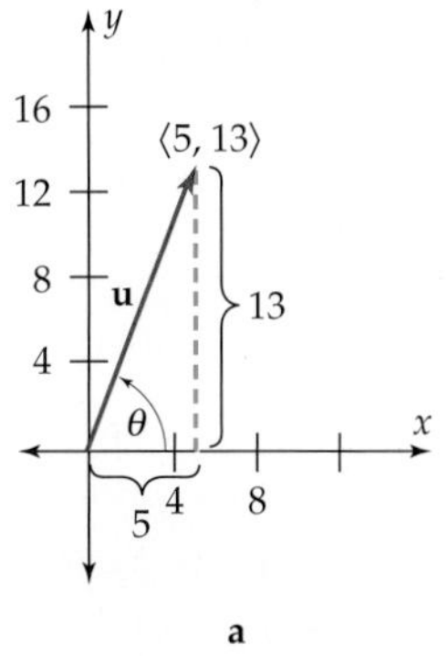

a. The direction angle θ of **u** satisfies

$$\tan \theta = \frac{b}{a} = \frac{13}{5} = 2.6.$$

Using the TAN^{-1} key on a calculator indicates that $\theta \approx 68.96°$. The vector **u** is shown in Figure 10.6-3.

b. The direction angle θ of **v** satisfies

$$\tan \theta = \frac{b}{a} = \frac{7}{-10} = -0.7.$$

Because **v** lies in the second quadrant, θ must be between 90° and 180°. A calculator shows that $t \approx -34.99°$ has a tangent that is approximately equal to -0.7. The period of tangent is 180°, so

$$\tan t = \tan(t + 180°)$$

for every t. Therefore,

$$\theta \approx -34.99° + 180° = 145.01°$$

is the angle between 90° and 180° such that $\tan \theta \approx -0.7$. The vector **v** is shown in Figure 10.6-4.

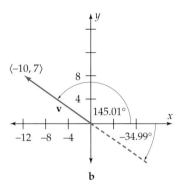

Figure 10.6-4

Vector Applications

A common application of vectors is in modeling a system of forces acting on an object. Every force has direction and magnitude, therefore, each can be represented by a vector. The sum of all the forces acting on an object is called the **resultant force.**

Example 5 Resultant Force

An object at the origin is acted upon by two forces. A 150-pound force makes an angle of 20° with the positive x-axis, and the other force of 100 pounds makes an angle of 70° with the positive x-axis, as shown in Figure 10.6-5. Find the direction and magnitude of the resultant force.

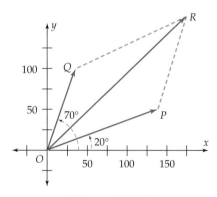

Figure 10.6-5

Solution

The forces acting upon the object are:

$$\overrightarrow{OP} = (150 \cos 20°)\mathbf{i} + (150 \sin 20°)\mathbf{j}$$
$$\overrightarrow{OQ} = (100 \cos 70°)\mathbf{i} + (100 \sin 70°)\mathbf{j}$$

The resultant force $\overrightarrow{OR}$ is the sum of $\overrightarrow{OP}$ and $\overrightarrow{OQ}$.

$$\overrightarrow{OR} = (150 \cos 20°)\mathbf{i} + (150 \sin 20°)\mathbf{j} + (100 \cos 70°)\mathbf{i} + (100 \sin 70°)\mathbf{j}$$
$$\overrightarrow{OR} \approx 175.16\mathbf{i} + 145.27\mathbf{j}$$

The magnitude of the resultant force $\overrightarrow{OR}$ is

$$\|\overrightarrow{OR}\| \approx \sqrt{175.16^2 + 145.27^2} \approx 227.56.$$

The direction angle θ of the resultant force satisfies

$$\tan \theta \approx \frac{145.27}{175.16} \approx 0.8294$$

A calculator in degree mode shows that $\theta \approx 39.67°$. ∎

Example 6 Resultant Force

A 200-pound box lies on a ramp that makes an angle of 24° with the horizontal. A rope is tied to the box from a post at the top of the ramp to keep it in position (see Figure 10.6-6). Ignoring friction, how much force is being exerted on the rope by the box?

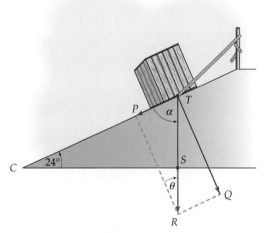

Figure 10.6-6

Solution

Because of gravity, the box exerts a 200-pound weight straight down (vector $\overrightarrow{TR}$). As Figure 10.6-6 shows, $\overrightarrow{TR}$ is the sum of $\overrightarrow{TP}$ and $\overrightarrow{TQ}$. The force on the rope is represented by $\overrightarrow{TP}$, the vector of the force pulling the box down the ramp, and $\|\overrightarrow{TP}\|$ represents the magnitude of the force.

In right triangle TSC, $\alpha + 24° = 90°$, and in right triangle TRP, $\alpha + \theta = 90°$. Therefore,

$$\alpha + \theta = \alpha + 24°$$
$$\theta = 24°$$

The box weighs 200 pounds, so $\|\overrightarrow{TR}\| = 200$. Use $\sin \theta$ to find $\|\overrightarrow{TP}\|$.

$$\sin \theta = \frac{\|\overrightarrow{TP}\|}{\|\overrightarrow{TR}\|}$$

$$\sin 24° = \frac{\|\overrightarrow{TP}\|}{200}$$

$$\|\overrightarrow{TP}\| = 200 \sin 24° \approx 81.35$$

The force on the rope is about 81.35 pounds.

◼

Example 7   Resultant Force

An airplane is traveling in the direction 50° with an air speed of 300 miles per hour, and there is a 35-mile-per-hour wind from the direction 120°, as represented by the vectors **p** and **w** in Figures 10.6-7, which shows the angles using aerial navigation orientation. Find the *course* and *ground speed* of the plane (that is, its direction and speed relative to the ground).

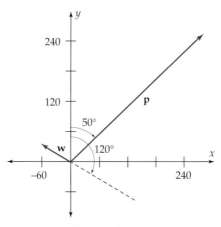

Figure 10.6-7

Solution

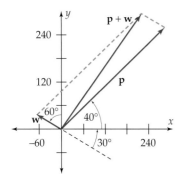

Figure 10.6-8

Figure 10.6-8 shows **p**, **w**, and **p** + **w**. The course of the plane is the direction angle of the vector **p** + **w**, and its ground speed is the magnitude of **p** + **w**.

The direction angle of **p** (the angle it makes with the positive x-axis) is $90° - 50° = 40°$. The angle that **w** makes with the positive y-axis is

$180° − 120° = 60°$, so the direction angle of **w**, as measured from the positive x-axis, is $60° + 90° = 150°$. Therefore,

$$\mathbf{p} = (300 \cos 40°)\mathbf{i} + (300 \sin 40°)\mathbf{j}$$
$$\mathbf{w} = (35 \cos 150°)\mathbf{i} + (35 \sin 150°)\mathbf{j}$$
$$\mathbf{p} + \mathbf{w} = [(300 \cos 40°)\mathbf{i} + (300 \sin 40°)\mathbf{j}] + [(35 \cos 150°)\mathbf{i}$$
$$+ (35 \sin 150°)\mathbf{j}]$$
$$= (300 \cos 40° + 35 \cos 150°)\mathbf{i} + (300 \sin 40° + 35 \sin 150°)\mathbf{j}$$
$$\approx 199.50\mathbf{i} + 210.34\mathbf{j}$$

The direction angle of $\mathbf{p} + \mathbf{w}$ is

$$\tan \theta = \frac{210.34}{199.50}$$
$$\tan \theta \approx 1.0543$$
$$\theta \approx 46.5°$$

The course of the plane is the angle between $\mathbf{p} + \mathbf{w}$ and true north.

$$90° − 46.5° = 43.5°$$

The ground speed of the plane is $\|\mathbf{p} + \mathbf{w}\|$.

$$\|\mathbf{p} + \mathbf{w}\| = \sqrt{199.50^2 + 210.34^2} \approx 289.9$$

Thus, the plane's course is about $43.5°$ and its ground speed is about 289.9 miles per hour.

■

Exercises 10.6

In Exercises 1–5, find $\mathbf{u} + \mathbf{v}$, $\mathbf{u} − \mathbf{v}$, and $3\mathbf{u} − 2\mathbf{v}$.

1. $\mathbf{u} = \mathbf{i} − \mathbf{j}, \mathbf{v} = 2\mathbf{i} + \mathbf{j}$

2. $\mathbf{u} = 8\mathbf{i}, \mathbf{v} = 2(3\mathbf{i} − 2\mathbf{j})$

3. $\mathbf{u} = −4(−\mathbf{i} + \mathbf{j}), \mathbf{v} = −3\mathbf{i}$

4. $\mathbf{u} = −\left(2\mathbf{i} + \frac{3}{2}\mathbf{j}\right), \mathbf{v} = \frac{3}{4}\mathbf{i}$

5. $\mathbf{u} = \sqrt{2}\mathbf{j}, \mathbf{v} = \sqrt{3}\mathbf{i}$

In Exercises 6–11, find the components of the given vector, where $\mathbf{u} = \mathbf{i} − 2\mathbf{j}$, $\mathbf{v} = 3\mathbf{i} + \mathbf{j}$, and $\mathbf{w} = −4\mathbf{i} + \mathbf{j}$.

6. $\mathbf{u} + 2\mathbf{w}$

7. $\frac{1}{2}(3\mathbf{v} + \mathbf{w})$

8. $\frac{1}{2}\mathbf{w}$

9. $−2\mathbf{u} + 3\mathbf{v}$

10. $\frac{1}{4}(8\mathbf{u} + 4\mathbf{v} − \mathbf{w})$

11. $3(\mathbf{u} − 2\mathbf{v}) − 6\mathbf{w}$

In Exercises 12–19, find the component form of the vector v whose magnitude and direction angle θ are given.

12. $\|\mathbf{v}\| = 4, \theta = 0°$

13. $\|\mathbf{v}\| = 5, \theta = 30°$

14. $\|\mathbf{v}\| = 10, \theta = 225°$

15. $\|\mathbf{v}\| = 20, \theta = 120°$

16. $\|\mathbf{v}\| = 6, \theta = 40°$

17. $\|\mathbf{v}\| = 8, \theta = 160°$

18. $\|\mathbf{v}\| = \frac{1}{2}, \theta = 250°$

19. $\|\mathbf{v}\| = 3, \theta = 310°$

In Exercises 20–27, find the magnitude and direction angle of the vector v.

20. $\mathbf{v} = \langle 4, 4 \rangle$

21. $\mathbf{v} = \langle 5, 5\sqrt{3} \rangle$

22. $\mathbf{v} = \langle −8, 0 \rangle$

23. $\mathbf{v} = \langle 4, 5 \rangle$

24. $\mathbf{v} = 6\mathbf{j}$

25. $\mathbf{v} = 4\mathbf{i} − 8\mathbf{j}$

26. $\mathbf{v} = −2\mathbf{i} + 8\mathbf{j}$

27. $\mathbf{v} = −15\mathbf{i} − 10\mathbf{j}$

In Exercises 28–31, find a unit vector that has the same direction as the given vector.

28. $\langle 4, -5 \rangle$ **29.** $-7\mathbf{i} + 8\mathbf{j}$

30. $5\mathbf{i} + 10\mathbf{j}$ **31.** $-3\mathbf{i} - 9\mathbf{j}$

In Exercises 32–35, an object at the origin is acted upon by two forces **u** and **v**, with direction angle θ_u and θ_v, respectively. Find the direction and magnitude of the resultant force.

32. $\mathbf{u} = 30$ pounds, $\theta_u = 0°$; $\mathbf{v} = 90$ pounds, $\theta_v = 60°$

33. $\mathbf{u} = 6$ pounds, $\theta_u = 45°$; $\mathbf{v} = 6$ pounds, $\theta_v = 120°$

34. $\mathbf{u} = 12$ kilograms, $\theta_u = 130°$; $\mathbf{v} = 20$ kilograms, $\theta_v = 250°$

35. $\mathbf{u} = 30$ kilograms, $\theta_u = 300°$; $\mathbf{v} = 80$ kilograms, $\theta_v = 40°$

36. Two ropes are tied to a wagon. A child pulls one with a force of 20 pounds, while another child pulls the other with a force of 30 pounds. See the figure. If the angle between the two ropes is 28°, how much force must be exerted by a third child, standing behind the wagon, to keep the wagon from moving? *Hint:* Assume the wagon is at the origin and one rope runs along the positive x-axis. Proceed as in Example 5 to find the resultant force on the wagon from the ropes. The third child must use the same amount in the opposite direction.

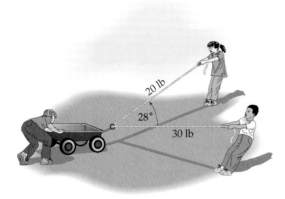

37. Two circus elephants, Bessie and Maybelle, are dragging a large wagon, as shown in the figure. If Bessie pulls with a force of 2200 pounds and Maybelle with a force of 1500 pounds and the wagon moves along the dashed line, what is angle θ?

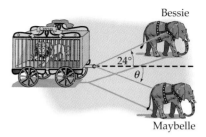

Exercises 38–41 deal with an object on an inclined plane. The situation is similar to that in Figure 10.6-6 of Example 6, where $\|\overrightarrow{TP}\|$ is the component of the weight of the object parallel to the plane and $\|\overrightarrow{TQ}\|$ is the component of the weight perpendicular to the plane.

38. An object weighing 50 pounds lies on an inclined plane that makes a 40° angle with the horizontal. Find the components of the weight parallel and perpendicular to the plane. *Hint:* Solve an appropriate triangle.

39. Do Exercise 38 when the object weighs 200 pounds and the inclined plane makes a 20° angle with the horizontal.

40. If an object on an inclined plane weighs 150 pounds and the component of the weight perpendicular to the plane is 60 pounds, what angle does the plane make with the horizontal?

41. A force of 500 pounds is needed to pull a cart up a ramp that makes a 15° angle with the ground. Assuming that no friction is involved, find the weight of the cart. *Hint:* Draw a picture similar to Figure 10.6-6; the 500-pound force is parallel to the ramp.

In Exercises 42–47, find the course and ground speed of the plane under the given conditions. See Example 7. All angle measurements are given as aerial navigation directions. See Exercise 55 of Section 6.2.

42. air speed 250 miles per hour in the direction 60°; wind speed 40 miles per hour from the direction 330°

43. air speed 400 miles per hour in the direction 150°; wind speed 30 miles per hour from the direction 60°

44. air speed 300 miles per hour in the direction 300°; wind speed 50 miles per hour in (not from) the direction 30°

45. air speed 500 miles per hour in the direction 180°; wind speed 70 miles per hour in the direction 40°

46. The course and ground speed of a plane are 70° and 400 miles per hour respectively. There is a 60-mile-per-hour wind blowing south. Find the approximate direction and air speed of the plane.

47. A plane is flying in the direction 200° with an air speed of 500 miles per hour. Its course and ground speed are 210° and 450 miles per hour, respectively. What is the direction and speed of the wind?

48. A river flows from east to west. A swimmer on the south bank wants to swim to a point on the opposite shore directly north of her starting point. She can swim at 2.8 miles per hour, and there is a 1-mile-per-hour current in the river. In what direction should she swim in order to travel directly north (that is, what angle should her path make with the south bank of the river)?

49. A river flows from west to east. A swimmer on the north bank swims at 3.1 miles per hour along a straight course that makes a 75° angle with the north bank of the river and reaches the south bank at a point directly south of his starting point. How fast is the current in the river?

50. A 400-pound weight is suspended by two cables (see the following figure). What is the force (tension) on each cable? *Hint:* Imagine that the weight is at the origin and that the dashed line is the x-axis. Then cable **v** is represented by the vector

$$(c \cos 65°)\mathbf{i} + (c \sin 65°)\mathbf{j}$$

which has magnitude c. (Why?) Represent cable **u** similarly, denoting its magnitude as d. Use the fact that $\mathbf{u} + \mathbf{v} = 0\mathbf{i} + 400\mathbf{j}$ (why?) to set up a system of two equations in the unknowns c and d.

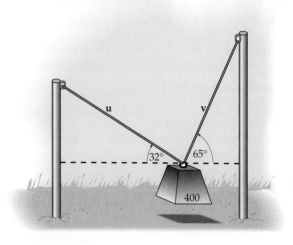

51. A 175-pound high-wire artist stands balanced on a tightrope, which sags slightly at the point where he is standing. The rope in front of him makes a 6° angle with the horizontal and the rope behind him makes a 4° angle with the horizontal. Find the force on each end of the rope. *Hint:* Use a picture and procedure similar to that in Exercise 50.

52. Let **v** be the vector with initial point (x_1, y_1) and terminal point (x_2, y_2), and let k be any real number.
   a. Show that $\tan \theta = \tan \beta$ where θ is the direction angle of **v** and β is the direction angle of $k\mathbf{v}$. Use the fact that $\tan t = \tan(t + 180°)$ to conclude that **v** and $k\mathbf{v}$ have either the same or opposite directions.
   b. Use the fact that (c, d) and $(-c, -d)$ lie on the same straight line on opposite sides of the origin to verify that **v** and $k\mathbf{v}$ have the same direction if $k > 0$ and opposite directions if $k < 0$.

53. Let $\mathbf{u} = \langle a, b \rangle$ and $\mathbf{v} = \langle c, d \rangle$. In Exercise 34 of Section 10.5, $\|\mathbf{u} - \mathbf{v}\| = \|\mathbf{w}\|$ was shown (see the figure with Exercise 34 of Section 10.5). Show that $\mathbf{u} - \mathbf{v}$ is equivalent to the vector **w** with initial point (c, d) and terminal point (a, b) by now showing that $\mathbf{u} - \mathbf{v}$ and **w** have the same direction.

10.6.A

Excursion: The Dot Product

Objectives

- Find the dot product of two vectors and the angle between two vectors

- Determine projection and component vectors and use them in physical applications

Unlike multiplication of real numbers where there is only one type of multiplication, vector operations include three types of multiplication: scalar multiplication, dot products, and cross products. This section discusses the vector operation called the **dot product.** Unlike scalar multiplication of vectors, the dot product is not a vector.

The dot product of two vectors is a *real number.*

Dot Product
○

The *dot product* of vectors $\mathbf{u} = \langle a, b \rangle = a\mathbf{i} + b\mathbf{j}$ and $\mathbf{v} = \langle c, d \rangle = c\mathbf{i} + d\mathbf{j}$ is denoted $\mathbf{u} \cdot \mathbf{v}$ and is defined to be the real number $ac + bd$. Thus,

$$\mathbf{u} \cdot \mathbf{v} = ac + bd.$$

NOTE The dot product of two vectors is found by multiplying corresponding components and finding the sum of the products.

Example 1 Find Dot Product of Two Vectors

Find the dot product $\mathbf{u} \cdot \mathbf{v}$ for the given vectors $\mathbf{u}$ and $\mathbf{v}$.

a. $\mathbf{u} = \langle 5, 3 \rangle$ and $\mathbf{v} = \langle -2, 6 \rangle$
b. $\mathbf{u} = 4\mathbf{i} - 2\mathbf{j}$ and $\mathbf{v} = 3\mathbf{i} - \mathbf{j}$
c. $\mathbf{u} = \langle 2, -4 \rangle$ and $\mathbf{v} = \langle 6, 3 \rangle$

Solution

a. $\mathbf{u} \cdot \mathbf{v} = \langle 5, 3 \rangle \cdot \langle -2, 6 \rangle = 5(-2) + 3(6) = 8$
b. $\mathbf{u} \cdot \mathbf{v} = (4\mathbf{i} - 2\mathbf{j}) \cdot (3\mathbf{i} - \mathbf{j}) = 4(3) + (-2)(-1) = 14$
c. $\mathbf{u} \cdot \mathbf{v} = \langle 2, -4 \rangle \cdot \langle 6, 3 \rangle = 2(6) + (-4)(3) = 0$

The dot product has a number of useful properties.

Properties of the Dot Product
○

If $\mathbf{u}$, $\mathbf{v}$, and $\mathbf{w}$ are vectors, and k is a real number, then:

1. $\mathbf{u} \cdot \mathbf{u} = \|\mathbf{u}\|^2$
2. $\mathbf{u} \cdot \mathbf{v} = \mathbf{v} \cdot \mathbf{u}$ *commutative*
3. $\mathbf{u} \cdot (\mathbf{v} + \mathbf{w}) = \mathbf{u} \cdot \mathbf{v} + \mathbf{u} \cdot \mathbf{w}$ *distributive*
4. $k\mathbf{u} \cdot \mathbf{v} = k(\mathbf{u} \cdot \mathbf{v}) = \mathbf{u} \cdot k\mathbf{v}$
5. $\mathbf{0} \cdot \mathbf{u} = 0$

Proof Let a, b, c, and d be real numbers.

1. If $\mathbf{u} = \langle a, b \rangle$, then $\|\mathbf{u}\| = \sqrt{a^2 + b^2}$. Therefore,

$$\mathbf{u} \cdot \mathbf{u} = \langle a, b \rangle \cdot \langle a, b \rangle = a(a) + b(b) = a^2 + b^2 = \left(\sqrt{a^2 + b^2} \right)^2 = \|\mathbf{u}\|^2.$$

2. If $\mathbf{u} = \langle a, b \rangle$ and $\mathbf{v} = \langle c, d \rangle$, then

$$\mathbf{u} \cdot \mathbf{v} = \langle a, b \rangle \cdot \langle c, d \rangle = ac + bd = ca + db = \langle c, d \rangle \cdot \langle a, b \rangle = \mathbf{v} \cdot \mathbf{u}.$$

The proofs of the last three statements are asked for in the exercises.

Angles Between Vectors

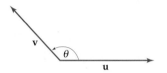

Figure 10.6.A-1

If $\mathbf{u} = \langle a, b \rangle$ and $\mathbf{v} = \langle c, d \rangle$ are any nonzero vectors, then **the angle between u and v** is the smallest angle θ formed by these two vectors, as shown in Figure 10.6.A-1. The clockwise or counterclockwise rotation is ignored, and the angle between $\mathbf{v}$ and $\mathbf{u}$ is considered to be the same as the angle between $\mathbf{u}$ and $\mathbf{v}$. Thus, the radian measure of θ is in the interval $[0, \pi]$.

Nonzero vectors $\mathbf{u}$ and $\mathbf{v}$ are said to be **parallel** if the angle between them is either 0 or π radians. In other words, $\mathbf{u}$ and $\mathbf{v}$ are parallel if they lie on the same straight line through the origin and have either the same or opposite directions. The zero vector $\mathbf{0}$ is considered to be parallel to every vector.

Any scalar multiple of $\mathbf{u}$ is parallel to $\mathbf{u}$ because it lies on the same straight line as $\mathbf{u}$. Conversely, if $\mathbf{v}$ is parallel to $\mathbf{u}$, it is easy to show that $\mathbf{v}$ must be a scalar multiple of $\mathbf{u}$. This is shown in the exercises.

Parallel Vectors

> Vectors **u** and **v** are parallel exactly when
>
> $$\mathbf{v} = k\mathbf{u}, \text{ for some real number } k.$$

Example 2   Determine Parallel Vectors

Determine whether the vectors $\mathbf{u} = \langle 2, 3 \rangle$ and $\mathbf{v} = \langle 8, 12 \rangle$ are parallel.

Solution

Vector $\mathbf{v}$ is a scalar multiple of $\mathbf{u}$.

$$\mathbf{v} = \langle 8, 12 \rangle = 4\langle 2, 3 \rangle = 4\mathbf{u}$$

Thus, vectors $\mathbf{u}$ and $\mathbf{v}$ are parallel.

The angle between nonzero vectors $\mathbf{u}$ and $\mathbf{v}$ is closely related to their dot product.

Angle Theorem

If θ is the angle between the nonzero vectors **u** and **v**, then

$$\mathbf{u} \cdot \mathbf{v} = \|\mathbf{u}\| \, \|\mathbf{v}\| \cos \theta,$$

or equivalently,

$$\cos \theta = \frac{\mathbf{u} \cdot \mathbf{v}}{\|\mathbf{u}\| \, \|\mathbf{v}\|}.$$

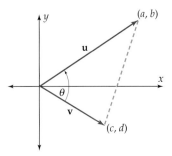

Figure 10.6.A-2

Proof Let a, b, c, and d be real numbers, and suppose that $\|\mathbf{u}\| \neq 0$ and $\|\mathbf{v}\| \neq 0$. If $\mathbf{u} = \langle a, b \rangle$, $\mathbf{v} = \langle c, d \rangle$, and the angle θ is not 0 or π, then **u** and **v** form two sides of a triangle, as shown in Figure 10.6.A-2.

The lengths of two sides of the triangle are $\|\mathbf{u}\| = \sqrt{a^2 + b^2}$ and $\|\mathbf{v}\| = \sqrt{c^2 + d^2}$. The distance formula shows that the length of the third side (opposite angle θ) is $\sqrt{(a - c)^2 + (b - d)^2}$. Therefore, the Law of Cosines produces the following result.

$$\left[\sqrt{(a - c)^2 + (b - d)^2} \right]^2 = \|\mathbf{u}\|^2 + \|\mathbf{v}\|^2 - 2\|\mathbf{u}\| \, \|\mathbf{v}\| \cos \theta$$
$$(a - c)^2 + (b - d)^2 = (a^2 + b^2) + (c^2 + d^2) - 2\|\mathbf{u}\| \, \|\mathbf{v}\| \cos \theta$$
$$a^2 - 2ac + c^2 + b^2 - 2bd + d^2 = a^2 + b^2 + c^2 + d^2 - 2\|\mathbf{u}\| \, \|\mathbf{v}\| \cos \theta$$
$$-2ac - 2bd = -2\|\mathbf{u}\| \, \|\mathbf{v}\| \cos \theta$$
$$-2(ac + bd) = -2\|\mathbf{u}\| \, \|\mathbf{v}\| \cos \theta$$
$$ac + bd = \|\mathbf{u}\| \, \|\mathbf{v}\| \cos \theta$$
$$\mathbf{u} \cdot \mathbf{v} = \|\mathbf{u}\| \, \|\mathbf{v}\| \cos \theta \qquad \mathbf{u} \cdot \mathbf{v} = ac + bd$$
$$\frac{\mathbf{u} \cdot \mathbf{v}}{\|\mathbf{u}\| \|\mathbf{v}\|} = \cos \theta \qquad \blacksquare$$

The proof when θ is 0 or π is exercise 41.

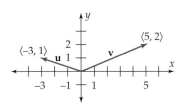

Figure 10.6.A-3

Example 3   Find the Angle Between Vectors

Find the angle θ between the vectors $\langle -3, 1 \rangle$ and $\langle 5, 2 \rangle$, which are shown in Figure 10.6.A-3.

Solution

Apply the formula from the Angle Theorem with $\mathbf{u} = \langle -3, 1 \rangle$ and $\mathbf{v} = \langle 5, 2 \rangle$.

$$\cos \theta = \frac{\mathbf{u} \cdot \mathbf{v}}{\|\mathbf{u}\| \|\mathbf{v}\|} = \frac{(-3)(5) + 1(2)}{(\sqrt{(-3)^2 + 1^2})(\sqrt{5^2 + 2^2})} = \frac{-13}{\sqrt{10}\,\sqrt{29}} = \frac{-13}{\sqrt{290}}$$

Using the $\mathbf{COS}^{-1}$ key shows that

$$\theta \approx 2.4393 \text{ radians, or } \approx 139.76°.$$

$\blacksquare$

The Angle Theorem has several useful consequences. For instance, taking the absolute value of each side of $\mathbf{u} \cdot \mathbf{v} = \|\mathbf{u}\| \, \|\mathbf{v}\| \cos \theta$, and using the fact that $|\|\mathbf{u}\|\,\|\mathbf{v}\|| = \|\mathbf{u}\|\,\|\mathbf{v}\|$ (because $\|\mathbf{u}\|\,\|\mathbf{v}\|$ is always positive), produces the following results.

$$|\mathbf{u}\cdot\mathbf{v}| = |\,\|\mathbf{u}\|\,\|\mathbf{v}\|\cos\theta\,| = |\,\|\mathbf{u}\|\,\|\mathbf{v}\|\,|\,|\cos\theta| = \|\mathbf{u}\|\,\|\mathbf{v}\|\,|\cos\theta|$$

For any angle θ, $|\cos\theta| \le 1$; therefore,

$$|\mathbf{u}\cdot\mathbf{v}| = \|\mathbf{u}\|\,\|\mathbf{v}\|\,|\cos\theta| \le \|\mathbf{u}\|\,\|\mathbf{v}\|.$$

This proves the Schwarz inequality.

Schwarz Inequality

For any vectors u and v,
$$|\mathbf{u}\cdot\mathbf{v}| \le \|\mathbf{u}\|\,\|\mathbf{v}\|.$$

Vectors **u** and **v** are said to be **orthogonal** (or perpendicular) if the angle between them is $\frac{\pi}{2}$ radians (90°), or if at least one of them is **0**. The key fact about orthogonal vectors follows.

Orthogonal Vectors

Let u and v be vectors. Then
u and **v** are orthogonal exactly when $\mathbf{u}\cdot\mathbf{v} = 0$.

Proof If **u** or **v** is 0, then $\mathbf{u}\cdot\mathbf{v} = 0$. If **u** and **v** are nonzero orthogonal vectors, then by the Angle Theorem:

$$\mathbf{u}\cdot\mathbf{v} = \|\mathbf{u}\|\,\|\mathbf{v}\|\cos\theta = \|\mathbf{u}\|\,\|\mathbf{v}\|\cos\frac{\pi}{2} = \|\mathbf{u}\|\,\|\mathbf{v}\|(0) = 0$$

Conversely, if **u** and **v** are vectors such that $\mathbf{u}\cdot\mathbf{v} = 0$, then Exercise 42 asks for a proof that **u** and **v** are orthogonal. ∎

Example 4　Find Orthogonal Vectors

Determine whether the given vectors are orthogonal.

a. $\mathbf{u} = \langle 2,-6\rangle$ and $\mathbf{v} = \langle 9,3\rangle$ 　　**b.** $\mathbf{u} = \frac{1}{2}\mathbf{i} + 5\mathbf{j}$ and $\mathbf{v} = 10\mathbf{i} - \mathbf{j}$

Solution

a. $\mathbf{u}\cdot\mathbf{v} = \langle 2,-6\rangle\cdot\langle 9,3\rangle$ 　　**b.** $\mathbf{u}\cdot\mathbf{v} = \left(\frac{1}{2}\mathbf{i}+5\mathbf{j}\right)\cdot(10\mathbf{i}-\mathbf{j})$

$$= 2(9)+(-6)(3) \qquad\qquad = \frac{1}{2}(10)+5(-1)$$

$$= 18 - 18 = 0 \qquad\qquad = 5 - 5 = 0$$

Vectors **u** and **v** are orthogonal.　　Vectors **u** and **v** are orthogonal.

Projections and Components

If **u** and **v** are nonzero vectors, and θ is the angle between them, construct the perpendicular line segment from the terminal point P of **u** to the straight line on which **v** lies. This perpendicular segment intersects the line at a point Q. The three possibilities are shown in Figure 10.6.A-4.

The vector $\overrightarrow{OQ}$ is called the **projection of u onto v** and is denoted $\text{proj}_v\mathbf{u}$. A useful description of $\text{proj}_v\mathbf{u}$ follows.

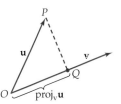 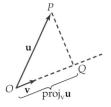 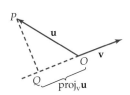

Figure 10.6.A-4

Projection of u *onto* v

If u and v are nonzero vectors, then the projection of u onto v is the vector

$$\text{proj}_v\mathbf{u} = \left(\frac{\mathbf{u}\cdot\mathbf{v}}{\|\mathbf{v}\|^2}\right)\mathbf{v}.$$

Proof Because $\text{proj}_v\mathbf{u}$ and **v** lie on the same straight line, they are parallel. Therefore, $\text{proj}_v\mathbf{u} = k\mathbf{v}$ for some real number k. Construct the orthogonal vector from a point Q on **v** through point P, the terminal point of **u**. Let **w** be the vector with its initial point at the origin and the same length and direction as $\overrightarrow{QP}$, as in the two cases shown in Figure 10.6.A-5.

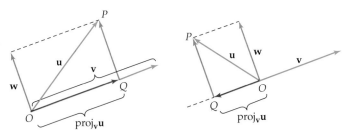

Figure 10.6.A-5

Because **w** is parallel to $\overrightarrow{QP}$ it is orthogonal to **v**. As shown in Figure 10.6.A-5, $\mathbf{u} = \text{proj}_v\mathbf{u} + \mathbf{w} = k\mathbf{v} + \mathbf{w}$. Consequently, by the properties of the dot product:

$$\mathbf{u} \cdot \mathbf{v} = (k\mathbf{v} + \mathbf{w}) \cdot \mathbf{v} \qquad \textit{substitution}$$
$$= (k\mathbf{v}) \cdot \mathbf{v} + \mathbf{w} \cdot \mathbf{v} \qquad \textit{distributive}$$
$$= k(\mathbf{v} \cdot \mathbf{v}) + \mathbf{w} \cdot \mathbf{v}$$
$$= k\|\mathbf{v}\|^2 + \mathbf{w} \cdot \mathbf{v} \qquad \mathbf{v} \cdot \mathbf{v} = \|\mathbf{v}\|^2$$

But $\mathbf{w} \cdot \mathbf{v} = 0$ because $\mathbf{w}$ and $\mathbf{v}$ are orthogonal. So,

$$\mathbf{u} \cdot \mathbf{v} = k\|\mathbf{v}\|^2 \quad \text{or equivalently,} \quad k = \frac{\mathbf{u} \cdot \mathbf{v}}{\|\mathbf{v}\|^2}.$$

Finally, multiplying both sides of the last statement by $\mathbf{v}$, and substituting $\text{proj}_\mathbf{v}\mathbf{u}$ for $k\mathbf{v}$, the desired result is proved.

$$\text{proj}_\mathbf{v}\mathbf{u} = k\mathbf{v} = \left(\frac{\mathbf{u} \cdot \mathbf{v}}{\|\mathbf{v}\|^2}\right)\mathbf{v} \qquad ■$$

Example 5   Find Projection Vectors

If $\mathbf{u} = 8\mathbf{i} + 3\mathbf{j}$ and $\mathbf{v} = 4\mathbf{i} - 2\mathbf{j}$, find $\text{proj}_\mathbf{v}\mathbf{u}$ and $\text{proj}_\mathbf{u}\mathbf{v}$.

Solution

$$\mathbf{u} \cdot \mathbf{v} = 8(4) + 3(-2) = 26 = \mathbf{v} \cdot \mathbf{u}$$
$$\|\mathbf{v}\|^2 = \mathbf{v} \cdot \mathbf{v} = 4^2 + (-2)^2 = 20 \quad \text{and} \quad \|\mathbf{u}\|^2 = \mathbf{u} \cdot \mathbf{u} = 8^2 + 3^2 = 73$$

Therefore,

$$\text{proj}_\mathbf{v}\mathbf{u} = \left(\frac{\mathbf{u} \cdot \mathbf{v}}{\|\mathbf{v}\|^2}\right)\mathbf{v} = \left(\frac{26}{20}\right)(4\mathbf{i} - 2\mathbf{j}) = \frac{26}{5}\mathbf{i} - \frac{13}{5}\mathbf{j}$$

and

$$\text{proj}_\mathbf{u}\mathbf{v} = \left(\frac{\mathbf{v} \cdot \mathbf{u}}{\|\mathbf{u}\|^2}\right)\mathbf{u} = \left(\frac{26}{73}\right)(8\mathbf{i} + 3\mathbf{j}) = \frac{208}{73}\mathbf{i} + \frac{78}{73}\mathbf{j} \qquad ■$$

The projection vectors from Example 5 are shown in Figure 10.6.A-6.

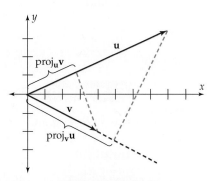

Figure 10.6.A-6

Projections and Components

Recall from Section 10.6 that $\dfrac{1}{\|\mathbf{v}\|}\mathbf{v}$ is a unit vector in the direction of $\mathbf{v}$. Then, $\text{proj}_\mathbf{v}\mathbf{u}$ can be expressed as a scalar multiple of this unit vector.

$$\text{proj}_\mathbf{v}\mathbf{u} = \left(\frac{\mathbf{u}\cdot\mathbf{v}}{\|\mathbf{v}\|^2}\right)\mathbf{v} = \left(\frac{\mathbf{u}\cdot\mathbf{v}}{\|\mathbf{v}\|}\right)\left(\frac{1}{\|\mathbf{v}\|}\mathbf{v}\right)$$

The scalar $\dfrac{\mathbf{u}\cdot\mathbf{v}}{\|\mathbf{v}\|}$ is called the **component of u along v**, and is denoted $\text{comp}_\mathbf{v}\mathbf{u}$.

$$\text{proj}_\mathbf{v}\mathbf{u} = \left(\frac{\mathbf{u}\cdot\mathbf{v}}{\|\mathbf{v}\|}\right)\left(\frac{1}{\|\mathbf{v}\|}\mathbf{v}\right) = \text{comp}_\mathbf{v}\mathbf{u}\left(\frac{1}{\|\mathbf{v}\|}\mathbf{v}\right)$$

Because $\dfrac{1}{\|\mathbf{v}\|}\mathbf{v}$ is a unit vector, it can be used to find the length of $\text{proj}_\mathbf{v}\mathbf{u}$.

$$\|\text{proj}_\mathbf{v}\mathbf{u}\| = \left\|\text{comp}_\mathbf{v}\mathbf{u}\left(\frac{1}{\|\mathbf{v}\|}\mathbf{v}\right)\right\| = |\text{comp}_\mathbf{v}\mathbf{u}|\left\|\left(\frac{1}{\|\mathbf{v}\|}\mathbf{v}\right)\right\| = |\text{comp}_\mathbf{v}\mathbf{u}|.$$

Also, because $\mathbf{u}\cdot\mathbf{v} = \|\mathbf{u}\|\,\|\mathbf{v}\|\cos\theta$, where θ is the angle between $\mathbf{u}$ and $\mathbf{v}$,

$$\begin{aligned}\text{comp}_\mathbf{v}\mathbf{u} &= \frac{\mathbf{u}\cdot\mathbf{v}}{\|\mathbf{v}\|}\\ &= \frac{\|\mathbf{u}\|\,\|\mathbf{v}\|\cos\theta}{\|\mathbf{v}\|}\\ &= \|\mathbf{u}\|\cos\theta\end{aligned}$$

This result is stated formally as follows.

Projections and Components

> If $\mathbf{u}$ and $\mathbf{v}$ are nonzero vectors, and θ is the angle between them, then
>
> $$\text{comp}_\mathbf{v}\mathbf{u} = \frac{\mathbf{u}\cdot\mathbf{v}}{\|\mathbf{v}\|} = \|\mathbf{u}\|\cos\theta$$
>
> and
>
> $$\|\text{proj}_\mathbf{v}\mathbf{u}\| = |\,\text{comp}_\mathbf{v}\mathbf{u}\,|.$$

Example 6 **Find Component Vectors**

If $\mathbf{u} = 2\mathbf{i} + 3\mathbf{j}$ and $\mathbf{v} = -5\mathbf{i} + 2\mathbf{j}$, find $\text{comp}_\mathbf{v}\mathbf{u}$ and $\text{comp}_\mathbf{u}\mathbf{v}$.

Solution

$$\mathbf{u}\cdot\mathbf{v} = 2(-5) + 3(2) = -4 = \mathbf{v}\cdot\mathbf{u}$$
$$\|\mathbf{v}\| = \sqrt{(-5)^2 + 2^2} = \sqrt{29} \quad\text{and}\quad \|\mathbf{u}\| = \sqrt{2^2 + 3^2} = \sqrt{13}$$

Therefore,

$$\text{comp}_\mathbf{v}\mathbf{u} = \frac{\mathbf{u} \cdot \mathbf{v}}{\|\mathbf{v}\|} = \frac{-4}{\sqrt{29}} \quad \text{and} \quad \text{comp}_\mathbf{u}\mathbf{v} = \frac{\mathbf{v} \cdot \mathbf{u}}{\|\mathbf{u}\|} = \frac{-4}{\sqrt{13}}$$

Applications

Vectors and the dot product can be used to solve a variety of problems.

Example 7   Find Forces Due to Gravity

A 4000-pound automobile is on an inclined ramp that makes a 15° angle with the horizontal. Find the force required to keep it from rolling down the ramp, assuming that the only force that must be overcome is that due to gravity.

Solution

The situation is shown in Figure 10.6.A-7, where the coordinate system is chosen so that the car is at the origin, the vector **F** representing the downward force of gravity is on the *y*-axis, and **v** is a unit vector from the origin down the ramp.

Because the car weighs 4000 pounds, $\mathbf{F} = -4000\mathbf{j}$. The angle between **v** and **F** is $90° - 15° = 75°$. The vector $\text{proj}_\mathbf{v}\mathbf{F}$ is the force pulling the car down the ramp, so a force of the same magnitude in the opposite direction is needed to keep the car motionless.

$$\begin{aligned}
\|\text{proj}_\mathbf{v}\mathbf{F}\| &= |\text{comp}_\mathbf{v}\mathbf{F}| \\
&= |\|\mathbf{F}\| \cos 75°| \\
&= 4000 \cos 75° \\
&\approx 1035.3
\end{aligned}$$

Therefore, a force of 1035.3 pounds is required to hold the car in place.

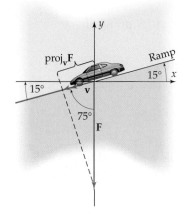

Figure 10.6.A-7

If a constant force **F** is applied to an object, pushing or pulling it a distance *d* in the direction of the force, as shown in Figure 10.6.A-8, the amount of **work** done by the force is defined to be the product of the magnitude of the force and the distance.

$$W = (\text{magnitude of force})(\text{distance}) = \|\mathbf{F}\|(d)$$

If the magnitude of **F** is measured in pounds and *d* in feet, then the units for *W* are foot-pounds. For example, if you push a car for 35 feet along a level driveway by exerting a constant force of 110 pounds, the amount of work done is $110(35) = 3850$ foot-pounds.

When a force **F** moves an object in the direction of a vector **d** rather than in the direction of **F**, as shown in Figure 10.6.A-9, then the motion of the object can be considered as the result of the vector $\text{proj}_\mathbf{d}\mathbf{F}$, which is a force in the same direction as **d**.

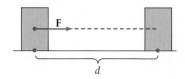

Figure 10.6.A-8

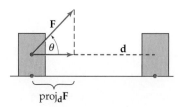

Figure 10.6.A-9

NOTE This formula reduces to the previous one when **F** and **d** have the same direction because in that case, $\cos \theta = \cos 0 = 1$, so that $W = \|\mathbf{F}\| \|\mathbf{d}\| = $ magnitude of force times distance moved.

Therefore, the amount of work done by **F** is the same as the amount of work done by $\text{proj}_\mathbf{d}\mathbf{F}$, as shown below.

$$W = \|\text{proj}_\mathbf{d}\mathbf{F}\| \|\mathbf{d}\|$$
$$= |\text{comp}_\mathbf{d}\mathbf{F}| \|\mathbf{d}\|$$
$$= \|\mathbf{F}\| (\cos \theta) \|\mathbf{d}\|$$
$$= \mathbf{F} \cdot \mathbf{d} \qquad \textit{See note.}$$

Consequently, work can be described as follows.

Work

> The work W done by a constant force **F** as its point of application moves along the vector **d** is
>
> $$W = |\text{comp}_\mathbf{d}\mathbf{F}| \|\mathbf{d}\| \qquad \text{or equivalently,} \qquad W = \mathbf{F} \cdot \mathbf{d}.$$

Example 8   **Compute Work**

How much work is done by a child who pulls a sled 100 feet over level ground by exerting a constant 20-pound force on a rope that makes a 45° angle with the ground?

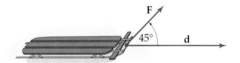

Figure 10.6.A-10

Solution

The situation is shown in Figure 10.6.A-10, where force **F** on the rope has magnitude 20, and the sled moves along vector **d** of length 100.

$$W = \mathbf{F} \cdot \mathbf{d}$$
$$= \|\mathbf{F}\| \|\mathbf{d}\| \cdot \cos \theta$$
$$= 20 \cdot 100 \cdot \frac{\sqrt{2}}{2}$$
$$= 1000\sqrt{2}$$
$$\approx 1414.2$$

Therefore, the work done is 1414.2 foot-pounds.

Exercises 10.6.A

In Exercises 1–6, find u · v, u · u, and v · v.

1. $u = \langle 3, 4 \rangle, v = \langle -5, 2 \rangle$

2. $u = \langle -1, 6 \rangle, v = \left\langle -4, \frac{1}{3} \right\rangle$

3. $u = 2i + j, v = 3i$

4. $u = i - j, v = 5j$

5. $u = 3i + 2j, v = 2i + 3j$

6. $u = 4i - j, v = -i + 2j$

In Exercises 7–12, find the dot product when $u = \langle 2, 5 \rangle, v = \langle -4, 3 \rangle$, and $w = \langle 2, -1 \rangle$.

7. $u \cdot (v + w)$

8. $u \cdot (v - w)$

9. $(u + v) \cdot (v + w)$

10. $(u + v) \cdot (u - v)$

11. $(3u + v) \cdot 2w$

12. $(u + 4v) \cdot (2u + w)$

In Exercises 13–18, find the angle between vectors u and v.

13. $u = \langle 4, -3 \rangle, v = \langle 1, 2 \rangle$

14. $u = \langle 2, 4 \rangle, v = \langle 0, -5 \rangle$

15. $u = 2i - 3j, v = -i$

16. $u = 2j, v = 4i + j$

17. $u = \sqrt{2}\,i + \sqrt{2}\,j, v = i - j$

18. $u = 3i - 5j, v = -2i + 3j$

In Exercises 19–24, determine whether the vectors u and v are parallel, orthogonal, or neither.

19. $u = \langle 2, 6 \rangle, v = \langle 3, -1 \rangle$

20. $u = \langle -5, 3 \rangle, v = \langle 2, 6 \rangle$

21. $u = \langle 9, -6 \rangle, v = \langle -6, 4 \rangle$

22. $u = -i + 2j, v = 2i - 4j$

23. $u = 2i - 2j, v = 5i + 8j$

24. $u = 6i - 4j, v = 2i + 3j$

In Exercises 25–28, find a real number k such that vectors u and v are orthogonal.

25. $u = 2i + 3j, v = 3i - kj$

26. $u = -3i + j, v = 2ki - 4j$

27. $u = i - j, v = ki + \sqrt{2}\,j$

28. $u = -4i + 5j, v = 2i + 2kj$

In Exercises 29–32, find $proj_u v$ and $proj_v u$.

29. $u = 3i - 5j, v = 6i + 2j$

30. $u = 2i - 3j, v = i + 2j$

31. $u = i + j, v = i - j$

32. $u = 5i + j, v = -2i + 3j$

In Exercises 33–36, find $comp_v u$.

33. $u = 10i + 4j, v = 3i - 2j$

34. $u = i - 2j, v = 3i + j$

35. $u = 3i + 2j, v = -i + 3j$

36. $u = i + j, v = -3i - 2j$

In Exercises 37–39, let $u = \langle a, b \rangle, v = \langle c, d \rangle$ and $w = \langle r, s \rangle$. Verify that the given property of dot products is valid by calculating the quantities on each side of the equal sign.

37. $u \cdot (v + w) = u \cdot v + u \cdot w$

38. $ku \cdot v = k(u \cdot v) = u \cdot kv$

39. $0 \cdot u = 0$

40. Suppose $u = \langle a, b \rangle$ and $v = \langle c, d \rangle$ are nonzero parallel vectors.
   a. If $c \neq 0$, show that u and v lie on the same nonvertical straight line through the origin.
   b. If $a \neq 0$, show that $v = \frac{c}{a}\,u$ (that is, v is a scalar multiple of u). *Hint:* The equation of the line on which u and v lie is $y = mx$ for some constant m (why?), which implies that $b = ma$ and $d = mc$.
   c. If $c = 0$, show that v is a scalar multiple of u. *Hint:* If $c = 0$ then $a = 0$ (why?) and so $b \neq 0$ (otherwise $u = 0$).

41. Prove the Angle Theorem in the case when θ is 0 or π.

42. If **u** and **v** are nonzero vectors such that $\mathbf{u} \cdot \mathbf{v} = 0$, show that **u** and **v** are orthogonal. *Hint:* If θ is the angle between **u** and **v**, what is $\cos \theta$ and what does this say about θ?

43. Show that $(1, 2), (3, 4), (5, 2)$ are the vertices of a right triangle by considering the sides of the triangle as vectors.

44. Find a number x such that the angle between the vectors $\langle 1, 1 \rangle$ and $\langle x, 1 \rangle$ is $\dfrac{\pi}{4}$ radians.

45. Find nonzero vectors **u**, **v**, and **w** such that $\mathbf{u} \cdot \mathbf{v} = \mathbf{u} \cdot \mathbf{w}$, $\mathbf{v} \neq \mathbf{w}$, and neither **v** nor **w** is orthogonal to **u**.

46. If **u** and **v** are nonzero vectors, show that the vectors $\|\mathbf{u}\|\mathbf{v} + \|\mathbf{v}\|\mathbf{u}$, $\|\mathbf{u}\|\mathbf{v} - \|\mathbf{v}\|\mathbf{u}$ are orthogonal.

47. A 600-pound trailer is on an inclined ramp that makes a 30° angle with the horizontal. Find the force required to keep it from rolling down the ramp, assuming that the only force that must be overcome is due to gravity.

48. In Example 7, find the vector that represents the force necessary to keep the car motionless.

In Exercises 49–52, find the work done by a constant force F as the point of application of F moves along the vector $\overrightarrow{PQ}$.

49. $\mathbf{F} = 2\mathbf{i} + 5\mathbf{j}$, $P = (0, 0)$, $Q = (4, 1)$

50. $\mathbf{F} = \mathbf{i} - 2\mathbf{j}$, $P = (0, 0)$, $Q = (-5, 2)$

51. $\mathbf{F} = 2\mathbf{i} + 3\mathbf{j}$, $P = (2, 3)$, $Q = (5, 9)$ *Hint:* Find the component form of $\overrightarrow{PQ}$.

52. $\mathbf{F} = 5\mathbf{i} + \mathbf{j}$, $P = (-1, 2)$, $Q = (4, -3)$

53. A lawn mower handle makes an angle of 60° with the ground. A woman pushes on the handle with a force of 30 pounds. How much work is done as she moves the lawn mower a distance of 75 feet on level ground?

54. A child pulls a wagon along a level sidewalk by exerting a force of 18 pounds on the wagon handle, which makes an angle of 25° with the horizontal. How much work is done as she pulls the wagon 200 feet?

55. A 40-pound cart is pushed 100 feet up a ramp that makes a 20° angle with the horizontal. How much work is done against gravity? *Hint:* The amount of work done against gravity is the negative of the amount of work done by gravity. Position the cart on a coordinate plane so that the cart is at the origin. Then the cart moves along vector $\mathbf{d} = (100 \cos 20°)\mathbf{i} + (100 \sin 20°)\mathbf{j}$ and the downward force of gravity is $\mathbf{F} = 0\mathbf{i} - 40\mathbf{j}$.

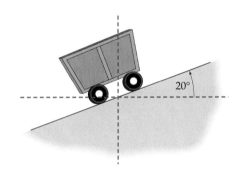

56. Suppose the child in Exercise 54 is pulling the wagon up a hill that makes an angle of 20° with the horizontal, and all other conditions remain the same. How much work is done in pulling the wagon 150 feet?

CHAPTER 10 REVIEW

Important Concepts

Important Facts and Formulas

Law of Cosines $a^2 = b^2 + c^2 - 2bc \cos A$

Law of Cosines, *Alternate Form:* $\cos A = \dfrac{b^2 + c^2 - a^2}{2bc}$

Law of Sines $\dfrac{a}{\sin A} = \dfrac{b}{\sin B} = \dfrac{c}{\sin C}$

Area of triangle ABC: $\dfrac{ab \sin C}{2}$

Heron's Formula Area of triangle $ABC = \sqrt{s(s-a)(s-b)(s-c)}$, where $s = \dfrac{1}{2}(a + b + c)$.

$|a + bi| = \sqrt{a^2 + b^2}$

$a + bi = r(\cos \theta + i \sin \theta)$, where
$$r = \sqrt{a^2 + b^2}, a = r \cos \theta, b = r \sin \theta$$

$r_1(\cos \theta_1 + i \sin \theta_1) \cdot r_2(\cos \theta_2 + i \sin \theta_2) =$
$$r_1 r_2 [\cos(\theta_1 + \theta_2) + i \sin(\theta_1 + \theta_2)]$$

$\dfrac{r_1(\cos \theta_1 + i \sin \theta_1)}{r_2(\cos \theta_2 + i \sin \theta_2)} = \dfrac{r_1}{r_2}[\cos(\theta_1 - \theta_2) + i \sin(\theta_1 - \theta_2)]$

DeMoivre's Theorem
$$[r(\cos \theta + i \sin \theta)]^n = r^n[\cos n\theta + i \sin n\theta]$$

The distinct nth roots of $r(\cos \theta + i \sin \theta)$ are:
$$\sqrt[n]{r}\left[\cos\left(\frac{\theta + 2k\pi}{n}\right) + i \sin\left(\frac{\theta + 2k\pi}{n}\right)\right] \qquad (k = 0, 1, 2, \ldots, n - 1)$$

The distinct nth roots of unity are:
$$\cos \frac{2k\pi}{n} + i \sin \frac{2k\pi}{n} \qquad (k = 0, 1, 2, \ldots, n - 1)$$

If $P = (x_1, y_1)$ and $Q = (x_2, y_2)$, then $\overrightarrow{PQ} = \langle x_2 - x_1, y_2 - y_1 \rangle$.

$\|\langle a, b \rangle\| = \sqrt{a^2 + b^2}$

If $\mathbf{u} = \langle a, b \rangle$ and k is a scalar, then $k\mathbf{u} = \langle ka, kb \rangle$.

If $\mathbf{u} = \langle a, b \rangle$ and $\mathbf{v} = \langle c, d \rangle$, then
$$\mathbf{u} + \mathbf{v} = \langle a + c, b + d \rangle \text{ and } \mathbf{u} - \mathbf{v} = \langle a - c, b - d \rangle.$$

Properties of Vector Addition and Scalar Multiplication
For any vectors **u**, **v**, and **w** and any scalars r and s:

1. $\mathbf{u} + (\mathbf{v} + \mathbf{w}) = (\mathbf{u} + \mathbf{v}) + \mathbf{w}$
2. $\mathbf{u} + \mathbf{v} = \mathbf{v} + \mathbf{u}$
3. $\mathbf{v} + \mathbf{0} = \mathbf{v} = \mathbf{0} + \mathbf{v}$
4. $\mathbf{v} + (-\mathbf{v}) = \mathbf{0}$
5. $r(\mathbf{u} + \mathbf{v}) = r\mathbf{u} + r\mathbf{v}$
6. $(r + s)\mathbf{v} = r\mathbf{v} + s\mathbf{v}$
7. $(rs)\mathbf{v} = r(s\mathbf{v}) = s(r\mathbf{v})$
8. $1\mathbf{v} = \mathbf{v}$
9. $0\mathbf{v} = \mathbf{0} = r\mathbf{0}$

If $\mathbf{u} = \langle a, b \rangle = a\mathbf{i} + b\mathbf{j}$, then

$$a = \|\mathbf{u}\| \cos\theta \quad \text{and} \quad b = \|\mathbf{u}\| \sin\theta,$$

where θ is the direction angle of **u**.

If $\mathbf{u} = \langle a, b \rangle = a\mathbf{i} + b\mathbf{j}$ and $\mathbf{v} = \langle c, d \rangle = c\mathbf{i} + d\mathbf{j}$, then

$$\mathbf{u} \cdot \mathbf{v} = ac + bd.$$

If θ is the angle between nonzero vectors **u** and **v**, then

$$\mathbf{u} \cdot \mathbf{v} = \|\mathbf{u}\|\|\mathbf{v}\| \cos\theta.$$

Schwarz Inequality $|\mathbf{u} \cdot \mathbf{v}| \leq \|\mathbf{u}\|\|\mathbf{v}\|$

Vectors **u** and **v** are orthogonal exactly when $\mathbf{u} \cdot \mathbf{v} = 0$.

$$\text{proj}_{\mathbf{v}}\mathbf{u} = \left(\frac{\mathbf{u} \cdot \mathbf{v}}{\|\mathbf{v}\|^2}\right)\mathbf{v}$$

$$\text{comp}_{\mathbf{v}}\mathbf{u} = \frac{\mathbf{u} \cdot \mathbf{v}}{\|\mathbf{v}\|} = \|\mathbf{u}\| \cos\theta, \text{ where } \theta \text{ is the angle between } \mathbf{u} \text{ and } \mathbf{v}.$$

Properties of Dot Products
If **u**, **v**, and **w** are vectors, and k is a real number, then:

1. $\mathbf{u} \cdot \mathbf{u} = \|\mathbf{u}\|^2$
2. $\mathbf{u} \cdot \mathbf{v} = \mathbf{v} \cdot \mathbf{u}$
3. $\mathbf{u} \cdot (\mathbf{v} + \mathbf{w}) = \mathbf{u} \cdot \mathbf{v} + \mathbf{u} \cdot \mathbf{w}$
4. $k\mathbf{u} \cdot \mathbf{v} = k(\mathbf{u} \cdot \mathbf{v}) = \mathbf{u} \cdot k\mathbf{v}$
5. $\mathbf{0} \cdot \mathbf{u} = 0$

Review Exercises

Note: Standard notation is used for triangles.

Section 10.1

In Exercises 1–6, use the Law of Cosines to solve triangle *ABC*.

1. $a = 12, b = 10, c = 15$

2. $a = 7.5, b = 3.2, c = 6.4$

3. $a = 10, c = 14, B = 130°$

4. $a = 7, b = 8.6, C = 72.4°$

5. $a = 5, c = 8, B = 76°$

6. $a = 90, b = 70, c = 40$

7. Two trains depart simultaneously from the same station. The angle between their two tracks is 120°. One train travels at an average speed of 45 miles per hour and the other at 70 miles per hour. How far apart are the trains after 3 hours?

8. A 40-foot flagpole sits on the side of a hill. The hillside makes a 17° angle with the horizontal. How long is a wire that runs from the top of the pole to a point 72 feet downhill from the base of the pole?

9. Find angle *ABC* in the figure below.

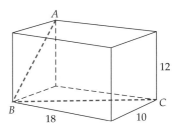

10. A surveyor stakes out points *A* and *B* on opposite sides of a building. Point *C* is 300 feet from *A* and 440 feet from *B*. Angle *ACB* measures 38°. What is the distance from *A* to *B*?

Section 10.2

In Exercises 11–18, use the Law of Sines to solve triangle *ABC*.

11. $B = 124°, C = 31°, c = 3.5$

12. $A = 96°, B = 44°, b = 12$

13. $a = 75, c = 84, C = 62°$

14. $a = 5, c = 2.5, C = 30°$

15. $a = 3.5, b = 4, A = 60°$

16. $a = 3.8, c = 2.8, C = 41°$

17. $A = 48°, B = 57°, b = 47$

18. $A = 67°, c = 125, a = 100$

19. Find the area of triangle *ABC* if $b = 24, c = 15,$ and $A = 55°$.

20. Find the area of triangle *ABC* if $a = 10, c = 14,$ and $B = 75°$.

21. A boat travels for 8 kilometers in a straight line from the dock. It is then sighted from a lighthouse which is 6.5 kilometers from the dock. The angle determined by the dock, the lighthouse (vertex), and the boat is 25°. How far is the boat from the lighthouse?

22. A pole tilts 12° from the vertical, away from the sun, and casts a 34-foot shadow on level ground. The angle of elevation from the end of the shadow to the top of the pole is 64°. How long is the pole?

23. Two surveyors, Joe and Alice, are 240 meters apart on a riverbank. Each sights a flagpole on the opposite bank. The angle from the pole to Joe (vertex) to Alice is 63°. The angle from the pole to Alice (vertex) to Joe is 54°. How far are Joe and Alice from the pole?

24. A straight road slopes at an angle of 10° with the horizontal. When the angle of elevation of the sun is 62.5°, a telephone pole at the side of the road casts a 15-foot shadow downhill, parallel to the road. How high is the telephone pole?

25. A woman on the top of a 448-foot building spots a small plane. As she views the plane, its angle of elevation is 62°. At the same instant a man at the ground-level entrance to the building sees the plane and notes that its angle of elevation is 65°.
   a. How far is the woman from the plane?
   b. How far is the man from the plane?
   c. How high is the plane?

26. Use the Law of Sines to prove Engelsohn's equations given below: For any triangle ABC (standard notation),

$$\frac{a + b}{c} = \frac{\sin A + \sin B}{\sin C} \quad \text{and} \quad \frac{a - b}{c} = \frac{\sin A - \sin B}{\sin C}.$$

In Exercises 27–30, find the area of the triangle described.

27. angle of 30°, adjacent side lengths 5 and 8

28. angle of 40°, adjacent side lengths 3 and 12

29. side lengths 7, 11, and 14

30. side lengths 4, 8, and 10

Section   10.3   **31.** Simplify $|i(4 + 2i)| + |3 - i|$.

32. Simplify $|3 + 2i| - |1 - 2i|$.

33. Graph the equation $|z| = 2$ in the complex plane.

34. Graph the equation $|z - 3| = 1$ in the complex plane.

35. Express $1 + i\sqrt{3}$ in polar form.

36. Express $4 - 5i$ in polar form.

In Exercises 37–41, express the given number in the form $a + bi$.

37. $2\left(\cos\frac{\pi}{12} + i\sin\frac{\pi}{12}\right) \cdot 4\left(\cos\frac{\pi}{6} + i\sin\frac{\pi}{6}\right)$

38. $3\left(\cos\frac{\pi}{8} + i\sin\frac{\pi}{8}\right) \cdot 2\left(\cos\frac{3\pi}{8} + i\sin\frac{3\pi}{8}\right)$

39. $\dfrac{12\left(\cos \dfrac{7\pi}{12} + i \sin \dfrac{7\pi}{12}\right)}{3\left(\cos \dfrac{5\pi}{12} + i \sin \dfrac{5\pi}{12}\right)}$

Section 10.4

40. $\left(\cos \dfrac{\pi}{12} + i \sin \dfrac{\pi}{12}\right)^{18}$ **41.** $\left[\sqrt[3]{3}\left(\cos \dfrac{5\pi}{36} + i \sin \dfrac{5\pi}{36}\right)\right]^{12}$

In Exercises 42–46, solve the given equation in the complex number system, and express your answers in polar form.

42. $x^3 = i$ **43.** $x^6 = 1$ **44.** $x^8 = -\sqrt{3} - 3i$

45. $x^4 = i$ **46.** $x^3 = 1 - i$

Section 10.5

In Exercises 47–50, let $\mathbf{u} = \langle 3, -2 \rangle$ and $\mathbf{v} = \langle 8, 1 \rangle$. Find each of the following:

47. $\mathbf{u} + \mathbf{v}$ **48.** $\|-3\mathbf{v}\|$ **49.** $\|2\mathbf{v} - 4\mathbf{u}\|$ **50.** $3\mathbf{u} - \dfrac{1}{2}\mathbf{v}$

In Exercises 51–54, let $\mathbf{u} = -2\mathbf{i} + \mathbf{j}$ and $\mathbf{v} = 3\mathbf{i} - 4\mathbf{j}$. Find each of the following:

51. $4\mathbf{u} - \mathbf{v}$ **52.** $\mathbf{u} + 2\mathbf{v}$ **53.** $\|\mathbf{u} + \mathbf{v}\|$ **54.** $\|\mathbf{u}\| + \|\mathbf{v}\|$

55. Find the components of the vector $\mathbf{v}$ such that $\|\mathbf{v}\| = 5$ and the direction angle of $\mathbf{v}$ is $45°$.

Section 10.6

56. Find the magnitude and direction angle of $3\mathbf{i} + 4\mathbf{j}$.

57. Find a unit vector whose direction is opposite the direction of $3\mathbf{i} - 6\mathbf{j}$.

58. An object at the origin is acted upon by a 10-pound force with direction angle $90°$ and a 20-pound force with direction angle $30°$. Find the magnitude and direction of the resultant force.

59. A plane flies in the direction $120°$, with an air speed of 300 miles per hour. The wind is blowing from north to south at 40 miles per hour. Find the course and ground speed of the plane.

60. An object weighing 40 pounds lies on an inclined plane that makes a $30°$ angle with the horizontal. Find the components of the weight parallel and perpendicular to the plane.

Section 10.6.A

In Exercises 61–64, let $\mathbf{u} = \langle 3, -4 \rangle$, $\mathbf{v} = \langle -2, 5 \rangle$, and $\mathbf{w} = \langle 0, 3 \rangle$. Find each of the following:

61. $\mathbf{u} \cdot \mathbf{v}$ **62.** $\mathbf{u} \cdot \mathbf{u} - \mathbf{v} \cdot \mathbf{v}$ **63.** $(\mathbf{u} + \mathbf{v}) \cdot \mathbf{w}$

64. $(\mathbf{u} + \mathbf{w}) \cdot (\mathbf{w} - 3\mathbf{v})$

65. What is the angle between the vectors $5\mathbf{i} - 2\mathbf{j}$ and $3\mathbf{i} + \mathbf{j}$?

66. Is $3\mathbf{i} - 2\mathbf{j}$ orthogonal to $4\mathbf{i} + 6\mathbf{j}$?

In Exercises 67 and 68, let $\mathbf{u} = 4\mathbf{i} - 3\mathbf{j}$ and $\mathbf{v} = 2\mathbf{i} + \mathbf{j}$. Find each of the following:

67. $\text{proj}_{\mathbf{v}}\mathbf{u}$ **68.** $\text{comp}_{\mathbf{u}}\mathbf{v}$

69. If $\mathbf{u}$ and $\mathbf{v}$ have the same magnitude, show that $\mathbf{u} + \mathbf{v}$ and $\mathbf{u} - \mathbf{v}$ are orthogonal.

70. If $\mathbf{u}$ and $\mathbf{v}$ are nonzero vectors, show that the vector $\mathbf{u} - k\mathbf{v}$ is orthogonal to $\mathbf{v}$, where $k = \dfrac{\mathbf{u} \cdot \mathbf{v}}{\|\mathbf{v}\|^2}$.

71. A 3500-pound automobile is on an inclined ramp that makes a 30° angle with the horizontal. Find the force required to keep it from rolling down the ramp, assuming the only force that must be overcome is due to gravity.

72. A sled is pulled along level ground by a rope that makes a 50° angle with the horizontal. If a force of 40 pounds is used to pull the sled, how much work is done in pulling it 100 feet?

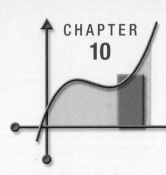

can do calculus
Euler's Formula

One of the most interesting and surprising identities in all of mathematics is one that relates the exponential function e^x to the trigonometric functions $\sin x$ and $\cos x$ and the imaginary number i.

$$e^{ix} = \cos x + i \sin x$$

The identity, known as Euler's formula, is named after the mathematician Leonhard Euler (1707–1783), who discovered it in 1748. The formula is used in many areas of calculus—most notably differential equations.

Euler's formula is true for any real number x, and many real numbers produce surprising results.

Example 1 Evaluating Euler's Formula

Evaluate $e^{i\pi}$.

Solution

Substitute π for x in the formula and simplify.

$$e^{i\pi} = \cos \pi + i \sin \pi = -1 + i(0) = -1$$

Therefore, $e^{i\pi} = -1$. ■

Rewriting the last equation connects the five most common constants of mathematics: $e, \pi, i, 0,$ and 1.

$$e^{i\pi} + 1 = 0$$

One of the most surprising aspects of this displayed equation is that raising an irrational number to an irrational power results in an *integer*. In fact, raising an imaginary number to an imaginary power can also give a real number, as shown in the next example.

Example 2 Imaginary Numbers Raised to Imaginary Powers

Show that $i = e^{\frac{\pi}{2}i}$ and find i^i.

Solution

Substitute $x = \dfrac{\pi}{2}$ into Euler's formula and simplify.

$$e^{\frac{\pi}{2}i} = \cos \frac{\pi}{2} + i \sin \frac{\pi}{2} = 0 + i(1) = i$$

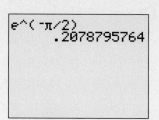

Figure 10.C-1

To find i^i, raise both sides of the identity $i = e^{\frac{\pi}{2}i}$ to the power i.

$$i^i = \left(e^{\frac{\pi}{2}i}\right)^i = e^{\frac{\pi}{2}i^2} = e^{\frac{\pi}{2}(-1)} = e^{-\frac{\pi}{2}}$$

A calculator computes the value of $e^{-\frac{\pi}{2}}$ to be 0.2078795764, as shown in Figure 10.C-1. So $i^i \approx 0.2079$.

Euler's formula can be used to define complex powers of e, that is, e^{x+iy}.

$$e^z = e^{x+iy} = e^x \cdot e^{iy} = e^x(\cos y + i\sin y)$$

The equation $e^{x+iy} = e^x(\cos y + i\sin y)$ defines a complex power of e in terms of a real power of e and the cosine and sine of a real number.

Example 3   Complex Power of e

Find the exact value and approximate value of $e^{\pi+2i}$.

Solution

Substitute $x = \pi$ and $y = 2$ into the formula $e^z = e^x(\cos y + i\sin y)$.

$$\begin{aligned} e^{\pi+2i} &= e^{\pi}(\cos 2 + i\sin 2) && \textit{exact value} \\ &\approx 23.14(-0.4161 + 0.9093i) \\ &\approx -9.629926 + 21.041772i && \textit{approximate value} \end{aligned}$$

Exercises

Find the exact value and the approximate value of the following powers of e.

1. $e^{-\pi i}e^{-\pi i}$

2. $\left(e^{3i}\right)^{3i}$

3. $e^{-i}e^{-i}$

4. $e^{\frac{\pi}{4}i}$

5. $e^{1+i\pi}$

6. $e^{2\pi i}$

7. $e^{1-\frac{\pi}{3}i}$

8. $e^{\pi+i}$

Analytic Geometry

You are there!

All planets travel in elliptical orbits around the sun, moons travel in elliptical orbits around planets, and satellites follow elliptical paths around the earth. Parabolic reflectors are used in spotlights, radar antennas, and satellite dishes. The long-range navigation system (LORAN) uses hyperbolas to enable a ship to determine its exact location. See Exercise 29 in Section 11.1.

Chapter Outline

can do calculus Arc Length of a Polar Graph

Interdependence of Sections

$$
\begin{array}{l}
11.1 \\
11.2 \\
11.3
\end{array} \Big\} \longrightarrow 11.4
$$

$$11.5 \longrightarrow 11.6$$

$$11.7$$

Sections 3.1, 3.2, and 3.4 are prerequisites for this chapter. Except for the discussion of standard equations for conics in Sections 11.1–11.4, Chapter 6 (Trigonometry) is also a prerequisite.

W‌hen a right circular cone is cut by a plane, the intersection is a curve called a **conic section,** as shown in the figure below. (A point, a line, or two intersecting lines are sometimes called **degenerate conic sections.)** Conic sections were studied by the ancient Greeks and are still of interest. For example, the orbits of planets are ellipses, parabolic mirrors are used in telescopes, and certain atomic particles follow hyperbolic paths.

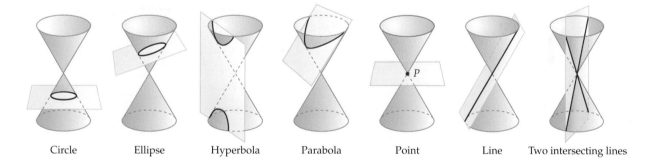

| Circle | Ellipse | Hyperbola | Parabola | Point | Line | Two intersecting lines |

Although the Greeks studied conic sections from a purely geometric point of view, the modern approach is to describe them in terms of the coordinate plane and distance, or as the graphs of certain types of equations. The study of the geometric properties of objects using a coordinate system is called **analytic geometry.** Circles are discussed in the appendix and used in prior sections. In this chapter, ellipses, hyperbolas, and parabolas are defined in terms of points and distances, and their equations are determined. The standard form of the equation of a conic includes the key information necessary for a rough sketch of its graph. Techniques for graphing conic sections with a calculator are discussed in the sections that define each conic section, and applications are given.

691

11.1   Ellipses

Objectives

- Define an ellipse
- Write the equation of an ellipse
- Identify important characteristics of ellipses
- Graph ellipses

An ellipse is a closed figure that can be thought of as a circle that has been elongated along a line of symmetry through its center. In this section, ellipses are defined in terms of points and distances, and then their equations are derived from the definition.

Definition of an Ellipse

Let P and Q be points in the plane and k a number greater than the distance from P to Q. The **ellipse** with **foci** (singular: **focus**) P and Q is

the set of all points X such that the *sum* of the distance from X to P and the distance from X to Q is k.

Written algebraically with X representing a point (x, y) on the ellipse,

$$XP + XQ = k$$

To draw the ellipse, pin the ends of a string of length k at points P and Q, as shown in Figure 11.1-1. Place a pencil against the string, and keep the string taut while moving the pencil.

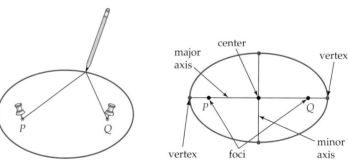

Figure 11.1-1   **Figure 11.1-2**

The midpoint of the segment $\overline{PQ}$ joining the foci is the **center** of the ellipse. The points where the line through the foci intercept the ellipse are its **vertices**. The segment connecting the vertices is the **major axis**, and the segment through the center of the ellipse perpendicular to the major axis is the **minor axis**, as shown in Figure 11.1-2.

If the points P and Q coincide, the ellipse generated is a circle with radius $\frac{k}{2}$. Thus, a circle is a special case of an ellipse.

Equation of an Ellipse

The simplest case is an ellipse centered at the origin, with its foci on the x- or y-axis. Suppose that the foci are on the x-axis at the points $P(-c, 0)$

and $Q(c, 0)$, where $c > 0$. Let $a = \dfrac{k}{2}$, so that $k = 2a$. Then (x, y) is on the ellipse exactly when

[distance from (x, y) to P] + [distance from (x, y) to Q] = $k = 2a$.

Written algebraically,

$$\sqrt{(x + c)^2 + (y - 0)^2} + \sqrt{(x - c)^2 + (y - 0)^2} = 2a$$

which can be rewritten as

$$\sqrt{(x + c)^2 + y^2} = 2a - \sqrt{(x - c)^2 + y^2}.$$

Square both sides and simplify the result.

$$a\sqrt{(x - c)^2 + y^2} = a^2 - cx$$

Square both sides again and simplify.

$$(a^2 - c^2)x^2 + a^2 y^2 = a^2(a^2 - c^2) \qquad \text{[1]}$$

To simplify the last equation, let $b = \sqrt{a^2 - c^2}$, so that

$$b^2 = a^2 - c^2$$

Equation [1] then becomes

$$b^2 x^2 + a^2 y^2 = a^2 b^2$$

Dividing both sides by $a^2 b^2$ shows that the coordinates of every point on the ellipse satisfy the equation

$$\frac{x^2}{a^2} + \frac{y^2}{b^2} = 1 \qquad \textit{Standard form of an ellipse}$$

Conversely, it can be shown that every point whose coordinates satisfy the equation is on the ellipse. The equation for an ellipse with foci $(0, c)$ and $(0, -c)$ on the y-axis is developed similarly.

Standard Equation of an Ellipse Centered at the Origin

Let a and b be real numbers such that $0 < b < a$. Then the graph of each of the following equations is an ellipse centered at the origin.

Foci on the x-axis:

$$\frac{x^2}{a^2} + \frac{y^2}{b^2} = 1$$

Foci on the y-axis:

$$\frac{x^2}{b^2} + \frac{y^2}{a^2} = 1$$

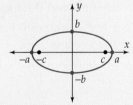

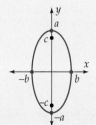

When the equation is in standard form, the x- and y-intercepts are easily found.

x-intercepts $(y = 0)$

$$\frac{x^2}{a^2} + \frac{0^2}{b^2} = 1$$

$$x^2 = a^2$$

$$x = \pm a$$

y-intercepts $(x = 0)$

$$\frac{0^2}{a^2} + \frac{y^2}{b^2} = 1$$

$$y^2 = b^2$$

$$y = \pm b$$

The characteristics of the graph of an ellipse centered at the origin are shown in the following box.

Characteristics of Ellipses

For $0 < b < a$,

Foci on the x-axis:

$$\frac{x^2}{a^2} + \frac{y^2}{b^2} = 1$$

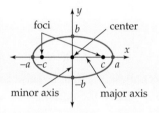

Foci on the y-axis:

$$\frac{x^2}{b^2} + \frac{y^2}{a^2} = 1$$

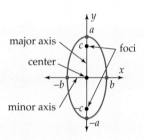

x-intercepts: $\pm a$
y-intercepts: $\pm b$
major axis is on the x-axis
vertices $(-a, 0)$ and $(a, 0)$
foci $(-c, 0)$ and $(c, 0)$, where
$$c = \sqrt{a^2 - b^2}$$

x-intercepts: $\pm b$
y-intercepts: $\pm a$
major axis is on the y-axis
vertices $(0, -a)$ and $(0, a)$
foci $(0, -c)$ and $(0, c)$, where
$$c = \sqrt{a^2 - b^2}$$

Notice the following facts in both cases.

- the foci are within the ellipse
- the major axis always contains the foci and is determined by which denominator is larger
- the distance between the foci is $2c$
- the center is the midpoint between the foci and the midpoint between the vertices
- the distance between the vertices is $2a$
- $c^2 = a^2 - b^2$

When the equation of an ellipse centered at the origin is in standard form, the denominator of the x term always gives the x-intercepts and the denominator of the y term always gives the y-intercepts.

Graphing an Ellipse

Example 1   Graph an Ellipse

Show that the graph of the equation $25x^2 + 16y^2 = 400$ is an ellipse. Label the foci, the vertices, the major axis, and the minor axis.

Solution

Put the equation in standard form by dividing both sides by 400.

$$\frac{x^2}{16} + \frac{y^2}{25} = 1$$

This is the equation of an ellipse with its center at the origin. The foci are on the y-axis because the denominator of y^2 is larger. Since $a^2 = 25$ and $b^2 = 16$, the x-intercepts are $\pm b = \pm 4$ and the y-intercepts are $\pm a = \pm 5$. To graph the ellipse, plot the intercepts and draw the ellipse, as shown in Figure 11.1-3.

To locate the foci, note that $c = \sqrt{25 - 16} = \sqrt{9} = 3$ and that the foci are on the y-axis. Therefore, the foci are $(0, -3)$ and $(0, 3)$.

The vertices are $(0, -5)$ and $(0, 5)$, and the major axis lies on the y-axis with endpoints at the vertices.

The minor axis lies on the x-axis, with endpoints $(-4, 0)$ and $(4, 0)$.

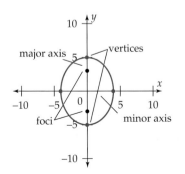

Figure 11.1-3

Example 2   Graph an Ellipse on a Calculator

Graph the ellipse with equation $4x^2 + 9y^2 = 36$ on a calculator.

Solution

Solve the equation for y.

$$9y^2 = 36 - 4x^2$$
$$y^2 = \frac{36 - 4x^2}{9}$$
$$y = \pm\sqrt{\frac{36 - 4x^2}{9}} = \pm\frac{2}{3}\sqrt{9 - x^2}$$

The ellipse is defined by the two functions

$$Y_1 = \frac{2}{3}\sqrt{9 - x^2} \quad \text{and} \quad Y_2 = -\frac{2}{3}\sqrt{9 - x^2},$$

whose graphs are shown in Figure 11.1-4.

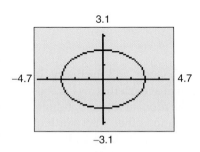

Figure 11.1-4

NOTE Graph all conic sections using a square window to see the correct shape.

Ellipse Equations

Example 3   Find the Equation of an Ellipse

Find the equation of the ellipse that has vertices at $(0, \pm 6)$ and foci at $(0, \pm 2\sqrt{6})$. Then sketch its graph by using the intercepts.

Solution

The foci of the ellipse lie on the y-axis, and its center is the origin. Thus, the equation has the form

$$\frac{x^2}{b^2} + \frac{y^2}{a^2} = 1$$

Find b by letting $a = 6$ and $c = 2\sqrt{6}$ and by using the relationship among the values for an ellipse.

$$c^2 = a^2 - b^2$$
$$(2\sqrt{6})^2 = (6)^2 - b^2$$
$$24 = 36 - b^2$$
$$b^2 = 12$$
$$b = \sqrt{12} \approx 3.5$$

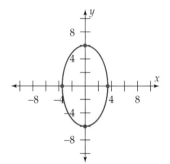

Figure 11.1-5

Thus, the equation is

$$\frac{x^2}{(\sqrt{12})^2} + \frac{y^2}{6^2} = 1 \qquad \text{or} \qquad \frac{x^2}{12} + \frac{y^2}{36} = 1$$

and the intercepts are $(0, \pm 6)$ and $(\pm\sqrt{12}, 0)$. See Figure 11.1-5.

Applications of Ellipses

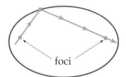

Figure 11.1-6

Elliptical surfaces have interesting reflective properties. A sound wave or light ray that passes through one focus and reflects off an ellipse will always pass through the other focus, as shown in Figure 11.1-6.

Example 4   Finding the Foci

The Whispering Gallery at the Museum of Science and Industry in Chicago is elliptical in shape, with a parabolic dish at each focus. (Parabolas are discussed in Section 11.3.) The shape of the room and two parabolic dishes carry the quietest sound from one focus to the other. The width of the ellipse is 13 feet 6 inches and the length of the ellipse is 47 feet 4 inches. Assume that the ellipse is centered at the origin. Find its equation, sketch its graph, and locate the foci.

> **NOTE** The area of an ellipse is $A = \pi ab$, where $2a$ is the length of the major axis and $2b$ is the length of the minor axis. See Exercise 24 for a method to estimate the circumference of an ellipse.

Solution

Because the length of the ellipse is 47 feet 4 inches, the value of a is half that amount, or $23\frac{2}{3}$ feet. Because the width is 13 feet 6 inches, the value of b is half that, or $6\dfrac{3}{4}$ feet. Therefore, the equation of the ellipse is

$$\frac{x^2}{\left(23\dfrac{2}{3}\right)^2} + \frac{y^2}{\left(6\dfrac{3}{4}\right)^2} = 1$$

$$\frac{x^2}{\dfrac{5041}{9}} + \frac{y^2}{\dfrac{729}{16}} = 1$$

$$\frac{9x^2}{5041} + \frac{16y^2}{729} = 1$$

The distance from the center to each focus is c, which is given by

$$c^2 = a^2 - b^2 = \frac{5041}{9} - \frac{729}{16} = \frac{74{,}095}{144}$$

$$c = \sqrt{\frac{74{,}095}{144}} \approx 22.7$$

Therefore, the foci are approximately $F_1(-22.7, 0)$ and $F_2(22.7, 0)$, as shown in Figure 11.1-7. ∎

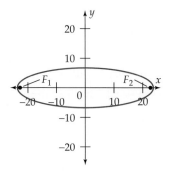

Figure 11.1-7

The planets and many comets have elliptical orbits, with the Sun at one focus. The Moon travels in an elliptical orbit with Earth at one focus, and man-made satellites usually travel in elliptical orbits around Earth.

Example 5   Elliptical Orbits

Earth's orbit around the Sun is an ellipse that is almost a circle. The Sun is at one focus, the major axis is 299,190,000 km in length, and the minor axis is 299,148,000 km in length. What are the minimum and maximum distances from Earth to the Sun?

Solution

Choose a coordinate system with the center of the ellipse at the origin and the Sun at the point $(c, 0)$ to get a diagram of the orbit. See Figure 11.1-8a.

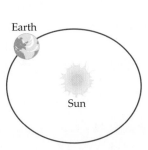

Figure 11.1-8a

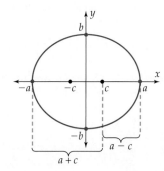

Figure 11.1-8b

The length of the major axis is $2a$ and the length of the minor axis is $2b$, so

$$2a = 299{,}190{,}000 \qquad 2b = 299{,}148{,}000$$
$$a = 149{,}595{,}000 \qquad b = 149{,}574{,}000$$

Therefore, the distance from each focus to the center is given by

$$c = \sqrt{a^2 - b^2} \approx 2{,}507{,}000$$

It can be proved algebraically that the minimum and maximum distances from a focus to a point on the ellipse are at the endpoints of the major axis. That is, the maximum distance is $a + c$ and the minimum distance is $a - c$. See Figure 11.1-8b.

- minimum distance $= a - c \approx 147{,}088{,}000$ km ≈ 91.2 million miles
- maximum distance $= a + c \approx 152{,}102{,}000$ km ≈ 94.3 million miles

---

Exercises 11.1

In Exercises 1–6, find the equation of the ellipse centered at the origin that satisfies the given conditions.

1. foci on x-axis; x-intercepts ± 7, y-intercepts ± 2

2. foci on y-axis; x-intercepts ± 1, y-intercepts ± 8

3. foci on x-axis; major axis of length 12; minor axis of length 8

4. foci on y-axis; major axis of length 20; minor axis of length 18

5. endpoints of major and minor axes: $(0, -7), (0, 7),$ $(-3, 0), (3, 0)$

6. vertices $(8, 0)$ and $(-8, 0)$, minor axis of length 8

In Exercises 7–12, match one of the following equations to the given graph.

$$\frac{x^2}{9} + \frac{y^2}{16} = 1 \qquad \frac{x^2}{16} + \frac{y^2}{9} = 1$$

$$\frac{x^2}{4} + \frac{y^2}{25} = 1 \qquad \frac{x^2}{25} + \frac{y^2}{4} = 1$$

$$2x^2 + y^2 = 12 \qquad x^2 + 6y^2 = 18$$

7.

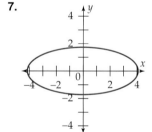

8.

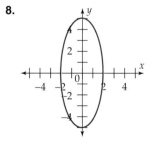

9.

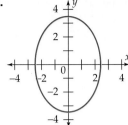

10.

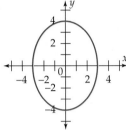

11.

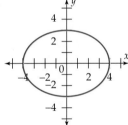

12.

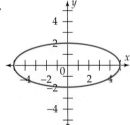

In Exercises 13–16, find a complete graph of the equation.

13. $\dfrac{x^2}{25} + \dfrac{y^2}{4} = 1$ **14.** $\dfrac{x^2}{6} + \dfrac{y^2}{16} = 1$

15. $4x^2 + 3y^2 = 12$ **16.** $9x^2 + 4y^2 = 72$

Calculus can be used to show that the area of the ellipse with equation $\dfrac{x^2}{a^2} + \dfrac{y^2}{b^2} = 1$ is πab. Use this fact to find the area of each ellipse in Exercises 17 – 22.

17. $\dfrac{x^2}{16} + \dfrac{y^2}{4} = 1$ **18.** $\dfrac{x^2}{9} + \dfrac{y^2}{5} = 1$

19. $3x^2 + 4y^2 = 12$ **20.** $7x^2 + 5y^2 = 35$

21. $6x^2 + 2y^2 = 14$ **22.** $5x^2 + y^2 = 5$

23. Washington, D.C. has a park located next to the White House called The Ellipse. Letting the center of the ellipse be at the origin of a coordinate system, the equation that defines the boundary of the park is

$$\frac{x^2}{562{,}500} + \frac{y^2}{409{,}600} = 1$$

Find how many square feet of grass is needed to cover the entire park.

24. The Indian mathematician Ramanujan is credited with developing the following formula that approximates the circumference of an ellipse. If $2a$ and $2b$ are the lengths of the major and minor axes of the ellipse, the circumference can be approximated by

$$\pi(3a + 3b) - \sqrt{(a + 3b)(b + 3a)}$$

Estimate the amount of fencing needed to enclose The Ellipse park described in Exercise 23.

25. Consider the ellipse whose equation is $\dfrac{x^2}{a^2} + \dfrac{y^2}{b^2} = 1$. Show that if $a = b$, then the graph is actually a circle.

26. Complete the derivation of the equation of the ellipse as follows.
   a. By squaring both sides, show that the equation

$$\sqrt{(x + c)^2 + y^2} = 2a - \sqrt{(x - c)^2 + y^2}$$

   may be simplified as

$$a\sqrt{(x - c)^2 + y^2} = a^2 - cx.$$

   b. Show that the last equation in part **a** may be further simplified as

$$(a^2 - c^2)x^2 + a^2 y^2 = a^2(a^2 - c^2).$$

27. Sketch the graph of $\dfrac{y^2}{4} + \dfrac{x^2}{b^2} = 1$ for $b = 2$, $b = 4$, $b = 8$, $b = 12$, and $b = 20$. What happens to the ellipse as b takes larger and larger values? Could the graph ever degenerate into a vertical line?

28. Halley's Comet has an elliptical orbit with the sun at one focus and a major axis of 1,636,484,848 miles. The closest the comet comes to the sun is 54,004,000 miles. What is the maximum distance from the comet to the sun?

29. The orbit of the Moon around Earth is an ellipse with Earth at one focus. If the length of the major axis of the orbit is 477,736 miles and the length of the minor axis is 477,078 miles, find the minimum and maximum distances from Earth to the Moon.

30. *Critical Thinking* An arched footbridge over a 100-foot river is shaped like half an ellipse. The maximum height of the bridge over the river is 20 feet. Find the height of the bridge over a point in the river exactly 25 feet from the center of the river.

31. *Critical Thinking* Find the length of the sides (in terms of a, b, and c) of triangle FOC in the following ellipse. Its equation is $\dfrac{x^2}{a^2} + \dfrac{y^2}{b^2} = 1$ and F is one focus. Justify your answer.

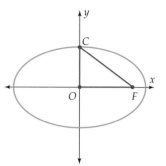

11.2 Hyperbolas

Objectives

- Define a hyperbola
- Write the equation of a hyperbola
- Identify important characteristics of hyperbolas
- Graph hyperbolas

Like an ellipse, a hyperbola has two foci, two vertices, and a center; but its shape is quite different.

Definition of a Hyperbola

Let P and Q be points in the plane and k be a positive number. The **hyperbola** with **foci** P and Q is the set of all points X such that

the absolute value of the *difference* of the distance from X to P and the distance from X to Q is k.

That is,

$$|XP - XQ| = k,$$

where X represents the point (x, y) and k is called the **distance difference**.

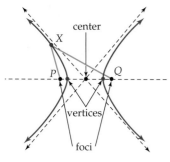

Figure 11.2-1

As shown in Figure 11.2-1, a hyperbola consists of two separate branches (shown in red). The distances XP and XQ are shown in blue. The dotted straight lines are the **asymptotes** of the hyperbola. The asymptotes are not part of the hyperbola but are useful in graphing. A hyperbola approaches its asymptotes, but it never touches them.

The midpoint of the segment joining the foci, $\overline{PQ}$, is the **center** of the hyperbola, and the line through P and Q is called the **focal axis.** The points where the focal axis intercepts the hyperbola are its **vertices.**

Equation of a Hyperbola

The simplest case is a hyperbola centered at the origin with its foci on the x- or y-axis. The equation of a hyperbola is derived by using the distance formula, and it is left as an exercise.

Standard Equation of a Hyperbola Centered at the Origin

Let a and b be positive real numbers. Then the graph of each of the following equations is a hyperbola centered at the origin.

foci on the x-axis:

$$\frac{x^2}{a^2} - \frac{y^2}{b^2} = 1$$

foci on the y-axis:

$$\frac{y^2}{a^2} - \frac{x^2}{b^2} = 1$$

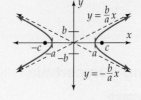

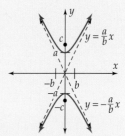

The characteristics of the graph of a hyperbola centered at the origin are shown in the following box. Notice in both cases that

- the hyperbola bends toward the foci
- the positive term determines which way the hyperbola opens
- the distance between the foci is $2c$
- the distance between the vertices is $2a$
- the center is the midpoint between the foci and the midpoint between the vertices
- $c^2 = a^2 + b^2$

When the equation is in standard form with the x term positive and y term negative, the hyperbola intersects the x-axis and opens left and right.

When the x term is negative and the y term is positive, the hyperbola intersects the y-axis and opens up and down.

Characteristics of Hyperbolas

For positive numbers a and b,

Foci on the x-axis:	Foci on the y-axis:
$$\frac{x^2}{a^2} - \frac{y^2}{b^2} = 1$$	$$\frac{y^2}{a^2} - \frac{x^2}{b^2} = 1$$

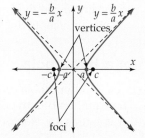 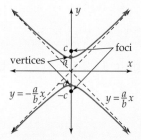

x-intercepts: $\pm a$	x-intercepts: none
y-intercepts: none	y-intercepts: $\pm a$
focal axis is on the x-axis	focal axis is on the y-axis
vertices $(-a, 0)$ and $(a, 0)$	vertices $(0, -a)$ and $(0, a)$
foci $(-c, 0)$ and $(c, 0)$, where	foci $(0, -c)$ and $(0, c)$, where
$c = \sqrt{a^2 + b^2}$	$c = \sqrt{a^2 + b^2}$
asymptotes: $y = \dfrac{b}{a}x$ and	asymptotes: $y = \dfrac{a}{b}x$ and
$y = -\dfrac{b}{a}x$	$y = -\dfrac{a}{b}x$

Graphing a Hyperbola

Example 1   **Graph a Hyperbola**

Show that the graph of the equation $9x^2 - 4y^2 = 36$ is a hyperbola. Graph it and its asymptotes. Find the equations of the asymptotes, and label the foci and the vertices.

Solution

Put the equation in standard form by dividing both sides by 36 and simplifying.

$$\frac{9x^2}{36} - \frac{4y^2}{36} = 1$$

$$\frac{x^2}{4} - \frac{y^2}{9} = 1$$

$$\frac{x^2}{2^2} - \frac{y^2}{3^2} = 1$$

Applying the fact in the box with $a = 2$ and $b = 3$ shows that the graph is a hyperbola centered at the origin with vertices $(2, 0)$ and $(-2, 0)$ and has asymptotes $y = \dfrac{3}{2}x$ and $y = -\dfrac{3}{2}x$. First plot the vertices and sketch the **auxiliary rectangle** determined by the vertical lines $x = \pm a = \pm 2$ and the horizontal lines $y = \pm b = \pm 3$. The asymptotes go through the origin and the corners of this rectangle, as shown on the left in Figure 11.2-2. It is then easy to sketch the hyperbola by drawing curves that are asymptotic to the dashed lines.

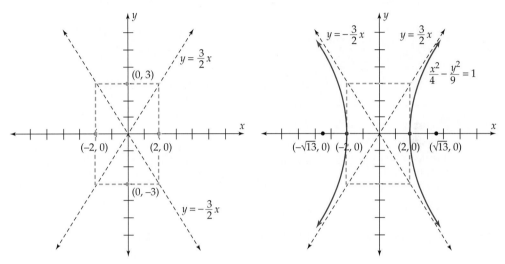

Figure 11.2-2

Locate the foci by using the formula $c = \sqrt{a^2 + b^2}$ with $a = 2$ and $b = 3$.

$$c = \sqrt{2^2 + 3^3}$$
$$= \sqrt{4 + 9} = \sqrt{13} \approx 3.6$$

Therefore, the foci are $\left(\sqrt{13}, 0\right)$ and $\left(-\sqrt{13}, 0\right)$, as shown on the graph on the right in Figure 11.2-2. ∎

Example 2 **Graph a Hyperbola on a Calculator**

Identify the graph of $4x^2 - 9y^2 = 36$, and then graph it on a calculator.

Solution

Dividing both sides of $4x^2 - 9y^2 = 36$ by 36 shows that it is the equation of a hyperbola.

$$\frac{x^2}{9} - \frac{y^2}{4} = 1$$

To graph this hyperbola on a calculator, solve the original equation for y.

$$9y^2 = 4x^2 - 36$$

$$y^2 = \frac{4x^2 - 36}{9}$$

$$y = \pm\sqrt{\frac{4x^2 - 36}{9}} = \pm\frac{2}{3}\sqrt{x^2 - 9}$$

The hyperbola is defined by the two functions

$$Y_1 = \frac{2}{3}\sqrt{x^2 - 9} \quad \text{and} \quad Y_2 = -\frac{2}{3}\sqrt{x^2 - 9}$$

whose graphs are shown in Figure 11.2-3.

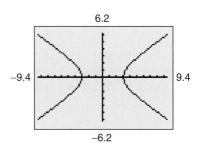

Figure 11.2-3

NOTE The two branches of the hyperbola in Figure 11.2-3 do not correspond to the two functions shown in Example 2. One function gives the part above the x-axis and the other gives the part below the x-axis.

Writing the Equation of a Hyperbola

Example 3 Find the Equation of a Hyperbola

Find the equation of the hyperbola that has vertices at $(0, 1)$ and $(0, -1)$ and passes through the point $(3, \sqrt{2})$. Then sketch its graph by using the asymptotes, and label the foci.

Solution

The vertices are on the y-axis and the equation has the form

$$\frac{y^2}{a^2} - \frac{x^2}{b^2} = 1,$$

with $a = 1$. Because $(3, \sqrt{2})$ is on the graph,

$$\frac{(\sqrt{2})^2}{1^2} - \frac{3^2}{b^2} = 1$$

$$2 - \frac{9}{b^2} = 1$$

$$b^2 = 9.$$

Therefore, $b = 3$ and the equation of the hyperbola is

$$\frac{y^2}{1^2} - \frac{x^2}{3^2} = 1 \quad \text{or} \quad y^2 - \frac{x^2}{9} = 1$$

The asymptotes of the hyperbola are the lines $y = \pm\frac{1}{3}x$.

The foci are on the y-axis c units away from the center, $(0, 0)$, where

$$c = \sqrt{1^2 + 3^3} = \sqrt{1 + 9} = \sqrt{10}$$

Thus, the foci are at $(0, \sqrt{10})$ and $(0, -\sqrt{10})$, as shown in Figure 11.2-4.

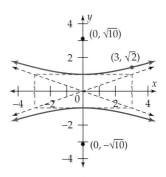

Figure 11.2-4

Applications of Hyperbolas

Applications modeled by hyperbolas occur in science, business, and economics. Unlike Halley's comet, which as an elliptical orbit, some comets have hyperbolic orbits. These comets pass through the solar system once and never return.

Additionally, the reflective properties of hyperbolas are used in the design of camera and telescope lenses. The Hubble Space Telescope incorporates a Cassegrain telescope (invented in 1672), which has both a hyperbolic mirror and a parabolic mirror. If a light ray passes through one focus of a hyperbola and reflects off the hyperbola at a point P, then the reflected ray moves along the straight line determined by P and the other focus, as shown in Figure 11.2-5.

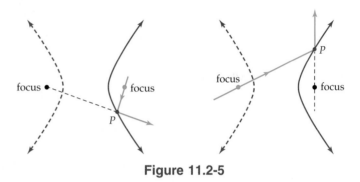

Figure 11.2-5

The next example illustrates the way hyperbolas are used in location systems.

Example 4   Determine Locations

An explosion was heard on a passenger ship and on a naval ship that are $\frac{1}{2}$ mile apart. Passengers on Ship A heard the sound $\frac{1}{2}$ second before sailors on Ship B. The speed of sound in air is approximately 1100 feet per second. Describe the possible locations of the explosion.

Solution

In $\frac{1}{2}$ second, the sound traveled $\frac{1}{2}(1100)$, or 550 feet. Therefore, the explosion occurred at a point 550 feet closer to ship A than to ship B. That is, the difference between the distance from the explosion to ship B and from the explosion to ship A is 550 feet. Whenever a difference is constant, a hyperbola is usually a good model.

Draw a coordinate system and place A and B on the x-axis equidistant from the origin. The locations of the ships are the foci of the hyperbola, and the hyperbola contains all possible locations of the explosion.

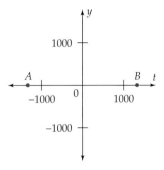

Figure 11.2-6a

Because the distance from A to B is $\frac{1}{2}$ mile, or 2640 feet, the coordinates of A and B are $(-1320, 0)$ and $(1320, 0)$, as shown in Figure 11.2-6a.

The explosion occurred on one branch of the hyperbola with foci $(-1320, 0)$ and $(1320, 0)$ such that $|XB - XA| = 550$ for every point X on the hyperbola.

Let V_1 be the vertex of the hyperbola closer to focus A. Because V_1 is on the hyperbola, the difference between the distances AV_1 and BV_1 is 550 feet. As shown in Figure 11.2-6b,

$$|BV_1 - AV_1| = 550$$
$$|(c + a) - (c - a)| = 550$$
$$|2a| = 550$$

Because $a > 0$, $\qquad a = 275$

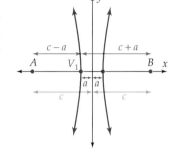

Figure 11.2-6b

Thus, $a = 275, c = 1320$, and

$$b^2 = c^2 - a^2 = 1320^2 - 275^2$$
$$= 1,742,400 - 75,625$$
$$b^2 = 1,666,775$$

Therefore, the equation of the hyperbola is

$$\frac{x^2}{a^2} - \frac{y^2}{b^2} = \frac{x^2}{75,625} - \frac{y^2}{1,666,775} = 1.$$

The explosion occurred somewhere on the branch of the hyperbola closer to the passenger ship at A, as illustrated in Figure 11.2-6c.

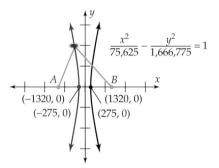

Figure 11.2-6c

To find the exact location of the explosion, the sound must be detected at a third location that is the focus of another hyperbola that shares one of the two foci given in the original problem. The intersection of the two hyperbolas will identify the precise location of the explosion, but the second hyperbola will not have its center at the origin. See Example 10 in Section 11.4, which gives the procedure for finding the exact location. ∎

Exercises 11.2

In Exercises 1–6, find the equation of the hyperbola centered at the origin that satisfies the given conditions.

1. x-intercepts ± 3, asymptote $y = 2x$

2. y-intercepts ± 12, asymptote $y = \dfrac{3x}{2}$

3. vertex $(2, 0)$, passing through $\left(4, \sqrt{3}\right)$

4. vertex $\left(0, \sqrt{12}\right)$, passing through $\left(2\sqrt{3}, 6\right)$

5. focus $(-3, 0)$ and vertex $(-2, 0)$

6. focus $(0, 4)$ and vertex $\left(0, \sqrt{12}\right)$

In Exercises 7–12, match one of the following equations to the given graph.

$$\frac{x^2}{9} + \frac{y^2}{4} = 1 \qquad\qquad \frac{y^2}{16} - \frac{x^2}{9} = 1$$

$$8x^2 + y^2 = 8 \qquad\qquad 8x^2 - y^2 = 8$$

$$\frac{x^2}{9} - \frac{y^2}{4} = 1 \qquad\qquad 16y^2 - \frac{25x^2}{9} = 1$$

7.

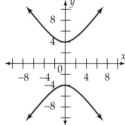

8.

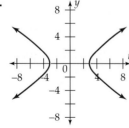

9.

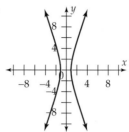

10.

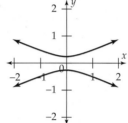

11.

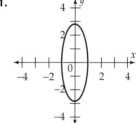

12.

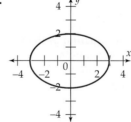

In Exercises 13–18, sketch a complete graph of the equation. Label the foci and the asymptote equations.

13. $\dfrac{x^2}{6} - \dfrac{y^2}{16} = 1$

14. $\dfrac{x^2}{4} - y^2 = 1$

15. $4x^2 - y^2 = 16$

16. $3y^2 - 5x^2 = 15$

17. $18y^2 - 8x^2 - 2 = 0$

18. $x^2 - 2y^2 = -1$

In Exercises 19–24, graph each equation using a graphing calculator.

19. $4x^2 - y^2 = 16$

20. $\dfrac{x^2}{4} - y^2 = 1$

21. $x^2 - 2y^2 = -1$

22. $\dfrac{x^2}{6} - \dfrac{y^2}{16} = 1$

23. $3y^2 - 5x^2 = 15$

24. $18y^2 - 8x^2 - 2 = 0$

25. Sketch the graph of $\dfrac{y^2}{4} - \dfrac{x^2}{b^2} = 1$ for $b = 2$, $b = 4$, $b = 8$, $b = 12$, and $b = 20$. What happens to the hyperbola as b takes larger and larger values? Could the graph ever degenerate into a pair of horizontal lines?

26. Sketch the graph of $\dfrac{y^2}{a^2} - \dfrac{x^2}{16} = 1$ for $a = 8$, $a = 4$, $a = 2$, $a = 1$, and $a = 0.5$. What happens to the hyperbola as a takes smaller and smaller values? Could the graph ever degenerate into a pair of vertical lines?

27. April and Marty, 2 miles apart, are talking on the phone when lightning strikes nearby. They each hear the thunder, but April hears it 2.4 seconds after Marty. Sketch a graph of the locations where the lightning could have struck. [Sound travels at approximately 1100 feet per second.]

28. In Exercise 27, suppose that later in the conversation Marty hears the thunder 3 seconds after April. Sketch a graph of the locations where the lightning could have struck.

For Exercises 29–30, write the equation of the tangent line to the given curve at the given point by using the following facts. The slope m of the tangent line to a hyperbola at the point (x, y) is

$$m = \frac{b^2 x}{a^2 y} \quad \text{for} \quad \frac{x^2}{a^2} - \frac{y^2}{b^2} = 1$$

$$m = \frac{a^2 x}{b^2 y} \quad \text{for} \quad \frac{y^2}{a^2} - \frac{x^2}{b^2} = 1$$

29. $\dfrac{x^2}{8} - \dfrac{y^2}{4} = 1$ at $(4, 2)$

30. $\dfrac{y^2}{8} - \dfrac{x^2}{36} = 1$ at $(6, 4)$

31. Show that the difference between the distance from each focus to any point on a hyperbola is equal to the distance between the vertices.

32. Derive the equation of a hyperbola centered at the origin as follows.
   a. Let $P(x, y)$ be a point on the hyperbola with foci $F_1(-c, 0)$ and $F_2(c, 0)$. Assume that $F_1 P > F_2 P$. By the definition of a hyperbola, the distance formula, and Exercise 32,

$$F_1 P - F_2 P = k$$
$$\sqrt{(x + c)^2 + y^2} - \sqrt{(x - c)^2 + y^2} = 2a$$

Show that the last equation simplifies as shown.

$$cx - a^2 = a\sqrt{(x - c)^2 + y^2}$$

   b. Show that the last equation in part **a** may be further simplified as shown.

$$x^2(c^2 - a^2) - a^2 y^2 = a^2(c^2 - a^2)$$

   c. Let $b^2 = c^2 - a^2$ and show that the equation in **b** simplifies to the standard form of a hyperbola centered at the origin.

33. *Critical Thinking* The following hyperbola is centered at the origin with vertex V and the auxiliary rectangle as shown. Use the length of one of the sides of triangle POV to locate the foci. Justify your answer.

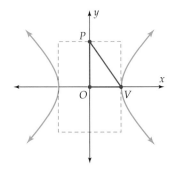

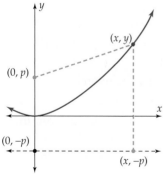

11.3 Parabolas

Objectives

- Define a parabola
- Write the equation of a parabola
- Identify important characteristics of parabolas
- Graph parabolas

Parabolas appeared in Section 3.3 as the graphs of quadratic functions, which are a special case of the following more general definition.

Definition of a Parabola

Let L be a line in the plane and P be a point not on L. If X is any point not on L, the distance from X to L is defined to be the length of the perpendicular line segment from X to L. The **parabola** with **focus** P and **directrix** L is the set of all points X such that

distance from X to P = distance from X to L

as shown in Figure 11.3-1.

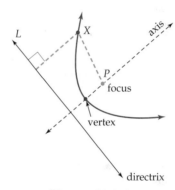

Figure 11.3-1

The line through P perpendicular to L is called the **axis.** The intersection of the axis with the parabola, which is the midpoint of the segment of the axis from P to L, is the **vertex of the parabola,** as shown in Figure 11.3-1.

Equation of a Parabola

Suppose that the focus is on the y-axis at the point $(0, p)$, where p is a nonzero constant, and that the directrix is the horizontal line $y = -p$. If (x, y) is any point on the parabola, then the distance from (x, y) to the horizontal line $y = -p$ is the length of the vertical segment from (x, y) to $(x, -p)$, as shown in Figure 11.3-2.

By the definition of a parabola,

$$\text{distance from } (x, y) \text{ to } (0, p) = \text{distance from } (x, y) \text{ to } y = -p$$
$$\text{distance from } (x, y) \text{ to } (0, p) = \text{distance from } (x, y) \text{ to } (x, -p)$$
$$\sqrt{(x - 0)^2 + (y - p)^2} = \sqrt{(x - x)^2 + [y - (-p)]^2}$$

Figure 11.3-2

Square both sides of the equation and simplify.

$$(x - 0)^2 + (y - p)^2 = (x - x)^2 + (y + p)^2$$
$$x^2 + y^2 - 2py + p^2 = 0^2 + y^2 + 2py + p^2$$
$$x^2 = 4py \qquad \textit{standard form of a parabola}$$

Conversely, it can be shown that every point whose coordinates satisfy this equation is on the parabola. A similar argument works for the parabola with focus $(p, 0)$ on the x-axis and directrix the vertical line $x = -p$, and leads to the following conclusion.

Standard Equation of a Parabola Centered at the Origin

Let p be a nonzero real number. Then the graph of each of the following equations is a parabola with vertex at the origin.

focus at $(0, p)$	focus at $(p, 0)$
directrix: $y = -p$	directrix: $x = -p$
$x^2 = 4py$	$y^2 = 4px$

NOTE The equations of a parabola in standard form can also be written as

$$y = \frac{1}{4p} x^2$$

and

$$x = \frac{1}{4p} y^2.$$

One of the variables is quadratic and the other variable is linear. When the y term is linear, the parabola opens up or down; when the x term is linear, the parabola opens left or right. The characteristics of the graph of a parabola with vertex at the origin are shown in the following box. Notice the following facts in both cases.

- the parabola bends toward the focus and away from the directrix
- the linear term determines the orientation of the parabola and the axis of symmetry—left/right or up/down
- the sign of p determines which way the parabola opens
- the distance between the focus and the directrix is $2p$
- the distance from the vertex to the focus and the distance from the vertex to the directrix is p
- the vertex is the midpoint of the line segment joining the focus and the directrix

Characteristics of Parabolas

For a nonzero real number p, parabolas have the following characteristics.

$$x^2 = 4py \qquad\qquad y^2 = 4px$$

- focus on the y axis at $(0, p)$
- directrix $y = -p$
- axis of symmetry is the y-axis

- focus on the x-axis at $(p, 0)$
- directrix $x = -p$
- axis of symmetry is the x-axis

- If $p > 0$, then the parabola:

opens up

opens right

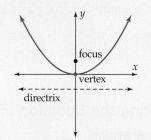

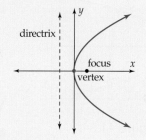

- If $p < 0$, then the parabola:

opens down

opens left

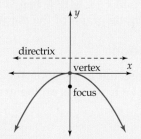

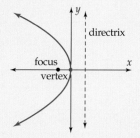

Example 1   Graphing a Parabola

Show that the graph of the equation $x^2 + 8y = 0$ is a parabola. Draw its graph, and then find and label its focus and directrix.

Solution

Write the equation in standard form: $x^2 = -8y$. This equation is of the form $x^2 = 4py$, so the graph is a parabola. To find the value of p, note that

$$4p = -8$$
$$p = -2$$

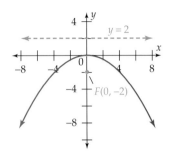

Figure 11.3-3

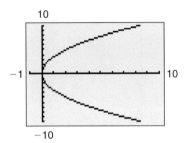

Figure 11.3-4

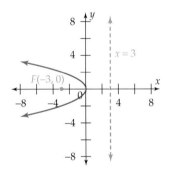

Figure 11.3-5

Therefore, the following statements are true, as shown in Figure 11.3-3.

- the focus is $(0, p) = (0, -2)$
- the directrix is $y = -p = -(-2) = 2$
- the parabola opens downward because p is negative

Example 2   Graph a Parabola on a Calculator

On a calculator, graph the parabola $y^2 = 12x$.

Solution

Solve the equation for y and enter both functions into a calculator.

$$y = \pm\sqrt{12x}$$

The graphs of $Y_1 = \sqrt{12x}$ and $Y_2 = -\sqrt{12x}$ are shown in Figure 11.3-4.

Writing the Equation of a Parabola

Example 3   Find the Equation of a Parabola

Find the focus, directrix, and equation of the parabola that passes through the point $\left(-1, \sqrt{12}\right)$, has vertex $(0, 0)$, and has its focus on the x-axis. Sketch the graph of the parabola, and label its focus and directrix.

Solution

Because the focus is on the x-axis, the equation has the form $y^2 = 4px$. Since $\left(-1, \sqrt{12}\right)$ is on the graph,

$$\left(\sqrt{12}\right)^2 = 4p(-1)$$
$$12 = -4p$$
$$-3 = p$$

Therefore, the focus is $(-3, 0)$ and the directrix is the vertical line $x = 3$. The equation of the parabola is $y^2 = -12x$, whose graph is shown in Figure 11.3-5.

Applications of Parabolas

Projectiles follow a parabolic curve, a fact that is used in the design of water slides in which the rider slides down a sharp incline, then up and over a hill, before plunging downward into a pool. At the peak of the hill, the rider shoots up along a parabolic arc several inches above the slide, experiencing a sensation of weightlessness.

Certain laws of physics show that sound waves or light rays from a source at the focus of a parabola will reflect off the parabola in rays parallel to the axis of the parabola, as shown in Figure 11.3-6. This is the reason that parabolas are used in automobile headlights and searchlights.

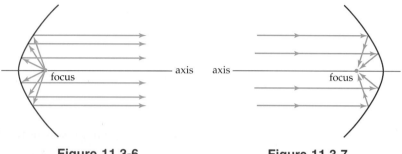

Figure 11.3-6   Figure 11.3-7

Conversely, a sound wave or light ray coming toward a parabola will be reflected into the focus, as shown in Figure 11.3-7. This fact is used in the design of radar antennas, satellite dishes, and field microphones used at outdoor sporting events to pick up conversations on the field.

Example 4 Parabola Application

A radio telescope in the Very Large Array at Socorro, New Mexico, shown in Figure 11.3-8a, has the shape of a parabolic dish (a cross section through the center of the dish is a parabola). It is approximately 12 feet deep at the center and has a diameter of 82 feet. How far from the vertex of the parabolic dish should the receiver be placed in order to "catch" all the radio waves that hit the dish?

Figure 11.3-8a

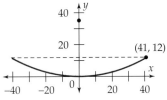

Figure 11.3-8b

All radio waves hitting the dish are reflected into the focus, so the receiver should be located there. To find the focus, draw a cross section of the dish, with the vertex at the origin, as shown in Figure 11.3-8b. The equation of this parabola is of the form $x^2 = 4py$. Because the point (41, 12) is on the parabola,

$$x^2 = 4py$$
$$41^2 = 4p(12) \qquad \textit{Substitute}$$
$$41^2 = 48p \qquad \textit{Simplify}$$
$$p = \frac{41^2}{48} \qquad \textit{Divide both sides by 48}$$
$$p = \frac{1681}{48} \approx 35 \text{ feet}$$

The focus is the point $(0, p)$, which is p units from the vertex $(0, 0)$. Therefore, the receiver should be placed about 35 feet from the vertex.

Exercises 11.3

In Exercises 1–6, find the equation of the parabola with vertex at the origin that satisfies the given condition.

1. axis $x = 0$, passing through (2, 12)

2. axis $y = 0$, passing (2, 12)

3. focus $(5, 0)$

4. focus $(0, 3.5)$

5. directrix $x = -2$

6. directrix $y = 3$

In Exercises 7–10, match one of the following equations to the given graph.

$$6x = y^2 \qquad y^2 = -4x$$

$$y = \frac{x^2}{4} \qquad x^2 = -8y$$

7.

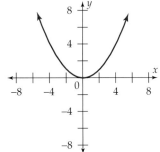

8.

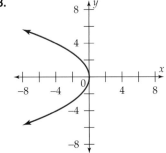

9.

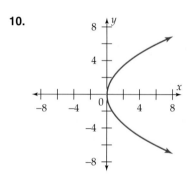

10.

In Exercises 11–14, sketch a complete graph of the equation.

11. $x = -6y^2$

12. $\frac{1}{2}y^2 = 2x$

13. $8x = 2y^2$

14. $4y = x^2$

In Exercises 15–18, find the focus and directrix of the parabola.

15. $y = 3x^2$

16. $x = \frac{1}{2}y^2$

17. $y = \frac{1}{4}x^2$

18. $x = -6y^2$

In Exercises 19–22, find the equation of the parabola centered at the origin passing through the given points.

19. $(-1, 2)$ and $(1, 2)$

20. $\left(3, -\frac{3}{2}\right)$ and $\left(3, \frac{3}{2}\right)$

21. $(-1, -2)$ and $(-1, 2)$

22. $(-2, -5)$ and $(2, -5)$

23. Find the point on the graph of $y^2 = 8x$ that is closest to the focus of the parabola.

24. Find the point on the graph of $x^2 = -3y$

The receiver in a parabolic television dish is 2 feet from the vertex and is located at the focus. Find an equation of a cross section of the receiver. (Assume that the dish is directed to the right and that the vertex is at the origin.)

26. The receiver in a parabolic television dish is 1.5 feet from the vertex and is located at the focus. Find an equation of a cross section of the receiver. (Assume that the dish is directed upward and that the vertex is at the origin.)

27. The filament of a flashlight bulb is located at the focus, which is $\frac{1}{2}$ inch from the vertex of a parabolic reflector. Find an equation of a cross section of the reflector. (Assume that the flashlight is directed to the left and that the vertex is at the origin.)

28. The filament of a flashlight bulb is located at the focus, which is $\frac{1}{2}$ inch from the vertex of a parabolic reflector. Find an equation of a cross section of the reflector. (Assume that the flashlight is directed downward and that the vertex is at the origin.)

11.4 Translations and Rotations of Conics

Objectives

- Write the equation of a translated conic
- Graph a translated conic
- Determine the shape of a translated conic without graphing
- Apply translated conics to real-world problems

Now that you are familiar with conic sections centered at the origin, the discussion will be expanded to include both conics centered at other points in the plane and ones with axes that may not be parallel to the coordinate axes.

As you saw in Section 3.4, replacing a variable x with $x - 5$ in the rule of a function $y = f(x)$ shifts the graph of the function 5 units to the right, whereas replacing x with $x + 5$, that is, $x - (-5)$, shifts the graph 5 units to the left. Similarly, if the rule of a function is given by $y = f(x)$, then replacing y with $y - 4$ shifts the graph 4 units upward, because $y - 4 = f(x)$ is equivalent to $y = f(x) + 4$. For equations that are not functions, a similar result applies.

Horizontal and Vertical Shifts

Let h and k be constant. Replacing x with $x - h$ and y with $y - k$ in an equation shifts the graph of the equation:

- $|h|$ units to the right for positive h and to the left for negative h
- $|k|$ units upward for positive k and downward for negative k

The process of writing the equation of a conic is the same as that discussed in Sections 11.1 through 11.3, except that x and y are replaced with $x - h$ and $y - k$, where (h, k) is the vertex of a parabola or the center of an ellipse or a hyperbola.

Example 1   Graph a Translated Conic

Identify and sketch the graph of

$$\frac{(x - 5)^2}{9} + \frac{(y + 4)^2}{36} = 1$$

and find its center, major axis, and minor axis.

Solution

The given equation can be obtained from the equation $\dfrac{x^2}{9} + \dfrac{y^2}{36} = 1$, whose graph is known to be an ellipse, as follows:

replace x by $x - 5$ and   replace y by $y - (-4) = y + 4$.

This is the situation described in the previous box with $h = 5$ and $k = -4$. Therefore, the graph is the ellipse $\dfrac{x^2}{9} + \dfrac{y^2}{36} = 1$ shifted 5 units to the right and 4 units downward, as shown in Figure 11.4-1.

- The center of the ellipse is $(5, -4)$.
- The major axis lies on the vertical line $x = 5$.
- The minor axis is on the horizontal line $y = -4$.

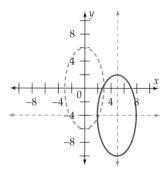

Figure 11.4-1

Before identifying a conic section and determining its characteristics, the corresponding equation should be rewritten in standard form.

Example 2   Identify a Conic

Identify and sketch the graph of

$$4x^2 + 9y^2 - 32x - 90y + 253 = 0.$$

Solution

Rewrite the equation as

$$(4x^2 - 32x) + (9y^2 - 90y) = -253$$
$$4(x^2 - 8x) + 9(y^2 - 10y) = -253$$

Complete the square in $x^2 - 8x$ and $y^2 - 10y$.

$$4(x^2 - 8x + 16) + 9(y^2 - 10y + 25) = -253 + ? + ?$$

Be careful here: 16 and 25 were not added to the left side of the equation. Actually $4 \cdot 16 = 64$ and $9 \cdot 25 = 225$ were added, when the left side is multiplied out. Therefore, to leave the original equation unchanged, 64 and 225 must be added to the right side.

$$4(x^2 - 8x + 16) + 9(y^2 - 10y + 25) = -253 + 64 + 225$$
$$4(x - 4)^2 + 9(y - 5)^2 = 36$$
$$\frac{4(x - 4)^2}{36} + \frac{9(y - 5)^2}{36} = 1$$
$$\frac{(x - 4)^2}{9} + \frac{(y - 5)^2}{4} = 1$$

NOTE Review the technique of completing the square in Section 2.2, if needed.

The graph of this equation is the ellipse $\dfrac{x^2}{9} + \dfrac{y^2}{4} = 1$ shifted 4 units to the right and 5 units upward. Its center is at $(4, 5)$, its major axis lies on the horizontal line $y = 5$, and its minor axis lies on the vertical line $x = 4$, as shown in Figure 11.4-2.

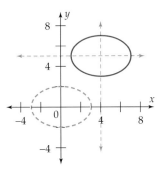

Figure 11.4-2

Example 3   **Writing the Equation of a Translated Conic**

Find the equation of an ellipse with center at $(5, -4)$ such that the endpoints of its major and minor axes are $(5, 2)$, $(5, -10)$, $(2, -4)$, and $(8, -4)$. Find the coordinates of the foci.

Solution

The major axis has length 12 and is parallel to the y-axis. The minor axis has length 6 and is parallel to the x-axis. Therefore, $a = 6$, $b = 3$, and the equation of the ellipse has the form

$$\frac{(x - h)^2}{3^2} + \frac{(y - k)^2}{6^2} = 1$$

Because it has its center at $(5, -4)$, the equation of the ellipse has the form

$$\frac{(x - 5)^2}{3^2} + \frac{(y - (-4))^2}{6^2} = 1$$

$$\frac{(x - 5)^2}{9} + \frac{(y + 4)^2}{36} = 1.$$

Since $a = 6$ and $b = 3$, and in an ellipse, $c = \sqrt{a^2 - b^2}$,

$$c = \sqrt{6^2 - 3^2} = \sqrt{36 - 9} = \sqrt{27} = 3\sqrt{3}$$

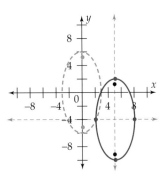

Figure 11.4-3

The foci of $\dfrac{(x - 5)^2}{9} + \dfrac{(y + 4)^2}{36} = 1$ are $3\sqrt{3}$ units from the center $(5, -4)$ on the major axis. That is, the foci are $\left(5, -4 + 3\sqrt{3}\right)$ and $\left(5, -4 - 3\sqrt{3}\right)$, as shown in Figure 11.4-3.

Example 4 **Identify a Translated Conic**

Identify and sketch the graph of $x = 2y^2 + 12y + 14$. Label all character-istics of the conic.

Solution

Rewrite the equation and complete the square in y, being careful to add the appropriate amounts to both sides of the equation.

$$2y^2 + 12y = x - 14$$
$$2(y^2 + 6y) = x - 14$$
$$2(y^2 + 6y + 9) = x - 14 + 2(9)$$
$$2(y + 3)^2 = x + 4$$
$$(y + 3)^2 = \frac{1}{2}(x + 4)$$
$$(y - (-3))^2 = \frac{1}{2}(x - (-4))$$

Thus, the graph is the graph of the parabola $y^2 = \frac{1}{2}x$ shifted 4 units to the left and 3 units downward, as shown in Figure 11.4-4.

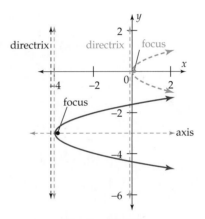

Figure 11.4-4

The parabola $y^2 = \frac{1}{2}x$ has its vertex at $(0, 0)$, the x-axis as its axis of sym-metry, $\left(\frac{1}{8}, 0\right)$ as its focus, and $x = -\frac{1}{8}$ as its directrix. After the graph is shifted, the parabola will have its vertex at $(-4, -3)$ and the horizontal line $y = -3$ as its axis.

The translated parabola has its focus at $\left(\frac{1}{8} - 4, -3\right)$, or $\left(-\frac{31}{8}, -3\right)$ and directrix $x = -\frac{1}{8} - 4 = -\frac{33}{8}$.

The following is a summary of the standard equations of conic sections whose axes are parallel to the coordinate axes.

Standard Equations of Conic Sections

Let (h, k) be any point in the plane.

- If a and b are real numbers with $a > b > 0$, then the graph of each of the following equations is an ellipse with center (h, k).

$$\frac{(x - h)^2}{a^2} + \frac{(y - k)^2}{b^2} = 1$$

$\begin{cases} \text{major axis on the horizontal line } y = k \\ \text{minor axis on the vertical line } x = h \\ \text{vertices: } (h \pm a, k) \\ \text{foci: } (h - c, k) \text{ and } (h + c, k), \text{ where} \\ \qquad c = \sqrt{a^2 - b^2} \end{cases}$

$$\frac{(x - h)^2}{b^2} + \frac{(y - k)^2}{a^2} = 1$$

$\begin{cases} \text{major axis on the vertical line } x = h \\ \text{minor axis on the horizontal line } y = k \\ \text{vertices: } (h, k \pm a) \\ \text{foci: } (h, k - c) \text{ and } (h, k + c), \text{ where} \\ \qquad c = \sqrt{a^2 - b^2} \end{cases}$

- If a and b are positive real numbers, then the graph of each of the following equations is a hyperbola with center (h, k).

$$\frac{(x - h)^2}{a^2} - \frac{(y - k)^2}{b^2} = 1$$

$\begin{cases} \text{focal axis on the horizontal line } y = k \\ \text{vertices: } (h - a, k) \text{ and } (h + a, k) \\ \text{foci: } (h - c, k) \text{ and } (h + c, k), \text{ where} \\ \qquad c = \sqrt{a^2 + b^2} \\ \text{asymptotes: } y = \pm\frac{b}{a}(x - h) + k \end{cases}$

$$\frac{(y - k)^2}{a^2} - \frac{(x - h)^2}{b^2} = 1$$

$\begin{cases} \text{focal axis on the vertical line } x = h \\ \text{vertices: } (h, k - a) \text{ and } (h, k + a) \\ \text{foci: } (h, k - c) \text{ and } (h, k + c), \text{ where} \\ \qquad c = \sqrt{a^2 + b^2} \\ \text{asymptotes: } y = \pm\frac{a}{b}(x - h) + k \end{cases}$

- If p is a nonzero real number, then the graph of each of the following equations is a parabola with vertex (h, k).

$$(x - h)^2 = 4p(y - k)$$

$\begin{cases} \text{focus: } (h, k + p) \\ \text{directrix: the horizontal line } y = k - p \\ \text{axis: the vertical line } x = h \\ \text{opens upward if } p > 0, \text{ downward if } p < 0 \end{cases}$

$$(y - k)^2 = 4p(x - h)$$

$\begin{cases} \text{focus: } (h + p, k) \\ \text{directrix: the vertical line } x = h - p \\ \text{axis: the horizontal line } y = k \\ \text{opens to right if } p > 0, \text{ to left if } p < 0 \end{cases}$

When the equation of a conic section is in standard form, the techniques in previous sections can be used to obtain its graph on a calculator.

Technology Tip

The Casio 9850 has a conic section grapher, on the main menu, that produces the graphs of equations in standard form when the various coefficients are entered.

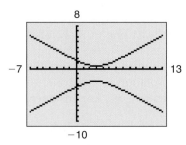

Figure 11.4-5

Example 5 **Calculator Graph of a Conic**

Graph the equation $\dfrac{(y + 1)^2}{2} - \dfrac{(x - 3)^2}{4} = 1$.

Solution

The graph is a hyperbola centered at $(3, -1)$. To graph on a calculator, solve the equation for y.

$$\frac{(y + 1)^2}{2} = 1 + \frac{(x - 3)^2}{4}$$

$$(y + 1)^2 = 2\left[1 + \frac{(x - 3)^2}{4}\right] = 2 + \frac{(x - 3)^2}{2}$$

$$y + 1 = \pm\sqrt{2 + \frac{(x - 3)^2}{2}}$$

$$Y_1 = \sqrt{2 + \frac{(x - 3)^2}{2}} - 1 \quad \text{or} \quad Y_2 = -\sqrt{2 + \frac{(x - 3)^2}{2}} - 1$$

Graph the last two functions on the same screen. The graph of the first is the top half and the graph of the second is the bottom half of the graph of the original equation, as shown in Figure 11.4-5. ∎

When a second-degree equation is not in standard form, the fastest way to graph it is to use the method in Example 5, modified as in the next example.

Example 6 **Graph a Conic Not in Standard Form**

Graph the equation $x^2 + 8y^2 + 6x + 9y + 4 = 0$ without putting it in standard form.

Solution

Write the equation as

$$8y^2 + 9y + (x^2 + 6x + 4) = 0.$$

This is a quadratic equation of the form $ay^2 + by + c = 0$, with

$$a = 8, \qquad b = 9, \qquad \text{and} \qquad c = x^2 + 6x + 4,$$

which can be solved by using the quadratic formula.

$$y = \frac{-b \pm \sqrt{b^2 - 4ac}}{2a}$$

$$= \frac{-9 \pm \sqrt{9^2 - 4 \cdot 8(x^2 + 6x + 4)}}{2 \cdot 8}$$

$$= \frac{-9 \pm \sqrt{81 - 32(x^2 + 6x + 4)}}{16}$$

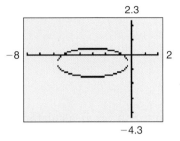

Figure 11.4-6

The graphs of both of the functions

$$Y_1 = \frac{-9 + \sqrt{81 - 32(x^2 + 6x + 4)}}{16} \text{ and}$$

$$Y_2 = \frac{-9 - \sqrt{81 - 32(x^2 + 6x + 4)}}{16}$$

are shown on the same screen in Figure 11.4-6. The conic is an ellipse. ∎

Rotations and Second-Degree Equations

A second-degree equation in x and y is one that can be written in the form

$$Ax^2 + Bxy + Cy^2 + Dx + Ey + F = 0 \qquad \text{[1]}$$

for some constants A, B, C, D, E, and F, with at least one of A, B, or C nonzero. Every conic section is the graph of a second-degree equation. The terms Dx, Ey, and F determine the translation of the conic from the origin. When $B \neq 0$, the term Bxy determines a rotation of the conic so that its axes are no longer parallel to the coordinate axes. For instance, the ellipse equation $\dfrac{x^2}{4} + \dfrac{(y-3)^2}{6} = 1$ can be written as

$$12\left(\frac{x^2}{4}\right) + 12\left[\frac{(y-3)^2}{6}\right] = 12$$

$$3x^2 + 2(y-3)^2 = 12$$

$$3x^2 + 2(y^2 - 6y + 9) = 12$$

$$3x^2 + 2y^2 - 12y + 18 = 12$$

$$3x^2 + 2y^2 - 12y + 6 = 0$$

The last equation above has the form of equation [1] with $A = 3, B = 0, C = 2, D = 0, E = -12,$ and $F = 6$.

Conversely, it can be shown that the graph of every second-degree equation is a conic section (possibly degenerate—see page 691). When the equation has an xy term, the conic may be rotated from standard position such that its axis or axes are not parallel to the coordinate axes.

Example 7   Identify a Conic

Graph the equation $3x^2 + 6xy + y^2 + x - 2y + 7 = 0$ and identify the conic.

Solution

Rewrite the equation as

$$y^2 + 6xy - 2y + 3x^2 + x + 7 = 0$$

$$y^2 + (6x - 2)y + (3x^2 + x + 7) = 0$$

The last equation has the form $ay^2 + by + c = 0$, with $a = 1, b = 6x - 2,$ and $c = 3x^2 + x + 7$. It can be solved for y by using the quadratic formula.

$$y = \frac{-b \pm \sqrt{b^2 - 4ac}}{2a}$$

$$y = \frac{-(6x - 2) \pm \sqrt{(6x - 2)^2 - 4 \cdot 1 \cdot (3x^2 + x + 7)}}{2 \cdot 1}$$

Half of the graph is obtained by graphing

$$Y_1 = \frac{-(6x - 2) + \sqrt{(6x - 2)^2 - 4 \cdot 1 \cdot (3x^2 + x + 7)}}{2}$$

and the other half by graphing

$$Y_2 = \frac{-(6x - 2) - \sqrt{(6x - 2)^2 - 4 \cdot 1 \cdot (3x^2 + x + 7)}}{2}$$

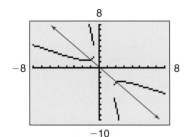

Figure 11.4-7

The graph is a hyperbola whose focal axis is tilted.

The Discriminant

The following fact makes it easy to identify the graphs of second-degree equations without graphing.

Graphs of Second-Degree Equations

> The graph of the equation
>
> $Ax^2 + Bxy + Cy^2 + Dx + Ey + F = 0$, with A, B, C not all zero,
>
> • is a circle, an ellipse, or a point, if $B^2 - 4AC < 0$
> • is a parabola, a line, or two parallel lines, if $B^2 - 4AC = 0$
> • is a hyperbola or two intersecting lines, if $B^2 - 4AC > 0$
>
> The expression $B^2 - 4AC$ is called the discriminant.

Example 8   Identify a Conic

Identify the graph of $2x^2 - 4xy + 3y^2 + 5x + 6y - 8 = 0$ and confirm your conclusions by graphing.

Solution

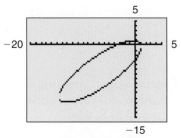

Figure 11.4-8

Compute the discriminant with $A = 2$, $B = -4$, and $C = 3$.

$$B^2 - 4AC = (-4)^2 - 4 \cdot 2 \cdot 3 = 16 - 24 = -8$$

Hence, the graph is an ellipse, a circle, or a single point. Use the quadratic formula to solve for y.

$$3y^2 + (-4x + 6)y + (2x^2 + 5x - 8) = 0$$

Graph both solutions on the same screen, as shown in Figure 11.4–8.

$$y = \frac{-(-4x + 6) \pm \sqrt{(-4x + 6)^2 - 4 \cdot 3 \cdot (2x^2 + 5x - 8)}}{2 \cdot 3}$$

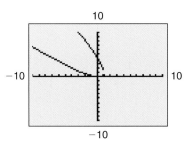

Figure 11.4-9a

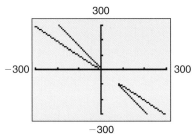

Figure 11.4-9b

Example 9 Use the Discriminant

Identify the graph of $3x^2 + 5xy + 2y^2 - 8y - 1 = 0$, and sketch a complete graph.

Solution

The discriminant of the equation is $B^2 - 4AC = 5^2 - 4 \cdot 3 \cdot 2 = 1$. So the graph is a hyperbola—or two intersecting lines in the degenerate case.

To graph the equation, write the equation in quadratic form in y.

$$3x^2 + 5xy + 2y^2 - 8y - 1 = 0$$
$$2y^2 + 5xy - 8y + 3x^2 - 1 = 0$$
$$2y^2 + (5x - 8)y + (3x^2 - 1) = 0$$

Then use the quadratic formula to solve for y.

$$y = \frac{-(5x - 8) \pm \sqrt{(5x - 8)^2 - 4 \cdot 2 \cdot (3x^2 - 1)}}{4}$$

Graphing these two functions in the standard window produces Figure 11.4-9a, which looks like a parabola. This cannot be correct: because the discriminant is positive, the graph must be a hyperbola. A different viewing window is needed for a complete graph of this hyperbola, which is shown in Figure 11.4-9b.

Applications

The long-range navigation system (LORAN) uses hyperbolas to enable a ship to determine its exact location by radio, as illustrated in the following example.

Example 10 LORAN Application

Three LORAN radio transmitters Q, P, and R are located 200 miles apart along a straight line and simultaneously transmit signals at regular intervals. These signals travel at a speed of 980 feet per microsecond, the speed of light. Ship S receives a signal from P and, 528 microseconds later, a signal from Q. It also receives a signal from R 305 microseconds after the one from P. Determine the ship's location.

Solution

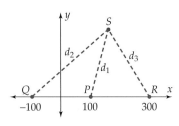

Figure 11.4-10

Let the x-axis be the line through the LORAN stations, with the origin located midway between Q and P, so that the situation looks like Figure 11.4-10. If the signal takes t microseconds to go from P to S, then

$$d_1 = 980t \qquad \text{and} \qquad d_2 = 980(t + 528)$$

so that

$$|d_1 - d_2| = |980t - 980(t + 528)| = 980 \cdot 528 = 517{,}440 \text{ feet.}$$

Since one mile is 5280 feet,

$$|d_1 - d_2| = \frac{517{,}440}{5280} = 98 \text{ miles.}$$

In other words,

$$|(\text{distance from } P \text{ to } S) - (\text{distance from } Q \text{ to } S)| = 98 \text{ miles.}$$

This is the definition of a hyperbola given in Section 11.2; thus, S is on the hyperbola with foci $P = (100, 0)$ and $Q = (-100, 0)$ and distance difference $r = 98$. This hyperbola has an equation of the form

$$\frac{x^2}{a^2} - \frac{y^2}{b^2} = 1,$$

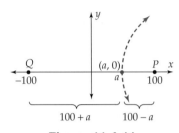

Figure 11.4-11

where $(\pm a, 0)$ are the vertices, $(\pm c, 0) = (\pm 100, 0)$ are the foci and $c^2 = a^2 + b^2$.

Figure 11.4-11 and the fact that the vertex $(a, 0)$ is on the hyperbola show that

$$|[\text{distance from } P \text{ to } (a, 0)] - [\text{distance } Q \text{ to } (a, 0)]| = r = 98$$
$$|(100 - a) - (100 + a)| = 98$$
$$|-2a| = 98$$
$$|a| = 49$$

Consequently, $a^2 = 49^2 = 2401$ and $b^2 = c^2 - a^2 = 100^2 - 49^2 = 7599$. Thus, the ship lies on the hyperbola

$$\frac{x^2}{2401} - \frac{y^2}{7599} = 1. \qquad [2]$$

A similar argument using P and R as foci shows that the ship also lies on the hyperbola with foci $P = (100, 0)$ and $R = (300, 0)$ and center $(200, 0)$, whose distance difference r is

$$|d_1 - d_3| = 980 \cdot 305 = 298{,}900 \text{ feet} \approx 56.61 \text{ miles.}$$

As before, you can verify that $a = \dfrac{56.61}{2} = 28.305$ and $a^2 = 28.305^2 = 801.17$. This hyperbola has center $(200, 0)$ and its foci are $(200 - c, k) = (100, 0)$ and $(200 + c, k) = (300, 0)$, which implies that $c = 100$.

$$b^2 = c^2 - a^2 = 100^2 - 801.17 = 9198.83$$

The ship also lies on the hyperbola

$$\frac{(x - 200)^2}{801.17} - \frac{y^2}{9198.83} = 1. \qquad [3]$$

Since the ship lies on both hyperbolas, its coordinates are solutions of both equations [2] and [3]. They can be found algebraically by solving each of the equations for y^2, setting the results equal, and solving for x. They can be found geometrically by graphing both hyperbolas and finding the points of intersection. Since the signal from P was received first, the ship is closer to P. So it is located at the point S in Figure 11.4–12 or at the intersection point directly below it. A graphical intersection finder shows that point S is at approximately $(130.48, 215.14)$, where the coordinates are in miles from the origin.

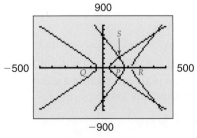

Figure 11.4-12

Exercises 11.4

In Exercises 1–16, find the equation of the conic sections satisfying the given conditions.

1. ellipse with center $(2, 3)$; endpoints of major and minor axes: $(2, -1), (0, 3), (2, 7), (4, 3)$

2. ellipse with center $(-5, 2)$ endpoints of major and minor axes: $(0, 2), (-5, 17), (-10, 2), (-5, -13)$

3. ellipse with center $(7, -4)$ foci on the line $x = 7$; major axis of length 12; minor axis of length 5

4. ellipse with center $(-3, -9)$; foci on the line $y = -9$; major axis of length 15; minor axis of length 7

5. hyperbola with center $(-2, 3)$; vertex $(-2, 1)$; passing through $\left(-2 + 3\sqrt{10}, 11\right)$

6. hyperbola with center $(-5, 1)$; vertex $(-3, 1)$; passing through $\left(-1, 1 - 4\sqrt{3}\right)$

7. hyperbola with center $(4, 2)$; vertex $(7, 2)$; asymptote $3y = 4x - 10$

8. hyperbola with center $(-3, -5)$; vertex $(-3, 0)$; asymptote $6y = 5x - 15$

9. parabola with vertex $(1, 0)$; axis $x = 1$; passing through $(2, 13)$

10. parabola with vertex $(-3, 0)$; axis $y = 0$; passing through $(-1, 1)$

11. parabola with vertex $(2, 1)$; axis $y = 1$; passing through $(5, 0)$

12. parabola with vertex $(1, -3)$; axis $y = -3$; passing through $(-1, -4)$

13. ellipse with center $(3, -2)$; passing through $(3, -6)$ and $(9, -2)$

14. ellipse with center $(2, 5)$; passing through $(2, 4)$ and $(-3, 5)$

15. parabola with vertex $(-3, -2)$ and focus $\left(-\frac{47}{16}, -2\right)$

16. parabola with vertex $(-5, -5)$ and focus $\left(-5, -\frac{99}{20}\right)$

In Exercises 17–22, assume that the graph of the equation is a nondegenerate conic section. Without graphing, determine whether the graph is a circle, ellipse, hyperbola, or parabola.

17. $x^2 - 2xy + 3y^2 - 1 = 0$

18. $xy - 1 = 0$

19. $x^2 + 2xy + y^2 + 2\sqrt{2}x - 2\sqrt{2}y = 0$

20. $2x^2 - 4xy + 5y^2 - 6 = 0$

21. $17x^2 - 48xy + 31y^2 + 50 = 0$

22. $2x^2 - 4xy - 2y^2 + 3x + 5y - 10 = 0$

In Exercises 23–34, sketch a complete graph of each conic section.

23. $\dfrac{(x - 1)^2}{4} + \dfrac{(y - 5)^2}{9} = 1$

24. $\dfrac{(x - 2)^2}{16} + \dfrac{(y + 3)^2}{12} = 1$

25. $\dfrac{(x + 1)^2}{16} + \dfrac{(y - 4)^2}{8} = 1$

26. $\dfrac{(x + 5)^2}{4} + \dfrac{(y + 2)^2}{12} = 1$

27. $y = 4(x - 1)^2 + 2$ 28. $y = 3(x - 2)^2 - 3$

29. $x = 2(y - 2)^2$ 30. $x = -3(y - 1)^2 - 2$

31. $\dfrac{(y + 3)^2}{25} - \dfrac{(x + 1)^2}{16} = 1$

32. $\dfrac{(y + 1)^2}{9} - \dfrac{(x - 1)^2}{25} = 1$

33. $\dfrac{(x + 3)^2}{1} - \dfrac{(y - 2)^2}{4} = 1$

34. $\dfrac{(y + 5)^2}{9} - \dfrac{(x - 2)^2}{1} = 1$

In Exercises 35–52, use the discriminant to identify the conic section whose equation is given, and find a viewing window that shows a complete graph.

35. $9x^2 + 4y^2 + 54x - 8y + 49 = 0$

36. $4x^2 + 5y^2 - 8x + 30y + 29 = 0$

37. $4y^2 - x^2 + 6x - 24y + 11 = 0$

38. $x^2 - 16y^2 = 0$

39. $3y^2 - x - 2y + 1 = 0$

40. $x^2 - 6x + y + 5 = 0$

41. $41x^2 - 24xy + 34y^2 - 25 = 0$

42. $x^2 + 2\sqrt{3}xy + 3y^2 + 8\sqrt{3}x - 8y + 32 = 0$

43. $17x^2 - 48xy + 31y^2 + 49 = 0$

44. $52x^2 - 72xy + 73y^2 = 200$

45. $9x^2 + 24xy + 16y^2 + 90x - 130y = 0$

46. $x^2 + 10xy + y^2 + 1 = 0$

47. $23x^2 + 26\sqrt{3}xy - 3y^2 - 16x + 16\sqrt{3}y + 128 = 0$

48. $x^2 + 2xy + y^2 + 12\sqrt{2}x - 12\sqrt{2}y = 0$

49. $17x^2 - 12xy + 8y^2 - 80 = 0$

50. $11x^2 - 24xy + 4y^2 + 30x + 40y - 45 = 0$

51. $3x^2 + 2\sqrt{3}xy + y^2 + 4x - 4\sqrt{3}y - 16 = 0$

52. $3x^2 + 2\sqrt{2}xy + 2y^2 - 12 = 0$

In Exercises 53 and 54, find the equations of two distinct ellipses satisfying the given conditions.

53. Center at $(-5, 3)$; major axis of length 14; minor axis of length 8.

54. Center at $(2, -6)$; major axis of length 15; minor axis of length 6.

55. *Critical Thinking* Show that the asymptotes of the hyperbola $\dfrac{x^2}{a^2} - \dfrac{y^2}{a^2} = 1$ are perpendicular to each other.

56. Find a number k such that $(-2, 1)$ is on the graph of $3x^2 + ky^2 = 4$. Then graph the equation.

57. Find the number b such that the vertex of the parabola $y = x^2 + bx + c$ lies on the y-axis.

58. Find the number d such that the parabola $(y + 1)^2 = dx + 4$ passes through $(-6, 3)$.

59. Find the points of intersection of the parabola $4y^2 + 4y = 5x - 12$ and the line $x = 9$.

60. Find the points of intersection of the parabola $4x^2 - 8x = 2y + 5$ and the line $y = 15$.

In Exercises 61–64, write the resulting equation in standard form.

61. Translate the hyperbola defined by the equation $3y^2 + 20x = 23 + 5x^2 + 12y$ up 3 units and to the right 5 units.

62. Translate the hyperbola defined by the equation $16x^2 - 9y^2 + 64x = 89 - 18y$ down 2 units and to the right 3 units.

63. Translate the hyperbola defined by the equation $4x^2 - 9y^2 - 8x + 54y = 113$ up 1 unit and to the left 4 units.

64. Translate the hyperbola defined by the equation $7x^2 - 5y^2 = 48 - 20y - 14x$ down 5 units and to the left 4 units.

65. Suppose a golf ball driven off the tee travels 210 yards down the fairway. During flight it reaches a maximum height of 55 yards. Find an equation that describes the ball's parabolic path if the tee is at the origin and the positive x-axis is along the ground in the direction of the drive.

66. Suppose a golf ball driven off the tee travels 175 yards down the fairway. During flight it reaches a maximum height of 40 yards. Find an equation that describes the ball's parabolic path if the tee is at the origin and the positive x-axis is along the ground in the direction of the drive.

67. Two listening stations 1 mile apart record an explosion. One microphone receives the sound 2 seconds after the other does. Use the line through the microphones as the x-axis, with the origin midway between the microphones, and the fact that sound travels at 1100 feet/second to find the equation of the hyperbola on which the explosion is located. Can you determine the exact location of the explosion?

68. Two transmission stations P and Q are located 200 miles apart on a straight shoreline. A ship 50 miles from shore is moving parallel to the shoreline. A signal from Q reaches the ship 400 microseconds after a signal from P. If the signals travel at 980 feet per microsecond, find the location of the ship (in terms of miles) in the coordinate system with x-axis through P and Q, and origin midway between them.

Excursion: Rotation of Axes

Objectives

- Write the equation of a rotated conic section in terms of *u* and *v*

- Determine the angle of rotation of a rotated conic section

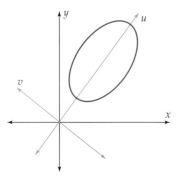

Figure 11.4.A-1

The graph of an equation of the form

$$Ax^2 + Bxy + Cy^2 + Dx + Ey + F = 0,$$

with $B \neq 0$, is a conic section that is rotated so that its axes are not parallel to the coordinate axes, as in Figure 11.4.A-1. Although the graph is readily obtained with a calculator, as in Examples 7–9 of Section 11.4, useful information about the center, vertices, etc., cannot be read directly from the equation, as it can be with an equation in standard form. However, if the *xy* coordinate system is replaced by a new coordinate system, as indicated by the blue *uv* axes in Figure 11.4.A-1, then the conic is not rotated in the new system and has a *uv* equation in standard form that will provide the desired information.

Rotation Equations

In order to use this approach, first determine the relationship between the *xy* coordinates of a point and its coordinates in the *uv* system. Suppose the *uv* coordinate system is obtained by rotating the *xy* axes about the origin, counterclockwise through an angle θ. If a point *P* has coordinates (x, y) in the *xy* system, its coordinates (u, v) can be found in the rotated coordinate system by using Figure 11.4.A-2.

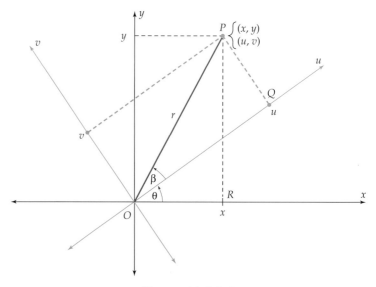

Figure 11.4.A-2

Triangle OPQ shows that

$$\cos \beta = \frac{OQ}{OP} = \frac{u}{r} \quad \text{and} \quad \sin \beta = \frac{PQ}{OP} = \frac{v}{r}$$

Therefore,

$$u = r \cos \beta \quad \text{and} \quad v = r \sin \beta$$

Similarly, triangle OPR shows that

$$\cos(\theta + \beta) = \frac{OR}{OP} = \frac{x}{r} \quad \text{and} \quad \sin(\theta + \beta) = \frac{PR}{OP} = \frac{y}{r}$$

so that

$$x = r \cos(\theta + \beta) \quad \text{and} \quad y = r \sin(\theta + \beta)$$

Applying the addition identity for cosine shows that

$$
\begin{aligned}
x &= r \cos(\theta + \beta) \\
&= r(\cos \theta \cos \beta - \sin \theta \sin \beta) \\
&= (r \cos \beta)\cos \theta - (r \sin \beta)\sin \theta \\
&= u \cos \theta - v \sin \theta
\end{aligned}
$$

A similar argument with $y = r \sin(\theta + \beta)$ and the addition identity for sine leads to the following result.

The Rotation Equations

> If the xy coordinate axes are rotated through an angle θ to produce the uv coordinate axes, then the coordinates (x, y) and (u, v) of a point are related by the following equations.
>
> $$x = u \cos \theta - v \sin \theta$$
> $$y = u \sin \theta + v \cos \theta$$

Example 1   **A Rotated Conic in the *uv* System**

If the xy axes are rotated $\dfrac{\pi}{6}$ radians, find the equation relative to the uv axes of the graph of

$$3x^2 + 2\sqrt{3}xy + y^2 + x - \sqrt{3}y = 0$$

Identify and graph the equation.

Solution

NOTE Recall that $\dfrac{\pi}{6}$ represents about 0.5236 radians, or 30°.

Because $\sin \dfrac{\pi}{6} = \dfrac{1}{2}$ and $\cos \dfrac{\pi}{6} = \dfrac{\sqrt{3}}{2}$, the rotation equations are

$$x = u \cos \frac{\pi}{6} - v \sin \frac{\pi}{6} = \frac{\sqrt{3}}{2}u - \frac{1}{2}v$$

$$y = u \sin \frac{\pi}{6} + v \cos \frac{\pi}{6} = \frac{1}{2}u + \frac{\sqrt{3}}{2}v$$

Substitute these expressions into the original equation.

$$3x^2 + 2\sqrt{3}xy + y^2 + x - \sqrt{3}y = 0$$

$$3\left(\frac{\sqrt{3}}{2}u - \frac{1}{2}v\right)^2 + 2\sqrt{3}\left(\frac{\sqrt{3}}{2}u - \frac{1}{2}v\right)\left(\frac{1}{2}u + \frac{\sqrt{3}}{2}v\right)$$

$$+ \left(\frac{1}{2}u + \frac{\sqrt{3}}{2}v\right)^2 + \left(\frac{\sqrt{3}}{2}u - \frac{1}{2}v\right) - \sqrt{3}\left(\frac{1}{2}u + \frac{\sqrt{3}}{2}v\right) = 0$$

Then multiply out the result.

$$3\left(\frac{3}{4}u^2 - \frac{\sqrt{3}}{2}uv + \frac{1}{4}v^2\right) + 2\sqrt{3}\left(\frac{\sqrt{3}}{4}u^2 + \frac{1}{2}uv - \frac{\sqrt{3}}{4}v^2\right)$$

$$+ \left(\frac{1}{4}u^2 + \frac{\sqrt{3}}{2}uv + \frac{3}{4}v^2\right) + \left(\frac{\sqrt{3}}{2}u - \frac{1}{2}v\right) - \sqrt{3}\left(\frac{1}{2}u + \frac{\sqrt{3}}{2}v\right) = 0$$

You can verify that the last equation simplifies to

$$4u^2 - 2v = 0 \qquad \text{or equivalently,} \quad u^2 = \frac{1}{2}v = 4\left(\frac{1}{8}\right)v$$

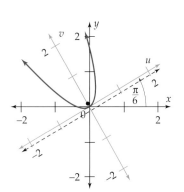

Figure 11.4.A-3

In the uv system, $u^2 = \frac{1}{2}v$, is the equation of an upward-opening parabola with vertex at $(0, 0)$ focus at $\left(0, \frac{1}{8}\right)$, and directrix $v = -\frac{1}{8}$, as shown in Figure 11.4.A-3.

■

Rotation Angle to Eliminate *xy* Term

Rotating the axes in the preceding example changed the original equation, which included an xy term, to an equation that had no uv term. This can be done for any second-degree equation by choosing an angle of rotation that will eliminate the xy term.

Rotation Angle

> The equation $Ax^2 + Bxy + Cy^2 + Dx + Ey + F = 0$ $(B \neq 0)$ can be rewritten as $A'u^2 + C'v^2 + D'u + E'v + F = 0$ by rotating the xy axes through an angle θ such that
>
> $$\cot 2\theta = \frac{A - C}{B} \qquad \left(0 < \theta < \frac{\pi}{2}\right)$$

The restriction $0 < \theta < \frac{\pi}{2}$ insures that $0 < 2\theta < \pi$.

Example 2   Find the Rotation Angle

What angle of rotation will eliminate the xy term in the equation

$$153x^2 + 192xy + 97y^2 - 1710x - 1470y + 5625 = 0,$$

and what are the rotation equations?

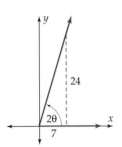

Figure 11.4.A-4

Solution

Letting $A = 153, B = 192$, and $C = 97$, the figure should be rotated through an angle of θ, where

$$\cot 2\theta = \frac{153 - 97}{192} = \frac{56}{192} = \frac{7}{24}$$

Because $0 < 2\theta < \pi$ and $\cot 2\theta$ is positive, the terminal side of the angle 2θ lies in the first quadrant, as shown in Figure 11.4.A-4. The hypotenuse of the triangle shown has length $\sqrt{7^2 + 24^2} = \sqrt{625} = 25$.

Hence, $\cos 2\theta = \frac{7}{25}$. The half-angle identities show that

$$\sin \theta = \sqrt{\frac{1 - \cos 2\theta}{2}} = \sqrt{\frac{1 - \frac{7}{25}}{2}} = \sqrt{\frac{9}{25}} = \frac{3}{5}$$

$$\cos \theta = \sqrt{\frac{1 + \cos 2\theta}{2}} = \sqrt{\frac{1 + \frac{7}{25}}{2}} = \sqrt{\frac{16}{25}} = \frac{4}{5}$$

Using $\sin \theta = \frac{3}{5}$ and the SIN^{-1} key on a calculator, the angle θ of rotation is approximately 0.6435 radians, or about 36.87°. The rotation equations are

$$x = u \cos \theta - v \sin \theta = \frac{4}{5}u - \frac{3}{5}v$$

$$y = u \sin \theta + v \cos \theta = \frac{3}{5}u + \frac{4}{5}v.$$

Identifying Rotated Conics

The rotation equations can be used to find the equation of the rotated conic in the uv coordinate system. Substitute the x rotation equation for x and the y rotation equation for y, and simplify the result to eliminate the xy term.

Example 3   Graph a Rotated Conic

Graph the equation without using a calculator.

$$153x^2 + 192xy + 97y^2 - 1710x - 1470y + 5625 = 0$$

Solution

The angle θ and the rotation equations for eliminating the xy term were found in the preceding example. Substitute the rotation equations into the given equation and simplify the result to eliminate the xy term.

$$153x^2 + 192xy + 97y^2 - 1710x - 1470y + 5625 = 0$$

$$153\left(\frac{4}{5}u - \frac{3}{5}v\right)^2 + 192\left(\frac{4}{5}u - \frac{3}{5}v\right)\left(\frac{3}{5}u + \frac{4}{5}v\right)$$

$$+ 97\left(\frac{3}{5}u + \frac{4}{5}v\right)^2 - 1710\left(\frac{4}{5}u - \frac{3}{5}v\right) - 1470\left(\frac{3}{5}u + \frac{4}{5}v\right) + 5625 = 0$$

$$153\left(\frac{16}{25}u^2 - \frac{24}{25}uv + \frac{9}{25}v^2\right) + 192\left(\frac{12}{25}u^2 + \frac{7}{25}uv - \frac{12}{25}v^2\right)$$

$$+ 97\left(\frac{9}{25}u^2 + \frac{24}{25}uv + \frac{16}{25}v^2\right) - 2250u - 150v + 5625 = 0$$

$$225u^2 + 25v^2 - 2250u - 150v + 5625 = 0$$

$$9u^2 + v^2 - 90u - 6v + 225 = 0$$

$$9(u^2 - 10u) + (v^2 - 6v) = -225$$

Finally, complete the square in u and v by adding the appropriate amounts to the right side so as not to change the equation.

$$9(u^2 - 10u + 25) + (v^2 - 6v + 9) = -225 + 9(25) + 9$$

$$9(u - 5)^2 + (v - 3)^2 = 9$$

$$\frac{(u - 5)^2}{1} + \frac{(v - 3)^2}{9} = 1$$

Therefore, the graph is an ellipse centered at (5, 3) in the uv coordinate system, as shown in Figure 11.4.A-5.

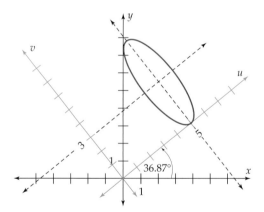

Figure 11.4.A-5

Exercises 11.4.A

In Exercises 1–4, rotate the axes through the given angle to form the uv coordinate system. Express the given equation in terms of the uv coordinate system.

1. $\theta = \dfrac{\pi}{4}$; $xy = 1$

2. $\theta = \dfrac{\pi}{4}$; $13x^2 + 10xy + 13y^2 = 72$

3. $\theta = \dfrac{\pi}{6}$; $7x^2 - 6\sqrt{3}xy + 13y^2 - 16 = 0$

4. $\sin\theta = \dfrac{1}{\sqrt{5}}$; $x^2 - 4xy + 4y^2 + 5\sqrt{5}y + 1 = 0$

In Exercises 5–8 find the angle of rotation that will eliminate the xy term of the equation and list the rotation equations in this case.

5. $41x^2 - 24xy + 34y^2 - 25 = 0$

6. $x^2 + 2\sqrt{3}xy + 3y^2 + 8\sqrt{3}x - 8y + 32 = 0$

7. $17x^2 - 48xy + 31y^2 + 49 = 0$

8. $52x^2 - 72xy + 73y^2 = 200$

9. *Critical Thinking*
  a. Given an equation
$$Ax^2 + Bxy + Cy^2 + Dx + Ey + F = 0$$
   with $B \neq 0$ and an angle θ, use the rotation equations to rewrite the equation in the form
$$A'u^2 + B'uv + C'v^2 + D'u + E'v + F' = 0,$$
   where $A', \ldots, F'$ are expressions involving $\sin\theta$, $\cos\theta$ and the constants $A, \ldots, F$.
  b. Verify that
   $B' = 2(C - A)\sin\theta\cos\theta + B(\cos^2\theta - \sin^2\theta)$
  c. Use the double-angle identities to show that
   $B' = (C - A)\sin 2\theta + B\cos 2\theta$
  d. If θ is chosen so that $\cos 2\theta = \dfrac{A - C}{B}$, show that $B' = 0$. This proves the rotation angle formula.

10. *Critical Thinking* Assume that the graph of $A'u^2 + C'v^2 + D'u + E'v + F' = 0$ (with at least one of A' or C' nonzero) in the uv coordinate system is a nondegenerate conic. Show that its graph is an ellipse if $A'C' > 0$ (A' and C' have the same sign), a hyperbola if $A'C' < 0$ (A' and C' have opposite signs), or a parabola if $A'C' = 0$.

11. *Critical Thinking* Assume the graph of
$$Ax^2 + Bxy + Cy^2 + Dx + Ey + F = 0$$
   is a nondegenerate conic section. Prove the statement in the box on page 723 as follows.
  a. In Exercise 9 **a.** show that
   $(B')^2 - 4A'C' = B^2 - 4AC.$
  b. Assume θ has been chosen so that $B' = 0$. Use Exercise 10 to show that the graph of the original equation is
   an ellipse if $B^2 - 4AC < 0$,
   a parabola if $B^2 - 4AC = 0$, and
   a hyperbola if $B^2 - 4AC > 0$.

12. *Critical Thinking* Suppose an xy- and uv-coordinate system have the same origin and θ is the angle between the positive x-axis and the positive u-axis. Show that the point (u, v) in the rotated system is related to the point (x, y) by the following equations. *Hint:* If the rotation from the xy-coordinate system to the uv-coordinate system is positive, then the rotation from the uv-coordinate system to the xy-coordinate system is negative.
$$u = x\cos\theta + y\sin\theta$$
$$v = y\cos\theta - x\sin\theta.$$

In Exercises 13–16, find the new coordinates of the point when the coordinate axes are rotated through the given angle by using the equations in Exercise 12.

13. $(3, 2)$; $\theta = \dfrac{\pi}{4}$

14. $(-2, 4)$; $\theta = \dfrac{\pi}{3}$

15. $(1, 0)$; $\theta = \dfrac{\pi}{6}$

16. $(3, 3)$; $\sin\theta = \dfrac{5}{13}$

11.5 Polar Coordinates

Objectives

- Locate points in a polar coordinate system

- Convert between coordinates in rectangular and polar systems

- Create graphs of equations in polar coordinates

- Recognize equations and graphs of:

  cardioid

  rose

  circle

  lemniscate

  limaçon

The coordinate system most commonly used is the rectangular coordinate system, which is based on two perpendicular axes. However, other coordinate systems are possible.

The Polar Coordinate System

Choose a point O in the plane, called the **origin**, or **pole.** The horizontal ray extending to the right with endpoint O is called the **polar axis.** A point P in the plane has **polar coordinates**

$$(r, \theta)$$

where r is the length of $\overline{OP}$ and θ is the angle with the polar axis as its initial side and $\overline{OP}$ as its terminal side, as shown in Figure 11.5-1. Unless otherwise stated, θ will be measured in radians.

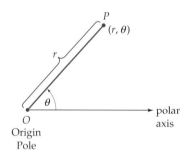

Figure 11.5-1

> **NOTE** The coordinates of the origin can be written as $(0, \theta)$, where θ is any angle.

The θ-coordinate may be either positive or negative, depending on whether it is measured as a counterclockwise or clockwise rotation. Figure 11.5-2 shows some points in a polar coordinate system, and the "circular grid" that a polar coordinate system imposes on the plane.

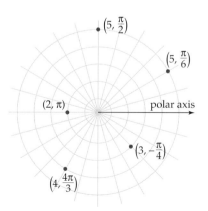

Figure 11.5-2

The polar coordinates of a point P are *not* unique. For example, because $\frac{\pi}{3}$, $\frac{7\pi}{3}$, and $\frac{-5\pi}{3}$ are coterminal angles, the coordinates $\left(2, \frac{\pi}{3}\right), \left(2, \frac{7\pi}{3}\right)$, and $\left(2, \frac{-5\pi}{3}\right)$ all represent the same point, as shown in Figure 11.5-3.

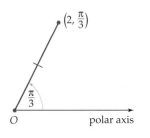
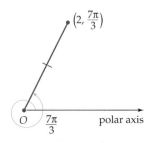
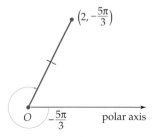

Figure 11.5-3

The r-coordinate may also be negative, as shown in Figure 11.5-4. For $r > 0$, the point $(-r, \theta)$ lies on the line containing the terminal side of θ at a distance r from the origin—but on the *opposite* side of the origin from the point (r, θ).

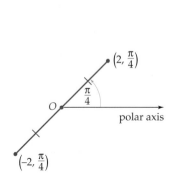
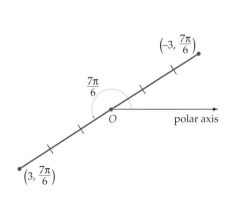
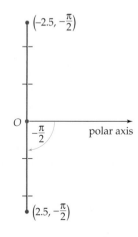

Figure 11.5-4

Example 1   **Polar Coordinates of a Point**

Determine if the given coordinates represent the same point as $\left(3, \frac{\pi}{6}\right)$ in a polar coordinate system.

a. $\left(3, \frac{13\pi}{6}\right)$ **b.** $\left(3, \frac{-5\pi}{6}\right)$ **c.** $\left(-3, \frac{7\pi}{6}\right)$

Solution

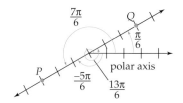

Figure 11.5-5

The point labeled Q in Figure 11.5-5 can be represented by the coordinates $\left(3, \dfrac{\pi}{6}\right), \left(3, \dfrac{13\pi}{6}\right)$, or $\left(-3, \dfrac{7\pi}{6}\right)$. The point labeled P can be represented by the coordinates $\left(3, \dfrac{-5\pi}{6}\right)$. Thus, the coordinates in **a** and **c** represent the same point as $\left(3, \dfrac{\pi}{6}\right)$, but the coordinates in **b** do not. ∎

Polar and Rectangular Coordinates

Suppose that a polar and rectangular system of coordinates are drawn in the same plane, with the origins at the same point, so that the polar axis is the positive x-axis, and the polar line $\theta = \dfrac{\pi}{2}$ is the y-axis. The coordinates of point P in the plane can be written as (r, θ) or as (x, y), as shown in Figure 11.5-6.

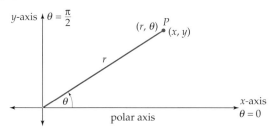

Figure 11.5-6

Let r be as shown in Figure 11.5-6, with r positive. Since r is the distance from $(0, 0)$ to (x, y), the distance formula shows that

$$r = \sqrt{x^2 + y^2}$$

Also, by the definitions of the trigonometric functions in the coordinate plane,

$$\cos \theta = \frac{x}{r} \qquad \sin \theta = \frac{y}{r} \qquad \tan \theta = \frac{y}{x}$$

These equations can be used to obtain the relationship between polar and rectangular coordinates.

Coordinate Conversion Formulas

> **Polar → Rectangular**
> Point P with polar coordinates (r, θ) has rectangular coordinates (x, y), where
> $$x = r \cos \theta \quad \text{and} \quad y = r \sin \theta$$
>
> **Rectangular → Polar**
> Point P with rectangular coordinates (x, y) has polar coordinates (r, θ), where
> $$r^2 = x^2 + y^2 \quad \text{and} \quad \tan \theta = \frac{y}{x}$$

Technology Tip

Keys to convert from rectangular to polar coordinates, or vice versa, are in the TI-83 **ANGLE** menu, in the **OPS** submenu of the TI-86 **VECTOR** menu, in the **ANGLE** submenu of the TI-89 **MATH** menu, in the **CONV** submenu of the Sharp 9600 **MATH** menu, and in the **ANGLE** submenu of the Casio 9850 **OPTN** menu. Conversions programs for HP-38 are in the Program Appendix.

The conversion formulas from polar to rectangular coordinates give a unique solution for all values of r and θ.

Example 2   Polar → Rectangular

Convert each point from polar coordinates to rectangular coordinates.

a. $\left(2, \dfrac{\pi}{6}\right)$ **b.** $(3, 4)$

Solution

a. For $\left(2, \dfrac{\pi}{6}\right)$, apply the conversion formulas using $r = 2$ and $\theta = \dfrac{\pi}{6}$.

$$x = 2 \cos \frac{\pi}{6} = 2 \cdot \frac{\sqrt{3}}{2} = \sqrt{3}$$

$$y = 2 \sin \frac{\pi}{6} = 2 \cdot \frac{1}{2} = 1$$

So the rectangular coordinates are $\left(\sqrt{3}, 1\right)$.

b. For $(3, 4)$, apply the conversion formulas using $r = 3$ and $\theta = 4$.

$$x = 3 \cos 4 \approx -1.96$$
$$y = 3 \sin 4 \approx -2.27$$

So the approximate rectangular coordinates are $(-1.96, -2.27)$.

Figure 11.5-7 displays the rectangular coordinates of the points in part **a** and part **b**, along with both a rectangular grid and a polar grid.

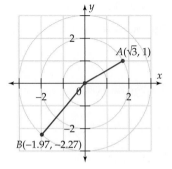

Figure 11.5-7

The conversion formulas from rectangular to polar coordinates do not have unique solutions for r and θ. In particular, the equation $\tan \theta = \dfrac{y}{x}$ has no solutions when $x = 0$ and infinitely many solutions when $x \neq 0$.

$$\theta = \tan^{-1}\frac{y}{x} + k\pi \qquad\qquad (k \text{ is any integer})$$

Not every solution works for a specific point P. To find solutions that represent the point P, you need to know which quadrant contains P. $\theta = \tan^{-1}\frac{y}{x}$ can be used for points in Quadrants I and IV because it would be an angle between $-\frac{\pi}{2}$ and $\frac{\pi}{2}$. Similarly, $\theta = \tan^{-1}\frac{y}{x} + \pi$ can be used for points in Quadrants II and III because it would be an angle between $\frac{\pi}{2}$ and $\frac{3\pi}{2}$.

Example 3   Rectangular → Polar

Convert each point from rectangular coordinates to polar coordinates.

a. $(2, -2)$ **b.** $(-3, -5)$ **c.** $(0, -5)$ **d.** $(-2, 4)$

Solution

a. For $(2, -2)$, the second set of equations of the coordinate conversion formulas with $x = 2$ and $y = -2$ shows that

$$r = \sqrt{2^2 + (-2)^2} = \sqrt{8} = 2\sqrt{2} \qquad \text{and} \qquad \tan\theta = \frac{-2}{2} = -1, \qquad \text{or}$$

$\theta = \tan^{-1}\frac{-2}{2} = -\frac{\pi}{4}$. The point is in Quadrant IV, so two possible answers are $\left(2\sqrt{2}, -\frac{\pi}{4}\right)$ or $\left(2\sqrt{2}, \frac{7\pi}{4}\right)$.

b. For $(-3, -5)$, $r = \sqrt{(-3)^2 + (-5)^2} = \sqrt{34}$. A calculator shows that

$$\tan^{-1}\frac{-5}{-3} \approx 1.0304$$

Because the point $(-3, -5)$ is in Quadrant III, $\theta \approx 1.0304 + \pi \approx 4.17$. Therefore, one possible answer is $\left(\sqrt{34}, 4.17\right)$.

c. For $(0, -5)$, $r = \sqrt{0^2 + (-5)^2} = 5$. Because the point is on the negative y-axis, $\theta = \frac{3\pi}{2}$. Therefore, two possible answers are $\left(5, \frac{3\pi}{2}\right)$ or $\left(5, -\frac{\pi}{2}\right)$.

d. For $(-2, 4)$, $r = \sqrt{(-2)^2 + 4^2} = \sqrt{4 + 16} = \sqrt{20} = 2\sqrt{5}$.

$\tan\theta = -\frac{4}{2} = -2$, and $\tan^{-1}(-2) \approx -1.11$, which is in Quadrant IV.

Because $(-2, 4)$ is in Quadrant II, $\theta \approx -1.11 + \pi \approx 2.03$.

Therefore, one possible answer is $(2\sqrt{5}, 2.03)$.

Figure 11.5-8 displays the polar coordinates of the points in parts **a–d**, along with both a rectangular grid and a polar grid.

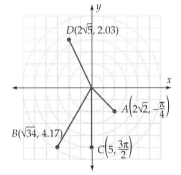

Figure 11.5-8

Polar Graphs

An equation like $r = 2\cos\theta$, where r and θ are the variables, is a **polar equation.** Equations in x and y are called **rectangular** or **Cartesian equations.** Many useful curves have simple polar equations, although they may have complicated rectangular equations.

Like other graphs, the graph of a polar equation in r and θ is the set of points (r, θ) in the plane that make the equation true. It is possible to write a polar equation in rectangular form or a rectangular equation in polar form by using the coordinate conversion formulas, definitions, and basic facts about trigonometric functions.

Graphs of the Form $r = a$ and $\theta = b$

Several types of graphs have equations that are simpler in polar form than in rectangular form. For example, the graph of $r = 1$ consists of points of the form $(1, \theta)$, which is all points that are 1 unit from the pole. That is, the graph of $r = 1$ is the unit circle centered at the pole. The equation $\theta = \dfrac{\pi}{4}$ consists of all points of the form $\left(r, \dfrac{\pi}{4}\right)$. That is, all points that lie on the line that makes a $\dfrac{\pi}{4}$, or 45°, angle with the polar axis.

Example 4   **Polar Graphs**

Graph each polar equation below.

a. $r = 3$

b. $\theta = \dfrac{\pi}{6}$

Solution

a. The graph consists of all points $(3, \theta)$, that is, all points whose distance from the pole is 3. So, the graph is a circle of radius 3 with its center at the pole.

b. The graph consists of all points $\left(r, \dfrac{\pi}{6}\right)$. These points lie on the straight line that contains the terminal side of an angle of $\dfrac{\pi}{6}$ radians, whose initial side is the polar axis.

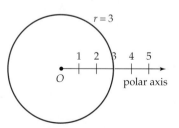

Figure 11.5-9

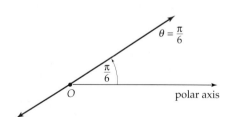

Figure 11.5-10

Graphs of Other Polar Equations

Other types of graphs have simple equations in polar form. Several types of polar graphs have specific forms that can be classified by special names like cardioid, limaçon, and rose.

Many polar equations are functions, with independent variable θ, and dependent variable r. Therefore, polar functions are written as $r = f(\theta)$.

Example 5   Polar Graphs

Graph $r = 1 + \sin \theta$.

Solution

Consider the behavior of $\sin \theta$ in each quadrant.

As θ increases from 0 to $\frac{\pi}{2}$, $\sin \theta$ increases from 0 to 1. So $r = 1 + \sin \theta$ increases from 1 to 2.

As θ increases from $\frac{\pi}{2}$ to π, $\sin \theta$ decreases from 1 to 0. So $r = 1 + \sin \theta$ decreases from 2 to 1.

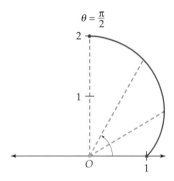

As θ increases from π to $\frac{3\pi}{2}$, $\sin \theta$ decreases from 0 to -1. So $r = 1 + \sin \theta$ decreases from 1 to 0.

As θ increases from $\frac{3\pi}{2}$ to 2π, $\sin \theta$ increases from -1 to 0. So $r = 1 + \sin \theta$ increases from 0 to 1.

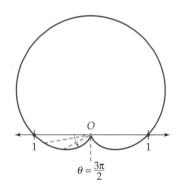
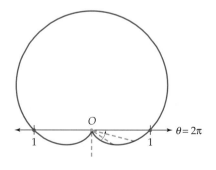

Figure 11.5-11

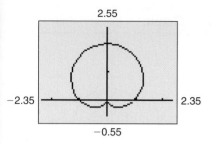

2.55

−2.35   2.35

−0.55

Figure 11.5-12

For $\theta > 2\pi$ and $\theta < 0$, $\sin\theta$ repeats the same pattern, so the full graph, as shown in the lower right drawing of Figure 11.5-11, is called a **cardioid**. The graph of $r = 1 + \sin\theta$ displayed on a graphing calculator is shown in Figure 11.5-12.

The easiest way to graph a polar function of the form $r = f(\theta)$ is to use a calculator in polar graphing mode. The following Tip should be helpful.

Technology Tip

The viewing window of a calculator in polar graphing mode has the usual settings for the x- and y-values, and also θ min, θ max, and θ step. (The Casio 9850 has θ pitch instead of θ step.) For a complete graph of a polar equation that contains a trigonometric function, the interval from θ min to θ max should be at least as large as the period of the function.

The value of θ step determines the number of points plotted by the calculator. A smaller value of θ step will generally result in a more accurate curve but will also take longer to graph.

To view the polar coordinates using the Trace feature, from the Format menu choose PolarGC on TI models and PolarCoord on Sharp 9600. Casio 9850 and HP 38G automatically display coordinates for the type of graph shown.

Graphing Exploration

Graph $r = 2 + 4\cos\theta$ on a calculator in polar graphing mode. Experiment with the size of the window and the values of θ min, θ max, and θ step to find (approximately) the graph shown in Figure 11.5-13. What window settings did you use to obtain the graph?

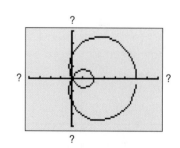

?

?   ?

?

Figure 11.5-13

Common Polar Graphs

The following is a summary of commonly encountered polar graphs. In each case, a and b are constants, and θ is measured in radians.

Depending on the plus or minus sign and whether sine or cosine is used, the basic shape of each graph may differ from those shown by a rotation, reflection, or horizontal or vertical shift.

Equation	Name of Graph	Shape of Graph
$r = a\theta \quad (\theta \geq 0)$ $r = a\theta \quad (\theta \leq 0)$	Archimedian spiral	
$r = a\,(1 \pm \sin\theta)$ $r = a\,(1 \pm \cos\theta)$	cardioid	
$r = a \sin n\theta$ $r = a \cos n\theta$ $(n \geq 2)$	rose For n odd, there are n petals. For n even, there are $2n$ petals.	
$r = a \sin \theta$ $r = a \cos \theta$	circle	

Equation	Name of Graph	Shape of Graph
$r^2 = \pm a^2 \sin 2\theta$ $r^2 = \pm a^2 \cos 2\theta$	lemniscate	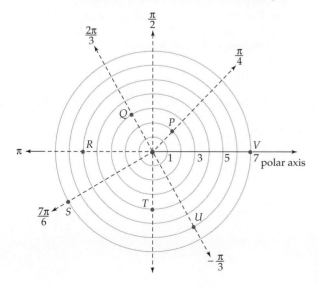
$r = a + b \sin \theta$ $r = a + b \sin \theta$ $(a, b > 0, a \neq b)$	limaçon	

(Shape of Graph for lemniscate row, labeled) $r^2 = a^2 \sin 2\theta$ $r^2 = a^2 \cos 2\theta$

(Shape of Graph for limaçon row, labeled)
$a < b$ $b < a < 2b$ $a \geq 2b$
$r = a + b \cos \theta$ $r = a + b \sin \theta$ $r = a - b \sin \theta$

Exercises 11.5

1. What is one possible pair of polar coordinates of each of the points P, Q, R, S, T, U, V in the figure?

In Exercises 2–6, list four other pairs of polar coordinates for the given point, each with a different combination of signs (that is, $r > 0$, $\theta > 0$; $r > 0$, $\theta < 0$; $r < 0$, $\theta > 0$; and $r < 0$, $\theta < 0$).

2. $\left(3, \dfrac{\pi}{3}\right)$ **3.** $(-5, \pi)$ **4.** $\left(2, -\dfrac{2\pi}{3}\right)$

5. $\left(-1, -\dfrac{\pi}{6}\right)$ **6.** $\left(\sqrt{3}, \dfrac{3\pi}{4}\right)$

In Exercises 7–10, convert the polar coordinates to rectangular coordinates.

7. $\left(3, \dfrac{\pi}{3}\right)$ **8.** $\left(-2, \dfrac{\pi}{4}\right)$

9. $\left(-1, \dfrac{5\pi}{6}\right)$ **10.** $(2, 0)$

In Exercises 11–16, convert the rectangular coordinates to polar coordinates.

11. $\left(3\sqrt{3}, -3\right)$ **12.** $\left(2\sqrt{3}, -2\right)$ **13.** $(2, 4)$

14. $(3, -2)$ **15.** $(-5, 2.5)$ **16.** $(-6.2, -3)$

In Exercises 17–22, sketch the graph of the equation without using a calculator.

17. $r = 4$ **18.** $r = -1$ **19.** $\theta = -\dfrac{\pi}{3}$

20. $\theta = \dfrac{5\pi}{6}$ **21.** $\theta = 1$ **22.** $\theta = -4$

In Exercises 23–46, sketch the graph of the equation.

23. $r = \theta$ $(\theta \leq 0)$ **24.** $r = 3\theta$ $(\theta \geq 0)$

25. $r = 1 - \sin \theta$ **26.** $r = 3 - 3 \cos \theta$

27. $r = -2 \cos \theta$ **28.** $r = -6 \sin \theta$

29. $r = \cos 2\theta$ **30.** $r = \cos 3\theta$

31. $r = \sin 3\theta$ **32.** $r = \sin 4\theta$

33. $r^2 = 4 \cos 2\theta$ **34.** $r^2 = \sin 2\theta$

35. $r = 2 + 4 \cos \theta$ **36.** $r = 1 + 2 \cos \theta$

37. $r = \sin \theta + \cos \theta$ **38.** $r = 4 \cos \theta + 4 \sin \theta$

39. $r = \sin \dfrac{\theta}{2}$ **40.** $r = 4 \tan \theta$

41. $r = \sin \theta \tan \theta$ (cissoid)

42. $r = 4 + 2 \sec \theta$ (conchoid)

43. $r = e^{\theta}$ (logarithmic spiral)

44. $r^2 = \dfrac{1}{\theta}$ **45.** $r = \dfrac{1}{\theta}$ $(\theta > 0)$ **46.** $r^2 = \theta$

47. a. Find a complete graph of $r = 1 - 2 \sin 3\theta$.
  b. Predict what the graph of $r = 1 - 2 \sin 4\theta$ will look like. Then check your prediction with a calculator.
  c. Predict what the graph of $r = 1 - 2 \sin 5\theta$ will look like. Then check your prediction with a calculator.

48. a. Find a complete graph of $r = 1 - 3 \sin 2\theta$.
  b. Predict what the graph of $r = 1 - 3 \sin 3\theta$ will look like. Then check your prediction with a calculator.
  c. Predict what the graph of $r = 1 - 3 \sin 4\theta$ will look like. Then check your prediction with a calculator.

49. If a and b are constants such that $ab \neq 0$, show that the graph of $r = a \sin \theta + b \cos \theta$ is a circle. *Hint*: Multiply both sides by r and convert to rectangular coordinates.

50. *Critical Thinking* Prove that the coordinate conversion formulas are valid when $r < 0$. *Hint*: If P has coordinates (x, y) and (r, θ), with $r < 0$, verify that the point Q with rectangular coordinates $(-x, -y)$ has polar coordinates $(-r, \theta)$. Since $r < 0$, $-r$ is positive and the conversion formulas proved in the text apply to Q. For instance, $-x = -r \cos \theta$, which implies that $x = r \cos \theta$.

51. *Critical Thinking* Distance Formula for Polar Coordinates: Prove that the distance from (r, θ) to (s, β) is $\sqrt{r^2 + s^2 - 2rs \cos (\theta - \beta)}$. *Hint*: If $r > 0$, $s > 0$, and $\theta > \beta$, then the triangle with vertices (r, θ), (s, β), $(0, 0)$ has an angle of $\theta - \beta$, whose sides have lengths r and s. Use the Law of Cosines.

52. *Critical Thinking* Explain why the following symmetry tests for the graphs of polar equations are valid.
  a. If replacing θ by $-\theta$ produces an equivalent equation, then the graph is symmetric with respect to the line $\theta = 0$ (the x-axis).
  b. If replacing θ by $\pi - \theta$ produces an equivalent equation, then the graph is symmetric with respect to the line $\theta = \pi/2$ (the y-axis).
  c. If replacing r by $-r$ produces an equivalent equation, then the graph is symmetric with respect to the pole (origin).

11.6   Polar Equations of Conics

Objectives

• Define eccentricity of an ellipse, a parabola, and a hyperbola

• Develop and use the general polar equation of a conic section

In a rectangular coordinate system, each type of conic section has a different definition. By using polar coordinates, it is possible to give a unified treatment of conics and their equations. A key concept in this development is *eccentricity*.

Eccentricity

Recall that ellipses and hyperbolas are defined in terms of two foci, and both have two vertices that lie on the line through the foci. The **eccentricity,** *e*, of an ellipse or a hyperbola is the ratio

$$e = \frac{\text{distance between the foci}}{\text{distance between the vertices}}$$

NOTE Do not confuse the eccentricity of a conic section, which is denoted as *e* and whose value varies, with the number *e*, which is the constant 2.718281828.... The meaning should be clear in context.

If a conic is centered at the origin with foci on the *x*-axis, the situation is as follows.

Ellipse	**Hyperbola**
$\dfrac{x^2}{a^2} + \dfrac{y^2}{b^2} = 1$	$\dfrac{x^2}{a^2} - \dfrac{y^2}{b^2} = 1$

For $a > b$,

foci: $(\pm c, 0)$ vertices: $(\pm a, 0)$ foci: $(\pm c, 0)$ vertices: $(\pm a, 0)$

$c = \sqrt{a^2 - b^2}$ $c = \sqrt{a^2 + b^2}$

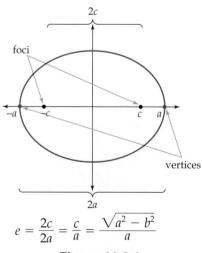

$$e = \frac{2c}{2a} = \frac{c}{a} = \frac{\sqrt{a^2 - b^2}}{a}$$

Figure 11.6-1

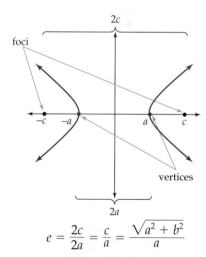

$$e = \frac{2c}{2a} = \frac{c}{a} = \frac{\sqrt{a^2 + b^2}}{a}$$

Figure 11.6-2

A similar analysis shows that the formulas for e are also valid for conics whose foci lie on the y-axis. These formulas can be used to compute the eccentricity of any ellipse or hyperbola whose equation is in standard form.

As Figure 11.6-1 shows, the distance between the foci of an ellipse is always less than the distance between its vertices, so that

$$0 < e < 1 \text{ for all ellipses.}$$

Similarly, the distance between the foci of a hyperbola is greater than the distance between its vertices, as shown in Figure 11.6-2, so that

$$e > 1 \text{ for all hyperbolas.}$$

Example 1   Eccentricity of a Conic

Find the eccentricity of each given conic.

a. $\dfrac{y^2}{4} - \dfrac{x^2}{21} = 1$ **b.** $4x^2 + 9y^2 - 32x - 90y + 253 = 0$

Solution

a. $\dfrac{y^2}{4} - \dfrac{x^2}{21} = 1$ represents a hyperbola with $a^2 = 4$ and $b^2 = 21$, so

$$e = \frac{\sqrt{a^2 + b^2}}{a} = \frac{\sqrt{4 + 21}}{2} = \frac{\sqrt{25}}{2} = \frac{5}{2} = 2.5$$

b. From Example 2 in Section 11.4, $4x^2 + 9y^2 - 32x - 90y + 253 = 0$ can be written in standard form, as

$$\frac{(x - 4)^2}{9} + \frac{(y - 5)^2}{4} = 1$$

The graph of this equation has the same shape as the ellipse

$$\frac{x^2}{9} + \frac{y^2}{4} = 1$$

with a horizontal and a vertical shift. Since the distances between the foci or vertices are the same in both ellipses, the eccentricity is the same for both. Using $a^2 = 9$ and $b^2 = 4$, the eccentricity is

$$e = \frac{\sqrt{a^2 - b^2}}{a} = \frac{\sqrt{9 - 4}}{3} = \frac{\sqrt{5}}{3} \approx 0.745$$

■

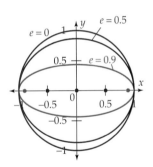

Figure 11.6-3

The eccentricity of an ellipse measures its distortion from a circle, which is a special case of an ellipse. In a circle, the two foci coincide at the center, so the distance between the foci is 0 and its eccentricity is 0. As the foci move farther apart, the eccentricity increases, and the ellipse becomes more distorted from a circle. In Figure 11.6-3, the foci and eccentricities are shown in the same color as the corresponding ellipse.

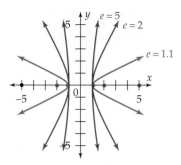

Figure 11.6-4

In Figure 11.6-4, colors of the foci and the eccentricities correspond to each hyperbola. As the foci move farther from the vertices, the branches of the hyperbola become straighter and approach vertical lines.

The preceding discussion does not apply to parabolas because they have only one focus. For reasons explained below, the eccentricity of any parabola is defined to be the number 1.

Alternate Definition of Conics

The following description, whose proof is omitted, is sometimes used to define the conic sections because it provides a unified approach instead of the variety of descriptions given in Sections 11.1, 11.2, and 11.3. It is also used to determine the polar equations of conic sections.

Alternate Definition of Conic Sections

Let L be a fixed line called a directrix, P a fixed point not on L, and e a positive constant. The set of all points X in the plane such that

$$\frac{\text{distance between } X \text{ and the fixed point}}{\text{distance between } X \text{ and the fixed line}} = \frac{XP}{XL} = e$$

is a conic section with P as one focus.

- For $0 < e < 1$, the conic is an ellipse.
- For $e = 1$, the conic is a parabola.
- For $e > 1$, the conic is a hyperbola.

NOTE Recall that the distance from a point to a line is measured along the perpendicular segment from the point to the line.

Recall that the definition of a parabola was all points equidistant from a fixed point and a fixed line. Therefore, the alternate definition coincides with the original definition given in Section 11.3. Examples of this definition are shown in the following diagram.

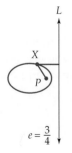

$e = \dfrac{3}{4}$

$$\frac{XP}{XL} = \frac{3}{4} \rightarrow XP = \frac{3}{4}XL$$

The distance from X to P is $\dfrac{3}{4}$ the distance from X to L. The conic is an ellipse.

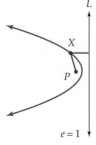

$e = 1$

$$\frac{XP}{XL} = 1 \rightarrow XP = XL$$

The distance from X to P equals the distance from X to L. The conic is a parabola.

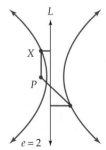

$e = 2$

$$\frac{XP}{XL} = 2 \rightarrow XP = 2XL$$

The distance from X to P is twice the distance from X to L. The conic is a hyperbola.

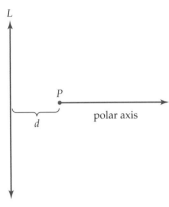

Figure 11.6-5

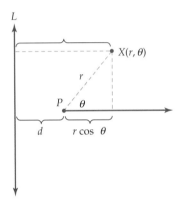

Figure 11.6-6

Polar Equations of Conics

To generate polar equations of conics from the alternate definition, let P be the pole, and L be a vertical line d units to the left of the pole, as shown in Figure 11.6-5.

A point $X = (r, \theta)$ on a general conic satisfies the condition

$$\frac{XP}{XL} = e$$

By the definition of polar coordinates, the r-coordinate of X, shown in Figure 11.6–6, is the distance from the origin to X.

$$XP = r$$

Figure 11.6-6 also shows that

$$XL = d + r \cos \theta$$

So the polar equation of the conic is given by

$$\frac{XP}{XL} = \frac{r}{d + r \cos \theta} = e$$
$$r = ed + e r \cos \theta$$
$$r - e r \cos \theta = ed$$
$$r(1 - e \cos \theta) = ed$$
$$r = \frac{ed}{1 - e \cos \theta}$$

If L is to the right of the polar axis, it can be shown that

$$r = \frac{ed}{1 + e \cos \theta}$$

If L is a horizontal line, it can also be shown that

$$r = \frac{ed}{1 - e \sin \theta} \quad \text{or} \quad r = \frac{ed}{1 + e \sin \theta}$$

depending on whether L is below the pole or above it.

If an equation has another value in place of 1, divide both numerator and denominator by that number to rewrite the equation in the desired form. When the constant term in the denominator is 1, the eccentricity is the coefficient of the trigonometric function. For example, suppose a conic is given by

$$r = \frac{20}{4 - 8 \cos \theta}$$

Divide both numerator and denominator by 4.

$$r = \frac{5}{1 - 2 \cos \theta}$$

The conic is a hyperbola because the eccentricity is 2.

Polar Equations of Conic Sections

NOTE d is the distance from the focus at the pole to the directrix.

Equations	Graph	Example
$r = \dfrac{ed}{1 + e \cos \theta}$ $r = \dfrac{ed}{1 - e \cos \theta}$	$0 < e < 1$ *Ellipse* • Vertices $\theta = 0$ and $\theta = \pi$ • One focus at $(0, 0)$	
	$e = 1$ *Parabola* • Vertex $\theta = 0$ or $\theta = \pi$; r is not defined for the other value of θ • Focus at $(0, 0)$	
	$e > 1$ *Hyperbola* • Vertices $\theta = 0$ and $\theta = \pi$ • One focus at $(0, 0)$	
$r = \dfrac{ed}{1 + e \sin \theta}$ $r = \dfrac{ed}{1 - e \sin \theta}$	$0 < e < 1$ *Ellipse* • Vertices $\theta = \dfrac{\pi}{2}$ and $\theta = \dfrac{3\pi}{2}$ • One focus at $(0, 0)$	
	$e = 1$ *Parabola* • Vertices $\theta = \dfrac{\pi}{2}$ or $\theta = \dfrac{3\pi}{2}$; r is not defined for the other value of θ • Focus at $(0, 0)$	
	$e > 1$ *Hyperbola* • Vertices $\theta = \dfrac{\pi}{2}$ and and $\theta = \dfrac{3\pi}{2}$ • One focus at $(0, 0)$	

Example 2   Polar Equations of Conic Sections

Find a complete graph of $r = \dfrac{3e}{1 + e \cos \theta}$ for the following eccentricities.

a. $e = 0.7$ **b.** $e = 1$ **c.** $e = 2$

Solution

From the first equation in the preceding chart, with $d = 3$, the graphs are an ellipse, a parabola, and a hyperbola, respectively, as shown in Figure 11.6-7. In each case, $0 \le \theta \le 2\pi$.

a. $e = 0.7$

$$r = \frac{3(0.7)}{1 + 0.7 \cos \theta} = \frac{2.1}{1 + 0.7 \cos \theta}$$
ellipse

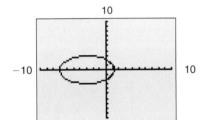

b. $e = 1$

$$r = \frac{3(1)}{1 + 1 \cdot \cos \theta} = \frac{3}{1 + \cos \theta}$$
parabola

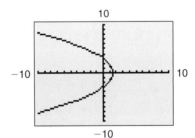

c. $e = 2$

$$r = \frac{3(2)}{1 + 2 \cos \theta} = \frac{6}{1 + 2 \cos \theta}$$
hyperbola

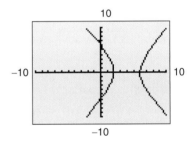

Figure 11.6-7

Example 3   Polar Equations of Conic Sections

Identify the conic section that is the graph of

$$r = \frac{20}{4 - 10 \sin \theta}$$

and find its eccentricity and vertices.

Solution

First, rewrite the equation in one of the forms listed in the preceding box.

$$r = \frac{20}{4 - 10 \sin \theta} = \frac{20}{4(1 - 2.5 \sin \theta)} = \frac{5}{1 - 2.5 \sin \theta}$$

According to the equation, $e = 2.5$. Thus, the graph is a hyperbola with eccentricity 2.5.

The vertices occur when $\theta = \dfrac{\pi}{2}$ and $\theta = \dfrac{3\pi}{2}$. To find the r-coordinates, substitute into the original equation.

$$\theta = \frac{\pi}{2} \;\rightarrow\; r = \frac{20}{4 - 10\sin\dfrac{\pi}{2}} = \frac{20}{4 - 10 \cdot 1} = \frac{20}{-6} = -\frac{10}{3}$$

$$\theta = \frac{3\pi}{2} \;\rightarrow\; r = \frac{20}{4 - 10\sin\dfrac{3\pi}{2}} = \frac{20}{4 - 10(-1)} = \frac{20}{14} = \frac{10}{7}$$

The vertices are $\left(-\dfrac{10}{3}, \dfrac{\pi}{2}\right)$ and $\left(\dfrac{10}{7}, \dfrac{3\pi}{2}\right)$. ∎

Graphing Exploration

Find a viewing window that shows a complete graph of the hyperbola in Example 3.

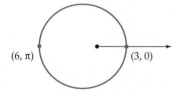

Figure 11.6-8

Example 4 **Polar Equations of Conic Sections**

Find a polar equation of the ellipse with one focus at $(0, 0)$ and vertices $(3, 0)$ and $(6, \pi)$.

Solution

Because the vertices occur when $\theta = 0$ and $\theta = \pi$, the polar equation is of the form

$$r = \frac{ed}{1 + e\cos\theta} \qquad \text{or} \qquad r = \frac{ed}{1 - e\cos\theta}.$$

Select one of these equations, say

$$r = \frac{ed}{1 + e\cos\theta}$$

and proceed as follows. If the selected equation leads to a contradiction, start again with the other form.

Substitute the values of r and θ given by the vertices to obtain two equations.

$$(3, 0) \qquad\qquad\qquad\qquad (6, \pi)$$

$$3 = \frac{ed}{1 + e\cos 0} \qquad\qquad 6 = \frac{ed}{1 + e\cos \pi}$$

$$3 = \frac{ed}{1 + e} \qquad\qquad\qquad 6 = \frac{ed}{1 - e}$$

$$3(1 + e) = ed \qquad \text{and} \qquad 6(1 - e) = ed$$

Therefore,

$$3(1 + e) = 6(1 - e)$$
$$3 + 3e = 6 - 6e$$
$$9e = 3$$
$$e = \frac{1}{3}$$

Substituting this value of e into the equation $3(1 + e) = ed$ and solving for d shows that $d = 12$. Hence, $ed = 4$ and the equation of the ellipse is

$$r = \frac{4}{1 + \frac{1}{3}\cos\theta} \qquad \text{or equivalently,} \qquad r = \frac{12}{3 + \cos\theta}$$

If you had started this process with the equation $r = \dfrac{ed}{1 - e\cos\theta}$, you would have obtained $e = -\dfrac{1}{3}$, which is impossible since the eccentricity is always positive.

Exercises 11.6

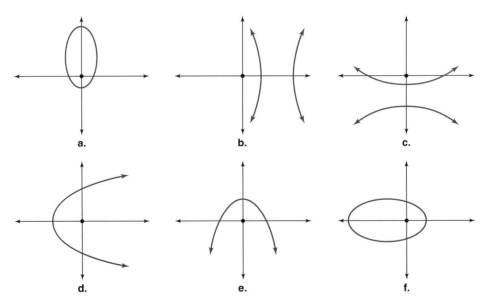

a.   b.   c.

d.   e.   f.

In Exercises 1–6, which of the graphs a–f above could be the graph of the given equation?

1. $r = \dfrac{3}{1 - \cos\theta}$

2. $r = \dfrac{6}{2 + \cos\theta}$

3. $r = \dfrac{6}{2 - 4\sin\theta}$

4. $r = \dfrac{15}{1 + 4\cos\theta}$

5. $r = \dfrac{6}{3 - 2\sin\theta}$

6. $r = \dfrac{6}{\dfrac{3}{2} + \dfrac{3}{2}\sin\theta}$

In Exercises 7–12, identify the conic section whose equation is given; if it is an ellipse or hyperbola, state its eccentricity.

7. $r = \dfrac{12}{3 + 4 \sin \theta}$

8. $r = \dfrac{-10}{2 + 3 \cos \theta}$

9. $r = \dfrac{8}{3 + 3 \sin \theta}$

10. $r = \dfrac{20}{5 - 10 \sin \theta}$

11. $r = \dfrac{2}{6 - 4 \cos \theta}$

12. $r = \dfrac{-6}{5 + 2 \cos \theta}$

In Exercises 13–18, find the eccentricity of the conic whose equation is given.

13. $\dfrac{x^2}{100} + \dfrac{y^2}{99} = 1$

14. $\dfrac{(x - 4)^2}{18} + \dfrac{(y + 5)^2}{25} = 1$

15. $\dfrac{(x - 6)^2}{10} - \dfrac{y^2}{40} = 1$

16. $4x^2 + 9y^2 - 24x + 36y + 36 = 0$

17. $16x^2 - 9y^2 - 32x + 36y + 124 = 0$

18. $4x^2 - 5y^2 - 16x - 50y + 71 = 0$

19. a. Using a square viewing window, graph these ellipses on the same screen, if possible.

$$\dfrac{x^2}{16} + \dfrac{y^2}{1} = 1 \quad \dfrac{x^2}{16} + \dfrac{y^2}{6} = 1 \quad \dfrac{x^2}{16} + \dfrac{y^2}{14} = 1$$

b. Compute the eccentricity of each ellipse in part **a.**
c. Based on parts **a** and **b**, how is the shape of an ellipse related to its eccentricity?

20. a. Graph these hyperbolas on the same screen, if possible.

$$\dfrac{y^2}{4} - \dfrac{x^2}{1} = 1 \quad \dfrac{y^2}{4} - \dfrac{x^2}{12} = 1 \quad \dfrac{y^2}{4} - \dfrac{x^2}{96} = 1$$

b. Compute the eccentricity of each hyperbola in part **a.**
c. Based on parts **a** and **b**, how is the shape of a hyperbola related to its eccentricity?

In Exercises 21–32, sketch the graph of the equation and label the vertices.

21. $r = \dfrac{8}{1 - \cos \theta}$

22. $r = \dfrac{5}{3 + 2 \sin \theta}$

23. $r = \dfrac{4}{2 - 4 \cos \theta}$

24. $r = \dfrac{5}{1 + \cos \theta}$

25. $r = \dfrac{10}{4 - 3 \sin \theta}$

26. $r = \dfrac{12}{3 + 4 \sin \theta}$

27. $r = \dfrac{15}{3 - 2 \cos \theta}$

28. $r = \dfrac{32}{3 + 5 \sin \theta}$

29. $r = \dfrac{3}{1 + \sin \theta}$

30. $r = \dfrac{10}{3 + 2 \cos \theta}$

31. $r = \dfrac{10}{2 + 3 \sin \theta}$

32. $r = \dfrac{15}{4 - 4 \cos \theta}$

In Exercises 33–46, find the polar equation of the conic section that has focus (0, 0) and satisfies the given conditions.

33. parabola; vertex $(3, \pi)$

34. parabola; vertex $\left(2, \dfrac{\pi}{2}\right)$

35. ellipse; vertices $\left(2, \dfrac{\pi}{2}\right)$ and $\left(8, \dfrac{3\pi}{2}\right)$

36. ellipse; vertices $(2, 0)$ and $(4, \pi)$

37. hyperbola; vertices $(1, 0)$ and $(-3, \pi)$

38. hyperbola; vertices $\left(-2, \dfrac{\pi}{2}\right)$ and $\left(4, \dfrac{3\pi}{2}\right)$

39. eccentricity 4; directrix $r = -2 \sec \theta$

40. eccentricity 2; directrix $r = 4 \csc \theta$

41. eccentricity 1; directrix $r = -3 \csc \theta$

42. eccentricity 1; directrix $r = 5 \sec \theta$

43. eccentricity $\dfrac{1}{2}$; directrix $r = 2 \sec \theta$

44. eccentricity $\dfrac{4}{5}$; directrix $r = 3 \csc \theta$

45. hyperbola; vertical directrix to the left of the pole; eccentricity 2; $\left(1, \dfrac{2\pi}{3}\right)$ is on the graph.

46. hyperbola; horizontal directrix above the pole; eccentricity 2; $\left(1, \dfrac{2\pi}{3}\right)$ is on the graph.

47. A comet travels in a parabolic orbit with the sun as the focus. When the comet is 60 million miles from the sun, the line segment from the sun to the comet makes an angle of $\dfrac{\pi}{3}$ radians with the axis of the parabolic orbit. Using the sun as the pole and assuming the axis of the orbit lies along the polar axis, find a polar equation for the orbit.

48. Halley's Comet has an elliptical orbit, with eccentricity 0.97 and the sun as a focus. The length of the major axis of the orbit is 3364.74 million miles. Using the sun as the pole and assuming the major axis of the orbit is perpendicular to the polar axis, find a polar equation for the orbit.

11.7 Plane Curves and Parametric Equations

Objectives

- Define plane curves and parameterizations
- Find parametric equations for projectile motion and cycloids

Many curves in the plane cannot be represented as the graph of a function $y = f(x)$. Parametric graphing makes it possible to represent such curves in terms of functions and also provides a formal definition of a curve in the plane.

Plane Curves

Consider an object moving in the plane during a particular time interval. In order to describe both the path of the object and its location at a particular time, three variables are needed: the time t, and the coordinates (x, y) of the object at time t. For example, the coordinates might be given by

$$x = 4 \cos t + 5 \cos 3t \quad \text{and} \quad y = \sin 3t + t$$

During the time interval $0 \le t \le 12.5$, the object traces out the curve shown in Figure 11.7-1. The points labeled on the graph show the location of the point at various times. Note that the object may be at the same location at different times, the points where the graph crosses itself.

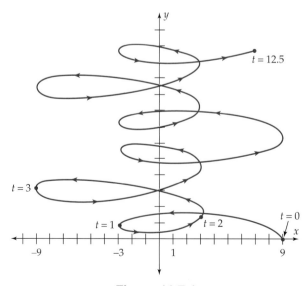

Figure 11.7-1

Definition of a Plane Curve

> Let f and g be continuous functions of t on an interval I. The set of all points (x, y), where
>
> $$x = f(t) \quad \text{and} \quad y = g(t)$$
>
> is called a *plane curve*. The variable t is called a *parameter* and the equations that define x and y are called *parametric equations*.

A pair of parametric equations that describe a given curve is called a **parameterization** of the curve. More than one parameterization is possible for a given curve.

Example 1   Parameterizations of a Line

Find three parameterizations of the line through $(1, -3)$ with slope -2.

Solution

The equation of the line in rectangular coordinates is

$$y + 3 = -2(x - 1) \quad \text{or equivalently} \quad y = -2x - 1 \qquad \text{[1]}$$

Choose three expressions in terms of t to represent x, and substitute each into equation [1] to find corresponding expressions for y.

a. $x = t$

$y = -2t - 1$

for any t

b. $x = t + 1$

$y = -2(t + 1) - 1$

$= -2t - 3$

for any t

c. $x = \tan t$

$y = -2\tan t - 1$

$-\dfrac{\pi}{2} < t < \dfrac{\pi}{2}$

Notice in **a** and **b** that when t runs through all real numbers, both x and y take on all real numbers as well. In **c** when t runs from $-\dfrac{\pi}{2}$ to $\dfrac{\pi}{2}$, $x = \tan t$ takes all possible real number values, and hence so does y. Therefore, each parameterization represents the entire line.

CAUTION

Not every substitution of an expression for x gives a complete parameterization of the graph. For example, the parametric equations

$$x = t^2$$
$$y = -2t^2 - 1$$

give a nonnegative x-coordinate and a negative y-coordinate for every value of t, so the parameterization produces only part of the graph.

Graphing Parametric Equations

Parametric equations may be graphed by hand by plotting points, or by using a calculator in parametric mode. When choosing a viewing window, you must specify values not only for x and y, but also for t. You must also choose a t-step (or t-pitch), which determines how much t changes each time a point is plotted. A t-step between 0.05 and 0.15 usually produces a relatively smooth graph in a reasonable amount of time.

Technology Tip

Graphing Exploration ●

Graph the curve shown in Figure 11.7-1 at the beginning of this sec-tion using the window

$$0 \leq t \leq 12.5 \qquad -10 \leq x \leq 10 \qquad 0 \leq y \leq 15$$

and t-step 0.1. Does the graph look like Figure 11.7-1? Now change the t-step to 1.5 and graph the equations again. Now how does the graph look? Experiment with different t-steps to see how they affect the graph.

Example 2   **Parameterization of a Parabola**

By hand, graph the curve given by

$$x = -2t \qquad \text{and} \qquad y = 4t^2 - 4, \qquad -1 \leq t \leq 2.$$

Confirm your sketch by using the parametric mode on a calculator.

Solution

For $-1 \leq t \leq 2$, there is a value of x and a value of y that corresponds to each specific value of t. Find several points by picking values for t, find-ing the corresponding values of x and y, plotting the points, and connecting the points in the order determined by the least to greatest values of t.

t	$x = -2t$	$y = 4t^2 - 4$	(x, y)
-1	2	0	$(2, 0)$
0	0	-4	$(0, -4)$
1	-2	0	$(-2, 0)$
2	-4	12	$(-4, 12)$

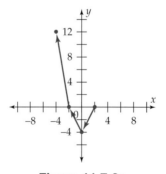

Figure 11.7-2a

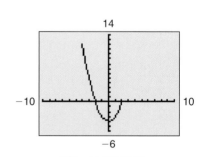

Figure 11.7-2b

The points are plotted and the direction of the curve is indicated in Figure 11.7-2a, and a calculator-generated graph is shown in Figure 11.7-2b.

The direction in which a parametric curve is traced is called its **orientation.**

Eliminating the Parameter

Some curves given by parametric equations can also be expressed as part of the graph of an equation in x and y. The process for doing this, called **eliminating the parameter,** is as follows.

> **Solve one of the parametric equations for the parameter t and substitute this result in the other parametric equation.**

Example 3   **Eliminate the Parameter**

Consider the curve given in Example 2.

$$x = -2t \qquad \text{and} \qquad y = 4t^2 - 4, \qquad -1 \le t \le 2$$

Find an equation in x and y whose graph includes the graph of the given curve.

Solution

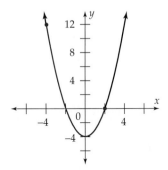

Figure 11.7-3

Solve one of the parametric equations for t and substitute the result into the other equation. Solving $x = -2t$ for t shows that $t = -\dfrac{x}{2}$. Substituting this into the equation for y and simplifying the result will eliminate t.

$$y = 4t^2 - 4 = 4\left(-\frac{x}{2}\right)^2 - 4 = 4\left(\frac{x^2}{4}\right) - 4 = x^2 - 4$$

The graph of $y = x^2 - 4$ is the parabola shown in Figure 11.7-3.

Every point on the curve given by the parametric equations is also on the graph of $y = x^2 - 4$. However, the curve given by the parametric equation is *not* the entire parabola, but only the part shown in red, which joins the points $(2, 0)$ and $(-4, 12)$. These points correspond to the minimum and maximum values of t, $t = -1$ and $t = 2$.

Example 4   **Parameterization of Transformations**

Given the parent relation $x = y^2$, write a set of parametric equations to represent the relation, and sketch the graph.

Then write the parametric equations of the following successive transformations of the parent relation, and sketch each graph.

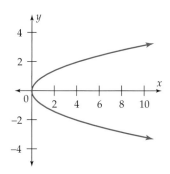

Figure 11.7-4a

a. a horizontal stretch by a factor of 5

b. then a horizontal shift 3 units to the right

c. then a vertical shift down 2 units

Finally, find the focus and a parameterization of the directrix of the parabola found in step **c.**

Solution

The parent relation can be parameterized as

$$x = t^2 \quad \text{and} \quad y = t \quad t \text{ any real number,}$$

whose graph is shown in Figure 11.7-4.

a. A horizontal stretch by a factor of 5

$$x = 5t^2$$
$$y = t$$
for any t

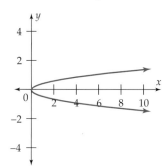

Figure 11.7-4b

b. Then a horizontal shift 3 units to the right

$$x = 5t^2 + 3$$
$$y = t$$
for any t

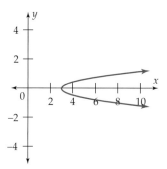

Figure 11.7-4c

c. Then a vertical shift down 2 units

$$x = 5t^2 + 3$$
$$y = t - 2$$
for any t

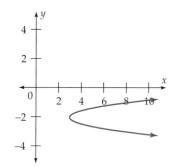

Figure 11.7-4d

Recall that the equation of a parabola has the form $y^2 = 4px$. Solving for x, the equation can be written as

$$x = \frac{1}{4p} y^2$$

Therefore, the coefficient of the squared term can be used to find the value of p, which in turn can be used to find both the focus and the directrix of the parabola.

Setting the coefficient of the squared term, 5, equal to $\frac{1}{4p}$ yields

$$5 = \frac{1}{4p} \quad \text{or} \quad p = \frac{1}{20}$$

Note that the vertex has been translated to $(3, -2)$ and that the focus is $\frac{1}{20}$ of a unit to the right of the vertex. Thus, the focus is at $\left(3 + \frac{1}{20}, -2\right)$, or $\left(\frac{61}{20}, -2\right)$. The directrix is the vertical line that is $\frac{1}{20}$ of a unit to the left of the vertex, that is, $x = 3 - \frac{1}{20} = \frac{59}{20}$.

■

Applications

Example 5   Application of Parameterization of a Parabola

A golfer hits a ball with an initial velocity of 140 feet per second so that its path as it leaves the ground makes an angle of 31° with the horizontal.

a. When does the ball hit the ground?

b. How far from its starting point does it land?

c. What is the maximum height of the ball during its flight?

Solution

Imagine that the golf ball starts at the origin and travels in the direction of the positive x-axis. If there were no gravity, the distance traveled by the ball in t seconds would be $140t$ feet. As shown in Figure 11.7-5a, the coordinates (x, y) of the ball would satisfy

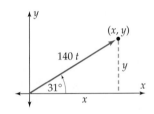

Figure 11.7-5a

$$\frac{x}{140t} = \cos 31° \qquad \frac{y}{140t} = \sin 31°$$
$$x = (140 \cos 31°)t \qquad y = (140 \sin 31°)t.$$

However, gravity at time t exerts a force of $16t^2$ feet per second per second downward, that is, in the negative direction on the y-axis. Consequently, the coordinates of the golf ball at time t are

$$x = (140 \cos 31°)t \qquad \text{and} \qquad y = (140 \sin 31°)t - 16t^2.$$

The path given by these parametric equations is shown in Figure 11.7-5b.

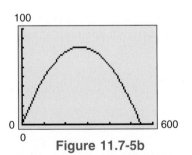

Figure 11.7-5b

a. The ball is on the ground when $y = 0$, that is, at the x-intercepts of the graph, which can be found geometrically by using trace and zoom-in. To find the intercepts algebraically, set $y = 0$ and solve for t.

$$(140 \sin 31°)t - 16t^2 = 0$$
$$t(140 \sin 31° - 16t) = 0$$
$$t = 0 \quad \text{or} \quad 140 \sin 31° - 16t = 0$$
$$t = \frac{140 \sin 31°}{16} \approx 4.5066$$

Thus, the ball hits the ground after approximately 4.5066 seconds.

b. The horizontal distance traveled by the ball is given by the x-coordinate of the second intercept. The x-coordinate when $t \approx 4.5066$ is

$$x = (140 \cos 31°)(4.5066) \approx 540.81 \text{ feet.}$$

c. The graph in Figure 11.7-5 looks like a parabola—and it is, as you can verify by eliminating the parameter t (see Exercise 40). The y-coordinate of the vertex is the maximum height of the ball. It can be found graphically by using trace and zoom-in, or algebraically as follows.

The vertex occurs halfway between the two x-intercepts at $x = 0$ and $x = 540.81$, that is, when $x \approx \dfrac{0 + 540.81}{2} = 270.405$.

$$(140 \cos 31°)t = x = 270.405$$

$$t = \frac{270.405}{140 \cos 31°}$$

$$\approx 2.2533$$

Therefore, the y-coordinate of the vertex, which is the maximum height of the ball, is

$$y = (140 \sin 31°)(2.2533) - 16(2.2533)^2 \approx 81.237 \text{ feet.}$$

Technology Tip

The graphical root finder and maximum finder do not operate in parametric mode.

Example 6   Projectile Motion

A batter hits a ball that is 3 feet above the ground. The ball leaves the bat with an initial velocity of 138 feet per second, making an angle of 26° with the horizontal and heading toward a 25-foot fence that is 400 feet away. Will the ball go over the fence?

Solution

Suppose that home plate is at the origin and that the ball travels in the direction of the positive x-axis. The vertical and horizontal distances traveled by the ball, disregarding gravity, are

$$\frac{x}{138t} = \cos 26° \qquad \frac{y - 3}{138t} = \sin 26°$$

$$x = (138 \cos 26°)t \qquad y = (138 \sin 26°)t + 3,$$

as shown in Figure 11.7-6a.

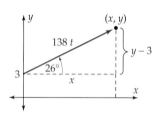

Figure 11.7-6a

Allowing for the effect of gravity on the y-coordinate, the ball's path is given by the parametric equations

$$x = (138 \cos 26°)t \qquad \text{and} \qquad y = (138 \sin 26°)t + 3 - 16t^2.$$

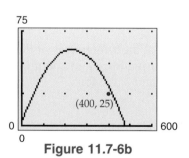

Figure 11.7-6b

The graph of the ball's path, shown in Figure 11.7-6b, was made with the grid-on feature and vertical tick marks 25 units apart. It shows that the y-coordinate of the ball is greater than 25 when its x-coordinate is 400. So, the ball goes over the fence.

The procedure used in Example 6 applies to the general case. Replacing 3 by k, 26° by θ, and 138 by v leads to the following conclusion.

Projectile Motion

When a projectile

- **is fired from the position $(0, k)$ on the positive y-axis at an angle θ with the horizontal,**
- **in the direction of the positive x-axis,**
- **with initial velocity v feet per second,**
- **with negligible air resistance,**

then its position at time t seconds is given by the parametric equations

$$x = (v \cos \theta)t \qquad \text{and} \qquad y = (v \sin \theta)t + k - 16t^2.$$

Technology Tip

In parametric graphing zoom-in can be very time-consuming. It is often more effective to limit the t range to the values near the points you are interested in and set the t step very small. The picture may be hard to read, but trace can be used to determine coordinates.

Graphing Exploration

Will the ball in Example 5 go over the fence if its initial velocity is 135 feet per second? Use degree mode and the viewing window of Figure 11.7-6b with $0 \le t \le 4$ and t step = 0.1 to graph the ball's path. You may need to use trace if the graph is hard to read. If the answer still is not clear, try changing the t step to 0.02.

Cycloids

Imagine a bug that is sitting at a point P at the edge of a wheel. The path traced out by the bug as the wheel rolls is a curve called a **cycloid**, as shown in Figure 11.7-7.

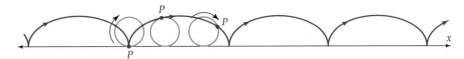

Figure 11.7-7

Cycloids have a number of interesting applications. For example, of all the possible paths joining P and Q in Figure 11.7-8, an arch of an inverted cycloid (in red) is the curve along which a particle subject only to gravity will slide from P to Q in the shortest possible time.

The Dutch physicist Christiaan Huygens, who invented the pendulum clock, proved that a particle takes the same amount of time to slide to the bottom point, Q, of an inverted cycloid (see Figure 11.7-9) starting from *any* point P on the curve.

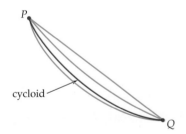

Figure 11.7-8

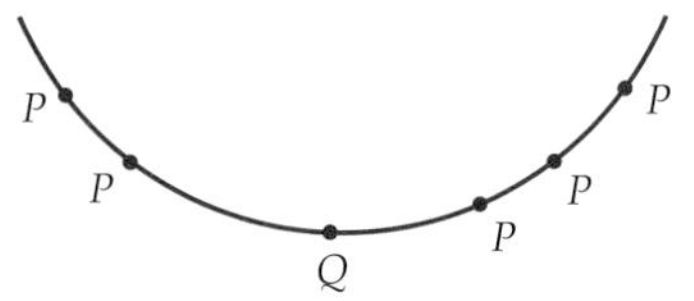

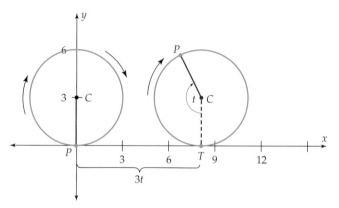

Figure 11.7-9

Example 7 **Parameterization of a Cycloid**

Find a parameterization of a cycloid generated by point P on a circle of radius 3 that rolls along the x-axis.

Solution

Begin with P at the origin and the center C of the circle at $(0, 3)$. As the circle rolls along the x-axis, the segment $\overline{CP}$ rotates through an angle of t radians, as shown in Figure 11.7-10.

Figure 11.7-10

The distance from T to the origin is the length of the arc of the circle from T to P. From the formula for arc length in Section 6.3, $\ell = r\theta = 3t$.

Therefore, the center C has coordinates $(3t, 3)$. For $0 < t < \dfrac{\pi}{2}$, triangle PQC in Figure 11.7-11 shows that

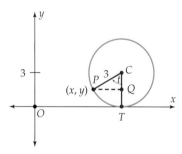

Figure 11.7-11

$$\sin t = \frac{PQ}{3} \qquad \text{and} \qquad \cos t = \frac{CQ}{3}$$

or, equivalently,

$$PQ = 3 \sin t \qquad \text{and} \qquad CQ = 3 \cos t$$

Thus, the point (x, y) in Figure 11.7-11 has the following coordinates.

$$x = OT - PQ = 3t - 3\sin t = 3(t - \sin t)$$
$$y = CT - CQ = 3 - 3\cos t = 3(1 - \cos t)$$

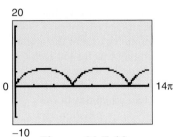

Figure 11.7-12

A similar analysis for other values of t shows that these equations are valid for all values of t. (See Exercises 47–51.) Therefore, the parametric equations of the cycloid are

$$x = 3(t - \sin t) \quad \text{and} \quad y = 3(1 - \cos t), \text{ for any } t.$$

In general, a cycloid generated by a point on a circle of radius r has the following parameterization.

$$x = r\,(t - \sin t) \quad \text{and} \quad y = r\,(1 - \cos t), \quad \text{for any } t$$

Exercises 11.7

In Exercises 1–14, find a viewing window that shows a complete graph of the curve.

1. $x = t^2 - 4, \quad y = \dfrac{t}{2}, \quad -2 \le t \le 3$

2. $x = 3t^2, \quad y = 2 + 5t, \quad 0 \le t \le 2$

3. $x = 2t, \quad y = t^2 - 1, \quad -1 \le t \le 2$

4. $x = t - 1, \quad y = \dfrac{t+1}{t-1}, \quad t \ge 1$

5. $x = 4 \sin 2t + 9, \quad y = 6 \cos t - 8, \quad 0 \le t \le 2\pi$

6. $x = t^3 - 3t - 8, \quad y = 3t^2 - 15, \quad -4 \le t \le 4$

7. $x = 6 \cos t + 12 \cos^2 t, \quad y = 8 \sin t + 8 \sin t \cos t,$
$\quad 0 \le t \le 2\pi$

8. $x = 12 \cos t, \quad y = 12 \sin 2t, \quad 0 \le t \le 2\pi$

9. $x = 6 \cos t + 5 \cos 3t, \quad y = 6 \sin t - 5 \sin 3t,$
$\quad 0 \le t \le 2\pi$

10. $x = 3t^2 + 10, \quad y = 4t^3, \quad t$ any real number

11. $x = 12 \cos 3t \cos t + 6, \quad y = 12 \cos 3t \sin t - 7,$
$\quad 0 \le t \le 2\pi$

12. $x = 2 \cos 3t - 6, \quad y = 2 \cos 3t \sin t + 7,$
$\quad 0 \le t \le 2\pi$

13. $x = t \sin t, \quad y = t \cos t, \quad 0 \le t \le 8\pi$

14. $x = 9 \sin t, \quad y = 9t \cos t, \quad 0 \le t \le 20$

In Exercises 15–24, the given curve is part of the graph of an equation in x and y. Eliminate the parameter by solving one equation for t and substituting the result into the other equation.

15. $x = t - 3, \quad y = 2t + 1, \quad t \ge 0$

16. $x = t + 5, \quad y = \sqrt{t}, \quad t \ge 0$

17. $x = -2 + t^2, \quad y = 1 + 2t^2, \quad \text{for any } t$

18. $x = t^2 + 1, \quad y = t^2 - 1, \quad \text{for any } t$

19. $x = e^t, \quad y = t, \quad \text{for any } t$

20. $x = 2e^t, \quad y = 1 - e^t, \quad t \ge 0$

21. $x = 3 \cos t, \quad y = 3 \sin t, \quad 0 \le t \le 2\pi$

22. $x = 4 \sin 2t, \quad y = 2 \cos 2t, \quad 0 \le t \le 2\pi$

23. $x = 3 \cos t, \quad y = 4 \sin t, \quad 0 \le t \le 2\pi$

24. $x = 2 \sin t - 3, \quad y = 2 \cos t + 1, \quad 0 \le t \le \pi$

In Exercises 25 and 26, sketch the graphs of the given curves and compare them. Do they differ? If so, how?

25. a. $x = -4 + 6t, \quad y = 7 - 12t, \quad 0 \le t \le 1$
   b. $x = 2 - 6t, \quad y = -5 + 12t, \quad 0 \le t \le 1$

26. a. $x = t, \quad y = t^2, \quad \text{for any } t$
   b. $x = \sqrt{t}, \quad y = t, \quad \text{for any } t$
   c. $x = e^t, \quad y = e^{2t}, \quad \text{for any } t$

27. By eliminating the parameter, show that the curve with parametric equations
$$x = a + (c - a)t, \quad y = b + (d - b)t$$
$$\text{for any } t$$
is a straight line.

In Exercises 28–30, find a parameterization of the given curve. Confirm your answer by graphing.

28. line segment from $(14, -5)$ to $(5, -14)$ *Hint*: See Exercise 27.

29. line segment from $(-6, 12)$ to $(12, -10)$

30. line segment from $(18, 4)$ to $(-16, 14)$

In Exercises 31–34, locate all local maxima and minima (other than endpoints) of the curve.

31. $x = 4t - 6$, $\quad y = 3t^2 + 2$, $\quad -10 \le t \le 10$

32. $x = t^3 + \sin t + 4$, $\quad y = \cos t$, $\quad -1.5 \le t \le 2$

33. $x = 4t^3 - t + 4$, $\quad y = -3t^2 + 5$, $\quad -2 \le t \le 2$

34. $x = 4t^3 - \cos t - 5$, $\quad y = 3t^2 - 8$, $\quad -2 \le t \le 2$

35. Show that the ball's path in Example 5 is a parabola by eliminating the parameter in the parametric equations below.
$$x = (140 \cos 31°)t$$
$$y = (140 \sin 31°)t - 16t^2$$

In Exercises 36–41, use a calculator in degree mode, and assume that air resistance is negligible.

36. A ball is thrown from a height of 5 feet above the ground with an initial velocity of 60 feet/second at an angle of 50° with the horizontal.
 a. Graph the ball's path.
 b. When and where does the ball hit ground?

37. A medieval bowman shoots an arrow which leaves the bow 4 feet above the ground with an initial velocity of 88 feet/second at an angle of 48° with the horizontal.
 a. Graph the arrow's path.
 b. Will the arrow go over the 40-foot-high castle wall that is 200 feet from the archer?

38. A golfer at a driving range stands on a platform 2 feet above the ground and hits the ball with an initial velocity of 120 feet/second at an angle of 39° with the horizontal. There is a 32-foot-high fence 400 feet away. Will the ball fall short, hit the fence, or go over it?

39. A golf ball is hit off the tee at an angle of 30° and lands 300 feet away. What was its initial velocity? *Hint*: The ball lands when $x = 300$ and $y = 0$. Use this fact and the parametric equations for the ball's path to find two equations in the variables t and v. Solve for v.

40. A football kicked from the ground has an initial velocity of 75 feet/second.
 a. Set up the parametric equations that describe the ball's path. Experiment graphically with different angles to find the smallest angle (within one degree) needed so that the ball travels at least 150 feet.
 b. Use algebra and trigonometry to find the angle needed for the ball to travel exactly 150 feet. *Hint*: The ball lands when $x = 150$ and $y = 0$. Use this fact and the parametric equations for the ball's path to find two equations in the variables t and θ. Solve the "x equation" for t and substitute this result into the other one; then solve for θ. The double-angle identity may be helpful for putting this equation into a form that is easy to solve.

41. A skeet is fired from the ground with an initial velocity of 110 feet/second at an angle of 28°.
 a. Graph the skeet's path.
 b. How long is the skeet in the air?
 c. How high does it go?

42. A golf ball is hit off the ground at an angle of θ degrees with an initial velocity of 100 feet/second.
 a. Graph the path of the ball when $\theta = 30°$ and when $\theta = 60°$. In which case does the ball land farthest away?
 b. Do part **a** when $\theta = 25°$ and $\theta = 65°$.
 c. Experiment further and make a conjecture as to the results when the sum of the two angles is 90°.
 d. Prove your conjecture algebraically. *Hint*: Find the value of t at which a ball hit at angle θ hits the ground (which occurs when $y = 0$); this value of t will be an expression involving θ. Find the corresponding value of x (which is the distance of the ball from the starting point). Then do the same for an angle of $90° - \theta$, and use the cofunction identities (in degrees) to show that you get the same value of x.

43. A golf ball is hit off the ground at an angle of θ degrees with an initial velocity of 100 feet/second.
 a. Graph the path of the ball when $\theta = 20°$, $\theta = 40°$, $\theta = 60°$, and $\theta = 80°$.
 b. For what angle in part **a** does the ball land farthest from where it started?
 c. Experiment with different angles, as in parts **a** and **b**, and make a conjecture as to which angle results in the ball landing farthest from its starting point.

In Exercises 44–46, complete the derivation of the parametric equations of the cycloid in Example 7.

44. a. If $\dfrac{\pi}{2} < t < \pi$, verify that angle θ in the figure has measure $t - \dfrac{\pi}{2}$ and that

$$x = OT - CQ = 3t - 3\cos\left(t - \frac{\pi}{2}\right)$$

$$y = CT + PQ = 3 + 3\sin\left(t - \frac{\pi}{2}\right).$$

b. Use the addition and subtraction identities for sine and cosine to show that in this case
$x = 3(t - \sin t)$ and $y = 3(1 - \cos t)$.

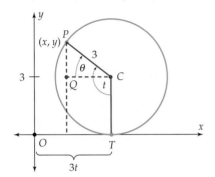

45. a. If $\frac{3\pi}{2} < t < 2\pi$, verify that angle θ in the

figure has measure $t - \frac{3\pi}{2}$ and that

$$x = OT + CQ = 3t + 3\cos\left(t - \frac{3\pi}{2}\right)$$

$$y = CT - PQ = 3 - 3\sin\left(t - \frac{3\pi}{2}\right).$$

b. Use the addition and subtraction identities for sine and cosine to show that in this case
$x = 3(t - \sin t)$ and $y = 3(1 - \cos t)$.

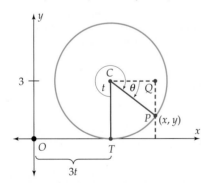

46. a. If $\pi < t < \frac{3\pi}{2}$, verify that angle θ in the figure

measures $\frac{3\pi}{2} - t$ and that

$$x = OT + CQ = 3t + 3\cos\left(\frac{3\pi}{2} - t\right)$$

$$y = CT + PQ = 3 + 3\sin\left(\frac{3\pi}{2} - t\right).$$

b. Use the addition and subtraction identities for sine and cosine to show that in this case

$$x = 3(t - \sin t) \text{ and } y = 3(1 - \cos t).$$

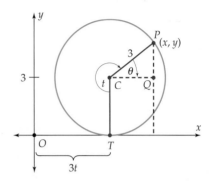

47. *Critical Thinking* Set your calculator for radian mode and for simultaneous graphing mode. Check your instruction manual for how to do this. Particles A, B, and C are moving in the plane, with their positions at time t seconds given by:
A: $x = 8\cos t$ and $y = 5\sin t$
B: $x = 3t$ and $y = 5t$
C: $x = 3t$ and $y = 4t$

a. Graph the paths of A and B in the window with $0 \le x \le 12$, $0 \le y \le 6$, and $0 \le t \le 2$. The paths intersect, but do the particles actually collide? That is, are they at the same point at the same time? For slow motion, choose a very small t-step, such as 0.01.

b. Set t-step $= 0.05$ and trace to estimate the time at which A and B are closest to each other.

c. Graph the paths of A and C and determine geometrically, as in part **b**, whether they collide. Approximately when are they closest?

d. Confirm your answers in part **c** as follows. Explain why the distance between particles A and C at time t is given by

$$d = \sqrt{(8\cos t - 3t)^2 + (5\sin t - 4t)^2}.$$

A and C will collide if $d = 0$ at some time. Using function graphing mode, graph this distance function when $0 \le t \le 2$. Zoom-in if necessary, and show that d is always positive. Find the value of t for which d is smallest.

48. *Critical Thinking* A particle moves on the horizontal line $y = 3$. Its x-coordinate at time t seconds is given by $x = 2t^3 - 13t^2 + 23t - 8$. This exercise explores the motion of the particle.

a. Graph the path of the particle in the viewing window with $-10 \le x \le 10$, $-2 \le y \le 4$, $0 \le t \le 4.3$, and t-step $= 0.05$. Note that the calculator seems to pause before completing the graph.

b. Use trace (starting with $t = 0$) and watch the path of the particle as you press the right arrow key at regular intervals. How many times does it change direction? When does it appear to be moving the fastest?

c. At what times t does the particle change direction? What are its x-coordinates at these times?

11.7.A   *Excursion:* **Parameterizations of Conic Sections**

Objectives

• Define parametric equations for a circle, an ellipse, a hyperbola, and a parabola

Conic sections can often be graphed more conveniently in parametric mode. Parameterizations for conic sections can be found by using Pythagorean identities, as shown in the following examples.

Circles

Example 1   Parameterization of a Circle

The equation of the circle with center (4, 1) and radius 3 is

$$(x - 4)^2 + (y - 1)^2 = 9.$$

Show that the following equations provide a parameterization of this circle.

$$x = 3 \cos t + 4 \quad \text{and} \quad y = 3 \sin t + 1, \quad 0 \le t \le 2\pi \quad \textbf{[1]}$$

Solution

To show that the parametric equations satisfy the circle equation, substitute into the equation of the circle and use the Pythagorean identity.

$$\begin{aligned}
(x - 4)^2 + (y - 1)^2 &= (3 \cos t + 4 - 4)^2 + (3 \sin t + 1 - 1)^2 \\
&= (3 \cos t)^2 + (3 \sin t)^2 \\
&= 9 \cos^2 t + 9 \sin^2 t \\
&= 9 (\cos^2 t + \sin^2 t) \\
&= 9(1) \\
&= 9
\end{aligned}$$

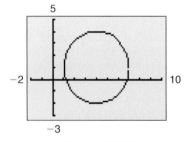

Figure 11.7.A-1

With this parameterization the circle is traced out in a counterclockwise direction from the point (7, 1), as shown in Figure 11.7.A-1. Another parameterization is given by

$$x = 3 \cos 2t + 4 \quad \text{and} \quad y = -3 \sin 2t + 1, \quad 0 \le t \le \pi$$

Verify that this last parameterization traces out the circle in a clockwise direction twice as fast as the parameterization given in [1], because t runs from 0 to π, rather than to 2π.

NOTE When the values of t are given in radian measure, such as 2π, make sure your calculator is in radian mode when graphing.

Parametric Equations of a Circle

The circle with center (c, d) and radius r is given by the parametric equations

$$x = r \cos t + c \quad \text{and} \quad y = r \sin t + d \quad (0 \le t \le 2\pi).$$

The procedure used in Example 1 works in the general case. Example 1 is the special case where $r = 3$ and $(c, d) = (4, 1)$.

Ellipses

Because an ellipse is a generalization of a circle, a similar parameterization can be used.

Example 2 Parameterization of an Ellipse

Find a parameterization of the following ellipse.

$$\frac{x^2}{25} + \frac{y^2}{4} = 1$$

Solution

Let

$$x = 5 \cos t \quad \text{and} \quad y = 2 \sin t, \quad 0 \le t \le 2\pi.$$

Use the Pythagorean identity to show that these parametric equations satisfy the equation of an ellipse.

$$\frac{x^2}{25} + \frac{y^2}{4} = \frac{(5 \cos t)^2}{25} + \frac{(2 \sin t)^2}{4}$$

$$= \frac{25 \cos^2 t}{25} + \frac{4 \sin^2 t}{4}$$

$$= \cos^2 t + \sin^2 t$$

$$= 1$$

The graph is shown in Figure 11.7.A-2. Its major axis has length $2 \cdot 5 = 10$, and its minor axis has length $2 \cdot 2 = 4$.

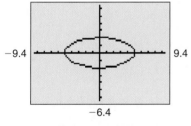

6.4

−9.4   9.4

−6.4

Figure 11.7.A-2

The parameterization in Example 2, where the center of the ellipse is at $(0, 0)$, can be extended to the general case.

Parametric Equations of an Ellipse

The ellipse with center (c, d) and a horizontal axis of length $2a$ and a vertical axis of length $2b$ is given by the parametric equations

$$x = a \cos t + c \quad \text{and} \quad y = b \sin t + d \quad (0 \le t \le 2\pi).$$

Hyperbolas

The hyperbola centered at (c, d) with equation

$$\frac{(x - c)^2}{a^2} - \frac{(y - d)^2}{b^2} = 1$$

can be obtained from the following parameterization.

$$x = a \sec t + c \qquad y = b \tan t + d, \qquad 0 \le t \le 2\pi$$

By a Pythagorean identity, $1 + \tan^2 t = \sec^2 t$. Therefore,

$$\frac{(x - c)^2}{a^2} - \frac{(y - d)^2}{b^2} = \frac{(a \sec t + c - c)^2}{a^2} - \frac{(b \tan t + d - d)^2}{b^2}$$

$$= \frac{(a \sec t)^2}{a^2} - \frac{(b \tan t)^2}{b^2}$$

$$= \frac{a^2 \sec^2 t}{a^2} - \frac{b^2 \tan^2 t}{b^2}$$

$$= \sec^2 t - \tan^2 t = 1$$

A similar argument works for other hyperbolas and leads to the following conclusion.

Parametric Equations of a Hyperbola

Hyperbolas with center at (c, d) have the following parameterizations.

Equation	*Parameterization*
$\dfrac{(x - c)^2}{a^2} - \dfrac{(y - d)^2}{b^2} = 1$	$x = a \sec t + c \qquad y = b \tan t + d$
	$(0 \le t \le 2\pi)$
$\dfrac{(y - d)^2}{a^2} - \dfrac{(x - c)^2}{b^2} = 1$	$x = b \tan t + c \qquad y = a \sec t + d$
	$(0 \le t \le 2\pi)$

Example 3 Parameterization of a Conic

Identify the conic section whose equation is given below, and find a parameterization for it.

$$\frac{(y - 5)^2}{9} - \frac{(x + 2)^2}{16} = 1$$

Solution

The equation is a hyperbola with center at $(-2, 5)$. It has the same form as the second equation in the preceding box, with $a = 3, b = 4$, and $(c, d) = (-2, 5)$. Therefore, its parametric equations are

$$x = 4 \tan t - 2 \qquad y = 3 \sec t + 5, \qquad 0 \le t \le 2\pi.$$

Parametric Equations of a Parabola

When a parabola has an equation such as

$$y = 4(x - 5)^2 + 7,$$

in which y is a function of x, then it can be graphed on a calculator either in function mode or in parametric mode with

$$x = t \quad \text{and} \quad y = 4(t - 5)^2 + 7.$$

A parabola with an equation such as

$$x = 2(y + 3)^2 - 4,$$

in which x is a function of y, cannot be graphed (by using a single equation) in function mode on a calculator, but it can be graphed in parametric mode by letting

$$x = 2(t + 3)^2 - 4 \quad \text{and} \quad y = t.$$

Similar techniques work for other parabolas.

Exercises 11.7.A

In Exercises 1–4, find a parameterization of the given curve. Confirm your answer by graphing.

1. circle with center $(9, 12)$ and radius 5

2. $x^2 + y^2 - 14x + 8y + 29 = 0$ *Hint:* see Example 2 in Section 11.4.

3. $x^2 + y^2 - 4x - 6y + 9 = 0$

4. circle with center $(7, -4)$ and radius 6

In Exercises 5–26, find parametric equations for the curve whose equation is given, and use these parametric equations to find a complete graph of the curve.

5. $\dfrac{x^2}{10} - 1 = \dfrac{-y^2}{36}$

6. $\dfrac{y^2}{49} + \dfrac{x^2}{81} = 1$

7. $4x^2 + 4y^2 = 1$

8. $x^2 + 4y^2 = 1$

9. $\dfrac{x^2}{10} - \dfrac{y^2}{36} = 1$

10. $\dfrac{y^2}{9} - \dfrac{x^2}{16} = 1$

11. $x^2 - 4y^2 = 1$

12. $2x^2 - y^2 = 4$

13. $8x = 2y^2$

14. $4y = x^2$

15. $\dfrac{(x - 1)^2}{4} + \dfrac{(y - 5)^2}{9} = 1$

16. $\dfrac{(x - 2)^2}{16} + \dfrac{(y + 3)^2}{12} = 1$

17. $\dfrac{(x + 1)^2}{16} + \dfrac{(y - 4)^2}{8} = 1$

18. $\dfrac{(x + 5)^2}{4} + \dfrac{(y + 2)^2}{12} = 1$

19. $y = 4(x - 1)^2 + 2$

20. $y = 3(x - 2)^2 - 3$

21. $x = 2(y - 2)^2$

22. $x = -3(y - 1)^2 - 2$

23. $\dfrac{(y + 3)^2}{25} - \dfrac{(x + 1)^2}{16} = 1$

24. $\dfrac{(y + 1)^2}{9} - \dfrac{(x - 1)^2}{25} = 1$

25. $\dfrac{(x + 3)^2}{1} - \dfrac{(y - 2)^2}{4} = 1$

26. $\dfrac{(y + 5)^2}{9} - \dfrac{(x - 2)^2}{1} = 1$

CHAPTER

11

REVIEW

Important Concepts

Important Facts and Formulas

Equation of an **ellipse** with center (h, k) and axes on the lines $x = h, y = k$:

$$\frac{(x - h)^2}{a^2} + \frac{(y - k)^2}{b^2} = 1$$

Equation of a **hyperbola** with center (h, k) and vertices on the line $y = k$:

$$\frac{(x - h)^2}{a^2} - \frac{(y - k)^2}{b^2} = 1$$

Equation of **hyperbola** with center (h, k) and vertices on the line $x = h$:

$$\frac{(y - k)^2}{a^2} - \frac{(x - h)^2}{b^2} = 1$$

Equation of a **parabola** with vertex (h, k) and axis $x = h$:

$$(x - h)^2 = 4p(y - k)$$

Equation of a **parabola** with vertex (h, k) and axis $y = k$:

$$(y - k)^2 = 4p(x - h)$$

Rotation equations:

$$x = u \cos \theta - v \sin \theta$$
$$y = u \sin \theta + v \cos \theta$$

Rotation Angle:

To eliminate the xy term in $Ax^2 + Bxy + Cy^2 + Dx + Ey + F = 0$, rotate the axes through an angle θ such that $\cot 2\theta = \dfrac{A - C}{B}$.

The rectangular and polar coordinates of a point are related by

$$x = r \cos \theta \qquad \text{and} \qquad y = r \sin \theta$$
$$r^2 = x^2 + y^2 \qquad \text{and} \qquad \tan \theta = \frac{y}{x}$$

If e and d are constants with $e > 0$, then the graph of a polar equation of the form

$$r = \frac{ed}{1 \pm e \cos \theta} \qquad or \qquad r = \frac{ed}{1 \pm e \sin \theta}$$

is an ellipse if $0 < e < 1$, a parabola if $e = 1$, and a hyperbola if $e > 1$.

Review Exercises

In Exercises 1–10, find the foci and vertices of the conic, and find a viewing window that shows a complete graph of the equation.

Section 11.1

1. $\dfrac{x^2}{16} + \dfrac{y^2}{20} = 1$

2. $\dfrac{x^2}{4} + \dfrac{y^2}{25} = 1$

3. $25x^2 + 4y^2 = 100$

4. $4x^2 + 9y^2 = 36$

5. Find the equation of the ellipse with center at the origin, one vertex at $(0, 4)$, passing through $\left(\sqrt{3}, 2\sqrt{3}\right)$.

6. Find the equation of the ellipse with center at the origin, one vertex at $(3, 0)$, passing through $\left(1, \dfrac{2\sqrt{2}}{3}\right)$.

Section 11.2

7. $\dfrac{x^2}{9} - \dfrac{y^2}{16} = 1$

8. $\dfrac{x^2}{16} - \dfrac{y^2}{4} = 1$

9. Find the equation of the hyperbola with center at the origin, one vertex at $(0, -2)$, passing through $\left(-1, 2\sqrt{2}\right)$.

10. Find the equation of the hyperbola with center at the origin, one vertex at $(3, 0)$, passing through $\left(5, -\dfrac{8}{3}\right)$.

Section 11.3

In Exercises 11–16, find the equation of the parabola with vertex at the origin that satisfies the given condition

11. axis $x = 0$, passing through $(-1, 5)$

12. axis $y = 0$, passing through $(-1, 5)$

13. focus $(-4, 0)$

14. focus $(0, -3)$

15. directrix $x = -4$

16. directrix $y = 2$

17. Find the focus and directrix of the parabola $10y = 7x^2$.

18. Find the focus and directrix of the parabola $3y^2 - x - 4y + 4 = 0$.

Section 11.4

In Exercises 19–28, sketch the graph of the equation and identify the conic. If there are asymptotes, give their equations and label all characteristic points.

19. $\dfrac{(x-1)^2}{7} + \dfrac{(y-3)^2}{16} = 1$

20. $3x^2 = 1 + 2y^2$

21. $\dfrac{(x-3)^2}{9} + \dfrac{(y+5)^2}{4} = 1$

22. $\dfrac{(y+4)^2}{25} - \dfrac{(x-1)^2}{4} = 1$

23. $4x^2 - 9y^2 = 144$

24. $x^2 + 4y^2 - 10x + 9 = 0$

25. $2y = 4(x-3)^2 + 6$

26. $3y = 6(x+1)^2 - 9$

27. $x = y^2 + 2y + 2$

28. $y = x^2 - 2x + 3$

29. What is the center of the ellipse $4x^2 + 3y^2 - 32x + 36y + 124 = 0$?

30. Find the equation of the hyperbola with center at the origin, one vertex at $(0, 5)$, passing through $(1, 3\sqrt{5})$.

31. Find the equation of the hyperbola with center at $(3, 0)$, one vertex at $(3, 2)$, passing through $(1, \sqrt{5})$.

32. Find the equation of the parabola with vertex $(2, 5)$, axis $x = 2$, passing through $(3, 12)$.

33. Find the equation of the parabola with vertex $\left(\dfrac{3}{2}, -\dfrac{1}{2}\right)$, axis $y = -\dfrac{1}{2}$, passing through $(-3, 1)$.

34. Find the equation of the parabola with vertex $(5, 2)$ that passes through the points $(7, 3)$ and $(9, 6)$.

35. Find the equation of the ellipse with center at $(3, 1)$, one vertex at $(1, 1)$, passing through $\left(2, 1 + \sqrt{\dfrac{3}{2}}\right)$.

In Exercises 36–39, assume that the graph of the equation is a nondegenerate conic. Use the discriminant to identify the graph.

36. $x^2 + y^2 - xy - 4y = 0$

37. $4xy - 3x^2 - 20 = 0$

38. $4x^2 - 4xy + y^2 - \sqrt{5}x - 2\sqrt{5}y = 0$

39. $3x^2 + 2\sqrt{2}xy + 2y^2 - 12 = 0$

In Exercises 40–45, find a viewing window that shows a complete graph of the equation.

40. $x^2 + xy + y^2 - 3y - 6 = 0$

41. $x^2 + xy - 2 = 0$

42. $x^2 - 4xy + y^2 + 5 = 0$

43. $x^2 + 3xy + y^2 - 2\sqrt{2}x + 2\sqrt{2}y = 0$

44. $x^2 + 2xy + y^2 - 4\sqrt{2}y = 0$

45. $x^2 - xy + y^2 - 6 = 0$

Section 11.4.A

In Exercises 46–47, find the rotation equations when the x- and y-axes are rotated through the given angle.

46. $45°$

47. $60°$

In Exercises 48–49, find the angle through which the x- and y-axes should be rotated to eliminate the xy term in the equation.

48. $x^2 - 4xy + y^2 + 5 = 0$

49. $x^2 + xy + y^2 - 3y - 6 = 0$

Section 11.5

50. List four other pairs of polar coordinates for the point $\left(-2, \dfrac{\pi}{4}\right)$.

51. Plot the points $\left(2, \dfrac{3\pi}{4}\right)$ and $\left(-3, -\dfrac{2\pi}{3}\right)$ on a polar coordinate graph.

In Exercises 52–61, sketch the graph of the polar equation.

52. $r = -2$

53. $\theta = \dfrac{2\pi}{3}$

54. $\theta = -\dfrac{5\pi}{6}$

55. $r = 2\theta \ (\theta \le 0)$

56. $r = 4\cos\theta$

57. $r = 2 - 2\sin\theta$

58. $r = \cos 3\theta$

59. $r^2 = \cos 2\theta$

60. $r = 1 + 2\sin\theta$

61. $r = 5$

62. Convert $\left(3, \sqrt{3}\right)$ from rectangular to polar coordinates.

63. Convert $\left(3, -\dfrac{2\pi}{3}\right)$ from polar to rectangular coordinates.

Section 11.6

64. What is the eccentricity of the ellipse $24x^2 + 30y^2 = 120$?

65. What is the eccentricity of the ellipse $3x^2 + y^2 = 84$?

In Exercises 66–69, sketch the graph of the equation, labeling the vertices and identifying the conic.

66. $r = \dfrac{14}{7 + 7\cos\theta}$

67. $r = \dfrac{-24}{3 - 9\cos\theta}$

68. $r = \dfrac{10}{3 + 4\sin\theta}$

69. $r = \dfrac{12}{2 - \sin\theta}$

In Exercises 70–73, find a polar equation of the conic that has focus $(0, 0)$ and satisfies the given conditions.

70. hyperbola; vertices $\left(5, \dfrac{\pi}{2}\right)$ and $\left(-3, \dfrac{3\pi}{2}\right)$

71. eccentricity 1; directrix $r = 2\sec\theta$

72. eccentricity 0.75; directrix $r = -3\csc\theta$

73. ellipse; vertices $(4, 0)$ and $(6, \pi)$

In Exercises 74–77, find a viewing window that shows a complete graph of the curve with the given parametric equations.

74. $x = [64 \cos (\pi/6)]t$ and $y = -16t^2 + \left[64 \sin \dfrac{\pi}{6}\right]t, \;\; 0 \le t \le \pi$

75. $x = t^3 + t + 1$ and $y = t^2 + 2t, \;\; -3 \le t \le 3$

76. $x = t^2 - t + 3$ and $y = t^3 - 5t, \;\; -3 \le t \le 3$

77. $x = 8 \cos t + \cos 8t$ and $y = 8 \sin t - \sin 8t, \;\; 0 \le t \le 2\pi$

Section 11.7

In Exercises 78–81, sketch the graph of the curve whose parametric equations are given, and by eliminating the parameter, find an equation in x and y whose graph contains the given curve.

78. $x = 3 \cos t, \;\; y = 5 \sin t, \;\; 0 \le t \le 2\pi$

79. $x = \cos t, \;\; y = 2 \sin^2 t, \;\; 0 \le t \le 2\pi$

80. $x = e^t, \;\; y = \sqrt{t + 1}, \;\; t \ge 1$

81. $x = 2t - 1, \;\; y = 2 - t, \;\; -3 \le t \le 3$

82. Which of the following is not a parameterization of the curve $x = y^2 + 1$?
   a. $x = t^2 + 1,$ $y = t,$ any real number t
   b. $x = \sin^2 t + 1,$ $y = \sin t,$ any real number t
   c. $x = t^4 + 1,$ $y = t^2,$ any real number t
   d. $x = t^6 + 1,$ $y = t^3,$ any real number t

83. Which of the curves in Questions 74–77 appear to be the graphs of functions of the form $y = f(x)$?

Section 11.7.A

In Exercises 84–87, find a parameterization of the given curve. Confirm your answer by graphing.

84. circle with center $(3, -2)$ and radius 4

85. circle with center $(-3, 5)$ and radius 5

86. $9x^2 + 4y^2 - 54x + 16y + 61 = 0$ **87.** $4x^2 + y^2 + 16x - 6y + 21 = 0$

In Exercises 88–97, find parametric equations for the curve whose equation is given, and use these parametric equations to find a complete graph of the curve.

88. $9x^2 + 9y^2 = 1$ **89.** $4x^2 + 9y^2 = 1$

90. $16x^2 - y^2 = 1$ **91.** $x^2 - 36y^2 = 1$

92. $\dfrac{(x - 3)^2}{9} + \dfrac{(y + 4)^2}{25} = 1$ **93.** $\dfrac{(x + 2)^2}{49} + \dfrac{(y - 5)^2}{64} = 1$

94. $\dfrac{(x - 2)^2}{81} - \dfrac{(y - 5)^2}{100} = 1$ **95.** $\dfrac{(y + 3)^2}{4} - \dfrac{(x - 2)^2}{12} = 1$

96. $y = 3(x + 2)^2 - 5$ **97.** $x = -32(y + 4)^2 - 5$

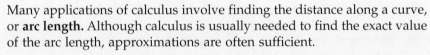

can do calculus
Arc Length of a Polar Graph

Many applications of calculus involve finding the distance along a curve, or **arc length**. Although calculus is usually needed to find the exact value of the arc length, approximations are often sufficient.

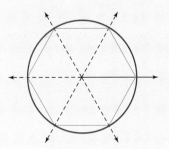

A curve may be approximated by straight segments with endpoints on the curve, as shown in Figure 11.C-1. In polar coordinates, the curve, which is a circle, can be represented by the function $r = c$ for some constant c. The circumference of the circle is $2\pi c \approx 6.28c$. The length of each blue segment is also c, since the dashed lines form equilateral triangles. Thus, the approximate length of the curve is the total length of the blue segments, or $6c$.

Figure 11.C-1

In general, the Law of Cosines may be used to find the length of a segment with two endpoints on the curve, as shown in the following example.

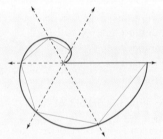

Figure 11.C-2

| Example 1 | Estimating the Length of a Curve |

Estimate the length of the spiral with the equation $r = 2\theta$ from 0 to 2π.

Solution

The dashed lines in Figure 11.C-2 divide the spiral into triangles with an angle of $\dfrac{\pi}{3}$ at the origin. The table below shows the value of r for each value of θ that is an endpoint of a segment.

θ	0	$\dfrac{\pi}{3}$	$\dfrac{2\pi}{3}$	π	$\dfrac{4\pi}{3}$	$\dfrac{5\pi}{3}$	2π
r	0	$\dfrac{2\pi}{3}$	$\dfrac{4\pi}{3}$	2π	$\dfrac{8\pi}{3}$	$\dfrac{10\pi}{3}$	4π

The first segment has one endpoint at the origin, so its length is the value of r at the other endpoint, which is $\dfrac{2\pi}{3}$.

Every remaining segment is the side of a triangle that is opposite an angle at the origin of $\dfrac{\pi}{3}$, as shown in Figure 11.C-3.

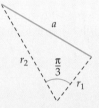

Figure 11.C-3

By the Law of Cosines,

$$a^2 = r_1^2 + r_2^2 - 2r_1r_2 \cos\frac{\pi}{3}$$
$$a = \sqrt{r_1^2 + r_2^2 - r_1r_2}$$

The lengths of the segments can be calculated using this formula.

Segment from $\theta = 0$ to $\theta = \dfrac{\pi}{3}$: $\quad \dfrac{2\pi}{3} \approx 2.09$

Segment from $\theta = \dfrac{\pi}{3}$ to $\theta = \dfrac{2\pi}{3}$: $\sqrt{\left(\dfrac{2\pi}{3}\right)^2 + \left(\dfrac{4\pi}{3}\right)^2 - \left(\dfrac{2\pi}{3}\right)\left(\dfrac{4\pi}{3}\right)} \approx 3.63$

Segment from $\theta = \dfrac{2\pi}{3}$ to $\theta = \pi$: $\sqrt{\left(\dfrac{4\pi}{3}\right)^2 + (2\pi)^2 - \left(\dfrac{4\pi}{3}\right)(2\pi)} \approx 5.54$

Segment from $\theta = \pi$ to $\theta = \dfrac{4\pi}{3}$: $\sqrt{(2\pi)^2 + \left(\dfrac{8\pi}{3}\right)^2 - (2\pi)\left(\dfrac{8\pi}{3}\right)} \approx 7.55$

Segment from $\theta = \dfrac{4\pi}{3}$ to $\theta = \dfrac{5\pi}{3}$: $\sqrt{\left(\dfrac{8\pi}{3}\right)^2 + \left(\dfrac{10\pi}{3}\right)^2 - \left(\dfrac{8\pi}{3}\right)\left(\dfrac{10\pi}{3}\right)} \approx 9.60$

Segment from $\theta = \dfrac{5\pi}{3}$ to $\theta = 2\pi$: $\sqrt{\left(\dfrac{10\pi}{3}\right)^2 + (4\pi)^2 - \left(\dfrac{10\pi}{3}\right)(4\pi)} \approx 11.66$

The approximate length of the spiral is the sum of the segments.

$$\text{arc length} \approx 2.09 + 3.63 + 5.54 + 7.55 + 9.60 + 11.66 \approx 40.07$$

Exercises

In Exercises 1–4, approximate each curve for $0 \le \theta \le 2\pi$ by six segments and estimate each arc length.

1. $r = 1.5\theta$

2. $r = 3 + 2\cos\theta$

3. $r = 1 + \cos\theta$

4. $r = \dfrac{1}{2 + \sin\theta}$

5. Use the figure to estimate the length of the cardioid with the equation $r = 1 + \sin\theta$.

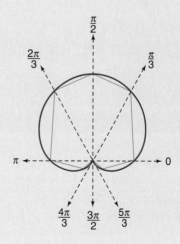

6. Use Heron's formula for the area of a triangle (see page 633) and your results from Exercise 5 to estimate the area of the cardioid with the equation $r = 1 + \sin\theta$

777

CHAPTER 12

Systems and Matrices

Is this a diamond in the rough?

The structure of certain crystals can be defined by a large system of linear equations with more than a hundred equations and variables. A variety of resource allocation problems involving many variables can be handled by solving an appropriate system of equations. The fastest solution methods involve matrices and are easily implemented on a computer or calculator. See Exercise 36 in Section 12.2.

Chapter Outline

Interdependence of Sections

Readers who are familiar with solving systems of linear equations may omit section 12.1.

$$12.1 \rightarrow 12.2 \rightarrow 12.3 \rightarrow 12.4$$
$$\searrow$$
$$12.5$$

Real-world situations often require a common solution to several equations with multiple variables. Such a collection of equations is known as a *system of equations.* Solutions to a system of equations in two or three variables may be represented geometrically by intersections of lines or planes. In this chapter, systems will be solved graphically, algebraically by substitution or elimination, and by two matrix methods: row reduction and inverse matrices.

12.1 Solving Systems of Equations

Objectives

- Solve systems of equations by graphing, substitution, and elimination

- Recognize consistent, inconsistent, and dependent systems

- Solve applications using systems

A **system of equations** is a set of two or more equations in two or more variables. When a system has 3 equations in 2 variables, it is called a 3×2 system. In the examples of systems of equations shown below, the first is a 3×3 system, the second is a 3×4 system, and the third is a 2×2 system.

$$
\begin{aligned}
2x - 5y + 3z &= 1 \\
x + 2y - z &= 2 \\
3x + y + 2z &= 11
\end{aligned}
\qquad
\begin{aligned}
2x + 5y + z + w &= 0 \\
2y - 4z + 41w &= 5 \\
3x + 7y + 5z - 8w &= -6
\end{aligned}
\qquad
\begin{aligned}
x^2 + y^2 &= 25 \\
x^2 - y &= 7
\end{aligned}
$$

   Three equations in   *Three equations in*   *Two equations in*
    three variables   *four variables*   *two variables*

The first two systems above are called **linear systems** because the variables in each equation are all to the power of one, thus they are all linear. The third is a **nonlinear system** because at least one equation is nonlinear—in this case, quadratic.

779

Figure 12.1-1

Solutions of a System of Equations

A **solution of a system of equations** is a set of values that satisfy all the equations in the system. In the first system of equations on the previous page, substituting $x = 1$, $y = 2$, and $z = 3$ gives the following:

$$2x - 5y + 3z = 2(1) - 5(2) + 3(3) = 2 - 10 + 9 = 1$$
$$x + 2y - z = (1) + 2(2) - 3 = 1 + 4 - 3 = 2$$
$$3x + y + 2z = 3(1) + (2) + 2(3) = 3 + 2 + 6 = 11$$

Because the set of values $x = 1$, $y = 2$, $z = 3$ makes all equations true, the set is a solution of the system. The set of values $x = 0$, $y = 7$, $z = 12$ is a solution of the first two equations, but not the third, so it is not a solution of the system.

Solutions of systems of equations in two variables can be found numerically by comparing tables of values for the equations.

Example 1   Solving a System Numerically

Find a solution of the system of equations below by using tables of values for the equations.

$$2x - y = 1$$
$$3x + 2y = 12$$

Solution

First, solve each equation for y. Then create a table of values for each equation. The table in Figure 12.1-1 shows solutions to each equation. To solve the system, find a common output.

$$y = 2x - 1$$
$$y = -\frac{3}{2}x + 6$$

Notice that at $x = 2$, the y-values are the same for the two equations. Thus, $x = 2$, $y = 3$ is a solution of the system of equations. ∎

Solving systems numerically has several disadvantages. First, there is no way of knowing whether all possible solutions have been found. Second, many values may have to be checked before a solution is found. And third, if a solution lies between the values in the table, it may be missed.

Solving Systems with Graphs

One method of solving systems of equations in two variables is graphing the equations and finding the point(s) of intersection. Since the graph of each equation represents all possible solutions of that equation, a point of intersection of two graphs represents a solution of both equations. The advantage of solving a system graphically is that the solution is shown visually, but solving systems graphically is limited to two-variable systems.

Example 2   Graphical Solutions of a Linear System

Find a solution of the system of equations below by graphing the equations.

$$2x - y = 1$$
$$3x + 2y = 4$$

Solution

Solve each equation for y, graph each equation, and find the coordinates of all points of intersection.

$$y = 2x - 1$$
$$y = -\frac{3}{2}x + 2$$

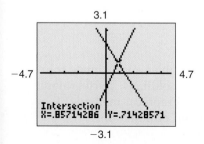

Figure 12.1-2

The system of equations has exactly one solution, $x \approx 0.86$ and $y \approx 0.71$, as shown in Figure 12.1-2.   ∎

Type of System and Number of Solutions

Systems of equations may be classified according to the number of solutions. A system with no solutions is called **inconsistent,** and a system with at least one solution is called **consistent.**

Linear Systems

Because the graphs in a linear system with two variables are lines, there are exactly three geometric possibilities.

* the lines can be parallel and have no point of intersection
* the lines can intersect at a single point
* the lines can coincide

Each of these possibilities leads to a different number of solutions for the system. The three types of 2 × 2 linear systems are shown below.

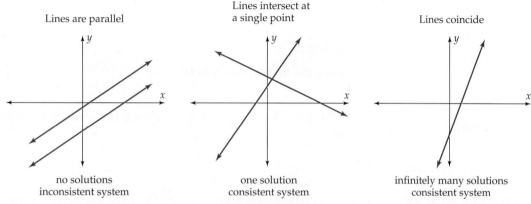

Figure 12.1-3

Number of Solutions of a Linear System

There are exactly three possibilities for the number of solutions of a 2 × 2 system of *linear* equations.

- no solutions (inconsistent system)
- one solution (consistent system)
- infinitely many solutions (consistent system)

Solving Systems Algebraically

Solving systems of equations by graphing often gives approximate solutions, while algebraic methods produce exact solutions. Furthermore, algebraic methods are often as easy to use as graphical methods. Two common algebraic methods are **substitution** and **elimination.**

Substitution Method

Solving Systems with Substitution

To solve a system using the substitution method:

1. Solve one equation for x (or y).
2. Substitute the expression for x (or y) into the other equation.
3. Solve for the remaining variable.
4. Substitute the value found in Step 3 into one of the original equations, and solve for the other variable.
5. Verify the solution in each equation.

Example 3 Solving a System by Substitution

Solve the system of equations below by substitution.

$$3x - y = 12$$
$$2x + 3y = 2$$

Solution

Solve the first equation for y.

$$y = 3x - 12$$

Substitute the expression $3x - 12$ for y in the second equation and solve for x.

$$2x + 3(3x - 12) = 2$$
$$2x + 9x - 36 = 2$$
$$11x = 38$$
$$x = \frac{38}{11} \approx 3.45$$

CAUTION

When solving a system of equations, remember to find values for *all* of the variables.

To find the value of y, substitute $\dfrac{38}{11}$, the value of x, into $y = 3x - 12$ and simplify.

$$y = 3\left(\frac{38}{11}\right) - 12 = -\frac{18}{11} \approx -1.64$$

The exact solution to the system is $x = \dfrac{38}{11}$, $y = -\dfrac{18}{11}$, and the approximate solution is $x \approx 3.45$, $y \approx -1.64$. ∎

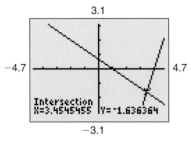

3.1

−4.7   4.7

Intersection
X=3.4545455 Y=-1.636364

−3.1

Figure 12.1-4

The solution may be confirmed by graphing, as shown in Figure 12.1-4, where $x \approx 3.45$ and $y \approx -1.64$.

Elimination Method

Elimination is another algebraic method used to solve systems.

Solving Systems by Elimination

To solve a system using the elimination method:

1. **Multiply one or both of the equations by a nonzero constant so that the coefficients of x (or y) are opposites of each other.**
2. **Eliminate x (or y) by adding the equations, and solve for the remaining variable.**
3. **Substitute the value found in Step 2 into one of the original equations, and solve for the other variable.**
4. **Verify the solution in each equation.**

Example 4   Solving a System by Elimination

Solve the system of equations below by elimination.

$$x - 3y = 4$$
$$2x + y = 1$$

Solution

Multiply the first equation by -2.

$$-2x + 6y = -8$$
$$2x + y = 1$$

Add the equations to eliminate x, and solve the resulting equation.

$$
\begin{array}{r}
-2x + 6y = -8 \\
+\quad 2x + y = 1 \\
\hline
7y = -7 \\
y = -1
\end{array}
$$

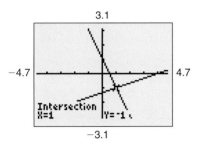

Figure 12.1-5

Substitute -1 for y in one of the original equations and solve for x.

$$x - 3(-1) = 4$$
$$x = 1$$

The solution of the system is $x = 1$, $y = -1$. The solution is confirmed graphically in Figure 12.1-5.

Solutions of Consistent and Inconsistent Systems

The following examples show how the elimination method may be used to solve consistent systems with infinitely many solutions or inconsistent systems.

Example 5   Recognizing an Inconsistent System

Solve the system of equations below by elimination.

$$2x - 3y = 5$$
$$4x - 6y = 1$$

Solution

Multiply the first equation by -2, then add the two equations.

$$-4x + 6y = -10$$
$$+ \quad 4x - 6y = \quad 1$$
$$\overline{\qquad\quad 0 = \quad -9}$$

The last statement, $0 = -9$, is always false. This indicates that the original system has no solutions. Thus, the system is inconsistent.

Graphing Exploration ●

Confirm the result of Example 5 geometrically by graphing the two equations in the system. Do the lines intersect, or are they parallel?

Example 6   Recognizing a System with Infinitely Many Solutions

Solve the system of equations below by elimination.

$$2x - 4y = \quad 6$$
$$-3x + 6y = -9$$

Solution

Multiply the first equation by 3 and the second equation by 2, then add the two equations.

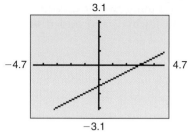

Figure 12.1-6

$$6x - 12y = 18$$
$$+ \, -6x + 12y = -18$$
$$\overline{ 0 = 0}$$

The last equation, $0 = 0$, is always true. This indicates that the two equations represent the same line, and every ordered pair that satisfies the first equation must also satisfy the second equation. Thus, the system has infinitely many solutions. ∎

Using a Parameter to Write Solutions

It is common to represent solutions of consistent systems that have infinitely many solutions in terms of a variable called a **parameter,** which represents any real number. In Example 6, let $y = t$ and substitute this value into one of the equations.

$$2x - 4t = 6 \qquad \textit{t is any real number.}$$
$$x = 3 + 2t \qquad \textit{Solve for x.}$$

The solutions can be written as $x = 3 + 2t$, $y = t$. Individual numerical solutions can be found by substituting real values for t, as follows.

$$t = 1 \qquad x = 5, y = 1$$
$$t = -2 \qquad x = -1, y = -2$$
$$t = 0 \qquad x = 3, y = 0$$

Solving Larger Systems by Elimination

It is possible to use elimination to solve larger systems. Equations are combined in pairs to create a system of equations with one fewer variable that can be solved using the techniques discussed in this section. The solutions of the reduced system are then substituted back into the original equations to find the remaining variables.

Example 7   **Solving a 3 × 3 System by Elimination**

Solve the system of equations below by elimination.

$$2x + y - z = -1 \qquad [1]$$
$$-x - 3y + z = 5 \qquad [2]$$
$$x + 4y - 2z = -10 \qquad [3]$$

Solution

Eliminate z by adding equations [1] and [2].

$$2x + y - z = -1 \qquad [1]$$
$$+ \, -x - 3y + z = 5 \qquad [2]$$
$$\overline{x - 2y = 4 \qquad [4]}$$

Eliminate *the same* variable, in this case z, by combining two other equations. One possible way is to multiply equation [2] by 2 and add it to equation [3].

$$
\begin{array}{rll}
-2x - 6y + 2z = & 10 & 2 \cdot [2] \\
+ \quad x + 4y - 2z = & -10 & [3] \\
\hline
-x - 2y \quad\quad\;\; = & 0 & [5]
\end{array}
$$

The two resulting equations, [4] and [5], form a system of two equations in two variables, which can be solved by elimination, substitution, or graphing.

$$
\begin{array}{rll}
x - 2y = & 4 & [4] \\
+ \quad -x - 2y = & 0 & [5] \\
\hline
-4y = & 4 & \\
y = & -1 &
\end{array}
$$

Find the value of x by substituting $y = -1$ into equation [4].

$$
\begin{aligned}
x - 2(-1) &= 4 \\
x \quad\quad &= 2
\end{aligned}
$$

To find the value of z, substitute the values $x = 2$ and $y = -1$ into equation [1] from the original system, and solve.

$$
\begin{aligned}
2(2) + (-1) - z &= -1 \\
z &= 4
\end{aligned}
$$

The solution is $x = 2$, $y = -1$, $z = 4$.

The solution should be checked in *all* equations of the original system. ∎

Applications of Systems

Systems of equations occur in many real-world applications. The simplest situations involve two quantities and two linear relationships between these quantities, as shown in the following example.

Example 8   2 × 2 Linear System Application

A ball game is attended by 575 people, and total ticket sales are $2575. If tickets cost $5 for adults and $3 for children, how many adults and how many children attended the game?

Solution

Let x be the number of adults and y be the number of children. The first equation is based on the total number of people at the game.

$$
\underset{\text{number of adults}}{x} + \underset{\text{number of children}}{y} = \underset{\text{total attendance}}{575}
$$

The second equation is based on the ticket sales. Notice that the term for each type of ticket sales is found by multiplying the price per ticket by the number of tickets sold, and total ticket sales is the sum of the sales of the different types of tickets.

adult ticket sales   +   child ticket sales   =   total ticket sales

$$\left(\begin{array}{c} price \\ per \\ ticket \end{array}\right)\left(\begin{array}{c} number \\ of \\ adults \end{array}\right) \qquad \left(\begin{array}{c} price \\ per \\ child \end{array}\right)\left(\begin{array}{c} number \\ of \\ children \end{array}\right)$$

$$5x \qquad + \qquad 3y \qquad = \qquad 2575$$

Solve the system of equations.

$$\begin{array}{ll} x + y = 575 & \text{\textit{number of tickets}} \\ 5x + 3y = 2575 & \text{\textit{total ticket sales}} \end{array}$$

Multiply the first equation by -3 and add the result to the second equation.

$$\begin{array}{rl} -3x - 3y = & -1725 \\ + \quad 5x + 3y = & 2575 \\ \hline 2x = & 850 \\ x = & 425 \end{array}$$

So 425 adults and $y = 575 - 425 = 150$ children attended the game. Confirm by graphing, as shown in Figure 12.1-7. ∎

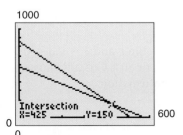

Figure 12.1-7

Example 9   Mixture Application

A cafe sells two kinds of coffee in bulk. The Costa Rican sells for $4.50 per pound, and the Kenyan sells for $7.00 per pound. The owner wishes to mix a blend that would sell for $5.00 per pound. How much of each type of coffee should be used in the blend?

Solution

Let x be the amount of Costa Rican coffee and y be the amount of Kenyan coffee in each pound of the blend. The first equation is based on the weight of the coffee.

weight of Costa   +   weight of   =   one pound of blend
Rican   Kenyan

$$x \qquad + \qquad y \qquad = \qquad 1$$

The second equation is based on the price of the coffee.

price of Costa Rican   +   price of Kenyan   =   price of blend

$$\left(\begin{array}{c} price \\ per \\ pound \end{array}\right)\left(\begin{array}{c} weight \\ of \\ coffee \end{array}\right) \qquad \left(\begin{array}{c} price \\ per \\ pound \end{array}\right)\left(\begin{array}{c} weight \\ of \\ coffee \end{array}\right)$$

$$4.50x \qquad + \qquad 7.00y \qquad = \qquad \$5.00$$

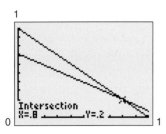

Figure 12.1-8

Solve the system of equations.

$$x + y = 1$$
$$4.5x + 7y = 5$$

Multiply the first equation by -7 and add it to the second equation.

$$
\begin{array}{rcl}
-7x - 7y &=& -7 \\
+ \quad 4.5x + 7y &=& 5 \\
\hline
-2.5x \qquad\ \ &=& -2 \\
x \qquad\quad &=& 0.8
\end{array}
$$

The owner should use 0.8 pounds of Costa Rican coffee and $1 - 0.8 = 0.2$ pounds of Kenyan coffee in each pound of blend, or 80% Costa Rican and 20% Kenyan. See Figure 12.1-8 for graphical confirmation. ∎

Exercises 12.1

In Exercises 1–6, determine whether the given values of x, y, and z are a solution of the system of equations.

1. $x = -1, y = 3$

$$2x + y = 1$$
$$-3x + 2y = 9$$

2. $x = 3, y = 4$

$$2x + 6y = 30$$
$$x + 2y = 11$$

3. $x - 2, y = -1$

$$\frac{1}{3}x + \frac{1}{2}y = \frac{1}{6}$$
$$\frac{1}{2}x + \frac{1}{3}y = \frac{2}{3}$$

4. $x = 0.4, y = 0.7$

$$3.1x - 2y = -0.16$$
$$5x - 3.5y = -0.48$$

5. $x = \frac{1}{2}, y = 3, z = -1$

$$2x - y + 4z = -6$$
$$3y + 3z = 6$$
$$2z = 2$$

6. $x = 2, y = \frac{3}{2}, z = -\frac{1}{2}$

$$3x + 4y - 2z = 13$$
$$x - 3y + 5z = -5$$
$$\frac{1}{2}x \qquad + 8z = -3$$

In Exercises 7–14, use substitution to solve the system.

7. $x - 2y = 5$
$\quad\ 2x + y = 3$

8. $3x - y = 1$
$\quad -x + 2y = 4$

9. $3x - 2y = 4$
$\quad\ 2x + y = -1$

10. $5x - 3y = -2$
$\quad\ -x + 2y = 3$

11. $r + s = 0$
$\quad\ r - s = 5$

12. $t = 3u + 5$
$\quad\ t = u + 5$

13. $x + y = c + d$ (where c, d are constants)
$\quad x - y = 2c - d$

14. $x + 3y = c - d$ (where c, d are constants)
$\quad 2x - y = c + d$

In Exercises 15–34, use the elimination method to solve the system.

15. $2x - 2y = 12$
$\quad -2x + 3y = 10$

16. $3x + 2y = -4$
$\quad\ 4x - 2y = -10$

17. $x + 3y = -1$
$\quad\ 2x - y = 5$

18. $4x - 3y = -1$
$\quad\ x + 2y = 19$

19. $2x + 3y = 15$
$\quad\ 8x + 12y = 40$

20. $2x + 5y = 8$
$\quad\ 6x + 15y = 18$

21. $3x - 2y = 4$
$\quad\ 6x - 4y = 8$

22. $2x - 8y = 2$
$\quad\ 3x - 12y = 3$

23. $12x - 16y = 8$
$\quad\ 42x - 56y = 28$

24. $\frac{1}{3}x + \frac{2}{5}y = \frac{1}{6}$
$\quad 20x + 24y = 10$

25. $9x - 3y = 1$
$\quad\ 6x - 2y = -5$

26. $8x + 4y = 3$
$\quad\ 10x + 5y = 1$

27. $\frac{x}{3} - \frac{y}{2} = -3$
$\quad \frac{2x}{5} + \frac{y}{5} = -2$

28. $\frac{x}{3} + \frac{3y}{5} = 4$
$\quad \frac{x}{6} - \frac{y}{2} = -3$

29.
$$\frac{x+y}{4} - \frac{x-y}{3} = 1$$
$$\frac{x+y}{4} + \frac{x-y}{2} = 9$$

30.
$$\frac{x-y}{4} + \frac{x+y}{3} = 1$$
$$\frac{x+2y}{3} + \frac{3x-y}{2} = -2$$

31. $3.5x - 2.18y = 2.00782$
$1.92x + 6.77y = -3.86928$

32. $463x - 80y = -13781.6$
$0.0375x + 0.912y = 50.79624$

33. $2x - 4y + z = 14$
$-2x + y - 6z = -31$
$x - 3y + 2z = 14$

34. $x + 3y - 2z = 8$
$-4x - 3y + z = 3$
$5x - y - 6z = 20$

In Exercises 35 and 36, find the values of *c* and *d* for which both given points lie on the given straight line. *Hint*: Substitute the *x*- and *y*-values of each of the given points into the equation to create a 2 × 2 system.

35. $cx + dy = 2;\ (0, 4)$ and $(2, 16)$

36. $cx + dy = -6;\ (1, 3)$ and $(-2, 12)$

37. Bill and Ann plan to install a heating system for their swimming pool. They have gathered the following cost information.

System	Installation cost	Monthly operational cost
Electric	$2000	$80.00
Solar	$14,000	$ 9.50

   a. Write a linear equation for each heating system that expresses its total cost y in terms of x, the number of years of operation.
   b. What is the five-year total cost of electric heat? of solar heat?
   c. In what year will the total cost of the two heating systems be the same? Which is the cheapest system before that time?

38. One parcel of land is worth $100,000 now and is increasing in value at the rate of $3000 per year. A second parcel is now worth $60,000 and is increasing in value at the rate of $7500 per year.
   a. For each parcel of land, write an equation that expresses the value y of the land in year x.
   b. Graph the equations in part **a**.
   c. Where do the lines intersect? What is the significance of this point?
   d. Which parcel will be worth more in five years? in 15 years?

39. A toy company makes dolls, as well as collector cases for each doll. To make x cases costs the company $5000 in fixed overhead, plus $7.50 per case. An outside supplier has offered to produce any desired volume of cases for $8.20 per case.
   a. Write an equation that expresses the company's cost to make x cases itself.
   b. Write an equation that expresses the cost of buying x cases from the outside supplier.
   c. Graph both equations on the same axes and determine when the two costs are the same.
   d. When should the company make the cases themselves, and when should they buy them from the outside supplier?

40. The sum of two numbers is 40. The difference of twice the first number and the second is 11. What are the numbers?

41. A 200-seat theater charges $3 for adults and $1.50 for children. If all seats were filled and the total ticket income was $510, how many adults and how many children were in the audience?

42. A theater charges $4 for main floor seats and $2.50 for balcony seats. If all seats are sold, the ticket income is $2100. At one show, 25% of the main floor seats and 40% of the balcony seats were sold, and ticket income was $600. How many seats are on the main floor and how many in the balcony?

43. An investor has part of her money in an account that pays 2% annual interest, and the rest in an account that pays 4% annual interest. If she has $4000 less in the higher paying account than in the lower paying one and her total annual interest income is $1010, how much does she have invested in each account?

44. The death rate per 100,000 population y in year x for heart disease and cancer is approximated by these equations:

$$\text{Heart Disease:} \quad 6.9x + 2y = 728.4$$
$$\text{Cancer:} \quad -1.3x + \ y = 167.5,$$

where $x = 0$ corresponds to 1970. If the equations remain accurate, when will the death rates for heart disease and cancer be the same? (Source: U.S. Department of Health and Human Services)

45. At a certain store, cashews cost $4.40 per pound and peanuts cost $1.20 per pound. If you want to buy exactly 3 pounds of nuts for $6.00, how many pounds of each kind of nuts should you buy? *Hint:* If you buy x pounds of cashews and y pounds of peanuts, then $x + y = 3$. Find a second equation by considering cost and solve the resulting system.

46. A store sells deluxe tape recorders for $150. The regular model costs $120. The total tape recorder inventory would sell for $43,800. But during a

recent month the store actually sold half of its deluxe models and two-thirds of the regular models and took in a total of $26,700. How many of each kind of tape recorder did they have at the beginning of the month?

47. How many cubic centimeters (cm³) of a solution that is 20% acid and of another solution that is 45% acid should be mixed to produce 100 cm³ of a solution that is 30% acid?

48. How many grams of a 50%-silver alloy should be mixed with a 75%-silver alloy to obtain 40 grams of a 60%-silver alloy?

49. A machine in a pottery factory takes 3 minutes to form a bowl and 2 minutes to form a plate. The material for a bowl costs $0.25 and the material for a plate costs $0.20. If the machine runs for 8 hours straight and exactly $44 is spent for material, how many bowls and plates can be produced?

Excursion: Graphs in Three Dimensions

Objectives

- Plot points in three dimensions

- Graph planes in three dimensions

- Use graphs of planes to visualize the number of solutions to a 3 × 3 system of equations

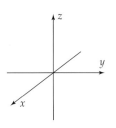

Figure 12.1.A-1

In section 12.1, two-dimensional graphs were used to interpret and solve systems of equations in two variables. Systems of equations in three variables can be represented by three-dimensional graphs, as shown in this excursion. However, finding the solutions of such systems requires algebraic techniques that are presented in the following sections.

Three-Dimensional Coordinates

Just as ordered pairs of real numbers (x, y) are identified with points in a plane, ordered triples (x, y, z) of real numbers can be identified with points in three-dimensional space. To do this, draw three coordinate axes as shown in Figure 12.1.A-1. The axes in three-dimensional space are usually called the x-axis, the y-axis, and the **z-axis.** In three-dimensional coordinates, the arrowhead on each axis indicates the positive direction.

Each pair of axes determines a **coordinate plane,** which is named by the axes that determine it. There are three coordinate planes, the xy-plane, the yz-plane, and the xz-plane, which divide the three-dimensional space into eight regions, called **octants,** shown in Figure 12.1.A-2. The octant in which all coordinates are positive is called the **first octant.**

NOTE The octants can be considered as the regions above and below each quadrant of the *xy*-plane.

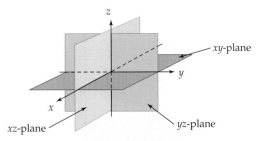

Figure 12.1.A-2

Plotting Points in Three Dimensions

To plot the point (a, b, c) in a three-dimensional coordinate system, move a units from the origin along the *x*-axis, move b units parallel to the *y*-axis, then move c units parallel to the *z*-axis. Dashed lines are used to indicate the distances parallel to the *y*- and *z*-axes.

Example 1   Points in Space

Plot the given points in a three-dimensional coordinate system.

$$(1, 3, 4), (0, -2, 0), (2, -2, -3)$$

Solution

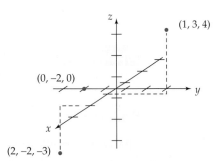

Figure 12.1.A-3

Graphs in Three Dimensions

A function in three dimensions can be written in terms of x, y, and z, or as a function of two variables, x and y. The graph of a linear equation in three dimensions is a plane. A comparison of two-dimensional and three-dimensional forms follows.

Two dimensions		Three dimensions	
$y = mx + b$ $f(x) = mx + b$	slope-intercept form of a line	$z = mx + ny + b$ $F(x, y) = mx + ny + b$	slope-intercept form of a plane
$m = \dfrac{y_2 - y_1}{x_2 - x_1}$	slope	$m = \dfrac{z_2 - z_1}{x_2 - x_1}$	slope in x-direction
b	y-intercept	$n = \dfrac{z_2 - z_1}{y_2 - y_1}$	slope in y-direction
		b	z-intercept
$Ax + By = C$	general form of a line	$Ax + By + Cz = D$	general form of a plane
$y - y_0 = m(x - x_0)$	point-slope form of a line	$z - z_0 = m(x - x_0) + n(y - y_0)$	point-slope form of a plane
$x = 0$ $y = 0$	y-axis x-axis	$x = 0$ $y = 0$ $z = 0$	yz-plane xz-plane xy-plane
$x = a$ $y = b$	vertical line horizontal line	$x = a$ $y = b$ $z = c$	plane: parallel to yz-plane parallel to xz-plane parallel to xy-plane

Graphing Planes

One method of graphing a plane in three dimensions is to find the x-, y-, and z-intercepts, plot the intercepts on the axes, and then sketch the plane. To find the x-intercept, set y and z equal to 0, and solve for x. The y-intercept and z-intercept are found in a similar manner.

Example 2   Graphing a Plane in General Form

Graph the plane $2x + 3y + 4z = 12$.

Solution

First, find the intercepts.

x-intercept: $2x + 3(0) + 4(0) = 12$
$\phantom{x\text{-intercept:}\quad}x = 6$

y-intercept: $2(0) + 3y + 4(0) = 12$
$\phantom{y\text{-intercept:}\quad 2(0) +}y = 4$

z-intercept: $2(0) + 3(0) + 4z = 12$
$\phantom{z\text{-intercept:}\quad 2(0) + 3(0) +}z = 3$

Plot the intercepts, and sketch the plane that contains them, as shown in Figure 12.1.A-4.

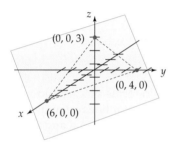

Figure 12.1.A-4

Example 3   Graphing a Plane in Slope-Intercept Form

Graph the plane $F(x, y) = x + 2y - 2$.

Solution

First, find the intercepts. Use the fact that $z = F(x, y)$ to find the z-intercept.

x-intercept: $0 = x + 2(0) - 2$
$$x = 2$$

y-intercept: $0 = 0 + 2y - 2$
$$y = 1$$

z-intercept: $z = 0 + 2(0) - 2$
$$z = -2$$

Plot the intercepts and sketch the plane that contains them, as shown in Figure 12.1.A-5.

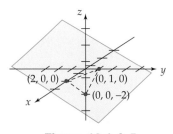

Figure 12.1.A-5

Example 4   Graphing a Plane Parallel to an Axis

Graph the plane $z - 4 = 2(x - 1)$.

Solution

First, find the intercepts. There is no y term; thus, the plane has no y-intercept. It is parallel to the y-axis.

x-intercept: $0 - 4 = 2(x - 1)$
$$x = -1$$

z-intercept: $z - 4 = 2(0 - 1)$
$$z = 2$$

Plot the intercepts and sketch the plane that contains them, as shown in Figure 12.1.A-6.

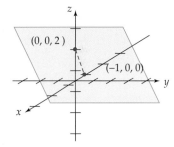

Figure 12.1.A-6

Graphical Representations of 3 × 3 Systems

A linear system of equations in three variables is represented graphically by three planes. A solution of a 3 × 3 linear system is a point of intersection of *all three* planes. As in two variables, a linear system in three variables can have no solutions, one solution, or infinitely many solutions.

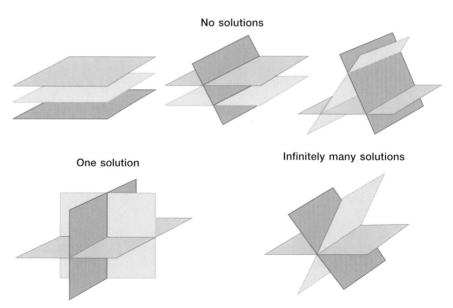

Figure 12.1.A-7

All remaining possibilities not shown are listed below:

- three planes coincide (infinitely many solutions)
- two planes coincide and the third plane intersects them (infinitely many solutions)
- two planes coincide and the third plane is parallel (no solutions)

Exercises 12.1.A

In Exercises 1–8, plot the given point in a three-dimensional coordinate system.

1. $(1, 4, 5)$ **2.** $(-3, 2, 4)$

3. $(0, 2, -3)$ **4.** $(4, 0, 6)$

5. $(3, 0, 0)$ **6.** $(0, 0, -4)$

7. $(2, -3, -1)$ **8.** $(-3, -1, 5)$

In Exercises 9–20, graph the plane described by the given equation.

9. $x + 3y - z = 6$ **10.** $5x + 2y - 4z = 10$

11. $3x - 4y + 6z = 9$ **12.** $-2x + 4y + 5z = 8$

13. $z = x + y - 3$ **14.** $z = 2x - y + 6$

15. $F(x, y) = 2x + 4y - 8$ **16.** $F(x, y) = 3x - 5y + 9$

17. $z + 6 = 3(x - 2)$ **18.** $z - 8 = 4(y - 3)$

19. $3x + 2z = -6$ **20.** $4x + z = 2$

21. *Critical Thinking* Describe the possibilities for the number of solutions of a linear system of equations with 2 equations in 3 variables. Explain your answers in terms of intersections of two planes. You may include a sketch in your answer.

12.2 Matrices

Objectives

- Represent systems of equations by augmented matrices
- Solve systems of equations by row reduction
- Solve systems by using a calculator to obtain reduced row echelon form matrices
- Solve applications by using matrices

Augmented Matrices

It is often convenient to use an array of numbers, called a **matrix,** as a method to represent a system of equations. For example, the system

$$x + 2y = -2$$
$$2x + 6y = 2$$

is written in matrix form as

$$\begin{pmatrix} 1 & 2 & -2 \\ 2 & 6 & 2 \end{pmatrix}$$

In this shorthand, only the coefficients of the variables are written. This representation is called an **augmented matrix** where each row of the matrix represents an equation of the system. The numbers in the first column are coefficients of x, the numbers in the second column are coefficients of y, and the third column's numbers are the constant terms. A vertical dashed line is often used to represent the equal signs.

Example 1 **Writing a System as an Augmented Matrix**

Write an augmented matrix for the system of equations.

$$x + 2y + 3z = -2$$
$$2y - 5z = 6$$
$$3x + 3y + 10z = -2$$

Solution

The augmented matrix is $\begin{pmatrix} 1 & 2 & 3 & -2 \\ 0 & 2 & -5 & 6 \\ 3 & 3 & 10 & -2 \end{pmatrix}$.

Notice that 0 is the x-coefficient in the second equation. ∎

Solving Systems Using Augmented Matrices

Recall that in the elimination method, an equation may be multiplied by a nonzero constant, or two equations may be added together. Also, the order of the equations is irrelevant, so equations may be interchanged. Performing any of these operations produces an **equivalent system,** that is, a system with the same solutions.

Augmented matrices can be used to solve linear systems. When dealing with matrices, operations similar to those used in the elimination method are called **elementary row operations.**

Elementary Row Operations

Performing any of the following operations on an augmented matrix produces an augmented matrix of an equivalent system:

- Interchange any two rows.
- Replace any row by a nonzero constant multiple of itself.
- Replace any row by the sum of itself and a nonzero constant multiple of another row.

Example 2 shows the use of the elementary row operations in solving a system. To solve a system of two equations in two variables using elementary row operations, produce an equivalent matrix that has one row with an x-coefficient of 1 and a y-coefficient of 0, and the other row with an x-coefficient of 0 and a y-coefficient of 1. The desired equivalent matrix and its corresponding system are shown below.

$$\begin{pmatrix} 1 & 0 & | & a \\ 0 & 1 & | & b \end{pmatrix} \longleftrightarrow \begin{array}{l} x = a \\ y = b \end{array}$$

Example 2   Using an Augmented Matrix

Solve the system of equations $\quad \begin{array}{l} x + 2y = -2 \\ 2x + 6y = 2 \end{array}$

Solution

The system is solved below by using elementary row operations in the elimination method on the left and the augmented matrix method on the right. Compare the steps performed in each method.

$$\begin{array}{l} x + 2y = -2 \\ 2x + 6y = 2 \end{array} \qquad \begin{pmatrix} 1 & 2 & | & -2 \\ 2 & 6 & | & 2 \end{pmatrix}$$

Replace the second row by the sum of itself and -2 times the first row.

$$-2r_1 + r_2 \to r_2$$

$$\begin{array}{l} x + 2y = -2 \\ 2y = 6 \end{array} \qquad \begin{pmatrix} 1 & 2 & | & -2 \\ 0 & 2 & | & 6 \end{pmatrix}$$

Multiply the second row by $\dfrac{1}{2}$.

$$\dfrac{1}{2} r_2 \to r_2$$

$$\begin{array}{l} x + 2y = -2 \\ y = 3 \end{array} \qquad \begin{pmatrix} 1 & 2 & | & -2 \\ 0 & 1 & | & 3 \end{pmatrix}$$

Replace the first row by the sum of itself and -2 times the second row.

$$-2r_2 + r_1 \to r_1$$

$$\begin{array}{l} x = -8 \\ y = 3 \end{array} \qquad \begin{pmatrix} 1 & 0 & | & -8 \\ 0 & 1 & | & 3 \end{pmatrix}$$

NOTE In previous methods, the step to replace a row with the sum of itself and a multiple of another row was done in two or more steps.

This last augmented matrix $\begin{pmatrix} 1 & 0 & -8 \\ 0 & 1 & 3 \end{pmatrix}$ represents the same solution of the system as the solution obtained by using the elimination method. The solution of the system is $x = -8$, $y = 3$. ∎

Reduced Row-Echelon Form

The last matrix of Example 2 is in **reduced row-echelon form,** which is summarized as follows.

Reduced Row-Echelon Form

A matrix is in reduced row-echelon form if it satisfies the following conditions.

- All rows consisting entirely of zeros (if any) are at the bottom.
- The first nonzero entry in each nonzero row is a 1 (called a *leading* 1).
- Any column containing a leading 1 has zeros as all other entries.
- Each leading 1 appears to the right of leading 1's in any preceding row.

Gauss-Jordan Elimination

The method of using elementary row operations to produce an equivalent matrix in reduced row-echelon form is called **Gauss-Jordan elimination.** When an augmented matrix is in reduced row-echelon form, the solutions of the system it represents can be read immediately, as in the last step of Example 2.

Example 3   Using Gauss-Jordan Elimination

The matrices below are in reduced row-echelon form. Write the system represented by each matrix, find the solutions, if any, and classify each system as consistent, consistent with infinitely many solutions, or inconsistent.

a. $\begin{pmatrix} 1 & -3 & 4 \\ 0 & 0 & 0 \end{pmatrix}$ **b.** $\begin{pmatrix} 1 & 0 & 0 & 3 \\ 0 & 1 & 0 & -7 \\ 0 & 0 & 1 & 4 \end{pmatrix}$ **c.** $\begin{pmatrix} 1 & 2 & -1 \\ 0 & 0 & 3 \end{pmatrix}$

Solution

a. The system represented by the augmented matrix is

$$x - 3y = 4$$
$$0x + 0y = 0$$

NOTE A matrix can represent a system of equations that has variables other than x, y, and z. When given a matrix without the corresponding system, the choice of letters used to represent the variables is arbitrary. Another common choice is x_1, x_2, and x_3.

The second equation, $0 = 0$, is always true. The system is consistent with infinitely many solutions. All solutions lie on the line represented by $x - 3y = 4$.

Represent the solutions of the system using the parameter t. Letting $y = t$ yields $x - 3t = 4$, so $x = 4 + 3t$. Individual solutions may then be found by substituting real values for t.

t (a real number)	$x = 4 + 3t$	$y = t$
$t = 1$	$x = 7$	$y = 1$
$t = -2$	$x = -2,$	$y = -2$
$t = 0$	$x = 4$	$y = 0$

b. The system represented by the matrix is

$$\begin{aligned} x & = 3 \\ &y = -7 \\ &z = 4 \end{aligned}$$

The solution of the system is $x = 3$, $y = -7$, $z = 4$, so the system is consistent.

c. The system represented by the matrix is

$$\begin{aligned} x + 2y &= -1 \\ 0x + 0y &= 3 \end{aligned}$$

The second equation, $0 = 3$, is always false. This indicates that the system is inconsistent because it has no solutions. ∎

Technology Tip

Check your calculator manual to learn how to enter and store matrices in the matrix memory.

To put a matrix in reduced row echelon form, use rref in the MATH or OPS submenu of TI-83/86 MATRIX menu, or in the MATRIX submenu of the TI-89 or HP-38 MATH menu; or use rrowEF in the MATH submenu of the Sharp 9600 MATRIX menu.

Calculators and Reduced Row-Echelon Form

Most graphing calculators have a command that uses elementary row operations to put a given matrix into reduced row-echelon form.

Example 4 Using Reduced Row-Echelon Form

Solve the following systems of equations using a calculator's reduced row-echelon form feature:

a. $\begin{aligned} 2x + y &= 0 \\ -4x + y &= 18 \end{aligned}$

b. $\begin{aligned} -x + 2y - 3z &= 5 \\ 3x - y + 5z &= -3 \\ y - 2z &= 6 \end{aligned}$

Solution

Write the augmented matrix for each system, enter each system into a calculator as a matrix, then reduce to reduced row-echelon form (see Technology Tip).

a. $\left(\begin{array}{cc|c} 2 & 1 & 0 \\ -4 & 1 & 18 \end{array} \right)$

b. $\left(\begin{array}{ccc|c} -1 & 2 & -3 & 5 \\ 3 & -1 & 5 & -3 \\ 0 & 1 & -2 & 6 \end{array} \right)$

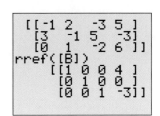

Figure 12.2-1a   Figure 12.2-1b

The solution is $x = -3, y = 6$.   The solution is $x = 4, y = 0, z = -3$.

Example 5   **Calculator Solution to an Inconsistent System**

Solve the system of equations.

$$x + y + 2z = 1$$
$$2x + 4y + 5z = 2$$
$$3x + 5y + 7z = 4$$

$$\begin{pmatrix} 1 & 1 & 2 & \vdots & 1 \\ 2 & 4 & 5 & \vdots & 2 \\ 3 & 5 & 7 & \vdots & 4 \end{pmatrix}$$

Solution

Write the augmented matrix for the system, enter the matrix into a calculator, then reduce to reduced row-echelon form, as shown in Figure 12.2-2.

```
[[1  1  2  1]
 [2  4  5  2]
 [3  5  7  4]]
rref([A])
 [[1  0  1.5  0]
  [0  1  .5   0]
  [0  0  0    1]]
```

The last row of the reduced matrix represents the equation

$$0x + 0y + 0z = 1.$$

Because the equation has no solution, the original system has no solution and is therefore inconsistent.

Figure 12.2-2

Example 6   **Calculator Solution of a System**

Solve the system of equations below.

$$2x + 5y + z + 3w = 0$$
$$2y - 4z + 6w = 0$$
$$2x + 17y - 23z + 40w = 0$$

$$\begin{pmatrix} 2 & 5 & 1 & 3 & \vdots & 0 \\ 0 & 2 & -4 & 6 & \vdots & 0 \\ 2 & 17 & -23 & 40 & \vdots & 0 \end{pmatrix}$$

Solution

Notice that all of the constant terms in the system are zero. A system like this has at least one solution, namely, $x = 0, y = 0, z = 0, w = 0$, which is called the *trivial solution*. However, there may be nonzero solutions as well.

```
rref([A])
 [[1  0  5.5  0  0]
  [0  1  -2   0  0]
  [0  0  0    1  0]]
```

Write the augmented matrix for the system, then enter and reduce it to reduced row-echelon form using a calculator, as shown in Figure 12.2-3.

Figure 12.2-3

The system corresponding to the reduced matrix is

$$
\begin{aligned}
x + 5.5z &= 0 \\
y - 2z &= 0 \\
w &= 0
\end{aligned}
$$

The system is consistent with infinitely many solutions. The value of w is always 0, and the first two equations can be solved for x and y in terms of z.

$$
\begin{aligned}
x &= -5.5z \\
y &= 2z \\
w &= 0
\end{aligned}
$$

Letting $z = t$, the solutions of the system all have the form

$$
x = -5.5t, \qquad y = 2t, \qquad z = t, \qquad w = 0.
$$

Individual solutions may be found by substituting real values for t.

$$
\begin{aligned}
t &= 0 & x &= 0, & y &= 0, & z &= 0, & w &= 0 \\
t &= 1 & x &= -5.5, & y &= 2, & z &= 1, & w &= 0 \\
t &= -3 & x &= 16.5, & y &= -6, & z &= -3, & w &= 0
\end{aligned}
$$

■

Example 7 Application Using Calculator Reduced Row-Echelon Form

Charlie is starting a small business and borrows $10,000 on three different credit cards, with annual interest rates of 18%, 15%, and 9%, respectively. He borrows three times as much on the 15% card as he does on the 18% card, and his total annual interest on all three cards is $1244.25. How much did he borrow on each credit card?

Solution

Let x be the amount borrowed on the 18% card, y the amount borrowed on the 15% card, and z the amount borrowed on the 9% card. The total amount borrowed is $10,000.

$$
x + y + z = 10{,}000
$$

Total interest is the sum of the amounts of interest on the three cards.

Interest on 18% card		Interest on 15% card		Interest on 9% card		Total interest
$0.18x$	$+$	$0.15y$	$+$	$0.09z$	$=$	1244.25

The amounts on the cards are related by a third equation.

Amount on 15% card		3 times amount on 18% card
y	$=$	$3x$

The equation $y = 3x$ is equivalent to $3x - y = 0$. Therefore, the system of equations is

$$
\begin{array}{rcrcrcl}
x &+& y &+& z &=& 10{,}000 \\
0.18x &+& 0.15y &+& 0.09z &=& 1244.25 \\
3x &-& y & & &=& 0
\end{array}
$$

The corresponding matrix and its reduced row-echelon form are shown in Figure 12.2-4.

$$
\begin{pmatrix}
1 & 1 & 1 & 10{,}000 \\
0.18 & 0.15 & 0.09 & 1244.25 \\
3 & -1 & 0 & 0
\end{pmatrix}
$$

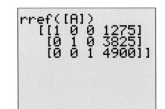

Figure 12.2-4

The solution is $x = 1275$, $y = 3825$, and $z = 4900$. Charlie borrowed \$1275 on the 18% card, \$3825 on the 15% card, and \$4900 on the 9% card.

Exercises 12.2

In Exercises 1–4, write the augmented matrix of the system.

1. $2x - 3y + 4z = 1$
 $x + 2y - 6z = 0$
 $3x - 7y + 4z = -3$

2. $x + 2y - 3w + 7z = -5$
 $2x - y - 3w + 2z = 4$
 $3x + 2y + 7w - 6z = 0$

3. $x - \dfrac{1}{2}y + \dfrac{7}{4}z = 0$

 $2x - \dfrac{3}{2}y + 5z = 0$

 $-2y + \dfrac{1}{3}z = 0$

4. $2x - \dfrac{1}{2}y + \dfrac{7}{2}w - 6z = 1$

 $\dfrac{1}{4}x - 6y + 2w - z = 2$

 $4y - \dfrac{1}{2}w + 6z = 3$

 $2x + 3y - 2w + \dfrac{1}{2}z = 4$

In Exercises 5–8, the augmented matrix of a system of equations is given. Express the system in equation notation.

5. $\begin{pmatrix} 2 & -3 & 1 \\ 4 & 7 & 2 \end{pmatrix}$

6. $\begin{pmatrix} 2 & 3 & 5 & 2 \\ 1 & 6 & 9 & 0 \end{pmatrix}$

7. $\begin{pmatrix} 1 & 0 & 1 & 0 & 1 \\ 1 & -1 & 4 & -2 & 3 \\ 4 & 2 & 5 & 0 & 2 \end{pmatrix}$

8. $\begin{pmatrix} 1 & 7 & 0 & 4 \\ 2 & 3 & 1 & 6 \\ -1 & 0 & 2 & 3 \end{pmatrix}$

In Exercises 9–12, the reduced row-echelon form of the augmented matrix of a system of equations is given. Find the solutions of the system.

9. $\begin{pmatrix} 1 & 0 & 0 & 0 & \frac{3}{2} \\ 0 & 1 & 0 & 0 & 5 \\ 0 & 0 & 1 & 0 & -2 \\ 0 & 0 & 0 & 1 & 0 \end{pmatrix}$

10. $\begin{pmatrix} 1 & 0 & 0 & 0 & 0 & 5 \\ 0 & 1 & 0 & 0 & 0 & 4 \\ 0 & 0 & 1 & 0 & 0 & 3 \\ 0 & 0 & 0 & 0 & 1 & 2 \\ 0 & 0 & 0 & 0 & 0 & 1 \end{pmatrix}$

11. $\begin{pmatrix} 1 & 0 & 0 & 1 & 2 \\ 0 & 1 & 0 & 2 & -3 \\ 0 & 0 & 1 & 0 & 4 \\ 0 & 0 & 0 & 0 & 0 \end{pmatrix}$

12. $\begin{pmatrix} 1 & 0 & 0 & 0 & 7 \\ 0 & 1 & 0 & 0 & 1 \\ 0 & 0 & 1 & 0 & -5 \\ 0 & 0 & 0 & 1 & 4 \\ 0 & 0 & 0 & 0 & 0 \\ 0 & 0 & 0 & 0 & 0 \end{pmatrix}$

In Exercises 13–20, use Gauss-Jordan elimination to solve the system.

13.
$$-x + 3y + 2z = 0$$
$$-2x - 3y - 2z = 3$$
$$x + 2y + 3z = 0$$

14.
$$3x + 7y + 9z = 0$$
$$x + 2y + 3z = 2$$
$$x + 4y + z = 2$$

15.
$$x + 2y + 2z = 1$$
$$x - 2y + 2z = 4$$
$$2x - 2y + 3z = 5$$

16.
$$2x - y + 2z = 1$$
$$3x + y + 2z = 0$$
$$7x - y + 3z = 2$$

17.
$$x - 2y + 4z = 6$$
$$x + y + 13z = 6$$
$$-2x + 6y - z = -10$$

18.
$$x - y + 5z = -6$$
$$3x + 3y - z = 10$$
$$x + 3y + 2z = 5$$

19.
$$x + y + z = 200$$
$$x - 2y + 2z = 0$$
$$2x + 3y + 5z = 600$$
$$2x - y + z = 200$$

20.
$$3x - y + z = 6$$
$$x + 2y - z = 0$$

In Exercises 21–36, solve the system by any method.

21.
$$11x + 10y + 9z = 5$$
$$x + 2y + 3z = 1$$
$$3x + 2y + z = 1$$

22.
$$-x + 2y - 3z + 4w = 8$$
$$2x - 4y + z + 2w = -3$$
$$5x - 4y + z + 2w = -3$$

23.
$$x + y = 3$$
$$5x - y = 3$$
$$9x - 4y = 1$$

24.
$$2x - y + 2z = 3$$
$$-x + 2y - z = 0$$
$$x + y - z = 1$$

25.
$$x - 4y - 13z = 4$$
$$x - 2y - 3z = 2$$
$$-3x + 5y + 4z = 2$$

26.
$$2x - 4y + z = 3$$
$$x + 3y - 7z = 1$$
$$-2x + 4y - z = 10$$

27.
$$4x + y + 3z = 7$$
$$x - y + 2z = 3$$
$$3x + 2y + z = 4$$

28.
$$x + 4y + z = 3$$
$$-x + 2y + 2z = 0$$
$$2x + 2y - z = 3$$

29.
$$x + y + z = 0$$
$$3x - y + z = 0$$
$$-5x - y + z = 0$$

30.
$$x + y + z = 0$$
$$x - y - z = 0$$
$$x - y + z = 0$$

31.
$$2x + y + 3z - 2w = -6$$
$$4x + 3y + z - w = -2$$
$$x + y + z + w = -5$$
$$-2x - 2y + 2z + 2w = -10$$

32.
$$x + y + z + w = -1$$
$$-x + 4y + z - w = 0$$
$$x - 2y + z - 2w = 11$$
$$-x - 2y + z + 2w = -3$$

33.
$$x - 2y - z - 3w = 18$$
$$-x + y + 3z - 3w = 7$$
$$4y + 3z - 2w = 8$$
$$2x - 2y + 3z + w = -7$$

34.
$$3x - y + 2z + 5w = 0$$
$$-x + 3y + 2z + 5w = 0$$
$$x + 2y + 5z - 4w = 0$$
$$2x - y + 5z + 3w = 0$$

35.
$$\frac{1}{x + 1} - \frac{2}{y - 3} + \frac{3}{z - 2} = 4$$
$$\frac{5}{y - 3} - \frac{10}{z - 2} = -5$$
$$\frac{-3}{x + 1} + \frac{4}{y - 3} - \frac{1}{z - 2} = -2$$

Hint: Let $u = \dfrac{1}{x + 1}$, $v = \dfrac{1}{y - 3}$, $w = \dfrac{1}{z - 2}$.

36. A matrix can be used to represent a set of points in space, with the x-coordinates in the first column, the y-coordinates in the second column, and the z-coordinates in the third column. Each row represents a point. A *crystal lattice* is used to represent the atomic structure of a crystal. The two matrices below represent simple cubic and A10 crystal lattices, in which the atoms of the crystal are at the points represented by the rows of the matrix.

Simple Cubic

x	y	z
0	0	0
3.35	0	0
0	3.35	0
3.35	3.35	0
0	0	3.35
3.35	0	3.35
0	3.35	3.35
3.35	3.35	3.35

A10

x	y	z
0	0	0
2.93	0.48	0.48
0.48	2.93	0.48
0.48	0.48	2.93
3.40	3.40	0.95
3.40	0.95	3.40
0.95	3.40	3.40
3.88	3.88	3.88

In two different three-dimensional coordinate systems, plot the points in each matrix and connect them to form two prisms. How are the two lattices alike? How are they different?

37. A collection of nickels, dimes, and quarters totals $6.00. If there are 52 coins altogether and twice as many dimes as nickels, how many of each kind of coin are there?

38. A collection of nickels, dimes, and quarters totals $8.20. The number of nickels and dimes together is twice the number of quarters. The value of the nickels is one-third of the value of the dimes. How many of each kind of coin are there?

39. Lillian borrows $10,000. She borrows some from her friend at 8% annual interest, twice as much as that from her bank at 9%, and the remainder from her insurance company at 5%. She pays a total of $830 in interest for the first year. How much did she borrow from each source?

40. An investor puts a total of $25,000 into three stocks. She invests some of it in stock A and $2000 more than one-half that amount in stock B. The remainder is invested in stock C. Stock A rises 16% in value, stock B 20%, and stock C 18%. Her investment in the three stocks is now worth $29,440. How much was originally invested in each stock?

41. An investor has $70,000 invested in a mutual fund, bonds, and a fast food franchise. She has twice as much invested in bonds as in the mutual fund. Last year the mutual fund paid a 2% dividend, the bonds 10%, and the fast food franchise 6%; her dividend income was $4800. How much is invested in each of the three investments?

42. Tickets to a concert cost $2 for children, $3 for teenagers, and $5 for adults. When 570 people attended the concert, the total ticket receipts were $1950. Three-fourths as many teenagers as children attended. How many children, adults, and teenagers attended?

43. A company sells three models of humidifiers: the bedroom model weighs 10 pounds and comes in an 8-cubic-foot box; the living room model weighs 20 pounds and comes in an 8-cubic-foot box; the whole-house model weighs 60 pounds and comes in a 28-cubic-foot box. Each of their delivery vans has 248 cubic feet of space and can hold a maximum of 440 pounds. In order for a van to be as fully loaded as possible, how many of each model should it carry?

44. Peanuts cost $3 per pound, almonds $4 per pound, and cashews $8 per pound. How many pounds of each should be used to produce 140 pounds of a mixture costing $6 per pound, in which there are twice as many peanuts as almonds?

45. If Tom, George, and Mario work together, they can paint a large room in 4 hours. When only George and Mario work together, it takes 8 hours to paint the room. Tom and George, working together, take 6 hours to paint the room. How long would it take each of them to paint the room alone? *Hint:* If x is the amount of the room painted in 1 hour by Tom, y is the amount painted by George, and z the amount painted by Mario, then $x + y + z = \dfrac{1}{4}$.

46. Pipes R, S, and T are connected to the same tank. When all three pipes are running, they can fill the tank in 2 hours. When only pipes S and T are running, they can fill the tank in 4 hours. When only R and T are running, they can fill the tank in 2.4 hours. How long would it take each pipe running alone to fill the tank?

47. A furniture manufacturer has 1950 hours available each week in the cutting department, 1490 hours in the assembly department, and 2160 in the finishing department. Manufacturing a chair requires 0.2 hours of cutting, 0.3 hours of assembly, and 0.1 hours of finishing. A chest requires 0.5 hours of cutting, 0.4 hours of assembly, and 0.6 hours of finishing. A table requires 0.3 hours of cutting, 0.1 hours of assembly, and 0.4 hours of finishing. How many chairs, chests, and tables should be produced in order to use all the available production capacity?

48. A stereo equipment manufacturer produces three models of speakers, R, S, and T, and has three kinds of delivery vehicles: trucks, vans, and station wagons. A truck holds 2 boxes of model R, 1 of model S, and 3 of model T. A van holds 1 box of model R, 3 of model S, and 2 of model T. A station wagon holds 1 box of model R, 3 of model S, and 1 of model T. If 15 boxes of model R, 20 of model S, and 22 of model T are to be delivered, how many vehicles of each type should be used so that all operate at full capacity?

49. A company produces three camera models: A, B, and C. Each model A requires 3 hours of lens polishing, 2 hours of assembly time, and 2 hours of finishing time. Each model B requires 2, 2, and 1 hours of lens polishing, assembly, and finishing time, and each model C requires 1, 3, and 1 hours, respectively. There are 100 hours available for lens polishing, 100 hours for assembly, and 65 hours for finishing each week. How many of each model should be produced if all available time is used?

12.3

Matrix Operations

Objectives

- Add and subtract matrices
- Multiply a matrix by a scalar factor
- Multiply two matrices
- Use matrix multiplication to solve problems
- Use matrices to represent directed networks

Matrices were used in Section 12.2 to solve systems of linear equations. However, matrices are also useful for organizing data. The arithmetic of matrices has practical applications in the natural sciences, engineering, the social sciences, and management. Matrices are now considered in a more general setting.

A matrix has been defined as an array of numbers. The **dimensions** of a matrix indicate the number of rows and columns in the matrix. An $m \times n$ **matrix** has m rows and n columns. For example:

$$A = \begin{pmatrix} 3 & 2 & -5 \\ 6 & 1 & 7 \\ -2 & 0 & 5 \end{pmatrix} \qquad B = \begin{pmatrix} \frac{3}{2} \\ -5 \\ 0 \\ 12 \end{pmatrix}$$

3×3 *matrix* 4×1 *matrix*
3 rows, 3 columns   *4 rows, 1 column*

Each entry of a matrix can be located by stating the row and column in which it appears. An entry a_{ij} is the entry in row i and column j of its corresponding matrix. In the matrices above, $a_{13} = -5$ and $b_{41} = 12$. Two matrices are said to be **equal** if they have the same dimensions and the corresponding entries are equal.

The general form of a matrix can be written as shown below.

$$A = \begin{pmatrix} a_{11} & a_{12} & a_{13} & \cdots & a_{1n} \\ a_{21} & a_{22} & a_{23} & \cdots & a_{2n} \\ a_{31} & a_{32} & a_{33} & \cdots & a_{3n} \\ \vdots & \vdots & \vdots & & \vdots \\ a_{m1} & a_{m2} & a_{m3} & \cdots & a_{mn} \end{pmatrix}$$

Matrix Addition and Subtraction

Matrices may be added or subtracted, but unlike real numbers, not all sums and differences are defined. It is only possible to add or subtract matrices that have the same dimensions.

Matrix Addition and Subtraction

Matrices that have the same dimensions may be added or subtracted by adding or subtracting the corresponding entries.

For matrices that have different dimensions, addition and subtraction are not defined.

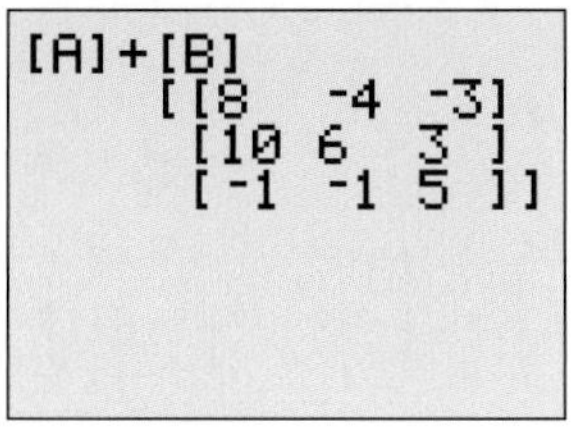

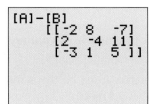

Figure 12.3-1a

Figure 12.3-1b

Example 1   Adding and Subtracting Matrices

For the given matrices, find $A + B$ and $A - B$.

$$A = \begin{pmatrix} 3 & 2 & -5 \\ 6 & 1 & 7 \\ -2 & 0 & 5 \end{pmatrix} \qquad B = \begin{pmatrix} 5 & -6 & 2 \\ 4 & 5 & -4 \\ 1 & -1 & 0 \end{pmatrix}$$

Solution

Both are 3×3 matrices, so add or subtract the corresponding entries.

$$A + B = \begin{pmatrix} 3 & 2 & -5 \\ 6 & 1 & 7 \\ -2 & 0 & 5 \end{pmatrix} + \begin{pmatrix} 5 & -6 & 2 \\ 4 & 5 & -4 \\ 1 & -1 & 0 \end{pmatrix} = \begin{pmatrix} 8 & -4 & -3 \\ 10 & 6 & 3 \\ -1 & -1 & 5 \end{pmatrix}$$

$$A - B = \begin{pmatrix} 3 & 2 & -5 \\ 6 & 1 & 7 \\ -2 & 0 & 5 \end{pmatrix} - \begin{pmatrix} 5 & -6 & 2 \\ 4 & 5 & -4 \\ 1 & -1 & 0 \end{pmatrix} = \begin{pmatrix} -2 & 8 & -7 \\ 2 & -4 & 11 \\ -3 & 1 & 5 \end{pmatrix}$$

The results are confirmed in Figures 12.3-1a and 12.3-1b. ∎

Multiplication and Matrices

Scalar Multiplication

There are two different types of multiplication associated with matrices: scalar multiplication and matrix multiplication. **Scalar multiplication** is the product of a real number and a matrix, while **matrix multiplication** is the product of two matrices.

Scalar Multiplication

Scalar multiplication is the product of a *scalar*, or real number, and a matrix. If A is an $m \times n$ matrix and k is a real number, then kA is the $m \times n$ matrix formed by multiplying each entry of A by k.

$$k \begin{pmatrix} a_{11} & \cdots & a_{1n} \\ \vdots & \ddots & \vdots \\ a_{m1} & \cdots & a_{mn} \end{pmatrix} = \begin{pmatrix} ka_{11} & \cdots & ka_{1n} \\ \vdots & \ddots & \vdots \\ ka_{m1} & \cdots & ka_{mn} \end{pmatrix}$$

Example 2   Scalar Multiplication

For the matrix $A = \begin{pmatrix} 3 & 2 & -5 \\ 6 & 1 & 7 \\ -2 & 0 & 5 \end{pmatrix}$, find $3A$.

```
3[A]
   [[9  6 -15]
    [18  3 21 ]
    [-6  0 15 ]]
```

Figure 12.3-2

Solution

Multiply each entry of A by 3.

$$3A = 3\begin{pmatrix} 3 & 2 & -5 \\ 6 & 1 & 7 \\ -2 & 0 & 5 \end{pmatrix} = \begin{pmatrix} 3(3) & 3(2) & 3(-5) \\ 3(6) & 3(1) & 3(7) \\ 3(-2) & 3(0) & 3(5) \end{pmatrix} = \begin{pmatrix} 9 & 6 & -15 \\ 18 & 3 & 21 \\ -6 & 0 & 15 \end{pmatrix}$$

The results are confirmed in Figure 12.3-2.   ■

Matrix Multiplication

To multiply two matrices, multiply the rows of the first matrix by columns of the second matrix.

The number of entries in each row of the first matrix must be the same as the number of entries in each column of the second matrix.

To multiply a row by a column, multiply the corresponding entries, then add the results. In the following illustration, row 2 of the first matrix is multiplied by column 1 of the second matrix to produce the entry in row 2 column 1 of the product matrix. Note that the product of a row and a column is a single number.

$$\begin{pmatrix} * & * & * \\ 3 & 1 & 2 \\ * & * & * \end{pmatrix}\begin{pmatrix} 2 & * & * \\ 0 & * & * \\ 1 & * & * \end{pmatrix} = \begin{pmatrix} & & * & & & * & * \\ 3\cdot2 & + & 1\cdot0 & + & 2\cdot1 & * & * \\ & & * & & & * & * \end{pmatrix} = \begin{pmatrix} * & * & * \\ 8 & * & * \\ * & * & * \end{pmatrix}$$

$$\underset{a_{21}b_{11}}{\uparrow} \qquad \underset{a_{22}b_{21}}{\uparrow} \qquad \underset{a_{23}b_{31}}{\uparrow}$$

Matrix Multiplication

The product AB is defined only when the number of columns of A is the same as the number of rows of B.

If A is an $m \times n$ matrix and B is an $n \times p$ matrix, then AB is an $m \times p$ matrix C where the entry in the ith row, jth column is

$$c_{ij} = a_{i1}b_{1j} + a_{i2}b_{2j} + \ldots + a_{in}b_{nj}$$

The following diagram shows how the dimensions of the product matrix are related to the dimensions of the factor matrices:

$$(m \times n \text{ matrix}) \cdot (n \times p \text{ matrix}) = (m \times p \text{ matrix})$$

CAUTION

Before finding the entries of a product matrix, check the dimensions of the factor matrices to make sure that the product is defined.

Example 3   Matrix Multiplication

For the given matrices, find AB, BA, AC, and CA when defined.

$$A = \begin{pmatrix} 3 & 1 & 2 \\ -1 & 0 & 4 \end{pmatrix} \qquad B = \begin{pmatrix} 2 & -3 \\ 0 & 5 \\ 1 & 8 \end{pmatrix} \qquad C = \begin{pmatrix} 1 & 3 \\ 0 & -1 \end{pmatrix}$$

Solution

First, verify that each product is defined.

A is 2×3 and B is 3×2, so AB is defined.

B is 3×2 and A is 2×3, so BA is defined.

A is 2×3 and C is 2×2, so AC is *not* defined.

C is 2×2 and A is 2×3, so CA is defined.

AB is a 2×2 matrix.

> **CAUTION**
>
> Matrix multiplication is not commutative, that is, $AB \neq BA$ in general. AB and BA may have different dimensions, as in Example 3, or BA may not be defined when AB is. Even when AB and BA are both defined and have the same dimensions, they may not be equal.

$$AB = \begin{pmatrix} 3 & 1 & 2 \\ -1 & 0 & 4 \end{pmatrix}\begin{pmatrix} 2 & -3 \\ 0 & 5 \\ 1 & 8 \end{pmatrix}$$

$$= \begin{pmatrix} \overbrace{3(2) + 1(0) + 2(1)}^{\text{row 1 of } A \times \text{ column 1 of } B} & \overbrace{3(-3) + 1(5) + 2(8)}^{\text{row 1 of } A \times \text{ column 2 of } B} \\ \underbrace{(-1)2 + 0(0) + 4(1)}_{\text{row 2 of } A \times \text{ column 1 of } B} & \underbrace{(-1)(-3) + 0(5) + 4(8)}_{\text{row 2 of } A \times \text{ column 2 of } B} \end{pmatrix}$$

$$= \begin{pmatrix} 8 & 12 \\ 2 & 35 \end{pmatrix}$$

BA is a 3×3 matrix.

$$BA = \begin{pmatrix} 2 & -3 \\ 0 & 5 \\ 1 & 8 \end{pmatrix}\begin{pmatrix} 3 & 1 & 2 \\ -1 & 0 & 4 \end{pmatrix}$$

$$= \begin{pmatrix} 2(3) + (-3)(-1) & 2(1) + (-3)(0) & 2(2) + (-3)(4) \\ 0(3) + 5(-1) & 0(1) + 5(0) & 0(2) + 5(4) \\ 1(3) + 8(-1) & 1(1) + 8(0) & 1(2) + 8(4) \end{pmatrix}$$

$$= \begin{pmatrix} 9 & 2 & -8 \\ -5 & 0 & 20 \\ -5 & 1 & 34 \end{pmatrix}$$

Note that $AB \neq BA$.

AC is not defined.

CA is a 2×3 matrix.

$$CA = \begin{pmatrix} 1 & 3 \\ 0 & -1 \end{pmatrix} \begin{pmatrix} 3 & 1 & 2 \\ -1 & 0 & 4 \end{pmatrix}$$

$$= \begin{pmatrix} 1(3) + & 3(-1) & 1(1) + & 3(0) & 1(2) + & 3(4) \\ 0(3) + (-1)(-1) & 0(1) + (-1)(0) & 0(2) + (-1)(4) \end{pmatrix}$$

$$= \begin{pmatrix} 0 & 1 & 14 \\ 1 & 0 & -4 \end{pmatrix}$$

Matrices can also be multiplied on a calculator, as shown below.

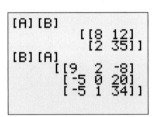

Figure 12.3-3

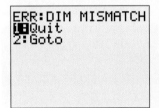

Technology Tip

To multiply matrices on a calculator, enter the matrices in the memory and recall them as needed. If the product of two matrices is not defined, the calculator will give an error message.

Figure 12.3-4

Applications

Matrices are a convenient way to handle data that is grouped into categories. If the categories of the rows of one matrix are the same as those of the columns of another, the matrices can often be multiplied to form a meaningful product.

Example 4   **Using Matrix Multiplication**

A furniture restorer refinishes chairs, tables, and dressers. The amount of time required to complete each step of refinishing and the cost per hour of each step are given by the following matrices. Find the product of the two matrices and interpret the result.

	Hours				cost per hour
	removing finish	sanding	finishing		
chair	0.5 hr	2.5 hr	1 hr	removing finish	$7
table	1 hr	4 hr	1.5 hr	sanding	$18
dresser	3 hr	7 hr	4.5 hr	finishing	$10

[A] [B]
[[58.5]
[94]
[192]]

Figure 12.3-5

Solution

The first matrix is 3 × 3 and the second is 3 × 1, so multiplication of the first matrix by the second matrix is defined, and the product is a 3 × 1 matrix. In the product of a row and a column, the amount of time for each step is multiplied by the cost per hour for that step, giving the cost for that step. The costs are then added, giving the total cost for the item. The product matrix will give the total cost for refinishing each item.

$$\begin{pmatrix} 0.5\,\text{hr} & 2.5\,\text{hr} & 1\,\text{hr} \\ 1\,\text{hr} & 4\,\text{hr} & 1.5\,\text{hr} \\ 3\,\text{hr} & 7\,\text{hr} & 4.5\,\text{hr} \end{pmatrix} \begin{pmatrix} \$7 \\ \$18 \\ \$10 \end{pmatrix} = \begin{matrix} \text{chair} \\ \text{table} \\ \text{dresser} \end{matrix} \overset{\text{total cost}}{\begin{pmatrix} \$58.50 \\ \$94 \\ \$192 \end{pmatrix}}$$

Directed Networks

The following figure is a **directed network.** The points that are labeled by capital letters are called **vertices,** and the arrows indicate the direction in which the paths between the vertices can be traveled. For example, from vertex L there is 1 path to M and 2 paths to K, but from K, there are 0 paths to L or to M.

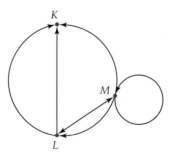

Figure 12.3-6

From	To	Number of paths
K	K	0
K	L	0
K	M	0
L	K	2
L	L	0
L	M	1
M	K	1
M	L	2
M	M	1

An **adjacency matrix** can be used to represent the connections between the vertices, as shown at right. The entries in the matrix are the number of direct paths, called **one-stage paths,** from one vertex to another.

$$\begin{array}{c} \\ \text{From:} \end{array} \begin{array}{c} \\ K \\ L \\ M \end{array} \overset{\displaystyle \begin{array}{ccc} & \text{To:} & \\ K & L & M \end{array}}{\begin{pmatrix} 0 & 0 & 0 \\ 2 & 0 & 1 \\ 1 & 2 & 1 \end{pmatrix}}$$

Multiplying Adjacency Matrices

If A is the adjacency matrix of a network, then the product $A \times A = A^2$ is a matrix for the number of two-stage paths, that is, paths from one vertex to another through one intermediate vertex.

Example 5 Using an Adjacency Matrix

Find the matrix for the number of two-stage paths for the directed network on page 809, and interpret the result.

Solution

The matrix for the number of two-stage paths is

$$\begin{pmatrix} 0 & 0 & 0 \\ 2 & 0 & 1 \\ 1 & 2 & 1 \end{pmatrix}^2 = \begin{pmatrix} 0 & 0 & 0 \\ 2 & 0 & 1 \\ 1 & 2 & 1 \end{pmatrix}\begin{pmatrix} 0 & 0 & 0 \\ 2 & 0 & 1 \\ 1 & 2 & 1 \end{pmatrix} = \begin{pmatrix} 0 & 0 & 0 \\ 1 & 2 & 1 \\ 5 & 2 & 3 \end{pmatrix}$$

The matrix gives the number of two-stage paths, which are given in the table below.

NOTE Two different two-stage paths may pass through the same vertices in the same order, as shown below.

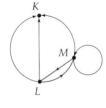

From	To	Number of two-stage paths	Paths
K	K	0	none
K	L	0	none
K	M	0	none
L	K	1	$L \to M \to K$
L	L	2	$L \to M \to L; L \to M \to L$ (see Note)
L	M	1	$L \to M \to M$
M	K	5	$M \to L \to K; M \to L \to K; M \to L \to K$ $M \to L \to K; M \to M \to K$
M	L	2	$M \to M \to L; M \to M \to L$
M	M	3	$M \to L \to M; M \to L \to M; M \to M \to M$

Example 6 Food Webs

A *food web* shows the relationships between certain predators and prey in an ecosystem. A directed network can be used to represent a food web, with the arrows pointing in the direction of prey to predator. Write an adjacency matrix for the following food web.

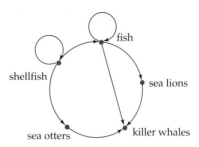

Figure 12.3-7

Solution

The matrix is given below.

To:

		s	f	so	sl	kw
From:	s	1	1	1	0	0
	f	0	1	0	1	1
	so	0	0	0	0	1
	sl	0	0	0	0	1
	kw	0	0	0	0	0

Exercises 12.3

In Exercises 1–6, refer to matrices A, B, and C below.

$$A = \begin{pmatrix} 2 & -6 & 3 \\ 4 & -2 & 1 \\ 3 & 5 & -5 \end{pmatrix} \qquad B = \begin{pmatrix} -4 & 4 & 7 \\ 5 & 3 & 2 \\ -1 & -6 & 6 \end{pmatrix}$$

$$C = \begin{pmatrix} 4 & 3 & -5 \\ -2 & -1 & 7 \\ 4 & 6 & 1 \end{pmatrix}$$

Find each of the following:

1. $A + B$

2. AB

3. $A + C$

4. $3A$

5. $2C$

6. $2B + 3C$

In Exercises 7–12, determine if the product AB or BA is defined. If a product is defined, state its dimensions. Do not calculate the products.

7. $A = \begin{pmatrix} 3 & 6 & 7 \\ 8 & 0 & 1 \end{pmatrix}$ $B = \begin{pmatrix} 2 & 5 & 9 & 1 \\ 7 & 0 & 0 & 6 \\ -1 & 3 & 8 & 7 \end{pmatrix}$

8. $A = \begin{pmatrix} -1 & -2 & -5 \\ 9 & 2 & -1 \\ 10 & 34 & 5 \end{pmatrix}$ $B = \begin{pmatrix} 17 & -9 \\ -6 & 12 \\ 3 & 5 \end{pmatrix}$

9. $A = \begin{pmatrix} 1 & 0 \\ 1 & 1 \\ 0 & 1 \end{pmatrix}$ $B = \begin{pmatrix} 5 & 6 & 11 \\ 7 & 8 & 15 \end{pmatrix}$

10. $A = \begin{pmatrix} 1 & -5 & 7 \\ 2 & 4 & 8 \\ 1 & -1 & 2 \end{pmatrix}$ $B = \begin{pmatrix} -2 & 4 & 9 \\ 13 & -2 & 1 \\ 5 & 25 & 0 \end{pmatrix}$

11. $A = \begin{pmatrix} -4 & 15 \\ 3 & -7 \\ 2 & 10 \end{pmatrix}$ $B = \begin{pmatrix} 1 & 2 \\ 3 & 4 \end{pmatrix}$

12. $A = \begin{pmatrix} 10 & 12 \\ -6 & 0 \\ 1 & 23 \\ -4 & 3 \end{pmatrix}$ $\qquad B = \begin{pmatrix} 1 & 2 & 3 \\ 3 & 2 & 1 \end{pmatrix}$

In Exercises 13–18, find AB.

13. $A = \begin{pmatrix} 3 & 2 \\ 2 & 4 \end{pmatrix}$ $\qquad B = \begin{pmatrix} 1 & -2 & 3 \\ 0 & 3 & 1 \end{pmatrix}$

14. $A = \begin{pmatrix} -1 & 2 & 3 \\ 0 & -1 & 2 \\ 1 & 2 & 0 \end{pmatrix}$ $\qquad B = \begin{pmatrix} 3 & -2 & -1 \\ 1 & 0 & 5 \\ 1 & -1 & -1 \end{pmatrix}$

15. $A = \begin{pmatrix} 1 & 0 & -4 \\ 0 & 2 & -1 \\ 2 & 3 & 4 \end{pmatrix}$ $\qquad B = \begin{pmatrix} 1 & 1 \\ 1 & 0 \\ 0 & 1 \end{pmatrix}$

16. $A = \begin{pmatrix} 1 & -2 \\ 3 & 0 \\ 0 & -1 \\ 2 & 1 \end{pmatrix}$ $\qquad B = \begin{pmatrix} -1 & 3 & -2 & 0 \\ 6 & 1 & 0 & -2 \end{pmatrix}$

17. $A = \begin{pmatrix} 2 & 0 & -1 \\ 1 & 1 & 2 \\ 0 & 2 & -3 \\ 2 & 3 & 0 \end{pmatrix}$ $\qquad B = \begin{pmatrix} 1 & 0 & 1 & 1 \\ 1 & 1 & 0 & 1 \\ 1 & 1 & 1 & 0 \end{pmatrix}$

18. $A = \begin{pmatrix} 10 & 0 & 1 & 0 \\ -1 & 1 & 0 & 1 \end{pmatrix}$ $\qquad B = \begin{pmatrix} 2 & -1 & 0 & 1 \\ -2 & 3 & 1 & -4 \\ 3 & 5 & 2 & -5 \end{pmatrix}$

In Exercises 19–22, show that AB is not equal to BA by computing both products.

19. $A = \begin{pmatrix} 3 & 2 \\ 5 & 1 \end{pmatrix}$ $\qquad B = \begin{pmatrix} 7 & -5 \\ -2 & 6 \end{pmatrix}$

20. $A = \begin{pmatrix} \frac{3}{2} & 2 \\ 4 & \frac{7}{2} \end{pmatrix}$ $\qquad B = \begin{pmatrix} 1 & -\frac{3}{2} \\ \frac{5}{2} & 1 \end{pmatrix}$

21. $A = \begin{pmatrix} 4 & 2 & -1 \\ 0 & 1 & 2 \\ -3 & 0 & 1 \end{pmatrix}$ $\qquad B = \begin{pmatrix} 1 & 7 & -5 \\ 2 & -2 & 6 \\ 0 & 0 & 0 \end{pmatrix}$

22. $A = \begin{pmatrix} 1 & 1 & -1 & 1 \\ 2 & 0 & 3 & 2 \\ -3 & 0 & 0 & 1 \\ 1 & -1 & 1 & 2 \end{pmatrix}$ $\qquad B = \begin{pmatrix} 0 & 1 & 7 & 7 \\ 2 & 3 & -2 & 1 \\ 5 & 0 & 1 & 0 \\ -1 & 0 & 1 & 0 \end{pmatrix}$

23. Write an adjacency matrix for the directed network below.

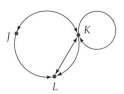

24. Write an adjacency matrix for the directed network below.

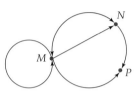

25. Find a matrix for the directed network in Exercise 23 that represents the number of two-stage paths.

26. Find a matrix for the directed network in Exercise 24 that represents the number of two-stage paths.

27. A bakery sells giant cookies, sheet cakes, and 3-tiered cakes. The time required for each step is given in the matrix below.

	baking	decorating
giant cookie	0.5 hr	0.25 hr
sheet cake	0.75 hr	0.5 hr
3-tiered cake	1.5 hr	1.25 hr

The cost per hour for baking and decorating is given by the matrix below. Find the product of the two matrices and interpret the result.

	cost per hour
baking	$4
decorating	$7

28. A boutique sells shirts, pants, and dresses. The time required for each step is given in the matrix below.

	cutting	sewing
shirt	1 hr	1 hr
pants	1.5 hr	1.25 hr
dress	2 hr	1.75 hr

The cost per hour for cutting and sewing is given by the matrix below. Find the product of the two matrices and interpret the result.

$$\begin{array}{c} \text{cost per} \\ \text{hour} \end{array}$$

$$\begin{array}{c} \text{cutting} \\ \text{sewing} \end{array} \begin{pmatrix} \$5 \\ \$9 \end{pmatrix}$$

29. A small college offers lecture and lab courses. The class sizes are given in the matrix below.

	freshman level	sophomore level	junior level	senior level
lecture	150	100	75	50
lab	30	25	25	20

The tuition for each course is given by the matrix below. Find the product of the two matrices. Interpret all meaningful entries in the product.

	lecture	lab
freshman level	$200	$40
sophomore level	$240	$48
junior level	$280	$56
senior level	$320	$64

30. A store sells trail mixes made of nuts and dried fruit. The nutritional information per serving is given in the matrix below.

	nuts	fruit
fat	1 g	52 g
protein	3 g	20 g
carbohydrates	65 g	21 g

The percent of fruit and nuts per serving in each mix is given below. Find the product of the two matrices, and interpret the result.

	mix A	mix B
nuts	30%	45%
fruit	70%	55%

31. Write an adjacency matrix for the food web represented by the directed network below.

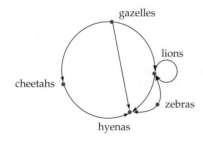

32. Write an adjacency matrix for the food web represented by the directed network below.

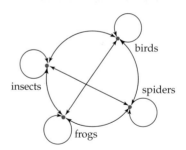

33. An airline offers nonstop flights between certain cities, as shown on the directed network below.

a. Write an adjacency matrix A for the directed network above.
b. Find the matrix A^2, which represents the number of flights between cities with exactly 1 layover. Find the matrix A^3, which represents the number of flights between cities with exactly 2 layovers.
c. Find the matrix $A + A^2 + A^3$, and interpret the result.

34. A delivery company ships packages between certain locations, as shown by the directed network below.

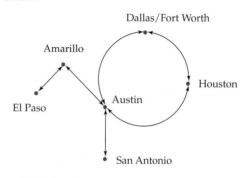

a. Write an adjacency matrix A for the directed network above.
b. Find the matrix $A + A^2 + A^3$, and interpret the result.

Matrix Methods for Square Systems

12.4

Objectives

- Define the $n \times n$ identity matrix

- Find the inverse of an invertible matrix

- Solve square systems of equations using inverse matrices

A system of equations that has the same number of equations as variables is called a **square system.** There is a method of solving this type of system that does not require row reduction. This method only works if the system has a unique solution.

Examine the system of equations below.

$$\left.\begin{array}{rcr} x + y + z &=& 2 \\ 2x + 3y &=& 5 \\ x + 2y + z &=& -1 \end{array}\right\} \qquad [1]$$

Instead of using a single matrix to represent the system, we can consider the system as having three parts: the coefficients, the variables, and the constants. A matrix can be used to represent each part.

$$A = \begin{pmatrix} 1 & 1 & 1 \\ 2 & 3 & 0 \\ 1 & 2 & 1 \end{pmatrix} \qquad X = \begin{pmatrix} x \\ y \\ z \end{pmatrix} \qquad B = \begin{pmatrix} 2 \\ 5 \\ -1 \end{pmatrix}$$

$\qquad\qquad$ *coefficients* $\qquad\qquad$ *variables* $\qquad\qquad$ *constants*

The relationship between the three matrices and the system is shown in the following example.

Example 1   A Matrix Equation

For the system of equations and the three matrices above, verify that $AX = B$.

Solution

By the definition of matrix multiplication:

$$AX = \begin{pmatrix} 1 & 1 & 1 \\ 2 & 3 & 0 \\ 1 & 2 & 1 \end{pmatrix}\begin{pmatrix} x \\ y \\ z \end{pmatrix} = \begin{pmatrix} x + y + z \\ 2x + 3y \\ x + 2y + z \end{pmatrix}$$

According to the system of equations [1], the entries of the matrix AX are equal to the corresponding entries of B, so the two matrices are equal, that is, $AX = B$.

Example 1 shows that a square system can be represented by the **matrix equation** $AX = B$, where A is the matrix of the system's coefficients and B is the matrix of the system's constants. Thus, the system can be solved by solving the corresponding matrix equation. Solving the equation $AX = B$ means finding the entries of the matrix X, which are the variables of the system.

Identity Matrices and Inverse Matrices

To solve a matrix equation $AX = B$, it is necessary to "undo" the matrix multiplication. One method of solving similar equations with real numbers is by multiplying both sides of the equation by the inverse of a.

$$ax = b$$
$$a^{-1}ax = a^{-1}b \qquad [2]$$
$$x = a^{-1}b$$

The solution of equation [2] depends on the fact that $aa^{-1} = 1$, which is the identity for multiplication of real numbers. Thus, in order to define the inverse of a matrix, we must first define the identity for matrix multiplication.

The $n \times n$ **identity matrix** I_n is the matrix with n rows and n columns that has 1's on the diagonal from the top left to the bottom right and 0's as all its other entries.

$$I_2 = \begin{pmatrix} 1 & 0 \\ 0 & 1 \end{pmatrix} \qquad I_3 = \begin{pmatrix} 1 & 0 & 0 \\ 0 & 1 & 0 \\ 0 & 0 & 1 \end{pmatrix} \qquad I_4 = \begin{pmatrix} 1 & 0 & 0 & 0 \\ 0 & 1 & 0 & 0 \\ 0 & 0 & 1 & 0 \\ 0 & 0 & 0 & 1 \end{pmatrix}$$

The identity matrix, I_n, is the identity for multiplication of $n \times n$ matrices.

Identity Matrix

For any $n \times n$ matrix A,

$$AI_n = I_nA = A.$$

Example 2   Verifying the Identity Matrix Property

For matrix C, verify that $CI_2 = I_2C = C$.

$$C = \begin{pmatrix} 3 & 2 \\ 5 & 7 \end{pmatrix}$$

Solution

By the definition of matrix multiplication,

$$CI_2 = \begin{pmatrix} 3 & 2 \\ 5 & 7 \end{pmatrix}\begin{pmatrix} 1 & 0 \\ 0 & 1 \end{pmatrix} = \begin{pmatrix} 3(1) + 2(0) & 3(0) + 2(1) \\ 5(1) + 7(0) & 5(0) + 7(1) \end{pmatrix} = \begin{pmatrix} 3 & 2 \\ 5 & 7 \end{pmatrix} = C$$

$$I_2C = \begin{pmatrix} 1 & 0 \\ 0 & 1 \end{pmatrix}\begin{pmatrix} 3 & 2 \\ 5 & 7 \end{pmatrix} = \begin{pmatrix} 1(3) + 0(5) & 1(2) + 0(7) \\ 0(3) + 1(5) & 0(2) + 1(7) \end{pmatrix} = \begin{pmatrix} 3 & 2 \\ 5 & 7 \end{pmatrix} = C$$

Inverse Matrices

An $n \times n$ matrix A is called **invertible**, or **nonsingular**, if there exists an $n \times n$ matrix B such that $AB = I_n$. (In this case it is also true that $BA = I_n$.)

The matrix B is called the **inverse** of A, and is written as A^{-1}, where $AA^{-1} = A^{-1}A = I_n$. Not all matrices have a multiplicative inverse.

Example 3   Verifying an Inverse Matrix

For the given matrices, verify that B is the inverse of A.

$$A = \begin{pmatrix} 2 & 1 \\ 3 & 1 \end{pmatrix} \qquad B = \begin{pmatrix} -1 & 1 \\ 3 & -2 \end{pmatrix}$$

Solution

By the definition of matrix multiplication,

$$AB = \begin{pmatrix} 2 & 1 \\ 3 & 1 \end{pmatrix}\begin{pmatrix} -1 & 1 \\ 3 & -2 \end{pmatrix} = \begin{pmatrix} 2(-1) + 1(3) & 2(1) + 1(-2) \\ 3(-1) + 1(3) & 3(1) + 1(-2) \end{pmatrix} = \begin{pmatrix} 1 & 0 \\ 0 & 1 \end{pmatrix} = I_2$$

Notice also that

$$BA = \begin{pmatrix} -1 & 1 \\ 3 & -2 \end{pmatrix}\begin{pmatrix} 2 & 1 \\ 3 & 1 \end{pmatrix} = \begin{pmatrix} (-1)(2) + 1(3) & (-1)(1) + 1(1) \\ 3(2) + (-2)(3) & 3(1) + (-2)(1) \end{pmatrix}$$

$$= \begin{pmatrix} 1 & 0 \\ 0 & 1 \end{pmatrix} = I_2$$

There are several methods of finding the inverse of an invertible matrix.

Example 4   Finding an Inverse Matrix

Find the inverse of matrix $A = \begin{pmatrix} 2 & 6 \\ 1 & 4 \end{pmatrix}$.

Solution

Suppose $A^{-1} = \begin{pmatrix} x & u \\ y & v \end{pmatrix}$. Then $AA^{-1} = I_2$.

$$AA^{-1} = \begin{pmatrix} 2 & 6 \\ 1 & 4 \end{pmatrix}\begin{pmatrix} x & u \\ y & v \end{pmatrix} = \begin{pmatrix} 2x + 6y & 2u + 6v \\ x + 4y & u + 4v \end{pmatrix} = \begin{pmatrix} 1 & 0 \\ 0 & 1 \end{pmatrix} = I_2$$

Setting the corresponding entries of AA^{-1} and I_n equal to each other results in two systems of equations, one for each column.

$$\begin{array}{ll} 2x + 6y = 1 & \quad 2u + 6v = 0 \\ x + 4y = 0 & \quad u + 4v = 1 \end{array}$$

The solutions of the two systems are $x = 2$, $y = -\dfrac{1}{2}$ and $u = -3$, $v = 1$.

Thus, $A^{-1} = \begin{pmatrix} 2 & -3 \\ -\frac{1}{2} & 1 \end{pmatrix}$. Check this by verifying that $AA^{-1} = I_2$.

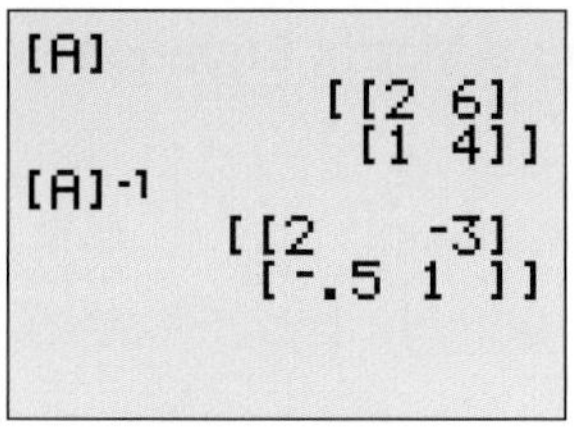

```
[A]
       [[2 6]
        [1 4]]
[A]-1
       [[2    -3]
        [-.5  1 ]]
```

Figure 12.4-1

Most graphing calculators can also be used to find inverse matrices directly by using the x^{-1} key, as shown in Figure 12.4-1.

Solving Square Systems Using Inverse Matrices

Recall that the need for inverse matrices arose out of the matrix equation $AX = B$, which represents a square system of equations. The equation can now be easily solved by multiplying both sides by the inverse of the coefficient matrix A.

$$AX = B$$
$$A^{-1}AX = A^{-1}B \qquad \textit{Multiply both sides by } A^{-1}.$$
$$I_nX = A^{-1}B \qquad A^{-1}A = I_n \textit{ by definition of inverse.}$$
$$X = A^{-1}B \qquad I_nX = X \textit{ by definition of identity.}$$

Thus, the solution of a square system of equations with an invertible coefficient matrix A and constant matrix B is $X = A^{-1}B$.

CAUTION

Because matrix multiplication is not commutative, it is important to always multiply in the same order on both sides of the equation.

Matrix Solution of a Square System

Suppose that a square system of equations can be represented by the matrix equation $AX = B$, where A is the matrix of the coefficients, X is the matrix of the variables, and B is the matrix of the constants. If A is invertible, then the unique solution of the system is

$$X = A^{-1}B$$

If A is not invertible, then the system is either consistent with infinitely many solutions or inconsistent. Its solutions (if any) may be found by using Gauss-Jordan elimination.

Example 5 **Solving a 2 × 2 System Using a Matrix Equation**

Use an inverse matrix to solve
$$\begin{aligned} x + y &= 2 \\ 2x - 9y &= 15 \end{aligned}$$

```
[A]-1[B]
       [[3 ]
        [-1]]
```

Solution

The coefficient matrix $A = \begin{pmatrix} 1 & 1 \\ 2 & -9 \end{pmatrix}$ and the constant matrix $B = \begin{pmatrix} 2 \\ 15 \end{pmatrix}$. Then $X = A^{-1}B = \begin{pmatrix} 3 \\ -1 \end{pmatrix}$, so the solution is $x = 3, y = -1$.

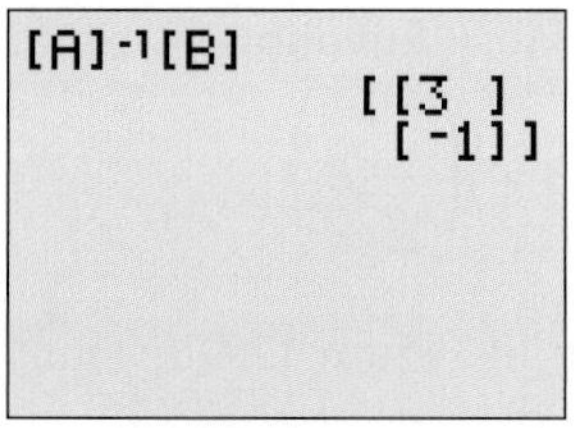

Figure 12.4-2

Example 6 Solving a 3 × 3 System Using a Matrix Equation

Use an inverse matrix to solve
$$\begin{aligned} x + y + z &= 2 \\ 2x + 3y &= 5 \\ x + 2y + z &= -1 \end{aligned}$$

Solution

The coefficient matrix is $A = \begin{pmatrix} 1 & 1 & 1 \\ 2 & 3 & 0 \\ 1 & 2 & 1 \end{pmatrix}$ and the constant matrix is

$B = \begin{pmatrix} 2 \\ 5 \\ -1 \end{pmatrix}$. Then $X = A^{-1}B = \begin{pmatrix} 7 \\ -3 \\ -2 \end{pmatrix}$, so the solution is $x = 7$, $y = -3$,

$z = -2$, as shown in Figure 12.4-3.

```
[A]-1[B]
        [[7 ]
         [-3]
         [-2]]
```

Figure 12.4-3

Curve Fitting

Just as two points determine a unique line, three noncollinear points determine a unique parabola. In general, a polynomial of degree n can be determined by $n + 1$ noncolinear points, a circle by three non-collinear points, and a general conic by five noncollinear points. Matrix methods can be used to find curves that pass through a given set of points.

Example 7 Finding the Parabola Through Three Points

Find the equation of the parabola that passes through the points $(1, -4)$, $(-1, -10)$, and $(4, -25)$.

Solution

The equation of a parabola can be written as $y = ax^2 + bx + c$.

Substitute the values of x and y from each point into the equation to form a system of equations with the variables a, b, and c.

$$\begin{array}{rcl} (x, y) & & y = ax^2 + bx + c \\ (1, -4) & -4 = & a + b + c \\ (-1, -10) & -10 = & a - b + c \\ (4, -25) & -25 = & 16a + 4b + c \end{array}$$

Find the values of a, b, and c by solving the matrix equation $AX = B$.
$$A = \begin{pmatrix} 1 & 1 & 1 \\ 1 & -1 & 1 \\ 16 & 4 & 1 \end{pmatrix}, X = \begin{pmatrix} a \\ b \\ c \end{pmatrix}, \text{ and } B = \begin{pmatrix} -4 \\ -10 \\ -25 \end{pmatrix}$$

```
[A]-1[B]
        [[-2]
         [3 ]
         [-5]]
```

The solution is $a = -2$, $b = 3$, $c = -5$, as shown in Figure 12.4-4. Thus, the equation of the parabola is $y = -2x^2 + 3x - 5$.

Figure 12.4-4

Exercises 12.4

In Exercises 1–4, write the identity matrix I_n for each matrix, and verify that $CI_n = I_nC = C$.

1. $C = \begin{pmatrix} 3 & -2 \\ 1 & 4 \end{pmatrix}$

2. $C = \begin{pmatrix} 6 & 4 \\ -3 & 2 \end{pmatrix}$

3. $C = \begin{pmatrix} 2 & 1 & 0 \\ 0 & 3 & 2 \\ 4 & -1 & 0 \end{pmatrix}$

4. $C = \begin{pmatrix} 0 & 0 & 1 \\ -2 & 4 & 1 \\ 1 & 3 & 5 \end{pmatrix}$

In Exercises 5–8, verify that B is the inverse of A.

5. $A = \begin{pmatrix} 3 & 1 \\ 5 & 2 \end{pmatrix}$ $B = \begin{pmatrix} 2 & -1 \\ -5 & 3 \end{pmatrix}$

6. $A = \begin{pmatrix} 4 & 8 \\ 2 & 6 \end{pmatrix}$ $B = \begin{pmatrix} \frac{3}{4} & -1 \\ -\frac{1}{4} & \frac{1}{2} \end{pmatrix}$

7. $A = \begin{pmatrix} 1 & 0 & 1 \\ -1 & 0 & 1 \\ 1 & 1 & -1 \end{pmatrix}$ $B = \begin{pmatrix} \frac{1}{2} & -\frac{1}{2} & 0 \\ 0 & 1 & 1 \\ \frac{1}{2} & \frac{1}{2} & 0 \end{pmatrix}$

8. $A = \begin{pmatrix} 2 & 1 & 0 \\ 1 & 2 & 2 \\ 1 & 0 & 0 \end{pmatrix}$ $B = \begin{pmatrix} 0 & 0 & 1 \\ 1 & 0 & -2 \\ -1 & \frac{1}{2} & \frac{3}{2} \end{pmatrix}$

In Exercises 9–12, write a set of systems of equations that represent the solution of the matrix equation $AA^{-1} = I_n$. (See Example 4.) Do not solve the systems.

9. $A = \begin{pmatrix} 2 & 0 \\ 4 & 1 \end{pmatrix}$

10. $A = \begin{pmatrix} -1 & 3 \\ 2 & -5 \end{pmatrix}$

11. $A = \begin{pmatrix} 1 & 2 & -1 \\ 0 & 1 & 2 \\ 3 & 2 & 1 \end{pmatrix}$

12. $A = \begin{pmatrix} 4 & -3 & 2 \\ 2 & 0 & 1 \\ -1 & 0 & 5 \end{pmatrix}$

In Exercises 13–20, find the inverse of the matrix, if it exists.

13. $\begin{pmatrix} 1 & 2 \\ 3 & 4 \end{pmatrix}$

14. $\begin{pmatrix} 3 & 5 \\ 1 & 4 \end{pmatrix}$

15. $\begin{pmatrix} 3 & -1 \\ -6 & 2 \end{pmatrix}$

16. $\begin{pmatrix} 1 & -1 & 0 \\ 1 & 0 & -1 \\ 6 & -2 & -3 \end{pmatrix}$

17. $\begin{pmatrix} 1 & 2 & 0 \\ 3 & -1 & 2 \\ -2 & 3 & -2 \end{pmatrix}$

18. $\begin{pmatrix} 1 & -3 & 4 \\ 2 & -5 & 7 \\ 0 & -1 & 1 \end{pmatrix}$

19. $\begin{pmatrix} 5 & 0 & 2 \\ 2 & 2 & 1 \\ -3 & 1 & -1 \end{pmatrix}$

20. $\begin{pmatrix} -1 & 3 & 1 \\ 2 & 5 & 0 \\ 3 & 1 & -2 \end{pmatrix}$

In Exercises 21–26, solve the system of equations by using inverse matrices. (See Examples 5 and 6.)

21. $\begin{aligned} 3x + 5y &= 4 \\ 2x - 6y &= 12 \end{aligned}$

22. $\begin{aligned} 3x - 5y &= -23 \\ -8x + 6y &= 10 \end{aligned}$

23. $\begin{aligned} -x + y &= 1 \\ -x + z &= -2 \\ 6x - 2y - 3z &= 3 \end{aligned}$

24. $\begin{aligned} x + 2y + 3z &= 1 \\ 2x + 5y + 3z &= 0 \\ x + 8z &= -1 \end{aligned}$

25. $\begin{aligned} 2x + y &= 0 \\ -4x - y - 3z &= 1 \\ -3x + y + 2z &= 2 \end{aligned}$

26. $\begin{aligned} -3x - 3y - 4z &= 2 \\ y + z &= 1 \\ 4x + 3y + 4z &= 3 \end{aligned}$

In Exercises 27–34, solve the system by any method.

27. $\begin{aligned} x + y + 2w &= 3 \\ 2x - y + z - w &= 5 \\ 3x + 3y + 2z - 2w &= 0 \\ x + 2y + z &= 2 \end{aligned}$

28. $\begin{aligned} x - 2y + 3z &= 1 \\ y - z + w &= -2 \\ -2x + 2y - 2z + 4w &= 5 \\ 2y - 3z + w &= 8 \end{aligned}$

29. $\begin{aligned} x + 2y + 4z &= 6 \\ y + z &= 1 \\ x + 3y + 5z &= 10 \end{aligned}$

30. $\begin{aligned} x + 4y + 5z + 2w &= 0 \\ 2x + y + 4z - 2w &= 0 \\ -x + 7y + 10z + 5w &= 0 \\ -4x + 2y + z + 5w &= 0 \end{aligned}$

31. $\begin{aligned} x + 2y + 3z &= 6 \\ 3x + 2y + 4z &= 9 \\ 2x + 6y + 8z + w &= 17 \\ 2x + 2z - 2w &= 2 \end{aligned}$

32. $\begin{aligned} x + 3w &= -2 \\ x - 4y - z + 3w &= -7 \\ 4y + z &= 5 \\ -x + 12y + 3z - 3w &= 17 \end{aligned}$

33. $\begin{aligned} x + 2y + 2z - 2w &= -23 \\ 4x + 4y - z + 5w &= 7 \\ -2x + 5y + 6z + 4w &= 0 \\ 5x + 13y + 7z + 12w &= -7 \end{aligned}$

34. $x + 2y + 5z - 2v + 4w = 0$
$2x - 4y + 6z + v + 4w = 0$
$5x + 2y - 3z + 2v + 3w = 0$
$6x - 5y - 2z + 5v + 3w = 0$
$x + 2y - z - 2v + 4w = 0$

35. *Critical Thinking* Consider the two systems of equations below.

$x - 2y = 3$ $\qquad$ $x - 2y = 4$
$-3x + 6y = -9$ $\qquad$ $-3x + 6y = -7$

    a. Write a matrix equation that represents each system. Which matrices in the two equations are the same? Does either matrix equation have a solution?

    b. Solve each system by any method. Make a conjecture about the relationship between the existence of an inverse coefficient matrix and the nature of the solutions to any system with those coefficients.

36. *Critical Thinking* Consider the system of equations below.

$$x + 2y - 3z = -4$$
$$2x + 4y + z = -1$$
$$x - 5y + 2z = 15$$

    a. Write an augmented matrix that represents the system, and reduce it to reduced row echelon form.

    b. Write a matrix equation that represents the system, and solve it using an inverse matrix.

    c. Describe your results in part **a** in terms of the matrix equation from part **b**.

In Exercises 37–40, find constants a, b, c such that the three given points lie on the parabola $y = ax^2 + bx + c$. (See Example 7.)

37. $(1, 0)$, $(2, 3)$, $(3, 8)$ $\qquad$ **38.** $(1, 1)$, $(2, 1)$, $(3, 2)$

39. $(3, 2)$, $(1, 1)$, $(2, 1)$ $\qquad$ **40.** $(1, 6)$, $(2, 3)$, $(4, 25)$

In Exercises 41–43, write a system of equations that determines the polynomial of the given type that passes through the given points. Do not solve the system.

41. cubic; $(0, 5)$, $(2, 1)$, $(4, -7)$, $(8, 3)$

42. cubic; $(-3, 1)$, $(-1, -2)$, $(0, 6)$, $(3, 0)$

43. quartic; $(-5, -1)$, $(-2, 0)$, $(1, 3)$, $(2, 5)$, $(10, -4)$

44. Concentrations of the greenhouse gas carbon dioxide, CO_2, have increased quadratically over the past half century. The concentration y of CO_2, in parts per million, in year x is given by an equation of the form

$$y = ax^2 + bx + c.$$

    a. Let $x = 0$ correspond to 1958 and use the following data to find a, b, and c.

Year	1958	1979	2001
CO_2 Concentration	315	337	371

    b. Use this equation to estimate the CO_2 concentration in the years 1983, 1993, and 2003. For comparison purposes, the actual concentrations in 1983 and 1993 were 343 ppm and 357 ppm respectively.

45. Find constants a, b, and c such that the points $(0, -2)$ $(\ln 2, 1)$, and $(\ln 4, 4)$ lie on the graph of $f(x) = ae^x + be^{-x} + c$. (See Example 7.)

46. Find constants a, b, and c such that the points $(0, -1)$ $(\ln 2, 4)$, and $(\ln 3, 7)$ lie on the graph of $f(x) = ae^x + be^{-x} + c$.

47. A conic section has the equation $Ax^2 + Bxy + Cy^2 + Dx + Ey + F = 0$. Find the values of A, B, C, D, E, and F for the conic section that passes through the six given points: $(3, 4)$, $(6, 2)$, $(2, 6)$, $(12, 1)$, $(4, 3)$, $(1, 12)$. Write the equation and identify the type of conic section.

48. A candy company produces three types of gift boxes: A, B, and C. A box of variety A contains 0.6 lb of chocolates and 0.4 lb of mints. A box of variety B contains 0.3 lb of chocolates, 0.4 lb of mints, and 0.3 lb of caramels. A box of variety C contains 0.5 lb of chocolates, 0.3 lb of mints, and 0.2 lb of caramels. The company has 41,400 lb of chocolates, 29,400 lb of mints, and 16,200 lb of caramels in stock. How many boxes of each kind should be made in order to use up all their stock?

49. Certain circus animals are fed the same three food mixes: R, S, and T. Lions receive 1.1 units of mix R, 2.4 units of mix S, and 3.7 units of mix T each day. Horses receive 8.1 units of mix R, 2.9 units of mix S, and 5.1 units of mix T each day. Bears receive 1.3 units of mix R, 1.3 units of mix S, and 2.3 units of mix T each day. If 16,000 units of mix R, 28,000 units of mix S, and 44,000 units of mix T are available each day, how many of each type of animal can be supported?

12.5

Nonlinear Systems

Objectives

- Solve nonlinear systems algebraically

- Solve nonlinear systems graphically

The matrix methods discussed in Section 12.2 and Section 12.4 can only be used for linear systems. Sometimes, however, it is necessary to solve nonlinear systems. Some nonlinear systems may be solved algebraically, by substitution or elimination.

Example 1 Solving a Nonlinear System by Elimination

Solve the system of equations.

$$x^2 - y^2 = 5$$
$$x^2 + y^2 = 13$$

Solution

This system can easily be solved by elimination. Add the two equations to eliminate y^2, and solve the resulting equation.

$$
\begin{array}{rl}
x^2 - y^2 =& 5 \\
+\quad x^2 + y^2 =& 13 \\
\hline
2x^2 \qquad =& 18 \\
x^2 \qquad =& 9 \\
x \qquad =& \pm 3
\end{array}
$$

NOTE Nonlinear systems can have any number of solutions, including solutions with the same x-value but different y-values—and vice versa. Thus, it is convenient to write the solutions as ordered pairs, (x, y).

Substitute each value of x into one of the original equations and solve for y. The x term is squared in both equations, so it is not necessary to substitute both 3 and -3, because $3^2 = (-3)^2$.

$$
\begin{array}{rl}
3^2 - y^2 =& 5 \\
y^2 =& 4 \\
y =& \pm 2
\end{array}
$$

The system has four solutions: $x = 3, y = 2$; $x = 3, y = -2$; $x = -3, y = 2$; and $x = -3$, $y = -2$. Written as ordered pairs, the solutions are $(3, 2)$, $(3, -2)$, $(-3, 2)$, and $(-3, -2)$.

Example 2 Solving a Nonlinear System by Substitution

Solve the system of equations.

$$2x^2 - y^2 = 1$$
$$x + y = 12$$

Solution

This system can be solved by substitution. Solve the second equation for y, and substitute into the first equation.

$$y = 12 - x$$
$$2x^2 - (12 - x)^2 = 1$$
$$2x^2 - 144 + 24x - x^2 = 1$$
$$x^2 + 24x - 145 = 0$$
$$x = 5 \text{ or } x = -29$$

If these values of x are substituted back into the second equation, the resulting solutions are $y = 7$ or $y = 41$, respectively. This gives two solutions, $(5, 7)$ and $(-29, 41)$.

Notice that if the values for x were substituted into the first equation instead, the resulting solutions would be $y = \pm 7$ or $y = \pm 41$. This would give 4 solutions, $(5, 7)$, $(5, -7)$, $(-29, 41)$, and $(-29, -41)$. However, the solutions $(5, -7)$ and $(-29, -41)$ do not satisfy the second equation; they are extraneous.

Thus, the solutions of the system are $(5, 7)$ and $(-29, 41)$. ∎

> **CAUTION**
>
> When solving non-linear systems algebraically, extraneous solutions can result. Check all solutions in all of the original equations.

Solving Nonlinear Systems Graphically

Consider the system below.

$$y = x^4 - 4x^3 + 9x - 1$$
$$y = 3x^2 - 3x - 7$$

Substitution may seem like an appropriate method for solving the system. However, if the expression for y in the first equation is substituted for y in the second equation, the result is

$$x^4 - 4x^3 + 9x - 1 = 3x^2 - 3x - 7$$
$$x^4 - 4x^3 - 3x^2 + 12x + 6 = 0$$

This fourth-degree equation cannot be readily solved algebraically, so a graphical approach is appropriate.

Example 3   Solving a Nonlinear System Graphically

Solve the following system of equations graphically.

$$y = x^4 - 4x^3 + 9x - 1$$
$$y = 3x^2 - 3x - 7$$

Solution

Graph both equations on the same screen. Trace or use an intersection finder to determine the coordinates of the intersections.

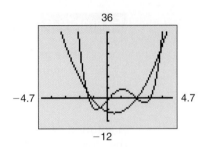

Figure 12.5-1

The graphs intersect at four points. The approximate solutions are $(-1.5, 4.4)$, $(-0.5, -4.8)$, $(2.1, 0.1)$, and $(3.9, 26.3)$. ∎

Example 4 Solving a Nonlinear System Graphically

Solve the following system of equations graphically.

$$2x^2 \qquad + 3y^2 = 30$$
$$2x^2 - xy - y^2 = \; 8$$

Solution

In order to graph the equations, they must both be solved for y.

$$2x^2 + 3y^2 = 30$$

$$y^2 = 10 - \frac{2}{3}x^2$$

$$y = \pm\sqrt{10 - \frac{2}{3}x^2}$$

To solve the second equation for y, use the quadratic formula with y as the variable.

$$2x^2 - xy - y^2 = 8$$
$$-y^2 - xy + (2x^2 - 8) = 0$$

$$a = -1, b = -x, \text{ and } c = 2x^2 - 8$$

$$y = \frac{x \pm \sqrt{x^2 + 4(2x^2 - 8)}}{-2}$$

$$= \frac{x \pm \sqrt{9x^2 - 32}}{-2}$$

Graph the four equations and then trace or use an intersection finder.

There are four solutions: $(3, 2)$, $(-3, -2)$, $(-2.2, 2.6)$, and $(2.2, -2.6)$. The first two are exact solutions, a fact that can be confirmed by substituting the values into the original equations. ∎

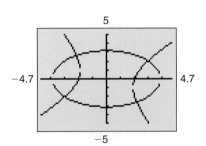

Figure 12.5-2

Example 5 Application of a Nonlinear System

The revenue and cost (in dollars) for manufacturing x bicycles are given by the following equations:

$$\text{cost:} \quad y = 85x + 120{,}000$$
$$\text{revenue:} \quad y = -0.04x^2 + 320x$$

A solution of this system is called a *break-even point*, which occurs when the cost and revenue are equal. Find all break-even points of this system.

Solution

Graph both equations on the same screen. To choose a window, notice that the graph of the revenue equation is a parabola with vertex (4000, 640,000).

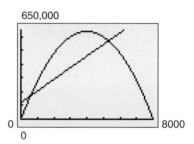

Figure 12.5-3

There are two break-even points: approximately $(565, 168{,}022)$ and $(5310, 571{,}353)$. This means that if the manufacturer makes and sells 565 or 5310 bicycles, the cost and revenue will be the same. That is, the manufacturer will break even. From the graph, you can see that between 565 and 5310, the revenue is greater than the cost, so the manufacturer will make a profit when producing between 565 and 5310 bicycles.

Exercises 12.5

In Exercises 1–12, solve the system algebraically.

1. $x^2 - y = 0$
   $-2x + y = 3$

2. $x^2 - y = 0$
   $-3x + y = -2$

3. $x^2 - y = 0$
   $x^2 + 3y = 6$

4. $x^2 - y = 0$
   $x^2 + 4y = 4$

5. $x + y = 10$
   $xy = 21$

6. $2x + y = 4$
   $xy = 2$

7. $xy + 2y^2 = 8$
   $x - 2y = 4$

8. $xy + 4x^2 = 3$
   $3x + y = 2$

9. $x^2 + y^2 - 4x - 4y = -4$
   $x - y = 2$

10. $x^2 + y^2 - 4x - 2y = -1$
   $x + 2y = 2$

11. $x^2 + y^2 = 25$
   $x^2 + y = 19$

12. $x^2 + y^2 = 1$
   $x^2 - y = 5$

In Exercises 13–28, solve the system by any means.

13. $y = x^3 - 3x^2 + 4$
   $y = -0.5x^2 + 3x - 2$

14. $y = -x^3 + 3x^2 + x - 3$
   $y = -2x^2 + 5$

15. $y = x^3 - 3x + 2$
   $y = \dfrac{3}{x^2 + 3}$

16. $y = 0.25x^4 - 2x^2 + 4$
$y = x^3 - x^2 - 2x + 1$

17. $y = x^3 + x + 1$
$y = \sin x$

18. $y = x^2 - 4$
$y = \cos x$

19. $25x^2 - 16y^2 = 400$
$-9x^2 + 4y^2 = -36$

20. $9x^2 + 16y^2 = 140$
$-x^2 + 4y^2 = -4$

21. $5x^2 + 3y^2 - 20x + 6y = -8$
$x - y = 2$

22. $4x^2 + 9y^2 = 36$
$2x - y = -1$

23. $x^2 + 4xy + 4y^2 - 30x - 90y + 450 = 0$
$x^2 + x - y + 1 = 0$

24. $3x^2 + 4xy + 3y^2 - 12x + 2y + 7 = 0$
$x^2 - 10x - y + 21 = 0$

25. $4x^2 - 6xy + 2y^2 - 3x + 10y = 6$
$4x^2 + y^2 = 64$

26. $5x^2 + xy + 6y^2 - 79x - 73y + 196 = 0$
$x^2 - 2xy + y^2 - 8x - 8y + 48 = 0$

27. $x^2 + 3xy + y^2 = 2$
$3x^2 - 5xy + 3y^2 = 7$

28. $2x^2 - 8xy + 8y^2 + 2x - 5 = 0$
$16x^2 - 24xy + 9y^2 + 100x - 200y + 100 = 0$

In Exercises 29–32, find the center (h, k) and radius r of the circle $(x - h)^2 + (y - k)^2 = r^2$ that passes through the three given points.

29. $(0, 5)$, $(3, 4)$, $(4, 3)$ **30.** $(3, 4)$, $(2, 5)$, $(3, 6)$

31. $(5, 25)$, $(17, 21)$, $(2, 24)$

32. $(8, 12)$, $(14, 4)$, $(6.4, 12.8)$

33. Find the break-even points for the following revenue and cost functions. (See Example 5.)

$$\text{cost: } \quad y = 30x + 25{,}000$$
$$\text{revenue: } \quad y = -0.03x^2 + 100x$$

34. A 52-foot-long piece of wire is to be cut into three pieces, two of which are the same length. The two equal pieces are to be bent into circles and the third piece into a square. What should the length of each piece be if the total area enclosed by the two circles and the square is 100 square feet?

35. A rectangular box (including top) with square ends and a volume of 16 cubic meters is to be constructed from 40 square meters of cardboard. What should its dimensions be?

36. A rectangular sheet of metal is to be rolled into a circular tube. If the tube is to have a surface area (excluding ends) of 210 square inches and a volume of 252 cubic inches, what size of metal sheet should be used? (Recall that the circumference of a circle with radius r is $2\pi r$ and that the volume of a cylinder with radius r and height h is $\pi r^2 h$.)

37. Find two real numbers whose sum is -16 and whose product is 48.

38. Find two real numbers whose sum is 34.5 and whose product is 297.

39. Find two positive real numbers whose difference is 1 and whose product is 4.16.

40. Find two real numbers whose difference is 25.75 and whose product is 127.5.

41. Find two real numbers whose sum is 3 such that the sum of their squares is 369.

42. Find two real numbers whose sum is 2 such that the difference of their squares is 60.

43. Find the dimensions of a rectangular room whose perimeter is 58 feet and whose area is 204 square feet.

44. Find the dimensions of a rectangular room whose perimeter is 53 feet and whose area is 165 square feet.

45. A rectangle has an area of 120 square inches and a diagonal 17 inches in length. What are its dimensions?

46. A right triangle has an area of 225 square centimeters and a hypotenuse 35 centimeters in length. To the nearest tenth of a centimeter, how long are the legs of the triangle?

47. Find the equation of the straight line that intersects the parabola $y = x^2$ only at the point $(3, 9)$. *Hint:* What condition on the discriminant guarantees that a quadratic equation has exactly one real solution?

Excursion: Systems of Inequalities

Objectives

- Solve inequalities in two variables
- Solve systems of inequalities by graphing
- Solve linear programming problems

Inequalities in two variables are solved by graphing. The solution to an inequality in two variables is the region in the coordinate plane consisting of all points whose coordinates satisfy the inequality.

Example 1   Solving an Inequality in Two Variables

Solve the inequality $y \geq 2x + 2$.

Solution

First, graph the line $y = 2x + 2$. The solution to the inequality is the set of all points on the line, plus all points in either the region above or the region below the line. To determine which region is the solution, choose a point that is not on the line, such as $(0, 0)$, and test it in the inequality.

$$0 \overset{?}{\geq} 2(0) + 2 \qquad \textit{False}$$

The inequality is false for the test point, so shade the region that does not contain that point—in this case, the region above the line. ∎

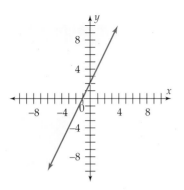

Figure 12.5.A-1

The method used in Example 1 can be summarized as follows.

Test-Point Method for Solving Inequalities in Two Variables

Replace the inequality symbol by an equal sign, and graph the resulting line.

- For $\leq$ and $\geq$ inequalities, use a solid line to indicate that the line is part of the solution.
- For $>$ and $<$ inequalities, use a dashed line to indicate that the line is *not* part of the solution.

Choose a test point that is not on the line, and substitute its coordinates in the inequality.

- If the coordinates of the test point make the inequality true, then the solution includes the region on the side of the line containing the test point.
- If the coordinates of the test point make the inequality false, then the solution includes the region on the side of the line that does not contain the test point.

The test-point method can be used to solve any inequality, but the following technique for linear inequalities with two variables is often easier, especially when using a calculator.

Example 2   Solving a Linear Inequality

Solve the inequality $6x + 3y < 6$.

Solution

First, solve the inequality for y.

$$3y < -6x + 6$$
$$y < -2x + 2$$

If the point (x, y) satisfies this inequality, then it lies below the line $y = -2x + 2$. Thus, the solution of the inequality is the set of all points that lie below the line $y = -2x + 2$, as shown in Figure 12.5.A-2. The line $y = -2x + 2$ is not part of the solution.

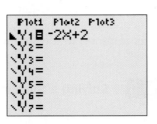
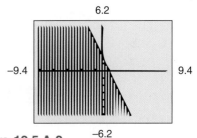

Figure 12.5.A-2

CAUTION

Graphing calculators do not display a dashed line with the shade feature. The line in Figure 12.5.A-2 is not part of the solution.

The solution method used in Example 2 can be summarized as follows.

Solving Linear Inequalities in Two Variables

Solve the inequality for y so that it has one of the following forms:

$$y > mx + b \qquad y \geq mx + b \qquad y < mx + b \qquad y \leq mx + b$$

- The solution of $y > mx + b$ is the half-plane *above* the line.
- The solution of $y < mx + b$ is the half-plane *below* the line.

For $y \geq mx + b$ and $y \leq mx + b$, the line $y = mx + b$ is also part of the solution.

Technology Tip

To display shading on TI models, select the graph style for a function by moving the cursor to the left of the equal sign in the function editor to the graph's style icon, shown in the first column. Press ENTER repeatedly to rotate through the graph styles until the desired style is shown. Then graph the function as usual. There is also a SHADE option in the DRAW menu.

In the function memory of CASIO 9850, select Type(F3) ▶(F6) and then the inequality sign desired. The SHADE menu is in the DRAW menu of the SHARP 9600. Refer to the manual for specific instructions. HP-38 does not have a shade feature.

Systems of Inequalities in Two Variables

The solution of a system of inequalities in two variables is found by graphing all the inequalities on the same coordinate plane. The solution is the region that is common to the solutions of all the graphs.

Example 3 **Solving a System of Inequalities**

Solve the system of inequalities.

$$y \leq \ x + 3$$
$$y > -x + 1$$

Solution

Graph the two inequalities together, as shown in Figure 12.5.A-3. Figure 12.5.A-4 shows a calculator screen with regions shaded.

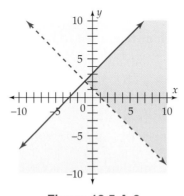

Figure 12.5.A-3

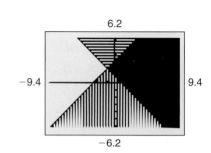

Figure 12.5.A-4

The area where the shaded regions intersect is the solution of the system. Any point in this shaded region of the plane is a solution of both inequalities. For example, the point (5, 2) in the solution satisfies both inequalities, as shown below.

$$2 \leq \quad 5 + 3 = 8$$
$$2 > -5 + 1 = -4$$

Linear Programming

Linear programming is a process that involves finding the maximum or minimum output of a linear function, called the **objective function,** subject to certain restrictions, called **constraints.**

For linear programming problems in two variables, the objective function has the form $F(x, y) = ax + by$, and the constraints are linear inequalities. The solution of the system of linear inequalities formed by the constraints is called the **feasible region.**

The feasible region is a region in the plane that is bounded by straight lines, such as those shown in Figure 12.5.A-5. The first figure is bounded on all four sides and the two other figures have one side that is not bounded.

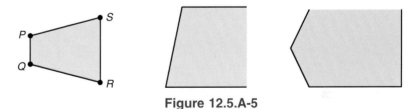

Figure 12.5.A-5

A **corner point** of such a region is any point where two of the sides intersect, such as points P, Q, R, and S in the first region in Figure 12.5.A-5.

The key to solving linear programming problems is the following theorem, which will not be proved here.

Fundamental Theorem of Linear Programming

The maximum value or minimum value of the objective function (if it exists) always occurs at one or more of the corner points of the feasible region. Thus, the solution may be found by graphing the feasible region, and testing the coordinates of the corner points in the objective function to find the maximum or minimum value of the function.

To see why the Fundamental Theorem above is true, notice that the graph of the objective function is a plane in three dimensions. The portion of the plane that lies above the feasible region must have its high point and low point at a corner, as shown in Figure 12.5.A-6.

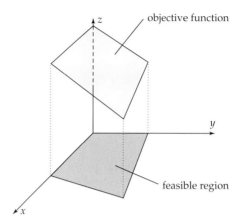

Figure 12.5.A-6

Example 4   A Linear Programming Problem

Find the maximum value of the function $F(x, y) = 3x + 2y$ subject to the constraints below.

$$\begin{cases} x + 4y \le 18 \\ 2x - y \le 9 \\ x \ge 0 \\ y \ge 0 \end{cases}$$

Solution

First, graph the feasible region. This is the solution of the system of inequalities.

NOTE In linear programming problems with a feasible region that is unbounded on one or more sides, there may be a minimum or maximum value of the objective function, but (usually) not both.

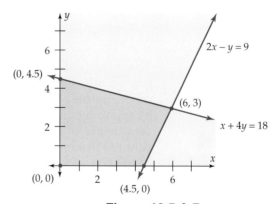

Figure 12.5.A-7

Second, find the corner points of the feasible region from the graph. They are (0, 0), (0, 4.5), (4.5, 0), and (6, 3).

Third, evaluate the objective function at each of the corner points.

Corner point	$F(x, y) = 3x + 2y$
(0, 0)	$3(0) + 2(0) = 0$
(0, 4.5)	$3(0) + 2(4.5) = 9$
(4.5, 0)	$3(4.5) + 2(0) = 13.5$
(6, 3)	$3(6) + 2(3) = 24$

The solution is the corner point (6, 3), which yields the largest value of the objective function, 24. This is the maximum value of the objective function.

■

Example 5   Application

Carla is making earrings and necklaces to sell at a craft fair. The profit from each pair of earrings is $3, and the profit from each necklace is $5. She has 12 hours to make all of the jewelry she plans to sell. Each pair of earrings takes 15 minutes to make, and each necklace takes 40 minutes to make. She also has $80 for supplies. The supplies for a pair of earrings cost $2, and the supplies for a necklace cost $4. How many pairs of earrings and how many necklaces should she make to maximize her profit?

Solution

Let x be the number of pairs of earrings and y be the number of necklaces. The objective function, which represents the profit, is $P(x, y) = 3x + 5y$. The constraints are inequalities involving time and cost. In addition, there is an implied constraint that neither quantity can be negative. This gives the following linear programming problem:

$$\text{Maximize } P(x, y) = 3x + 5y$$

$$\text{Subject to: } \begin{cases} 15x + 40y \le 720 & \textit{time} \\ 2x + 4y \le 80 & \textit{cost} \\ x \ge 0 \\ y \ge 0 \end{cases}$$

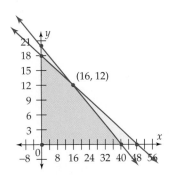

Figure 12.5.A-8

The feasible region is shown in Figure 12.5.A-8.

The corner points are shown below, with the objective function evaluated at each point.

Corner point	$P(x, y) = 3x + 5y$
(0, 0)	$3(0) + 5(0) = 0$
(0, 18)	$3(0) + 5(18) = 90$
(40, 0)	$3(40) + 5(0) = 120$
(16, 12)	$3(16) + 5(12) = 108$

The maximum value occurs at (40, 0). To make the maximum profit, Carla should make 40 pairs of earrings and 0 necklaces. Her maximum profit will be $120.

Summary: Solving Linear Programming Problems

To solve a linear programming problem:

- Graph the feasible region. This is the solution of the system of inequalities formed by the constraints.
- Find the corner points of the feasible region from the graph.
- Evaluate the objective function at each corner point.
- Choose the corner point which yields the greatest (or least) value of the objective function. This is the maximum (or minimum) value of the function on the feasible region.

Exercises 12.5.A

In Exercises 1–12, solve the system of inequalities.

1. $y \le 2x + 4$
$y > x - 2$

2. $y \ge x - 3$
$y \ge 4x + 2$

3. $y > 3x - 1$
$y < \frac{1}{2}x + 3$

4. $y \le \frac{1}{4}x + 1$
$y > 4x - 1$

5. $2x + 3y > 6$
$x - 2y \le 5$

6. $2x + 4y \le 5$
$3x + 2y \le 8$

7. $7 \ge 2x + 1$
$y \le x$

8. $y \ge x$
$y < 2x + 3$

9. $y > 2x - 1$
$x + y < 16$

10. $y \le x + 3$
$x - y < 1$

11. $y \le 1$
$x \le -1$

12. $4x + 9y \le 36$
$4y - x < 16$

In Exercises 13–16, graph the feasible region described by the system of inequalities, and find all of its corner points.

13. $3x + 4y \le 24$
$9x - 2y \le 30$
$x \ge 0$
$y \ge 0$

14. $x + y \le 7$
$7x + 2y \le 24$
$x \ge 0$
$y \ge 0$

15. $x + 2y \le 8$
$3x - y \le 6$
$x \ge 0$
$y \ge 0$

16. $2x + 3y \le 12$
$5x + 2y \le 10$
$x \ge 0$
$y \ge 0$

Solve the following linear programming problems.

17. Maximize: $F(x, y) = 2x + 5y$
Subject to: $\begin{cases} x + y \le 6 \\ x - y \le 4 \\ x \ge 0 \\ y \ge 0 \end{cases}$

18. Maxmimize: $F(x, y) = 3x + 7y$
Subject to: $\begin{cases} -x + 2y \le 10 \\ 7x + 11y \le 105 \\ x \ge 0 \\ y \ge 0 \end{cases}$

19. Minimize: $F(x, y) = \frac{1}{2}x + \frac{3}{4}y$
Subject to: $\begin{cases} 3x + 4y \le 32 \\ 4x + 2y \le 36 \\ x \ge 0 \\ y \ge 0 \end{cases}$

20. Minimize: $F(x, y) = 4x + 2y$
Subject to: $\begin{cases} -3x + 12y \le 60 \\ 8x - 5y \le 56 \\ x \ge 0 \\ y \ge 0 \end{cases}$

21. A lunch counter sells two types of sandwiches, roast beef and chicken salad. The profit on the sandwiches is $2 for chicken salad and $3 for roast beef. The amount of bread available is enough for 30 sandwiches. There are 4 hours available to prepare sandwiches. If chicken salad sandwiches take 7 minutes to prepare and roast beef sandwiches take 10 minutes, how many of each type of sandwich should be prepared to maximize the profit?

22. A dealer has a lot that can hold 30 vehicles. In this lot, there are two available models, A and B. The dealer normally sells at least twice as many model A cars as model B cars. If the dealer makes a profit of $1300 on model A cars and $1700 on model B cars, how many of each car should the dealer have in the lot?

23. A 30-acre orchard is to contain two types of trees, peach and almond. The profit per year is $16.80 per peach tree and $21.60 per almond tree. An acre can sustain 1080 peach trees or 900 almond trees. If the grower has available labor to plant a maximum of 30,000 trees, how many of each type of tree should be planted?

24. An investor has $12,000 to invest into two different funds. Fund A, which is a high-risk fund, yields an average return of 14%. Fund B, which is a low-risk fund, yields an average return of 6%. To reduce the risk, the investor wants the amount in fund B to be at least twice the amount in fund A. How much should be invested in each fund to maximize the return? What is the maximum return?

CHAPTER 12 REVIEW

Important Concepts

Review Exercises

Section **12.1**

In Exercises 1–10, solve the system of linear equations by any method.

1. $-5x + 3y = 4$
$2x - y = -3$

2. $3x - y = 6$
$2x + 3y = 7$

3. $3x - 5y = 10$

$4x - 3y = 6$

4. $\dfrac{1}{4}x - \dfrac{1}{3}y = -\dfrac{1}{4}$

$\dfrac{1}{10}x + \dfrac{2}{5}y = \dfrac{2}{5}$

5. $3x + y - z = 13$
$x + y + 2z = 9$
$-3x - y + 2z = 9$

6. $x + 2y + 3z = 1$
$4x + 4y + 4z = 2$
$10x + 8y + 5z = 4$

7. $4x + 3y - 3z = 2$
$5x - 3y + 2z = 10$
$2x - 2y + 3z = 14$

8. $x + y - 4z = 0$
$2x + y - 3z = 2$
$-3x - y + 2z = -4$

9. $x - 2y - 3z = 1$

$5y + 10z = 0$

$8x - 6y - 4z = 8$

10. $4x - y - 2z = 4$

$x - y - \dfrac{1}{2}z = 1$

$2x - y - z = 8$

11. The sum of one number and three times a second number is -20. The sum of the second number and two times the first number is 55. Find the two numbers.

12. You are given \$144 in \$1, \$5, and \$10 bills. There are 35 bills. There are two more \$10 bills than \$5 bills. How many bills of each type do you have?

13. Let L be the line with equation $4x - 2y = 6$ and M the line with equation $-10x + 5y = -15$. Which of the following statements is true?
a. L and M do not intersect.
b. L and M intersect at a single point.
c. L and M are the same line.
d. All of the above are true.
e. None of the above are true.

14. Which of the following statements about the given system of equations are *false*?

$$\begin{array}{rcrcrcr} x & & & + & z & = & 2 \\ 6x & + & 4y & + & 14z & = & 24 \\ 2x & + & y & + & 4z & = & 7 \end{array}$$

a. $x = 2, y = 3, z = 0$ is a solution.
b. $x = 1, y = 1, z = 1$ is a solution.
c. $x = 1, y = -3, z = 3$ is a solution.
d. The system has an infinite number of solutions.
e. $x = 2, y = 5, z = -1$ is not a solution.

15. Tickets to a lecture cost \$1 for students, \$1.50 for faculty, and \$2 for others. Total attendance at the lecture was 460, and the total income from tickets was \$570. Three times as many students as faculty attended. How many faculty members attended the lecture?

16. An alloy containing 40% gold and an alloy containing 70% gold are to be mixed to produce 50 pounds of an alloy containing 60% gold. How much of each alloy is needed?

Section 12.2

For Exercises 17–20, write the system of linear equations represented by the augmented matrix.

17. $\begin{pmatrix} 2 & 6 & \vdots & 16 \\ 2 & 3 & \vdots & 7 \end{pmatrix}$

18. $\begin{pmatrix} 2 & -1 & \vdots & 4 \\ 3 & 2 & \vdots & -1 \end{pmatrix}$

19. $\begin{pmatrix} 2 & 0 & 3 & \vdots & -2 \\ 4 & -3 & 7 & \vdots & 1 \\ 8 & -9 & 10 & \vdots & -3 \end{pmatrix}$

20. $\begin{pmatrix} 1 & 1 & -5 & \vdots & 2 \\ 1 & 0 & -2 & \vdots & 0 \\ 2 & -1 & -1 & \vdots & 1 \end{pmatrix}$

For Exercises 21–26, write the system represented by each matrix, find the solutions, if any, and classify each system as consistent, inconsistent, or dependent.

21. $\begin{pmatrix} 4 & -2 & \vdots & 14 \\ 1 & -5 & \vdots & 9 \end{pmatrix}$

22. $\begin{pmatrix} 9 & -6 & \vdots & 3 \\ -12 & 8 & \vdots & -4 \end{pmatrix}$

23. $\begin{pmatrix} 1 & 1 & -1 & \vdots & 1 \\ 1 & -2 & 3 & \vdots & -3 \\ 4 & 1 & 0 & \vdots & 2 \end{pmatrix}$

24. $\begin{pmatrix} -1 & 2 & 1 & \vdots & 4 \\ 1 & 3 & 0 & \vdots & 2 \\ 3 & -5 & -1 & \vdots & 0 \end{pmatrix}$

25. $\begin{pmatrix} 2 & 3 & -1 & \vdots & 4 \\ 1 & -4 & 1 & \vdots & 7 \end{pmatrix}$

26. $\begin{pmatrix} 1 & 1 & \vdots & 2 \\ 2 & -3 & \vdots & 3 \\ 1 & -1 & \vdots & 4 \end{pmatrix}$

Section 12.3

In Exercises 27–30, perform the indicated matrix multiplication or state that the product is not defined.

$$A = \begin{pmatrix} -1 & 0 \\ 0 & -1 \end{pmatrix} \qquad B = \begin{pmatrix} 2 & -3 \\ 4 & 1 \end{pmatrix} \qquad C = \begin{pmatrix} 3 & 2 \\ 2 & 4 \end{pmatrix}$$

$$D = \begin{pmatrix} -3 & 1 & 2 \\ 1 & 0 & 4 \end{pmatrix} \qquad E = \begin{pmatrix} 1 & 2 \\ -3 & 4 \\ 0 & 5 \end{pmatrix} \qquad E = \begin{pmatrix} 2 & 3 \\ 6 & 3 \\ 6 & 1 \end{pmatrix}$$

27. AB
28. CD
29. AE
30. DF

In Exercises 31–34, find the inverse of the matrix, if it exists.

31. $\begin{pmatrix} 3 & -7 \\ 4 & -9 \end{pmatrix}$

32. $\begin{pmatrix} 2 & 6 \\ 1 & 3 \end{pmatrix}$

33. $\begin{pmatrix} 3 & 2 & 6 \\ 1 & 1 & 2 \\ 2 & 2 & 5 \end{pmatrix}$

34. $\begin{pmatrix} 1 & -1 & 1 \\ 2 & -3 & 2 \\ -4 & 6 & 1 \end{pmatrix}$

Section 12.4

In Exercises 35–38, use matrix inverses to solve the system.

35.
$$\begin{aligned} x - 2y + 3z &= 4 \\ 2x + y - 4z &= 3 \\ -3x + 4y - z &= -2 \end{aligned}$$

36.
$$\begin{aligned} 2x - y - 2z + 2u &= 0 \\ x + 3y - 2z + u &= 0 \\ -x + 4y + 2z - 3u &= 0 \\ x + y + z + u &= 0 \end{aligned}$$

37.
$$x \quad\quad + 2z + 6w = 2$$
$$3x + 4y - 2z - \quad w = 0$$
$$5x \quad\quad + 2z - 5w = -4$$
$$4x - 4y + 2z + 3w = 1$$

38.
$$2x + \quad y + 2z + \quad u \quad\quad = 2$$
$$x + 3y - 4z - 2u + 2v = -2$$
$$2x + 3y + 5z - 4u + \quad v = 1$$
$$x \quad\quad - 2z \quad\quad + 4v = 4$$
$$2x \quad\quad + 6z \quad\quad - 5v = 0$$

39. Find the equation of the parabola passing through the points $(-3, 52)$, $(2, 17)$, $(8, 305)$.

40. The table shows the number of hours spent per person per year on home video games. Find a quadratic equation that contains this data, with $x = 6$ corresponding to 1996.

Year	1996	2000	2004
Hours	25	76	161

[*Source: Statistical Abstract of the U.S.: 2001*]

Section 12.5

In Exercises 41–46, solve the system.

41. $x^2 - y = 0$
$y - 2x = 3$

42. $x^2 + y^2 = 25$
$x^2 + y = 19$

43. $x^2 + y^2 = 16$
$x + y = 2$

44. $6x^2 + 4xy + 3y^2 = 36$
$x^2 - xy + y^2 = 9$

45. $x^3 + y^3 = 26$
$x^2 + y = 6$

46. $x^2 - 3xy + 2y^2 - y + x = 0$
$5x^2 - 10xy + 5y^2 = 8$

Section 12.5.A

47. Minimize and maximize $F(x, y) = 30x + 10y$

subject to $\begin{cases} 2x + 2y \geq 4 \\ x + y \leq 36 \\ 2x + y \leq 10 \\ x \geq 0 \\ y \geq 0 \end{cases}$

48. Minimize and maximize $F(x, y) = 8x + 7y$

subject to $\begin{cases} 4x + 3y \geq 24 \\ 3x + 4y \geq 8 \\ x \geq 0 \\ y \geq 0 \end{cases}$

49. Animal feed is to be made from corn and soybeans. One pound of corn has 30 units of fat and 20 units of protein, and one pound of soybeans has 20 units of fat and 40 units of protein. What is the minimum total weight of feed to supply a daily requirement of 2800 units of fat and 2200 units of protein?

50. A home supply store sells two models of dehumidifiers, standard and deluxe. The standard model comes in a 10-ft^3 box and weighs 10 lb, and the deluxe model comes in a 9-ft^3 box and weighs 12 lb. The store's delivery van has 248 ft^3 of space and can hold a maximum of 440 lb. If the store makes a profit of $20 on the standard model and $30 on the deluxe model, how many boxes of each model can the van carry to maximize the profit for each load?

can do calculus

Partial Fractions

In calculus it is sometimes necessary to write a complicated rational expression as the sum of simpler ones. Two forms of rational expressions whose sum is a rational expression will be introduced in this section: denominators with nonrepeated factors and those with repeated factors.

| Example 1 | Denominators with Nonrepeated Factors |

Find the constants A and B such that $\dfrac{7x - 6}{x^2 - x - 6} = \dfrac{A}{x + 2} + \dfrac{B}{x - 3}$.

Solution

The denominators on the right side of the equation are linear factors of the denominator on the left side. Multiply both sides of the equation by the common denominator, $(x + 2)(x - 3)$, and collect like terms.

$$7x - 6 = A(x - 3) + B(x + 2)$$
$$= Ax - 3A + Bx + 2B$$
$$= Ax + Bx - 3A + 2B$$
$$= (A + B)x + (-3A + 2B)$$

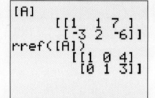

Figure 12.C-1

Because the polynomials on the left and right sides of the last equation are equal, their coefficients must be equal term by term.

$$A + B = 7 \qquad \text{\textit{Coefficient of x}}$$
$$-3A + 2B = -6 \qquad \text{\textit{Constant term}}$$

The two equations above form a system of equations with unknowns A and B. Solving the system yields $A = 4$ and $B = 3$. Therefore,

$$\frac{7x - 6}{x^2 - x - 6} = \frac{4}{x + 2} + \frac{3}{x - 3}$$

In Example 1, $\dfrac{4}{x + 2} + \dfrac{3}{x - 3}$ is called the **partial fraction decomposition,** or simply the partial fractions, of $\dfrac{7x - 6}{x^2 - x - 6}$.

Nonrepeated Linear Factor Denominators

If the denominator of a rational expression can be expressed as a product of nonrepeated linear factors, each term of the decomposition has the form $\dfrac{A}{x - a}$.

When a factor of the denominator is repeated, every power less than or equal to the multiplicity of the factor must be considered.

Example 2   Repeated Linear Factors

Find the partial fraction decomposition of $\dfrac{2x^2 + 15x + 10}{x^3 + 3x^2 - 4}$.

Solution

The denominator can be factored into $(x - 1)(x + 2)^2$, as shown in Figure 12.C-2. Because $(x + 2)^2$ is a repeated factor, both $x + 2$ and $(x + 2)^2$ must be considered as possible denominators of the decomposition. The process of finding the numerators is the same as that shown in Example 1.

Multiply both sides of the equation by the common denominator, $(x - 1)(x + 2)^2$, and collect like terms on the right side.

$$
\begin{aligned}
2x^2 + 15x + 10 &= A(x + 2)^2 + B(x - 1)(x + 2) + C(x - 1) \\
&= A(x^2 + 4x + 4) + B(x^2 + x - 2) + C(x - 1) \\
&= Ax^2 + 4Ax + 4A + Bx^2 + Bx - 2B + Cx - C \\
&= (A + B)x^2 + (4A + B + C)x + (4A - 2B - C)
\end{aligned}
$$

The polynomials on the left and right sides are equal, so coefficients must be equal term by term.

$$
\begin{array}{ll}
A + B = 2 & \textit{Coefficient of } x^2 \\
4A + B + C = 15 & \textit{Coefficient of } x \\
2A - 2B - C = 10 & \textit{Constant term}
\end{array}
$$

This is a system of equations with unknowns A, B, and C. The augmented matrix of the system and an equivalent reduced row echelon form matrix are shown in Figure 12.C-3.

Therefore, $A = 3$, $B = -1$, $C = 4$, and

$$
\frac{2x^2 + 15x + 10}{(x - 1)(x + 2)^2} = \frac{3}{x - 1} + \frac{-1}{x + 2} + \frac{4}{(x + 2)^2}
$$

∎

In theory, any polynomial with real coefficients can be written as a product of real linear factors and real quadratic factors. (See Section 4.2.)

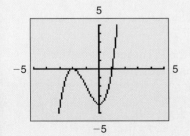

Figure 12.C-2

```
[[1  1   0   2 ]
 [4  1   1  15]
 [4 -2  -1  10]]
rref([D])
 [[1  0   0   3 ]
  [0  1   0  -1]
  [0  0   1   4 ]]
```

Figure 12.C-3

Nonrepeated Quadratic Factor Denominators

> If the denominator contains a nonrepeated quadratic factor, then the decomposition will contain a term of the form $\dfrac{Ax + B}{ax^2 + bx + c}$, where $ax^2 + bx + c$ is irreducible over the set of real numbers.

Like repeated linear factors, if an irreducible quadratic factor is repeated, every power less than or equal to the multiplicity of the factor must be considered. The numerator of all quadratic factors has the form $Ax + B$.

Example 3 Nonrepeated Quadratic Factor

Find the partial fraction decomposition of $\dfrac{x-2}{x^3+6x^2+10x+8}$.

Solution

The denominator has the nonrepeated linear factor $x+4$, as shown in Figure 12.C-4, and the nonrepeated quadratic factor x^2+2x+2 found by using synthetic division. Thus, the partial fraction decomposition has the form $\dfrac{x-2}{x^3+6x^2+10x+8}=\dfrac{A}{x+4}+\dfrac{Bx+C}{x^2+2x+2}$.

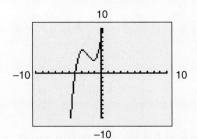

Figure 12.C-4

Multiplying both sides of the equation by the common denominator, $(x+4)(x^2+2x+2)$, and collecting like terms yields

$$x-2=A(x^2+2x+2)+(Bx+C)(x+4)$$
$$=Ax^2+2Ax+2A+Bx^2+Cx+4Bx+4C$$
$$=(A+B)x^2+(2A+4B+C)x+(2A+4C)$$

Because there is no x^2 term in the original rational expression, the corresponding coefficient must be 0. Therefore,

$$
\begin{aligned}
A+B &= 0 && \textit{Coefficient of } x^2\\
2A+4B+C &= 1 && \textit{Coefficient of } x\\
2A\qquad+4C &= -2 && \textit{Constant term}
\end{aligned}
$$

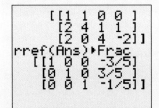

Figure 12.C-5

The solution of the system is $A=-\dfrac{3}{5}$, $B=\dfrac{3}{5}$, and $C=-\dfrac{1}{5}$, as shown in Figure 12.C-5.

$$\frac{x-2}{x^3+6x^2+10x+8}=\frac{-\dfrac{3}{5}}{x+4}+\frac{\dfrac{3}{5}x-\dfrac{1}{5}}{x^2+2x+2}=\frac{1}{5}\left(\frac{-3}{x+4}+\frac{3x-1}{x^2+2x+2}\right)$$ ∎

All the rational expressions in the previous examples have been proper fractions, which means the degree of the numerator was less than the degree of the denominator. If the rational expression is improper, then divide the numerator by the denominator and decompose the remainder that is a proper fraction.

Example 4 Decomposing an Improper Rational Expression

Find the partial fraction decomposition of $\dfrac{x^3-x+3}{x^2+x-2}$.

$$
\begin{array}{r}
x-1\\
x^2+x-2\,\overline{)\,x^3+0x^2-x+3}\\
\underline{x^3+x^2-2x}\\
-x^2+x+3\\
\underline{-x^2-x+2}\\
2x+1
\end{array}
$$

Solution

The rational expression is an improper fraction because the degree of the numerator is greater than the degree of the denominator. Therefore, divide the numerator by the denominator (shown in the margin) and write the remainder as a fraction of the divisor.

$$\frac{x^3 - x + 3}{x^2 + x - 2} = x - 1 + \frac{2x + 1}{x^2 + x - 2}$$

Now decompose $\frac{2x + 1}{x^2 + x - 2}$ into $\frac{A}{x + 2} + \frac{B}{x - 1}$ by using the procedure discussed in Example 1.

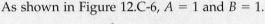

$$\begin{aligned} 2x + 1 &= A(x - 1) + B(x + 2) \\ &= Ax - A + Bx + 2B \\ &= (A + B)x + (-A + 2B) \end{aligned}$$

$$\begin{aligned} A + B &= 2 \\ -A + 2B &= 1 \end{aligned}$$

Figure 12.C-6

As shown in Figure 12.C-6, $A = 1$ and $B = 1$.

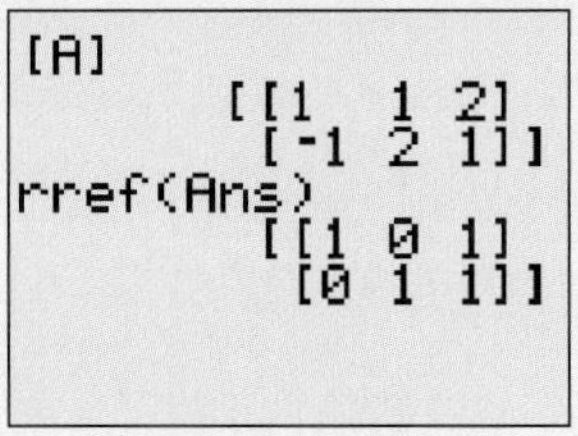

$$\frac{x^3 - x + 3}{x^2 + x - 2} = x - 1 + \frac{1}{x + 2} + \frac{1}{x - 1}$$

When the denominator contains a power of a linear or a quadratic factor, every integral power of that factor must be taken into consideration when finding partial fractions, as outlined below.

Decomposition into Partial Fractions

1. **Divide numerator by denominator if the fraction is improper, and find partial fractions of the remainder.**
2. **Factor the denominator into factors of the form $(px + q)^m$ and $(ax^2 + bx + c)^n$, where $ax^2 + bx + c$ is irreducible over the set of real numbers.**
3. **For each linear factor of the form $(px + q)^m$, the partial fraction must include the following sum:**

$$\frac{A_1}{px + q} + \frac{A_2}{(px + q)^2} + \cdots + \frac{A_m}{(px + q)^m}$$

4. **For each quadratic factor of the form $(ax^2 + bx + c)^n$, the partial fraction must include the following sum:**

$$\frac{B_1x + C_1}{ax^2 + bx + c} + \frac{B_2x + C_2}{(ax^2 + bx + c)^2} + \cdots \frac{B_nx + C_n}{(ax^2 + bx + c)^n}$$

Exercises

In Exercises 1–7, find the partial fraction decomposition of each expression.

1. $\frac{x}{x^2 + 3x + 2}$

2. $\frac{1}{x^2 - 1}$

3. $\frac{2x + 1}{x^3 - 4x^2 - 3x + 18}$

4. $\frac{x^2 - x - 21}{2x^3 - x^2 + 8x - 4}$

5. $\frac{5x^2 + 1}{x^3 + 1}$

6. $\frac{x - 2}{x^3 + 6x^2 + 10x + 8}$

7. $\frac{2x^3 - 4x^2 - x - 3}{x^2 - 2x - 3}$

CHAPTER 13

Statistics and Probability

What are the odds?

Suppose a dart player can hit the bulls-eye about 25% of the time. How likely is the event shown above? The number of bulls-eyes in a given number of tries can be described as a *binomial experiment,* and the probabilities can be easily calculated. See Exercises 5–8 in Section 13.4.A.

Chapter Outline

Interdependence of Sections

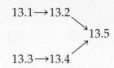

Statistics and probability are essential tools for understanding the modern world. Both involve studying a group of individuals or objects, known as a **population,** and a subset of the population, known as a **sample.** In statistics, information from a sample is used to draw conclusions about the population. In probability, information from the population is used to draw conclusions about a sample.

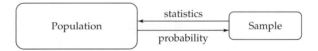

Basic Statistics

Objectives

- Identify data types
- Create displays of qualitative and quantitative data
- Describe the shape of a distribution

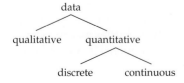

Statistics is used to make sense of information, or **data,** by using techniques to organize, summarize, and draw conclusions from the data. Most statistical data is gathered by taking a **random sample** of the population. In a random sample, all members of the population and all groups of members of a given size have an equal chance of being in the sample.

Data can be divided into two types: **qualitative** and **quantitative.** Quantitative data is numerical, such as "the number of hours spent studying each night" or "the distance from home to school." Qualitative data can be divided into categories, such as "liberal," "moderate," "conservative," or "blue eyes," "brown eyes."

Quantitative data can be further classified as either **discrete** or **continuous.** If the difference between two values can be arbitrarily small, the data is continuous. If there is a minimum increment between two different values, the data is discrete.

843

Example 1 **Types of Data**

In each example, identify the data as either qualitative or quantitative. If quantitative, then identify it as discrete or continuous.

a. the height of each player on a basketball team

b. the style of shoes worn by each student in a classroom

c. the number of people in each household in the United States

Solution

a. The data is quantitative, because each value can be written as a number, such as 68.32 inches. It is continuous, because there is no minimum difference between two values; two players could have heights 68.32 inches and 68.33 inches, or 68.323 inches and 68.324 inches.

b. The data is qualitative, since it can be grouped into categories, such as tennis shoes, sandals, and high heels.

c. The data is quantitative, because each value is a number. It is discrete, because there is a minimum difference of 1 between two different values; two households could have 4 and 5 members, but not 4 and 4.1 members.

NOTE Continuous data is sometimes treated as discrete, and vice versa. For example, heights are usually rounded to the nearest inch, so there is a minimum difference of 1 inch between measurements. In the discrete case, for amounts of money, the minimum increment of $0.01 is so small that the data can often be treated as continuous.

Data Displays

One of the most important uses of statistics is to organize data and display it visually. Most displays show the data values or categories and some measure of how often each value or category occurs.

The number of times a value occurs is known as the **frequency** of that value. If the frequency is divided by the total number of responses, the result is the **relative frequency** of that value, which can be expressed as a fraction, a decimal, or a percent. A **frequency table** displays the categories with frequencies, relative frequencies, or both.

Example 2 **Frequency Table**

A group of 30 people were asked their favorite flavor of ice cream. Of these, 6 chose vanilla, 12 chose chocolate, 4 chose butter pecan, and 8 chose mint chocolate chip. Create a table with frequencies and relative frequencies for each flavor.

Solution

Flavor	Frequency	Relative frequency
Vanilla	6	$\frac{6}{30} = \frac{1}{5} = 0.2 = 20\%$
Chocolate	12	$\frac{12}{30} = \frac{2}{5} = 0.4 = 40\%$
Butter pecan	4	$\frac{4}{30} = \frac{2}{15} \approx 0.13 \approx 13\%$
Mint chocolate chip	8	$\frac{8}{30} = \frac{4}{15} \approx 0.27 \approx 27\%$

■

Displaying Qualitative Data

Two common ways of displaying qualitative data are *bar graphs* and *pie charts*. A **bar graph** displays the categories on a horizontal axis and the frequencies or relative frequencies on a vertical axis, or vice versa. The height or length of each bar shows the frequency of the value. All bars should have the same width.

Example 3 **Bar Graph**

Use the data in the frequency table from Example 2 to make a bar graph.

Solution

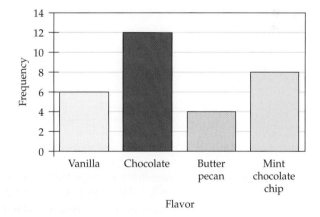

■

A **pie chart** displays the categories and their relative frequencies. The "pie" is divided into sectors whose central angle measure equals the fraction of 360° represented by the relative frequency of each category.

The central angle measure of the sector that represents a category with relative frequency r is $r \cdot 360°$.

| **Example 4** | **Pie Chart** |

Create a pie chart using the data in the frequency table from Example 2. Label each sector with the category and its relative frequency.

Solution

The central angle measures of the categories of the sectors are:

Vanilla: $0.2 \cdot 360° = 72°$

Chocolate: $0.4 \cdot 360° = 144°$

Butter pecan: $0.13 \cdot 360° \approx 47°$

Mint chocolate chip:
$0.27 \cdot 360° \approx 97°$

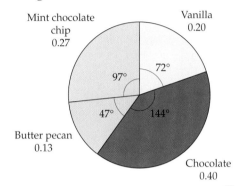

NOTE Before statistical analysis, numerical data is usually arranged in order from the lowest value to the highest value. An arrangement of numerical data is called a **distribution**.

Displaying Quantitative Data

Numerical data can also be displayed in a variety of ways to indicate each value and its frequency. The shape of a smooth curve over the display indicates characteristics of the data values. The most common distribution shapes are shown below.

Common Distribution Shapes

Uniform: All the data values have approximately the same frequency.

Symmetric: The right and left sides of the distribution have frequencies that are mirror images of each other.

Skewed right: The right side of the distribution has much lower frequencies than the left.

Skewed left: The left side of the distribution has much lower frequencies than the right.

NOTE If an outlier is caused by an error in measurement or other type of error, it is usually removed from the data set before further analysis. In general, an outlier should not be removed without justification.

An **outlier** is a data value that is far removed from the rest of the data, which usually indicates that the value needs investigation. Outliers may be caused by errors or by unusual members of the population.

Example 5 The Shape of Data

From the four given shapes, choose the best distribution for the data.

a. the last digit of each number in the phone book
b. the salaries of the employees of a corporation
c. the age of retirement for all people in the U.S.
d. the heights of all adult women in the U.S.

Solution

a. The last four digits of a phone number are assigned randomly, so all digits have about the same frequency. The distribution is uniform.
b. In a typical corporation, most employees earn relatively low salaries while a few executives make high salaries. The distribution is skewed right.
c. Few people make enough money to retire young, and most people retire in their 60's or later. The distribution is skewed left.
d. The average height of an adult woman is at the middle of the distribution, which is symmetric with respect to this value.

Two common displays of quantitative data are the *stem plot* and the *histogram*. A **stem plot** is commonly used to display small data sets.

The data below shows 31 test scores for a class exam:

$$32, 67, 89, 90, 87, 72, 75, 88, 95, 83, 97, 72, 85, 93, 79, 63$$
$$70, 87, 74, 86, 98, 100, 97, 85, 77, 88, 92, 94, 81, 76, 64$$

The stem plot for the class test data is shown below:

```
 3 | 2
 4 |
 5 |
 6 | 3 4 7
 7 | 0 2 2 4 5 6 7 9
 8 | 1 3 5 5 6 7 7 8 8 9
 9 | 0 2 3 4 5 7 7 8
10 | 0
```

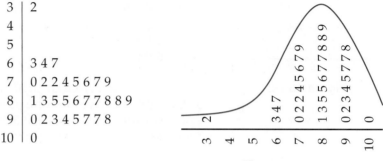

Figure 13.1-1

The entry 3 | 2 represents the score 32. Similarly, the row 6 | 3 4 7 represents the scores 63, 64, and 67. There are 31 scores represented.

Note that the score of 32 is far below the remaining data and so it could be an outlier in this distribution. It may be the score of a student who didn't study for the test. However, it is most likely not an error in measurement, so the value cannot be removed from the data set. The distribution is skewed left (Figure 13.1-1).

Creating a Stem Plot

To create a stem plot:

1. **Choose the leading digit or digits to be the *stems*. Arrange the stems vertically from lowest to highest value from top to bottom.**

2. **The last digit is the *leaf*. Record a leaf for each data value on the same horizontal line as its corresponding stem. Arrange the leaves from lowest to highest value from left to right.**

3. **Provide a key that indicates the total number of data elements and an interpretation of one stem and leaf indicating appropriate units.**

Example 6   Stem Plot

A company uses a 3-minute recorded phone message to advertise its product. A random sample of 40 calls is used to determine how much of the message was heard before the listener hung up. Create a stem plot of the data below and discuss its shape.

2.4, 0.2, 3.0, 2.8, 1.5, 1.9, 0.7, 1.0, 2.5, 1.3,
0.8, 2.1, 3.0, 0.4, 1.2, 3.0, 1.1, 0.3, 0.7, 1.8,
0.3, 1.0, 2.1, 3.0, 2.9, 0.5, 1.4, 3.0, 2.8, 1.2,
0.5, 0.5, 1.5, 0.9, 1.8, 0.6, 0.6, 0.7, 0.8, 0.8

Solution

```
0 | 2 3 3 4 5 5 5 6 6 7 7 7 8 8 8 9
1 | 0 0 1 2 2 3 4 5 5 8 8 9
2 | 1 1 4 5 8 8 9
3 | 0 0 0 0 0
```

Key: 2|8 represents a time of 2.8 minutes.
40 times are represented.

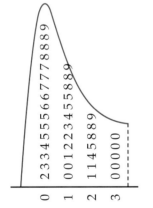

Figure 13.1-2

The distribution is skewed right, as shown in Figure 13.1-2. The values on the right side have lower frequencies than the values on the left. Notice that the distribution is cut off at 3, because no phone calls last longer than 3 minutes, the length of the entire message.

A **histogram,** which can be thought of as a bar graph with no gap between adjacent bars, is often used with large sets of quantitative data. First, the data is divided into a convenient number of intervals of equal width. The frequencies (or relative frequencies) of the data in the intervals are the heights of the rectangles. For example, the test scores given on page 847 can be represented by the histogram in Figure 13.1-3.

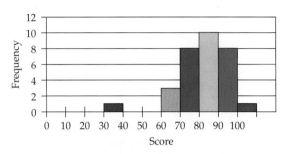

Figure 13.1-3

Here, the test scores have been divided into 10-point intervals, 0 through 9, 10 through 19, and so on. The histogram indicates, for example, that there are no scores between 50 and 59, eight scores between 70 and 79, and one score of 100. Each bar on the graph has width 10, so the **class interval** is said to be 10.

Creating a Histogram

To create a histogram:

1. **Divide the range of the data into classes of equal width, so that each data value is in exactly one class. The width of these intervals is called the *class interval*.**

2. **Draw a horizontal axis and indicate the first value in each class interval.**

3. **Draw a vertical scale and label it with either frequencies or relative frequencies.**

4. **Draw rectangles with a width equal to the class interval and height equal to the frequency of the data within each interval.**

Example 7   **Histogram**

Create a histogram of the following SAT scores.

580, 490, 590, 390, 410, 370, 470, 540, 490, 660, 500, 670, 430, 670, 490, 720, 580, 680, 590, 480, 560, 480, 400, 440, 560, 540, 330, 490, 540, 540, 520, 650, 540, 600, 630, 580, 540, 500, 270, 600, 390, 540, 300, 350, 600, 540, 510, 410, 370, 390, 200, 500, 740, 510, 540, 560, 510, 430, 440, 590, 560, 510, 600, 460, 450, 510, 420, 430, 560, 680, 610, 600, 600, 520, 480, 490, 320, 450, 500, 490

Solution

The smallest value is 197 and the largest value is 741, so the range of the data is 544 points. A convenient choice for the classes is 150 through 199, 200 through 249, 250 through 299, and so on—a class interval of 50 points. The frequency table below shows how many data values are in each class.

Class	150–199	200–249	250–299	300–349	350–399	400–449	450–499	500–549	550–599	600–649	650–699	700–749
Frequency	0	1	1	3	6	9	13	20	11	8	6	2

The histogram is shown in Figure 13.1-4. The shape is approximately symmetric.

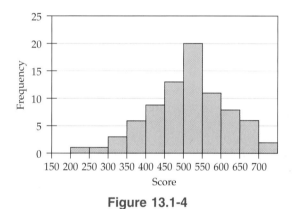

Figure 13.1-4

Figure 13.1-5 shows three histograms of the data in Example 7, created on a calculator. Notice that the choice of the scale on the *x*-axis determines the width of the class intervals. Which do you think is the best representation of the data?

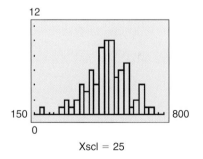

Xscl = 25

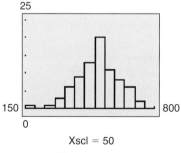

Xscl = 50

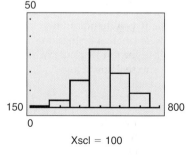

Xscl = 100

Figure 13.1-5

Remember that it is more important to be able to interpret a distribution than it is to simply produce the display. Technology can easily produce a histogram, but the purpose of the display is to help interpret the data.

Exercises 13.1

In Exercises 1–4, identify the population and the sample.

1. There are three schedule options for classes at a high school: 90-minute classes every other day for a year, 90-minute classes every day for a semester, or 45-minute classes every day for a year. Out of 1200 students, 50 students from each grade level are chosen at random and asked their preference.

2. The manager of a convenience store wishes to determine how many cartons of eggs are damaged in shipment and delivery. For ten shipments of 1000 cartons of eggs, she examines every 50th carton to see how many cartons contain cracked eggs.

3. A survey is taken to determine the number of pets in the typical American family. A computer is used to randomly select 5 states, then 10 counties in each state, then 50 families in each county. Each of these families is asked how many pets they own.

4. A biologist tranquilizes 400 wild elephants and measures the lengths of their tusks to determine their ages.

Use the descriptions in Exercises 1–4 to answer Exercises 5–10.

5. Determine whether the data in each description is qualitative or quantitative. If the data is quantitative, determine whether it is continuous or discrete.

6. Describe two ways in which the data from Exercise 1 could be displayed.

7. How large is the sample in Exercise 2?

8. Describe two ways in which the data from Exercise 2 could be displayed.

9. How large is the sample in Exercise 3?

10. Which would be more appropriate to display the data from Exercise 4: a stem plot or a histogram? Explain your reasoning.

The following frequency table gives the preferred type of exercise for 50 women at a local gym.

Exercise	Frequency	Relative frequency
Aerobics	20	?
Kickboxing	8	?
Tai chi	8	?
Stationary bike	14	?

11. Complete the table to show the relative frequency for each category.

12. Create a bar graph for the data with the vertical axis showing the frequencies.

13. Create a bar graph with the vertical axis showing the relative frequencies.

14. Create a pie chart for the data.

For Exercises 15–18, suppose 25 people are asked their favorite color. The results are: 6 red, 8 blue, 5 purple, 4 green, 1 yellow, and 1 orange.

15. Create a frequency table for the given data. Include relative frequencies.

16. Create a bar graph for the data with the vertical axis showing the frequencies.

17. Create a bar graph with the vertical axis showing the relative frequencies.

18. Create a pie chart for the data.

In Exercises 19–24, state whether the shape of the distribution is best described as uniform, symmetric, skewed right, or skewed left.

19. The scores of a national standardized test

20. The age at which students get a driver's license

21.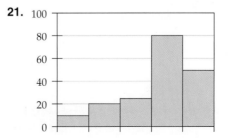

22.
```
1 | 0 2 5 6 8
2 | 3 5 6 9
3 | 1 4 7 8 8
4 | 2 3 5 5
5 | 4 6 7 9
```

23. The position of the second hand of a clock at 100 randomly chosen times in a 12-hour period

24.
```
 8 | 2
 9 | 3 5
10 | 2 5 6 8
11 | 0 1 4
12 | 7
```

In Exercises 25–28, create a stem plot for the given data.

25. 23, 45, 38, 41, 24, 67, 42, 46, 51, 33, 43, 47, 54, 49, 47, 36, 27, 33, 41, 29

26. 1.8, 2.0, 1.4, 5.6, 1.1, 2.6, 0.8, 1.5, 1.4, 2.6, 0.7, 1.6, 0.4, 1.1, 0.5, 1.3

27. 98, 87, 100, 86, 92, 78, 56, 100, 90, 88, 93, 99, 76, 83, 86, 91, 72, 85, 79, 81, 82, 91, 86, 70, 84

During summer semester, a community college surveyed its students to determine travel time to campus. A random sample of 30 students gave the following times in minutes:

12	25	48	45	6	90
15	55	75	60	27	30
32	40	18	35	22	8
42	65	17	25	35	40
12	28	42	37	45	55

During fall semester, the survey was repeated. The new times in minutes are:

63	52	43	48	32	14
46	40	29	20	75	48
9	25	40	20	46	37
35	31	69	86	63	17
104	7	52	55	29	14

28. Create a stem plot of the summer semester data.

29. Does the data set of the summer semester times contain any outliers? Explain.

30. Create a stem plot of the fall semester data.

31. Compare the shape of the two data sets. Which type of distribution do you think best describes these data sets? What might explain the differences in these data sets?

32. Create a histogram with a class interval of 10 for the data below.
68, 84, 59, 72, 62, 76, 61, 63, 68, 56, 70, 79, 54, 65, 66, 71, 70, 58, 63, 68, 84, 63, 53, 68, 63, 76, 66, 66, 70, 72, 88, 68, 75, 63, 76, 58, 86, 65, 66, 73, 53, 76, 59, 81, 59, 65, 67, 73, 62, 75, 89, 58

33. Create a histogram for the following ACT scores. Be sure to choose an appropriate class interval.
14, 25, 15, 18, 17, 11, 15, 10, 25, 6, 11, 4, 12, 24, 19, 14, 20, 13, 23, 19, 13, 20, 14, 24, 10, 18, 30, 22, 16, 26, 10, 23, 22, 19, 23, 21, 16, 18, 18, 20, 25, 14, 19, 7, 16, 18, 31, 14, 7, 10, 16, 13, 18, 10

34. Create a histogram with a class interval of 5 for the data in the stem plot below.

```
5 | 7 8 8 9 9 9
6 | 0 0 0 1 1 2 2 2 3 3 4 5 7 9
7 | 0 1 2 2 4 5 5 6 7 7 8
8 | 0 0 0 1 1
```

35. *Critical Thinking* How does the shape of the histogram you created in Exercise 34 compare to the shape of the data in the stem plot? Which do you think is a better representation of the data, and why?

13.2 Measures of Center and Spread

Objectives

- Calculate measures of center
- Calculate measures of spread
- Choose the most appropriate measure of center or spread
- Create and interpret a box plot

While the shape of a stem plot or a histogram gives a picture of a data set, numerical measures are more precise and can be calculated easily (using technology for large data sets). These measures help to further summarize and interpret data. Two quantities are commonly used to describe a data set: a measure of the "center" of the data and a measure of how spread out the data is.

Measures of Center

A sample may contain hundreds, or even thousands of data values. This information is often summarized by one value that represents the center, or central tendency, of the data. The three most common measures of center are *mean*, *median*, and *mode*.

Mean

The **mean** is more commonly known as the *average*. The mean is calculated by adding all values and dividing by the total number of values. Recall from Chapter 1, the symbol Σ is used to indicate the sum of a set of values.

$$\text{mean:} \quad \overline{x} = \frac{x_1 + x_2 + \ldots + x_n}{n} = \frac{\Sigma x_i}{n}$$

The mean is represented by $\overline{x}$, read as "x bar." The x is used to represent the data variable, while each data value is represented as x_1, x_2, x_3, and so on. The sum is divided by n, the number of data elements.

Example 1 Mean Number of Accidents

A six-month study of a busy intersection reports the number of accidents per month as 3, 8, 5, 6, 6, 10. Find the mean number of accidents per month at the site.

Solution

$$x_1 = 3, x_2 = 8, x_3 = 5, x_4 = 6, x_5 = 6, x_6 = 10$$

$$\overline{x} = \frac{\Sigma x_i}{n} = \frac{3 + 8 + 5 + 6 + 6 + 10}{6} = \frac{38}{6} \approx 6.3$$

The data shows an average of 6.3 accidents per month at the given intersection.

One problem with the mean as a measure of center is that it may be distorted by extreme values, as shown in the following example.

Example 2   **Mean Home Prices**

In the real-estate section of the Sunday paper, the following houses were listed:

2-bedroom fixer-upper:	$98,000
2-bedroom ranch:	$136,700
3-bedroom colonial:	$210,000
3-bedroom contemporary:	$289,900
4-bedroom contemporary:	$315,500
8-bedroom mansion:	$2,456,500

Find the mean price, and discuss how well it represents the center of the data.

Solution

$$\bar{x} = \frac{\Sigma x_i}{n} = \frac{98,000 + 136,700 + 210,000 + 289,900 + 315,500 + 2,456,500}{6}$$

$$= \frac{3,506,600}{6} \approx 584,433.33$$

In the data set, 5 out of the 6 values are below $350,000, but the mean is over $550,000, so the mean does not seem to be a very good representation of the center of the data set. Notice that the value $2,456,500 is more than twice the rest of the data combined. Thus, it has a very large affect on the mean, "pulling" it away from the other values.

■

Median

As shown in Example 2, the mean is not always the best way to represent the center of a distribution. If the distribution is skewed or contains extreme values, the **median,** or middle value of the data set is often used. To determine the median, the data must be in order from smallest to largest (or largest to smallest).

If the number of values is odd, then one number will be the middle number, as shown below.

3, 4, 7, 8, 9, 11, 15

There are 7 values, and the median, which is in the 4th position, is 8. Notice that three values are less than the median and three values are greater than the median.

If the number of values is even, there are two middle numbers, as shown below.

17, 22, 24, 30, 35, 40

There are 6 values, and the median is the average of the middle numbers, which are in the 3rd and 4th positions. So the median is $\frac{24 + 30}{2} = 27$.

Notice that three values are less than the median and three values are greater than the median.

Median

> If $x_1, x_2, x_3 \ldots x_n$ are ordered from smallest to largest, then the median is the middle entry when n is odd and the average of the two middle entries when n is even.
>
> $$\text{median} = \begin{cases} \text{for } n \text{ odd, the value in the } \dfrac{n+1}{2} \text{ position} \\ \text{for } n \text{ even, the average of the values in} \\ \text{the } \dfrac{n}{2} \text{ and } \dfrac{n}{2}+1 \text{ positions} \end{cases}$$

The median is said to be a more *resistant* measure of center than the mean, since it is less affected by a skewed distribution or extreme values in a data set.

Example 3 Median Home Prices

Find the median of the data in Example 2, and discuss how well it represents the center of the data.

Solution

The data is already in order from smallest to largest, with $n = 6$.

| 98,000 | 136,700 | 210,000 | 289,900 | 315,500 | 2,456,500 |
| 1st position | 2nd position | 3rd position | 4th position | 5th position | 6th position |

The median is the average of the values in positions $\dfrac{n}{2} = 3$ and $\dfrac{n}{2}+1 = 4$, which are 210,000 and 289,900, so

$$\text{median} = \frac{210,000 + 289,900}{2} = \frac{499,900}{2} = 249,950$$

A price of $249,950 is much more representative of the houses in this listing. The most expensive house does not have the same strong effect that it had in the calculation of the mean.

Mode

The **mode** is the data value with the highest frequency. It is most often used for qualitative data, for which the mean and median are undefined. The mode can be thought of as the "most typical" value in the data set.

NOTE If every value in a data set occurs the same number of times, there is no mode. If two or more scores have equal frequencies that are higher than those of all other values, the data set is called *bimodal* (two modes), *trimodal* (three modes), or *multimodal*.

Example 4 Mode of a Data Set

Find the mode of the data represented by the bar graph below.

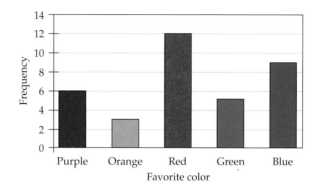

Solution

The height of each bar represents the frequency, so the mode is the category with the tallest bar, which is red. ∎

Mean, Median, and Mode of a Distribution

Recall the shapes of symmetric, skewed left, and skewed right distributions.

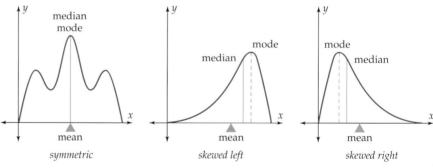

Figure 13.2-1

The mean is the balance point of a distribution. Notice that on a skewed distribution, the mean moves toward the tail to balance out the "weight" of the outlying data. The median divides the area under the distribution into 2 equal areas. The mode is the highest point on the distribution.

- **If a distribution is symmetric, then the mean and median are equal.**
- **If a distribution is skewed left, then the mean is to the left of the median.**
- **If a distribution is skewed right, then the mean is to the right of the median.**

Technology Tip

If necessary, see the Technology Appendix to learn how to find the mean and median of a data set.

┌───┐
│ ── **Calculator Exploration** ●──────────────────   │
│   │
│ Use the statistics functions of your calculator to find the mean and │
│ median of the data represented by the following stem plot.   │
│   │
│ 3 │ 2   │
│ 4 │ 8   Key: 6│7 represents a score of 67 points. │
│ 5 │ 2 3   43 scores are represented.   │
│ 6 │ 3 5 6 7 9   │
│ 7 │ 0 2 2 4 5 6 7 9   │
│ 8 │ 1 3 5 5 6 7 7 8 8 9   │
│ 9 │ 0 2 2 3 4 5 5 5 5 7 7 8   │
│ 10 │ 0 0 0 0   │
└───┘

Measures of Spread

Finding the shape and center of a data set still gives an incomplete picture of the data. The following stem plots show three data sets with a symmetric distribution and center 105.

NOTE If the mean and median of a distribution are the same value, as in the data sets represented by the stem plots at right, their value is often referred to as the **center**.

```
 6 │              6 │ 5            6 │
 7 │              7 │              7 │
 8 │ 5            8 │ 1 9          8 │
 9 │ 1 9          9 │              9 │ 1 5
10 │ 1 5 9       10 │ 1 5 9       10 │ 1 3 5 7 9
11 │ 1 9         11 │             11 │ 5 9
12 │ 5           12 │ 1 9         12 │
13 │             13 │             13 │
14 │             14 │ 5           14 │
```

The data has a different spread in each stem plot. The spread of the data, or **variability,** is an important characteristic of a data set. The second plot has the most variability because the data is very spread out, while the third has the least because the date is clustered very near the center. The three most common measures of spread are the *standard deviation,* the *range,* and the *interquartile range.*

Standard Deviation

The **standard deviation** of a data set is the most common measure of variability. It is best used if the data is symmetric about a mean. Standard deviation measures the average distance of a data element from the mean.

The **deviation** of a data value x_i from the mean $\bar{x}$ is the difference, $x_i - \bar{x}$. Consider the following data set:

$$2, 5, 7, 8, 10$$

The mean of the data is $\dfrac{2 + 5 + 7 + 8 + 10}{5} = 6.4$. The points are shown with their deviations on a number line in Figure 13.2-2.

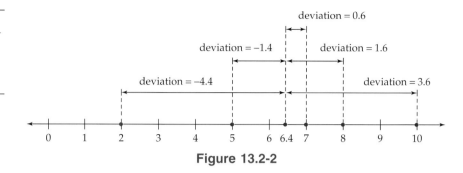

Figure 13.2-2

The average of the deviations is $\dfrac{-4.4 + (-1.4) + 0.6 + 1.6 + 3.6}{5} = 0$, because the positive and negative values cancel each other out. To avoid this, each deviation is squared, then the average is found. This quantity is called the **variance.** The square root of the variance is the **standard deviation,** denoted by the Greek letter σ (sigma).

For the data set {2, 5, 7, 8, 10}, first square each deviation.

$$\{(-4.4)^2, (1.4)^2, 0.6^2, 1.6^2, 3.6^2\} = \{19.36, 1.96, 0.36, 2.56, 12.96\}$$

Average the squared deviations to find the variance, σ^2:

$$\sigma^2 = \frac{19.36 + 1.96 + 0.36 + 2.56 + 12.96}{5} = 7.44$$

Take the square root of the variance to find the standard deviation:

$$\sigma = \sqrt{7.44} \approx 2.73$$

Population versus Sample If data is taken from a sample instead of the entire population, it is common to divide by $n - 1$ instead of n when averaging the squared deviations. The result is called the **sample standard deviation** and is denoted by s. For large data sets, the sample standard deviation is very close to the population standard deviation.

Standard Deviation

To find the standard deviation of a data set with n values,

1. Subtract each value from the mean to find the deviation.
2. Square each deviation, and find the mean of the squared deviations. If the data is from a sample, divide by $n - 1$ instead of n. The result is called the *variance.*
3. Take the square root of the variance.

These steps are summarized in the following formulas:

Population standard deviation

$$\sigma = \sqrt{\frac{\Sigma(x_i - \overline{x})^2}{n}}$$

Sample standard deviation

$$s = \sqrt{\frac{\Sigma(x_i - \overline{x})^2}{n - 1}}$$

Example 5   Standard Deviation

Find the population standard deviation of the data in the first stem plot on page 857 using the formula. Then use a calculator to find the population standard deviations of the data in the other two plots.

Solution

For the first stem plot, $\bar{x} = 105$ and $n = 9$. The following table shows the squared deviations.

x_i	85	91	99	101	105	109	111	119	125
$x_i - \bar{x}$	-20	-14	-6	-4	0	4	6	14	20
$(x_i - \bar{x})^2$	400	196	36	16	0	16	36	196	400

$$\sigma = \sqrt{\frac{400 + 196 + 36 + 16 + 0 + 16 + 36 + 196 + 400}{9}} = \sqrt{\frac{1296}{9}} = 12$$

An informal interpretation is that the average distance from the data values to the mean is 12 units.

The population standard deviations of the data in the second and third stem plots are shown in Figure 13.2-3.

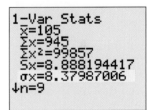

Figure 13.2-3

Notice that the second stem plot, which is the most spread out, has the largest standard deviation, and the third stem plot, which is the most clustered together, has the smallest standard deviation.

Range

The **range** is the difference between the maximum and minimum data values. The main advantage of the range is that it is easy to compute.

Example 6   The Range

Find the range of the data in each stem plot on page 857.

Solution

The range of the data in the first stem plot is $125 - 85 = 40$.
The range of the data in the second stem plot is $145 - 65 = 80$.
The range of the data in the third stem plot is $119 - 91 = 28$.

Interquartile Range

Like the mean, the standard deviation and range are strongly affected by extreme values in the data. The **interquartile range** is a measure of variability that is resistant to extreme values, yet gives a good indication of the spread of the data.

Recall that the median is the middle value of the data set. Thus, the median divides the data into two halves, the **lower half** and the **upper half.** The **quartiles** further divide the data into fourths. The **1st quartile,** Q_1, is the median of the lower half. The **3rd quartile,** Q_3, is the median of the upper half. (The median may be considered to be the 2nd quartile.)

Figure 13.2-4 shows the quartiles for n even or n odd.

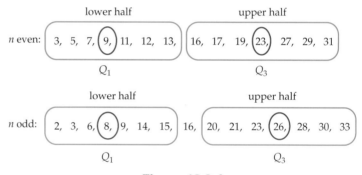

Figure 13.2-4

The **interquartile range** is the difference between the quartiles,

$$IQR = Q_3 - Q_1$$

which represents the spread of the middle 50% of the data.

A value that is less than $Q_1 - 1.5(IQR)$ or greater than $Q_3 + 1.5(IQR)$ is considered an outlier, as shown in Figure 13.2-5.

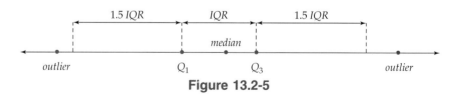

Figure 13.2-5

Example 7 Interquartile Range

Find the interquartile range of the data in the first stem plot on page 857.

Solution

The quartiles of the data in the first stem plot are shown below.

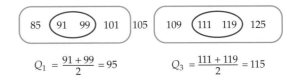

$$Q_1 = \frac{91 + 99}{2} = 95 \qquad Q_3 = \frac{111 + 119}{2} = 115$$

The interquartile range is $115 - 95 = 20$.

Calculator Exploration

Use a graphing calculator to find the interquartile range of the data in each of the other two stem plots on page 857.

Five-Number Summary and Box Plots

The **five-number summary** of a data set is the following list:

minimum, Q_1, median, Q_3, maximum

These values are used to construct a display called a **box plot,** as follows:

1. Construct a number line and locate each value of the five-number summary.

2. Construct a rectangle whose length equals the interquartile range, with a vertical line to indicate the median.

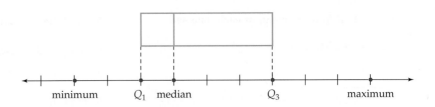

Technology Tip

See the technology appendix, if necessary, for instruction on constructing a box plot using a graphing calculator.

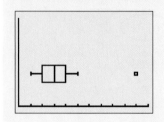

3. Construct horizontal whiskers to the minimum and maximum values.

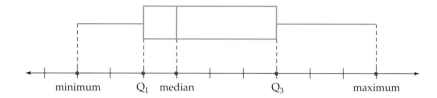

If a data element is an outlier, it may be marked with a ★ or other mark. The whiskers then extend to the farthest value on each side that is not an outlier.

Example 8   Constructing a Box Plot

Construct a box plot for the data in the first stem plot on page 857.

Solution

The five-number summary of the data is 85, 95, 105, 115, 125. The box plot is shown below.

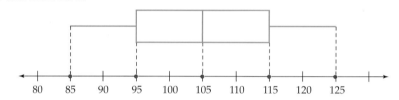

Calculator Exploration ●

Use a graphing calculator to construct a box plot for the data in each of the other two stem plots on page 857.

Exercises 13.2

In Exercises 1–4, find the mean of each data set.

1. 23, 25, 38, 42, 54, 57, 65

2. 3, 5, 6, 2, 10, 9, 7, 5, 11, 6, 4, 2, 5, 4

3. 3.6, 7.2, 5.9, 2.8, 21.6, 4.4

4. 78, 93, 87, 82, 90

5. Find the median of the data set in Exercise 1.

6. Find the median of the data set in Exercise 2.

7. Find the median of the data set in Exercise 3.

8. Find the median of the data set in Exercise 4.

9. Find the mean, median, and mode of the following data set:
13, 13, 12, 6, 14, 9, 11, 19, 13, 9, 7, 16, 11, 12, 15, 12, 11, 12, 14, 9, 11, 13, 17, 13, 13

In Exercises 10–13, find the mode of the data set represented by each display.

10.

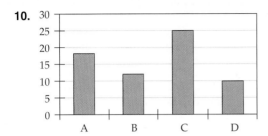

11.
```
3 | 2 5 5
4 | 0 6 6 7 9
5 | 3 3 3 6
6 | 1 2 4 7 8 8
```

12.

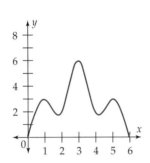

13.

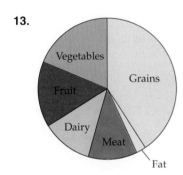

For each distribution shape, indicate whether the mean is larger, the median is larger, or the mean and median are equal.

14. symmetric

15. skewed left

16. skewed right

17. uniform

Find the population standard deviation of the following data sets without using a calculator.

18. 8, 9, 10, 11, 12

19. 6, 8, 10, 12, 14

20. 10, 10, 10, 10, 10

21. 0, 5, 10, 15, 20

Use a calculator to find the population and sample standard deviations of the following data sets.

22. 3, 6, 3, 5, 7, 8, 2, 6, 3, 6, 8, 4, 8, 2, 6, 9

23. 24, 17, 18, 18, 19, 26, 19, 8, 25, 15, 17, 11, 27, 20

24. 6, 8, 4, 11, 8, 8, 9, 6, 6, 8, 8, 12, 10, 10, 7

25. 50, 72, 86, 92, 86, 77, 57, 80, 93, 74, 53, 69, 65, 57, 73, 60, 66, 94, 81, 81

26. Find the range of the data set in Exercise 18.

27. Find the range of the data set in Exercise 19.

28. Find the range of the data set in Exercise 20.

29. Find the range of the data set in Exercise 21.

30. Find the interquartile range of the data set in Exercise 18.

31. Find the interquartile range of the data set in Exercise 19.

32. Find the interquartile range of the data set in Exercise 20.

33. Find the interquartile range of the data set in Exercise 21.

34. Find the five-number summary of the data set in Exercise 18, and create a box plot for the data.

35. Find the five-number summary of the data set in Exercise 19, and create a box plot for the data.

36. Find the five-number summary of the data set in Exercise 20, and create a box plot for the data.

37. Find the five-number summary of the data set in Exercise 21, and create a box plot for the data.

For Exercises 38–43, the wait times of 30 people in a doctor's office are given below, rounded to the nearest five minutes:

40, 35, 65, 40, 40, 5, 50, 85, 30, 50, 60, 60, 10, 65, 15, 45, 20, 40, 45, 70, 70, 25, 40, 45, 70, 65, 45, 25, 15, 25

38. Construct a histogram of the data. Describe the shape of the data set. Based on the shape, discuss the relative positions of the mean and median.

39. Find the mean and median of the data set.

40. Which measure of central tendency is preferred for this data set? Why?

41. Find the sample standard deviation, range, and interquartile range of the data set.

42. Construct a box-plot of the data.

43. Explain why the sample standard deviation is or is not a good measure of dispersion for this data set.

44. During a baseball game, 9 players had 1 hit each, 3 players had 2 hits each, and 6 players had no hits. Find the mean number of hits per player.

45. A teacher has two sections of the same course. The average on an exam was 94 for one class with 20 students, while the average was 88 for the other class with 30 students. Find the combined average exam score.

46. The mean score of a class exam was 78, and the median score was 82. Sketch a possible distribution of the scores.

47. Over the last year, 350 lawsuits for punitive damages were settled with a mean settlement of $750,000 and a median settlement of $60,000. Sketch a possible distribution of the settlements.

48. A restaurant employs six chefs with the salaries in dollars shown below:
25,000, 27,000, 35,000, 105,000, 40,000, 45,000
Determine the mean and median salaries.

49. Which measure of center more accurately describes the "typical" salary at the restaurant in Exercise 48?

50. The speed of a computer is primarily determined by a chip in the CPU. A manufacturer tested 12 chips and reported the following speeds in megahertz units:
    11.6, 11.9, 12.0, 12.0, 14.0, 15.2,
    13.0, 14.3, 13.6, 13.8, 12.8, 12.9

Find the sample standard deviation and the population standard deviation of the data, and interpret your results.

51. Create two data sets of five numbers each that have the same mean but different standard deviations.

52. Create two data sets of five numbers each that have the same standard deviations but different means.

53. *Critical Thinking* How is the mean of a data set affected if a constant k is added to each value?

54. *Critical Thinking* How is the standard deviation of a data set affected if a constant k is added to each value?

55. *Critical Thinking* How is the mean of a data set affected if each value is multiplied by a constant k?

56. *Critical Thinking* How is the standard deviation of a data set affected if each value is multiplied by a constant k?

57. *Critical Thinking* What must be true about a data set in order for the standard deviation to equal 0?

13.3

Basic Probability

Objectives

- Define probability and use properties of probability

- Find the expected value of a random variable

- Use probability density functions to estimate probabilities

Definitions

In the study of probability, an **experiment** is any process that generates one or more observable outcomes. The set of all possible outcomes is called the **sample space** of the experiment. Some examples of experiments and their sample spaces are shown in the following table.

Figure 13.3-1

Experiment	Sample space
tossing a coin	heads and tails, written as {H, T}
rolling a number cube (Figure 13.3-1)	{1, 2, 3, 4, 5, 6}
choosing a name from the phone book	all the names in the phone book
counting the number of fish in a lake	the set of non-negative integers

An **event** is any outcome or set of outcomes in the sample space. For example, in the experiment of rolling a number cube, the set {1, 3, 5} is an event, which can be described as "rolling a 1, 3, or 5," or simply "rolling an odd number."

The **probability** of an event is a number from 0 to 1 (or 0% to 100%) inclusive that indicates how likely the event is to occur.

- A probability of 0 (or 0%) indicates that the event cannot occur.
- A probability of 1 (or 100%) indicates that the event must occur.

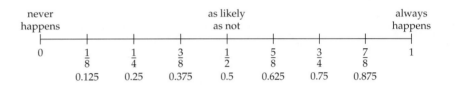

- The sum of the probabilities of all outcomes in the sample space is 1.
- The probability of an event is the sum of the probabilities of the outcomes in the event.

Probability Distributions

The probability of an event E can be described by a function P, where the domain of the function is the sample space and the range of the function is the closed interval [0, 1]. $P(X)$ denotes the probability of the outcome X, and $P(E)$ denotes the probability of the event E.

The rule of the function P can be described by a table, called a **probability distribution.**

Example 1   Probability Distribution

Suppose that 100 marbles are placed in a bag; 50 red, 30 blue, 10 yellow, and 10 green. An experiment consists of drawing one marble out of the bag and observing its color.

a. What is the sample space of the experiment?

NOTE Probabilities expressed as percents are often called **chances.** According to this probability distribution, there is a 50% chance of drawing a red marble, a 30% chance of drawing a blue marble, a 10% chance of drawing a yellow marble, and a 10% chance of drawing a green marble.

b. Write out a reasonable probability distribution for this experiment, and verify that the sum of the probabilities of the outcomes is 1.

c. What is the probability that a blue or green marble will be drawn?

Solution

a. The sample space is all possible outcomes:

$$\{\text{red, blue, yellow, green}\}$$

b. A reasonable probability distribution is shown below, which is based on the relative frequency of marbles of each color.

Color of marble	Red	Blue	Yellow	Green
Probability	$\frac{50}{100} = 0.5$	$\frac{30}{100} = 0.3$	$\frac{10}{100} = 0.1$	$\frac{10}{100} = 0.1$

The sum of the probabilities of the outcomes is

$$0.5 + 0.3 + 0.1 + 0.1 = 1$$

c. The event "a blue or green marble will be drawn" can be written as the set of outcomes {blue, green}. The probability of the event is the sum of the probabilities for blue and green.

$$P(\{\text{blue, green}\}) = P(\text{blue}) + P(\text{green}) = 0.3 + 0.1 = 0.4$$

Mutually Exclusive Events

Two events are **mutually exclusive** if they have no outcomes in common. Two mutually exclusive events cannot both occur in the same trial of an experiment. If two events E and F are mutually exclusive, then the probability of the event (E or F) is the sum of the individual probabilities, $P(E) + P(F)$.

The **complement** of an event is the set of all outcomes that are *not* contained in the event. The complement of event E can be thought of as "the event that E does not occur." An event and its complement are always mutually exclusive, and together they contain all the outcomes in the sample space. Thus, the probability of an event and the probability of its complement must add to 1, which leads to the following fact.

Probability of a Complement

If an event E has probability p, then the complement of the event has probability $1 - p$.

Example 2   **Mutually Exclusive Events**

An experiment consists of spinning the spinner in Figure 13.3-2. The following table shows the probability distribution for the experiment.

Outcome	A	S	C	E
Probability	0.4	0.3	0.2	0.1

a. Which of the following pairs of events E and F are mutually exclusive?

$E = \{A, C, E\}$ $F = \{C, S\}$
$E =$ (a vowel) $F =$ (in the first five letters of the alphabet)
$E =$ (a vowel) $F = \{C\}$

b. What is the complement of the event $\{A, S\}$?

c. What is the probability of the event "the spinner does not land on A?"

Figure 13.3-2

Solution

a. The events $E = \{A, C, E\}$ and $F = \{C, S\}$ are not mutually exclusive because they have a common outcome, C.

The events $E =$ (a vowel) and $F =$ (in the first five letters of the alphabet) are not mutually exclusive because they have two common outcomes, A and E.

The events $E =$ (a vowel) and $F = \{C\}$ are mutually exclusive because they have no common outcome.

b. The complement of the event $\{A, S\}$ is the set of outcomes that are not in the event, $\{C, E\}$.

c. The complement of the event "the spinner does not land on A" is $\{A\}$, which has a probability of 0.4. Thus, the probability of the event is $1 - 0.4 = 0.6$.

◼

Independent Events

Two events are **independent** if the occurrence or non-occurrence of one event has no effect on the probability of the other event. For example, if an experiment is repeated several times under exactly the same conditions, the outcomes of the individual trials are independent. If two events E and F are independent, then the probability of the event (E and F) is the product of the individual probabilities, $P(E) \cdot P(F)$.

NOTE The terms *mutually exclusive* and *independent* are often confused. Some important differences are detailed below.

Mutually exclusive	Independent
The term often refers to two possible results for a *single trial* of a given experiment.	The term often refers to the results from *two or more trials* of an experiment or from different experiments.
The word "or" is often used to describe a pair of mutually exclusive events.	The word "and" is often used to describe a pair of independent events.
For mutually exclusive events E and F, $$P(E \text{ or } F) = P(E) + P(F)$$	For independent events E and F, $$P(E \text{ and } F) = P(E) \cdot P(F)$$

If two events are mutually exclusive, they cannot be independent, because the occurrence of one would cause the other to have a probability of 0.

Example 3   **Independent Events**

The probability of winning a certain game is 0.1. Suppose the game is played on two different occasions. What is the probability of

a. winning both times?

b. losing both times?

c. winning once and losing once?

Solution

a. The results of the two different trials are independent, so the probability of winning both times can be found by multiplying the probability of winning each time.
$$P(\text{winning both games}) = 0.1 \cdot 0.1 = 0.01$$

b. Since losing is the complement of winning, the probability of losing is $1 - 0.1 = 0.9$. The probability of losing both times can be found by multiplying the probability of losing each time.
$$P(\text{losing both games}) = 0.9 \cdot 0.9 = 0.81$$

c. The complement of the event (winning once and losing once) is the set of the two events in parts **a** and **b**. The events in parts **a** and **b** are mutually exclusive, because it is impossible to win both times *and* lose both times, so their probabilities may be added.
$$P(\text{winning once and losing once}) = 1 - (0.01 + 0.81) = 0.18$$

Random Variables

In many cases, the characteristics of an experiment that are being studied are numerical, such as the total on a roll of two number cubes. In other cases, the outcomes of an experiment may be assigned numbers, such as heads = 1, tails = 0.

A **random variable** is a function that assigns a number to each outcome in the sample space of an experiment.

Example 4   Random Variable

An experiment consists of rolling two number cubes. A random variable assigns the total of the faces shown to each outcome.

a. Write out the sample space for the experiment.

b. Find the range of the random variable.

c. List the outcomes to which the value 7 is assigned.

Solution

a. The sample space may be written as a set of ordered pairs.

(1, 1)	(1, 2)	(1, 3)	(1, 4)	(1, 5)	(1, 6)
(2, 1)	(2, 2)	(2, 3)	(2, 4)	(2, 5)	(2, 6)
(3, 1)	(3, 2)	(3, 3)	(3, 4)	(3, 5)	(3, 6)
(4, 1)	(4, 2)	(4, 3)	(4, 4)	(4, 5)	(4, 6)
(5, 1)	(5, 2)	(5, 3)	(5, 4)	(5, 5)	(5, 6)
(6, 1)	(6, 2)	(6, 3)	(6, 4)	(6, 5)	(6, 6)

b. The smallest possible value is 2, which is assigned to the outcome (1, 1). The largest possible value is 12, which is assigned to the outcome (6, 6). The range is the set of integers from 2 to 12.

c. The outcomes (1, 6), (2, 5), (3, 4), (4, 3), (5, 2), and (6, 1) are assigned to the value 7. ■

Number of trials	Average sum of two number cubes
100	7.3
200	6.98
300	7.26
400	7.005
500	6.978

Figure 13.3-3

Expected Value of a Random Variable

The **expected value,** or **mean,** of a random variable is the average value of the outcomes. In the experiment of rolling two number cubes, suppose the experiment was repeated 10 times, resulting in the following values for the random variable:

$$8, 5, 8, 6, 11, 11, 3, 9, 9, 7$$

The average value is $\dfrac{8 + 5 + 8 + 6 + 11 + 11 + 3 + 9 + 9 + 7}{10} = 7.7$. If the experiment is repeated a large number of times, the average approaches the expected value. A simulation was used to run a large number of trials, and the results are shown in Figure 13.3-3. The averages seem to be approaching 7, which is a reasonable estimate of the expected value.

To calculate the expected value of a random variable from a probability distribution, multiply each value by its probability, and add the results.

Example 5 Expected Value

A probability distribution for the random variable in the experiment in Example 4 is given below. Find the expected value of the random variable.

Sum of faces	2	3	4	5	6	7	8	9	10	11	12
Probability	$\frac{1}{36}$	$\frac{1}{18}$	$\frac{1}{12}$	$\frac{1}{9}$	$\frac{5}{36}$	$\frac{1}{6}$	$\frac{5}{36}$	$\frac{1}{9}$	$\frac{1}{12}$	$\frac{1}{18}$	$\frac{1}{36}$

Solution

Multiply each value by its probability, and add.

$$2\left(\frac{1}{36}\right) + 3\left(\frac{1}{18}\right) + 4\left(\frac{1}{12}\right) + 5\left(\frac{1}{9}\right) + 6\left(\frac{5}{36}\right) + 7\left(\frac{1}{6}\right)$$
$$+ 8\left(\frac{5}{36}\right) + 9\left(\frac{1}{9}\right) + 10\left(\frac{1}{12}\right) + 11\left(\frac{1}{18}\right) + 12\left(\frac{1}{36}\right) = 7$$

The expected value is not always in the range of the random variable, as shown in the following example.

Example 6 Expected Value of a Lottery Ticket

The probability distribution for a \$1 instant-win lottery ticket is given below. Find the expected value and interpret the result.

Solution

Win	\$0	\$3	\$5	\$10	\$20	\$40	\$100	\$400	\$2500
Probability	0.882746	0.06	0.04	0.01	0.005	0.002	0.0002	0.00005	0.000004

$$0(0.882746) + 3(0.06) + 5(0.04) + 10(0.01) + 20(0.005) + 40(0.002)$$
$$+ 100(0.0002) + 400(0.00005) + 2500(0.000004) = 0.71$$

The *average* amount won is \$0.71, though it is not possible to win exactly 71 cents on one ticket. However, since the ticket costs \$1, there is an average net *loss* of \$1 − \$0.71 = \$0.29 per play.

Probability Density Functions

In Example 1, colored marbles were drawn from a bag and the probability of each color being drawn was determined by its relative frequency.

red: 0.5   blue: 0.3   yellow: 0.1   green: 0.1

This probability distribution is displayed in a bar graph in Figure 13.3-4, in which each bar is 1 unit wide. Thus the area of each rectangular bar represents the probability of the corresponding color. The sum of the areas of the bars is 1.

If rectangles in the bar graph have width 1 unit, then the area of each rectangle represents the probability of the corresponding category.

A function with the property that the area under the graph corresponds to a probability distribution is called a **probability density function.**

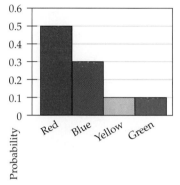

Figure 13.3-4

Example 7   **Discrete Probability Density Functions**

Draw a probability density function for the distribution in Example 5.

Solution

The probability density function is a piecewise-defined function, shown in Figure 13.3-5, where the height of each piece is the probability of the value on the left endpoint of the interval. The area of the shaded rectangle represents the probability that the sum is 9.

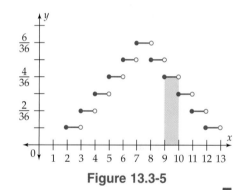

Figure 13.3-5

When a random variable has infinitely many values within a certain interval, the probability distribution can be represented by a continuous density function, as in the following example.

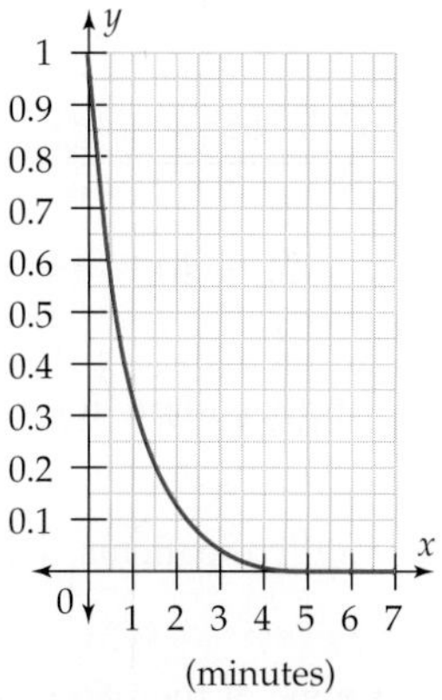

Example 8   **Continuous Probability Density Function**

The probability density function in Figure 13.3-6 can be used to estimate the probability that a customer calling a company's customer service line will have to wait for a given amount of time. The area of each square on the grid is $0.5 \cdot 0.05 = 0.025$, and the total area under the curve is 1. Estimate the probability that a customer will have to wait between 2 and 3 minutes.

(minutes)

Figure 13.3-6

Solution

The probability is the area under the curve between 2 and 3, which is shaded in Figure 13.3-7. The area is approximately $3\frac{1}{2}$ squares on the grid, or

$$3\frac{1}{2}(0.025) = 0.0875$$

Thus, the probability that a customer will have to wait between 2 and 3 minutes is about 0.0875.

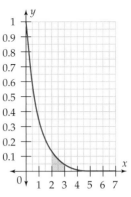

Figure 13.3-7

Exercises 13.3

Use the following probability distribution for Exercises 1–4.

Outcome	A	B	C	D
Probability	0.5	0.3	?	?

1. List the sample space for the probability distribution.

2. Suppose that outcomes C and D have the same probability. Complete the probability distribution.

3. What is the probability of the outcome (A or B)?

4. What is the probability of the outcome (not A)?

Exercises 5–8 refer to the spinner at the right. The probability of landing on black is $\frac{1}{2}$, and the probability of landing on red is $\frac{1}{3}$.

5. Create a probability distribution for the experiment of spinning the spinner.

Suppose the experiment is repeated three times. Assume the trials are independent.

6. What is the probability it will land on black all three times?

7. What is the probability it will land on white all three times?

8. What is the probability of the outcome (black, white, red)? of the outcome (black, red, white)? What is the probability that it will land once on each color?

A doctor has assigned the following chances to a medical procedure:

full recovery	55%
condition improves	24%
no change	17%
condition worsens	4%

Suppose the procedure is performed on 5 patients. Assume that the procedure is independent for each patient.

9. What is the probability that all five patients will recover completely?

10. What is the probability that none of the patients will get worse?

A bag contains red and blue marbles, such that the probability of drawing a blue marble is $\frac{3}{8}$. An experiment consists of drawing a marble, replacing it, and drawing another marble. The two draws are independent. A random variable assigns the number of blue marbles to each outcome.

11. What is the range of the random variable?

12. What is the probability that the random variable has an output of 2?

13. What is the probability that the random variable has an outcome of 0?

14. What is the probability that the random variable has an outcome of 3?

15. Create a probability distribution for the random variable.

16. Calculate the expected value of the random variable.

In Exercises 17–20, find the expected value of the random variable with the given probability distribution.

17.

Outcome	0	1	5	10	1000
Probability	0.43	0.32	0.24	0.10	0.01

18.

Outcome	0	1	2	3
Probability	0.25	0.25	0.25	0.25

19.

Outcome	15	16	17	18	19	20
Probability	0.1	0.3	0.2	0.2	0.1	0.1

20.

Outcome	2	3	4
Probability	$\frac{1}{4}$	$\frac{1}{2}$	$\frac{1}{4}$

An office employs 5 people. A random variable is assigned to the number of people absent on a given day. The probability distribution is given below.

Absent	0	1	2	3	4	5
Probability	0.59	0.33	0.07	0.01	0	0

21. What is the probability that at least one person is absent?

22. Find the expected value of the random variable, and interpret the result.

An experiment consists of planting four seeds. A random variable assigns the number of seeds that sprout to each outcome.

23. Complete the following probability distribution for the experiment.

Sprouted	0	1	2	3	4
Probability	?	0.154	0.345	0.345	0.130

24. Find the expected value of the random variable, and interpret the result.

25. Draw a probability density function for the random variable. Shade an area of the graph that corresponds to the probability that 3 or more seeds will sprout.

26. Use the probability distribution to determine the probability that each seed will sprout, assuming that they are independent. *Hint:* if the probability that one seed will sprout is p, what is the probability that all four seeds will sprout?

A random variable with a *uniform* distribution has a probability density function that is constant over the range of the variable, and 0 everywhere else. Use the graph of the probability density function shown below for Exercises 27–30.

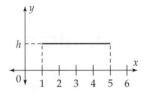

27. What is the range of the random variable?

28. What is the height h of the probability density function?

29. What is the probability that the random variable is between 2 and 4?

30. What is the probability that the random variable is greater than 4?

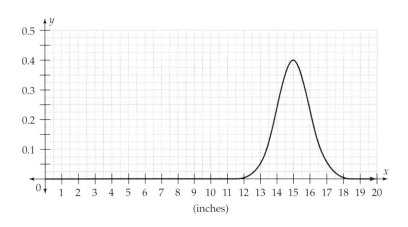

(inches)

(minutes)

The probability density function at left above models the number of inches of rainfall per year for a certain location. The area of each square on the grid is 0.01.

31. Estimate the probability that the rainfall for a certain year is between 14 and 16 inches.

32. Estimate the probability that the rainfall for a certain year is greater than 17 inches.

33. The median of a probability density function is the point that divides the area under the curve into two equal areas. Estimate the median rainfall, based on the given probability density function.

In commuting to work, Joshua takes one bus, then transfers to another bus. The probability density function at right above models the total length of time that he has to wait for both buses.

34. What is the height of the probability density function at $t = 5$ minutes?

35. What is the probability that Joshua has to wait for less than 5 minutes?

36. What is the probability that Joshua has to wait for between 3 and 6 minutes?

Determining Probabilities

Objectives

- Estimate probability using experimental methods
- Estimate probability using theoretical methods

The exact probability of a real event can never be known. Probabilities are estimated in two ways: experimentally and theoretically.

Experimental Estimates of Probability

Suppose an outcome of an experiment has a probability of 0.3. If the experiment were repeated many times, that outcome would occur in approximately 30% of the trials. In 100 trials, for example, it might occur 30 times, or maybe 28 times or 34 times. Statistical analysis shows, however, that it is unlikely that it would occur fewer than 20 times or more than 40 times.

The basis for experimental estimates of probability may be summarized as follows:

As the number of trials of an experiment increases, the relative frequency of an outcome approaches the probability of the outcome.

Thus, if an experiment is repeated n times, the experimental estimate of the probability of an event is

$$P(E) \approx \frac{\text{number of trials with an outcome in } E}{n}$$

Figure 13.4-1

| Example 1 | **Experimental Estimate of Probability** |

An experiment consists of throwing a dart at the target in Figure 13.4-1. Suppose the experiment is repeated 200 times, with the following results:

red	43
yellow	86
blue	71

Write a probability distribution for the experiment.

Solution

The probabilities may be estimated using the experimental formula.

Outcome	red	yellow	blue
Probability	$\frac{43}{200} \approx 0.2$	$\frac{86}{200} \approx 0.4$	$\frac{71}{200} \approx 0.4$

■

Probability Simulations

In order to estimate probability using the experimental approach, a large number of trials is needed. Because this approach is often time-consuming, computer simulations that duplicate the conditions of a single trial are often used.

Most graphing calculators have random number generators that can be used to simulate simple probability experiments. To simulate an experiment with a large number of trials, it is easiest to use a program that can keep track of the frequency of each outcome.

Suppose an experiment consists of tossing three coins and counting the number of heads, and that the probability of heads for each coin is 0.5. The possible outcomes of the experiment are 0 heads, 1 head, 2 heads, or 3 heads. One trial can be simulated by a command that randomly generates three values, which can be either 0 or 1, and adds them (see the Technology Tip on page 876). The three random integers represent the three coins, where 1 represents heads and 0 represents tails.

Technology Tip

To randomly generate three values that can be 0 or 1 and add them:

TI-83 and TI-86	sum (randInt (0, 1, 3))
TI-89 and TI-92	sum ({rand(2) − 1, rand(2) − 1, rand(2) − 1})
Sharp 9600	sum (int (2 random 3))
Casio 9850	Sum {Int 2Ran#, Int 2Ran#, Int 2Ran#}
HP-38	ΣList ({INT (2 RANDOM), INT (2 RANDOM), INT (2 RANDOM),})

The following is a sample program for running a simulation with n trials of the experiment. The program displays a list of the probabilities for 0 heads, 1 head, 2 heads, and 3 heads.

```
Prompt N                          N is the number of trials.
0 → A: 0 → B: 0 → C: 0 → D
For (K, 1, N, 1)
sum (randInt (0, 1, 3)) → T       T is the outcome of a single trial.
If T = 0
A + 1 → A                         A is the number of trials with 0 heads.
If T = 1
B + 1 → B                         B is the number of trials with 1 head.
If T = 2
C + 1 → C                         C is the number of trials with 2 heads.
If T = 3
D + 1 → D                         D is the number of trials with 3 heads.
End
{A/N, B/N, C/N, D/N}
```

Example 2   **Probability Simulation**

Use the program to create a probability distribution for the experiment of tossing 3 coins and counting the number of heads. Assume that $P(\text{heads}) = P(\text{tails}) = 0.5$ for each coin.

Solution

The results will vary each time the program is run. Using the results from Figure 13.4-2, one approximate distribution is shown below.

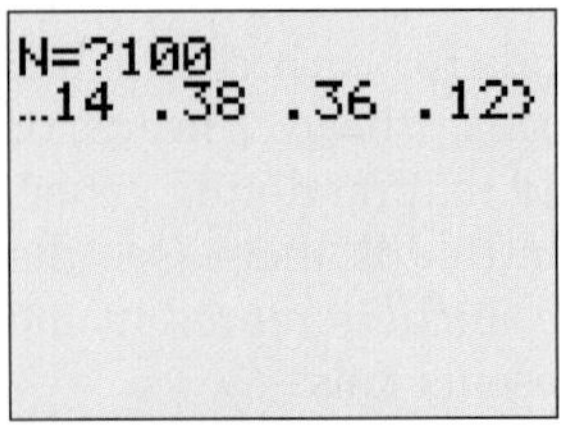

```
N=?100
...14 .38 .36 .12}
```

Figure 13.4-2

Outcome	0 heads	1 head	2 heads	3 heads
Probability	0.14	0.38	0.36	0.12

Calculator Exploration ●

Run the probability simulation in Example 2, using 100 trials. Are your results similar to those in the example? Compare your results to those of your classmates.

NOTE The assumption that all outcomes are equally likely was used in the probability simulation in Example 2. If $P(\text{heads}) = P(\text{tails}) = 1$, then heads and tails are equally likely. Also, for the given calculator commands, the outcomes 0 and 1 are equally likely each time.

Theoretical Estimates of Probability

In the theoretical approach, certain assumptions are made about the outcomes of the experiment. Then, the properties of probability are used to determine the probability of each outcome.

The most common assumption is that all outcomes are **equally likely,** that is, they have the same probability of occurring. For example, in tossing a coin it is usually assumed that heads and tails are equally likely. Since the probabilities must add to 1, the probability of each outcome must equal $\frac{1}{2}$. This idea is used to develop the following formula.

Probability for Equally Likely Outcomes

○

Suppose an experiment has a sample space of n outcomes, all of which are equally likely. Then the probability of each outcome is $\frac{1}{n}$, and the probability of an event E is given by

$$P(E) = \frac{\text{number of outcomes in } E}{n}$$

Example 3 **Rolling a Number Cube**

An experiment consists of rolling a number cube. Suppose that all outcomes are equally likely.

a. Write the probability distribution for the experiment.
b. Find the probability of the event that an even number is rolled.

Solution

a. The sample space consists of the 6 outcomes {1, 2, 3, 4, 5, 6}. If the outcomes are equally likely, then the probability of each is $\frac{1}{6}$. The probability distribution for the experiment is

Outcome	1	2	3	4	5	6
Probability	$\frac{1}{6}$	$\frac{1}{6}$	$\frac{1}{6}$	$\frac{1}{6}$	$\frac{1}{6}$	$\frac{1}{6}$

b. The event that an even number is rolled consists of the 3 outcomes
{2, 4, 6}. Thus, the probability that an even number is rolled is
$\frac{3}{6} = \frac{1}{2}$.

Of course, the outcomes of an experiment are not always equally likely.
Based on the probability simulation of tossing 3 coins in Example 2, the
outcomes 0, 1, 2, and 3 heads do not seem to be equally likely. However,
it is possible to determine the probability theoretically by considering each
coin separately.

Example 4   **Theoretical Probability**

Use properties of probability to write a theoretical probability distribution for the experiment in Example 2.

Solution

Each coin has no effect on the other coins, so the outcomes of the coins
are independent. Thus, the probabilities can be multiplied.

The only outcome with 0 heads is TTT. The probability of tails for each
coin is 0.5, so the probability of the outcome TTT is

T T T
0.5(0.5)(0.5) = 0.125

There are three outcomes with 1 head: HTT, THT, and TTH. Each outcome has a probability of the 0.125. For example,

H T T
0.5(0.5)(0.5) = 0.125

The probabilities of the three outcomes can be added, so the probability
of 1 head is 0.125 + 0.125 + 0.125 = 0.375.

There are three outcomes with 2 heads: HHT, HTH, and THH. The probability of 2 heads is also 0.125 + 0.125 + 0.125 = 0.375.

There is one outcome with 3 heads, HHH, which also has a probability
of 0.125.

The probability distribution is shown below.

Outcome	0 heads	1 head	2 heads	3 heads
Probability	0.125	0.375	0.375	0.125

How do the theoretical probabilities obtained in Example 4 compare to
the experimental ones you found in Example 2?

Counting Techniques

The probability formula for equally likely outcomes uses the size of the sample space. In simple experiments, this may be easily determined, but some experiments require more sophisticated counting techniques.

The basis of most counting techniques is the Fundamental Counting Principle, which is also known as the Multiplication Principle.

Fundamental Counting Principle

Consider a set of k experiments. Suppose the first experiment has n_1 outcomes, the second has n_2 outcomes, and so on. Then the total number of outcomes is $n_1 \cdot n_2 \cdot \ ... \ \cdot n_k$ for all k experiments.

Example 5 **Using the Fundamental Counting Principle**

A catalog offers chairs in a choice of 2 heights, regular and tall. There are 10 colors available for the finish, and 12 choices of fabric for the seats. The chair back has 4 different possible designs. How many different chairs can be ordered?

Solution

Each option can be considered as an experiment. The number of choices for each option is the number of outcomes. According to the Fundamental Counting Principle, the number of different chairs is

$$2 \cdot 10 \cdot 12 \cdot 4 = 960$$

Consider the following experiment: Each letter of the alphabet is written on a piece of paper, and three letters are chosen at random. There are two important questions in determining the nature of the experiment:

1. Is each letter replaced before the next letter is chosen?

2. Does the order of the letters matter in the result?

If the answer to Question 1 is *yes*, the letters are said to be chosen **with replacement.** In this case, letters may be repeated in the result. Also, the number of letters to choose from is always the same. If the answer is *no*, then the letters are said to be chosen **without replacement.** In this case, there will be no repeated letters, and the number of letters to choose from decreases by 1 for each letter chosen.

If the answer to Question 2 is *yes*, the result is said to be **order important.** In this case, the outcome CAT is considered to be different from the outcome ACT. If the answer is *no*, the result is said to be in **any order.** In this case, the six outcomes CAT, CTA, TAC, TCA, ACT, ATC are considered to be the same.

NOTE Many times, it is necessary to use the context of the experiment to determine whether it is with replacement, or if order is important.

Three of the four possible cases are shown in the table below. The fourth case, with replacement and in any order, will not be discussed. Use the Fundamental Counting Principle to explain the number of outcomes in each case.

With replacement Order important	Without replacement Order important	Without replacement Any order
$26 \cdot 26 \cdot 26 = 17{,}576$	$26 \cdot 25 \cdot 24 = 15{,}600$	$\dfrac{26 \cdot 25 \cdot 24}{3 \cdot 2 \cdot 1} = 2600$

Example 6　3 Coin Toss

Use the Fundamental Counting Principle to verify the probability distribution in Example 4.

Solution

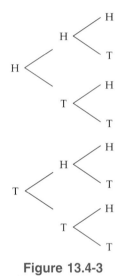

Figure 13.4-3

There are two possible outcomes for each coin: heads and tails. Thus, the number of outcomes for tossing three coins is $2 \cdot 2 \cdot 2 = 8$. To find the 8 different outcomes, it is helpful to use a tree diagram, as shown in Figure 13.4-3. The outcomes are given below.

HHH	HHT	HTH	HTT	THH	THT	TTH	TTT
3 heads	*2 heads*	*2 heads*	*1 head*	*2 heads*	*1 head*	*1 head*	*0 heads*

Each of these outcomes is equally likely, so the probability distribution is

Outcome	0 heads	1 head	2 heads	3 heads
Probability	$\frac{1}{8} = 0.125$	$\frac{3}{8} = 0.375$	$\frac{3}{8} = 0.375$	$\frac{1}{8} = 0.125$

Permutations and Combinations

The two cases without replacement are called **permutations** (order important) and **combinations** (any order). In order to write a formula for permutations and combinations, $n!$—read "n **factorial**"—is used to describe the product of all the integers from 1 to n.

$$n! = n(n - 1)(n - 2) \ldots (3)(2)(1)$$

In the example of drawing 3 letters without replacement where order is important, the number of permutations can be written using factorials as

$$26 \cdot 25 \cdot 24 = \frac{26 \cdot 25 \cdot 24 \cdot 23 \cdot 22 \cdot \ldots \cdot 3 \cdot 2 \cdot 1}{23 \cdot 22 \cdot \ldots \cdot 3 \cdot 2 \cdot 1} = \frac{26!}{23!}$$

In the case where order is not important, the number of combinations can be written as

$$\frac{26 \cdot 25 \cdot 24}{3 \cdot 2 \cdot 1} = \frac{26!}{(3 \cdot 2 \cdot 1)23!} = \frac{26!}{3! \cdot 23!}$$

Permutation and combination formulas are also written using factorials.

Permutations and Combinations

Permutations

If *r* items are chosen in order without replacement from *n* possible items, the number of permutations is

$$_nP_r = \frac{n!}{(n-r)!}$$

Combinations

If *r* items are chosen in any order without replacement from *n* possible items, the number of combinations is

$$_nC_r = \frac{n!}{r!(n-r)!}$$

If each item is equally likely to be chosen, the permutations and combinations are all equally likely for a given value of *r*.

Note: $_nP_r$ may also be written as $P_{n,r}$ or $P(n, r)$, and $_nC_r$ may be written as $C_{n,r}$, $C(n, r)$, or $\binom{n}{r}$.

Technology Tip

Permutations and combinations are located on the PROB, PRB, or PROBABILITY submenu of the MATH menu on TI-83, TI-86, TI-89, Sharp 9600, and HP-38, and on the PROB submenu of the OPTN menu on Casio 9850.

Example 7 Matching Problem

Suppose you have four personalized letters and four addressed envelopes. If the letters are randomly placed in the envelopes, what is the probability that all four letters will go to the correct addresses?

Solution

For all four letters to go to the correct addresses, they must be chosen in the exact same order as the envelopes. The size of the sample space is the number of permutations, $_4P_4$.

$$_4P_4 = \frac{4!}{(4-4)!} = \frac{4!}{0!} = 24$$

Thus, the probability is $\frac{1}{24} \approx 0.04$.

Example 8 Pick-6 Lottery

In a "pick-6" lottery, 54 numbered balls are used. Out of these, 6 are randomly chosen. To win, at least 3 balls must be matched in any order. What is the probability of winning the jackpot (all 6 balls)? What is the probability of matching any 5 balls? any 4 balls? any 3 balls?

Solution

The size of the sample space is the number of combinations.

$$_{54}C_6 = 25{,}827{,}165$$

The probability of winning the jackpot is

$$\frac{1}{25{,}827{,}165} \approx 0.00000004$$

The event of matching 5, 4, or 3 numbers can be determined as follows:

$$P(\text{matching } k \text{ numbers}) = \frac{\text{number of combinations that match } k \text{ numbers}}{_{54}C_6}$$

There are $_6C_k$ ways to match k numbers out of 6. The remaining $6 - k$ numbers do *not* match any of the 6 winning numbers, so there are 48 numbers to choose from, giving $_{48}C_{6-k}$ ways to choose the remaining numbers. By the Fundamental Counting Principle, there are $_6C_k \cdot {_{48}C_{6-k}}$ combinations that match k numbers.

$$P(\text{matching } k \text{ numbers}) = \frac{_6C_k \cdot {_{48}C_{6-k}}}{_{54}C_6}$$

$$P(\text{matching 5 numbers}) = \frac{_6C_5 \cdot {_{48}C_1}}{_{54}C_6} = \frac{6 \cdot 48}{25{,}827{,}165} \approx 0.00001$$

$$P(\text{matching 4 numbers}) = \frac{_6C_4 \cdot {_{48}C_2}}{_{54}C_6} = \frac{15 \cdot 1128}{25{,}827{,}165} \approx 0.0007$$

$$P(\text{matching 3 numbers}) = \frac{_6C_3 \cdot {_{48}C_3}}{_{54}C_6} = \frac{20 \cdot 17296}{25{,}827{,}165} \approx 0.01$$

```
54 nCr 6
            25827165
Ans-1
     3.87189225e-8
```

Figure 13.4-4

Exercises 13.4

For Exercises 1–4, an experiment consists of drawing a marble out of a bag, observing the color, and then placing it back in the bag. Suppose the experiment is repeated 75 times, with the following results:

red	38
blue	23
green	11
yellow	3

1. Write a probability distribution of the experiment using the experimental formula.

2. Based on your distribution from Exercise 1, what is the probability of drawing either a blue or green marble?

3. Based on your distribution from Exercise 1, what is the probability of drawing two yellow marbles in a row?

4. Suppose it is known that there is a total of 300 marbles in the bag. Estimate the number of each color of marble.

A dreidel is a top with four sides, used in a Hanukah game. The sides are labeled with the Hebrew letters *nun, gimel, hay,* and *shin.* A dreidel is spun 100 times, with the following results:

nun	10
gimel	45
hay	24
shin	21

dreidel

5. Write a probability distribution for the dreidel.

6. A player wins tokens if the dreidel lands on either *gimel* or *hay*. What is the probability of winning tokens?

7. A player loses tokens if the dreidel lands on *nun*. What is the probability of losing four times in a row?

Exercises 8–11 refer to the following experiment: two number cubes are rolled, and a random variable assigns the sum of the faces to each outcome.

8. The following commands generate two random integers from 1 to 6 and add them.
TI-83/86: sum(randInt(1, 6, 2))
TI-89/92: sum({rand(6), rand(6)})
Sharp 9600: sum(int(6random(2)) + 1)
Casio 9850: Sum{Int 6Ran# + 1, Int 6Ran# + 1}
HP-38: ΣLIST({INT(6 RANDOM) + 1,
       INT(6 RANDOM) + 1})
Run 5 trials of the experiment and list your results.

9. Run a simulation of the experiment with at least 50 trials, and create a probability distribution.

10. Use your probability distribution from Exercise 9 to find the probabilities for the following values of the random variable.
a. greater than 9
b. less than 6
c. at least 4

11. Use your probability distribution from Exercise 9 to find the expected value of the random variable.

12. A bag contains 3 red marbles and 4 blue marbles. Suppose each marble is equally likely to be chosen. What is the probability of the event of drawing a red marble?

13. Suppose that a person's birthday is equally likely to be any day of the year. What is the probability that a randomly chosen person has the same birthday as you?

A teacher writes the name of each of her 25 students on a slip of paper and places the papers in a box. To call on a student, she draws a slip of paper from the box. Each paper is equally likely to be drawn, and the papers are replaced in the box after each draw.

14. What is the probability of calling on a particular student?

15. What is the probability of calling on the same student twice in a row?

16. If there are 9 students in the last row, what is the probability of calling on a student in the last row?

17. If the class contains 11 boys and 14 girls, what is the probability of calling on a girl? What is the probability of calling on 3 girls in a row?

18. A clothing store offers a shirt in 5 colors, in long or short sleeves, with a choice of three different collars. How many ways can the shirt be designed?

19. A quiz has 5 true-false questions and 3 multiple choice questions with 4 options each. How many possible ways are there to answer the 8 questions?

20. A license plate has 3 digits from 0 to 9, followed by 3 letters. How many different license plates are possible?

21. A gallery has 25 paintings in its permanent collection, with display space for 10 at one time. How many different collections can be shown?

22. A committee of 8 people randomly chooses 3 people in order to be president, vice president, and treasurer. In how many ways can the officers be chosen?

23. A baseball team has 9 players. How many different batting orders are there?

24. A small library contains 700 novels. In how many ways can you check out 3 novels?

25. A manufacturer is testing 4 brands of soda in a blind taste test. The participants know the brands being tested but do not know which is which. What is the probability that a participant will identify all 4 brands correctly by guessing?

26. A researcher is studying the abilities of people who claim to be able to read minds. He chooses 6 numbers between 1 and 50 (inclusive), and asks each participant to guess the numbers in order. What is the probability of guessing all 6 correctly?

A botanist is testing two kinds of seeds. She divides a plot of land into 16 equal areas numbered from 1 to 16. She then randomly chooses 8 of these areas to plant seed A, and she plants seed B in the remaining areas.

1	2	3	4
5	6	7	8
9	10	11	12
13	14	15	16

27. How many ways are there to choose 8 plots out of 16?

A	A	A	A
A	A	A	A
B	B	B	B
B	B	B	B

28. What is the probability of the event shown at right?

29. What is the probability that all of the areas with seed A will form a 4 × 2 rectangle on one side of the plot, and all of the areas with seed B will form a 4 × 2 rectangle on the other side?

Critical Thinking **Exercises 30–35 refer to a famous probability problem: suppose a certain number of people are in a room. What is the probability that two or more people in the room will have the same birthday?**

30. Suppose each day of the year is equally likely to be a person's birthday. How many ways are there to name one date per person (not necessarily all different) for each of 3 people? of 20 people? of n people?

31. The complement of the event "two or more people will have the same birthday" is

"everybody has a different birthday." How many ways are there to name a *different* date for each of 3 people? of 20 people? of n people?

32. The probability that everybody has a different birthday can be written as

$$\frac{\text{Number of ways to name } n \text{ different dates}}{\text{Number of ways to name } n \text{ dates}}$$

Use your results from Exercises 30 and 31 to write a formula in terms of n for the probability that everybody has a different birthday.

33. Use your results from Exercise 32 to write a formula in terms of n for the probability that two or more people have the same birthday. Find the probability for $n = 3$, for $n = 20$, and for $n = 35$.

34. How many people must be in the room for the probability to be approximately $\frac{1}{2}$ that two or more have the same birthday?

35. How many people must be in the room for the probability to be 1 that two or more have the same birthday? *Hint:* do not use the formula.

Excursion: Binomial Experiments

Objectives

- Calculate the probability of a binomial experiment

Many experiments can be described in terms of just two outcomes, such as winning or losing, heads or tails, boy or girl. These experiments determine a group of problems called **binomial or Bernoulli experiments,** named after Jacob Bernoulli, a Swiss mathematician who studied these distributions extensively in the late 1600's.

Binomial Experiments

Here is a typical binomial experiment: in a basketball contest, each contestant is allowed 3 free-throws. If a certain individual has a 70% chance of making each free-throw, what is the probability of making exactly 2 out of 3?

The essential elements in a binomial experiment are given below.

Binomial Experiment

A set of n trials is called a binomial experiment if the following are true.

1. The trials are independent.
2. Each trial has only 2 outcomes, which may be designated as *success* (S) and *failure* (F).
3. The probability of success p is the same for each trial. The probability of failure is $q = 1 - p$.

NOTE The terms "success" and "failure" are often used in experiments to designate outcomes such as heads or tails, even if neither outcome is preferred.

In the example of the basketball contest, the outcome *SFS* indicates that the first free-throw is a success, the second a failure, and the third a success. The trials are independent, so the probability of the outcome *SFS* is the product of the probabilities for each trial.

$$P(SFS) = P(S) \cdot P(F) \cdot P(S) = (0.7)(0.3)(0.7) = 0.147$$

Example 1 **Basketball Contest**

Refer to the basketball contest described on page 884. Suppose that the probability of making each free-throw is 0.7. What is the probability of making exactly 2 free-throws in 3 tries?

Solution

The outcomes in the event "2 free-throws in 3 tries" are *SSF, SFS, FSS*. The probability of the event is the sum of the probabilities of the three outcomes.

$$P(SSF) = P(S) \cdot P(S) \cdot P(F) = (0.7)(0.7)(0.3) = 0.147$$
$$P(SFS) = P(S) \cdot P(F) \cdot P(S) = (0.7)(0.3)(0.7) = 0.147$$
$$P(FSS) = P(F) \cdot P(S) \cdot P(S) = (0.3)(0.7)(0.7) = 0.147$$
$$P(2 \text{ free-throws}) = P(SSF) + P(SFS) + P(FSS)$$
$$= 0.147 + 0.147 + 0.147 = 0.441$$

In Example 1, note that the probability of *SSF* is the same as the probability of *SFS* or *FSS*. In general, the probability of any outcome with r successes and $n{-}r$ failures in n trials is

$$\underbrace{(pp \dots p)}_{(r \text{ times})}\underbrace{(qq \dots q)}_{(n - r \text{ times})} = p^r q^{n-r}$$

To develop a general formula for the probability of r successes in n trials, it is necessary to determine how many different outcomes have r successes. Consider the number of outcomes with 3 successes in 5 trials, as shown below. For clarity, the F's are left as blanks.

SSS _ _ SS _ S _ SS _ _ S S _ SS _ S _ S _ S

S _ _ SS _ SSS _   _ SS _ S _ S _ SS _ _ SSS

The number of outcomes is the same as the number of ways to choose 3 positions for the S out of 5 possible positions. The order of the S's does not matter, because they are all the same. This is the number of combinations, $_5C_3 = 10$.

Probability of a Binomial Experiment

In a binomial experiment,

$$P(r \text{ successes in } n \text{ trials}) = {_nC_r}p^rq^{n-r}$$

where p is the probability of success, and $q = 1 - p$ is the probability of failure.

Example 2   Lottery Tickets

A lottery consists of choosing a number from 000 to 999. All digits of the number must be matched in order, so the probability of winning is $\frac{1}{1000} = 0.001$. A ticket costs \$1, and the prize is \$500. Suppose you play the lottery 1000 times in a row.

a. Write a probability distribution for the number of wins.

b. What is the probability that you will break even or better?

Solution

a. The number of wins could be anything from 0 to 1000. However, the probability of winning more than a few times is so small that it is essentially 0. Thus, the sample space will be considered as 0, 1, 2, 3, 4, and 5 or more wins. The probabilities are calculated using the binomial probability formula, with $n = 1000$ and $p = 0.001$.

$P(0 \text{ wins}) = {_{1000}C_0}(0.001)^0(0.999)^{1000} \approx 0.3677$
$P(1 \text{ win}) = {_{1000}C_1}(0.001)^1(0.999)^{999} \approx 0.3681$
$P(2 \text{ wins}) = {_{1000}C_2}(0.001)^2(0.999)^{998} \approx 0.1840$
$P(3 \text{ wins}) = {_{1000}C_3}(0.001)^3(0.999)^{997} \approx 0.0613$
$P(4 \text{ wins}) = {_{1000}C_4}(0.001)^4(0.999)^{996} \approx 0.0153$
$P(5 \text{ or more wins}) \approx 1 - 0.3677 - 0.3681 - 0.1840 - 0.0613 - 0.0153$
≈ 0.0036

Outcome	0 wins	1 win	2 wins	3 wins	4 wins	5 or more wins
Probability	0.3677	0.3681	0.1840	0.0613	0.0153	0.0036

b. In order to break even or better, you must win 2 or more times. The probability is the sum of the probabilities of winning 2, 3, 4, or 5 or more times.

$$P(\text{break even or better}) \approx 0.1840 + 0.0613 + 0.0153 + 0.0036 \approx 0.2642$$

Technology Tip

● The command binom-pdf(in the DISTR menu of the TI-83 finds the probability for r successes in n trials of a binomial experiment, given n, p and r. The command binomcdf (finds the cumulative probability for r or fewer successes in n trials.

```
binompdf(10,0.25
,6)
       .0162220001
binomcdf(10,0.25
,4)
       .9218730926
```

Figure 13.4.A-1

Example 3   Multiple Choice Exam

Morgan is taking a 10-question multiple choice test but has not studied. Each question has 4 possible responses, only one of which is correct. Find the probability of getting the results below if he answers all questions randomly.

a. exactly 6 questions correct

b. 4 or fewer questions correct

c. 8 or more questions correct

Solution

The probability of getting each question correct is $p = \dfrac{1}{4} = 0.25$.

a. $P(6 \text{ correct}) = {}_{10}C_6(0.25)^6(0.75)^4 \approx 0.016$

b. $P(4 \text{ or fewer correct}) = {}_{10}C_0(0.25)^0(0.75)^{10} + {}_{10}C_1(0.25)^1(0.75)^9 + {}_{10}C_2(0.25)^2(0.75)^8 + {}_{10}C_3(0.25)^3(0.75)^7 + {}_{10}C_4(0.25)^4(0.75)^6 \approx 0.922$

c. $P(8 \text{ or more correct}) = {}_{10}C_8(0.25)^8(0.75)^2 + {}_{10}C_9(0.25)^9(0.75)^1 + {}_{10}C_{10}(0.25)^{10}(0.75)^0 \approx 0.0004$

Binomial Distributions

Consider the following binomial experiment: a coin is tossed 4 times, and the probability of heads on each toss is $\dfrac{1}{2}$. A probability distribution for the number of heads is shown below.

Number of heads	0	1	2	3	4
Probability	$\dfrac{1}{16}$	$\dfrac{1}{4}$	$\dfrac{3}{8}$	$\dfrac{1}{4}$	$\dfrac{1}{16}$

A probability density function that represents this distribution is shown in Figure 13.4.A-2. Notice that the shape of the graph is symmetric.

The expected value of this distribution is

$$0\left(\frac{1}{16}\right) + 1\left(\frac{1}{4}\right) + 2\left(\frac{3}{8}\right) + 3\left(\frac{1}{4}\right) + 4\left(\frac{1}{16}\right) = 2$$

which is the (approximate) center of the probability distribution.

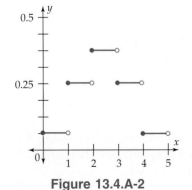

Figure 13.4.A-2

For large values of n or when p is near $\frac{1}{2}$, the shape of a binomial distribution is approximately symmetric, with its center at the expected value. For small values of n if p is different from $\frac{1}{2}$, the distribution will be skewed. However, as n increases, the distribution becomes more symmetric. The graphs in Figure 13.4.A-3 show the distributions of a binomial experiment with $p = \frac{1}{3}$ for $n = 3, 10,$ and 30. The shape of the distribution approaches a special curve, called the *normal curve*, which is developed in the next section.

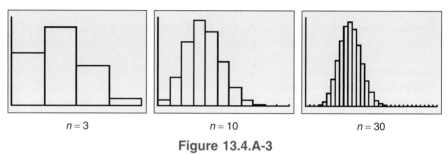

$n = 3$ $n = 10$ $n = 30$

Figure 13.4.A-3

Characteristics of a Binomial Distribution

The distribution of a binomial experiment with n trials and probability of success p is approximately symmetric for large values of n. The center of the distribution is the expected value.

The expected value of the binomial distribution is np.

The standard deviation of the binomial distribution is $\sqrt{npq}$.

Example 4   Multiple Choice Exam

Find the expected value and standard deviation of the number of questions correct on the multiple choice exam in Example 3.

Solution

In this case, $n = 10$, $p = 0.25$, and $q = 0.75$. The expected value is

$$np = 10(0.25) = 2.5$$

and the standard deviation is

$$\sqrt{npq} = \sqrt{10(0.25)(0.75)} \approx 1.4.$$

This means that if a large number of students guessed on the exam, the average number correct would be 2.5, with a standard deviation of 1.4. A graph of the distribution is shown in Figure 13.4.A-4.

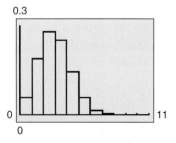

Figure 13.4.A-4

Exercises 13.4.A

For Exercises 1–4, a binomial experiment consists of planting 4 seeds. The probability of success (that a given seed will sprout) is $p = 0.65$. The sample outcome *SFSS* means that the first seed sprouted, the second seed did not sprout, and the third and fourth seeds sprouted.

1. What is the probability of failure?

2. Write out the $_4C_2 = 6$ outcomes that have exactly two successes.

3. Complete the probability distribution below.

Sprouted	0	1	2	3	4
Probability	?	?	?	?	?

4. Find the expected value of the number of seeds that will sprout, and interpret the result.

For Exercises 5–8, suppose the probability of a certain dart player hitting a bulls-eye is 0.25.

5. Write a probability distribution for the number of bulls-eyes in 4 tries.

6. What is the probability of hitting at least 3 bulls-eyes in 4 tries?

7. What is the probability of hitting less than 2 bulls-eyes in 4 tries?

8. What is the expected value of the number of bulls-eyes in 4 tries?

A true-false exam has 100 questions, and for each question $P(\text{true}) = P(\text{false}) = 0.5$. What is the probability of answering

9. 50 questions correct?

10. 70 questions correct?

11. 30 questions correct?

12. 90 questions correct?

13. Find the expected value and standard deviation of the number of correct answers.

An experiment consists of rolling a number cube 30 times. The outcome 6 is considered a success, and all other outcomes are considered failures. Assume all faces are equally likely, so that $p = P(\text{success}) = \dfrac{1}{6}$.

14. Find the expected value μ of the probability distribution. What is the probability of e successes?

15. What is the probability of $\mu + 1$ successes? What is the probability of $\mu - 1$ successes?

16. Find the standard deviation σ of the probability distribution. What is the probability that the outcome is between $\mu + \sigma$ and $\mu - \sigma$?

13.5 Normal Distributions

Objectives

- Draw a normal distribution given its mean and standard deviation

- Use normal distributions to find probabilities

To statisticians, the most important probability density function is the **normal curve** (sometimes called the bell curve). **Normal distributions** are used to predict the outcomes of many events, such as the probability that a student scores a 750 on the SAT, or the probability that you will grow to be 67 inches tall. For statisticians, it is also a valuable tool for predicting if an outcome is statistically significant or just caused by chance.

Properties of the Normal Curve

A normal distribution is bell-shaped and symmetric about its mean. The x-axis is a horizontal asymptote, and the area under the curve and above the x-axis is 1. The maximum value occurs at the mean, and the curve has two points of inflection, at 1 standard deviation to the right and left of the mean.

Because a normal distribution is symmetric, the mean, median, and mode have the same value. This value is also called the *center*. The Greek letter μ (mu) is used to represent the mean of a normally distributed population. Also, the population standard deviation σ is used for the standard deviation.

Figure 13.5-1 shows three normal curves, with μ and σ labeled.

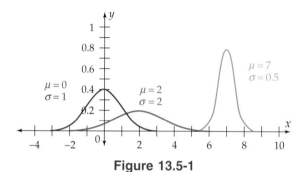

Figure 13.5-1

The normal curve with a mean of 0 and standard deviation of 1 is called the **standard normal curve.** The equation of the standard normal curve is

$$y = \frac{1}{\sqrt{2\pi}} e^{\frac{-x^2}{2}}$$

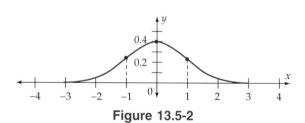

Figure 13.5-2

The standard normal curve can be thought of as a parent function for all normal curves.

- A change in μ results in a horizontal translation of the curve.
- A change in σ results in a horizontal stretch and vertical compression of the curve, or vice versa, so that the resulting area is still 1.

Graphing Exploration ●

The normal curves below have the same value of σ and different values of μ. Graph the curves in the same viewing window and describe the results.

$$y = \frac{1}{\sqrt{2\pi}}\, e^{\frac{-x^2}{2}} \qquad y = \frac{1}{\sqrt{2\pi}}\, e^{\frac{-(x-3)^2}{2}} \qquad y = \frac{1}{\sqrt{2\pi}}\, e^{\frac{-(x+4)^2}{2}}$$

The normal curves below have the same value of μ and different values of σ. Graph the curves below in the same viewing window and describe the results.

$$y = \frac{1}{\sqrt{2\pi}}\, e^{\frac{-x^2}{2}} \qquad y = \frac{1}{3\sqrt{2\pi}}\, e^{\frac{-x^2}{18}} \qquad y = \frac{3}{\sqrt{2\pi}}\, e^{\frac{-9x^2}{2}}$$

Equation of Normal Curve ○

A random variable is said to have a normal distribution with mean μ and standard deviation σ if its density function is given by the equation

$$y = \frac{1}{\sigma\sqrt{2\pi}}\, e^{\frac{-(x-\mu)^2}{2\sigma^2}}$$

Most of the time, the mean and standard deviation of an entire population cannot be measured. The population mean and standard deviation are often estimated by using a sample.

Example 1   Using Sample Information

A paper in *Animal Behavior* gives 11 sample distances, in cm, from which a bat can first detect a nearby insect. The bat does this by sending out high-pitched sounds and listening for the echoes. Assume the population is normally distributed.

$$62, 23, 27, 56, 52, 34, 42, 40, 68, 45, 83$$

a. Compute the mean and standard deviation of this sample.

b. Draw a normal curve to represent the distribution.

Solution

a. The mean is 48.36 and the sample standard deviation is 18.08, as shown in Figure 13.5-3.

b. The normal curve is shown in Figure 13.5-4.

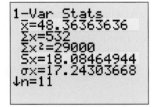

```
1-Var Stats
 x̄=48.36363636
 Σx=532
 Σx²=29000
 Sx=18.08464944
 σx=17.24303668
↓n=11
```

Figure 13.5-3

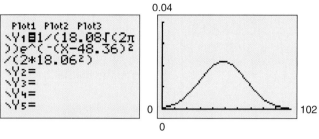

Figure 13.5-4

The Empirical Rule

Consider the intervals formed by one, two, and three standard deviations on either side of the mean, as shown below. The **empirical rule** describes the areas under the normal curve over these intervals.

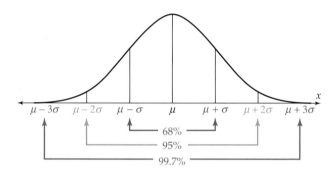

Empirical Rule

In a normal distribution:

- **about 68% of the data values are within one standard deviation of the mean.**
- **about 95% of the data values are within two standard deviations of the mean.**
- **about 99.7% of the data values are within three standard deviations of the mean.**

NOTE Each percentage in the empirical rule can also be interpreted as the probability that a data value chosen at random will lie within one, two, or three standard deviations of the mean.

Example 2 Running Shoes

A pair of running shoes lasts an average of 450 miles, with a standard deviation of 50 miles. Use the empirical rule to find the probability that a new pair of shoes will have the following lifespans, in miles.

a. between 400 and 500 miles

b. more than 550 miles

Solution

Figure 13.5-5 shows the normal distribution with the intervals of one, two, and three standard deviations on either side of the mean.

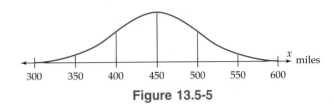

Figure 13.5-5

a. The area under the curve between 400 and 500 miles is approximately 68% of the total area. Since the area under a density function corresponds to the probability, the probability that a pair of shoes will last between 400 and 500 miles is about 0.68.

b. The area under the curve between 350 and 550 miles is 95% of the total area, which leaves 5% for the area less than 350 and greater than 550. Since the normal curve is symmetric, the area greater than 550 is exactly half of this, or 2.5%. Thus, the probability that a pair of shoes will last more than 550 miles is about 0.025.

The Standard Normal Curve

In general, determining the area under a normal curve is very difficult. Because of this, it is common to **standardize** data to match the normal curve with a mean of 0 and standard deviation of 1, for which these areas are known.

Comparing Data Sets

Sarah and Megan are high school juniors. Sarah scored 660 on the SAT, and Megan scored 29 on the ACT. Who did better? Although the scores on both tests are normally distributed, the mean and standard deviation are very different. One way to compare the distributions is to adjust the scales of the axes, as shown in Figure 13.5-6.

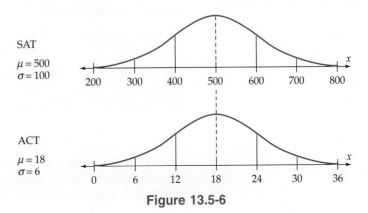

Figure 13.5-6

A more precise way to compare two scores from different data sets is to use the standard deviation as a unit of measurement. Each score is represented by the number of standard deviations above or below the mean.

Example 3 Comparing Scores

Use the standard deviation as a unit of measurement to compare the SAT and ACT scores for Sarah and Megan.

Solution

Sarah's score of 660 is 160 points above the mean, which is 500. The standard deviation is 100, so Sarah's score is $\frac{160}{100} = 1.6$ standard deviations above the mean.

Megan's score of 29 is 11 points above the mean, which is 18. The standard deviation is 6, so Megan's score is $\frac{11}{6} \approx 1.83$ standard deviations above the mean. Thus, Megan's score is better than Sarah's score. ∎

The number of standard deviations that a data value is above the mean is called the **z-value**. In Example 3, Sarah's z-value is 1.58 and Megan's z-value is 1.83. For a normal distribution, the z-values correspond to values on the standard normal curve, as shown in Figure 13.5-7.

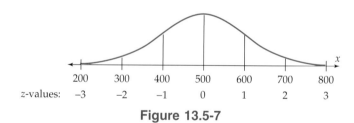

Figure 13.5-7

z-Values

The *z-value* of the value x in a data set with mean μ and standard deviation σ is

$$z = \frac{x - \mu}{\sigma}$$

The area under a normal curve between $x = a$ and $x = b$ is equal to the area under the standard normal curve between the z-value of a and the z-value of b.

Once z-values are determined, corresponding areas under the normal curve are often found using a table. Because of the symmetry of the normal curve, it is only necessary to include positive z-values in the table.

The following table gives the area under the normal curve between 0 and the given z-values, as shown in Figure 13.5-8.

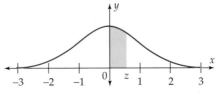

Figure 13.5-8

z	0.1	0.2	0.3	0.4	0.5	0.6	0.7	0.8	0.9	1
Area	0.04	0.08	0.12	0.16	0.19	0.23	0.26	0.29	0.32	0.34

Example 4   Using z-Values to Determine Area

A normally distributed data set has a mean of 25 and a standard deviation of 5. Find the probability that a data value chosen at random is between 23 and 28.

Solution

First, find the z-values for 23 and 28, given $\mu = 25$ and $\sigma = 5$.

$$z = \frac{23 - 25}{5} = -0.4 \qquad z = \frac{28 - 25}{5} = 0.6$$

Divide the area into two parts: the area from -0.4 to 0, and the area from 0 to 0.6, as shown in Figure 13.5-9. The areas are found in the table above. Because the normal curve is symmetric with respect to $x = 0$, the area from -0.4 to 0 is the same as the area from 0 to 0.4, or 0.16. The area from 0 to 0.6 is 0.23. The total area is the sum of the two areas, 0.39. Thus, the probability that a randomly chosen data value is between 23 and 28 is 0.39.

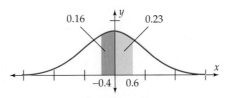

Figure 13.5-9

Technology Tip

Normalcdf under the DISTR menu of the TI-83 will calculate the area under the normal curve in a given interval. The parameters are Normalcdf (lower bound, upper bound, μ, σ).

Example 5   Response Times

The EMT response time for an emergency is the difference between the time the call is received and the time the ambulance arrives on the scene. Suppose the response times for a given city have a normal distribution with $\mu = 6$ minutes and $\sigma = 1.2$ minutes. For a randomly received call, estimate the probability of the following response times.

a. between 6 and 7 minutes   **b.** less than 5 minutes

c. less than 7 minutes

Solution

a. The z-values are $z = \dfrac{6-6}{1.2} = 0$ and $z = \dfrac{7-6}{1.2} \approx 0.8$. The probability of a response time between 6 and 7 minutes is the area under the standard normal curve from 0 to 0.8, which is approximately 0.29.

b. The z-value is $z = \dfrac{5-6}{1.2} \approx -0.8$. The area from 0 to -0.8 is approximately 0.29, so the probability of a response time under 5 minutes is about $0.5 - 0.29 = 0.21$ (see Figure 13.5-10).

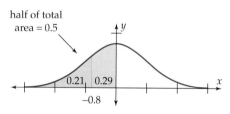

Figure 13.5-10

c. The area under the curve from 0 to 6 minutes is 0.5. From part **a**, the area under the curve from 6 to 7 minutes is 0.29. Thus, the probability of a response time under 7 minutes is $0.5 + 0.29 = 0.79$.

Exercises 13.5

In Exercises 1–4, refer to the normal curve below. The area of each square of the grid is 0.01.

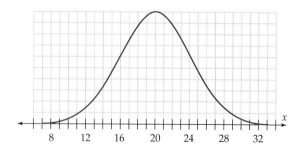

1. Find μ.   **2.** Estimate σ.

3. Estimate the area under the curve from 16 to 24.

4. Estimate the area under the curve from 12 to 28.

Graph the normal curves for the following values of μ and σ.

5. $\mu = 10, \sigma = 12$ **6.** $\mu = 40, \sigma = 12$

7. $\mu = 500, \sigma = 100$ **8.** $\mu = 3, \sigma = 5$

Suppose the heights of adult men are normally distributed. The heights of a sample of 30 men are shown below, in inches.

65, 83, 69, 67, 69, 67, 67, 72, 85, 68, 73, 65, 67, 65, 72, 71, 67, 73, 68, 72, 61, 75, 66, 78, 65, 71, 68, 76, 67, 68

9. Compute the mean and standard deviation of this sample.

10. Draw a normal curve that represents the distribution of adult male heights, based on the sample.

Suppose that the heights of adult women are normally distributed with $\mu = 65$ inches and $\sigma = 2.5$ inches. Use the properties of the normal curve and the Empirical Rule to find the probability that a randomly chosen woman is within the given range.

11. taller than 65 inches

12. shorter than 67.5 inches

13. between 62.5 inches and 67.5 inches

14. between 60 inches and 70 inches

15. between 57.5 inches and 67.5 inches

16. A student took two national standardized tests while applying for college. On the first test, $\mu = 475$ and $\sigma = 75$, and on the second test, $\mu = 32$ and $\sigma = 6$. If he scored 630 on the first test and 45 on the second, on which test did he do better?

17. Four students took a national standardized test for which the mean was 500 and the standard deviation was 100. Their scores were 560, 450, 640, and 530. Determine the z-value for each student.

18. If a student's z-value was 1.75 on the test described in problem 17, what was the student's score?

19. A sample of restaurants in a city showed that the average cost of a glass of iced tea is \$1.25 with a standard deviation of 7¢. Three of the restaurants charge 95¢, \$1.00, and \$1.35. Determine the z-value for each restaurant.

20. If a new restaurant charges a price for iced tea that has a z-value of -1.25 (see Exercise 19), then what is the tea's actual cost?

At a certain restaurant, the wait time for a table is normally distributed with $\mu = 30$ minutes and $\sigma = 10$ minutes. Use the table on page 895 to estimate the following:

21. the probability that the wait time for a table is between 30 and 35 minutes

22. the probability that the wait time for a table is between 24 and 30 minutes

23. the probability that the wait time for a table is between 25 and 38 minutes

24. the probability that the wait time for a table is less than 22 minutes

Daytime high temperatures in New York in February are normally distributed with an average of 30.2° and a standard deviation of 8.5°.

25. Estimate the probability that the temperature on a given day in February is 39° or higher.

26. Estimate the probability that the temperature on a given day in February is 22° or lower.

27. Estimate the probability that the temperature on a given day in February is between 13° and 39°.

28. Estimate the probability that the temperature on a given day in February is between 25° and 30°.

29. Estimate the probability that the temperature on a given day in February is between 27° and 38°.

The *quartiles* of a normal distribution are the values that divide the area under the curve into fourths.

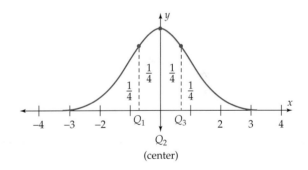

The 1st and 3rd quartiles are approximately 0.675σ to the left and right of the mean, or

$$Q_1 = \mu - 0.675\sigma \qquad \text{and} \qquad Q_3 = \mu + 0.675\sigma$$

30. Find Q_1 and Q_3 for a distribution with $\mu = 20$ and $\sigma = 4$.

31. Suppose the scores on an exam are normally distributed with $\mu = 70$ and $\sigma = 10$. Find Q_1 and Q_3, and interpret the result.

32. For the exam in Exercise 31, what exam score would place a student in the top 25% of the class?

CHAPTER

13

REVIEW

Important Concepts

Important Facts and Formulas

mean: $\bar{x} = \dfrac{\Sigma x_i}{n}$

If $x_1, x_2, x_3, \ldots x_n$ are ordered from smallest to largest, then the median is the middle entry when n is odd and the average of the two middle entries when n is even.

$$\text{median} = \begin{cases} \text{for } n \text{ odd, the value in the } \dfrac{n+1}{2} \text{ position} \\ \text{for } n \text{ even, the average of the values in} \\ \quad \text{the } \dfrac{n}{2} \text{ and } \dfrac{n}{2}+1 \text{ positions} \end{cases}$$

Population standard deviation

$$\sigma = \sqrt{\dfrac{\Sigma(x_i - \bar{x})^2}{n}}$$

Sample standard deviation

$$s = \sqrt{\dfrac{\Sigma(x_i - \bar{x})^2}{n-1}}$$

Suppose an experiment has a sample space of n outcomes, all of which are equally likely. Then the probability of each outcome is $\dfrac{1}{n}$, and the probability of an event E is given by

$$P(E) = \dfrac{\text{number of outcomes in } E}{n}$$

Fundamental Counting Principle

Consider a set of k experiments. Suppose the first experiment has n_1 outcomes, the second has n_2 outcomes, and so on. Then the total number of outcomes is $n_1 \cdot n_2 \cdot \ldots \cdot n_k$ for all k experiments.

Permutations

If r items are chosen in order without replacement from n possible items, the number of permutations is

$$_nP_r = \dfrac{n!}{(n-r)!}$$

Combinations

If r items are chosen in any order without replacement from n possible items, the number of combinations is

$$_nC_r = \dfrac{n!}{r!(n-r)!}$$

In a binomial experiment, $P(r \text{ successes in } n \text{ trials}) = {}_nC_r p^r q^{n-r}$ where p is the probability of success, and $q = 1 - p$ is the probability of failure. The expected value of a binomial distribution is np, and the standard deviation is $\sqrt{npq}$.

A random variable is said to have a normal distribution with mean μ and standard deviation σ if its density function is given by the equation

$$y = \frac{1}{\sigma\sqrt{2\pi}}e^{-\frac{(x-\mu)^2}{2\sigma^2}}$$

Empirical Rule

In a normal distribution:

- about 68% of the data values are within one standard deviation of the mean.

- about 95% of the data values are within two standard deviations of the mean.

- about 99.7% of the data values are within three standard deviations of the mean.

The z-value of the value x in a data set with mean μ and standard deviation σ is $z = \frac{x - \mu}{\sigma}$.

Review Exercises

Exercises 1–4 refer to the following description: A group of bird-watchers is trying to determine what types of birds are common to their area. The group observed 21 sparrows, 15 purple finches, 10 chickadees, 5 cardinals, and 2 blue jays.

Section 13.1

1. Is the data qualitative or quantitative?

2. Create a frequency table for the data.

3. Create a bar graph for the data.

4. Create a pie chart for the data.

Exercises 5–17 refer to the following description: a study is done to determine the average commuting time of employees at a company. A total of 34 employees are surveyed, with the following results (in minutes).

31.9, 34, 30.7, 39, 33.1, 35.2, 30.5, 32.7, 29.4, 33.4, 22.3, 31.9, 32.3, 29.4, 33, 18.2, 29.1, 32.5, 22.2, 36.1, 27.7, 36, 31.9, 26, 31.7, 23.2, 30.7, 24.4, 33, 28.4, 28.8, 23.3, 32.2, 22.8

5. Is the data qualitative or quantitative?

6. Is the data discrete or continuous?

7. Create a stem plot for the data.

8. Create a histogram for the data with class intervals of 5 minutes.

9. Use your histogram from Exercise 8 to describe the shape of the data.

Section   13.2

10. Find the mean of the data.

11. Find the median of the data.

12. Find the mode of the data.

13. Find the sample standard deviation of the data.

14. Find the range of the data.

15. Find the first and third quartiles of the data.

16. Find the interquartile range of the data.

17. Create a box plot for the data.

Section   13.3

Exercises 18–22 refer to the following probability distribution:

Outcome	1	2	3	4	5
Probability	0.1	?	0.4	?	0.1

18. List the sample space for the probability distribution.

19. Suppose the probabilities are the same for outcomes 2 and 4. Complete the probability distribution.

20. What is the probability that the outcome is an even number?

21. What is the probability that the outcome is greater than 2?

22. Suppose the experiment with the given probability distribution is repeated 3 times. Assuming the trials are independent, what is the probability of the outcome {1, 2, 3}?

An experiment consists of spinning the spinner at left 3 times. A probability distribution for the outcomes is given below. (W = white, R = red)

Outcome	WWW	WWR	WRW	RWW	WRR	RWR	RRW	RRR
Probability	0.512	0.128	0.128	0.128	0.032	0.032	0.032	0.008

A random variable is assigned to the number of times the spinner lands on red.

23. What is the range of the random variable?

24. What is the probability that the value of the random variable is 2?

25. Create a probability distribution for the random variable.

26. Find the expected value of the random variable, and interpret the result.

27. Graph the probability density function of the random variable, and shade the area of the graph that corresponds to the probability that the spinner lands on white 3 times.

Section **13.4**

28. Suppose the experiment is repeated 25 times, with the following results: WRW, RRW, WWW, WWW, WWW, WWW, WWR, RWW, WWW, WRW, WWW, WWR, WWW, RWW, WWW, RWR, WWW, WRW, WWW, RWW, WWW, WWW, WRW, WWW, WWR

Write a probability distribution of the random variable, based on the experimental results. How do the probabilities compare to your results in Exercise 25?

Exercises 29–33 refer to the following experiment: A sock drawer contains 6 identical black socks, 8 identical white socks, and 1 blue sock. A sock is chosen randomly from the drawer. Assume all socks are equally likely to be chosen.

29. What is the probability of choosing a black sock? a white sock? a blue sock?

30. Suppose a black sock is chosen. What is the probability that the next sock chosen will also be black? *Hint:* how many of each color are left in the drawer?

31. Suppose a white sock is chosen. What is the probability that the next sock chosen will also be white? *Hint:* how many of each color are left in the drawer?

32. Suppose a blue sock is chosen. What is the probability that the next sock chosen will also be blue? *Hint:* how many of each color are left in the drawer?

33. Use your results from Exercises 30 – 32 to determine the probability of choosing a pair if two socks are chosen randomly from the drawer.

34. A lottery ticket involves matching 5 numbers between 1 and 50 in any order. What is the probability of matching all 5 numbers? What is the probability of matching any 4 numbers?

35. Suppose there are 4 people on a subcommittee, and you do not know their last names. If you have a list of 10 last names of all of the people in the committee, what is the probability of correctly guessing the last names of the people in the subcommittee?

Section   13.4.A

A binomial experiment consists of randomly choosing 7 tiles imprinted with letters of the alphabet. An outcome of a vowel is considered a success, and a consonant is considered a failure. The probability of success is $p = 0.44$.

36. Complete the probability distribution below for the number of vowels.

Number of vowels	0	1	2	3	4	5	6	7
Probability	?	?	?	?	?	?	?	?

37. Find the expected value and standard deviation of the number of vowels.

Suppose the scores on an exam are normally distributed with $\mu = 75$ and $\sigma = 8$. Use properties of the normal curve, the empirical rule, and the table on page 895 to answer Exercises 38–46.

38. Write the equation of the normal curve for the distribution of the scores.

39. Graph the normal curve for the distribution of the scores.

40. Estimate the probability that a randomly chosen score is greater than 75.

41. Estimate the probability that a randomly chosen score is between 67 and 83.

42. Estimate the probability that a randomly chosen score is greater than 59.

43. Estimate the probability that a randomly chosen score is less than 99.

44. Estimate the probability that a randomly chosen score is between 75 and 78.

45. Estimate the probability that a randomly chosen score is between 70 and 82.

Section   13.5

46. Estimate the probability that a randomly chosen score is less than 74.

can do calculus

Area Under a Curve

Many applications of calculus involve finding the area under a curve. In probability, for example, it is often necessary to find areas under a normal curve or other probability density function. In other areas, such as physics, the area under a curve can be used to determine total distance traveled or the total amount of force on an object. In this section, properties of probability are used to estimate the area under a curve.

Example 1 Area Model for Probability

Consider the graph in Figure 13.C-1. Suppose a point in the rectangle is chosen randomly. If A is the area of the shaded region, write a formula in terms of A, a, b, and h for the probability that the point is in the shaded region.

Figure 13.C-1

Solution

If the point is chosen randomly, then all points in the sample space are equally likely to be chosen. The sample space is all points in the rectangle, and the event above can be described as the set of all points in the shaded area, both of which are infinite. Since it is impossible to divide the number of outcomes in the event by the number of outcomes in the sample space, the areas of the regions are used instead. The area of the rectangle is $h(b - a)$.

$$P(E) = \frac{\text{area of shaded region}}{\text{area of rectangle}} = \frac{A}{h(b - a)}$$

A probability simulation can also be used to find the probability in Example 1. Suppose $n = 1000$ points in the rectangle are chosen randomly, and 470 of them are in the shaded region. Recall that the experimental estimate of the probability of an event is

$$P(E) \approx \frac{\text{number of trials with an outcome in } E}{n} \approx \frac{470}{1000} \approx 0.47$$

By setting the two probability estimates equal to each other and solving, a formula can be found for the area A in terms of a, b, and h.

$$\frac{A}{h(b - a)} \approx 0.47$$
$$A \approx 0.47\, h(b - a)$$

Area Under a Curve

In general, the area A under a curve between the x-values a and b with $a < b$ may be estimated as follows:

1. Draw a rectangle with a base of length $b - a$ that contains the desired area. Let h be the height of the rectangle.

2. Randomly choose n points in the rectangle, using a calculator or computer. Determine the number of points e that lie in the desired area.

3. The area is approximated by the formula below.

$$A \approx \frac{e}{n} h(b - a)$$

Using Probability Simulations

To generate a large number of points and determine the number of points that lie under a curve, a calculator or computer program is usually used. A sample program is given below. The equation of the graph must be entered in Y_1, and the calculator window should contain the desired region. Note: the choice of window will not affect the answer.

Prompt A	*A is the left bound of the rectangle.*
Prompt B	*B is the right bound of the rectangle.*
Prompt H	*H is the height of the rectangle.*
Prompt N	*N is the number of points in the rectangle.*
$0 \to E$	*E is the number of points in the shaded region.*
For (K, 1, N)	
$(B - A)\text{rand} + A \to X$	*This command generates an x-coordinate, X.*
$H \text{ rand} \to Y$	*This command generates a y-coordinate, Y.*
Pt-On (X, Y)	*This command displays the point (X, Y).*
If $Y \leq Y_1(X)$	*The point is tested to determine whether it is*
$E + 1 \to E$	*under the curve.*
End	
Disp $(E/N)H(B - A)$	*This command displays the estimate of the area.*

Example 2   Area of a Quarter-Circle

Use a probability simulation to estimate the area under the curve with equation $y = \sqrt{1 - x^2}$ from 0 to 1. Since this region is one-fourth of a circle with radius 1, the area should be $\frac{\pi}{4} \approx 0.785$.

Solution

The result of a simulation with $n = 500$ points is shown in Figure 13.C-2. The area estimate is 0.782, which is very close to the predicted area.

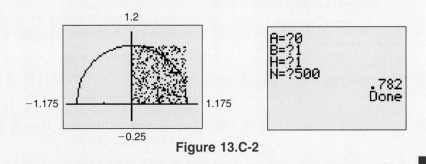

Figure 13.C-2

This method can also be used to find areas under a normal curve.

Example 3   Area Under a Normal Curve

a. Use a probability simulation to estimate the area under the normal curve with $\mu = 70$ and $\sigma = 10$ between $a = 85$ and $b = 95$.

b. Suppose the scores on an exam are normally distributed with $\mu = 70$ and $\sigma = 10$. Estimate the probability that a randomly chosen score is between 85 and 95.

Solution

a. The normal curve has the equation $y = 0.03989e^{-0.005(x-70)^2}$. Trace to find a good value of h. The closer the value of h is to the maximum value of the function over the given interval, the better the estimate will be. A good choice of h is 0.014. The result of a simulation with $n = 500$ points is shown in Figure 13.C-3. The area estimate is 0.0616.

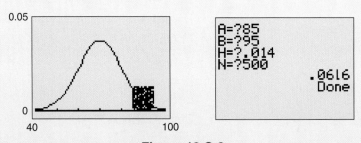

Figure 13.C-3

b. The probability that a randomly chosen score is between 85 and 95 is approximately the area under the normal curve, or about 0.06.

Exercises

In Exercises 1–6, estimate the area under the given curve between the given values of a and b.

1. $y = x^2$ $\qquad$ $a = 0, b = 1$

2. $y = \sin x$ $\qquad$ $a = 0, b = \pi$

3. $y = -x^2 + 5x - 4$ $\qquad$ $a = 1, b = 4$

4. $y = e^{-x}$ $\qquad$ $a = 2, b = 10$

5. $y = \dfrac{1}{x}$ $\qquad$ $a = 3, b = 5$

6. $y = \sqrt{x}$ $\qquad$ $a = 7, b = 9$

7. Suppose the weights of apples from a certain tree are normally distributed with $\mu = 138$ g and $\sigma = 18$ g. Estimate the probability that a randomly chosen apple weighs between 100 g and 150 g.

8. The function $y = \dfrac{1}{\sqrt{x}}$ is not defined at $x = 0$, and the graph has a vertical asymptote. However, calculus can be used to show that the area under the curve from 0 to 1 is finite. Use a probability simulation to estimate the area by letting $a = 0$ and $b = 1$. Compare the value of the area estimates for $h = 3, 4$, and 5. Run the simulation at least twice for each value of h to be sure you have a good estimate.

9. Use a probability simulation to verify that the area under the standard normal curve is 1. *Hint:* according to the Empirical Rule, 99.7% of the area under a normal curve is within 3σ of the mean.

Limits and Continuity

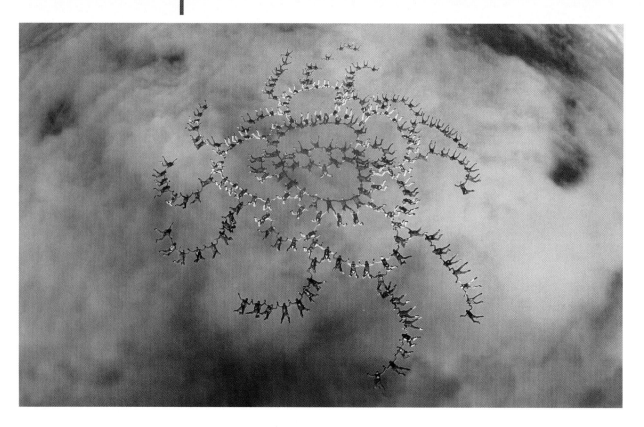

Terminal Velocity

Parachutists have two forces acting on them, as does any free-falling body. One force is gravity, which causes the body to speed up as it falls, and the other is air resistance, which causes the body to slow down. As the body moves faster, the air resistance builds until it nearly balances the gravitational force. So the body speeds up very little after it has fallen some distance. Terminal velocity is achieved when the air resistance approaches the gravitational pull. See Exercise 43 in Section 14.5.

Chapter Outline

Interdependence of Sections

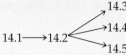

The mathematics presented in previous chapters deals with static problems, such as

> What is the size of the angle?
>
> What is the average speed of a car between $t = 0$ and $t = 5$ minutes?

Calculus, on the other hand, deals with dynamic problems, such as

> At what rate is the angle increasing in size?
>
> How fast is the car going at time $t = 4.2$ minutes?

The key to dealing with such dynamic problems is the concept of limit, which is introduced in this chapter.

Limits of Functions

Many mathematical problems involve the behavior of a function at a particular number:

> What is the value of the function $f(x)$ when $x = c$?

The underlying idea of **limit,** however, is the behavior of the function *near* $x = c$ rather than *at* $x = c$. You have dealt with limits informally in previous chapters, but this section will discuss limits in more detail and give the notation used when talking about them.

Suppose you want to describe the behavior of

$$f(x) = \frac{0.1x^4 - 0.8x^3 + 1.6x^2 + 2x - 8}{x - 4}$$

when x is very close to 4. Notice that the function is not defined when $x = 4$. To see what happens to the values of $f(x)$ when x is very close to 4, observe the graph of the function in the viewing window shown in Figure 14.1-1. (See the Technology Tip about how to produce a graph that shows the hole.)

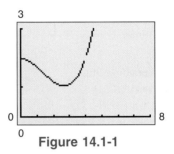

Figure 14.1-1

To further explore the behavior of the function near $x = 4$, perform the following Graphing Exploration.

Graphing Exploration

Graph $f(x)$ in the viewing window with $3.5 \leq x \leq 4.5$ and $0 \leq y \leq 3$. Use the trace feature to move along the graph, and examine the values of $f(x)$ when x takes values close to 4. Your results should be consistent with the following table of values.

	x approaches 4 from the left				*x approaches 4 from the right*		
x	3.9	3.99	3.999	4	4.001	4.01	4.1
$f(x)$	1.8479	1.9841	1.9984	*	2.0016	2.0161	2.168

The exploration and the table suggest that as x gets closer and closer to 4 from either side, the corresponding values of $f(x)$ get closer and closer to 2. Furthermore, by taking x close enough to 4, the corresponding values can be made *as close as you want to* 2.

For instance,

$$f(3.99999) = 1.999984 \quad \text{and} \quad f(4.00001) = 2.000016$$

Notation

The statement above is usually expressed by saying

"The limit of $f(x)$ as x approaches 4 is 2,"

which is written symbolically as

$$\lim_{x \to 4} f(x) = 2 \quad \text{or} \quad \lim_{x \to 4} \frac{0.1x^4 - 0.8x^3 + 1.6x^2 + 2x - 8}{x - 4} = 2$$

Informal Definition of Limit

The following definition of "limit" in the general case is similar to the situation previously described, but now f is any function, c and L are fixed real numbers, and the phrase "arbitrarily close" means "as close as you want." In the previous discussion, $c = 4$ and $L = 2$.

Informal Definition of Limit

> Let f be a function and let c be a real number such that $f(x)$ is defined for all values of x near $x = c$, except possibly at $x = c$ itself. Suppose that
>
> > whenever x takes values closer and closer but not equal to c (on both sides of c), the corresponding values of $f(x)$ get very close to, and possibly equal, to the same real number L
>
> and that
>
> > the values of $f(x)$ can be made arbitrarily close to L by taking values of x close enough to c, but not equal to c.
>
> Then it is said that
>
> > The limit of the function $f(x)$ as x approaches c is the number L,
>
> which is written
>
> $$\lim_{x \to c} f(x) = L$$

NOTE The limit in Example 1 is very important in calculus.

Example 1   **Limit of a Function**

If $f(x) = \dfrac{\sin x}{x}$, find $\lim_{x \to 0} f(x)$.

Solution

Although $f(x)$ is not defined when $x = 0$, a calculator's trace feature can be used with the graph of the function to examine the values of $f(x)$ when x is very close to 0. The table feature can also be used.

Calculator Exploration ●

Create a table of values for $f(x) = \dfrac{\sin x}{x}$ with values of x both smaller than and larger than $x = 0$. Are the function values approaching the same value as x approaches 0 from both sides?

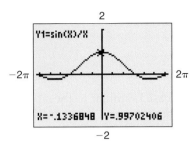

2

Y1=sin(X)/X

-2π 2π

X=-.1336848 Y=.99702406

-2

Figure 14.1-2

The exploration should suggest that

$$\lim_{x \to 0} f(x) = 1 \text{ or equivalently, } \lim_{x \to 0} \frac{\sin x}{x} = 1,$$

a fact that will be proved in calculus.

Example 2   **Limit of a Function**

Find $\lim_{x \to 2} f(x)$, where f is the function given by the following two-part rule.

$$f(x) = \begin{cases} 0 \text{ if } x \text{ is an integer} \\ 1 \text{ if } x \text{ is not an integer} \end{cases}$$

Solution

A calculator is not much help here, but the function is easily graphed by hand.

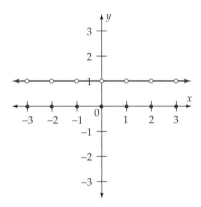

Figure 14.1-3

When x is a number very close but not equal to 2 (either greater than 2 or less than 2), the corresponding value of $f(x)$ is 1, and this is true no matter how close x is to 2. Thus,

$$\lim_{x \to 2} f(x) = 1.$$

Because $f(2) = 0$ by definition, the limit of f as x approaches 2 is *not* the same as the value of the function f at $x = 2$.

Limits and Function Values

> If the limit of a function f as x approaches c exists, this limit may *not* be equal to $f(c)$. In fact, $f(c)$ may not even be defined.

Very often the limit of a function as x approaches a point is equal to the value of the function at that point.

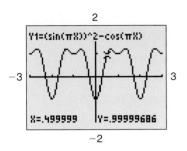

Figure 14.1-4

Example 3 Limit of a Function and a Function Value

If $f(x) = \sin^2 \pi x - \cos \pi x$, find $f(0.5)$ and $\lim_{x \to 0.5} f(x)$.

Solution

$$f(0.5) = f\left(\frac{1}{2}\right) = \sin^2 \frac{\pi}{2} - \cos \frac{\pi}{2} = 1^2 - 0 = 1.$$

Using the trace feature on the graph of $f(x)$, shown in Figure 14.1-4, suggests that the limit is a number near 1.

A much narrower viewing window is needed to determine the limit more precisely.

Graphing Exploration •

Graph $f(x)$ in a viewing window with $0.49 \le x \le 0.51$ and $0.99 \le y \le 1.01$. Use the trace feature to move along the graph on both sides of $x = 0.5$ and confirm that as x gets closer and closer to 0.5, $f(x)$ gets closer and closer to 1.

The Exploration suggests that

$$\lim_{x \to 0.5} f(x) = 1 = f(0.5).$$

Thus, the value of the function at $x = 0.5$ is the same as the limit as x approaches 0.5. ∎

NOTE Whenever a calculator was used in preceding examples, it was said that the information provided by the calculator *suggested* that the limit of the function was a particular number. Although such calculator explorations provide strong evidence, they do not constitute a proof and in some instances can be very misleading. (See Exercise 36.) Nevertheless, a calculator can help you develop an intuitive understanding for limits, which is needed for a rigorous treatment of the concept.

Nonexistence of Limits

Not every function has a limit at every number. Limits can fail to exist for several reasons.

Nonexistence of Limits

The limit of a function f as x approaches c may fail to exist if:

1. $f(x)$ becomes infinitely large or infinitely small as x approaches c from either side

2. $f(x)$ approaches L as x approaches c from the right and $f(x)$ approaches M, with $M \neq L$, as x approaches c from the left

3. $f(x)$ oscillates infinitely many times between two numbers as x approaches c from either side

The examples that follow illustrate each of these possibilities.

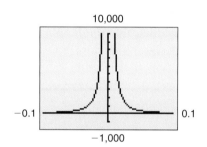

Figure 14.1-5

Example 4 A Function that Approaches Infinity

Discuss the existence of $\lim\limits_{x \to 0} \dfrac{1}{x^2}$.

Solution

Figure 14.1-5 shows the graph of $f(x) = \dfrac{1}{x^2}$ near $x = 0$. As x approaches 0 from the left or right, the corresponding values of $f(x)$ become larger and larger without bound—rather than approaching one particular number—which can be verified by using the trace feature. Therefore, $\lim\limits_{x \to 0} \dfrac{1}{x^2}$ does not exist.

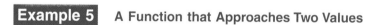

Figure 14.1-6a

Example 5 A Function that Approaches Two Values

Find $\lim\limits_{x \to 0} \dfrac{|x|}{x}$, if it exists.

Solution

The function $f(x) = \dfrac{|x|}{x}$ is not defined when $x = 0$.

According to the definition of absolute value, $|x| = x$ when $x > 0$ and $|x| = -x$ when $x < 0$. There are two possibilities.

$$\text{If } x > 0, \text{ then } f(x) = \frac{|x|}{x} = \frac{x}{x} = 1.$$

$$\text{If } x < 0, \text{ then } f(x) = \frac{|x|}{x} = \frac{-x}{x} = -1$$

Consequently, the graph of f looks like Figure 14.1-6a. A table of values for $f(x)$ is shown in Figure 14.1-6b.

If x approaches 0 from the right, that is, through positive values, then the

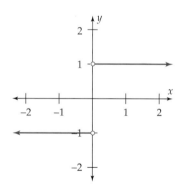

Figure 14.1-6b

corresponding value of $f(x)$ is always 1. If x approaches 0 from the left, that is, from negative values, then the corresponding value of $f(x)$ is always -1. Thus, as x approaches 0 from both sides of 0, the corresponding values of $f(x)$ do not approach the same real number, as required by the definition of limit. Therefore, the limit does not exist. ∎

Example 6 An Oscillating Function

Find $\lim\limits_{x \to 0} \sin \frac{\pi}{x}$, if it exists.

Solution

To understand the behavior of $f(x) = \sin \frac{\pi}{x}$, consider what happens when x is close to 0.

As x takes values:	Then $\frac{\pi}{x}$ takes values:
from $\frac{1}{2}$ to $\frac{1}{4}$	2π to 4π
from $\frac{1}{4}$ to $\frac{1}{6}$	4π to 6π
from $\frac{1}{6}$ to $\frac{1}{8}$	6π to 8π

Thus, the graph of $\sin \frac{\pi}{x}$ completes one period of the sine function from $x = \frac{1}{2}$ to $x = \frac{1}{4}$, another from $x = \frac{1}{4}$ to $x = \frac{1}{6}$, and so on. A similar phenomenon occurs for negative values of x. Consequently, the graph of f oscillates infinitely often between -1 and 1, with the waves becoming more and more compressed as x approaches 0, as shown in Figure 14.1-7.

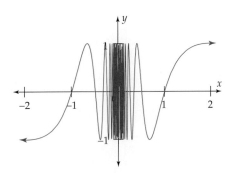

Figure 14.1-7

As x approaches 0, the function takes every value between -1 and 1 infinitely many times. In particular, $f(x)$ does not approach one particular real number. Therefore, $\lim\limits_{x \to 0} \sin \frac{\pi}{x}$ does not exist. ∎

Exercises 14.1

In Exercises 1–10, complete the table and use the result to estimate the given limit.

1. $\lim\limits_{x \to 3} \dfrac{x-3}{x^2-2x-3}$

x	2.9	2.99	2.999	3.001	3.01	3.1
$f(x)$						

2. $\lim\limits_{x \to 3} \dfrac{x-3}{x^2-9}$

x	2.9	2.99	2.999	3.001	3.01	3.1
$f(x)$						

3. $\lim\limits_{x \to 0} \dfrac{\sqrt{x+2}-\sqrt{2}}{x}$

x	−0.1	−0.01	−0.001	0.001	0.01	0.1
$f(x)$						

4. $\lim\limits_{x \to 0} \dfrac{\sqrt{x+5}-\sqrt{5}}{x}$

x	−0.1	−0.01	−0.001	0.001	0.01	0.1
$f(x)$						

5. $\lim\limits_{x \to -7} \dfrac{\sqrt{2-x}-3}{x+7}$

x	−7.1	−7.01	−7.001	−6.999	−6.99	−6.9
$f(x)$						

6. $\lim\limits_{x \to 0} \dfrac{\sqrt{1-x}-1}{x}$

x	−0.1	−0.01	−0.001	0.001	0.01	0.1
$f(x)$						

7. $\lim\limits_{x \to 1} \dfrac{\dfrac{1}{x+2}-\dfrac{1}{3}}{x-1}$

x	0.9	0.99	0.999	1.001	1.01	1.1
$f(x)$						

8. $\lim\limits_{x \to -1} \dfrac{\dfrac{1}{x+3}-\dfrac{1}{2}}{x+1}$

x	−1.1	−1.01	−1.001	−0.999	−0.99	−0.9
$f(x)$						

9. $\lim\limits_{x \to 0} \dfrac{\cos x - 1}{x}$

x	−0.1	−0.01	−0.001	0.001	0.01	0.1
$f(x)$						

10. $\lim\limits_{x \to \frac{\pi}{4}} \dfrac{\tan x - 1}{x - \dfrac{\pi}{4}}$

x	0.78	0.785	0.7853	0.7854	0.7855	0.786
$f(x)$						

In Exercises 11–26, use a calculator to find a reasonable estimate of the limit. If the limit does not exist, explain why.

11. $\lim\limits_{x \to -1} \dfrac{x^6-1}{x^4-1}$

12. $\lim\limits_{x \to 2} \dfrac{x^5-32}{x^3-8}$

13. $\lim\limits_{x \to 3} \dfrac{x^2-x-6}{x^2-2x-3}$

14. $\lim\limits_{x \to 1} \dfrac{x^2-1}{x^2+x-2}$

15. $\lim\limits_{x \to 1} \dfrac{x^3-1}{x^2-1}$

16. $\lim\limits_{x \to -2} \dfrac{x^2+5x+6}{x^2-x-6}$

17. $\lim\limits_{x \to 0} \dfrac{\tan x - x}{x^3}$

18. $\lim\limits_{x \to 0} \dfrac{\tan x}{x + \sin x}$

19. $\lim\limits_{x \to 0} \dfrac{x - \tan x}{x - \sin x}$

20. $\lim\limits_{x \to 0} \dfrac{x + \sin 2x}{x - \sin 2x}$

21. $\lim\limits_{x \to 3} \dfrac{\sqrt{x}-\sqrt{3}}{x-3}$

22. $\lim\limits_{x \to 25} \dfrac{\sqrt{x}-5}{x-25}$

23. $\lim\limits_{x \to 0} \dfrac{x}{\ln|x|}$

24. $\lim\limits_{x \to 0} \dfrac{e^{2x}-1}{x}$

25. $\lim\limits_{x\to 0} \dfrac{e^x - 1}{\sin x}$

26. $\lim\limits_{x\to 0}\left(x\sin\dfrac{1}{x}\right)$

In Exercises 27–32, use the graph of the function f to determine the following:

$$\lim\limits_{x\to -3} f(x) \qquad \lim\limits_{x\to 0} f(x) \qquad \lim\limits_{x\to 2} f(x)$$

27.

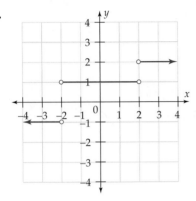

28.

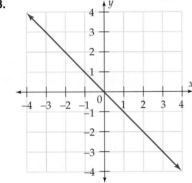

29.

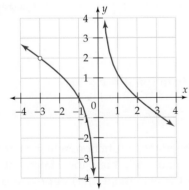

30.

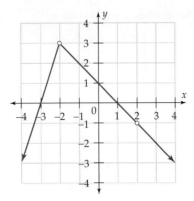

31.

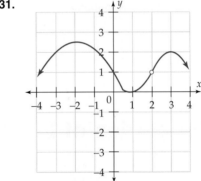

32.

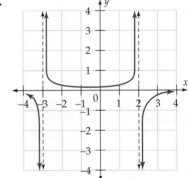

33. a. Graph the function f whose rule is

$$f(x) = \begin{cases} 3 - x & \text{if } x < -2 \\ x + 2 & \text{if } -2 \le x < 2 \\ 1 & \text{if } x = 2 \\ 4 - x & \text{if } x > 2 \end{cases}$$

Use the graph in part **a** to evaluate the following limits.

b. $\lim\limits_{x\to -2} f(x)$ **c.** $\lim\limits_{x\to 1} f(x)$ **d.** $\lim\limits_{x\to 2} f(x)$

34. a. Graph the function g whose rule is

$$g(x) = \begin{cases} x^2 & \text{if } x < -1 \\ x + 2 & \text{if } -1 \le x < 1 \\ 2 & \text{if } x = 1 \\ 3 - x & \text{if } x > 1 \end{cases}$$

Use the graph in part **a** to evaluate the following limits.

b. $\lim\limits_{x \to -1} g(x)$ **c.** $\lim\limits_{x \to 0} g(x)$ **d.** $\lim\limits_{x \to 1} g(x)$

35. *Critical Thinking* Consider the function t whose rule is

$$t(x) = \begin{cases} 0 \text{ if } x \text{ is rational} \\ 1 \text{ if } x \text{ is irrational} \end{cases}$$

Explain why $\lim\limits_{x \to c} t(x)$ does not exist for every value of c.

36. *Critical Thinking* If $f(x) = \dfrac{1 - \cos x^6}{x^{12}}$, then

$\lim\limits_{x \to 0} f(x) = \dfrac{1}{2}$, as is shown in calculus. A calculator or computer, however, may indicate otherwise. Graph $f(x)$ in a viewing window with $-0.1 \le x \le 0.1$, and use the trace feature to determine the values of $f(x)$ when x approaches 0. What does this suggest that the limit is?

14.2 Properties of Limits

Objectives

- Find the limit of
  the constant function
  the identity function

- Use the properties of limits

- Find the limit of
  polynomial functions
  rational functions

- Use the Limit Theorem

Most of the functions that appear in calculus are combinations of simpler functions, such as sums, products, quotients, and compositions. This section presents rules for finding limits of combinations of functions without a table or a graph.

There are two easy, but important, cases where the limit of a function may be found by evaluating the function. The first occurs with constant functions, such as $f(x) = 5$. To find $\lim\limits_{x \to 3} f(x)$, that is, $\lim\limits_{x \to 3} 5$, note that as x approaches 3, the corresponding value of $f(x)$ is *always* the number 5, so that $\lim\limits_{x \to 3} f(x) = \lim\limits_{x \to 3} 5 = 5$. Thus, $\lim\limits_{x \to 3} f(x)$ is the number $f(3) = 5$. The same thing is true for any constant function.

Limit of a Constant

If d is a constant, then $\lim\limits_{x \to c} d = d$.

The same phenomenon occurs with the identity function, which is given by the rule $I(x) = x$. If c is any real number, then the statement "x approaches c" is exactly the same as the statement "$I(x)$ approaches c" because $I(x) = x$ for every x. Thus,

Limit of the Identity Function

For every real number c, $\lim\limits_{x \to c} x = c$.

Properties of Limits

There are a number of facts that greatly simplify the computation of limits. Rigorous proofs of these properties will not be given, knowing the central idea is more important now. For instance, suppose that as x approaches c, the values of a function f approach a number L and the values of a function g approach a number M. Then it is plausible that as x approaches c, the values of the function $f + g$ approach $L + M$ and that the values of the function $f \cdot g$ approach $L \cdot M$. Following is a formal statement in terms of limits.

Properties of Limits

If f and g are functions and c, L, and M are numbers such that

$$\lim_{x \to c} f(x) = L \quad \text{and} \quad \lim_{x \to c} g(x) = M,$$

then

1. $\lim_{x \to c} (f + g)(x) = \lim_{x \to c}[f(x) + g(x)]$
$$= L + M$$

2. $\lim_{x \to c} (f - g)(x) = \lim_{x \to c}[f(x) - g(x)]$
$$= L - M$$

3. $\lim_{x \to c} (f \cdot g)(x) = \lim_{x \to c}[f(x) \cdot g(x)]$
$$= L \cdot M$$

4. $\lim_{x \to c} \left(\frac{f}{g}\right)(x) = \lim_{x \to c}\left(\frac{f(x)}{g(x)}\right)$
$$= \frac{L}{M} \quad \text{(for } M \neq 0)$$

5. $\lim_{x \to c} \sqrt{f(x)} = \sqrt{L}$ (provided $f(x) \geq 0$ for all x near c)

NOTE In Property 4, $\lim_{x \to c}\left(\frac{f}{g}\right)(x)$ does not exist if $M = 0$ and $L \neq 0$. If $M = 0$ and $L = 0$, the limit may or may not exist.

These properties are often stated somewhat differently. For instance, because $\lim_{x \to c} f(x) = L$ and $\lim_{x \to c} g(x) = M$, Property 1 can be written as

$$\lim_{x \to c} (f + g)(x) = \lim_{x \to c} f(x) + \lim_{x \to c} g(x)$$

and similarly for the other properties.

Limits of Polynomial Functions

Properties 1–3, together with the facts about limits of constants and the identity function presented at the beginning of the section, now make it easy to find the limit of any polynomial function.

Example 1   Limit of a Polynomial Function

If $f(x) = x^2 - 2x + 3$, find $\lim_{x \to -4} f(x) = \lim_{x \to -4} (x^2 - 2x + 3)$.

Solution

$$\lim_{x \to -4} (x^2 - 2x + 3) = \lim_{x \to -4} x^2 - \lim_{x \to -4} 2x + \lim_{x \to -4} 3 \qquad \textit{Properties 1 and 2}$$

$$= \lim_{x \to -4} x \cdot \lim_{x \to -4} x - \lim_{x \to -4} 2 \cdot \lim_{x \to -4} x + \lim_{x \to -4} 3 \qquad \textit{Property 3}$$

$$= \lim_{x \to -4} x \cdot \lim_{x \to -4} x - 2 \lim_{x \to -4} x + 3 \qquad \textit{Limit of a constant}$$

$$= (-4)(-4) - \qquad 2(-4) \quad + 3 \qquad \textit{Limit of } x$$

$$= 16 - (-8) + 3$$

$$= 27$$

Note that the limit of $f(x) = x^2 - 2x + 3$ at $x = -4$ is the same as the value of the function at $x = -4$, namely, $f(-4) = (-4)^2 - 2(-4) + 3 = 27$. ∎

Because any polynomial function consists of sums and products of constants and x, the same argument used in Example 1 works for any polynomial function and leads to the following conclusion.

Limits of Polynomial Functions

If $f(x)$ is a polynomial function and c is any real number, then

$$\lim_{x \to c} f(x) = f(c).$$

In other words, the limit is the value of the polynomial function f at $x = c$.

Limits of Rational Functions

The fact in the previous box and Property 4 of limits make it easy to compute limits of many rational functions.

Example 2 Limit of a Rational Function

If $f(x) = \dfrac{x^3 - 3x^2 + 10}{x^2 - 6x + 1}$, find $\lim_{x \to 2} f(x)$.

Solution

The graph of f near $x = 2$ suggests that the limit is a number near -0.86, as shown in Figure 14.2-1. You can determine the limit exactly by noting that $f(x)$ is the quotient of the two functions

$$g(x) = x^3 - 3x^2 + 10 \qquad \text{and} \qquad h(x) = x^2 - 6x + 1.$$

As x approaches 2, the limit of each can be found by evaluation of the functions at $x = 2$. Therefore,

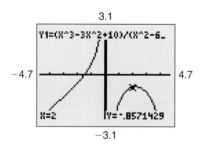

3.1

Y1=(X^3-3X^2+10)/(X^2-6.

−4.7   4.7

X=2   Y=-.8571429

−3.1

Figure 14.2-1

$$\lim_{x \to 2} f(x) = \lim_{x \to 2} \frac{x^3 - 3x^2 + 10}{x^2 - 6x + 1}$$

$$= \frac{\lim\limits_{x \to 2} x^3 - 3x^2 + 10}{\lim\limits_{x \to 2} x^2 - 6x + 1} \qquad \textit{limit property 4}$$

$$= \frac{2^3 - 3 \cdot 2^2 + 10}{2^2 - 6 \cdot 2 + 1} \qquad \textit{limits of polynomial functions}$$

$$= \frac{6}{-7} = -\frac{6}{7} \approx -0.857$$

Note that the limit of $f(x)$ as x approaches 2 is the number $f(2)$. ∎

The procedure in Example 2 works for other rational functions as well.

Limits of Rational Functions

Let $f(x)$ be a rational function and let c be a real number such that $f(c)$ is defined. Then

$$\lim_{x \to c} f(x) = f(c).$$

In other words, the limit of a rational function as x approaches c is the value of the function at $x = c$, if the function is defined there.

When a rational function is not defined at a number, different techniques must be used to find its limit there—if it exists.

Example 3   Limit of a Rational Function

If $f(x) = \dfrac{x^2 - 2x - 3}{x - 3}$, find $\lim\limits_{x \to 3} f(x)$.

Solution

Because $f(x)$ is not defined when $x = 3$, the limit cannot be found by evaluating the function. Although it could be estimated graphically, it can be found by using algebraic methods. Begin by factoring the numerator.

$$\frac{x^2 - 2x - 3}{x - 3} = \frac{(x + 1)(x - 3)}{x - 3}$$

Because the numerator and denominator have a common factor, the rational expression may be reduced.

$$\frac{(x + 1)(x - 3)}{x - 3} = x + 1, \text{ for all } x \neq 3.$$

The definition of the limit as x approaches 3 involves only the behavior of the function *near* $x = 3$ and not *at* $x = 3$. The preceding equation shows that both $f(x)$ and the function $g(x) = x + 1$ have exactly the same

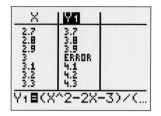

Figure 14.2-2

values at all numbers except $x = 3$. So they must have the same limit as x approaches 3.

$$\lim_{x \to 3} \frac{x^2 - 2x - 3}{x - 3} = \lim_{x \to 3} (x + 1) = 3 + 1 = 4,$$

as illustrated in Figure 14.2-2.

The technique illustrated in Example 3 applies in many cases. When two functions have identical behavior, except possibly at $x = c$, they will have the same limit as x approaches c.

Limit Theorem

> If f and g are functions that have limits as x approaches c and
>
> $$f(x) = g(x) \qquad \text{for all } x \neq c,$$
>
> then
>
> $$\lim_{x \to c} f(x) = \lim_{x \to c} g(x).$$

Recall that the difference quotient of a function f is given by

$$\frac{f(x + h) - f(x)}{h}$$

NOTE Do not confuse the variable h with the function h. The meaning should be clear in context.

The difference quotient can be evaluated for a specific value of x, say $x = c$, to obtain a new form.

$$\frac{f(c + h) - f(c)}{h}$$

Limits of the difference quotient of a function f play an important role in calculus. When computing such limits, the variable is often the quantity h, as in the following example.

Example 4 Limit of a Difference Quotient

If $f(x) = x^2$, find $\lim\limits_{h \to 0} \dfrac{f(5 + h) - f(5)}{h}$.

Solution

Using algebra, write the difference quotient as follows:

$$\begin{aligned} \frac{f(5 + h) - f(5)}{h} &= \frac{(5 + h)^2 - 5^2}{h} \\ &= \frac{(25 + 10h + h^2) - 25}{h} \\ &= \frac{10h + h^2}{h} \end{aligned}$$

When the difference quotient is written this way, it is easy to see that it is a function of h, and the function is not defined when $h = 0$. Find the limit of the difference quotient as h approaches 0.

$$\lim_{h \to 0} \frac{f(5 + h) - f(5)}{5} = \lim_{h \to 0} \frac{10h + h^2}{h}$$

$$= \lim_{h \to 0} \frac{h(10 + h)}{h} \qquad \textit{Factor the numerator.}$$

$$= \lim_{h \to 0} (10 + h) \qquad \textit{Limit Theorem}$$

$$= 10 + 0 = 10 \qquad \textit{limit of a polynomial function}$$

Exercises 14.2

In Exercises 1–8, use the following facts about the functions f, g, and h to find the required limit.

$$\lim_{x \to 4} f(x) = 5 \quad \lim_{x \to 4} g(x) = 0 \quad \lim_{x \to 4} h(x) = -2$$

1. $\lim_{x \to 4} (f + g)(x)$

2. $\lim_{x \to 4} (g - h)(x)$

3. $\lim_{x \to 4} \dfrac{f}{g}(x)$

4. $\lim_{x \to 4} \dfrac{g}{h}(x)$

5. $\lim_{x \to 4} (fg)(x)$

6. $\lim_{x \to 4} [h(x)]^2$

7. $\lim_{x \to 4} \left(\dfrac{3h}{2f + g} \right)(x)$

8. $\lim_{x \to 4} \left(\dfrac{f - 2g}{4h} \right)(x)$

In Exercises 9–23, find the limit, if it exists. If the limit does not exist, explain why.

9. $\lim_{x \to 2} (6x^3 - 2x^2 + 5x - 3)$

10. $\lim_{x \to -1} (x^7 + 2x^5 - x^4 + 3x + 4)$

11. $\lim_{x \to -2} \dfrac{3x - 1}{2x + 3}$

12. $\lim_{x \to 3} \dfrac{x^2 + x + 1}{x^2 - 2x}$

13. $\lim_{x \to 1} \sqrt{x^3 + 6x^2 + 2x + 5}$

14. $\lim_{x \to 2} \sqrt{x^2 + x + 3}$

15. $\lim_{x \to 0} \left(\dfrac{\dfrac{1}{x + 5} - \dfrac{1}{5}}{x} \right)$

16. $\lim_{x \to 0} \left(\dfrac{\dfrac{2}{x + 6} - \dfrac{1}{3}}{x} \right)$

17. $\lim_{x \to 1} \left(\dfrac{1}{x - 1} - \dfrac{2}{x^2 - 1} \right)$

18. $\lim_{x \to -2} \left[\dfrac{x^2}{x + 2} + \dfrac{2x}{x + 2} \right]$

19. $\lim_{x \to 0} \dfrac{x^2}{|x|}$

20. $\lim_{x \to -2} |x + 2|$

21. $\lim_{x \to 0} \dfrac{\sqrt{2 - x} - \sqrt{2}}{x}$

22. $\lim_{x \to 0} \left[\dfrac{|x|}{x} - \dfrac{x}{|x|} \right]$

23. $\lim_{x \to -3} \dfrac{|x + 3|}{x + 3}$

In Exercises 24–27, find

$$\lim_{h \to 0} \frac{f(2 + h) - f(2)}{h}.$$

24. $f(x) = x^2$

25. $f(x) = x^3$

26. $f(x) = x^2 + x + 1$

27. $f(x) = \sqrt{x}$

In Exercises 28–29, use a unit circle diagram to explain why the given statement is true.

28. $\lim_{t \to \frac{\pi}{2}} \sin t = 1$

29. $\lim_{t \to \frac{\pi}{2}} \cos t = 0$

Exercises 30–34 involve the greatest integer function, $f(x) = [x]$, which is defined to be the greatest integer that is less than or equal to a given number x. See Section 3.1. Use a calculator as an aid in analyzing these problems.

30. For $h(x) = [x] - [-x]$, find $\lim_{x \to 2} h(x)$, if the limit exists.

31. For $g(x) = x - [-x]$, find $\lim_{x \to 2} g(x)$, if the limit exists.

32. For $r(x) = \dfrac{[x] + [-x]}{x}$, find $\lim_{x \to 3} r(x)$, if the limit exists.

33. For $k(x) = \dfrac{x}{[x] + [-x]}$, find $\lim\limits_{x \to 1} k(x)$, if the limit exists.

34. For $f(x) = x|x|$, find $\lim\limits_{h \to 0} \dfrac{f(0 + h) - f(0)}{h}$.

35. *Critical Thinking* Give an example of functions f and g and a number c such that neither $\lim\limits_{x \to c} f(x)$ nor $\lim\limits_{x \to c} g(x)$ exists, but $\lim\limits_{x \to c} (f + g)(x)$ does exist.

36. *Critical Thinking* Given an example of functions f and g and a number c such that neither $\lim\limits_{x \to c} f(x)$ nor $\lim\limits_{x \to c} g(x)$ exists, but $\lim\limits_{x \to c} (fg)(x)$ does exist.

Excursion: One-Sided Limits

Objectives

• Find one-sided limits

The function whose graph is shown in Figure 14.2.A-1 is defined for all values of x except $x = 4$.

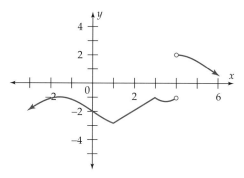

Figure 14.2.A-1

As x approaches 4 from the right, that is, takes values larger than but close to 4, the graph shows that the corresponding values of $f(x)$ get very close to 2. Consequently, "the limit of $f(x)$ as x approaches 4 from the right is 2."

$$\lim_{x \to 4^+} f(x) = 2$$

The small plus sign on 4 indicates that only the values of x with $x > 4$ are considered. Similarly, as x approaches 4 from the left, the graph shows that the corresponding values of $f(x)$ get very close to -1. Consequently, "the limit of $f(x)$ as x approaches 4 from the left is -1.

$$\lim_{x \to 4^-} f(x) = -1$$

The small minus sign indicates that only values of x with $x < 4$ are considered.

These "one-sided" limits are a bit different than the "two sided" limits discussed in Section 14.2. When x approaches 4 from the left and from the right, the corresponding values of $f(x)$ do not approach a single number, so the limit as x approaches 4, as defined in Section 14.2, does not exist.

The same notation and terminology are used in the general case, where f is any function and c and L are real numbers. The definition of the "right-hand limit,"

$$\lim_{x \to c^+} f(x) = L,$$

is obtained by inserting "$x > c$" in place of the phrase "on both sides of c" in the definition of limit in Section 14.2. The function f need not be defined when $x < c$.

Similarly, inserting "$x < c$" in place of "on both sides of c" in the same definition produces the definition of the "left-hand limit."

$$\lim_{x \to c^-} f(x) = L$$

Again, the function f need not be defined when $x > c$.

Example 1   One-Sided Limit

Find $\lim\limits_{x \to 3^+} \sqrt{x - 3} + 1$.

Solution

The function $f(x) = \sqrt{x - 3} + 1$ is defined only when $x \geq 3$, that is, for values of x to the right of 3. The graph of $f(x)$ is shown in Figure 14.2.A-2a, and a table of values is shown in 14.2.A-2b.

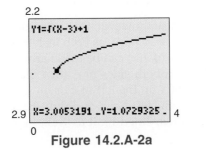

Figure 14.2.A-2a

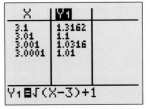

Figure 14.2.A-2b

The values of $f(x)$ approach 1 as x approaches 3 from the right. Therefore, $\lim\limits_{x \to 3^+} \sqrt{x - 3} + 1 = 1$.

Computing One-Sided Limits

The computation of one-sided limits is greatly facilitated by the following fact.

All the results about limits in Section 14.2, such as the properties of limits, limits of polynomial functions, and the Limit Theorem, remain valid if "$x \to c$" is replaced by either "$x \to c^+$" or "$x \to c^-$."

Example 2 Using Properties of Limits

Find $\lim\limits_{x \to 3^-} \sqrt{9 - x^2}$.

Solution

The function $f(x) = \sqrt{9 - x^2}$ is defined only when $-3 \le x \le 3$, because the quantity under the radical is negative for other values of x. Compute the limit of $f(x)$ as x approaches 3 from the left by using the properties of limits:

$$\lim_{x \to 3^-} \sqrt{9 - x^2} = \sqrt{\lim_{x \to 3^-}(9 - x^2)} \qquad \textit{property 5}$$

$$= \sqrt{\lim_{x \to 3^-} 9 - \lim_{x \to 3^-} x^2} \qquad \textit{property 2}$$

$$= \sqrt{\lim_{x \to 3^-} 9 - \left(\lim_{x \to 3^-} x\right)\left(\lim_{x \to 3^-} x\right)} \qquad \textit{property 3}$$

$$= \sqrt{9 - 3^2} = 0 \qquad \begin{array}{l}\textit{limit of a constant}\\ \textit{limit of the identity function}\end{array}$$

Three Types of Limits

Notice that there are three kinds of limits: left-hand limits, right-hand limits, and "two-sided" limits as defined in Section 14.1. Example 1 exhibits a function that has a right-hand limit at $x = 3$, but no left-hand or two sided limit. Even when a function has both a left-hand and a right-hand limit at $x = c$, these limits may not be the same, as was shown in the introduction of this *Excursion*.

It is clear, however, that a function which has a two-sided limit L at $x = c$ necessarily has L as both its left-hand and right-hand limit at $x = c$. If the values of $f(x)$ can be made arbitrarily close to L by taking x close enough to c on both sides of c, then the same thing is true if you take only values of x on the left of c or on the right of c. Conversely, if a function has the same left-hand and right-hand limits at $x = c$, then this number must be a two-sided limit as well. In summary,

Two-sided Limits

Let f be a function and let c and L be real numbers. Then

$$\lim_{x \to c} f(x) = L \quad \text{exactly when} \quad \lim_{x \to c^-} f(x) = L \text{ and } \lim_{x \to c^+} f(x) = L.$$

Example 3   Limits

From the following graph, find

a. $\lim\limits_{x \to 2^-} f(x)$ **b.** $\lim\limits_{x \to 2^-} f(x)$ **c.** $\lim\limits_{x \to 2^+} f(x)$

d. $\lim\limits_{x \to 6^-} f(x)$ **e.** $\lim\limits_{x \to 6^+} f(x)$

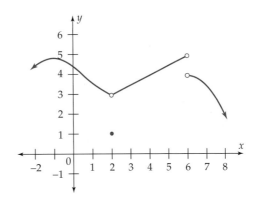

Solution

The graph shows that

a. $\lim\limits_{x \to 2} f(x) = 3$ **b.** $\lim\limits_{x \to 2^-} f(x) = 3$ **c.** $\lim\limits_{x \to 2^+} f(x) = 3$

d. $\lim\limits_{x \to 6^-} f(x) = 5$ **e.** $\lim\limits_{x \to 6^+} f(x) = 4$

Exercises 14.2.A

In Exercises 1–6, use a calculator to find a reasonable
estimate of the limit.

1. $\lim\limits_{x \to \pi^-} \dfrac{\sin x}{1 - \cos x}$ **2.** $\lim\limits_{x \to \frac{\pi}{2}^-} (\sec x - \tan x)$

3. $\lim\limits_{x \to 0^+} \sqrt{x}\,(\ln x)$ **4.** $\lim\limits_{x \to 0^+} \left(\dfrac{1}{x}\right)^x$

5. $\lim\limits_{x \to 0^-} \dfrac{\sin 6x}{x}$ **6.** $\lim\limits_{x \to 0^+} \dfrac{\sin 3x}{1 + \sin 4x}$

In Exercises 7–10, use the graph of the function f to
determine the required limits.

a. $\lim\limits_{x \to -2^-} f(x)$ **b.** $\lim\limits_{x \to 0^+} f(x)$

c. $\lim\limits_{x \to 3^-} f(x)$ **d.** $\lim\limits_{x \to 3^+} f(x)$

7.

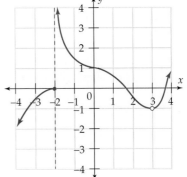

8.

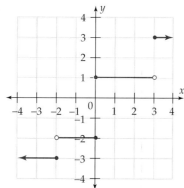

9.

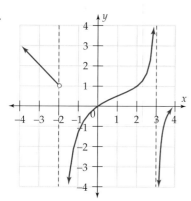

10.

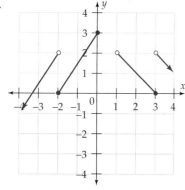

11. In Exercise 33a of Section 14.1, find
  a. $\lim_{x \to -2^-} f(x)$ **b.** $\lim_{x \to -2^+} f(x)$
  c. $\lim_{x \to 2^-} f(x)$ **d.** $\lim_{x \to 2^+} f(x)$

12. In Exercise 34a of Section 14.1, find
  a. $\lim_{x \to -1^-} g(x)$ **b.** $\lim_{x \to -1^+} g(x)$
  c. $\lim_{x \to 1^-} g(x)$ **d.** $\lim_{x \to 1^+} g(x)$

In Exercises 13–22, find the limit.

13. $\lim_{x \to 1^+} \left(\sqrt{x - 1} + 3 \right)$ **14.** $\lim_{x \to 3^-} \sqrt{-3 - x}$

15. $\lim_{x \to 4^-} \dfrac{x - 4}{x^2 - 16}$ **16.** $\lim_{x \to 2^+} \dfrac{|x - 2|}{x - 2}$

17. $\lim_{x \to 3^+} \dfrac{3}{x^2 - 9}$ **18.** $\lim_{x \to 2^-} \dfrac{x + 1}{x^2 - x - 2}$

19. $\lim_{x \to -2.5^+} \left(\sqrt{5 + 2x} + x \right)$

20. $\lim_{x \to 3^+} \left(\sqrt{x - 3} + \sqrt{3x} \right)$

21. $\lim_{x \to -3^+} \left(\dfrac{|x + 3|}{x + 3} + \sqrt{x + 3} + 1 \right)$

22. $\lim_{x \to -4^-} \left(\sqrt{|x| - 4} + x^2 \right)$

Exercises 23 and 24 involve the greatest integer function, $f(x) = [x]$. See Exercise 30 in Section 14.2.

23. Find $\lim_{x \to 2^+} [x]$ and $\lim_{x \to 2^-} [x]$.

24. Find $\lim_{x \to 3^-} (x - [x])$ and $\lim_{x \to 3^+} (x - [x])$.

14.3 The Formal Definition of Limit (Optional)

Objectives

- Use the formal definition of limit

The informal definition of limit in Section 14.1 is quite adequate for understanding the basic properties of limits and for calculating the limits of many familiar functions. This definition, or one very much like it, was used for more than a century and played a crucial role in the development of calculus. Nevertheless, the informal definition is not entirely satisfactory; it is based on ideas that have been illustrated by examples but not precisely defined.

Mathematical intuition, as exemplified in the informal definition of limit, is a valuable guide; but it is not infallible. On several occasions in the history of mathematics, what first seemed intuitively plausible has turned out to be false. In the long run, the only way to guarantee the accuracy of mathematical results is to base them on rigorously precise definitions and theorems. This section takes the first step in building this rigorous foundation by developing a formal definition of limit.

In order to keep the discussion as concrete as possible, suppose f is a function such that $\lim_{x \to 5} f(x) = 12$. You do not need to know the rule of f or anything else about it to understand the following discussion.

The informal definition of the statement "$\lim_{x \to 5} f(x) = 12$" that was given in Section 14.1 has two components:

A. As x takes values very close to but not equal to 5, the corresponding values of $f(x)$ get very close—and possibly are equal—to 12.

B. The value of $f(x)$ can be made arbitrarily close (as close as you want) to 12 by taking x sufficiently close (but not equal) to 5.

In a sense, Component **A** is unnecessary because it is included in Component **B**: If the values of $f(x)$ can be made *arbitrarily close* to 12 by taking x close enough to 5, then presumably $f(x)$ can be made to get very close to 12 by taking values of x very close to 5.

Consequently, to obtain the formal definition of limit, begin with Component B of the informal definition.

> $\lim_{x \to 5} f(x) = 12$ **means that the value of $f(x)$ can be made as close as you want to 12 by taking x close enough to 5.**   [1]

The definition above, referred to as Definition [1], will be modified step by step until the formal definition of limit is reached.

Definition [1] says, in effect, that there is a two-step process involved in finding a limit, if it exists:

1. Know how close you want $f(x)$ to be to 12,

2. Determine how close x must be to 5 to guarantee this.

Definition [1] can now be restated as Definition [2].

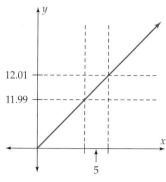

x is in this interval when
$11.99 < f(x) < 12.01$

Figure 14.3-1

$\lim_{x \to 5} f(x) = 12$ **means that whenever you specify how close**
$f(x)$ **should be to 12, you know how close x must be to**   [2]
5 to guarantee it.

For example, if you want $f(x)$ to be within 0.01 of 12, that is, between 11.99 and 12.01, you can find how close x must be to 5 to guarantee that

$$11.99 < f(x) < 12.01.$$

Any value of x in the interval around 5 shown in Figure 14.3-1 will produce $11.99 < f(x) < 12.01$.

But "arbitrarily close" implies much more. You must be able to find how close x is to 5 regardless of how close you want $f(x)$ to be to 12. If you want $f(x)$ to be within 0.002 of 12, or 0.0001 of 12, or within any distance of 12, you must be able to find how close x must be to 5 in each case to accomplish this. So, Definition [2] can be restated as follows:

$\lim_{x \to 5} f(x) = 12$ **means that no matter what positive number**
you specify in measuring how close you want $f(x)$ to be
to 12, you must be able to find how close x must be to   [3]
5 in order to guarantee that $f(x)$ is that close to 12.

Hereafter, the small positive number you specify in measuring how close $f(x)$ should be to 12 will be denoted by the Greek letter ε (epsilon). When you know how close x should be to 5 to accomplish this, denote the number by the Greek letter δ (delta). Presumably the number δ, which measures how close x must be to 5, will depend on the number ε, which measures how close you want $f(x)$ to be to 12. Using this language, Definition [3] becomes Definition [4].

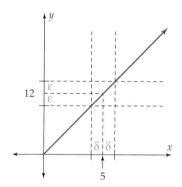

Figure 14.3-2

$\lim_{x \to 5} f(x) = 12$ **means that for every positive number ε**
there is a positive number δ that depends on ε with
this property: [4]
If x is within δ of 5 but not equal to 5, then
$f(x)$ is within ε of 12, and possibly equal to 12.

Although Definition [4] is essentially the formal definition, somewhat briefer notation is usually used.

If you think of $f(x)$ and 12 as numbers on the number line, then the statement

$$f(x) \text{ is within } \varepsilon \text{ of } 12$$

means that

the distance from $f(x)$ to 12 is less than ε.

Because distance on the number line is measured by absolute value (see Sections 2.4 and 2.5.A), the last statement can be written as

$$|f(x) - 12| < \varepsilon.$$

Similarly, saying that x is within δ of 5 and not equal to 5 means that the distance from x to 5 is less than δ but greater than 0, that is

$$0 < |x - 5| < \delta.$$

NOTE Epsilon, ε, and delta, δ, are Greek letters that are often used to represent small amounts.

Using this notation, Definition [4] becomes the desired formal definition.

$\lim\limits_{x \to 5} f(x) = 12$ **means that for each positive number** ε,
there is a number δ **that depends on** ε, **such that**   [5]
if $0 < |x - 5| < \delta$, **then** $|f(x) - 12| < \varepsilon$.

Definition [5] is sufficiently rigorous because the imprecise terms "arbitrarily close" and "close enough" in the informal definition have been replaced by a precise statement using inequalities that can be verified in specific cases, as will be shown in the examples that follow. There is nothing special about 5 and 12 in the preceding discussion; the entire analysis applies equally well in the general case and leads to the formal definition of limit, which is just Definition [5] with c in place of 5, L in place of 12, and f for any function.

Definition of Limit

Let f be a function and let c be a real number such that $f(x)$ is defined for all x, except possibly $x = c$, in some open interval containing c. The limit of $f(x)$ as x approaches c is L, which is written

$$\lim_{x \to c} f(x) = L,$$

provided that for each positive number ε, there is a positive number δ that depends on ε with the property

if $0 < |x - c| < \delta$,   then $|f(x) - L| < \varepsilon$.

This definition is often called the ε-δ definition of limits.

Example 1   **Proving a Limit**

Let $f(x) = 4x - 8$ and prove that $\lim\limits_{x \to 5} f(x) = 12$.

Solution

Apply the definition of limit with $c = 5$, $L = 12$, and $f(x) = 4x - 8$. Figure 14.3-3 illustrates the situation. Suppose that ε is any positive number. Find a positive number δ with the property

If $0 < |x - 5| < \delta$,   then $|f(x) - 12| < \varepsilon$.

Let δ be the number $\dfrac{\varepsilon}{4}$, and show that this δ will work. For now, do not worry about how $\delta = \dfrac{\varepsilon}{4}$ was found; just verify that the following argument is valid.

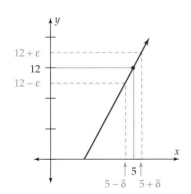

Figure 14.3-3

If $|x - 5| < \delta$, then

$$|x - 5| < \frac{\varepsilon}{4} \qquad \delta = \frac{\varepsilon}{4}$$

$$4|x - 5| < \varepsilon \qquad \textit{Multiply both sides by 4.}$$

$$|4||x - 5| < \varepsilon \qquad 4 = |4|$$

$$|4(x - 5)| < \varepsilon \qquad |a||b| = |ab|$$

$$|4x - 20| < \varepsilon$$

$$|(4x - 8) - 12| < \varepsilon \qquad \textit{Rewrite } -20 \textit{ as } -8 - 12.$$

$$|f(x) - 12| < \varepsilon \qquad f(x) = 4x - 8$$

This verifies that for each $\varepsilon > 0$, there is a positive δ with the property

$$\text{If } 0 < |x - 5| < \delta, \quad \text{then} \quad |f(x) - 12| < \varepsilon.$$

This completes the proof that $\lim\limits_{x \to 5} f(x) = 12$. ∎

Proofs like the one in Example 1 often seem mysterious to beginners. Although they can follow the argument after δ has been found, they do not see how to find δ. Example 2 gives a fuller picture of the processes used in proving statements about limits.

Example 2 proves that for any positive number ε, there exists δ such that

$$|f(x) - 9| < \varepsilon \text{ whenever } 0 < |x - 1| < \delta.$$

Example 2 Use the ε-δ Definition of Limit

Prove that $\lim\limits_{x \to 1} (2x + 7) = 9$.

Solution

In this case, $f(x) = 2x + 7, c = 1$, and $L = 9$. Let ε be a positive number and find a δ with the property

$$\text{If } 0 < |x - 1| < \delta, \quad \text{then} \quad |(2x + 7) - 9| < \varepsilon.$$

In order to get some idea which δ might have this property, *work backwards* from the desired conclusion, namely,

$$|(2x + 7) - 9| < \varepsilon.$$

The last statement is equivalent to

$$|2x - 2| < \varepsilon,$$

which in turn is equivalent to each of the following statements.

$$|2(x - 1)| < \varepsilon$$
$$|2||x - 1| < \varepsilon$$
$$2|x - 1| < \varepsilon$$
$$|x - 1| < \frac{\varepsilon}{2}$$

When the conclusion is written this way, it suggests that the number $\frac{\varepsilon}{2}$ would be a good choice for δ.

Everything up to here has been "scratch work." Now give the actual proof, written forwards.

Given a positive number ε, let δ be the number $\frac{\varepsilon}{2}$. If $0 < |x - 1| < \delta$, then

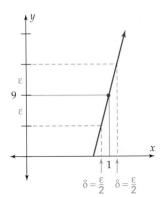

$$|x - 1| < \frac{\varepsilon}{2} \qquad \delta = \frac{\varepsilon}{2}$$
$$2|x - 1| < \varepsilon \qquad \textit{Multiply both sides by 2.}$$
$$|2||x - 1| < \varepsilon \qquad 2 = |2|$$
$$|2(x - 1)| < \varepsilon \qquad |a||b| = |ab|$$
$$|2x - 2| < \varepsilon$$
$$|(2x + 7) - 9| < \varepsilon \qquad \textit{Rewrite } -2 \textit{ as } 7 - 9.$$
$$|f(x) - 9| < \varepsilon \qquad f(x) = 2x + 7$$

Figure 14.3-4

Therefore, $\delta = \frac{\varepsilon}{2}$ has the required property, and the proof is complete. ∎

Proving Limit Properties

Once the algebraic scratch work was done in Examples 1 and 2, the limit proofs were relatively easy. In most cases, however, a more involved argument is required. In fact, it can be quite difficult to prove directly from the definition, for example, that $\lim\limits_{x \to 3} \dfrac{x^2 - 4x + 1}{x^3 - 2x^2 - x} = -\dfrac{1}{3}$. Fortunately, such complicated calculations can often be avoided by using the various limit properties given in Section 14.2. Of course, these properties must first be proved using the definition. Surprisingly, the proofs are comparatively easy.

Example 3 Proving Limit Properties

Let f and g be functions such that

$$\lim_{x \to c} f(x) = L \quad \text{and} \quad \lim_{x \to c} g(x) = M.$$

Prove that $\lim\limits_{x \to c} (f(x) + g(x)) = L + M$.

Solution

Scratch Work: If ε is any positive number, find a positive δ with the property

$$\text{If } 0 < |x - c| < \delta, \quad \text{then} \quad |(f(x) + g(x)) - (L + M)| < \varepsilon.$$

Note the following result of the triangle inequality. (See Section 2.4.)

$$|(f(x) + g(x)) - (L + M)| = |(f(x) - L) + (g(x) - M)|$$
$$\leq |f(x) - L| + |g(x) - M|$$

If there is a δ with the property

If $0 < |x - c| < \delta$, then $|f(x) - L| + |g(x) - M| < \varepsilon$,

then the smaller quantity $|(f(x) + g(x)) - (L + M)|$ will also be less than ε when $0 < |x - c| < \delta$. Such a δ can be found as follows.

Proof Let ε be any positive number. Because $\lim\limits_{x \to c} f(x) = L$, apply the definition of limit with $\dfrac{\varepsilon}{2}$ in place of ε:

there is a positive number δ_1 with the property

If $0 < |x - c| < \delta_1$, then $|f(x) - L| < \dfrac{\varepsilon}{2}$.

Similarly, because $\lim\limits_{x \to c} g(x) = M$,

there is a positive number δ_2 with the property

If $0 < |x - c| < \delta_2$, then $|g(x) - M| < \dfrac{\varepsilon}{2}$.

Now let δ be the smaller of the two numbers δ_1 and δ_2, so that $\delta \leq \delta_1$ and $\delta \leq \delta_2$. Then if $0 < |x - c| < \delta$, it must be true that

$$0 < |x - c| < \delta_1 \quad \text{and} \quad 0 < |x - c| < \delta_2.$$

Therefore,

$$|f(x) - L| < \frac{\varepsilon}{2} \quad \text{and} \quad |g(x) - M| < \frac{\varepsilon}{2}.$$

Consequently, if $0 < |x - c| < \delta$, then

$$|(f(x) + g(x)) - (L + M)| = |(f(x) - L) + (g(x) - M)|$$
$$\leq |f(x) - L| + |g(x) - M|$$
$$< \frac{\varepsilon}{2} + \frac{\varepsilon}{2}$$
$$= \varepsilon$$

It has been shown that for any $\varepsilon > 0$, there is a $\delta > 0$ with the property:

If $0 < |x - c| < \delta$,   then $|(f(x) + g(x)) - (L + M)| < \varepsilon$.

Therefore, $\lim\limits_{x \to c} (f(x) + g(x)) = L + M$.

■

The proofs of the other limit properties and theorems of Section 14.2 are introduced in calculus.

One-Sided Limits

The formal definition of limit may easily be carried over to one-sided limits, as defined informally in *Excursion* 14.2.A, by using the following fact:

$$|x - c| < \delta \qquad \text{exactly when} \qquad -\delta < x - c < \delta,$$

which is equivalent to

$$|x - c| < \delta \qquad \text{exactly when} \qquad c - \delta < x < c + \delta.$$

Thus, the numbers between c and $c + \delta$ lie to the right of c, within distance δ of c, and the numbers between $c - \delta$ and c lie to the left of c, within distance δ of c.

Consequently, the formal definition of right-hand limits can be obtained from the definition above by replacing the phrase "if $0 < |x - c| < \delta$" with "$c < x < c + \delta$." For a formal definition of the left-hand limits, replace the phrase "if $0 < |x - c| < \delta$" with "if $c - \delta < x < c$."

Exercises 14.3

In Exercises 1–12, use the formal definition of limit to prove the given statement, as in Example 1.

1. $\lim_{x \to 3} (3x - 2) = 7$

2. $\lim_{x \to 1} (4x + 2) = 6$

3. $\lim_{x \to 5} x = 5$

4. $\lim_{x \to 0} (x + 2) = 2$

5. $\lim_{x \to 2} (6x + 3) = 15$

6. $\lim_{x \to 7} (-2x + 19) = 5$

7. $\lim_{x \to 1} 4 = 4$

8. $\lim_{x \to 2} \pi = \pi$

9. $\lim_{x \to 4} (x - 6) = -2$

10. $\lim_{x \to 1} (2x - 7) = -5$

11. $\lim_{x \to -2} (2x + 5) = 1$

12. $\lim_{x \to -3} (2x - 4) = -10$

In Exercises 13 and 14, use the formal definition of limit to prove the statement.

13. $\lim_{x \to 0} x^2 = 0$

14. $\lim_{x \to 0} x^3 = 0$

In Exercises 15 and 16, let f and g be functions such that

$$\lim_{x \to c} f(x) = L \text{ and } \lim_{x \to c} g(x) = M.$$

15. *Critical Thinking* Prove that
$\lim_{x \to c} (f(x) - g(x)) = L - M$. *Hint:* see Example 3.

16. *Critical Thinking* If k is a constant, prove that
$\lim_{x \to c} k f(x) = kL$.

14.4 Continuity

Objectives

- Determine if a function is continuous at a point

- Determine if a function is continuous on an interval

- Apply properties of continuous functions

Calculus deals in large part with continuous functions, and the properties of continuous functions are essential for understanding many of the key theorems in calculus. This section presents the intuitive idea of continuity, its formal definition, and the various properties of continuity—which were used in the work with graphs in earlier chapters.

Continuity Informally

Let c be a real number in the domain of a function f. Informally, the function f is **continuous** at $x = c$ if you can draw the graph of f at and near the point $(c, f(c))$ without lifting your pencil from the paper. For example, each of the four graphs in Figure 14.4-1 is the graph of a function that is continuous at $x = c$.

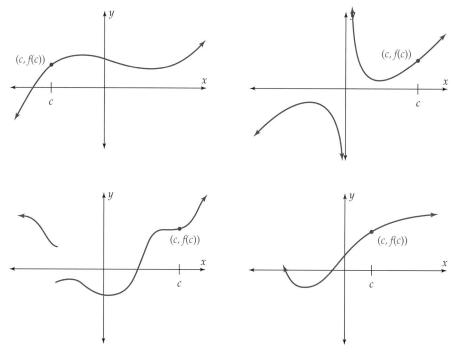

Figure 14.4-1

Thus, a function is continuous at $x = c$ if its graph around the point $(c, f(c))$ is connected and unbroken.

On the other hand, none of the functions whose graphs are shown in Figure 14.4-2 is continuous at $x = c$. Try to draw one of these graphs near $x = c$ without lifting your pencil from the paper.

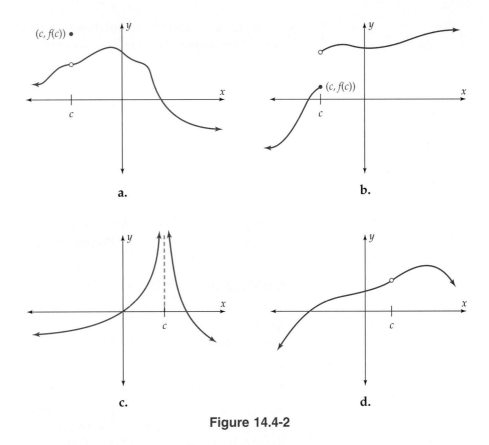

Figure 14.4-2

Figure 14.4-2 shows that a function is **discontinuous,** that is, not continuous, at $x = c$ if the graph has a break, gap, hole, or jump when $x = c$.

Calculators and Discontinuity

When a calculator uses "connected" mode to graph a function, it plots a number of points and then connects them with line segments to produce a curve. Thus, the calculator *assumes* that the function is continuous at any point it plots. For example, a calculator may not show the hole in graph **d** of Figure 14.4-2, or it may insert a vertical line segment where the graph jumps in graph **b** of Figure 14.4-2. Consequently, a calculator may present misleading information about the continuity of a function.

Analytic Description of Continuity

The goal is to find a mathematical description of continuity at a point that does not depend on having the graph given in advance. This is done by expressing in analytic terms the intuitive geometric idea of continuity given above.

If the graph of f can be drawn at and near a point $(c, f(c))$ without lifting pencil from paper, then there are two possibilities:

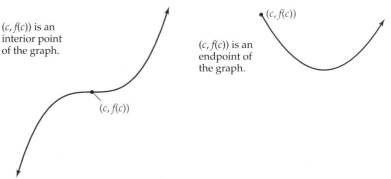

(c, f(c)) is an interior point of the graph.

(c, f(c)) is an endpoint of the graph.

(c, f(c))

Figure 14.4-3

Continuity at an Interior Point

If the point $(c, f(c))$ is an interior point of the graph, and the graph can be drawn around the point $(c, f(c))$ without lifting pencil from paper, then at the very least, the following two statments are true.

- $f(x)$ must be defined for $x = c$
- $f(x)$ must be defined for $x = t$, when t is any number near c

For if $f(t)$ is not defined for some t near c, there will be a hole in the graph at the point $(t, f(t))$, which would require lifting the pencil when drawing the graph. See graphs **c** and **d** of Figure 14.4-2 for functions that are not defined at $x = c$. The situation can be described more precisely by saying:

> **$f(x)$ is defined for all x in some open interval containing c. In other words, there are numbers a and b with $a < c < b$ such that $f(x)$ is defined for all x with $a < x < b$. In particular, $f(c)$ is defined.**   [1]

Although condition [1] is necessary in order for f to be continuous at $x = c$, this condition by itself does not *guarantee* continuity. For instance, $x = c$ and the graphs **a** and **b** in Figure 14.4-2 show functions whose graphs are defined for all values of x near c, but are *not* continuous at $x = c$.

If $f(c)$ is defined, there are two conditions that can *prevent* a function from being continuous at $x = c$:

- There is a jump at $x = c$, that is, the limit of $f(x)$ as x approaches c does not exist.
- There is a hole in the graph at $x = c$, that is, limit of $f(x)$ exists at $x = c$, but it is not equal to $f(c)$.

The conditions that prevent a function from being continuous at a point are shown in Figure 14.4-4. Notice the reason that the graph is not continuous at $x = a$, at $x = b$, and at $x = c$.

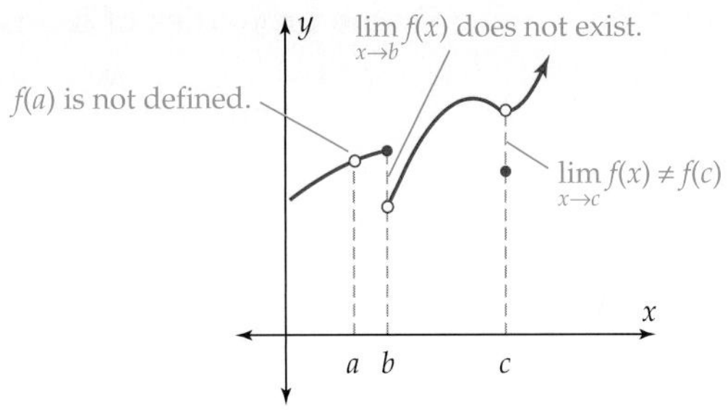

Figure 14.4-4

The preceding analysis leads to the following formal definition of continuity for interior points.

Definition of Continuity

> Let f be a function that is defined for all x in some open interval containing c. Then f is said to be *continuous* at $x = c$ under the following conditions:
>
> 1. $f(c)$ is defined
> 2. $\lim\limits_{x \to c} f(x)$ exists
> 3. $\lim\limits_{x \to c} f(x) = f(c)$

Example 1   Continuity at a Point

Without graphing, show that the function

$$f(x) = \frac{\sqrt{x^2 - x + 1}}{x - 5}$$

is continuous at $x = -3$.

Solution

To show continuity of f at $x = -3$, show that

$$f(-3) = \lim_{x \to -3} \frac{\sqrt{x^2 - x + 1}}{x - 5}.$$

$$f(-3) = \frac{\sqrt{(-3)^2 - (-3) + 1}}{(-3) - 5}$$

$$= -\frac{\sqrt{13}}{8}$$

By the properties of limits given in Section 14.2,

$$\lim_{x \to -3} f(x) = \lim_{x \to -3} \frac{\sqrt{x^2 - x + 1}}{x - 5}$$

$$= \frac{\lim_{x \to -3} \sqrt{x^2 - x + 1}}{\lim_{x \to -3} (x - 5)} \qquad \textit{limit of a quotient}$$

$$= \frac{\sqrt{\lim_{x \to -3} x^2 - x + 1}}{\lim_{x \to -3} (x - 5)} \qquad \textit{limit of a root}$$

$$= \frac{\sqrt{(-3)^2 - (-3) + 1}}{(-3) - 5} \qquad \textit{limit of a polynomial}$$

$$= -\frac{\sqrt{13}}{8}$$

Therefore, $\lim_{x \to -3} f(x) = f(-3)$ and f is continuous at $x = -3$. ∎

The facts about limits presented in Sections 14.1 and 14.2 and the definition of continuity provide justification for several assumptions about graphs that were made earlier in this book.

Continuity of Special Functions

Every polynomial function is continuous at every real number.

Every rational function is continuous at every real number in its domain.

Every exponential function is continuous at every real number.

Every logarithmic function is continuous at every *positive* real number.

$f(x) = \sin x$ and $g(x) = \cos x$ are continuous at every real number.

$h(x) = \tan x$ is continuous at every real number in its domain.

NOTE One-sided limits, which were discussed in Section 14.2.A, are a prerequisite for the material on continuity on an interval.

Continuity on an Interval

Consider continuity at an endpoint of the graph of a function f, such as $(a, f(a))$ or $(b, f(b))$ shown in Figure 14.4-5.

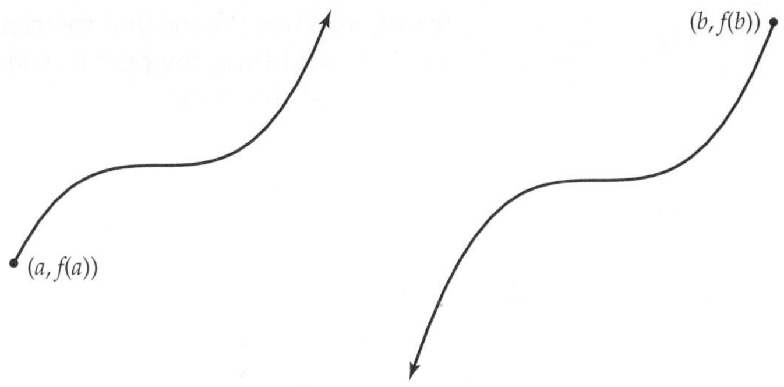

Figure 14.4-5

The intuitive idea of continuity at $(a, f(a))$ is that the graph of f can be drawn at $x = a$ and to the right of the point $(a, f(a))$ without lifting the pencil from the paper. Essentially the same analysis that was given above can be made here if we consider only values of x to the right of $x = a$. In short, continuity at the endpoint $(a, f(a))$ means that $\lim_{x \to a^+} f(x) = f(a)$. An analogous discussion applies to the endpoint $(b, f(b))$, which leads to the formal definition.

Continuity from the Left and Right

A function f is *continuous from the right* at $x = a$ provided that
$$\lim_{x \to a^+} f(x) = f(a).$$

A function f is *continuous from the left* at $x = b$ provided that
$$\lim_{x \to b^-} f(x) = f(b).$$

Example 2 Continuity at an Endpoint

Show that $f(x) = \sqrt{x}$ is continuous from the right at $x = 0$.

Solution

The function $f(x) = \sqrt{x}$, which is not defined when $x < 0$, is continuous from the right at $x = 0$ because $f(0) = \sqrt{0} = 0$, and

$$\lim_{x \to 0^+} f(x) = \lim_{x \to 0^+} \sqrt{x} = 0 = f(0).$$

The most useful functions are those that are continuous at every point in an interval. Consider the following three examples.

- $h(x) = \tan x$ is continuous at every number in the interval $\left(-\dfrac{\pi}{2}, \dfrac{\pi}{2} \right)$

- $g(x) = \ln x$ is continuous at every number in $(0, \infty)$
- $f(x) = \sin x$ is continuous at every number in $(-\infty, \infty)$

Intuitively, this means that their graphs can be drawn over the entire interval without lifting the pencil from the paper. Most of the functions in this book are of this type.

Continuity on an Interval

A function f is said to be *continuous on an open interval* (a, b) provided that f is continuous at every value in the interval.

A function f is said to be *continuous on a closed interval* $[a, b]$ provided that f is continuous from the right at $x = a$, continuous from the left at $x = b$, and continuous at every value in the open interval (a, b).

Analogous definitions may be given for continuity on intervals of the form $[a, b), (a, b], (a, \infty), [a, \infty), (-\infty, b), (-\infty, b]$, and $(-\infty, \infty)$.

Example 3 Continuity of a Function

Discuss the continuity of the function shown in Figure 14.4-6.

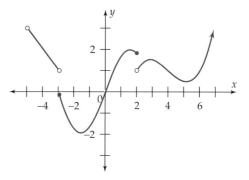

Figure 14.4-6

Solution

The function is discontinuous at $x = -3$ and $x = 2$, but it is continuous on each of the intervals $(-5, -3), [-3, 2], (2, \infty)$.

Properties of Continuous Functions

Using the definition is not always the most convenient way to show that a particular function is continuous. It is often easier to establish continuity by using the following facts.

Properties of Continuous Functions

> If the functions f and g are continuous at $x = c$, then each of the following functions is also continuous at $x = c$:
>
> 1. the sum function $f + g$
> 2. the difference function $f - g$
> 3. the product function fg
> 4. the quotient function $\dfrac{f}{g}$, $g(c) \neq 0$

Proof By the definition of the sum function, $(f + g)(x) = f(x) + g(x)$. Because f and g are continuous at $x = c$,

$$\lim_{x \to c} f(x) = f(c) \quad \text{and} \quad \lim_{x \to c} g(x) = g(c).$$

Therefore, by the first property of limits,

$$\begin{aligned}
\lim_{x \to c} (f + g)(x) &= \lim_{x \to c} (f(x) + g(x)) \\
&= \lim_{x \to c} f(x) + \lim_{x \to c} g(x) \\
&= f(c) + g(c) \\
&= (f + g)(c)
\end{aligned}$$

This says that $f + g$ is continuous at $x = c$.

The remaining statements are proved similarly, using limit properties 2, 3, and 4.   ∎

Example 4   Continuity of Functions

Assume that $f(x) = \sin x$ and $g(x) = x^3 + 5x - 2$ are continuous at $x = 0$. Prove that the following functions are continuous at $x = 0$.

a. $\sin x + (x^3 + 5x - 2)$ **b.** $\sin x - (x^3 + 5x - 2)$

c. $(\sin x)(x^3 + 5x - 2)$ **d.** $\dfrac{\sin x}{x^3 + 5x - 2}$

Solution

Because f an g are continuous at $x = 0$, each of the following functions are continuous at $x = 0$ by the listed property of continuous functions.

a. $\sin x + (x^3 + 5x - 2) = (f + g)(x)$ *sum of continuous functions*

b. $\sin x - (x^3 + 5x - 2) = (f - g)(x)$ *difference of continuous functions*

c. $(\sin x)(x^3 + 5x - 2) = fg(x)$ *product of continuous functions*

d. $\dfrac{\sin x}{x^3 + 5x - 2} = \left(\dfrac{f}{g}\right)(x)$ *quotient of continuous functions*

Composite Functions

Composition of functions is often used to construct new functions from given ones.

Continuity of Composite Functions

If the function f is continuous at $x = c$ and the function g is continuous at $x = f(c)$, then the composite function $g \circ f$ is continuous at $x = c$.

Example 5   Continuity of Composite Functions

Show that $h(x) = \sqrt{x^3 - 3x^2 + x + 7}$ is continuous at $x = 2$.

Solution

The polynomial function $f(x) = x^3 - 3x^2 + x + 7$ is continuous at $x = 2$ and $f(2) = 2^3 - 3(2)^2 + 2 + 7 = 5$. The function $g(x) = \sqrt{x}$ is continuous at 5 because by limit property 5

$$\lim_{x \to 5} \sqrt{x} = \sqrt{\lim_{x \to 5} x} = \sqrt{5} = g(5).$$

By the box above, with $c = 2$ and $f(c) = 5$, the composite function $g \circ f$, which is given by

$$(g \circ f)(x) = g(f(x)) = g(x^3 - 3x^2 + x + 7) = \sqrt{x^3 - 3x^2 + x + 7}$$

is also continuous at $x = 2$. ∎

The Intermediate Value Theorem

This section's introduction to continuity will close by mentioning, without proof, a very important property of continuous functions.

The Intermediate Value Theorem

If the function f is continuous on the closed interval $[a, b]$ and k is any number between $f(a)$ and $f(b)$, then there exists at least one number c between a and b such that $f(c) = k$.

The truth of the Intermediate Value Theorem can be understood geometrically by remembering that since f is continuous on $[a, b]$, the graph of f can be drawn from the point $(a, f(a))$ to the point $(b, f(b))$ without lifting the pencil from the paper. As suggested in Figure 14.4-7, there is no way that this can be done unless the graph crosses the horizontal line $y = k$, where $f(a) < k < f(b)$.

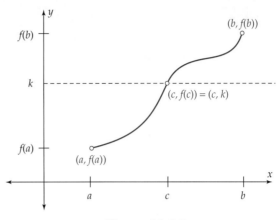

Figure 14.4-7

The first coordinate of the point where the graph crosses this line is some number c between a and b, and its second coordinate is $f(c)$ because the point is on the graph of f. But $(c, f(c))$ is also on the line $y = k$, so its second coordinate must be k; that is, $f(c) = k$.

The Intermediate Value Theorem further explains why the graph of a continuous function is connected and unbroken. If the function f is continuous on the interval $[a, b]$, then its graph cannot go from the point $(a, f(a))$ to the point $(b, f(b))$ without moving through all the y values between $f(a)$ and $f(b)$.

The graphical method of solving equations that has been used throughout this book is based on the Intermediate Value Theorem, as are some root-finding features on calculators. If f is continuous on the interval $[a, b]$ and $f(a)$ and $f(b)$ have opposite signs, then 0 is a number between $f(a)$ and $f(b)$. Consequently, by the Intermediate Value Theorem, with $k = 0$, there is at least one number c between a and b such that $f(c) = 0$. In other words, $x = c$ is a solution of the equation $f(x) = 0$.

So when a calculator shows that the graph of a continuous function f has points above and below the x-axis, there really is an x-intercept between these points, that is, a solution of $f(x) = 0$. Zoom-in uses this fact by looking at smaller and smaller viewing windows that contain points of the graph on both sides of the x-axis. The closer together the points are horizontally, the better the approximation of the x-intercept, or solution, that can be read from the graph.

Exercises 14.4

In Exercises 1 and 2, use the graph to find all the numbers at which the function is not continuous.

1.

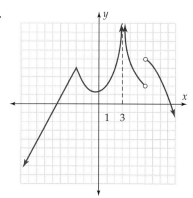

2.

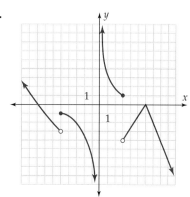

In Exercises 3–6, determine whether the function whose graph is given is continuous at $x = -2$, at $x = 0$, and at $x = 3$.

3.

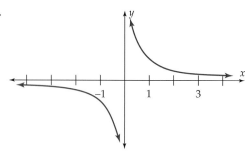

4.

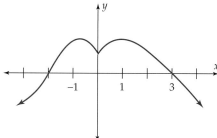

5.

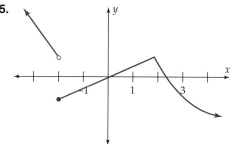

6.

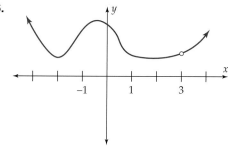

In Exercises 7–12, use the definition of continuity and the properties of limits to show that the function is continuous at the given number.

7. $f(x) = x^2 + 5(x - 2)^7, x = 3$

8. $g(x) = (x^2 - 3x - 10)(x^2 + 2x^2 - 5x + 4), x = -1$

9. $f(x) = \dfrac{x^2 - 9}{(x^2 - x - 6)(x^2 + 6x + 9)}, x = 2$

10. $h(x) = \dfrac{x + 3}{(x^2 - x - 1)(x^2 + 1)}, x = -2$

11. $f(x) = \dfrac{x\sqrt{x}}{(x - 6)^2}, x = 36$

12. $k(x) = \dfrac{\sqrt{8 - x^2}}{2x^2 - 5}, x = -2$

In Exercises 13–18, explain why the function is not continuous at the given number.

13. $f(x) = \dfrac{1}{(x-3)^3}$, $x = 3$

14. $h(x) = \dfrac{x^2 + 4}{x^2 - x - 2}$, $x = 2$

15. $f(x) = \dfrac{x^2 + 4x + 3}{x^2 - x - 2}$, $x = -1$

16. $g(x) = \begin{cases} \sin\dfrac{\pi}{x} & \text{if } x \neq 0 \\ 1 & \text{if } x = 0 \end{cases}$, $x = 0$

17. $f(x) = \begin{cases} x^2 & \text{if } x \neq 0 \\ 1 & \text{if } x = 0 \end{cases}$, $x = 0$

18. $f(x) = \dfrac{\sqrt{2+x} - \sqrt{2}}{x}$, $x = 0$

In Exercises 19–24, determine whether or not the function is continuous at the given number.

19. $f(x) = \begin{cases} -2x + 4 & \text{if } x \leq 2 \\ 2x - 4 & \text{if } x > 2 \end{cases}$, $x = 2$

20. $g(x) = \begin{cases} 2x + 5 & \text{if } x < -1 \\ -2x + 1 & \text{if } x \geq -1 \end{cases}$, $x = -1$

21. $f(x) = \begin{cases} x^2 - x & \text{if } x \leq 0 \\ 2x^2 & \text{if } x > 0 \end{cases}$, $x = 0$

22. $g(x) = \begin{cases} x^3 - x + 1 & \text{if } x < 2 \\ 3x^2 - 2x - 1 & \text{if } x \geq 2 \end{cases}$, $x = 2$

23. $f(x) = |x - 3|$, $x = 3$

24. $k(x) = -|x + 2| + 3$, $x = -2$

In Exercises 25–28, determine all numbers at which the function is continuous.

25. $f(x) = \begin{cases} \dfrac{x^2 + x - 2}{x^2 - 4x + 3} & \text{if } x \neq 1 \\ -\dfrac{3}{2} & \text{if } x = 1 \end{cases}$

26. $g(x) = \begin{cases} \dfrac{x^2 - x - 6}{x^2 - 4} & \text{if } x \neq -2 \\ \dfrac{4}{5} & \text{if } x = -2 \end{cases}$

27. $f(x) = \begin{cases} x^2 + 1 & \text{if } x < 0 \\ x & \text{if } 0 < x \leq 2 \\ -2x + 3 & \text{if } x > 2 \end{cases}$

28. $h(x) = \begin{cases} \dfrac{1}{x} & \text{if } x < 1 \text{ and } x \neq 0 \\ x^2 & \text{if } x \geq 1 \end{cases}$

29. *Critical Thinking* For what values of b is the following function continuous at $x = 3$?

$$f(x) = \begin{cases} bx + 4 & \text{if } x \leq 3 \\ bx^2 - 2 & \text{if } x > 3 \end{cases}$$

30. *Critical Thinking* Show that $f(x) = \sqrt{|x|}$ is continuous at $x = 0$.

A function f that is not defined at $x = c$ is said to have a removable discontinuity at $x = c$ if there is a function g such that $g(c)$ is defined, g is continuous at $x = c$, and $g(x) = f(x)$ for $x \neq c$. In Exercises 31–34, show that the function f has a removable discontinuity by finding an appropriate function g.

31. $f(x) = \dfrac{x - 1}{x^2 - 1}$

32. $f(x) = \dfrac{x^2}{|x|}$

33. $f(x) = \dfrac{2 - \sqrt{x}}{4 - x}$

34. $f(x) = \dfrac{\sin x}{x}$ *Hint:* See Example 1 of Section 14.1.

35. Show that the function $f(x) = \dfrac{|x|}{x}$ has a discontinuity at $x = 0$ that is *not* removable.

Limits Involving Infinity

Objectives

- Define limits involving infinity
- Use properties of limits at infinity
- Use the Limit Theorem

In the discussion that follows, it is important to remember that

There is no real number called "infinity," and the symbol ∞, which is usually read "infinity," does not represent any real number.

Nevertheless, the word "infinity" and the symbol ∞ are often used as a convenient shorthand to describe the way some functions behave under certain circumstances. Generally speaking, "infinity" indicates a situation in which some numerical quantity gets larger and larger without bound, meaning that it can be made larger than any given number. Similarly, "negative infinity," $-\infty$, indicates a situation in which a numerical quantity gets smaller and smaller without bound, meaning that it can be made smaller than any given negative number.

In Section 14.1, several ways were discussed in which a function might fail to have a limit as x approaches a number c. The word "infinity" is often used to describe one such situation. Consider the function f whose graph is shown in Figure 14.5-1.

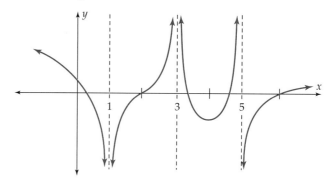

Figure 14.5-1

The graph shows that as x approaches 3 from the left or right, the corresponding values of $f(x)$ do not get closer and closer to a particular number. Instead, they become larger and larger without bound. Although there is no limit as defined in Section 14.1, it is convenient to describe this situation symbolically by writing

$$\lim_{x \to 3} f(x) = \infty,$$

which is read "the limit of $f(x)$ as x approaches 3 is infinity." Similarly, f does not have a limit as x approaches 1 from the left or right, because the corresponding values of $f(x)$ get smaller and smaller without bound. We say that "the limit of $f(x)$ as x approaches 1 is negative infinity" and write

$$\lim_{x \to 1} f(x) = -\infty.$$

NOTE *Excursion* 14.2.A is a prerequisite for some of the material that follows.

Near $x = 5$, the values of $f(x)$ get very large on the left side of 5 and very small on the right side of 5, so we write

$$\lim_{x \to 5^-} f(x) = \infty \quad \text{and} \quad \lim_{x \to 5^+} f(x) = -\infty,$$

which are read "The limit as x approaches 5 from the left is infinity" and "the limit as x approaches 5 from the right is negative infinity."

There are many cases like the ones illustrated above in which the language of limits and the word "infinity" can be useful for describing the behavior of a function that actually does not have a limit in the sense of Section 14.1.

Example 1   Infinite Limits

Describe the behavior of $f(x) = -\dfrac{5}{x^4}$ near $x = 0$.

Solution

The graph of f is shown in Figure 14.5-2. The trace feature indicates that the values of $f(x)$ get small without bound as x approaches 0 from the left or from the right.

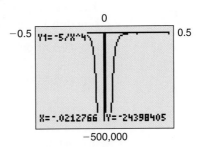

Figure 14.5-2

Therefore, $\lim\limits_{x \to 0} -\dfrac{5}{x^4} = -\infty$.

Example 2   Infinite Limits

Describe the behavior of the function $g(x) = \dfrac{8}{x^2 - 2x - 8}$ near $x = -2$.

Solution

As shown in Figure 14.5-3, the graph of g is not continuous at $x = -2$. To the left of $x = -2$, the values of $g(x)$ get large without bound, and the values of $g(x)$ to the right of $x = -2$ get small without bound.

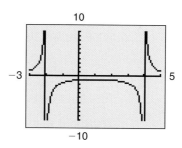

10

−3   5

−10

Figure 14.5-3

Therefore, $\displaystyle\lim_{x \to -2^-} \frac{8}{x^2 - 2x - 8} = \infty$ and $\displaystyle\lim_{x \to -2^+} \frac{8}{x^2 - 2x - 8} = -\infty.$ ∎

Infinite Limits and Vertical Asymptotes

The "infinite limits" considered in Figure 14.5-1 and in Examples 1 and 2 can be interpreted geometrically: Each such limit corresponds to a vertical asymptote of the graph.

Vertical Asymptotes

The vertical line $x = c$ is a *vertical asymptote* of the graph of the function f if at least one of the following is true.

$$\lim_{x \to c^-} f(x) = \infty \qquad \lim_{x \to c^+} f(x) = \infty \qquad \lim_{x \to c} f(x) = \infty$$

$$\lim_{x \to c^-} f(x) = -\infty \qquad \lim_{x \to c^+} f(x) = -\infty \qquad \lim_{x \to c} f(x) = -\infty$$

Limits at Infinity

Whenever the word "limit" has been used up to now, it referred to the behavior of a function when x was near a particular number c. Now, the behavior of a function when x takes very large or very small values will be considered. That is, the end behavior of a function will be discussed.

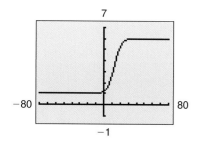

7

−80   80

−1

Figure 14.5-4

The graph of $f(x) = \dfrac{5}{1 + 24e^{-\frac{x}{4}}} + 1$ is shown in Figure 14.5-4.

┌─── **Graphing Exploration** ●───

Produce the graph shown in Figure 14.5-4 and use the trace feature to find values of $f(x)$ as x gets larger and larger. Are the values approaching a single value?

As you move to the right, the graph gets very close to the horizontal line $y = 6$. In other words, as x gets larger and larger, the corresponding values of $f(x)$ get closer and closer to 6, which can be expressed symbolically as

$$\lim_{x \to \infty} f(x) = 6.$$

The last statement is read "the limit of $f(x)$ as x approaches infinity is 6."

Toward the left the graph gets very close to the horizontal line $y = 1$; that is, as x gets smaller and smaller, the corresponding values of $f(x)$ get closer and closer to 1. (See note.) It is said that "the limit of $f(x)$ as x approaches negative infinity is 1," which is written

$$\lim_{x \to -\infty} f(x) = 1.$$

The types of limits when x gets large or small without bound are similar to those in Section 14.1 in that the values of the function do approach a fixed number. The definition in the general case is similar: f is any function, L is a real number, and the phrase "arbitrarily close" means "as close as you want."

NOTE Due to rounding, the trace feature on most calculators will display $y = 1$ when x is smaller than approximately -60. However, the value of the function is always greater than 1. Why?

Limits at Infinity

> Let f be a function that is defined for all $x > a$ for some number a. If
>
> > as x takes larger and larger positive values, increasing without bound, the corresponding values of $f(x)$ get very close, and possibly are equal, to a single real number L
>
> and
>
> > the values of $f(x)$ can be made arbitrarily close (as close as you want) to L by taking large enough values of x,
>
> then
>
> > the limit of $f(x)$ as x approaches infinity is L,
>
> which is written
>
> $$\lim_{x \to \infty} f(x) = L.$$

Limits as x approaches negative infinity are defined analogously by replacing "$x > a$" with "$x < a$", "increasing" with "decreasing", and "larger and larger positive" with "smaller and smaller negative" in the preceding definition. These definitions are informal because such phrases as "arbitrarily close" have not been precisely defined. Rigorous definitions, similar to those in Section 14.3 for ordinary limits, are discussed in Exercises 49–50.

Horizontal Asymptotes and Limits at Infinity

Limits as x approaches infinity or negative infinity correspond to horizontal asymptotes of the graph of the function.

Horizontal Asymptotes

The line $y = L$ is a *horizontal asymptote* of the graph of the function f if either

$$\lim_{x \to \infty} f(x) = L \quad \text{or} \quad \lim_{x \to -\infty} f(x) = L.$$

Example 3   Limits at Infinity

Discuss the behavior of $f(x) = \dfrac{1}{x}$ as x approaches infinity and as x approaches negative infinity.

Solution

When x is a very large positive number, $\dfrac{1}{x}$ is a positive number that is very close to 0. Similarly, when x is a very small negative number—which is large in absolute value—such as $-5{,}000{,}000$, $\dfrac{1}{x}$ is a negative number that is very close to 0. These facts suggest that $y = 0$ is a horizontal asymptote, or

$$\lim_{x \to \infty} f(x) = 0 \quad \text{and} \quad \lim_{x \to -\infty} f(x) = 0,$$

as confirmed in Figure 14.5-5.

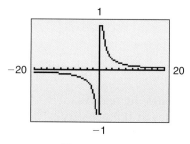

Figure 14.5-5

Example 4   Limits at Positive and Negative Infinity

Discuss the behavior of $f(x) = x^3 - 10x - 5$ as x approaches infinity and as x approaches negative infinity.

Solution

As shown in Figure 14.5-6, $f(x)$ does not approach a single value as x approaches infinity or as x approaches negative infinity.

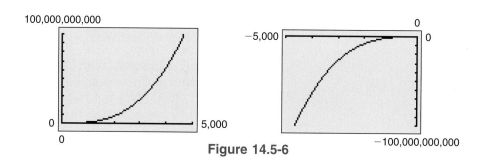

Figure 14.5-6

Thus, $\lim\limits_{x \to \infty} f(x)$ and $\lim\limits_{x \to -\infty} f(x)$, as defined in Section 14.1, do not exist. However, the situations are often described by writing

$$\lim_{x \to \infty} f(x) = \infty \quad \text{and} \quad \lim_{x \to -\infty} f(x) = -\infty$$

In fact, no polynomial graph has a horizontal asymptote. That is, no polynomial function has a limit as x approaches infinity or negative infinity.

Limit of a Constant Function

The limits of constant functions are easily found. Consider, for example, the function $f(x) = 5$. As x approaches infinity or negative infinity, the corresponding value of $f(x)$ is *always* the number 5, so $\lim\limits_{x \to \infty} f(x) = 5$ and $\lim\limits_{x \to -\infty} f(x) = 5$. A similar argument works for any constant function.

Limit of a Constant

If c is a constant, then $\lim\limits_{x \to \infty} c = c$ and $\lim\limits_{x \to -\infty} c = c$.

Properties of Limits

Infinite limits have the same useful properties that ordinary limits have. For instance, suppose that as x approaches infinity, the values of a function f approach a number L, and the values of a function g approach a number M. Then it is plausible that the values of $(f + g)(x)$ approach $L + M$, the values of $(fg)(x)$ approach $L \cdot M$, and so forth. Similar remarks apply when x approaches negative infinity.

Properties of Limits at Infinity

If f and g are functions and L and M are numbers such that

$$\lim_{x \to \infty} f(x) = L \quad \text{and} \quad \lim_{x \to \infty} g(x) = M,$$

then

1. $\lim\limits_{x \to \infty} (f + g)(x) = \lim\limits_{x \to \infty} (f(x) + g(x)) = \lim\limits_{x \to \infty} f(x) + \lim\limits_{x \to \infty} g(x) = L + M$

2. $\lim\limits_{x \to \infty} (f - g)(x) = \lim\limits_{x \to \infty} (f(x) - g(x)) = \lim\limits_{x \to \infty} f(x) - \lim\limits_{x \to \infty} g(x) = L - M$

3. $\lim\limits_{x \to \infty} (fg)(x) = \lim\limits_{x \to \infty} (f(x) \cdot g(x)) = \left(\lim\limits_{x \to \infty} f(x)\right)\left(\lim\limits_{x \to \infty} g(x)\right) = L \cdot M$

4. $\lim\limits_{x \to \infty} \left(\dfrac{f}{g}\right)(x) = \lim\limits_{x \to \infty} \left(\dfrac{f(x)}{g(x)}\right) = \dfrac{\lim\limits_{x \to \infty} f(x)}{\lim\limits_{x \to \infty} g(x)} = \dfrac{L}{M}, \ M \neq 0$

5. $\lim\limits_{x \to \infty} \sqrt{f(x)} = \sqrt{L}$, provided $f(x) \geq 0$ for all large x

Properties 1–5 also hold with $-\infty$ in place of ∞, provided that for property 5, $f(x) \geq 0$ for all small x.

Limit of $\dfrac{c}{x^n}$

If c is a constant, then Property 3 and Example 3 show that

$$\lim_{x\to\infty} \frac{c}{x} = \lim_{x\to\infty}\left(c \cdot \frac{1}{x}\right) = \left(\lim_{x\to\infty} c\right) \cdot \left(\lim_{x\to\infty} \frac{1}{x}\right) = c \cdot 0 = 0.$$

Repeatedly using Property 3 with this fact and Example 3, note that the result holds for any integer $n \geq 2$.

$$\lim_{x\to\infty} \frac{c}{x^n} = \lim_{x\to\infty}\left(\frac{c}{x} \cdot \frac{1}{x} \cdot \frac{1}{x} \cdot \cdots \cdot \frac{1}{x}\right)$$

$$= \left(\lim_{x\to\infty} \frac{c}{x}\right)\left(\lim_{x\to\infty} \frac{1}{x}\right)\left(\lim_{x\to\infty} \frac{1}{x}\right)\cdots\left(\lim_{x\to\infty} \frac{1}{x}\right)$$

$$= 0 \cdot 0 \cdot 0 \cdot \cdots \cdot 0$$

$$= 0$$

A similar argument works with $-\infty$ in place of ∞ and produces this useful result, which is essentially a formal statement of half of the Big-Little Concept discussed in Section 4.4.

Limit Theorem

If c is a constant, then for each positive integer n,

$$\lim_{x\to\infty} \frac{c}{x^n} = 0 \qquad \text{and} \qquad \lim_{x\to-\infty} \frac{c}{x^n} = 0$$

The Limit Theorem and the limit properties now make it possible to determine the limit, if it exists, of any rational function as x approaches infinity or negative infinity.

Example 5   End Behavior of a Rational Function

Describe the end behavior of $f(x) = \dfrac{3x^2 - 2x + 1}{2x^2 + 4x - 5}$ and justify your conclusion.

Solution

If you graph $f(x) = \dfrac{3x^2 - 2x + 1}{2x^2 + 4x - 5}$, to the right of the y-axis you will see that there appears to be a horizontal asymptote close to $y = 1.5$, as shown in Figure 14.5-7. This can be confirmed algebraically by computing

$$\lim_{x\to\infty} \frac{3x^2 - 2x + 1}{2x^2 + 4x - 5}.$$

Property 4 cannot be used directly because neither the numerator nor denominator have a finite limit as x approaches infinity, as discussed in Example 4. To rewrite the expression in an equivalent form, divide both

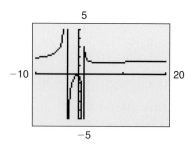

Figure 14.5-7

numerator and denominator by the highest power of x that appears, namely x^2. Dividing both by x^2 is the same as multiplying by $\dfrac{\frac{1}{x^2}}{\frac{1}{x^2}}$, a form of 1, so the value of the fraction is not changed.

$$\lim_{x \to \infty} \frac{3x^2 - 2x + 1}{2x^2 + 4x - 5} = \lim_{x \to \infty} \frac{\dfrac{3x^2 - 2x + 1}{x^2}}{\dfrac{2x^2 + 4x - 5}{x^2}}$$

$$= \lim_{x \to \infty} \frac{\dfrac{3x^2}{x^2} - \dfrac{2x}{x^2} + \dfrac{1}{x^2}}{\dfrac{2x^2}{x^2} + \dfrac{4x}{x^2} - \dfrac{5}{x^2}}$$

$$= \lim_{x \to \infty} \frac{3 - \dfrac{2}{x} + \dfrac{1}{x^2}}{2 + \dfrac{4}{x} - \dfrac{5}{x^2}}$$

$$= \frac{\displaystyle\lim_{x \to \infty}\left(3 - \dfrac{2}{x} + \dfrac{1}{x^2}\right)}{\displaystyle\lim_{x \to \infty}\left(2 + \dfrac{4}{x} - \dfrac{5}{x^2}\right)} \qquad \text{\textit{property 4}}$$

$$= \frac{\displaystyle\lim_{x \to \infty} 3 - \lim_{x \to \infty} \dfrac{2}{x} + \lim_{x \to \infty} \dfrac{1}{x^2}}{\displaystyle\lim_{x \to \infty} 2 + \lim_{x \to \infty} \dfrac{4}{x} - \lim_{x \to \infty} \dfrac{5}{x^2}} \qquad \text{\textit{property 1, 2}}$$

$$= \frac{3 - \displaystyle\lim_{x \to \infty} \dfrac{2}{x} + \lim_{x \to \infty} \dfrac{1}{x^2}}{2 + \displaystyle\lim_{x \to \infty} \dfrac{4}{x} - \lim_{x \to \infty} \dfrac{5}{x^2}} \qquad \text{\textit{limit of constant}}$$

$$= \frac{3 - 0 + 0}{2 + 0 - 0} \qquad \text{\textit{limit theorem}}$$

$$= \frac{3}{2}$$

A slight variation on the last example can be used to compute certain limits involving square roots.

Example 6   **Limits at Infinity**

Find each limit.

a. $\displaystyle\lim_{x \to \infty} \frac{\sqrt{3x^2 + 1}}{2x + 3}$ **b.** $\displaystyle\lim_{x \to -\infty} \frac{\sqrt{3x^2 + 1}}{2x + 3}$

Solution

a. Only positive values of x need to be considered when finding the limit as x approaches infinity. When x is positive, $\sqrt{x^2} = x$. Therefore,

$$\lim_{x \to \infty} \frac{\sqrt{3x^2 + 1}}{2x + 3} = \lim_{x \to \infty} \frac{\dfrac{\sqrt{3x^2 + 1}}{x}}{\dfrac{2x + 3}{x}} \qquad \textit{multiply by } \dfrac{\frac{1}{x}}{\frac{1}{x}}$$

$$= \lim_{x \to \infty} \frac{\dfrac{\sqrt{3x^2 + 1}}{\sqrt{x^2}}}{\dfrac{2x + 3}{x}} \qquad \textit{$\sqrt{x^2} = x$, for $x > 0$}$$

$$= \lim_{x \to \infty} \frac{\sqrt{\dfrac{3x^2 + 1}{x^2}}}{\dfrac{2x + 3}{x}} \qquad \textit{$\dfrac{\sqrt{a}}{\sqrt{b}} = \sqrt{\dfrac{a}{b}}$}$$

$$= \lim_{x \to \infty} \frac{\sqrt{3 + \dfrac{1}{x^2}}}{2 + \dfrac{3}{x}}$$

$$= \frac{\lim\limits_{x \to \infty} \sqrt{3 + \dfrac{1}{x^2}}}{\lim\limits_{x \to \infty} \left(2 + \dfrac{3}{x}\right)} \qquad \textit{property 4}$$

$$= \frac{\sqrt{\lim\limits_{x \to \infty} \left(3 + \dfrac{1}{x^2}\right)}}{\lim\limits_{x \to \infty} \left(2 + \dfrac{3}{x}\right)} \qquad \textit{property 5}$$

$$= \frac{\sqrt{\lim\limits_{x \to \infty} 3 + \lim\limits_{x \to \infty} \dfrac{1}{x^2}}}{\lim\limits_{x \to \infty} 2 + \lim\limits_{x \to \infty} \dfrac{3}{x}} \qquad \textit{property 1}$$

$$= \frac{\sqrt{3 + 0}}{2 + 0} \qquad \textit{constant limit and limit theorem}$$

$$= \frac{\sqrt{3}}{2}$$

b. To compute the limit as x approaches negative infinity, you need only consider negative values of x and use the fact that when x is negative, $x = -\sqrt{x^2}$. For instance, $-2 = \sqrt{(-2)^2} = -\sqrt{4}$. Then an argument similar to the one in part **a** shows that

$$\lim_{x \to -\infty} \frac{\sqrt{3x^2 + 1}}{2x + 3} = -\frac{\sqrt{3}}{2}$$

Although the properties of limits and some algebraic ingenuity can often by used to compute limits, as in the preceding examples, more sophisticated techniques are needed to determine certain limits. This is the case, for example, with the proof that $\lim\limits_{n\to\infty}\left(1+\dfrac{1}{n}\right)^n$ exists and is the number e.

Exercises 14.5

In Exercises 1–8, use a calculator to estimate the limit.

1. $\lim\limits_{x\to\infty}\left[\sqrt{x^2+1}-(x+1)\right]$

2. $\lim\limits_{x\to\infty}\left[\sqrt{x^2+x+1}+x\right]$

3. $\lim\limits_{x\to-\infty}\dfrac{x^{\frac{2}{3}}-x^{\frac{4}{3}}}{x^3}$

4. $\lim\limits_{x\to\infty}\dfrac{x^{\frac{5}{4}}+x}{2x-x^{\frac{5}{4}}}$

5. $\lim\limits_{x\to-\infty}\sin\dfrac{1}{x}$

6. $\lim\limits_{x\to\infty}\dfrac{\sin x}{x}$

7. $\lim\limits_{x\to\infty}\dfrac{\ln x}{x}$

8. $\lim\limits_{x\to\infty}\dfrac{5}{1+(1.1)^{-\frac{x}{20}}}$

In Exercises 9–14, list the vertical asymptotes of the graph, if any exist. Then use the graph of the function to find

$$\lim\limits_{x\to\infty}f(x)\quad\text{and}\quad\lim\limits_{x\to-\infty}f(x).$$

9.

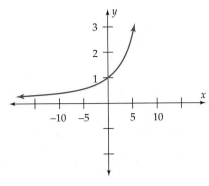

10.

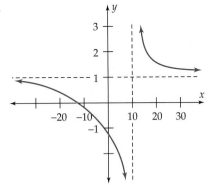

11.

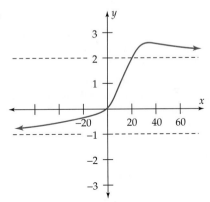

12.

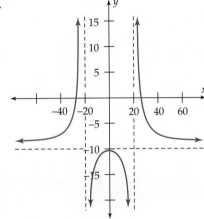

13.

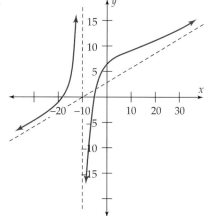

14.

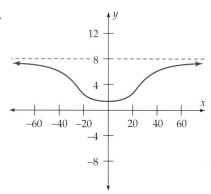

In Exercises 15–20, use the limit theorem and the properties of limits to find the horizontal asymptotes of the graph of the given function.

15. $f(x) = \dfrac{3x^2 + 5}{4x^2 - 6x + 2}$

16. $g(x) = \dfrac{x^2}{x^2 - 2x + 1}$

17. $h(x) = \dfrac{2x^2 - 6x + 1}{2 + x - x^2}$

18. $k(x) = \dfrac{3x + x^2 - 4}{2x - x^3 + x^2}$

19. $f(x) = \dfrac{3x^4 - 2x^3 + 5x^2 - x + 1}{7x^3 - 4x^2 + 6x - 12}$

20. $g(x) = \dfrac{2x^5 - x^3 + 2x - 9}{5 - x^5}$

In Exercises 21–39, use the limit theorem and the properties of limits to find the limit.

21. $\displaystyle\lim_{x \to -\infty} \dfrac{(x - 3)(x + 2)}{2x^2 + x + 1}$

22. $\displaystyle\lim_{x \to \infty} \dfrac{(2x + 1)(3x - 2)}{3x^2 + 2x - 5}$

23. $\displaystyle\lim_{x \to \infty} \left(3x - \dfrac{1}{x^2}\right)$ **24.** $\displaystyle\lim_{x \to -\infty} (3x^2 + 1)^{-2}$

25. $\displaystyle\lim_{x \to -\infty} \left(\dfrac{3x}{x + 2} + \dfrac{2x}{x - 1}\right)$

26. $\displaystyle\lim_{x \to \infty} \left(\dfrac{x}{x^2 + 1} + \dfrac{2x^2}{x^3 + x}\right)$

27. $\displaystyle\lim_{x \to \infty} \dfrac{2x}{\sqrt{x^2 - 2x}}$ **28.** $\displaystyle\lim_{x \to -\infty} \dfrac{x}{\sqrt{x^2 - 1}}$

29. $\displaystyle\lim_{x \to -\infty} \dfrac{3x - 2}{\sqrt{2x^2 + 1}}$ **30.** $\displaystyle\lim_{x \to \infty} \dfrac{3x - 2}{\sqrt{2x^2 + 1}}$

31. $\displaystyle\lim_{x \to \infty} \dfrac{\sqrt{2x^2 + 1}}{3x - 5}$ **32.** $\displaystyle\lim_{x \to -\infty} \dfrac{\sqrt{2x^2 + 1}}{3x - 5}$

33. $\displaystyle\lim_{x \to -\infty} \dfrac{\sqrt{3x^2 + 3}}{x + 3}$ **34.** $\displaystyle\lim_{x \to \infty} \dfrac{\sqrt{3x^2 + 2x}}{2x + 1}$

35. $\displaystyle\lim_{x \to -\infty} \dfrac{x^2 + 2x + 1}{\sqrt{x^4 + 2x}}$ **36.** $\displaystyle\lim_{x \to \infty} \dfrac{\sqrt{x^6 - x^2}}{2x^3}$

37. $\displaystyle\lim_{x \to \infty} \dfrac{1 - \sqrt{x}}{1 + \sqrt{x}}$ *Hint:* Rationalize the denominator.

38. $\displaystyle\lim_{x \to \infty} \dfrac{\sqrt{x} + 2}{\sqrt{x} - 3}$

39. $\displaystyle\lim_{x \to \infty} \left(\sqrt{x^2 + 1} - x\right)$

     Hint: Multiply by $\dfrac{\sqrt{x^2 + 1} + x}{\sqrt{x^2 + 1} + x}$.

In Exercises 40–42, find the limit by adapting the hint from Exercise 39.

40. $\displaystyle\lim_{x \to -\infty} \left(x + \sqrt{x^2 + 4}\right)$

41. $\displaystyle\lim_{x \to \infty} \left(\sqrt{x^2 - 1} - \sqrt{x^2 + 1}\right)$

42. $\displaystyle\lim_{x \to -\infty} \left(\sqrt{x^2 + 5x + 5} + x + 1\right)$

43. A free-falling body has two forces acting on it: gravity, which causes the body to speed up as it falls, and air resistance, which causes the body to slow down. Assuming that a free-falling body has an initial velocity of zero and that its velocity is proportional to the force due to air resistance, the velocity of a falling object can be written as a function of the amount of elapsed time.

$$\text{velocity} = f(t) = \frac{mg}{k}\left(1 - e^{-\frac{k}{m}t}\right)$$

The variable m represents the mass of the body, g is acceleration due to gravity ($\approx$32 feet per second per second), and k is the contant of proportionality. For a fall with a parachute, $k = 1.6m$; without a parachute, $k = 0.18m$.

When the air resistance has built until it nearly balances the gravitational force, the body speeds up very little. Upon reaching this condition, the body continues to move downward with a constant maximum speed called *terminal velocity*. Find the terminal velocity of falling bodies with a parachute and without a parachute by finding the limit as t approaches infinity.

In Exercises 44–45, find the limit.

44. *Critical Thinking* $\displaystyle\lim_{x \to \infty} \frac{x}{|x|}$

45. *Critical Thinking* $\displaystyle\lim_{x \to -\infty} \frac{|x|}{|x| + 1}$

46. *Critical Thinking* Let $[x]$ denote the greatest integer function and find

   a. $\displaystyle\lim_{x \to \infty} \frac{[x]}{x}$ **b.** $\displaystyle\lim_{x \to -\infty} \frac{[x]}{x}$

47. *Critical Thinking* Find $\displaystyle\lim_{x \to \infty} \frac{\sqrt{x + \sqrt{x + \sqrt{x}}}}{\sqrt{x + 1}}$.

48. *Critical Thinking* Let $f(x)$ be a nonzero polynomial with leading coefficient a, and let $g(x)$ be a nonzero polynomial with leading coefficient c. Prove that

   a. if degree $f(x) <$ degree $g(x)$, then $\displaystyle\lim_{x \to \infty} \frac{f(x)}{g(x)} = 0$.

   b. if degree $f(x) =$ degree $g(x)$, then $\displaystyle\lim_{x \to \infty} \frac{f(x)}{g(x)} = \frac{a}{c}$.

   c. if degree $f(x) >$ degree $g(x)$, then $\displaystyle\lim_{x \to \infty} \frac{f(x)}{g(x)}$ does not exist.

Formal definitions of limits at infinity and negative infinity are given in Exercises 49 and 50. Adapt the discussion in Section 14.3 to explain how these definitions are derived from the informal definitions in this section.

49. *Critical Thinking* Let f be a function and L be a real number. Then the statement $\displaystyle\lim_{x \to \infty} f(x) = L$ means that for each positive number ε, there is a positive real number k that depends on ε with the following property:

   If $x > k$, then $|f(x) - L| < \varepsilon$

   Hint: Concentrate on the second part of the informal definition. The number k measures "large enough," that is, how large the values of x must be in order to guarantee that $f(x)$ is as close as you want to L.

50. *Critical Thinking* Let f be a function and L be a real number. Then the statement $\displaystyle\lim_{x \to -\infty} f(x) = L$ means that for each positive number ε, there is a negative real number n that depends on ε with the following property:

   If $x < n$, then $|f(x) - L| < \varepsilon$

CHAPTER

14

REVIEW

Important Concepts

Review Exercises

Section 14.1

In Exercises 1–2, use a calculator to estimate the limit.

1. $\lim\limits_{x \to 0} \dfrac{3x - \sin x}{x}$

2. $\lim\limits_{x \to \frac{\pi}{2}} \dfrac{1 - \sin x}{1 + \cos 2x}$

In Exercises 3–4, use the graph of the function to determine the limit.

3. $\lim\limits_{x \to 2} f(x)$

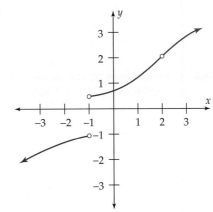

4. $\lim\limits_{x \to -1} f(x)$

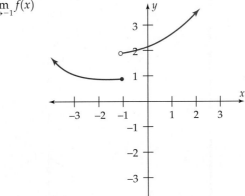

Section 14.2

In Exercises 5–6, assume that $\lim\limits_{x \to 3} f(x) = 5$ and $\lim\limits_{x \to 3} g(x) = -2$.

5. Find $\lim\limits_{x \to 3} \dfrac{f(x)g(x) - 2f(x)}{[g(x)]^2}$

6. Find $\lim\limits_{x \to 3} \dfrac{\sqrt{f(x)} - 2g(x)}{f(x) + g(x)}$

In Exercises 7–10, find the limit if it exists. If the limit does not exist, explain why.

7. $\lim\limits_{x \to 1} \dfrac{x^2 - 1}{x^2 - 3x + 2}$

8. $\lim\limits_{x \to -2} \dfrac{x^2 - x - 6}{x^2 + x - 2}$

9. $\lim\limits_{x \to 0} \dfrac{\sqrt{1 + x} - 1}{x}$

10. $\lim\limits_{x \to 2} \dfrac{x^2 - 2x - 3}{x^2 - 6x + 9}$

11. If $f(x) = x^2 + 1$, find $\displaystyle\lim_{h \to 0} \frac{f(2 + h) - f(2)}{h}$.

12. If $f(x) = 3x - 2$ and c is a constant, find $\displaystyle\lim_{h \to 0} \frac{f(c + h) - f(c)}{h}$.

Section 14.2.A

13. $\displaystyle\lim_{x \to -5^+} \frac{|x + 5|}{x + 5}$

14. $\displaystyle\lim_{x \to 7^-} \left(\sqrt{7 - x^2 + 6x} + 2 \right)$

Section 14.3

In Exercises 15–16, use the formal definition of limit to prove the statement.

15. $\displaystyle\lim_{x \to 3} (2x + 1) = 7$

16. $\displaystyle\lim_{x \to 2} \left(\frac{1}{2}x + 3 \right) = 4$

Section 14.4

In Exercises 17–18, determine whether the function whose graph is given is continuous at $x = -3$ and $x = 2$.

17.

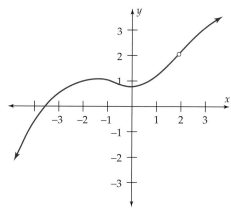

18.

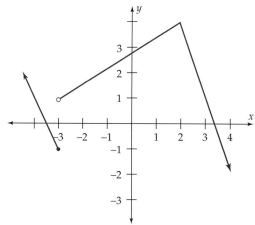

19. Show that $f(x) = \dfrac{x^2 - x - 6}{x^2 - 9}$ has the given traits.

     a. continuous at $x = 2$ **b.** discontinuous at $x = 3$

20. Is the function given by

$$f(x) = \begin{cases} 3x - 2 & \text{if } x \le 3 \\ 10 - x & \text{if } x > 3 \end{cases}$$

continuous at $x = 3$? Justify your answer.

Section 14.5

In Exercises 21–22, find the vertical asymptotes of the graph of the given function, and state whether the graph moves upward or downward on each side of each asymptote.

21. $f(x) = \dfrac{x^2 + 1}{x^2 - x - 2}$

22. $g(x) = \dfrac{x^2 - 1}{x^2 - 3x + 2}$

In Exercises 23–26, find the limit.

23. $\displaystyle\lim_{x \to \infty} \dfrac{2x^3 - 3x^2 + 5x - 1}{4x^3 + 2x^2 - x + 10}$

24. $\displaystyle\lim_{x \to -\infty} \dfrac{4 - 3x - 2x^2}{x^3 + 2x + 5}$

25. $\displaystyle\lim_{x \to -\infty} \left(\dfrac{2x + 1}{x - 3} + \dfrac{4x - 1}{3x} \right)$

26. $\displaystyle\lim_{x \to \infty} \dfrac{\sqrt{3x^2 + 2}}{4x + 1}$

In Exercises 27–28, find the horizontal asymptotes of the graph of the given function algebraically, and verify your results graphically with a calculator.

27. $f(x) = \dfrac{x^2 - x + 7}{2x^2 + 5x + 7}$

28. $f(x) = \dfrac{x - 9}{\sqrt{4x^2 + 3x + 2}}$

can do calculus
Riemann Sums

Calculus deals with rates of change, such as the speed of a car, and problems such as the following:

> If you know the continuously changing speed of a car at any instant, can you determine how far the car has traveled?

A special case of this question will be answered in this section by using Riemann sums.

Time (sec)	Velocity (ft/sec)
0	14
1	29
2	61
3	128
4	268

Example 1 Total Distance Given Velocities

Suppose a racecar is moving with increasing velocity. The velocity of the car at various times is given in the table. Estimate the total distance traveled in the 4-second interval.

Solution

Because the velocity is increasing, the car has gone at least 14 feet during the first second, at least 29 feet during the second, at least 61 feet during the third second, and at least 128 feet during the fourth second. During the four-second interval, the car has traveled at least

$$14 + 29 + 61 + 128 = 232 \text{ feet} \qquad \textit{underestimate}$$

Therefore, 232 feet is an underestimate of the total distance traveled.

An overestimate can be found by noting that the car travels no more than 29 feet in the first second, no more than 61 feet in the next second, no more than 128 in the third second, and no more than 268 feet in the last second. Altogether, the car traveled no more than

$$29 + 61 + 128 + 268 = 486 \text{ feet} \qquad \textit{overestimate}$$

Therefore, the total distance traveled is between 232 feet and 486 feet. ∎

The lower and upper estimates can be represented on a graph, where the velocity is shown as a smooth curve passing through each point given in the table, and the estimates of the distance traveled each second are represented by the area of rectangles. See Figure 14.C-1. The darker rectangles represent the underestimate for each second and the darker and lighter rectangles stacked together represent the overestimate.

Because the time interval between each measurement is 1 second, each rectangle is 1 unit wide. Each height corresponds to how far the car could have traveled during each time interval. Therefore, the areas of the darker rectangles are 14, 29, 61, and 128, and the sum of the areas represents the total underestimate of 232.

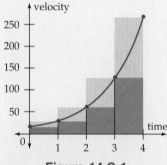

Figure 14.C-1

Similarly, the sum of the areas of the darker and lighter rectangles, which represents the overestimate, is 486.

There is a difference of 486 − 232 = 254 feet between the estimates. This difference can also be found by adding the areas of the lighter rectangles.

A Better Estimate

To get a better estimate of how far the car traveled during the 4-second interval, the velocity is measured for each half second, as shown in the table. The graph shown in Figure 14.C-2 displays the new data.

In the first half second, the car travels at least $14\left(\dfrac{1}{2}\right) = 7$ feet and at most $20\left(\dfrac{1}{2}\right) = 10$ feet. The distance traveled in each half second is calculated for both the underestimate and the overestimate as

$$v_i(\Delta t)$$

where v_i represents the velocity as measured at one end of the time interval and Δt represents length of each the time interval.

$$\text{Underestimate } = 14\left(\frac{1}{2}\right) + 20\left(\frac{1}{2}\right) + 29\left(\frac{1}{2}\right) + 42\left(\frac{1}{2}\right)$$

$$+ 61\left(\frac{1}{2}\right) + 88\left(\frac{1}{2}\right) + 128\left(\frac{1}{2}\right) + 185\left(\frac{1}{2}\right) = 283.5 \text{ feet}$$

$$\text{Overestimate } = 20\left(\frac{1}{2}\right) + 29\left(\frac{1}{2}\right) + 42\left(\frac{1}{2}\right) + 61\left(\frac{1}{2}\right)$$

$$+ 88\left(\frac{1}{2}\right) + 128\left(\frac{1}{2}\right) + 185\left(\frac{1}{2}\right) + 268\left(\frac{1}{2}\right) = 410.5 \text{ feet}$$

The difference between the estimates is again shown as the area of the lighter rectangles. This difference is

$$410.5 - 283.5 = 127.$$

Notice that the difference between the better estimates is half what it was in Example 1. By halving the intervals of measurement, the difference between the estimates is halved. Similarly, if the interval of measurement was given for every tenth of a second, the estimates would differ by $254(0.1) = 25.4$ feet, and if the interval of measurement was every thousandth of a second, the difference between the estimates would be $254(0.001) = 0.254$.

Time (sec)	Velocity (ft/sec)
0	14
0.5	20
1	29
1.5	42
2	61
2.5	88
3	128
3.5	185
4	268

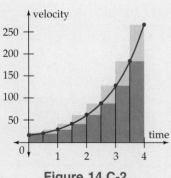

Figure 14.C-2

Example 2 Accuracy of Estimates

How frequently must the velocity be measured to ensure that the estimated distances traveled by the race car are within 5 feet of each other?

Solution

The difference between the velocity at the beginning and end of the measurements is $268 - 14 = 254$. If the time between each measurement is Δt, then the difference between the estimates is $254(\Delta t)$. For the differences of the estimates to be within 5 feet,

$$254(\Delta t) < 5 \quad \text{or} \quad \Delta t < 0.0196850394 \text{ seconds.}$$

As the length of the intervals of measurement become smaller and smaller, the underestimate and overestimate approach the same number—the area under the curve—which represents the total distance traveled.

Riemann Sums

Suppose that velocity is given as an increasing function of time: $v = f(t)$. To find the total distance traveled by a moving object over the time interval $a < t < b$, divide the interval into n equally spaced times $t_0 = a, t_1, \ldots, t_n = b$, where each time interval is $\Delta t = \dfrac{b-a}{n}$ in duration.

During each time interval, the velocity is given by $f(t_i)$, so the estimated distance traveled during each interval is velocity times the length of each time interval.

$$f(t_i)\Delta t \qquad \textit{distance at each } \Delta t$$

Both the underestimate and the overestimate of the total distance traveled can be written as the sum of the individual distances. The underestimate sum begins with $f(t_0)\Delta t$ and the overestimate sum begins with $f(t_1)\Delta t$

$$f(t_1))\Delta t + f(t_2))\Delta t + \cdots f(t_n))\Delta t = \sum_{i=1}^{n} f(t_i)\Delta t \qquad \textit{overestimate}$$

$$f(t_0))\Delta t + f(t_1))\Delta t + \cdots f(t_{n-1}))\Delta t = \sum_{i=0}^{n-1} f(t_i)\Delta t \qquad \textit{underestimate}$$

$$\text{Total distance traveled} = \lim_{n \to \infty} f(t_1)\Delta t + f(t_2)\Delta t + \cdots + f(t_n)\Delta t$$

$$= \lim_{n \to \infty} \sum_{i=1}^{n} f(t_i)\Delta t$$

As Examples 1 and 2 show, these estimates will be very close to each other when n is very large and the correspoding Δt is very small. In fact, the actual total distance can be found by taking the limit of one of these sums as n gets very large without bound, written $n \to \infty$.

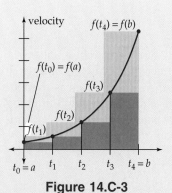

Figure 14.C-3

This limit can be interpreted geometrically as the area between the graph of f and the horizontal axis from $t = a$ to $t = b$. The sum $\sum_{i=1}^{n} f(t_i)\Delta t$ is called a **Riemann sum.** The limit of the Riemann sums

$$\lim_{n \to \infty} \sum_{i=1}^{n} f(t_i)\Delta t$$

is called the **definite integral** of f from a to b and is denoted by

$$\int_{a}^{b} f(t)dt.$$

Definite integrals are studied fully in calculus. They have a wide variety of other applications, including determining the lengths of curves and the volumes of irregularly shaped solids, finding the amount of work done by a force, and making sophisticated probability calculations.

Exercises

1. A driver slams on the brakes and comes to a stop in five seconds. The following velocities are recorded after the brakes are applied.

Time (sec)	0	1	2	3	4	5
Velocity (ft/sec)	102	70	46	29	12	0

  a. Find an upper and lower estimate of the distance traveled by the car after the brakes were applied.
  b. Sketch the graph of velocity versus time, and show the upper and lower estimates and the difference between them.
  c. How often would the velocity need to be measured to assure that the estimates differ by less than 5 feet? by less than 1 foot?

2. Use the grid to estimate the area of the region bounded by the curve, the horizontal axis, and the lines $x = \pm 4$. Get an upper and a lower estimate that are within 4 square units of one another. Explain your procedure.

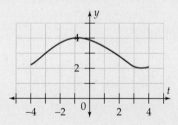

3. a. For the diagram below, estimate the shaded area with an error of at most 0.1.
   b. How can the shaded area be approximated to any desired degree of accuracy?

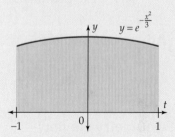

4. Estimate the total distance an object travels between $t = 0$ and $t = 10$ if the graph below represents the velocity v of the object in ft/sec.

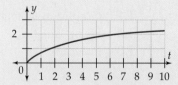

5. Suppose the velocity of an object is given by $v(t) = \cos t$ for $0 \le t \le 1.5$. Estimate the distance traveled during the 1.5-second interval, accurate to one decimal place.

6. A snail is crawling at a velocity given by $v(t) = \dfrac{1}{t}$, where $1 \le t \le 2$ hours and v is in feet per hour. Estimate the distance that the snail crawls during the second hour.

Appendix

ALGEBRA REVIEW

This appendix reviews the fundamental algebraic facts that are used frequently in this book. You must be able to handle these algebraic manipulations in order to succeed in this course and in calculus.

A.1 Integral Exponents

Exponents provide a convenient shorthand for certain products. If c is a real number, then c^2 denotes cc and c^3 denotes ccc. More generally, for any positive integer n

$$c^n \text{ denotes the product } ccc \cdots c \quad (n \text{ factors}).$$

In this notation c^1 is just c, so we usually omit the exponent 1.

Example 1

$3^4 = 3 \cdot 3 \cdot 3 \cdot 3 = 81$ and

$$(-2)^5 = (-2)(-2)(-2)(-2)(-2) = -32.$$

For every positive integer n, $0^n = 0 \cdots 0 = 0$. ∎

Example 2

To find $(2.4)^9$ use the $\wedge$ (or a^b or x^y) key on your calculator:*

$$2.4 \wedge 9 \text{ ENTER*}$$

which produces the (approximate) answer 2641.80754. ∎

Because exponents are just shorthand for multiplication, it is easy to determine the rules they obey. For instance,

$$c^3 c^5 = (ccc)(ccccc) = c^8, \qquad \text{that is,} \qquad c^3 c^5 = c^{3+5}.$$

$$\frac{c^7}{c^4} = \frac{ccccccc}{cccc} = \frac{\cancel{ccccccc}}{\cancel{cccc}} = ccc = c^3, \qquad \text{that is,} \qquad \frac{c^7}{c^4} = c^{7-4}.$$

*The ENTER key is labeled EXE on Casio calculators.

Similar arguments work in the general case:

To multiply c^m by c^n, add the exponents: $c^m c^n = c^{m+n}$.

To divide c^m by c^n, subtract the exponents: $\dfrac{c^m}{c^n} = c^{m-n}$.

Example 3

$$4^2 \cdot 4^7 = 4^{2+7} = 4^9 \qquad \text{and} \qquad \frac{2^8}{2^3} = 2^{8-3} = 2^5.$$

The notation c^n can be extended to the cases when n is zero or negative as follows:

If $c \neq 0$, then c^0 is defined to be the number 1.

If $c \neq 0$ and n is a positive integer, then

$$c^{-n} \text{ is defined to be the number } \frac{1}{c^n}.$$

Note that 0^0 and negative powers of 0 are *not* defined (negative powers of 0 would involve division by 0). The reason for choosing these definitions of c^{-n} for nonzero c is that the multiplication and division rules for exponents remain valid. For instance,

$$c^5 \cdot c^0 = c^5 \cdot 1 = c^5, \qquad \text{so that} \qquad c^5 c^0 = c^{5+0}.$$
$$c^7 c^{-7} = c^7 \left(\frac{1}{c^7} \right) = 1 = c^0, \qquad \text{so that} \qquad c^7 c^{-7} = c^{7-7}.$$

Example 4

$6^{-3} = \dfrac{1}{6^3} = \dfrac{1}{216}$ and $(-2)^{-5} = \dfrac{1}{(-2)^5} = -\dfrac{1}{32}$. A calculator shows that $(0.287)^{-12} \approx 3{,}201{,}969.857.$*

If c and d are nonzero real numbers and m and n are integers (positive, negative, or zero), then we have these

Exponent Laws

1. $c^m c^n = c^{m+n}$
2. $\dfrac{c^m}{c^n} = c^{m-n}$
3. $(c^m)^n = c^{mn}$
4. $(cd)^n = c^n d^n$
5. $\left(\dfrac{c}{d} \right)^n = \dfrac{c^n}{d^n}$
6. $c^{-n} = \dfrac{1}{c^n}$

* $\approx$ means "approximately equal to."

Example 5

Here are examples of each of the six exponent laws.

1. $\pi^{-5}\pi^2 = \pi^{-5+2} = \pi^{-3} = \dfrac{1}{\pi^3}.$ **4.** $(2x)^5 = 2^5x^5 = 32x^5.$

2. $\dfrac{x^9}{x^4} = x^{9-4} = x^5.$ **5.** $\left(\dfrac{7}{3}\right)^{10} = \dfrac{7^{10}}{3^{10}}.$

3. $(5^{-3})^2 = 5^{(-3)2} = 5^{-6}.$ **6.** $\dfrac{1}{x^{-5}} = \dfrac{1}{\left(\dfrac{1}{x^5}\right)} = x^5.$

CAUTION

$(2x)^5$ is not the same as $2x^5$. Part 4 of Example 5 shows that $(2x)^5 = 32x^5$ and not $2x^5$.

The exponent laws can often be used to simplify complicated expressions.

Example 6

a. $(2x^2y^3z)^4 = 2^4(x^2)^4(y^3)^4z^4 = 16x^8y^{12}z^4.$
   $\uparrow$ $\uparrow$
   Law (4)   *Law (3)*

b. $(r^{-3}s^2)^{-2} = (r^{-3})^{-2}(s^2)^{-2} = r^6s^{-4} = \dfrac{r^6}{s^4}.$
   $\uparrow$ $\uparrow$
   Law (4)   *Law (3)*

c. $\dfrac{x^5(y^2)^3}{(x^2y)^2} = \dfrac{x^5y^6}{(x^2y)^2} = \dfrac{x^5y^6}{(x^2)^2y^2} = \dfrac{x^5y^6}{x^4y^2} = x^{5-4}y^{6-2} = xy^4.$
         $\uparrow$ $\uparrow$ $\uparrow$ $\uparrow$
        Law (3)   *Law (4)*   *Law (3) Law (2)*

It is usually more efficient to use the exponent laws with the negative exponents rather than first converting to positive exponents. If positive exponents are required, the conversion can be made in the last step.

Example 7

Simplify and express without negative exponents

$$\frac{a^{-2}(b^2c^3)^{-2}}{(a^{-3}b^{-5})^2c}.$$

Solution

$$\frac{a^{-2}(b^2c^3)^{-2}}{(a^{-3}b^{-5})^2c} = \frac{a^{-2}(b^2)^{-2}(c^3)^{-2}}{(a^{-3})^2(b^{-5})^2c} = \frac{a^{-2}b^{-4}c^{-6}}{a^{-6}b^{-10}c}$$
           $\uparrow$ $\uparrow$
        Law (4)   *Law (3)*

$$= a^{-2-(-6)}b^{-4-(-10)}c^{-6-1} = a^4b^6c^{-7} = \frac{a^4b^6}{c^7}.$$
    $\uparrow$
  Law (2)

Since $(-1)(-1) = +1$, any even power of -1, such as $(-1)^4$ or $(-1)^{12}$, will be equal to 1. Every odd power of -1 is equal to -1; for instance $(-1)^5 = (-1)^4(-1) = 1(-1) = -1$. Consequently, for every positive number c

$$(-c)^n = [(-1)c]^n = (-1)^n c^n = \begin{cases} c^n & \text{if } n \text{ is even} \\ -c^n & \text{if } n \text{ is odd} \end{cases}.$$

Example 8

$(-3)^4 = 3^4 = 81$ and $(-5)^3 = -5^3 = -125$.

CAUTION

Be careful with negative bases. For instance, if you want to compute $(-12)^4$, which is a positive number, but you key in $(-)$ 12 $\wedge$ 4 ENTER the calculator will interpret this as $-(12^4)$ and produce a negative answer. To get the correct answer, you must key in the parentheses:

$$(\, (-)\, 12 \,) \wedge 4 \text{ ENTER}.$$

Exercises A.1

In Exercises 1–18, evaluate the expression.

1. $(-6)^2$

2. -6^2

3. $5 + 4(3^2 + 2^3)$

4. $(-3)2^2 + 4^2 - 1$

5. $\dfrac{(-3)^2 + (-2)^4}{-2^2 - 1}$

6. $\dfrac{(-4)^2 + 2}{(-4)^2 - 7} + 1$

7. $\left(\dfrac{-5}{4}\right)^3$

8. $-\left(\dfrac{7}{4} + \dfrac{3}{4}\right)^2$

9. $\left(\dfrac{1}{3}\right)^3 + \left(\dfrac{2}{3}\right)^3$

10. $\left(\dfrac{5}{7}\right)^2 + \left(\dfrac{2}{7}\right)^2$

11. $2^4 - 2^7$

12. $3^3 - 3^{-7}$

13. $(2^{-2} + 2)^2$

14. $(3^{-1} - 3^3)^2$

15. $2^2 \cdot 3^{-3} - 3^2 \cdot 2^{-3}$

16. $4^3 \cdot 5^{-2} + 4^2 \cdot 5^{-1}$

17. $\dfrac{1}{2^3} + \dfrac{1}{2^{-4}}$

18. $3^2\left(\dfrac{1}{3} + \dfrac{1}{3^{-2}}\right)$

In Exercises 19–38, simplify the expression. Each letter represents a nonzero real number and should appear at most once in your answer.

19. $x^2 \cdot x^3 \cdot x^5$

20. $y \cdot y^4 \cdot y^6$

21. $(0.03)y^2 \cdot y^7$

22. $(1.3)z^3 \cdot z^5$

23. $(2x^2)^3 3x$

24. $(3y^3)^4 5y^2$

25. $(3x^2y)^2$

26. $(2xy^3)^3$

27. $(a^2)(7a)(-3a^3)$

28. $(b^3)(-b^2)(3b)$

29. $(2w)^3(3w)(4w)^2$

30. $(3d)^4(2d)^2(5d)$

31. $a^{-2}b^3a^3$

32. $c^4d^5c^{-3}$

33. $(2x)^{-2}(2y)^3(4x)$

34. $(3x)^{-3}(2y)^{-2}(2x)$

35. $(-3a^4)^2(9x^3)^{-1}$

36. $(2y^3)^3(3y^2)^{-2}$

37. $(2x^2y)^0(3xy)$

38. $(3x^2y^4)^0$

In Exercises 39–42, express the given number as a power of 2.

39. $(64)^2$

40. $\left(\dfrac{1}{8}\right)^3$

41. $(2^4 \cdot 16^{-2})^3$

42. $\left(\dfrac{1}{2}\right)^{-8}\left(\dfrac{1}{4}\right)^4\left(\dfrac{1}{16}\right)^{-3}$

In Exercises 43–60, simplify and write the given expression without negative exponents. All letters represent nonzero real numbers.

43. $\dfrac{x^4(x^2)^3}{x^3}$

44. $\left(\dfrac{z^2}{t^3}\right)^4 \cdot \left(\dfrac{z^3}{t}\right)^5$

45. $\left(\dfrac{e^6}{c^4}\right)^2 \cdot \left(\dfrac{c^3}{e}\right)^3$

46. $\left(\dfrac{x^7}{y^6}\right)^2 \cdot \left(\dfrac{y^2}{x}\right)^4$

47. $\left(\dfrac{ab^2c^3d^4}{abc^2d}\right)^2$

48. $\dfrac{(3x)^2(y^2)^3x^2}{(2xy^2)^3}$

49. $\left(\dfrac{a^6}{b^{-4}}\right)^2$

50. $\left(\dfrac{x^{-2}}{y^{-2}}\right)^2$

51. $\left(\dfrac{c^5}{d^{-3}}\right)^{-2}$

52. $\left(\dfrac{x^{-1}}{2y^{-1}}\right)\left(\dfrac{2y}{x}\right)^{-2}$

53. $\left(\dfrac{3x}{y^2}\right)^{-3}\left(\dfrac{-x}{2y^3}\right)^2$

54. $\left(\dfrac{5u^2v}{2uv^2}\right)^2\left(\dfrac{-3uv}{2u^2v}\right)^{-3}$

55. $\dfrac{(a^{-3}b^2c)^{-2}}{(ab^{-2}c^3)^{-1}}$

56. $\dfrac{(-2cd^2e^{-1})^3}{(5c^{-3}de)^{-2}}$

57. $(c^{-1}d^{-2})^{-3}$

58. $[(x^2y^{-1})^2]^{-3}$

59. $a^2(a^{-1}+a^{-3})$

60. $\dfrac{a^{-2}}{b^{-2}}+\dfrac{b^2}{a^2}$

In Exercises 61–66, determine the sign of the given number without calculating the product.

61. $(-2.6)^3(-4.3)^{-2}$

62. $(4.1)^{-2}(2.5)^{-3}$

63. $(-1)^9(6.7)^5$

64. $(-4)^{12}6^9$

65. $(-3.1)^{-3}(4.6)^{-6}(7.2)^7$

66. $(45.8)^{-7}(-7.9)^{-9}(-8.5)^{-4}$

In Exercises 67–72, r, s, and t are positive integers and a, b, and c are nonzero real numbers. Simplify and write the given expression without negative exponents.

67. $\dfrac{3^{-r}}{3^{-s-r}}$

68. $\dfrac{4^{-(t+1)}}{4^{2-t}}$

69. $\left(\dfrac{a^6}{b^{-4}}\right)^t$

70. $\dfrac{c^{-t}}{(6b)^{-s}}$

71. $\dfrac{(c^{-r}b^s)^t}{(c^tb^{-s})^r}$

72. $\dfrac{(a^rb^{-s})^{-t}}{(b^tc^r)^{-s}}$

In Exercises 73–80, give an example to show that the statement may be false for some numbers.

73. $a^r + b^r = (a + b)^r$

74. $a^ra^s = a^{rs}$

75. $a^rb^s = (ab)^{r+s}$

76. $c^{-r} = -c^r$

77. $\dfrac{c^r}{c^s} = c^{\frac{r}{s}}$

78. $(a + 1)(b + 1) = ab + 1$

79. $(-a)^2 = -a^2$

80. $(-a)(-b) = -ab$

A.2   Arithmetic of Algebraic Expressions

Expressions such as

$$b + 3c^2, \qquad 3x^2 - 5x + 4, \qquad \sqrt{x^3 + z}, \qquad \dfrac{x^3 + 4xy - \pi}{x^2 + xy}$$

are called **algebraic expressions.** Each expression represents a number that is obtained by performing various algebraic operations (such as addition or taking roots) on one or more numbers, some of which may be denoted by letters.

A letter that denotes a particular real number is called a **constant;** its value remains unchanged throughout the discussion. For example, the Greek letter π has long been used to denote the number $3.14159 \cdots$. Sometimes a constant is a fixed but unspecified real number, as in "an angle of k degrees" or "a triangle with base of length b."

A letter that can represent *any* real number is called a **variable.** In the expression $2x + 5$, for example, the variable x can be any real number. If $x = 3$, then $2x + 5 = 2 \cdot 3 + 5 = 11$. If $x = \frac{1}{2}$, then $2x + 5 = 2 \cdot \frac{1}{2} + 5 = 6$, and so on.*

Constants are usually denoted by letters near the beginning of the alphabet and variables by letters near the end of the alphabet. Consequently, in expressions such as $cx + d$ and $cy^2 + dy$, it is understood that c and d are constants and x and y are variables.

The usual rules of arithmetic are valid for algebraic expressions:

Commutative Laws:

$$a + b = b + a \quad \text{and} \quad ab = ba$$

Associative Laws:

$$(a + b) + c = a + (b + c) \quad \text{and} \quad (ab)c = a(bc)$$

Distributive Laws:

$$a(b + c) = ab + ac \quad \text{and} \quad (b + c)a = ba + ca.$$

Example 1

Use the distributive law to *combine like terms*; for instance,

$$3x + 5x + 4x = (3 + 5 + 4)x = 12x.$$

In practice, you do the middle part in your head and simply write $3x + 5x + 4x = 12x$.

Example 2

In more complicated expressions, eliminate parentheses, use the commutative law to group like terms together, and then combine them.

$$\left(a^2b - 3\sqrt{c}\right) + \left(5ab + 7\sqrt{c}\right) + 7a^2b = a^2b - 3\sqrt{c} + 5ab + 7\sqrt{c} + 7a^2b$$

Regroup: $\quad = a^2b + 7a^2b - 3\sqrt{c} + 7\sqrt{c} + 5ab$

Combine like terms: $\quad = 8a^2b + 4\sqrt{c} + 5ab.$

CAUTION

Be careful when parentheses are preceded by a minus sign: $-(b + 3) = -b - 3$ and not $-b + 3$. Here's the reason: $-(b + 3)$ means $(-1)(b + 3)$, so that by the distributive law,

$$-(b + 3) = (-1)(b + 3) = (-1)b + (-1)3 = -b - 3.$$

Similarly, $-(7 - y) = -7 - (-y) = -7 + y.$

---

*We assume any conditions on the constants and variables necessary to guarantee that an algebraic expression does represent a real number. For instance, in $\sqrt{z}$ we assume $z \geq 0$ and in $\frac{1}{c}$ we assume $c \neq 0$.

The examples in the Caution Box illustrate the following.

Rules for Eliminating Parentheses

> **Parentheses preceded by a plus sign (or no sign) may be deleted.**
>
> **Parentheses preceded by a minus sign may be deleted *if* the sign of every term within the parentheses is changed.**

The usual method of multiplying algebraic expressions is to use the distributive laws repeatedly, as shown in the following examples. The net result is to *multiply every term in the first sum by every term in the second sum.*

Example 3

To compute $(y - 2)(3y^2 - 7y + 4)$, we first apply the distributive law, treating $(3y^2 - 7y + 4)$ as a single number:

$$(y - 2)(3y^2 - 7y + 4) = y(3y^2 - 7y + 4) - 2(3y^2 - 7y + 4)$$

Distributive law: $\quad = 3y^3 - 7y^2 + 4y - 6y^2 + 14y - 8$

Regroup: $\quad = 3y^3 - 7y^2 - 6y^2 + 4y + 14y - 8$

Combine like terms: $\quad = 3y^3 - 13y^2 + 18y - 8.$

Example 4

We follow the same procedure with $(2x - 5y)(3x + 4y)$:

$$(2x - 5y)(3x + 4y) = 2x(3x + 4y) - 5y(3x + 4y)$$
$$= 2x \cdot 3x + 2x \cdot 4y + (-5y) \cdot 3x + (-5y) \cdot 4y$$
$$= 6x^2 + 8xy - 15xy - 20y^2$$
$$= 6x^2 - 7xy - 20y^2.$$

Observe the pattern in the second line of Example 4 and its relationship to the terms being multiplied:

$$(2x - 5y)(3x + 4y) = 2x \cdot 3x + 2x \cdot 4y + (-5y) \cdot 3x + (-5y) \cdot 4y$$

First terms

$(2x - 5y)(3x + 4y)$

Outside terms

$(2x - 5y)(3x + 4y)$

Inside terms

$(2x - 5y)(3x + 4y)$

Last terms

This pattern is easy to remember by using the acronym FOIL (**F**irst, **O**utside, **I**nside, **L**ast). The FOIL method makes it easy to find products such as this one mentally, without the necessity of writing out the intermediate steps.

Example 5

$$(3x + 2)(x + 5) = 3x^2 + 15x + 2x + 10 = 3x^2 + 17x + 10.$$

First Outside Inside Last

Exercises A.2

In Exercises 1–54, perform the indicated operations and simplify your answer.

1. $x + 7x$

2. $5w + 7w - 3w$

3. $6a^2b + (-8b)a^2$

4. $-6x^3\sqrt{t} + 7x^3\sqrt{t} + 15x^3\sqrt{t}$

5. $(x^2 + 2x + 1) - (x^3 - 3x^2 + 4)$

6. $\left[u^4 - (-3)u^3 + \dfrac{u}{2} + 1\right] + \left(u^4 - 2u^3 + 5 - \dfrac{u}{2}\right)$

7. $\left[u^4 - (-3)u^3 + \dfrac{u}{2} + 1\right] - \left(u^4 - 2u^3 + 5 - \dfrac{u}{2}\right)$

8. $\left(6a^2b + 3a\sqrt{c} - 5ab\sqrt{c}\right) + \left(-6ab^2 - 3ab + 6ab\sqrt{c}\right)$

9. $[4z - 6z^2w - (-2)z^3w^2] + (8 - 6z^2w - zw^3 + 4z^3w^2)$

10. $(x^5y - 2x + 3xy^3) - (-2x - x^5y + 2xy^3)$

11. $(9x - x^3 + 1) - [2x^3 + (-6)x + (-7)]$

12. $\left(x - \sqrt{y} - z\right) - \left(x + \sqrt{y} - z\right) - \left(\sqrt{y} + z - x\right)$

13. $(x^2 - 3xy) - (x + xy) - (x^2 + xy)$

14. $2x(x^2 + 2)$

15. $(-5y)(-3y^2 + 1)$

16. $x^2y(xy - 6xy^2)$

17. $3ax(4ax - 2a^2y + 2ay)$

18. $2x(x^2 - 3xy + 2y^2)$

19. $6z^3(2z + 5)$

20. $-3x^2(12x^6 - 7x^5)$

21. $3ab(4a - 6b + 2a^2b)$

22. $(-3ay)(4ay - 5y)$

23. $(x + 1)(x - 2)$

24. $(x + 2)(2x - 5)$

25. $(-2x + 4)(-x - 3)$

26. $(y - 6)(2y + 2)$

27. $(y + 3)(y + 4)$

28. $(w - 2)(3w + 1)$

29. $(3x + 7)(-2x + 5)$

30. $(ab + 1)(a - 2)$

31. $(y - 3)(3y^2 + 4)$

32. $(y + 8)(y - 8)$

33. $(x + 4)(x - 4)$

34. $(3x - y)(3x + y)$

35. $(4a + 5b)(4a - 5b)$

36. $(x + 6)^2$

37. $(y - 11)^2$

38. $(2x + 3y)^2$

39. $(5x - b)^2$

40. $(2s^2 - 9y)(2s^2 + 9y)$

41. $(4x^3 - y^4)^2$

42. $(4x^3 - 5y^2)(4x^3 + 5y^2)$

43. $(-3x^2 + 2y^4)^2$

44. $(c - 2)(2c^2 - 3c + 1)$

45. $(2y + 3)(y^2 + 3y - 1)$

46. $(x + 2y)(2x^2 - xy + y^2)$

47. $(5w + 6)(-3w^2 + 4w - 3)$

48. $(5x - 2y)(x^2 - 2xy + 3y^2)$

49. $2x(3x + 1)(4x - 2)$

50. $3y(-y + 2)(3y + 1)$

51. $(x - 1)(x - 2)(x - 3)$

52. $(y - 2)(3y + 2)(y + 2)$

53. $(x + 4y)(2y - x)(3x - y)$

54. $(2x - y)(3x + 2y)(y - x)$

In Exercises 55–64, find the coefficient of x^2 in the given product. Avoid doing any more multiplying than necessary.

55. $(x^2 + 3x + 1)(2x - 3)$ **56.** $(x^2 - 1)(x + 1)$

57. $(x^3 + 2x - 6)(x^2 + 1)$ **58.** $(\sqrt{3} + x)(\sqrt{3} - x)$

59. $(x + 2)^3$ **60.** $(x^2 + x + 1)(x - 1)$

61. $(x^2 + x + 1)(x^2 - x + 1)$

62. $(2x^2 + 1)(2x^2 - 1)$

63. $(2x - 1)(x^2 + 3x + 2)$

64. $(1 - 2x)(4x^2 + x - 1)$

In Exercises 65–70, perform the indicated multiplication and simplify your answer if possible.

65. $(\sqrt{x} + 5)(\sqrt{x} - 5)$

66. $(2\sqrt{x} + \sqrt{2y})(2\sqrt{x} - \sqrt{2y})$

67. $(3 + \sqrt{y})^2$ **68.** $(7w - \sqrt{2x})^2$

69. $(1 + \sqrt{3}x)(x + \sqrt{3})$ **70.** $(2y + \sqrt{3})(\sqrt{5}y - 1)$

In Exercises 71–76, compute the product and arrange the terms of your answer according to decreasing powers of x, with each power of x appearing at most once.

Example: $(ax + b)(4x - c) = 4ax^2 + (4b - ac)x - bc$.

71. $(ax + b)(3x + 2)$ **72.** $(4x - c)(dx + c)$

73. $(ax + b)(bx + a)$ **74.** $rx(3rx + 1)(4x - r)$

75. $(x - a)(x - b)(x - c)$ **76.** $(2dx - c)(3cx + d)$

In Exercises 77–82, assume that all exponents are non-negative integers and find the product.

Example: $2x^k(3x + x^{n+1}) = (2x^k)(3x) + (2x^k)(x^{n+1})$
$$= 6x^{k+1} + 2x^{k+n+1}.$$

77. $3^r 3^4 3^t$ **78.** $(2x^n)(8x^k)$

79. $(x^m + 2)(x^n - 3)$ **80.** $(y^r + 1)(y^s - 4)$

81. $(2x^n - 5)(x^{3n} + 4x^n + 1)$

82. $(3y^{2k} + y^k + 1)(y^k - 3)$

In Exercises 83–92, find a numerical example to show that the given statement is false. Then find the mistake in the statement and correct it.

Example: *The statement* $-(b + 2) = -b + 2$ *is false when* $b = 5$, *since* $-(5 + 2) = -7$ *but* $-5 + 2 = -3$. *The mistake is the sign on the 2. The correct statement is* $-(b + 2) = -b - 2$.

83. $3(y + 2) = 3y + 2$

84. $x - (3y + 4) = x - 3y + 4$

85. $(x + y)^2 = x + y^2$ **86.** $(2x)^3 = 2x^3$

87. $(7x)(7y) = 7xy$ **88.** $(x + y)^2 = x^2 + y^2$

89. $y + y + y = y^3$ **90.** $(a - b)^2 = a^2 - b^2$

91. $(x - 3)(x - 2) = x^2 - 5x - 6$

92. $(a + b)(a^2 + b^2) = a^3 + b^3$

In Exercises 93 and 94, explain algebraically why each of these parlor tricks always works.

93. *Critical Thinking* Write down a nonzero number. Add 1 to it and square the result. Subtract 1 from the original number and square the result. Subtract this second square from the first one. Divide by the number with which you started. The answer is 4.

94. *Critical Thinking* Write down a positive number. Add 4 to it. Multiply the result by the original number. Add 4 to this result and then take the square root. Subtract the number with which you started. The answer is 2.

95. *Critical Thinking* Invent a similar parlor trick in which the answer is always the number with which you started.

Factoring

Factoring is the reverse of multiplication: We begin with a product and find the factors that multiply together to produce this product. Factoring skills are necessary to simplify expressions, to do arithmetic with fractional expressions, and to solve equations and inequalities.

The first general rule for factoring is

Common Factors

If there is a common factor in every term of the expression, factor out the common factor of highest degree.

Example 1

In $4x^6 - 8x$, for example, each term contains a factor of $4x$, so that $4x^6 - 8x = 4x(x^5 - 2)$. Similarly, the common factor of highest degree in $x^3y^2 + 2xy^3 - 3x^2y^4$ is xy^2 and

$$x^3y^2 + 2xy^3 - 3x^2y^4 = xy^2(x^2 + 2y - 3xy^2).$$

You can greatly increase your factoring proficiency by learning to recognize multiplication patterns that appear frequently. Here are the most common ones.

Quadratic Factoring Patterns

Difference of Squares	$u^2 - v^2 = (u + v)(u - v)$
Perfect Squares	$u^2 + 2uv + v^2 = (u + v)^2$
	$u^2 - 2uv + v^2 = (u - v)^2$

Example 2

a. $x^2 - 9y^2$ can be written $x^2 - (3y)^2$, a difference of squares. Therefore, $x^2 - 9y^2 = (x + 3y)(x - 3y)$.

b. $y^2 - 7 = y^2 - (\sqrt{7})^2 = (y + \sqrt{7})(y - \sqrt{7})$.*

c. $36r^2 - 64s^2 = (6r)^2 - (8s)^2 = (6r + 8s)(6r - 8s)$
$= 2(3r + 4s)2(3r - 4s) = 4(3r + 4s)(3r - 4s).$

*When a polynomial has integer coefficients, we normally look only for factors with integer coefficients. But when it is easy to find other factors, as here, we shall do so.

Example 3

Since the first and last terms of $4x^2 - 36x + 81$ are perfect squares, we try to use the perfect square pattern with $u = 2x$ and $v = 9$:

$$4x^2 - 36x + 81 = (2x)^2 - 36x + 9^2$$
$$= (2x)^2 - 2 \cdot 2x \cdot 9 + 9^2 = (2x - 9)^2.$$

Cubic Factoring Patterns

Difference of Cubes	$u^3 - v^3 = (u - v)(u^2 + uv + v^2)$
Sum of Cubes	$u^3 + v^3 = (u + v)(u^2 - uv + v^2)$
Perfect Cubes	$u^3 + 3u^2v + 3uv^2 + v^3 = (u + v)^3$
	$u^3 - 3u^2v + 3uv^2 - v^3 = (u - v)^3$

Example 4

a. $\quad x^3 - 125 = x^3 - 5^3 = (x - 5)(x^2 + 5x + 5^2)$
$$= (x - 5)(x^2 + 5x + 25).$$

b. $\quad x^3 + 8y^3 = x^3 + (2y)^3 = (x + 2y)[x^2 - x \cdot 2y + (2y)^2]$
$$= (x + 2y)(x^2 - 2xy + 4y^2).$$

c. $\quad x^3 - 12x^2 + 48x - 64 = x^3 - 12x^2 + 48x - 4^3$
$$= x^3 - 3x^2 \cdot 4 + 3x \cdot 4^2 - 4^3$$
$$= (x - 4)^3.$$

When none of the multiplication patterns applies, use trial and error to factor quadratic polynomials. If a quadratic has two first-degree factors, then the factors must be of the form $ax + b$ and $cx + d$ for some constants a, b, c, d. The product of such factors is

$$(ax + b)(cx + d) = acx^2 + adx + bcx + bd$$
$$= acx^2 + (ad + bc)x + bd.$$

Note that *ac is the coefficient of* x^2 and *bd is the constant term* of the product polynomial. This pattern can be used to factor quadratics by reversing the FOIL process.

Example 5

If $x^2 + 9x + 18$ factors as $(ax + b)(cx + d)$, then we must have $ac = 1$ (coefficient of x^2) and $bd = 18$ (constant term). Thus, $a = \pm 1$ and $c = \pm 1$ (the only integer factors of 1). The only possibilities for b and d are

$$\pm 1, \pm 18 \quad \text{or} \quad \pm 2, \pm 9 \quad \text{or} \quad \pm 3, \pm 6.$$

We mentally try the various possibilities, using FOIL as our guide. For example, we try $b = 2$, $d = 9$ and check this factorization: $(x + 2)(x + 9)$. The sum of the outside and inside terms is $9x + 2x = 11x$, so this product can't be $x^2 + 9x + 18$. By trying other possibilities we find that $b = 3$, $d = 6$ leads to the correct factorization: $x^2 + 9x + 18 = (x + 3)(x + 6)$.

Example 6

To factor $6x^2 + 11x + 4$ as $(ax + b)(cx + d)$, we must find numbers a and c whose product is 6, the coefficient of x^2, and numbers b and d whose product is the constant term 4. Some possibilities are

$ac = 6$

a	±1	±2	±3	±6
c	±6	±3	±2	±1

$bd = 4$

b	±1	±2	±4
d	±4	±2	±1

Trial and error shows that $(2x + 1)(3x + 4) = 6x^2 + 11x + 4$.

Occasionally the patterns above can be used to factor expressions involving larger exponents than 2.

Example 7

a. $x^6 - y^6 = (x^3)^2 - (y^3)^2 = (x^3 + y^3)(x^3 - y^3)$
$\qquad = (x + y)(x^2 - xy + y^2)(x - y)(x^2 + xy + y^2)$.

b. $x^8 - 1 = (x^4)^2 - 1 = (x^4 + 1)(x^4 - 1)$
$\qquad\qquad = (x^4 + 1)(x^2 + 1)(x^2 - 1)$
$\qquad\qquad = (x^4 + 1)(x^2 + 1)(x + 1)(x - 1)$.

Example 8

To factor $x^4 - 2x^2 - 3$, let $u = x^2$. Then,

$$x^4 - 2x^2 - 3 = (x^2)^2 - 2x^2 - 3$$
$$= u^2 - 2u - 3 = (u + 1)(u - 3)$$
$$= (x^2 + 1)(x^2 - 3)$$
$$= \left(x^2 + 1\right)\left(x + \sqrt{3}\right)\left(x - \sqrt{3}\right).$$

Example 9

$3x^3 + 3x^2 + 2x + 2$ can be factored by regrouping and using the distributive law to factor out a common factor:

$$(3x^3 + 3x^2) + (2x + 2) = 3x^2(x + 1) + 2(x + 1)$$
$$= (3x^2 + 2)(x + 1).$$

Exercises A.3

In Exercises 1–58, factor the expression.

1. $x^2 - 4$

2. $x^2 + 6x + 9$

3. $9y^2 - 25$

4. $y^2 - 4y + 4$

5. $81x^2 + 36x + 4$

6. $4x^2 - 12x + 9$

7. $5 - x^2$

8. $1 - 36u^2$

9. $49 + 28z + 4z^2$

10. $25u^2 - 20uv + 4v^2$

11. $x^4 - y^4$

12. $x^2 - \dfrac{1}{9}$

13. $x^2 + x - 6$

14. $y^2 + 11y + 30$

15. $z^2 + 4z + 3$

16. $x^2 - 8x + 15$

17. $y^2 + 5y - 36$

18. $z^2 - 9z + 14$

19. $x^2 - 6x + 9$

20. $4y^2 - 81$

21. $x^2 + 7x + 10$

22. $w^2 - 6w - 16$

23. $x^2 + 11x + 18$

24. $x^2 + 3xy - 28y^2$

25. $3x^2 + 4x + 1$

26. $4y^2 + 4y + 1$

27. $2z^2 + 11z + 12$

28. $10x^2 - 17x + 3$

29. $9x^2 - 72x$

30. $4x^2 - 4x - 3$

31. $10x^2 - 8x - 2$

32. $7z^2 + 23z + 6$

33. $8u^2 + 6u - 9$

34. $2y^2 - 4y + 2$

35. $4x^2 + 20xy + 25y^2$

36. $63u^2 - 46uv + 8v^2$

37. $x^3 - 125$

38. $y^3 + 64$

39. $x^3 + 6x^2 + 12x + 8$

40. $y^3 - 3y^2 + 3y - 1$

41. $8 + x^3$

42. $z^3 - 9z^2 + 27z - 27$

43. $-x^3 + 15x^2 - 75x + 125$

44. $27 - t^3$

45. $x^3 + 1$

46. $x^3 - 1$

47. $8x^3 - y^3$

48. $(x - 1)^3 + 1$

49. $x^6 - 64$

50. $x^5 - 8x^2$

51. $y^4 + 7y^2 + 10$

52. $z^4 - 5z^2 + 6$

53. $81 - y^4$

54. $x^6 + 16x^3 + 64$

55. $z^6 - 1$

56. $y^6 + 26y^3 - 27$

57. $x^4 + 2x^2y - 3y^2$

58. $x^8 - 17x^4 + 16$

In Exercises 59–64, factor by regrouping and using the distributive law (as in Example 9).

59. $x^2 - yz + xz - xy$

60. $x^6 - 2x^4 - 8x^2 + 16$

61. $a^3 - 2b^2 + 2a^2b - ab$

62. $u^2v - 2w^2 - 2uvw + uw$

63. $x^3 + 4x^2 - 8x - 32$

64. $z^8 - 5z^7 + 2z - 10$

65. *Critical Thinking* Show that there do *not* exist real numbers c and d such that $x^2 + 1 = (x + c)(x + d)$.

A.4 Fractional Expressions

Quotients of algebraic expressions are called **fractional expressions**. A quotient of two polynomials is sometimes called a **rational expression**. The basic rules for dealing with fractional expressions are essentially the same as those for ordinary numerical fractions. For instance, $\dfrac{2}{4} = \dfrac{3}{6}$ and the "cross products" are equal: $2 \cdot 6 = 4 \cdot 3$. In the general case we have

Properties of Fractions

1. **Equality rule:** $\dfrac{a}{b} = \dfrac{c}{d}$ exactly when $ad = bc$.*

2. **Cancellation property:** If $k \neq 0$, then $\dfrac{ka}{kb} = \dfrac{a}{b}$.

The cancellation property follows directly from the equality rule because $(ka)b = (kb)a$.

Example 1

Here are examples of the two properties:

1. $\dfrac{x^2 + 2x}{x^2 + x - 2} = \dfrac{x}{x - 1}$ because the cross products are equal:

$$(x^2 + 2x)(x - 1) = x^3 + x^2 - 2x = (x^2 + x - 2)x.$$

2. $\dfrac{x^4 - 1}{x^2 + 1} = \dfrac{(x^2 + 1)(x^2 - 1)}{(x^2 + 1)} = \dfrac{x^2 - 1}{1} = x^2 - 1.$

A fraction is in **lowest terms** if its **numerator** (top) and **denominator** (bottom) have no common factors except ± 1. To express a fraction in lowest terms, factor numerator and denominator and cancel common factors.

Example 2

$$\frac{x^2 + x - 6}{x^2 - 3x + 2} = \frac{(x - 2)(x + 3)}{(x - 2)(x - 1)} = \frac{x + 3}{x - 1}.$$

To add two fractions with the same denominator, simply add the numerators as in ordinary arithmetic: $\dfrac{a}{b} + \dfrac{c}{b} = \dfrac{a + c}{b}$. Subtraction is done similarly.

Example 3

$$\frac{7x^2 + 2}{x^2 + 3} - \frac{4x^2 + 2x - 5}{x^2 + 3} = \frac{(7x^2 + 2) - (4x^2 + 2x - 5)}{x^2 + 3}$$

$$= \frac{7x^2 + 2 - 4x^2 - 2x + 5}{x^2 + 3}$$

$$= \frac{3x^2 - 2x + 7}{x^2 + 3}.$$

*Throughout this section we assume that all denominators are nonzero.

To add or subtract fractions with different denominators, you must first find a common denominator. One common denominator for a/b and c/d is the product of the two denominators bd because both fractions can be expressed with this denominator:

$$\frac{a}{b} = \frac{ad}{bd} \quad \text{and} \quad \frac{c}{d} = \frac{bc}{bd}.$$

Consequently,

$$\frac{a}{b} + \frac{c}{d} = \frac{ad}{bd} + \frac{bc}{bd} = \frac{ad + bc}{bd} \quad \text{and} \quad \frac{a}{b} - \frac{c}{d} = \frac{ad}{bd} - \frac{bc}{bd} = \frac{ad - bc}{bd}.$$

Example 4

$$
\begin{aligned}
\frac{2x + 1}{3x} - \frac{x^2 - 2}{x - 1} &= \frac{(2x + 1)(x - 1)}{3x(x - 1)} - \frac{3x(x^2 - 2)}{3x(x - 1)} \\
&= \frac{(2x + 1)(x - 1) - 3x(x^2 - 2)}{3x(x - 1)} \\
&= \frac{2x^2 - x - 1 - 3x^3 + 6x}{3x^2 - 3x} \\
&= \frac{-3x^3 + 2x^2 + 5x - 1}{3x^2 - 3x}.
\end{aligned}
$$

Although the product of the denominators can always be used as a common denominator, it's often more efficient to use the *least common denominator*. The least common denominator can be found by factoring each denominator completely (with integer coefficients) and then taking the product of the highest power of each of the distinct factors.

Example 5

In the sum $\dfrac{1}{100} + \dfrac{1}{120}$, the denominators are $100 = 2^2 \cdot 5^2$ and $120 = 2^3 \cdot 3 \cdot 5$. The distinct factors are 2, 3, 5. The highest exponent of 2 in either denominator is 3, the highest of 3 is 1, and the highest of 5 is 2. So the least common denominator is $2^3 \cdot 3 \cdot 5^2 = 600$

$$\frac{1}{100} + \frac{1}{120} = \frac{6}{600} + \frac{5}{600} = \frac{11}{600}.$$

Example 6

To find the least common denominator of $\dfrac{1}{x^2 + 2x + 1}$, $\dfrac{5x}{x^2 - x}$, and $\dfrac{3x - 7}{x^4 + x^3}$, factor each of the denominators completely:

$$(x + 1)^2, \qquad x(x - 1), \qquad x^3(x + 1),$$

The distinct factors are x, $x + 1$, and $x - 1$. The least common denominator is determined by the highest power of each factor:

$$x^3(x + 1)^2(x - 1).$$

To express one of several fractions in terms of the least common denominator, multiply its numerator and denominator by those factors in the common denominator that *don't* appear in the denominator of the fraction.

Example 7

The preceding example shows the least common denominator (LCD) of $\dfrac{1}{(x + 1)^2}$, $\dfrac{5x}{x(x - 1)}$, and $\dfrac{3x - 7}{x^3(x + 1)}$ to be $x^3(x + 1)^2(x - 1)$. Therefore,

$$\frac{1}{(x + 1)^2} = \frac{1}{(x + 1)^2} \cdot \frac{x^3(x - 1)}{x^3(x - 1)} = \frac{x^3(x - 1)}{x^3(x + 1)^2(x - 1)}$$

$$\frac{5x}{x(x - 1)} = \frac{5x}{x(x - 1)} \cdot \frac{x^2(x + 1)^2}{x^2(x + 1)^2} = \frac{5x^3(x + 1)^2}{x^3(x + 1)^2(x - 1)}$$

$$\frac{3x - 7}{x^3(x + 1)} = \frac{3x - 7}{x^3(x + 1)} \cdot \frac{(x + 1)(x - 1)}{(x + 1)(x - 1)} = \frac{(3x - 7)(x + 1)(x - 1)}{x^3(x + 1)^2(x - 1)}.$$

Example 8

To find $\dfrac{1}{z} + \dfrac{3z}{z + 1} - \dfrac{z^2}{(z + 1)^2}$ we use the LCD $z(z + 1)^2$:

$$\frac{1}{z} + \frac{3z}{z + 1} - \frac{z^2}{(z + 1)^2} = \frac{(z + 1)^2}{z(z + 1)^2} + \frac{3z^2(z + 1)}{z(z + 1)^2} - \frac{z^3}{z(z + 1)^2}$$

$$= \frac{(z + 1)^2 + 3z^2(z + 1) - z^3}{z(z + 1)^2}$$

$$= \frac{z^2 + 2z + 1 + 3z^3 + 3z^2 - z^3}{z(z + 1)^2}$$

$$= \frac{2z^3 + 4z^2 + 2z + 1}{z(z + 1)^2}.$$

Multiplication of fractions is easy: Multiply corresponding numerators and denominators, then simplify your answer.

Example 9

$$\frac{x^2 - 1}{x^2 + 2} \cdot \frac{3x - 4}{x + 1} = \frac{(x^2 - 1)(3x - 4)}{(x^2 + 2)(x + 1)}$$

$$= \frac{(x - 1)(x + 1)(3x - 4)}{(x^2 + 2)(x + 1)} = \frac{(x - 1)(3x - 4)}{x^2 + 2}.$$

Division of fractions is given by the rule:

Invert the divisor and multiply: $\quad \dfrac{a}{b} \div \dfrac{c}{d} = \dfrac{a}{b} \cdot \dfrac{d}{c} = \dfrac{ad}{bc}.$

Example 10

$$\frac{x^2 + x - 2}{x^2 - 6x + 9} \div \frac{x^2 - 1}{x - 3} = \frac{x^2 + x - 2}{x^2 - 6x + 9} \cdot \frac{x - 3}{x^2 - 1}$$

$$= \frac{(x + 2)(x - 1)}{(x - 3)^2} \cdot \frac{x - 3}{(x - 1)(x + 1)}$$

$$= \frac{x + 2}{(x - 3)(x + 1)}.$$

Division problems can also be written as fractions. For instance, $\dfrac{8}{2}$ means

$8 \div 2 = 4$. Similarly, the compound fraction $\dfrac{\dfrac{a}{b}}{\dfrac{c}{d}}$ means $\dfrac{a}{b} \div \dfrac{c}{d}$. So,

the basic rule for simplifying compound fractions is: *Invert the denominator and multiply it by the numerator.*

Example 11

a. $\dfrac{\dfrac{16y^2z}{8yz^2}}{\dfrac{yz}{6y^3z^3}} = \dfrac{16y^2z}{8yz^2} \cdot \dfrac{6y^3z^3}{yz} = \dfrac{16 \cdot 6 \cdot y^5z^4}{8y^2z^3}$

$$= 2 \cdot 6 \cdot y^{5-2}z^{4-3} = 12y^3z.$$

b. $\dfrac{\dfrac{y^2}{y + 2}}{y^3 + y} = \dfrac{y^2}{y + 2} \cdot \dfrac{1}{y^3 + y} = \dfrac{y^2}{(y + 2)(y^3 + y)}$

$$= \frac{y^2}{(y + 2)y(y^2 + 1)}$$

$$= \frac{y}{(y + 2)(y^2 + 1)}.$$

Exercises A.4

In Exercises 1–10, express the fraction in lowest terms.

1. $\dfrac{63}{49}$ **2.** $\dfrac{121}{33}$ **3.** $\dfrac{13 \cdot 27 \cdot 22 \cdot 10}{6 \cdot 4 \cdot 11 \cdot 12}$

4. $\dfrac{x^2 - 4}{x + 2}$ **5.** $\dfrac{x^2 - x - 2}{x^2 + 2x + 1}$ **6.** $\dfrac{z + 1}{z^3 + 1}$

7. $\dfrac{a^2 - b^2}{a^3 - b^3}$ **8.** $\dfrac{x^4 - 3x^2}{x^3}$

9. $\dfrac{(x + c)(x^2 - cx + c^2)}{x^4 + c^3x}$ **10.** $\dfrac{x^4 - y^4}{(x^2 + y^2)(x^2 - xy)}$

In Exercises 11–28, perform the indicated operations.

11. $\dfrac{3}{7} + \dfrac{2}{5}$ **12.** $\dfrac{7}{8} - \dfrac{5}{6}$ **13.** $\left(\dfrac{19}{7} + \dfrac{1}{2}\right) - \dfrac{1}{3}$

14. $\dfrac{1}{a} - \dfrac{2a}{b}$ **15.** $\dfrac{c}{d} + \dfrac{3c}{e}$ **16.** $\dfrac{r}{s} + \dfrac{s}{t} + \dfrac{t}{r}$

17. $\dfrac{b}{c} - \dfrac{c}{b}$ **18.** $\dfrac{a}{b} + \dfrac{2a}{b^2} + \dfrac{3a}{b^3}$ **19.** $\dfrac{1}{x+1} - \dfrac{1}{x}$

20. $\dfrac{1}{2x+1} + \dfrac{1}{2x-1}$

21. $\dfrac{1}{x+4} + \dfrac{2}{(x+4)^2} - \dfrac{3}{x^2+8x+16}$

22. $\dfrac{1}{x} + \dfrac{1}{xy} + \dfrac{1}{xy^2}$ **23.** $\dfrac{1}{x} - \dfrac{1}{3x-4}$

24. $\dfrac{3}{x-1} + \dfrac{4}{x+1}$ **25.** $\dfrac{1}{x+y} + \dfrac{x+y}{x^3+y^3}$

26. $\dfrac{6}{5(x-1)(x-2)^2} + \dfrac{x}{3(x-1)^2(x-2)}$

27. $\dfrac{1}{4x(x+1)(x+2)^3} - \dfrac{6x+2}{4(x+1)^3}$

28. $\dfrac{x+y}{(x^2-xy)(x-y)^2} - \dfrac{2}{(x^2-y^2)^2}$

In Exercises 29–42, express in lowest terms.

29. $\dfrac{3}{4} \cdot \dfrac{12}{5} \cdot \dfrac{10}{9}$ **30.** $\dfrac{10}{45} \cdot \dfrac{6}{14} \cdot \dfrac{1}{2}$

31. $\dfrac{3a^2c}{4ac} \cdot \dfrac{8ac^3}{9a^2c^4}$ **32.** $\dfrac{6x^2y}{2x} \cdot \dfrac{y}{21xy}$

33. $\dfrac{7x}{11y} \cdot \dfrac{66y^2}{14x^3}$ **34.** $\dfrac{ab}{c^2} \cdot \dfrac{cd}{a^2b} \cdot \dfrac{ad}{bc^2}$

35. $\dfrac{3x+9}{2x} \cdot \dfrac{8x^2}{x^2-9}$ **36.** $\dfrac{4x+16}{3x+15} \cdot \dfrac{2x+10}{x+4}$

37. $\dfrac{5y-25}{3} \cdot \dfrac{y^2}{y^2-25}$ **38.** $\dfrac{6x-12}{6x} \cdot \dfrac{8x^2}{x-2}$

39. $\dfrac{u}{u-1} \cdot \dfrac{u^2-1}{u^2}$

40. $\dfrac{t^2-t-6}{t^2-6t+9} \cdot \dfrac{t^2+4t-5}{t^2-25}$

41. $\dfrac{2u^2+uv-v^2}{4u^2-4uv+v^2} \cdot \dfrac{8u^2+6uv-9v^2}{4u^2-9v^2}$

42. $\dfrac{2x^2-3xy-2y^2}{6x^2-5xy-4y^2} \cdot \dfrac{6x^2+6xy}{x^2-xy-2y^2}$

In Exercises 43–60, compute the quotient and express in lowest terms.

43. $\dfrac{5}{12} \div \dfrac{4}{14}$ **44.** $\dfrac{\dfrac{100}{52}}{\dfrac{27}{26}}$ **45.** $\dfrac{uv}{v^2w} \div \dfrac{uv}{u^2v}$

46. $\dfrac{3x^2y}{(xy)^2} \div \dfrac{3xyz}{x^2y}$ **47.** $\dfrac{\dfrac{x+3}{x+4}}{\dfrac{2x}{x+4}}$ **48.** $\dfrac{\dfrac{(x+2)^2}{(x-2)^2}}{\dfrac{x^2+2x}{x^2-4}}$

49. $\dfrac{x+y}{x+2y} \div \left(\dfrac{x+y}{xy}\right)^2$ **50.** $\dfrac{\dfrac{u^3+v^3}{u^2-v^2}}{\dfrac{u^2-uv+v^2}{u+v}}$

51. $\dfrac{(c+d)^2}{c^2-d^2}$ **52.** $\dfrac{\dfrac{1}{x} - \dfrac{3}{2}}{\dfrac{2}{x-2} + \dfrac{5}{x}}$ **53.** $\dfrac{\dfrac{1}{x^2} - \dfrac{1}{y^2}}{\dfrac{1}{x} + \dfrac{1}{y}}$

54. $\dfrac{\dfrac{x}{x+1} + \dfrac{1}{x}}{\dfrac{1}{x} + \dfrac{1}{x+1}}$ **55.** $\dfrac{\dfrac{6}{y} - 3}{1 - \dfrac{1}{y-1}}$

56. $\dfrac{\dfrac{1}{3x} - \dfrac{1}{4y}}{\dfrac{5}{6x^2} + \dfrac{1}{y}}$ **57.** $\dfrac{\dfrac{1}{x+h} - \dfrac{1}{x}}{h}$

58. $\dfrac{\dfrac{1}{(x+h)^2} - \dfrac{1}{x^2}}{h}$ **59.** $(x^{-1} + y^{-1})^{-1}$

60. $\dfrac{(x+y)^{-1}}{x^{-1} + y^{-1}}$

In Exercises 61–67, find a numerical example to show that the given statement is false. Then find the mistake in the statement and correct it.

61. $\dfrac{1}{a} + \dfrac{1}{b} = \dfrac{1}{a+b}$ **62.** $\dfrac{x^2}{x^2+x^6} = 1 + x^3$

63. $\left(\dfrac{1}{\sqrt{a} + \sqrt{b}}\right)^2 = \dfrac{1}{a+b}$ **64.** $\dfrac{r+s}{r+t} = 1 + \dfrac{s}{t}$

65. $\dfrac{u}{v} + \dfrac{v}{u} = 1$ **66.** $\dfrac{\dfrac{1}{x}}{\dfrac{1}{y}} = \dfrac{1}{xy}$

67. $\left(\sqrt{x} + \sqrt{y}\right) \dfrac{1}{\sqrt{x} + \sqrt{y}} = x + y$

The Coordinate Plane

The Distance Formula

We shall often identify a point with its coordinates and refer, for example, to the point (2, 3). When dealing with several points simultaneously, it is customary to label the coordinates of the first point (x_1, y_1), the second point (x_2, y_2), the third point (x_3, y_3), and so on.* Once the plane is coordinatized, it's easy to compute the distance between any two points:

The Distance Formula

> **The distance between points (x_1, y_1) and (x_2, y_2) is**
> $$\sqrt{(x_1 - x_2)^2 + (y_1 - y_2)^2}.$$

Before proving the distance formula, we shall see how it is used.

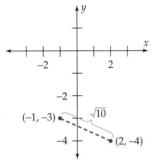

Figure A.5-1

Example 1

To find the distance between the points $(-1, -3)$ and $(2, -4)$ in Figure A.5-1, substitute $(-1, -3)$ for (x_1, y_1) and $(2, -4)$ for (x_2, y_2) in the distance formula.

Distance formula: $\quad \text{distance} = \sqrt{(x_1 - x_2)^2 + (y_1 - y_2)^2}$

Substitute: $\quad\quad\quad\quad\quad = \sqrt{(-1 - 2)^2 + (-3 - (-4))^2}$

Simplify: $\quad\quad\quad\quad\quad\quad = \sqrt{(-3)^2 + (-3 + 4)^2}$

$\quad\quad\quad\quad\quad\quad\quad\quad = \sqrt{9 + 1} = \sqrt{10}$

The order in which the points are used in the distance formula doesn't make a difference. If we substitute $(2, -4)$ for (x_1, y_1) and $(-1, -3)$ for (x_2, y_2), we get the same answer:

$$\sqrt{[2 - (-1)]^2 + [-4 - (-3)]^2} = \sqrt{3^2 + (-1)^2} = \sqrt{10}.$$

■

CAUTION

$\sqrt{a^2 + 4b^2}$ cannot be simplified. In particular, it is *not* equal to $a + 2b$.

Example 2

To find the distance from (a, b) to $(2a, -b)$, where a and b are fixed real numbers, substitute a for x_1, b for y_1, $2a$ for x_2, and $-b$ for y_2 in the distance formula:

$$\sqrt{(x_1 - x_2)^2 + (y_1 - y_2)^2} = \sqrt{(a - 2a)^2 + (b - (-b))^2}$$
$$= \sqrt{(-a)^2 + (b + b)^2} = \sqrt{a^2 + (2b)^2}$$
$$= \sqrt{a^2 + 4b^2}$$

■

---

*"x_1" is read "x-one" or "x-sub-one"; it is a *single symbol* denoting the first coordinate of the first point, just as c denotes the first coordinate of (c, d). Analogous remarks apply to y_1, x_2, and so on.

Proof of the Distance Formula Figure A.5-2 shows typical points P and Q in the plane. We must find length d of line segment PQ.

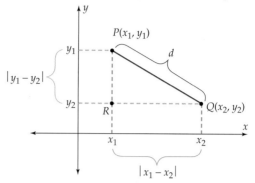

Figure A.5-2

As shown in Figure A.5-2, the length of RQ is the same as the distance from x_1 to x_2 on the x-axis (number line), namely, $|x_1 - x_2|$. Similarly, the length of PR is the same as the distance from y_1 to y_2 on the y-axis, namely, $|y_1 - y_2|$. According to the Pythagorean Theorem* the length d of PQ is given by:

$$(\text{Length } PQ)^2 = (\text{length } RQ)^2 + (\text{length } PR)^2$$

$$d^2 = |x_1 - x_2|^2 + |y_1 - y_2|^2$$

Since $|c|^2 = |c| \cdot |c| = |c^2| = c^2$ (because $c^2 \geq 0$), this equation becomes:

$$d^2 = (x_1 - x_2)^2 + (y_1 - y_2)^2$$

Since the length d is nonnegative, we must have

$$d = \sqrt{(x_1 - x_2)^2 + (y_1 - y_2)^2}$$

The distance formula can be used to prove the following useful fact (see Exercise 54).

The Midpoint Formula

The midpoint of the line segment from (x_1, y_1) to (x_2, y_2) is

$$\left(\frac{x_1 + x_2}{2}, \frac{y_1 + y_2}{2} \right)$$

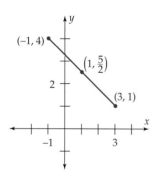

Figure A.5-3

Example 3

To find the midpoint of the segment joining $(-1, 4)$ and $(3, 1)$, use the formula in the box with $x_1 = -1$, $y_1 = 4$, $x_2 = 3$, and $y_2 = 1$. The midpoint is

$$\left(\frac{x_1 + x_2}{2}, \frac{y_1 + y_2}{2} \right) = \left(\frac{-1 + 3}{2}, \frac{4 + 1}{2} \right) = \left(1, \frac{5}{2} \right)$$

as shown in Figure A.5-3. ∎

*See the Geometry Review Appendix.

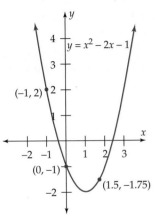

$y = x^2 - 2x - 1$

$(-1, 2)$

$(0, -1)$

$(1.5, -1.75)$

Figure A.5-4

Graphs

A **graph** is a set of points in the plane. Some graphs are based on data points. Other graphs arise from equations, as follows. A **solution** of an equation in variables x and y is a pair of numbers such that the substitution of the first number for x and the second for y produces a true statement. For instance, $(3, -2)$ is a solution of $5x + 7y = 1$ because

$$5 \cdot 3 + 7(-2) = 1$$

and $(-2, 3)$ is *not* a solution because $5(-2) + 7 \cdot 3 \neq 1$. The **graph of an equation** in two variables is the set of points in the plane whose coordinates are solutions of the equation. Thus the graph is a *geometric picture of the solutions.*

Example 4

The graph of $y = x^2 - 2x - 1$ is shown in Figure A.5-4. You can readily verify that each of the points whose coordinates are labeled is a solution of the equation. For instance, $(0, -1)$ is a solution because $-1 = 0^2 - 2(0) - 1$.

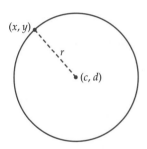

(x, y)

r

(c, d)

Figure A.5-5

Circles If (c, d) is a point in the plane and r a positive number, then the **circle with center (c, d) and radius r** consists of all points (x, y) that lie r units from (c, d), as shown in Figure A.5-5. According to the distance formula, the statement that "the distance from (x, y) to (c, d) is r units" is equivalent to:

$$\sqrt{(x - c)^2 + (y - d)^2} = r$$

Squaring both sides shows that (x, y) satisfies this equation:

$$(x - c)^2 + (y - d)^2 = r^2$$

Reversing the procedure shows that any solution (x, y) of this equation is a point on the circle. Therefore,

Circle Equation

> The circle with center (c, d) and radius r is the graph of
> $$(x - c)^2 + (y - d)^2 = r^2.$$

We say that $(x - c)^2 + (y - d)^2 = r^2$ is the **equation of the circle** with center (c, d) and radius r. If the center is at the origin, then $(c, d) = (0, 0)$ and the equation has a simpler form:

Circle at the Origin

> The circle with center $(0, 0)$ and radius r is the graph of
> $$x^2 + y^2 = r^2.$$

Example 5

a. Letting $r = 1$ shows that the graph of $x^2 + y^2 = 1$ is the circle of radius 1 centered at the origin, as shown in Figure A.5-6. This circle is called the **unit circle.**

b. The circle with center $(-3, 2)$ and radius 2, shown in Figure A.5-7, is the graph of the equation

$$((x - (-3))^2 + (y - 2)^2 = 2^2$$

or equivalently,

$$(x + 3)^2 + (y - 2)^2 = 4.$$

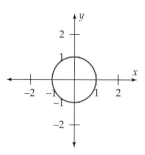

Figure A.5-6

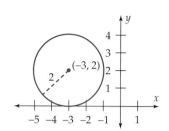

Figure A.5-7

Example 6

Find the equation of the circle with center $(3, -1)$ that passes through $(2, 4)$.

Solution

We must first find the radius. Since $(2, 4)$ is on the circle, the radius is the distance from $(2, 4)$ to $(3, -1)$ as shown in Figure A.5-8, namely,

$$\sqrt{(2 - 3)^2 + (4 - (-1))^2} = \sqrt{1 + 25} = \sqrt{26}$$

The equation of the circle with center at $(3, -1)$ and radius $\sqrt{26}$ is

$$(x - 3)^2 + (y - (-1))^2 = \left(\sqrt{26}\right)^2$$
$$(x - 3)^2 + (y + 1)^2 = 26$$
$$x^2 - 6x + 9 + y^2 + 2y + 1 = 26$$
$$x^2 + y^2 - 6x + 2y - 16 = 0.$$

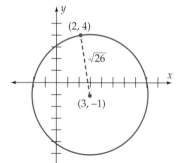

Figure A.5-8

The equation of any circle can always be written in the form

$$x^2 + y^2 + Bx + Cy + D = 0$$

for some constants B, C, D, as in Example 6 (where $B = -6$, $C = 2$, $D = -16$). Conversely, the graph of such an equation can always be determined.

Example 7

To find the graph of $3x^2 + 3y^2 - 12x - 30y + 45 = 0$, we divide both sides by 3 and rewrite the equation as

$$(x^2 - 4x) + (y^2 - 10y) = -15.$$

Next we complete the square in both expressions in parentheses (see page 91). To complete the square in $x^2 - 4x$, we add 4 (the square of half the coefficient of x) and to complete the square in $y^2 - 10y$ we add 25 (why?). In order to have an equivalent equation we must add these numbers to *both* sides:

$$(x^2 - 4x + 4) + (y^2 - 10y + 25) = -15 + 4 + 25$$
$$(x - 2)^2 + (y - 5)^2 = 14$$

Since $14 = (\sqrt{14})^2$, this is the equation of the circle with center $(2, 5)$ and radius $\sqrt{14}$. ∎

Exercises A.5

In Exercises 1–8, find the distance between the two points and the midpoint of the segment joining them.

1. $(-3, 5), (2, -7)$ **2.** $(2, 4), (1, 5)$

3. $(1, -5), (2, -1)$ **4.** $(-2, 3), (-3, 2)$

5. $(\sqrt{2}, 1), (\sqrt{3}, 2)$ **6.** $(-1, \sqrt{5}), (\sqrt{2}, -\sqrt{3})$

7. $(a, b), (b, a)$ **8.** $(s, t), (0, 0)$

9. According to the Information Technology Industry Council, there were about 12 million personal computers sold in the United States in 1992 and about 36 million in 1998.
 a. Represent the data graphically by two points.
 b. Find the midpoint of the line segment joining these points.
 c. How might this midpoint be interpreted? What assumptions, if any, are needed to make this interpretation?

10. A standard baseball diamond (which is actually a square) is shown in the figure at right. Suppose it is placed on a coordinate plane with home plate at the origin, first base on the positive x-axis, and third base on the positive y-axis. The unit of measurement is feet.
 a. Find the coordinates of first, second, and third base.
 b. If the left fielder is at the point $(50, 325)$, how far is he from first base?
 c. How far is the left fielder in part **b** from the right fielder, who is at the point $(280, 20)$?

In Exercises 11–14, find the equation of the circle with given center and radius r.

11. $(-3, 4)$; $r = 2$ **12.** $(-2, -1)$; $r = 3$

13. $(0, 0)$; $r = \sqrt{2}$ **14.** $(5, -2)$; $r = 1$

In Exercises 15–18, sketch the graph of the equation.

15. $(x - 2)^2 + (y - 4)^2 = 1$

16. $(x + 1)^2 + (y - 3)^2 = 9$

17. $(x - 5)^2 + (y + 2)^2 = 5$

18. $(x + 6)^2 + y^2 = 4$

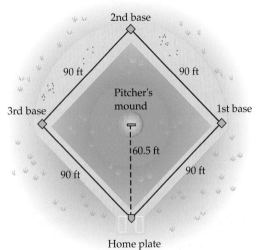

In Exercises 19–24, find the center and radius of the circle whose equation is given.

19. $x^2 + y^2 + 8x - 6y - 15 = 0$

20. $15x^2 + 15y^2 = 10$

21. $x^2 + y^2 + 6x - 4y - 15 = 0$

22. $x^2 + y^2 + 10x - 75 = 0$

23. $x^2 + y^2 + 25x + 10y = -12$

24. $3x^2 + 3y^2 + 12x + 12 = 18y$

In Exercises 25–27, show that the three points are the vertices of a right triangle, and state the length of the hypotenuse. [You may assume that a triangle with sides of lengths a, b, c is a right triangle with hypotenuse c provided that $a^2 + b^2 = c^2$.]

25. $(0, 0), (1, 1), (2, -2)$

26. $\left(\dfrac{\sqrt{2}}{2}, 0\right), \left(\dfrac{\sqrt{2}}{2}, \dfrac{\sqrt{2}}{2}\right), (0, 0)$

27. $(3, -2), (0, 4), (-2, 3)$

28. What is the perimeter of the triangle with vertices $(1, 1)$, $(5, 4)$, and $(-2, 5)$?

In Exercises 29–36, find the equation of the circle.

29. Center $(2, 2)$; passes through the origin.

30. Center $(-1, -3)$; passes through $(-4, -2)$.

31. Center $(1, 2)$; intersects x-axis at -1 and 3.

32. Center $(3, 1)$; diameter 2.

33. Center $(-5, 4)$; tangent (touching at one point) to the x-axis.

34. Center $(2, -6)$; tangent to the y-axis.

35. Endpoints of diameter are $(3, 3)$ and $(1, -1)$.

36. Endpoints of diameter are $(-3, 5)$ and $(7, -5)$.

37. One diagonal of a square has endpoints $(-3, 1)$ and $(2, -4)$. Find the endpoints of the other diagonal.

38. Find the vertices of all possible squares with this property: Two of the vertices are $(2, 1)$ and $(2, 5)$. *Hint:* There are three such squares.

39. Do Exercise 38 with (c, d) and (c, k) in place of $(2, 1)$ and $(2, 5)$.

40. Find the three points that divide the line segment from $(-4, 7)$ to $(10, -9)$ into four parts of equal length.

41. Find all points P on the x-axis that are 5 units from $(3, 4)$. *Hint:* P must have coordinates $(x, 0)$ for some x and the distance from P to $(3, 4)$ is 5.

42. Find all points on the y-axis that are 8 units from $(-2, 4)$.

43. Find all points with first coordinate 3 that are 6 units from $(-2, -5)$.

44. Find all points with second coordinate -1 that are 4 units from $(2, 3)$.

45. Find a number x such that $(0, 0)$, $(3, 2)$, and $(x, 0)$ are the vertices of an isosceles triangle, neither of whose two equal sides lie on the x-axis.

46. Do Exercise 45 if one of the two equal sides lies on the positive x-axis.

47. Show that the midpoint M of the hypotenuse of a right triangle is equidistant from the vertices of the triangle. *Hint:* Place the triangle in the first quadrant of the plane, with right angle at the origin so that the situation looks like the figure.

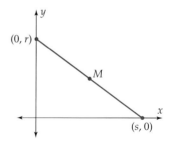

48. Show that the diagonals of a parallelogram bisect each other. *Hint:* Place the parallelogram in the first quadrant with a vertex at the origin and one side along the x-axis, so that the situation looks like the figure.

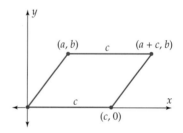

49. Show that the diagonals of a rectangle have the same length. *Hint:* Place the rectangle in the first quadrant of the plane and label its vertices appropriately, as in Exercises 47–48.

50. If the diagonals of a parallelogram have the same length, show that the parallelogram is actually a rectangle. *Hint:* See Exercise 48.

51. *Critical Thinking* For each nonzero real number k, the graph of $(x - k)^2 + y^2 = k^2$ is a circle. Describe all possible such circles.

52. *Critical Thinking* Suppose every point in the coordinate plane is moved 5 units straight up.
   a. To what point does each of these points go: $(0, -5), (2, 2), (5, 0), (5, 5), (4, 1)$?
   b. Which points go to each of the points in part **a**?
   c. To what point does (a, b) go?
   d. To what point does $(a, b - 5)$ go?
   e. What point goes to $(-4a, b)$?
   f. What points go to themselves?

53. *Critical Thinking* Let (c, d) be any point in the plane with $c \neq 0$. Prove that (c, d) and $(-c, -d)$ lie on the same straight line through the origin, on opposite sides of the origin, the same distance from the origin. *Hint:* Find the midpoint of the line segment joining (c, d) and $(-c, -d)$.

54. *Critical Thinking* *Proof of the Midpoint Formula* Let P and Q be the points (x_1, y_1) and (x_2, y_2) respectively and let M be the point with coordinates

$$\left(\frac{x_1 + x_2}{2}, \frac{y_1 + y_2}{2} \right).$$

Use the distance formula to compute the following:
   a. the distance d from P to Q;
   b. the distance d_1 from M to P;
   c. the distance d_2 from M to Q.
   d. Verify that $d_1 = d_2$.
   e. Show that $d_1 + d_2 = d$. *Hint:* Verify that

$$d_1 = \frac{1}{2}d \text{ and } d_2 = \frac{1}{2}d.$$

   f. Explain why parts **d** and **e** show that M is the midpoint of PQ.

ADVANCED TOPICS

B.1 The Binomial Theorem

The Binomial Theorem provides a formula for calculating the product $(x + y)^n$ for any positive integer n. Before we state the theorem, some preliminaries are needed.

Let n be a positive integer. The symbol $n!$ (read **n factorial**) denotes the product of all the integers from 1 to n. For example,

$$2! = 1 \cdot 2 = 2, \qquad 3! = 1 \cdot 2 \cdot 3 = 6, \qquad 4! = 1 \cdot 2 \cdot 3 \cdot 4 = 24,$$
$$5! = 1 \cdot 2 \cdot 3 \cdot 4 \cdot 5 = 120,$$
$$10! = 1 \cdot 2 \cdot 3 \cdot 4 \cdot 5 \cdot 6 \cdot 7 \cdot 8 \cdot 9 \cdot 10 = 3,628,800.$$

In general, we have this result:

n Factorial

Let n be a positive integer. Then

$$n! = 1 \cdot 2 \cdot 3 \cdot 4 \cdots (n - 2)(n - 1)n.$$

0! is defined to be the number 1.

Learn to use your calculator to compute factorials. You will find ! in the PROB (or PRB) submenu of the MATH or OPTN menu.

> **Calculator Exploration**
>
> 15! is such a large number your calculator will switch to scientific notation to express it. What is this approximation? Many calculators cannot compute factorials larger than 69! If yours does compute larger ones, how large a one can you compute without getting an error message [or on HP-38, getting the number 9.9999 ⋯ E499]?

If r and n are integers with $0 \le r \le n$, then

Binomial Coefficients

Either of the symbols $\binom{n}{r}$ or $_nC_r$ denotes the number $\dfrac{n!}{r!(n-r)!}$.

$\binom{n}{r}$ is called a *binomial coefficient*.

For example,

$$_5C_3 = \binom{5}{3} = \frac{5!}{3!(5-3)!} = \frac{5!}{3!2!} = \frac{1 \cdot 2 \cdot 3 \cdot 4 \cdot 5}{(1 \cdot 2 \cdot 3)(1 \cdot 2)} = \frac{4 \cdot 5}{2} = 10$$

$$_4C_2 = \binom{4}{2} = \frac{4!}{2!(4-2)!} = \frac{4!}{2!2!} = \frac{1 \cdot 2 \cdot 3 \cdot 4}{(1 \cdot 2)(1 \cdot 2)} = \frac{3 \cdot 4}{2} = 6.$$

Binomial coefficients can be computed on a calculator by using $_nC_r$ or Comb in the PROB (or PRB) submenu of the MATH or OPTN menu.

Calculator Exploration

Compute $_{56}C_{47} = \binom{56}{47}$. Although calculators cannot compute $457!$, they can compute many binomial coefficients, such as $\binom{475}{400}$, because most of the factors cancel out (as in the previous example). Check yours. Will it also compute $\binom{475}{50}$?

The preceding examples illustrate a fact whose proof will be omitted: *Every binomial coefficient is an integer.* Furthermore, for every nonnegative integer n,

$$\binom{n}{0} = 1 \quad \text{and} \quad \binom{n}{n} = 1$$

because

$$\binom{n}{0} = \frac{n!}{0!(n-0)!} + \frac{n!}{0!n!} = \frac{n!}{n!} = 1 \quad \text{and}$$

$$\binom{n}{n} = \frac{n!}{n!(n-n)!} = \frac{n!}{n!0!} = \frac{n!}{n!} = 1.$$

If we list the binomial coefficients for each value of n in this manner, we find that they form a rectangular array.

$$n = 0 \qquad \binom{0}{0}$$

$$n = 1 \qquad \binom{1}{0} \qquad \binom{1}{1}$$

$$n = 2 \qquad \binom{2}{0} \qquad \binom{2}{1} \qquad \binom{2}{2}$$

$$n = 3 \qquad \binom{3}{0} \qquad \binom{3}{1} \qquad \binom{3}{2} \qquad \binom{3}{3}$$

$$n = 4 \qquad \binom{4}{0} \qquad \binom{4}{1} \qquad \binom{4}{2} \qquad \binom{4}{3} \qquad \binom{4}{4}$$

$$\vdots \qquad \cdots \qquad \ddots$$

Calculating each binomial coefficient, we obtain the following array of numbers:

row 0					1				
row 1				1		1			
row 2			1		2		1		
row 3		1		3		3		1	
row 4	1		4		6		4		1

$$\vdots \qquad \cdots \qquad \ddots$$

This array is called **Pascal's triangle.** Its pattern is easy to remember. Each entry (except the 1's at the beginning or end of a row) is the sum of the two closest entries in the row above it. In the fourth row, for instance, 6 is the sum of the two 3's above it, and each 4 is the sum of the 1 and 3 above it. See Exercise 47 for a proof.

In order to develop a formula for calculating $(x + y)^n$, we first calculate these products for small values of n to see if we can find some kind of pattern:

$$
\begin{array}{lll}
& n = 0 & (x + y)^0 = \qquad\qquad 1 \\
& n = 1 & (x + y)^1 = \qquad\quad 1x + 1y \\
(*) & n = 2 & (x + y)^2 = \qquad 1x^2 + 2xy + 1y^2 \\
& n = 3 & (x + y)^3 = \quad 1x^3 + 3x^2y + 3xy^2 + 1y^3 \\
& n = 4 & (x + y)^4 = 1x^4 + 4x^3y + 6x^2y^2 + 4xy^3 + 1y^4
\end{array}
$$

One pattern is immediately obvious: the coefficients here (shown in color) are the top part of Pascal's triangle! In the case $n = 4$, for example, this means that the coefficients are the numbers

$$1 \quad 4 \quad 6 \quad 4 \quad 1$$

$$\binom{4}{0}, \ \binom{4}{1}, \ \binom{4}{2}, \ \binom{4}{3}, \ \binom{4}{4}.$$

If this pattern holds for larger n, then the coefficients in the expansion of $(x + y)^n$ are

$$\binom{n}{0}, \binom{n}{1}, \binom{n}{2}, \binom{n}{3}, \ldots, \binom{n}{n-1}, \binom{n}{n}.$$

As for the xy-terms associated with each of these coefficients, look at the pattern in (∗) above: the exponent of x goes down by 1 and the exponent of y goes up by 1 as you go from term to term, which suggests that the terms of the expansion of $(x + y)^n$ (without the coefficients) are:

$$x^n, \qquad x^{n-1}y, \qquad x^{n-2}y^2, \qquad x^{n-3}y^3, \ldots, xy^{n-1}, \quad y^n.$$

Combining the patterns of coefficients and xy-terms and using the fact that $\binom{n}{0} = 1$ and $\binom{n}{n} = 1$ suggests that the following result is true about the expansion of $(x + y)^n$.

The Binomial Theorem

> **For each positive integer n,**
>
> $$(x + y)^n = x^n + \binom{n}{1}x^{n-1}y + \binom{n}{2}x^{n-2}y^2 +$$
>
> $$\binom{n}{3}x^{n-3}y^3 + \cdots + \binom{n}{n-1}xy^{n-1} + y^n.$$

Using summation notation and the fact that $\binom{n}{0} = 1 = \binom{n}{n}$, we can write the Binomial Theorem compactly as

$$(x + y)^n = \sum_{j=0}^{n} \binom{n}{j}x^{n-j}y^j.$$

The Binomial Theorem will be proved in Section B.2 by means of mathematical induction. We shall assume its truth for now and illustrate some of its uses.

Example 1

Expand $(x + y)^8$.

Solution

We apply the Binomial Theorem in the case $n = 8$:

$$(x + y)^8 = x^8 + \binom{8}{1}x^7y + \binom{8}{2}x^6y^2 + \binom{8}{3}x^5y^3$$

$$+ \binom{8}{4}x^4y^4 + \binom{8}{5}x^3y^5 + \binom{8}{6}x^2y^6 + \binom{8}{7}xy^7 + y^8.$$

The coefficients can be computed individually by hand or by using $_nC_r$ (or COMB) on a calculator; for instance,

$$_8C_2 = \binom{8}{2} = \frac{8!}{2!6!} = 28 \qquad \text{or} \qquad _8C_3 = \binom{8}{3} = \frac{8!}{3!5!} = 56.$$

Alternatively, you can display all the coefficients at once by making a table of values for the function $f(x) = {}_8C_x$, as shown in Figure B.1-1.

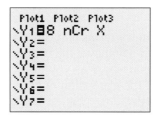 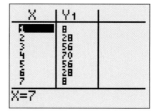

Figure B.1-1

Substituting these values in the preceding expansion, we have

$$(x + y)^8 = x^8 + 8x^7y + 28x^6y^2$$
$$+ 56x^5y^3 + 70x^4y^4 + 56x^3y^5 + 28x^2y^6 + 8xy^7 + y^8.$$

Example 2

Expand $(1 - z)^6$.

Solution

Note that $1 - z = 1 + (-z)$ and apply the Binomial Theorem with $x = 1$, $y = -z$, and $n = 6$:

$$(1 - z)^6 = 1^6 + \binom{6}{1}1^5(-z) + \binom{6}{2}1^4(-z)^2 + \binom{6}{3}1^3(-z)^3$$
$$+ \binom{6}{4}1^2(-z)^4 + \binom{6}{5}1(-z)^5 + (-z)^6$$
$$= 1 - \binom{6}{1}z + \binom{6}{2}z^2 - \binom{6}{3}z^3 + \binom{6}{4}z^4 - \binom{6}{5}z^5 + z^6$$
$$= 1 - 6z + 15z^2 - 20z^3 + 15z^4 - 6z^5 + z^6.$$

Example 3

Expand $(x^2 + x^{-1})^4$.

Solution

Use the Binomial Theorem with x^2 in place of x and x^{-1} in place of y:

$$(x^2 + x^{-1})^4 = (x^2)^4 + \binom{4}{1}(x^2)^3(x^{-1})$$
$$+ \binom{4}{2}(x^2)^2(x^{-1})^2 + \binom{4}{3}(x^2)(x^{-1})^3 + (x^{-1})^4$$

Technology Tip

Binomial expansions, such as those in Examples 1–3, can be done on TI-89 by using EXPAND in the ALGEBRA menu.

$$= x^8 + 4x^6x^{-1} + 6x^4x^{-2} + 4x^2x^{-3} + x^{-4}$$
$$= x^8 + 4x^5 + 6x^2 + 4x^{-1} + x^{-4}.$$

Example 4

Show that $(1.001)^{1000} > 2$ without using a calculator.

Solution

We write 1.001 as $1 + .001$ and apply the Binomial Theorem with $x = 1$, $y = .001$, and $n = 1000$:

$$(1.001)^{1000} = (1 + .001)^{1000}$$

$$= 1^{1000} + \binom{1000}{1} 1^{999}(.001) + \text{other positive terms}$$

$$= 1 + \binom{1000}{1}(.001) + \text{other positive terms.}$$

But $\binom{1000}{1} = \dfrac{1000!}{1!999!} = \dfrac{1000 \cdot 999!}{999!} = 1000.$ Therefore, $\binom{1000}{1}(.001) = 1,000(.001) = 1$ and $(1.001)^{1000} = 1 + 1 + \text{other positive terms} = 2 + \text{other positive terms.}$

Hence, $(1.001)^{1000} > 2.$

Sometimes we need to know only one term in the expansion of $(x + y)^n$. If you examine the expansion given by the Binomial Theorem, you will see that in the second term y has exponent 1, in the third term y has exponent 2, and so on. Thus,

Properties of the Binomial Expansion

In the binomial expansion of $(x + y)^n$,

The exponent of y is always one less than the number of the term.

Furthermore, in each of the middle terms of the expansion,

The coefficient of the term containing y^r is $\binom{n}{r}$.

The sum of the x exponent and the y exponent is n.

For instance, in the *ninth* term of the expansion of $(x + y)^{13}$, y has exponent 8, the coefficient is $\binom{13}{8}$, and x must have exponent 5 (since $8 + 5 = 13$). Thus, the ninth term is $\binom{13}{8}x^5y^8$.

Example 5

Find the ninth term of the expansion of $\left(2x^2 + \dfrac{\sqrt[4]{y}}{\sqrt{6}} \right)^{13}$.

Solution

We shall use the Binomial Theorem with $n = 13$ and with $2x^2$ in place of x and $\dfrac{\sqrt[4]{y}}{\sqrt{6}}$ in place of y. The remarks on the previous page show that the ninth term is

$$\binom{13}{8}(2x^2)^5 \left(\frac{\sqrt[4]{y}}{\sqrt{6}} \right)^8.$$

Since $\sqrt[4]{y} = y^{\frac{1}{4}}$ and $\sqrt{6} = \sqrt{3}\sqrt{2} = 3^{\frac{1}{2}}2^{\frac{1}{2}}$, we can simplify as follows:

$$\binom{13}{8}(2x^2)^5 \left(\frac{\sqrt[4]{y}}{\sqrt{6}} \right)^8 = \binom{13}{8}2^5(x^2)^5 \frac{(y^{\frac{1}{4}})^8}{(3^{\frac{1}{2}})^8(2^{\frac{1}{2}})^8} = \binom{13}{8}2^5 x^{10} \frac{y^2}{3^4 \cdot 2^4}$$

$$= \binom{13}{8}\frac{2}{3^4}x^{10}y^2 = \frac{13 \cdot 12 \cdot 11 \cdot 10 \cdot 9}{5 \cdot 4 \cdot 3 \cdot 2} \cdot \frac{2}{3^4}x^{10}y^2$$

$$= \frac{286}{9}x^{10}y^2.$$

Exercises B.1

In Exercises 1–10, evaluate the expression.

1. $6!$ **2.** $\dfrac{11!}{8!}$ **3.** $\dfrac{12!}{9!3!}$ **4.** $\dfrac{9! - 8!}{7!}$

5. $\dbinom{5}{3} + \dbinom{5}{2} - \dbinom{6}{3}$ **6.** $\dbinom{12}{11} - \dbinom{11}{10} + \dbinom{7}{0}$

7. $\dbinom{6}{0} + \dbinom{6}{1} + \dbinom{6}{2} + \dbinom{6}{3} + \dbinom{6}{4} + \dbinom{6}{5} + \dbinom{6}{6}$

8. $\dbinom{6}{0} - \dbinom{6}{1} + \dbinom{6}{2} - \dbinom{6}{3} + \dbinom{6}{4} - \dbinom{6}{5} + \dbinom{6}{6}$

9. $\dbinom{100}{96}$ **10.** $\dbinom{75}{72}$

In Exercises 11–16, expand the expression.

11. $(x + y)^5$ **12.** $(a + b)^7$ **13.** $(a - b)^5$

14. $(c - d)^8$ **15.** $(2x + y^2)^5$ **16.** $(3u - v^3)^6$

In Exercises 17–26, use the Binomial Theorem to expand and (where possible) simplify the expression.

17. $(\sqrt{x} + 1)^6$ **18.** $(2 - \sqrt{y})^5$

19. $(1 - c)^{10}$ **20.** $\left(\sqrt{c} + \dfrac{1}{\sqrt{c}} \right)^7$

21. $(x^{-3} + x)^4$ **22.** $(3x^{-2} - x^2)^6$

23. $(1 + \sqrt{3})^4 + (1 - \sqrt{3})^4$

24. $(\sqrt{3} + 1)^6 - (\sqrt{3} - 1)^6$

25. $(1 + i)^6$, where $i^2 = -1$

26. $(\sqrt{2} - i)^4$, where $i^2 = -1$

In Exercises 27–32, find the indicated term of the expansion of the given expression.

27. third, $(x + y)^5$ **28.** fourth, $(a + b)^6$

29. fifth, $(c - d)^7$ **30.** third, $(a + 2)^8$

31. fourth, $\left(u^{-2} + \dfrac{u}{2} \right)^7$ **32.** fifth, $(\sqrt{x} - \sqrt{2})^7$

33. Find the coefficient of x^5y^8 in the expansion of $(2x - y^2)^9$.

34. Find the coefficient of $x^{12}y^6$ in the expansion of $(x^3 - 3y)^{10}$.

35. Find the coefficient of $\dfrac{1}{x^3}$ in the expansion of $\left(2x + \dfrac{1}{x^2}\right)^6$.

36. Find the constant term in the expansion of $\left(y - \dfrac{1}{2y}\right)^{10}$.

37. a. Verify that $\dbinom{9}{1} = 9$ and $\dbinom{9}{8} = 9$.

b. Prove that for each positive integer n, $\dbinom{n}{1} = n$

and $\dbinom{n}{n-1} = n$. *Note:* Part **a** is just the case when $n = 9$ and $n - 1 = 8$.

38. a. Verify that $\dbinom{7}{2} = \dbinom{7}{5}$.

b. Let r and n be integers with $0 \le r \le n$. Prove that $\dbinom{n}{r} = \dbinom{n}{n-r}$. *Note:* Part **a** is just the case when $n = 7$ and $r = 2$.

39. Prove that for any positive integer n,

$$2^n = \dbinom{n}{0} + \dbinom{n}{1} + \dbinom{n}{2} + \cdots + \dbinom{n}{n}.$$

Hint: $2 = 1 + 1$.

40. Prove that for any positive integer n,

$$\dbinom{n}{0} - \dbinom{n}{1} + \dbinom{n}{2} - \dbinom{n}{3} + \dbinom{n}{4} - \cdots$$
$$+ (-1)^k \dbinom{n}{k} + \cdots + (-1)^n \dbinom{n}{n} = 0.$$

41. Use the Binomial Theorem with $x = \sin\theta$ and $y = \cos\theta$ to find $(\cos\theta + i\sin\theta)^4$ where $i^2 = -1$.

42. a. Use DeMoivre's Theorem on page 441 to find

$$(\cos\theta + i\sin\theta)^4.$$

b. Use the fact that the two expressions obtained in part **a** and in Exercise 41 must be equal to express $\cos 4\theta$ and $\sin 4\theta$ in terms of $\sin\theta$ and $\cos\theta$.

43. a. Let f be the function given by $f(x) = x^5$. Let h be a nonzero number and compute $f(x + h) - f(x)$ (but leave all binomial coefficients in the form $\dbinom{5}{r}$ here and below).

b. Use part **a** to show that h is a factor of $f(x + h) - f(x)$ and find $\dfrac{f(x+h) - f(x)}{h}$.

c. If h is *very* close to 0, find a simple approximation of the quantity $\dfrac{f(x+h) - f(x)}{h}$. See part **b**.

44. Do Exercise 43 with $f(x) = x^8$ in place of $f(x) = x^5$.

45. Do Exercise 43 with $f(x) = x^{12}$ in place of $f(x) = x^5$.

46. Let n be a fixed positive integer. Do Exercise 43 with $f(x) = x^n$ in place of $f(x) = x^5$.

47. Let r and n be integers such that $0 \le r \le n$.
a. Verify that $(n - r)! = (n - r)[n - (r + 1)]!$
b. Verify that $(n - r)! = [(n + 1) - (r + 1)]!$
c. Prove that $\dbinom{n}{r+1} + \dbinom{n}{r} = \dbinom{n+1}{r+1}$ for any $r \le n - 1$. *Hint:* Write out the terms on the left side and use parts **a** and **b** to express each of them as a fraction with denominator $(r + 1)!(n - r)!$. Then add these two fractions, simplify the numerator, and compare the result with $\dbinom{n+1}{r+1}$.

d. Use part **c** to explain why each entry in Pascal's triangle (except the 1's at the beginning or end of a row) is the sum of the two closest entries in the row above it.

48. a. Find these numbers and write them one *below* the next: 11^0, 11^1, 11^2, 11^3, 11^4.
b. Compare the list in part **a** with rows 0 to 4 of Pascal's triangle. What's the explanation?
c. What can be said about 11^5 and row 5 of Pascal's triangle?
d. Calculate all integer powers of 101 from 101^0 to 101^8, list the results one under the other, and compare the list with rows 0 to 8 of Pascal's triangle. What's the explanation? What happens with 101^9?

Mathematical Induction

Mathematical induction is a method of proof that can be used to prove a wide variety of mathematical facts, including the Binomial Theorem, DeMoivre's Theorem, and statements such as:

The sum of the first n positive integers is the number $\dfrac{n(n+1)}{2}$.

$2^n > n$ for every positive integer n.

For each positive integer n, 4 is a factor of $7^n - 3^n$.

All of the preceding statements have a common property. For example, a statement such as

The sum of the first n positive integers is the number $\dfrac{n(n+1)}{2}$

or, in symbols,

$$1 + 2 + 3 + \cdots + n = \frac{n(n+1)}{2}$$

is really an infinite sequence of statements, one for each possible value of n:

$$n = 1: \qquad 1 = \frac{1(2)}{2}$$

$$n = 2: \qquad 1 + 2 = \frac{2(3)}{2}$$

$$n = 3: \qquad 1 + 2 + 3 = \frac{3(4)}{2}$$

and so on. Obviously, there isn't time enough to verify every one of the statements on this list, one at a time. But we can find a workable method of proof by examining how each statement on the list is *related* to the *next* statement on the list.

For example, for $n = 50$, the statement is

$$1 + 2 + 3 + \cdots + 50 = \frac{50(51)}{2}.$$

At the moment, we don't know whether or not this statement is true. But just *suppose* that it were true. What could then be said about the next statement, the one for $n = 51$:

$$1 + 2 + 3 + \cdots + 50 + 51 = \frac{51(52)}{2}?$$

Well, *if* it is true that

$$1 + 2 + 3 + \cdots + 50 = \frac{50(51)}{2}$$

then adding 51 to both sides and simplifying the right side would yield these equalities:

$$1 + 2 + 3 + \cdots + 50 + 51 = \frac{50(51)}{2} + 51$$

$$1 + 2 + 3 + \cdots + 50 + 51 = \frac{50(51)}{2} + \frac{2(51)}{2} = \frac{50(51) + 2(51)}{2}$$

$$1 + 2 + 3 + \cdots + 50 + 51 = \frac{(50 + 2)51}{2}$$

$$1 + 2 + 3 + \cdots + 50 + 51 = \frac{51(52)}{2}.$$

Since this last equality is just the original statement for $n = 51$, we conclude that

If the statement is true for $n = 50$, *then* it is also true for $n = 51$.

We have *not* proved that the statement actually *is* true for $n = 50$, but only that *if* it is, then it is also true for $n = 51$.

We claim that this same conditional relationship holds for any two consecutive values of n. In other words, we claim that for any positive integer k,

① **If the statement is true for $n = k$, *then* it is also true for $n = k + 1$.**

The proof of this claim is the same argument used earlier (with k and $k + 1$ in place of 50 and 51): *If* it is true that

$$1 + 2 + 3 + \cdots + k = \frac{k(k + 1)}{2} \qquad \textit{[Original statement for n = k]}$$

then adding $k + 1$ to both sides and simplifying the right side produces these equalities:

$$1 + 2 + 3 + \cdots + k + (k + 1) = \frac{k(k + 1)}{2} + (k + 1)$$

$$1 + 2 + 3 + \cdots + k + (k + 1) = \frac{k(k + 1)}{2} + \frac{2(k + 1)}{2} = \frac{k(k + 1) + 2(k + 1)}{2}$$

$$1 + 2 + 3 + \cdots + k + (k + 1) = \frac{(k + 2)(k + 1)}{2}$$

$$1 + 2 + 3 + \cdots + k + (k + 1) = \frac{(k + 1)[(k + 1) + 1]}{2}.$$

[Original statement for n = k + 1]

We have proved that claim ① is valid for each positive integer k. We have *not* proved that the original statement is true for any value of n, but only that *if* it is true for $n = k$, then it is also true for $n = k + 1$. Applying this fact when $k = 1, 2, 3, \ldots$, we see that a recursive pattern emerges. Beginning with the smallest positive integer, 1,

$$
②
\begin{cases}
\text{\textit{If} the statement is true for } n = 1, \quad \text{\textit{then} it is also true for} \\
\quad n = 1 + 1 = 2; \\[6pt]
\text{\textit{If} the statement is true for } n = 2, \quad \text{\textit{then} it is also true for} \\
\quad n = 2 + 1 = 3; \\[6pt]
\text{\textit{If} the statement is true for } n = 3, \quad \text{\textit{then} it is also true for} \\
\quad n = 3 + 1 = 4; \\[6pt]
\vdots \\[6pt]
\text{\textit{If} the statement is true for } n = 50, \quad \text{\textit{then} it is also true for} \\
\quad n = 50 + 1 = 51; \\[6pt]
\text{\textit{If} the statement is true for } n = 51, \quad \text{\textit{then} it is also true for} \\
\quad n = 51 + 1 = 52; \\[6pt]
\vdots
\end{cases}
$$

and so on.

We are finally in a position to *prove* the original statement: $1 + 2 + 3 + \cdots + n = n(n + 1)/2$. Obviously, it *is* true for $n = 1$ since $1 = 1(2)/2$. Now apply in turn each of the propositions on list ②. Since the statement *is* true for $n = 1$, it must also be true for $n = 2$, and hence for $n = 3$, and hence for $n = 4$, and so on, for every value of n. Therefore, the original statement is true for *every* positive integer n.

The preceding proof is an illustration of the following principle:

Principle of Mathematical Induction

> Suppose there is given a statement involving the positive integer n and that:
>
> (i) The statement is true for $n = 1$.
>
> (ii) If the statement is true for $n = k$ (where k is any positive integer), then the statement is also true for $n = k + 1$.
>
> Then the statement is true for every positive integer n.

Property (i) is simply a statement of fact. To verify that it holds, you must prove the given statement is true for $n = 1$. This is usually easy, as in the preceding example.

Property (ii) is a *conditional* property. It does not assert that the given statement *is* true for $n = k$, but only that *if* it is true for $n = k$, then it is also true for $n = k + 1$. So to verify that property (ii) holds, you need only prove this conditional proposition:

If the statement is true for $n = k$, *then* it is also true for $n = k + 1$.

In order to prove this, or any conditional proposition, you must proceed as in the previous example: Assume the "if" part and use this assumption to prove the "then" part. As we saw earlier, the same argument will usually work for any possible k. Once this conditional proposition has been proved, you can use it *together* with property (i) to conclude that the given statement is necessarily true for every n, just as in the preceding example.

Thus proof by mathematical induction reduces to two steps:

Step 1

Prove that the given statement is true for $n = 1$.

Step 2

Let k be a positive integer. Assume that the given statement is true for $n = k$. Use this assumption to prove that the statement is true for $n = k + 1$.

Step 2 may be performed before step 1 if you wish. Step 2 is sometimes referred to as the **inductive step.** The assumption that the given statement is true for $n = k$ in this inductive step is called the **induction hypothesis.**

Example 1

Prove that $2^n > n$ for every positive integer n.

Solution

Here the statement involving n is $2^n > n$.

Step 1

When $n = 1$, we have the statement $2^1 > 1$. This is obviously true.

Step 2

Let k be any positive integer. We assume that the statement is true for $n = k$, that is, we assume that $2^k > k$. We shall use this assumption to prove that the statement is true for $n = k + 1$, that is, that $2^{k+1} > k + 1$.

We begin with the induction hypothesis:* $2^k > k$. Multiplying both sides of this inequality by 2 yields:

$$2 \cdot 2^k > 2k$$

③
$$2^{k+1} > 2k.$$

Since k is a positive integer, we know that $k \geq 1$. Adding k to each side of the inequality $k \geq 1$, we have

$$k + k \geq k + 1$$
$$2k \geq k + 1.$$

Combining this result with inequality ③, we see that

$$2^{k+1} > 2k \geq k + 1.$$

---

*This is the point at which you usually must do some work. Remember that what follows is the "finished proof." It does not include all the thought, scratch work, false starts, and so on that were done before this proof was actually found.

The first and last terms of this inequality show that $2^{k+1} > k + 1$. Therefore, the statement is true for $n = k + 1$. This argument works for any positive integer k. Thus, we have completed the inductive step. By the Principle of Mathematical Induction, we conclude that $2^n > n$ for every positive integer n.

Example 2

Simple arithmetic shows that

$$7^2 - 3^2 = 49 - 9 = 40 = 4 \cdot 10$$

and

$$7^3 - 3^3 = 343 - 27 = 316 = 4 \cdot 79.$$

In each case, 4 is a factor. These examples suggest that

For each positive integer n, 4 is a factor of $7^n - 3^n$.
This conjecture can be proved by induction as follows.

Step 1

When $n = 1$, the statement is "4 is a factor of $7^1 - 3^1$." Since $7^1 - 3^1 = 4 = 4 \cdot 1$, the statement is true for $n = 1$.

Step 2

Let k be a positive integer and assume that the statement is true for $n = k$, that is, that 4 is a factor of $7^k - 3^k$. Let us denote the other factor by D, so that the induction hypothesis is: $7^k - 3^k = 4D$. We must use this assumption to prove that the statement is true for $n = k + 1$, that is, that 4 is a factor of $7^{k+1} - 3^{k+1}$. Here is the proof:

$$
\begin{aligned}
7^{k+1} - 3^{k+1} &= 7^{k+1} - 7 \cdot 3^k + 7 \cdot 3^k - 3^{k+1} &&[\textit{Since } -7 \cdot 3^k + 7 \cdot 3^k = 0] \\
&= 7(7^k - 3^k) + (7 - 3)3^k &&[\textit{Factor}] \\
&= 7(4D) + (7 - 3)3^k &&[\textit{Induction hypothesis}] \\
&= 7(4D) + 4 \cdot 3^k &&[7 - 3 = 4] \\
&= 4(7D + 3^k). &&[\textit{Factor out 4}]
\end{aligned}
$$

From this last line, we see that 4 is a factor of $7^{k+1} - 3^{k+1}$. Thus, the statement is true for $n = k + 1$, and the inductive step is complete. Therefore, by the Principle of Mathematical Induction the conjecture is actually true for every positive integer n.

Another example of mathematical induction, the proof of the Binomial Theorem, is given at the end of this section.

Sometimes a statement involving the integer n may be false for $n = 1$ and (possibly) other small values of n, but true for all values of n beyond a particular number. For instance, the statement $2^n > n^2$ is false for $n = 1$, 2, 3, 4. But it is true for $n = 5$ and all larger values of n. A variation on the Principle of Mathematical Induction can be used to prove this fact and similar statements. See Exercise 28 for details.

A Common Mistake with Induction

It is sometimes tempting to omit step 2 of an inductive proof when the given statement can easily be verified for small values of n, especially if a clear pattern seems to be developing. As the next example shows, however, *omitting step 2 may lead to error.*

Example 3

An integer (>1) is said to be *prime* if its only positive integer factors are itself and 1. For instance, 11 is prime since its only positive integer factors are 11 and 1. But 15 is not prime because it has factors other than 15 and 1 (namely, 3 and 5). For each positive integer n, consider the number

$$f(n) = n^2 - n + 11.$$

You can readily verify that

$$f(1) = 11, \quad f(2) = 13, \quad f(3) = 17, \quad f(4) = 23, \quad f(5) = 31$$

and that *each of these numbers is prime.* Furthermore, there is a clear pattern: The first two numbers (11 and 13) differ by 2; the next two (13 and 17) differ by 4; the next two (17 and 23) differ by 6; and so on. On the basis of this evidence, we might conjecture:

For each positive integer n, the number $f(n) = n^2 - n + 11$ is prime.

We have seen that this conjecture is true for $n = 1, 2, 3, 4, 5$. Unfortunately, however, it is *false* for some values of n. For instance, when $n = 11$,

$$f(11) = 11^2 - 11 + 11 = 11^2 = 121.$$

But 121 is obviously *not* prime since it has a factor other than 121 and 1, namely, 11. You can verify that the statement is also false for $n = 12$ but true for $n = 13$.

In the preceding example, the proposition

If the statement is true for $n = k$, then it is true for $n = k + 1$

is false when $k = 10$ and $k + 1 = 11$. If you were not aware of this and tried to complete step 2 of an inductive proof, you would not have been able to find a valid proof for it. Of course, the fact that you can't find a proof of a proposition doesn't always mean that no proof exists. But when you are unable to complete step 2, you are warned that there is a possibility that the given statement may be false for some values of n. This warning should prevent you from drawing any wrong conclusions.

Proof of the Binomial Theorem

We shall use induction to prove that for every positive integer n,

$$(x + y)^n = x^n + \binom{n}{1} x^{n-1} y$$

$$+ \binom{n}{2} x^{n-2} y^2 + \binom{n}{3} x^{n-3} y^3 + \cdots + \binom{n}{n-1} xy^{n-1} + y^n.$$

This theorem was discussed and its notation explained in Section B.1.

Step 1

When $n = 1$, there are only two terms on the right side of the preceding equation, and the statement reads $(x + y)^1 = x^1 + y^1$. This is certainly true.

Step 2

Let k be any positive integer and assume that the theorem is true for $n = k$, that is, that

$$(x + y)^k = x^k + \binom{k}{1}x^{k-1}y + \binom{k}{2}x^{k-2}y^2 + \cdots$$

$$+ \binom{k}{r}x^{k-r}y^r + \cdots + \binom{k}{k-1}xy^{k-1} + y^k.$$

[On the right side of this equation, we have included a typical middle term $\binom{k}{r}x^{k-r}y^r$. The sum of the exponents is k, and the bottom part of the binomial coefficient is the same as the y exponent.] We shall use this assumption to prove that the theorem is true for $n = k + 1$, that is, that

$$(x + y)^{k+1} = x^{k+1} + \binom{k+1}{1}x^k y + \binom{k+1}{2}x^{k-1}y^2 + \cdots$$

$$+ \binom{k+1}{r+1}x^{k-r}y^{r+1} + \cdots + \binom{k+1}{k}xy^k + y^{k+1}.$$

We have simplified some of the terms on the right side; for instance, $(k + 1) - 1 = k$ and $(k + 1) - (r + 1) = k - r$. But this is the correct statement for $n = k + 1$: The coefficients of the middle terms are $\binom{k+1}{1}$, $\binom{k+1}{2}$, $\binom{k+1}{3}$, and so on; the sum of the exponents of each middle term is $k + 1$, and the bottom part of each binomial coefficient is the same as the y exponent.

In order to prove the theorem for $n = k + 1$, we shall need this fact about binomial coefficients: For any integers r and k with $0 \le r < k$,

④
$$\binom{k}{r+1} + \binom{k}{r} = \binom{k+1}{r+1}.$$

A proof of this fact is outlined in Exercise 47 on page 1001.

To prove the theorem for $n = k + 1$, we first note that

$$(x + y)^{k+1} = (x + y)(x + y)^k.$$

Applying the induction hypothesis to $(x + y)^k$, we see that

$$(x + y)^{k+1} = (x + y)\left[x^k + \binom{k}{1}x^{k-1}y + \binom{k}{2}x^{k-2}y^2 + \cdots + \binom{k}{r}x^{k-r}y^r\right.$$

$$\left. + \binom{k}{r+1}x^{k-(r+1)}y^{r+1} + \cdots + \binom{k}{k-1}xy^{k-1} + y^k\right]$$

$$= x\left[x^k + \binom{k}{1}x^{k-1}y + \cdots + y^k\right] + y\left[x^k + \binom{k}{1}x^{k-1}y + \cdots + y^k\right].$$

Next we multiply out the right-hand side. Remember that multiplying by x increases the x exponent by 1 and multiplying by y increases the y exponent by 1.

$$(x + y)^{k+1} = \left[x^{k+1} + \binom{k}{1}x^k y + \binom{k}{2}x^{k-1}y^2 + \cdots + \binom{k}{r}x^{k-r+1}y^r \right.$$
$$+ \binom{k}{r+1}x^{k-r}y^{r+1} + \cdots + \binom{k}{k-1}x^2 y^{k-1} + xy^k \Big]$$
$$+ \left[x^k y + \binom{k}{1}x^{k-1}y^2 + \binom{k}{2}x^{k-2}y^3 + \cdots + \binom{k}{r}x^{k-r}y^{r+1} \right.$$
$$+ \binom{k}{r+1}x^{k-(r+1)}y^{r+2} + \cdots + \binom{k}{k-1}xy^k + y^{k+1} \Big]$$
$$= x^{k+1} + \left[\binom{k}{1} + 1 \right]x^k y + \left[\binom{k}{2} + \binom{k}{1} \right]x^{k-1}y^2 + \cdots$$
$$+ \left[\binom{k}{r+1} + \binom{k}{r} \right]x^{k-r}y^{r+1} + \cdots + \left[1 + \binom{k}{k-1} \right]xy^k + y^{k+1}.$$

Now apply statement ④ to each of the coefficients of the middle terms.

For instance, with $r = 1$, statement ④ shows that $\binom{k}{2} + \binom{k}{1} = \binom{k+1}{2}$.

Similarly, with $r = 0$, $\binom{k}{1} + 1 = \binom{k}{1} + \binom{k}{0} = \binom{k+1}{1}$, and so on. Then the expression above for $(x + y)^{k+1}$ becomes

$$(x + y)^{k+1} = x^{k+1} + \binom{k+1}{1}x^k y + \binom{k+1}{2}x^{k-1}y^2 + \cdots$$
$$+ \binom{k+1}{r+1}x^{k-r}y^{r+1} + \cdots + \binom{k+1}{k}xy^k + y^{k+1}.$$

Since this last statement says the theorem is true for $n = k + 1$, the inductive step is complete. By the Principle of Mathematical Induction the theorem is true for every positive integer n.

Exercises B.2

In Exercises 1–18, use mathematical induction to prove that each of the given statements is true for every positive integer n.

1. $1 + 2 + 2^2 + 2^3 + 2^4 + \cdots + 2^{n-1} = 2^n - 1$

2. $1 + 3 + 3^2 + 3^3 + 3^4 + \cdots + 3^{n-1} = \dfrac{3^n - 1}{2}$

3. $1 + 3 + 5 + 7 + \cdots + (2n - 1) = n^2$

4. $2 + 4 + 6 + 8 + \cdots + 2n = n^2 + n$

5. $1^2 + 2^2 + 3^2 + \cdots + n^2 = \dfrac{n(n + 1)(2n + 1)}{6}$

6. $\dfrac{1}{2} + \dfrac{1}{4} + \dfrac{1}{8} + \cdots + \dfrac{1}{2^n} = 1 - \dfrac{1}{2^n}$

7. $\dfrac{1}{1 \cdot 2} + \dfrac{1}{2 \cdot 3} + \dfrac{1}{3 \cdot 4} + \cdots + \dfrac{1}{n(n + 1)} = \dfrac{n}{n + 1}$

8. $\left(1 + \dfrac{1}{1}\right)\left(1 + \dfrac{1}{2}\right)\left(1 + \dfrac{1}{3}\right) \cdots \left(1 + \dfrac{1}{n}\right) = n + 1$

9. $n + 2 > n$ **10.** $2n + 2 > n$

11. $3^n \geq 3n$ **12.** $3^n \geq 1 + 2n$

13. $3n > n + 1$ **14.** $\left(\dfrac{3}{2}\right)^n > n$

15. 3 is a factor of $2^{2n+1} + 1$

16. 5 is a factor of $2^{4n-2} + 1$

17. 64 is a factor of $3^{2n+2} - 8n - 9$

18. 64 is a factor of $9^n - 8n - 1$

19. Let c and d be fixed real numbers. Prove that
$$c + (c + d) + (c + 2d) + (c + 3d) + \cdots$$
$$+ [c + (n-1)d] = \frac{n[2c + (n-1)d]}{2}$$

20. Let r be a fixed real number with $r \neq 1$. Prove that
$$1 + r + r^2 + r^3 + \cdots + r^{n-1} = \frac{r^n - 1}{r - 1}.$$

Remember: $1 = r^0$; so when $n = 1$ the left side reduces to $r^0 = 1$.

21. a. Write *each* of $x^2 - y^2$, $x^3 - y^3$, and $x^4 - y^4$ as a product of $x - y$ and another factor.
   b. Make a conjecture as to how $x^n - y^n$ can be written as a product of $x - y$ and another factor. Use induction to prove your conjecture.

22. Let $x_1 = \sqrt{2}$; $x_2 = \sqrt{2 + \sqrt{2}}$;
$x_3 = \sqrt{2 + \sqrt{2 + \sqrt{2}}}$; and so on. Prove that $x_n < 2$ for every positive integer n.

In Exercises 23–27, if the given statement is true, prove it. If it is false, give a counterexample.

23. Every odd positive integer is prime.

24. The number $n^2 + n + 17$ is prime for every positive integer n.

25. $(n + 1)^2 > n^2 + 1$ for every positive integer n.

26. 3 is a factor of the number $n^3 - n + 3$ for every positive integer n.

27. 4 is a factor of the number $n^4 - n + 4$ for every positive integer n.

28. Let q be a *fixed* integer. Suppose a statement involving the integer n has these two properties:
   i. The statement is true for $n = q$.
   ii. *If* the statement is true for $n = k$ (where k is any integer with $k \geq q$), then the statement is also true for $n = k + 1$.
   Then we claim that the statement is true for every integer n greater than or equal to q.
   a. Give an informal explanation that shows why this claim should be valid. Note that when $q = 1$, this claim is precisely the Principle of Mathematical Induction.
   b. The claim made before part **a** will be called the *Extended Principle of Mathematical Induction.*

State the two steps necessary to use this principle to prove that a given statement is true for all $n \geq q$. (See discussion on page 1005.)

In Exercises 29–34, use the Extended Principle of Mathematical Induction (Exercise 28) to prove the given statement.

29. $2n - 4 > n$ for every $n \geq 5$. (Use 5 for q here.)

30. Let r be a fixed real number with $r > 1$. Then $(1 + r)^n > 1 + nr$ for every integer $n \geq 2$. (Use 2 for q here.)

31. $n^2 > n$ for all $n \geq 2$

32. $2^n > n^2$ for all $n \geq 5$

33. $3^n > 2^n + 10n$ for all $n \geq 4$

34. $2n < n!$ for all $n \geq 4$

35. Let n be a positive integer. Suppose that there are three pegs and on one of them n rings are stacked, with each ring being smaller in diameter than the one below it (see the figure). We want to transfer the stack of rings to another peg according to these rules: (i) Only one ring may be moved at a time; (ii) a ring can be moved to any peg, provided it is never placed on top of a smaller ring; (iii) the final order of the rings on the new peg must be the same as the original order on the first peg.

a. What is the smallest possible number of moves when $n = 2$? $n = 3$? $n = 4$?
b. Make a conjecture as to the smallest possible number of moves required for any n. Prove your conjecture by induction.

36. The basic formula for compound interest $T(x) = P(1 + r)^x$ was discussed in Chapter 5. Prove by induction that the formula is valid whenever x is a positive integer. [*Note:* P and r are assumed to be constant.]

37. Use induction to prove DeMoivre's Theorem: For any complex number $z = r(\cos \theta + i \sin \theta)$ and any positive integer n,
$$z^n = r^n[\cos(n\theta) + i \sin(n\theta)].$$

GEOMETRY REVIEW

Geometry Concepts

An **angle** consists of two half-lines that begin at the same point P, as in Figure G.1-1. The point P is called the **vertex** of the angle and the half-lines the **sides** of the angle.

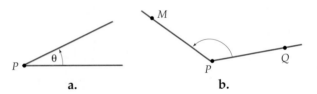

Figure G.1-1

An angle may be labeled by a Greek letter, such as angle θ in Figure G.1-1**a**, or by listing three points (a point on one side, the vertex, a point on the other side), such as angle QPM in Figure G.1-1**b**.

In order to measure the size of an angle, we must assign a number to each angle. Here is the classical method for doing this:

1. Construct a circle whose center is the vertex of the angle.

2. Divide the circumference of the circle into 360 equal parts (called **degrees**) by marking 360 points on the circumference, beginning with the point where one side of the angle intersects the circle. Label these points 0°, 1°, 2°, 3°, and so on.

3. The label of the point where the second side of the angle intersects the circle is the degree measure of the angle.

For example, Figure G.1-2 on the next page shows an angle θ of measure 25 degrees (in symbols, 25°) and an angle β of measure 135°.

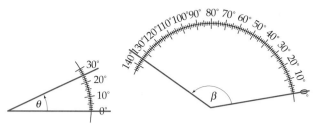

Figure G.1-2

An **acute angle** is an angle whose measure is strictly between 0° and 90°, such as angle θ in Figure G.1-2. A **right angle** is an angle that measures 90°. An **obtuse angle** is an angle whose measure is strictly between 90° and 180°, such as angle β in Figure G.1-2.

A **triangle** has three sides (straight line segments) and three angles, formed at the points where the various sides meet. When angles are measured in degrees,

> the sum of the measures of all three angles of a triangle is *always* 180°.

For instance, see Figure G.1-3.

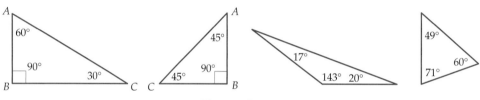

Figure G.1-3

A **right triangle** is a triangle, one of whose angles is a right angle, such as the first two triangles shown in Figure G.1-3. The side of a right triangle that lies opposite the right angle is called the **hypotenuse.** In each of the right triangles in Figure G.1-3, side AC is the hypotenuse.

Pythagorean Theorem

If the sides of a right triangle have lengths a and b and the hypotenuse has length c, then

$$c^2 = a^2 + b^2.$$

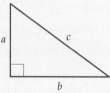

Example 1

Consider the right triangle with sides of lengths 5 and 12, as shown in Figure G.1-4.

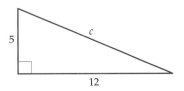

Figure G.1-4

According to the Pythagorean Theorem the length c of the hypotenuse satisfies the equation: $c^2 = 5^2 + 12^2 = 25 + 144 = 169$. Since $169 = 13^2$, we see that c must be 13.

Theorem I

If two angles of a triangle are equal, then the two sides opposite these angles have the same length.

Example 2

Suppose the hypotenuse of the right triangle shown in Figure G.1-5 has length 1 and that angles B and C measure $45°$ each.

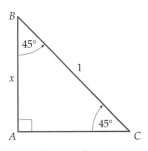

Figure G.1-5

Then by Theorem I, sides AB and AC have the same length. If x is the length of side AB, then by the Pythagorean Theorem:

$$x^2 + x^2 = 1^2$$
$$2x^2 = 1$$
$$x^2 = \frac{1}{2}$$
$$x = \sqrt{\frac{1}{2}} = \frac{1}{\sqrt{2}} = \frac{\sqrt{2}}{2}.$$

(We ignore the other solution of this equation, namely, $x = -\sqrt{\frac{1}{2}}$, since x represents a length here and thus must be nonnegative.) Therefore, the sides of a $90°-45°-45°$ triangle with hypotenuse 1 are each of length $\frac{\sqrt{2}}{2}$. ∎

Theorem II

> In a right triangle that has an angle of 30°, the length of the side opposite the 30° angle is one-half the length of the hypotenuse.

Example 3

Suppose that in the right triangle shown in Figure G.1-6 angle B is 30° and the length of hypotenuse BC is 2.

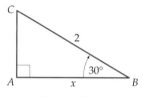

Figure G.1-6

By Theorem II the side opposite the 30° angle, namely, side AC, has length 1. If x denotes the length of side AB, then by the Pythagorean Theorem:

$$1^2 + x^2 = 2^2$$
$$x^2 = 3$$
$$x = \sqrt{3}.$$

∎

Example 4

The right triangle shown in Figure G.1-7 has a 30° angle at C, and side AC has length $\frac{\sqrt{3}}{2}$.

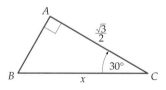

Figure G.1-7

Let x denote the length of the hypotenuse BC. By Theorem II, side AB has length $\frac{1}{2}x$. By the Pythagorean Theorem:

$$\left(\frac{1}{2}x\right)^2 + \left(\frac{\sqrt{3}}{2}\right)^2 = x^2$$

$$\frac{x^2}{4} + \frac{3}{4} = x^2$$

$$\frac{3}{4} = \frac{3}{4}x^2$$

$$x^2 = 1$$

$$x = 1.$$

Therefore, the triangle has hypotenuse of length 1 and sides of lengths $\frac{1}{2}$ and $\frac{\sqrt{3}}{2}$.

Two triangles, as in Figure G.1-8, are said to be **similar** if their corresponding angles are equal (that is, $\angle A = \angle D$; $\angle B = \angle E$; and $\angle C = \angle F$). Thus, similar triangles have the same *shape* but not necessarily the same *size*.

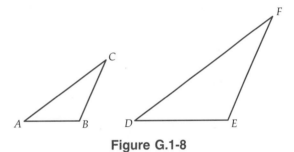

Figure G.1-8

Theorem III

Suppose triangle *ABC* with sides *a*, *b*, *c* is similar to triangle *DEF* with sides *d*, *e*, *f* (that is, $\angle A = \angle D$; $\angle B = \angle E$; $\angle C = \angle F$).

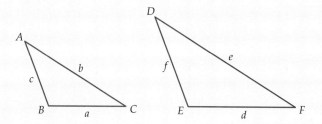

Then

$$\frac{a}{d} = \frac{b}{e} = \frac{c}{f}.$$

These equalities are equivalent to:

$$\frac{a}{b} = \frac{d}{e}, \quad \frac{b}{c} = \frac{e}{f}, \quad \frac{a}{c} = \frac{d}{f}.$$

The equivalence of the equalities in the conclusion of the theorem is easily verified. For example, since

$$\frac{a}{d} = \frac{b}{e}$$

we have

$$ae = db.$$

Dividing both sides of this equation by *be* yields:

$$\frac{ae}{be} = \frac{db}{be}$$

$$\frac{a}{b} = \frac{d}{e}.$$

The other equivalences are proved similarly.

Example 5

Suppose the triangles in Figure G.1-9 are similar and that the sides have the lengths indicated.

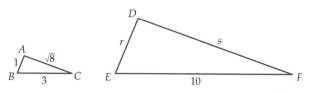

Figure G.1-9

Then by Theorem III,

$$\frac{\text{length } AC}{\text{length } DF} = \frac{\text{length } BC}{\text{length } EF}$$

In other words,

$$\frac{\sqrt{8}}{s} = \frac{3}{10}$$

so that

$$3s = 10\sqrt{8}$$
$$s = \left(\frac{10}{3}\right)\sqrt{8}.$$

Similarly, by Theorem III,

$$\frac{\text{length } AB}{\text{length } DE} = \frac{\text{length } BC}{\text{length } EF}$$

so that

$$\frac{1}{r} = \frac{3}{10}$$
$$3r = 10$$
$$r = \frac{10}{3}.$$

Therefore the sides of triangle DEF are of lengths 10, $\frac{10}{3}$, and $\frac{10}{3}\sqrt{8}$.

Technology

This appendix describes calculator features used throughout the book. The first section focuses on graphing functions and sequences, and the second section presents procedures for creating lists, statistics, statistical plots, and regression equations. Students who are unfamiliar with a graphing calculator should complete the entire appendix; all students may use it as a reference to specific features seen in the text.

T.1 Graphs and Tables

Graphing calculators have a MODE or SET UP feature that allows you to set different modes for number format, type of angle measure, graph type, and drawing mode. Select the following modes by using the procedures explained in detail below for TI-83, Sharp 9600, Casio 9850, and HP-38.

Number format:	Float or Standard
Angle measure:	Degree
Graph type:	function or rect
Drawing mode:	connected or connect

TI-83 Press MODE, then use the up or down arrow keys to move from one row to another and the left or right arrow keys to move to a desired selection. When the cursor is on a desired selection, press ENTER to choose that option. After all selections have been made, press 2nd QUIT to return to the home screen.

Sharp 9600 Press SET UP (or 2nd F BS) to view the current mode settings. The current settings are shown when menu A is selected. Use the up/down arrows to move among mode types listed as menus B through G. Use the right arrow and then the up/down arrows to access particular settings for each mode type. When the desired setting is highlighted, press ENTER.

Casio 9850 From the MAIN MENU, select RUN ENTER. Then press SHIFT SET UP. Use the up/down arrow key to select the different types of modes. Use the F1 through F6 buttons to select the desired setting for each mode.

HP 38G Press MODES (■HOME) to access the angle measure and number format settings. Select **Degree** and **Standard** by pressing CHOOS and then using the down arrow key to highlight the desired choice. Press OK when your preference is displayed. Select LIB/Function/START (or ENTER) to select the function applet. Press PLOT SETUP (■PLOT) to display the PLOT SETUP screen, then PAGE ∇ to scroll to the next page. Use the down arrow key to highlight CONNECT and press ✓CHK to insert a check mark, if needed.

Solutions and Graphs

The **graph of an equation** in two variables is the set of points in the plane whose coordinates are solutions of the equation. Thus, the graph is a *geometric picture of the solutions.*

The graph of $y = x^2$ consists of all points (x, x^2), where x is a real number. A table of values for this function is shown below along with the graphical representation of the points. See Figure T1-1a. The points suggest that the graph looks like Figure T1-1b, which is obtained by connecting the plotted points and extending the graph.

x	$y = x^2$
-2	4
-1.5	2.25
-1	1
-0.5	0.25
0	0
0.5	0.25
1	1
1.5	2.25
2	4

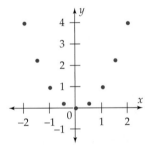

Figure T1-1a

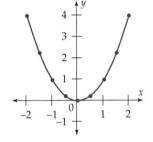

Figure T1-1b

Using Technology to Graph Functions

Technology improves graphing speed and accuracy by plotting a large number of points quickly. A graphing calculator graphs in the same way you would graph by hand, but it uses many more points.

Viewing Windows

The first step in graphing with technology is to choose a preliminary **viewing window,** or **viewing rectangle,** which is the portion of the coordinate plane that will appear on the screen. Using an inappropriate viewing window may display no portion of a graph or may misrepresent its important characteristics.

The viewing window for the graph in Figure T1-2a is the rectangular region indicated by the dashed blue lines. It includes all points (x, y) whose coordinates satisfy $-4 \leq x \leq 5$ and $-3 \leq y \leq 6$. To display this viewing window on a calculator, press the WINDOW (or RANGE or V-WINDOW or PLOT SETUP) key, and enter the appropriate numbers, as shown in Figure T1-2b for the TI-83. Other calculators are similar. The settings Xscl = 1 and Yscl = 1 put the tick marks 1 unit apart on the respective axes. This is usually the best setting for small viewing windows but not for large ones.

Technology

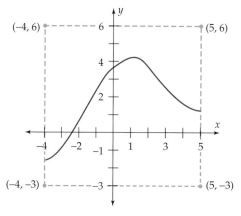

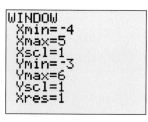

Figure T1-2a   Figure T1-2b

Resolution   Xres sets the pixel resolution for function graphs. When Xres is 1, functions are evaluated and graphed at each **pixel** (point) along the *x*-axis. At 10, functions are evaluated and graphed at every 10th pixel along the *x*-axis. Some calculators do not have a Xres setting, and on those that do, it should normally be set at 1 (or at "detail" on HP 38G).

Graphing Functions

The following example outlines the procedure for graphing an equation.

Example 1   **Using Technology to Graph a Function**

Use technology to graph the relation $2u^3 - 8u - 2v + 4 = 0$.

Solution

Step 1

Choose a preliminary viewing window.
If it is unknown where the graph lies in the plane, start with a viewing window with $-10 \le x \le 10$ and $-10 \le y \le 10$. This window setting is called the **standard window,** or **default window,** on most calculators. The window may be adjusted to fit the functions after graphing.

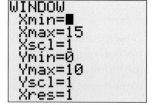

Figure T1-3a

To display the viewing **window editor** on a calculator, press Window (Range, V-Window, or Plot Setup) and enter the appropriate numbers, as shown in Figure T1-3a.

Xscl and Yscl determine where the tick marks will be displayed on the axes. Setting both to 1 is usually best for small viewing windows but not for large ones.

Step 2

Solve for the output variable, if necessary.
Calculators can only graph *functions* in a form where the output variable is expressed as a function of the input variable. In this example, assume that the output variable is v and solve the given equation for v:

$$2u^3 - 8u - 2v + 4 = 0$$
$$-2v = -2u^3 + 8u - 4 \qquad \textit{Rearrange terms.}$$
$$v = u^3 - 4u + 2 \qquad \textit{Divide by } -2.$$

Figure T1-3b

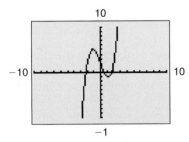

Figure T1-3c

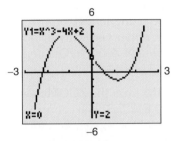

Figure T1-3d

Because the calculator graphs functions of the form $y = f(x)$, replace v with y and replace u with x. The function can be represented as the following.

$$y = x^3 - 4x + 2$$

Step 3

Enter the function by selecting the following.

TI and **Sharp 9600**	Y=
Casio 9850	GRAPH from the MAIN MENU
HP38G	SYMB

Key in the function, as shown in Figure T1-3b.

Display the graph by pressing GRAPH (or DRAW or PLOT). The graph of the function is shown in Figure T1-3c.

Step 4

If necessary, adjust the viewing window for a better view.

Notice that the point where the graph crosses the y-axis is not clear in the standard window. Changing the viewing window and displaying the graph again shows that the graph crosses the y-axis at 2. Figure T1-3d shows the graph after TRACE—which is discussed below—was pressed and the arrow keys were used to move the cursor to the y-intercept. ∎

Graphing Relations

Some relations must be written as two separate functions before they can be graphed. The method used to graph the function in Example 1 can be used to graph any equation that can be solved for y.

Example 2 Graphing a Relation

Graph the relation given by the equation $12x^2 - 4y^2 + 16x + 12 = 0$.

Solution

Solve the equation $12x^2 - 4y^2 + 16x + 12 = 0$ for y:

$$4y^2 = 12x^2 + 16x + 12$$
$$y^2 = 3x^2 + 4x + 3$$
$$y = \pm\sqrt{3x^2 + 4x + 3}$$

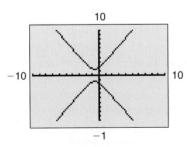

Figure T1-4

The graph is shown in Figure T1-4, where $y = \sqrt{3x^2 + 4x + 3}$ represents the upper portion of the graph and $y = -\sqrt{3x^2 + 4x + 3}$ represents the lower portion. ∎

Other Graphing Calculator Features

Trace

The trace feature allows you to display the coordinates of points on a graph of a function by using the left/right arrow keys, as illustrated in

Technology Tip

When you get a blank screen, press TRACE and use the left/right arrow keys. The coordinates of points on the graph will be displayed at the bottom of the screen, even though they are not in the current window. Use these coordinates as a guide for selecting a viewing window in which the graph does appear.

Technology

Figure T1-3d. The TRACE feature is located on the different calculators as follows.

TI and **Sharp 9600**	Trace is on the keyboard.
Casio 9850	Trace is the 2nd function above F1.
HP 38G	Trace is enabled/disabled by pressing the button under the menu shown when a function is plotted. TRACE is enabled when TRACE ■ is displayed and disabled when TRACE alone is displayed.

Zoom

Using the ZOOM feature of a graphing calculator will change the viewing window. ZOOM IN may be used to obtain better approximations for the coordinates of a point, while ZOOM OUT may be used to view a larger portion of the graph.

TI-83, Sharp 9600, and **Casio 9850**	ZOOM is on the keyboard.
HP 38G	ZOOM is a submenu of the PLOT menu. You may zoom in/out both vertically and horizontally by selecting In/Out, or you may zoom in/out either vertically or horizontally by selecting X-Zoom In/Out and Y-Zoom In/Out.

To use the ZOOM feature, select ZOOM-IN (or IN) from the ZOOM menu, move the cursor to the desired point, and press ENTER. The coordinates of the cursor's position are shown at the bottom of the screen. Repeatedly using ZOOM-IN will give better approximations of the coordinates of points.

The **scaling factors** used to ZOOM-IN or ZOOM-OUT may be adjusted on most calculators. To set the ZOOM factors, look for FACT or ZFACT or SET FACTORS in the ZOOM menu or in the MEMORY submenu of ZOOM of TI-83.

Maximums and Minimums

There are several ways to approximate the coordinates of a high point or a low point: using the TRACE feature as discussed in Example 1, using the ZOOM feature, and using the **maximum finder.** The maximum/minimum finder automatically finds the highest/lowest point with the calculator's greatest degree of accuracy. On some calculators, left and right bounds and an initial guess must be indicated. On other calculators, the cursor must be placed near the maximum point. The **minimum finder** works in a similar way. The maximum finder is referenced by the term in the first column of the chart and can be found in the menu referred to in the second column. Minimum finders are found in the same menu.

Model	Reference	Menu(s)
TI 83	maximum	CALC (2nd TRACE)
Sharp 9600	Maximum	CALC (2nd TRACE)
Casio	MAX	G-SOLVE
HP 38G	EXTREMUM	PLOT FCN menu

Graphing Exploration

In a standard viewing window, graph the relation

$$12x^2 - 4y^2 + 16x + 12 = 0,$$

which was given in Example 2. Use TRACE, ZOOM, and the maximum and minimum finders to find the coordinates of the maximum and minimum points of the relation. Use the up/down arrow keys to switch between the functions that represent the relation. Compare the values you get from each feature and determine which is the most accurate, which is the fastest, and which is easiest to use.

The relative maximum point's exact coordinates are $\left(-\dfrac{2}{3}, -\sqrt{\dfrac{5}{3}}\right)$, and the relative minimum point's exact coordinates are $\left(-\dfrac{2}{3}, \sqrt{\dfrac{5}{3}}\right)$.

Technology Tip

To use a square viewing window, use SQUARE, ZSQUARE, ZOOMSQR, or SQR in the ZOOM menu. This will adjust the x scale while keeping the y scale fixed.

Technology Tip

For a decimal window that is also square, use ZDECIMAL or ZOOMDEC in the TI-83/89 ZOOM menu, DECIMAL in the Sharp 9600 ZOOM menu and the HP 38G VIEWS menu, and INIT in the Casio 9850 V-WINDOW menu. In the TI-86 ZOOM menu, ZDECIMAL gives a decimal window that is not square.

Square Windows

Another useful screen is one in which one-unit segments on the x-axis are the same one-unit segments on the y-axis. This type of window is called a **square window.** Because calculator screens are wider than they are high, the y-axis in a square window must be shorter than the x-axis. On many calculators, such as the TI-83, the ratio of height to width is about $\dfrac{2}{3}$, so an x-axis with 20 units will have on its y-axis about $\dfrac{2}{3}(20) = 13$ units when square. Therefore, a square window with $-10 \leq x \leq 10$ could have $-6 \leq y \leq 7$, or $0 \leq y \leq 13$, on a screen that has a $2:3$ height-to-width ratio. Check your calculator's height-to-width ratio by looking at the scales after producing a square window. A square window should be used to display circles and perpendicular lines.

Graphing Exploration

The lines $y = 0.5x$ and $y = -2x + 2$ are perpendicular because the product of their slopes is -1. Graph both in the standard viewing window, and then graph them in a square window. Describe the different appearances of the lines in both window types.

Decimal Window

When using the TRACE feature, a calculator typically displays points as 2.34042519, for example, rather than as 2.3 or 2.34. A screen in which the points represent values with one or two decimal places is called a **decimal window**. A decimal window is appropriate when accuracy to one or two decimal places is desired.

Choosing a viewing window carefully can make the trace feature much more convenient, as the following Exploration demonstrates.

Graphing Exploration

- Graph $y = \dfrac{5}{9}(x - 32)$, which relates the temperature x in degrees Fahrenheit and the temperature y in degrees Celsius.
- Use a viewing window with $-40 \le y \le 40$ and $0 \le x \le k$, where k is one less than the number of pixels, or points, on your calculator screen divided by 10. On a TI-83, for example, $k = \dfrac{95 - 1}{10} = 9.4$. (See Technology Tip at left.)
- Use the TRACE feature to determine the Celsius temperatures corresponding to 20°F and 77°F.
- Set the window to $32 - \dfrac{k}{20} \le x \le 32 + \dfrac{k}{20}$, where k is the same as above. This is a decimal window with (32, 0) at its center.
- Graph the equation again, and use TRACE to determine the Celsius equivalent of 33.8°F.

Figure T1-5a

Figure T1-5b

Function Tables

Table of Function Values

The **table feature** of a calculator is a convenient way to display points and evaluate functions. By setting the initial input value and the increment value, a table of values may be displayed for functions stored in the memory. If more than one function is in the function memory, the output values for each are stored in separate columns of a table. To access the table setup screen, select the following.

TI 83 and **Sharp 9600**	TBLSET on the keyboard
Casio 9850	RANG in the TABLE menu
HP 38G	NUM SETUP on the keyboard

The increment is labeled ΔTBL on TI-83, TBLSTEP on Sharp 9600, NUMSTEP on HP-38, and PITCH on Casio 9850.

The screens shown in Figure T1-5a and T1-5b are a setup screen and a table of values for the function $y = x^3 - 4x + 2$, which is stored as Y1.

Graphs On and Off

An equation stays in the equation memory until you delete it. If there are several equations in memory and you want to graph only some of them, turn those equations "on" and the others "off." On most calculators an equation is "on" if its equal sign is shaded and "off" if its equal sign is clear. On HP 38G, an equation that is "on" has a check mark next to it.

Graphing Conventions

1. Unless directed otherwise, use a calculator for graphing.

2. Complete graphs are required unless a viewing window is specified or the context of a problem indicates that a partial graph is acceptable.

3. If the directions say "obtain the graph," "find the graph," or "graph the equation," you need not actually draw the graph on paper. For review purposes, however, it may be helpful to record the viewing window used.

4. The directions "sketch the graph" mean to draw the graph on paper, indicating the scale on each axis. This may involve simply copying the display that is on the calculator screen, or it may require graphing if the calculator display is misleading.

Calculator Investigation

1. Tick Marks
   a. Set Xscl = 1 so that adjacent tick marks on the x-axis are one unit apart. Find the largest range of x values such that the tick marks on the x-axis are clearly distinguishable and appear to be equally spaced.
   b. Do part a with y in place of x.

2. Viewing Window Look in the ZOOM menu, or the VIEWS menu on HP-38, to find out how many built-in viewing windows your calculator has. Take a look at each one.

3. Maximum/Minimum Finders Use your minimum finder to approximate the x-coordinates of the lowest point on the graph of $y = x^3 - 2x + 5$ in the window with $0 \le x \le 5$ and $-3 \le y \le 8$.

The correct answer is $x = \sqrt{\dfrac{2}{3}} \approx 0.81649658$.

How good is your approximation?

4. Square Windows Find a square viewing window on your calculator that has $-4 \le x \le 4$.

5. Dot Graphing Mode To see the points plotted by a calculator without the connecting segments, set your calculator to Dot or DrawDot mode, then graph $y = 0.5x^3 - 2x^2 + 1$ in the standard window. Try some other equations as well.

Sequence Graphing

Many calculators can produce a table of values and graph functions that are defined by recursive and nonrecursive sequences. In a recursive sequence, the nth term is defined in relation to a previous term or terms, such as $u(n) = u(n - 1) - 6$ or $u(n) = 3u(n - 2) - u(n - 1) + 4$. In a nonrecursive sequence, the nth term is a function of the variable n, such as $u(n) = 2n - 5$.

To enter, display a table of values for, and graph a sequence, select the following. In general, first set the mode to sequence and enter the sequence rule.

- Set the window parameters, set the drawing mode (dot or connected), and graph the sequence.
- Choose the table settings, and display the table.

TI-83   MODE   Seq

Sharp 9600   SETUP   COORD   Seq

Y= access the sequence editor screen

     nMin   the minimum n value evaluated

     u(n)   the rule of the sequence

     u(nMin)   the value of the sequence at the minimum n value (recursive sequence only)

WINDOW

     nMin   the smallest n value evaluated; must be an integer;

     nMax   the largest n value evaluated

     PlotStart   first term plotted

     PlotStep   incremental n value (graphing only); designates which points are plotted; does not affect sequence evaluation

   Xmin, Xmax, Xscl, Ymin, Ymax, Yscl same as function graphing values

GRAPH   displays the graph of sequences stored in memory

TBLSET   table settings

     TblStart smallest n value

     ΔTBL (TblStep) increment

TABLE   displays a table of values of sequences stored in memory

Casio 9850   RECUR   TYPE

     a_n general term of the sequence $\{u_n\}$

     a_{n+1} linear recursion between two terms

     a_{n+2} linear recursion between three terms

Rang   displays table range settings

     Start   starting value of n

     End   ending value of n

     a_1, b_1 value of first term

     (the value of n increments by 1)

EXIT

TABL   displays a table of values

     G-PLT   displays a graph of the data in the table.

Press EXIT to return to the table and EXIT again to return to the sequence editor.

NOTE nMax, PlotStart, and PlotStep must be integers greater than 1.

NOTE TI-83 Both Indpnt and (independent) and Depend (dependent) values may be set by the user or the calculator.

Sharp 9600 Input can be set by the user or the calculator.

Auto: the calculator enters values

Ask: the user enters values

Technology

HP38G	LIB	Sequence	SYM

U1(1)   first term of the sequence U1
U1(2)   second term of the sequence U1
U1(N)   rule of the sequence

PLOT SETUP

SEQPLOT CHOOS

Stairstep plots n on the horizontal axis and U_n on the vertical axis

Cobweb plots U_{n-1} on the horizontal axis and U_n on the vertical axis

NRNG, XRNG, and YRNG minimum/maximum values for the plotting window

NUM displays a table of values of each sequence in memory

T.2 Lists, Statistics, Plots, and Regression

Most calculators allow you to store one or more lists that can be used with statistical operations and graphs. Although the procedures needed to create the statistical values seen in this book are shown below, refer to your calculator's manual for a complete guide.

This section outlines the procedures to create the following items:

- statistical lists for 1-variable and 2-variable data
- statistics for 1-variable and 2-variable data
- histograms and box plots for 1-variable data
- scatter plots of 2-variable data
- regression equations of 2-variable data

Refer to Sections 1.5, 4.3.A, 5.7, and 13.1 for examples that involve lists and regression.

Lists

NOTE Words printed in all caps refer to buttons to be pressed or menu choices to be selected. For example, STAT   EDIT directs you to press the STAT button and then to select EDIT from the options shown.

Call up the **list editor** to enter data into lists by using the commands below.

TI-83 and Sharp 9600 STAT   EDIT
Lists are L1, L2, . . ., L6.

Casio 9850 STAT
Lists are List 1, List 2, . . ., List 6.

HP-38G LIB STATISTICS
Lists are C1, C2, . . ., C0. Press the button under 1VAR/2VAR until the appropriate setting appears.

Press ENTER (or EXE) after each entry in a list to proceed to the next position. Use the left/right arrow keys to move among lists and the up/down arrow keys to move within a list.

One-Variable Statistics

Data for 1-variable statistics can be entered into the list editor in two ways:

- Each value is entered into a single list.
- Each value is entered into one list and its frequency into the corresponding position of a second list to create a frequency table.

The symbols commonly used to represent the statistics for 1-variable data are as follows:

n, $N\Sigma$	sample number
$\bar{x}$, , MEAN	mean
Sx, sx, $x\sigma n-1$, SSDEVΣ	standard deviation from the sample
σx $x\sigma n$ PSDEV	population standard deviation from the sample
Σx, or TOTΣ	sum of the data
Σx^2	sum of squares of the data
minX, xmin, MINΣ	smallest value of the data
Q_1	value of the first quartile
Med, MEDIAN	median of the data
Q_3	value of the third quartile
maxX, xmax, MAXΣ	largest value of the data

HP 38G only:

PVARΣ	population variance of the data
SVARΣ	sample variance of the data

To compute 1-variable statistics, use the following procedures.

TI-83 and Sharp 9600   STAT   CALC   1: 1-Var Stats

- If the data is contained in one list, enter the list name by pressing the list name shown above the number keys 1 through 6.
- If the data was entered as a frequency table, enter the list name of the data, press [,] (comma), and enter the name of the list that contains the frequency.

Casio 9850   STAT   EXE   CALC   SET (F6)

NOTE Directions for Casio 9850 begin from the main menu screen.

- If the data is contained in one list:
  1. Set XList to the list that contains the data by pressing the key below the appropriate list name.
  2. Use the down arrow key to highlight 1Var Freq and set 1Var Freq to 1 by pressing F1.
- If the data is contained in a frequency table.
  1. Set 1Var XList to the list that contains the data by pressing the key below the appropriate list name.
  2. Set 1Var Freq to the list that contains the frequency of the data.

Press EXIT to return to the list editor.
Press 1Var (F1) to display the statistics.

HP 38G   LIB   Statistics   START   1Var

- SYMB Define which data columns make up the data set. Enter the name of the list that contains the data by pressing the button below C and entering the appropriate number.

- Use the right arrow key to highlight the second column, which contains the reference for the frequency of the data.

    If the data is contained in one list, enter 1 as the frequency. If the data is entered as a frequency table, enter the name of the list that contains the frequency by pressing the button below **C** and entering the appropriate number.

- STATS

Histograms and Box Plots (1-Variable Graphs)

A histogram is a bar graph that displays 1-variable data values on the x-axis and represents each corresponding frequency as the height of the box above the x-axis. A box plot and a modified box plot display the values Q1 to Q3 as a box with a vertical line at the median. A box plot displays the values of xMin to Q1 and of Q3 to xMax as whiskers at either end of the box, and a modified box plot displays outliers (values less than 1.5 * Q1 and greater than 1.5 * Q3) as points beyond the whiskers.

To create a graph of 1-variable data, enter the data into a single list or into a frequency table, and use the procedures to create a histogram or a box plot.

> **TI-83 and Sharp 9600** Because TI-83 and the Sharp 9600 have similar directions, the following applies to both unless otherwise stated.

- STAT PLOT   PLOT(1, 2 or 3)   ENTER
- Highlight **ON** and press **ENTER**.

    > **TI-83** Highlight the desired graph type by using the arrow keys, and press **ENTER**.

    > **Sharp 9600** Select **X** to signify 1-variable data.

- Use the down arrow key to select **XList** (or **ListX:**). Enter the name of the list that contains the data by using the keys **L1** through **L6**, which are the 2nd functions above the number keys 1 through 6.

    > **TI-83**

    > - Move the cursor to **FREQ** and enter 1 if the data is contained in a single list, or enter the name of the list that contains the frequency.

    > **Sharp 9600**

    > - Move the cursor to **FREQ** and enter the name of the list that contains the frequency.
    > - Move the cursor to **GRAPH**, press **STAT PLOT**, and select the graph type.

- If a modified box plot is selected, select the type of symbol that will denote outliers.
- Set the window values for **xMin** and **xMax**, and if creating a histogram, set the **yMin** and **yMax** values. Box plots ignore **yMin** and **yMax** values.
- GRAPH

Casio 9850   STAT   EXE

- GRPH (F1)   SET (F6)
- Select the StatGraph area desired by choosing GPH1 (F1), GPH2 (F2), or GPH3 (F3).
- Use the down arrow key to highlight Graph Type. Press F6 (▷) to display the graph type options. Choose Hist, Box (MedBox), or Box (MeanBox). MedBox shows the distribution of the data items that are grouped within Q1, Med, and Q3. MeanBox shows the distribution of the data around the mean when there is a large number of data items, and a vertical line is drawn at the mean.
- Select XList and enter the name of the list that contains the data.
- Select Frequency and enter 1 if the data is in one list or the name of the list that contains the frequency of the data.
- Choose the graph color.
- Press EXIT.
- Press GPH1 (2 or 3) to display the StatGraph area. Press EXIT to return to the previous screen.

HP 38G   LIB   Statistics   ENTER

- While the data lists are visible (numeric view), make sure that 1VAR is shown at the bottom right of the screen.
- PLOT SETUP (■PLOT)
- Highlight STATPLOT:, press CHOOS, and select the desired graph type.
- Set XRNG and YRNG. HWIDTH specifies the width of a histogram bar, and HRNG specifies the range of values for a set of histogram bars.
- PLOT

Two-Variable Statistics and Graphs

Two-variable statistics for both the x-variable and the y-variable include all the statistics listed for 1-variable statistics; that is, the mean of the y-variable data is denoted as $\bar{y}$, the minimum value of the y-variable data is denoted by yMin or MinY, and so forth. Additionally, Σxy, the sum of the product of corresponding data pairs, is also given.

To compute 2-variable statistics, use the following procedure after entering the data pairs into two lists.

TI-83 and Sharp 9600   STAT   CALC   2–Var Stats (2–Stats)

- Enter the list names that contain the data pairs separated by a comma, and press ENTER. The first named list is the x-list, and the second named list is the y-list.

Casio 9850   STAT   CALC   SET

- Use the down arrow key to select 2VAR XList, and enter the name of the list that contains the x-data. Similarly, enter the name of the list that contains the y-data. 2Var Freq specifies the list where paired-variable frequency values are located. Enter 1 if the data pairs are entered separately in the XList, and set 2Var Freq to 1 if the data pairs are entered separately in the XList and the Ylist.

- EXIT 2VAR (F2)

HP-38G   LIB   Statistics   NUM

- Set the correct menu label for 2VAR.
- STAT

Scatter Plots

Scatter plots graph the data points from XList and Ylist as coordinate pairs. The general procedure for graphing 2-variable data contained in two lists is as follows.

- Define the statistical plot.
- Define the viewing window.
- Display the graph.

TI-83 and Sharp 9600

- STAT PLOT, select the desired stat plot editor, highlight ON, and press ENTER.

    TI-83 Select the icon that represents the type of graph desired and press ENTER.

    Sharp 9600 Select XY to denote 2-variable data.
- Enter the names of the lists that contain the x-data and the y-data.

    Sharp 9600 STAT PLOT (2nd Y=)

    Choose the graph type and point symbol.

    Option GS.D. represents a scatter plot.
- GRAPH

Casio 9850   STAT   GPH   Set

- Select the graph number: GPH1, GPH2, or GPH3.
- Highlight Graph Type and choose Scat.
- Enter the names of the lists that contain the x-data and the y-data, enter the frequency of the data pairs, choose the mark type and the graph color. EXIT
- V-Window, enter the viewing window values, EXIT
- GPH, select the graph number that contains the desired settings

HP-38G   LIB   Statistics   ENTER

- 2Var should be selected
- SYMB, enter the names of the lists containing the data into rows S1 through S5, and press ✓CHK to select the set.
- PLOT

    If no regression curve is desired, press MENU and press Fit/Fit■ to display Fit.

Regression Equations

Most graphing calculators can compute the following types of regression equations.

Regression Type	Model	Reference
linear	$y = ax + b$	LinReg or Rg_ax+b
quadratic	$y = ax^2 + bx + c$	QuadReg or Rg_x^2
cubic	$y = ax^3 + bx^2 + cx + d$	CubicReg or Rg_x^3
quartic (not HP)	$y = ax^4 + bx^3 + cx^2 + dx + e$	QuartReg or Rg_x^4
logarithmic	$y = a \ln x$	LnReg, LogReg, or Rg_ln
exponential	$y = ae^{bx}$	ExpReg or Rg_ae^{bx}
power	$y = ax^n$	PwrReg or Rg_ax^b
logistic	$y = \dfrac{c}{1 + ae^{-bx}}$	Logistic or Rg_logistic
sinusoidal (not HP)	$y = a \sin(bx + c) + d$	SinReg or Rg_sin

The procedure to compute regression equations follows. Enter the data into two lists.

TI-83 STAT CALC

Select the regression model by using the up/down arrow keys. Enter the names of the lists separated by a comma by using the L1 through L6 keys, which are the 2nd functions for the numerals 1 through 6. The default is L1, L2.

Sharp 9600 STAT REG

Select the regression model by using the up/down arrow keys. Enter the names of the lists within parentheses separated by a comma by using the L1 through L6 keys, which are the second function for numerals 1 through 6. The default is (L1, L2).

Casio 9850 While viewing the lists, press CALC REG.

Select the regression model by pressing the corresponding F key. Additional models are accessed by pressing F6.

HP 38G LIB Statistics SYMB

In Numeric View (NUM) make sure that 2VAR is selected.

For the data set defined in S1, highlight Fit1, press ■SYMB, select S1FIT, and press CHOOS. Use the up/down arrow keys to highlight the desired model and press OK. A similar procedure is used for data defined in S2 through S5.

The regression model coefficients are displayed after the statistics are computed for the data set. Therefore, press NUM and STATS OK to compute the statistics, and then press SYMB. The regression model is shown next to Fit1.

Displaying a Regression Equation's Graph

Set the bounds of the display window by selecting the following.

TI-83 and Sharp 9600	WINDOW
Casio 9850	V-Window
HP-38G	SETUP PLOT (■ PLOT)

TI-83 and Sharp There are two methods for entering a regression equation into the Y= editor for display: automatic and manual. Note that each time a regression equation is found, the contents of RegEQ are overwritten with the new regression equation.

- *Automatic* The calculator can automatically place the regression equation into the Y= editor as Y3 when computing a regression equation. The following entry places the linear regression equation for the lists L1 and L2 into Y3 in the Y= editor.

  TI-83   LinReg L1,L2,Y3

  Sharp 9600   Rg_ax+b(L1,L2,Y3)

- *Manual* Whenever a regression model is found, the calculator places the regression equation into the variable RegEQ (or RegEqn), which can be entered into the Y= editor.

  TI-83   Press VARS Statistics EQ RegEQ from the Y= editor screen.

  Sharp 9600   VARS STAT REGEQN RegEqn

  A regression equation is displayed using the procedure to graph any type of equation.

Casio 9850

- While viewing the data lists, press GRPH.
- Select GPH1, GPH2, or GPH3 to view the desired graph type. (Press SET to change the options.)
- Choose the type of regression model desired (X represents linear regression.)

  DRAW   graphs the displayed regression equation

  COPY   lets you store the displayed regression equation as a function in the Y= editor. Use the up/down arrow keys to select the desired Y variable.

HP 38G

- Once the data has been entered (Numeric view), the data set defined (Symbolic view), the Fit model for 2-variable data selected (Symbolic setup view), and the data displayed as a scatter plot (Plot view), then the regression equation that is determined by the Fit model can be drawn by pressing MENU and choosing Fit■.
- The equation can be seen by pressing SYMB, highlighting the Fit model, and pressing SHOW.

Regression Coefficients

When some regression models are created, values of r (or corr on HP 38G), the correlation coefficient, and r^2 (or R^2), the coefficient of determination, are computed and stored as values. Values of r and r^2 are computed for the following regression models: linear, logarithmic, power, and exponential. The value of R^2 is computed for the following regression models: quadratic, cubic, and quartic. No correlation coefficient or coefficient of determination is given for logistic and sinusoidal regression models.

TI-83	The variables r, r^2, and R^2 are displayed when a regression equation is computed by executing the DiagnosticOn instruction, which is found in the CATALOG menu. When DiagnosticOff is set, the values for r, r^2, and R^2 are not displayed.
Sharp 9600	The values of r and r^2, or R^2 are automatically shown with the coefficients of a regression equation, as appropriate.
Casio9850	Neither form of a coefficient of determination is computed on a Casio.
HP 38G	The value of corr represents the linear fit only of the data, regardless of the Fit chosen. It is displayed with 2-variable statistics.

Scatter Plots of Residuals

Residuals, also called relative error, are stored as a list of values in a variable named Resid or RelErr on some calculators. Scatter plots of the residuals can be graphed but may not be visible in the same viewing window as the data. Adjust the window to view the scatter plot of the residuals.

TI-83 From a PLOT*n* screen set the following:

    ON

    Scatter Plot

    XList   L*n* (the list that contains the input data)

    Ylist   RESID (which is found in LIST NAMES)

    Mark   as desired

    GRAPH

Sharp 9600 From a PLOT*n* screen, set the following:

    ON

    DATA   XY

    ListX   L*n*   (the list that contains the input data)

    ListY   resid   (which is found in VARS STAT REGEQN)

Select the graph type by moving the cursor to GRAPH, pressing STAT PLOT, then S.D., and choosing the desired point symbol.

    GRAPH

Casio 9850 Residuals are not automatically computed when a regression equation is found.

HP 38G   LIB   Statistics   SYMB

- Select the desired data set by highlighting S*n* and pressing ✓CHK.
- Enter the name of the list that contains the input data into the first column.
- Enter RelErr as the name of the list in the second column.
- Set the size of the viewing window and press PLOT.

Programs

The programs listed here are of two types: programs to give older calculators some of the features that are built-in on newer ones (such as a table maker) and programs to do specific tasks discussed in this book (such as synthetic division). Each program is preceded by a *Description*, which describes, in general terms, how the program operates and what it does. Some programs require that certain things be done before the program is run (such as entering a function in the function memory); these requirements are listed as *Preliminaries*. Occasionally, italic remarks appear in brackets after a program step; they are *not* part of the program, but are intended to provide assistance when you are entering the program into your calculator. A remark such as "[*MATH NUM menu*]" means that the symbols or commands needed for that step of the program are in the NUM submenu of the MATH menu.

Fraction Conversion
(Built-in on TI-82/83/85/86 and HP-38)

Description: Enter a repeating decimal; the program converts it into a fraction. The denominator is displayed on the last line and the numerator on the line above.

Sharp 9600

Input N	If fpart (round $(N \times D, 7)) \neq 0$ Goto 1 [*MATH NUM menu*]
$0 \to D$	int$(N \times D + .5) \to N$
Label 1	Print N
$D + 1 \to D$	Print D

Casio 9850

Fix 7	Rnd [*MATH NUM menu*]
"N = "? $\to N$	(Frac Ans) $\neq 0 \Rightarrow$ Goto 1 [*MATH NUM menu*]
$0 \to D$	(Ans + .5) $\to N$
Lbl 1	Norm [*DISP menu*]
$D + 1 \to D$	(Int N)◢
$N \times D$	D

TI-82/83 Quadratic Formula

(Built-in on other calculators)

Description: Enter the coefficients of the quadratic equation $ax^2 + bx + c = 0$; the program finds all real solutions.

:ClrHome [*Optional*]

:Disp "AX^2 + BX + C = 0" [*Optional*]

:Prompt A

:Prompt B

:Prompt C

:(B^2 − 4AC) → S

:If S < 0

:Goto 1

:Disp $(-B + \sqrt{S})/2A$

:Disp $(-B - \sqrt{S})/2A$

:Stop

:Lbl 1

:Disp "NO REAL ROOTS"

TI-85 Table Maker

(Built-in on other calculators)

Preliminaries: Enter the function to be evaluated in the function memory as Y_1.

Description: Select a starting point and an increment (the amount by which adjacent x entries differ); the program displays a table of function values. To scroll through the table a page at a time, press "down" or "up." Press "quit" to end the program. [*Note:* An error message will occur if the calculator attempts to evaluate the function at a number for which it is not defined. In this case, change the starting point or increment to avoid the undefined point.]

:Lbl SETUP

:ClLCD [*Optional*]

:Disp " "TABLE SETUP"

:Input "TblMin = ", tblmin

:Input "ΔTbl = ", dtbl   [*CHAR GREEK menu*]

:tblmin → x   [*Use the x-var key for x.*]

:Lbl CONTD

:ClLCD

:Output(1,1,"x")   [*I/O menu*]

:Output(1,10,"y$_1$")

:For (cnt,2,7,1)

:Output(cnt,1,x)

:Output(cnt,8," ")

:Output(cnt,9,y$_1$)

:x + dtbl → x

:End

:Menu(1, "Down",CONTD, 2,"UP",CONTU, 4, "Setup," SETUP, 5, "quit", TQUIT)

:Lbl CONTU

:x − 12*dtbl → x

:Goto CONTD

:Lbl TQUIT

:ClLCD

:Stop

Synthetic Division

(Built-in on TI-89/92)

Preliminaries: Enter the coefficients of the dividend $F(x)$ (in order of decreasing powers of x, putting in zeros for missing coefficients) as list L_1 (or List 1). If the coefficients are 1, 2, 3, for example, key in {1, 2, 3,} and store it in L_1. The symbols { } are on the keyboard or in the LIST menu. The list name L_1 is on the keyboard of TI-82/83 and Sharp 9600. On TI-85/86 and HP-38, type in L1. On Casio 9850, use "List" in the LIST submenu of the OPTN menu to type in List 1.

Description: Write the divisor in the form $x - a$ and enter a. The program displays the degree of the quotient $Q(x)$, the coefficients of $Q(x)$ (in order of decreasing powers of x), and the remainder. If the program pauses before it has displayed all these items, you can use the arrow keys to scroll through the display; then press ENTER (or OK) to continue.

TI-82/83/85/86

:ClrHome [ClLCD on TI-85/86]
:Disp "DIVISOR IS X − A"
:Prompt A
:$L_1 \rightarrow L_2$ [*See Preliminaries for how to enter list names*]
:dim $L_1 \rightarrow N$ [dimL L_1 on TI-85/86]   [*LIST OPS menu*]
:For (K, 2, N)
:$(L_1(K) + A \times L_2(K - 1)) \rightarrow L_2(K)$
:End

:round($L_2(N),9) \rightarrow R$ [*MATH NUM menu*]
:$(N - 1) \rightarrow$ dim L_2
:Disp "DEGREE OF QUOTIENT"
:Disp dim $L_2 - 1$
:Disp "COEFFICIENTS"
:Pause L_2
:Disp "REMAINDER"
:Disp R

Sharp 9600

Clr T
Print "DIVISOR IS X − A"
Input A
$L_1 \rightarrow L_2$ [*See Preliminaries for how to enter list names*]
dim $(L_1) \rightarrow N$ [*LIST OPE menu*]
$2 \rightarrow K$
Label 1
$(L_1(K) + A \times L_2(K - 1)) \rightarrow L_2(K)$
$K + 1 \rightarrow K$
If $K \leq N$ Goto 1

round($L_2(N),9) \rightarrow R$ [*MATH NUM menu*]
$(N - 1) \rightarrow$ dim L_2
Clr T
Print "DEGREE OF QUOTIENT"
Print dim $L_2 - 1$
Print "COEFFICIENTS"
Print L_2
Print "REMAINDER"
Print R

Casio 9850

"DIVISOR IS X − A"

"A = "? → A

List 1 → List 2   [See Preliminaries for how to enter list names]

dim List 1 → N   [OPTN LIST menu]

2 → K

Lbl 1

(List 1[K] + A × List 2 [K − 1]) → List 2 [K]

K + 1 → K

K ≤ N ⇒ Goto 1

Fix 9   [SETUP DISP menu]

List 2 [N]

Rnd   [OPTN MATH NUM menu]

Ans → R

Norm   [SETUP DISP menu]

Seq(List 2 [X], X, 1, N − 1, 1) → List 2
[OPTN LIST menu]

"DEGREE OF QUOTIENT"

dim List 2 − 1◢

"COEFFICIENTS"

List 2◢

"REMAINDER"

R

HP-38

Input A; "SYNDIV", "X − A"; "ENTER A"; 0:

$L_1 → L_2$:   [See Preliminaries for how to enter list names]

Size(L_2) → N: [MATH LIST menu]

For C = 1 to (N − 1)   Step 1; L_2(C) × A + L_2(C + 1) → L_2(C + 1) End:

Makelist (L_2(J), J, 1, N − 1, 1) → L_3:   [MATH LIST menu]

Msgbox "DEGREE OF QUOTIENT" Size(L_3) − 1:

Msgbox "COEFFICIENTS" L_3:

Msgbox "REMAINDER" L_2(N):

HP-38 Rectangular/Polar Conversion Program

Description: Enter the rectangular coordinates of a point in the plane; the program displays the polar coordinates of the point.

Input X; "RECTANGULAR TO POLAR"; "X = "; "ENTER X"; 0:

Input Y: "RECTANGULAR TO POLAR"; "Y = "; "ENTER Y"; 0:

If X > 0

Then (ATAN(Y/X)) → C

Else (ATAN(X,Y) + π) → C:

End:

MSGBOX "R = " $\sqrt{X^2 + Y^2}$ "θ = " C:

HP-38 Polar/Rectangular Conversion Program

Description: Enter the polar coordinates of a point in the plane; the program displays the rectangular coordinates of the point.

Input R; "POLAR TO RECTANGULAR"; "R = "; "ENTER R"; 0:

Input θ; "POLAR TO RECTANGULAR"; "θ = "; "ENTER θ"; 0: [CHARS menu]

MSGBOX "X = " R(cos θ) "Y = " R(sin θ):

Glossary

absolute value (of a complex number)
$|a + bi| = \sqrt{a^2 + b^2}$ (p. 638)

absolute value of a number   For any real number c, if $c \geq 0$, then $|c| = c$ and if $c < 0$, then $|c| = -c$ (algebraic definition). $|c|$ is the distance from c to 0 on the number line (geometric definition). (p. 107, 108)

absolute-value inequalities   For a positive number k and any real number r, $|r| \leq k$ is equivalent to $-k \leq r \leq k$ and $|r| \geq k$ is equivalent to $r \leq -k$ or $r \geq k$. (p. 129)

acute angle   an angle with a degree measure of less than 90° (p. 414)

addition and subtraction identities   trigonometric identities involving a function of the sum or difference of two angle measures (p. 582)

adjacency matrix   a matrix used to represent the connections between vertices in a directed network (p. 809)

adjacent side (of a right triangle)   abbreviated adj, the side of a given acute angle in a right triangle that is *not* the hypotenuse (p. 415)

ambiguous case   When the measures of two sides of a triangle and the angle opposite one of them are known, there may be one, two, or no triangles that satisfy the given measures. (p. 627)

amplitude   The amplitude of a sinusoidal function is one-half of the difference between the maximum and minimum function values and is always positive. (p. 497) See also *sinusoidal function*.

analytic geometry   the study of geometric properties of objects using a coordinate system (p. 691)

angle   a figure formed by two rays and a common endpoint (p. 413)

angle of depression   the angle formed by a horizontal line and a line below it (p. 427)

angle of elevation   the angle formed by a horizontal line and a line above it (p. 426)

angle of inclination   If L is a nonhorizontal straight line in a coordinate plane, then the angle of inclination of L is the angle formed by the part of L above the x-axis and the x-axis in the positive direction. (p. 589)

Angle of Inclination Theorem   If L is a nonvertical line with angle of inclination θ, then $\tan \theta = $ slope of L. (p. 589)

Angle Theorem   If θ is the angle between nonzero vectors $\mathbf{u}$ and $\mathbf{v}$, then $\mathbf{u} \cdot \mathbf{v} = \|\mathbf{u}\| \|\mathbf{v}\| \cos \theta$ and
$\cos \theta = \dfrac{\mathbf{u} \cdot \mathbf{v}}{\|\mathbf{u}\| \|\mathbf{v}\|}$. (p. 672)

angular speed   a measure of speed of a point rotating at a constant rate around the center of a circle, given as the angle through which the point rotates over time (p. 440)

approach infinity   Output values of a function that get larger and larger without bound as input values increase are said to approach infinity. (p. 201)

arc   an unbroken part of a circle (p. 434)

arc length   the length of an arc, which is equal to the radius times the radian measure of the central angle of the arc (p. 435, 439)

arccosine function   the inverse cosine function, denoted by $g(x) = \arccos x$ (p. 533)

arcsine function   the inverse sine function, denoted by $g(x) = \arcsin x$ (p. 530)

arctangent function   the inverse tangent function, denoted by $g(x) = \arctan x$ (p. 535)

area of a triangle formula   The area of any triangle ABC in standard notation is $\dfrac{1}{2}ab \sin C$. (p. 632)

argument the angle θ in a trigonometric expression (p. 639)

arithmetic progression See *arithmetic sequence.*

arithmetic sequence a sequence in which the difference between each term and the preceding term is always constant (p. 22)

asymptotes of a hyperbola two lines intersecting at the center of a hyperbola which the hyperbola approaches but never touches (p. 701)

augmented matrix a matrix in which each row represents an equation of a system and contains the coefficients of the variables in the equation (p. 795)

average See *mean.*

average rate of change For any function f, the average rate of change of $f(x)$ with respect to x as x changes from a to b is the value $\dfrac{\text{change in } f(x)}{\text{change in } x} = \dfrac{f(b) - f(a)}{b - a}$. (p. 216)

axes (singular: axis) the number lines in a coordinate system (p. 5)

axis of a parabola the line through the focus of a parabola perpendicular to the directrix of the parabola (p. 709)

bar graph a visual display of qualitative data in which categories are displayed on the horizontal axis and frequencies or relative frequencies on the vertical axis (p. 845)

Basic Properties of Logarithms $\log_b x$ is defined only for $x > 0$; $\log_b 1 = 0$ and $\log_b b = 1$; $\log_b b^k = k$ for all real k; and $b^{\log_b x} = x$ for all $x > 0$. (p. 364, 372)

bell curve See *normal curve.*

Bernoulli experiment See *binomial experiment.*

Big-Little Concept If c is a number far from 0, then $\dfrac{1}{c}$ is a number close to 0. Conversely, if c is a number close to 0, then $\dfrac{1}{c}$ is a number far from 0. (p. 280)

binomial distribution the probability distribution for a binomial experiment (p. 888)

binomial experiment A probability experiment that can be described in terms of just two outcomes is a binomial experiment, also known as a *Bernoulli experiment.* It must meet the following conditions: the experiment consists of n trials whose outcomes are either successes or failures, and the trials are identical and independent with a constant probability of success, p, and a constant probability of failure, $q = 1 - p$. (p. 885)

bounds test a test used to determine the lower and upper bounds for the real zeros of a polynomial function (p. 256)

Cartesian coordinate system a two-dimensional coordinate system that corresponds ordered pairs of real numbers with locations in a coordinate plane (p. 5)

center of a hyperbola the midpoint of the segment that has the foci of the hyperbola as endpoints (p. 701)

center of an ellipse the midpoint of the segment that has the foci of the ellipse as endpoints (p. 692)

central angle an angle whose vertex is at the center of a circle (p. 434)

central tendency a value that is used to represent the center of an entire data set (p. 853)

change in x the horizontal distance moved from one point to another point in a coordinate plane; sometimes denoted Δx, and read "delta x" (p. 31)

change in y the vertical distance moved from one point to another point in a coordinate plane; sometimes denoted Δy, and read "delta y" (p. 31)

Change-of-Base Formula For any positive number x, $\log_b x = \dfrac{\log x}{\log b}$ and $\log_b x = \dfrac{\ln x}{\ln b}$. (p. 374)

closed interval an interval of numbers in which both endpoints of the interval are included in the set; denoted with two brackets (p. 118)

coefficient the numerical factor of a term in a polynomial (p. 239)

coefficient of determination a statistical measure, often denoted by r^2, that is the proportion of variation in y that can be attributed to a linear relationship between x and y in a data set (p. 47)

Cofunction Identities trigonometric identities that relate the sine, secant, and tangent functions to the cosine, cosecant, and cotangent functions, respectively (p. 586)

combination an arrangement of objects in which order is *not* important; a collection of objects (p. 880)

common difference the constant number, usually denoted by d, that is the difference between each term and the preceding term in an arithmetic sequence (p. 22)

common logarithm (of *x*)   the value of $g(x) = \log x$ at the number x, denoted $\log x$ (p. 356)

common logarithmic function   the inverse of the exponential function $f(x) = 10^x$, denoted $g(x) = \log x$ (p. 356)

common ratio   the constant value, denoted by r, given by the quotient of consecutive terms in a geometric sequence (p. 58)

complement of an event   the set of all outcomes that are not contained in the event (p. 866)

complete graph   a graph that shows all of its important features, including all peaks and valleys, points where it touches an axis, and suggests the general shape of the portions of the graph that are not in view (p. 82)

completely factored (over the set of real numbers) a polynomial written as the product of irreducible factors with real coefficients (p. 253)

completing the square   a process used to change an expression of the form $x^2 + bx$ into a perfect square by adding a suitable constant (p. 92)

complex number system   the number system that consists of real and nonreal numbers (p. 293)

complex numbers   numbers of the form $a + bi$, where a is a real number and bi is an imaginary number (p. 294)

complex plane   a coordinate plane with the horizontal axis labeled for real numbers and the vertical axis labeled for imaginary numbers (p. 301, 638)

components (of a vector)   the numbers a and b in the vector $\mathbf{u} = \langle a, b \rangle$, where $\mathbf{u}$ is a vector with initial point at the origin and terminal point at (a, b) (p. 655)

composite functions   If f and g are functions, then the composite function of f and g is $(g \circ f)(x) = g(f(x))$, read "g circle f" or "f followed by g." (p. 193)

composition of functions   a way of combining functions in which the output of one function is used as the input of another function (p. 193)

compound interest   This interest on an investment is compounded, or becomes part of the investment, at a particular interest rate per time period. If P dollars is invested at annual interest rate r per time period (expressed as a decimal), then the amount A after t time periods is $A = P(1 + r)t$. (p. 345)

concave down   a description of the way a curve bends if for any two points in a given interval that lie on the curve, the segment that connects them is *below* the curve (p. 154)

concave up   a description of the way a curve bends if for any two points in a given interval that lie on the

curve, the segment that connects them is *above* the curve (p. 154)

concavity   a description of the way that a curve bends, such as *concave up* or *concave down* (p. 154)

conic section   a curve that is formed by the intersection of a plane and a double-napped right circular cone (p. 691); Let L be a fixed line, called a directrix, P a fixed point not on L, and e a positive constant. The set of all points X in the plane such that
$$\frac{\text{distance between } X \text{ and the fixed point}}{\text{distance between } X \text{ and the fixed line}} = \frac{XP}{XL} = e \text{ is a}$$
conic section with P as one of its foci. (p. 747)

conjugate   The *conjugate* of the complex number $a + bi$ is the number $a - bi$, and the *conjugate* of $a - bi$ is $a + bi$. (p. 296, 309)

conjugate pairs   complex numbers $a + bi$ and $a - bi$ (p. 296)

Conjugate Zero Theorem   For every polynomial function f, if the complex number z is a zero of f, then its conjugate, $\bar{z}$, is also a zero of f. (p. 309)

consistent system   a system of equations with at least one solution (p. 781)

constant function   A function is said to be constant on an interval if its graph is a horizontal line over the interval; that is, if its output values are always constant as the input values are increasing. (p. 152)

constant polynomial   a polynomial that consists of only a constant term (p. 240)

constant term   the coefficient a_0 in a polynomial that is written in the form $a_n x^n + a_{n-1}x^{n-1} + \cdots + a_1 x + a_0$ (p. 239)

constraints   restrictions, represented by inequalities, that exist in linear programming (p. 829)

continuous compounding   This compound interest is compounded infinitely many times during a time period. If P dollars is invested at annual interest rate r and compounded continuously, then the amount A after t years is $A = Pe^{rt}$. (p. 348)

continuous function   a function whose graph is an unbroken curve with no jumps, gaps, or holes (p. 261, 939)

convergent series   a geometric series in which the terms $S_1, S_2, S_3, \ldots$ of the sequence of partial sums get closer and closer to a particular real number S in such a way that the partial sum S_k is arbitrarily close to S when k is large enough; a geometric series with common ratio r such that $|r| < 1$ (p. 77)

coordinate plane   See *Cartesian coordinate system*.

coordinate system   a system of locating points in a plane or in space by using ordered pairs or ordered triples, respectively, of real numbers (p. 5)

corner point   any point of a feasible region where at least two of the graphs of the constraints intersect (p. 829)

correlation coefficient   a statistical measure, often denoted by r, of how well the least squares regression line fits the data points that it models (p. 47)

cosecant ratio   For a given acute angle θ in a right triangle, the cosecant of θ is written as $\csc \theta$ and is equal to the reciprocal of the sine ratio of the given angle. (p. 416)

cosine ratio   For a given acute angle θ in a right triangle, the cosine of θ is written as $\cos \theta$ and is equal to the ratio of the adjacent side length to the length of the hypotenuse. (p. 416)

cotangent ratio   For a given acute angle θ in a right triangle, the cotangent of θ is written as $\cot \theta$ and is equal to the reciprocal of the tangent ratio of the given angle. (p. 416)

coterminal angles   angles formed by different rotations that have the same initial and terminal sides (p. 434)

cubic function   a third-degree polynomial function (p. 240)

cycle (of a periodic function)   a portion of the graph of a periodic function in which the function goes through one period (p. 493)

data   information gathered in a statistical experiment (p. 843)

decreasing function   A function is said to be decreasing on an interval if its graph always falls as you move from left to right over the interval; that is, its output values are always decreasing as the input values are increasing. (p. 152)

degenerate conic section   a point, line, or intersecting lines formed by the intersection of a plane and a double-napped right circular cone (p. 691)

degree (measure)   a unit of angle measure that equals $\frac{1}{360}$ of a circle, denoted with the degree symbol (°) (p. 414)

degree (of a polynomial)   the exponent of the highest power of the variable that appears with a nonzero coefficient in a polynomial (p. 240)

delta   See *change in x* or *change in y*.

DeMoivre's Theorem   For any complex number, $z = r(\cos \theta + i \sin \theta)$, and for any positive integer n, $z^n = r^n (\cos n\theta + i \sin n\theta)$. (p. 644)

denominator   the expression in a fraction that lies below the fraction bar (p. 4)

deviation (of a data value)   the difference of a data value from the mean of the data set (p. 857)

difference function   For any functions $f(x)$ and $g(x)$, their difference function is the new function $(f - g)(x) = f(x) - g(x)$. (p. 191)

difference quotient   the quantity $\dfrac{f(x + h) - f(x)}{h}$ for a function f (p. 219)

differential calculus   a method of calculating the changes in one variable produced by changes in a related variable (p. 138)

dimensions of a matrix   used to indicate the number of rows and columns in a matrix (Example: an $m \times n$ matrix has m rows and n columns) (p. 804)

directed network   a finite set of connected points in which permissible directions of travel between the points are indicated (p. 809)

direction (of a vector)   the angle that the directed line segment representing a vector $\langle a, b \rangle$ makes with the positive x-axis (p. 662)

directrix of a parabola   the line in the formation of a parabola such that its distance from any point on the parabola is equal to the distance from that point to the focus of the parabola (p. 709)

discontinuous function   a function that has one or more jumps, gaps, or holes (p. 937)

discriminant   the expression $b^2 - 4ac$ in the quadratic formula, used to determine the number of real solutions of a quadratic equation $ax^2 + bx + c = 0$ (p. 93)

distance (between real numbers)   The distance on the number line between real numbers c and d is $|c - d|$. (p. 108)

distance difference   the constant difference between the distances from each focus of a hyperbola to a point on the hyperbola (p. 700)

distribution   an arrangement of numerical data in order (usually ascending) (p. 846)

divergent series   a geometric series that is not convergent; a geometric series with common ratio r such that $|r| \geq 1$ (p. 77)

Division Algorithm   If a polynomial $f(x)$ is divided by a nonzero polynomial $h(x)$, then there is a quotient polynomial $q(x)$ and a remainder polynomial $r(x)$ such that $f(x) = h(x) \cdot q(x) + r(x)$, where either $r(x) = 0$ or $r(x)$ has a degree less than the degree of the divisor, $h(x)$. (p. 243)

DMS form   a form of degree measure expression which includes degrees, minutes, and seconds (p. 414)

domain   the set of first numbers in the ordered pairs of a relation (p. 6, 142)

domain convention   Unless information to the contrary is given, the domain of a function f includes every real number input for which the function rule produces a real number output. (p. 145)

dot product   a real number produced by multiplying corresponding components of two vectors and adding the products (p. 670)

Double-Angle Identities   trigonometric identities involving a function of an angle multiplied by 2 (p. 593)

eccentricity (of an ellipse or hyperbola)   the ratio $e = \dfrac{\text{distance between the foci}}{\text{distance between the vertices}}$, where $0 < e < 1$ for all ellipses and $e > 1$ for all hyperbolas (p. 745)

elementary row operations   operations used on an augmented matrix that produce an augmented matrix of an equivalent system (p. 796)

eliminating the parameter   expressing a curve that is given by parametric equations as part of the graph of an equation in x and y (p. 757)

ellipse   For any points P and Q in the plane and any number k greater than the distance from P to Q, an ellipse, with foci P and Q, is the set of all points (x, y) such that the sum of the distance from (x, y) to P and the distance from (x, y) to Q is k. (p. 692) a conic section with eccentricity between 0 and 1, not inclusive (p. 747)

empirical rule   a rule that describes the areas under the normal curve over intervals of one, two, and three standard deviations on either side of the mean in terms of percentages of the number of data values (p. 892)

end behavior   the shape of the graph of a function at the far left and far right of the coordinate plane when $|x|$ is large (p. 262, 287)

endpoints (of an interval)   the numbers c and d in a set of numbers that can be expressed as an interval from c to d (p. 118)

equal matrices   two or more matrices that have the same dimensions and equal corresponding entries (p. 804)

equivalent equations   equations that have the same solutions (p. 81)

equivalent inequalities   inequalities that have the same solutions (p. 119)

equivalent systems   systems of equations with the same solutions (p. 795)

equivalent vectors   vectors, such as $\mathbf{u}$ and $\mathbf{v}$, that have the same magnitude and direction, denoted $\mathbf{u} = \mathbf{v}$ (p. 654)

Euler's Formula   the identity $e^{ix} = \cos x + i \sin x$ (p. 688)

even function   a function f for which $f(-x) = f(x)$ for all x in its domain, its graph symmetric with respect to the y-axis (p. 188, 482)

event   any outcome or collection of outcomes in the sample space of an experiment (p. 865)

eventually fixed point   the number c for which the orbit of c for a given function eventually produces constant output values (p. 202)

eventually periodic point   the number c for which the orbit of c for a given function eventually produces repeating output values (p. 202)

expected value of a random variable   the average value of the outcome values for a random variable (p. 869)

experiment   in probability, any process that generates one or more observable outcomes (p. 864)

explicit form of a geometric sequence   In a geometric sequence $\{u_n\}$ with common ratio r, $u_n = r^{n-1}u_1$ for all $n \geq 1$. (p. 60)

explicit form of an arithmetic sequence   In an arithmetic sequence $\{u_n\}$ with common difference d, $u_n = u_1 + (n - 1)d$ for all $n \geq 2$. (p. 23)

exponential decay   decay that can be represented by a function of the form $f(x) = Pa^x$, where $f(x)$ is the quantity at time x, P is the initial quantity when $x = 0$, and $0 < a < 1$ is the factor by which the quantity decreases when x increases by 1 (p. 351)

exponential function (with base a)   a function whose rule is $f(x) = a^x$, where a is any positive real number, and whose domain is all real numbers (p. 336)

exponential growth   growth that can be represented by a function of the form $f(x) = Pa^x$, where $f(x)$ is the quantity at time x, P is the initial quantity when $x = 0$, and $a > 1$ is the factor by which the quantity increases when x increases by 1 (p. 349)

exponential model an exponential function used to represent the trend in a data set (p. 389)

extended inequality an inequality that compares more than two quantities and contains more than one inequality symbol (p. 118)

extraneous roots See *extraneous solutions*.

extraneous solutions solutions of a derived equation that are not solutions of the original equation (p. 110)

Factor Theorem A polynomial $f(x)$ has a linear factor $(x - a)$ if and only if $f(a) = 0$. (p. 245)

factorial The notation $n!$ is read "n factorial" and describes the product of all the integers from 1 through n. (p. 520, 880)

feasible region the region of the coordinate plane that is the intersection of the graphs of the constraints in linear programming (p. 829)

Fibonacci sequence the sequence $\{a_n\}$ discovered by Leonardo Fibonacci in the thirteenth century in which $a_1 = 1$, $a_2 = 1$, and for $n \geq 3$, a_n is the sum of the two preceding terms; $a_n = a_{n-1} + a_{n-2}$ (p. 21)

finite differences the differences between each y-value and the preceding one in a table of values (p. 43)

first octant the octant of a three-dimensional coordinate system in which all coordinates are positive (p. 790)

first quartile See *quartiles*.

five-number summary (of a data set) the following list of values: minimum, first quartile, second quartile, third quartile, and maximum (p. 861)

fixed point (of an orbit) the number c for which the orbit of c for a given function produces constant output values (p. 202)

focal axis of a hyperbola the line through the foci of a hyperbola (p. 701)

foci (singular, focus) of a hyperbola the points in the formation of hyperbola such that the difference of the distances from each focus to a point on the hyperbola is constant (p. 701)

foci (singular, focus) of an ellipse the points in the formation of an ellipse such that the sum of the distances from each focus to a point on the ellipse is constant (p. 692)

focus of a parabola the point in the formation of a parabola such that its distance from any point on the parabola is equal to the distance from that point to the directrix (p. 709)

Formula for Roots of Unity For each positive integer n, the n distinct nth roots of unity are
$$\cos \frac{2k\theta}{n} + i \sin \frac{2k\theta}{n} \text{ for } k = 0, 1, 2, \ldots, \text{ and } n - 1.$$
(p. 648)

fractional equation an equation formed by a fractional expression equal to 0 (p. 114)

fractional expression the quotient $\dfrac{f(x)}{g(x)}$, where $f(x)$ and $g(x)$ are algebraic expressions and $g(x) \neq 0$ (p. 114)

frequency (of a sound wave) the reciprocal of the period of the sinusoidal function that represents a sound wave (p. 558)

function a special type of relation in which each member of the domain corresponds to one and only one member of the range (p. 7) A function consists of a set of inputs called the domain, a rule by which each input determines one and only one output, and a set of outputs called the range. (p. 142)

function notation There is a customary method of denoting a function in abbreviated form. If f denotes a function and a denotes a number in the domain, then $f(a)$ denotes the output of the function f produced by input a. (p. 9)

function rule a set of operations that defines a function (p. 7)

Fundamental Counting Principle In a set of k experiments, if the first experiment has n_1 outcomes, the second has n_2 outcomes, $\ldots$, and the kth has n_k outcomes, then the total number of outcomes for all k experiments is $n_1 \cdot n_2 \cdot \ldots \cdot n_k$. (p. 879)

Fundamental Theorem of Algebra Every nonconstant polynomial has a zero in the complex number system. (p. 307)

Fundamental Theorem of Linear Programming The maximum or minimum of the objective function (if it exists) always occurs at one or more of the corner points of the feasible region. (p. 829)

Gauss-Jordan elimination the method of using elementary row operations on an augmented matrix to produce a matrix in reduced row-echelon form that represents an equivalent system (p. 797)

general form (of a line) a linear equation in the form $Ax + By - C = 0$, where A and B are not both equal to zero (p. 39)

geometric progression See *geometric sequence.*

geometric sequence a sequence in which terms are formed by multiplying a preceding term by a nonzero constant (p. 58)

graph a visual display of a set of points (p. 30)

graph of an equation the set of points whose coordinates are solutions of the equation (p. 30)

graphical zero finder the calculation performed by a graphics calculator in which the x-intercepts of the graph of a function are identified; labeled ROOT, ZERO, or X-INCPT in the TI-83 and Sharp 9600 CALC menu, the Casio 9850 G-SOLVE menu, the MATH submenu of TI-86/89 GRAPH menu, and the FCN submenu of the HP-38 PLOT menu (p. 84)

greatest integer function a piecewise-defined function denoted as $f(x) = [x]$ that converts a real number x into the largest integer that is less than or equal to x (p. 147)

Half-Angle Identities trigonometric identities involving a function of an angle divided by 2 (p. 596)

half-open interval an interval of numbers in which one endpoint of the interval is included in the set and the other endpoint of the interval is not included; denoted with one bracket and one parenthesis, respectively (p. 118)

Heron's Formula The area of any triangle ABC in standard notation is $\sqrt{s(s-a)(s-b)(s-c)}$, where $s = \frac{1}{2}(a + b + c)$. (p. 633)

Hertz the unit of measure for the frequency of a sound wave, where one Hertz is one cycle per second (p. 559)

histogram a display of quantitative data in which the data is divided into classes of equal size and displayed along the horizontal axis and frequencies or relative frequencies on the vertical axis (p. 848)

hole in a graph A point is omitted in the graph of a function and is not contained by an asymptote. For any rational function $f(x) = \dfrac{g(x)}{h(x)}$ and number d that produces both a zero numerator and a zero denominator, if the multiplicity of d as a zero of the related function g is greater than or equal to the multiplicity of d as a zero of the related function h, then the graph of f has a hole at $x = d$. (p. 283)

horizontal asymptote a horizontal line that the graph of a function approaches but never touches or crosses as $|x|$ gets large (p. 284, 952)

horizontal compression For any positive number $c > 1$, the graph of $y = f(cx)$ is the graph of f compressed horizontally, toward the y-axis, by a factor of $\frac{1}{c}$. (p. 179)

horizontal line a line that has a slope of zero and an equation of the form $y = b$, where b is the y-intercept (p. 37)

horizontal shifts For any positive number c, the graph of $y = f(x + c)$ is the graph of f shifted c units to the left, and the graph of $y = f(x - c)$ is the graph of f shifted c units to the right. (p. 175)

horizontal stretch For any positive number $c < 1$, the graph of $y = f(cx)$ is the graph of f stretched horizontally, away from the y-axis, by a factor of $\frac{1}{c}$. (p. 179)

horizontal line test A function f is one-to-one if and only if no horizontal line intersects the graph of f more than once. (p. 209)

hyperbola For any points P and Q in the plane and any positive number k, a hyperbola with foci P and Q is the set of all points (x, y) such that the absolute value of the difference of the distance from (x, y) to P and the distance from (x, y) to Q is k. (p. 700) a conic section with eccentricity greater than 1 (p. 700)

hypotenuse abbreviated hyp, the side of a right triangle that is across from the right angle (p. 415)

identities involving $\pi - t$ $\cos(\pi - t) = -\cos t$, $\sin(\pi - t) = \sin t$, $\tan(\pi - t) = -\tan t$ (p. 459)

identity an equation that is true for all values of the variable for which every term of the equation is defined (p. 454)

identity matrix The $n \times n$ matrix, denoted I_n, has 1s on the diagonal from the top left to the bottom right and 0s in all other entries. For any $n \times n$ matrix A, $AI_n = I_nA = A$. (p. 815)

imaginary axis the vertical axis in the complex plane where each imaginary number $0 + bi$ corresponds to the point $(0, b)$ (p. 638)

imaginary numbers a number of the form bi, where b is a real number and i is the imaginary unit (p. 294) The number $i = \sqrt{-1}$. (p. 294, 297)

inconsistent system a system of equations with no solutions (p. 781)

increasing function A function is said to be increasing on an interval if its graph always rises as you move from left to right over the interval, that is, if its output values are always increasing as the input values are increasing. (p. 152)

independent events two events such that the occurrence or non-occurrence of one event has no effect on the probability of the other event (p. 867)

infinite geometric series the infinite series $a_1 + a_2 + a_3 + \cdots$, where $\{a_n\}$ is a geometric sequence with common ratio r (p. 77)

infinite limit a limit of infinity as x approaches some constant c; corresponds to a vertical asymptote (p. 949)

infinite sequence a sequence with an infinite number of terms (p. 13)

infinite series the sum of terms of a sequence that continues without end, or an infinite sequence; an expression of the form $a_1 + a_2 + a_3 + \cdots$, in which a_n is a real number; also denoted by $\sum\limits_{n=1}^{\infty} a_n$ (p. 76)

inflection point a point where the graph of a function changes concavity (p. 154, 266)

initial point (of a vector) the point P in a vector that extends from point P to point Q (p. 653)

initial side the starting position of a ray that is rotated around its vertex (p. 433)

input (of a relation) the values denoted by the first numbers in the ordered pairs of a relation (p. 7)

instantaneous rate of change the rate of change of a function at a particular point (p. 234)

integers the set of numbers that consists of whole numbers and their opposites: $\ldots, -3, -2, -1, 0, 1, 2, 3, \ldots$ (p. 3)

integral calculus a method of calculating quantities such as distance, area, and volume (p. 138)

intercepts (of a rational function) If the graph of a rational function, f, has a y-intercept, it occurs at $f(0)$, and the x-intercepts occur at the numbers that are zeros of the numerator and *not* zeros of the denominator. (p. 279)

intercepts (of polynomial functions) The graph of a polynomial function of degree n has one y-intercept, which is equal to the constant term, and at most n x-intercepts. (p. 264)

interest a fee paid for the use of borrowed money; calculated as a percentage of the principal (p. 100)

Intermediate Value Theorem If the function f is continuous on the closed interval $[a, b]$ and k is any number between $f(a)$ and $f(b)$, then there exists at least

one number c between a and b such that $f(c) = k$. (p. 944)

interquartile range a measure of variability resistant to outliers; the difference between the first and third quartiles (p. 860)

intersection method a method of solving an equation of the form $f(x) = g(x)$ by graphing $y_1 = f(x)$ and $y_2 = g(x)$ on the same screen of a graphics calculator and finding the x-coordinate of each point of intersection (p. 82)

interval (of numbers) the set of all numbers lying between two fixed numbers (p. 118)

interval notation There is a customary method of denoting an interval of numbers. For real numbers c and d with $c < d$: $[c, d]$ denotes all real numbers x such that $c \leq x \leq d$; (c, d) denotes all real numbers x such that $c < x < d$; $[c, d)$ denotes all real numbers x such that $c \leq x < d$; and $(c, d]$ denotes all real numbers x such that $c < x \leq d$. (p. 118)

interval of convergence the set of values of x for which an infinite series converges to a function (p. 520)

inverse cosine function the inverse of the cosine function with a domain restricted to $[-1, 1]$, denoted by $g(x) = \cos^{-1} x$ (p. 533)

inverse function an inverse relation that is a function (p. 205)

inverse of a matrix For an $n \times n$ matrix A, the inverse of A is an $n \times n$ matrix B, also denoted A^{-1}, such that $AB = I_n$ and $BA = I_n$, or equivalently, $AA^{-1} = I_n$ and $A^{-1}A = I_n$. (p. 816)

inverse relation the result of exchanging the input and output values of a function or relation (p. 205)

inverse sine function the inverse of the sine function with a domain restricted to $\left[-\dfrac{\pi}{2}, \dfrac{\pi}{2}\right]$, denoted by $g(x) = \sin^{-1} x$ (p. 530)

inverse tangent function the inverse of the tangent function with a domain restricted to $\left[-\dfrac{\pi}{2}, \dfrac{\pi}{2}\right]$, denoted by $g(x) = \tan^{-1} x$ (p. 535)

invertible matrix an $n \times n$ matrix for which there exists an inverse matrix (p. 815)

irrational number the set of real numbers that cannot be expressed as a fraction of integers (p. 4)

irreducible (polynomial) a polynomial that cannot be written as the product of polynomials of lesser degree (p. 253)

iterations (of a function) the repeated compositions of a function with itself (p. 199)

kth partial sum the sum of the first k terms of a sequence $\{u_n\}$, where k is a positive integer (p. 26)

Law of Cosines For any triangle ABC in standard notation, $a^2 = b^2 + c^2 - 2bc \cos A$, $b^2 = a^2 + c^2 - 2ac \cos B$, and $c^2 = a^2 + b^2 - 2ab \cos C$. (p. 617)

Law of Sines For any triangle ABC in standard notation, $\dfrac{a}{\sin A} = \dfrac{b}{\sin B} = \dfrac{c}{\sin C}$. (p. 625)

Laws of Exponents For any nonnegative real numbers c and d and any rational numbers r and s,
$c^r c^s = c^{r+s}, \dfrac{c^r}{c^s} = c^{r-s} \, (c \neq 0), (c^r)^s = c^{rs}, (cd)^r = c^r d^r$,
$\left(\dfrac{c}{d}\right)^r = \dfrac{c^r}{d^r} \, (d \neq 0)$, and $c^{-r} = \dfrac{1}{c^r} \, (c \neq 0)$. (p. 330)

leading coefficient the nonzero coefficient of the highest power of the variable in a polynomial (p. 240)

least-squares regression line the one and only one line for which the sum of the squares of the residuals for a set of data is as small as possible (p. 47)

length (of a vector) the distance from point P to point Q in a vector that extends from point P to point Q, denoted $\|\overrightarrow{PQ}\|$ (p. 653)

limit a number (or infinity) that a function value approaches but never reaches as the domain values of that function approach a particular value or infinity (p. 909, 931)

limit at infinity a real number limit as x gets large or small without bound; corresponds to a horizontal asymptote (p. 951)

limit of a constant If d is a constant, then $\lim_{x \to c} d = d$. (p. 918)

limit of a constant at infinity If c is a constant, then $\lim_{x \to \infty} c = c$ and $\lim_{x \to -\infty} c = c$. (p. 953)

limit of a polynomial function If $f(x)$ is a polynomial function and c is any real number, then $\lim_{x \to c} f(x) = f(c)$. (p. 920)

limit of a rational function If $f(x)$ is a rational function and c is any real number such that $f(c)$ is defined, then $\lim_{x \to c} f(x) = f(c)$. (p. 921)

limit of the identity function For every real number c, $\lim_{x \to c} x = c$. (p. 918)

Limit Theorem If f and g are functions that have limits as x approaches c and $f(x) = g(x)$ for all $x \neq c$, then $\lim_{x \to c} f(x) = \lim_{x \to c} g(x)$. (p. 922, 954)

linear combination The vector $\mathbf{v} = a\mathbf{i} + b\mathbf{j}$ is said to be a linear combination of $\mathbf{i}$ and $\mathbf{j}$, where $\mathbf{i} = \langle 1, 0 \rangle$ and $\mathbf{j} = \langle 0, 1 \rangle$ are unit vectors. (p. 662)

linear function a first-degree polynomial function (p. 240)

linear programming a process that involves finding the maximum or minimum output of a linear function, called the objective function, subject to certain restrictions called constraints (p. 829)

linear regression the computational process for finding the least-squares regression line for a set of data (p. 47)

linear speed a measure of speed of a point rotating at a constant rate around the center of a circle, given as the distance that the point travels over time (p. 440)

linear system a system of equations in which all equations are linear (p. 779)

local extremum (plural: extrema) either a local maximum or a local minimum (p. 266)

local maximum (plural: local maxima) A function is said to have a local maximum of $f(c)$ at $x = c$ if the graph of f has a peak at the point $(c, f(c))$; that is, $f(x) < f(c)$ for all x near c. (p. 153)

local minimum (plural: local minima) A function is said to have a local minimum of $f(d)$ at $x = d$ if the graph of f has a valley at the point $(d, f(d))$; that is, $f(x) > f(d)$ for all x near d. (p. 153)

logarithm to the base b (of x) the value of $g(x) = \log_b x$ at the number x, denoted $\log_b x$ (p. 371)

logarithmic function to the base b the inverse of the exponential function $f(x) = b^x$, denoted $g(x) = \log_b x$, where b is a fixed positive number and $b > 1$ (p. 371)

logarithmic model a logarithmic function used to represent the trend in a data set (p. 389)

logarithmic scale a scale of numbers, such as the Richter scale, that is determined by a logarithmic function to measure logarithmic growth, which is very gradual and slow (p. 368)

logistic model a logistic function of the form $y = \dfrac{a}{1 + be^{-kx}}$, where a, b, and k are constant, used to represent the trend in a data set (p. 389)

lower bound (for the real zeros of a polynomial function) the number r such that all the real zeros of a polynomial function $f(x)$ are between r and s, where r and s are real numbers and $r < s$ (p. 255)

magnitude (of a vector) The length of a vector $\mathbf{v} = \langle a, b \rangle$ is $\|\mathbf{v}\| = \sqrt{a^2 + b^2}$. (p. 653)

major axis of an ellipse the segment connecting the vertices of an ellipse (p. 692)

Mandelbrot Set the set of complex numbers c such that the orbit of 0 under the function $f(x) = z^2 + c$ does not approach infinity (p. 304)

mathematical model a mathematical description or structure, such as an equation or graph, which illustrates a relationship between real-world quantities and which is often used to predict the likely value of an unknown quantity (p. 43)

matrix an array of numbers often used to represent a system of equations (p. 795)

matrix addition addition of corresponding entries of matrices that have the same dimensions (p. 804)

matrix equation a matrix equation in the form $AX = B$ that represents a system of equations, where A contains the coefficients of the equations in the system, X contains the variables of the system, and B contains the constants of the equations (p. 814)

matrix multiplication a method of multiplying two compatible matrices to produce a product matrix (p. 806)

matrix subtraction subtraction of corresponding entries of matrices that have the same dimensions (p. 804)

mean a measure of central tendency—also known as the *average*, denoted by $\bar{x}$ and read "*x* bar"—that is calculated by adding the data values and then dividing the sum by the number of data values (p. 853)

mean of a random variable See *expected value of a random variable.*

median a measure of central tendency that is, or indicates, the middle of a data set when the data values are arranged in ascending order (p. 855)

minor axis of an ellipse the segment through the center of the ellipse, perpendicular to the major axis, and with points of the ellipse as endpoints (p. 692)

minute a unit of degree measure equal to $\frac{1}{60}$ of a degree (p. 414)

mode a measure of central tendency that is given by the data value that occurs most frequently in a data set (p. 855)

modulus See *absolute value of a complex number.*

Multiplication Principle See *Fundamental Counting Principle.*

multiplicity (of a zero) If $x - a$ is a factor that occurs m times in the complete factorization of a polynomial, then a is called a zero with multiplicity m of the related polynomial function. (p. 265)

mutually exclusive events two events in a sample space that do not have outcomes in common (p. 866)

natural logarithm (of x) the value of $g(x) = \ln x$ at the number x, denoted $\ln x$ (p. 358)

natural logarithmic function the inverse of the natural exponential function $f(x) = e^x$, denoted $g(x) = \ln x$ (p. 358)

natural numbers The set of numbers that consists of counting numbers: 1, 2, 3, ... (p. 3)

Negative Angle Identities $\cos(-t) = \cos t$, $\sin(-t) = -\sin t$, $\tan(-t) = -\tan t$ (p. 459)

negative correlation the relationship between two real-world quantities when the slope of the least-squares regression line that represents the relationship is negative, that is, as one quantity increases, the other quantity decreases (p. 52)

no correlation the relationship between two real-world quantities when the correlation coefficient, r, for a least-squares regression line that represents the relationship is close to zero; no apparent trend in the data (p. 52)

nonlinear system a system of equations in which at least one equation is nonlinear (p. 779)

nonnegative integers the set of whole numbers: 0, 1, 2, 3, ... (p. 3)

nonsingular matrix See *invertible matrix.*

norm (of a vector) See *magnitude.*

normal curve the graph of a probability density function that corresponds to a normal distribution: bell-shaped and symmetric about the mean, with the x-axis as a horizontal asymptote (p. 889)

normal distribution a distribution of data that varies about the mean in such a way that the graph of its probability density function is a normal curve (p. 889)

nth root of a complex number The nth root of $a + bi$ is any of the n solutions of the equation $z^n = a + bi$. (p. 645)

nth roots For any real number c and any positive integer n, the nth root of c is denoted by either $\sqrt[n]{c}$ or

$c^{\frac{1}{n}}$ and is defined to be the solution of $x^n = c$ when n is odd or the nonnegative solution of $x^n = c$ when n is even and nonnegative. (p. 328)

numerator the expression in a fraction that lies above the fraction bar (p. 4)

numerical derivative A calculator term for the instantaneous rate of change at a given input value; denoted nDeriv, nDer, d/dx, dY/dX, or ∂. (p. 237)

objective function a linear function of which a minimum or maximum is obtained in linear programming (p. 829)

oblique asymptote See *slant asymptote.*

oblique triangle a triangle that does not contain a right angle (p. 617)

octant one of eight regions into which a three-dimensional coordinate system is divided by the intersection of the three coordinate planes (p. 790)

odd function a function f for which $f(-x) = -f(x)$ for all x in its domain, its graph symmetric with respect to the origin (p. 189, 483)

one-stage path (of a network) a direct path from one vertex to another in a directed network (p. 809)

one-to-one function a function f in which $f(a) = f(b)$ only when $a = b$; a function whose inverse relation is a function (p. 208)

open interval an interval of numbers in which neither endpoint of the interval is included in the set; denoted with two parentheses (p. 118)

opposite side (of a right triangle) abbreviated opp, the side of a right triangle that is across from a given acute angle of the triangle (p. 415)

orbit (of a number) the sequence of output values produced by iterating a given function with that number; the orbit of a number c for a given function is c, $f(c)$, $f^2(c)$, $f^3(c)$, $f^4(c)$, ... (p. 200)

ordered pair A pair of real numbers in parentheses, separated by a comma, is used to locate or represent a point in a coordinate plane. The first number represents the horizontal distance from the origin and the second number represents the vertical distance from the x-axis. (p. 5)

ordered set of numbers a set of numbers such that for any two numbers a and b in the set, exactly one of the following statements is true: $a < b$, $a = b$, or $a > b$ (p. 118)

orientation (of a parametric curve) the direction that a parametric curve is traced out (p. 757)

origin the point of intersection of the axes in a coordinate system (p. 5)

origin symmetry A graph is symmetric with respect to the origin if whenever (x, y) is on the graph, then $(-x, -y)$ is also on it. (p. 187)

orthogonal vectors perpendicular vectors; vectors $\mathbf{u}$ and $\mathbf{v}$ such that $\mathbf{u} \cdot \mathbf{v} = 0$ (p. 673)

outlier a data value that shows a strong deviation from the general trend of the distribution (p. 847)

output (of a relation) the values denoted by the second numbers in the ordered pairs of a relation (p. 7)

parabola the shape of the graph of a quadratic function (p. 165) For any line L in the plane and any point P not on line L, a parabola with focus P and directrix L is the set of points such that the distance from X to P is equal to the distance from X to line L. (p. 709) a conic section with eccentricity equal to 1 (p. 709)

parabolic asymptote a parabolic curve that the graph of a function approaches as $|x|$ gets large (p. 286)

parallel lines In a plane, these lines have the same slope. All vertical lines are also parallel. (p. 38)

parallel vectors vectors that are scalar multiples of each other (p. 671)

parameter the third variable used as input for the two functions that form a pair of parametric equations (p. 157, 785)

parameterization a pair of parametric equations that describe a given curve (p. 755)

parametric equations a pair of continuous functions that define the x- and y-coordinates of points in a coordinate plane in terms of a third variable, the parameter (p. 157)

parametric graphing graphing parametric equations (p. 157)

parent function a function with a certain shape that has the simplest algebraic rule for that shape (p. 172)

partial fraction decomposition See *partial fractions.*

partial fractions When a fraction is decomposed (broken down) and written as the sum of fractions, the terms of the sum are called partial fractions, and the sum is called the partial fraction decomposition of the original fraction. (p. 838)

partial sums of a geometric sequence For each positive integer k, the kth partial sum of a geometric sequence $\{u_n\}$ with common ratio $r \neq 1$ is

$$\sum_{n=1}^{k} u_n = u_1\left(\frac{1 - r^k}{1 - r}\right). \text{ (p. 61)}$$

partial sums of an arithmetic sequence For each positive integer k, the kth partial sum of an arithmetic sequence $\{u_n\}$ with common difference d is

$$\sum_{n=1}^{k} u_n = ku_1 + \frac{k(k-1)}{2}d \text{ or } \sum_{n=1}^{k} u_n = \frac{k}{2}(u_1 + u_k). \text{ (p. 27)}$$

period (of a function) the smallest value of k in a function f for which there exists some constant k such that $f(t) = f(t + k)$ for every number t in the domain of f (p. 457, 498) See also *sinusoidal function*.

periodic function a nonconstant function that repeats its values at regular intervals; a function f for which there exists some constant k such that $f(t) = f(t + k)$ for every number t in the domain of f (p. 457)

periodic orbit an orbit for a given function that produces repeating output values (p. 202)

periodic point (of an orbit) the number c for which the orbit of c for a given function produces repeating output values (p. 202)

periodicity identities $\sin t = \sin(t \pm 2\pi)$, $\cos t = \cos(t \pm 2\pi)$, $\tan t = \tan(t \pm \pi)$ (p. 458)

permutation an arrangement of objects in a specific order (p. 880)

perpendicular lines In a plane, two lines are perpendicular when their slopes are negative reciprocals (having a product of -1). Vertical lines and horizontal lines are perpendicular to each other. (p. 38)

phase shift a number representing the horizontal translation of a sinusoidal graph (p. 502) See also *sinusoidal function*.

pie chart a visual display of qualitative data in which categories are displayed in sectors of a circle, where the central angle of each sector is the product of the relative frequency of that category and $360°$ (p. 845)

piecewise-defined function a function whose rule includes several formulas, each of which is applied to certain values of the domain, as specified in the definition of the function (p. 146)

plane curve the set of all points (x, y) such that $x = f(t)$ and $y = g(t)$ and that f and g are continuous functions of t on an interval I (p. 755)

point-slope form a linear equation in the form $y - y_1 = m(x - x_1)$, where m represents the slope and (x_1, y_1) is a point on the line (p. 36)

polar axis the horizontal ray extending to the right from the pole in a polar coordinate system (p. 734)

polar coordinates coordinates (r, θ) of a point in the polar coordinate system, where r gives the distance from the point to the pole, and θ is the measure of the angle with the polar axis as its initial side and the segment from the pole to the point as its terminal side (p. 734)

polar form of a complex number For the complex number $a + bi$, the polar form is $r(\cos\theta + i\sin\theta)$, where $r = |a + bi|$, $a = r\cos\theta$, and $b = r\sin\theta$. (p. 639)

pole the origin of a polar coordinate system (p. 734)

polynomial an algebraic expression that can be written in the form $a_n x^n + a_{n-1}x^{n-1} + \cdots + a_3 x^3 + a_2 x^2 + a_1 x + a_0$, where n is a nonnegative integer, x is a variable, and each of $a_0, a_1, \ldots, a_n$ is a constant (p. 239)

polynomial equation (of degree n) an equation that can be written in the form $a_n x^n + a_{n-1}x^{n-1} + \cdots + a_1 x + a_0 = 0$, where n is a nonnegative integer, x is a variable, and each of $a_0, a_1, \ldots, a_n$ is a constant (p. 94)

polynomial form of a quadratic function a quadratic function in the form $f(x) = ax^2 + bx + c$, where a, b, and c are real numbers and $a \neq 0$ (p. 164)

polynomial function a function whose rule is given by a polynomial (p. 240)

polynomial model a polynomial function used to represent the trend in a data set (p. 273)

population a group of individuals or objects studied in a statistical experiment (p. 843)

positive correlation the relationship between two real-world quantities when the slope of the least-squares regression line that represents the relationship is positive, that is, as one quantity increases, the other quantity increases (p. 52)

positive integers the set of natural numbers: 1, 2, 3, ... (p. 3)

Power Law of Logarithms For all positive b and v, and all k, and $b \neq 1$, $\log_b(v^k) = k(\log_b v)$. (p. 366, 373)

power model a power function of the form $y = ax^r$, where a and r are constant, used to represent the trend in a data set (p. 389)

Power Principal If both sides of an equation are raised to the same positive integer power, then every solution of the original equation is a solution of the derived equation. However, the derived equation may have solutions that are not solutions of the original equation. (p. 112)

power-reducing identities trigonometric identities that relate second-degree expressions to first-degree expressions (p. 595)

prime number an integer greater than 1 whose only factors are itself and 1 (p. 20)

principal an amount of money that is deposited or borrowed (p. 100)

probability (of an event) a number from 0 to 1 (or 0% to 100%) that indicates how likely an event is to occur; calculated by dividing the number of elements in the event by the number of elements in the sample space (p. 865)

probability density function A function with the property that the area under the graph corresponds to a probability distribution. (p. 871)

probability distribution a table that describes the rule of a function $P(E)$ that gives the probability of an event, where the domain of the function is the sample space and the range of the function is the closed interval [0, 1] (p. 865)

probability of a binomial experiment $P(r$ successes in n trials$) = {}_nC_rp^rq^{n-r}$, where p is the probability of success, and $q = 1 - p$ is the probability of failure. (p. 886)

probability of a complement If an event E has probability p, then the complement of the event has probability $1 - p$. (p. 866)

product function For any functions $f(x)$ and $g(x)$, their product function is the new function $(fg)(x) = f(x) \cdot g(x)$. (p. 192)

Product Law of Logarithms For all positive b, v, and w, and $b \neq 1$, $\log_b(vw) = \log_b v + \log_b w$. (p. 365, 373)

product-to-sum trigonometric identities involving the product of two functions (p. 599)

projection vector A vector $\overrightarrow{OQ}$, called the projection of **u** on v, determined by constructing a segment from the terminal point of a vector **u** perpendicular to another vector **v** at a point Q on the vector, where point O is the initial point of both vectors, denoted $\text{proj}_v \, \mathbf{u}$. (p. 674)

Pythagorean identities the identity $\sin^2 t + \cos^2 t = 1$ and the identities derived from it (p. 456)

Pythagorean Theorem In a right triangle with legs a and b and hypotenuse c, $a^2 + b^2 = c^2$. (p. 421)

quadrants the four regions into which a coordinate plane is divided by its axes, usually indicated by Roman numerals I, II, III, and IV (p. 5)

quadratic equation an equation that can be written in the form $ax^2 + bx + c = 0$, where a, b, and c are real constants and $a \neq 0$ (p. 88)

quadratic formula The solutions of a quadratic equation $ax^2 + bx + c = 0$ are $x = \dfrac{-b \pm \sqrt{b^2 - 4ac}}{2a}$. (p. 92)

quadratic function a function whose rule is a second-degree polynomial (p. 163, 240)

qualitative data data that is categorical in nature, such as "liberal," "moderate," and "conservative" (p. 843)

quantitative data numerical data (p. 843)

quartic function a fourth-degree polynomial function (p. 240)

quartiles These values divide a data set into fourths. The median, or *second quartile* Q_2, divides the data into a *lower half* and an *upper half*; the *first quartile* Q_1 is the median of the lower half; and the third quartile Q_3 is the median of the upper half. (p. 860)

quotient function For any functions $f(x)$ and $g(x)$, their quotient function is the new function $\left(\dfrac{f}{g}\right)(x) = \dfrac{f(x)}{g(x)}$. (p. 192)

quotient identities $\tan t = \dfrac{\sin t}{\cos t}$ and $\cot t = \dfrac{\cos t}{\sin t}$ (p. 455)

Quotient Law of Logarithms For all positive b, v, and w, and $b \neq 1$, $\log_b\left(\dfrac{v}{w}\right) = \log_b v - \log_b w$. (p. 366, 373)

radian measure The radian measure of an angle in standard position is the length of the arc along the unit circle from the point (1, 0) on the initial side to the point P where the terminal side intersects the unit circle. (p. 436)

radical equations equations that contain roots (such as square roots, cube roots, etc.) of expressions that contain variables (p. 111)

radioactive decay decay in the amount of a radioactive substance that can be modeled by the function $f(x) = P(0.5)^{\frac{x}{h}}$, where P is the initial amount of the substance, $x = 0$ corresponds to when the decay began, and h is the half-life of the substance (p. 352)

radiocarbon dating a process of determining the age of an organic object by using the amount of carbon-14 remaining in the object (p. 352)

random sample a sample in which all members of the population and all groups of members of a given size have an equal chance of being in the sample (p. 843)

random variable a function that assigns a number to each element in the sample space of an experiment (p. 869)

range (of a data set) the difference between the maximum and minimum data values in a data set (p. 859)

range (of a function) the set of second numbers in the ordered pairs of a relation (p. 6, 142, 447)

rational exponent A rational exponent is a rational number with a nonzero denominator; for any positive real number c and rational number $\frac{t}{k}$ with positive denominator, $c^{\frac{t}{k}} = (c^t)^{\frac{1}{k}} = (c^{\frac{1}{k}})^t$ or $c^{\frac{t}{k}} = \sqrt[k]{c^t} = (\sqrt[k]{c})^t$. (p. 330)

rational function a function whose rule is the quotient of two polynomials, defined only for input values that produce a nonzero denominator (p. 278)

rational number the set of real numbers that can be expressed as a fraction of an integer numerator and an integer denominator, where the denominator is not equal to zero (p. 4)

Rational Zero Test If a rational number $\frac{r}{s}$, written in lowest terms, is a zero of the polynomial function $f(x) = a_n x^n + \cdots + a_1 x + a_0$, where the coefficients $a_n, \ldots, a_1$ are integers with $a_n \neq 0$ and $a_0 \neq 0$, then r is a factor of the constant term, a_0, and s is a factor of the leading coefficient, a_n. (p. 251)

rational zeros zeros of a function that are rational numbers (p. 250)

rationalizing (a denominator) writing equivalent fractions with no radicals in the denominator (p. 332)

real axis the horizontal axis in the complex plane where each real number $a + 0i$ corresponds to the point $(a, 0)$ (p. 638)

real numbers the set of numbers that consists of rational numbers and irrational numbers (p. 3)

real solutions solutions of an equation that are real numbers (p. 88)

real zeros solutions of an equation of the form $f(x) = 0$ that are real numbers (p. 245)

reciprocal identities identities that relate trigonometric functions and their reciprocals (p. 455)

rectangular coordinate system See *Cartesian coordinate system.*

recursive form of a geometric sequence In a geometric sequence $\{u_n\}$, $u_n = r u_{n-1}$ for some nonzero constant r and all $n \geq 2$. (p. 59)

recursive form of a sequence a method of defining a sequence when given the first term and the procedure for determining each term by using the preceding term (p. 15)

recursive form of an arithmetic sequence In an arithmetic sequence $\{u_n\}$, $u_n = u_{n-1} + d$ for some constant d and all $n \geq 2$. (p. 22)

reduced row-echelon form This form of an augmented matrix satisfies the following conditions: all rows consisting entirely of zeros (if any) are at the bottom; the first nonzero entry in each nonzero row is a 1 (called *leading 1*); any column containing a leading 1 has zeros in all other entries; and each leading 1 appears to the right of leading 1s in any preceding row. (p. 797)

reference angle the positive acute angle formed by the terminal side of θ in standard position and the x-axis (p. 449)

reflections The graph of $y = -f(x)$ is the graph of f reflected across the x-axis, and the graph of $y = f(-x)$ is the graph of f reflected across the y-axis. (p. 177)

relation a correspondence between two sets; a set of ordered pairs (p. 6)

Remainder Theorem If a polynomial $f(x)$ is divided by $(x - c)$, then the remainder is $f(c)$. (p. 244)

residual a measure of the error between an actual data value and the corresponding value given by a model; $r - y$, where (x, r) is a data point and (x, y) is a point contained by the model (p. 44)

Richter scale a logarithmic scale used to measure the magnitude of an earthquake (p. 368)

right angle an angle with a degree measure of $90°$ (p. 414)

roots solutions of an equation of the form $f(x) = 0$ and equal to the zeros of f (p. 83)

roots of unity the n distinct nth roots of 1 (the solutions of $z^n = 1$) (p. 648)

rotation equations equations that relate a point in a coordinate plane to the corresponding point in the plane after a rotation (p. 729)

rule of the function See *function rule.*

sample a subset of the population studied in a statistical experiment, whose information is used to draw conclusions about the population (p. 843)

Glossary

sample space the set of all possible outcomes in an experiment (p. 864)

scalar a real number, often denoted by k, used in scalar multiplication (p. 655)

scalar multiplication (with vectors) an operation in which a scalar k is multiplied by a vector $\mathbf{v}$ to produce another vector, denoted by $k\mathbf{v}$ (p. 655)

scalar multiplication with matrices multiplication of each entry in a matrix by a real number (p. 805)

scatter plot a graphical display of statistical data plotted as points on a coordinate plane to show the relationship between two quantities (p. 5)

Schwartz Inequality For any vectors $\mathbf{u}$ and $\mathbf{v}$, $|\mathbf{u} \cdot \mathbf{v}| \le \|\mathbf{u}\| \|\mathbf{v}\|$. (p. 673)

secant line (of a function) the straight line determined by two points on the graph of a function; the slope of the secant line joining points $(a, f(a))$ and $(b, f(b))$ on the graph of a function, equal to the average rate of change of the function from a to b (p. 218)

secant ratio For a given acute angle θ in a right triangle, the secant of θ is written as sec θ and is equal to the reciprocal of the cosine ratio of the given angle. (p. 416)

second a unit of degree measure equal to $\frac{1}{60}$ of a minute, or $\frac{1}{3600}$ of a degree (p. 414)

second quartile See *quartiles*.

second-degree equation See *quadratic equation*.

self-similar the property possessed by fractals that every subdivision of the fractal has a structure similar to the structure of the whole (p. 305)

sequence an ordered list of numbers (p. 13)

sequence notation a customary method of denoting a sequence or terms of a sequence in abbreviated form: $u_1, u_2, u_3, \dots, u_n$ (p. 14)

series the sum of the terms of a sequence (p. 76)

sides (of an angle) the two rays, segments, or lines that form an angle (p. 413)

Sigma notation See *summation notation*.

simple harmonic motion motion that can be described by a function of the form $f(x) = a \sin(bt + c) + d$ or $f(x) = a \cos(bt + c) + d$ (p. 549)

simple interest interest that is generally used when a loan or a bank balance is less than 1 year; calculated by $I = Prt$, where I is the simple interest, P is the principal, r is the annual interest, and t is time in years (p. 100)

sine ratio For a given acute angle θ in a right triangle, the sine of θ is written as sin θ and is equal to the ratio of the opposite side length to the length of the hypotenuse. (p. 416)

sinusoid the wave shape of the graph of a sine or cosine function (p. 510, 548)

sinusoidal function A function whose graph is the shape of a sinusoid and can be expressed in the form $f(x) = a \sin(bt + c) + d$ or $f(x) = a \cos(bt + c) + d$, where $|a|$ is the amplitude, $\frac{2\pi}{b}$ is the period, $-\frac{c}{b}$ is the phase shift, and d is the vertical shift. (p. 548)

skewed distribution a type of distribution in which the right or left side of its display indicate frequencies that are much greater than those of the other side (p. 846)

slant asymptote a nonvertical and nonhorizontal line that the graph of a function approaches as $|x|$ gets large (p. 286)

slope of a line The value of the ratio $\frac{\Delta y}{\Delta x} = \frac{y_2 - y_1}{x_2 - x_1}$, where (x_1, y_1) and (x_2, y_2) are points contained by the line and $x_1 \ne x_2$. (p. 32)

slope-intercept form a linear equation in the form $y = mx + b$, where m represents the slope and b represents the y-intercept (p. 33)

solution of a system of equations a set of values that satisfy all the equations in the system (p. 780)

solution of an equation the value(s) of the variable(s) that make the equation true (p. 30)

solution to an inequality (in two variables) the region in the coordinate plane consisting of all points whose coordinates satisfy the inequality (p. 827)

solving a triangle finding the lengths of all three sides and the measures of all three angles in a triangle when only some of these measures are known (p. 424)

sound waves periodic air pressure waves created by vibrations (p. 558)

special angles angles of degree measure 30°, 45°, or 60° (p. 418)

square root of squares For every real number c, $\sqrt{c^2} = |c|$. (p. 109)

square system a system of equations that has the same number of equations as variables (p. 814)

standard deviation a measure of variability that describes the average distance of data values from the mean, given by the square root of the variance (p. 857)

standard equation of a hyperbola For any point (h, k) in the plane and positive real numbers a and b,

Glossary

$$\frac{(x-h)^2}{a^2} - \frac{(y-k)^2}{b^2} = 1 \text{ or } \frac{(x-h)^2}{b^2} - \frac{(y-k)^2}{a^2} = 1.$$
(p. 701, 720)

standard equation of a parabola   For any point (h, k) in the plane and nonzero real number p, $(x-h)^2 = 4\,p(y-k)$ or $(y-k)^2 = 4\,p(x-h)$. (p. 710, 720)

standard equation of an ellipse   For any point (h, k) in the plane and real numbers a and b with $a > b > 0$, $\frac{(x-h)^2}{a^2} + \frac{(y-k)^2}{b^2} = 1$ or $\frac{(x-h)^2}{b^2} + \frac{(y-k)^2}{a^2} = 1.$ (p. 693, 720)

standard form (of a line)   used to display the equation of a line without fractions, a linear equation in the form $Ax + By = C$, where A and B are not both equal to zero (p. 39)

standard normal curve   a normal curve with a mean of 0 and a standard deviation of 1 (p. 890)

standard notation (of triangles)   a method of labeling triangles in which each vertex is labeled with a capital letter to denote the angle at that vertex, and the length of the side opposite that vertex is denoted by the same letter in lower case (p. 617)

standard position (of an angle)   an angle in the coordinate plane with its vertex at the origin and its initial side on the positive x-axis (p. 434)

standard viewing window   the window or screen of a graphics calculator that displays $-10 \le x \le 10$ and $-10 \le y \le 10$, listed in the ZOOM menu of most graphics calculators (p. 84)

standardize (data)   to adjust the scale of data that is normally distributed in order to match the standard normal curve (p. 893)

stem plot   a display of quantitative data in a tabular format consisting of the initial digit(s) of the data values, called *stems*, on the left and the remaining digits of the data values, called *leaves*, on the right; commonly used to display small data sets (p. 847)

step function   a function, such as the greatest-integer function, whose graph consists of horizontal line segments resembling steps (p. 157)

sum function   For any functions $f(x)$ and $g(x)$, their sum function is the new function $(f + g)(x) = f(x) + g(x)$. (p. 191)

sum of an infinite geometric series   The sum $S = \dfrac{a_1}{1-r}$, where $a_1 + ra_1 + r^2a_1 + r^3a_1 + \cdots$ is a convergent geometric series with common ratio r such that $|r| < 1$. (p. 77)

sum-to-product   trigonometric identities involving $\sin x \pm \sin y$ or $\cos x \pm \cos y$ (p. 599)

summation notation   a customary method of denoting the sum of terms by using the Greek letter Sigma (Σ) as follows: $\displaystyle\sum_{k=1}^{m} c_k = c_1 + c_2 + c_3 + \cdots + c_m$ (p. 25)

supplementary angle identity   For any acute angle θ, $\sin\theta = \sin(180° - \theta)$. (p. 628)

symmetric distribution   a type of distribution in which the right and left sides of its display indicate frequencies that are mirror images of each other (p. 846)

synthetic division   an abbreviated notation for performing polynomial division when the divisor is a first-degree polynomial (p. 241)

system of equations   a set of two or more equations in two or more variables (p. 779)

tangent line (of a function)   a line that touches the graph of a function at exactly one point; the slope of the tangent line to a curve at a point, equal to the instantaneous rate of change of the function at that point (p. 235)

tangent ratio   For a given acute angle θ in a right triangle, the tangent of θ is written as $\tan\theta$ and is equal to the ratio of the opposite side length to the adjacent side length. (p. 416)

term (of a sequence)   a number in a sequence (p. 13)

terminal point (of a vector)   the point Q in a vector that extends from point P to point Q (p. 653)

terminal side   the final position of a ray that is rotated around its vertex (p. 433)

third quartile   See *quartiles.*

transformation form of a quadratic function   a quadratic function in the form $f(x) = a(x - h)^2 + k$, where a, h, and k are real numbers and $a \ne 0$ (p. 164)

Triangle Sum Theorem   The sum of the measures of the angles in a triangle is $180°$. (p. 421)

trigonometric form of a complex number   See *polar form of a complex number.*

trigonometric functions of a real variable   a function whose rule is a trigonometric ratio in the coordinate plane with domain values in radian measure (p. 445)

trigonometric ratios (in a triangle)   the six possible combinations of side length ratios of a right triangle (p. 415)

trigonometric ratios (in the coordinate plane) the six trigonometric ratios defined in terms of a triangle determined by the coordinates of a point on the terminal side of an angle in standard position and the origin (p. 444)

two-stage path (of a network) a path in a directed network from one vertex to another with exactly one intermediate vertex (p. 810)

uniform distribution a type of distribution in which all of the data values have approximately the same frequency; its display is level (p. 846)

unit circle the circle of radius 1 centered at the origin of the coordinate plane (p. 435)

unit vector a vector with a length of 1 (p. 661)

upper bound (for the real zeros of a polynomial function) the number s such that all the real zeros of a polynomial function $f(x)$ are between r and s, where r and s are real numbers and $r < s$ (p. 255)

variability the spread of a data set (p. 857)

variance a measure of variability given by the average of squared deviations (p. 858)

vector a quantity that involves both magnitude and direction; represented geometrically by a directed line segment or arrow and denoted by using its endpoints, such as $\overrightarrow{PQ}$, or by a boldface lowercase letter, such as **u** (p. 653)

vector addition If $\mathbf{u} = \langle a, b \rangle$ and $\mathbf{v} = \langle c, d \rangle$, then $\mathbf{u} + \mathbf{v} = \langle a + c, b + d \rangle$. (p. 657)

vector subtraction If $\mathbf{u} = \langle a, b \rangle$ and $\mathbf{v} = \langle c, d \rangle$, then $\mathbf{u} - \mathbf{v} = \langle a - c, b - d \rangle$. (p. 658)

vertex (of an angle) the common endpoint of the two rays, segments, or lines that form an angle (p. 413)

vertex of a parabola the intersection of the axis of a parabola and the parabola; the midpoint of the segment from the focus of the parabola to the directrix (p. 709)

vertical asymptotes a vertical line that the graph of a function approaches but never touches or crosses because it is not defined there (p. 284, 950)

vertical compression For any positive number $c < 1$, the graph of $y = c \cdot f(x)$ is the graph of f compressed vertically, toward the x-axis, by a factor of c. (p. 179)

vertical line a line that has an undefined slope and an equation of the form $x = c$, where c is a constant real number (p. 37)

vertical shifts For any positive number c, the graph of $y = f(x) + c$ is the graph of f shifted upward c units, and the graph of $y = f(x) - c$ is the graph of f shifted downward c units. (p. 174) See also *sinusoidal function.*

vertical stretch For any positive number $c > 1$, the graph of $y = c \cdot f(x)$ is the graph of f stretched vertically, away from the x-axis, by a factor of c. (p. 179)

vertical line test A graph in a coordinate plane represents a function if and only if no vertical line intersects the graph more than once. (p. 151)

vertices of a hyperbola the points where the line through the foci intercepts the hyperbola (p. 701)

vertices of a network the points that are connected in a network (p. 809)

vertices of an ellipse the points where the line through the foci intercepts the ellipse (p. 692)

whole numbers the set of numbers that consists of natural numbers and zero: 0, 1, 2, ... (p. 3)

work The work W done by a constant force **F** as its point of application moves along the vector **d** is $W = \mathbf{F} \cdot \mathbf{d}$. (p. 678)

x-axis often the name of the horizontal axis of a coordinate plane with the positive direction to the right and the negative direction to the left (p. 5)

x-axis symmetry A graph is symmetric with respect to the x-axis if whenever (x, y) is on the graph, then $(x, -y)$ is also on it. (p. 185)

x-coordinate usually the first real number in an ordered pair (p. 5)

x-intercept the x-coordinate of a point where a graph crosses the x-axis; the x-intercepts of the graph of f, equal to the zeros of f and the solutions of $f(x) = 0$ (p. 83)

x-intercept form of a quadratic function a quadratic function in the form $f(x) = a(x - s)(x - t)$, where a, x, s, and t are real numbers and $a \neq 0$ (p. 164)

x-intercept method a method of solving an equation of the form $f(x) = 0$ by graphing $y = f(x)$ and finding the x-intercepts (p. 84)

y-axis often the name of the vertical axis of a coordinate plane with the positive direction up and the negative direction down (p. 5)

y-axis symmetry A graph is symmetric with respect to the y-axis if whenever (x, y) is on the graph, then $(-x, y)$ is also on it. (p. 184)

y-coordinate usually the second real number in an ordered pair (p. 5)

z-axis the vertical axis in a three-dimensional coordinate system with positive direction upward (p. 790)

zero polynomial the constant polynomial 0 (p. 240)

Zero Product Property If a product of real numbers is zero, then at least one of the factors is zero; if $ab = 0$, then $a = 0$ or $b = 0$. (p. 89)

zeros of a function inputs of the function that produce an output of zero (p. 83)

z-value a value that gives the number of standard deviations that a data value in a normal distribution is located above the mean (p. 894)

Acknowledgments

Photo Credits: page 2, Ron Behrmann/International Stock Photography; page 80, Orion Press/Natural Selection; page 140, Peter Van Steen/HRW Photo; page 326, Laurence Parent; page 412, Todd Gipstein/National Geographic Society Image Collection; page 472, Peter Van Steen/HRW Photo/Courtesy Jim Reese at KVET, Austin, Tx; page 522, Coco McCoy/Rainbow/PictureQuest; page 570, Telegraph Color Library/FPG International; page 616, Scott Barrow/International Stock Photography; page 690, Stone; page 778, Tom McHugh/Photo Researchers, Inc.; page 842, SuperStock; page 908, Tom Sanders/Photri/The Stock Market

Illustration Credits: Abbreviations used: (t) top, (c) center, (b) bottom, (l) left, (r) right, (bkgd) background

All work, unless otherwise noted, contributed by Holt, Rinehart and Winston.

Chapter Four: page 306 (tc), Pronk&Associates;
Chapter Six: page 470 (cl), NETS; page 471 (br), NETS. Chapter Eleven: page 713 (b), NETS. Chapter Thirteen: page 882 (br), NETS.

Answers to Selected Exercises

Chapter 1

Section 1.1, page 10

1. $A(-3, 3)$; $B(-1.5, 3)$; $C(-2.5, 0)$; $D(-1.5, -3)$;
$E(0, 2)$; $F(0, 0)$; $G(2, 0)$; $H(3, 1)$; $I(3, -1)$

3. $P(-6, 3)$ **5.** $P(4, 2)$

7.

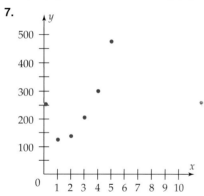

9. a. About $0.94 in 1987 and $1.19 in 1995.
  b. About 26.6%
  c. In the first third of 1985 and from 1989 onward.

11. a. Quadrant IV   **b.** Quadrants III or IV

13. a.

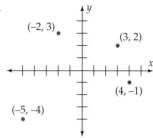

b.

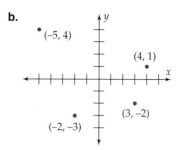

c. They are mirror images of each other, with the x-axis being the mirror. In other words, they lie on the same vertical line, on opposite sides of the x-axis, the same distance from the axis.

15. Yes. Each input produces only one output.

17. No. The value -5 produces two outputs.

19. (500, 0); (1509, 0); (3754, 35.08); (6783, 119.15);
(12500, 405); (55342, 2547.10)

21. Each input (income) yields only one output (tax).

23. Postage is a function of weight since each weight determines one and only one postage amount. But weight is *not* a function of postage since a given postage amount may apply to several different weights. For instance, *all* letters under 1 oz use just one first-class stamp.

25. Domain: all real numbers between -3 and 3, inclusive; range: all real numbers between -4 and 3, inclusive

27. 2 is output of $\frac{1}{2}$; 0 of $\frac{5}{2}$; and -3 of $-\frac{5}{2}$.

29. -1 is output of -2; 3 of 0; 2 of 1; -1 of 2.5; and 0 of -1.5.

31. 1 is output of -2; -3 of -1; -1 of 0; 1 (approximately) of $\frac{1}{2}$; and 1.5 of 1.

33. a. $[-3, 4]$ **b.** $[-2, 3]$ **c.** -2
     d. 0.5   **e.** 1   **f.** -1

Section 1.2, page 19

1. 20

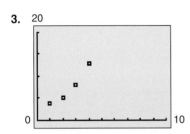

3. 20

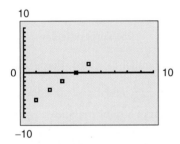

5. $u_1 = -6$ and $u_n = u_{n-1} + 2$

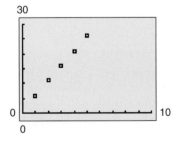

7. $u_1 = 6$ and $u_n = u_{n-1} + 5$

30

10

9. $u_1 = 4$
$u_2 = 2 \cdot 4 + 3 = 11$
$u_3 = 2 \cdot 11 + 3 = 25$
$u_4 = 2 \cdot 25 + 3 = 53$
$u_5 = 2 \cdot 53 + 3 = 109$

11. $u_1 = 1$
$u_2 = -2$
$u_3 = 3$
$u_4 = 1 - 2 + 3 = 2$
$u_5 = -2 + 3 + 2 = 3$

13. $u_0 = 400$; $u_n = 0.8u_{n-1}$; $u_6 \approx 104.858$ cm

15. For 2 rays: $u_2 = 1$; for 3 rays: $u_3 = 3$; for 4 rays: $u_4 = 6$; $u_n = u_{n-1} + n - 1$ for $n \geq 3$

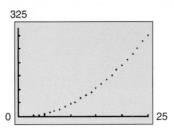

$u_{25} = 300$

17. $u_1 = 12$, $u_n = u_{n-1} + 2$ for $2 \leq n \leq 35$; $u_{30} = 70$ seats

19. $u_0 = 30{,}000$, $u_n = 1.06u_{n-1}$ for $n \geq 1$; $u_{10} = \$53{,}725.43$

21. $u_0 = 35{,}000$, $u_n = 0.75u_{n-1} + 6500$, for $n \geq 1$; $u_8 = 26{,}901$ students

23. $u_0 = 50{,}000$, $u_n = 0.9u_{n-1} + 4000$ for $n \geq 1$; $u_{20} = 41{,}216$; $u_{35} = 40{,}250$.

25. a. The items listed are the first ten primes. Every other number less than 29 can be factored into a product of smaller integers.
b. 59, 61, 67, 71

27. 4, 9, 25, 49, 121   **29.** 3, 7, 13, 19, 23

31. 1, 1, 2, 3, 5, 8, 13, 21, 34, 55

33. $n = 1: 5(1)^2 + 4(-1)^1 = 1 = 1^2$
$n = 2: 5(1)^2 + 4(-1)^2 = 9 = 3^2$
$n = 3: 5(2)^2 + 4(-1)^3 = 16 = 4^2$
$n = 4: 5(3)^2 + 4(-1)^4 = 49 = 7^2$
$n = 5: 5(5)^2 + 4(-1)^5 = 121 = 11^2$
$n = 6: 5(8)^2 + 4(-1)^6 = 324 = 18^2$
$n = 7: 5(13)^2 + 4(-1)^7 = 841 = 29^2$
$n = 8: 5(21)^2 + 4(-1)^8 = 2209 = 47^2$
$n = 9: 5(34)^2 + 4(-1)^9 = 5776 = 76^2$
$n = 10: 5(55)^2 + 4(-1)^{10} = 15{,}129 = 123^2$

Section 1.3, page 29

1. 13; $u_n = 2n + 3$

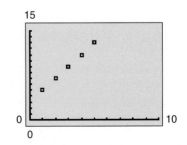

3. $5; u_n = \dfrac{n}{4} + \dfrac{15}{4}$

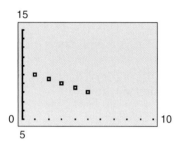

5. $8; u_n = -\dfrac{n}{2} + \dfrac{21}{2}$

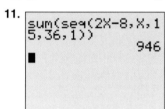

7. 45   **9.** 224

11.

```
sum(seq(2X-8,X,1
5,36,1))
            946
■
```

13. 87   **15.** $-\dfrac{21}{4}$ **17.** 30

19. $u_n - u_{n-1} = (3 - 2n) - [3 - 2(n - 1)] = -2$;
arithmetic with $d = -2$

21. $u_n - u_{n-1} = \dfrac{5 + 3n}{2} - \dfrac{5 + 3(n - 1)}{2} = \dfrac{3}{2}$;

arithmetic with $d = \dfrac{3}{2}$

23. $u_n - u_{n-1} = (c + 2n) - [c + 2(n - 1)] = 2$;
arithmetic with $d = 2$

25. $u_5 = 14; u_n = 2n + 4$

27. $u_5 = 25; u_n = 7n - 10$

29. $u_5 = 0; u_n = -\dfrac{15}{2} + \dfrac{3n}{2}$

31. 710   **33.** $156\dfrac{2}{3}$ **35.** 2550   **37.** 20,100

39. $77,500 in tenth year; $437,500 over ten years

41. 428   **43.** 23.25, 22.5, 21.75, 21, 20.25, 19.5, 18.75

Section 1.4, page 40

1. a. C **b.** B **c.** B **d.** D

3. Slope, 2; y-intercept, $b = 5$

5. Slope, $-\dfrac{3}{7}$; y-intercept, $b = -\dfrac{11}{7}$

7. Slope, $\dfrac{5}{2}$ **9.** Slope, 4   **11.** $t = 22$ **13.** $t = \dfrac{12}{5}$

15.

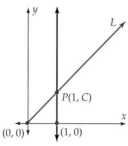

Slope of $L = \dfrac{C - 0}{1 - 0} = C$

17. $y = x + 2$ **19.** $y = -x + 8$ **21.** $y = -x - 5$

23. $y = -\dfrac{7}{3}x + \dfrac{34}{9}$ **25.** Perpendicular

27. Parallel   **29.** Parallel   **31.** Perpendicular

33. Yes. The slopes are $\dfrac{9}{8}, \dfrac{2}{5}$, and $-\dfrac{5}{2}$. Two sides
perpendicular result in a right triangle.

35. $y = 3x + 7$ **37.** $y = \dfrac{3}{2}x$ **39.** $y = x - 5$

41. $y = -x + 2$ **43.** $k = -\dfrac{11}{3}$

45. $u_n = u_1 + (n - 1)d$
$\qquad = -2 + (n - 1)4$
$u_n = 4n - 6$ or $y = 4x - 6$

47. The common difference is -6.
$u_n = u_1 + (n - 1)d$
$\qquad = 7 + (n - 1)(-6)$
$u_n = -6n + 13$ or $y = -6x + 13$

49. $u_n = u_1 + (n - 1)d$
$\qquad = -2 + (n - 1)8$
$u_n = 8n - 10$ or $y = 8x - 10$
The slope is $m = 8$ and the y-intercept is $b = -10$.

51. Both have slope $-\dfrac{A}{B}$ and different y-intercepts.

53. a. $y = 449x + 9287$
     b. $x = 9; y = $13,328$ (1990)
        $x = 24; y = $20,063$ (2005)

55. $375,000; $60,000

57. a. $y = 5x + 150$
     b. $x = -5, y = 125$ pounds (5 ft);
        $x = 7, y = 185$ pounds (6 ft)

59. a. $c(x) = 50x + 110,000$ **b.** $r(x) = 72x$
     c. $p(x) = 22x - 110,000$ **d.** $x = 5000$

61. a. $y = 8.50x + 50{,}000$ **b.** $11, $9.50, $9 per hat

63. a. $x = 10$ **b.** $x = 30$

Section 1.5, page 53

1. a. $y = \dfrac{3}{4}x + \dfrac{5}{4}$

   b. Sum of squares $= 3$

     Model B still has least error.

3. a. Slope $= 1.0564054$

   b. $y = 1.0564054x + 21.077892$

   c. Line described in **b** predicts a higher number of workers.

5. negative correlation

7. very little correlation

9. a. 0.09, 0.17, 1.22, 3.13, 5.14, 8.26

   b. not linear;

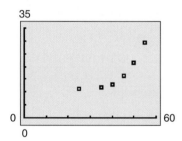

11. a. 4.6, 8.3, 14.3, 23.5, 37.2, 56.9, 84.3, 121.4, 170.7, 234.2

   b. not linear;

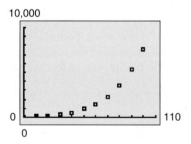

13. a. 446.9, 405.2, 515.8, 785.3, 298, 413

   b. linear; positive correlation

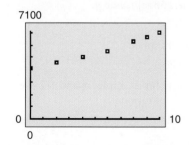

15. No High School Diploma

$y_2 = 12.31x + 238$

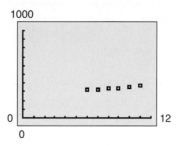

High School Graduate

$y_4 = 15.17x + 354$

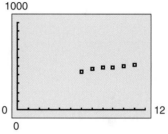

Some College

$y_1 = 20.74x + 392$

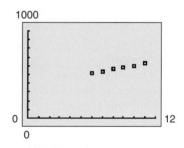

College Graduate

$y_3 = 34.86x + 543$

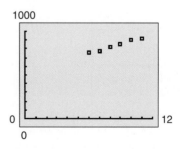

17. a. $y = -0.0292x + 4.0149$

   b. $y = 0.4078x + 16.8494$

   c. The income of the rich is increasing faster than the income of the poor is decreasing.

   d. The income gap will increase.

19. a. $y = -4x + 82$
b. The amount of federal money in loans is increasing and the amount in grants and work-study is decreasing.

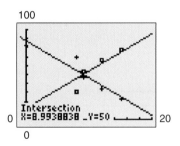

- ■ Loan data
- + Grant/work-study data
c. ≈1983

21. a.

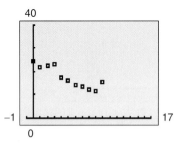

b. $y = -1.27x + 23.8318$
c. The model gives a negative median time for approval in 2005, and it will not be useful for data extrapolation.

23. a. $y = -0.08586x + 22.62286$
b. ≈14.72 for 1992, a terrific prediction.
c. This model may not remain valid for any future dates. The rate of improvement seems to be slowing down.
d. $r \approx -0.9797$
e. The data appears to be linear because the residuals do not form a pattern.

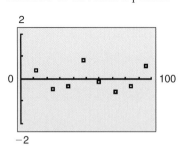

Section 1.6, page 63
1. Arithmetic   **3.** Geometric
5. Arithmetic   **7.** Geometric
9. $u_6 = 160; u_n = 2^{n-1} \cdot 5$
11. $u_6 = \dfrac{1}{256}; u_n = \dfrac{1}{4^{n-2}}$

13. $u_6 = -\dfrac{5}{16}; u_n = \dfrac{(-1)^{n-1} \cdot 5}{2^{n-2}}$

15. $\dfrac{315}{32}$ **17.** 381

19. $\dfrac{u_n}{u_{n-1}} = \dfrac{\left(-\dfrac{1}{2}\right)^n}{\left(-\dfrac{1}{2}\right)^{n-1}} = -\dfrac{1}{2}$; geometric with $r = -\dfrac{1}{2}$

21. $\dfrac{u_n}{u_{n-1}} = \dfrac{5^{n+2}}{5^{(n-1)+2}} = 5$; geometric with $r = 5$

23. $u_5 = 1; u_n = \dfrac{(-1)^{n-1}64}{4^{n-2}} = \dfrac{(-1)^{n-1}}{4^{n-5}}$

25. $u_5 = \dfrac{1}{16}; u_n = \dfrac{1}{4^{n-3}}$ **27.** $u_5 = -\dfrac{8}{25}; u_n = -\dfrac{2^{n-2}}{5^{n-3}}$

29. 254   **31.** $-\dfrac{4921}{19{,}683}$ **33.** $\dfrac{665}{8}$

35. a. Since for all n, the ratio r is
$$\dfrac{u_{n+1}}{u_n} = \dfrac{1.71(1.191^{n+1})}{1.71(1.191^n)} =$$
$$\dfrac{1.71(1.191^n)(1.191)}{1.71(1.191^n)} = 1.191,$$
the sequence is geometric.
b. $217.47

37. 23.75 ft

39. $\displaystyle\sum_{n=1}^{31} 2^{n-1} = \dfrac{1 - 2^{31}}{1 - 2} = (2^{31} - 1)$ cents $= $21,474,836.47$

41. $1898.44

43. $u_n = u_1 r^{n-1}$. $\log u_n = \log(u_1 r^{n-1}) = \log u_1 + \log(r^{n-1}) = \log u_1 + (n-1)\log r$

45. The sequence is $\{2^{n-1}\}$ and $r = 2$. So for any k, the kth term is 2^{k-1}, and the sum of the preceding terms is the $(k-1)$th partial sum of the sequence,
$$\sum_{n=1}^{k-1} 2^{n-1} = \dfrac{1 - 2^{k-1}}{1 - 2} = 2^{k-1} - 1.$$

47. 37 payments

Chapter 1 Review, page 67
1. $\sqrt{3}$ is an irrational number.
3. $e \approx 2.718$ is an irrational number.
5. 0 is a whole number.
7. $\sqrt{121}$ is a natural number.
9. 5 is a natural number.
11. Answers may vary; for example, π and $\sqrt{2}$ are real numbers that are not rational.
13. This is not a function; the input 2 has more than one output.
15. This is a function; for each input there is exactly one output.

17. all real numbers greater than or equal to 2 and not equal to 3

19. $r \geq 4$

21. a. $f(t) = 50\sqrt{t}$
   b. $g(t) = 2500\pi t$
   c. radius: 150 meters; area: 70,685.83 square meters
   d. 12.73 hr

23. $x \geq -3$ **25.** $x = 0$ and $4 \leq x \leq 5$

27. $-4 \leq x \leq 5$ **29.** 3 **31.** false

33. false **35.** \$1862.96. **37.** 12.5 cm

39. a. ≈ 1.618
   b. $1.618033989 \ldots$

41. $-4, -10, -28, -82, -244$ **43.** $u_n = 9 - 6n$

45. $u_n = 6n - 11$ **47.** 78

49.

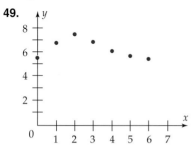

51. a. 1 **b.** $\dfrac{4}{5}$

53. $y = 3x - 7$

55. a. y-intercept is $\left(0, \dfrac{4}{3}\right)$; **b.** $y = \dfrac{5}{3}x + \dfrac{4}{3}$

57. $x - 5y = -29$ **59.** $m = 5$

61. true **63.** false

65. true **67. (d)** **69. (e)** **71.** $\dfrac{5}{3}$

73. a. $y = 0.25x + 62.9$ **b.** $x = 40, y = 72.9$ yrs.

75. c; $m = 75$ **77.** d; $m = 20$

79. a.

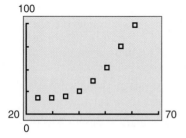

   b. Nonlinear

c. $20.10 - 19.58 = 0.52$ $20.79 - 20.10 = 0.69$
$25.23 - 20.79 = 4.44$ $34.89 - 25.23 = 9.66$
$48.55 - 34.89 = 13.66$ $69.17 - 48.55 = 20.62$
$98.92 - 69.17 = 29.75$
The finite differences show that the data is not linear.

81. a.

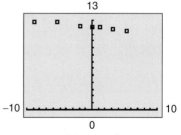

Managerial

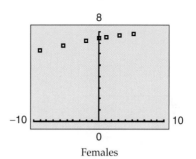

Females

Males

   b. Managerial, y_2 (negative slope, y-intercept at 11.74); Female, y_1 (positive slope, y-intercept at 7.34); Male, y_3 (negative slope, y-intercept at 15.48)

83. a. $y = 0.3654x + 10.6741$
   b. \$11.77, \$14.33; Both answers are close to actual amounts.
   c. \$15.79

85. $u_n = 2 \cdot 3^{n-1}$ **87.** $u_n = 384\left(\dfrac{1}{2}\right)^{n-1}$

89. -55 **91.** $\dfrac{315}{32}$

93. Second method is better.

Selected Answers

Chapter 1 can do calculus page 79

1. 1

2. $-\dfrac{3}{7}$

3. $\dfrac{0.06}{0.94} = \dfrac{3}{47}$

4. $\dfrac{2}{3}$

5. $\dfrac{500}{0.6} = 833\dfrac{1}{3}$

6. ≈ 5.7058

7. $4 + 2\sqrt{2}$

8. $\dfrac{1}{2}$

9. $\dfrac{2}{9}$

10. $\dfrac{37}{99}$

11. $\dfrac{597}{110}$

12. $\dfrac{8428}{99}$

13. $\dfrac{10{,}702}{4995}$

14. $\dfrac{18{,}564}{4995}$

15. Because there are infinitely many terms that are getting larger and larger, the sum cannot converge to a finite number.

16. The sum approaches $-\dfrac{1}{3}$.

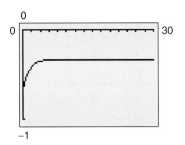

Chapter 2

Section 2.1, page 87

1. 3

3. 3

5. 2

7. $x \approx -2.426$

9. $x \approx -1.453,\ 1.164$

11. $x \approx -1.475,\ 1.237$

13. $x = 0,\ x \approx -1.750,\ 1.192$

15. $x \approx -1.379,\ 1.603$

17. $x \approx -1.601,\ 0.507,\ 1.329$

19. $x \approx -2.115,\ 0.254,\ 1.861$

21. $x \approx 2.102$

23. $x \approx -1.752$

25. $x \approx 0.951$

27. $x = 0,\ x \approx 2.207$

29. $x \approx 2.390$

31. $x \approx -0.651,\ 1.151$

33. $x \approx 7.033$

35. $x = \dfrac{2}{3}$

37. $x = \dfrac{1}{12}$

39. $x = \sqrt{3}$

41. 2004

43. 1999

Section 2.2, page 95

1. $x = 3$ or 5

3. $x = -2$ or 7

5. $y = \dfrac{1}{2}$ or -3

7. $t = -2$ or $-\dfrac{1}{4}$

9. $u = 1$ or $-\dfrac{4}{3}$

11. $x = \dfrac{1}{4}$ or $-\dfrac{4}{3}$

13. $x^2 = 9;\ x = \pm 3$

15. $x^2 = 40;\ x = \pm\sqrt{40} \approx \pm 6.325$

17. $3x^2 = 12;\ x^2 = 4;\ x = \pm 2$

19. $-5s^2 = -30;\ s^2 = 6;\ s = \pm\sqrt{6} \approx \pm 2.449$

21. $25x^2 - 4 = 0;\ x^2 = \dfrac{4}{25};\ x = \pm\dfrac{2}{5}$

23. $-3w^2 + 8 = -20;\ w^2 = \dfrac{28}{3};\ w = \pm\sqrt{\dfrac{28}{3}} \approx \pm 3.055$

25. $x = 1 \pm \sqrt{13}$

27. $w = \dfrac{(1 + \sqrt{5})}{2}$ or $\dfrac{(1 - \sqrt{5})}{2}$

29. $x = 2 \pm \sqrt{3}$

31. $x = -3 \pm \sqrt{2}$

33. No real number solutions

35. $x = \dfrac{1}{2} \pm \sqrt{2}$

37. $x = \dfrac{2 \pm \sqrt{3}}{2}$

39. $u = \dfrac{-4 \pm \sqrt{6}}{5}$

41. 2

43. 2

45. 1

47. $x = -3$ or -6

49. $x = \dfrac{-1 \pm \sqrt{2}}{2}$

51. $x = 5$ or $-\dfrac{3}{2}$

53. No real number solutions

55. No real number solutions

57. $x \approx 1.824$ or 0.470

59. $x = 13.79$

61. $y = \pm 1$ or $\pm\sqrt{6}$

63. $x = \pm\sqrt{7}$

65. $y = \pm 2$ or $\pm\dfrac{1}{\sqrt{2}}$

67. $x = \pm\dfrac{1}{\sqrt{5}}$

69. $k = 10$ or -10

71. $k = 16$

73. $k = 4$

Section 2.3, page 105

1. The two numbers: x and y; their sum is 15: $x + y = 15$; the difference of their squares is 5: $x^2 - y^2 = 5$.

3.

English Language	Mathematical Language
Length of rectangle	x
Width of rectangle	y
Perimeter is 45	$x + y + x + y = 45$ or $2x + 2y = 45$
Area is 112.5	$xy = 112.5$

5. Let x be the old salary. Then the raise is 8% of x. Hence,

$$\text{old salary} + \text{raise} = \$1600$$
$$x + (8\% \text{ of } x) = 1600$$
$$x + 0.08x = 1600.$$

7. The circle has radius $r = \dfrac{16}{2} = 8$, so its area is $\pi r^2 = \pi \cdot 8^2 = 64\pi$. Let x be the amount by which the radius is to be reduced. Then $r = 8 - x$ and the new area is $\pi(8 - x)^2$, which must be 48π less than the original area, that is, $\pi(8 - x)^2 = 64\pi - 48\pi$, or equivalently, $\pi(8 - x)^2 = 16\pi$.

9. \$366.67 at 12% and \$733.33 at 6%

11. $2\frac{2}{3}$ qt   **13.** 65 mph

15. 34.75 and 48   **17.** Approximately 1.75 ft

19. Red Riding Hood, 54 mph; wolf, 48 mph

21. a. ≈ 6.3 sec   **b.** ≈ 4.9 sec

23. a. Approximately 4.4 sec   **b.** After 50 sec

25. 23 cm by 24 cm by 25 cm   **27.** $r = 4.658$

29. $x = 2.234$ **31.** 2.2 by 4.4 by 4 ft high

Section 2.4, page 116

1. $|y - 2| = 4$

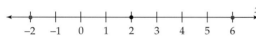

$y = -2, 6$

3. $|3w - 2| = 8$

Since $3w = -6$ or 10, dividing by 3, $w = -2, 3\frac{1}{3}$.

5. $|-2x - 4| = 5$

Since $-2x = -1$ or 9, dividing by -2, $x = \frac{1}{2}, -\frac{9}{2}$.

7. $|-3x - (-2)| = 5$ or $|-3x + 2| = 5$

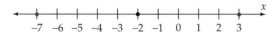

Since $-3x = -7$ or 3, dividing by -3, $x = \frac{7}{3}, -1$.

9. $x = -6$ or 3   **11.** $x = \frac{3}{2}$ **13.** $x = 2$

15. $x = \frac{3}{2}$ **17.** $x = -5$ or 1 or -3 or -1

19. $x = 1$ or 4 or $\frac{5 + \sqrt{33}}{2}$ or $\frac{5 - \sqrt{33}}{2}$

21. For any real number x, the distance between $2x^2$ and $-3x$ cannot be a negative number. Therefore, $|2x^2 + 3x| = -12$ has no real number solution.

23. Let x = Joan's ideal body weight. The difference between Joan's actual weight and her ideal weight is $x - 120$.

Therefore, $|x - 120| = 0.05x$.
$$x - 120 = 0.05x \text{ or } x - 120 = -0.05x$$
$$0.95x = 120 \qquad 1.05x = 120$$
$$x \approx 126.3 \qquad x \approx 114.3$$
To the nearest pound, Joan's ideal weight is either 114 pounds or 126 pounds.

25. If the true wind speed differs by 5 feet per second from the measured speed, let x = true wind speed and $|x - 20| = 5$
$$x - 20 = -5 \qquad \text{or} \qquad x - 20 = 5$$
$$x = 15 \qquad \text{or} \qquad x = 25$$
The true wind speed is between 15 and 25 feet per second.

27. $CL \approx -0.0097 = 0$ (in practice) and ≈ 0.0497

29. $x = 4$ **31.** $x = -2$ **33.** $x = \pm3$

35. $x = -1$ or 2   **37.** $x = 9$ **39.** $x = \frac{1}{2}$

41. $x = \frac{1}{2}$ or -4 **43.** $x \approx \pm0.73$

45. $x \approx -1.17$ or 2.59 or $x = -1$ **47.** $x \approx 1.658$

49. $x = 6$ **51.** $x = 3$ or 7   **53.** No solutions

55. $x \approx -0.457$ or 1.40   **57.** $x = 7$

59. $x = \frac{3 \pm \sqrt{41}}{4}$ **61.** $x = 1$ **63.** $x = -1$

65. $u = \sqrt{\dfrac{x^2}{1 - K^2}}$ **67.** $b = \sqrt{\dfrac{a^2}{A^2 - 1}}$

69. a. $I = \dfrac{x}{(x^2 + 1024)^{\frac{3}{2}}}$ **b.** 22.63 ft

Section 2.5, page 124

1. $x \geq 0$ **3.** $c \leq 3$

5.
```
   -2    0    2    4    6    8
```

7.
```
   -3 -2 -1  0  1  2  3
```

9.
```
        -4    -2    0  1
```

11. $[5, 8]$ **13.** $(-3, 14)$ **15.** $[-8, \infty)$

17. $\left(-\infty, \dfrac{3}{2}\right]$ **19.** $(-2, \infty)$ **21.** $\left(-\infty, -\dfrac{8}{5}\right]$

23. $(1, \infty)$ **25.** $(2, 4)$ **27.** $\left[-3, \dfrac{5}{2}\right)$

29. $\left(-\infty, \dfrac{4}{7}\right)$ **31.** $\left[-\dfrac{7}{17}, \infty\right)$ **33.** $\left[-1, \dfrac{1}{8}\right)$

35. $[5, \infty)$ **37.** $x < \dfrac{b + c}{a}$

39. $c < x < a + c$ **41.** $1 \leq x \leq 3$

43. $x \le \dfrac{-9 - \sqrt{21}}{2}$ or $x \ge \dfrac{-9 + \sqrt{21}}{2}$

45. $x \le \dfrac{1 - \sqrt{33}}{2}$ or $x \ge \dfrac{1 + \sqrt{33}}{2}$

47. $-1 \le x \le 0$ or $x \ge 1$

49. $x < -1$ or $0 < x < 3$

51. $-2 < x < -1$ or $1 < x < 2$

53. $-2.26 \le x \le 0.76$ or $x \ge 3.51$

55. $0.5 < x < 0.84$ **57.** $x < -\dfrac{1}{3}$ or $x > 2$

59. $-2 < x < -1$ or $1 < x < 3$

61. $x > 1$ **63.** $x \le -\dfrac{9}{2}$ or $x > -3$

65. $-3 < x < 1$ or $x \ge 5$

67. $-\sqrt{7} < x < \sqrt{7}$ or $x > 5.34$

69. $x < -3$ or $\dfrac{1}{2} < x < 5$

71. $x > -1.43$ **73.** $x \le -3.79$ or $x \ge 0.79$

75. Approximately 8.608 cents per kwh

77. More than \$12,500 **79.** Between \$4000 and \$5400

81. $1 < x < 19$ and $y = 20 - x$

83. $10 < x < 35$ **85.** $1 \le t \le 4$ **87.** $2 < t < 2.25$

Section 2.5.A, page 131

1. $-\dfrac{4}{3} \le x \le 0$ **3.** $\dfrac{7}{6} < x < \dfrac{11}{6}$

5. $x < -2$ or $x > -1$ **7.** $x \le -\dfrac{11}{20}$ or $x \ge -\dfrac{1}{4}$

9. $x < -\dfrac{53}{40}$ or $x > -\dfrac{43}{40}$ **11.** $x \le -\dfrac{7}{2}$ or $x \ge -\dfrac{5}{4}$

13. $x < -5$ or $-5 < x < -\dfrac{4}{3}$ or $x > 6$

15. $-\dfrac{1}{7} < x < 3$

17. $-\sqrt{3} < x < -1$ or $1 < x < \sqrt{3}$

19. $x < -\sqrt{6}$ or $x > \sqrt{6}$

21. $x \le -2$ or $-1 \le x \le 0$ or $x \ge 1$

23. $0 < x < \dfrac{2}{3}$ or $2 < x < \dfrac{8}{3}$

25. $-1.43 < x < 1.24$ **27.** $x < -0.89$ or $x > 1.56$

29. $x \le 2$ or $x \ge \dfrac{14}{3}$

31. $-1.13 < x < 1.35$ or $1.35 < x < 1.67$

33. If $|x - 3| < \dfrac{E}{5}$, then multiplying both sides by 5

shows that $5|x - 3| < E$. But
$5|x - 3| = |5| \cdot |x - 3| = |5(x - 3)| =$

$|5x - 15| = |(5x - 4) - 11|$. Thus,
$|(5x - 4) - 11| < E$.

Chapter 2 Review, page 135

1. $x = 2.7644$ **3.** $x = 3.2678$

5. $x = -3.2843$ **7.** $x = 1.6511$

9. No real solutions **11.** $z = \dfrac{-3 \pm 2\sqrt{11}}{5}$

13. $x = 3$ or -3 or $\sqrt{2}$ or $-\sqrt{2}$ **15.** 2

17. gold, $\dfrac{3}{11}$ oz; silver, $\dfrac{8}{11}$ oz

19. $2\dfrac{2}{9}$ hrs **21.** 9.6 ft **23.** 4 ft

25. 25 **27.** $(b - 1)^2$ **29.** $x = -\dfrac{1}{2}$ or $-\dfrac{11}{2}$

31. $|3x - 1| = 4$

$\qquad 3x - 1 = 4$ or $3x - 1 = -4$

$\qquad\qquad 3x = 5 \qquad\qquad 3x = -3$

$\qquad\qquad\quad x = \dfrac{5}{3} \qquad\qquad\quad x = -1$

33. $\sqrt{x^2 - x - 2} = 0$

Squaring both sides,

$\qquad x^2 - x - 2 = 0$

$\qquad (x - 2)(x + 1) = 0$

$\qquad\qquad\qquad\quad x = 2, -1$

Both of these check in the original equation.

35. $\dfrac{x^2 - 6x + 8}{x - 1} = 0$

Set the numerator equal to 0.

$\qquad x^2 - 6x + 8 = 0$

$\qquad (x - 2)(x - 4) = 0$

$\qquad\qquad\qquad\quad x = 2, 4$

Neither solution causes the denominator to be 0.

37. $x = \dfrac{5 - \sqrt{5}}{2}$ **39.** No solutions

41. a. $(-8, \infty)$ **b.** $(-\infty, 5]$ **43.** $\left[\dfrac{7}{4}, \infty\right)$

45. $(-\infty, -2)$ and $\left(-\dfrac{1}{3}, \infty\right)$

47. $x \le -1$ or $0 \le x \le 1$ **49.** e

51. $\left[-4, -\dfrac{5}{8}\right)$ **53.** $x \le -7$ or $x > -4$

55. $x < -2\sqrt{3}$ or $-3 < x < 2\sqrt{3}$

57. $x < \dfrac{1 - \sqrt{13}}{6}$ or $x > \dfrac{1 + \sqrt{13}}{6}$

59. $y \le -17$ or $y \ge 13$

61. $x \le -\dfrac{4}{3}$ or $x \ge 0$

Selected Answers

1. *Numerical Method*

a. Each base must be greater than 0 and less than 10 yards. The *nr* in the chart indicates that no rectangle can be formed with a base length of 5 yards or more because the opposite bases of a rectangle are the same length, and, since $5 + 5 = 10$, there would be no wire left to make the sides of a rectangle.

b.

length	1 yd	1.5 yd	2 yd	2.5 yd	3 yd	3.5 yd	4 yd	4.5 yd	5 yd	5.5 yd
height	4 yd	3.5 yd	3 yd	2.5 yd	2 yd	1.5 yd	1 yd	0.5 yd	*nr*	*nr*
area	4 yd^2	5.25 yd^2	6 yd^2	6.25 yd^2	6 yd^2	5.25 yd^2	4 yd^2	2.25 yd^2	—	—

c.

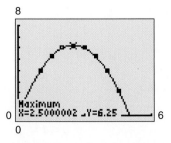

d. The maximum area 6.25 yd^2 appears to occur when the base length is 2.5 yd.

Analytical and Graphical Method

$$2l + 2w = 10$$
$$2w = 10 - 2l$$
$$w = 5 - l$$

$$A = l \times w$$
$$A = l(5 - l)$$
$$A = 5l - l^2$$
$$A = -l^2 + 5l$$

Using the maximum finder on a graphing calculator indicates that the maximum area of 6.25 yd^2 occurs at approximately 2.5 yd.

2. *Numerical Method*

a. The base must be greater than 0 and less than 6 units. The *nr* in the table indicates that no rectangle can be formed with a base of 6 or more units because $y = \sqrt{36 - x^2}$ would not exist if $x > 6$.

b.

x	1	2	3	4	5	6
y	5.92	5.66	5.20	4.47	3.32	*nr*
area	5.92	11.32	15.6	17.88	16.6	—

c.

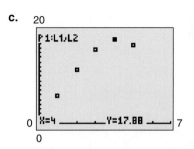

d. A maximum area 17.88 square units appears to occur when x is 4.

Analytical and Graphical Method

$$y = \sqrt{36 - x^2}$$

$$A = x \times y$$
$$A = x \times \sqrt{36 - x^2}$$

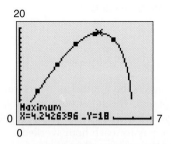

Using the maximum finder on a graphing calculator indicates that the maximum area of 18 square units occurs when x is approximately 4.24.

3. *Numerical Method*

a. The base must be greater than 0 and less than 4 units. The *nr* in the table indicates that no rectangle with a base of 4 or more units because $y \leq 0$ if $x \geq 4$.

Selected Answers

b.

x	0.5	1.0	1.5	2.0	2.5	3.0	3.5	4.0
y	1.75	1.5	1.25	1	0.75	0.5	0.25	nr
area	0.875	1.5	1.875	2.0	1.875	1.5	0.875	—

c.

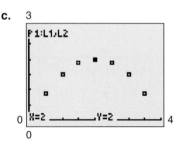

d. A maximum area of 2 square units appears to occur at $x = 2$.

Analytical and Graphing Method

$$A = x \times y$$

$$y = \frac{(4 - x)}{2} \qquad A = x \times \frac{(4 - x)}{2}$$

$$A = \frac{4x - x^2}{2}$$

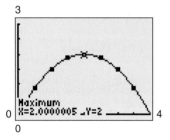

Using the maximum finder on a graphing calculator indicates that the maximum area is 2 when x is approximately 2.

Chapter 3

Section 3.1, page 148

1. The set of inputs is the number of hours you work in each pay period. The set of outputs is the amounts of your paychecks. The function rule is the amount of pay for each hour worked multiplied by the number of hours worked.

3. The set of inputs is temperatures of gas. The set of outputs is pressures of gas. The function rule is the formula $P = \frac{k}{T}$.

5. y is a function of x.

7. y is not a function of x.

9. y is a function of x.

11. y is not a function of x.   **13.** $\sqrt{3} + 1 \approx 2.73$

15. $\sqrt{\sqrt{2} + 3} - \sqrt{2} + 1 \approx 1.69$

17. 4   **19.** $\dfrac{34}{3}$ **21.** $\dfrac{59}{12}$

23. $(a + k)^2 + \dfrac{1}{a + k} + 2$

25. $(2 - x)^2 + \dfrac{1}{2 - x} + 2 = 6 - 4x + x^2 + \dfrac{1}{2 - x}$

27. 8   **29.** -1 **31.** $(s + 1)^2 - 1 = s^2 + 2s$

33. $t^2 - 1$ **35.** 1   **37.** 3

39. $-2x - h + 1$ **41.** $\dfrac{1}{\sqrt{x + h} + \sqrt{x}}$

43. All real numbers   **45.** All real numbers

47. All nonnegative real numbers

49. All nonzero real numbers

51. All real numbers

53. All real numbers except -2 and 3

55. $[6, 12]$

57. a. $f(0) = [0]$; the greatest integer less than or equal to 0 is 0.
b. $f(1.6) = [1.6] = 1$
c. $f(-2.3) = [-2.3] = -3$
d. $f(5 - 2\pi) = [5 - 2\pi] \approx [-1.283] = -2$
e. The domain of f is all real numbers.

59. a. $f(0) = 0$ **b.** $f(1.6) = 5.76$
c. $f(-2.3) = 0.69$ **d.** $f(5 - 2\pi) \approx -0.920$
e. The domain of f is all real numbers ≤ 20.

61. a. $f(0) = -5$ **b.** $f(1.6) = -3.4$
c. $f(-2.3) = -7.6$ **d.** $f(5 - 2\pi) \approx -5.566$
e. The domain of f is all real numbers.

63. a. $A = \pi r^2$ **b.** $A = \dfrac{1}{4}\pi d^2$

65. $V = 4x^3$

67. a. $C(x) = 5.75x + \dfrac{45,000}{x}$
b. The domain is $x > 0$.

69. a. Let t be the number of hours since he started

$$d(t) = \begin{cases} 3t & 0 \leq t \leq \dfrac{3}{4} \\ 2.25 + 5\left(t - \dfrac{3}{4}\right) & \dfrac{3}{4} < t \leq 2 \\ 8.5 & 2 < t \leq 2.5 \\ 8.5 + 3(t - 2.5) & 2.5 < t \leq 4 \end{cases}$$

b. The domain is t such that $0 \leq t \leq 4$.

71. Let x = amount of annual income and $f(x)$ = amount of tax.

$$f(x) = \begin{cases} 0 & \text{if } x < 2000 \\ 0.02(x - 2000) & \text{if } 2000 \leq x \leq 6000 \\ 80 + 0.05(x - 6000) & \text{if } x > 6000 \end{cases}$$

The domain is $x \geq 0$.

1. $f(-5) = 7$

3. The domain is $[-6, 9]$.

5. $g(1) = 2$

7. The domain is $[-7, 8]$.

9. This is not a function; for example, there are three output values for an input value of 4.

11. This is not a function; for example, there are three output values for an input value of 2.

13. This is a function.

15. Increasing on $(-2.5, 0)$ and $(1.7, 4)$; decreasing on $(-6, -2.5)$ and $(0, 1.7)$

17. Constant on $(-\infty, -1]$ and $[1, \infty)$; decreasing on $(-1, 1)$.

19. Increasing on $(-5.8, 0.5)$; decreasing on $(-\infty, -5.8)$ and $(0.5, \infty)$

21. Increasing on $(0, 0.867)$ and $(2.883, \infty)$; decreasing on $(-\infty, 0)$ and $(0.867, 2.883)$

23. Minimum at $x = 0.57735$; maximum at $x = -0.57735$

25. Minimum at $x = -1$; maximum at $x = 1$

27. Minimum at $x = 0.7633$; maximum at $x = 0.4367$

29. a. $A(x) = 50x - x^2$
    b. To maximize area each side should be 25 in. long.

31. a. $SA(x) = 2x^2 + \dfrac{3468}{x}$
    b. Base is approximately 9.5354 in. × 9.5354 in.; height is same (that is, 9.5354 in.).

33.

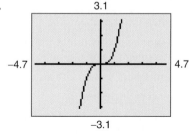

This function is concave up over the interval $(0, \infty)$ and concave down over the interval $(-\infty, 0)$. Therefore, the point of inflection is at $(0, 0)$.

35.

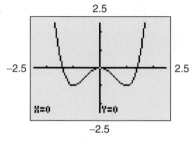

The function is concave up over the approximate intervals $(-\infty, -0.6)$ and $(0.6, \infty)$ and concave down over the approximate interval $(-0.6, 0.6)$.

Therefore, the points of inflection are approximately at $(-0.6, -0.6)$ and $(0.6, -0.6)$.

37. a.

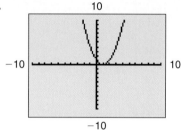

b. This function is increasing over the interval $(1, \infty)$ and decreasing over the interval $(-\infty, 1)$.
c. There is a local minimum at the point $(1, 0)$.
d. This function is concave up over the interval $(-\infty, \infty)$.
e. There is no point of inflection.

39. a.

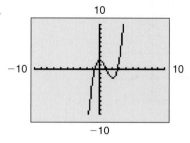

b. This function is increasing over the intervals $(-\infty, 0)$ and $(2, \infty)$ and decreasing over the interval $(0, 2)$.
c. There is a local maximum at the point $(0, 2)$ and a local minimum at the point $(2, -2)$.
d. This function is concave upward over the interval $(1, \infty)$ and concave downward over the interval $(-\infty, 1)$.
e. There is a point of inflection at $(1, 0)$.

41.

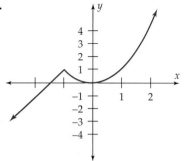

43.

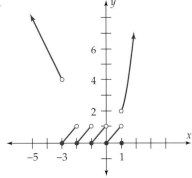

45. a. $f(x) = \begin{cases} x + 2 & x \geq 0 \\ -x + 2 & x < 0 \end{cases}$

b.

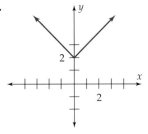

47. a. $h(x) = \begin{cases} \dfrac{x}{2} - 2 & x \geq 0 \\ -\dfrac{x}{2} - 2 & x < 0 \end{cases}$

b.

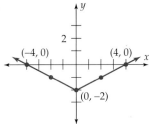

49. a. $f(x) = \begin{cases} x - 5 & x \geq 5 \\ 5 - x & x < 5 \end{cases}$

b.

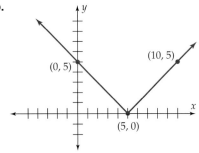

51.

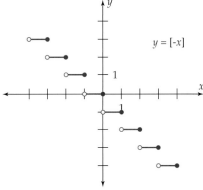

$y = [-x]$

53.

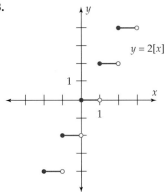

$y = 2[x]$

55. When $0 \leq x \leq 2$, x is positive and $x - 2$ is negative, so $|x| = x$ and $|x - 2| = -(x - 2)$. Therefore, $|x| + |x - 2| = x - (x - 2) = x - x + 2 = 2$ when $0 \leq x \leq 2$.

57. Domain: all real numbers x such that $x \leq -2$ or $x \geq 2$; range: all nonnegative real numbers

59. Domain: all real numbers; range: all real numbers

61. Many correct answers, including

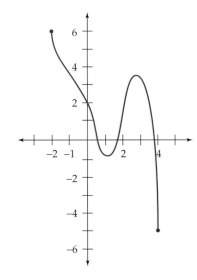

63. Entire graph:

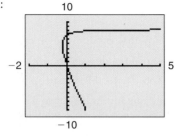

near the origin:

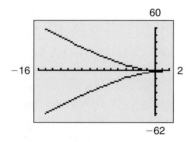

65. Entire graph:

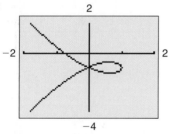

near the origin:

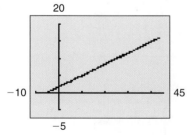

67.

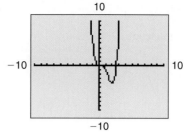

69.

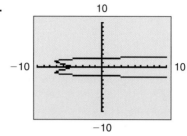

$x = t, y = t^4 - 3t^3 + t^2$

71.

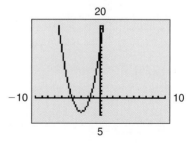

$x = t^4 - 3t^2 - 5, y = t$

Section 3.3, page 170

1. $(5, 2)$, upward   **3.** $(1, 2)$, downward

5. y-intercept $= 3$ The parabola opens upward.

7. y-intercept $= 5$ The parabola opens downward.

9. The x-intercepts are $x = 2$ and $x = -3$. The parabola opens upward.

11. The x-intercepts are $x = \dfrac{3}{4}$ and $x = \dfrac{1}{2}$. The parabola opens upward.

13. Vertex is $(-3, -4)$.
y-intercept $= 14$.
The x-intercepts are $x = -3 + \sqrt{2}$, $x = -3 - \sqrt{2}$ or $x \approx -1.586, -4.414$.

15. Vertex is $(-1, 4)$.
y-intercept $= 5$
there are no x-intercepts.

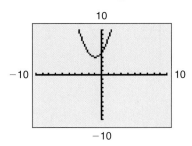

17. Vertex is $(4, 14)$
y-intercept $= -2$.
The x-intercepts are at approximately 0.258 and 7.742.

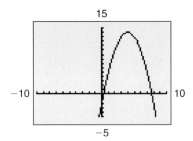

19. Vertex is $(1, -4)$.
y-intercept $= -3$.
The x-intercepts are -1 and 3.

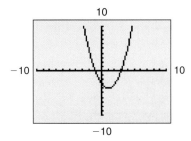

21. Vertex is $(-0.5, -24.5)$.
y-intercept is -24.
The x-intercepts are 3 and -4.

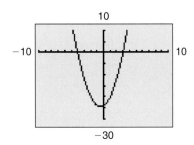

23. $g(x) = -2x^2 + 14x - 20$

1072 **Answers to Selected Exercises**

25. $f(x) = -\frac{1}{2}x^2 - 4x - 13$

27. $h(x) = -(2x + 1)(x - 7)$

29. $f(x) = 2(3x - 1)(x - 1)$

31. $f(x) = -3(x - 1)^2 + 2$

33. $g(x) = 2\left(x + \frac{5}{2}\right)^2 - \frac{49}{2}$

35. $f(x) = -2x^2 + 1$ **37.** $b = -4, c = 8$

39. $b = 0$ **41.** $a = -\frac{1}{2}$

43. Minimum product is -4; numbers are 2 and -2

45. Two 50-ft sides and one 100-ft side

47. $3.50   **49.** 30 salespeople   **51.** 1 second; 22 ft

53. The maximum height of 35,156.25 feet is reached 46.875 seconds after the bullet is fired.

Section 3.4, page 182

1. $f(x) = x^3$ **3.** $f(x) = 1$ **5.** $g(x) = \frac{1}{x}$

7. $h(x) = [x]$ **9.** $h(x) = x^2$

11.

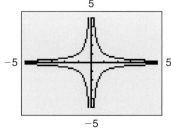

$h(x) = -\frac{1}{x}, h(x) = \frac{1}{x}$

13.

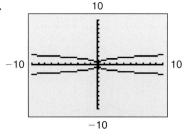

$h(x) = \sqrt[3]{-x}, h(x) = \sqrt[3]{x}$

15.

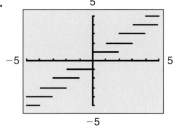

$g(x) = [x] + 1, g(x) = [x]$

17.

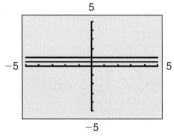

$$h(x) = |x - 2|, h(x) = |x|$$

19.

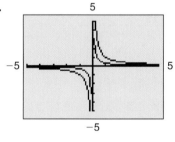

$$f(x) = \frac{1}{2}, f(x) = 1$$

21.

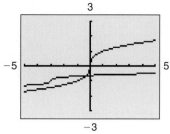

$$h(x) = \frac{1}{3x}, h(x) = \frac{1}{x}$$

23. $g(x) = -\sqrt{x} + 3$

25. $g(x) = -\dfrac{1}{2}|x + 3|$ **27.** $g(x) = 1.5(-x + 3)^2$

29. Shift the graph 4 units to the right and 1 unit upward; reflect the graph across the x-axis, and stretch it vertically by a factor of 3.

31. Reflect the graph across the y-axis, shift it 2 units to the left, stretch vertically by a factor of 4, and shift 3 units downward.

33. Compress the graph horizontally by a factor of $\dfrac{1}{1.3}$, shift it ≈ 3.23 units to the right, and shift 0.4 units upward.

35.

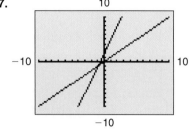

$$g(x) = \frac{1}{4}\sqrt[3]{x + 3} - 1, g(x) = \sqrt[3]{x}$$

37.

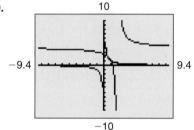

$$h(x) = 3(x - 1) + 5, y = x$$

39.

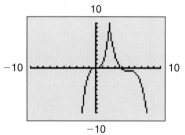

$$f(x) = \frac{-3}{2 - x} + 4, f(x) = \frac{1}{x}$$

41.

$$g(x) = \frac{2}{5}(5 - x)^3 - \frac{3}{5}, g(x) = x^3$$

43.

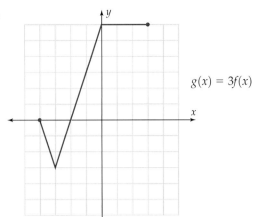

$g(x) = 3f(x)$

45.

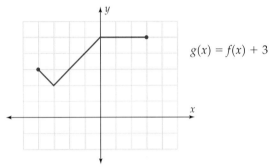

$g(x) = f(x) + 3$

47.

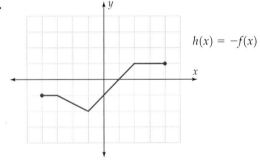

$h(x) = -f(x)$

49.

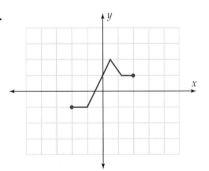

$h(x) = f(-2x)$

51.

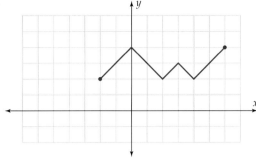

$g(x) = f(x - 2) + 3$

53.

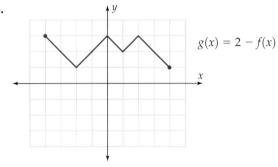

$g(x) = 2 - f(x)$

55.

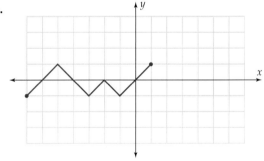

$g(x) = f(x + 3)$

57.

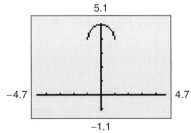

$g(x) = \sqrt{1 - x^2} + 4$

59.

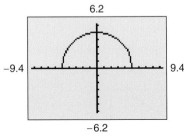

$g(x) = 3\sqrt{1 - x^2}$

61.

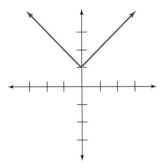

$g(x) = 5\sqrt{1 - \left(\dfrac{1}{5}x\right)^2}$

63. a. Shifts upward by 28 units
b. The graph is stretched vertically by a factor of 1.00012.

Section 3.4.A, page 189

1. Symmetric with respect to the y-axis

3. The graph does not have symmetry with respect to the x-axis, y-axis, or origin. However, it is symmetric with respect to the point $(0, 2)$.

5. $y = \dfrac{\sqrt[3]{x}}{x^2}$ Symmetric with respect to the origin.

7. Yes   **9.** Yes   **11.** Yes

13. No   **15.** Yes   **17.** Yes

19. Origin   **21.** Origin   **23.** y-axis   **25.** Odd

27. Even   **29.** Even   **31.** Even   **33.** Neither

35.

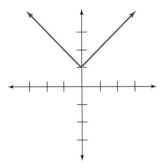

37.

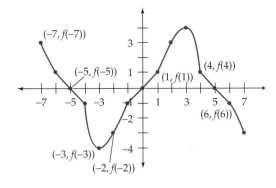

39. Many correct graphs, including the one shown here:

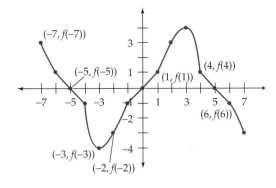

41. Suppose the graph is symmetric to the x-axis and the y-axis. If (x, y) is on the graph, then $(x, -y)$ is on the graph by x-axis symmetry. Hence, $(-x, -y)$ is on the graph by y-axis symmetry. Therefore, (x, y) on the graph implies that $(-x, -y)$ is on the graph, so the graph is symmetric with respect to the origin. Next suppose that the graph is symmetric to the y-axis and the origin. If (x, y) is on the graph, then $(-x, y)$ is on the graph by y-axis symmetry. Hence, $(-(-x), -y) = (x, -y)$ is on the graph by origin symmetry. Therefore, (x, y) on the graph implies that $(x, -y)$ is on the graph, so the graph is symmetric with respect to the x-axis. The proof of the third case is similar to that of the second case.

Section 3.5, page 196

1. $(f + g)(x) = x^3 - 3x + 2$;
$(f - g)(x) = -x^3 - 3x + 2$;
$(g - f)(x) = x^3 + 3x - 2$; domain for each is all real numbers

3. $(f + g)(x) = \dfrac{1}{x} + x^2 + 2x - 5$; $(f - g)(x) = \dfrac{1}{x} - x^2 - 2x + 5$; $(g - f)(x) = x^2 + 2x - 5 - \dfrac{1}{x}$; domain for each is all real numbers except 0

5. $(fg)(x) = -3x^4 + 2x^3$;
$\left(\dfrac{f}{g}\right)(x) = \dfrac{-3x + 2}{x^3}$; $\left(\dfrac{g}{f}\right)(x) = \dfrac{x^3}{-3x + 2}$

7. $(fg)(x) = x^2\sqrt{x-3} - 3\sqrt{x-3}$

$$\left(\frac{f}{g}\right)(x) = \frac{x^2 - 3}{\sqrt{x-3}}$$

$$\left(\frac{g}{f}\right)(x) = \frac{\sqrt{x-3}}{x^2 - 3}$$

9. Domain of fg: all real numbers except 0; domain of $\frac{f}{g}$: all real numbers except 0

11. The domain of fg is $\left[-\frac{4}{3}, 2\right]$. The domain of $\frac{f}{g}$ is $\left(-\frac{4}{3}, 2\right]$.

13. 49; 1; -8 **15.** -3; -3; 0   **17.** 1   **19.** 30

21. $(f \circ g)(x) = (x+3)^2$; $(g \circ f)(x) = x^2 + 3$; domain of $f \circ g$ and $g \circ f$ is all real numbers.

23. $(f \circ g)(x) = \frac{1}{\sqrt{x}}$; $(g \circ f)(x) = \frac{1}{\sqrt{x}}$; domain of $f \circ g$ and $g \circ f$ is $(0, \infty)$.

25. $(ff)(x) = x^6$; $(f \circ f)(x) = x^9$

27. $(ff)(x) = \frac{1}{x^2}$; $(f \circ f)(x) = x$

29. $(f \circ g)(x) = f\left(\frac{x-2}{9}\right) = 9\left(\frac{x-2}{9}\right) + 2 = x$ and

$(g \circ f)(x) = g(9x+2) = \frac{(9x+2)-2}{9} = x$

31. $(f \circ g)(x) = f(x-2)^3 = \sqrt[3]{(x-2)^3} + 2 = x$ and
$(g \circ f)(x) = g(\sqrt[3]{x} + 2) = (\sqrt[3]{x} + 2 - 2)^3 = x$

33. $f(x) = (B \circ A)(x)$, where $A(x) = x^2 + 2$, $B(x) = \sqrt[3]{x}$

35. $h(x) = (B \circ A)(x)$, where $A(x) = 7x^3 - 10x + 17$, $B(x) = x^7$

37. $f(x) = (B \circ A)(x)$, where $A(x) = 3x^2 + 5x - 7$, $B(x) = \frac{1}{x}$

39.

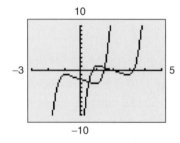

41.

x	1	2	3	4	5
$(g \circ f)(x)$	4	2	5	4	4

43.

x	1	2	3	4	5
$(f \circ f)(x)$	1	3	3	5	1

45.

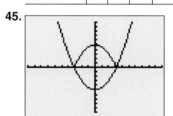

$f(x) = 0.5x^2 - 5$, $g \circ f = |f(x)| = |0.5x^2 - 5|$

47.

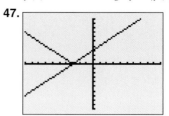

$f(x) = x + 3$, $g \circ f = |f(x)| = |x + 3|$

49. a. $(g \circ f)(x) = |f(x)|$ By the definition of absolute value,

$$|f(x)| = \begin{cases} f(x) & \text{if } f(x) \geq 0 \\ -f(x) & \text{if } f(x) < 0 \end{cases}$$

b. When $f(x) \geq 0$ the graph of $g \circ f$ is the same as the graph of f. When $f(x) < 0$, the graph of f is below the x-axis, but the graph of $-f$ is the reflection of f across the x-axis; therefore, the graph will be above the x-axis.

51.

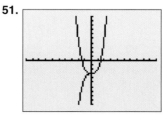

$y_1 = x^3 - 3$, $y_2 = f \circ g = f(|x|) = |x|^3 - 3$

53.

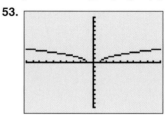

$y_1 = \sqrt{x-1}$, $y_2 = f \circ g = f(|x|) = \sqrt{|x|} - 1$

55. $f \circ I = I \circ f = f$

57. a. $f(x^2) = 2x^6 + 5x^2 - 1$
  b. $(f(x))^2 = (2x^3 + 5x - 1)^2$
  $= 4x^6 + 20x^4 - 4x^3 + 25x^2 - 10x + 1$
  c. No; $f(x^2) \neq (f(x))^2$ in general

59. $V = \dfrac{256\pi t^3}{3}$; 17,157.28 cm^3 **61.** $s = \dfrac{10t}{3}$

63. One such function is $f(x) = \dfrac{x-1}{x}$.

Section 3.5.A, page 203

1. 2, 2.16, 2.3328, 2.5194, 2.7210, 2.9387, 3.1737, 3.4276

3. 0.2, 0.64, 0.9216, 0.2890, 0.8219, 0.5854, 0.9708, 0.1133

5. 0.5, −0.375, 0.3223, −0.2888, 0.2647, −0.2462, 0.2312, −0.2189

7. approaches infinity

9. converges to 0   **11.** converges to 0

13. The fixed points are 3 and −2.

15. The fixed points are 0, 1, and −1.

17. The fixed points are $\dfrac{2 + \sqrt{8}}{2}$ and $\dfrac{2 - \sqrt{8}}{2}$.

19. Any real number greater than or equal to 0 is a fixed point. Any negative number is an eventually fixed point.

21. a. $f(x) = |x - 1|$ and $x = 0.5$; terms of orbit: 0.5, 0.5, 0.5, . . . ; 0.5 is a fixed point. $f(x) = |x - 1|$ and $x = -0.5$; terms of orbit: 1.5, 0.5, 0.5, . . . ; −0.5 is an eventually fixed point.
  b. $f(x) = |x - 1|$ and $x = 0$; terms of orbit: 1, 0, 1, 0, . . . ; 0 is a periodic point. $f(x) = |x - 1|$ and $x = 1$; terms of orbit: 0, 1, 0, 1, . . . ; 1 is a periodic point.

Section 3.6, page 212

1.

y	$f(y)$
4	1
2	2
3	3
6	4
1	5

3.

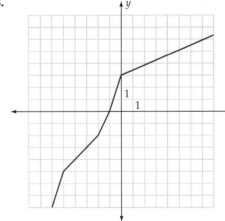

3 sample points on the inverse: $(-2, -2)$, $(0, 3)$, $(8, 6)$

5.

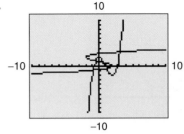

$x_1 = t$
$y_1 = t^3 - 3t^2 + 2$
$x_2 = t^3 - 3t^2 + 2$
$y_2 = t$

7.

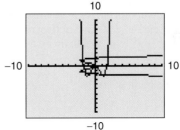

$x_1 = t$
$y_1 = t^4 - 3t^2$
$x_2 = t^4 - 3t^2$
$y_2 = t$

9. $g(x) = -x$ **11.** $x = 5y^2 - 4,\ y = \pm\sqrt{\dfrac{x+4}{5}}$

13. $g(x) = \sqrt[3]{\dfrac{5-x}{2}}$ **15.** $g(x) = \dfrac{x^2 + 7}{4},\ (x \geq 0)$

17. $g(x) = \dfrac{1}{x}$ **19.** $x = \dfrac{1}{2y^2 + 1},\ y = \pm\sqrt{\dfrac{1-x}{2x}}$

21. $g(x) = \sqrt[3]{\dfrac{5x+1}{1-x}}$

23. No   **25.** Yes   **27.** Yes   **29.** No

31.

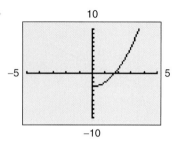

33.

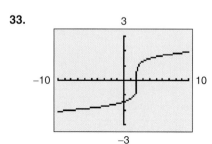

35.

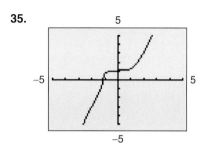

37. One restricted function is $h(x) = |x|$ with $x \geq 0$ (so that $h(x) = x$); inverse function $g(x) = x$.

39. One restricted function is $h(x) = -x^2$ with $x \leq 0$; inverse function $g(x) = -\sqrt{-x}$. Another restricted function is $h(x) = -x^2$ with $x \geq 0$; inverse function $g(x) = \sqrt{-x}$.

41. One restricted function is $h(x) = \dfrac{x^2 + 6}{2}$ with $x \geq 0$; inverse function $g(x) = \sqrt{2x - 6}$.

43. One restricted function is $f(x) = \dfrac{1}{x^2 + 1}$ with $x \leq 0$; inverse function
$$g(x) = -\sqrt{\frac{1}{x} - 1} = -\sqrt{\frac{1 - x}{x}}.$$

45. $(f \circ g)(x) = f(g(x)) = f(x - 1) = (x - 1) + 1 = x$ and $(g \circ f)(x) = g(f(x)) = g(x + 1) = (x + 1) - 1 = x$

47. $(f \circ g)(x) = f\left(\dfrac{1 - x}{x}\right) = \dfrac{1}{\left(\dfrac{1 - x}{x}\right) + 1} =$
$$\dfrac{1}{\dfrac{(1 - x) + x}{x}} = x \text{ and } (g \circ f)(x) = g\left(\dfrac{1}{x + 1}\right) =$$

$$\dfrac{1 - \dfrac{1}{x + 1}}{\dfrac{1}{x + 1}} = \dfrac{\dfrac{(x + 1) - 1}{x + 1}}{\dfrac{1}{x + 1}} = x$$

49. $(f \circ g)(x) = f(\sqrt[5]{x}) = (\sqrt[5]{x})^5 = x \, f \text{ and } (g \circ f)(x) = g(x^5) = \sqrt[5]{x^5} = x$

51. $(f \circ f)(x) = f(f(x)) = \dfrac{2f(x) + 1}{3f(x) - 2} =$
$$\dfrac{2\left[\dfrac{2x + 1}{3x - 2}\right] + 1}{3\left[\dfrac{2x + 1}{3x - 2}\right] - 2} = \dfrac{\dfrac{2(2x + 1) + (3x - 2)}{3x - 2}}{\dfrac{3(2x + 1) - 2(3x - 2)}{3x - 2}} =$$

$$\dfrac{\dfrac{7x}{3x - 2}}{\dfrac{7}{3x - 2}} = x$$

53. Let $y = f(x) = mx + b$. Since $m \neq 0$, we can solve for x and obtain $x = \dfrac{y - b}{m}$. Hence, the rule of the inverse function g is $g(x) = \dfrac{x - b}{m}$, and we have:
$$(f \circ g)(x) = f(g(x)) = f\left(\dfrac{x - b}{m}\right) =$$
$$m\left(\dfrac{x - b}{m}\right) + b = x \text{ and } (g \circ f)(x) = g(f(x)) =$$
$$g(mx + b) = \dfrac{(mx + b) - b}{m} = x.$$

55. a. Slope $= \dfrac{a - b}{b - a} = \dfrac{-(b - a)}{b - a} = -1$.

b. The line $y = x$ has slope 1 and by (a), line PQ has slope -1. Since the product of their slopes is -1, the lines are perpendicular.

c. Length $PR = \sqrt{(a - c)^2 + (b - c)^2}$
$$= \sqrt{a^2 - 2ac + c^2 + b^2 - 2bc + c^2}$$
$$= \sqrt{a^2 + b^2 + 2c^2 - 2ac - 2bc};$$
Length $RQ = \sqrt{(c - b)^2 + (c - a)^2}$
$$= \sqrt{c^2 - 2bc + b^2 + c^2 - 2ac + a^2}$$
$$= \sqrt{a^2 + b^2 + 2c^2 - 2ac - 2bc}.$$
Since the two lengths are the same, $y = x$ is the perpendicular bisector of segment PQ.

Section 3.7, page 220

1. a. 14 ft/sec   **b.** 54 ft/sec   **c.** 112 ft/sec
d. $93\dfrac{1}{3}$ ft/sec

3. a. 0.709 gal/in.   **b.** 2.036 gal/in.

5. a. 250 ties/mo   **b.** 438 ties/mo
c. 500 ties/mo   **d.** 563 ties/mo
e. -188 ties/mo   **f.** -750 ties/mo
g. -1500 ties/mo   **h.** -375 ties/mo

7. a. -55.5 **b.** -92.5 **c.** -462.5

9. -2 **11.** -1 **13.** 1.5858 **15.** 1

17. $2x + h$ **19.** $2t + h - 8000$ **21.** $2\pi r + \pi h$

23. a. Average rate of change is -7979.9, which means that water is leaving the tank at a rate of 7979.9 gal/min.
  b. -7979.99 gal/min.   **c.** -7980 gal/min.

25. a. 6.5π **b.** 6.2π **c.** 6.1π **d.** 6π
  e. It's the same.

27. a. C, 62.5 ft/sec; D, 75 ft/sec
  b. Approximately $t = 4$ to $t = 9.8$ sec
  c. The average speed of car D from $t = 4$ to $t = 10$ sec is the slope of the secant line joining the (approximate) points $(4, 100)$ and $(10, 600)$, namely, $\dfrac{600 - 100}{10 - 4} \approx 83.33$ ft/sec. The average speed of car C is the slope of the secant line joining the (approximate) points $(4, 475)$ and $(10, 800)$, namely, $\dfrac{800 - 475}{10 - 4} \approx 54.17$ ft/sec.

29. a. From day 0 until any day up to day 94, the average growth rate is positive.
  b. From day 0 to day 95
  c. -28, meaning that the population is decreasing at a rate of 28 chipmunks per day
  d. 20, -20, and 0 chipmunks per day

Chapter 3 Review, page 226

1. $f(-2) = 11$ $f(2) = 3$
  $f(-1) = 9$ $f(t) = 7 - 2t$
  $f(0) = 7$ $f(b + 1) = 5 - 2b$
  $f(1) = 5$ $f(x - h) = 7 - 2x - 2h$

3. $2\left(\dfrac{x}{2}\right)^3 + \left(\dfrac{x}{2}\right) + 1 = \dfrac{x^3}{4} + \dfrac{x}{2} + 1$

5. All real numbers ≥ 2 except for 3.

7. a. For 20 miles, it costs $150. For 30 miles, it costs $202.50
  b. 39 miles

9. $f(0) = 0, f(-1) = -1, f\left(\dfrac{1}{2}\right) = 1, f\left(-\dfrac{3}{2}\right) = -2$

11. $[-3, 3.5]$ **13.** -3

15. No local maxima; minimum at $x = -0.5$; increasing on $(-0.5, \infty)$; decreasing on $(-\infty, -0.5)$ This function is concave up for all values of x; there are no points of inflection.

17. Maximum at $x \approx -5.0704$; minimum at $x \approx -0.2629$. Increasing on $(-\infty, -5.0704)$ and $(-0.2629, \infty)$; decreasing on $(-5.0704, -0.2629)$ This function is concave up on the interval $\left(-\dfrac{8}{3}, \infty\right)$ and concave down on the interval $\left(-\infty, -\dfrac{8}{3}\right)$. There is a point of inflection at $x = -\dfrac{8}{3}$.

19. a. The graph is not one-to-one; therefore, it does not represent a function of x.

b. The graph represents a function of x because it is one-to-one.

21.

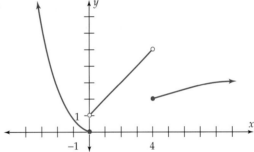

23.

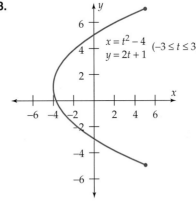

$x = t^2 - 4$
$y = 2t + 1$ $(-3 \leq t \leq 3)$

25. $g(x) = (x - 4)^2 + 1$

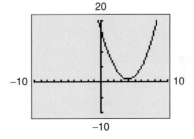

Vertex is $(4, 1)$.
The y-intercept is 17.
There are no x-intercepts.

27. $f(x) = -x^2 - 2x - 7$

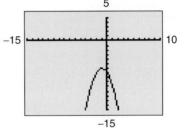

Vertex is $(-1, -6)$.   The y-intercept is -7.
There are no x-intercepts.

29.

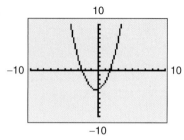

Vertex is $(-0.35, -4.2025)$.
The y-intercept is -4.08.
The x-intercepts are -2.4 and 1.7.

31. $f(x) = \left(x - \dfrac{3}{2}\right)^2 - \dfrac{25}{4}$ (transformation form)

   $f(x) = (x - 4)(x + 1)$ (x-intercept form)

33. parent function: $f(x) = \sqrt{x}$

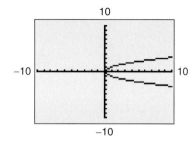

35. parent function: $g(x) = |x|$

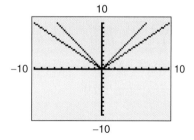

37. parent function: $f(x) = x^2$

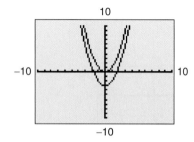

39. Compress the graph of g toward the x-axis by a factor of 0.25, then shift the graph vertically 2 units upward.

41. Shift the graph of g horizontally 7 units to the right; then stretch it away from the x-axis by a factor of 3; then reflect it across the x-axis; finally, shift the graph vertically 2 units upward.

43. e

45.

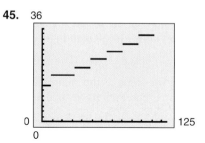

Note: the right endpoint of each segment is a part of the graph; the left endpoint is *not* a part of the graph.

47. x-axis, y-axis, origin

49. Even   **51.** Odd

53. a. -1 **b.** -1 **c.** 2

55. $-4x$ **57.** $\dfrac{82}{27}$ **59.** $\dfrac{1}{x^3} + 3$ **61.** $\dfrac{1}{4}$

63. $f(x) = x^2, g(x) = 2x + 1$

65. 2, 1, 0, 1, 0, 1, 0, 1

67.

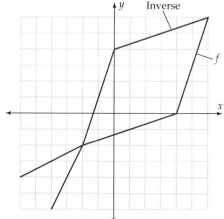

69. $x = 1 - y^2, y = \pm\sqrt{1 - x}$

71. $x = 2y + 1, f^{-1}(x) = \dfrac{x - 1}{2}$

73. $x = \sqrt[5]{y^3 + 1}, f^{-1}(x) = \sqrt[3]{x^5 - 1}$

75. The graph of f passes the horizontal line test and hence has an inverse function. It is easy to verify either geometrically [by reflecting the graph of f across the line $y = x$] or algebraically [by calculating $f(f(x))$] that f is its own inverse function.

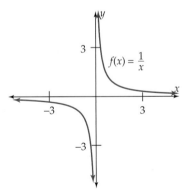

$f(x) = \dfrac{1}{x}$

77. $(g \circ f)(x) = 0.25(4x - 6) + 1.5 = x - 1.5 + 1.5 = x$
$(f \circ g)(x) = 4(0.25x + 1.5) - 6 = x + 6 - 6 = x$

79. $(g \circ f)(x) = \dfrac{3\left(\dfrac{2x + 1}{x - 3}\right) + 1}{\left(\dfrac{2x + 1}{x - 3}\right) - 2}$

$= \dfrac{\dfrac{3(2x + 1) + 1(x - 3)}{x - 3}}{\dfrac{2x + 1 - 2(x - 3)}{x - 3}} = \dfrac{\dfrac{7x}{x - 3}}{\dfrac{7}{x - 3}}$

$= \dfrac{7x}{x - 3} \cdot \dfrac{x - 3}{7} = x$

$(f \circ g)(x) = \dfrac{2\left(\dfrac{3x + 1}{x - 2}\right) + 1}{\left(\dfrac{3x + 1}{x - 2}\right) - 3}$

$= \dfrac{\dfrac{2(3x + 1) + 1(x - 2)}{x - 2}}{\dfrac{3x + 1 - 3(x - 2)}{x - 2}} = \dfrac{\dfrac{7x}{x - 2}}{\dfrac{7}{x - 2}}$

$= \dfrac{7x}{x - 2} \cdot \dfrac{x - 2}{7} = x$

81. a. $-\dfrac{1}{3}$ **b.** $\dfrac{5}{8}$

83. 6   **85.** 3   **87.** $2x + h$

89. a. For example, from -3 to 1
    b. For example, from 1 to 2
    c. For example, from 6 to 8
    d. Both intervals are portions of the same line, so their slopes are the same.

91. a. \$290/ton   **b.** \$230/ton   **c.** \$212/ton

Chapter 3 can do calculus, page 237

1. $s(t) = -16t^2 + 20t + 75$
-44 feet per second

2. 0.625 seconds   The instantaneous velocity of the ball is 0 when the ball reaches its maximum height. Thus, the maximum height of the ball will be 81.25 feet.

3. $s(t) = -16t^2 + 300$; -96 feet per second

4. 14   **5.** -0.111111 **6.** 3   **7.** $2a$

8. instantaneous rate of change $= -16$; equation of tangent line at $t = 4$: $y = -16t + 76$

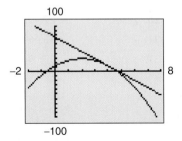

9. instantaneous rate of change $= 25.132741$
When $r = 1$, for each change of 1 unit in the radius, the surface area of the sphere will increase by approximately 25.132741 square units.

10. instantaneous rate of change $= 100$ dollars per phone   When $x = 1000$, for every additional phone sold, the profit increases by approximately \$100.

Chapter 4

Section 4.1, page 248

1. Polynomial of degree 3; leading coefficient 1; constant term 1

3. Polynomial of degree 3; leading coefficient 1; constant term -1

5. Polynomial of degree 2; leading coefficient 1; constant term -3

7. Not a polynomial

9.

$$\begin{array}{r|rrrrr}
2 & 3 & -8 & 0 & 9 & 5 \\
  &   & 6 & -4 & -8 & 2 \\
\hline
  & 3 & -2 & -4 & 1 & \boxed{7}
\end{array}$$

quotient $3x^3 - 2x^2 - 4x + 1$; remainder 7

11.

$$\begin{array}{r|rrrrr}
-3 & 2 & 5 & 0 & -2 & -8 \\
   &   & -6 & 3 & -9 & 33 \\
\hline
   & 2 & -1 & 3 & -11 & \boxed{25}
\end{array}$$

quotient $2x^3 - x^2 + 3x - 11$; remainder 25

13.

$$\begin{array}{r|rrrrr}
7 & 5 & 0 & -3 & -4 & 6 \\
  &   & 35 & 245 & 1,694 & 11,830 \\
\hline
  & 5 & 35 & 242 & 1,690 & \boxed{11,836}
\end{array}$$

quotient $5x^3 + 35x^2 + 242x + 1690$; remainder 11,836

15.

$$\begin{array}{r|rrrrr} 2 & 1 & -6 & 4 & 2 & -7 \\ & & 2 & -8 & -8 & -12 \\ \hline & 1 & -4 & -4 & -6 & \boxed{-19} \end{array}$$

quotient $x^3 - 4x^2 - 4x - 6$;
remainder -19

17. Quotient $3x^3 - 3x^2 + 5x - 11$; remainder 12

19. Quotient $x^2 + 2x - 6$; remainder $-7x + 7$

21. Quotient $5x^2 + 5x + 5$; remainder 0

23. No   **25.** Yes   **27.** 0, 2

29. $2\sqrt{2}, -1$ **31.** 2   **33.** 6

35. -30 **37.** 170,802   **39.** 5,935,832

41. No   **43.** No   **45.** Yes

47. $(x + 4)(2x - 7)(3x - 5)$

49. $(x - 3)(x + 3)(2x + 1)^2$

51. $f(x) = (x + 2)(x + 1)(x - 1)(x - 2)(x - 3)$
$\qquad = x^5 - 3x^4 - 5x^3 + 15x^2 + 4x - 12$

53. $f(x) = x(x + 1)(x - 1)(x - 2)(x - 3)$
$\qquad = x^5 - 5x^4 + 5x^3 + 5x^2 - 6x$

55. Many correct answers, including $f(x) \neq$
$(x - 1)(x - 7)(x + 4)$

57. Many correct answers, including $f(x) \neq$
$(x - 1)(x - 2)^2(x - \pi)^3$

59. $f(x) = \dfrac{17}{100}(x - 5)(x - 8)x$

61. $k = 1$ **63.** $k = 1$

65. If $x - c$ were a factor of $x^4 + x^2 + 1$, then c would
be a solution of $x^4 + x^2 + 1 = 0$, that is, c would
satisfy $c^4 + c^2 = -1$. But $c^4 \geq 0$ and $c^2 \geq 0$, so that
is impossible. Hence, $x - c$ is not a factor.

67. a. Many possible answers, including: if $n = 3$ and
$c = 1$, then $x + 1 = x - (-1)$ is not a factor of
$x^3 - 1$ since -1 is not a solution of $x^3 - 1 = 0$.
b. Since n is odd $(-c)^n = -c^n$ and hence $-c$ is a
solution of $x^n + c^n = 0$. Thus, $x - (-c) = x + c$
is a factor of $x^n + c^n$ by the Factor Theorem.

69. $k = 5$ **71.** $d = -5$

Section 4.2, page 258

1. $x = \pm 1$ or -3 **3.** $x = \pm 1$ or -5

5. $x = -4, 0, 1$ or $\dfrac{1}{2}$ **7.** $x = -3$ or 2

9. $x = 2$ **11.** $x = -5, 2$, or 3

13. $(x - 2)(2x^2 + 1)$ **15.** $x^3(x^2 + 3)(x + 2)$

17. $(x - 2)(x - 1)^2(x^2 + 3)$

19. Lower -5; upper 2   **21.** Lower -7; upper 3

23. $x = 1, 2$, or $-\dfrac{1}{2}$ **25.** $x = 1, \dfrac{1}{2}$, or $\dfrac{1}{3}$

27. $x = 2$ or $\dfrac{-5 \pm \sqrt{37}}{2}$ **29.** $x = \dfrac{1}{2}$ or $\pm\sqrt{2}$ or $\pm\sqrt{3}$

31. $x = -1, 5$, or $\pm\sqrt{3}$ **33.** $x = \dfrac{1}{3}$ or -1.8393

35. $x = -2.2470$ or -0.5550 or 0.8019 or 50

37. a. The only possible rational zeros of
$f(x) = x^2 - 2$ are ± 1 or ± 2 (why?). But $\sqrt{2}$ is a
zero of $f(x)$ and $\sqrt{2} \neq \pm 1$ or ± 2. Hence, $\sqrt{2}$ is
irrational.
b. $\sqrt{3}$ is a zero of $x^2 - 3$ whose only possible
rational zeros are ± 1 or ± 3 (why?). But
$\sqrt{3} \neq \pm 1$ or ± 3.

39. a. 8.6378 people per 100,000
b. 1995   **c.** 1991

41. 2 by 2 in.

43. a. $6°$/day at the beginning; $6.6435°$/day at the end
b. Day 2.0330 and day 10.7069
c. Day 5.0768 and day 9.6126
d. Day 7.6813

Section 4.3, page 269

1. Yes   **3.** Yes   **5.** No

7. Degree 3, yes; degree 4, no; degree 5, yes

9. No

11. Degree 3, no; degree 4, no; degree 5, yes

13. The graphs have the same *shape* in the window
with $-40 \leq x \leq 40$ and $-1000 \leq y \leq 5000$ but
don't look identical.

15. -2 is a zero of odd multiplicity, as are 1 and 3

17. -2 and -1 are zeros of odd multiplicity; 2 is a
zero of even multiplicity.

19. (e)   **21.** (f)   **23.** (c)

25. The graph in the standard viewing window does
not rise at the far right as does the graph of the
highest degree term x^3, so it is not complete.

27. The graph in the standard viewing window does
not rise at the far left and far right as does the
graph of the highest degree term $0.005x^4$, so it is
not complete.

29. $-9 \leq x \leq 3$ and $-20 \leq y \leq 40$

31. $-6 \leq x \leq 6$ and $-60 \leq y \leq 320$

33. $-3 \leq x \leq 4$ and $-35 \leq y \leq 20$

35. Left half: $-33 \leq x \leq -2$ and $-50{,}000 \leq y \leq$
$250{,}000$; right half: $-2 \leq x \leq 3$ and $-20 \leq y \leq 30$

37. $-90 \leq x \leq 120$ and $-15{,}000 \leq y \leq 5000$

39. Overall: $-3 \leq x \leq 3$ and $-20 \leq y \leq 20$; near
y-axis: $-0.1 \leq x \leq 0.2$ and $4.997 \leq y \leq 5.001$

41. a. The graph of a cubic polynomial (degree 3) has at
most $3 - 1 = 2$ local extrema. When $|x|$ is large,

the graph resembles the graph of ax^3, that is, one end shoots upward and the other end downward. If the graph had only one local extremum, both ends of the graph would go in the same direction (both up or down). Thus, the graph of a cubic polynomial has either two local extrema or none.

b. These are the only possible shapes for a graph that has 0 or 2 local extrema, 1 point of inflection, and resembles the graph of ax^3 when $|x|$ is large.

43. a. Odd **b.** Positive **c.** $-2, 0, 4,$ and 6 **d.** 5

45. (d)

47.

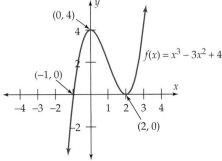

$f(x) = x^3 - 3x^2 + 4$

49.

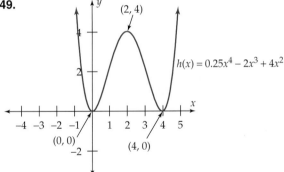

$h(x) = 0.25x^4 - 2x^3 + 4x^2$

51.

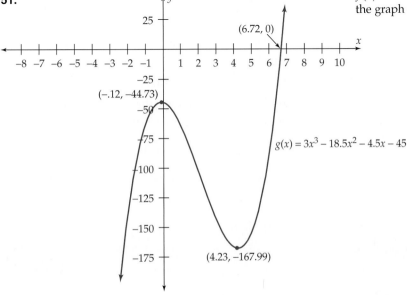

$g(x) = 3x^3 - 18.5x^2 - 4.5x - 45$

53.

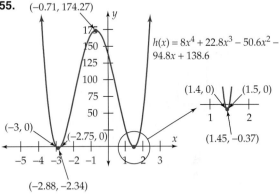

$f(x) = x^5 - 3x^3 + x + 1$

55.

$h(x) = 8x^4 + 22.8x^3 - 50.6x^2 - 94.8x + 138.6$

57. a. The solutions are zeros of
$g(x) - 4 = 0.01x^3 - 0.06x^2 + 0.12x - 0.08$. This polynomial has degree 3 and hence has at most 3 zeros.

b. $1 \leq x \leq 3$ and $3.99 \leq y \leq 4.01$

c. Suppose $f(x)$ has degree n. If the graph of $f(x)$ had a horizontal segment lying on the line $y = k$ for some constant k, then the equation $f(x) = k$ would have infinitely many solutions (why?). But the polynomial $f(x) - k$ has degree n (why?) and thus has at most n roots. Hence the equation $f(x) = k$ has at most n solutions, which means the graph cannot have a horizontal segment.

59. a. The general shape of the graph should be as shown here. The graph should cross the x-axis at the points specified, and bounce off the axis at 2.

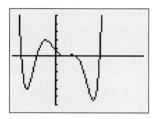

b. On the TI-83, only 3 of the roots are shown. 2 is skipped over entirely.

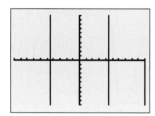

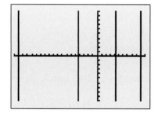

c. Again, $x = 2$ is missed.
d. Try the windows $-20 \leq x \leq -3$, $-5,000,000 \leq y \leq 1,000,000$. Then try $-3 \leq x \leq 2$, $-5000 \leq y \leq 60,000$. For the third part $1 \leq x \leq 5$, $-5000 \leq y \leq 5000$ and lastly $5 \leq x \leq 11$, $-100,000 \leq y \leq 100,000$

Section 4.3.A, page 276

1. Cubic   **3.** Quadratic

5. a. $y = -0.634335011x^3 + 11.79490831x^2 - 51.88599279x + 4900.867065$
b. 1987: 4898.0 per 100,000; 1995: 4635.6
c. 3138.2
d. Answers vary.

7. a.

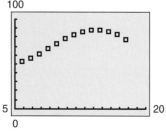

b. $y = -0.5179820180x^2 + 14.65684316x - 20.88711289$
c. Noon: 80°; 9 A.M.: 69°; 2 P.M.: 83°

9. a.

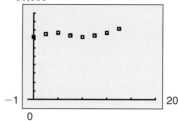

b. Quartic
c. $y = -1.595348011x^4 + 58.04379735x^3 - 630.033381x^2 + 2131.441153x + 36466.9811$
d. $42,545.95
e. According to this model, income will drop steeply after 2002.

11. a.

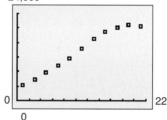

b. $y = -0.084189248x^4 - 0.528069153x^3 + 66.26642628x^2 + 397.2751554x + 3965.686061$
c. 1996: $19,606; The estimate is lower.

Section 4.4, page 290

1. All real numbers except $-\dfrac{5}{2}$

3. All real numbers except $3 + \sqrt{5}$ and $3 - \sqrt{5}$

5. All real numbers except $-\sqrt{2}$, 1, and $\sqrt{2}$

7. Vertical asymptotes $x = -1$ and $x = 6$

9. Hole at $x = 0$; vertical asymptote $x = -1$

11. Vertical asymptotes $x = -2$ and $x = 2$

13. $y = 3$; any window with $-115 \leq x \leq 110$

15. $y = -1$; any window with $-31 \leq x \leq 35$

17. $y = \dfrac{5}{2}$; any window with $-40 \leq x \leq 42$

19. Asymptote: $y = x$; window: $-14 \leq x \leq 14$ and $-15 \leq y \leq 15$

21. Asymptote: $y = x^2 - x$; window: $-15 \leq x \leq 6$ and $-40 \leq y \leq 240$

23.

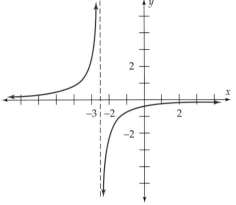

vertical asymptote $x = -5$
horizontal asymptote $y = 0$

25.

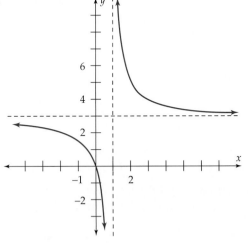

vertical asymptote $x = -2.5$
horizontal asymptote $y = 0$

27.

vertical asymptote $x = 1$
horizontal asymptote $y = 3$

29.

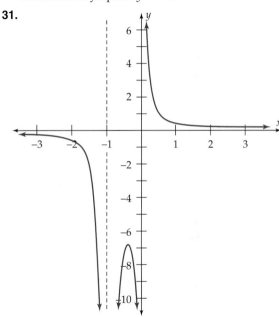

vertical asymptote $x = 3$
horizontal asymptote $y = -1$

31.

vertical asymptotes $x = -1, x = 0$
horizontal asymptote $y = 0$

33.

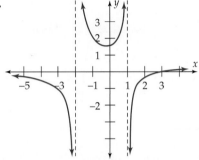

vertical asymptotes $x = -2, x = 1$
horizontal asymptote $y = 0$

35.

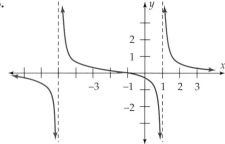

vertical asymptotes $x = -5, x = 1$
horizontal asymptote $y = 0$

37.

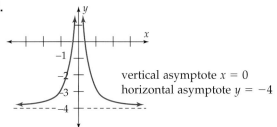

vertical asymptote $x = 0$
horizontal asymptote $y = -4$

39.

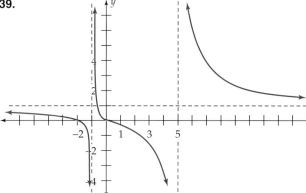

vertical asymptotes $x = -1, x = 5$
horizontal asymptote $y = 1$

41.

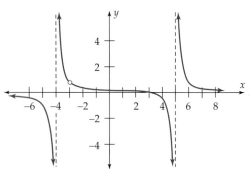

vertical asymptotes $x = -4, x = 5$
hole at $x = -3$
horizontal asymptote $y = 0$

43.

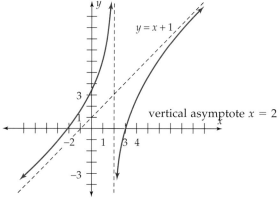

oblique asymptote $y = x + 1$

45.

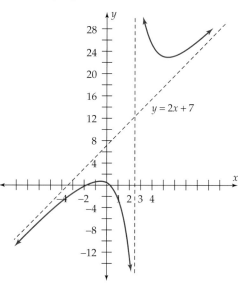

vertical asymptote $x = \dfrac{5}{2}$
oblique asymptote $y = 2x + 7$

47.

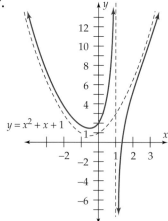

vertical asymptote $x = 1$
parabolic asymptote $y = x^2 + x + 1$

49.

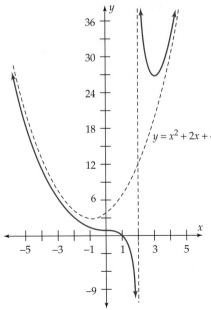

$y = x^2 + 2x + 4$

vertical asymptote $x = 2$
parabolic asymptote $y = x^2 + 2x + 4$

51. Overall: $-5 \leq x \leq 4.4$ and $-8 \leq y \leq 4$; hidden area near origin: $-2 \leq x \leq 2$ and $-0.5 \leq y \leq 0.5$; hidden area near $x = -5$: $-15 \leq x \leq -3$ and $-0.07 \leq y \leq 0.02$

53. $-9.4 \leq x \leq 9.4$ and $-4 \leq y \leq 4$; there is a hole at $x = 2$.

55. Overall: $-4.7 \leq x \leq 4.7$ and $-2 \leq y \leq 2$; there is a hole at $x = -1$; to see the vertical asymptote, use $0.65 \leq x \leq 0.75$ and $-3 \leq y \leq 3$.

57. For vertical asymptotes and x-intercepts: $-4.7 \leq x \leq 4.7$ and $-8 \leq y \leq 8$; to see graph get close to the horizontal asymptote: $-40 \leq x \leq 35$ and $-2 \leq y \leq 3$

59. Overall: $-4.7 \leq x \leq 4.7$ and $-2 \leq y \leq 2$; hidden area near $x = 4$: $3 \leq x \leq 15$ and $-0.02 \leq y \leq 0.01$

61. $-15.5 \leq x \leq 8.5$ and $-16 \leq y \leq 8$

63. $-4.7 \leq x \leq 4.7$ and $-12 \leq y \leq 8$

65. Overall: $-13 \leq x \leq 7$ and $-20 \leq y \leq 20$; hidden area near the origin: $-2.5 \leq x \leq 1$ and $-0.02 \leq y \leq 0.02$

67. b. Stretch the graph of $f(x)$ away from the x-axis by a factor of 2.
  c. The graph of $h(x)$ is the graph of $f(x)$ shifted vertically 4 units upward; the graph of $k(x)$ is the graph of $f(x)$ shifted horizontally 3 units to the right; the graph of $t(x)$ is the graph of $f(x)$ shifted horizontally 2 units to the left.
  d. Shift the graph of $f(x)$ horizontally 3 units to the right, stretch vertically by a factor of 2, then shift vertically 4 units upward.

e. $p(x) = \dfrac{4x - 10}{x - 3}$

f. Shift the graph of $f(x)$ horizontally $|s|$ units (to the left if $s > 0$; to the right if $s < 0$); stretch (or shrink) the graph by a factor of $|r|$ (away from the x-axis if $|r| > 1$, toward the x-axis if $0 < |r| < 1$); also if $r < 0$, reflect the graph in the x-axis; then shift vertically $|t|$ units (upward if $t > 0$; downward if $t < 0$).

g. $q(x) = \dfrac{tx + (r + ts)}{x + s}$

69. a. $\dfrac{-1}{x(x + h)}$

  b. $-\dfrac{1}{4.2} \approx -0.2381$; $-\dfrac{1}{4.02} \approx -0.2488$; $-\dfrac{1}{4.002} \approx -0.2499$; instantaneous rate of change $-\dfrac{1}{4} = -0.25$

  c. $-\dfrac{1}{9.3} \approx -0.1075$; $-\dfrac{1}{9.03} \approx -0.1107$; $-\dfrac{1}{9.003} \approx -0.1111$; instantaneous rate of change $-\dfrac{1}{9} = -0.1111 \cdots$

  d. They are the same.

71. a. $y = \dfrac{x - 1}{x - 2}$ **b.** $y = \dfrac{x - 1}{-x - 2}$
  c. Graph (a) has a vertical asymptote at $x = 2$ and graph (b) has a vertical asymptote at $x = -2$.

73. a. $C(x) = \dfrac{3}{100}(2x^2) + \dfrac{1.25}{100}\left(4x \cdot \dfrac{1000}{x^2}\right) = 0.06x^2 + \dfrac{50}{x}$
  b. $x \approx 16.85$ in.

75. a. $c(x) = \dfrac{20 + x}{50 + x}$
  b. between 25 gallons and 100 gallons
  c. $x = 50$ gallons

77. a. $a(x) = \dfrac{c(x)}{x} = \dfrac{40{,}000 + 2.60x}{x}$
  b. 100,000

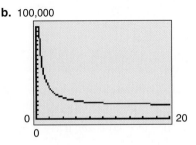

  c. $y = 2.60$; the average cost can never be below $2.60.

79. a. $v = \dfrac{50u}{u - 50}$
  b. $v = 50$

c.

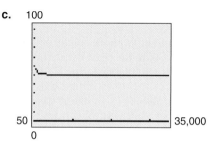

100

50   35,000

0

d. If the object is close, a small change in u leads to a large change in v. However, when u is large, a small change in u leads to nearly no change in v, so that u may change substantially while the object stays in focus.

Section 4.5, page 300

1. $8 + 2i$

3. $-2 - 10i$

5. $-\dfrac{1}{2} - 2i$

7. $\left(\dfrac{\sqrt{2} - \sqrt{3}}{2}\right) + 2i$

9. $1 + 13i$

11. $-10 + 11i$

13. $-21 - 20i$ **15.** 4 **17.** $-i$ **19.** i **21.** i

23. $\dfrac{5}{29} + \dfrac{2}{29}i$ **25.** $-\dfrac{1}{3}i$ **27.** $\dfrac{12}{41} - \dfrac{15}{41}i$

29. $\dfrac{-5}{41} - \dfrac{4}{41}i$ **31.** $\dfrac{10}{17} - \dfrac{11}{17}i$ **33.** $\dfrac{7}{10} + \dfrac{11}{10}i$

35. $-\dfrac{113}{170} + \dfrac{41}{170}i$ **37.** $6i$

39. $\sqrt{14}i$ **41.** $-4i$

43. $11i$ **45.** $\left(\sqrt{15} - 3\sqrt{2}\right)i$

47. $\dfrac{2}{3}$ **49.** $-41 - i$

51. $\left(2 + 5\sqrt{2}\right) + \left(\sqrt{5} - 2\sqrt{10}\right)i$

53. $\dfrac{1}{3} - \dfrac{\sqrt{2}}{3}i$ **55.** $x = 2, y = -2$

57. $x = -\dfrac{3}{4}, y = \dfrac{3}{2}$ **59.** $x = \dfrac{1}{3} \pm \dfrac{\sqrt{14}}{3}i$

61. $x = -\dfrac{1}{2} \pm \dfrac{\sqrt{7}}{2}i$ **63.** $x = \dfrac{1}{4} \pm \dfrac{\sqrt{31}}{4}i$

65. $x = \dfrac{3 \pm \sqrt{3}}{2}$

67. $x = 2, -1 + \sqrt{3}i, -1 - \sqrt{3}i$

69. $x = 1, -1, i, -i$ **71.** -1

73. If $z = a + bi$, with a, b real numbers, then $z - \bar{z} = (a + bi) - (a - bi) = 2bi$. If $z = a + bi$ is real, then $b = 0$ and hence, $z - \bar{z} = 2bi = 0$. Therefore, $z = \bar{z}$. Conversely, if $z = \bar{z}$, then $0 = z - \bar{z} = 2bi$, which implies that $b = 0$. Hence, $z = a$ is real.

75. $\dfrac{1}{z} = \left(\dfrac{a}{a^2 + b^2}\right) + \left(\dfrac{-b}{a^2 + b^2}\right)i$

Section 4.5.A, page 306

1. $f^1(0) = 0.3; f^2(0) = 0.39; f^3(0) = 0.4521;$
$d = \sqrt{(0.4521)^2 + 0^2} = 0.4521.$

3. $f^1(0) = 0.5 + 0.5i; f^2(0) = 0.5 + i;$
$f^3(0) = -0.25 + 1.5i; d \approx 1.5207$

5. $f^1(0) = -1.2 + 0.5i; f^2(0) = -0.01 - 0.7i;$
$f^3(0) = -1.6899 + 0.514i; d \approx 1.7663.$

7. The seventh iteration is more than 2 units from the origin.

9. The thirteenth iteration is more than 2 units from the origin.

11. The eighth iteration is more than 2 units from the origin.

13. i is the Mandelbrot set.

15. 1 is not in the Mandelbrot set.

17. The cycle approaches approximately $-0.275 + 0.387i$. The number $-0.2 + 0.6i$ is in the Mandelbrot set.

Section 4.6, page 313

1. $g(x)$ is not a factor of $f(x)$.

3. $g(x)$ is not a factor of $f(x)$.

5. $g(x)$ is not a factor of $f(x)$.

7. $x = 0$ (multiplicity 54); $x = -\dfrac{4}{5}$ (multiplicity 1)

9. $x = 0$ (multiplicity 15); $x = \pi$ (multiplicity 14); $x = \pi + 1$ (multiplicity 13)

11. $x = 1 + 2i$ or $1 - 2i$;
$f(x) = (x - 1 - 2i)(x - 1 + 2i)$

13. $x = -\dfrac{1}{3} + \dfrac{2\sqrt{5}}{3}i$ or $-\dfrac{1}{3} - \dfrac{2\sqrt{5}}{3}i$;
$f(x) = \left(x + \dfrac{1}{3} - \dfrac{2\sqrt{5}}{3}i\right)\left(x + \dfrac{1}{3} + \dfrac{2\sqrt{5}}{3}i\right)$

15. $x = 3$ or $-\dfrac{3}{2} + \dfrac{3\sqrt{3}}{2}i$ or $-\dfrac{3}{2} - \dfrac{3\sqrt{3}}{2}i$;
$f(x) = (x - 3)\left(x + \dfrac{3}{2} - \dfrac{3\sqrt{3}}{2}i\right)\left(x + \dfrac{3}{2} + \dfrac{3\sqrt{3}}{2}i\right)$

17. $x = -2$ or $1 + \sqrt{3}i$ or $1 - \sqrt{3}i$;
$f(x) = (x + 2)(x - 1 - \sqrt{3}i)(x - 1 + \sqrt{3}i)$

19. $x = 1$ or i or -1 or $-i$;
$f(x) = (x - 1)(x - i)(x + 1)(x + i)$

21. $x = \sqrt{5}$ or $-\sqrt{5}$ or $\sqrt{2}i$ or $-\sqrt{2}i$;
$f(x) = \left(x - \sqrt{5}\right)\left(x + \sqrt{5}\right)\left(x - \sqrt{2}i\right)\left(x + \sqrt{2}i\right)$

23. Many correct answers, including
$f(x) = (x - 1)(x - 7)(x + 4)$

25. Many correct answers, including
$f(x) = (x - 1)(x - 2)^2(x - \pi)^3$

27. $f(x) = 2x(x - 4)(x + 3)$

29. $f(x) = x^2 - 4x + 5$

31. $f(x) = (x - 2)(x^2 - 4x + 5)$

33. $f(x) = (x + 3)(x^2 - 2x + 2)(x^2 - 2x + 5)$

35. $f(x) = x^2 - 2x + 5$

37. $f(x) = (x - 4)^2(x^2 - 6x + 10)$

39. $f(x) = (x^4 - 3x^3)(x^2 - 2x + 2)$

41. $f(x) = 3x^2 - 6x + 6$

43. $f(x) = -2x^3 + 2x^2 - 2x + 2$

45. Many correct answers, including
$f(x) = x^2 - (1 - i)x + (2 + i)$

47. Many correct answers, including
$f(x) = x^3 - 5x^2 + (7 + 2i)x - (3 + 6i)$

49. $3, -\dfrac{1}{2} + \dfrac{\sqrt{3}}{2}i, -\dfrac{1}{2} - \dfrac{\sqrt{3}}{2}i$ **51.** $i, -i, -1, -2$

53. $1, 2i, -2i$ **55.** $i, -i, 2 + i, 2 - i$

57. a. Since $z + w = (a + c) + (b + d)i$,
$\overline{z + w} = (a + c) - (b + d)i$. Since $\bar{z} = a - bi$ and
$\bar{w} = c - di$, $\bar{z} + \bar{w} = (a - bi) + (c - di) = (a + c) - (b + d)i$. Hence $\overline{z + w} = \bar{z} + \bar{w}$.
b. Since $zw = (ac - bd) + (ad + bc)i$,
$\overline{zw} = (ac - bd) - (ad + bc)i$. Since $\bar{z} = a - bi$
and $\bar{w} = c - di$, $\bar{z} \cdot \bar{w} = (a - bi)(c - di) = (ac - bd) - (ad + bc)i$. Hence $\overline{zw} = \bar{z} \cdot \bar{w}$.

59. a. $\overline{f(z)} = \overline{az^3 + bz^2 + cz + d}$ (definition of $f(z)$)
$= \overline{az^3} + \overline{bz^2} + \overline{cz} + \bar{d}$ (Exercise 57(a))
$= \bar{a}\,\overline{z^3} + \bar{b}\,\overline{z^2} + \bar{c}\,\bar{z} + \bar{d}$ (Exercise 57(b))
$= a\overline{z^3} + b\overline{z^2} + c\bar{z} + d$ ($r = \bar{r}$ for r real)
$= a\bar{z}^3 + b\bar{z}^2 + c\bar{z} + d$ (Exercise 57(b))
$= f(\bar{z})$ (definition of f)
b. Since $f(z) = 0$, we have $0 = \bar{0} = \overline{f(z)} = f(\bar{z})$.
Hence $\bar{z}$ is a zero of $f(x)$.

61. If $f(z)$ is a polynomial with real coefficients, then
$f(z)$ can be factored as $g_1(z)g_2(z)g_3(z) \cdots g_k(z)$, where
each $g_i(z)$ is a polynomial with real coefficients
and degree 1 or 2. The rules of polynomial
multiplication show that the degree of $f(z)$ is the
sum: degree $g_1(z)$ + degree $g_2(z)$ + degree
$g_3(z)$ + $\cdots$ + degree $g_k(z)$. If all of the $g_i(z)$ have
degree 2, then this last sum is an even number.
But $f(z)$ has odd degree, so this can't occur.
Therefore, at least one of the $g_i(z)$ is a first-degree
polynomial and hence must have a real zero. This
zero is also a zero of $f(z)$.

Chapter 4 Review, page 317

1. (a), (c), (e), (f)   **3.** 0

5.
$$
\begin{array}{r|rrrrrrr}
2 & 1 & -5 & 8 & 1 & -17 & 16 & -4 \\
  &   & 2 & -6 & 4 & 10 & -14 & 4 \\
\hline
  & 1 & -3 & 2 & 5 & -7 & 2 & \boxed{0}
\end{array}
$$
other factor: $x^5 - 3x^4 + 2x^3 + 5x^2 - 7x + 2$

7. $x = \dfrac{44}{7}$

9. $f(x) = (x - 2)\big((x - (3 + 2\sqrt{3}))\big)\big(x - (3 - 2\sqrt{3})\big)$

11. $-2, \dfrac{4 \pm \sqrt{3}}{3}$ **13.** -1

15. a. There are no rational zeros
b. An irrational zero lies between -3 and -2.
Another lies between -1 and 0. A third is
between 1 and 2.

17. 3   **19.** d

21. When $x^4 - 4x^3 + 15$ is divided by $x + 1$
synthetically, the last row, $1 \ {-5} \ 5 \ {-5} \ 20$, has
alternating signs. Therefore, -1 is a lower bound
for the real zeros.

23. rational zeros: -1 and 4; irrational zero: ≈ -1.328

25. -3 is a zero of multiplicity 2; 4 is a zero of
multiplicity 1; -3 is a zero of multiplicity 1; 3 is a
zero of multiplicity 1

27. Answers may vary.

29. i, iv, and v are false.

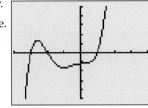

31. Use $-10 \leq x \leq 20$ and $-10,000 \leq y \leq 500$ for the
overall graph and $-2 \leq x \leq 2$ and $-10 \leq y \leq 5$
for behavior around the origin.

33. Use $0.2 \leq x \leq 2$ and $20 \leq y \leq 40$; $-1 \leq x \leq 0.2$,
$-20 \leq y \leq 20$

35. Use $-2 \leq x \leq 3$ and $-5 \leq y \leq 5$. There is an
x-intercept at $(-1, 0)$, a local maximum at $(0, 3)$,
and a local minimum at $\left(\dfrac{4}{3}, \dfrac{49}{27}\right)$.

37. Use $-3 \leq x \leq 3$ and $-5 \leq y \leq 5$. There are
x-intercepts at $x \approx -0.618, 1.618$ and a local
minimum at $x \approx 0.909$.

39. a. 120,000

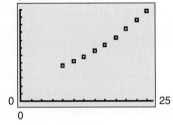

b. $y = 0.04x^4 + 0.19x^3 + 62.06x^2 + 1615.35x + 29{,}552.18$; \$78,882 in 2007 and \$125,721 in 2015

41. Use $-4.7 \leq x \leq 4.7$ and $-3.1 \leq y \leq 3.1$. There is a
vertical asymptote at $x = 2$ and a horizontal
asymptote at $y = -1$.

43. Use $-4.7 \le x \le 4.7$ and $-3.1 \le y \le 3.1$. There is a vertical asymptote at $x = 1$, a hole at $x = -1$, and the x-axis is the horizontal asymptote.

45. vertical asymptotes: $x = \pm\sqrt{3}$; parabolic asymptote: $y = x^2 - 6x + 5$

47. Use $-4.7 \le x \le 4.7$ and $-10 \le y \le 10$. vertical asymptote $x = 1$; horizontal asymptote $y = 0$; x-intercepts at $x = -2$, $x = 3$; for hidden behavior $-15 \le x \le 10$, $-0.5 \le y \le 0.5$

49. Use $-30 \le x \le 30$ and $-1000 \le y \le 1000$. For hidden behavior use $-7 \le x \le 7$, $-5 \le y \le 5$.

51. $x = \dfrac{-3 \pm \sqrt{31}i}{2}$

53. $x = \dfrac{3 \pm \sqrt{31}i}{10}$

55. $x = \sqrt{\dfrac{2}{3}}$ or $-\sqrt{\dfrac{2}{3}}$ or i or $-i$

57. $x = -2$ or $1 + \sqrt{3}i$ or $1 - \sqrt{3}i$

59. $i, -i, 2, -1$

61. Many correct answers, including $f(x) = x^4 - 2x^3 + 2x^2$

63. a fixed orbit of one point: $\left(\dfrac{3}{5}, \dfrac{4}{5}\right)$.

65. $(x - 1)(x - 2)(x - 3); (x - 1)(x - 2)(x - 3)$.

67. $(x + 1)(x - 2)(x^2 + 1); (x + 1)(x - 2)(x + i)(x - i)$.

69. $(x^2 + 1)(x^2 + 1); (x + i)(x - i)(x + i)(x - i)$

Chapter 4 can do calculus, page 325

1. a. $(-1, 4)$ **b.** $(-1, 4)$ and $(2, 4)$ **c.** $(3, 20)$

2. a. $(1, 0)$ **b.** $(-2, 0)$ or $(1, 0)$ **c.** $(-3, -16)$

3. a. approximately 3.785 cm $\times$ 6.980 cm or 8.560 cm $\times$ 1.365 cm
b. $V \approx 126.49$ cm^3 when side length is approximately 6.324 cm and height is approximately 3.163 cm.

4. a. approximately 4.427 inches by 4.427 inches.
b. The largest volume occurs when $x = \dfrac{10}{3}$.

5. a. $r \approx 4.09977$ **b.** $r \approx 1.996$; ≈ 37.566 in^2

6. a. Approximately 206 units are produced.
b. The minimum value of about 577 dollars per unit occurs when about 269 units are produced.

7. $r \approx 1.769, h = \dfrac{58}{\pi r^2} \approx 5.8996$

8. The maximum area of about 220.18 square feet occurs when x is about 9.31 feet.

9. 4 sq. units

10. $5 - x^2 \approx 1.5$. The point that is closest to $(0, 1)$ has the exact value of $\left(\sqrt{\dfrac{7}{2}}, \dfrac{3}{2}\right)$, but approximations are okay.

Chapter 5

Section 5.1, page 334

1. 12 **3.** 2 **5.** 0.09

7. 0.2 **9.** 0.125 **11.** 81

13. 16 **15.** $\dfrac{1}{64}$ **17.** $12^5\left(\sqrt[3]{12}\right)$

19. 11^{14} **21.** $(0.4)^6$ **23.** $16\sqrt{3}$

25. -8 **27.** $\dfrac{\sqrt{3}}{21}$ **29.** $-\dfrac{3}{4}$

31. $2\sqrt{5}$ **33.** 7 **35.** $22 - 8\sqrt{5}$

37. $15\sqrt{5}$ **39.** 1 **41.** $4\dfrac{a^4}{b}$

43. $\dfrac{d^5}{2\sqrt{c}}$ **45.** $(4x + 2y)^2$ **47.** $x^{\frac{9}{2}}$

49. $c^{\frac{42}{5}}d^{\frac{10}{3}}$ **51.** $\dfrac{a^{\frac{1}{2}}}{49b^{\frac{5}{2}}}$ **53.** $\dfrac{2^{\frac{9}{2}}a^{\frac{12}{5}}}{3^4b^4}$

55. a^x **57.** $(a^2 + b^2)^{\frac{1}{3}}$ **59.** $a^{\frac{3}{16}}$

61. $4t^{\frac{27}{10}}$ **63.** $\dfrac{1}{x^{\frac{1}{5}}y^{\frac{2}{5}}}$ **65.** 1

67. $x^{\frac{7}{6}} - x^{\frac{11}{6}}$ **69.** $x - y$

71. $x + y - (x + y)^{\frac{3}{2}}$ **73.** $\dfrac{3\sqrt{2}}{4}$

75. $\dfrac{3\sqrt{3} - 3}{4}$ **77.** $\dfrac{2\sqrt{x} - 4}{x - 4}$

79. $\left(x^{\frac{1}{3}} + 3\right)\left(x^{\frac{1}{3}} - 2\right)$ **81.** $\left(x^{\frac{1}{2}} + 3\right)\left(x^{\frac{1}{2}} + 1\right)$

83. $\left(x^{\frac{2}{5}} + 9\right)\left(x^{\frac{1}{5}} + 3\right)\left(x^{\frac{1}{5}} - 3\right)$

85. $\dfrac{1}{\sqrt{x + h + 1} + \sqrt{x + 1}}$

87. $\dfrac{2x + h}{\sqrt{(x + h)^2 + 1} + \sqrt{x^2 + 1}}$

89. a. The square (or any even power) of a real number is never negative. Graphically these equations lie strictly above or on the x-axis.
b. $\sqrt[3]{-8} = -2$, whereas $\sqrt[6]{(-8)^2} = 2$

91. $\sqrt[n]{\sqrt[m]{c}} = \sqrt[mn]{c}$; $\sqrt[m]{cd} = \sqrt[m]{c}\sqrt[m]{d}$; $\sqrt[m]{\dfrac{c}{d}} = \dfrac{\sqrt[m]{c}}{\sqrt[m]{d}}$

93. When n is an odd positive integer, if $a < b$, $a^n < b^n$. Therefore, $f(x) = x^n$ is an increasing function and thus is one-to-one. Therefore, $f(x) = x^n$ has an inverse if n is an odd positive integer. The inverse is $g(x) = \sqrt[n]{x}$.

95. about 19° F **97.** 49 mph

99.

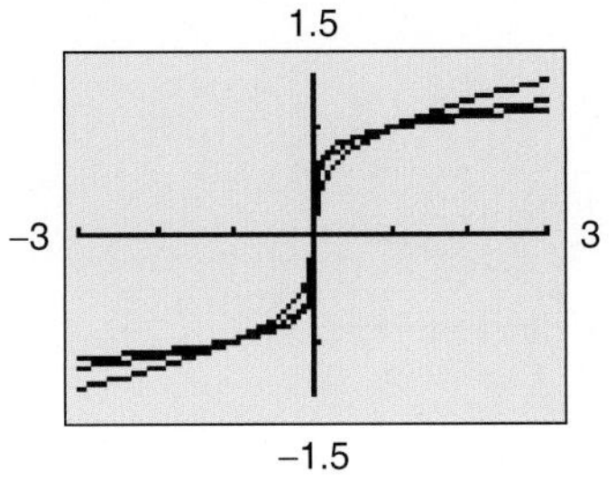

a. $x^{\frac{1}{3}} < x^{\frac{1}{5}} < x^{\frac{1}{7}}$ **b.** $x^{\frac{1}{7}} < x^{\frac{1}{5}} < x^{\frac{1}{3}}$
c. $x^{\frac{1}{3}} < x^{\frac{1}{5}} < x^{\frac{1}{7}}$ **d.** $x^{\frac{1}{7}} < x^{\frac{1}{5}} < x^{\frac{1}{3}}$

101. a. g is the graph of f moved 3 units left
b. h is the graph of f moved 2 units down
c. k is the graph of f moved 3 units left, then 2 units down.

Section 5.2, page 343

1. Shift the graph of h vertically 5 units downward.

3. Stretch the graph of h vertically by a factor of 3.

5. Shift the graph of h horizontally 2 units to the left, then vertically 5 units downward.

7. Shift the graph of h vertically 4 units upward.

9. Compress the graph of h vertically by a factor of $\frac{1}{4}$.

11. Reflect the graph of h across the y-axis, then shift horizontally 2 units to the right.

13. Reflect the graph of h across the y-axis, stretch horizontally by a factor of $\frac{1}{0.15} = 6\frac{2}{3}$, then stretch vertically by a factor of 4.

15. $f(x) = \left(\frac{5}{2}\right)^{-x}$

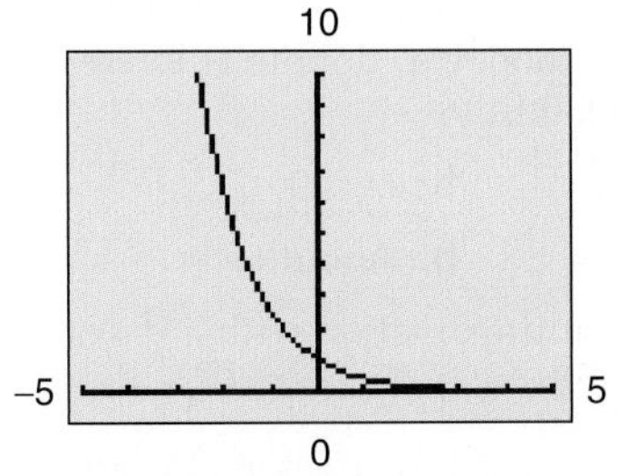

17. $g(x) = 3^{\frac{x}{2}}$

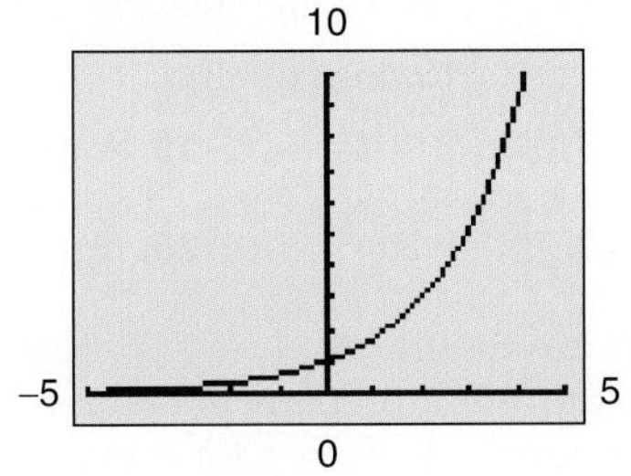

19. $g(x) = 2^{x-5}$

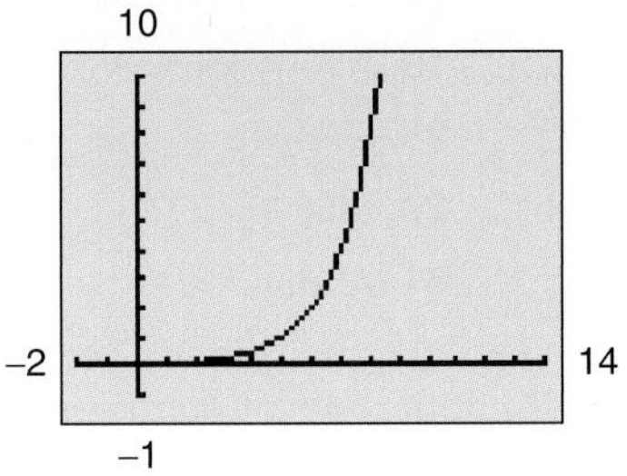

21. $f(x)$: B; $g(x)$: C; $h(x)$: A; $k(x)$: D

23. $-3 \leq x \leq 3$ and $0 \leq y \leq 1$

25. $-4 \leq x \leq 4$ and $-10 \leq y \leq 10$

27. $-4 \leq x \leq 4$ and $0 \leq y \leq 1$

29. $-5 \leq x \leq 20$ and $0 \leq y \leq 10$

31. Neither **33.** Odd

35. When x is large, $e^{-x} \approx 0$, so $e^x + e^{-x} \approx e^x + 0 = e^x$.

37. -4 **39.** $\dfrac{(e^{-1} - e^1) - (e^{-3} - e^3)}{2} \approx 8.84$

41. $\dfrac{5^{(x+h)^2} - 5^{x^2}}{h}$ **43.** $\dfrac{(e^{x+h} - e^{-x-h}) - (e^x - e^{-x})}{h}$

45. The x-axis is a horizontal asymptote; local maximum at (1.44,0.53).

47. No asymptotes; local minimum at (3, 0.0078).

49. No asymptotes; no extrema.

51. a. About 520 in 15 days; about 1559 in 25 days
b. in 29.3 days

53. a. 1980: 74.06; 2000: 76.34
b. 1930

55. a. 100,000 now; 83,527 in 2 months; 58,275 in 6 months
b. No. The graph continues to decrease toward zero.

57. a. The current population is 10, and in 5 years it will be about 149.
b. After about 9.55 years.

59. a. Not entirely
b. The graph of $f_8(x)$ appears to coincide with the graph of $g(x)$ on most calculator screens; when $-2.4 \leq x \leq 2.4$, the maximum error is at most 0.01.
c. Not at the right side of the viewing window; $f_{12}(x)$

Section 5.3, page 353

1. Annually: $1469.33; quarterly: $1485.95; monthly: $1489.85; weekly: $1491.37

3. $585.83 **5.** $610.40 **7.** $639.76

9. $563.75
11. $582.02
13. About $3325.29
15. About $3359.59
17. About $6351.16
19. About $568.59
21. Fund C
23. $385.18
25. About $1,162,003.14
27. $4000
29. About 5.00%
31. About 5.92%
33. a. About 9 years; about 9 years; about 9 years
b. Doubling time is not dependent on the amount invested, but on the rate at which it is invested.
35. About 9.9 years
37. a. About 12.6%
b. 12.6%; about 12.7%; about 12.7%
39. a. $f(x) = 6(3^x)$ or $f(x) = 18(3^{x-1})$
b. 3
c. No; yes
41. a. $g(x) = 100.4(1.014)^x$
b. 115.38 million
43. a. $E(x) = 5550(1.0368)^x$
b. $7966
c. In the sixth year
45. About 256; about 654
47. a. 6.705
b. 11.036
c. 16.242
49. a. $f(x) = (0.97)^x$
b. $0.86; $0.74
c. About 75 years
51. a. $f(t) = 20\left(0.5^{\frac{t}{140}}\right)$
b. About 11.892 mg; about 3.299 mg
c. About 325 days
53. About 5566 years old

Section 5.4, page 361

1. 4
3. -2.5
5. $10^3 = 1000$
7. $10^{2.8751} = 750$
9. $e^{1.0986} = 3$
11. $e^{-4.6052} = 0.01$
13. $e^{z+w} = x^2 + 2y$
15. $\log 0.01 = -2$
17. $\log 3 = 0.4771$
19. $\ln 25.79 = 3.25$
21. $\ln 5.5527 = \dfrac{12}{7}$
23. $\ln w = \dfrac{2}{r}$
25. $\sqrt{43}$
27. 15
29. $\dfrac{1}{2}$
31. 931
33. $x + y$
35. x^2
37. $(-1, \infty)$
39. $(-\infty, 0)$
41. They are exactly the same.
43. Stretch the graph of g away from the x-axis by a factor of 2. domain: all positive reals; range: all reals
45. Shift the graph of g horizontally 4 units to the right. domain: all reals > 4; range: all reals
47. Shift the graph of g horizontally 3 units to the left, then shift it vertically 4 units downward. domain: all reals > -3; range: all reals

49.
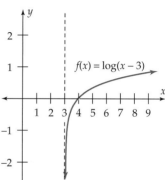

51.
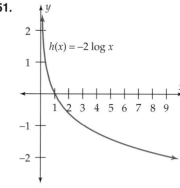

53. $0 \le x \le 9.4$ and $-6 \le y \le 6$ (vertical asymptote at $x = 1$)
55. $-10 \le x \le 10$ and $-3 \le y \le 3$
57. $0 \le x \le 20$ and $-6 \le y \le 3$
59. 0.5493
61. -0.2386
63. a. $\dfrac{\ln(3 + h) - \ln 3}{h}$
b. $h \approx 2.2$
65. a. About: 17.67, 11.90, 9.01, 6.12, 4.19, 3.22, 2.25
b. The rule of thumb is that the number of years it takes for your money to double at interest rate $r\%$ is 72 divided by r.
67. a. 77
b. 66; 59
69. a. 9.9 days
b. About 6986
71. $n = 30$ gives an approximation with a maximum error of 0.00001 when $-0.7 \le x \le 0.7$.

Section 5.5, page 369

1. 103
3. About -3.63
5. About 0.9030
7. About -0.1461
9. About -0.2219
11. $\ln(x^2 y^3)$
13. $\log(x - 3)$
15. $\ln(x^{-7})$
17. $3\ln(e - 1)$
19. $\log(20xy)$
21. $2u + 5v$
23. $\dfrac{1}{2}u + 2v$
25. $\dfrac{2}{3}u + \dfrac{1}{6}v$
27. a. For all $x > 0$
b. According to the fourth property of natural logarithms on page 364, $e^{\ln x} = x$ for every $x > 0$.

29. False; the right side is not defined when $x < 0$, but the left side is.

31. True by the Power Law

33. False; the graph of the left side differs from the graph of the right side.

35. Answers may vary: $\dfrac{\log 3}{\log 2} = 1.585$ and

$\log\left(\dfrac{3}{2}\right) = 0.1761$ thus $\dfrac{\log 3}{\log 2} \neq \log\left(\dfrac{3}{2}\right)$

37. $b = e$ **39.** $A = 3, B = 2$ **41.** 2

43. Approximately 2.54   **45.** 20 decibels

47. Approximately 66 decibels   **49.** 100 times

51. a. 1.2553   **b.** 3.9518   **c.** $\log x = \dfrac{\ln x}{\ln 10}$

Section 5.5.A, page 376

1. $\log 0.01 = -2$ **3.** $\log \sqrt[3]{10} = \dfrac{1}{3}$

5. $\log r = 7k$ **7.** $\log_7 5{,}764{,}801 = 8$

9. $\log_3\left(\dfrac{1}{9}\right) = -2$ **11.** $10^4 = 10{,}000$

13. $10^{2.8751} \approx 750$ **15.** $5^3 = 125$ **17.** $2^{-2} = \dfrac{1}{4}$

19. $10^{z+w} = x^2 + 2y$ **21.** $\sqrt{43}$ **23.** $\sqrt{x^2 + y^2}$

25. $\dfrac{1}{2}$ **27.** 6

29.

x	0	1	2	4
$f(x) = \log_4 x$	Not defined	0	0.5	1

31.

x	$\dfrac{1}{36}$	$\dfrac{1}{6}$	1	216
$h(x) = \log_6 x$	-2	-1	0	3

33.

x	0	$\dfrac{1}{7}$	$\sqrt{7}$	49
$f(x) = 2\log_7 x$	Not defined	-2	1	4

35.

x	-2.75	-1	1	29
$h(x) = 3\log_2(x + 3)$	-6	3	6	15

37. $b = 3$ **39.** $b = 20$

41. 5   **43.** 3   **45.** 4   **47.** $\log \dfrac{x^2 y^3}{z^6}$

49. $\log (x^2 - 3x)$ **51.** $\log_2(5c)$ **53.** $\log_4\left(\dfrac{1}{49c^2}\right)$

55. $\ln\left(\dfrac{(x + 1)^2}{x + 2}\right)$ **57.** $\log_2(x)$ **59.** $\ln(e^2 - 2e + 1)$

61. 3.3219   **63.** 0.8271   **65.** 1.1115   **67.** 1.6199

69. Horizontal shift of $\dfrac{4}{3}$ units to the right, then compress horizontally by a factor of $\dfrac{1}{3}$.

Domain: all real numbers $> \dfrac{4}{3}$

Range: all real numbers

71. Compress the graph vertically by a factor of $\dfrac{1}{3}$, then a horizontal translation of 1 unit to the right, then a vertical translation of 7 units upward.
Domain: all real numbers > 1
Range: all real numbers

73. True   **75.** True   **77.** False   **79.** 397^{398}

81. $\log_b u = \dfrac{\log_a u}{\log_a b}$ **83.** $\log_{10} u = 2\log_{100} u$

85. $\log_b x = \dfrac{1}{2}\log_b v + 3 = \log_b \sqrt{v} + \log_b b^3 =$

$\log_b\left(b^3 \cdot \sqrt{v}\right)$; hence $x = b^3 \sqrt{v}$.

87. $f(x) = g(x)$ only when $x \approx 0.123$, so the statement is false.

89.

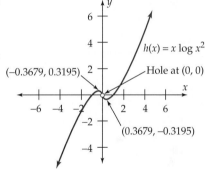

Section 5.6, page 386

1. $x = 4$ **3.** $x = \dfrac{1}{9}$ **5.** $x = \dfrac{1}{2}$ or -3

7. $x = -2$ or $-\dfrac{1}{2}$ **9.** $x = \dfrac{\ln 5}{\ln 3} \approx 1.465$

11. $x = \dfrac{\ln 3}{\ln 1.5} \approx 2.7095$

13. $x = \dfrac{\ln 3 - 5\ln 5}{\ln 5 + 2\ln 3} \approx -1.825$

15. $x = \dfrac{\ln 2 - \ln 3}{3\ln 2 + \ln 3} \approx -0.1276$

17. $x = \dfrac{(\ln 5)}{2} \approx 0.805$ **19.** $x = \dfrac{(-\ln 3.5)}{1.4} \approx -0.895$

21. $x = \dfrac{2\ln\left(\dfrac{5}{2.1}\right)}{\ln 3} \approx 1.579$ **23.** $x = 0$ or 1

25. $x = \ln 2 \approx 0.693$ or $x = \ln 3 \approx 1.099$

27. $x = \ln 3 \approx 1.099$

29. $x = \dfrac{\ln 2}{\ln 4} = \dfrac{1}{2}$ or $x = \dfrac{\ln 3}{\ln 4} \approx 0.792$

31. $x = \ln\left(t + \sqrt{t^2 + 1}\right)$

33. If $\ln u = \ln v$, then $e^{\ln u} = e^{\ln v}$, so $u = v$

35. $x = 9$ **37.** $x = 5$ **39.** $x = 6$ **41.** $x = 3$

43. $x = \dfrac{-5 + \sqrt{37}}{2}$ **45.** $x = \dfrac{9}{(e - 1)}$ **47.** $x = 5$

49. $x = \pm\sqrt{10001}$ **51.** $x = \sqrt{\dfrac{e + 1}{e - 1}}$

53. Approximately 3689 years old

55. Approximately 950.35 years ago

57. Approximately 444,000,000 years

59. Approximately 10.413 years

61. Approximately 9.853 days

63. Approximately 6.99%

65. a. Approximately 22.5 years
b. Approximately 22.1 years

67. $3197.05   **69.** 79.36 years

71. a. About 1.3601%   **b.** In the year 2027

73. a. $k \approx 21.459$ **b.** $t \approx 0.182$

75. a. There are 20 bacteria at the beginning and 2500 three hours later.

b. $\dfrac{\ln 2}{\ln 5} \approx 0.43$

77. a. At the outbreak: 200 people; after 3 weeks: about 2717 people
b. In about 6.09 weeks

79. a. $k \approx 0.229, c \approx 83.3$
b. 12.43 weeks

Section 5.7, page 396

1. Cubic, exponential, logistic

3. Exponential, quadratic, cubic

5. Exponential, logarithmic, quadratic, cubic

7. Quadratic, cubic   **9.** Quadratic, cubic

11. Ratios: 5.07, 5.06, 5.06, 5.08, 5.05; exponential is appropriate

13. a. For large values of x the term $56.33e^{-0.0216x}$ is close to zero so the quantity $(1 + 56.33e^{-0.0216x})$ is slightly larger than 1, which means

$\dfrac{442.1}{1 + 56.33e^{-0.0216x}}$ is always less than (but very close to) 442.1.

b.

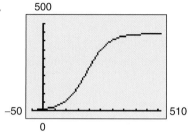

15. a.

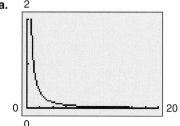

b.

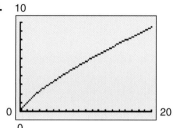

c.

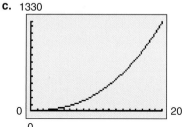

17. $\{(\ln x, \ln y)\}$ appears the most linear. Power model

19. $\{(\ln x, \ln y)\}$ and $\{(\ln x, y)\}$ are both nearly linear. Power or logarithmic model

21. a.

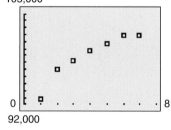

b. 105,000

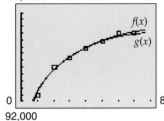

92,000

c.

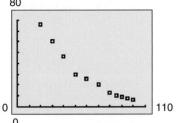

d. The logarithmic model predicts continued but slowing growth while the logistic predicts a cap of about 102,520. Therefore, the logarithmic model seems the better one for the long haul.

23. a. 80

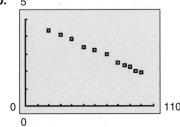

b. 5

c. Exponential.
$y = 152.22(0.97^x)$

175

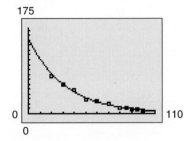

25. a. 1800

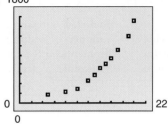

b. $y = 7.05x^2 - 78.34x + 398.73$

c. $y = \dfrac{6413.2}{1 + 107.2e^{-0.1815x}}$

d. 2325.01, 2419.97

e. The quadratic model will give an ever increasing number of kids, and the rate of increase will continue to increase. Before too terribly long the number of kids home schooled by the quadratic model will exceed the number of kids in the world. The logistic model, on the other hand, gives us a maximum that can never be exceeded.

27. a. $y = 17.5945 + 13.4239 \ln x$
   b. 77.4 years
   c. 2012

29. a. 85

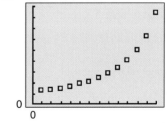

   b. $y = 10.48(1.16^x)$

c.-d.

Year	Worldwide shipments (thousands)	Predicted number shipments (thousands)	Worldwide shipments ratio (current to previous)
1985	14.7	12.2	
			1.03
1986	15.1	14.1	
			1.11
1987	16.7	16.4	
			1.08
1988	18.1	19	
			1.18
1989	21.3	22	
			1.11
1990	23.7	25.5	
			1.14
1991	27	29.6	
			1.2
1992	32.4	34.4	
			1.20
1993	38.9	39.9	
			1.23
1994	47.9	46.2	
			1.26
1995	60.2	53.6	
			1.18
1996	70.9	62.2	
			1.19
1997	84.3	72.2	

e. An exponential model may not be appropriate.

Chapter 5 Review, page 403

1. c^2 **3.** $a^{\frac{10}{3}}b^{\frac{42}{5}}$ **5.** $u^{\frac{1}{2}} - v^{\frac{1}{2}}$ **7.** $\dfrac{c^2 d^4}{2}$

9. $\dfrac{2}{\sqrt{2x + 2h + 1} + \sqrt{2x + 1}}$

11. Reflection across the x-axis, stretch vertically by a factor of 2

13. Reflection across the y-axis, stretch horizontally by a factor of 2

15. Vertical translation of 4 units upward

17. $-3 \le x \le 3$ and $0 \le y \le 2$

19. a. 62,000   33,708
       63,000   35,730
       64,000   37,874
  b. $S = 60,000 + 1000(t - 1)$ $S = 30,000(1.06)^{t-1}$
  c. Compunote is the best choice
  d. Calcuplay will be paying more this time, but your total earnings will be more from Compunote

21. a. About $1341.68   **b.** $541.68

23. a. About $2357.90
  b. After about 32.65 years

25. $f(x) = 56,000(1.065)^x$

27. About 3.75 grams

29. $\ln 756 = 6.628$ **31.** $\ln (u + v) = r^2 - 1$

33. $\log 756 = 2.8785$ **35.** $e^{7.118} = 1234$

37. $e^t = rs$ **39.** Undefined

41. Reflection across the y-axis, horizontal translation of 4 units to the right; Domain: all real numbers <4; Range: all real numbers

43. Vertical stretch by a factor of 3, vertical translation of 5 units downward; Domain: all positive real numbers; Range: all real numbers

45. 3   **47.** $\dfrac{3}{4}$ **49.** $2\ln x$ **51.** $\ln\left(\dfrac{9y}{x^2}\right)$ **53.** (c)

55. The domain consists of those values of x for which $\dfrac{x}{x - 1}$ is positive; $(-\infty, 0) \cup (1, \infty)$

57. $d^w = uv$ **59.** 2   **61.** (c)

63. $x = \dfrac{3 \pm \sqrt{57}}{4}$ **65.** $x = -\dfrac{1}{2}$

67. $x = e^{\frac{(u-c)}{d}}$ **69.** $x = 2$

71. $x = 101$ **73.** About 1.64 mg

75. Approximately 12 years

77. $452.89   **79.** 7.6

81. a. 11° F

  b.

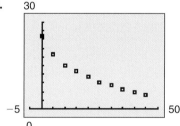

  c. The points $(x, \ln (y))$ are approximately linear.
  d. $y = 22.42(0.967^x)$
  e. 10.27° F

Chapter 5 can do calculus, page 411

 1. $y = -x + 1$;

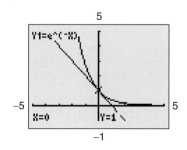

2. $y = -e^{-1}(x - 1) + e^{-1}$

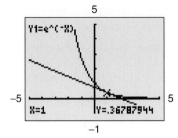

3. $y = -e^{-2}(x - 2) + e^{-2}$

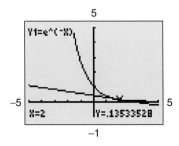

4. $y = -e^2(x + 2) + e^2$

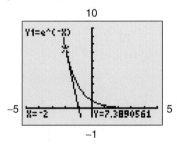

5. $y = x + 3$

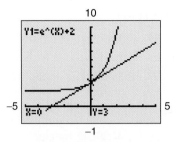

6. $y = e(x - 1) + e + 2$

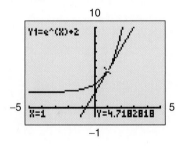

7. $y = e^2(x - 2) + e^2 + 2$

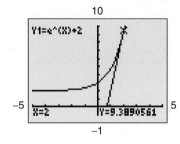

8. $y = e^{-2}(x + 2) + e^{-2} + 2$

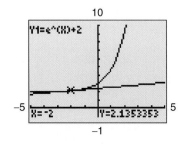

9. $y = (\ln 3)x + 1$

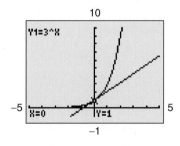

10. $y = (3 \ln 3)(x - 1) + 3$

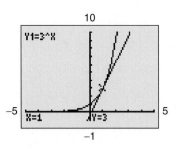

11. $y = (9 \ln 3)(x - 2) + 9$

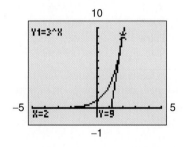

12. $y = \left(\frac{1}{9}\ln 3\right)(x + 2) + \frac{1}{9}$

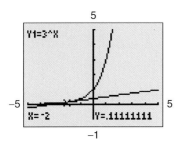

Chapter 6

Section 6.1, page 419

1. $47.26°$ **3.** $15.4125°$

5. $23°9'36''$ **7.** $4°12'27''$

9. $\sin\theta = \sqrt{\frac{2}{11}}$, $\cos\theta = \frac{3}{\sqrt{11}}$, $\tan\theta = \frac{\sqrt{2}}{3}$

$\cot\theta = \frac{3}{\sqrt{2}}$, $\sec\theta = \frac{\sqrt{11}}{3}$, $\csc\theta = \sqrt{\frac{11}{2}}$

11. $\sin\theta = \sqrt{\frac{3}{7}}$, $\cos\theta = \frac{2}{\sqrt{7}}$, $\tan\theta = \frac{\sqrt{3}}{2}$

$\cot\theta = \frac{2}{\sqrt{3}}$, $\sec\theta = \frac{\sqrt{7}}{2}$, $\csc\theta = \sqrt{\frac{7}{3}}$

13. $\sin\theta = \frac{h}{m}$, $\cos\theta = \frac{d}{m}$, $\tan\theta = \frac{h}{d}$

$\cot\theta = \frac{d}{h}$, $\sec\theta = \frac{m}{d}$, $\csc\theta = \frac{m}{h}$

15. $\sin 32° \approx 0.5299$ **17.** $\tan 6° \approx 0.1051$

19. $\sec 47° \approx 1.4663$ **21.** $\theta = 30°$

23. $\theta = 45°$ **25.** $\theta = 60°$

27. $\frac{1}{2}$ **29.** $\frac{3}{8}$ **31.** $\frac{16}{7}$

33. False;

$\sin 50° \approx 0.7660 \neq 2\sin 25° \approx 0.8452$

35. True;

$(\cos 28°)^2 \approx 0.7796 = 1 - (\sin 28°)^2 \approx 0.7796$

37. False;

$\tan 75° \approx 3.7321 \neq \tan 30° + \tan 45° \approx 1.5774$

39.

θ	$\sin\theta$	$\cos\theta$
$1°$	0.0175	0.9998
$0.1°$	0.00175	0.999998
$0.01°$	0.000175	0.99999998
$0.0001°$	0.0000175	0.9999999998

$\sin 0° = 0$; $\cos 0° = 1$ Since no triangle has an angle of $0°$, the right triangle definitions do not apply.

41. The area of the triangle is $\frac{1}{2}a \cdot h$. The altitude h forms a right triangle with side b as the hypotenuse and side h opposite θ, so $\sin\theta = \frac{b}{h} \to h = b\sin\theta$. Thus, the area of the triangle is $\frac{1}{2}a \cdot h = \frac{1}{2}a(b\sin\theta) = \frac{1}{2}ab\sin\theta$.

43. $A \approx 4320.123$ **45.** $A \approx 33.246$

Section 6.2, page 429

1. $c = 36$ **3.** $c = 36$ **5.** $c = 8.4$

7. $h = \frac{25\sqrt{2}}{2}$ **9.** $h = 300$ **11.** $h = 50\sqrt{3}$

13. $c = \frac{4\sqrt{3}}{3}$ **15.** $a = \frac{10\sqrt{3}}{3}$

17. $\angle A = 40°$, $a = 10\cos 50° = 6.4$, $c = 10\sin 50° = 7.7$

19. $\angle C = 76°$, $b = \frac{6}{\sin 14°} = 24.8$, $c = \frac{6}{\tan 14°} = 24.1$

21. $\angle C = 25°$, $a = 5\tan 65° = 10.7$, $b = \frac{5}{\cos 65°} = 11.8$

23. $\angle C = 18°$, $a = 3.5\sin 72° = 3.3$, $c = 3.5\cos 72° = 1.1$

25. About $48.59°$ **27.** About $48.19°$

29. $\angle A = 33.7°$, $\angle C = 56.3°$

31. $\angle A = 44.4°$, $\angle C = 45.6°$

33. $\angle A = 48.2°$, $\angle C = 41.8°$

35. $\angle A = 60.8°$, $\angle C = 29.2°$

37. a. $\cong 23.18$ feet.
  b. $\cong 6.21$ feet.

39. 460.2 ft **41.** 8598.3 ft **43.** No

45. Approximately 263.44 feet

47. 351.1 m **49.** 10.1 ft **51.** 1.6 mi

53. a. 56.7 ft **b.** 9.7 ft

55. 173.2 mi **57.** 52.5 mph **59.** 449.1 ft

Section 6.3, page 441

1. $40°$, $\frac{2\pi}{9}$ radians **3.** $20°$, $\frac{\pi}{9}$ radians

5. $10°$, $\frac{\pi}{18}$ radians **7.** $240°$, $\frac{4\pi}{3}$ radians

9. $288°$, $\frac{8\pi}{5}$ radians

11. $36°$ **13.** $-18°$ **15.** $135°$ **17.** $4°$

19. $-75°$ **21.** $972°$ **23.** $\frac{\pi}{30}$ **25.** $-\frac{\pi}{15}$

27. $\dfrac{5\pi}{12}$ **29.** $\dfrac{3\pi}{4}$ **31.** $-\dfrac{5\pi}{4}$ **33.** $\dfrac{31\pi}{6}$

35. $\dfrac{5\pi}{3}$ **37.** $\dfrac{3\pi}{4}$ **39.** $\dfrac{3\pi}{5}$ **41.** $7 - 2\pi$

43. $\dfrac{9\pi}{4}, \dfrac{17\pi}{4}, -\dfrac{7\pi}{4}, -\dfrac{15\pi}{4}$

45. $\dfrac{11\pi}{6}, \dfrac{23\pi}{6}, -\dfrac{13\pi}{6}, -\dfrac{25\pi}{6}$

47. $\dfrac{4\pi}{3}$ **49.** $\dfrac{7\pi}{6}$ **51.** $\dfrac{41\pi}{6}$ **53.** 8π cm

55. $\dfrac{17}{4}$ **57.** $\dfrac{50}{9}$ **59.** 2000   **61.** 5

63. 8.75   **65.** 3490.66 mi   **67.** 942.48 mi

69. 7π **71.** 4π **73.** 42.5π **75.** $2\pi k$

77. 3 radians ($\approx 171.9°$)

79. a. 400π radians per min

b. 800π in. per min or $\dfrac{200\pi}{3}$ ft per min

81. a. 5π radians per sec
b. 6.69 mph

83. 15.92 ft   **85.** approximately 8.6 miles

Section 6.4, page 452

1. $\sin t = \dfrac{7}{\sqrt{53}}, \cos t = \dfrac{2}{\sqrt{53}}, \tan t = \dfrac{7}{2}$

3. $\sin t = \dfrac{-6}{\sqrt{61}}, \cos t = \dfrac{-5}{\sqrt{61}}, \tan t = \dfrac{6}{5}$

5. $\sin t = \dfrac{-10}{\sqrt{103}}, \cos t = \dfrac{\sqrt{3}}{\sqrt{103}}, \tan t = \dfrac{-10}{\sqrt{3}}$

7. $\sin t = \dfrac{1}{\sqrt{5}}, \cos t = -\dfrac{2}{\sqrt{5}}, \tan t = -\dfrac{1}{2}$

9. $\sin t = -\dfrac{4}{5}, \cos t = -\dfrac{3}{5}, \tan t = \dfrac{4}{3}$

11. $\sin \dfrac{13\pi}{6} = \dfrac{1}{2}; \cos \dfrac{13\pi}{6} = \dfrac{\sqrt{3}}{2}$

13. $\sin 16\pi = 0; \cos 16\pi = 1$

15. a. $\sin \dfrac{7\pi}{5} \approx -0.9511, \cos \dfrac{7\pi}{5} \approx -0.3090,$

$\tan \dfrac{7\pi}{5} \approx 3.0777$

b. Since the sine and cosine are both negative, the terminal side is in the third quadrant.

17. a. $\sin\left(\dfrac{-14\pi}{9}\right) \approx 0.9848, \cos\left(\dfrac{-14\pi}{9}\right) \approx 0.1736,$

$\tan\left(\dfrac{-14\pi}{9}\right) \approx 5.6713$

b. Since the sine and cosine are both positive, the terminal side is in the first quadrant.

19. a. $\sin \dfrac{10\pi}{3} \approx -0.8660, \cos \dfrac{10\pi}{3} = -0.5,$

$\tan \dfrac{10\pi}{3} \approx 1.7321$

b. Since the sine and cosine are both negative, the terminal side is in the third quadrant.

21. a. $\sin 9.5\pi = -1, \cos 9.5\pi = 0, \tan 9.5\pi$ is undefined

b. Since the sine is -1 and the cosine is 0, the terminal side is on the negative y-axis.

23. a. $\sin(-17) \approx 0.9614, \cos(-17) \approx -0.2752,$
$\tan(-17) \approx -3.4939$

b. Since the sine is positive and the cosine is negative, the terminal side is in the second quadrant.

25.

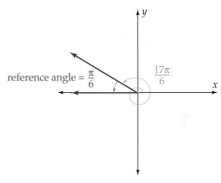

27.

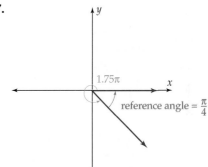

29.

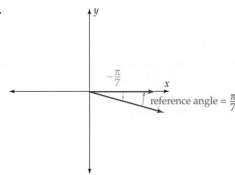

Answers to Selected Exercises   **1099**

31. $\sin\left(\dfrac{7\pi}{3}\right) = \dfrac{\sqrt{3}}{2}, \cos\left(\dfrac{7\pi}{3}\right) = \dfrac{1}{2}, \tan\left(\dfrac{7\pi}{3}\right) = \sqrt{3}$

33. $\sin\left(\dfrac{11\pi}{4}\right) = \dfrac{\sqrt{2}}{2}, \cos\left(\dfrac{11\pi}{4}\right) = -\dfrac{\sqrt{2}}{2},$

$\tan\left(\dfrac{11\pi}{4}\right) = -1$

35. $\sin\left(-\dfrac{3\pi}{2}\right) = 1, \cos\left(-\dfrac{3\pi}{2}\right) = 0, \tan\left(-\dfrac{3\pi}{2}\right) = \dfrac{\sin\theta}{\cos\theta}$
is undefined.

37. $\sin\left(-\dfrac{23\pi}{6}\right) = \dfrac{1}{2}, \cos\left(-\dfrac{23\pi}{6}\right) = \dfrac{\sqrt{3}}{2},$

$\tan\left(-\dfrac{23\pi}{6}\right)\dfrac{1}{\sqrt{3}} = \dfrac{\sqrt{3}}{3}$

39. $\sin\left(-\dfrac{19\pi}{3}\right) = -\dfrac{\sqrt{3}}{2}, \cos\left(-\dfrac{19\pi}{3}\right) = \dfrac{1}{2},$

$\tan\left(-\dfrac{19\pi}{3}\right) = -\sqrt{3}$

41. $\sin\left(-\dfrac{15\pi}{4}\right) = \dfrac{\sqrt{2}}{2}, \cos\left(-\dfrac{15\pi}{4}\right) = \dfrac{\sqrt{2}}{2},$

$\tan\left(-\dfrac{15\pi}{4}\right) = 1$

43. $\sin\left(\dfrac{5\pi}{6}\right) = \dfrac{1}{2}, \cos\left(\dfrac{5\pi}{6}\right) = -\dfrac{\sqrt{3}}{2}, \tan\left(\dfrac{5\pi}{6}\right) = \dfrac{-1}{\sqrt{3}}$

$= -\dfrac{\sqrt{3}}{3}$

45. $\sin\theta = 1, \cos\theta = 0,$ and $\tan\theta$ is undefined

47. $\sin\theta = 0, \cos\theta = 1,$ and $\tan\theta = 0$

49. $\dfrac{-\sqrt{2}}{2}$ **51.** $\dfrac{\sqrt{2}}{4}(1 - \sqrt{3})$ **53.** $\dfrac{-\sqrt{3}}{2}$

55. $\sin t = -\dfrac{5}{\sqrt{34}}, \cos t = \dfrac{3}{\sqrt{34}}, \tan t = -\dfrac{5}{3}$

57. $\sin t = \dfrac{1}{\sqrt{5}}, \cos t = -\dfrac{2}{\sqrt{5}}, \tan t = -\dfrac{1}{2}$

59. $\sin t = -\dfrac{3}{\sqrt{10}}, \cos t = \dfrac{1}{\sqrt{10}}, \tan t = -3$

61. $(r\cos t, r\sin t)$

63. Domain: all real numbers with $\theta \neq$ a multiple of π
Range: $(-\infty, -1) \cup (1, \infty)$

65. Domain: all real numbers with $\theta \neq$ a multiple of π
Range: all real numbers

Section 6.5, page 460

1. $\cos t$ **3.** 1 **5.** 1 **7.** $\csc^2 t$

9. $\cos t \approx 0.9457, \tan t \approx 0.3438, \cot t \approx 2.9089,$
$\sec t \approx 1.0574, \csc t \approx 3.0760$

11. $\sec t \approx 3.7646, \cos t \approx 0.2656, \sin t \approx 0.9641,$
$\cot t \approx 0.2755, \csc t \approx 1.0372$

13. $\sin t \approx 0.1601, \cos t \approx 0.9871, \tan t \approx 0.1622,$
$\cot t \approx 6.1668, \sec t \approx 1.0131$

15. $\sin^2 t - \cos^2 t$ **17.** $\cos t$

19. $\dfrac{1}{4}$ **21.** $\cos t + 2$ **23.** $\cos t$

25. $|\sin t \cos t|\sqrt{\sin t}$

27. even   **29.** even   **31.** odd

33. $\sin t = -\dfrac{\sqrt{3}}{2}$ **35.** $\sin t = \dfrac{\sqrt{3}}{2}$ **37.** $-\dfrac{3}{5}$

39. $-\dfrac{3}{5}$ **41.** $\dfrac{3}{4}$ **43.** $-\dfrac{3}{4}$

45. $-\dfrac{\sqrt{21}}{5}$ **47.** $-\dfrac{2}{5}$ **49.** $-\dfrac{\sqrt{21}}{5}$

51. $\dfrac{\sqrt{2 + \sqrt{2}}}{2}$ **53.** $\dfrac{\sqrt{2 - \sqrt{2}}}{2}$

55. possible   **57.** not possible   **59.** not possible

61. $\csc t = \csc(t \pm 2\pi); \sec t = \sec(t \pm 2\pi);$
$\cot t = \cot(t \pm \pi)$

Chapter 6 Review, page 464

1. $41.115°$ **3.** (d)   **5.** $\dfrac{4}{\sqrt{65}}$ **7.** $\dfrac{\sqrt{65}}{7}$

9. $\dfrac{4}{7}$ **11.** $C = 50°, a \approx 6.4, c \approx 7.7$

13. $C = 34°, b \approx 13.3, c \approx 7.4$ **15.** 225.9 ft

17. The boat has moved about 95.3 feet.

19. $255°$ **21.** $\dfrac{\pi}{5}$ **23.** $-\dfrac{3\pi}{4}$ **25.** $\dfrac{16\pi}{3}$

27. 2 revolutions per minute

29. $\dfrac{3}{5}$ **31.** 0 **33.** $-\dfrac{1}{2}$ **35.** $-\sqrt{3}$

37. $\dfrac{\sqrt{3}}{3}$ **39.** -2 **41.** $\dfrac{\sqrt{3}}{2}$

43. quadrants 2 and 3   **45.** $\dfrac{9}{4}$

47. $\dfrac{\dfrac{\sin t}{\cos t}}{\dfrac{\cos t}{\sin t}} = \tan^2 t$ **49.** e

51. $-\dfrac{3}{5}$ **53.** -1 **55.** b

Chapter 6 **can do calculus**, page 471

1. $f(t) = \sin t \cos t$

$\dfrac{\pi}{12}$

X	Y1
0	0
.2618	.25
.5236	.43301
.7854	.5
1.0472	.43301
1.309	.25
1.5708	0

Y1■sin(X)cos(X)

max of 0.5 when $x \approx 0.7854$

$\dfrac{\pi}{144}$

X	Y1
.71993	.49572
.74175	.4981
.76356	.49952
.78538	.5
.8072	.49952
.82901	.4981
.85083	.49572

Y1■sin(X)cos(X)

max of 0.5 when $x \approx 0.78538$

2. $f(t) = \sin t + 2 \cos t$

$\dfrac{\pi}{12}$

X	Y1
0	2
.2618	2.1907
.5236	2.2321
.7854	2.1213
1.0472	1.866
1.309	1.4836
1.5708	1

Y1■sin(X)+2cos(...

max of 2.2321 when $x \approx 0.5236$

$\dfrac{\pi}{144}$

X	Y1
.3927	2.2304
.41452	2.2334
.43633	2.2352
.45815	2.236
.47997	2.2358
.50178	2.2344
.5236	2.2321

Y1■sin(X)+2cos(...

max of 2.236 when $x \approx 0.45815$

3. $3 \sin t + \sin\left(\dfrac{\pi}{2} - t\right)$

$\dfrac{\pi}{12}$

X	Y1
0	1
.2618	1.7424
.5236	2.366
.7854	2.8284
1.0472	3.0981
1.309	3.1566
1.5708	3

Y1■3sin(X)+sin(...

max of 3.1566 when $x \approx 1.309$

$\dfrac{\pi}{144}$

X	Y1
1.1781	3.1543
1.1999	3.1585
1.2217	3.1611
1.2435	3.1622
1.2653	3.1619
1.2872	3.16
1.309	3.1566

Y1■3sin(X)+sin(...

max of 3.1622 when $x \approx 1.2435$

4. $f(t) = 2 \cos t - \dfrac{1}{1 + \sin t}$

$\dfrac{\pi}{12}$

X	Y1
0	1
.2618	1.1375
.5236	1.0654
.7854	.82843
1.0472	.4641
1.309	.00897
1.5708	-.5

Y1■2cos(X)-1/(1...

max of 1.1375 when $x \approx 0.2618$

$\dfrac{\pi}{144}$

X	Y1
.21817	1.1305
.23998	1.1347
.2618	1.1375
.28362	1.1387
.30543	1.1386
.32725	1.1371
.34907	1.1342

Y1■2cos(X)-1/(1...

max of 1.1387 when $x \approx 0.28362$

5. a. $200 \sin t \cos t$

b. $\dfrac{\pi}{4}$ radians; height $= 5\sqrt{2}$ meters and width $= 10\sqrt{2}$ meters

6. approximately 13.23 feet from the statue

7. a. road cost $= 10,000\left(10 - \dfrac{1}{\tan t}\right) + 20,000\left(\dfrac{1}{\sin t}\right)$

b. approximately \$117,321

Chapter 7

Section 7.1, page 483

1.

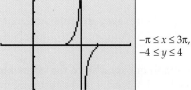

$-\pi \le x \le \dfrac{13\pi}{2}$, $-2 \le y \le 2$

3.

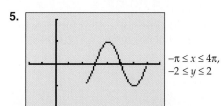

$-\pi \le x \le 3\pi$, $-4 \le y \le 4$

5.

$-\pi \le x \le 4\pi$, $-2 \le y \le 2$

7. $-\dfrac{3\pi}{2}, \dfrac{\pi}{2}$

9. 1

11. $-\dfrac{3\pi}{2}, -\dfrac{\pi}{2}, \dfrac{\pi}{2}, \dfrac{3\pi}{2}$

13. 1

15. $-\dfrac{\pi}{2} \le t \le \dfrac{\pi}{2}$

17. $-\dfrac{7\pi}{4} < t < -\dfrac{3\pi}{2}, -\dfrac{3\pi}{4} < t < -\dfrac{\pi}{2}, \dfrac{\pi}{4} < t < \dfrac{\pi}{2},$

and $\dfrac{5\pi}{4} < t < \dfrac{3\pi}{2}$

19. all values on the interval $[\pi, 2\pi]$ except $\dfrac{3\pi}{2}$

21. $t = \dfrac{\pi}{4} + 2n\pi$ or $t = \dfrac{3\pi}{4} + 2n\pi$, where n is any integer

23. $t = \dfrac{2\pi}{3} + 2n\pi$ or $t = \dfrac{4\pi}{3} + 2n\pi$, where n is any integer

25. $t = \dfrac{4\pi}{3} + 2n\pi$ or $t = \dfrac{5\pi}{3} + 2n\pi$, where n is any integer

27. $t = \dfrac{\pi}{6} + 2n\pi$ or $t = \dfrac{11\pi}{6} + 2n\pi$, where n is any integer

29. $t = \dfrac{\pi}{6} + 2n\pi$ or $t = \dfrac{5\pi}{6} + 2n\pi$, where n is any integer

31. $t = \dfrac{3\pi}{4} + 2n\pi$ or $t = \dfrac{5\pi}{4} + 2n\pi$, where n is any integer

33. $t = \dfrac{\pi}{3} + n\pi$, where n is any integer

35. Reflect the graph of f across the horizontal axis. domain: all real numbers; range: $-1 \le g(t) \le 1$

37. Shift the graph of f vertically 5 units upward. domain: all real numbers except odd multiples of $\dfrac{\pi}{2}$; range: all real numbers

39. Stretch the graph of f away from the horizontal axis by a factor of 3. domain: all real numbers; range: $-3 \le g(t) \le 3$

41. Stretch the graph of f away from the horizontal axis by a factor of 3, then shift the resulting graph vertically 2 units upward. domain: all real numbers; range: $-1 \le g(t) \le 5$

43. Shift the graph of f vertically 3 units upward. domain: all real numbers; range: $2 \le g(t) \le 4$

45.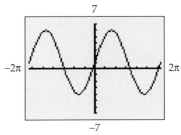

47.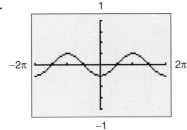

49. d   **51.** e   **53.** f

55. a. odd; $\sin(-t) = -\sin t$
b. even; $\cos(-t) = \cos t$
c. odd; $\tan(-t) = -\tan t$
d. even; $\sin(-t) = -\sin t$
e. odd; $\tan(-t) = -\tan t$

57. 1.4   **59.** 11

61.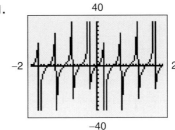

a. 0   **b.** 0
c. 15.4 yards   **d.** −3.6 yards
e. When $t = 0.25$, d is undefined. The beam is parallel to the wall at this time.

Section 7.2, page 490

1. The graph of $s(t) = 3 \sec t - 2$ is the graph of $g(t) = \sec t$ stretched vertically by a factor of 3 and shifted down 2 units.

3. The graph of $m(t) = \csc(t) + 4$ is the graph of $f(t) = \csc t$ shifted 4 units up.

5. The graph of $p(t) = \dfrac{1}{2} \sec t + 1$ is the graph of $g(t) = \sec t$ compressed vertically by a factor of $\dfrac{1}{2}$ and shifted up 1 unit.

7. The graph of $q(t) = \sec(-t) - 8$ is the graph of $g(t) = \sec t$ reflected across the vertical axis, and shifted 8 units down.

9. The graph of $v(t) = \pi \csc t$ is the graph of $f(t) = \csc t$ stretched vertically by a factor of π.

11. $g(t) = 3\sec(t + 1)$ **13.** $g(t) = -\dfrac{1}{4}\sec t$

15. $g(t) = \csc\left(t - \dfrac{\pi}{2}\right) - 5$ **17.** $g(t) = -\cot(-t)$

19. D **21.** B **23.** A **25.** A

27. B **29.** A **31.** A **33.** B

35.

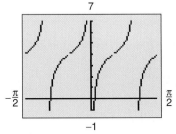

37.

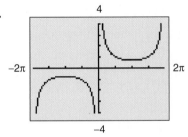

39. Look at the graph of $y = \sec t$ on page 488. If you draw in the line $y = t$, it will pass through $\left(-\dfrac{\pi}{2}, -\dfrac{\pi}{2}\right)$ and $\left(\dfrac{\pi}{2}, \dfrac{\pi}{2}\right)$, and obviously will not intersect the graph of $y = \sec t$ when $-\dfrac{\pi}{2} \le t \le \dfrac{\pi}{2}$. But it will intersect each part of the graph that lies above the horizontal axis, to the right of $t = \dfrac{\pi}{2}$; it will also intersect those parts that lie below the horizontal axis, to the left of $-\dfrac{\pi}{2}$. The first coordinate of each of these infinitely many intersection points will be a solution of $\sec t = t$.

Section 7.3, page 498

1. amplitude: 1; period: 2π

3. amplitude: 1; period: $\dfrac{2\pi}{3}$

5. amplitude: 4; period: 2π

7. amplitude: none; period: $\dfrac{\pi}{2}$

9. amplitude: 0.3; period: 6π

11. amplitude: $\dfrac{1}{2}$; period: $\dfrac{2\pi}{3}$

13. amplitude: 5; period: $\dfrac{20\pi}{17}$

15. amplitude: none; period: 4

17. a. 2 **b.** $t = \dfrac{1}{2}$ or $\dfrac{3}{2}$
 c. $t = 0$ or 2 **d.** $t = 1$

19. g is the graph of f horizontally compressed by a factor of $\dfrac{1}{5}$; amplitude: 1; period: $\dfrac{2\pi}{5}$.

21. g is the graph of f horizontally compressed by a factor of $\dfrac{1}{8}$; amplitude: 1; period: $\dfrac{\pi}{4}$.

23. g is the graph of f reflected across the y-axis; amplitude: none; period: π.

25. g is the graph of f horizontally compressed by a factor of $\dfrac{5}{8}$; amplitude: 1; period: $\dfrac{5\pi}{4}$.

27. g is the graph of f vertically stretched by a factor of 3; amplitude: 3; period: 2π.

29. g is the graph of f vertically compressed by a factor of $\dfrac{1}{3}$; amplitude: none; period: π.

31. g is the graph of f vertically stretched by a factor of 5 and horizontally compressed by a factor of $\dfrac{1}{2}$; amplitude: 5; period: π.

33. g is the graph of f reflected across the x-axis, vertically stretched by a factor of 2, and horizontally stretched by a factor of 5; amplitude: none; period: 5π.

35. g is the graph of f vertically compressed by a factor of $\dfrac{2}{5}$ and horizontally compressed by a factor of $\dfrac{1}{8}$; amplitude: $\dfrac{2}{5}$; period: $\dfrac{\pi}{4}$.

37. g is the graph of f vertically compressed by a factor of $\dfrac{1}{3}$ and horizontally compressed by a factor of $\dfrac{1}{\pi}$; amplitude: none; period: 1

39.

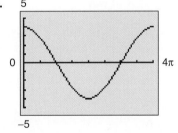

41.

12

$-\dfrac{\pi}{6}$ $\dfrac{\pi}{6}$

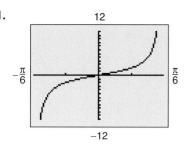

−12

43.

4

0   1

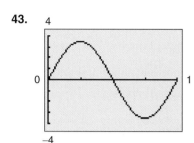

−4

45. d   **47.** b   **49.** f

51. $f(t) = 2 \sin \dfrac{t}{2}$ **53.** $f(t) = 1.8 \sin \dfrac{4t}{3}$

55. $f(t) = \dfrac{3}{2} \sin \dfrac{\pi t}{2}$ **57.** $f(t) = 2 \sin 4t$

59. $f(t) = -5 \sin(5t)$

61. local maximum of 1 at $t = 0$ and $t = \dfrac{2\pi}{3}$; local

minimum of -1 at $t = \dfrac{\pi}{3}$.

63. there is a local maximum of $\dfrac{\sqrt{3}}{2}$ at $t = \pi$; local

minimum of -1 at $t = -\dfrac{3\pi}{2}$.   **65.** $\dfrac{1}{900,000}$

Section 7.4, page 508

1. amplitude: 1; period: 2π; phase shift: -1; vertical shift: 0

3. amplitude: 5; period: π; phase shift: 0; vertical shift: 0

5. amplitude: 1; period: 2π; phase shift: π; vertical shift: -4

7. amplitude: 6; period: $\dfrac{2}{3}$; phase shift: $-\dfrac{1}{3\pi}$; vertical shift: 0

9. amplitude: 4; period: $\dfrac{2\pi}{3}$; phase shift: $\dfrac{\pi}{18}$; vertical shift: 1

11. amplitude: 7; period: $\dfrac{2\pi}{7}$; phase shift: $-\dfrac{1}{49}$; vertical shift: 0

13. amplitude: 3; period: π; phase shift: $\dfrac{5\pi}{8}$; vertical shift: 0

15. amplitude: 97; period: $\dfrac{\pi}{7}$; phase shift: $-\dfrac{5}{14}$; vertical shift: 0

17. amplitude: 1; period: 1; phase shift: 0; vertical shift: 7

19. amplitude: 3; period: 6; phase shift: $\dfrac{3}{\pi}$; vertical shift: 5

21. $f(t) = 3 \sin 8\left(t - \dfrac{\pi}{5}\right)$ or $f(t) = 3 \sin\left(8t - \dfrac{8\pi}{5}\right)$

23. $f(t) = \dfrac{2}{3} \sin \dfrac{2}{3}\left(t + \dfrac{2\pi}{3}\right) - 2$ or

$f(t) = \dfrac{2}{3} \sin\left(\dfrac{2}{3}t + \dfrac{4\pi}{9}\right) - 2$

25. $f(t) = 0.5 \sin 0.8\pi(t - 1.5) - 0.6$ or
$f(t) = 0.5 \sin(0.8\pi t - 1.2\pi) - 0.6$

27. $f(t) = 6 \sin \dfrac{6}{5}(t - 0) - 1$ or $f(t) = 6 \sin\left(\dfrac{6}{5}t\right) - 1$

29. $f(t) = \dfrac{5}{2} \sin \dfrac{10\pi}{9}(t - 0.2) + 0$ or

$f(t) = \dfrac{5}{2} \sin\left(\dfrac{10\pi}{9}t - \dfrac{2\pi}{9}\right)$

31. a. $f(t) = 12 \sin\left(10t - \dfrac{\pi}{2}\right)$

     b. $g(t) = -12 \cos 10t$

33. a. $f(t) = -\sin 2t$ **b.** $g(t) = -\cos\left(2t - \dfrac{\pi}{2}\right)$

35. a. $f(t) = \dfrac{1}{2} \sin 8t$ **b.** $g(t) = \dfrac{1}{2} \cos\left(8t - \dfrac{\pi}{2}\right)$

37. a. $f(t) = -4 \sin \dfrac{2}{3}t + 1$

     b. $f(t) = -4 \cos\left(\dfrac{2}{3}t - \dfrac{\pi}{2}\right) + 1$

39. a. $f(t) = -2 \sin\left(t - \dfrac{3\pi}{4}\right) + 6$

     b. $f(t) = 2 \cos\left(t - \dfrac{\pi}{4}\right) + 6$

41.

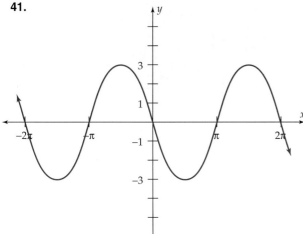

43.

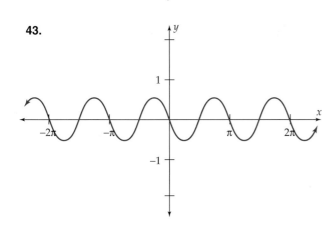

45.

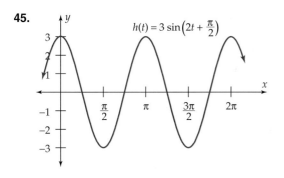

$h(t) = 3 \sin\left(2t + \frac{\pi}{2}\right)$

47.

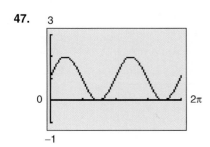

49. Local maximum at $t = \frac{5\pi}{6} \approx 2.6180$; local

minimum at $t = \frac{11\pi}{6} \approx 5.7596$

51. Local maxima at $t = \frac{\pi}{6} \approx 0.5236$, $t = \frac{5\pi}{6} \approx 2.6180$,

$t = \frac{3\pi}{2} \approx 4.7124$; local minima at $t = \frac{\pi}{2} \approx 1.5708$,

$t = \frac{7\pi}{6} \approx 3.6652$, $t = \frac{11\pi}{6} \approx 5.7596$

53. The graph of $f(t) = \sin^2 t + \cos^2 t$ is the same as the graph of $f(x) = 1$, a horizontal line intercepting the y-axis at 1.

55. Not an identity   **57.** Possibly an identity

59. $A \approx 3.8332$, $b = 4$, $c \approx 1.4572$

61. $A \approx 5.3852$, $b = 1$, $c \approx 1.1903$

63. All waves in the graph of g are of equal height, which is not the case with the graph of f. It cannot be constructed from a sine curve through translations, stretches, or contractions.

Section 7.4A, page 515

1. $f(t) = 2.2361 \sin(t + 1.1072)$

3. $f(t) = 5.3852 \sin(4t - 1.1903)$

5. $f(t) = 5.1164 \sin(3t - 0.7442)$

7. $0 \le t \le 2\pi$ and $-5 \le y \le 5$ (one period)

9. $-10 \le t \le 10$ and $-10 \le y \le 10$

11. $0 \le t \le \frac{\pi}{50}$ and $-2 \le y \le 2$ (one period)

13. $0 \le t \le 0.04$ and $-7 \le y \le 7$ (one period)

15. $0 \le t \le 10$ and $-6 \le y \le 10$ (one period)

17. To the left of the y-axis, the graph lies above the t-axis, which is a horizontal asymptote of the graph. To the right of the y-axis, the graph makes waves of amplitude 1, of shorter and shorter period.
Window: $-3 \le t \le 3.2$ and $-2 \le y \le 2$

19. The graph is symmetric with respect to the y-axis and consists of waves along the t-axis, whose amplitude slowly increases as you move farther from the origin in either direction.
Window: $-30 \le t \le 30$ and $-6 \le y \le 6$

21. There is a hole at point $(0, 1)$. The graph is symmetric with respect to the y-axis and consists of waves along the t-axis whose amplitude rapidly decreases as you move farther from the origin in either direction.
Window: $-30 \le t \le 30$ and $-0.3 \le y \le 1$

23. The function is periodic with period π. The graph lies on or below the t-axis because the logarithmic function is negative for numbers

between 0 and 1 and |cos *t*| is always between 0 and 1. The graph has vertical asymptotes when $t = \pm\frac{\pi}{2}, \pm\frac{3\pi}{2}, \pm\frac{5\pi}{2}, \pm\frac{7\pi}{2}, \ldots$ (cos *t* = 0 at these points and ln 0 is not defined).
Window: $-2\pi \le t \le 2\pi$ and $-3 \le y \le 1$ (two periods)

Chapter 7 Review, page 517

1. (c)

3.

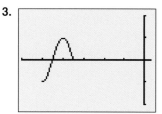

5. $0 + n2\pi$, where *n* is an integer

7. $-\frac{\pi}{3} + n\pi$, where *n* is an integer

9. The graph of *g* is the graph of *f* reflected across the horizontal axis and compressed horizontally by a factor of $\frac{1}{2}$. domain: all real numbers except $t = \frac{\pi}{4} + n\frac{\pi}{2}$, where *n* is an integer; range: all real numbers

11.

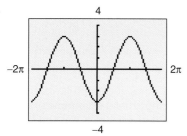

13.

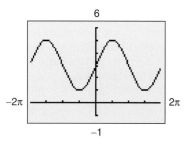

15. A   **17.** C

19.

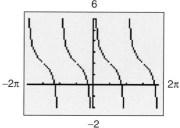

21.

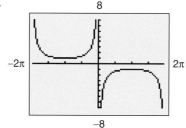

23. even

25.

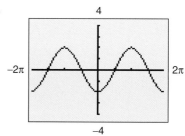

27.

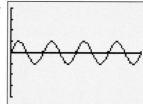

29. 400   **31.** C

33. $f(t) = 8\sin\left(\dfrac{2\pi t - 28\pi}{5}\right)$ **35.** $2\cos\left(\dfrac{5t}{2}\right)$

37.

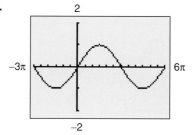

39. Not an identity   **41.** Possibly an identity

43. $f(t) = 10.5588 \sin(4t + 0.4580)$

45. $0 \le t \le \dfrac{\pi}{50}$ and $-5 \le y \le 5$ (one period)

Chapter 7 can do calculus, page 521

1. $2 + 6x + 18x^2 + 54x^3 + 162x^4 + \dots$; $-\dfrac{1}{6} \le x \le \dfrac{1}{6}$

2. $3 + 6x + 12x^2 + 24x^3 + 48x^4 + \dots$;
$-\dfrac{6}{16} \le x \le \dfrac{5}{16}$

3. $-2 + 2x - 2x^2 + 2x^3 - 2x^4 + \dots$; $-\dfrac{9}{16} \le x \le \dfrac{5}{8}$

4. $-3 + 6x - 12x^2 + 24x^3 - 48x^4 + \dots$;
$-\dfrac{1}{4} \le x \le \dfrac{11}{32}$

5. $\cos x$; $-\infty \le x \le \infty$

6. $\dfrac{1}{x}$; $0 \le x \le 2$ **7.** e^x; $-\infty \le x \le \infty$

Chapter 8

Section 8.1, page 528

1. $x = 0.5275 + k\pi$ or $1.6868 + k\pi$

3. $x = 0.4959 + 2k\pi$ or $1.2538 + 2k\pi$ or $1.5708 + 2k\pi$
or $1.8877 + 2k\pi$ or $2.6457 + 2k\pi$ or $4.7124 + 2k\pi$

5. $x = 0.1671 + 2k\pi$ or $1.8256 + 2k\pi$ or $2.8867 + 2k\pi$
or $4.5453 + 2k\pi$

7. $x = 1.2161 + 2k\pi$ or $5.0671 + 2k\pi$

9. $x = 2.4620 + 2k\pi$ or $3.8212 + 2k\pi$

11. $x = 0.5166 + 2k\pi$ or $5.6766 + 2k\pi$

13. a. The graph of $f(x) = \sin x$ on the interval from 0
to 2π shows that $\sin x = 1$ only when $x = \dfrac{\pi}{2}$.
Since $\sin x$ has period 2π, all other solutions are
obtained by adding or subtracting integer
multiples of 2π from $\dfrac{\pi}{2}$, that is,
$$\dfrac{\pi}{2} + 2\pi = \dfrac{5\pi}{2}, \dfrac{\pi}{2} + 2(2\pi) = \dfrac{9\pi}{2},$$
$$\dfrac{\pi}{2} + 3(2\pi) = \dfrac{13\pi}{2}, \text{ etc., and } \dfrac{\pi}{2} - 2\pi = -\dfrac{3\pi}{2},$$
$$\dfrac{\pi}{2} - 2(2\pi) = -\dfrac{7\pi}{2}, \dfrac{\pi}{2} - 3(2\pi) = -\dfrac{11\pi}{2}, \text{ etc.}$$

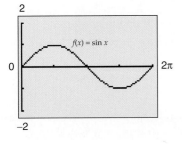

b. Similarly, the graph shows that $\sin x = -1$ only
when $x = \dfrac{3\pi}{2}$, so that all solutions are obtained
by adding or subtracting integer multiples of
2π from $\dfrac{3\pi}{2}$:
$$\dfrac{3\pi}{2} + 2\pi = \dfrac{7\pi}{2}, \dfrac{3\pi}{2} + 2(2\pi) = \dfrac{11\pi}{2},$$
$$\dfrac{3\pi}{2} + 3(2\pi) = \dfrac{15\pi}{2}, \text{ etc., and } \dfrac{3\pi}{2} - 2\pi = -\dfrac{\pi}{2},$$
$$\dfrac{3\pi}{2} - 2(2\pi) = -\dfrac{5\pi}{2}, \dfrac{3\pi}{2} - 3(2\pi) = -\dfrac{9\pi}{2}, \text{ etc.}$$

15. $x = 0.1193$ or 3.0223 **17.** $x = 1.3734$ or 4.5150

19. $\theta = 82.83°, 262.83°$ **21.** $\theta = 114.83°, 245.17°$

23. $\theta = 210°, 270°, 330°$

25. $\theta = 60°, 120°, 240°, 300°$

27. $\theta = 120°, 240°$ **29.** $\alpha = 65.38°$ **31.** $\alpha = 30°$

33. $\sin x = k$ and $\cos x = k$ have no solutions when
$k > 1$ or $k < -1$.

Section 8.2, page 536

1. $\dfrac{\pi}{2}$ **3.** $-\dfrac{\pi}{4}$ **5.** 0   **7.** $\dfrac{\pi}{6}$

9. $-\dfrac{\pi}{4}$ **11.** $-\dfrac{\pi}{3}$ **13.** $\dfrac{2\pi}{3}$ **15.** 0.3576

17. -1.2728 **19.** 0.7168   **21.** -0.8584 **23.** 2.2168

25. $\cos u = \dfrac{1}{2}$; $\tan u = -\sqrt{3}$

27. $\dfrac{\pi}{2}$ **29.** $\dfrac{5\pi}{6}$ **31.** $-\dfrac{\pi}{3}$ **33.** $\dfrac{\pi}{3}$

35. $\dfrac{\pi}{6}$ **37.** $\dfrac{4}{5}$ **39.** $\dfrac{4}{5}$ **41.** $\dfrac{5}{12}$

43. $\cos(\sin^{-1} v) = \sqrt{1 - v^2}$ $(-1 \le v \le 1)$

45. $\tan(\sin^{-1} v) = \dfrac{v}{\sqrt{1 - v^2}}$ $(-1 < v < 1)$

47.

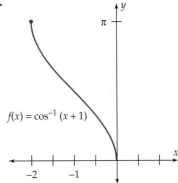

$f(x) = \cos^{-1}(x + 1)$

49.

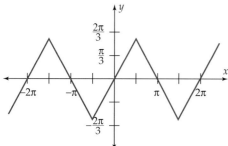

51. a. $\theta = \sin^{-1}\left(\dfrac{40}{x}\right)$ **b.** $\approx 9.2°$

53. $y = \csc x$

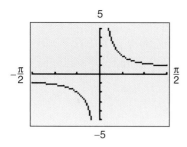

The graph of $y = \csc x$ is one-to-one and has an inverse.

$y = \csc^{-1} x$

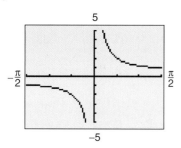

55. a. Let $\cos u = w$ with $0 \le u \le \pi$. Then $u = \cos^{-1} w$, and $\cos^{-1}(\cos u) = \cos^{-1} w = u$. Let $u = \cos^{-1} v$. Then $\cos u = v$, and $\cos(\cos^{-1} v) = \cos u = v$.

b. Let $\tan u = w$ with $-\dfrac{\pi}{2} \le u \le \dfrac{\pi}{2}$. Then $u = \tan^{-1} w$, and $\tan^{-1}(\tan u) = \tan^{-1} w = u$. Let $u = \tan^{-1} v$. Then $\tan u = v$, and $\tan(\tan^{-1} v) = \tan u = v$.

57. a. $\theta = \tan^{-1}\left(\dfrac{4}{x}\right) + \tan^{-1}\left(\dfrac{2}{x}\right)$ **b.** $x \approx 9.13$ feet

Section 8.3, page 545

1. $x = \dfrac{\pi}{3} + 2k\pi$ or $\dfrac{2\pi}{3} + 2k\pi$ **3.** $x = -\dfrac{\pi}{3} + k\pi$

5. $x = \pm\dfrac{5\pi}{6} + 2k\pi$ **7.** $x = -\dfrac{\pi}{6} + 2k\pi$ or $\dfrac{7\pi}{6} + 2k\pi$

9. $27.57°$ **11.** $14.18°$

13. $x = -0.4836 + 2k\pi$ or $3.6252 + 2k\pi$

15. $x = \pm 2.1700 + 2k\pi$ **17.** $x = -0.2327 + k\pi$

19. $x = 0.4101 + k\pi$ **21.** $x = \pm 1.9577 + 2k\pi$

23. $x = -\dfrac{\pi}{6} + 2k\pi$ or $\dfrac{2\pi}{3} + k\pi$ **25.** $x = \pm\dfrac{\pi}{2} + 4k\pi$

27. $x = -\dfrac{\pi}{9} + \dfrac{k\pi}{3}$ **29.** $x = \pm 0.7381 + \dfrac{2k\pi}{3}$

31. $x = 2.2143 + 2k\pi$ **33.** $x = 3.4814, 5.9433$

35. $x = \dfrac{3\pi}{4}, \dfrac{7\pi}{4}, 2.1588, 5.3004$

37. $x = \dfrac{\pi}{4}, \dfrac{\pi}{2}, \dfrac{5\pi}{4}, \dfrac{3\pi}{2}$ **39.** $x = \dfrac{\pi}{6}, \dfrac{\pi}{2}, \dfrac{5\pi}{6}, \dfrac{3\pi}{2}$

41. $x = 0.8481, 1.7682, 2.2935, 4.9098$

43. $x = 0.8213, 2.3203$

45. $x = 0.3649, 1.2059, 3.5065, 4.3475$

47. $x = 1.0591, 2.8679, 4.2007, 6.0095$

49. $x = \dfrac{\pi}{4}, \dfrac{3\pi}{4}, \dfrac{5\pi}{4}, \dfrac{7\pi}{4}$

51. $x = \dfrac{\pi}{4}, \dfrac{5\pi}{4}$ **53.** $x = \dfrac{\pi}{4}, \dfrac{5\pi}{4}$

55. $t = \dfrac{\tan^{-1} 4}{6} + \dfrac{k\pi}{6} \approx 1.2682, 0.7446, 0.2210, 1.7918$

57. not possible   **59.** $16.0°$ or $74.0°$ **61.** No solution

63. $x = \dfrac{\pi}{6n} + \dfrac{2k\pi}{n}, \dfrac{5\pi}{6n} + \dfrac{2k\pi}{n}$

Section 8.4, page 555

1. $f(t) = 125 \sin\left(\dfrac{\pi t}{5}\right)$

3. $f(t) = \cos 20\pi t + \sqrt{16 - \sin^2(20\pi t)}$

5. $h(t) = 6 \sin\left(\dfrac{\pi t}{2}\right)$ **7.** $h(t) = 6 \cos\left(\dfrac{\pi t}{2}\right)$

9. $d(t) = 10 \sin\left(\dfrac{\pi t}{2}\right)$

11. a.

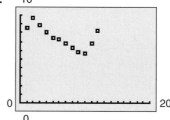

b. Roughly periodic;
$y = 1.358 \sin(0.4778x + 0.569) + 7.636$

c. No, the unemployment total will only be predicted in the range 6.2781 to 8.9944.

13. a. $y = 2.9138 \sin(0.400x + 1.809) + 2.376$

b. About 15.7, which is somewhat reasonable but may not be the best model to use.

c.

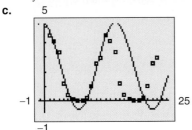

The model is not a good fit in the second year.

d. $y = 2.1663 \sin(0.513x + 1.051) + 1.71$

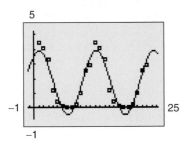

e. About 12.2
This model provides a much better fit.

Section 8.4.A, page 562

1.

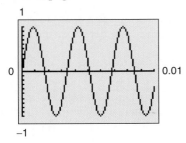

$y = \sin(294 \cdot 2\pi x)$

3.

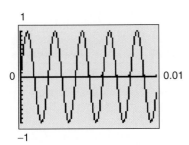

$y = \sin(440 \cdot 2\pi x)$

5. (graph of C-major chord: C + E + G)

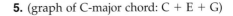
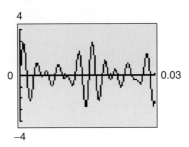

$y = \sin(262 \cdot 2\pi x) + \sin(330 \cdot 2\pi x) + \sin(392 \cdot 2\pi x)$

Chapter 8 Review, page 564

1. $x = k\pi$, where k is an integer.

3. $x = 0.8419 + 2k\pi$ or $2.2997 + 2k\pi$ or $4.1784 + 2k\pi$ or $5.2463 + 2k\pi$

5. $x \approx 0.5236 + 2k\pi$ or $2.6180 + 2k\pi$ or $4.7124 + 2k\pi$

7. $\tan 3t = \dfrac{3}{5}$, $3t = \tan^{-1}\left(\dfrac{3}{5}\right) + k\pi$,

$t = \dfrac{\tan^{-1}\left(\dfrac{3}{5}\right)}{3} + \dfrac{k\pi}{3}$. In the first 2 seconds the solutions are 0.1801, 1.2273.

9. $\dfrac{\pi}{3}$ **11.** $\dfrac{\pi}{3}$ **13.** 0   **15.** 2   **17.** $\dfrac{3\pi}{4}$

19. $\dfrac{\pi}{2}$

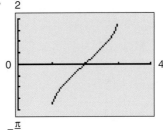

21. $-\dfrac{2}{5\sqrt{5}}$ **23.** $\approx 75°$ or $\approx 255°$

25. $x = \dfrac{\pi}{6} + 2k\pi$ or $x = \dfrac{11\pi}{6} + 2k\pi$

27. $x = \dfrac{4\pi}{9} + \dfrac{2k\pi}{3}$ or $x = \dfrac{5\pi}{9} + \dfrac{2k\pi}{3}$

29. $x \approx 2.49809 + 2k\pi$ or $x \approx 3.78509 + 2k\pi$

31. $x = \tan^{-1}\left(\dfrac{5}{2}\right) + k\pi \approx 1.19029 + k\pi$

33. $x = \dfrac{\pi}{4} + k\pi$ or $\dfrac{3\pi}{4} + k\pi$ **35.** $x = \pm\dfrac{\pi}{3} + k\pi$

37. $x \approx 0.8959 + 2k\pi$ or $2.2457 + 2k\pi$

39. $9.06°$ or $80.94°$

41. a. 19 feet

    b. 3 ft below water

    c. 20 seconds

    d. Answers may vary: $g(t) = 11\cos\left(\dfrac{\pi}{10}t\right) + 8$

    e. Answers may vary:

$$h(t) = 11\sin\left(\dfrac{\pi}{10}t - \dfrac{\pi}{2}\right) + 8$$

    f. $t \approx 4.418 + 20k$ and $t \approx 15.582 + 20k$ seconds, where k is any integer.

43. Using approximate values,
$y = 0.006\cos(2094.768x - 8.379)$

Chapter 8 can do calculus, page 569

1. 1   **2.** 0   **3.** does not exist

4. 1   **5.** 1   **6.** 1

7. does not exist   **8.** does not exist

9. 1   **10.** 1   **11.** 0.75   **12.** $\dfrac{8}{7}$

13. does not exist   **14.** 3   **15.** does not exist

16. does not exist   **17.** 6   **18.** -4

19. does not exist   **20.** -0.5 **21.** 5

22. does not exist   **23.** 3   **24.** 0

25. $\lim\limits_{x\to 0} \dfrac{\sin bx}{\sin cx} = \dfrac{b}{c}$

Chapter 9

Section 9.1, page 580

1. Possibly an identity

3. Possibly an identity

5. b   **7.** e

9. $\tan x \cos x = \left(\dfrac{\sin x}{\cos x}\right)\cos x = \sin x$

11. $\cos x \sec x = \cos x\left(\dfrac{1}{\cos x}\right) = 1$

13. $\tan x \csc x = \left(\dfrac{\sin x}{\cos x}\right)\left(\dfrac{1}{\sin x}\right) = \dfrac{1}{\cos x} = \sec x$

15. $\dfrac{\tan x}{\sec x} = \dfrac{\frac{\sin x}{\cos x}}{\frac{1}{\cos x}} = \sin x$

17. $(1 + \cos x)(1 - \cos x) = 1 - \cos^2 x = \sin^2 x$

19. Not an identity

21. $\dfrac{\sin(-x)}{\cos(-x)} = \dfrac{-\sin x}{\cos x} = -\tan x$

23. $\cot(-x) = \dfrac{\cos(-x)}{\sin(-x)} = \dfrac{\cos x}{-\sin x} = -\cot x$

25. Not an identity

27. $\sec^2 x - \csc^2 x = (1 + \tan^2 x) - (1 + \cot^2 x) = \tan^2 x - \cot^2 x$

29. $\sin^2 x(\cot x + 1)^2 = [\sin x(\cot x + 1)]^2 = (\cos x + \sin x)^2 = [\cos x(1 + \tan x)]^2 = \cos^2 x(\tan x + 1)^2$

31. $\sin^2 x - \tan^2 x = \sin^2 x - \dfrac{\sin^2 x}{\cos^2 x} =$

$\sin^2 x\left(1 - \dfrac{1}{\cos^2 x}\right) = \sin^2 x(1 - \sec^2 x) =$

$\sin^2 x(-\tan^2 x) = -\sin^2 x \tan^2 x$

33. $(\cos^2 x - 1)(\tan^2 x + 1) = (-\sin^2 x)(\sec^2 x) =$

$(-\sin^2 x)\left(\dfrac{1}{\cos^2 x}\right) = -\tan^2 x$

35. $\dfrac{\sec x}{\csc x} = \dfrac{\frac{1}{\cos x}}{\frac{1}{\sin x}} = \dfrac{\sin x}{\cos x} = \tan x$

37. $\cos^4 x - \sin^4 x = (\cos^2 x - \sin^2 x)(\cos^2 x + \sin^2 x) = \cos^2 x - \sin^2 x$

39. Not an identity

41. $\dfrac{\sec x}{\csc x} + \dfrac{\sin x}{\cos x} = \dfrac{\frac{1}{\cos x}}{\frac{1}{\sin x}} + \tan x = \dfrac{\sin x}{\cos x} +$

$\tan x = \tan x + \tan x = 2\tan x$

43. $\dfrac{\sec x + \csc x}{1 + \tan x} = \dfrac{\frac{1}{\cos x} + \frac{1}{\sin x}}{1 + \frac{\sin x}{\cos x}} \cdot \dfrac{\sin x \cos x}{\sin x \cos x} =$

$\dfrac{\sin x + \cos x}{\sin x \cos x + \sin^2 x} = \dfrac{\sin x + \cos x}{\sin x(\cos x + \sin x)}$

$= \dfrac{1}{\sin x} = \csc x$

45. $\dfrac{1}{\csc x - \sin x} = \dfrac{1}{\frac{1}{\sin x} - \sin x} \cdot \dfrac{\sin x}{\sin x} = \dfrac{\sin x}{1 - \sin^2 x}$

$= \dfrac{\sin x}{\cos^2 x} = \left(\dfrac{1}{\cos x}\right)\left(\dfrac{\sin x}{\cos x}\right)$

$= \sec x \tan x$

47. Not an identity

49. Conjecture: $\cos x$. Proof: $1 - \dfrac{\sin^2 x}{1 + \cos x} =$

$\dfrac{1 + \cos x - \sin^2 x}{1 + \cos x} = \dfrac{\cos x + (1 - \sin^2 x)}{1 + \cos x} =$

$\dfrac{\cos x + \cos^2 x}{1 + \cos x} = \dfrac{\cos x(1 + \cos x)}{1 + \cos x} = \cos x$

51. Conjecture: $\tan x$: Proof:

$(\sin x + \cos x)(\sec x + \csc x) - \cot x - 2 =$

$\sin x \sec x + \sin x \csc x + \cos x \sec x +$

$\cos x \csc x - \cot x - 2 = \sin x \cdot \dfrac{1}{\cos x} +$

$$\sin x \cdot \frac{1}{\sin x} + \cos x \cdot \frac{1}{\cos x} + \cos x \cdot \frac{1}{\sin x} -$$

$$\cot x - 2 = \frac{\sin x}{\cos x} + 1 + 1 + \frac{\cos x}{\sin x} - \cot x - 2$$

$$= \tan x + \cot x - \cot x = \tan x$$

53. $\dfrac{1 - \sin x}{\sec x} = \dfrac{1 - \sin x}{\sec x} \cdot \dfrac{(1 + \sin x)}{(1 + \sin x)}$

$$= \frac{1 - \sin^2 x}{\sec x(1 + \sin x)} = \frac{\cos^2 x}{\frac{1}{\cos x}(1 + \sin x)} = \frac{\cos^3 x}{1 + \sin x}$$

55. $\dfrac{\cos x}{1 - \sin x} \cdot \dfrac{1 + \sin x}{1 + \sin x} = \dfrac{\cos x(1 + \sin x)}{1 - \sin^2 x}$

$$= \frac{\cos x(1 + \sin x)}{\cos^2 x} = \frac{1 + \sin x}{\cos x} = \frac{1}{\cos x} + \frac{\sin x}{\cos x}$$

$$= \sec x + \tan x$$

57. $\dfrac{\cos x \cot x}{\cot x - \cos x} \cdot \dfrac{\sin x}{\sin x} = \dfrac{\cos x \cos x}{\cos x - \cos x \sin x}$

$$= \frac{\cos^2 x}{\cos x(1 - \sin x)} = \frac{\cos x}{1 - \sin x} \cdot \frac{1 + \sin x}{1 + \sin x}$$

$$= \frac{\cos x(1 + \sin x)}{1 - \sin^2 x} = \frac{\cos x + \sin x \cos x}{\cos^2 x} \cdot \frac{\frac{1}{\sin x}}{\frac{1}{\sin x}}$$

$$= \frac{\frac{\cos x}{\sin x} + \cos x}{\cos x \left(\frac{\cos x}{\sin x}\right)} = \frac{\cot x + \cos x}{\cos x \cot x}$$

59. $\cot x = \dfrac{1}{\tan x}$, so $\log_{10}(\cot x) = \log_{10}\left(\dfrac{1}{\tan x}\right)$

$$= \log_{10}(\tan x)^{-1} = -\log_{10}(\tan x)$$

61. $\csc x + \cot x = (\csc x + \cot x) \cdot \dfrac{(\csc x - \cot x)}{(\csc x - \cot x)}$

$$= \frac{\csc^2 x - \cot^2 x}{\csc x - \cot x} = \frac{1}{\csc x - \cot x};$$

so, $\log_{10}(\csc x + \cot x) = \log_{10}\left(\dfrac{1}{\csc x - \cot x}\right)$

$$= \log_{10}(\csc x - \cot x)^{-1} = -\log_{10}(\csc x - \cot x)$$

63. $-\tan x \tan y(\cot x - \cot y)$

$$= -\tan y(\tan x \cot x) + \tan x(\tan y \cot y)$$

$$= -\tan y + \tan x = \tan x - \tan y$$

65. $\dfrac{\cos x - \sin y}{\cos y - \sin x} \cdot \dfrac{\cos x + \sin y}{\cos x + \sin y}$

$$= \frac{\cos^2 x - \sin^2 y}{(\cos y - \sin x)(\cos x + \sin y)}$$

$$= \frac{(1 - \sin^2 x) - (1 - \cos^2 y)}{(\cos y - \sin x)(\cos x + \sin y)}$$

$$= \frac{\cos^2 y - \sin^2 x}{(\cos y - \sin x)(\cos x + \sin y)}$$

$$= \frac{(\cos y - \sin x)(\cos y + \sin x)}{(\cos y - \sin x)(\cos x + \sin y)} = \frac{\cos y + \sin x}{\cos x + \sin y}$$

Section 9.2, page 587

1. $\dfrac{\sqrt{6} - \sqrt{2}}{4}$ **3.** $2 - \sqrt{3}$ **5.** $2 - \sqrt{3}$

7. $-2 - \sqrt{3}$ **9.** $-2 - \sqrt{3}$ **11.** $\dfrac{\sqrt{6} + \sqrt{2}}{4}$

13. $\cos x$ **15.** $-\sin x$ **17.** $-1/\cos x$

19. $-\sin 2$ **21.** $\cos x$ **23.** $-2\sin x \sin y$

25. $\dfrac{4 + \sqrt{2}}{6}$ **27.** $\dfrac{2\sqrt{6} - \sqrt{3}}{10}$ **29.** -0.393

31. 0.993 **33.** -2.34

35. $\dfrac{f(x + h) - f(x)}{h} = \dfrac{\cos(x + h) - \cos x}{h}$

$$= \frac{(\cos x \cos h - \sin x \sin h) - \cos x}{h}$$

$$= \frac{\cos x \cos h - \cos x}{h} - \frac{\sin x \sin h}{h}$$

$$= \cos x\left(\frac{\cos h - 1}{h}\right) - \sin x\left(\frac{\sin h}{h}\right)$$

37. $\sin(x + y) = -\dfrac{44}{125}$; $\tan(x + y) = \dfrac{44}{117}$; $x + y$ is in the third quadrant.

39. $\cos(x + y) = -\dfrac{56}{65}$; $\tan(x + y) = \dfrac{33}{56}$; $x + y$ is in the third quadrant.

41. $\sin(u + v + w) = \sin u \cos v \cos w$
$\qquad + \cos u \sin v \cos w$
$\qquad + \cos u \cos v \sin w - \sin u \sin v \sin w$

43. Since $y = \dfrac{\pi}{2} - x$, $\sin y = \sin\left(\dfrac{\pi}{2} - x\right) = \cos x$.
Hence, $\sin^2 x + \sin^2 y = \sin^2 x + \cos^2 x = 1$

45. $\sin(x - \pi) = \sin x \cos \pi - \cos x \sin \pi$
$\qquad = (\sin x)(-1) - (\cos x)(0) = -\sin x$

47. $\cos(\pi - x) = \cos \pi \cos x + \sin \pi \sin x$
$\qquad = (-1)\cos x + (0)\sin x = -\cos x$

49. $\sin(x + \pi) = \sin x \cos \pi + \cos x \sin \pi$
$\qquad = (\sin x)(-1) + (\cos x)(0) = -\sin x$

51. By Exercises 49 and 50, $\tan(x + \pi) = \dfrac{\sin(x + \pi)}{\cos(x + \pi)}$

$$= \frac{-\sin x}{-\cos x} = \tan x$$

53. $\dfrac{1}{2}[\cos(x - y) - \cos(x + y)] = \dfrac{1}{2}[(\cos x \cos y +$
$\qquad \sin x \sin y) - (\cos x \cos y - \sin x \sin y)]$

$$= \frac{1}{2}(2 \sin x \sin y) = \sin x \sin y$$

55. $\cos(x + y)\cos(x - y)$
$\qquad = (\cos x \cos y - \sin x \sin y)(\cos x \cos y + \sin x \sin y)$
$\qquad = (\cos x \cos y)^2 - (\sin x \sin y)^2$
$\qquad = \cos^2 x \cos^2 y - \sin^2 x \sin^2 y$

57. $\dfrac{\cos(x - y)}{\sin x \cos y} = \dfrac{\cos x \cos y + \sin x \sin y}{\sin x \cos y}$

$$= \frac{\cos x}{\sin x} + \frac{\sin y}{\cos y} = \cot x + \tan y$$

59. Not an identity

61. $\dfrac{\sin(x + y)}{\sin(x - y)}$

$$= \dfrac{\sin x \cos y + \cos x \sin y}{\sin x \cos y - \cos x \sin y} \cdot \dfrac{\dfrac{1}{\cos x \cos y}}{\dfrac{1}{\cos x \cos y}}$$

$$= \dfrac{\dfrac{\sin x}{\cos x} + \dfrac{\sin y}{\cos y}}{\dfrac{\sin x}{\cos x} - \dfrac{\sin y}{\cos y}} = \dfrac{\tan x + \tan y}{\tan x - \tan y}$$

63. Not an identity   **65.** Not an identity

Section 9.2.A, page 592

1. 0.64 radians   **3.** 2.47 radians   **5.** $\dfrac{\pi}{2}$

7. 1.37 radians or 1.77 radians   **9.** $\dfrac{\pi}{4}$ or $\dfrac{3\pi}{4}$

11. 1.39 radians or 1.75 radians

Section 9.3, page 600

1. $\dfrac{\sqrt{2 + \sqrt{2}}}{2}$ **3.** $\dfrac{\sqrt{2 + \sqrt{2}}}{2}$

5. $2 - \sqrt{3}$ **7.** $\dfrac{\sqrt{2 + \sqrt{3}}}{2}$

9. $\dfrac{\sqrt{2 - \sqrt{2}}}{2}$ **11.** $-\sqrt{2} + 1$

13. $\dfrac{1}{2}\sin 10x - \dfrac{1}{2}\sin 2x$ **15.** $\dfrac{1}{2}\cos 6x + \dfrac{1}{2}\cos 2x$

17. $\dfrac{1}{2}\cos 20x - \dfrac{1}{2}\cos 14x$ **19.** $2\sin 4x \cos x$

21. $2\sin 2x \cos 7x$

23. $\sin 2x = \dfrac{120}{169}, \cos 2x = \dfrac{119}{169}, \tan 2x = \dfrac{120}{119}$

25. $\sin 2x = \dfrac{24}{25}, \cos 2x = -\dfrac{7}{25}, \tan 2x = -\dfrac{24}{7}$

27. $\sin 2x = \dfrac{24}{25}, \cos 2x = \dfrac{7}{25}, \tan 2x = \dfrac{24}{7}$

29. $\sin 2x = \dfrac{\sqrt{15}}{8}, \cos 2x = \dfrac{7}{8}, \tan 2x = \dfrac{\sqrt{15}}{7}$

31. $\sin \dfrac{x}{2} = 0.5477, \cos \dfrac{x}{2} = 0.8367, \tan \dfrac{x}{2} = 0.6547$

33. $\sin \dfrac{x}{2} = \dfrac{1}{\sqrt{10}}, \cos \dfrac{x}{2} = \dfrac{-3}{\sqrt{10}}, \tan \dfrac{x}{2} = \dfrac{-1}{3}$

35. $\sin \dfrac{x}{2} = \sqrt{\dfrac{\sqrt{5} + 2}{2\sqrt{5}}}, \cos \dfrac{x}{2} = -\sqrt{\dfrac{\sqrt{5} - 2}{2\sqrt{5}}},$
$\tan \dfrac{x}{2} = -\sqrt{9 + 4\sqrt{5}} = -\sqrt{5} - 2$

37. $\sin 2x = 0.96$ **39.** $\cos 2x = 0.28$

41. $\sin \dfrac{x}{2} = 0.3162$ **43.** $\cos 3x = 4\cos^3 x - 3\cos x$

45. $\cos x$ **47.** $\sin 4y$ **49.** 1

51. $\sin 16x = \sin[2(8x)] = 2\sin 8x \cos 8x$

53. $\cos^4 x - \sin^4 x = (\cos^2 x - \sin^2 x)(\cos^2 x + \sin^2 x) = \cos^2 x - \sin^2 x = \cos 2x$

55. Not an identity

57. $\dfrac{1 + \cos 2x}{\sin 2x} = \dfrac{1 + (2\cos^2 x - 1)}{2\sin x \cos x} = \dfrac{2\cos^2 x}{2\sin x \cos x} =$
$\dfrac{\cos x}{\sin x} = \cot x$

59. $\sin 3x = \sin(2x + x) = \sin 2x \cos x + \cos 2x \sin x$
$= (2\sin x \cos x)\cos x + (1 - 2\sin^2 x)\sin x$
$= 2\sin x \cos^2 x + \sin x - 2\sin^3 x$
$= 2\sin x(1 - \sin^2 x) + \sin x - 2\sin^3 x$
$= \sin x(2 - 2\sin^2 x + 1 - 2\sin^2 x)$
$= \sin x(3 - 4\sin^2 x)$

61. Not an identity

63. $\csc^2\left(\dfrac{x}{2}\right) = \dfrac{1}{\sin^2\left(\dfrac{x}{2}\right)} = \dfrac{1}{\dfrac{1 - \cos x}{2}} = \dfrac{2}{1 - \cos x}$

65. $\dfrac{\sin x - \sin 3x}{\cos x + \cos 3x} = \dfrac{2\cos 2x \sin(-x)}{2\cos 2x \cos(-x)} = \dfrac{-\sin x}{\cos x}$
$= -\tan x$

67. $\dfrac{\sin 4x + \sin 6x}{\cos 4x - \cos 6x} = \dfrac{2\sin 5x \cos(-x)}{-2\sin 5x \sin(-x)} = \dfrac{\cos x}{\sin x}$
$= \cot x$

69. $\dfrac{\sin x + \sin y}{\cos x - \cos y} = \dfrac{2\sin\left(\dfrac{x + y}{2}\right)\cos\left(\dfrac{x - y}{2}\right)}{-2\sin\left(\dfrac{x + y}{2}\right)\sin\left(\dfrac{x - y}{2}\right)}$

$$= \dfrac{-\cos\left(\dfrac{x - y}{2}\right)}{\sin\left(\dfrac{x - y}{2}\right)} = -\cot\left(\dfrac{x - y}{2}\right)$$

71. a. $\dfrac{1 - \cos x}{\sin x} = \dfrac{(1 - \cos x)(1 + \cos x)}{\sin x(1 + \cos x)}$
$= \dfrac{1 - \cos^2 x}{\sin x(1 + \cos x)} = \dfrac{\sin^2 x}{\sin x(1 + \cos x)} = \dfrac{\sin x}{1 + \cos x}$
b. By the half-angle identity proved in the text
and part (a), $\tan \dfrac{x}{2} = \dfrac{1 - \cos x}{\sin x} = \dfrac{\sin x}{1 + \cos x}$

73. $R = vt \cos \alpha$
$R = v\left(\dfrac{2v \sin \alpha}{g}\right)\cos \alpha$
$R = \dfrac{2v^2 \sin \alpha \cos \alpha}{g}$
$R = \dfrac{v^2 \sin 2\alpha}{g}$

75. $2\left(\sin^2\frac{1}{2}\alpha - \sin^2\frac{1}{2}\theta\right)$

$= 2\left(\dfrac{1 - \cos 2\left(\frac{1}{2}\alpha\right)}{2} - \dfrac{1 - \cos 2\left(\frac{1}{2}\theta\right)}{2}\right)$

$= 2\left(\dfrac{1 - \cos\alpha - 1 + \cos\theta}{2}\right)$

$= \cos\theta - \cos\alpha$

Section 9.4, page 608

1. no solution

3. $x = 0, \pi, 2\pi, \dfrac{7\pi}{6}, \dfrac{11\pi}{6}$

5. $x = \dfrac{\pi}{2}, \dfrac{3\pi}{2}$

7. $x = 0, 2\pi$

9. $x = \dfrac{\pi}{2}, \dfrac{3\pi}{2}$

11. $x = \dfrac{3\pi}{8}, \dfrac{7\pi}{8}, \dfrac{11\pi}{8}, \dfrac{15\pi}{8}$

13. $x = \dfrac{\pi}{4}, \dfrac{3\pi}{4}, \dfrac{5\pi}{4}, \dfrac{7\pi}{4}, \dfrac{\pi}{12}, \dfrac{5\pi}{12}, \dfrac{13\pi}{12}, \dfrac{17\pi}{12}$

15. $x = \dfrac{\pi}{4}, \dfrac{3\pi}{4}, \dfrac{5\pi}{4}, \dfrac{7\pi}{4}$

17. $x = \dfrac{\pi}{3}, \dfrac{5\pi}{3}$

19. $x = \dfrac{3\pi}{4}, \dfrac{7\pi}{4}$

21. $x = \dfrac{\pi}{3}, \dfrac{5\pi}{3}, \pi$

23. $x = \dfrac{3\pi}{4}, \dfrac{7\pi}{4}$

25. $x = \dfrac{\pi}{3}, \dfrac{5\pi}{3}$

27. $x = \dfrac{5\pi}{12}, \dfrac{13\pi}{12}$

29. $x = -\pi, 0, \pi$

31. $x = \dfrac{\pi}{3}, -\pi, \pi$

33. $x = \dfrac{2\pi}{5}, \dfrac{6\pi}{5}, 2\pi, 0, \dfrac{4\pi}{3}$

35. $x = \dfrac{\pi}{4}, \dfrac{3\pi}{4}, \dfrac{5\pi}{4}, \dfrac{7\pi}{4}, 0, \pi, 2\pi$

37. a. $f(x) = 2\sin\left(x + \dfrac{\pi}{3}\right)$

  b. 2

  c. $x = \dfrac{\pi}{6}$

39. a. $f(x) = \sqrt{2}\sin\left(x + \dfrac{7\pi}{4}\right)$

  b. $f(x) = \sqrt{2}$

  c. $x = \dfrac{3\pi}{4}$

Chapter 9 Review, page 611

1. $\dfrac{1}{3} + \cot t$

3. $\sin^4 x$

5. $\sin^4 t - \cos^4 t = (\sin^2 t - \cos^2 t)(\sin^2 t + \cos^2 t) =$
$[\sin^2 t - (1 - \sin^2 t)](1) = 2\sin^2 t - 1$

7. $\dfrac{\sin t}{1 - \cos t} = \dfrac{\sin t}{1 - \cos t} \cdot \dfrac{(1 + \cos t)}{(1 + \cos t)}$

$= \dfrac{\sin t(1 + \cos t)}{1 - \cos^2 t} = \dfrac{\sin t(1 + \cos t)}{\sin^2 t} = \dfrac{1 + \cos t}{\sin t}$

9. Not an identity

11. $(\sin x + \cos x)^2 - \sin 2x$
$= \sin^2 x + 2\sin x\cos x + \cos^2 x - 2\sin x\cos x$
$= \sin^2 x + \cos^2 x = 1$

13. $\dfrac{\cos^4 x - \sin^4 x}{1 - \tan^4 x} = \dfrac{(\cos^2 x - \sin^2 x)(\cos^2 x + \sin^2 x)}{(1 - \tan^2 x)(1 + \tan^2 x)}$

$= \dfrac{\cos^2 x - \sin^2 x}{(1 - \tan^2 x)\sec^2 x} = \dfrac{(\cos^2 x - \sin^2 x)}{\left(1 - \dfrac{\sin^2 x}{\cos^2 x}\right)\dfrac{1}{\cos^2 x}}$

$= \dfrac{(\cos^2 x - \sin^2 x)\cos^4 x}{\cos^2 x - \sin^2 x} = \cos^4 x$

15. $\sec x - \cos x = \dfrac{1}{\cos x} - \cos x$

$= \dfrac{1 - \cos^2 x}{\cos x} = \dfrac{\sin^2 x}{\cos x}$

$= \sin x\dfrac{\sin x}{\cos x} = \sin x\tan x$

17. (a)

19. $\cos(x + y)\cos(x - y)$
$= [\cos x\cos y - \sin x\sin y][\cos x\cos y + \sin x\sin y]$
$= \cos^2 x\cos^2 y - \sin^2 x\sin^2 y$
$= \cos^2 x(1 - \sin^2 y) - (1 - \cos^2 x)\sin^2 y$
$= \cos^2 x - \cos^2 x\sin^2 y - \sin^2 y + \cos^2 x\sin^2 y$
$= \cos^2 x - \sin^2 y$

21. a. $-\dfrac{3}{5}$ **b.** $\dfrac{117}{44}$ **c.** $\dfrac{44}{125}$

23. $-\dfrac{120}{169}$ **25.** $\dfrac{\sqrt{42} + 2\sqrt{2}}{10}$

27. $-\dfrac{1}{\cos x}$ **29.** ≈ 1.23 radians

31. $\dfrac{1 - \cos 2x}{\tan x} = \dfrac{1 - (1 - 2\sin^2 x)}{\tan x} = \dfrac{2\sin^2 x}{\tan x}$

$= \dfrac{2\sin^2 x}{\dfrac{\sin x}{\cos x}} = \dfrac{2\sin^2 x\cos x}{\sin x}$

$= 2\sin x\cos x = \sin 2x$

33. $2\cos x - 2\cos^3 x = 2\cos x(1 - \cos^2 x)$
$= 2\cos x(\sin^2 x) = \sin x(2\sin x\cos x)$

35. $\dfrac{120}{169}$

37. Yes. $\sin 2x = 2\sin x\cos x = 2(0)\cos x = 0$

39. $\cos\left(\dfrac{\pi}{12}\right) = \cos\left[\dfrac{1}{2}\left(\dfrac{\pi}{6}\right)\right]$

$= \sqrt{\dfrac{1 + \cos\dfrac{\pi}{6}}{2}} = \sqrt{\dfrac{1 + \dfrac{\sqrt{3}}{2}}{2}}$

$= \sqrt{\dfrac{2 + \sqrt{3}}{4}} = \dfrac{\sqrt{2 + \sqrt{3}}}{2}; \cos\left(\dfrac{\pi}{12}\right) =$

$$\cos\left(\frac{\pi}{4} - \frac{\pi}{6}\right) = \cos\frac{\pi}{4}\cos\frac{\pi}{6} + \sin\frac{\pi}{4}\sin\frac{\pi}{6}$$

$$= \frac{\sqrt{2}}{2}\left(\frac{\sqrt{3}}{2}\right) + \frac{\sqrt{2}}{2}\left(\frac{1}{2}\right) = \frac{\sqrt{6} + \sqrt{2}}{4}. \text{ So,}$$

$$\frac{\sqrt{2} + \sqrt{3}}{2} = \frac{\sqrt{6} + \sqrt{2}}{4} \text{ or } \sqrt{2} + \sqrt{3} = \frac{\sqrt{2} + \sqrt{6}}{2}$$

41. 0.96   **43.** $x = k\pi$ **45.** $x \approx 2.0344 + k\pi$

Chapter 9 can do calculus, page 615

1. a. 1; $\sin x$ is changing at a rate of 1 unit per increase in x when $x = 0$.

b. $\frac{\sqrt{2}}{2}$; $\sin x$ is increasing approximately 0.7071 per unit increase in x when $x = \frac{\pi}{4}$.

c. 0; $\sin x$ is not changing per unit increase in x when $x = \frac{\pi}{2}$

d. $\frac{\sqrt{3}}{2}$; $\sin x$ is increasing approximately 0.8660 per unit increase in x when $x = \frac{\pi}{6}$.

2. $-\sin x$

3. a. 0; $\cos x$ is not changing per unit increase in x when $x = 0$.

b. $-\frac{\sqrt{2}}{2}$; $\cos x$ is decreasing approximately 0.7071 units per unit increase in x when $x = \frac{\pi}{4}$.

c. -1; $\cos x$ is decreasing 1 unit per unit increase in x when $x = \frac{\pi}{2}$.

d. $-\frac{1}{2}$; $\cos x$ is decreasing $\frac{1}{2}$ unit per unit increase in x when $x = \frac{\pi}{6}$.

Chapter 10

Section 10.1, page 622

1. $a = 4.2$, $\angle B = 125.0°$, $\angle C = 35.0°$

3. $c = 13.9$, $\angle A = 22.5°$, $\angle B = 39.5°$

5. $a = 24.4$, $\angle B = 18.4°$, $\angle C = 21.6°$

7. $c = 21.5$, $\angle A = 33.5°$, $\angle B = 67.9°$

9. $\angle A = 120°$, $\angle B = 21.8°$, $\angle C = 38.2°$

11. $\angle A = 24.1°$, $\angle B = 30.8°$, $\angle C = 125.1°$

13. $\angle A = 38.8°$, $\angle B = 34.5°$, $\angle C = 106.7°$

15. $\angle A = 34.1°$, $\angle B = 50.5°$, $\angle C = 95.4°$

17. 54.2° at vertex $(0, 0)$; 48.4° at vertex $(5, -2)$; 77.4° at vertex $(1, -4)$

19. 334.9 km   **21.** 63.7 ft

23. 84.9°   **25.** 8.4 km

27. 231.9 ft   **29.** 154.5 ft

31. 4.7 cm and 9.0 cm   **33.** 33.44°

35. 978.7 mi

37. $AB = 24.27$, $AC = 21.23$, $BC = 19.5$, $\angle A = 50.2°$, $\angle B = 56.8°$, $\angle C = 73.0°$

39. 16.99 m

Section 10.2, page 634

1. $\angle C = 110°$, $b = 2.5$, $c = 6.3$

3. $\angle B = 14°$, $b = 2.2$, $c = 6.8$

5. $\angle A = 88°$, $a = 17.3$, $c = 12.8$

7. $\angle C = 41.5°$, $b = 9.7$, $c = 10.9$

9. 7.3   **11.** 32.5   **13.** 82.3   **15.** 31.4

17. No solution

19. $\angle A_1 = 55.2°$, $\angle C_1 = 104.8°$, $c_1 = 14.1$; $\angle A_2 = 124.8°$, $\angle C_2 = 35.2°$, $c_2 = 8.4$

21. No solution

23. $\angle B_1 = 65.8°$, $\angle A_1 = 58.2°$, $a_1 = 10.3$; $\angle B_2 = 114.2°$, $\angle A_2 = 9.8°$, $a_2 = 2.1$

25. $\angle C = 72°$, $b = 14.7$, $c = 15.2$

27. $a = 9.8$, $\angle B = 23.3°$, $\angle C = 81.7°$

29. $\angle A = 18.6°$, $\angle B = 39.6°$, $\angle C = 121.9°$

31. $c = 13.9$, $\angle A = 60.1°$, $\angle B = 72.9°$

33. $\angle C = 39.8°$, $\angle A = 77.7°$, $a = 18.9$

35. No solution   **37.** 6.5   **39.** About 7691

41. 135.5 m   **43.** 5.4°   **45.** 5 ft

47. 5.3°   **49.** 30.1 km   **51.** About 9642 ft

53. a. Use the Law of Cosines in triangle ABD to find $\angle ABD$; then $\angle EBA$ is $180° - \angle ABD$. (Why?) Use the Law of Cosines in triangle ABC to find $\angle CAB$; then $\angle EAB$ is $180° - \angle CAB$. You now have two of the angles in triangle EAB and can easily find the third. Use these angles, side AB, and the Law of Sines to find AE.

b. 94.24 ft

55. 13.36 m   **57.** 5.8 gal   **59.** 11.18 sq units

61. No such triangle exists because the sum of the lengths of any two sides of a triangle must be greater than the length of the third side, which is not the case here.

1.–7.

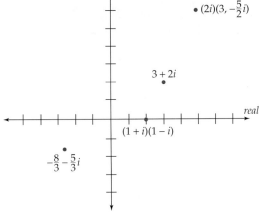

9. 13　　　　**11.** $\sqrt{3}$　　　　**13.** 12

15. Many correct answers, including $z = 2i$, $w = i$

17.

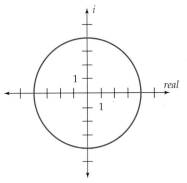

19.

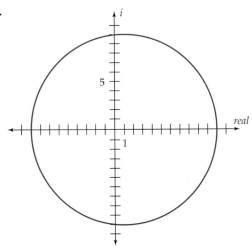

21.

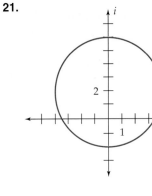

23.

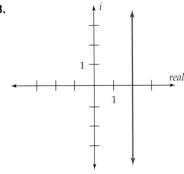

25. $5(\cos 0.9273 + i \sin 0.9273)$

27. $13(\cos 5.1072 + i \sin 5.1072)$

29. $\sqrt{5}(\cos 1.1071 + i \sin 1.1071)$

31. $\sqrt{18.5}(\cos 2.1910 + i \sin 2.1910)$

33. $6\left(\cos \dfrac{2\pi}{3} + i \sin \dfrac{2\pi}{3}\right) = -3 + 3\sqrt{3}i$

35. $42\left(\cos \dfrac{7\pi}{6} + i \sin \dfrac{7\pi}{6}\right) = -21\sqrt{3} - 21i$

37. $\dfrac{3}{2}\left(\cos \dfrac{\pi}{4} + i \sin \dfrac{\pi}{4}\right) = \left(\dfrac{3\sqrt{2}}{4}\right) + \left(\dfrac{3\sqrt{2}}{4}\right)i$

39. $2\sqrt{2}\left(\cos \dfrac{7\pi}{12} + i \sin \dfrac{7\pi}{12}\right)$

41. $\cos \dfrac{\pi}{2} + i \sin \dfrac{\pi}{2}$

43. $12\left(\cos \dfrac{2\pi}{3} + i \sin \dfrac{2\pi}{3}\right)$

45. $2\sqrt{2}\left(\cos \dfrac{19\pi}{12} + i \sin \dfrac{19\pi}{12}\right)$

47. The polar form of i is $1(\cos 90° + i \sin 90°)$. Hence, by the Polar Multiplication Rule

$$zi = r \cdot 1(\cos(\theta + 90°) + i \sin(\theta + 90°)).$$

You can think of z as lying on a circle with center at the origin and radius r. Then zi lies on the same circle (since it too is r units from the origin), but 90° farther around the circle (in a counterclockwise direction).

Selected Answers

49. a. $\dfrac{b}{a}$ **b.** $\dfrac{d}{c}$ **c.** $y - b = \left(\dfrac{d}{c}\right)(x - a)$

d. $y - d = \dfrac{b}{a}(x - c)$

f. $(a + c, b + d)$ lies on L since $(b + d) - b = \dfrac{d}{c}[(a + c) - a]$ and $(a + c, b + d)$ lies on M since $(b + d) - d = \dfrac{b}{a}[(a + c) - c]$.

51. a. $r_2(\cos\theta_2 + i\sin\theta_2)(\cos\theta_2 - i\sin\theta_2)$
$= r_2(\cos^2\theta_2 + \sin^2\theta_2) = r_2$

b. $r_1(\cos\theta_1 + i\sin\theta_1)(\cos\theta_2 - i\sin\theta_2)$
$= r_1[(\cos\theta_1\cos\theta_2 + \sin\theta_1\sin\theta_2) + i(\sin\theta_1\cos\theta_2 - \cos\theta_1\sin\theta_2)]$
$= r_1[\cos(\theta_1 - \theta_2) + i\sin(\theta_1 - \theta_2)]$

Section 10.4, page 652

1. i **3.** $\dfrac{-243\sqrt{3}}{2} - \dfrac{243}{2}i$ **5.** -64

7. $\dfrac{1}{2} - \dfrac{\sqrt{3}}{2}i$ **9.** i **11.** $1, -1, i, -i$

13. $4\left(\cos\dfrac{\pi}{15} + i\sin\dfrac{\pi}{15}\right)$, $4\left(\cos\dfrac{11\pi}{15} + i\sin\dfrac{11\pi}{15}\right)$, $4\left(\cos\dfrac{7\pi}{5} + i\sin\dfrac{7\pi}{5}\right)$

15. $3\left(\cos\dfrac{\pi}{48} + i\sin\dfrac{\pi}{48}\right)$, $3\left(\cos\dfrac{25\pi}{48} + i\sin\dfrac{25\pi}{48}\right)$, $3\left(\cos\dfrac{49\pi}{48} + i\sin\dfrac{49\pi}{48}\right)$, $3\left(\cos\dfrac{73\pi}{48} + i\sin\dfrac{73\pi}{48}\right)$

17. $\left(\cos\dfrac{\pi}{5} + i\sin\dfrac{\pi}{5}\right)$, $\left(\cos\dfrac{3\pi}{5} + i\sin\dfrac{3\pi}{5}\right)$, $(\cos\pi + i\sin\pi)$, $\left(\cos\dfrac{7\pi}{5} + i\sin\dfrac{7\pi}{5}\right)$, $\left(\cos\dfrac{9\pi}{5} + i\sin\dfrac{9\pi}{5}\right)$

19. $\left(\cos\dfrac{\pi}{10} + i\sin\dfrac{\pi}{10}\right)$, $\left(\cos\dfrac{\pi}{2} + i\sin\dfrac{\pi}{2}\right)$, $\left(\cos\dfrac{9\pi}{10} + i\sin\dfrac{9\pi}{10}\right)$, $\left(\cos\dfrac{13\pi}{10} + i\sin\dfrac{13\pi}{10}\right)$, $\left(\cos\dfrac{17\pi}{10} + i\sin\dfrac{17\pi}{10}\right)$

21. $\sqrt[4]{2}\left(\cos\dfrac{\pi}{8} + i\sin\dfrac{\pi}{8}\right)$, $\sqrt[4]{2}\left(\cos\dfrac{9\pi}{8} + i\sin\dfrac{9\pi}{8}\right)$

23. $x = \dfrac{\sqrt{3}}{2} + \dfrac{1}{2}i$ or $\dfrac{\sqrt{3}}{2} - \dfrac{1}{2}i$ or $-\dfrac{\sqrt{3}}{2} + \dfrac{1}{2}i$ or $-\dfrac{\sqrt{3}}{2} - \dfrac{1}{2}i$ or i or $-i$

25. $\dfrac{\sqrt{3}}{2} + \dfrac{1}{2}i$ or $-\dfrac{\sqrt{3}}{2} + \dfrac{1}{2}i$ or $-i$

27. $x = 3i$ or $\dfrac{3\sqrt{3}}{2} - \dfrac{3}{2}i$ or $-\dfrac{3\sqrt{3}}{2} - \dfrac{3}{2}i$

29. $\sqrt[4]{2}\left(\dfrac{\sqrt{3}}{2} + \dfrac{1}{2}i\right)$ or $\sqrt[4]{2}\left(-\dfrac{1}{2} + \dfrac{\sqrt{3}}{2}i\right)$ or $\sqrt[4]{2}\left(-\dfrac{\sqrt{3}}{2} - \dfrac{1}{2}i\right)$ or $\sqrt[4]{2}\left(\dfrac{1}{2} - \dfrac{\sqrt{3}}{2}i\right)$

31. $1, 0.6235 \pm 0.7818i, -0.2225 \pm 0.9749i, -0.9010 \pm 0.4339i$

33. $\pm 1, \pm i, 0.7071 \pm 0.7071i, -0.7071 \pm 0.7071i$

35. $1, 0.7660 \pm 0.6428i, 0.1736 \pm 0.9848i, -0.5 \pm 0.8660i, -0.9397 \pm 0.3420i$

37. $x^6 - 1 = (x - 1)(x^5 + x^4 + x^3 + x^2 + x + 1)$, so the solutions of $x^5 + x^4 + x^3 + x^2 + x + 1 = 0$ are the sixth roots of unity other than 1; namely, $-1, \dfrac{1}{2} + \dfrac{\sqrt{3}}{2}i, \dfrac{1}{2} - \dfrac{\sqrt{3}}{2}i, -\dfrac{1}{2} + \dfrac{\sqrt{3}}{2}i, -\dfrac{1}{2} - \dfrac{\sqrt{3}}{2}i$.

39. 12

41. For each i, u_i is an nth root of unity, so $(u_i)^n = 1$. Hence $(vu_i)^n = (v^n)(u_i)^n = v^n \cdot 1 = r(\cos\theta + i\sin\theta)$ and vu_i is a solution of the equation. If $vu_i = vu_j$, then multiplying both sides by $\dfrac{1}{v}$ shows that $u_i = u_j$. In other words, if u_i is not equal to u_j, then $vu_i \neq vu_j$. Thus, the solution $vu_1, \ldots, vu_n$ are all distinct.

Section 10.5, page 660

1. $3\sqrt{5}$ **3.** $\sqrt{34}$ **5.** $\langle 6, 6\rangle$

7. $\langle -6, 10\rangle$ **9.** $\left\langle \dfrac{13}{5}, -\dfrac{2}{5}\right\rangle$

11. $\mathbf{u} + \mathbf{v} = \langle 4, 5\rangle$; $\mathbf{u} - \mathbf{v} = \langle -8, 3\rangle$; $3\mathbf{u} - 2\mathbf{v} = \langle -18, 10\rangle$

13. $\mathbf{u} + \mathbf{v} = \langle 3 + 4\sqrt{2}, 1 + 3\sqrt{2}\rangle$; $\mathbf{u} - \mathbf{v} = \langle 3 - 4\sqrt{2}, -1 + 3\sqrt{2}\rangle$; $3\mathbf{u} - 2\mathbf{v} = \langle 9 - 8\sqrt{2}, -2 + 9\sqrt{2}\rangle$

15. $\mathbf{u} + \mathbf{v} = \left\langle -\dfrac{23}{4}, 13\right\rangle$; $\mathbf{u} - \mathbf{v} = \left\langle -\dfrac{9}{4}, 7\right\rangle$; $3\mathbf{u} - 2\mathbf{v} = \left\langle -\dfrac{17}{2}, 24\right\rangle$

17. $\|\mathbf{u} - \mathbf{v}\| = \sqrt{130}$

19. $\|\mathbf{v} + \mathbf{w}\| = 10\sqrt{2}$

21. $\|-2(\mathbf{w} + 2\mathbf{u})\| = 0$

23. $\left\|\dfrac{7}{6}\mathbf{v} - \dfrac{2}{3}\mathbf{v}\right\| = 2\sqrt{5}$

25. $\mathbf{u}_1 + \mathbf{u}_2 + \mathbf{u}_3 + \mathbf{u}_4 = \langle -3, 9\rangle$, $\mathbf{v} = \langle 3, -9\rangle$

27. $\mathbf{v} + (-\mathbf{v}) = \langle c, d\rangle + \langle -c, -d\rangle = \langle 0, 0\rangle = \mathbf{0}$

29. $(r + s)\mathbf{v} = (r + s)\langle c, d\rangle = \langle (r + s)c, (r + s)d\rangle$
$= \langle rc, rd\rangle + \langle sc, sd\rangle = r\mathbf{v} + s\mathbf{v}$

31. $1\mathbf{v} = 1\langle c, d\rangle = \langle c, d\rangle = \mathbf{v}$, $0\mathbf{v} = 0\langle c, d\rangle = \langle 0, 0\rangle = \mathbf{0}$

33. a. $\sqrt{(a + c - a)^2 + (b + d - b)^2} = \sqrt{c^2 + d^2} = \|\mathbf{v}\|$

b. $\sqrt{(a + c - c)^2 + (b + d - d)^2} = \sqrt{a^2 + b^2} = \|\mathbf{u}\|$

c. The slope is $\dfrac{d}{c}$, which is the same as the slope of the vector **v**.

d. The slope of the line is $\dfrac{b}{a}$, which is the same as the slope of the vector **u**.

Section 10.6, page 667

1. $\mathbf{u} + \mathbf{v} = 3\mathbf{i}, \mathbf{u} - \mathbf{v} = -\mathbf{i} - 2\mathbf{j}, 3\mathbf{u} - 2\mathbf{v} = -\mathbf{i} - 5\mathbf{j}$

3. $\mathbf{u} + \mathbf{v} = \mathbf{i} - 4\mathbf{j}, \mathbf{u} - \mathbf{v} = 7\mathbf{i} - 4\mathbf{j}$,
$3\mathbf{u} - 2\mathbf{v} = 18\mathbf{i} - 12\mathbf{j}$

5. $\mathbf{u} + \mathbf{v} = \sqrt{3}\,\mathbf{i} + \sqrt{2}\,\mathbf{j}, \mathbf{u} - \mathbf{v} = -\sqrt{3}\,\mathbf{i} + \sqrt{2}\,\mathbf{j}$,
$3\mathbf{u} - 2\mathbf{v} = -2\sqrt{3}\,\mathbf{i} + 3\sqrt{2}\,\mathbf{j}$

7. $\dfrac{5}{2}\mathbf{i} + 2\mathbf{j}$ **9.** $7\mathbf{i} + 7\mathbf{j}$

11. $9\mathbf{i} - 18\mathbf{j}$ **13.** $\mathbf{v} = \left\langle \dfrac{5\sqrt{3}}{2}, \dfrac{5}{2} \right\rangle$

15. $\mathbf{v} = \langle -10, 10\sqrt{3} \rangle$ **17.** $\mathbf{v} \approx \langle -7.5175, 2.7362 \rangle$

19. $\mathbf{v} \approx \langle 1.9284, -2.2981 \rangle$

21. $\|\mathbf{v}\| = 10, \theta = 60°$

23. $\|\mathbf{v}\| = \sqrt{41} \approx 6.4031, \theta \approx 51.34°$

25. $\|\mathbf{v}\| = 4\sqrt{5}, \theta \approx 296.6°$

27. $\|\mathbf{v}\| = 5\sqrt{13}, \theta \approx 213.7°$

29. $-\dfrac{7}{\sqrt{113}}\mathbf{i} + \dfrac{8}{\sqrt{113}}\mathbf{j}$ **31.** $-\dfrac{1}{\sqrt{10}}\mathbf{i} - \dfrac{3}{\sqrt{10}}\mathbf{j}$

33. Direction: 82.5°; magnitude: 9.52 lb

35. Direction: 18.4°; magnitude: 80.4 kg

37. $\theta = \sin^{-1}\left(\dfrac{-894.8}{1500}\right) \approx -36.6°$

39. Parallel to plane: 68.4 lb; perpendicular to plane: 187.9 lb

41. 1931.85 pounds

43. Ground speed: 401.1 mph; course: 154.3°

45. Ground speed: 448.7 mph; course: 174.2°

47. Air speed: 96.6 mph; direction: 326°

49. 0.8023 mph

51. 1005 lb on 6°; 1002 lb on 4°

53. $\mathbf{u} - \mathbf{v}$ lies on the straight line through $(0, 0)$ and $(a - c, b - d)$ which has slope
$\dfrac{(a - c) - 0}{(b - d) - 0} = \dfrac{a - c}{b - d}$. Similarly, **w** lies on the line through (a, b) and (c, d), which also has slope $\dfrac{a - c}{b - d}$. So, $\mathbf{u} - \mathbf{v}$ and **w** are parallel. Verify that they actually have the same direction by considering the relative positions of (a, b), (c, d), and $(a - c, b - d)$. For instance, if $\mathbf{u} - \mathbf{v}$ points

upward to the right, then (a, b) lies to the right and above (c, d). Hence $c < a$ and $d < b$, so that $a - c > 0$ and $b - d > 0$, which means that the endpoint of **w** lies in the first quadrant, that is, **w** points upward to the right.

Section 10.6.A, page 679

1. $\mathbf{u} \cdot \mathbf{v} = -7, \mathbf{u} \cdot \mathbf{u} = 25, \mathbf{v} \cdot \mathbf{v} = 29$

3. $\mathbf{u} \cdot \mathbf{v} = 6, \mathbf{u} \cdot \mathbf{u} = 5, \mathbf{v} \cdot \mathbf{v} = 9$

5. $\mathbf{u} \cdot \mathbf{v} = 12, \mathbf{u} \cdot \mathbf{u} = 13, \mathbf{v} \cdot \mathbf{v} = 13$

7. 6   **9.** 20   **11.** -28 **13.** 1.75065 radians

15. 2.1588 radians   **17.** $\dfrac{\pi}{2}$ radians

19. Orthogonal   **21.** Parallel   **23.** Neither

25. $k = 2$ **27.** $k = \sqrt{2}$

29. $\text{proj}_{\mathbf{u}}\mathbf{v} = \left\langle \dfrac{12}{17}, -\dfrac{20}{17} \right\rangle; \text{proj}_{\mathbf{v}}\mathbf{u} = \left\langle \dfrac{6}{5}, \dfrac{2}{5} \right\rangle$

31. $\text{proj}_{\mathbf{u}}\mathbf{v} = \langle 0, 0 \rangle; \text{proj}_{\mathbf{v}}\mathbf{u} = \langle 0, 0 \rangle$

33. $\text{comp}_{\mathbf{v}}\mathbf{u} = \dfrac{22}{\sqrt{13}}$ **35.** $\text{comp}_{\mathbf{v}}\mathbf{u} = \dfrac{3}{\sqrt{10}}$

37. $\mathbf{u} \cdot (\mathbf{v} + \mathbf{w}) = \langle a, b \rangle \cdot (\langle c, d \rangle + \langle r, s \rangle)$
$= \langle a, b \rangle \cdot \langle c + r, d + s \rangle = a(c + r) + b(d + s)$
$= ac + ar + bd + bs$
$\mathbf{u} \cdot \mathbf{v} + \mathbf{u} \cdot \mathbf{w} = \langle a, b \rangle \cdot \langle c, d \rangle + \langle a, b \rangle \cdot \langle r, s \rangle$
$= (ac + bd) + (ar + bs) = ac + ar + bd + bs$

39. $0 \cdot \mathbf{u} = \langle 0, 0 \rangle \cdot \langle a, b \rangle = 0a + 0b = 0$

41. If $\theta = 0$ or π, then **u** and **v** are parallel, so $\mathbf{v} = k\mathbf{u}$ for some real number k. We know that $\|\mathbf{v}\| = |k|\|\mathbf{u}\|$. If $\theta = 0$, then $\cos \theta = 1$ and $k > 0$. Since $k > 0$, $|k| = k$ and so $\|\mathbf{v}\| = k\|\mathbf{u}\|$. Therefore, $\mathbf{u} \cdot \mathbf{v} = \mathbf{u} \cdot k\mathbf{u} = k\mathbf{u} \cdot \mathbf{u} = k\|\mathbf{u}\|^2 = \|\mathbf{u}\|(k\|\mathbf{u}\|) = \|\mathbf{u}\|\|\mathbf{v}\| = \|\mathbf{u}\|\|\mathbf{v}\| \cos \theta$. On the other hand, if $\theta = \pi$, then $\cos \theta = -1$ and $k < 0$. Since $k < 0$, $|k| = -k$ and so $\|\mathbf{v}\| = -k\|\mathbf{u}\|$. Then $\mathbf{u} \cdot \mathbf{v} = \mathbf{u} \cdot k\mathbf{u}, = k\mathbf{u} \cdot \mathbf{u} = k\|\mathbf{u}\|^2 = \|\mathbf{u}\|(-k\|\mathbf{u}\|) = -\|\mathbf{u}\|\|\mathbf{v}\| = \|\mathbf{u}\|\|\mathbf{v}\| \cos \theta$. In both cases we have shown $\mathbf{u} \cdot \mathbf{v} = \|\mathbf{u}\|\|\mathbf{v}\| \cos \theta$.

43. If $A = (1, 2)$, $B = (3, 4)$, and $C = (5, 2)$, then the vector $\overrightarrow{AB} = \langle 2, 2 \rangle$, $\overrightarrow{AC} = \langle 4, 0 \rangle$, and $\overrightarrow{BC} = \langle 2, -2 \rangle$. Since $\overrightarrow{AB} \cdot \overrightarrow{BC} = 0$, $\overrightarrow{AB}$ and $\overrightarrow{BC}$ are perpendicular, so the angle at vertex B is a right angle.

45. Many possible answers: One is $\mathbf{u} = \langle 1, 0 \rangle$, $\mathbf{v} = \langle 1, 1 \rangle$, and $\mathbf{w} = \langle 1, -1 \rangle$.

47. 300 lb ($= 600 \cos 60°$)

49. 13   **51.** 24

53. The force in the direction of the lawnmower's motion is $30 \cos 60° = 15$ lb. Thus, the work done is $15(75) = 1125$ ft-lb.

55. 1368 ft-lb

Chapter 10 Review, page 684

1. $A = 52.9°, B = 41.6°, C = 85.5°$

3. $A = 20.6°, b = 21.8, C = 29.4°$

5. $A = 35.5°, b = 8.3, C = 68.5°$

7. Approximately 301 mi

9. 71.89°

11. $A = 25°, a = 2.9, b = 5.6$

13. $A = 52.03°, B = 65.97°, b = 86.9$

15. $B = 81.8°, C = 38.2°, c = 2.5$ and
    $B = 98.2°, C = 21.8°, c = 1.5$

17. $a = 41.6; C = 75°, c = 54.1$

19. 147.4   21. 13.4 km

23. Joe is 217.9 m from the pole and Alice is 240 m from the pole.

25. **a.** 3617.65 ft   **b.** 4018.71 ft   **c.** 3642.19 ft

27. 10   29. 37.95

31. $\sqrt{10} + \sqrt{20}$

33. The graph is a circle of radius 2 centered at the origin.

35. $2\left(\cos\dfrac{\pi}{3} + i\sin\dfrac{\pi}{3}\right)$ 37. $4\sqrt{2} + 4\sqrt{2}i$

39. $2\sqrt{3} + 2i$ 41. $\dfrac{81}{2} - \dfrac{81\sqrt{3}}{2}i$

43. $1, \cos\dfrac{\pi}{3} + i\sin\dfrac{\pi}{3}, \cos\dfrac{2\pi}{3} + i\sin\dfrac{2\pi}{3}, -1,$

    $\cos\dfrac{4\pi}{3} + i\sin\dfrac{4\pi}{3}, \cos\dfrac{5\pi}{3} + i\sin\dfrac{5\pi}{3}$

45. $\cos\dfrac{\pi}{8} + i\sin\dfrac{\pi}{8}, \cos\dfrac{5\pi}{8} + i\sin\dfrac{5\pi}{8},$

    $\cos\dfrac{9\pi}{8} + i\sin\dfrac{9\pi}{8}, \cos\dfrac{13\pi}{8} + i\sin\dfrac{13\pi}{8}$

47. $\langle 11, -1 \rangle$ 49. $2\sqrt{29}$ 51. $-11\mathbf{i} + 8\mathbf{j}$

53. $\sqrt{10}$ 55. $\left\langle \dfrac{5\sqrt{2}}{2}, \dfrac{5\sqrt{2}}{2} \right\rangle$

57. $-\dfrac{1}{\sqrt{5}}\mathbf{i} + \dfrac{2}{\sqrt{5}}\mathbf{j}$

59. Ground speed: 321.87 mph; course: 126.18°

61. −26   63. 3   65. 0.70 radians

67. $\text{proj}_v\mathbf{u} = \mathbf{v} = 2\mathbf{i} + \mathbf{j}$

69. $(\mathbf{u} + \mathbf{v}) \cdot (\mathbf{u} - \mathbf{v}) = \mathbf{u} \cdot \mathbf{u} - \mathbf{u} \cdot \mathbf{v} + \mathbf{v} \cdot \mathbf{u} - \mathbf{v} \cdot \mathbf{v} =$
    $\mathbf{u} \cdot \mathbf{u} - \mathbf{v} \cdot \mathbf{v} = \|\mathbf{u}^2\| - \|\mathbf{v}^2\| = 0$ since $\mathbf{u}$ and $\mathbf{v}$ have the same magnitude.

71. 1750 lb

Chapter 10 can do calculus, page 689

1. 1   2. $\cos(3) + i\sin(3); -0.9900 + 0.1411i$

3. $\cos(-2) + i\sin(-2); -0.4161 - 0.9093i$

---

4. $\cos\left(\dfrac{\pi}{4}\right) + i\sin\left(\dfrac{\pi}{4}\right); 0.7071 + 0.7071i$

5. $e(\cos\pi + i\sin\pi); -2.7183$

6. 1

7. $e\left(\cos -\dfrac{\pi}{3} + i\sin -\dfrac{\pi}{3}\right); 1.3591 - 2.3541i$

8. $e^\pi(\cos 1 + i\sin 1); 12.5030 + 19.4722i$

Chapter 11

Section 11.1, page 698

1. $\dfrac{x^2}{49} + \dfrac{y^2}{4} = 1$ 3. $\dfrac{x^2}{36} + \dfrac{y^2}{16} = 1$

5. $\dfrac{x^2}{9} + \dfrac{y^2}{49} = 1$ 7. $x^2 + 6y^2 = 18$

9. $2x^2 + y^2 = 12$ 11. $\dfrac{x^2}{16} + \dfrac{y^2}{9} = 1$

13. Ellipse

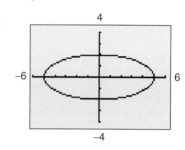

15. Ellipse

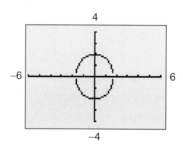

17. 8π 19. $2\sqrt{3}\pi$ 21. $\dfrac{7\pi}{\sqrt{3}}$

23. approximately 1,507,964 sq. ft.

25. If $a = b$, then $\dfrac{x^2}{a^2} + \dfrac{y^2}{a^2} = 1$. Multiplying both sides by a^2 gives $x^2 + y^2 = a^2$, the equation of a circle of radius a with center at the origin.

27. As b gets larger, the ellipse becomes more elongated horizontally. As b gets closer to 0, the graph becomes very close to being a vertical line. However, it will never be a vertical line, because b cannot have a value of 0.

29. Approximately 226,335 mi and 251,401 mi

31. b = length of OC; c = length of OF; since $c = \sqrt{a^2 - b^2}$, $c^2 = a^2 - b^2$ or $a^2 = b^2 + c^2$; by the Pythagorean Theorem a = length of CF.

Section 11.2, page 707

1. $\dfrac{x^2}{9} - \dfrac{y^2}{36} = 1$

3. $\dfrac{x^2}{4} - y^2 = 1$

5. $\dfrac{x^2}{4} - \dfrac{y^2}{5} = 1$

7. $\dfrac{y^2}{16} - \dfrac{x^2}{9} = 1$

9. $\dfrac{x^2}{1} - \dfrac{y^2}{8} = 1$ or $8x^2 - y^2 = 8$

11. $\dfrac{x^2}{1} + \dfrac{y^2}{8} = 1$ or $8x^2 + y^2 = 8$

13.

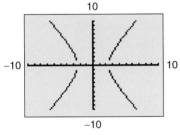

foci are at $\left(\sqrt{22}, 0\right)$ and $\left(-\sqrt{22}, 0\right)$; asymptotes are $y = \pm\dfrac{b}{a}x$; $y = \dfrac{4}{\sqrt{6}}x$ and $y = -\dfrac{4}{\sqrt{6}}x$

15.

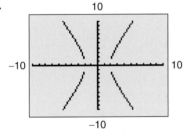

foci are at $\left(\sqrt{20}, 0\right)$ and $\left(-\sqrt{20}, 0\right)$; asymptotes are $y = \pm\dfrac{b}{a}x$; $y = 2x$ and $y = -2x$

17.

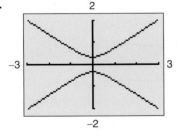

foci are at $\left(0, \dfrac{\sqrt{13}}{6}\right)$ and $\left(0, -\dfrac{\sqrt{13}}{6}\right)$; asymptotes are $y = \pm\dfrac{a}{b}x$; $y = \dfrac{2}{3}x$ and $y = -\dfrac{2}{3}x$

19. Hyperbola

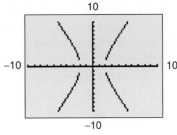

Because of limited resolution, this calculator-generated graph does not show that the top and bottom halves of the graph are connected.

21.

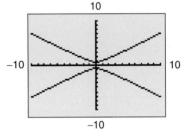

23.

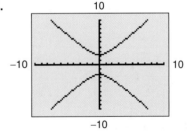

25. The two branches of the hyperbola are very "flat" when b is large. With very large b and a small viewing window, the hyperbola may look like two horizontal lines, but it isn't because its asymptotes $y = \pm\dfrac{2}{b}x$ are not horizontal (their slopes, $\pm\dfrac{2}{b}$, are close to, but not equal to, 0 when b is large).

27.

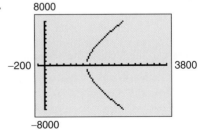

29. $y = x - 2$

31. The distance between the vertices is $2a$. One point on the hyperbola is the vertex at $(a, 0)$. This point is the distance $c - a$ from the closest focus and a distance $c + a$ from the other focus. The

Answers to Selected Exercises **1119**

differences of these distances is $c + a - (c - a) =$ $2a$. Therefore, by the definition of a hyperbola, when the difference of the distances from any point on the hyperbola to the two foci is constant, this constant difference is $2a$; this is the distance between the two vertices.

33. $OV = a$, $OP = b$; since in the right triangle $a^2 + b^2 = c^2$ and in the equation of a hyperbola $c^2 = a^2 + b^2$, $PV = c$, which is the distance from each focus to the center O.

Section 11.3, page 714

1. $y = 3x^2$ **3.** $y^2 = 20x$ **5.** $y^2 = 8x$

7. $y = \dfrac{x^2}{4}$ **9.** $x^2 = -8y$

11. Parabola

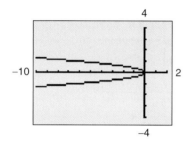

13. Parabola

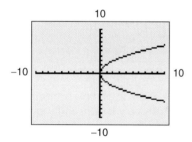

15. Focus: $\left(0, \dfrac{1}{12}\right)$; directrix: $y = -\dfrac{1}{12}$

17. Focus: $(0, 1)$; directrix: $y = -1$

19. $x^2 = \dfrac{1}{2}y$ **21.** $y^2 = -4x$

23. The point closest to the focus is the vertex at $(0, 0)$.

25. $y^2 = 8x$ **27.** $y^2 = -2x$

Section 11.4, page 726

1. $\dfrac{(x - 2)^2}{4} + \dfrac{(y - 3)^2}{16} = 1$

3. $\dfrac{4(x - 7)^2}{25} + \dfrac{(y + 4)^2}{36} = 1$

5. $\dfrac{(y - 3)^2}{4} - \dfrac{(x + 2)^2}{6} = 1$

7. $\dfrac{(x - 4)^2}{9} - \dfrac{(y - 2)^2}{16} = 1$

9. $y = 13(x - 1)^2$ **11.** $x - 2 = 3(y - 1)^2$

13. $\dfrac{(x - 3)^2}{36} + \dfrac{(y + 2)^2}{16} = 1$

15. $x + 3 = 4(y + 2)^2$

17. Ellipse   **19.** Parabola   **21.** Hyperbola

23.

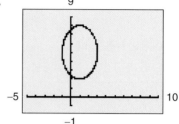

25.

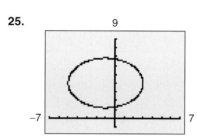

27.

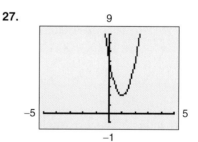

29.

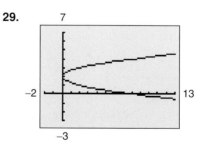

31.

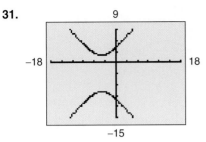

33.

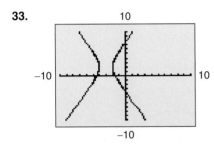

35. Ellipse; $-6 \le x \le 3$ and $-2 \le y \le 4$

37. Hyperbola; $-7 \le x \le 13$ and $-3 \le y \le 9$

39. Parabola; $-1 \le x \le 8$ and $-3 \le y \le 3$

41. Ellipse; $-1.5 \le x \le 1.5$ and $-1 \le y \le 1$

43. Hyperbola; $-15 \le x \le 15$ and $-10 \le y \le 10$

45. Parabola; $-19 \le x \le 2$ and $-1 \le y \le 13$

47. Hyperbola; $-15 \le x \le 15$ and $-15 \le y \le 15$

49. Ellipse; $-6 \le x \le 6$ and $-4 \le y \le 4$

51. Parabola; $-9 \le x \le 4$ and $-2 \le y \le 10$

53. $\dfrac{(x+5)^2}{49} + \dfrac{(y-3)^2}{16} = 1$ or $\dfrac{(x+5)^2}{16} + \dfrac{(y-3)^2}{49} = 1$

55. The asymptotes of $\dfrac{x^2}{a^2} - \dfrac{y^2}{a^2} = 1$ are $y = \pm\dfrac{a}{a}x$ or $y = \pm x$, with slopes $+1$ and -1. Since $(+1)(-1) = -1$, these lines are perpendicular.

57. $b = 0$

59. $\left(9, -\dfrac{1}{2} \pm \dfrac{1}{2}\sqrt{34}\right)$

61. $\dfrac{(y-5)^2}{5} - \dfrac{(x-7)^2}{3} = 1$

63. $\dfrac{(x+12)^2}{144} - \dfrac{(y-4)^2}{64} = 1$

65. $(x-105)^2 = -200.45(y-55)$

67. $\dfrac{x^2}{1,210,000} - \dfrac{y^2}{5,759,600} = 1$ (measurement in feet). The exact location cannot be determined from the given information.

Section 11.4A, page 733

1. $\dfrac{u^2}{2} - \dfrac{v^2}{2} = 1$

3. $\dfrac{u^2}{4} + v^2 = 1$

5. $\theta \approx 53.13°$; $x = \dfrac{3}{5}u - \dfrac{4}{5}v$; $y = \dfrac{4}{5}u + \dfrac{3}{5}v$

7. $\theta \approx 36.87°$; $x = \dfrac{4}{5}u - \dfrac{3}{5}v$; $y = \dfrac{3}{5}u + \dfrac{4}{5}v$

9. a. $(A \cos^2 \theta + B \cos \theta \sin \theta + C \sin^2 \theta)u^2 + (B \cos^2 \theta - 2A \cos \theta \sin \theta + 2C \cos \theta \sin \theta - B \sin^2 \theta)uv + (C \cos^2 \theta - B \cos \theta \sin \theta + A \sin^2 \theta)v^2 + (D \cos \theta + E \sin \theta)u + (E \cos \theta - D \sin \theta)v + F = 0$

b. $B' = B \cos^2 \theta - 2A \cos \theta \sin \theta + 2C \cos \theta \sin \theta - B \sin^2 \theta = 2(C - A)\sin \theta \cos \theta + B(\cos^2 \theta - \sin^2 \theta)$ since B' is the coefficient of uv

c. Since $\sin 2\theta = 2 \sin \theta \cos \theta$ and $\cos 2\theta = \cos^2 \theta - \sin^2 \theta$, $B' = (C - A) \sin 2\theta + B \cos 2\theta$.

d. If $\cot 2\theta = \dfrac{A - C}{B}$ then $A - C = B \cot 2\theta$ and we have $B' = (-B \cot 2\theta) \sin 2\theta + B \cos 2\theta = -B \cos 2\theta + B \cos 2\theta = 0$.

11. a. From Exercise 9 (a) we have $(B')^2 - 4A'C' = (B \cos^2 \theta - 2A \cos \theta \sin \theta + 2C \cos \theta \sin \theta - B \sin^2 \theta)^2 - 4(A \cos^2 \theta + B \cos \theta \sin \theta + C \sin^2 \theta)(C \cos^2 \theta - B \cos \theta \sin \theta + A \sin^2 \theta) = [B(\cos^2 \theta - \sin^2 \theta) + 2(C - A) \cos \theta \sin \theta]^2 - 4(A \cos^2 \theta + B \cos \theta \sin \theta + C \sin^2 \theta)(C \cos^2 \theta - B \cos \theta \sin \theta + A \sin^2 \theta) = B^2(\cos^2 \theta - \sin^2 \theta)^2 + 4(C - A)^2 \cos^2 \theta \sin^2 \theta + 4B(C - A)(\cos^2 \theta - \sin^2 \theta) \cos \theta \sin \theta - [4AC(\cos^4 \theta + \sin^4 \theta) + 4(A^2 + C^2 - B^2) \cos^2 \theta \sin^2 \theta - 4AB(\cos^3 \theta \sin \theta - \cos \theta \sin^3 \theta) + 4BC(\cos^3 \theta \sin \theta - \cos \theta \sin^3 \theta)] = B^2(\cos^4 \theta - 2 \cos^2 \theta \sin^2 \theta + \sin^4 \theta + 4 \cos^2 \theta \sin^2 \theta) - 4AC(2 \cos^2 \theta \sin^2 \theta + \cos^4 \theta + \sin^4 \theta)$ (everything else cancels) $= (B^2 - 4AC)(\cos^4 \theta + 2 \cos^2 \theta \sin^2 \theta + \sin^4 \theta) = (B^2 - 4AC)(\cos^2 \theta + \sin^2 \theta)^2 = B^2 - 4AC$

b. If $B^2 - 4AC < 0$, then also $(B')^2 - 4A'C' < 0$. Since $B' = 0$, $-4A'C' < 0$ and so $A'C' > 0$. By Exercise 10, the graph is an ellipse. The other two cases are proved in the same way.

13. $\left(\dfrac{5\sqrt{2}}{2}, -\dfrac{\sqrt{2}}{2}\right)$

15. $\left(\dfrac{\sqrt{3}}{2}, -\dfrac{1}{2}\right)$

Section 11.5, page 743

1. $P = \left(2, \dfrac{\pi}{4}\right)$, $Q = \left(3, \dfrac{2\pi}{3}\right)$, $R = (5, \pi)$, $S = \left(7, \dfrac{7\pi}{6}\right)$, $T = \left(4, \dfrac{3\pi}{2}\right)$, $U = \left(6, -\dfrac{\pi}{3}\right)$ or $\left(6, \dfrac{5\pi}{3}\right)$, $V = (7, 0)$

3. $(5, 2\pi)$, $(5, -2\pi)$, $(-5, 3\pi)$, $(-5, -\pi)$, and others

5. $\left(1, \dfrac{5\pi}{6}\right)$, $\left(1, -\dfrac{7\pi}{6}\right)$, $\left(-1, \dfrac{11\pi}{6}\right)$, $\left(-1, -\dfrac{13\pi}{6}\right)$, and others

7. $\left(\dfrac{3}{2}, \dfrac{3\sqrt{3}}{2}\right)$

9. $\left(\dfrac{\sqrt{3}}{2}, -\dfrac{1}{2}\right)$

11. $\left(6, -\dfrac{\pi}{6}\right)$

13. $\left(2\sqrt{5}, 1.1071\right)$

15. $\left(\sqrt{31.25}, 2.6779\right)$

17.

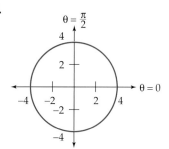

19.

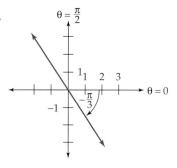

21.

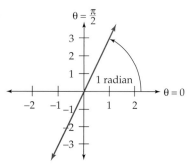

23.

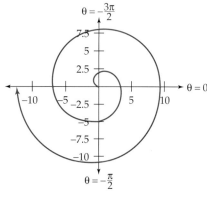

25.

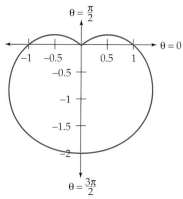

27.

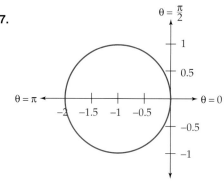

29.

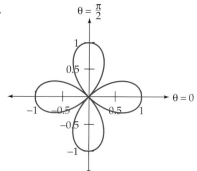

31.

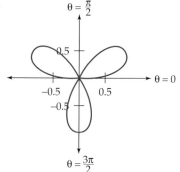

33.

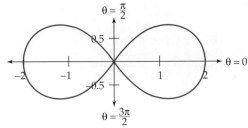

35.

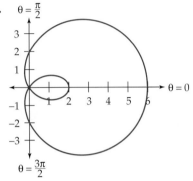

37.

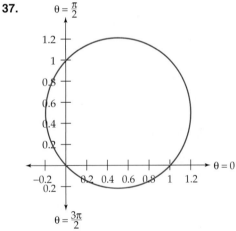

39.

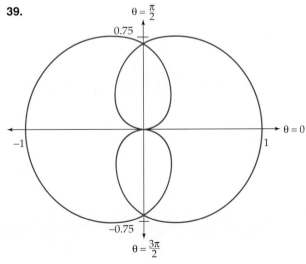

41.

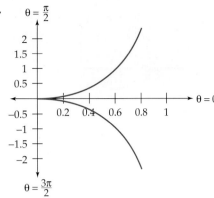

43.

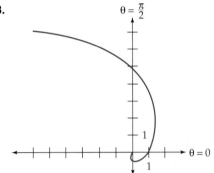

45.

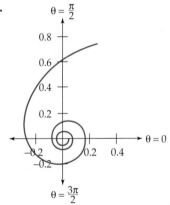

47. a.

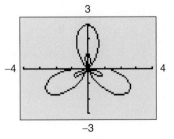

b.

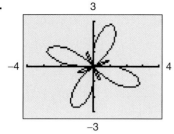

c.

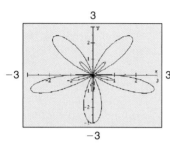

49. $r = a \sin \theta + b \cos \theta \Rightarrow r^2 = ar \sin \theta + br \cos \theta \Rightarrow$
$x^2 + y^2 = ay + bx \Rightarrow x^2 - bx + y^2 - ay = 0 \Rightarrow$

$$\left(x^2 - bx + \frac{b^2}{4} \right) + \left(y^2 - ay + \frac{a^2}{4} \right) = \frac{(a^2 + b^2)}{4} \Rightarrow$$

$$\left(x - \frac{b}{2} \right)^2 + \left(y - \frac{a}{2} \right)^2 = \frac{(a^2 + b^2)}{4}, \text{ a circle with}$$

center $\left(\dfrac{b}{2}, \dfrac{a}{2} \right)$ and radius $\dfrac{\sqrt{a^2 + b^2}}{2}$.

51. Using the Law of Cosines in the following
diagram, $d^2 = r^2 + s^2 - 2rs \cos(\theta - \beta)$, so
$d = \sqrt{r^2 + s^2 - 2rs \cos(\theta - \beta)}$.

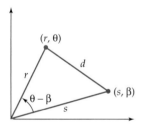

Section 11.6, page 752

1. (d)   **3.** (c)   **5.** (a)

7. Hyperbola, $e = \dfrac{4}{3}$ **9.** Parabola, $e = 1$

11. Ellipse, $e = \dfrac{2}{3}$ **13.** 0.1   **15.** $\sqrt{5}$ **17.** $\dfrac{5}{4}$

19. a.

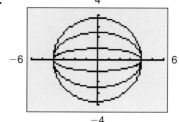

b. $\dfrac{\sqrt{15}}{4}, \dfrac{\sqrt{10}}{4}, \dfrac{\sqrt{2}}{4}$

c. The smaller the eccentricity, the closer the shape
is to circular.

21.

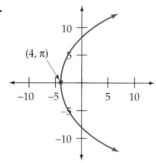

23.

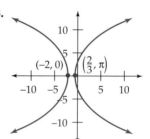

25.

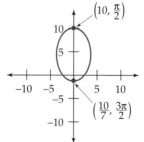

27.

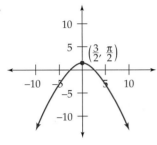

29.

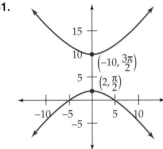

31.

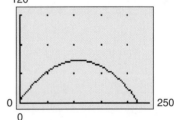

33. $r = \dfrac{6}{1 - \cos\theta}$ **35.** $r = \dfrac{16}{5 + 3\sin\theta}$

37. $r = \dfrac{3}{1 + 2\cos\theta}$ **39.** $r = \dfrac{8}{1 - 4\cos\theta}$

41. $r = \dfrac{3}{1 - \sin\theta}$ **43.** $r = \dfrac{2}{2 + \cos\theta}$

45. $r = \dfrac{2}{1 - 2\cos\theta}$ **47.** $r = \dfrac{3 \cdot 10^7}{1 - \cos\theta}$

Section 11.7, page 763

1. $-5 \le x \le 6$ and $-2 \le y \le 2$

3. $-3 \le x \le 4$ and $-2 \le y \le 3$

5. $0 \le x \le 14$ and $-15 \le y \le 0$

7. $-2 \le x \le 20$ and $-11 \le y \le 11$

9. $-12 \le x \le 12$ and $-12 \le y \le 12$

11. $-2 \le x \le 20$ and $-20 \le y \le 4$

13. $-25 \le x \le 22$ and $-25 \le y \le 26$

15. $y = 2x + 7$ **17.** $y = 2x + 5$ **19.** $y = \ln x$

21. $x^2 + y^2 = 9$ **23.** $16x^2 + 9y^2 = 144$

25. Both give a straight line segment between $P = (-4, 7)$ and $Q = (2, -5)$. The parametric equations in (a) move from P to Q, and the parametric equations in (b) move from Q to P.

27. Solving $x = a + (c - a)t$ for t gives $t = \dfrac{x - a}{c - a}$ and substituting in $y = b + (d - b)t$ then gives $y = b + (d - b)\dfrac{x - a}{c - a}$, or $y = b + \dfrac{d - b}{c - a}(x - a)$. This is a linear equation and therefore gives a straight line. You can check by substitution that (a, b) and (c, d) lie on this straight line; in fact, these points correspond to $t = 0$ and $t = 1$, respectively.

29. $x = -6 + 18t,\ y = 12 - 22t$ $(0 \le t \le 1)$

31. Local minimum at $(-6, 2)$

33. Local maximum at $(4, 5)$

35. Solve the first equation for $t = \dfrac{x}{140 \cos 31°}$. Substitute into the second to get
$$y = (140 \sin 31°)\left(\dfrac{x}{140 \cos 31°}\right) - 16\left(\dfrac{x}{140 \cos 31°}\right)^2,$$
which is the equation of a parabola.

37. a.

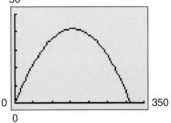

$x = (88 \cos 48°)t$
$y = (88 \sin 48°)t - 16t^2 + 4$
$0 \le t \le 4.5$
b. Yes

39. $v = 80\sqrt[4]{3} \approx 105.29$ ft/sec

41. a.

$x = (110 \cos 28°)t$
$y = (110 \sin 28°)t - 16t^2$
$0 \le t \le 3.5$
b. About 3.2 sec
c. 41.67 ft

43. a. 200

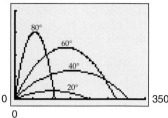

b. 40°

c. 200

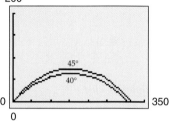

An angle of 45° seems to result in the longest distance.

45. a. Since $\angle TCQ = \frac{3\pi}{2}$, $t + \frac{3\pi}{2} + \theta$, $\theta = t - \frac{3\pi}{2}$.

Then $x = OT + CQ = 3t + 3\cos\theta = 3t + 3\cos\left(t - \frac{3\pi}{2}\right)$. And $y = CT - PQ = 3 - 3\sin\theta$

$= 3 - 3\sin\left(t - \frac{3\pi}{2}\right)$.

b. $\cos\left(t - \frac{3\pi}{2}\right) = \cos t \cos\frac{3\pi}{2} + \sin t \sin\frac{3\pi}{2}$

$= (\cos t)(0) + (\sin t)(-1) = -\sin t$. Therefore,

$3t + 3\cos\left(t - \frac{3\pi}{2}\right) = 3t - 3\sin t =$

$3(t - \sin t)$. $\sin\left(t - \frac{3\pi}{2}\right) = \sin t \cos\frac{3\pi}{2} -$

$\cos t \sin\frac{3\pi}{2} = (\sin t)(0) - (\cos t)(-1) = \cos t$.

Therefore, $3 - 3\sin\left(t - \frac{3\pi}{2}\right) = 3 - 3\cos t =$

$3(1 - \cos t)$.

47. a. 6

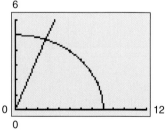

The particles do not collide.

b. $t \approx 1.1$

c. 6

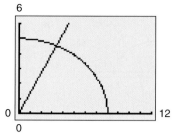

The particles do not collide; they are closest when $t \approx 1.13$.

d. 8

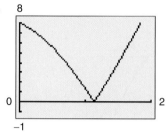

d is smallest when $t \approx 1.1322$.

Section 11.7A, page 769

1. $x = 9 + 5\cos t$, $y = 12 + 5\sin t$ $(0 \le t \le 2\pi)$

3. $x = 2\cos t + 2$, $y = 2\sin t + 3$ $(0 \le t \le 2\pi)$

5. $x = \sqrt{10}\cos t$, $y = 6\sin t$ $(0 \le t \le 2\pi)$

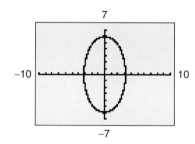

7. $x = \frac{1}{2}\cos t$, $y = \frac{1}{2}\sin t$ $(0 \le t \le 2\pi)$

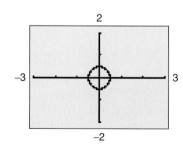

9. $x = \dfrac{\sqrt{10}}{\cos t}, y = 6 \tan t \quad (0 \le t \le 2\pi)$

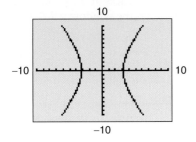

11. $x = \dfrac{1}{\cos t}, y = \dfrac{1}{2} \tan t \quad (0 \le t \le 2\pi)$

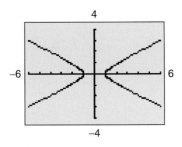

13. $x = \dfrac{t^2}{4}, y = t \quad$ (t any real number)

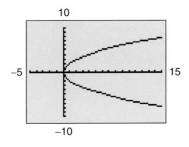

15. $x = 2 \cos t + 1, y = 3 \sin t + 5 \quad (0 \le t \le 2\pi)$

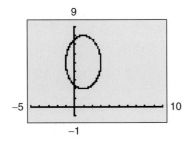

17. $x = 4 \cos t - 1, y = \sqrt{8} \sin t + 4 \quad (0 \le t \le 2\pi)$

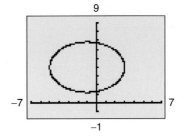

19. $x = t, y = 4(t - 1)^2 + 2 \quad$ (any real number t)

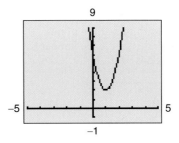

21. $x = 2(t - 2)^2, y = t \quad$ (any real number t)

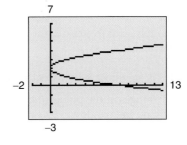

23. $x = 4 \tan t - 1, y = \dfrac{5}{\cos t} - 3 \quad (0 \le t \le 2\pi)$

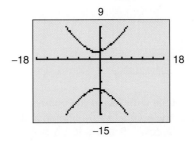

Selected Answers

25. $x = \dfrac{1}{\cos t} - 3, y = 2\tan t + 2 \quad (0 \le t \le 2\pi)$

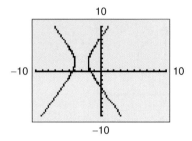

Chapter 11 Review, page 772

1. This is an ellipse with foci at the points $(0, \pm 2)$ and vertices at the points $(0, \pm 2\sqrt{5})$. Shown is the graph on the window $-9 \le x \le 9$, $-6 \le y \le 6$.

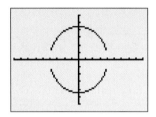

3. This is the same graph as in Exercise 2; the equations are equivalent.

5. $\dfrac{x^2}{12} + \dfrac{y^2}{16} = 1$; This is an ellipse with foci at the points $(0, \pm 2)$ and vertices at the points $(0, \pm 4)$. Shown is the graph on the window $-9 \le x \le 9$, $-6 \le y \le 6$.

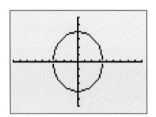

7. This is a hyperbola with foci at the points $(\pm 5, 0)$ and vertices at the points $(\pm 3, 0)$. Shown is the graph on the window $-9 \le x \le 9$, $-6 \le y \le 6$.

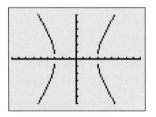

9. $\dfrac{y^2}{4} - \dfrac{x^2}{1} = 1$; This is a hyperbola with foci at the points $(0, \pm\sqrt{5})$ and vertices at the points $(0, \pm 2)$. Shown is the graph on the window $-9 \le x \le 9$, $-6 \le y \le 6$.

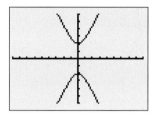

11. $y^2 = -25x$ **13.** $y^2 = -16x$ **15.** $y^2 = 16x$

17. Focus: $\left(0, \dfrac{5}{14}\right)$, directrix: $y = -\dfrac{5}{14}$

19. Ellipse, foci: $(1, 6)$, $(1, 0)$, vertices: $(1, 7)$, $(1, -1)$

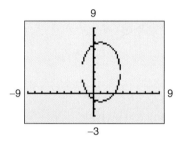

21. This is an ellipse with center at $(3, -5)$, vertices at the points $(0, -5)$ and $(6, -5)$ and foci at the points $(3 - \sqrt{5}, -5)$ and $(3 + \sqrt{5}, -5)$.

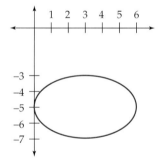

23. This is a hyperbola with center at $(0, 0)$, vertices at the points $(6, 0)$ and $(-6, 0)$ foci at the points $\left(\sqrt{52}, 0\right)$ and $\left(-\sqrt{52}, 0\right)$, and asymptotes $y = \pm\frac{2}{3}x$.

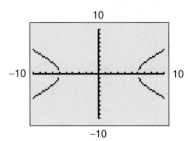

25. This is a parabola with vertex at the point $(3, 3)$, focus at the point $\left(3, \frac{25}{8}\right)$, and directrix $y = \frac{23}{8}$.

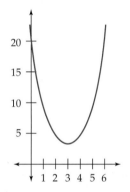

27. This is a parabola with vertex at the point $(1, -1)$, focus at the point $\left(\frac{5}{4}, -1\right)$, and directrix $x = \frac{3}{4}$.

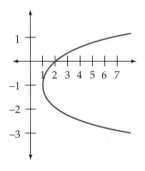

29. Center: $(4, -6)$

31. $\dfrac{y^2}{4} - \dfrac{(x-3)^2}{16} = 1$

33. $\left(y + \dfrac{1}{2}\right)^2 = -\dfrac{1}{2}\left(x - \dfrac{3}{2}\right)$

35. $\dfrac{(x-3)^2}{4} + \dfrac{(y-1)^2}{2} = 1$

37. Hyperbola   **39.** Ellipse

41. $-9 \le x \le 9$ and $-6 \le y \le 6$

43. $-15 \le x \le 10$ and $-10 \le y \le 20$

45. $-6 \le x \le 6$ and $-4 \le y \le 4$

47. $x = \dfrac{1}{2}u - \dfrac{\sqrt{3}}{2}v$

$y = \dfrac{\sqrt{3}}{2}u + \dfrac{1}{2}v$

49. $45°$

51.

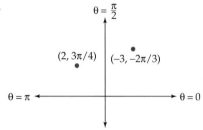

53.

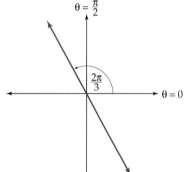

55.

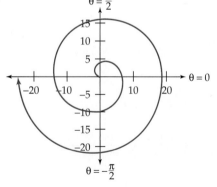

57.

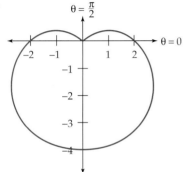

59.

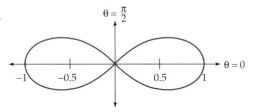

61.

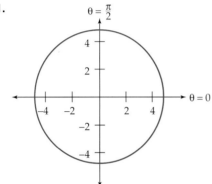

63. $\left(-\dfrac{3}{2}, -\dfrac{3\sqrt{3}}{2}\right)$ **65.** Eccentricity $= \sqrt{\dfrac{2}{3}} \approx 0.8165$

67. Hyperbola

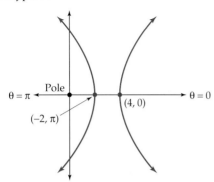

69. Ellipse

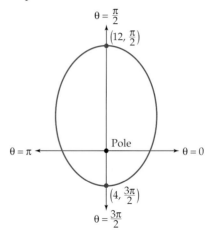

71. $r = \dfrac{2}{1 + \cos\theta}$ **73.** $r = \dfrac{24}{5 + \cos\theta}$

75. $-35 \le x \le 32$ and $-2 \le y \le 16$

77. $-15 \le x \le 15$ and $-10 \le y \le 10$

79. $y = -2x^2 + 2$

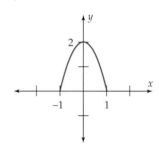

Point moves from $(1, 0)$ to $(-1, 0)$ as t goes from 0 to π. Then point retraces its path, moving from $(-1, 0)$ to $(1, 0)$ as t goes from π to 2π.

81. $x = 3 - 2y$ or $y = -\dfrac{1}{2}x + \dfrac{3}{2}$ **83.** numbers 74 and 75

85. $x = 5\cos t - 3, y = 5\sin t + 5, 0 \le t \le 2\pi$

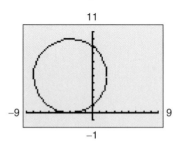

87. $x = \cos t - 2, y = 2\sin t + 3, 0 \le t \le 2\pi$

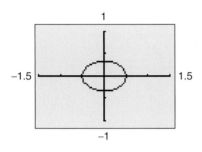

89. $x = \frac{1}{2}\cos t, y = \frac{1}{3}\sin t, 0 \le t \le 2\pi$

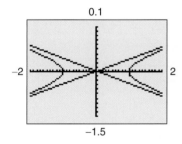

91. $x = \sec t, y = \frac{1}{36}\tan t, 0 \le t \le 2\pi$

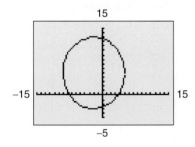

93. $x = 7\cos t - 2, y = 8\sin t + 5, 0 \le t \le 2\pi$

95. $x = \sqrt{12}\tan t + 2, y = 2\sec t - 3, 0 \le t \le 2\pi$

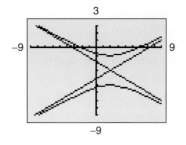

Note that the diagonal lines shown here are not part of the graph but are just about where the asymptotes should be.

97. $x = -32(t + 4)^2 - 5, y = t, -10 \le t \le 10$

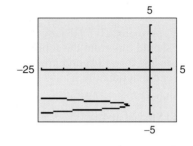

Chapter 11 can do calculus, page 777

1. approximately 30   **2.** approximately 20

3. approximately 8   **4.** approximately 4

5. approximately 10   **6.** approximately 5

Chapter 12

Section 12.1, page 788

1. Yes   **3.** Yes   **5.** No

7. $x = \frac{11}{5}, y = -\frac{7}{5}$ **9.** $x = \frac{2}{7}, y = -\frac{11}{7}$

11. $r = \frac{5}{2}, s = -\frac{5}{2}$ **13.** $x = \frac{3c}{2}, y = \frac{-c + 2d}{2}$

15. $x = 28, y = 22$ **17.** $x = 2, y = -1$

19. Inconsistent

21. $x = b, y = \frac{3b - 4}{2}$, where b is any real number

23. $x = b, y = \frac{3b - 2}{4}$, where b is any real number

25. Inconsistent

27. $x = -6, y = 2$ **29.** $x = \frac{66}{5}, y = \frac{18}{5}$

31. $x = 0.185, y = -0.624$

33. $x = 3, y = -1, z = 4$

35. $c = -3, d = \dfrac{1}{2}$

37. a. Electric: $y = 960x + 2000$;
  solar: $y = 114x + 14{,}000$
b. Electric: \$6800; solar: \$14,570
c. Costs same in fourteenth year; electric; solar

39. a. $y = 7.50x + 5000$
b. $y = 8.20x$
c. 130,000

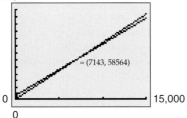

Costs equal at approximately 7143 cases.
d. The company should buy from the supplier any number of cases less than 7143 and produce their own beyond that quantity.

41. 140 adults, 60 children

43. \$19,500 at 2% and \$15,500 at 4%

45. $\dfrac{3}{4}$ lb cashews and $2\dfrac{1}{4}$ lb peanuts

47. 60cc of 20% and 40cc of 45%

49. 80 bowls; 120 plates

Section 12.1.A, page 794

1.

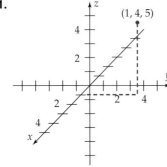

3.

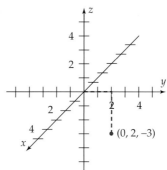

5.

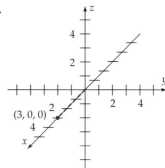

7.

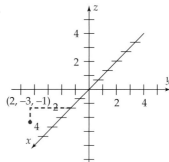

9.

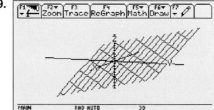

$$x = 6$$
$$\text{intercepts:} \quad y = 2$$
$$z = -6$$

11.

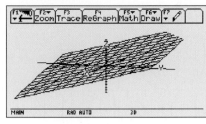

$$x = 3$$
intercepts: $y = -\dfrac{9}{4}$
$$z = \dfrac{3}{2}$$

13.

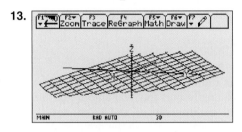

$$x = 3$$
intercepts: $y = 3$
$$z = -3$$

15.

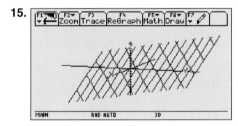

$$x = 4$$
intercepts: $y = 2$
$$z = -8$$

17.

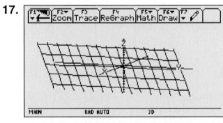

$$x = 4$$
intercepts: no y-intercept
$$z = -12$$

19.

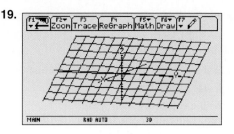

$$x = -2$$
intercepts: no y-intercept
$$z = -3$$

21. Each equation can be represented by a plane. Two planes are parallel, are coincident, or they intersect in a line. The system of equations either has no solution, an infinite number of solutions which lie on the plane, or an infinite number of solutions, all of which lie on a straight line.

Section 12.2, page 801

1. $\begin{pmatrix} 2 & -3 & 4 & 1 \\ 1 & 2 & -6 & 0 \\ 3 & -7 & 4 & -3 \end{pmatrix}$ **3.** $\begin{pmatrix} 1 & -\dfrac{1}{2} & \dfrac{7}{4} & 0 \\ 2 & -\dfrac{3}{2} & 5 & 0 \\ 0 & -2 & \dfrac{1}{3} & 0 \end{pmatrix}$

5. $2x - 3y = 1$
$4x + 7y = 2$

7. $\begin{aligned} x + z &= 1 \\ x - y + 4z - 2w &= 3 \\ 4x + 2y + 5z &= 2 \end{aligned}$

9. $x = \dfrac{3}{2}, y = 5, z = -2, w = 0$

11. $x = 2 - t, y = -3 - 2t, z = 4, w = t$, where t is any real number

13. $x = -1, y = -1, z = 1$

15. $x = -\dfrac{1}{2}, y = -\dfrac{3}{4}, z = \dfrac{3}{2}$

17. $x = -14, y = -6, z = 2$

19. No solution.

21. $z = t, y = \dfrac{1}{2} - 2t, x = t$, where t is any real number

23. $x = 1, y = 2$ **25.** No solutions

27. $z = t, y = t - 1, x = -t + 2$, for any real number t

29. $x = 0, y = 0, z = 0$

31. $x = -1, y = 1, z = -3, w = -2$

33. $x = 3, y = 1, z = -2, w = -5$.

35. $x = -\dfrac{3}{4}, y = \dfrac{10}{3}, z = \dfrac{5}{2}$

37. 10 quarters; 28 dimes; 14 nickels

39. $3000 from her friend; $6000 from the bank; $1000 from the insurance company

41. $15,000 in the mutual fund; $30,000 in bonds; $25,000 in food franchise

43. Three possible solutions:
18 bedroom, 13 living room, 0 whole house
16 bedroom, 8 living room, 2 whole house
14 bedroom, 3 living room, 4 whole house

45. Tom: 8 hours; George: 24 hours; Mario: 12 hours.

47. 2000 chairs; 1600 chests; 2500 tables

49. 20 model A; 15 model B; 10 model C

Section 12.3, page 811

1. $A + B = \begin{pmatrix} 2 + (-4) & -6 + 4 & 3 + 7 \\ 4 + 5 & -2 + 3 & 1 + 2 \\ 3 + (-1) & 5 + (-6) & -5 + 6 \end{pmatrix} = \begin{pmatrix} -2 & -2 & 10 \\ 9 & 1 & 3 \\ 2 & -1 & 1 \end{pmatrix}$

3. $A + C = \begin{pmatrix} 2 + 4 & -6 + 3 & 3 + (-5) \\ 4 + (-2) & -2 + (-1) & 1 + 7 \\ 3 + 4 & 5 + 6 & -5 + 1 \end{pmatrix} = \begin{pmatrix} 6 & -3 & -2 \\ 2 & -3 & 8 \\ 7 & 11 & -4 \end{pmatrix}$

5. $2C = \begin{pmatrix} 2(4) & 2(3) & 2(-5) \\ 2(-2) & 2(-1) & 2(7) \\ 2(4) & 2(6) & 2(1) \end{pmatrix} = \begin{pmatrix} 8 & 6 & -10 \\ -4 & -2 & 14 \\ 8 & 12 & 2 \end{pmatrix}$

7. AB defined, 2×4; BA not defined

9. AB defined, 3×3; BA defined, 2×2

11. AB defined, 3×2; BA not defined

13. $\begin{pmatrix} 3 & 0 & 11 \\ 2 & 8 & 10 \end{pmatrix}$

15. $\begin{pmatrix} 1 & -3 \\ 2 & -1 \\ 5 & 6 \end{pmatrix}$

17. $\begin{pmatrix} 1 & -1 & 1 & 2 \\ 4 & 3 & 3 & 2 \\ -1 & -1 & -3 & 2 \\ 5 & 3 & 2 & 5 \end{pmatrix}$

19. $AB = \begin{pmatrix} 17 & -3 \\ 33 & -19 \end{pmatrix}$; $BA = \begin{pmatrix} -4 & 9 \\ 24 & 2 \end{pmatrix}$

21. $AB = \begin{pmatrix} 8 & 24 & -8 \\ 2 & -2 & 6 \\ -3 & -21 & 15 \end{pmatrix}$; $BA = \begin{pmatrix} 19 & 9 & 8 \\ -10 & 2 & 0 \\ 0 & 0 & 0 \end{pmatrix}$

23.

$$\begin{array}{cc} & \text{To:} \\ & \begin{array}{ccc} J & K & L \end{array} \\ \text{From: } \begin{array}{c} J \\ K \\ L \end{array} & \begin{pmatrix} 0 & 1 & 1 \\ 1 & 1 & 2 \\ 0 & 1 & 0 \end{pmatrix} \end{array}$$

25. $\begin{pmatrix} 0 & 1 & 1 \\ 1 & 1 & 2 \\ 0 & 1 & 0 \end{pmatrix}^2 = \begin{pmatrix} 0 & 1 & 1 \\ 1 & 1 & 2 \\ 0 & 1 & 0 \end{pmatrix}\begin{pmatrix} 0 & 1 & 1 \\ 1 & 1 & 2 \\ 0 & 1 & 0 \end{pmatrix} = \begin{pmatrix} 1 & 2 & 2 \\ 1 & 4 & 3 \\ 1 & 1 & 2 \end{pmatrix}$

27. $\begin{pmatrix} 3.75 \\ 6.5 \\ 14.75 \end{pmatrix}$

The total cost to bake and decorate each giant cookie is $3.75; sheet cake: $6.50; 3-tiered cake: $14.75.

29. $\begin{pmatrix} 91000 & 18200 \\ 25400 & 5080 \end{pmatrix}$; $a_{11} = $91,000$ represents the total amount of tuition the college got from lecture; $a_{22} = 5080 represents the total amount of tuition the college got from lab; a_{12} and a_{21} are not meaningful in the context of the problem.

31.

$$\begin{array}{c} \\ C \\ G \\ H \\ L \\ Z \end{array} \begin{array}{ccccc} C & G & H & L & Z \end{array} \begin{pmatrix} 0 & 0 & 1 & 0 & 0 \\ 1 & 0 & 1 & 1 & 0 \\ 0 & 0 & 0 & 0 & 0 \\ 0 & 0 & 1 & 1 & 0 \\ 0 & 0 & 1 & 1 & 0 \end{pmatrix}$$

33. a.

$$\begin{array}{c} \\ C \\ Ma \\ Mil \\ Min \\ SL \end{array} \begin{array}{ccccc} C & Ma & Mil & Min & SL \end{array} \begin{pmatrix} 0 & 1 & 1 & 1 & 1 \\ 1 & 0 & 1 & 1 & 0 \\ 1 & 1 & 0 & 0 & 1 \\ 1 & 1 & 0 & 0 & 1 \\ 1 & 0 & 1 & 1 & 0 \end{pmatrix}$$

b. $A^2 = \begin{pmatrix} 4 & 2 & 2 & 2 & 2 \\ 2 & 3 & 1 & 1 & 3 \\ 2 & 1 & 3 & 3 & 1 \\ 2 & 1 & 3 & 3 & 1 \\ 2 & 3 & 1 & 1 & 3 \end{pmatrix}$, $A^3 = \begin{pmatrix} 8 & 8 & 8 & 8 & 8 \\ 8 & 4 & 8 & 8 & 4 \\ 8 & 8 & 4 & 4 & 8 \\ 8 & 8 & 4 & 4 & 8 \\ 8 & 4 & 8 & 8 & 4 \end{pmatrix}$

c. $A + A^2 + A^3 = \begin{pmatrix} 12 & 11 & 11 & 11 & 11 \\ 11 & 7 & 10 & 10 & 7 \\ 11 & 10 & 7 & 7 & 10 \\ 11 & 10 & 7 & 7 & 10 \\ 11 & 7 & 10 & 10 & 7 \end{pmatrix}$

This matrix represents the total number of flights that are direct, have one layover, or have two layovers between each pair of cities.

1134   **Answers to Selected Exercises**

1. $I_2 = \begin{pmatrix} 1 & 0 \\ 0 & 1 \end{pmatrix}$; $CI_2 = \begin{pmatrix} 3 & -2 \\ 1 & 4 \end{pmatrix}$; $I_2C = \begin{pmatrix} 3 & -2 \\ 1 & 4 \end{pmatrix}$

3. $I_3 = \begin{pmatrix} 1 & 0 & 0 \\ 0 & 1 & 0 \\ 0 & 0 & 1 \end{pmatrix}$; $CI_3 = \begin{pmatrix} 2 & 1 & 0 \\ 0 & 3 & 2 \\ 4 & -1 & 0 \end{pmatrix}$;

$I_3C = \begin{pmatrix} 2 & 1 & 0 \\ 0 & 3 & 2 \\ 4 & -1 & 0 \end{pmatrix}$

5. $A \cdot B = \begin{pmatrix} 3 & 1 \\ 5 & 2 \end{pmatrix}\begin{pmatrix} 2 & -1 \\ -5 & 3 \end{pmatrix} =$

$\begin{pmatrix} 3(2) + 1(-5) & 5(2) + 2(-5) \\ 3(-1) + 1(3) & 5(-1) + 2(3) \end{pmatrix}$

$= \begin{pmatrix} 1 & 0 \\ 0 & 1 \end{pmatrix}$

7. $A \cdot B = \begin{pmatrix} 1 & 0 & 1 \\ -1 & 0 & 1 \\ 1 & 1 & -1 \end{pmatrix}\begin{pmatrix} \frac{1}{2} & -\frac{1}{2} & 0 \\ 0 & 1 & 1 \\ \frac{1}{2} & \frac{1}{2} & 0 \end{pmatrix} = \begin{pmatrix} 1 & 0 & 0 \\ 0 & 1 & 0 \\ 0 & 0 & 1 \end{pmatrix}$

9.
$$2x = 1 \qquad 2u = 0$$
$$4x + y = 0 \qquad 4u + v = 1$$

11.
$$x + 2y - z = 1 \quad u + 2v - w = 0 \quad r + 2s - t = 0$$
$$y + 2z = 0 \qquad v + 2w = 1 \qquad s + 2t = 0$$
$$3x + 2y + z = 0 \quad 3u + 2v + w = 0 \quad 3r + 2s + t = 1$$

13. $\begin{pmatrix} -2 & 1 \\ \frac{3}{2} & -\frac{1}{2} \end{pmatrix}$

15. No inverse

17. No inverse

19. $\begin{pmatrix} -3 & 2 & -4 \\ -1 & 1 & -1 \\ 8 & -5 & 10 \end{pmatrix}$

21. $x = 3, y = -1$

23. $x = -1, y = 0, z = -3$

25. $x = -8, y = 16, z = 5$

27. $x = -0.5, y = -2.1, z = 6.7, w = 2.8$

29. no solution

31. $x = 2 - t, y = 3.5 - 2.5t, z = -1 + 2t$, where t is any real number.

33. $x = -\frac{1149}{161}, y = \frac{426}{161}, z = -\frac{1124}{161}, w = \frac{579}{161}$

35. a.
$$\begin{pmatrix} 1 & -2 \\ -3 & 6 \end{pmatrix}\begin{pmatrix} x \\ y \end{pmatrix} = \begin{pmatrix} 3 \\ -9 \end{pmatrix}; \begin{pmatrix} 1 & -2 \\ -3 & 6 \end{pmatrix}\begin{pmatrix} x \\ y \end{pmatrix} = \begin{pmatrix} 4 \\ -7 \end{pmatrix}$$
The A matrix and X matrix are the same; no
b. The first system has an infinite number of solutions of the form $x = t, y = \frac{1}{2}t - \frac{3}{2}$; the second system has no solution.
If a coefficient matrix does not have an inverse, then any system with those coefficients will have an infinite number of solutions or no solution.

37. $a = 1, b = 0, c = -1; y = x^2 - 1$

39. $a = 0.5, b = -1.5, c = 2; y = 0.5x^2 - 1.5x + 2.$

41. (x, y) $y = ax^3 + bx^2 + cx + d$
$(0, 5)$ $5 = d$
$(2, 1)$ $1 = 8a + 4b + 2c + d$
$(4, -7)$ $-7 = 64a + 16b + 4c + d$
$(8, 3)$ $3 = 512a + 64b + 8c + d$

43. (x, y) $y = ax^4 + bx^3 + cx^2 + dx + e$
$(-5, -1)$ $-1 = 625a - 125b + 25c - 5d + e$
$(-2, 0)$ $0 = 16a - 8b + 4c - 2d + e$
$(1, 3)$ $3 = a + b + c + d + e$
$(2, 5)$ $5 = 16a + 8b + 4c + 2d + e$
$(10, -4)$ $-4 = 10{,}000a + 1000b + 100c + 10d + e$

45. $a = 1, b = -4, c = 1; y = e^x - 4e^{-x} + 1$

47. $A = 0, B = -\frac{1}{12}F, C = 0, D = 0, E = 0,$ and $F = t,$ where t is any real number. The equation is $-\frac{t}{12}xy + t = 0,$ which reduces to $xy = 12;$ hyperbola

49. $l \approx 10{,}128.2, h \approx 224.4, b \approx 2339.7$

Section 12.5, page 824

1. $x = 3, y = 9$ or $x = -1, y = 1$

3. $x = \sqrt{\frac{3}{2}}, y = \frac{3}{2}$ or $x = -\sqrt{\frac{3}{2}}, y = \frac{3}{2}$

5. $x = 7, y = 3$ or $x = 3, y = 7$

7. $x = 0, y = -2$ or $x = 6, y = 1$

9. $x = 2, y = 0$ or $x = 4, y = 2$

11. $x = 4, y = 3$ or $x = -4, y = 3$ or $x = \sqrt{21}, y = -2$ or $x = -\sqrt{21}, y = -2$

Selected Answers

13. $x = -1.6237$, $y = -8.1891$ or $x = 1.3163$, $y = 1.0826$ or $x = 2.8073$, $y = 2.4814$

15. $x = -1.9493$, $y = 0.4412$ or $x = 0.3634$, $y = 0.9578$ or $x = 1.4184$, $y = 0.5986$

17. $x = -0.9519$, $y = -0.8145$

19. No solutions

21. $x = \dfrac{13 - \sqrt{105}}{8}$, $y = \dfrac{-3 - \sqrt{105}}{8}$ or $x = \dfrac{13 + \sqrt{105}}{8}$, $y = \dfrac{-3 + \sqrt{105}}{8}$

23. $x = -4.8093$, $y = 19.3201$ or $x = -3.1434$, $y = 7.7374$ or $x = 2.1407$, $y = 7.7230$ or $x = 2.8120$, $y = 11.7195$

25. $x = -3.8371$, $y = -2.2596$ or $x = -0.9324$, $y = -7.7796$

27. $x = -1.4873$, $y = 0.0480$ or $x = -0.0480$, $y = 1.4873$ or $x = 0.0480$, $y = -1.4873$ or $x = 1.4873$, $y = -0.0480$

29. center $(0, 0)$; $r = 5$

31. center $(7.5, 12.5)$; $r \approx 12.75$

33. $(440.2, 38205.5)$ and $(1493.1, 81794.5)$.

35. Two possible boxes: one is 2 by 2 by 4 m and the other is approximately 3.123 by 3.123 by 1.640 m.

37. -4 and -12 **39.** 1.6 and 2.6

41. 15 and -12 **43.** 12 ft by 17 ft

45. 8×15 inches   **47.** $y = 6x - 9$

Section 12.5.A, page 832

1. $-10 \le x \le 10$; $-10 \le y \le 10$

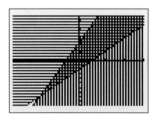

3. $-10 \le x \le 10$; $-10 \le y \le 10$

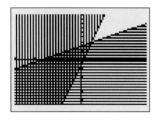

5. $-10 \le x \le 10$; $-10 \le y \le 10$

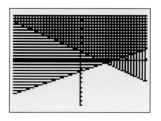

7. $-10 \le x \le 10$; $-10 \le y \le 10$

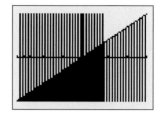

9. $-10 \le x \le 10$; $-10 \le y \le 20$

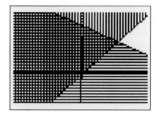

11. $-10 \le x \le 10$; $-10 \le y \le 10$

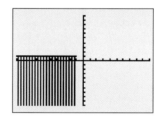

13. $0 \le x \le 10$; $0 \le y \le 10$

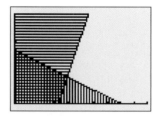

corner points: $(0, 0)$, $(0, 6)$, $\left(3\tfrac{1}{3}, 0\right)$, $(4, 3)$

15. $0 \le x \le 10; 0 \le y \le 10$

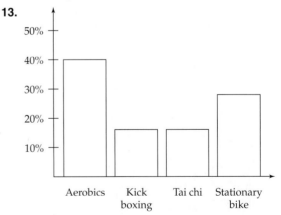

corner points: $(0, 0), (0, 4), (2, 0), \left(\dfrac{20}{7}, \dfrac{18}{7}\right)$

17. At $(0, 6)$, the objective function has a value of 30.

19. At $(0, 0)$, the objective function has a value of 0.

21. 24 roast beef sandwiches for a profit of $72

23. 3000 peach trees and 27,000 almond trees

Chapter 12 Review Exercises, page 835

1. $x = -5, y = -7$ **3.** $x = 0, y = -2$

5. $x = 35, y = -70, z = 22$ **7.** $x = 2, y = 4, z = 6$

9. $x = -t + 1, y = -2t, z = t$ for any real number t

11. 37 and -19 **13.** (c)   **15.** 100

17. $2x + 6y = 16$
$2x + 3y = 7$

19. $2x + 3z = -2$
$4x - 3y + 7z = 1$
$8x - 9y + 10z = -3$

21. $x = \dfrac{26}{9}, y = -\dfrac{11}{9}$; consistent

23. no solution; inconsistent

25. $x = \dfrac{1}{11}t + \dfrac{37}{11}, y = \dfrac{3}{11}t - \dfrac{10}{11}, z = t$, for any real number t; consistent

27. $\begin{pmatrix} -2 & 3 \\ -4 & -1 \end{pmatrix}$ **29.** Not defined

31. $\begin{pmatrix} -9 & 7 \\ -4 & 3 \end{pmatrix}$ **33.** $\begin{pmatrix} 1 & 2 & -2 \\ -1 & 3 & 0 \\ 0 & -2 & 1 \end{pmatrix}$

35. $x = 4, y = 3, z = 2$

37. $x = -\dfrac{1}{85}, y = -\dfrac{14}{85}, z = -\dfrac{21}{34}, w = \dfrac{46}{85}$

39. $y = 5x^2 - 2x + 1$

41. $x = 3, y = 9$ or $x = -1, y = 1$

43. $x = 1 - \sqrt{7}, y = 1 + \sqrt{7}$ or
$x = 1 + \sqrt{7}, y = 1 - \sqrt{7}$

45. $x = -1.692, y = 3.136$ or $x = 1.812, y = 2.717$

47. maximum is 150 at $(5, 0)$; minimum is 20 at $(0, 2)$

49. minimum of 97.5 pounds at $(85, 12.5)$

Chapter 12 can do calculus, page 841

1. $\dfrac{-1}{x + 1} + \dfrac{2}{x + 2}$ **2.** $\dfrac{-\dfrac{1}{2}}{x + 1} + \dfrac{\dfrac{1}{2}}{x - 1}$

3. $\dfrac{-\dfrac{3}{25}}{x + 2} + \dfrac{\dfrac{3}{25}}{x - 3} + \dfrac{\dfrac{7}{5}}{(x - 3)^2}$

4. $\dfrac{-5}{2x - 1} + \dfrac{3x + 1}{x^2 + 4}$ **5.** $\dfrac{2}{x + 1} + \dfrac{3x - 1}{x^2 - x + 1}$

6. $\dfrac{-\dfrac{3}{5}}{x + 4} + \dfrac{\dfrac{3}{5}x - \dfrac{1}{5}}{x^2 + 2x + 2}$

7. $2x + \dfrac{\dfrac{1}{2}}{x + 1} + \dfrac{\dfrac{9}{2}}{x - 3} = 2x + \dfrac{1}{2}\left(\dfrac{1}{x + 1} + \dfrac{9}{x - 3}\right)$

Chapter 13

Section 13.1, page 851

1. The population is the entire student body; the sample is 50 students from each grade level.

3. The population is the total number of American families; the sample is 50 families in each of 10 counties in each of 5 states.

5. In #1 the data is qualitative.
In #2 the data is qualitative.
In #3 the data is quantitative and discrete.
In #4 the data is quantitative and continuous.

7. 200 cartons.   **9.** 2500 families.

11.

Exercise	Relative frequency
Aerobics	40%
Kick boxing	16%
Tai chi	16%
Stationary bike	28%

13.

15.

Color	Frequency	Relative frequency
red	6	24%
blue	8	32%
purple	5	20%
green	4	16%
yellow	1	4%
orange	1	4%

17.

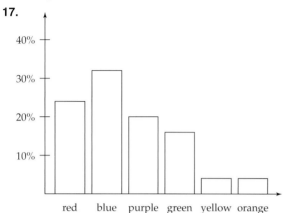

19. symmetric   **21.** skewed left   **23.** uniform

25.

```
2 | 3  4  7  9
3 | 3  3  6  8
4 | 1  1  2  3  5  6  7  7  9   Key: 2|3 represents 23
5 | 1  4
6 | 7
```

27.

```
 5 | 6
 6 |
 7 | 0  2  6  8  9
 8 | 1  2  3  4  5  6  6  6  7  8   Key: 5|6 represents 56
 9 | 0  1  1  2  3  8  9
10 | 0  0
```

29. The number 90 is an outlier since it is quite a distance from the rest of the data.

31. The shape of the fall semester data is basically symmetric; the summer semester data is skewed right. It may be that in the summer enrolled students live closer to campus.

33.

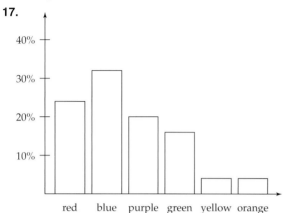

35. Sample answer: the histogram is not as symmetric as the stem plot. The histogram more accurately shows the distribution of the data due to the smaller class interval of 5.

Section 13.2, page 862

1. approximately 43.429

3. approximately 7.583

5. 42   **7.** 5.15

9. mean: 12.2
median: 12
mode: 13

11. 53   **13.** Grains

15. The median is larger than the mean.

17. The mean and the median are the same.

19. approximately 2.828

21. approximately 7.071

23. $\sigma = 5.249$; $s = 5.447$

25. $\sigma = 13.176$; $s = 13.518$

27. 19   **29.** 44

31. 7   **33.** 21

35. five-number summary: 8, 17, 18.5, 24, 27

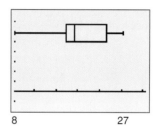

37. five-number summary: 50, 62.5, 73.5, 83.5, 94

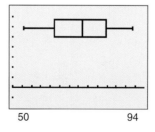

39. mean: 43.167   median: 42.5

41. standard deviation: 20.3
range: 80
interquartile range: 35

43. The sample standard deviation is a good measure of dispersion because the data set is relatively small.

45. 90.4

47.

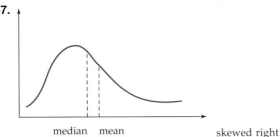

median   mean   skewed right

49. The median more accurately describes the "typical" salary, since the outlier of 105,000 has a large effect on the mean.

51. Answers may vary. Sample:

data	mean	standard deviation
26,28,30,32,34	30	3.162
20,25,30,35,40	30	7.906

53. The mean will increase by the value of k.

55. The mean will be multiplied by the constant k.

57. All data values must be the same.

Section 13.3, page 872

1. {A, B, C, D}   **3.** 0.8

5.

Outcome	black	red	white
Probability	$\frac{1}{2}$	$\frac{1}{3}$	$\frac{1}{6}$

7. $\frac{1}{216}$ **9.** approximately 0.05 or 5%

11. {0, 1, 2}   **13.** approximately 39%

15.

Number of blue	0	1	2
Probability	$\frac{25}{64}$	$\frac{30}{64} = \frac{15}{32}$	$\frac{9}{64}$

17. 12.52   **19.** 17.2   **21.** 0.41   **23.** 0.026

25.

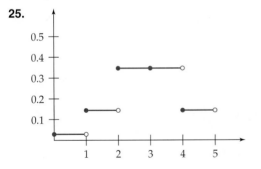

27. 1 to 5   **29.** $\frac{1}{2}$

31. approximately 0.55

33. The median appears to occur at 15 inches of rain.

35. $\frac{5}{10}$ or 50%

1.

Outcome	red	blue	green	yellow
Probability	≈0.50	≈0.31	≈0.15	≈0.04

3. 0.0016

5.

Outcome	nun	gimel	hay	shin
Probability	0.1	0.45	0.24	0.21

7. 0.0001

9. Answers may vary. Sample:

Outcome	2	3	4	5	6	7	8	9	10	11	12
Probability	$\frac{1}{50}$	$\frac{4}{50}$	$\frac{6}{50}$	$\frac{6}{50}$	$\frac{5}{50}$	$\frac{7}{50}$	$\frac{6}{50}$	$\frac{5}{50}$	$\frac{5}{50}$	$\frac{4}{50}$	$\frac{1}{50}$

11. Answers may vary. Sample: 6.89

13. approximately 0.0027   **15.** 0.0016

17. 0.44; approximately 0.085   **19.** 2048

21. 3,268,760   **23.** 362,880

25. approximately 0.04   **27.** 12,870

29. approximately 3.108×10^{-4}

31. 48,228,180; 1.03669×10^{51}; $\dfrac{365!}{(365 - n)!}$

33. probability $= 1 - \dfrac{_{365}P_n}{365^n}$

$n = 3$: approximately 0.008
$n = 20$: approximately 0.411
$n = 35$: approximately 0.814

35. 366 people

Section 13.4A, page 889

1. 0.35

3. $P(0) \approx 0.015$
$P(1) \approx 0.111$
$P(2) \approx 0.311$
$P(3) \approx 0.384$
$P(4) \approx 0.179$

5. $P(0) \approx 0.316$
$P(1) \approx 0.422$
$P(2) \approx 0.211$
$P(3) \approx 0.047$
$P(4) \approx 0.004$

7. approximately 0.738

9. approximately 0.0796

11. approximately 0.000023

13. expected value: 50; standard deviation: 5

15. approximately 0.160; approximately 0.185

Section 13.5, page 896

1. 20   **3.** approximately 0.68

5.

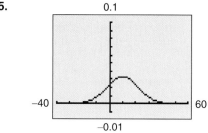

7.

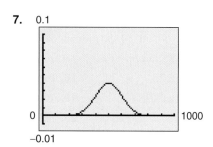

9. the mean is 70. The standard deviation is 5.228.

11. 0.5   **13.** 0.68   **15.** 0.8385

17. $560 \rightarrow 0.6$ z-value
$450 \rightarrow -0.5$ z-value
$640 \rightarrow 1.4$ z-value
$530 \rightarrow 0.3$ z-value

19. $\$0.95 \rightarrow -4.29$ z-value
$\$1.00 \rightarrow -3.57$ z-value
$\$1.35 \rightarrow 1.43$ z-value

21. 0.19   **23.** 0.48   **25.** 0.16

27. 0.815   **29.** 0.48

31. $Q_1 = 63.25$; $Q_3 = 76.75$; Fifty percent of the scores fall between 63.25 and 76.75.

Chapter 13 Review, page 900

1. qualitative

3.

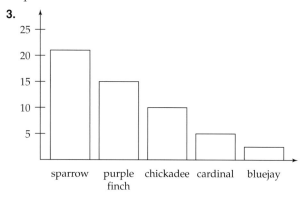

5. quantitative

7.

18	2			
19				
20				
21				
22	2	3	8	
23	2	3		
24	4			
25				
26	0			
27	7			
28	4	8		
29	1	4	4	
30	5	7	7	
31	7	9	9	9
32	2	3	5	7
33	0	0	1	4
34	0			
35	2			
36	0	1		
37				
38				
39	0			

Key 18|2 represents 18.2

9. The distribution is skewed left.

11. 31.2   **13.** 4.72   **15.** $Q_1 = 27.7$; $Q_3 = 33$

17.

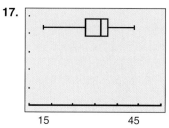

19.

Outcome	1	2	3	4	5
Probability	0.1	0.2	0.4	0.2	0.1

21. 0.7   **23.** 0 to 3

25.

Number of red	0	1	2	3
Probability	0.512	0.384	0.096	0.008

27.

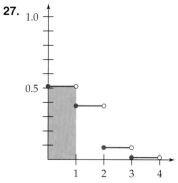

29. 0.4; 0.53; 0.07   **31.** 0.5   **33.** 0.86

35. approximately 0.0048   **37.** 3.08; 1.3

39.

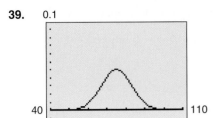

41. 0.68 **43.** 99.85% **45.** 0.55

Chapter 13 can do calculus, page 907

In Exercises 1–6, estimates may vary.

1. $\approx \frac{1}{3}$ **2.** ≈ 2 **3.** ≈ 4.5

4. ≈ 0.14 **5.** ≈ 0.51 **6.** ≈ 5.67

7. Your answer should be close to 0.7301. A sample is shown of the program using the normal curve with equation $y = \frac{1}{18\sqrt{2\pi}} e^{-\frac{(x-138)^2}{648}}$; $a = 100$, $b = 150$, and $h = 0.025$.

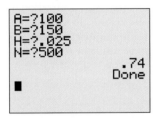

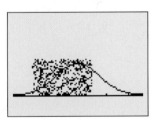

(Scales $84 \le X \le 192$, $-0.01 \le Y \le 0.05$)

8. Samples of the program are shown

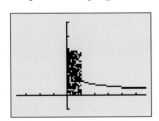

for $h = 3$; area ≈ 1.74

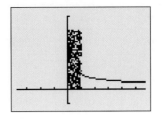

for $h = 4$; area ≈ 1.856

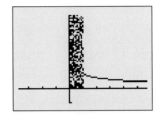

for $h = 5$; area ≈ 2.02
(Scales $-3.7 \le x \le 5.7$, $-1 \le y \le 5$)
The area estimates get larger for larger values of h. The value for $h = 5$ is close to 2, which is the exact area under the curve from 0 to 1.

9. A sample is shown of the program using the equation of the standard normal curve with $a = -3$, $b = 3$, and $h = 0.5$. The estimate is very close to the expected area of 0.997, or 99.7% of the area under the curve.

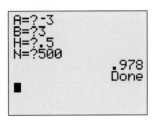

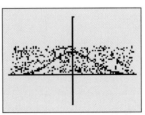

(Scales $-3 \le x \le 3$, $-0.5 \le y \le 1$)

Chapter 14

Section 14.1, page 916

1.

x	2.9	2.99	2.999
$f(x)$	0.25641	0.25063	0.25006

x	3.001	3.01	3.1
$f(x)$	0.24994	0.24938	0.2439

$\lim_{x \to 3} = 0.25$

3.

x	-0.1	-0.01	-0.001
$f(x)$	0.35809	0.354	0.3536

x	0.001	0.01	0.1
$f(x)$	0.35351	0.35311	0.34924

$\lim_{x \to 0} = 0.3535$

5.

x	-7.1	-7.01	-7.001
$f(x)$	-0.1662	-0.1666	-0.1667

x	-6.999	-6.99	-6.9
$f(x)$	-0.1667	-0.1667	-0.1671

$\lim_{x \to -7} = -0.1667$

7.

x	0.9	0.99	0.999
$f(x)$	-0.1149	-0.1115	-0.1111

x	1.001	1.01	1.1
$f(x)$	-0.1111	-0.1107	-0.1075

$\lim_{x \to 1} = -0.1111$

9.

x	-0.1	-0.01	-0.001
$f(x)$	0.04996	0.005	0.0005

x	0.001	0.01	0.1
$f(x)$	-0.0005	-0.005	-0.05

$\lim_{x \to 0} = 0$

11. 1.5 **13.** 1.25 **15** 1.5 **17.** 0.333

19. -2 **21.** 0.2887 **23.** 0 **25.** 1

27. $\lim_{x \to -3} f(x) = -1$; $\lim_{x \to 0} f(x) = 1$; $\lim_{x \to 2} f(x)$ does not exist

29. $\lim_{x \to -3} f(x) = 2$; $\lim_{x \to 0} f(x)$ does not exist; $\lim_{x \to 2} f(x) = 0$

31. $\lim_{x \to -3} f(x) = 2$; $\lim_{x \to 0} f(x) = 1$; $\lim_{x \to 2} f(x) = 1$

33. a.

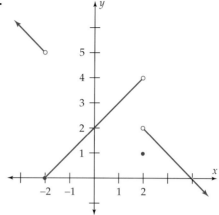

b. $\lim_{x \to -2} f(x)$ does not exist.

c. $\lim_{x \to 1} f(x) = 3$ **d.** $\lim_{x \to 2} f(x)$ does not exist.

35. No matter how close x gets to c, there are still an infinite number of both rational and irrational numbers between x and c, so t(x) will take the values 0 and 1 an infinite number of times, but never get close to a *single* number for all values of x that are very close to c.

Section 14.2, page 923

1. 5 **3.** Limit does not exist.

5. 0 **7.** $-\dfrac{3}{5}$ **9.** 47 **11.** 7

13. $\sqrt{14}$ **15.** $-\dfrac{1}{25}$

17. $\dfrac{1}{2}$ **19.** 0 **21.** $-\dfrac{1}{2\sqrt{2}}$

23. The limit does not exist. Values of x less than -3 are mapped by the function to -1 and values of x more than -3 are mapped by the function to 1.

25. 12 **27.** $\dfrac{1}{2\sqrt{2}}$

29. As the angle t in standard position gets closer to $\dfrac{\pi}{2}$, the x-coordinate of the point at which the terminal side of t crosses the unit circle gets closer to 0. Since this x-coordinate is the cosine of the angle t, we have $\lim_{t \to \frac{\pi}{2}} \cos t = 0$.

31. Using the function $g(x) = x + [-x]$, when x is close to 2 but slightly more than 2, we have $x \approx 2$, $[-x] = -3$. When x is close to 2 but slightly less than 2 we have $x \approx 2$, $[-x] = -2$. In this case, the difference is either 5 or 4 depending on whether x is more than 2 or less than 2 and so the limit doesn't exist.

33. -1

35. Many correct answers, including $f(x) = \dfrac{|x|}{x}$, $g(x) = \dfrac{-x}{|x|}$, and $c = 0$. In this case, $\lim\limits_{x \to 0} f(x)$ does not exist by Example 10; a similar argument shows that $\lim\limits_{x \to 0} g(x)$ does not exist. But $\lim\limits_{x \to 0} (f + g)(x) = 0$ by Exercise 22.

Section 14.2A, page 927

1. 0 **3.** 0 **5.** 6

7. a. 0 **b.** 1 **c.** -1 **d.** -1

9. a. 1 **b.** 0 **c.** Limit does not exist.
d. Limit does not exist.

11. a. 5 **b.** 0 **c.** 4 **d.** 2

13. 3 **15.** $\dfrac{1}{8}$ **17.** Limit does not exist.

19. -2.5 **21.** 2 **23.** $\lim\limits_{x \to 2^+} [x] = 2$ and $\lim\limits_{x \to 2} [x] = 1$

Section 14.3, page 935

The symbol $\Rightarrow$ means "implies."

1. Given $\varepsilon > 0$, let $\delta = \dfrac{\varepsilon}{3}$. Then $0 < |x - 3| < \delta \Rightarrow$

$|x - 3| < \dfrac{\varepsilon}{3} \Rightarrow 3|x - 3| < \varepsilon \Rightarrow |3(x - 3)| < \varepsilon \Rightarrow$
$|3x - 9| < \varepsilon \Rightarrow |(3x - 2) - 7| < \varepsilon \Rightarrow$
$|f(x) - 7| < \varepsilon$

3. Given $\varepsilon > 0$, let $\delta = \varepsilon$. Then $0 < |x - 5| < \delta \Rightarrow$
$|x - 5| < \varepsilon \Rightarrow |f(x) - 5| < \varepsilon$

5. Given $\varepsilon > 0$, let $\delta = \dfrac{\varepsilon}{6}$. Then $0 < |x - 2| < \delta \Rightarrow$

$|x - 2| < \dfrac{\varepsilon}{6} \Rightarrow 6|x - 2| < \varepsilon \Rightarrow |6(x - 2)| < \varepsilon \Rightarrow$
$|6x - 12| < \varepsilon \Rightarrow |(6x + 3) - 15| < \varepsilon \Rightarrow$
$|f(x) - 15| < \varepsilon$

7. Given $\varepsilon > 0$, let δ be any positive number. Then for every number x (including those satisfying $0 < |x - 1| < \delta$), $|f(x) - 4| = |4 - 4| = 0 < \varepsilon$

9. Given $\varepsilon > 0$, let $\delta = \varepsilon$. Then $0 < |x - 4| < \delta \Rightarrow$
$|x - 4| < \varepsilon \Rightarrow |(x - 6) - (-2)| < \varepsilon \Rightarrow$
$|f(x) - (-2)| < \varepsilon$

11. Given $\varepsilon > 0$, let $\delta = \dfrac{\varepsilon}{2}$. Then

$0 < |x - (-2)| < \delta \Rightarrow |x - (-2)| < \dfrac{\varepsilon}{2} \Rightarrow$
$2|x - (-2)| < \varepsilon \Rightarrow |2(x - (-2))| < \varepsilon \Rightarrow$
$|2x + 4| < \varepsilon \Rightarrow |(2x + 5) - 1| < \varepsilon \Rightarrow$
$|f(x) - 1| < \varepsilon$

13. Given $\varepsilon > 0$, let $\delta = \sqrt{\varepsilon}$. Then
$0 < |x - 0| < \delta \Rightarrow 0 < |x| < \sqrt{\varepsilon} \Rightarrow |x|^2 < \varepsilon \Rightarrow$
$|x^2| < \varepsilon \Rightarrow |x^2 - 0| < \varepsilon \Rightarrow |f(x) - 0| < \varepsilon$

15. Let $\varepsilon > 0$. Then there exist positive numbers δ_1, δ_2

such that if $0 < |x - c| < \delta_1$, then $|f(x) - L| < \dfrac{\varepsilon}{2}$

and if $0 < |x - c| < \delta_2$, then $|g(x) - M| < \dfrac{\varepsilon}{2}$.
Choose δ to be the smaller of δ_1, δ_2. Then if

$0 < |x - c| < \delta$, we have both $|f(x) - L| < \dfrac{\varepsilon}{2}$

and $|g(x) - M| < \dfrac{\varepsilon}{2}$. Then

$|f(x) - L| + |g(x) - M| < \dfrac{\varepsilon}{2} + \dfrac{\varepsilon}{2} = \varepsilon$. This can be

rewritten as $|f(x) - L| + |M - g(x)| < \varepsilon$.
Now using the triangle inequality we have
$|f(x) - g(x) - (L - M)| < \varepsilon$. Therefore,
$\lim\limits_{x \to c} (f(x) - g(x)) = L - M$.

Section 14.4, page 946

1. $x = 3, x = 6$

3. Continuous at $x = -2$ and $x = 3$; discontinuous at $x = 0$

5. Continuous at $x = 0$ and $x = 3$; discontinuous at $x = -2$

7. $\lim\limits_{x \to 3} f(x) = \lim\limits_{x \to 3} (x^2 + 5(x - 2)^7) = \lim\limits_{x \to 3} x^2 +$
$\lim\limits_{x \to 3} (5(x - 2)^7) = \lim\limits_{x \to 3} x^2 + (\lim\limits_{x \to 3} 5)(\lim\limits_{x \to 3} (x - 2))^7 =$
$9 + 5(3 - 2)^7 = 14 = f(3)$

9. $\lim\limits_{x \to 2} f(x) = \lim\limits_{x \to 2} \dfrac{x^2 - 9}{(x^2 - x - 6)(x^2 + 6x + 9)} =$

$\dfrac{\lim\limits_{x \to 2} (x^2 - 9)}{\lim\limits_{x \to 2} (x^2 - x - 6) \cdot \lim\limits_{x \to 2} (x^2 + 6x + 9)} =$

$\dfrac{2^2 - 9}{(2^2 - 2 - 6)(2^2 + 6 \cdot 2 + 9)} = \dfrac{-5}{(-4)(25)} =$

$\dfrac{1}{20} = f(2)$

11. $\displaystyle \lim_{x\to 36} f(x) = \frac{\displaystyle\lim_{x\to 36}(x\sqrt{x})}{\displaystyle\lim_{x\to 36}(x-6)^2} =$

$$\frac{\displaystyle\lim_{x\to 36}x \cdot \lim_{x\to 36}\sqrt{x}}{\displaystyle\lim_{x\to 36}(x-6)\cdot\lim_{x\to 36}(x-6)} = \frac{36\sqrt{36}}{(36-6)(36-6)} =$$

$$\frac{36\cdot 6}{30\cdot 30} = \frac{216}{900} = \frac{6}{25} = f(36)$$

13. f is not defined at $x = 3$.

15. f is not defined at $x = -1$.

17. $\displaystyle\lim_{x\to 0}f(x) = 0$, but $f(0) = 1$; hence $\displaystyle\lim_{x\to 0}f(x) \neq f(0)$

19. Continuous   **21.** Continuous

23. Continuous

25. Continuous at every real number except $x = 3$

27. Continuous at every real number except $x = 0$ and $x = 2$

29. $b = 1$

31. $g(x) = \dfrac{1}{x+1}$ f has a removable discontinuity at $x = 1$.

33. $g(x) = \dfrac{1}{2 + \sqrt{x}}$ f has a removable discontinuity at $x = 4$.

35. If $g(x) = f(x)$ for all $x \neq 0$, then $g(x) = 1$ for all $x > 0$ and $g(x) = -1$ for all $x < 0$. Thus $\displaystyle\lim_{x\to 0}g(x)$ does not exist. Hence the definition of continuity cannot be satisfied, no matter what $g(0)$ is.

Section 14.5, page 957

1. -1 **3.** 0   **5.** 0   **7.** 0

9. No vertical asymptotes; $\displaystyle\lim_{x\to\infty}f(x) = \infty$;

$\displaystyle\lim_{x\to -\infty}f(x) = 0$

11. No vertical asymptotes; $\displaystyle\lim_{x\to\infty}f(x) = 2$;

$\displaystyle\lim_{x\to -\infty}f(x) = -1$

13. Vertical asymptote $x = -10$; $\displaystyle\lim_{x\to\infty}f(x) = \infty$;

$\displaystyle\lim_{x\to -\infty}f(x) = -\infty$

15. $y = \dfrac{3}{4}$ **17.** $y = -2$

19. No horizontal asymptote   **21.** $\dfrac{1}{2}$

23. ∞ **25.** 5   **27.** 2   **29.** $-\dfrac{3}{\sqrt{2}}$ **31.** $\dfrac{\sqrt{2}}{3}$

33. $-\sqrt{3}$ **35.** 1   **37.** -1 **39.** 0   **41.** 0

43. With a parachute: 20 ft/sec
Without a parachute: 177.78 ft/sec

45. 1   **47.** 1

49. The first part of the informal definition is included in the second part, which says "the values of $f(x)$ can be made arbitrarily close to L by taking large enough values of x." This means that whenever you specify how close $f(x)$ should be to L, we can tell you how large x must be to guarantee this. In other words, you specify how close you want $f(x)$ to be to L by giving a positive number ε and we tell you how large x must be to guarantee that $f(x)$ is within ε of L, that is, to guarantee that $|f(x) - L| < \varepsilon$. We do this by giving a positive number k such that $|f(x) - L| < \varepsilon$ whenever $x > k$. This can be reworded as follows: For every positive number ε, there is a positive number k (depending on ε) with this property:

If $x > k$, then $|f(x) - L| < \varepsilon$.

Chapter 14 Review, page 961

1. 2   **3.** 2   **5.** -5 **7.** -2

9. $\dfrac{1}{2}$ **11.** 4   **13.** 1

15. Given $\varepsilon > 0$, let $\delta = \dfrac{\varepsilon}{2}$. Then $0 < |x - 3| < \delta \Rightarrow$

$|x - 3| < \dfrac{\varepsilon}{2} \Rightarrow 2|x - 3| < \varepsilon \Rightarrow |2(x - 3)| < \varepsilon \Rightarrow$

$|2x - 6| < \varepsilon \Rightarrow |(2x + 1) - 7| < \varepsilon \Rightarrow$
$|f(x) - 7| < \varepsilon$

17. Continuous at $x = -3$; discontinuous at $x = 2$

19. a. $\displaystyle\lim_{x\to 2}f(x) = \lim_{x\to 2}\dfrac{x^2 - x - 6}{x^2 - 9} =$

$\dfrac{\displaystyle\lim_{x\to 2}(x^2 - x - 6)}{\displaystyle\lim_{x\to 2}(x^2 - 9)} = \dfrac{2^2 - 2 - 6}{2^2 - 9} = \dfrac{-4}{-5} =$

$\dfrac{4}{5} = f(2)$

b. f is not defined at $x = 3$ and hence is discontinuous there.

21. Vertical asymptotes at $x = -1$ and $x = 2$. The graph moves upward as x approaches -1 from the left and downward as x approaches -1 from the right. The graph moves downward as x approaches 2 from the left and upward as x approaches 2 from the right.

23. $\dfrac{1}{2}$ **25.** $\dfrac{10}{3}$ **27.** $y = \dfrac{1}{2}$

Chapter 14 can do calculus, page 967

1. a. upper estimate: 259 ft.
lower estimate: 157 ft.

b. 110

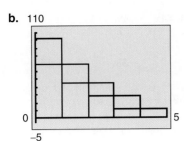

c. less than 5 ft: $\Delta t < 0.04902$ sec.
less than 1 ft: $\Delta t < 0.0098$ sec.

2. Lower estimate: 21
Upper estimate: 25
For the lower estimate, count all of the complete squares beneath the curve. For the upper estimate, count all of the complete squares below the curve and estimate the number of partial squares below the curve.

3. a. 1.798 **b.** The degree of accuracy can be increased by lowering the Δt.

4. between 15 and 17 ft. **5.** 1.0

6. between 0.67 and 0.72 ft.

Algebra Review

Section A.1, page 972

1. 36 **3.** 73 **5.** -5

7. $-\dfrac{125}{64}$ **9.** $\dfrac{1}{3}$ **11.** -112

13. $\dfrac{81}{16}$ **15.** $-\dfrac{211}{216}$ **17.** $\dfrac{129}{8}$

19. x^{10} **21.** $0.03y^9$ **23.** $24x^7$

25. $9x^4y^2$ **27.** $-21a^6$ **29.** $384w^6$

31. ab^3 **33.** $8x^{-1}y^3$ **35.** a^8x^{-3}

37. $3xy$ **39.** 2^{12} **41.** 2^{-12}

43. x^7 **45.** ce^9 **47.** $b^2c^2d^6$

49. $a^{12}b^8$ **51.** $\dfrac{1}{(c^{10}d^6)}$ **53.** $\dfrac{1}{(108x)}$

55. $\dfrac{a^7c}{b^6}$ **57.** c^3d^6 **59.** $a + \dfrac{1}{a}$

61. Negative **63.** Negative **65.** Negative

67. 3^s **69.** $a^{6t}b^{4t}$ **71.** $\dfrac{b^{rs+st}}{c^{2rt}}$

73. Many possible examples, including
$3^2 + 4^2 = 9 + 16 = 25$, but $(3 + 4)^2 = 7^2 = 49$

75. Many possible examples, including
$3^2 \cdot 2^3 = 9 \cdot 8 = 72$; but $(3 \cdot 2)^{2+3} = 6^5 = 7776$

77. Many possible examples, including $\dfrac{2^6}{2^3} = \dfrac{64}{8} = 8$,
but $2^{\frac{6}{3}} = 2^2 = 4$

79. False for all nonzero a; for instance,
$(-3)^2 = (-3)(-3) = 9$, but $-3^2 = -9$

Section A.2, page 976

1. $8x$ **3.** $-2a^2b$

5. $-x^3 + 4x^2 + 2x - 3$ **7.** $5u^3 + u - 4$

9. $4z - 12z^2w + 6z^3w^2 - zw^3 + 8$

11. $-3x^3 + 15x + 8$ **13.** $-5xy - x$ **15.** $15y^3 - 5y$

17. $12a^2x^2 - 6a^3xy + 6a^2xy$

19. $12z^4 + 30z^3$ **21.** $12a^2b - 18ab^2 + 6a^3b^2$

23. $x^2 - x - 2$ **25.** $2x^2 + 2x - 12$

27. $y^2 + 7y + 12$ **29.** $-6x^2 + x + 35$

31. $3y^3 - 9y^2 + 4y - 12$ **33.** $x^2 - 16$

35. $16a^2 - 25b^2$ **37.** $y^2 - 22y + 121$

39. $25x^2 - 10bx + b^2$ **41.** $16x^6 - 8x^3y^4 + y^8$

43. $9x^4 - 12x^2y^4 + 4y^8$ **45.** $2y^3 + 9y^2 + 7y - 3$

47. $-15w^3 + 2w^2 + 9w - 18$

49. $24x^3 - 4x^2 - 4x$ **51.** $x^3 - 6x^2 + 11x - 6$

53. $-3x^3 - 5x^2y + 26xy^2 - 8y^3$

55. 3 **57.** -6 **59.** 6 **61.** 1 **63.** 5

65. $x - 25$ **67.** $9 + 6\sqrt{y} + y$

69. $\sqrt{3}x^2 + 4x + \sqrt{3}$ **71.** $3ax^2 + (3b + 2a)x + 2b$

73. $abx^2 + (a^2 + b^2)x + ab$

75. $x^3 - (a + b + c)x^2 + (ab + ac + bc)x - abc$

77. 3^{4+r+t} **79.** $x^{m+n} + 2x^n - 3x^m - 6$

81. $2x^{4n} - 5x^{3n} + 8x^{2n} - 18x^n - 5$

83. Example: if $y = 4$, then $3(4 + 2) \neq (3 \cdot 4) + 2$;
correct statement: $3(y + 2) = 3y + 6$

85. Example: if $x = 2$, $y = 3$, then $(2 + 3)^2 \neq 2 + 3^2$;
correct statement: $(x + y)^2 = x^2 + 2xy + y^2$

87. Example: if $x = 2$, $y = 3$, then $(7 \cdot 2)(7 \cdot 3) \neq 7 \cdot 2 \cdot 3$; correct statement: $(7x)(7y) = 49xy$

89. Example: if $y = 2$, then $2 + 2 + 2 \neq 2^3$; correct statement: $y + y + y = 3y$

91. Example: if $x = 4$, then $(4 - 3)(4 - 2) \neq 4^2 - 5 \cdot 4 - 6$; correct statement: $(x - 3)(x - 2) = x^2 - 5x + 6$

93. If x is the chosen number, then adding 1 and squaring the result gives $(x + 1)^2$. Subtracting 1 from the original number x and squaring the result gives $(x - 1)^2$. Subtracting the second of these squares from the first yields: $(x + 1)^2 - (x - 1)^2 = (x^2 + 2x + 1) - (x^2 - 2x + 1) = 4x$. Dividing by the original number x now gives $\dfrac{4x}{x} = 4$. So the answer is always 4, no matter what number x is chosen.

95. Many correct answers

Section A.3, page 981

1. $(x + 2)(x - 2)$ **3.** $(3y + 5)(3y - 5)$

5. $(9x + 2)^2$ **7.** $(\sqrt{5} + x)(\sqrt{5} - x)$

9. $(7 + 2z)^2$ **11.** $(x^2 + y^2)(x + y)(x - y)$

13. $(x + 3)(x - 2)$ **15.** $(z + 3)(z + 1)$

17. $(y + 9)(y - 4)$ **19.** $(x - 3)^2$

21. $(x + 5)(x + 2)$ **23.** $(x + 9)(x + 2)$

25. $(3x + 1)(x + 1)$ **27.** $(2z + 3)(z + 4)$

29. $9x(x - 8)$ **31.** $2(x - 1)(5x + 1)$

33. $(4u - 3)(2u + 3)$ **35.** $(2x + 5y)^2$

37. $(x - 5)(x^2 + 5x + 25)$

39. $(x + 2)^3$ **41.** $(2 + x)(4 - 2x + x^2)$

43. $(-x + 5)^3$ **45.** $(x + 1)(x^2 - x + 1)$

47. $(2x - y)(4x^2 + 2xy + y^2)$

49. $(x^3 + 2^3)(x^3 - 2^3) =$
$\qquad (x + 2)(x^2 - 2x + 4)(x - 2)(x^2 + 2x + 4)$

51. $(y^2 + 5)(y^2 + 2)$ **53.** $(9 + y^2)(3 + y)(3 - y)$

55. $(z + 1)(z^2 - z + 1)(z - 1)(z^2 + z + 1)$

57. $(x^2 + 3y)(x^2 - y)$ **59.** $(x + z)(x - y)$

61. $(a + 2b)(a^2 - b)$

63. $(x^2 - 8)(x + 4) = \left(x + \sqrt{8}\right)\left(x - \sqrt{8}\right)(x + 4)$

65. If $x^2 + 1 = (x + c)(x + d) = x^2 + (c + d)x + cd$, then $c + d = 0$ and $cd = 1$. But $c + d = 0$ implies that $c = -d$ and hence that $1 = cd = (-d)d = -d^2$, or equivalently, that $d^2 = -1$. Since there is no real number with this property, $x^2 + 1$ cannot possibly factor in this way.

Section A.4, page 985

1. $\dfrac{9}{7}$ **3.** $\dfrac{195}{8}$ **5.** $\dfrac{x - 2}{x + 1}$

7. $\dfrac{a + b}{a^2 + ab + b^2}$ **9.** $\dfrac{1}{x}$ **11.** $\dfrac{29}{35}$

13. $\dfrac{121}{42}$ **15.** $\dfrac{ce + 3cd}{de}$ **17.** $\dfrac{b^2 - c^2}{bc}$

19. $\dfrac{-1}{x(x + 1)}$ **21.** $\dfrac{x + 3}{(x + 4)^2}$ **23.** $\dfrac{2x - 4}{x(3x - 4)}$

25. $\dfrac{x^2 - xy + y^2 + x + y}{x^3 + y^3}$

27. $\dfrac{-6x^5 - 38x^4 - 84x^3 - 71x^2 - 14x + 1}{4x(x + 1)^3(x + 2)^3}$

29. 2   **31.** $\dfrac{2}{(3c)}$ **33.** $\dfrac{3y}{x^2}$ **35.** $\dfrac{12x}{x - 3}$

37. $\dfrac{5y^2}{3(y + 5)}$ **39.** $\dfrac{u + 1}{u}$ **41.** $\dfrac{(u + v)(4u - 3v)}{(2u - v)(2u - 3v)}$

43. $\dfrac{35}{24}$ **45.** $\dfrac{u^2}{vw}$ **47.** $\dfrac{x + 3}{2x}$

49. $\dfrac{x^2 y^2}{(x + y)(x + 2y)}$ **51.** $\dfrac{cd(c + d)}{c - d}$ **53.** $\dfrac{y - x}{xy}$

55. $\dfrac{-3y + 3}{y}$ **57.** $\dfrac{-1}{x(x + h)}$ **59.** $\dfrac{xy}{x + y}$

61. Example: if $a = 1$, $b = 2$, then $\dfrac{1}{1} + \dfrac{1}{2} \neq \dfrac{1}{1 + 2}$; correct statement: $\dfrac{1}{a} + \dfrac{1}{b} = \dfrac{b + a}{ab}$

63. Example: if $a = 4$, $b = 9$, then $\left(\dfrac{1}{\sqrt{4} + \sqrt{9}}\right)^2 \neq \dfrac{1}{4 + 9}$; correct statement: $\left(\dfrac{1}{\sqrt{a} + \sqrt{b}}\right)^2 = \dfrac{1}{a + 2\sqrt{ab} + b}$

65. Example: if $u = 1$, $v = 2$, then $\dfrac{1}{2} + \dfrac{2}{1} \neq 1$; correct statement: $\dfrac{u}{v} + \dfrac{v}{u} = \dfrac{u^2 + v^2}{vu}$

67. Example: if $x = 4$, $y = 9$, then $\left(\sqrt{4} + \sqrt{9}\right) \cdot \dfrac{1}{\sqrt{4} + \sqrt{9}} \neq 4 + 9$; correct statement: $\left(\sqrt{x} + \sqrt{y}\right) \cdot \dfrac{1}{\sqrt{x} + \sqrt{y}} = 1$

Section A.5, page 991

1. $13; \left(-\dfrac{1}{2}, -1\right)$ **3.** $\sqrt{17}; \left(\dfrac{3}{2}, -3\right)$

5. $\sqrt{6 - 2\sqrt{6}} \approx 1.05; \left(\dfrac{\sqrt{2} + \sqrt{3}}{2}, \dfrac{3}{2}\right)$

7. $\sqrt{2}|a - b|; \left(\dfrac{a + b}{2}, \dfrac{a + b}{2}\right)$

9. a.

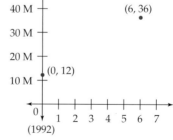

Selected Answers

b.

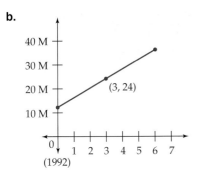

(1992)

c. In 1995, about 24 million personal computers were sold. We must assume that sales increased steadily.

11. $(x + 3)^2 + (y - 4)^2 = 4$

13. $x^2 + y^2 = 2$

15.

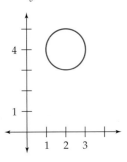

17.

19. Center $(-4, 3)$, radius $2\sqrt{10}$

21. Center $(-3, 2)$, radius $2\sqrt{7}$

23. Center $(-12.5, -5)$, radius $\sqrt{169.25}$

25. Hypotenuse from $(1, 1)$ to $(2, -2)$ has length $\sqrt{10}$; other sides have lengths $\sqrt{2}$ and $\sqrt{8}$. Since $\left(\sqrt{2}\right)^2 + \left(\sqrt{8}\right)^2 = \left(\sqrt{10}\right)^2$, this is a right triangle.

27. Hypotenuse from $(-2, 3)$ to $(3, -2)$ has length $\sqrt{50}$; other sides have lengths $\sqrt{5}$ and $\sqrt{45}$. Since $\left(\sqrt{5}\right)^2 + \left(\sqrt{45}\right)^2 = \left(\sqrt{50}\right)^2$, this is a right triangle.

29. $(x - 2)^2 + (y - 2)^2 = 8$

31. $(x - 1)^2 + (y - 2)^2 = 8$

33. $(x + 5)^2 + (y - 4)^2 = 16$

35. $x^2 + y^2 - 4x - 2y = 0$

37. $(-3, -4)$ and $(2, 1)$

39. Assume $k > d$. The other two vertices of one possible square are $(c + k - d, d)$, $(c + k - d, k)$; those of another square are $(c - (k - d), d)$, $(c - (k - d), k)$; those of a third square are $\left(c + \dfrac{k - d}{2}, \dfrac{k + d}{2}\right)$, $\left(c - \dfrac{k - d}{2}, \dfrac{k + d}{2}\right)$.

41. $(0, 0)$, $(6, 0)$

43. $\left(3, -5 + \sqrt{11}\right), \left(3, -5 - \sqrt{11}\right)$

45. $x = 6$

47. M has coordinates $\left(\dfrac{s}{2}, \dfrac{r}{2}\right)$ by the midpoint formula. Hence the distance from M to $(0, 0)$ is

$$\sqrt{\left(\frac{s}{2} - 0\right)^2 + \left(\frac{r}{2} - 0\right)^2} = \sqrt{\frac{s^2}{4} + \frac{r^2}{4}},$$

and the distance from M to $(0, r)$ is the same:

$$\sqrt{\left(\frac{s}{2} - 0\right)^2 + \left(\frac{r}{2} - r\right)^2} = \sqrt{\left(\frac{s}{2}\right)^2 + \left(-\frac{r}{2}\right)^2}$$
$$= \sqrt{\frac{s^2}{4} + \frac{r^2}{4}}$$

as is the distance from M to $(s, 0)$:

$$\sqrt{\left(\frac{s}{2} - s\right)^2 + \left(\frac{r}{2} - 0\right)^2} = \sqrt{\left(-\frac{s}{2}\right)^2 + \left(\frac{r}{s}\right)^2}$$
$$= \sqrt{\frac{s^2}{4} + \frac{r^2}{4}}.$$

49. Place one vertex of the rectangle at the origin, with one side on the positive x-axis and another on the positive y-axis. Let $(a, 0)$ be the coordinates of the vertex on the x-axis and $(0, b)$ the coordinates of the vertex on the y-axis. Then the fourth vertex has coordinates (a, b) (draw a picture!). One diagonal has endpoints $(0, b)$ and $(a, 0)$, so that its length is $\sqrt{(0 - a)^2 + (b - 0)^2} = \sqrt{a^2 + b^2}$. The other diagonal has endpoints $(0, 0)$ and (a, b) and hence has the same length: $\sqrt{(0 - a)^2 + (0 - b)^2} = \sqrt{a^2 + b^2}$.

51. The circle $(x - k)^2 + y^2 = k^2$ has center $(k, 0)$ and radius $|k|$ (the distance from $(k, 0)$ to $(0, 0)$). So the family consists of every circle that is tangent to the y-axis *and* has center on the x-axis.

53. The points are on opposite sides of the origin because one first coordinate is positive and one is negative. They are equidistant from the origin because the midpoint on the line segment joining them is

$$\left[\frac{c + (-c)}{2}, \frac{d + (-d)}{2}\right] = (0, 0).$$

Advanced Topics

Section B.1, page 1000

1. 720 **3.** 220 **5.** 0 **7.** 64 **9.** 3,921,225

11. $x^5 + 5x^4y + 10x^3y^2 + 10x^2y^3 + 5xy^4 + y^5$

13. $a^5 - 5a^4b + 10a^3b^2 - 10a^2b^3 + 5ab^4 - b^5$

15. $32x^5 + 80x^4y^2 + 80x^3y^4 + 40x^2y^6 + 10xy^8 + y^{10}$

17. $x^3 + 6x^2\sqrt{x} + 15x^2 + 20x\sqrt{x} + 15x + 6\sqrt{x} + 1$

19. $1 - 10c + 45c^2 - 120c^3 + 210c^4 - 252c^5 + 210c^6 - 120c^7 + 45c^8 - 10c^9 + c^{10}$

21. $x^{-12} + 4x^{-8} + 6x^{-4} + 4 + x^4$ **23.** 56

25. $-8i$ **27.** $10x^3y^2$ **29.** $35c^3d^4$

31. $\dfrac{35}{8}u^{-5}$ **33.** 4032 **35.** 160

37. a. $\dbinom{9}{1} = \dfrac{9!}{1!8!} = 9; \dbinom{9}{8} = \dfrac{9!}{8!1!} = 9$

b. $\dbinom{n}{1} = \dbinom{n}{n-1} = \dfrac{n!}{1!(n-1)!} = \dfrac{n(n-1)!}{(n-1)!} = n$

39. $2^n = (1+1)^n = 1^n + \dbinom{n}{1}1^{n-1} \cdot 1 +$

$\dbinom{n}{2}1^{n-2} \cdot 1^2 + \dbinom{n}{3}1^{n-3} \cdot 1^3 + \cdots +$

$\dbinom{n}{n-1}1^1 \cdot 1^{n-1} + 1^n = \dbinom{n}{0} + \dbinom{n}{1} +$

$\dbinom{n}{2} + \dbinom{n}{3} + \cdots + \dbinom{n}{n-1} + \dbinom{n}{n}$

41. $\cos^4 \theta + 4i \cos^3 \theta \sin \theta - 6 \cos^2 \theta \sin^2 \theta - 4i \cos \theta \sin^3 \theta + \sin^4 \theta$

43. a. $f(x+h) - f(x) = (x+h)^5 - x^5 =$

$\left[x^5 + \dbinom{5}{1}x^4h + \dbinom{5}{2}x^3h^2 + \dbinom{5}{3}x^2h^3 + \right.$

$\left. \dbinom{5}{4}xh^4 + h^5 \right] - x^5 = \dbinom{5}{1}x^4h +$

$\dbinom{5}{2}x^3h^2 + \dbinom{5}{3}x^2h^3 + \dbinom{5}{4}xh^4 + h^5$

b. $\dfrac{f(x+h) - f(x)}{h} = \dbinom{5}{1}x^4 + \dbinom{5}{2}x^3h +$

$\dbinom{5}{3}x^2h^2 + \dbinom{5}{4}xh^3 + h^4$

c. When h is *very* close to 0, so are the last four terms in part **b**, so $\dfrac{f(x+h) - f(x)}{h} \approx$

$\dbinom{5}{1}x^4 = 5x^4.$

45. $\dfrac{f(x+h) - f(x)}{h} = \dfrac{(x+h)^{12} - x^{12}}{h} = \dbinom{12}{1}x^{11} +$

$\dbinom{12}{2}x^{10}h + \dbinom{12}{3}x^9h^2 + \dbinom{12}{4}x^8h^3 + \cdots +$

$\dbinom{12}{10}x^2h^9 + \dbinom{12}{11}xh^{10} + h^{11} \approx \dbinom{12}{1}x^{11}$

$= 12x^{11}$, when h is very close to 0.

47. a. $(n - r)! =$

$(n - r)(n - r - 1)(n - r - 2)(n - r - 3) \cdots 2 \cdot 1$

$= (n - r)[n - (r + 1)][(n - (r + 1)) - 1] \cdots 2 \cdot 1$

$= (n - r)[n - (r + 1)]!$

b. Since $(n + 1) - (r + 1) = n - r$,

$[(n + 1) - (r + 1)]! = (n - r)!$

c. $\dbinom{n}{r+1} + \dbinom{n}{r} = \dfrac{n!}{(r+1)![n - (r+1)]!} +$

$\dfrac{n!}{r!(n-r)!} = \dfrac{n!(n - r) + n!(r + 1)}{(r + 1)!(n - r)!} =$

$\dfrac{n!(n + 1)}{(r + 1)!(n - r)!} =$

$\dfrac{(n + 1)!}{(r + 1)![(n + 1) - (r + 1)]!} = \dbinom{n + 1}{r + 1}$

d. For example, rows 2 and 3 of Pascal's triangle are

$\qquad 1 \qquad\qquad 2 \qquad\qquad 1$

$1 \qquad ③ \qquad\qquad 3 \qquad\qquad 1$

that is,

$\dbinom{2}{0} \qquad\qquad \dbinom{2}{1} \qquad\qquad \dbinom{2}{2}$

$\dbinom{3}{0} \qquad \dbinom{3}{1} \qquad \dbinom{3}{2} \qquad \dbinom{3}{3}$

The circled 3 is the sum of the two closest entries in the row above: $1 + 2$. But this just says that $\dbinom{3}{1} = \dbinom{2}{0} + \dbinom{2}{1}$, which is part **c** with $n = 2$ and $r = 0$. Similarly, in the general case, verify that the two closest entries in the row above $\dbinom{n + 1}{r + 1}$ are $\dbinom{n}{r}$ and $\dbinom{n}{r + 1}$ and use part **c**.

Section B.2, page 1009

1. *Step 1:* For $n = 1$ the statement is $1 = 2^1 - 1$, which is true. *Step 2:* Assume that the statement is true for $n = k$: that is,
$1 + 2 + 2^2 + 2^3 + \cdots + 2^{k-1} = 2^k - 1$. Add 2^k to both sides, and rearrange terms:

$1 + 2 + 2^2 + 2^3 + \cdots + 2^{k-1} + 2^k = 2^k - 1 + 2^k$

$1 + 2 + 2^2 + 2^3 + \cdots + 2^{k-1} + 2^{(k+1)-1} = 2(2^k) - 1$

$1 + 2 + 2^2 + 2^3 + \cdots + 2^{k-1} + 2^{(k+1)-1} = 2^{k+1} - 1$

But this last line says that the statement is true for $n = k + 1$. Therefore, by the Principle of Mathematical Induction the statement is true for every positive integer n.

Note: **Hereafter, in these answers, step 1 will be omitted if it is trivial (as in Exercise 1), and only the essential parts of step 2 will be given.**

3. Assume that the statement is true for $n = k$:
$1 + 3 + 5 + \cdots + (2k - 1) = k^2$.
Add $2(k + 1) - 1$ to both sides:
$1 + 3 + 5 + \cdots + (2k - 1) + [2(k + 1) - 1] = k^2 + 2(k + 1) - 1 = k^2 + 2k + 1 = (k + 1)^2$.
The first and last parts of this equation say that the statement is true for $n = k + 1$.

5. Assume that the statement is true for $n = k$:

$$1^2 + 2^2 + 3^2 + \cdots + k^2 = \frac{k(k + 1)(2k + 1)}{6}$$

Add $(k + 1)^2$ to both sides:
$1^2 + 2^2 + 3^2 + \cdots + k^2 + (k + 1)^2$

$$= \frac{k(k + 1)(2k + 1)}{6} + (k + 1)^2$$

$$= \frac{k(k + 1)(2k + 1) + 6(k + 1)^2}{6}$$

$$= \frac{(k + 1)[k(2k + 1) + 6(k + 1)]}{6}$$

$$= \frac{(k + 1)(2k^2 + 7k + 6)}{6}$$

$$= \frac{(k + 1)(k + 2)(2k + 3)}{6}$$

$$= \frac{(k + 1)[(k + 1) + 1][2(k + 1) + 1]}{6}$$

The first and last parts of this equation say that the statement is true for $n = k + 1$.

7. Assume that the statement is true for $n = k$:

$$\frac{1}{1 \cdot 2} + \frac{1}{2 \cdot 3} + \cdots + \frac{1}{k(k + 1)} = \frac{k}{k + 1}.$$

Adding $\dfrac{1}{(k + 1)[(k + 1) + 1]} = \dfrac{1}{(k + 1)(k + 2)}$ to both sides yields:

$$\frac{1}{1 \cdot 2} + \frac{1}{2 \cdot 3} + \cdots + \frac{1}{k(k + 1)} + \frac{1}{(k + 1)(k + 2)}$$

$$= \frac{k}{k + 1} + \frac{1}{(k + 1)(k + 2)}$$

$$= \frac{k(k + 2) + 1}{(k + 1)(k + 2)} = \frac{k^2 + 2k + 1}{(k + 1)(k + 2)}$$

$$= \frac{(k + 1)^2}{(k + 1)(k + 2)} = \frac{k + 1}{k + 2} = \frac{k + 1}{(k + 1) + 1}$$

The first and last parts of this equation show that the statement is true for $n = k + 1$.

9. Assume the statement is true for $n = k$: $k + 2 > k$. Adding 1 to both sides, we have: $k + 2 + 1 > k + 1$, or equivalently, $(k + 1) + 2 > (k + 1)$. Therefore, the statement is true for $n = k + 1$.

11. Assume the statement is true for $n = k$: $3^k \geq 3k$. Multiplying both sides by 3 yields: $3 \cdot 3^k \geq 3 \cdot 3k$, or equivalently, $3^{k+1} \geq 3 \cdot 3k$. Now since $k \geq 1$, we know that $3k \geq 3$ and hence that $2 \cdot 3k \geq 3$. Therefore, $2 \cdot 3k + 3k \geq 3 + 3k$, or equivalently, $3 \cdot 3k \geq 3k + 3$. Combining this last inequality with the fact that $3^{k+1} \geq 3 \cdot 3k$, we see that $3^{k+1} \geq 3k + 3$, or equivalently, $3^{k+1} \geq 3(k + 1)$. Therefore, the statement is true for $n = k + 1$.

13. Assume the statement is true for $n = k$: $3k > k + 1$. Adding 3 to both sides yields: $3k + 3 > k + 1 + 3$, or equivalently, $3(k + 1) > (k + 1) + 3$. Since $(k + 1) + 3$ is certainly greater than $(k + 1) + 1$, we conclude that $3(k + 1) > (k + 1) + 1$. Therefore, the statement is true for $n = k + 1$.

15. Assume the statement is true for $n = k$; then 3 is a factor of $2^{2k+1} + 1$; that is, $2^{2k+1} + 1 = 3M$ for some integer M. Thus, $2^{2k+1} = 3M - 1$. Now $2^{2(k+1)+1} = 2^{2k+2+1} = 2^{2+2k+1} = 2^2 \cdot 2^{2k+1} = 4(3M - 1) = 12M - 4 = 3(4M) - 3 - 1 = 3(4M - 1) - 1$. From the first and last terms of this equation we see that $2^{2(k+1)+1} + 1 = 3(4M - 1)$. Hence, 3 is a factor of $2^{2(k+1)+1} + 1$. Therefore, the statement is true for $n = k + 1$.

17. Assume the statement is true for $n = k$: 64 is a factor of $3^{2k+2} - 8k - 9$. Then $3^{2k+2} - 8k - 9 = 64N$ for some integer N so that $3^{2k+2} = 8k + 9 + 64N$. Now $3^{2(k+1)+2} = 3^{2k+2+2} = 3^{2+(2k+2)} = 3^2 \cdot 3^{2k+2} = 9(8k + 9 + 64N)$. Consequently, $3^{2(k+1)+2} - 8(k + 1) - 9 = 3^{2(k+1)+2} - 8k - 8 - 9$

$$= 3^{2(k+1)+2} - 8k - 17$$
$$= [9(8k + 9 + 64N)] - 8k - 17$$
$$= 72k + 81 + 9 \cdot 64N - 8k - 17$$
$$= 64k + 64 + 9 \cdot 64N = 64(k + 1 + 9N).$$

From the first and last parts of this equation we see that 64 is a factor of $3^{2(k+1)+2} - 8(k + 1) - 9$. Therefore, the statement is true for $n = k + 1$.

19. Assuming that the statement is true for $n = k$:
$c + (c + d) + (c + 2d) + \cdots + [c + (k - 1)d] = \dfrac{k[2c + (k - 1)d]}{2}$. Adding $c + kd$ to both sides, we have

$c + (c + d) + (c + 2d) + \cdots + [c + (k - 1)d] + (c + kd)$

$$= \frac{k[2c + (k - 1)d]}{2} + c + kd$$

$$= \frac{k[2c + (k - 1)d] + 2(c + kd)}{2}$$

$$= \frac{2ck + k(k - 1)d + 2c + 2kd}{2}$$

$$= \frac{2ck + 2c + kd(k-1) + 2kd}{2}$$

$$= \frac{(k+1)2c + kd(k-1+2)}{2}$$

$$= \frac{(k+1)2c + kd(k+1)}{2} = \frac{(k+1)(2c+kd)}{2}$$

$$= \frac{(k+1)(2c + [(k+1)-1]d)}{2}$$

Therefore, the statement is true for $n = k + 1$.

21. a. $x^2 - y^2 = (x - y)(x + y)$;
$x^3 - y^3 = (x - y)(x^2 + xy + y^2)$;
$x^4 - y^4 = (x - y)(x^3 + x^2y + xy^2 + y^3)$

b. *Conjecture:* $x^n - y^n = (x - y)(x^{n-1} + x^{n-2}y + x^{n-3}y^2 + \cdots + x^2y^{n-3} + xy^{n-2} + y^{n-1})$.
Proof: The statement is true for $n = 2, 3, 4$, by part **a**. Assume that the statement is true for $n = k$:

$x^k - y^k =$
$\quad (x - y)(x^{k-1} + x^{k-2}y + \cdots + xy^{k-2} + y^{k-1})$.
Now use the fact that $-yx^k + yx^k = 0$ to write $x^{k+1} - y^{k+1}$ as follows:

$x^{k+1} - y^{k+1} = x^{k+1} - yx^k + yx^k - y^{k+1}$
$\quad = (x^{k+1} - yx^k) + (yx^k - y^{k+1})$
$\quad = (x - y)x^k + y(x^k - y^k)$
$\quad = (x - y)x^k + y(x - y)(x^{k-1} + x^{k-2}y$
$\qquad + x^{k-3}y^2 + \cdots + xy^{k-2} + y^{k-1})$
$\quad = (x - y)x^k + (x - y)(x^{k-1}y +$
$\qquad x^{k-2}y^2 + x^{k-3}y^3 + \cdots + xy^{k-1} + y^k)$
$\quad = (x - y)[x^k + x^{k-1}y + x^{k-2}y^2 +$
$\qquad x^{k-3}y^3 + \cdots + xy^{k-1} + y^k]$

The first and last parts of this equation show that the conjecture is true for $n = k + 1$. Therefore, by mathematical induction, the conjecture is true for every integer $n \geq 2$.

23. False; counterexample: $n = 9$

25. True: *Proof:* Since $(1 + 1)^2 > 1^2 + 1$, the statement is true for $n = 1$. Assume the statement is true for $n = k$: $(k + 1)^2 > k^2 + 1$. Then $[(k + 1) + 1]^2 = (k + 1)^2 + 2(k + 1) + 1 > k^2 + 1 + 2(k + 1) + 1 = k^2 + 2k + 2 + 2 > k^2 + 2k + 2 = k^2 + 2k + 1 + 1 = (k + 1)^2 + 1$. The first and last terms of this inequality say that the statement is true for $n = k + 1$. Therefore, by induction the statement is true for every positive integer n.

27. False; counterexample: $n = 2$

29. Since $2 \cdot 5 - 4 > 5$, the statement is true for $n = 5$. Assume the statement is true for $n = k$ (with $k \geq 5$): $2k - 4 > k$. Adding 2 to both sides shows that $2k - 4 + 2 > k + 2$, or equivalently, $2(k + 1) - 4 > k + 2$. Since $k + 2 > k + 1$, we see that $2(k + 1) - 4 > k + 1$. So the statement is true for $n = k + 1$. Therefore, by the Extended

Principle of Mathematical Induction, the statement is true for all $n \geq 5$.

31. Since $2^2 > 2$, the statement is true for $n = 2$. Assume that $k \geq 2$ and that the statement is true for $n = k$: $k^2 > k$. Then $(k + 1)^2 = k^2 + 2k + 1 > k^2 + 1 > k + 1$. The first and last terms of this inequality show that the statement is true for $n = k + 1$. Therefore, by induction, the statement is true for all $n \geq 2$.

33. Since $3^4 = 81$ and $2^4 + 10 \cdot 4 = 16 + 40 = 56$, we see that $3^4 > 2^4 + 10 \cdot 4$. So the statement is true for $n = 4$. Assume that $k \geq 4$ and that the statement is true for $n = k$: $3^k > 2^k + 10k$. Multiplying both sides by 3 yields:
$3 \cdot 3^k > 3(2^k + 10k)$, or equivalently,
$3^{k+1} > 3 \cdot 2^k + 30k$. But

$$3 \cdot 2^k + 30k > 2 \cdot 2^k + 30k = 2^{k+1} + 30k.$$

Therefore, $3^{k+1} > 2^{k+1} + 30k$. Now we shall show that $30k > 10(k + 1)$. Since $k \geq 4$, we have $20k \geq 20 \cdot 4$, so that $20k > 80 > 10$. Adding $10k$ to both sides of $20k > 10$ yields: $30k > 10k + 10$, or equivalently, $30k > 10(k + 1)$. Consequently,

$$3^{k+1} > 2^{k+1} + 30k > 2^{k+1} + 10(k + 1).$$

The first and last terms of this inequality show that the statement is true for $n = k + 1$. Therefore, the statement is true for all $n \geq 4$ by induction.

35. a. 3 (that is, $2^2 - 1$) for $n = 2$; 7 (that is, $2^3 - 1$) for $n = 3$; 15 (that is, $2^4 - 1$) for $n = 4$.

b. *Conjecture:* The smallest possible number of moves for n rings is $2^n - 1$. *Proof:* This conjecture is easily seen to be true for $n = 1$ or $n = 2$. Assume it is true for $n = k$ and that we have $k + 1$ rings to move. In order to move the *bottom* ring from the first peg to another peg (say, the second one), it is first necessary to move the top k rings off the first peg *and* leave the second peg vacant at the end (the second peg will have to be used *during* this moving process). If this is to be done according to the rules, we will end up with the top k rings on the third peg in the *same* order they were on the first peg. According to the induction assumption, the least possible number of moves needed to do this is $2^k - 1$. It now takes one move to transfer the bottom ring [the $(k + 1)$st] from the first to the second peg. Finally, the top k rings now on the third peg must be moved to the second peg. Once again by the induction hypothesis, the least number of moves for doing this is $2^k - 1$. Therefore, the smallest total number of moves needed to transfer all $k + 1$ rings from the first to the second peg is $(2^k - 1) + 1 + (2^k - 1) = (2^k + 2^k) - 1 = 2 \cdot 2^k - 1 = 2^{k+1} - 1$. Hence, the conjecture is true for $n = k + 1$. Therefore, by induction it is true for all positive integers n.

37. *De Moivre's Theorem:* For any complex number $z = r(\cos\theta + i\sin\theta)$ and any positive integer n, $z^n = r^n[\cos(n\theta) + i\sin(n\theta)]$. *Proof:* The theorem is obviously true when $n = 1$. Assume that the theorem is true for $n = k$, that is, $z^k = r^k[\cos(k\theta) + i\sin(k\theta)]$. Then
$$z^{k+1} = z \cdot z^k =$$
$$[r(\cos\theta + i\sin\theta)](r^k[\cos(k\theta) + i\sin(k\theta)]).$$

According to the multiplication rule for complex numbers in polar form (multiply the moduli and add the arguments) we have:
$$z^{k+1} = r \cdot r^k[\cos(\theta + k\theta) + i\sin(\theta + k\theta)]$$
$$= r^{k+1}\{\cos[(k+1)\theta] + i\sin[(k+1)\theta]\}.$$

This statement says the theorem is true for $n = k + 1$. Therefore, by induction, the theorem is true for every positive integer n.

Index

common logarithmic functions, 356–357, 364

common ratios, 58–61, 66, 77

complements, event, 866–867

completing the square, 90–92, 169

complex numbers
    absolute values, 638–639
    arithmetic of, 295–296
    definition, 294
    equal, 294
    Euler's formula, 688–689
    factorization, 308, 310–313
    imaginary powers of, 688–689
    Mandelbrot set, 304–306
    nth roots, 645–651
    orbits, 301–304
    polar form, 639–640
    polar multiplication and
        division, 640–642
    polynomial coefficients, 307
    powers of, 644–645, 688–689
    properties, 293–294
    quotients of, 296
    real and imaginary parts, 300
    roots of unity, 648–651
    square roots, 297
    zeros, 308–310, 317

complex number system, 293–294

complex plane, 301, 637–642, 650

components, vector, 655, 676–677

composite functions, 193–195, 211–212

compound interest, 345–349, 360–361, 382, 402

compressions, 177–180

concavity, 154

conic sections
    definitions, 691, 747
    degenerate, 691
    discriminants, 723–724
    eccentricity, 745–748
    ellipses, 692–698, 716–722, 745–747, 767, 771–772
    horizontal and vertical shifts, 716–717
    hyperbolas, 700–706, 721–725, 745–750, 771–772
    identifying, 717–719, 722–723
    nonstandard equations, 721–722
    parabolas, 163, 709–714, 719, 756–760, 771–772
    parameterizations, 766–769
    polar equations, 745–752, 772
    rotations, 722–724, 728–732
    standard equations, 720

conjugate pairs, 296

conjugates, complex, 296, 309

conjugate solutions, 299

conjugate zeros, 309–313

Conjugate Zero Theorem, 309

consistent systems, 781

constant functions, 152, 173, 192, 953

constant polynomials, 240

constants, 239

constraints, 829

continuity
    analytic description, 937–939
    calculators and, 937
    composite functions, 944
    definition, 939
    at endpoints, 941–942
    informal definition, 936–937
    on intervals, 940–942
    from the left and right, 941
    at a point, 938–940
    polynomial equations, 261–262
    properties of continuous functions, 942–943
    removable discontinuities, 947
    of special functions, 940

continuous compounding, 347–349

convergence, 77, 200, 203, 520–521

coordinate planes, 5, 790

coordinates, 5

coordinate systems
    comparison of, 792
    conversions, 737–738
    polar, 734–743, 776–777
    rectangular, 5, 736–739
    three-dimensional, 790–793

corner points, 829, 831–832

correlation coefficients, 47, 52, 66

cosecants, 416–419, 444–446, 485–487, 490

cosines
    addition and subtraction identities, 610
    amplitude, 493–498, 516
    basic equations, 538–541
    coterminal angles, 451
    damping, 512–514
    definition, 416, 444–445
    domain and range, 447, 477–478, 483
    double-angle identities, 593–595, 602–603, 611
    exact values, 448–451, 536
    graphs of, 475–478, 497–498
    half-angle identities, 596–597, 611
    inverse function, 532–534, 539–541, 563
    law of, 617–622, 682
    oscillating behavior, 568
    periodicity, 456–458, 493–497, 516

cosines (*continued*)
    phase shifts, 501–505, 516, 549
    power-reducing identities, 595–596
    product-to-sum identities, 599
    property summary, 483
    restricted, 532–533
    roots of unity, 648–651, 682
    special angles, 418–419, 462
    sum-to-product identities, 599–600
    transformations, 481–482, 503–505
    trigonometric identities, 454–460, 463
    unit circle, 445–446

cotangents, 416–419, 444–446, 489–490

coterminal angles, 434, 436–437, 450–451

counting numbers, 3

counting techniques, 879–882, 899

Critical Thinking, 20, 21, 64, 132, 172, 214, 250, 259, 273, 300, 344, 363, 388, 420–421, 433, 453, 492, 529, 538, 547, 624, 637, 643–644, 652, 700, 708, 727, 733, 744, 765–766, 794, 820, 852, 864, 884, 935, 947, 959

crystal lattices, 802

cube root of one, 299

cubic functions, 173, 240

cubic models, 396

cubic regression, 274–276

curve fitting, 818. *see also* models; regression

cycles, 492, 559

cycloids, 761–763

cylinder surface area, 149, 324

D

damping, 512–514

data. *see also* statistics
    comparing, 893–894
    definition, 843
    displays of, 844–850
    distribution shapes, 846–847
    outliers, 847, 862
    qualitative, 843, 845–846
    quantitative, 843, 846–850
    standardized, 893
    types of, 843
    variability, 857
    z-values, 894–896

decomposition, partial fraction, 838–841

definite integrals, 967

degenerate conic sections, 691

degree measure, 94, 436–437, 462, 528

degree of a polynomial, 240–242, 260–261, 263, 313

DeMoivre's Theorem, 644–645, 682

denominators, partial fractions, 838–841

density functions, 871–872, 891, 898

depression, angles of, 425–429

derivatives, numerical, 237

deviations, data, 857–859

difference functions, 191, 943

difference of cubes, 298

difference quotients, 143–144, 219–220, 234–235, 408, 584, 922–923

differential calculus, 76

directed networks, 809–811

direction angles, 662–664

directrix, 709–711, 720

discriminants, 93–94, 172, 723–724

distance
  absolute value and, 108, 128
  applications, 101–102, 113–114
  average rates of change, 214–220
  between two moving objects, 619
  from velocities, 964–967

distance difference, 700

distributions
  binomial, 887–888, 898
  definition, 846
  mean, median, and mode, 856–857
  normal, 889–896
  probability, 865–866
  shapes, 846–847, 857

divergence, 77

division
  algorithm, 243
  checking, 242–243
  polar, of complex numbers, 640–642
  polynomial, 240–245
  remainders and factors, 243–245
  synthetic, 241–242

domains
  convention, 145–146
  exponential and logarithmic functions, 359–360, 375–376
  functions, 142
  inverse functions, 533
  rational functions, 279
  of relations, 6–7
  restricting, 210–211, 529–530, 532, 534–535

domains (*continued*)
  sequences, 14–15
  sum, difference, product, quotient functions, 192
  trigonometric functions, 447, 477, 480, 483, 486–488, 490

dot products
  angles between vectors, 671–673
  gravity, 677–678
  projections and components, 674–677
  properties, 670–671

double-angle identities, 593–595, 602–603, 611

dreidels, 882

dynamical systems, 199

E

e, 341, 347–349. *see also* exponential functions; logarithmic functions

eccentricity, 745–748

effective rate of interest, 354

elementary row operations, 795–796

elevation, angles of, 425–429

eliminating the parameter, 757–759

elimination method, 783–786, 797–798, 821

ellipses
  applications, 696–698
  characteristics, 694
  circumference, 699
  definitions, 692, 745–747
  eccentricity, 745–747
  equations, 692–694, 696, 720–722, 771–772
  graphing, 695
  parameterization, 767
  polar equations, 749
  translations, 716–718

empirical rule, 892–893, 899

end behavior, 262–264, 284–287, 289, 316, 954–955

endpoints, 118

Engelsohn's equations, 685

equations. *see also* quadratic equations; systems of equations; trigonometric equations
  absolute value, 109–111
  applications of, 97–104
  basic, 524–528, 538–542
  conditional, 523
  conic sections, 720

equations (*continued*)
  degrees, 94
  ellipses, 692–694, 696, 720–722, 770–771
  Engelsohn's, 685
  exponential, 379–384
  fractional, 114–115
  functions, 144–145
  graphical solutions, 81–86, 524–528
  hyperbolas, 701–702, 704, 720, 771–772
  linear, 33–37, 39
  logarithmic, 379, 384–386
  matrix, 814, 817–818
  normal curve, 891, 899
  number relations, 97–98
  parabolas, 709–710, 712, 720
  parametric, 157–159, 755–757, 767–769
  polar, 745–752, 772
  polynomial, 94–95, 260–262
  radical, 111–113
  rotation, 728–730
  second-degree, 722–724
  solutions in context, 98–100
  tangent lines, 236–237
  translated conics, 718

equivalent inequalities, 119

equivalent statements, 81, 134

equivalent systems, 795

equivalent vectors, 653–655

Euler's formula, 688–689

even degree, 261, 263, 313

even functions, 188, 482–483, 489–490

events, definition, 865. *see also* probability

eventually fixed points, 202–203

eventually periodic points, 202

expected values, 869–870

experiments
  binomial, 842, 884–888
  definition, 864–865
  probability estimates from, 874–877

exponential decay, 350–352, 402

exponential equations, 379–384

exponential functions. *see also* logarithmic functions
  applications, 345–352
  bases, 336–337, 371, 380, 402
  bases other than *e*, 410–411
  common logarithms and, 356–357
  compound interest, 345–347, 382
  graphs, 59, 336–342, 375

Index

Index

infinity (*continued*)
    limits approaching, 201,
        303–305, 914, 948–953
        negative, 948, 951–953, 956
        properties of limits, 953–957
        vertical asymptotes and, 950
inflection points, 154, 266, 317
initial point (vectors), 653
initial sides, of rays, 433
input, 7–9
instantaneous rates of change,
    234–237
integers, 3–4
integral calculus, 76
integrals, definite, 967
intensity, 562
interest applications, 100–101,
    339–340, 345–349, 354,
    360–361, 382, 404
Intermediate Value Theorem,
    944–945
interquartile range, 860–861
intersection method, 86, 127, 134,
    524–525
interval notation, 118–119
interval of convergence, 520–521
inverse functions
    composition of, 532
    cosine, 532–534, 538–539, 541,
        563
    definition, 210
    horizontal line test, 530
    restricting the domain, 210–211
    sine, 529–532, 539, 563
    tangent, 534–536, 540, 563
inverse matrices, 815–817
inverse relations
    algebraic representations,
        207–208, 534
    composite, 211–212
    definition, 205
    graphs, 205–207
    horizontal line test, 209–210, 226
    one-to-one functions, 208–211
    restricting the domain, 210–211,
        529, 532, 534
irrational exponents, 333
irrational numbers, 4, 341, 688
irreducible polynomials, 253, 315
iterations, 199–200

ladder safety, 426
latitude, 442
law of cosines, 617–622, 682

law of sines
    AAS information, 626
    ambiguous case, 627–628
    area of a triangle, 632–633
    ASA information, 631–632
    definition, 625, 682
    SSA information, 628–633
    supplementary angle identity,
        628
laws of exponents, 330–331, 402
laws of logarithms, 373–374, 402
least squares regression lines,
    47–52
lemniscate graphs, 743
length, maximum, 469
limaçon graphs, 743
limits of functions
    approaching infinity, 201,
        303–305, 914, 948–957
    approaching two values,
        914–915
    of constants, 918, 953
    definition, 909–913, 929–935
    difference quotients, 922–923
    function values, 912–913
    identity function, 918
    nonexistence of, 913–915
    notation, 910–911, 925, 931, 951
    one-sided, 924–927, 935
    oscillating functions, 915
    polynomial functions, 919–920
    properties of, 919, 933–934,
        953–957
    proving, 931–934
    rational functions, 920–923,
        954–957
    trigonometric functions, 566–
        568
    two-sided, 926–927
Limit Theorem, 922, 954
linear combinations of vectors, 662
linear depreciation, 35–36
linear equations, 33–37, 39
linear functions, 34–36, 240
linear inequalities, 119–120, 827
linear models
    corresponding function, 396
    finite differences, 43–44
    least squares regression lines,
        47–52
    modeling terminology, 44–46
    prediction from, 51–52
    residuals, 44–46, 49–51, 66
linear programming, 829–832
linear regression, 47–52
linear speed, 439–440
linear systems, 779, 781–782,
    796–797

lines. *see also* slope
    angles between intersecting,
        590–592
    arithmetic sequences and, 34
    least squares regression, 47–52
    parallel and perpendicular,
        38–39, 66
    parameterizations of, 755
    point-slope form, 36–37, 39, 66,
        792
    secant, 218–219, 408, 409
    slope-intercept form, 33–36, 39,
        66, 792–793
    standard form, 39, 66
    tangent, 235–237, 408–411
    vertical and horizontal, 37–38,
        66
local maxima, 153, 266
local minima, 153, 266
logarithmic equations, 379,
    384–386
logarithmic functions
    change-of-base formula,
        374–375, 402
    common, 356–357, 364
    graphs, 359–361, 375–376
    laws of, 373–374, 402
    natural, 358–359, 364
    other bases, 370–376
    Power Law, 367
    Product Law, 365
    properties, 363–364, 372–373
    Quotient Law, 366
    solving, 384–386
    transformations, 359–360,
        375–376
logarithmic models, 389, 394
logistic models, 342, 389, 391–392,
    395, 401
LORAN, 724–725
lottery probabilities, 870, 881–882,
    886–887
lower bounds, 255–256

Mach numbers, 529
magnitude, vector, 653, 655
Mandelbrot set, 304–306
mathematical models, definition,
    43. *see also* models
mathematical patterns, 13–19
matrices (singular: matrix)
    addition and subtraction,
        804–805
    adjacency, 809–810

Index

Index

radian/degree conversion, 436–437, 463

radian measure, 435–438, 444–445

radicals, 111–113, 327–329, 332–333. *see also* roots

radioactive decay, 340, 351–352, 402

radiocarbon dating, 352, 381–382

radio signals, 472, 500

radio telescopes, 713–714

Ramanujan, 699

random samples, definition, 843

random variables, 869–870

ranges
   definition, 142
   exponential and logarithmic functions, 359, 375
   relations, 6–7
   statistical, 859–860
   trigonometric functions, 446, 476, 479, 482, 486–489

rates of change
   average, 214–219, 226
   difference quotient, 219–220, 234
   instantaneous, 234–237, 614–615
   logistic models, 391
   slope of tangent lines, 235–237

rational exponents, 329–331, 402

rational functions
   complete graphs, 287–289
   definition, 278
   domains, 279
   end behavior, 284–285, 287, 289
   holes, 282–283, 289
   horizontal asymptotes, 284
   intercepts, 279–280, 288–289, 317
   limits, 920–923, 954–957
   maximum of, 322
   parabolic asymptotes, 286
   partial fractions, 838–841
   slant asymptotes, 285–286, 289
   trigonometric identities, 578–579
   vertical asymptotes, 281–282, 288–289, 317, 950

rational inequalities, 127–128

rationalizing denominators and numerators, 332–333

rational numbers, 4, 78–79

rational zeros, 250–254, 316

rays, rotation, 433

real axis, 638

real numbers, 3–4

real solutions, 89, 94

real zeros, 245, 248, 250–257

reciprocal identities, 455, 460, 463, 574

rectangles, 98–99, 703

rectangular box volume, 99–100, 323

rectangular coordinate systems, 5, 736–738

recursively defined sequences, 15, 66

reduced row echelon form, 797–801

reference angles, 449–451

reflections, 177, 206, 226, 481, 487, 501

refraction, 545

regression. *see also* models
   cubic, 274–276
   exponential, 390
   least squares, 47–52
   linear, 47–52
   polynomial, 273–276
   power, 394
   quadratic, 274–276
   quartic, 274–276, 392
   sinusoidal functions, 553–554

relations, 6–7, 97–98

relative frequency, 844–845

remainders, 244–245

Remainder Theorem, 244

removable discontinuities, 947

repeating decimals, 78–79

replacement, in counting, 879–880

residuals, 44–46, 48, 50–51, 66

response times, 895–896

restricted domains, 210–211, 529, 532, 534

resultant force, 664–667

Richter magnitudes, 368–369

Riemann sums, 964–967

right triangles, 415–418, 421–426

roots
   absolute value, 109
   of complex numbers, 646–648
   cube root of one, 299
   extraneous, 110–111
   graphical root finder, 84–85, 122
   limits at infinity, 955–957
   nth, 327–329, 645–651
   square, 90, 109, 297, 955–956
   of unity, 648–651, 682

roots of unity, 648–651, 682

rose graphs, 742

rotation angles, 730–731, 771

rotations, 722–723, 728–732, 771

rounding, 426, 525

rule of a relation, 7

rule of the function, 7

samples, definition, 843

sample space, definition, 864–865

sample standard deviation, 858, 899

scalar multiplication, 655–656, 659, 661, 683, 805–806

scatter plots, 5–7, 48, 50–51

Schwarz inequality, 673, 683

secant lines, 218–219, 408

secants, 408, 416–418, 444–445, 486–487, 489

second-degree equations, 722–724. *see also* quadratic equations

self-similar under magnification, 305

sequences
   applications, 17–19, 28–29
   arithmetic, 21–29, 34, 66
   definition, 13, 66
   explicit forms, 34, 66
   geometric, 58–63, 76–79
   graphs, 14–16
   notation, 14, 16–17
   partial sums, 26–29
   recursive forms, 15–16, 22, 66
   summation notation, 25

series, infinite geometric, 76–79, 520–521

shading on graphs, 827–828

side-angle-side (SAS) information, 618–621

side-side-angle (SSA) information, 627–631

side-side-side (SSS) information, 619, 633

sides of angles, 413, 422, 424

simple harmonic motion. *see also* sinusoidal functions
   bouncing springs, 551–553
   characteristics, 547
   definition, 549
   examples of, 522, 550–553
   rotating wheel, 550–551

simple interest, 100

sines
   addition and subtraction identities, 582–583, 604, 610
   amplitude, 497–498, 516
   basic equations, 539–540, 542

Index

uniform distributions, 846
unit circles, 445–446, 449, 473, 475, 478, 650
unit vectors, 661–664
upper bounds, 255–256

variability, 857–860
variance, 858
vectors
    angles between, 671–673, 681
    arithmetic, 655–659, 662, 681
    components, 674–677, 681
    components and magnitudes, 655
    direction angles, 662–664
    dot products, 670–678
    equivalent, 654–655
    gravity, 677–678
    linear combinations, 662
    notation, 653, 655, 662
    orthogonal, 673, 681
    parallel, 671
    projections, 674–677, 681
    properties, 659
    resultant force, 664–667
    Schwarz inequality, 673, 683
    unit, 661–664
    velocity, 663
    work calculation, 677–678
    zero, 658
velocity
    average, 235
    free-fall, 958–959
    instantaneous, 234–236
    terminal, 908, 959
    total distance from, 964–965
    vectors, 663
vertical asymptotes, 281–282, 288–289, 950
vertical lines, 37–38, 66, 792
vertical line test, 151–152, 186, 225
vertical shifts, 174, 481–482, 501, 504, 516
vertical stretches and
    compressions, 177–180, 339, 481, 487, 501
vertices (singular: vertex)
    directed matrices, 809–810

vertices (*continued*)
    ellipse, 692, 720
    hyperbolas, 701, 720
    parabolas, 709, 720
    quadratic functions, 163–166, 169, 225
    triangle, 415
Very Large Array (Socorro, New Mexico), 713–714
volume, 216, 323

waves, 493–498, 558–562
whole numbers, 3–4
wind chill, 335
work, 677–678

x-axis symmetry, 185–186, 188
x-coordinates, 5
x-coordinate transformations, 180–181
x-intercept form of quadratic functions, 164, 166–169, 225
x-intercept method, 84–86, 94, 112, 127–128, 134, 525–528
x-intercepts
    ellipses, 694
    hyperbolas, 702
    parabolas, 163
    polynomial functions, 264–265
    quadratic functions, 163–165, 169, 225
    rational functions, 279–280, 288–289
x-variables, 6

y-axis symmetry, 184–185, 188
y-coordinates, 5, 166
y-coordinate transformations, 178–179
y-intercepts
    ellipses, 694
    hyperbolas, 702
    parabolas, 163
    polynomial functions, 264

y-intercepts (*continued*)
    quadratic functions, 163–166, 169
    rational functions, 279, 288–289
    in three dimensions, 792
y-variables, 6

z-axis, 790
Zero Product Property, 89
zeros
    bounds, 254–256
    complex, 310–313, 317
    complex polynomials, 307–313
    conjugate, 309–313
    Factor Theorem and, 252–253
    multiplicity, 265, 283, 308–309
    orbits, 302–304
    polynomials, 240, 245–248, 250–257, 265, 308–313, 316–317
    rational, 250–254, 316
    of unity, 298–299
zero vectors, 658
z-values, 894–896, 900